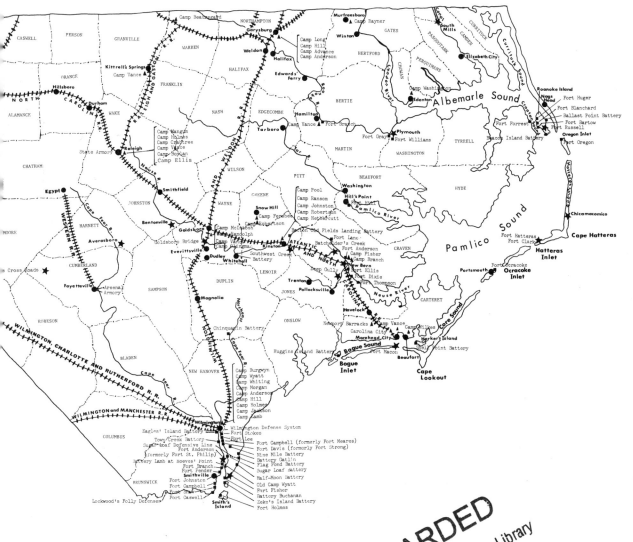

NORTH CAROLINA TROOPS

1861-1865

A ROSTER

Private Neill Alexander Maultsby, who eventually rose through the ranks to become 1st Sergeant of Company H, 51st Regiment, stands at attention with his British Enfield rifle-musket and bayonet. His accoutrements are a simple cartridge box and sling, cap box, and roller buckle waist belt. The short jacket and forage cap were popular with North Carolina troops. Private Maultsby was shot through the right lung near Cold Harbor, Virginia, on or about June 1, 1864, but clung to life for more than six weeks before dying at Petersburg. His service record appears on page 360 of this volume. Image furnished by Henry Mintz, Hallsboro, North Carolina.

North Carolina Troops
1861-1865
A Roster

COMPILED BY
WEYMOUTH T. JORDAN, JR.

UNIT HISTORIES BY
WEYMOUTH T. JORDAN, JR.

VOL. XII
INFANTRY

49TH-52ND
REGIMENTS

RALEIGH, NORTH CAROLINA
DIVISION OF ARCHIVES AND HISTORY
1990

Copyright, 1990, by the North Carolina Division of Archives and History

Typeset by
Advertising Communications Incorporated, Durham, North Carolina

Printed and Bound by
University Graphics, North Carolina State University, Raleigh

ISBN 0-86526-017-6 (Volume XII)
ISBN 0-86526-005-2 (Set)

PREFACE

North Carolina Troops, 1861-1865: A Roster commemorates, through the publication of their individual service records, the more than 125,000 North Carolinians, blacks and Indians as well as whites, who fought for the Confederacy and the Union during the Civil War. The project to publish this series was inaugurated in February, 1961, under the auspices of the North Carolina Confederate Centennial Commission and was transferred to the State Department of Archives and History (now the Department of Cultural Resources) when the commission was terminated in 1965. Through the years, thousands of military records and manuscripts have been abstracted and approximately 230 cubic feet of service record data on North Carolina's Civil War personnel have been accumulated. The publication of these data in the twelve volumes that have now appeared provides not only a vivid portrait of the men who served from our state but also an invaluable source of genealogical and statistical information.

North Carolina Troops has received a warm reception from scholars, two of whom have described it as "a magnificent achievement" and "the finest state roster ever produced." In this volume, which covers the Forty-ninth through the Fifty-second infantry regiments, readers will particularly enjoy the regimental histories, which are more detailed and comprehensive than those in earlier volumes and contain footnoted material from Civil War letters, diaries, newspapers, and a wide range of published works. Of particular interest are the accounts of the Forty-ninth Regiment's part in the battles of Sharpsburg and the Crater; the Fifty-first Regiment's courageous defense of Fort Wagner, in Charleston Harbor; and the decimation of the Fifty-second Regiment in the Pickett-Pettigrew Charge at Gettysburg.

North Carolina Troops is a fitting memorial to the devotion, courage, and sacrifice of the brave soldiers from our state who fought and died for the Confederacy and the Union. I am pleased to commend it to historians and students of the Civil War, to bibliophiles and genealogists, and—as a compendium of our Civil War heritage—to the people of North Carolina.

January 23, 1990

JAMES G. MARTIN
Governor of North Carolina

CONTENTS

Preface . . . . \ v

Introduction ix

49th Regiment N.C. Troops 1
    Field and Staff 26
    Company A 29
    1st Company B (Chatham Cossacks) 40
    2nd Company B (Cleveland Mountain Boys) 45
    Company C 54
    Company D 64
    Company E 72
    Company F (Mecklenburg Guards) 79
    Company G (Kings Mountain Tigers) 90
    Company H (Gaston Rangers) 102
    Company I (Catawba Marksmen) 116
    Company K (Pleasant Home Guards) 126
    Miscellaneous 138

50th Regiment N.C. Troops 140
    Field and Staff 149
    Company A 152
    Company B 163
    Company C 175
    Company D 187
    Company E 196
    Company F (Moore Sharpshooters) 204
    Company G (Rutherford Farmers) 215
    Company H 225
    Company I (Rutherford Regulars and Rutherford Regulators) 235
    Company K (Green River Rifles) 246
    Miscellaneous 256

51st Regiment N.C. Troops 258
    Field and Staff 276
    Company A 278
    Company B (Warsaw Sampsons) 288
    Company C (Duplin Stars) 298
    Company D (Scotch Tigers) 308
    Company E (Clay Valley Rangers) 319
    Company F (Ashpole True Boys) 331
    Company G 340
    Company H (Columbus Light Infantry) 353
    Company I 366
    Company K (Confederate Stars) 381
    Miscellaneous 392

52nd Regiment N.C. Troops 393
    Field and Staff 415
    Company A (Cabarrus Riflemen) 417
    Company B (Randolph Guards) 427
    Company C (Orapeake Guards) 438
    Company D (McCulloch's Avengers) 446
    Company E (Richmond Regulators) 454
    Company F (Wilkes Grays) 465
    Company G (Dry Pond Dixies) 480
    Company H (Spring Hill Guards) 490
    Company I (Stanly Rebels) 501
    Company K (Fighting Boys) 511
    Miscellaneous 520

Index 522

Illustrations appear on pages ii, xix, xx, and following pages 139, 257, and 392.
Map of Charleston Harbor appears on page 262.

INTRODUCTION

The principal source of information for the individual service records in this volume is the microfilm edition (M270) of the Civil War service record materials on file in the North Carolina section of Record Group 109 in the National Archives, Washington, D.C. The North Carolina section of Record Group 109, known officially as the Compiled Service Records of Confederate Soldiers Who Served in Organizations from the State of North Carolina, is composed of individual service record envelopes for each North Carolina soldier in which are filed data cards containing information abstracted from primary Civil War records. Envelopes are filed numerically by regiment or battalion and then alphabetically by surname. Primary records from which service record information was abstracted include company muster rolls, payrolls, rosters, appointment books, hospital registers, prison registers and rolls, parole registers, and inspection reports. Some envelopes contain primary documents such as enlistment and discharge papers, pay vouchers, requisitions, court-martial proceedings, and personal correspondence. In addition, the North Carolina Roll of Honor, compiled by the state adjutant general during the war and containing service record information on thousands of North Carolina soldiers, was loaned to federal authorities in Washington at the time Record Group 109 was compiled, and its contents were abstracted and incorporated into the record group.

A second National Archives source utilized in this volume is the Unfiled Papers and Slips Belonging to Confederate Compiled Service Records (M347). That collection consists of cards and papers collected and compiled for inclusion in Record Group 109 but not filed, for various reasons, in that collection. Other National Archives collections of which at least some use was made are the Compiled Records Showing Service of Military Units in Confederate Organizations (M861); Records Relating to Confederate Naval and Marine Personnel (M260); Compiled Service Records of Confederate Soldiers Who Served in Organizations Raised Directly by the Confederate Government (M258); Selected Records of the War Department Relating to Confederate Prisoners of War, 1861-1865 (M598); Register of Confederate Soldiers, Sailors, and Citizens Who Died in Federal Prisons and Military Hospitals in the North, 1861-1865 (M918); Confederate States Army Casualties: Lists and Narrative Reports, 1861-1865 (M836); Orders and Circulars Issued by the Army of the Potomac and the Army and Department of Northern Virginia, C.S.A., 1861-1865 (M921); and the compiled service records collections for the states of Virginia (M324), South Carolina (M267), Arkansas (M376), and Mississippi (M427).

Material obtained from the National Archives was supplemented by records in the North Carolina state archives. Those included muster rolls for periods not covered by muster rolls on file at the National Archives, bounty rolls, state pension applications filed by Confederate veterans and their widows, and records of the office of the state adjutant general. Pension applications filed by North Carolina soldiers with the states of Tennessee and Florida were also utilized. Information relative to Confederate service was abstracted from membership applications, Cross of Honor certificates, and Cross of Military Service certificates in the possession of the North Carolina Division of the United Daughters of the Confederacy as well as from Confederate gravestone records compiled by the same organization. Also utilized were published registers of Hollywood Cemetery, Richmond, Virginia; Stonewall Cemetery, Winchester, Virginia; and the cemeteries at Sharpsburg, Maryland; Gettysburg, Pennsylvania; and Elmira, New York.

Because of the shortcomings of the *Roster of North Carolina Troops in the War Between the States*, edited by John W. Moore (Raleigh: [State of North Carolina], 4 volumes, 1882), hereinafter cited as Moore's *Roster*, that source and local rosters compiled from it were not used except for auxiliary purposes such as cross-reference. However, service record information was abstracted from *Histories of the Several Regiments and Battalions from North Carolina in the Great War, 1861-'65* (Raleigh and Goldsboro: State of North Carolina, 5 volumes, 1901), by Walter Clark, hereinafter cited as Clark's *Regiments*. Casualty reports and obituaries were abstracted from 1861-1865 issues of various North Carolina newspapers, and service record information was received from descendants of Civil War veterans, from professional and lay historians, and from other private individuals. The recent publication of a master index to the 1860 federal census of North Carolina permitted extensive use of that valuable document for the first time in the history of the roster project. Also utilized were the *Confederate Veteran* magazine, *War of the Rebellion: A Compilation of the Official Records of the Union and Confederate Armies*, North Carolina militia records, and (for nonmilitary information such as birth dates, full names, and prewar occupations) published genealogies. In the latter category, the North Carolina county *Heritage Book* series was particularly helpful. Some service record information was obtained from letters and diaries in the North Carolina state archives, the Southern Historical Collection at the University of North Carolina (Chapel Hill), and the Duke University Manuscript Collection; however, many additional details of interest and significance concerning the military careers of North Carolina soldiers no doubt remain among the seemingly inexhaustible treasures in those three repositories.

Information abstracted from the foregoing sources was arranged and consolidated for each member of each unit for which a roster appears in this volume. The method adopted for presenting regimental rosters and listing the names and service records of individual soldiers is as follows:

Regimental field officers (Colonels, Lieutenant Colonels, Majors), as well as regimental staff officers (Adjutants, Assistant Quartermasters, Assistant Commissaries of Subsistence, Surgeons, Chaplains, Ensigns) and regimental noncommissioned officers (Sergeants Major, Quartermaster Sergeants, Commissary Sergeants, Ordnance Sergeants, Hospital Stewards) are grouped together by rank under a major heading entitled Field and Staff. Names and service records are listed chronologically by date of rank within these various groups. Members of regimental bands are listed alphabetically at the end of the Field and Staff section.

Rosters of the companies (usually ten in number) of which a regiment was composed follow the Field and Staff and are divided into two major sections consisting of (1) Officers and (2) Noncommissioned Officers and Privates. Within the Officers section are two subsections for (i) Captains and (ii) Lieutenants. Captains are listed chronologically by date of rank; lieutenants are listed alphabetically. All soldiers whose names and service records appear in the section for Noncommissioned Officers and Privates are listed alphabetically regardless of their date of rank and whether they were sergeants, corporals, or privates.

Following the last company roster is a miscellaneous section listing soldiers who were members of the regiment but whose records do not indicate the company in which they served.

The spelling of personal names, including given names as well as surnames, is based on a comparison of information in Record Group 109 with information from other sources such as Confederate pension applications, the 1860 federal census of North Carolina, family sources, published genealogies, and, in some cases, direct information from professional genealogists. Because genealogical sources and the 1860 census are now being utilized more extensively than in the past, this system represents an improvement over the one that was employed in earlier volumes. Even so, a number of oddities and corruptions have undoubtedly occurred, and the index has been extensively cross-referenced to assist the researcher in locating names that may appear in corrupted form.

In composing the service records contained in this volume, the editor has generally cited as the enlistment date for each soldier the date of enlistment that was recorded for him on the muster-in roll or earliest surviving muster roll of the company in which he served. The place of enlistment was usually derived from the same sources. Actually, there were at least five dates on which a soldier might be reported to have entered service: the date he enrolled for military service; the date he enlisted or was conscripted; the date he reported for duty; the date his unit was mustered into state service; and the date his unit was mustered into Confederate service. Similarly, the place of enlistment might be reported as the town or county where he enrolled or was conscripted; the town, county, or camp where he joined the unit to which he was assigned; or the camp of instruction to which he was assigned. No standard procedure was followed by company clerks in citing either date or place of enlistment, and individual clerks sometimes arbitrarily altered their previous procedure. It is a frequent occurrence, therefore, for several conflicting enlistment dates and places of enlistment to appear in the primary records for a single soldier. In such circumstances, the procedure outlined above for determining and standardizing enlistment dates and places of enlistment has been deemed the most satisfactory.

All references to counties are as of 1861-1865 boundaries. In instances where primary records indicate that a soldier was born in a county that had not been formed at the time of the soldier's birth, an asterisk appears after the county (e.g., Born in Alamance County*), and the assumption can generally be made that the individual in question was born at a locality that later became part of the county cited.

Records pertaining to the age at date of enlistment of soldiers have proved so contradictory and unreliable that, in the absence of a reason to favor one source over another, the editor has arbitrarily adopted the practice of selecting for inclusion in the service records in this volume the youngest age among the possibilities available. Although enlistment officers probably "rounded off" ages to the next birthday in some instances, and both enlistment officers and enlistees undoubtedly falsified ages on occasion, it also seems likely that ignorance of exact birth dates was not uncommon. The latter rarely appear in primary Civil War records, and the fact that North Carolina pension applications filed thirty years or more after the cessation of hostilities often reflect age discrepancies similar to those in wartime records is suggestive. The age-at-date-of-enlistment problem is further complicated by the fact that each soldier, like all mortals, was two different ages during any given calendar year depending on whether or not his birthday had already passed. Thus, a Confederate hospital record indicating that a soldier was 28 years old in May, 1864, does not reveal whether he was 24 or 25 when he enlisted in July, 1861. The editor's procedure in such cases is to quote the source in bracket's (e.g. [Confederate hospital records dated May, 1864, give his age as 28]). As a general cautionary principle, it must be stated that if a service record contains any single item of incorrect information it is most likely to be the soldier's age. Nevertheless, it is believed that a significant improvement in this area has resulted from the utilization of the 1860 federal census, published genealogical materials, and the expertise of professional genealogists, as indicated above.

Prewar occupations cited in service records are derived primarily from military records in the National Archives; however, utilization of the 1860 federal census, which contains more detailed information, has permitted a considerable qualitative improvement in this category. Men who are listed simply as "farmers" in military records can now be subdivided into farmers and farm laborers or even more precisely identified as turpentine workers and the like.

All references to cities and towns are as of their 1861-1865 designations; however, in instances where the place-name was later changed the 1861-1865 designation is followed by the current name in parentheses—e.g., Smithville (Southport). North Carolina counties, cities, towns, etc., are not followed by reference to the state except for clarity (e.g., Greensboro; but Washington, North Carolina). Counties and localities in other states are followed by the state only on the first occasion that they are mentioned in a service record. West Virginia place names are cited as being in West Virginia only if the date of the reference is on or subsequent to June 20, 1863, the date West Virginia was admitted to the Union. If the reference is prior to that date, the locality is cited as being in [West] Virginia. In a few cases it proved impossible to ascertain the state or county in which a hamlet or geographical feature was located, either because no such place could be identified or because two or more places with the same name were located in two or more states or counties and no evidence was available as to which of the places was the one intended. Such place names appear in quotation marks in this volume (e.g., "Table Knob," or "Warrenton").

Cause of death, reason for discharge, and other information that sometimes is unsavory or unheroic, and thus unwelcome to later generations, is presented in quotation marks in order to emphasize its authenticity and, perhaps, channel any dismay on the part of the soldier's descendants in the direction of the documentary source. Information that is ambiguous, contradictory, unverifiable, or of doubtful accuracy is also presented in quotation marks and will normally be found in brackets at the end of a service record. Brackets are used also to enclose editorial corrections, interpolations, comments, and cross-references, and they are employed at the end of some service records to convey information that would have been illogical or awkward to present in the body of the service record.

The phrase "on or about" is used when the dates derived from primary records seem doubtful or otherwise in need of qualification (e.g., Wounded at Gettysburg, Pennsylvania, on or about July 5, 1863). That phrase is used also when an event which is not a verified or verifiable historical fact is cited in primary records as having occurred on two or more dates that are more or less consecutive, the date cited being the one that seems most probably correct on the basis of available evidence (e.g., Died at Raleigh on or about April 8, 1864). In instances where there is no reason to favor one date over another, hyphenated dates are given if the dates are more or less consecutive (e.g., Died at Raleigh, April 2-8, 1864). When such dates are not more or less consecutive they are cited individually (e.g., Died at Raleigh on April 2 or June 5, 1864). Hyphenated dates preceded by "in" indicate a single event that occurred during the period in question (e.g., Hospitalized at Goldsboro in July-August, 1863); but dates preceded by "during" indicate a condition that prevailed throughout the period in question (e.g., Hospitalized at Goldsboro during July-August, 1864). Again, this system was found necessary because in many instances the exact date of an event could not be determined.

The phrase "present or accounted for" is used to indicate that a soldier was either present for duty or absent for reasons other than desertion or extended absence without leave. Desertion and absence without leave are terms that were often employed synonymously by company clerks; hence, a soldier who absented himself without authorization but returned of his own accord sixty days later might be listed as a deserter in the records of one company, while a soldier who absented himself from another company for the same period under identical circumstances might be listed as absent without leave. The editor has judged it best not to standardize those terms, however inequitable the contemporary "system" may now seem, and references to desertion or absence without leave that appear in this volume are, in the overwhelming majority of cases, quoted directly from primary sources. In previous volumes, reference was generally made to unauthorized absences of less than sixty days only in the case of chronic deserters. However, because of the interest and, to some degree, controversy concerning the question of North Carolina desertion rates, a more flexible policy has been adopted beginning with this volume: we will now include information concerning unauthorized absences in the 20-60 day range and also shorter absences that may have affected a regiment's combat capacity at critical moments.

With regard to North Carolina desertion rates in general, it will be evident from the foregoing discussion that the problem of even defining desertion presents major difficulties. These are further complicated by the fact that very few muster rolls are extant for the critical period from January through April, 1865. For most North Carolina regiments no rolls exist of later date than October, 1864, and for others only a few rolls survive for the entire war. A definitive statistical study of North Carolina desertion rates therefore does not seem possible. After almost twenty years of work in North Carolina Civil War history I have found no convincing evidence to refute the widely held conviction that North Carolina desertion rates were higher than those for other states. Indeed, whatever one might wish, the preponderance of evidence continues to be in the other direction. The real question, however, is not the fact of desertion but the reasons for it—such as the relative weakness of the North Carolina slavocracy and its values; a powerful current of latent pro-Unionism (including a sizable pro-Union minority); enforcement of the Conscription Act with a degree of rigor that seems to have exceeded that prevailing in other Confederate states; widespread disaffection toward the perceived abuses, neglect, and unfairness of the Confederate government; and a general conviction that North Carolina's duty was to defend the South rather than invade the North. It is worth remembering, too, that for much of the war troops from most other Confederate states were either fighting on their home ground or had little cause to fear for the well-being and safety of their families. This was not true in the case of the North Carolina soldier. Near anarchy prevailed in the North Carolina mountains, and much of the eastern third of the state was either Federally occupied or subject to destructive raids. That situation existed in large part because most of the state's troops had been dispatched to the defense of Virginia. A thorough investigation of these factors—not further inconclusive statistical studies or chauvinistic responses to those who imply that courage is somehow a function of state lines—is what is needed. Such studies will not diminish the reputation for bravery the North Carolina soldier won on the battlefield. On the contrary, they will almost certainly further enhance the pride that Tar Heels can justifiably take in the North Carolina soldier's contributions and sacrifices to a cause in which he had little stake and in which, in many instances, he may not have wholly believed.

The phrase "no further records" is used at the end of a service record when there is doubt as to the manner in which the soldier's military career terminated (e.g., Company muster rolls indicate he was discharged at Weldon on May 9, 1864; however, medical records indicate he died in hospital at Weldon on May 30, 1864. No further records). Use of this phrase does not indicate that there are literally no further records extant but that there are no further records pertaining to the most important aspects of a soldier's military career. Additional records pertaining to hospitalizations for minor complaints, authorized leaves of absence, issuance of clothing, and other comparatively insignificant episodes exist, often in quantity, for most of the soldiers whose service records appear in this volume.

During the twenty-nine years since the inception of the roster project, rules of capitalization, punctuation, and style have changed considerably; for example, it is no longer considered good form to capitalize an individual's title or rank unless it appears before his name. However, except in those few instances where a new system provided greater clarity or seemed distinctly advantageous, systems employed in earlier volumes have been retained. One particularly noticeable punctuation oddity that perhaps should be mentioned specifically involves the use in the possessive case of singular nouns ending in "s." Personal names are rendered "s's" (e.g., Jones's men), but, on the theory that the historic spelling of a place-name cannot be altered by a change in modern rules of punctuation, place-names ending in the possessive are rendered without the final "s" (e.g., Jones' Mill, Virginia).

The chronic editorial problem of cross-referencing the service records of soldiers who served in two or more units also would appear to merit discussion at this point. A specific case may serve best to illustrate the difficulties involved and the precautions that should be taken by users of *North Carolina Troops*. Private William T. Wood enlisted originally in Company B, 17th Regiment N.C. Troops (2nd Organization). In November, 1862, he was transferred to Company A, 8th Regiment N.C. State Troops. His service record in the roster for Company B, 17th Regiment, should conclude, therefore, with a statement that he was transferred to Company A, 8th Regiment, in November, 1862; his service record in the roster for Company A, 8th Regiment, should begin with a statement that he served previously in Company B, 17th Regiment, and was transferred to Company A, 8th Regiment, in November, 1862. Unfortunately, as often happens in the case of transferees, there was no record in the files of the 8th Regiment of Private Wood's previous service in the 17th Regiment, and the roster of the 8th Regiment was already in print when his previous service in the 17th Regiment was discovered in the records of the latter unit; hence, the appropriate cross-reference was omitted in the roster of the 8th Regiment. In an attempt to circumvent cross-referencing problems of the foregoing type, an effort was made to locate records of dual service for soldiers whose careers either began abruptly in mid-war or terminated inexplicably a year or more before the fighting ceased; however, for a variety of reasons it was not always possible to locate or conclusively identify additional records for such individuals. Therefore, until a revised edition of *North Carolina Troops* is published, reference should be made to the index to each volume in this series (or to the master index that will be published at its conclusion) whenever the service record of a soldier begins or terminates in a manner that does not preclude previous or later service in another unit.

I would like to express my sincere appreciation to those persons who have contributed to the publication of this volume:

—Jeffrey J. Crow, administrator of the Historical Publications Section, read one of the regimental histories in manuscript and provided both logistical support and sound professional advice.

—Bob High, of Whiteville, North Carolina, a highly able and extraordinarily industrious editor, researcher, and genealogist, contributed important information concerning the location and contents of dozens of newspaper casualty lists, obituaries, and articles. He also provided valuable personal data (full names, birth dates, prewar occupations, etc.) for men who served in two Columbus County units—Companies G and H of the 51st Regiment.

—Joe McLaurin, of Rockingham, North Carolina, whose work in the field of Richmond County genealogy has been widely and deservedly recognized and praised, reviewed the roster of Company E, 52nd Regiment (a Richmond County unit), and contributed much useful personal data concerning its members.

—Henry Mintz, of Hallsboro, North Carolina, located and obtained copies of the indispensable William J. Burney letters, which are cited in the history of the 51st Regiment and which had not been published previously or otherwise utilized. He also provided one of the photographic illustrations that appears in this volume.

—Ken Simpson, Joe Mobley, and Torrey McLean, Civil War specialists and respected colleagues on the staff of the North Carolina Division of Archives and History, each read one of the regimental histories in manuscript and contributed valuable criticisms, corrections, comments, and suggestions.

—Mickey Black, of Salisbury, North Carolina, a highly competent authority on Civil War weapons, uniforms, and photographs, once again (as with Volume XI) made a very significant and much appreciated contribution by composing the descriptions that appear beneath the illustrations.

—A. S. Perry, of Raleigh, provided valuable information concerning North Carolina soldiers who were executed for desertion.

—Raymond W. Watkins, of Falls Church, Virginia, who is undoubtedly the country's leading authority on Confederate cemeteries, continued his long-standing practice of providing information on burial sites and grave markers of North Carolina soldiers.

—Lisa Bailey, proofreader of the Historical Publications Section, read all four regimental histories and corrected a number of embarrassing technical errors.

—Susan M. Trimble, editorial secretary of the roster project (June, 1988-June, 1989), prepared the manuscript for the 51st and 52nd regiments, proofread the manuscript for the entire volume, typed thousands of cards containing information abstracted from newspaper casualty lists and obituaries, and gladdened the heart of the editor with her intelligence, efficiency, productivity, and cheerful cooperation. Mrs. Trimble's predecessor, Lisa K. Keenum (May, 1984-February, 1988), prepared the manuscript for the 49th and 50th regiments.

—Elizabeth N. Shipp, editorial assistant (September, 1988-June, 1989) and editorial secretary (July-September, 1989) did most of the work on the index, proofread the manuscript for the volume, and carried out all of her professional assignments with impressive industry and intelligence.

—Trudy M. Rayfield, acting editorial assistant (September, 1989, to date) assigned page numbers to all index entries. She and Ann W. Little, editorial secretary (February, 1990, to date) also proofread the page proof for the volume, thereby rescuing the editor, his versatility in such matters notwithstanding, from a variety of egregious blunders.

—Vanessa Goodman, who was editorial assistant during a difficult period (January-May, 1988) when the roster project was for the most part without secretarial help, learned how to operate complicated word processing equipment with remarkable ease while demonstrating admirable maturity, skill, and patience in all facets of her work. Her fine efforts are both remembered and appreciated. The hard work and important contributions of editorial assistants Jennifer Hubbard Peel (October, 1986-August, 1987) and Roberta A. Leighton (September-October, 1987) are also acknowledged with gratitude.

Weymouth T. Jordan, Jr.
Editor

March 8, 1990

NORTH CAROLINA TROOPS
1861-1865
A ROSTER

Cicero A. Durham served as Assistant Quartermaster of the 49th Regiment. His position as a regimental staff officer required the buff piping on his coat and vest. The three bars on his collar denote the rank of Captain. Although Assistant Quartermasters were theoretically noncombatants, Durham habitually pitched into any accessible battle with gusto. He was mortally wounded at Drewry's Bluff, Virginia, in May, 1864. His service record appears on page 26 of this volume. Image furnished by The Museum of the Confederacy, Richmond, Virginia.

Charles Duffy, Jr., Surgeon of the 49th Regiment, wears an unusual tunic with white collar and cuffs. His trousers and kepi are typical. He served with the regiment from the spring of 1864 until its surrender at Appomattox Court House on April 9, 1865. After the war Duffy went on to a distinguished medical career, founded a hospital in New Bern, and became one of the town's leading citizens. His service record appears on page 27 of this volume. Image furnished by Greg Mast, Roxboro, North Carolina.

49TH REGIMENT N.C. TROOPS

This regiment was organized at Camp Mangum, near Raleigh, on April 12, 1862, and was composed of men recruited primarily in the counties of Catawba, Chatham, Cleveland, Gaston, Iredell, Lincoln, McDowell, Mecklenburg, Moore, Rowan, and Rutherford. Its first colonel was Stephen Dodson Ramseur, a Lincoln County native and West Point graduate who had served previously as major of the 10th Regiment N.C. State Troops (1st Regiment N.C. Artillery). The men were issued uniforms, blankets, knapsacks, and canteens and, after being quartered briefly in log cabins built the previous winter, moved into "good wall tents."[1] A few days later the regiment moved its camp to a nearby open field and began its initiation into the skills, duties, and trials of soldiering. Private W. A. Day of Company I recalled the regimen at Camp Mangum as follows:

> [R]oll-call [was held at] about daylight, squad-drill from seven to eight, company drill from nine to eleven, battallion [*sic*] drill from one to three, dress parade at sundown, and roll call again at night, with the usual routine of guard duty.[2]

Rations consisted of flour, pickled beef and pork, peas, and rice. Although many of the married men "had the blues very badly" and there was considerable sickness in the camp—primarily measles and gastric disorders caused by bad water and poorly prepared food—most of the neophyte soldiers apparently "enjoyed [themselves] very well."[3] After a brief period of drilling with long, iron-tipped spears called "Confederate Pikes," the men were issued sixty-nine caliber muskets which, Private Day observed, seemingly dated, if not from "the Crusades," at least from "the Wars of Queen Anne."[4]

On May 2 the regiment was transferred from state to Confederate service. Two days later it was ordered to Goldsboro, which it reached by rail on May 5. There it set up camp just outside the town in a field near the railroad and was assigned to the division of Major General Theophilus H. Holmes. Drill continued six days a week. Sickness—attributed by Private Day to the "low and level" nature of the country and a diet of peas, "old bacon," and unsifted corn meal that was "not fit for a hog to eat"— plagued the regiment, and several men died.[5]

On May 21 the regiment was ordered to Petersburg, Virginia, where a powerful Federal army under Major General George B. McClellan was advancing up the peninsula between the James and York rivers and threatening Richmond, the Confederate capital. Reaching Weldon by rail at about midnight, the men took shelter under a railroad car shed that was to be their home for almost two weeks while they awaited a train to take them further north. On the morning of June 2 the men filed into boxcars and resumed their journey. They reached Petersburg shortly before noon the same day.

At Petersburg the 49th Regiment was assigned to the brigade of Brigadier General Robert Ransom, which also included the 24th Regiment N.C. Troops (14th Regiment N.C. Volunteers) and the 25th, 26th, 35th, and 48th Regiments N.C. Troops. The brigade then went into camp just north of the city. The ancient muskets with which the 49th had been

---

[1] W. A. Day, *A True History of Company I, 49th Regiment, North Carolina Troops, in the Great Civil War, Between the North and the South* (Newton, North Carolina: The Enterprise Job Office, 1893), 11, hereinafter cited as Day, *A True History Of Company I.*

[2] Day, *A True History of Company I,* 11.

[3] Day, *A True History of Company I,* 12.

[4] Day, *A True History of Company I,* 11-12.

[5] Day, *A True History of Company I,* 14.

armed were collected, and the men were issued Enfield, Springfield, and Fayetteville rifles. On June 17 the regiment saw its first action when it exchanged fire with Federal warships on the James River at City Point. Outgunned by the enemy, whose shots, according to Private Day, "flew all over us," the regiment fell back.[6] Its casualties, if any, were not reported. The men returned to Petersburg the next day.

On June 24 Ransom's brigade, including the 49th Regiment, was ordered to Richmond, where the long-anticipated battle with McClellan's advancing army appeared imminent. There the brigade was assigned to the command of Major General Benjamin Huger and placed in a reserve position on the Williamsburg Road. The next day the 49th was ordered forward to support Brigadier General A. R. Wright's Georgia brigade and lost three men wounded in a "heavy skirmish" near King's School House.[7]

The engagement at King's School House, inconsequential in itself, inaugurated a series of battles known as the Seven Days. During that bloody week the Confederate commander, General Robert E. Lee, launched a succession of ill-coordinated attacks against McClellan's right wing on the north side of the Chickahominy River and forced the gargantuan Federal army back from the gates of Richmond. Although only briefly under fire during the next five days, the 49th Regiment was almost constantly on the move, suffering severely from the stifling summer heat and a water shortage. By July 1 the Federals appeared to Lee to be in full retreat and so demoralized that one more attack might encompass their destruction. He therefore ordered an assault on a virtually impregnable Federal position at Malvern Hill.[8]

Although scarcely 100 feet high, Malvern Hill dominated the surrounding terrain, was protected on its flanks by swamps, creeks, and ravines, and was approachable only through a wide "clover field."[9] A fence and the edge of a marsh provided additional obstacles. Atop the hill 100 Federal cannon were in place, with another 150 on the flanks and in reserve. Lee, after trying unsuccessfully for most of the day to get his artillery into position, ordered an attack in the late afternoon in the mistaken belief that the Federals were withdrawing. The result was one of the war's more horrific slaughters. Rushing forward toward Malvern Hill's frowning, mile-and-a-half-long crest, the Confederates were scythed down in files by "sheets" of canister and case shot.[10] The 24th, 25th, and 35th regiments of Ransom's brigade, which were in reserve, were sent to the aid of Major General John B. Magruder's division on the Confederate right and were followed at about twilight by the 26th and 49th regiments.

[W]e moved out of the woods into the clover field [Private Day recalled], and were soon in full view of the hill. We moved rapidly across the field, keeping our lines in perfect order under the terrible fire from the batteries. . . . When we reached the fence a staff officer was there sitting on his horse crying at the top of his voice: "Lord God Almighty double quick, they are cutting our men all to pieces," and kept on repeating the words as long as we could hear him. In crossing the fence and swamp our lines were broken and, moving on to the foot of the hill where we were sheltered from the fire, we reformed our line. In a few moments the command to charge was

---

[6]Day, *A True History of Company I*, 16.

[7]Letter dated July 10, 1862, from 49th Regiment Adjutant Cicero A. Durham, published in *Wilmington Journal* (Weekly), July 24, 1862. See also R. N. Scott and others (eds.), *The War of the Rebellion: A Compilation of the Official Records of the Union and Confederate Armies* (Washington: Government Printing Office, 70 Volumes, 1880-1901), Series I, XI, Part II, 792, 805-806, hereinafter cited as *Official Records (Army)*; Day, *A True History of Company I*, 17-18.

[8]An overblown but basically accurate account of the activities and movements of Ransom's brigade during the Seven Days appears in the Charlotte *Daily Bulletin* of July 19, 1862. The writer, presumably a member of Ransom's brigade, signed himself "Rip Van Winkle."

[9]Day, *A True History of Company I*, 19.

[10]Day, *A True History of Company I*, 19.

given. We gave what the Yankees were pleased to call the "rebel yell," and started at a double quick up the hill, and were soon breasting the storm.[11]

Thirty feet from the batteries the Confederate infantrymen, "wrapped . . . in flames" by cannon fire that General Ransom categorized as "beyond description," staggered to a halt.

We . . . fired round after round at the Yankee artillerymen, whose faces shined by the flash of their guns [Day's account continued]. Our firing seemed to make no impression on them.[12]

Flinging themselves down, the men maintained their position for a few minutes and then retreated to the shelter of a swale at the foot of the hill. There, in the darkness and confusion, some members of the 49th failed to receive an order to fall back and spent a harrowing, rainy night listening to the moans and supplications of the wounded. During the night the Federal army continued its withdrawal to Harrison's Landing, on the James, leaving the Confederates in possession of the field. The 49th Regiment then marched about a mile through the woods and went into camp.

The timber was cut and slashed all to pieces [Private Day recalled] and in some places whole trees were cut down by the shells. The dead and wounded were lying all through the woods and fields and details of men were burying the dead and caring for the wounded. The surgeons were busy all day amputating limbs. We built fires and stood around them shivering, trying to get dry. It rained nearly all day. . . .[13]

Casualties in the 49th Regiment at Malvern Hill were officially reported as 18 men killed, 70 wounded, and 16 missing.[14]

Two days after the battle the 49th Regiment was sent to Turkey Bend, twenty miles below Richmond on the James River. On July 6 the men arrived back in Richmond after an exhausting march through searing heat. The next day they moved with the rest of the brigade to Drewry's Bluff, a fortified position on the James below Richmond that protected the Confederate capital from waterborne Federal attack. At Drewry's Bluff the men were set to work constructing breastworks. Guard duty, drill, and dress parade also occupied much of their time. Sickness, probably caused by brackish drinking water drawn from three-foot-deep wells, continued to plague the regiment. A number of deaths resulted, including that of Private Johann H. Stroup of Company H who fell across a doctor's lap and died during an examination.[15]

On July 29 the brigade was ordered to Petersburg, where it went into camp on the City Point Road "in a high level field."[16] There the men remained, building fortifications, until August 19, when they were ordered to Richmond. On the 23rd they moved briefly to Drewry's Bluff, returning to Richmond on the 26th. On that day the brigade entrained for Rapidan Station, about sixty miles northwest of Richmond near Orange Court House, where

[11]Day, *A True History of Company I*, 20.

[12]*Official Records (Army)*, Series I, XI, Part II, 795; Day, *A True History of Company I*, 20.

[13]Day, *A True History of Company I*, 21.

[14]*Official Records (Army)*, Series I, XI, Part II, 507, 509. The roster of the 49th Regiment compiled for this volume lists 30 men killed or mortally wounded, 72 wounded, and 12 captured at Malvern Hill. Adjutant Durham's letter cited above in footnote 7 indicates that the 49th Regiment lost 14 men killed, 79 wounded, and 14 missing. The letter also contains a brief account of the regiment's part in the battle.

[15]Day, *A True History of Company I*, 23.

[16]Day, *A True History of Company I*, 24.

it remained during the Confederate victory at Second Manassas on August 29-30. At about that time Ransom's brigade was placed in the division temporarily commanded by Brigadier General John G. Walker, and Walker's division was assigned to the command of Major General James Longstreet. The 48th Regiment had been transferred to Walker's former brigade on June 26, 1862, and the 26th Regiment was now transferred to Brigadier General James J. Pettigrew's new brigade. Thus Ransom's brigade was composed of the 24th, 25th, 35th, and 49th Regiments N.C. Troops.

On about September 5 Ransom's brigade joined the Army of Northern Virginia near Leesburg to take part in General Lee's impending Maryland campaign. Two days later the brigade crossed the Potomac River at the Leesburg fords and proceeded northward to Monocacy Junction, near Frederick, which it reached on September 8. On the 9th the brigade, with the rest of Walker's division, was ordered to march some ten miles southward to the mouth of the Monocacy River to destroy the aqueduct of the Chesapeake and Ohio Canal. The aqueduct was seized that evening after a brief skirmish with Federal pickets but proved, because of its "massive" masonry, impervious to Confederate demolition efforts.[17]

Walker then received orders to recross the Potomac and move westward to Harpers Ferry, where a large but vulnerable Federal garrison in the deep valley at the junction of the Potomac and Shenandoah rivers posed a threat to Lee's line of communications. After an arduous march two regiments of Walker's division, the 27th North Carolina and 30th Virginia, occupied Loudoun Heights, southeast of the town, on September 13. The remainder of the division, including the 49th Regiment, was placed "in a strong position to prevent the escape of the enemy down the south bank of the Potomac."[18] Maryland Heights, across the river, was seized by Confederate forces under Major General Lafayette McLaws, while to the west Major General Thomas J. Jackson's command occupied Bolivar Heights. Surrounded, the 12,000-man Federal garrison surrendered on the morning of September 15 after a brief bombardment.

In the meantime McClellan, having learned the exact nature of Lee's plans and dispositions from the famous "lost order," was advancing ponderously from the east, hoping to relieve the Harpers Ferry garrison, drive a wedge through the dangerously divided Confederate army, and destroy it piecemeal. First, however, he would have to cross South Mountain, a high ridge stretching approximately fifty miles northward from a point just northeast of Harpers Ferry. Beyond South Mountain Lee's army, whose extremities were about twenty-five miles apart, was strung out from Harpers Ferry to Hagerstown.

On September 14 the Confederate forces north of Harpers Ferry battled courageously at long odds to hold the South Mountain gaps but were finally forced from their positions after nightfall. Informed by a civilian sympathizer of the Federal discovery of the lost order, Lee instructed his scattered units to concentrate at Sharpsburg, where he planned to ford the Potomac. However, on the morning of the 15th news of the fall of Harpers Ferry arrived, and Lee decided to stand and fight.

A hard night march brought most of Jackson's command to Sharpsburg by the afternoon of the 16th. Walker's division, moving westward on the afternoon of the 15th, crossed the Shenandoah River, rested briefly, took up the march again about midnight, forded the Potomac (for the third time in ten days) on the morning of the 16th, and reached Sharpsburg that afternoon. About three o'clock that night the division was moved to the extreme right of the Confederate line along Antietam Creek, a deep little stream averaging about twenty-five yards in width that, scarcely a mile to the south of the division's position at Snavely's Ford,

---

[17]*Official Records (Army)*, Series I, XIX, Part I, 912.
[18]*Official Records (Army)*, Series I, XIX, Part I, 913.

emptied into the Potomac. McClellan, meantime, after inching his cautious way forward on the 15th, spent the 16th observing the Confederate lines and formulating plans—thereby squandering any opportunity to destroy Lee's army while it was still divided. By the morning of the 17th the Federals were ready to give battle.

Across Antietam Creek, Lee's line stretched for about four miles along a low ridge. Farm houses, corn fields, orchards, woods, meadows, and fences dotted the landscape, and natural defensive positions were provided by swales, hollows, ravines, and limestone outcroppings. In the middle of the line a sunken road ran north from the nondescript little town of Sharpsburg, whose apprehensive citizens were in flight or battening down in cellars or caves. Just west of the road, about a mile north of Sharpsburg, stood a small, whitewashed Dunker church. Four stone bridges spanned the Antietam, but the central and northern portions of Lee's line diverged from the creek so that only one bridge, called the Rohrbach Bridge after a local family, would be contested. Lee's army numbered about 40,000 men, barely half of the 75,000 commanded by McClellan. With the Potomac less than two miles in the Confederate rear and fordable only at Boteler's Ford, near the southern end of the Confederate line, loss of the battle would mean the probable destruction of the Army of Northern Virginia. Lee, however, planned to fight a defensive, opportunistic battle. He was also relying heavily on the congenital circumspection of McClellan, whose great organizational, managerial, and inspirational abilities were negated by an inability to improvise when faced with the unexpected, a disastrous tendency to overestimate the strength of his opponents, and an evident conviction that it was more important not to lose battles than to win them. McClellan's plan was to open with a heavy attack on the Confederate left in concert with a diversionary assault on the right, thereby forcing Lee to weaken the center of his line. A powerful thrust through the vulnerable Confederate center would then split and destroy Lee's army.

At daybreak on the misty morning of the 17th a Federal corps under Major General Joseph Hooker surged forward against the Confederate left, held by three divisions of Jackson's command. A desperate, seesaw battle ensued through woods, pastures, and a cornfield. First one side and then the other gained a temporary advantage as fresh units joined the fighting and artillery fire exacted a murderous toll. A large and potentially disastrous gap torn in Jackson's line was plugged at the last moment by the arrival of a reserve division under Brigadier General John B. Hood, whose attack drove Hooker back in confusion. After Hood's division was shot to pieces, a second, poorly led Federal corps under Brigadier General Joseph Mansfield pitched into the frazzled Confederates. When that attack lost steam, a division of Major General Edwin Sumner's corps stormed forward.

In the meantime, the diversionary attack planned by McClellan against the Confederate right had failed to materialize, permitting Lee to bring reinforcements to Jackson's tottering position. McLaws's division, ordered to Jackson's support, arrived in the vicinity of the Dunker church with other units in time to take Sumner's unsuspecting division in the flank with a series of crushing volleys that carpeted the ground with blue-clad bodies and sent the survivors flying. Pursuing the Federals into the open fields beyond the woods, the Confederates were brought up short by ravaging blasts from a line of Federal batteries. Walker's division, including the 49th Regiment, ordered over from the Confederate right, then stumbled into the maelstrom and repulsed a feeble Federal attack belatedly launched to assist Sumner.

The focus of the battle now shifted to the center, where a series of costly Federal assaults by Sumner's other two divisions finally routed units under Major General D. H. Hill from the sunken road, leaving the Confederate dead piled three deep and again threatening catastrophe. Improvising frantically, Longstreet organized a few batteries to hold back the swarming Federals while Hill, brandishing a musket, led a 200-man counterattack. To the north, in the vicinity of the Dunker church, a weak assault in which the 49th Regiment took part unexpectedly succeeded in driving the Federals from their hard-earned lodgment in the West Woods, creating a din to the rear that gave pause to the Federals advancing beyond the sunken road. Presently, the 49th found itself charging across a meadow into a "tornado of canister" pumped into its ranks by a row of Federal cannon.[19] Carrying their wounded, the men fell back to the West Woods, where they helped repel three Federal regiments that launched a rash and unsupported charge against the Dunker Church. During the remainder of the day the regiment remained prone in the woods, enduring a mind-numbing storm of artillery fire that "[tore] the trees asunder, lopp[ed] off huge branches, and fill[ed] the air with shrieks and explosions."[20]

Meantime, at the sunken road, ever after to be known as "Bloody Lane," the desperate efforts of Longstreet and Hill had bought sufficient time for the Confederates to emplace a powerful linc of cannon. In the face of stiffening Confederate opposition, the Federal attack lost momentum and receded. McClellan now looked to the depleted Confederate right, where the corps of Major General Ambrose E. Burnside, following three hours of frustration and mounting casualties, had at last forced a crossing of Antietam Creek. After pausing for two hours to perfect arrangements for an assault that, if delivered sooner, would almost certainly have destroyed Lee's army, Burnside ordered his men forward in a seemingly inexorable advance. Sweeping the weak Confederate opposition before them, the Federals were within a few hundred yards of entering Sharpsburg and cutting Lee's line of retreat to Boteler's Ford when Major General A. P. Hill's division, newly arrived on the battlefield after a frantic march from Harpers Ferry, struck them in the left flank and sent them reeling back to the west bank of the Antietam. Although possessing a two-to-one advantage over Hill, Burnside felt unable to resume the offensive without reinforcements. These McClellan declined to provide, although 20,000 men in two Federal corps had yet to see action. Twelve hours after it began, the fighting ended. The next day the two armies remained on the ghastly, corpse-strewn field without offering battle, and on the night of the 18th the Army of Northern Virginia recrossed the Potomac. Confederate casualties during the battle numbered 1,546 killed, 7,752 wounded, and 1,018 missing, for a total of 10,316; Federal losses numbered 2,108 killed, 9,549 wounded, and 753 missing, for a total of 12,410. The 49th Regiment was officially reported to have lost 16 men killed and 61 wounded, the most severe losses among the four regiments of Ransom's brigade.[21]

The Army of Northern Virginia retreated up the Shenandoah Valley to Martinsburg. On September 27th it moved to the vicinity of Winchester, where it remained for almost a month. On October 22 Walker's division, including the 49th Regiment, was ordered to cross the Blue Ridge Mountains at Ashby's Gap and take a position just east of the gap near Upperville. Four days later McClellan began crossing the Potomac and moving down the eastern slopes of the Blue Ridge in a halfhearted attempt, at the insistence of President Lincoln, to interpose his army between Lee and Richmond. On October 28 Lee ordered Longstreet's corps to move east of the mountains to Culpeper Court House; Jackson's corps was instructed to remain in the Shenandoah Valley, near Winchester, to threaten the Federal flank. Walker's division remained for the time being in the vicinity of Upperville. By November 3 McClellan had

---

[19]Milo M. Quaife (ed.), *From the Cannon's Mouth: The Civil War Letters of General Alpheus S. Williams* (Detroit: Wayne State University Press, 1959), 129.

[20]*Official Records (Army)*, Series I, XIX, Part I, 916. See also *Official Records (Army)*, Series I, XIX, Part I, 919-921.

[21]*Official Records (Army)*, Series I, XIX, Part I, 811. The roster of the 49th Regiment prepared for this volume lists 26 men killed or mortally wounded, 43 wounded, and 12 captured at Sharpsburg.

reached the area of Warrenton in his snail-like progress to find Longstreet blocking his route of advance. Exasperated beyond endurance by McClellan's delays and complaints, Lincoln sacked the Federal commander on November 7 and replaced him with the affable but unimaginative, obstinate, and self-doubting Burnside, who was instructed to get on with the war. Moving with unwonted decisiveness, Burnside quickly produced a plan: he would concentrate his army south of Warrenton, as if to attack Longstreet at Culpeper Court House, and then lunge suddenly southeastward against Fredericksburg, on the south bank of the Rappahannock River. From Fredericksburg, where he could receive supplies by water rather than by railroads vulnerable to the ubiquitous Jackson and his cavalry cohort, General J. E. B. Stuart, he proposed somewhat vaguely to "move . . . upon Richmond."[22]

On November 15 the Army of the Potomac advanced. Two days later it reached Falmouth, across and just upriver from Fredericksburg. Unable to cross the Rappahannock because of the nonarrival of bridging equipment he had requisitioned, Burnside was also fearful that one part of his army might become isolated from the other if he attempted to ford the frigid, rising river and seize the formidable but virtually undefended heights above Fredericksburg. He therefore settled down fretfully to await his pontoons.

In the meantime the 49th Regiment, with the rest of Walker's division, departed from Upperville on October 31 and after a three-day march rejoined Longstreet at Culpeper Court House on November 3. The next day the 49th moved about six miles south to Cedar Run. On the 8th the regiment left Cedar Run on a two-day march westward through flurrying snow to Madison Court House. Ten days later, after news was received of Burnside's presence on the Rappahannock, the men set out on a "forced march" to Fredericksburg.

> We marched sixteen miles the first day [Private Day of the 49th recalled]. . . . The weather was cold and rainy and the roads almost knee-deep in mud and water. We were on the march four days and suffered terribly. It rained three days in succession and one night when we were camped on the side of a hill it rained so hard that when we lay down the water would run under us. It rained our fires out and we had to rest the best we could.[23]

Longstreet's bedraggled, hollow-eyed men began arriving at Fredericksburg on November 20 and went into position on Marye's Heights, a long ridge whose open slopes afforded an excellent field of fire. Walker's former division, under the command of Robert Ransom since the transfer of Walker on November 7, was posted in a reserve position. Jackson's corps, on the march from Winchester since November 22, reached Fredericksburg on November 30 and was deployed downstream at various crossings and key points to intercept any attack that Burnside might launch against the vulnerable Confederate right. On November 25 Burnside's long-awaited pontoons began arriving, but by then the Federal commander, apprehensively watching the growing Confederate force atop Marye's Heights, was having second thoughts about a direct attack on Fredericksburg. Another week went by while the possibility of an attack downstream at Skinker's Neck was assessed. By then Jackson's men were in position, and Burnside was forced to think again. Convinced that the Marye's Heights position had been weakened to guard the Confederate flank, Burnside reverted to his original strategy: he would bridge the Rappahannock at Fredericksburg and launch a frontal assault.

At 2 a.m. on the morning of December 11 Federal engineers set to work assembling three pontoon bridges at Fredericksburg and two more a mile downstream, where a second Federal

---

[22]*Official Records (Army)*, Series I, XIX, Part II, 552. Colonel Ramseur was appointed brigadier general on November 1, 1862, and transferred. Lieutenant Colonel LeRoy M. McAfee, a Cleveland County attorney, was promoted to colonel in Ramseur's place and commanded the regiment for the remainder of the war.

[23]Day, *A True History of Company I*, 30-31.

force under Brigadier General William B. Franklin was to cross. As the sun rose and the morning mist burned off, a Mississippi brigade in the town opened fire on the bridge-builders from a distance of eighty yards, killing and wounding several and sending the remainder scrambling for cover. A Federal artillery barrage temporarily suppressed the sharpshooters, but when the fire lifted they opened up again. A new bombardment, this time by about 100 guns, set parts of the town ablaze but once more failed to subdue the stubborn Mississippians, whereupon Federal infantry were sent across the river in boats. A vicious little battle through the streets ensued as the Confederates fell back to a sunken road behind a stone wall at the foot of Marye's Heights.

His bridges in place at last, Burnside crossed the Rappahannock the next morning and began organizing for an attack. In the meantime Lee recalled Jackson's scattered divisions from their positions below Fredericksburg and positioned them on Longstreet's right. At 10 a.m. on the morning of the 13th Franklin's command assaulted Jackson. Shortly thereafter the Federal right wing advanced into a storm of musketry and cannon fire at Marye's Heights. As the Federal dead piled up before the stone wall, the suicidal nature of Burnside's plan seemingly became apparent to every Federal on the field except Burnside, who continued to hammer away. After seven ill-coordinated, division-strength Federal attacks were methodically shot to pieces by the incredulous and increasingly sickened Confederates, Burnside called a halt as darkness fell.

Meanwhile, on the Federal left, Franklin, pleading a lack of clarity in his orders, had been inactive for hours, permitting Lee to bring over reinforcements. In fact, however, there was not much need for them. Many of Longstreet's regiments, including the 49th North Carolina, saw little or no action. Several members of the 49th were wounded by a shell around 1:00 p.m. as the regiment moved up from a reserve position to an artillery redoubt just to the left of the junction of the sunken road and the Orange Court House Turnpike. There, Captain Henry Chambers of Company C noted in his diary, "we lay all day," taking a few more casualties while "the shells and rifle balls pass[ed] over us in showers."[24] On the night of the 14th the regiment was ordered to the sunken road, where a sudden flurry of firing on the picket line prompted a wild volley from the men of the 49th that wounded one of their own pickets. The Federals began withdrawing across the Rappahannock that night, and by the morning of the 16th the last of them were gone, leaving perhaps 2,000 dead buried on the field. Another 9,000 or so wounded remained behind in hospitals or rolled north in ambulances. Confederate casualties, most of which were sustained by Jackson's corps, numbered about 5,000. In the 49th Regiment one man, Private J. H. Putnam of Company G, was killed and thirteen wounded.[25]

The 49th Regiment remained in camp near Fredericksburg until January 3, 1863, when it was ordered to North Carolina with the rest of Ransom's brigade to guard the Wilmington and Weldon Railroad. Proceeding on foot, the regiment arrived at a point just north of Petersburg on January 7 and went into camp.[26] On the 17th it departed by rail for Weldon, which it

[24]T. H. Pearce and Selby A. Daniels (eds.), *Diary of Captain Henry A. Chambers* (Wendell, North Carolina: Broadfoot's Bookmark, 1983), 75, hereinafter cited as Pearce and Daniels, *Diary of Captain Chambers*.

[25]In his report on the battle in *Official Records (Army)*, Series I, XXI, 625-629, General Ransom reported the losses of the 49th Regiment at Fredericksburg as one man killed and eight wounded; however, five additional wounded were identified by the staff of the Civil War Roster Project in preparing a roster for the 49th.

[26]While at Petersburg, Company B of the 49th Regiment was transferred as a unit to the 15th Regiment N.C. Troops (5th Regiment N.C. Volunteers) in exchange for Company D of that regiment. The reasons for this exchange are uncertain but may have had something to do with the fact that the 49th Regiment was composed primarily of companies from the western part of the state and the 15th was made up principally of eastern-county companies. A Chatham County company (from the east) went to the 15th Regiment in exchange for a Cleveland County company (from the west).

reached late that afternoon. During the night the train proceeded to Goldsboro with the men "crowded and jammed" in the boxcars and suffering intensely from the "piercing" cold.[27] On the 18th the train continued on to Warsaw, where the regiment camped for three days before marching to Kenansville on the 22nd. There the men enjoyed a month's respite, drilling when the rainy weather permitted and performing picket duty but otherwise employed in such gratifying tasks as improving their winter quarters, consuming the ample rations with which they were blessed, writing letters, attending church, and courting the local belles. During this period a new regiment, the 56th North Carolina, was assigned to the brigade.

On February 22 the regiment boarded flatcars and moved to Wilmington. There the men remained for another quiet month, taking no part in D. H. Hill's abortive attempt to recapture New Bern. On March 25th and 26th the brigade moved by rail to Goldsboro. Eight days later, on April 2, the 49th and 56th regiments took the cars to Kinston, where they remained for two weeks. After Hill abandoned his unsuccessful siege of Washington, North Carolina, on April 16, the regiment was ordered to Wise's Forks, a few miles southeast of Kinston, where it was divided into several groups of two or three companies each and sent out to picket various roads. A few shots were exchanged with Federal artillery on the 17th, and on the 20th, at Sandy Ridge (Lenoir County), twenty-eight members of Companies A and B were captured after their outpost was overrun.[28] Three members of the 49th were wounded, one of whom, Private F. W. Cabaniss of Company B, died. Four days later the 49th was relieved by the 56th Regiment and returned to Wise's Forks.

On May 6 the regiment was sent to Moseley Creek, about nine miles northwest of Kinston, where it remained on picket duty until May 12. At Gum Swamp (Jones County), on the 22nd, the 25th and 56th regiments of Ransom's brigade were surprised and virtually surrounded by five Federal regiments and forced to fight their way out or flee into the swamps. More than 160 members of the 56th were captured. The 49th Regiment, sent to the aid of its sister units after several of its own companies narrowly evaded the Federal trap, helped force the Federals back toward New Bern. Led by the combative D. H. Hill, the pursuing Confederates overtook the Federals and shelled them out of their bivouac around midnight. Delaying only long enough to "fire the woods," the Federals beat a hasty retreat eastward.[29] Following another skirmish the next day at Core Creek, the regiment returned to its camp near Kinston on May 25.

On May 30 the regiment departed by rail for Petersburg, which it reached via Goldsboro and Weldon on the 31st. Although the men expected to rejoin the Army of Northern Virginia to take part in what proved to be Lee's ill-fated Gettysburg campaign, Ransom's entire brigade was retained in the Richmond-Petersburg area under orders of the War Department. On June 1 the brigade was sent down the Norfolk and Petersburg Railroad to Ivor Station, about thirty-five miles southeast of Petersburg near the Blackwater River. It returned to Petersburg on June 12 and was ordered to Drewry's Bluff. On June 17 the brigade moved back to Petersburg. Brigadier General Matt W. Ransom, assigned to command the brigade after the promotion of his brother Robert to the rank of major general, assumed his new duties the same day. Thus the 49th Regiment, with the 24th, 25th, 35th, and 56th regiments, was now in Matt Ransom's brigade of Robert Ransom's division.

---

[27]Pearce and Daniels, *Diary of Captain Chambers*, 86.
[28]*Official Records (Army)*, Series I, XVIII, 226, 239-240, 255.
[29]*Greensboro Patriot* (Weekly), June 4, 1863.

On June 21 the brigade, with the exception of the 35th Regiment, returned to Drewry's Bluff, where it remained for four days before marching on to Richmond. There, on July 2, the men were involved in a skirmish at Bottom's Bridge, on the Chickahominy River about twelve miles east of Richmond. The brigade then marched back to Richmond, where it remained for a few days before moving to Petersburg. On July 27, after the return of Lee's battered army from Gettysburg, the brigade was dispatched by rail to Weldon to protect the vital railroad bridge there from raiding Federal cavalrymen. On July 28 the Federals, vastly superior in numbers but poorly led, were repulsed by eight companies of the 49th Regiment and four of the 24th in a skirmish at Boone's Mill (Northampton County). Some of the Confederate defenders were enjoying an au naturel swim in the millpond and were forced by the sudden Federal attack to fight the battle in various degrees of undress.[30] One member of the 49th, Private John Drum of Company I, was killed and two slightly wounded.[31] After pursuing the enemy as far as Jackson, in Northampton County, the men marched to Garysburg, across the Roanoke River from Weldon.

On August 12 the 49th Regiment moved to Tarboro, and on the 15th the men marched to Rocky Mount. Four days later they returned by rail to Garysburg, where they remained for more than two months performing fatigue duty, drilling, and guarding the railroad bridge. On November 2 the regiment moved to Kinston, on the 29th it returned by rail to Weldon, and on December 3 it moved to Tarboro. An anticipated enemy raid having failed to materialize, the regiment returned to Weldon on December 4. There the men constructed "cabins" consisting of log walls about four feet high roofed with "flies" (tent squares).[32] About two weeks later the regiment was sent to Murfreesboro, in Hertford County, "to drive off or capture a large body of Yankees and negroes" who were "carrying on at a high rate" in that part of the state.[33] These irregulars, known as "Buffaloes," offered little resistance before scattering into the swamps. On December 23 the regiment returned once more to Weldon.

In late January and early February, 1864, Matt Ransom's brigade, including the 49th Regiment, took part in Major General George E. Pickett's attempt to recapture New Bern. Located at the confluence of the Neuse and Trent rivers, New Bern served as a base for Federal raiders whose depredations in the eastern part of the state had resulted in the destruction of large quantities of foodstuffs and other property and devastated civilian morale. Pickett, commanding a force of about 13,000 men concentrated at Kinston, planned a three-column attack. One column, under Brigadier General Robert F. Hoke, was to move directly against New Bern between the Neuse and Trent, "endeavor to surprise the troops on Batchelder's Creek, silence the guns in the Star fort and batteries near the Neuse, and penetrate the town in that direction."[34] A second column, commanded by Brigadier General Seth M. Barton and including Ransom's brigade, was to advance along the south bank of the Trent and capture the three forts defending New Bern's southern approaches. If practicable, Barton's column was to cross the Atlantic and North Carolina Railroad bridge into the town, and, if unable to capture it, prevent any reinforcements from arriving by land or water from Beaufort or Morehead City. The third column, under Colonel James Dearing, would move down the north bank of the Neuse, neutralize or capture Fort Anderson (across the Neuse

---

[30]Don Causey, Sr., "The Naked Battle," *The State*, XLVIII (March, 1981), 14-16. See also *Official Records (Army)*, Series I, XXVII, Part II, 982-983, 985; T. C. Parramore, "The Roanoke-Chowan Story (Chapter 8), Five Days in July, 1863," Ahoskie, North Carolina *Daily Roanoke-Chowan News*, Civil War Supplement, 1960, 92.

[31]Edward X. Phifer to his mother, July 31, 1863, Edward Phifer Papers, Southern Historical Collection, University of North Carolina Library at Chapel Hill, hereinafter cited as Phifer Papers.

[32]Day, *A True History of Company I*, 50.

[33]Pearce and Daniels, *Diary of Captain Chambers*, 159.

[34]*Official Records (Army)*, Series I, XXXIII, 1102.

from New Bern), and attempt to situate itself so as to open an enfilading fire on the works defending the town against Hoke. At the same time a naval force of fourteen cutters would descend the Neuse and attack any Federal gunboats that were encountered.

On the morning of January 30, 1864, Pickett's three columns set out toward their various objectives. Hoke's column crossed Batchelder's Creek on the morning of February 1, captured an enemy blockhouse, and then moved on to New Bern, where it halted to await Barton's attack from the south.[35] Barton's men, meanwhile, crossed the Trent on a pontoon bridge, and, moving via Trenton, reached a point two or three miles north of the deserted and "almost entirely destroyed" village of Pollocksville, where they camped on the night of the 31st.[36] "This country shows the sad effects of war," Captain Chambers noted in his diary.

> [We saw] large farms lying untilled and unattended, deserted negro quarters, dilapidated fences and outhouses and occasionally the charred vestiges of some residences where the vandal invaders had wreaked their vengeance upon some secessionist.[37]

On the morning of February 1 Barton arrived at his objective to find himself confronted by a seeming maze of breastworks, blockhouses, gun emplacements, forts, and felled trees set in terrain that was dangerously open in some places and impassably marshy in others. Convinced that the "serious" obstacles before him were "insurmountable" by any means at his disposal, Barton contented himself with the seizure of a Federal outpost and an exchange of artillery fire with the enemy while awaiting new instructions from Pickett.[38] On the night of February 2, under orders from Pickett, Barton began to withdraw. "Such a march we had last night!" Captain Chambers lamented in his diary.

> The road through this low, swampy country was bad enough as we went down, but now the rain and the constant passing and repassing of artillery, cavalry and the wagon trains had rendered it terrible. It was one vast mudhole about the consistency of batter and about shoemouth deep as a general thing, with frequent places of much greater depth. The night was dark and its darkness was enhanced by the thick swamp forest on either side of the road. This precluded all idea of avoiding the mud by taking the woods on either side, for if one left the mud he would be entangled in an almost inextricable network of bamboo briers. The orders were to keep the men well closed up, but this order was unnecessary as the discharge of firearms towards the rear answered every purpose. The men were pervaded with the [erroneous] belief that the enemy was close upon us and . . . no other means [was] necessary to urge them forward. On we went, plunging through the mud, sometimes at the shoemouth and sometimes up to our knees. Frequently, men would stick fast . . . and have to be pulled out by main force. Wagons stalled and several horses and mules were killed in the rush.[39]

Visibility improved somewhat after the men began setting fire to the turpentine-rich pine trees that lined the road and making torches from their branches. Floundering into

---

[35]*Official Records (Army)*, Series I, XXXIII, 96. See also Edward X. Phifer to his mother, February 4, [1864], Phifer Papers.

[36]Pearce and Daniels, *Diary of Captain Chambers*, 170. It appears probable that, contrary to the reports of Generals Pickett and Barton in *Official Records (Army)*, Series I, XXXIII, 92-94, 97-99, Barton's column did not set out from Kinston until the morning of January 31, 1864.

[37]Pearce and Daniels, *Diary of Captain Chambers*, 170.

[38]*Official Records (Army)*, Series I, XXXIII, 98.

[39]Pearce and Daniels, *Diary of Captain Chambers*, 173.

Pollocksville about midnight, the exhausted soldiers camped for the night before resuming their retreat the next morning. In the meantime, Colonel Dearing, across the Neuse, sent word to Pickett that Fort Anderson, his objective, was too powerful to attack. An angry and frustrated Pickett then canceled the entire operation and, calling for a court of inquiry into the conduct of the hapless Barton, ordered all three columns to withdraw to Kinston.[40]

Mud-caked and frazzled, the men of the 49th reached the vicinity of Kinston on the afternoon of February 4 after a frigid, fireless night in the swamps. The regiment returned to Weldon by rail on February 7 but was immediately ordered to Petersburg, where it arrived on the evening of February 8. Finding that its orders to proceed to Petersburg had been occasioned by a false alarm, the regiment returned to Weldon on February 10.

Two weeks later, on February 24, the 49th was sent by rail with the rest of the brigade to Franklin, Virginia, under orders to conduct a "foraging and destroying" expedition in the direction of Suffolk and the Dismal Swamp Canal.[41] On the 26th the brigade marched out of Franklin and, after passing through Gatesville, North Carolina, reached South Mills, in Camden County, North Carolina, on the morning of the 28th. Following a skirmish with the enemy near South Mills on March 1 during which ten prisoners—"mostly Dutch"—were captured, the brigade fell back toward Franklin on the 5th with "50,000 pounds of bacon and other stores of value."[42] On March 8th the men were diverted to Suffolk, where they captured the camp of a contingent of black Federal cavalrymen the next day, seized a large stock of clothing and blankets, and massacred a number of prisoners. In a letter published in the Charlotte *Daily Bulletin* of March 18, 1864, an unnamed member of Ransom's brigade recounted the day's bloody events as follows:

> We did not take *any* prisoners [during the capture of the camp]. Officers and men were perfectly enthusiastic in *killing* the "d....d rascals," as I heard many call them. Supposing that our force was a small one, ten negroes under a white officer, were placed in a house on the further extremity of town for the purpose of picking off our officers. When our line was formed near them to charge the Yanks they fired constantly upon us, killing two, and wounding some. They fought with desperation, seeing the hopelessness of their situation. A few minutes elapsed and the torch was applied to the dwelling. Soon the fire and smoke had its effect—suffocation commenced—one of the infernals leaped from the window to escape the horrible death of burning, a minute more and a dozen bayonets pierced his body; another, and another followed, and shared the same fate. Three stayed and met their doom with manly resolution. They were burned to cinders. After the flames enveloped the house, and immense clouds of smoke were issuing from . . . within, the crack of a rifle was heard above, and one of the artillery men fell severely wounded in the knee. This was the last fire from the house. Soon it fell and all was ashes. . . .
>
> Ransom's brigade never takes any negro prisoners. Our soldiers would not even bury the negroes—they were buried by negroes. If any of us should be captured by them, our fate would be hard.[43]

After holding Suffolk for two days, the brigade marched to Franklin, which it reached on the 12th. There the men boarded trains for Weldon, where they arrived the same day. During the Suffolk expedition Ransom's brigade lost two men killed and five wounded.[44]

---

[40]*Official Records (Army)*, Series I, XXXIII, 92-94.
[41]Day, *A True History of Company I*, 53.
[42]Charlotte *Daily Bulletin*, March 18, 1864.
[43]Charlotte *Daily Bulletin*, March 18, 1864. The exact number of "inhuman wretches [black cavalrymen]" who were killed at the camp is uncertain, but it appears that most of the Federals made their escape on horseback.
[44]Charlotte *Daily Bulletin*, March 18, 1864.

On March 30 the 49th Regiment, leaving the remainder of the brigade behind at Weldon, moved by rail to Boykin's Depot, just over the Virginia line about sixteen miles southwest of Franklin. It then marched, via Murfreesboro and Winton, to Harrellsville, in Hertford County, North Carolina. There it was assigned to picket duty on the Chowan River and along Albemarle Sound, taking no direct part in Hoke's recapture of Plymouth and Washington, North Carolina, but enjoying, in the rhapsodic words of one member of the regiment, "all the delights of springtime, beautiful scenery on sound and river, and in the opening life of woods and flowers. The fish and other delicacies of this favored region touched a tender spot in the make-up of veterans . . . and the period spent here marked a green spot in the memories of officers and men as the last space of repose and comfort, which fell to our lot during the struggle."[45]

This idyllic interlude came to an abrupt end on April 29 when the regiment departed from Harrellsville on a twenty-five mile march southwest in the direction of Windsor. On April 30 the regiment marched through Windsor and proceeded to Taylor's Ferry, where it forded the Roanoke River in the rain on May 1 and camped at Hamilton, in Martin County. The men then moved south to Greenville, crossed Contentnea Creek and the Neuse and Trent rivers, and proceeded to Trenton, which they reached on May 5. A planned attempt by Hoke to recapture New Bern was aborted when word was received the next day of Lieutenant General U. S. Grant's attack on Lee at the Wilderness, near Chancellorsville, Virginia. Responding to Lee's call for reinforcements, the 49th Regiment marched to Kinston and from there moved by rail to Weldon, where it arrived during the wee hours of May 9. It departed the same morning by rail for Jarratt's Station, about thirty miles south of Petersburg on the Weldon Railroad, to assist in driving off a Federal cavalry raid. The 49th then rejoined Ransom's brigade, which was now part of Hoke's division, at Petersburg on May 10.

During the week of May 5-11, 1864, while the Army of Northern Virginia and the Army of the Potomac were locked in deadly combat at the Wilderness and Spotsylvania Court House, a 39,000-man Federal army under Major General Benjamin F. Butler disembarked from transports a few miles northeast of Petersburg at City Point and Bermuda Hundred, a neck of land between the James and Appomattox rivers. After failing in an inept attempt to capture Petersburg and its vital railroad junctions, Butler began edging his way up the south bank of the James towards Richmond on the 12th. A Confederate force under General P. G. T. Beauregard, to which Ransom's brigade was assigned, fell back slowly before Butler to Drewry's Bluff, on the James. The 49th Regiment suffered moderate casualties on the 13th after it was nearly surrounded and forced to retreat through a swamp. An all-night rain followed during which the men "lay there in the mud and water, shivering without any fire."[46] More casualties were incurred the next day as the Federals, undeterred by the continuing downpour, raked the regiment's works with grape and canister while sharpshooters kept up a steady fire from a nearby woods. An unsuccessful attempt to dislodge the sharpshooters on the 15th resulted in additional losses.

---

[45]Walter Clark (ed.), *Histories of the Several Regiments and Battalions from North Carolina in the Great War, 1861-'65* (Raleigh and Goldsboro: State of North Carolina, 5 volumes, 1901), III, 134-135, hereinafter cited as Clark, *Histories of the North Carolina Regiments*. Although the 49th Regiment, having been selected to guard a flank, took no direct part in the attack on Plymouth, its popular, daredevil quartermaster, Cicero Durham, did. Durham's office in the 49th automatically excused him from combat, but he invariably pitched in with such relish that he became known as the "Fighting Quartermaster." At Plymouth he volunteered to command Ransom's skirmishers, a highly dangerous assignment. He was mortally wounded a few weeks later at Drewry's Bluff. See Edwin G. Moore, "Ransom's Brigade: Its Gallant Conduct in the Capture of Plymouth," *Southern Historical Society Papers*, XXXVI (1908), 363-367.

[46]Day, *A True History of Company I*, 65.

The next morning Beauregard launched an attack in an attempt to cut off Butler from his base at Bermuda Hundred. Beauregard's plan called for a heavy attack against the Federal right while the rest of his line conducted a vigorous demonstration to prevent the dispatch of reinforcements; however, lack of coordination among the Confederate commanders and a general disorientation resulting from a dense morning fog produced heavy fighting in the Confederate center as well. Matt Ransom's brigade was assigned to a reserve position near the center of the Confederate line, but the 24th and 49th regiments were soon ordered forward to the assistance of a brigade commanded by Brigadier General Bushrod R. Johnson. Moving at the double-quick through thick woods, the men of the 49th drove the Federals from a line of light fortifications before coming under an enfilading fire from the right. Facing to the right, the regiment charged and overran the Federal position, only to come up against a new and stronger line of battle. Its ranks considerably thinned by the "terrific" fire to which it had been subjected, the regiment fell back to the woods, where it remained until the success of Beauregard's attack on Butler's right caused a general retreat all along the Federal front.[47] Skirmishing continued on May 17, 18, and 19 as Butler completed his withdrawal. On May 20 the Confederates attacked again, thereby "corking" Butler's army in the Bermuda Hundred "bottle." During the fighting between May 14 and May 20 the 49th Regiment lost, according to information compiled by the regimental surgeon, 23 men killed, 117 wounded, and 3 missing.[48]

The 49th Regiment remained at Bermuda Hundred building fortifications and performing picket duty for the next two weeks. During that time it was assigned, along with the other regiments of Matt Ransom's brigade, to a newly formed division under Bushrod Johnson, who was promoted to the rank of major general. On the morning of June 2 a sortie by the regiment resulted in the capture of "many" prisoners and a line of rifle pits at a cost of 4 men killed or mortally wounded, 5 wounded, and 10 captured.[49] Two days later the brigade crossed the James on a pontoon bridge at Drewry's Bluff and marched to the vicinity of Bottom's Bridge. On June 5 the 49th and 56th regiments moved about a mile north and threw up rifle pits to protect the Richmond and York River Railroad bridge over the Chickahominy River. On June 11 the entire brigade was ordered to Chaffin's Bluff, about six miles south of Richmond on the James, where it arrived that afternoon. There, "almost oblivious" of the "distant roaring" of the guns to the north, the men enjoyed a few halcyon days, fishing and dining "magnificently" from the "luxuriant gardens" left behind by troops who had previously occupied the position.[50]

In the meantime, north of Richmond, Grant's Army of the Potomac, after a month of murderous fighting that culminated in a grisly bloodbath at Cold Harbor on June 3, prepared for another in a series of marches around the Army of Northern Virginia's right flank. On the night of June 12 Grant quietly pulled his men back and began a long southward sidle to the east of Richmond. Aware of Grant's departure but forced to remain north of the James to cover Richmond until he was certain that his opponent also intended to cross the river, Lee moved slowly south. On June 14 Grant began fording the James; at the same time a Federal

---

[47]Pearce and Daniels, *Diary of Captain Chambers*, 197.

[48]Raleigh *Daily Confederate*, May 26, 1864. The roster of the 49th Regiment prepared for this volume indicates that 42 men were killed or mortally wounded, 101 wounded, and 16 captured at Drewry's Bluff and Bermuda Hundred from May 13 through May 20, 1864. For a detailed account of the movements and activities of the 49th Regiment for the period April 29-May 21, 1864, see letter from Lieutenant Edward X. Phifer to his mother dated May 29, 1864, Phifer Papers.

[49]Pearce and Daniels, *Diary of Captain Chambers*, 201. Casualty figures are based on research for the roster prepared for this volume.

[50]Raleigh *Daily Confederate*, June 23, 1864.

corps under Major General W. F. Smith arrived by water to reinforce Butler. With Lee still north of the James, a vigorous attack the next day on Beauregard's ragtag force of 3,000 men manning the Petersburg fortifications would almost certainly have resulted in the capture of the city, isolating Richmond and changing the course of the war. However, the opportunity was bungled through delays, a reluctance to test the formidable Petersburg defenses after the butchery at Cold Harbor, and a series of tragicomic staff-work blunders. A Federal attack late in the day, although delivered with minimal determination, was more than sufficient to drive the Confederate defenders from a mile-long segment of their outer works. During the night Johnson's division, at Bermuda Hundred, was ordered to Petersburg, and Beauregard was further reinforced by the arrival of Hoke's division from north of the James, bringing his strength up to about 15,000 men. Major units of the Army of the Potomac also continued to arrive, and by sunrise on the 16th some 75,000 Federals were on the field.

Presented with their second opportunity in two days to fight what might well have been the decisive battle of the war, the Federals again failed to press their advantage. A series of disjointed attacks resulted in the capture of several redans and some trenches. These breakthroughs were not vigorously exploited, and Federal casualties were inordinately high. Expertly shifting his limited resources, Beauregard left whole segments of the ten-mile-long Petersburg fortifications virtually undefended, gambling that a coordinated assault would not be forthcoming.

The 49th Regiment, after an all-night march from Chaffin's Bluff, arrived at Petersburg on the morning of the 16th, made "a long double quick" through "a storm of shot and shell," and reached its assigned works near the Avery farm just in time to repulse a Federal attack.[51] Thereafter the men were subjected to, in the words of Captain Chambers, "the severest and closest shelling I ever experienced."[52] During the evening the 49th was rushed north of Petersburg to Swift Creek, where it arrived too late to assist the 56th Regiment and the brigade of Brigadier General Archibald Gracie in repulsing an unsuccessful attempt by Federal cavalry to cut communications between Petersburg and Richmond. The regiment was then sent marching northward on the Richmond turnpike to establish contact with the corps of Lieutenant General James Longstreet. Around midnight the weary men of the 49th went into bivouac, but early the next morning they moved by rail back to Petersburg and resumed their former position near the Avery farm. Most of Ransom's brigade was involved in heavy fighting that evening when the feisty Beauregard, still heavily outnumbered, launched a successful counterattack, but the 49th Regiment remained behind to hold the brigade's fortifications. Around midnight Beauregard ordered his men to fall back to a shorter line closer to Petersburg, and units of the Army of Northern Virginia at last began arriving on the field. Renewed attacks the next day against Lee's tough veterans produced severe losses but no significant gains for the Federals. The 49th Regiment was involved in a heavy skirmish and came under the fire of Federal sharpshooters but suffered few casualties. During the fighting near Petersburg on June 16-18 the 49th Regiment lost 4 men killed and 20 wounded.[53]

The exhausted men of the 49th were relieved, with the remainder of Ransom's brigade, on June 19 but returned to the trenches two days later. Most of the next six weeks was spent on duty in the lines east of Petersburg. Working primarily at night and sleeping during the day, the men constructed breastworks, traverses, "covered ways," picket trenches, and

---

[51]Pearce and Daniels, *Diary of Captain Chambers*, 203; Clark, *Histories of the North Carolina Regiments*, III, 139.
[52]Pearce and Daniels, *Diary of Captain Chambers*, 203.
[53]Raleigh *Daily Confederate*, June 23, July 23, 1864.

bombproofs.[54] Shelling and sharpshooting became, according to Captain Chambers, "the usual routine."[55] During the period from June 21 through July 1, Assistant Surgeon T. W. Dandridge of the 49th reported, sharpshooting—a "game" at which "our men . . . are satisfied that they hold a [f]air hand against the enemy"—cost the regiment ten men killed and ten wounded.[56]

In the meantime General Grant, convinced that a protracted siege was in the offing, ordered the construction of extensive fortifications. Somewhat contradictorily, he also authorized the irrepressible Burnside to attempt to breach the Confederate defenses with a gunpowder mine planted in a tunnel to be dug by a contingent of Pennsylvania coal miners. Working in around-the-clock shifts, the miners gouged out a 510-foot shaft in a matter of weeks, excavating some 18,000 cubic feet of dirt, clay, and sand in the process. Two lateral galleries, each forty feet long, stretched beneath the Confederate works from the end of the shaft. Three hundred twenty kegs containing four tons of gunpowder were then laboriously manhandled into the two galleries and several other magazines. By the morning of July 30 all was in readiness. The Federal plan, modified to its detriment since originally put forward, called for little more than exploding the mine, opening fire with massed Federal cannon, and then storming into the breach with four divisions, one of which was composed of inexperienced Negro soldiers officered by whites. The corps of Major Generals E. O. C. Ord and G. K. Warren would support the attack on its flanks.

At 4:40 a.m. on July 30 the mine went off with a roar beneath Brigadier General Stephen Elliott's South Carolina brigade of Bushrod Johnson's division, producing a crater 170 feet long, 60 to 80 feet wide, and 30 feet deep and blowing nine companies of South Carolinians into the air. "The astonishing . . . explosion," Johnson reported, "bursting like a volcano at the feet of the men," heaved up "an immense column of more than 100,000 cubic feet of earth to fall around in heavy masses, wounding, crushing, or burying everything within its reach. . . ."[57] While the stunned survivors bolted for the rear, more than 100 Federal cannon opened fire. Poorly led and almost as badly shocked by the explosion as the Confederates, Federal infantrymen straggled forward through the dust and, having clambered to the top of the twelve foot wall of dirt and debris produced by the explosion, stood gaping in amazement into the smoking chasm. Moving forward at last, the Federals found themselves in an incredible ruin of broken gun carriages, protruding timbers, wrecked cannon, and bloody, half-buried Confederates, some of whom were still alive and attempting to extricate themselves. The attack then lost what little cohesion it possessed as a majority of the Federals, disoriented by the unfamiliar contours of the crater and half blinded by the "torrents" of dust, milled about attempting to get their bearings or locate their officers.[58] Some paused to dig out injured Confederates or, unbelievably, to pick up souvenirs.

In the meantime the Confederate regiments adjacent to the crater, after giving ground, succeeded in containing the Federal incursion with the aid of reinforcements and withering blasts from several nearby artillery pieces. The 24th and 49th regiments, to the left of the crater, were rushed to Elliott's assistance and were instrumental in halting the Federal advance on that part of the line. "Two companies of the Forty-ninth North Carolina Regiment," Johnson reported, "posted in the covered way near the main line, poured a heavy volley on the flank of the enemy in rear, and our men of the Seventeenth South Carolina and

---

[54]W. A. Day, "In the Trenches at Petersburg," *Confederate Veteran*, XXXIV (January, 1926), 23.
[55]Pearce and Daniels, *Diary of Captain Chambers*, 207.
[56]Raleigh *Daily Confederate*, July 8, 1864.
[57]*Official Records (Army)*, Series I, XL, Part I, 788.
[58]*Official Records (Army)*, Series I, XL, Part I, 788.

Forty-ninth North Carolina Regiments, under cover of angles, boyaux, &c., drove back the charge along the trenches."[59]

Enraged by the black soldiers' shouts of "No quarter," the 49th Regiment clung to its works, Lieutenant Thomas R. Roulhac of Company D reported, with "the tenacity of despair" and "the fury of madmen."

> [A]s each rifle became too hot to be used [Roulhac continued] another gun was at work by one who took the place of the first, or supplied him with rifles which could be handled. From a redoubt to our left and rear Wright's Battery opened upon the crowded, panic-stricken foe, as they huddled together, an enfilading, plunging fire with five field pieces, and two mortars, every shot and shell tearing its way through living flesh.[60]

A lurid account of the fighting by Private Day, although containing inaccuracies, gives some idea of the frenzy that seized the combatants:

> [The] sight [that] met our eyes [when we reached the field was] enough to chill the warmest blood. The men who had been blown high in the air were lying around, the smoke was rising in great clouds out of the Crater, the field in front was full of the charging enemy, with their flags flying, negroes in front[?], the drunken[?] brutes shouting, "No quatah! No quatah!" and butchering every man they saw alive in the works. We saw the position we were in; to be captured meant death. It was said that their orders were to break through our lines at the Crater . . . [and] then send the negroes into the city. We thought of the old men, women, and children in Petersburg who would be at their mercy. The earth was quivering. In the city and far in our rear the shells from two hundred guns[?] were raining. Our officers ran up and down the line, waving their naked swords and shouting: "Hold them back, boys! Hold them back! By everything you hold dear on earth, hold them back!". . . Every man stood square to his post and fought with the heroism of men reduced to desperation. We shot and shot to kill; our targets a field full of men, distance forty yards. We mowed them down; they fell on top of each other in piles.[61]

Elsewhere around the perimeter the Federals also began to take severe casualties, and inside the crater the mortar shells referred to by Roulhac began to fall with devastating effect. Federal reinforcements sustained heavy losses as they crossed the open space between their lines and the crater, and on the Federal flanks the attacks of Generals Ord and Warren stalled. Around 8:30 a.m. two brigades of Confederate General William Mahone's division arrived at the scene and were preparing to attack when a weak line, composed primarily of Negro soldiers, charged their position. Although still in the process of forming their line of battle, Mahone's men charged into the midst of the courageous but unsupported and badly outnumbered Federals, driving them back to the warren of trenches on the crater's periphery. A new Confederate attack around 10 a.m. failed to regain any ground, but the Federal position was clearly hopeless. Confederate artillery continued to exact a murderous toll on the increasingly desperate men huddled in the crater, and the 100 yards of open ground separating them from the Federal line was now so thoroughly swept by Confederate fire that, according to Private Day, "we . . . dropped every man" who tried to run back.[62] At 1 p.m.

---

[59]*Official Records (Army)*, Series I, XL, Part I, 790.

[60]Clark, *Histories of the North Carolina Regiments*, III, 142.

[61]W. A. Day, "The Breastworks at Petersburg," *Confederate Veteran*, XXIX (May, 1921), 174, hereinafter cited as Day, "Petersburg."

[62]Day, "Petersburg," 175.

another attack by Mahone's men carried to the lip of the crater. There, Private Day reported,

> They halted on the brink and fired one volley into the surging mass, then turned the butts of their guns and jumped in among them. How the negroe's skulls cracked under the blows. Some of them ran over on our side and started for the rear, while others made a dash for their own lines. . . . I, boy like, ran up the line to see them. When I got there they had the ground covered with broken headed negroes, and were searching about among the bomb proofs for more, the officers were trying to stop them but they kept on until they finished up.[63]

Captain Chambers reported a "tremendous slaughter" had been perpetrated by Mahone's men who, infuriated by the shouts of "No quarter to the rebels," had "taken revenge" by granting "little quarter" themselves. For its part the 49th Regiment, Chambers continued, had done "most effective work" from its position to the left of the crater as the enemy "fled in one great confused and surging mass down the hill to their own works."[64] Remarkably, only nine members of the regiment had been killed and eleven wounded. Ransom's brigade as a whole was officially reported to have lost 14 men killed, 60 wounded, and 8 missing; total Confederate casualties were about 1,500. On the Federal side, almost 4,000 men were dead and wounded.[65]

For the 49th Regiment a dismal three-week period in or near Petersburg fortifications now followed.

> [W]e moved back to the position we occupied before [Private Day reported], and lay there until the 8th of August, then moved back to the reserve works. We were under the mortar fire and John H. German, of Company I was slightly wounded. We lay in reserve until the night of the 12th[,] then moved to the front. The next day we went out to the wagon yard to wash, and back again at night. On the 14th it rained hard all day, the water ran like a creek in the trenches and in one place in our front, it washed the yankee breast-works away. It rained every day for a week. Heavy cannonading and sharpshooting going on all the time. It seemed like the enemy was determined to give us no rest. On the night of the 18th they commenced at midnight and threw mortar shells into the works until day light. The trenches were almost knee deep in mud and it was still raining. Our clothes were covered with mud and soaked with rain, no place to sleep and nothing much to eat, and sixty-four pound mortar shells bursting all around.[66]

Ransom's brigade remained in the trenches until August 20 when it was moved south of Petersburg to the extreme right of the Confederate line. There, two days earlier, Grant had severed one of Lee's few remaining supply arteries by seizing Globe Tavern, three miles south of Petersburg on the Weldon Railroad. Heavy fighting on August 18 and 19 failed to dislodge the Federals, whereupon additional Confederate reinforcements, including the 49th Regiment, were called to the scene. On August 21 the Confederates, under A. P. Hill and William Mahone, tried again. A noisy but ineffective bombardment by thirty cannon was followed by a headlong Confederate assault that was wrecked by heavy artillery fire. Private Day reported the battle as follows:

---

[63]Day, *A True History of Company I*, 84. According to Day, Mahone's men "spared the white men as best they could, but negro skulls cracked under the blows like eggshells. They begged pitifully for their lives, but the answer was: 'No quarter this morning, no quarter now.' " Day, "Petersburg," 175.

[64]Pearce and Daniels, *Diary of Captain Chambers*, 210.

[65]*Official Records (Army)*, Series I, XL, Part I, 793. Casualties reported for the 49th Regiment are based on information compiled for the following regimental roster.

[66]Day, *A True History of Company I*, 86.

The command forward was given and we moved off promptly and crossing [a] swamp, we struck a ridge covered with a stunted growth of trees. A straight path ran through the woods and one of the men of Company G was killed by a sharpshooter firing down the path. We moved on slowly through the woods and soon came in sight of the enemy's breast-works. The command [to] charge was given, [and] we gave a cheer and started for their works. The enemy stood and watched us until we were within twenty five [*sic*] yards of them. . . . All at once they threw their guns across the works and fired a dreadful volley at our line, but owing to their haste they fired over our heads. Consequently our loss was light. We dashed on and carried the works, capturing a number of prisoners. The others started on a dead run for the rear.[67]

All had gone relatively well to this point, but the regiment now came upon an "old pine field" in which the Federals had cut down the trees, leaving the butts hanging to four-foot-high stumps.[68] On a ridge slightly to the rear of the pines was another line composed principally of artillery. Private Day's account continued:

We moved on to capture the second line but when we struck the pines we . . . got so badly tangled . . . we did not know what to do. All this time the enemy's gun[s] double shotted with grape and canister had been playing on us. Seeing that it was impossible to carry the work, orders were sent in to fall back to the first line. . . . As we were falling back our own artillery . . . opened on us . . . and continued their fire until a courier ran his horse over and stopped them. Several of our men were killed and wounded by their fire. Meantime the Yankee infantry had opened up on us and this, added to their artillery, made it a very warm place to stay. . . . The enemy gradually ceased their fire and everything became quiet except an occasional shot from a sharpshooter.[69]

Globe Tavern remained in Federal hands. Losses in the 49th Regiment, according to information compiled for this volume, were 8 men killed, 16 wounded, and 4 captured.

Ransom's brigade then returned to its former position in the lines east of Petersburg where it remained for six months, taking no part in the heavy fighting that flared at Jones' Farm, Burgess' Mill, or Hatcher's Run. Sharpshooting and artillery fire, particularly from the hated mortars, continued to take a toll. Conditions in the trenches, which had been sufficiently miserable during the summer, deteriorated further with the coming of cold weather.

We had no wood to make fires [Private Day recalled], and our shelters were holes in the ground, covered over with boards and dirt. Every time it rained they leaked muddy water on us. They were called boom-proofs [bombproofs] and sheltered us from minnie balls and pieces of shells very well, but were of no account when a sixty-four pounder struck them. The enemy kept shelling us . . . and when the nights were dark and rainy, they shelled us more than at any other time.[70]

In November, after the weather became so cold that the men could not survive without fires, small quantities of coal and wood were issued. Rations were reduced to what seemed "the lowest possible notch." Five consecutive days of rain during the middle of the month added further to the men's woes as the trenches became "nearly full" of mud and water.[71] On

---

[67]Day, *A True History of Company I*, 88.
[68]Day, *A True History of Company I*, 88.
[69]Day, *A True History of Company I*, 88-89.
[70]Day, *A True History of Company I*, 90.
[71]Day, *A True History of Company I*, 91.

December 9 a storm forced the men of the 49th into the frigid waters of a nearby creek where ice threatened to destroy a dam and flood their lines.

> We spent the Christmas of 1864 in the mud . . . under the fire of sharpshooters and mortars [Day remembered]. On January 2nd 1865, the citizens of Petersburg and Richmond gave the soldiers a dinner, but it had to pass through so many hands, that when it got to us, there was [almost] none of it [left]. One of the Sergeants of . . . Company I said our part was three bites of beef and a mouthful of chicken to the man, and one turnip and a cabbage head to the whole Company. At night it snowed and on the 10th it rained hard all day, and the breast-works had become soaked clear through, and began to wash away in places. The dam broke and the bombproofs fell in, leaving us without any shelter. We had to stand about in the rain almost knee deep in mud and water.[72]

Under these conditions the strength of the regiment slowly ebbed. Men died of disease or spent weeks and months in hospitals trying to recover their health, the deadly mortars and sharpshooters continued to take their toll, and desertions to the enemy became commonplace.

> It rained almost half the time, [Private Day recalled, and] sometimes it would freeze and everything would be covered with ice. The weather was very cold, and our uniforms and blankets wore out, and our Government [was] too poor to furnish us new ones, but our people at home sent us clothes which kept us from freezing to death and boxes of rations which kept us from starving. On the 10th of February we drew some clothing which was the last our Government ever gave us. We also drew some money, but it had depreciated in value so that we could scarcely buy anything with it. . . . A month's wages wouldn't buy a square meal.[73]

Infuriated by the discovery of a "plot" by several members of Company H to desert to the enemy, Colonel LeRoy McAfee of the 49th wrote a scathing letter to the Charlotte *Daily Bulletin* on March 1 laying the blame on defeatist letters from home and denouncing their authors and all who encouraged them as "low, miserable, white-livered scoundrels" who, "like dogs, submit and crawl upon their bellies and lick the rod that smites them." The "more guilty" of the Company H malefactors, McAfee reported, were under guard awaiting trial, and no doubt they were severely punished, but no combination of punishment, forgiveness, reward, or exhortation seemed sufficient to prevent the "crying evil" of desertion, which continued to drain the strength of the 49th and the entire Confederate army.[74]

On March 16 the 49th Regiment was withdrawn from the Petersburg lines and moved to a reserve position southwest of Petersburg, where it remained for over a week "luxuriating" in "excellent" shanties formerly occupied by some Virginia troops.[75] "That was the first day since the 12th of May, 1864 [Private Day observed plaintively], that we never heard a gun fire."[76] The men were "allowed to wash" on the 18th, and spent most of the next week drilling, standing inspection, and performing dress parade.[77] On the evening of the 24th the regiment, with the rest of Ransom's brigade, was sent back to its former position east of

---

[72]Day, *A True History of Company I*, 92-93.
[73]Day, *A True History of Company I*, 93-94.
[74]Charlotte *Daily Bulletin*, March 10, 1865.
[75]Pearce and Daniels, *Diary of Captain Chambers*, 251.
[76]Day, *A True History of Company I*, 94.
[77]Pearce and Daniels, *Diary of Captain Chambers*, 251.

Petersburg, where preparations for a desperate, forlorn-hope assault against a Federal bastion known as Fort Stedman were under way.

Lee's attack on Fort Stedman on the morning of March 25 was intended to force Grant to temporarily assume a defensive posture and shorten his constricting lines around Petersburg, thereby allowing part of the Army of Northern Virginia to join General Joseph E. Johnston in North Carolina. After crushing the advancing army of Major General William T. Sherman, the united Confederate armies would return to Virginia and defeat Grant. The prospects of success were exceedingly remote, not to say chimerical, but Lee believed that failure would leave him no worse off than if he did nothing and "quietly awaited [Sherman's] approach."[78]

About 4 a.m. on the morning of March 25 the Confederates moved silently forward and, taking the drowsy Federals by surprise, quickly captured Fort Stedman. Several Confederate columns then moved out toward what were believed to be three small auxiliary forts behind Stedman, the capture of which would provide platforms for attacks to widen the gap and permit reinforcements to enfilade the Federal rear. Unfortunately, it soon developed that the three auxiliary forts were nonexistent. The entire plan then began to unravel. The disoriented men fell back to Fort Stedman, where they began taking heavy battery and infantry fire. From its position slightly to the left of the fort the 49th Regiment came under enfilading infantry fire from its left. Shrapnel from shells fired from the right of Fort Stedman and from the front then began raking the regiment. Realizing that his attack had failed, Lee ordered a withdrawal. That order was enthusiastically obeyed by major portions of the assault force, but some units, including the 49th Regiment, did not get the word. Captain Chambers, in temporary command of the 49th, wrote in his diary that evening that he had "noticed" the "large quantity" of Confederate troops in Fort Stedman "going back to our lines" but thought that they were merely being sent "to re-enforce some weaker point."

> I had no idea [he continued] we were abandoning the works we had taken and felt no uneasiness until *all* the troops on my right were gone, and the enemy coming up to their works again. I then, for the first time, learned that the order to retire had been given sometime before. We would soon be surrounded by overwhelming numbers and captured. To retreat under the concentrated fire of all the enemy's batteries and rifles . . . looked like almost certain destruction. But try it we must. The order was given and we start[ed]. Good God what a time! It seemed as if the enemy's artillery opened with redoubled vigor and the minie balls came in showers. Many were wounded and as their unhurt comrades passed them would beg piteously to be carried out. The hearts of many failed them and they did not start at all. Others started but took shelter in the picket trenches and covered ways.[79]

"Such a storm of shot and shell as I never dreamed of before," Lieutenant B. F. Dixon of Company G recalled. "How any man escaped death I have never been able to see."[80] Running for their lives amid "a perfect storm" of grape, canister, mortar shells, and minie balls that raked them from three directions, the men reached their lines to find they had sustained "the [second] greatest loss . . . the Forty-ninth met with during the war."[81] At least 106 members of the regiment were captured, suggesting that the number of men who refused to brave the blistering Federal fire was even more substantial than Captain Chambers's account seems to

[78]Clifford Dowdey and Louis H. Manarin, *The Wartime Papers of R. E. Lee* (Boston: Little, Brown and Company, 1961), 917.
[79]Pearce and Daniels, *Diary of Captain Chambers*, 253.
[80]Clark, *Histories of the North Carolina Regiments*, III, 158.
[81]Day, *A True History of Company I*, 96; Clark, *Histories of the North Carolina Regiments*, III, 145.

suggest. Remarkably, only eight members of the regiment were killed and twenty-three wounded. It seems probable that the regiment, as a result of its losses at Fort Stedman, was reduced to about 300 men. Confederate losses as a whole numbered about 4,000, as opposed to 1,500 Federals.

On March 27 Federal General Phil Sheridan's victorious Army of the Shenandoah, having devastated the Shenandoah Valley and virtually destroyed the opposing army of Lieutenant General Jubal A. Early, joined Grant. Anticipating an immediate attack on the vital Southside Railroad, Lee concentrated most of his cavalry west of Petersburg and, on the evening of the 29th, ordered Confederate infantry units to join them. Major General George E. Pickett assumed command of the force.

On the 29th the expected Federal movement began with Sheridan's cavalrymen making a wide detour well to the southwest of Petersburg before turning northwest. At the same time, a powerful Federal infantry force advanced slowly west through rain and mud and crossed the Boydton Plank Road. Bushrod Johnson's division, of which the 49th Regiment and the other units of Ransom's brigade were still a part, was ordered forward to discover the identity and strength of the Federal infantry and was engaged in heavy skirmishing near Burgess' Mill on the afternoon of the 29th. The next day the 49th moved west in a torrential rain to Five Forks, where it bivouacked for the night. The Federal infantry force, under G. K. Warren, continued to inch westward, and Sheridan's cavalry reached the critical road junction at Five Forks before falling back in the face of Pickett's infantry. Severe fighting occurred on the 31st as Pickett drove Sheridan back to Dinwiddie Court House and Warren came under attack by troops under the command of Bushrod Johnson. The 49th Regiment advanced with Pickett's force toward Dinwiddie Court House but, although almost continuously on the move or in line of battle, remained on the periphery of the fight.

> After crossing [a rain-swollen creek and] . . . forming in line of battle [Captain Chambers wrote in his diary] we . . . passed through old pine field thickets and deep ravines. Occasionally we halted and listened to the contest going on below, the din of musketry, artillery and the savage yells of the struggling men. Now moving forward, now at a halt, now through the thickets of pine and now over ravines bordered by briers and brambles. Darkness at length came on us in line of battle. . . .[82]

After sleeping on their arms that night and skirmishing briefly with the enemy on the morning of April 1, the regiment fell back with the other units under Pickett's command to Five Forks. There the 49th and the other regiments of Ransom's brigade went into position on the extreme left of the Confederate line. Sheridan's cavalry followed close on Pickett's heels. Pickett formed a defensive line in the shape of an "L" with one arm facing south against Sheridan and the other, shorter arm facing east toward Warren. Apprehending no danger for the remainder of the day, Pickett retired with several of his generals at about two o'clock to the nearby banks of the Nottoway River, where a shad bake was planned. Shortly thereafter Warren's command arrived on the field and began forming for an attack.

Around 4:15 p.m. the Federals charged the Confederate left. At the same time, Sheridan's dismounted troopers advanced against the Confederate center and right. Abruptly, the 49th and the other regiments of Ransom's brigade found themselves under fire from the front, flank, and rear as Warren, having serendipitously miscalculated the location and length of the Confederate line, executed a classical turning movement. Ransom's brigade, at the vortex of

---

[82]Pearce and Daniels, *Diary of Captain Chambers*, 256.

an attack in which some 50,000 Federals surged forward against a defensive force of 19,000, quickly found itself trapped. An ill-advised attempt by the 49th Regiment to form a line to the rear was seized by some of the men as an opportunity to flee the field and left the 24th and 56th regiments so exposed that they were cut off from their sister units and captured. Those members of the 49th who could be rallied then attempted to return to their original position; others disappeared in whatever direction safety seemed to lie.

With the few noble fellows who still surrounded us [Captain Chambers wrote in his diary], joined by the remnants of [W. H.] Wallace's brigade and the 25th N. C. . . . we charged, driving the enemy before us. . . . We re-occupied our works but the position was untenable. Our men got on the outside of our works to protect themselves from the fire in the rear, which was much heavier than that from the front. . . . It was a terrible hour. . . . The musketry was deafening, the minie balls were coming from both front and rear seemingly as thick as hail, the poor wounded fellows were begging piteously to be carried off, and all this time the Yankee column in [our] rear was bearing down upon us.[83]

A new attempt to form a line to the rear, led by the gallant Chambers, collapsed before the withering fire of the enemy. "The hearts of many failed them," Chambers wrote. "Lying in the holes caused by throwing up the works, they were afraid to raise their heads either to fight or run."[84] "Penned in like rats," a few stalwart members of the regiment continued to put up a feeble resistance until the Federal infantry, coordinating their attack at last, rushed toward the low breastworks "like an avalanche."[85]

In but a few moments more the left flank of the regiment was driven back on the right [Lieutenant Roulhac recalled] . . . while the enemy's line in our former front came over the works, which had been stubbornly held by Captain J. C. Grier, of Company F. . . . We were overpowered and the few that were left were made prisoners, some being knocked down with the butts of rifles, and Captain Grier throwing away his empty pistol, as several bayonets were presented at his breast. . . .[86]

Pickett, in the meantime, had finally reached the field, but the battle was hopelessly and ruinously lost. An attack on the Confederate lines at Petersburg the next day forced Lee to abandon Richmond and begin retreating to the west in a desperate attempt to unite what remained of his shattered army with Johnston's. For at least 199 members of the 49th Regiment the war was over. Of that number, 1 man had been killed, 9 wounded, and 189 captured, figures that suggest not only the magnitude of the Five Forks debacle but also a dismal combat performance. Clearly, if understandably, many of the men, faced with overwhelming odds and under attack from several directions, had declined to get themselves killed under suicidal circumstances. In any case, it seems probable that fewer that 125 men remained for duty with the 49th Regiment after the battle.

Under orders from Lee, the remnants of the Army of Northern Virginia began concentrating at Amelia Court House, about thirty miles west of Petersburg. Although most of his units reached that pleasant little market town on the 4th, the nonarrival of rations Lee had ordered caused a delay of twenty-four hours while foraging parties scoured the

---

[83]Pearce and Daniels, *Diary of Captain Chambers*, 257-258.
[84]Pearce and Daniels, *Diary of Captain Chambers*, 258.
[85]Clark, *Histories of the North Carolina Regiments*, III, 147; Day, *A True History of Company I*, 99.
[86]Clark, *Histories of the North Carolina Regiments*, III, 147.

countryside for food and fodder. Meanwhile, Federal cavalry and infantry, paralleling Lee's line of retreat, slipped ahead of the Confederates and occupied Jetersville, thereby cutting the Richmond and Danville Railroad. Abandoning the railroad, Lee's weary, starving army moved out of Amelia Court House about noon on the 5th, looping to the northwest to avoid Jetersville. After marching all night in a driving rain the head of the Confederate column, under Longstreet, reached Rice's Station on the Southside Railroad around noon on the 6th.

In the meantime the Confederate rear guard, under Major General John B. Gordon, became separated from the center of the column, while the center, under Lieutenant Generals Richard S. Ewell and Richard H. Anderson, lost contact with the van. In what were in effect two separate engagements, Ewell, with about 3,000 men, and Anderson, with about 6,000, were brought to battle by the hard-driving Federals at Sayler's Creek on the late afternoon of April 6. Fighting without artillery, Ewell was overwhelmed after a brave but brief resistance and captured with most of his command. Anderson's corps, of which the vestiges of Ransom's brigade and the 49th Regiment were a part, held out a bit longer as units under Pickett, on the left, fended off several attacks before collapsing. Ransom, on the right, was flanked and routed. More than 3,000 of Anderson's men were made prisoners; the remainder, a disorganized mob, fled westward. Lee's rear guard, under Gordon, was also defeated in fighting near Sayler's Creek with the loss of another 2,000 men and most of the Confederate wagon train.

Harassed by Federal cavalry, the Army of Northern Virginia moved on, marching all night to reach Farmville, where boxcars loaded with provisions waited. In the midst of a hurried, half-cooked breakfast word was received of the approach of Federal cavalry and infantry, forcing a hasty retreat over the Farmville bridges to the north side of the rain-swollen Appomattox River. There, about three miles north of Farmville, the rear guard, now under General Mahone, was attacked on the morning of the 7th near Cumberland Church. Although lacking sufficient numbers to defeat Mahone, the attackers delayed the Confederate retreat for the rest of the day.

During the night of April 7 Lee's bone-weary soldiers were on the move again, this time toward Appomattox Station, on the Southside Railroad, where supplies sent from Lynchburg were waiting. The haggard, footsore army, disintegrating as men deserted, wandered away in search of food, or fell out from exhaustion, continued its desolate, hopeless march throughout the next day without serious interference; the enemy units in Lee's rear failed to overtake their quarry, while to the south the Federals were hurrying forward on a parallel track to get across Lee's line of retreat at Appomattox Station. Gordon's command, of which the last survivors of the 49th Regiment were now a part, took the lead while Longstreet's men formed the rear guard. Three miles short of Appomattox Station the army bivouacked for the night. At about 9 o'clock a short burst of cannon fire was heard from the southwest, followed by silence. Presently, it became clear that Federal forces had captured the vital supplies at Appomattox Station and were across Lee's line of march.

Later that night Lee and his generals held their last council of war. The essential questions now became: how strong was the Federal force that had seized Appomattox Station, and did it include infantry? Cavalry might be swept aside, but if infantry units were present in sizable numbers it would be impossible for Lee, with his wrecked, emaciated army, now reduced to an organized force of perhaps 12,000 men, to break through. In that case, surrender would be the only rational option.

On the morning of April 9 Confederate units under Gordon and Fitzhugh Lee attacked at Appomattox Station and succeeded in driving a line of Federal cavalrymen from their temporary breastworks. At that moment of apparent deliverance Federal infantry units, some of which had marched for twenty-one hours in the last twenty-four, began arriving on the field. Shortly, Gordon found himself under assault from three sides and cut off from Fitz Lee. In the Confederate rear, Longstreet's command also braced for an attack by a newly arrived Federal corps. Trapped and hopelessly outnumbered, Lee surrendered the Army of Northern Virginia at the nearby hamlet of Appomattox Court House that afternoon. On April 12, one hundred six members of the 49th Regiment were paroled.[87]

[87]Thousands of stragglers rejoined their commands at Appomattox Court House during the three days following Lee's surrender, more than doubling the number of men who were present on April 9. It is probable that no more than forty or fifty of the 106 men paroled on April 12 were present for duty on the 9th.

FIELD AND STAFF

COLONELS

RAMSEUR, STEPHEN DODSON
Previously served as Major of the 10th Regiment N.C. State Troops (1st Regiment N.C. Artillery). Promoted to Colonel and transferred to this regiment on April 12, 1862. Wounded in the right arm at Malvern Hill, Virginia, July 1, 1862. Appointed Brigadier General on November 1, 1862, and transferred.

McAFEE, LeROY MANGUM
Resided in Cleveland County and was by occupation a lawyer prior to enlisting at age 24. Appointed Major on April 12, 1862. Promoted to Lieutenant Colonel on June 19, 1862. Promoted to Colonel on November 1, 1862. Wounded at Drewry's Bluff, Virginia, May 16, 1864. Returned to duty on an unspecified date. Wounded at Fort Stedman, Virginia, March 25, 1865. Returned to duty prior to April 1, 1865, when he was wounded at Five Forks, Virginia. Survived the war.

LIEUTENANT COLONELS

ELIASON, WILLIAM ADLAI
Previously served as Assistant Quartermaster (Captain) of the 7th Regiment N.C. State Troops. Transferred to this regiment upon appointment as Lieutenant Colonel on April 12, 1862. Resigned on June 19, 1862, by reason of ill health.

FLEMMING, JOHN A.
Previously served as Captain of Company A of this regiment. Appointed Major on June 19, 1862, and transferred to the Field and Staff. Promoted to Lieutenant Colonel on November 1, 1862. "Shot through the head & instantly killed" at the Battle of the Crater on July 30, 1864.

DAVIS, JAMES TAYLOR
Previously served as Captain of Company F of this regiment. Appointed Major on September 16, 1863, and transferred to the Field and Staff. Promoted to Lieutenant Colonel on July 30, 1864. Wounded in the "bowels" at Fort Stedman, Virginia, March 25, 1865. Hospitalized at Petersburg, Virginia, where he died the same date. "He died as Christians do, with his Bible on his breast and his last words breathing of peace, home and God." [Charlotte *Western Democrat*, August 15, 1865.]

MAJORS

CHAMBERS, PINCKNEY BROWN
Previously served as Captain of Company C of this regiment. Appointed Major on November 1, 1862, and transferred to the Field and Staff. Resigned on September 16, 1863. His letter of resignation reads in part as follows: "I would respectfully state that I am owner of one hundred & fifteen negroes and on a recent visit home I found them in a state of insubordination[,] so much so that my family are unwilling to stay at home through fear of personal violence."

PETTY, CHARLES Q.
Previously served as Captain of Company H of this regiment. Appointed Major on August 5, 1864, and transferred to the Field and Staff. Wounded on December 14, 1864, "during a mortar shelling." Surrendered at Appomattox Court House, Virginia, April 9, 1865.

ADJUTANTS

RICHMOND, STEPHEN D.
Previously served as 1st Sergeant of Company C, 13th Regiment N.C. Troops (3rd Regiment N.C. Volunteers). Appointed Adjutant on or about April 12, 1862, and transferred to this regiment. Died at Raleigh on May 23, 1862, of "typhoid fever."

DURHAM, CICERO A.
Previously served as 1st Lieutenant of Company E, 12th Regiment N.C. Troops (2nd Regiment N.C. Volunteers). Appointed Adjutant (1st Lieutenant) of this regiment on July 8, 1862, to rank from May 15, 1862. Appointed Assistant Quartermaster (Captain) of this regiment on April 30, 1863, to rank from March 1, 1863.

DINKINS, HENRY H.
Previously served as Sergeant Major of this regiment. Appointed Adjutant (1st Lieutenant) on June 26, 1863, to rank from May 2, 1863. Was apparently absent sick during much of the last year of the war. Paroled at Jackson, Mississippi, May 14, 1865.

ASSISTANT QUARTERMASTERS

WILSON, JAMES W.
Previously served as Captain of Company F, 6th Regiment N.C. State Troops. Appointed Assistant Quartermaster (Captain) of this regiment on July 8, 1862, to rank from May 18, 1862. Appointed Quartermaster (Major) of General S. D. Ramseur's brigade on February 28, 1863.

DURHAM, CICERO A.
Previously served as Adjutant of this regiment. Appointed Assistant Quartermaster (Captain) on April 30, 1863, to rank from March 1, 1863. Wounded in the left arm (possibly also in the chest) at Drewry's Bluff, Virginia, May 13, 1864. Arm amputated. Died at Richmond, Virginia, on or about June 8, 1864, of wounds.

ASSISTANT COMMISSARY OF SUBSISTENCE

GEORGE, EDWARD PAYSON
Previously served as Private in Company K, 30th Regiment N.C. Troops. Appointed Assistant Commissary of Subsistence (Captain) on May 1, 1862, and transferred to this regiment. Dropped from the rolls of the regiment on or about July 31, 1863, after his office was abolished by an act of the Confederate Congress.

SURGEONS

BRUCE, S. C.
Appointed Surgeon of this regiment to rank from April 30, 1862. Declined the appointment.

RUFFIN, JOHN KIRKLAND
Previously served as Assistant Surgeon of the 5th Regiment N.C. State Troops. Appointed Surgeon of this regiment on May 28, 1862. Resigned on or about May 2, 1864. Reason he resigned not reported.

DUFFY, CHARLES, JR.
Previously served as Surgeon of the 54th Regiment N.C. Troops. Appointed Surgeon of this regiment on April 14, 1864. Surrendered at Appomattox Court House, Virginia, April 9, 1865.

ASSISTANT SURGEONS

MANN, JOSEPH B.
Appointed Assistant Surgeon to rank from April 1, 1862. Resigned on April 30, 1862.

WARD, JAMES H.
Appointed Assistant Surgeon on April 30, 1862. Resigned on an unspecified date because "the fatigues, labors & exposures of camp are too great for a man of my age (I am 46 years old)." Resignation accepted on June 28, 1862.

THORPE, H. R.
Appointed Assistant Surgeon on May 4, 1862. Captured at or near Sharpsburg, Maryland, on or about September 17, 1862. Confined at Fort McHenry, Maryland. Paroled and transferred to Aiken's Landing, James River, Virginia, where he was received on October 17, 1862, for exchange. Declared exchanged at Aiken's Landing on November 10, 1862. "Relieved from duty" on November 1, 1862.

GOODE, REGINALD H.
Appointed Assistant Surgeon on October 18, 1862, and was assigned to this regiment on November 11, 1862. Captured at Drewry's Bluff, Virginia, May 13, 1864. Confined at Point Lookout, Maryland, May 18, 1864. Confined at Fort Delaware, Delaware, June 28, 1864.

Paroled and transferred to Aiken's Landing, James River, Virginia, where he was received on August 12, 1864, for exchange. Surrendered at Appomattox Court House, Virginia, April 9, 1865.

CHAPLAINS

BARRETT, ROBERT G.
Appointed Chaplain on April 30, 1862. Resigned on August 7, 1862. Reason he resigned not reported. Resignation accepted on August 11, 1862.

NICHOLSON, PETER C.
Baptist. Appointed Chaplain on July 30, 1863, to rank from June 15, 1863. Resigned on an unspecified date. Reason he resigned not reported. Resignation accepted on November 17, 1864.

MENDENHALL, CYRUS ERASTUS
Served as Private in Company H of this regiment. Appointed Chaplain on June 26, 1863, to rank from June 22, 1863. Declined the appointment on July 13, 1863, on the grounds that there was already a Chaplain serving with the 49th Regiment. Later served as 2nd Lieutenant of Company H.

ENSIGN

LONDON, JOHN R.
Previously served as Sergeant in 2nd Company B of this regiment. Appointed Ensign (1st Lieutenant) on July 18, 1864, and transferred to the Field and Staff. Wounded in the left leg at or near Petersburg, Virginia, December 6, 1864. Hospitalized at Petersburg where he died on December 31, 1864, of wounds.

SERGEANTS MAJOR

PHIFER, GEORGE L.
Previously served as Musician (Bugler) in Company A, 10th Regiment N.C. State Troops (1st Regiment N.C. Artillery). Promoted to Sergeant Major and transferred to this regiment on April 21, 1862. Appointed 1st Lieutenant on December 22, 1862, and transferred to Company K of this regiment. Later served as Captain of Company K.

DINKINS, HENRY H.
Previously served as Sergeant in Company C, 18th Regiment Mississippi Infantry. Transferred to this regiment on December 29, 1862, with the rank of Sergeant Major. Appointed Adjutant (1st Lieutenant) of this regiment on June 26, 1863, to rank from May 2, 1863.

ROULHAC, THOMAS R.
Previously served as Private in Company A, 10th

Regiment N.C. State Troops (1st Regiment N.C. Artillery). Promoted to Sergeant Major and transferred to this regiment on August 31, 1863. Appointed 1st Lieutenant on June 15, 1864, and transferred to Company D of this regiment.

POOLE, JOHN W.

Resided in Pasquotank County. Place and date of enlistment not reported. First listed in the records of this company on February 22, 1865. Took the Oath of Allegiance at Norfolk, Virginia, June 15, 1865.

QUARTERMASTER SERGEANTS

GOUGER, JAMES H.

Resided in Rowan County and enlisted in Wayne County on May 25, 1862, for the war. Mustered in as Quartermaster Sergeant. Appointed Ordnance Sergeant of this regiment on March 1, 1863.

HOLLAND, JAMES R.

Previously served as Private in Company H of this regiment. Promoted to Quartermaster Sergeant on March 1, 1863, and transferred to the Field and Staff. Surrendered at Appomattox Court House, Virginia, April 9, 1865.

COMMISSARY SERGEANT

WHITE, JOHN B.

Previously served as Private in Company H of this regiment. Appointed Commissary Sergeant prior to August 2, 1862, and transferred to the Field and Staff. Reduced to ranks and transferred back to Company H prior to January 1, 1863. Appointed acting Commissary Sergeant in May-June, 1863, and transferred for temporary duty with the Field and Staff. Appointed to the permanent rank of Commissary Sergeant in July-August, 1864, and transferred for permanent duty with the Field and Staff.

ORDNANCE SERGEANTS

GOUGER, JAMES H.

Previously served as Quartermaster Sergeant of this regiment. Appointed Ordnance Sergeant on March 1, 1863. Reduced to ranks and transferred to Company F of this regiment in January-August, 1864.

MENDENHALL, CYRUS ERASTUS

Served as Private in Company H of this regiment. Reported on duty as acting Ordnance Sergeant in May-June, 1864. Later served as 2nd Lieutenant of Company H.

CAMERON, JOHN F.

Resided in Fairfield District, South Carolina. Place and date of enlistment not reported. Date of appointment as Ordnance Sergeant not reported. Captured near Petersburg, Virginia, April 2, 1865. Confined at Point Lookout, Maryland, April 5, 1865. Released at Point Lookout on June 21, 1865, after taking the Oath of Allegiance.

HOSPITAL STEWARDS

NEAGLE, JOHN L.

Previously served as Private in Company H of this regiment. Appointed Hospital Steward prior to January 1, 1863, and transferred to the Field and Staff. Appointed Assistant Surgeon on January 22, 1863, and transferred out of the regiment.

HALL, HARRISON

Previously served as Private in Company H of this regiment. Appointed acting regimental Hospital Steward on or about March 10, 1863, and transferred to the Field and Staff. Promoted to the permanent rank of Hospital Steward on November 11, 1864.

BAND

Because of the paucity of records for the Field and Staff of the 49th Regiment, the date on which the regimental band was organized and the names of the men who comprised it are uncertain. It is known, however, that the band was extant in October, 1863. The following soldiers served as Musicians in the 49th Regiment and may have been assigned at one time or another to the regimental band. For service record details, see the companies indicated:

ALBRIGHT, R. H., Musician
Company E.

ANTHONY, J. DAVID, Musician
2nd Company B.

BAILEY, MILAS ALEXANDER, Musician
Company E.

BRISON, JOSEPH W., Musician
Company H.

BROWN, ANDREW ELBERT, Musician
Company I.

CAROTHERS, THOMAS M., Musician
Company F.

CLARK, JAMES MEL, Musician
Company E.

DAVIS, ISAIAH I., Musician
Company K.

ELLIOTT, JULIUS A., Musician
Company C.

FARRIS, JOHN T., Musician
Company E.

GOFORTH, G. W., Musician
Company G.

HACKNEY, BASIL A., Musician
1st Company B.

HARMON, T. W., Musician
Company G.

HOPIS, JOEL, Musician
Company A.

HORDE, RICHARD M., Musician
2nd Company B (see Lieutenants' section).

JAMES, WILLIAM L., Musician
Company A.

LENTZ, ELI CRAWFORD, Drum Major
Company C.

McALLISTER, HENRY B., Musician
Company F.

McLEAN, JOHN CRAIG, Musician
Company H.

PATTERSON, PINKNEY D., Musician
Company G.

RIGGSBEE, JONES E., Musician
1st Company B.

SHELTON, MEACON J., Musician
Company I.

WILSON, JOSIAH J., Musician
Company H.

WILSON, SAMUEL M., Musician
Company H.

COMPANY A

This company was raised primarily in McDowell and
Rutherford counties and enlisted in McDowell County in
February-March, 1862. It was mustered into state service
at Camp Mangum, near Raleigh, on April 15, 1862, and
assigned to the 49th Regiment N.C. Troops as Company A.
After joining the regiment the company functioned as a part
of the regiment, and its history for the remainder of the war
is reported as a part of the regimental history.

The information contained in the following roster was
compiled primarily from a company muster-in and
descriptive roll dated April 15, 1862, and from company
muster rolls for November 1, 1862-December 31, 1863, and
May 1-August 31, 1864. No company muster rolls were
located for May 1-October 31, 1862; January 1-April 30,
1864; or for the period after August 31, 1864. Valuable
information was obtained from primary records such as the
North Carolina adjutant general's *Roll of Honor*, discharge
certificates, medical records, prisoner of war records, *The
War of the Rebellion: A Compilation of the Official Records
of the Union and Confederate Armies*, militia records,
newspaper casualty lists and obituaries, Confederate
pension applications filed with the state of North Carolina,
and the 1860 federal census of North Carolina. Secondary
sources such as postwar rosters and histories, cemetery
records, the *Confederate Veteran*, published genealogies,
and records of the United Daughters of the Confederacy
also provided useful information.

OFFICERS

CAPTAINS

FLEMMING, JOHN A.
Previously served as Private in Company E, 1st Regiment
N.C. Infantry (6 months, 1861). Elected Captain of this
company on February 15, 1862. Appointed Major on June
19, 1862, and transferred to the Field and Staff of this
regiment. Later served as Lieutenant Colonel of this
regiment.

LYTLE, GEORGE W.
Born in McDowell County* where he resided as a farmer
prior to enlisting in McDowell County at age 33. Elected
1st Lieutenant on February 15, 1862. Promoted to Captain
on June 19, 1862. Reported present or accounted for from
November, 1862, through December, 1863. Wounded at or
near Drewry's Bluff, Virginia, May 16, 1864.
Hospitalized at Richmond, Virginia, where he died on or
about May 17, 1864, of wounds.

HIGGINS, JAMES MARION
Born in McDowell County where he resided as a farmer
prior to enlisting in McDowell County at age 19. Elected
2nd Lieutenant on or about February 14, 1862. Promoted
to 1st Lieutenant on June 19, 1862. Reported present or
accounted for from November, 1862, through December,
1863. Promoted to Captain on May 16, 1864. Reported
present in July-August, 1864. Resigned on an unspecified
date by reason of ill health. Resignation accepted on or
about December 14, 1864. [May have served previously
as 1st Lieutenant of 1st Company D, 15th Regiment N.C.
Troops (5th Regiment N.C. Volunteers).]

SHERRILL, JAMES H.
Previously served as 1st Lieutenant of Company I of this
regiment. Promoted to Captain on March 1, 1865, and
transferred to this company. Surrendered at Appomattox

Court House, Virginia, April 9, 1865. [Wounded in two unspecified battles.]

LIEUTENANTS

CONLEY, H. CLAY, 2nd Lieutenant
Born in McDowell County where he resided as a student prior to enlisting in McDowell County at age 17, February 20, 1862. Appointed 3rd Lieutenant on July 18, 1862. Promoted to 2nd Lieutenant on October 6, 1862. Reported present or accounted for from November, 1862, through December, 1863. Killed at Drewry's Bluff, Virginia, May 16, 1864. [May have served previously as 2nd Lieutenant of 1st Company D, 15th Regiment N.C. Troops (5th Regiment N.C. Volunteers).]

FLEMING, JOHN H., 1st Lieutenant
Born in McDowell County* where he resided as a farmer prior to enlisting in McDowell County at age 23, March 14, 1862. Mustered in as Private. Promoted to 1st Sergeant on October 7, 1862, "for meritorious conduct." Reported present or accounted for from November, 1862, through December, 1863, and in May-August, 1864. Wounded near Petersburg, Virginia, in December, 1864. Returned to duty on an unspecified date. Appointed 1st Lieutenant on March 1, 1865. Captured at Five Forks, Virginia, April 1, 1865. Confined at Old Capitol Prison, Washington, D.C., April 5, 1865. Transferred to Johnson's Island, Ohio, April 9, 1865. Released at Johnson's Island on June 18, 1865, after taking the Oath of Allegiance.

FLEMMING, JAMES GREENLEE, 2nd Lieutenant
Born in McDowell County where he resided as a student prior to enlisting in McDowell County at age 18, February 15, 1862. Mustered in as 1st Sergeant. Elected 2nd Lieutenant on July 15, 1862. Killed at Sharpsburg, Maryland, September 17, 1862.

LYTLE, THOMAS Y., 2nd Lieutenant
Born in McDowell County and resided in Buncombe County where he was by occupation a student prior to enlisting in McDowell County at age 19, March 12, 1862. Mustered in as Sergeant. Appointed 3rd Lieutenant on July 15, 1862. Reported present or accounted for from November, 1862, through December, 1863. Promoted to 2nd Lieutenant on May 16, 1864. Wounded ("shocked by shell") at the Battle of the Crater, near Petersburg, Virginia, July 30, 1864. Returned to duty prior to September 1, 1864. Furloughed for eighteen days on January 1, 1865. Dropped from the rolls of the company for absence without leave on February 27, 1865.

NEAL, JOSEPH CAMP, 2nd Lieutenant
Previously served as Sergeant in Company B, 22nd Regiment N.C. Troops (12th Regiment N.C. Volunteers). Appointed 2nd Lieutenant of this company on or about May 2, 1862. Resigned on June 11, 1862, because "it [is] impossible to obtain a leave of absence and circumstances of the greatest importance to me require my immediate presence at home. . . ." Resignation accepted on July 2, 1862.

WHISNANT, ELI, 3rd Lieutenant
Born in Rutherford County where he resided as a farmer prior to enlisting in McDowell County at age 34, March 12, 1862. Mustered in as Sergeant. Reported present or accounted for from November, 1862, through December, 1863. Elected 3rd Lieutenant on June 15, 1864. Reported on duty as acting commander of the company in July-August, 1864. Dropped from the rolls of the company on February 27, 1865, "for incompetency" and/or "physical disability." Apparently continued to serve with the company in another capacity. Surrendered at Appomattox Court House, Virginia, April 9, 1865.

NONCOMMISSIONED OFFICERS AND PRIVATES

ADAMS, RICHARD, Private
Born in Burke County and resided in McDowell County where he was by occupation a laborer prior to enlisting in McDowell County at age 45, March 1, 1862. Died at Salisbury on November 1 or November 10, 1862, of disease.

BAXTER, AARON F., Private
Born in Lincoln County and resided in McDowell County where he was by occupation a carpenter prior to enlisting in McDowell County at age 41, March 10, 1862. Detailed for duty as a shoemaker at Richmond, Virginia, November 15, 1862. Reported on detail as a shoemaker at Richmond through August, 1864. Assigned to Company C, 2nd Battalion Virginia Local Defense Troops, while on duty at Richmond.

BEATY, JOHN W., Private
Born in Rutherford County where he resided as a laborer prior to enlisting in McDowell County at age 23, March 16, 1862. Killed at Sharpsburg, Maryland, September 17, 1862.

BIRD, JAMES A., Corporal
Resided in McDowell County where he enlisted at age 18, May 1, 1863, for the war. Mustered in as Private. Promoted to Corporal on October 1, 1863. Reported present through December, 1863, and in May-August, 1864. Survived the war.

BIRD, JAMES H., Private
Enlisted in McDowell County on December 1, 1863, for the war. Deserted from camp near Weldon on March 28, 1864. Arrested on or about April 10, 1864. Returned to duty on May 25, 1864. Reported present in July-August, 1864. Hospitalized at Richmond, Virginia, October 21, 1864, with an unspecified disability and was furloughed for sixty days on November 27, 1864. No further records.

BLALOCK, JOSEPH B., Private
Born in Burke County and resided in McDowell County where he was by occupation a laborer prior to enlisting in McDowell County at age 33, March 18, 1862. Reported absent without leave in November-December, 1862. Rejoined the company on February 10, 1863. Deserted on

May 24, 1863. Returned from desertion on June 27, 1863. Reported present in July-December, 1863. Deserted on March 28, 1864. Arrested on or about April 16, 1864. Returned to duty on June 25, 1864. Deserted while on duty as a wagon guard near Petersburg, Virginia, July 24, 1864.

BLANTON, JOSEPH R., Private

Born in Rutherford County where he resided as a minister prior to enlisting in McDowell County at age 32, March 24, 1862. Mustered in as Sergeant. Reported present in November, 1862-February, 1863. Furloughed on March 20, 1863. Furlough expired on April 20, 1863, and he was listed as a deserter. Reduced to ranks on an unspecified date. Returned from desertion on or about August 20, 1863. Reported present in September-December, 1863. No further records.

BLANTON, WILLIAM J., Private

Enlisted in McDowell County on October 13, 1863, for the war. Reported present in November-December, 1863. Captured at Bermuda Hundred, Virginia, June 2, 1864. Confined at Point Lookout, Maryland, June 12, 1864. Transferred to Elmira, New York, July 9, 1864. Died at Elmira on October 10, 1864, of "anasarca."

BOWERS, JOHN ANDERSON, Private

Born in Rutherford County where he resided as a laborer prior to enlisting in McDowell County at age 22, March 19, 1862. Reported present or accounted for from November, 1862, through December, 1863. Captured at Bermuda Hundred, Virginia, June 2, 1864. Confined at Point Lookout, Maryland, June 12, 1864. Transferred to Elmira, New York, July 9, 1864. Paroled at Elmira on March 2, 1865, and transferred to the James River, Virginia, for exchange. Hospitalized at Richmond, Virginia, March 7, 1865, with debilitas. Furloughed for thirty days on March 9, 1865.

BUTLER, ELISHA, Private

Born in McDowell County where he resided as a laborer prior to enlisting in McDowell County at age 18, March 11, 1862. Died in hospital at Petersburg, Virginia, August 8, 1862, of "ty[phoid] febris."

CAMP, RICHARD L., Private

Born in Cleveland County* and resided in McDowell County where he was by occupation a farmer prior to enlisting in McDowell County at age 34, February 27, 1862. Deserted on September 18, 1862. Returned from desertion on January 25, 1863. Reported present in March-December, 1863, and May-August, 1864. Deserted to the enemy on or about February 25, 1865. Confined at Washington, D.C., March 1, 1865. Released on an unspecified date after taking the Oath of Allegiance.

CANIPE, ELI, Private

Born in Cleveland County* and resided in McDowell County where he was by occupation a farmer prior to enlisting in McDowell County at age 23, March 12, 1862. Reported present from November, 1862, through August, 1863. Deserted at Weldon on or about September 24, 1863. Went over to the enemy on or about October 24, 1864. Sent to City Point, Virginia. Transferred to Camp Hamilton,

Virginia, where he arrived on November 1, 1864. Released at Camp Hamilton on November 12, 1864, after taking the Oath of Allegiance.

CARAWAY, DANIEL M., Private

Born in McDowell County* where he resided as a farmer prior to enlisting in McDowell County at age 25, March 6, 1862. Reported present from November, 1862, through December, 1863. Hospitalized at Petersburg, Virginia, June 22, 1864, with acute diarrhoea. Furloughed for thirty days on September 8, 1864. No further records.

CARAWAY, JAMES D. LAFAYETTE, Private

Born in McDowell County* where he resided as a farmer prior to enlisting in McDowell County at age 29, March 1, 1862. Died at Goldsboro on May 12 or May 20, 1862, of disease.

CHRISOWN, BURTON, Private

Born in Yancey County* where he resided as a farmer prior to enlisting in McDowell County at age 45, March 1, 1862. Deserted near Petersburg, Virginia, on or about August 15, 1862.

COGGINS, JOHN W., Private

Born in McDowell County* where he resided as a farmer prior to enlisting in McDowell County at age 22, March 12, 1862. Killed at Sharpsburg, Maryland, September 17, 1862.

CONDRY, DAVID C., Private

Born in McDowell County where he resided as a laborer prior to enlisting in McDowell County at age 18, March 6, 1862. Reported present or accounted for from November, 1862, through December, 1863. Captured at Bermuda Hundred, Virginia, June 2, 1864. Confined at Point Lookout, Maryland, June 12, 1864. Transferred to Elmira, New York, July 8, 1864. Released at Elmira on July 3, 1865, after taking the Oath of Allegiance.

CONDRY, JOSEPH, Private

Resided in McDowell County where he enlisted at age 18, February 9, 1863, for the war. Died in McDowell County on May 4, 1863, of disease.

CONNER, SAMUEL L., Private

Born in Haywood County and resided in McDowell County where he was by occupation a farmer prior to enlisting in McDowell County at age 23, March 3, 1862. Reported present or accounted for in November, 1862-February, 1863. Deserted at Kinston on or about May 15, 1863.

COX, EDWARD A., Private

Born in Yancey County where he resided as a farmer prior to enlisting in McDowell County at age 26, March 24, 1862. Deserted on August 15, 1862. Apprehended on an unspecified date and was court-martialed. Returned to duty on or about June 17, 1863. Reported present in July-December, 1863. Captured near Drewry's Bluff, Virginia, May 16, 1864. Confined at Point Lookout, Maryland, May 19, 1864. Transferred to Elmira, New York, August 16, 1864. Paroled at Elmira on March 14, 1865. Received at

Boulware's Wharf, James River, Virginia, on or about March 18, 1865, for exchange. Hospitalized at Richmond, Virginia, March 21, 1865, with scorbutus. Deserted on March 23, 1865.

COX, HARMON M., Corporal

Born in Yancey County where he resided as a farmer prior to enlisting in McDowell County at age 23, March 1, 1862. Mustered in as Corporal. Deserted on August 14, 1862.

CROW, JAMES L., Private

Born in Rutherford County where he resided as a farmer prior to enlisting in McDowell County at age 46, March 17, 1862. Reported present or accounted for from November, 1862, through February, 1863. Discharged on March 9, 1863, after providing Private John Crow of this company as a substitute.

CROW, JOHN, Private

Resided in Rutherford County and enlisted in McDowell County at age 16, March 8, 1863, for the war as a substitute for Private James L. Crow of this company. Died at Wilmington on May 17 or May 27, 1863. Cause of death not reported.

DAVIS, JOHN A., Private

Born in McDowell County where he resided as a farmer prior to enlisting in McDowell County at age 18, March 10, 1862. Reported present from November, 1862, through December, 1863. No further records.

DAVIS, LOGAN C., Private

Born in McDowell County where he resided as a farmer prior to enlisting in McDowell County at age 20, March 10, 1862. Died at Raleigh on May 10, 1862, of disease.

DAVIS, THOMAS A., Sergeant

Born in McDowell County* where he resided as a farmer prior to enlisting in McDowell County at age 25, March 10, 1862. Mustered in as Private. Wounded at Malvern Hill, Virginia, July 1, 1862. Returned to duty on an unspecified date. Reported present from November, 1862, through December, 1863. Promoted to Corporal on April 24, 1863. Reported present in May-August, 1864. Promoted to Sergeant in July-August, 1864. No further records.

DAVIS, WILLIAM B., Private

Born in McDowell County where he resided as a farmer prior to enlisting in McDowell County at age 20, March 10, 1862. Reported present from November, 1862, through December, 1863. Reported absent with leave in May-June, 1864. Reported absent without leave in July-August, 1864. "Noted for his coolness and undaunted bravery in action." [North Carolina pension records indicate that he was wounded at Sharpsburg, Maryland, in September, "1863."]

DAVIS, WILLIAM JASPER, Private

Born in McDowell County* where he resided as a farmer prior to enlisting in McDowell County at age 24, March 10, 1862. Died in hospital at Petersburg, Virginia, on or about July 31, 1862, of "meningitis."

DICKSON, JAMES JOSHUA, Corporal

Born in Burke County and resided in Mitchell or Yancey County where he was by occupation a farmer prior to enlisting in McDowell County at age 40, February 25, 1862. Mustered in as Private. Reported present from November, 1862, through February, 1863. Discharged on March 27, 1863, after providing Private William A. Dickson of this company as a substitute. Reenlisted in the company on April 29, 1864. Was apparently mustered in with the rank of Corporal. Reported present in May-August, 1864. Captured at Five Forks, Virginia, April 1, 1865. Confined at Point Lookout, Maryland, April 5, 1865. Released at Point Lookout on June 26, 1865, after taking the Oath of Allegiance.

DICKSON, WILLIAM A., Private

Resided in Yancey or Mitchell County and enlisted in McDowell County at age 17, February 25, 1863, for the war as a substitute for Private James Joshua Dickson. Reported present or accounted for in March-December, 1863, and May-August, 1864. Hospitalized at Richmond, Virginia, November 27, 1864, with colitis and returned to duty on December 29, 1864. Hospitalized at Richmond on March 9, 1865, with chronic diarrhoea. Captured in hospital at Richmond on April 3, 1865. Transferred to Newport News, Virginia, April 23, 1865. Released at Newport News on June 15, 1865, after taking the Oath of Allegiance.

EARLY, FRANK, Private

Born in McDowell County where he resided as a farmer prior to enlisting in McDowell County at age 18, March 11, 1862. Wounded at Malvern Hill, Virginia, July 1, 1862. Reported absent without leave in November-December, 1862. Returned to duty on January 25, 1863. Discharged on April 16, 1863, by reason of wounds received at Malvern Hill. [May have served later as Corporal in Company B, 22nd Regiment N.C. Troops (12th Regiment N.C. Volunteers).]

ENGLAND, JOHIAL, Private

Born in McDowell County* where he resided as a farmer prior to enlisting in McDowell County at age 29, March 10, 1862. Died at Goldsboro on May 14, 1862, of disease.

FINLAY, ROBERT W., Corporal

Born in McDowell County* where he resided as a farmer prior to enlisting in McDowell County at age 28, February 20, 1862. Mustered in as Private. Promoted to Corporal on July 1, 1862. Killed at Malvern Hill, Virginia, the same date.

FLEMMING, WILLIAM J., Sergeant

Born in McDowell County where he resided prior to enlisting in McDowell County at age 20, March 14, 1862. Mustered in as Private. Wounded in the right arm at Fredericksburg, Virginia, December 13, 1862. Promoted to Corporal prior to January 1, 1863. Promoted to Sergeant on July 1, 1863. Reported absent wounded or absent sick through December, 1863. Retired to the Invalid Corps on June 14, 1864.

GARDNER, JEREMIAH A., Private

Born in Cleveland County* and resided in McDowell

County where he enlisted at age 22, March 11, 1862. Died in hospital at Petersburg, Virginia, on or about August 5, 1862, of "febris remittens."

GARVIN, THOMAS W., Private
Born in McDowell County where he resided as a farmer prior to enlisting in McDowell County at age 19, March 1, 1862. Reported present from November, 1862, through March, 1863. Captured at Sandy Ridge (Lenoir County) on April 20, 1863. Confined at Fort Monroe, Virginia. Paroled and transferred to City Point, Virginia, where he was received on May 28, 1863, for exchange. Returned to duty prior to July 1, 1863. Reported present in July-December, 1863, and May-August, 1864. Deserted to the enemy on or about October 24, 1864. Confined at Camp Hamilton, Virginia, November 1, 1864. Released on November 12, 1864, after taking the Oath of Allegiance.

GOODSON, WILLIAM A., Private
Born in McDowell County* where he resided as a farmer prior to enlisting in McDowell County at age 26, March 14, 1862. Died at Goldsboro on June 6, 1862, of disease.

GRAYSON, ALFRED M., Private
Born in Rutherford County where he resided as a farmer prior to enlisting in McDowell County at age 24, March 16, 1862. Died in hospital at Petersburg, Virginia, on or about July 26, 1862, of "feb[ris] typh[oides]."

GRAYSON, JOHN S., Sergeant
Born in Rutherford County where he resided as a farmer prior to enlisting in McDowell County at age 26, March 16, 1862. Mustered in as Private. Reported absent without leave from July 1, 1862, until March 1, 1863. Sent to hospital on June 1, 1863. Reported present in July-December, 1863. Promoted to Corporal on October 1, 1863. Reported absent sick in July-August, 1864. Promoted to Sergeant subsequent to August 31, 1864. Deserted to the enemy on or about March 8, 1865. Confined at Washington, D.C., March 10, 1865. Released on an unspecified date after taking the Oath of Allegiance.

GREEN, HENRY, Private
Born in Cleveland County* and resided in McDowell County where he was by occupation a farmer prior to enlisting in McDowell County at age 30, March 14, 1862. Reported present in November-December, 1862. Reported absent sick in January-February, 1863. Deserted on May 29, 1863. Returned from desertion on June 27, 1863. Reported present in July-December, 1863, and May-August, 1864. Deserted to the enemy on or about February 25, 1865. Confined at Washington, D.C., on or about March 13, 1865. Released on an unspecified date after taking the Oath of Allegiance.

GRIST, COMMODORE D., Private
Born in McDowell County* where he resided as a farmer prior to enlisting in McDowell County at age 23, March 8, 1862. Reported present or accounted for from November, 1862, through November, 1863. Deserted on December 1, 1863. Returned to duty on an unspecified date. Reported present in May-August, 1864. Killed near Petersburg, Virginia, December 15, 1864.

GRIST, DOC, Private
Resided in McDowell County where he enlisted on October 2, 1863, for the war. Reported present in October-December, 1863, and May-August, 1864. Captured at Five Forks, Virginia, April 1, 1865. Confined at Point Lookout, Maryland, April 5, 1865. Released at Point Lookout on June 27, 1865, after taking the Oath of Allegiance.

GUFFY, ELIJAH P., Private
Born in McDowell County* and resided in Rutherford County where he was by occupation a farmer prior to enlisting in McDowell County at age 24, March 10, 1862. Reported present or accounted for from November, 1862, through December, 1863. Reported present in May-August, 1864. Surrendered at Appomattox Court House, Virginia, April 9, 1865.

HAMBY, MILLINGTON P., Sergeant
Born in Buncombe County where he resided as a farmer prior to enlisting in McDowell County at age 18, March 14, 1862. Mustered in as Private. Reported present or accounted for from November, 1862, through February, 1863. Captured at Sandy Ridge (Lenoir County) on April 20, 1863. Sent to Fort Monroe, Virginia. Received at City Point, Virginia, May 28, 1863, for exchange. Returned to duty in July-August, 1863. Reported present in September-December, 1863, and May-August, 1864. Promoted to Sergeant on April 30, 1864. Died at or near Petersburg, Virginia, on or about October 5, 1864. Cause of death not reported. "Noted for his coolness and undaunted bravery in action."

HANEY, WILLIAM, Private
Born in McDowell County and resided in Yancey County where he was by occupation a farmer prior to enlisting in McDowell County at age 18, March 1, 1862. Deserted on or about August 15, 1862.

HARRIS, FRANCIS M., Sergeant
Born in McDowell County* where he resided as a farmer prior to enlisting in McDowell County at age 25, March 14, 1862. Mustered in as Private. Promoted to Corporal prior to January 1, 1863. Reported present from November, 1862, through December, 1863. Promoted to Sergeant on April 24, 1863. Reported in confinement at Castle Thunder Prison, Richmond, Virginia, May 14, 1864. No further records.

HARRISON, J. W., Private
Enlisted in McDowell County on October 13, 1863, for the war. Reported present in November-December, 1863, and May-August, 1864. [May have been killed in action in Virginia prior to October 11, 1864.]

HOGAN, WILLIAM, Private
Born in McDowell County* where he resided as a farmer prior to enlisting in McDowell County at age 33, February 28, 1862. Reported present or accounted for from November, 1862, through February, 1863. Deserted on or about May 16, 1863. Returned from desertion on August 29, 1863. Reported present in September-December, 1863. Court-martialed on or about September 24, 1864.

Reason he was court-martialed not reported. No further records.

HOPIS, JOEL, Private

Born in McDowell County where he resided as a farmer prior to enlisting in McDowell County at age 18, March 20, 1862. Mustered in as Private. Reported present from November, 1862, through June, 1863. Appointed Musician (Drummer) on March 1, 1863. Reduced to ranks in July-August, 1863. Reported present or accounted for in July-December, 1863. No further records.

HUFFSTUTLER, ALBERT, Private

Born in McDowell County where he resided as a farmer prior to enlisting in McDowell County at age 20, February 28, 1862. Reported present from November, 1862, through December, 1863, and in May-June, 1864. Hospitalized at Petersburg, Virginia, December 1, 1864, with a gunshot wound of the head. Place and date wounded not reported. Died in hospital at Petersburg on December 8, 1864, of wounds.

HUFFSTUTLER, HENRY, Private

Born in Lincoln County and resided in McDowell County where he was by occupation a farmer prior to enlisting in McDowell County at age 47, February 28, 1862. Deserted on August 8, 1862. Returned from desertion on February 8, 1863. Reported present or accounted for from March, 1863, through June, 1864. Reported absent sick in July-August, 1864.

HURT, JAMES R., Private

Born in Montgomery County and resided in McDowell County where he was by occupation a stonemason prior to enlisting in McDowell County at age 34, March 11, 1862. Wounded at Malvern Hill, Virginia, on or about July 1, 1862. Died in hospital at Charlottesville, Virginia, November 23, 1862, of "febris typhoides."

JACKSON, GABRIEL, Private

Born in McDowell County where he resided as laborer prior to enlisting in McDowell County at age 19, March 8, 1862. Reported present from November, 1862, through December, 1863, and in May-August, 1864. Captured at Five Forks, Virginia, April 1, 1865. Confined at Point Lookout, Maryland, April 5, 1865. Released at Point Lookout on June 28, 1865, after taking the Oath of Allegiance.

JAMES, FRANCIS A., Sergeant

Born in Rowan County and resided in McDowell County where he was by occupation a tailor prior to enlisting in McDowell County at age 46, February 15, 1862. Mustered in as Corporal. Promoted to Sergeant on an unspecified date that was probably prior to July 1, 1862. Wounded in the hand or head at Malvern Hill, Virginia, July 1, 1862. Reported absent without leave in November-December, 1862. Reported absent sick in January-February, 1863. Discharged on May 9, 1863, by reason of disability from wounds received at Malvern Hill.

JAMES, WILLIAM L., Musician

Born in Spartanburg District, South Carolina, and resided in McDowell County where he was by occupation

a carpenter prior to enlisting at age 28, February 20, 1862. Mustered in as Corporal. Promoted to Sergeant prior to January 1, 1863. Reported present in November, 1862-December, 1863. Appointed Musician in July-August, 1863. Reported present in May-August, 1864. Survived the war.

JOHNSON, WILLIAM, Private

Resided in McDowell County. Place and date of enlistment not reported; however, he probably enlisted subsequent to August 31, 1864. Hospitalized at Petersburg, Virginia, March 27, 1865, with pneumonia. Captured in hospital at Petersburg on April 3, 1865. Transferred to a Federal hospital at Point of Rocks, Virginia, where he arrived on April 9, 1865. Transferred to Point Lookout, Maryland, on an unspecified date. Released at Point Lookout on June 28, 1865, after taking the Oath of Allegiance.

JONES, WILLIAM L., Private

Place and date of enlistment not reported. Surrendered at Appomattox Court House, Virginia, April 9, 1865.

JORDAN, JAMES M., Private

Born in McDowell County where he resided as a laborer prior to enlisting in McDowell County at age 18, March 8, 1862. Killed at Sharpsburg, Maryland, September 17, 1862.

JUSTICE, WILLIAM A., Private

Born in McDowell County where he resided as a farmer prior to enlisting in McDowell County at age 18, March 10, 1862. Died in hospital at Petersburg, Virginia, on or about July 9, 1862, of "typhoid febris."

KESTER, JOHN, Private

Resided in Rutherford County. Place and date of enlistment not reported; however, he probably enlisted subsequent to August 31, 1864. Captured at Five Forks, Virginia, April 1, 1865. Confined at Point Lookout, Maryland, April 5, 1865. Released at Point Lookout on June 28, 1865, after taking the Oath of Allegiance.

LEAKY, J. S., Private

Resided in McDowell County where he enlisted on October 10, 1863, for the war. Reported present in May-August, 1864. Hospitalized at Richmond, Virginia, September 18, 1864, with chronic diarrhoea. Furloughed for thirty days on October 6, 1864. Deserted to the enemy on an unspecified date. Took the Oath of Allegiance in Tennessee on December 14, 1864.

LEWIS, JAMES, Private

Born in McDowell County* where he resided as a farmer prior to enlisting in McDowell County at age 25, March 28, 1862. Wounded at Malvern Hill, Virginia, July 1, 1862. Reported absent wounded in November-December, 1862. Listed as a deserter on February 10, 1863. Reported absent disabled in March-October, 1863. Reported absent sick in November-December, 1863, and May-August, 1864.

LOWREY, ALEX W., Private

Born in Yancey County* and resided in McDowell County

where he was by occupation a farmer prior to enlisting in McDowell County at age 31, March 11, 1862. Wounded at Malvern Hill, Virginia, July 1, 1862. Hospitalized at Richmond, Virginia, where he died on or about July 6, 1862, of wounds.

LYTLE, M. P., Corporal

Resided in Buncombe County and was by occupation a farmer prior to enlisting in McDowell County at age 31, October 2, 1863, for the war. Mustered in as Private. Reported present in September-December, 1863, and May-August, 1864. Promoted to Corporal in July-August, 1864. No further records.

McCOY, DANIEL M., Private

Born in McDowell County and was by occupation a carpenter prior to enlisting in McDowell County at age 18, March 10, 1864, for the war. Captured near Drewry's Bluff, Virginia, May 16, 1864. Confined at Point Lookout, Maryland, May 28, 1864. Released at Point Lookout on May 30, 1864, after taking the Oath of Allegiance and joining the U.S. Army. Assigned to Company I, 1st Regiment U.S. Volunteer Infantry.

McCURRY, KAJA J., Private

Born in Rutherford County where he resided as a farmer prior to enlisting in McDowell County at age 18, March 17, 1862. Captured at or near Sharpsburg, Maryland, on or about September 17, 1862. Paroled on September 21 or October 4, 1862. Reported present from November, 1862, through March, 1863. Captured at Sandy Ridge (Lenoir County) on April 20, 1863. Sent to Fort Monroe, Virginia. Paroled and transferred to City Point, Virginia, where he was received on May 28, 1863, for exchange. Reported present in July-October, 1863. Reported absent without leave in November-December, 1863, and May-August, 1864. Deserted to the enemy on or about October 9, 1864. Confined at Washington, D.C., October 12, 1864. Released on an unspecified date after taking the Oath of Allegiance.

McFARLAND, JOHN M., Private

Born in Cleveland County* and resided in McDowell County where he was by occupation a farmer prior to enlisting in McDowell County at age 23, March 3, 1862. Reported present from November, 1862, through December, 1863. Wounded near Petersburg, Virginia, June 16-18, 1864. Returned to duty prior to July 1, 1864. Wounded in the wrist at Petersburg on October 10, 1864. Survived the war.

McKINNY, HENRY, JR., Private

Born in McDowell County where he resided as a farmer prior to enlisting in McDowell County at age 18, March 24, 1862. Reported present from November, 1862, through December, 1863. No further records.

McKINNY, HENRY, SR., Private

Born in McDowell County* where he resided as a farmer prior to enlisting in McDowell County at age 34, February 25, 1862. Deserted on August 8, 1862. Returned to duty on February 22, 1863. Reported present in March-December, 1863. No further records. Survived the war. [North Carolina pension records indicate that he was wounded at Malvern Hill, Virginia, in 1862.]

McKINNY, JOSEPH, Private

Born in McDowell County* where he resided as a farmer prior to enlisting in McDowell County at age 21, March 24, 1862. Discharged on May 18, 1862, by reason of "dislocation of the [right] hip joint of too long standing to be restored with safety to the patient." He received his injury in a railroad accident near Company Shops (Burlington).

McKINNY, SAMPSON, Private

Born in McDowell County* where he resided as a farmer prior to enlisting in McDowell County at age 25, March 24, 1862. Deserted on or about August 15, 1862. Returned to duty on December 5, 1863. No further records. Survived the war. [North Carolina pension records indicate that he was injured near Petersburg, Virginia, in 1863.]

MANN, BENJAMIN M., Private

Born in Yancey County and resided in McDowell County where he was by occupation a laborer prior to enlisting in McDowell County at age 20, March 14, 1862. Reported absent sick from November, 1862, through December, 1863, and in May-August, 1864. Surrendered at Appomattox Court House, Virginia, April 9, 1865.

MANORS, CRAYTER J., Private

Born in Rutherford County where he resided as a farmer prior to enlisting in McDowell County at age 26, February 26, 1862. Deserted on August 15, 1862. Returned from desertion on an unspecified date. Hospitalized at Petersburg, Virginia, September 17, 1862, with acute dysentery. Deserted on April 3, 1863. Court-martialed on or about September 24, 1864. No further records.

MANORS, JAMES B., Private

Born in Rutherford County where he resided as a farmer prior to enlisting in McDowell County at age 20, March 12, 1862. Deserted on August 15, 1862. Hospitalized at Richmond, Virginia, November 12, 1862. Died in hospital at Richmond on January 14, 1863, of disease.

MARLOW, ELIJAH W., Private

Born in Rutherford County and resided in McDowell County where he was by occupation a farmer prior to enlisting in McDowell County at age 28, February 28, 1862. Reported present from November, 1862, through February, 1863. Deserted on May 29, 1863. Returned from desertion on June 27, 1863. Reported present in July-December, 1863, and May-June, 1864. Captured at Globe Tavern, Virginia, August 21, 1864. Confined at Point Lookout, Maryland, August 24, 1864. Paroled at Point Lookout on March 14, 1865. Received at Boulware's Wharf, James River, Virginia, March 16, 1865, for exchange.

MASHBURN, BAXTER, Private

Born in Yancey County* and resided in McDowell County where he was by occupation a farmer prior to enlisting in McDowell County at age 39, March 1, 1862. Died in hospital at Petersburg, Virginia, on or about July 23, 1862, of "typhoid febris."

MEDFORD, WILLIAM RILEY, Private

Born in McDowell County* where he resided as a farmer prior to enlisting in McDowell County at age 32, March 11, 1862. Reported present from November, 1862, through June, 1863. Deserted on July 24, 1863. Returned from desertion on October 25, 1863. Reported present in November-December, 1863. Wounded in the face and/or jaw at Drewry's Bluff, Virginia, in May, 1864. Hospitalized at Richmond, Virginia, May 16, 1864. Furloughed for sixty days on June 1, 1864. No further records. Survived the war.

MELTON, ALFRED, Private

Resided in Rutherford County and was by occupation a farmer prior to enlisting in McDowell County at age 30, March 1, 1864, for the war. Killed near Petersburg, Virginia, June 16-18, 1864.

MELTON, ELIJAH R., Sergeant

Born in Rutherford County where he resided as a farmer prior to enlisting in McDowell County at age 20, March 10, 1862. Mustered in as Private. Captured at or near Sharpsburg, Maryland, on or about September 17-19, 1862. Confined at Fort McHenry, Maryland. Paroled and transferred to Aiken's Landing, James River, Virginia, where he was received on November 2, 1862, for exchange. Declared exchanged at Aiken's Landing on November 10, 1862. Returned to duty and was promoted to Corporal prior to January 1, 1863. Promoted to Sergeant on May 1, 1863. Reported present in January-August, 1863. Died at home in Rutherford County on September 21 or September 25, 1863, of disease.

MELTON, S. L., Private

Resided in McDowell County where he enlisted on January 1, 1864, for the war. Reported present in May-August, 1864. Deserted to the enemy on or about October 24, 1864. Confined at Camp Hamilton, Virginia, November 1, 1864. Released on an unspecified date after taking the Oath of Allegiance.

MELTON, SAMUEL, Private

Born in Rutherford County where he resided as a farmer prior to enlisting in McDowell County at age 17, March 10, 1862. Wounded (leg broken) and captured at Sharpsburg, Maryland, September 17, 1862. Paroled on September 27, 1862. Reported absent wounded through December, 1863. Returned to duty on an unspecified date. Reported present in May-August, 1864. Deserted to the enemy on or about January 26, 1865. Confined at Washington, D.C., February 1, 1865. Released on an unspecified date after taking the Oath of Allegiance.

MELTON, W. LANDRUM, Private

Resided in Rutherford County and enlisted in McDowell County at age 18, January 1, 1864, for the war. Reported present in July-August, 1864. Deserted to the enemy on or about January 26, 1865. Confined at Washington, D.C., February 1, 1865. Released on an unspecified date after taking the Oath of Allegiance.

MOFFETT, J. R., Private

Resided in McDowell County where he enlisted at age 42, September 14, 1863, for the war. Reported present in November-December, 1863. Deserted near Weldon on March 27, 1864. Arrested on or about April 10, 1864. Rejoined the company on May 25, 1864. Hospitalized at Petersburg, Virginia, June 17, 1864, with diarrhoea. Died on July 25, 1864. Place and cause of death not reported.

MOFFETT, WILLIAM P., Private

Resided in McDowell County and was by occupation a farmer prior to enlisting in McDowell County at age 31, October 1, 1863, for the war. Reported present in November-December, 1863. Reported absent on detached service in May-August, 1864. Deserted at Petersburg, Virginia, October 4, 1864. Took the Oath of Allegiance at Knoxville, Tennessee, March 14, 1865.

MOFFITT, JAMES J., Private

Born in McDowell County where he resided as a farmer prior to enlisting in McDowell County at age 18, March 14, 1862. Reported present from November, 1862, through February, 1863. Deserted on May 16, 1863. Returned to duty on June 27, 1863. Reported present in July-December, 1863. Deserted on March 28, 1864. Arrested on or about April 10, 1864. Rejoined the company on May 25, 1864. Reported absent sick in July-August, 1864. Deserted at Petersburg, Virginia, August 31, 1864. Took the Oath of Allegiance at Knoxville, Tennessee, March 31, 1865.

MOFFITT, JOHN N., Private

Resided in McDowell or Buncombe County and enlisted in McDowell County at age 40, May 1, 1863, for the war. Reported present through December, 1863. Deserted near Weldon on March 27, 1864. Arrested on or about April 10, 1864. Rejoined the company on May 25, 1864. Reported present in July-August, 1864. Captured at Fort Stedman, Virginia, March 25, 1865. Confined at Point Lookout, Maryland, March 28, 1865. Released at Point Lookout on June 29, 1865, after taking the Oath of Allegiance.

MOONEY, GEORGE W., Private

Resided in McDowell County and was by occupation a farmer prior to enlisting in McDowell County at age 37, October 2, 1863, for the war. Deserted on December 1, 1863. Arrested on January 27, 1864. Rejoined the company on May 25, 1864. Reported present in July-August, 1864. Furloughed for sixty days on November 22, 1864.

MOONEY, JOHN, Private

Resided in McDowell County where he enlisted at age 18, February 9, 1863, for the war. Reported present or accounted for in February-December, 1863. Wounded in the face near Petersburg, Virginia, June 21-July 1, 1864. Returned to duty on or about July 1, 1864. Deserted to the enemy on or about January 26, 1865. Confined at Washington, D.C., February 1, 1865. Released on an unspecified date after taking the Oath of Allegiance.

MOONEY, ROBERT J., Private

Born in Rutherford County and resided in McDowell County where he was by occupation a farmer prior to enlisting in McDowell County at age 21, March 10, 1862. Reported present from November, 1862, through March, 1863. Captured at Sandy Ridge (Lenoir County) on April

20, 1863. Exchanged on June 1, 1863. Returned to duty in July-August, 1863. Reported present or accounted for in September-December, 1863, and May-August, 1864. Deserted to the enemy on or about January 26, 1865. Confined at Washington, D.C., February 1, 1865. Released on an unspecified date after taking the Oath of Allegiance.

MOORE, R. H., Sergeant
Resided in McDowell County where he enlisted at age 28, August 1, 1863, for the war. Mustered in as Private. Promoted to Corporal on October 1, 1863. Reported present through December, 1863. Deserted on March 28, 1864. Arrested on or about April 10, 1864. Rejoined the company on May 25, 1864. Reduced to ranks prior to July 1, 1864. Reported absent sick in July-August, 1864. Promoted to Sergeant on an unspecified date. Surrendered at Appomattox Court House, Virginia, April 9, 1865.

MORGAN, JOHN D., _____
North Carolina pension records indicate that he served in this company.

MORRISON, I. M., Private
Place and date of enlistment not reported; however, he probably enlisted subsequent to August 31, 1864. Surrendered at Appomattox Court House, Virginia, April 9, 1865.

MORROW, McKIBBIN, Private
Born in McDowell County where he resided as a farmer prior to enlisting in McDowell County at age 20, February 25, 1862. Died in hospital at Petersburg, Virginia, on or about August 18, 1862, of "dysenteria acuta."

MOSS, ABNER C., Private
Born in Iredell County and resided in McDowell County where he was by occupation a farmer prior to enlisting in McDowell County at age 47, March 10, 1862. Hospitalized on July 30, 1862, with bronchitis. Returned to duty on September 15, 1862. Reported present from November, 1862, through February, 1863. Died at Raleigh on April 4, 1863, of "diarrhoea."

MURRAY, W. D., Private
Place and date of enlistment not reported; however, he probably enlisted subsequent to August 31, 1864. Captured at Five Forks, Virginia, April 1, 1865. Confined at Point Lookout, Maryland, April 5, 1865. Died at Point Lookout on May 17, 1865, of "pneumonia."

NEAL, JOSEPH GRAYSON, Private
Previously served as Corporal in Company B, 22nd Regiment N.C. Troops (12th Regiment N.C. Volunteers). Enlisted in this company on October 6, 1863, with the rank of Private. Appointed 2nd Lieutenant on September 15, 1864, and transferred to Company B, 35th Regiment N.C. Troops.

NESBITT, BENJAMIN, Private
Resided in McDowell County and was by occupation a farmer prior to enlisting in McDowell County at age 39,

October 2, 1863, for the war. Reported present in October-December, 1863, and May-August, 1864. Captured at Five Forks, Virginia, April 1, 1865. Confined at Point Lookout, Maryland, April 5, 1865. Released at Point Lookout on June 29, 1865, after taking the Oath of Allegiance.

O'BRIEN, JOHN, Private
Born in Ireland and resided in McDowell County where he was by occupation a farmer prior to enlisting in McDowell County at age 33, March 12, 1862. Deserted in Maryland on September 10-12, 1862.

OWENS, ADAM C., Private
Enlisted in McDowell County on or about October 13, 1863, for the war. Deserted on November 25, 1863.

PARKER, JOSEPH, Private
Enlisted in McDowell County on October 2, 1863, for the war. Reported present until he deserted at Weldon on December 1, 1863.

PATTON, WILLIAM, Private
Born in McDowell County* where he resided as a farmer prior to enlisting in McDowell County at age 47, March 10, 1862. Captured at Frederick, Maryland, September 12, 1862. Confined at Fort Delaware, Delaware. Paroled and transferred to Aiken's Landing, James River, Virginia, October 2, 1862. Declared exchanged at Aiken's Landing on November 10, 1862. Reported absent without leave until January 25, 1863, when he rejoined the company. Deserted on May 16, 1863. Returned to duty on June 27, 1863. Reported present in July-December, 1863. Deserted near Weldon on February 24, 1864. Returned to duty on May 25, 1864. Reported present in July-August, 1864. Surrendered at Appomattox Court House, Virginia, April 9, 1865.

PENDERGRASS, MICHAEL G., Private
Resided in McDowell County where he enlisted at age 18, October 2, 1863, for the war. Reported present in July-August, 1864. Captured at Fort Stedman, Virginia, March 25, 1865. Confined at Point Lookout, Maryland, March 28, 1865. Released at Point Lookout on June 16, 1865, after taking the Oath of Allegiance.

PINKERTON, JAMES R., Private
Born in Buncombe County and resided in McDowell County where he was by occupation a farmer prior to enlisting in McDowell County at age 29, March 3, 1862. Deserted on September 12, 1862. Returned from desertion on March 1, 1863. Reported present or accounted for through December, 1863. No further records.

POPE, ALBERT, Private
Enlisted in McDowell County on March 1, 1864, for the war. Reported present in May-June, 1864. Reported absent sick in July-August, 1864. No further records.

POPE, ELKANAH, Private
Born in Lincoln County and was by occupation a blacksmith prior to enlisting in McDowell County at age

32, February 28, 1862. Deserted on August 10, 1862. Apprehended and brought back on November 12, 1862. Reported present in January-June, 1863. Deserted on July 24, 1863. Apprehended on an unspecified date, court-martialed, and sentenced to be shot on October 8, 1864. Applied for a pardon on October 5, 1864; however, it is not clear whether a pardon was granted. No further records.

POPE, FRANKLIN G., Private
Born in Rutherford County and resided in Catawba County where he was by occupation a laborer prior to enlisting in McDowell County at age 19, February 22, 1862. Died in hospital at Petersburg, Virginia, on or about August 11, 1862, of "febris typhoides."

POPE, JOHN W., Private
Born in Rutherford County and enlisted in McDowell County at age 21, March 16, 1862. Wounded in the chin at King's School House, Virginia, June 25, 1862. Returned to duty on an unspecified date. Reported present from November, 1862, through February, 1863. Captured at Sandy Ridge (Lenoir County) on April 20, 1863. Confined at Fort Monroe, Virginia. Paroled and transferred to City Point, Virginia, where he was received on May 28, 1863, for exchange. Returned to duty prior to July 1, 1863. Reported present through December, 1863. Captured near Drewry's Bluff, Virginia, May 16, 1864. Confined at Point Lookout, Maryland, May 19, 1864. Transferred to Elmira, New York, August 16, 1864. Released at Elmira on July 3, 1865, after taking the Oath of Allegiance.

POTEET, FRANCIS M., Private
Resided in McDowell County and was by occupation a miller prior to enlisting in McDowell County at age 36, October 2, 1863, for the war. Deserted at Weldon on December 1, 1863. Arrested on January 27, 1864. Rejoined the company on May 25, 1864. Reported present in July-August, 1864.

PRICHARD, HENRY, Private
Born in Yancey County* and was by occupation a farmer prior to enlisting in McDowell County at age 34, February 26, 1862. Deserted near Richmond, Virginia, December 20, 1862.

QUEEN, GEORGE W., Private
Born in Rutherford County where he resided as a laborer prior to enlisting in McDowell County at age 21, March 11, 1862. Reported present in November-December, 1862. Died in hospital at Petersburg, Virginia, February 15, 1863, of "febris typhoides."

QUEEN, JEREMIAH M., _____
North Carolina pension records indicate that he served in this company.

QUEEN, WILLIAM, Private
Born in Rutherford County where he resided as a laborer prior to enlisting in McDowell County at age 18, March 11, 1862. Reported present or accounted for in November, 1862-February, 1863. Captured at Sandy Ridge (Lenoir County) on April 20, 1863. Confined at Fort Monroe,

Virginia. Paroled and transferred to City Point, Virginia, where he was received on May 28, 1863, for exchange. Sent to hospital on June 25, 1863. Returned to duty in July-August, 1863. Reported present in September-December, 1863, and May-August, 1864. Deserted to the enemy on or about January 26, 1865. Confined at Washington, D.C., February 1, 1865. Released on an unspecified date after taking the Oath of Allegiance.

REEL, JOHN H., Private
Resided in McDowell County where he enlisted at age 19, April 10, 1864, for the war. Reported present in May-August, 1864. Survived the war.

RHOM, ROBERT, Private
Born in Rutherford County and resided in McDowell County where he was by occupation a laborer prior to enlisting in McDowell County at age 36, March 11, 1862. Reported present from November, 1862, through February, 1863. Wounded in the left leg and captured at Sandy Ridge (Lenoir County) on April 20, 1863. Left leg amputated. Hospitalized at New Bern. Transferred to Fort Monroe, Virginia, on or about July 18, 1863. Paroled on August 4, 1863. Received on or about August 5, 1863, for exchange. Retired to the Invalid Corps on December 20, 1864.

ROSS, SPENCER, Corporal
Born in McDowell County* where he resided as a farmer prior to enlisting in McDowell County at age 22, March 14, 1862. Mustered in as Corporal. Died at Goldsboro on May 18, 1862, of disease.

RUMFELT, JAMES S., Private
Born in McDowell County* where he resided as a laborer prior to enlisting in McDowell County at age 22, February 28, 1862. Reported present or accounted for from November, 1862, through June, 1863. Deserted on July 24, 1863. Returned from desertion on December 17, 1863. Deserted on February 24, 1864. Returned from desertion on May 25, 1864. Reported present in July-August, 1864. Hospitalized at Danville, Virginia, March 30, 1865, with pneumonia. Survived the war. [North Carolina pension records indicate that he was wounded in the leg at Petersburg, Virginia, on an unspecified date.]

RUMFELT, JOHN L., Private
Born in McDowell County where he resided as a laborer prior to enlisting in McDowell County at age 20, February 28, 1862. Died in hospital at Petersburg, Virginia, June 29, 1862, of "pneumonia."

SANDLIN, GEORGE L., Private
Born in McDowell County where he resided as a laborer prior to enlisting in McDowell County at age 18, March 11, 1862. Captured at Frederick, Maryland, September 12, 1862. Confined at Fort Delaware, Delaware. Paroled and transferred to Aiken's Landing, James River, Virginia, October 2, 1862, for exchange. Declared exchanged at Aiken's Landing on November 10, 1862. Reported present through March, 1863. Captured at Sandy Ridge (Lenoir County) on April 20, 1863. Confined at Fort Monroe, Virginia. Paroled and transferred to City Point, Virginia, where he was received on May 28, 1863,

for exchange. Reported present in July-December, 1863, and May-August, 1864. Survived the war.

SHEHAN, EDWARD A., Private
Born in Lancaster District, South Carolina, and resided in McDowell County where he was by occupation a laborer prior to enlisting in McDowell County at age 53, February 26, 1862. Reported present in November-December, 1862. Discharged on January 29 or February 1, 1863, by reason of disability.

SHEHAN, HODGE, Private
Born in McDowell County where he resided as a laborer prior to enlisting in McDowell County at age 16, February 26, 1862. Reported present from November, 1862, through December, 1863, and in May-June, 1864. Killed near Petersburg, Virginia, July 5, 1864.

SHERRELL, W., Private
Place and date of enlistment not reported; however, he probably enlisted subsequent to August 31, 1864. Surrendered at Appomattox Court House, Virginia, April 9, 1865.

SMART, PHILOW WHITEFIELD, Private
Born in Rutherford County where he resided as a laborer prior to enlisting in McDowell County at age 22, February 15, 1862. Reported present from November, 1862, through June, 1863. Reported absent sick in July-December, 1863. Killed near Petersburg, Virginia, June 21-July 1, 1864.

SMART, WILLIAM G., Private
Born in Rutherford County where he resided as a laborer prior to enlisting in McDowell County at age 31, February 26, 1862. Reported present from November, 1862, through December, 1863, and in May-June, 1864. Transferred to the Reserve Corps in July-August, 1864.

STAFFORD, NATHANIEL, Private
Born in McDowell County* where he resided as a laborer prior to enlisting in McDowell County at age 22, March 3, 1862. Died in hospital at Richmond, Virginia, on or about June 25, 1862. Cause of death not reported.

STREET, DAVID D., Private
Born in Rutherford County and resided in McDowell County where he was by occupation a shoemaker prior to enlisting in McDowell County at age 25, March 11, 1862. Killed at Sharpsburg, Maryland, September 17, 1862.

TOWRY, JOSEPH, Private
Born in Rutherford County where he resided as a laborer prior to enlisting in McDowell County at age 18, March 16, 1862. Wounded at Malvern Hill, Virginia, on or about July 1, 1862. Furloughed for thirty days on July 5, 1862. Reported absent without leave in November-December, 1862. Listed as a deserter on February 10, 1863. Discharged on May 1 or May 4, 1863. Reason discharged not reported.

TOWRY, MARTIN S., Private
Born in Rutherford County where he resided as a

laborer prior to enlisting in McDowell County at age 28, March 16, 1862. Reported absent without leave in November-December, 1862. Listed as a deserter on February 10, 1863. Reported absent on sick furlough in May-October, 1863. Reported absent sick in November-December, 1863. Returned to duty on an unspecified date. Reported present in May-August, 1864. Hospitalized at Richmond, Virginia, October 7, 1864, with acute colitis[?] and returned to duty on November 25, 1864. Captured at Five Forks, Virginia, April 1, 1865. Confined at Point Lookout, Maryland, April 5, 1865. Released at Point Lookout on June 21, 1865, after taking the Oath of Allegiance.

WACASTER, STEPHEN M., Private
Born in McDowell County* where he resided as a fifer prior to enlisting in McDowell County at age 22, March 1, 1862. Reported present from November, 1862, through June, 1863. Deserted on July 24, 1863.

WACASTER, WILLIAM W., Private
Born in McDowell County* where he resided as a fifer prior to enlisting in McDowell County at age 35, March 8, 1862. Reported present from November, 1862, through June, 1863. Deserted on or about July 24, 1863. Returned to duty on July 1, 1864. Deserted on July 24, 1864.

WADKINS, JOHN M., Private
Born in Claiborne County, Tennessee, and resided in McDowell County where he was by occupation a miner prior to enlisting in McDowell County at age 38, March 1, 1862. Wounded at Sharpsburg, Maryland, September 17, 1862. Reported absent wounded or absent sick through December, 1863. Returned to duty on an unspecified date. Reported present in May-August, 1864.

WALKER, ALFRED, Private
Born in Rutherford County where he resided as a laborer prior to enlisting in McDowell County at age 32, March 12, 1862. Reported present from November, 1862, through December, 1863, and in May-August, 1864. Deserted to the enemy on or about February 26, 1865. Confined at Washington, D.C., March 1, 1865. Released on an unspecified date after taking the Oath of Allegiance.

WALKER, JAMES W., Private
Born in Rutherford County where he resided as a laborer prior to enlisting in McDowell County at age 22, March 12, 1862. Captured at Frederick, Maryland, September 12, 1862. Confined at Fort Delaware, Delaware. Paroled and transferred to Aiken's Landing, James River, Virginia, October 2, 1862, for exchange. Declared exchanged at Aiken's Landing on November 10, 1862. Reported absent without leave until January 11, 1863, when he returned to duty. Reported present in March-December, 1863, and May-August, 1864. Deserted to the enemy on or about February 26, 1865. Confined at Washington, D.C., March 1, 1865. Released on an unspecified date after taking the Oath of Allegiance. [North Carolina pension records indicate that he was wounded in the chest on June 20, 1863.]

WALKER, JERRY, SR., Private

Born in Rutherford County where he resided as a laborer prior to enlisting in McDowell County at age 20, March 12, 1862. Reported present or accounted for from November, 1862, through December, 1863. Wounded in the left shoulder and right leg at or near Drewry's Bluff, Virginia, on or about May 14, 1864. Hospitalized at Richmond, Virginia. Furloughed for forty days on or about June 5, 1864. Returned to duty on or about August 15, 1864. Survived the war.

WALKER, JERRY L., Corporal

Born in Rutherford County where he resided as a laborer prior to enlisting in McDowell County at age 19, February 27, 1862. Mustered in as Private. Wounded at Sharpsburg, Maryland, September 17, 1862. Returned to duty on an unspecified date. Reported present or accounted for from November, 1862, through December, 1863. Wounded in the head near Petersburg, Virginia, June 30, 1864. Returned to duty prior to August 31, 1864. Promoted to Corporal subsequent to August 31, 1864. Deserted to the enemy on or about March 8, 1865. Confined at Washington, D.C., March 10, 1865. Released on an unspecified date after taking the Oath of Allegiance.

WALKER, JOHN, Private

Born in Rutherford County where he resided as a laborer prior to enlisting in McDowell County at age 24, March 16, 1862. Reported present from November, 1862, through December, 1863. Captured at Bermuda Hundred, Virginia, June 2, 1864. Confined at Point Lookout, Maryland, June 10, 1864. Transferred to Elmira, New York, July 9, 1864. Paroled at Elmira on March 14, 1865. Received at Boulware's Wharf, James River, Virginia, on or about March 21, 1865, for exchange. Hospitalized at Richmond, Virginia, March 22, 1865, with debilitas. Deserted on March 23, 1865.

WALKER, JONATHAN, Private

Born in Rutherford County where he resided as a laborer prior to enlisting in McDowell County at age 23, March 16, 1862. Reported present from November, 1862, through December, 1863. Captured at Bermuda Hundred, Virginia, June 2, 1864. Confined at Fort Monroe, Virginia. Transferred to Point Lookout, Maryland, where he arrived on June 12, 1864. Transferred to Elmira, New York, July 9, 1864. Paroled at Elmira on February 20, 1865, and transferred for exchange. [North Carolina pension records indicate that he was wounded in the head at Petersburg, Virginia, May 7, 1864, and was wounded in the right leg at "Gettysburg, Pennsylvania, in October, 1864."]

WALKER, WASHINGTON, _____

Place and date of enlistment not reported. Name cancelled prior to April 15, 1862. No further records.

WARD, JETHRO, Private

Born in McDowell County where he resided as a laborer prior to enlisting in McDowell County at age 19, March 1, 1862. Reported absent sick in November-December, 1862. Listed as a deserter on February 10, 1863. Reported absent sick in March-December, 1863. Returned to duty on an unspecified date. Reported present in May-June,

1864. Reported absent sick in July-August, 1864. Survived the war.

WATKINS, GEORGE E., Private

Place and date of enlistment not reported. Wounded at Malvern Hill, Virginia, July 1, 1862. Returned to duty on an unspecified date. Killed at Sharpsburg, Maryland, September 17, 1862.

WEST, ALEXANDER, Private

Resided in McDowell County where he enlisted at age 17, May 15, 1862, for the war. Reported present or accounted for from November, 1862, through December, 1863, and in May-August, 1864. Captured at Five Forks, Virginia, April 1, 1865. Confined at Point Lookout, Maryland, April 5, 1865. Released at Point Lookout on June 21, 1865, after taking the Oath of Allegiance.

WEST, THOMAS, Private

Born in McDowell County where he resided as a laborer prior to enlisting in McDowell County at age 18, March 14, 1862. Reported absent without leave in November-December, 1862. Listed as a deserter on February 10, 1863. Died in McDowell County on April 9 or April 18, 1863, of disease.

WHISNANT, ELKANAH, Sergeant

Born in Rutherford County where he resided as a laborer prior to enlisting in McDowell County at age 24, March 11, 1862. Mustered in as Private. Wounded at Sharpsburg, Maryland, September 17, 1862. Returned to duty on an unspecified date. Promoted to Corporal on November 1, 1862. Reported present from November, 1862, through December, 1863. Promoted to Sergeant on October 1, 1863. Reported present in May-August, 1864. Deserted to the enemy on or about March 8, 1865. Confined at Washington, D.C., March 10, 1865. Released on an unspecified date after taking the Oath of Allegiance.

WHISNANT, EPHRAIM, Private

Resided in Rutherford County and was by occupation a farmer prior to enlisting in McDowell County at age 39, October 2, 1863, for the war. Reported present in October-December, 1863, and May-August, 1864. Wounded in both legs at Fort Stedman, Virginia, March 25, 1865. Hospitalized at Richmond, Virginia. Captured in hospital at Richmond on April 3, 1865. Transferred to Point Lookout, Maryland, May 9, 1865. Released at Point Lookout on or about June 28, 1865, after taking the Oath of Allegiance.

1ST COMPANY B

This company, known as the "Chatham Cossacks," was raised in Chatham County and enlisted in Chatham County in February-March, 1862. It was mustered into state service at Camp Mangum, near Raleigh, on April 21, 1862, and assigned to the 49th Regiment N.C. Troops as Company B. Inasmuch as it was the first of two companies to serve in the 49th Regiment as Company B, it was later referred to as 1st Company B. The company served with the 49th Regiment until January 9, 1863, when it was transferred to the 15th Regiment N.C. Troops (5th Regiment N.C. Volunteers) in exchange for Company D of the 15th. When this company joined the 15th Regiment, it was designated 2nd Company D.

The information contained in the following roster was compiled in part from a company muster-in and descriptive roll dated April 21, 1862, and from a company muster roll for November 1-December 31, 1862. No company muster rolls were found for May 1-October 31, 1862. Valuable information was obtained from primary sources such as the North Carolina adjutant general's *Roll of Honor*, discharge certificates, medical records, prisoner of war records, *The War of the Rebellion: A Compilation of the Official Records of the Union and Confederate Armies*, militia records, newspaper casualty lists and obituaries, Confederate pension applications filed with the state of North Carolina, and the 1860 federal census of North Carolina. Secondary sources such as postwar rosters and histories, cemetery records, the *Confederate Veteran*, published genealogies, and records of the United Daughters of the Confederacy also provided useful information.

The following roster covers only the period from February-March, 1862, through January 9, 1863. All service record information after that date appears in the roster of 2nd Company D, 15th Regiment N.C. Troops (5th Regiment N.C. Volunteers), in Volume V of this series.

OFFICERS

CAPTAINS

WARD, EDWARD H.
Born in Chatham County and was by occupation a physician prior to enlisting at age 31. Elected Captain on April 21, 1862. Resigned on May 26, 1862, by reason of "ill health & indisposition. . . ." Resignation accepted on May 31, 1862.

BENNETT, JEHU S.
Born in Chatham County where he resided as a farmer prior to enlisting at age 29. Appointed 1st Lieutenant on April 21, 1862. Promoted to Captain on May 31, 1862. Died in hospital at Petersburg, Virginia, August 10, 1862, of "febris typhoides."

OLDHAM, YOUNGER A.
Born in Chatham County where he resided as a farmer prior to enlisting at age 21. Elected 2nd Lieutenant on or about May 30, 1862. Elected 1st Lieutenant on May 31, 1862. Promoted to Captain on or about August 10, 1862. Transferred to 2nd Company D, 15th Regiment N.C. Troops (5th Regiment N.C. Volunteers), January 9, 1863.

LIEUTENANT

RIGGSBEE, JOHN M., 3rd Lieutenant
Born in Chatham County where he resided as a farmer

prior to enlisting at age 23. Appointed 3rd Lieutenant on or about April 21, 1862. Reduced to ranks on or about May 31, 1862, because there were not enough men in the company to entitle it to a full complement of officers. [Previously served as 2nd Lieutenant in the 49th Regiment N.C. Militia. See also his service record in the Noncommissioned Officers and Privates' section below.]

NONCOMMISSIONED OFFICERS AND PRIVATES

ANDREWS, WILLIAM H., Private
Born in Orange County where he resided as a carpenter prior to enlisting at age 29, March 8, 1862. Killed at Malvern Hill, Virginia, July 1, 1862.

AUSLEY, JAMES W., Private
Born in Chatham County where he resided as a farmer prior to enlisting at age 19, March 3, 1862. Reported present in November-December, 1862. Transferred to 2nd Company D, 15th Regiment N.C. Troops (5th Regiment N.C. Volunteers), January 9, 1863.

BENNETT, ALVIN, Private
Born in Chatham County where he resided as a farmer prior to enlisting at age 43, February 25, 1862. Captured at Frederick, Maryland, September 12, 1862. Confined at Fort Delaware, Delaware. Paroled and transferred to Aiken's Landing, James River, Virginia, October 2, 1862, for exchange. Received at Aiken's Landing on October 6, 1862. Died in hospital at Richmond, Virginia, October 9 or October 27, 1862, of "febris typhoides."

BENNETT, JAMES G., Private
Born in Chatham County where he resided as a farmer prior to enlisting at age 25, February 25, 1862. Reported absent without leave in November-December, 1862. Transferred to 2nd Company D, 15th Regiment N.C. Troops (5th Regiment N.C. Volunteers), January 9, 1863.

BENNETT, MANATH A., Private
Born in Chatham County where he resided as a farmer prior to enlisting at age 21, February 25, 1862. Died in hospital at Petersburg, Virginia, on or about November 17, 1862, of "pneumonia."

BENNETT, WILLIAM BENJAMIN, Private
Born in Chatham County where he resided as a farmer prior to enlisting at age 24, February 25, 1862. Wounded at Malvern Hill, Virginia, July 1, 1862. Returned to duty prior to December 13, 1862, when he was wounded in the face at Fredericksburg, Virginia. Hospitalized at Richmond, Virginia, December 16, 1862. Transferred to 2nd Company D, 15th Regiment N.C. Troops (5th Regiment N.C. Volunteers), January 9, 1863.

BLAKE, JOHN, Private
Born in Orange County and resided in Chatham County where he was by occupation a farmer prior to enlisting at age 16, March 11, 1862, as a substitute. Died on May 20, 1862, of disease. Place of death not reported.

BREWER, SAMUEL W., Private

Born in Chatham County where he resided as a farmer prior to enlisting at age 21, February 25, 1862. Captured at Frederick, Maryland, September 12, 1862. Confined at Fort Delaware, Delaware, on an unspecified date. Paroled at Fort Delaware and transferred to Aiken's Landing, James River, Virginia, October 2, 1862, for exchange. Declared exchanged at Aiken's Landing on November 10, 1862. Reported absent without leave on or about December 31, 1862. Transferred to 2nd Company D, 15th Regiment N.C. Troops (5th Regiment N.C. Volunteers), January 9, 1863.

BROWN, ALBERT, Sergeant

Born in Chatham County where he resided as a farmer prior to enlisting at age 21, March 23, 1862. Mustered in as Sergeant. Died in hospital at Petersburg, Virginia, July 23, 1862, of "meningitis."

BROWN, ELISHA B., Private

Born in Chatham County where he resided as a farmer prior to enlisting at age 27, March 1, 1862. Reported present in November-December, 1862. Transferred to 2nd Company D, 15th Regiment N.C. Troops (5th Regiment N.C. Volunteers), January 9, 1863.

BROWN, JOSEPH A., Private

Born in Chatham County where he resided as a farmer prior to enlisting at age 43, March 5, 1862. Discharged on October 10, 1862, by reason of disability.

CAVINESS, THOMAS, Private

Born in Chatham County where he resided prior to enlisting in Pitt County on March 18, 1862. Never reported for duty. Transferred to 2nd Company D, 15th Regiment N.C. Troops (5th Regiment N.C. Volunteers), January 9, 1863.

CLARK, THOMAS C., Private

Born in Chatham County where he resided as a farmer prior to enlisting at age 23, March 11, 1862. Reported present in November-December, 1862. Transferred to 2nd Company D, 15th Regiment N.C. Troops (5th Regiment N.C. Volunteers), January 9, 1863.

COLE, JAMES M., Private

Born in Chatham County where he resided as a farmer prior to enlisting at age 20, February 24, 1862. Wounded at Malvern Hill, Virginia, July 1, 1862. Reported present in November-December, 1862. Transferred to 2nd Company D, 15th Regiment N.C. Troops (5th Regiment N.C. Volunteers), January 9, 1863.

COLE, JOHN, Private

Born in Chatham County and was by occupation a farmer prior to enlisting at age 44, February 25, 1862. Never reported for duty. Transferred to 2nd Company D, 15th Regiment N.C. Troops (5th Regiment N.C. Volunteers), January 9, 1863.

COOK, WILLIAM P., Private

Born in Davidson County and resided in Chatham County prior to enlisting at age 30, February 24, 1862. Reported absent without leave in November-December, 1862. Transferred to 2nd Company D, 15th Regiment N.C. Troops (5th Regiment N.C. Volunteers), January 9, 1863.

COOPER, JAMES DANIEL, Private

Born in Chatham County where he resided as a farmer prior to enlisting at age 28, March 1, 1862. Reported present in November-December, 1862. Transferred to 2nd Company D, 15th Regiment N.C. Troops (5th Regiment N.C. Volunteers), January 9, 1863.

DAWSON, JOSEPH, Private

Born in Chatham or Orange County and resided in Chatham County where he was by occupation a farmer prior to enlisting at age 33, March 3, 1862. Died in hospital at Liberty, Virginia, November 20 or December 20, 1862, of "fever."

FOLTEGE, SAMUEL, Private

Resided in Davidson County and enlisted at age 24, July 15, 1862, for the war. Killed at Sharpsburg, Maryland, September 17, 1862.

GOODWIN, WESLEY, Sergeant

Born in Chatham County where he resided as a carpenter prior to enlisting at age 41, February 24, 1862. Mustered in as Sergeant. Discharged in April, 1862, by reason of disability.

GOODWIN, WINSHIP, Private

Born in Chatham County where he resided as a farmer prior to enlisting at age 19, March 3, 1862. Reported present in November-December, 1862. Transferred to 2nd Company D, 15th Regiment N.C. Troops (5th Regiment N.C. Volunteers), January 9, 1863.

HACKNEY, ALBERT J., Sergeant

Born in Chatham County where he resided as a farmer prior to enlisting at age 23, March 10, 1862. Mustered in as Sergeant. Reported absent sick in November-December, 1862. Transferred to 2nd Company D, 15th Regiment N.C. Troops (5th Regiment N.C. Volunteers), January 9, 1863.

HACKNEY, BASIL A., Private

Born in Chatham County where he resided as a farmer prior to enlisting at age 24, March 8, 1862. Mustered in as Musician (Drummer). Reduced to ranks prior to January 1, 1863. Reported absent sick in hospital in November-December, 1862. Transferred to 2nd Company D, 15th Regiment N.C. Troops (5th Regiment N.C. Volunteers), January 9, 1863.

HACKNEY, BASIL M., Private

Born in Chatham County where he resided as a farmer prior to enlisting at age 33, March 8, 1862. Reported absent without leave in November-December, 1862. Transferred to 2nd Company D, 15th Regiment N.C. Troops (5th Regiment N.C. Volunteers), January 9, 1863.

HACKNEY, JESSE E., Private

Born in Chatham County where he resided as a farmer prior to enlisting at age 19, March 11, 1862. Wounded at

Malvern Hill, Virginia, July 1, 1862. Returned to duty on an unspecified date. Reported present in November-December, 1862. Transferred to 2nd Company D, 15th Regiment N.C. Troops (5th Regiment N.C. Volunteers), January 9, 1863.

HACKNEY, JOSHUA H., Private
Born in Chatham County where he resided as a farmer prior to enlisting at age 25, March 10, 1862. Reported present in November-December, 1862. Transferred to 2nd Company D, 15th Regiment N.C. Troops (5th Regiment N.C. Volunteers), January 9, 1863.

HENDERSON, JOHN, Private
Born in Chatham County where he resided as a farmer prior to enlisting at age 50, March 14, 1862. Discharged on June 20, 1862, by reason of being overage.

HERNDON, SIDNEY LUCIEN, Corporal
Born in Chatham County where he resided as a farmer prior to enlisting at age 35, February 26, 1862. Mustered in as Corporal. Wounded at Malvern Hill, Virginia, July 1, 1862. Reported absent without leave in November-December, 1862. Transferred to 2nd Company D, 15th Regiment N.C. Troops (5th Regiment N.C. Volunteers), January 9, 1863.

HORTON, JAMES W., Sergeant
Born in Chatham County where he resided as a farmer prior to enlisting at age 25, March 6, 1862. Mustered in as Sergeant. Captured at Frederick, Maryland, September 12, 1862. Confined at Fort Delaware, Delaware. Paroled and transferred to Aiken's Landing, James River, Virginia, October 2, 1862. Declared exchanged at Aiken's Landing on November 10, 1862. Returned to duty prior to January 1, 1863. Transferred to 2nd Company D, 15th Regiment N.C. Troops (5th Regiment N.C. Volunteers), January 9, 1863. Later served as 3rd Lieutenant of that unit. [Prior to his service in 1st Company B, 49th Regiment N.C. Troops, he served as 1st Lieutenant in the 49th Regiment N.C. Militia.]

KIRBY, WILEY L., Private
Born in Chatham County where he resided as a farmer prior to enlisting at age 18, February 25, 1862. Wounded at Malvern Hill, Virginia, July 1, 1862. Returned to duty on an unspecified date. Reported present in November-December, 1862. Transferred to 2nd Company D, 15th Regiment N.C. Troops (5th Regiment N.C. Volunteers), January 9, 1863.

MANN, CARNEY C., Private
Born in Chatham County where he resided as a farmer prior to enlisting at age 21, March 11, 1862. Furloughed for sixty days on November 5, 1862. Transferred to 2nd Company D, 15th Regiment N.C. Troops (5th Regiment N.C. Volunteers), January 9, 1863.

MANN, HENRY A., Private
Born in Chatham County where he resided as a farmer prior to enlisting at age 18, February 24, 1862. Reported absent without leave in November-December, 1862. Transferred to 2nd Company D, 15th Regiment N.C. Troops (5th Regiment N.C. Volunteers), January 9, 1863.

MARKS, JAMES A., Private
Born in Stanly County* where he resided as a farmer prior to enlisting at age 23, March 5, 1862. Reported present in November-December, 1862. Transferred to 2nd Company D, 15th Regiment N.C. Troops (5th Regiment N.C. Volunteers), January 9, 1863.

MARKS, THOMAS B., Private
Born in Chatham County where he resided as a farmer prior to enlisting at age 26 on February 25, 1862. Reported present in November-December, 1862. Transferred to 2nd Company D, 15th Regiment N.C. Troops (5th Regiment N.C. Volunteers), January 9, 1863.

MORGAN, JOHN, Private
Born in Chatham County where he resided as a farmer prior to enlisting at age 16, February 28, 1862, as a substitute. Died on May 20, 1862, of disease. Place of death not reported.

NEAL, ELISHA M., Private
Born in Chatham County where he resided as a farmer prior to enlisting at age 30, March 3, 1862. Hospitalized at Richmond, Virginia, October 16, 1862, with chronic diarrhoea. Transferred to 2nd Company D, 15th Regiment N.C. Troops (5th Regiment N.C. Volunteers), January 9, 1863.

NEAL, WILLIAM A., Private
Born in Chatham County where he resided as a farmer prior to enlisting at age 18, March 3, 1862. Hospitalized at Culpeper, Virginia, November 3, 1862, with pneumonia. Transferred to hospital at Richmond, Virginia, on or about November 6, 1862. Furloughed for thirty days on November 25, 1862. Transferred to 2nd Company D, 15th Regiment N.C. Troops (5th Regiment N.C. Volunteers), January 9, 1863.

OLDHAM, THOMAS S., Corporal
Born in Chatham County where he resided as a farmer prior to enlisting at age 26, March 23, 1862. Mustered in as Corporal. Reported absent sick in November-December, 1862. Transferred to 2nd Company D, 15th Regiment N.C. Troops (5th Regiment N.C. Volunteers), January 9, 1863.

OLDHAM, WESLEY A., Private
Born in Chatham County where he resided as a farmer prior to enlisting at age 18, March 17, 1862. Died in hospital at Richmond, Virginia, December 17, 1862, of "c[hronic] diarrhoea" and/or "pneumonia."

OLDHAM, WILLIAM E., Sergeant
Born in Chatham County where he resided as a farmer prior to enlisting at age 23, February 25, 1862. Mustered in as Corporal. Reported present in November-December, 1862. Promoted to Sergeant prior to January 1, 1863. Transferred to 2nd Company D, 15th Regiment N.C. Troops (5th Regiment N.C. Volunteers), January 9, 1863. Later served as 1st Lieutenant of that unit.

OLIVE, CALVIN, Corporal
Born in Chatham County where he resided as a farmer prior to enlisting at age 41, February 25, 1862. Mustered in as Corporal. Reported absent sick in November-December, 1862. Transferred to 2nd Company D, 15th Regiment N.C. Troops (5th Regiment N.C. Volunteers), January 9, 1863.

PARTIN, BENJAMIN F., Private
Born in Orange County and resided in Chatham County where he was by occupation a farmer prior to enlisting at age 20, February 24, 1862. Hospitalized at Danville, Virginia, July 2, 1862, with bronchitis. Furloughed on September 27, 1862. Reported absent without leave in November-December, 1862. Transferred to 2nd Company D, 15th Regiment N.C. Troops (5th Regiment N.C. Volunteers), January 9, 1863.

PENNINGTON, JACKSON, Private
Born in Chatham County where he resided as a farmer prior to enlisting at age 19, March 30, 1862. Reported present in November-December, 1862. Transferred to 2nd Company D, 15th Regiment N.C. Troops (5th Regiment N.C. Volunteers), January 9, 1863.

PICKARD, ALVIS, Private
Born in Alamance County* where he resided prior to enlisting on March 4, 1862. Never reported for duty. Transferred to 2nd Company D, 15th Regiment N.C. Troops (5th Regiment N.C. Volunteers), January 9, 1863.

RAY, BRANTLEY M., Private
Born in Orange or Chatham County and resided in Orange County where he was by occupation a blacksmith prior to enlisting at age 27, February 24, 1862. Discharged on or about December 11, 1862, by reason of "hernia."

RAY, FRANCIS, Private
Born in Chatham County and resided in Orange County where he was by occupation a blacksmith prior to enlisting at age 30, March 18, 1862. Reported absent without leave in November-December, 1862. Transferred to 2nd Company D, 15th Regiment N.C. Troops (5th Regiment N.C. Volunteers), January 9, 1863.

REAVES, JOHN, Private
Born in Chatham County where he resided as a farmer prior to enlisting at age 39, February 25, 1862. Died in hospital at Petersburg, Virginia, July 20, 1862, of "typhoid febris."

RIGGSBEE, ALEXANDER J., Private
Born in Chatham County where he resided as a farmer prior to enlisting at age 18, February 25, 1862. Wounded at Malvern Hill, Virginia, July 1, 1862. Returned to duty prior to September 17, 1862, when he was wounded at Sharpsburg, Maryland. Returned to duty on an unspecified date. Reported present in November-December, 1862. Transferred to 2nd Company D, 15th Regiment N.C. Troops (5th Regiment N.C. Volunteers), January 9, 1863.

RIGGSBEE, ELBERT, Private
Born in Chatham County where he resided as a laborer

prior to enlisting at age 23, February 25, 1862. Reported present in November-December, 1862. Transferred to 2nd Company D, 15th Regiment N.C. Troops (5th Regiment N.C. Volunteers), January 9, 1863.

RIGGSBEE, JOHN ALVIS, 1st Sergeant
Born in Chatham County where he resided as a carpenter prior to enlisting at age 34, February 24, 1862. Mustered in as 1st Sergeant. Wounded at Malvern Hill, Virginia, July 1, 1862. Reported absent sick in hospital in November-December, 1862. Transferred to 2nd Company D, 15th Regiment N.C. Troops (5th Regiment N.C. Volunteers), January 9, 1863.

RIGGSBEE, JOHN M., Private
Previously served as 3rd Lieutenant of this company. [See Lieutenants' section above.] Reduced to ranks on or about May 31, 1862. Wounded at Malvern Hill, Virginia, July 1, 1862. Discharged on August 10, 1862, after providing a substitute.

RIGGSBEE, JOHN W., Private
Born in Chatham County where he resided as a farmer prior to enlisting at age 24, February 25, 1862. Reported present in November-December, 1862. Transferred to 2nd Company D, 15th Regiment N.C. Troops (5th Regiment N.C. Volunteers), January 9, 1863.

RIGGSBEE, JONES E., Private
Born in Chatham County where he resided as a laborer prior to enlisting at age 21, February 25, 1862. Mustered in as Musician (Fifer). Reduced to ranks on an unspecified date. Reported present in November-December, 1862. Transferred to 2nd Company D, 15th Regiment N.C. Troops (5th Regiment N.C. Volunteers), January 9, 1863.

RIGGSBEE, LARKINS J., Private
Resided in Chatham County and was by occupation a laborer prior to enlisting at age 24, June 20, 1862, for the war. Reported absent sick in hospital in November-December, 1862. Transferred to 2nd Company D, 15th Regiment N.C. Troops (5th Regiment N.C. Volunteers), January 9, 1863.

RIGGSBEE, REVEL, Private
Born in Chatham County where he resided as a farmer prior to enlisting at age 19, February 25, 1862. Reported present in November-December, 1862. Transferred to 2nd Company D, 15th Regiment N.C. Troops (5th Regiment N.C. Volunteers), January 9, 1863.

RIGGSBEE, THOMAS S., Private
Born in Chatham County where he resided as a farmer prior to enlisting at age 16, February 25, 1862. Discharged on or about September 20, 1862, by reason of being underage.

RIGGSBEE, WILLIAM L., Private
Born in Chatham County where he resided as a farmer prior to enlisting at age 35, February 25, 1862. Died in hospital at Petersburg, Virginia, July 28, 1862, of "febris typhoides."

RYLEY, JAMES, Private
Resided in Chatham County and enlisted at age 36, August 10, 1862, for the war as a substitute. Deserted at Petersburg, Virginia, August 20, 1862.

STEDMAN, ANDREW J., Sergeant
Born in Gates County where he resided as a lawyer prior to enlisting in Chatham County at age 32, March 18, 1862. Mustered in as Sergeant. Wounded at Malvern Hill, Virginia, July 1, 1862. Appointed Signal Officer (1st Lieutenant) on October 13, 1862, to rank from October 10, 1862, and transferred to the Signal Corps.

WADDLE, CAMULL D., Private
Born in Chatham County where he resided prior to enlisting in Chatham County at age 18, March 18, 1862. Appointed Drillmaster and transferred for duty at Camp Mangum, near Raleigh, in April, 1862.

WHITFIELD, CANNY L., Private
Born in Martin County where he resided as a carpenter prior to enlisting at age 34, March 3, 1862. Reported present in November-December, 1862. Transferred to 2nd Company D, 15th Regiment N.C. Troops (5th Regiment N.C. Volunteers), January 9, 1863.

WHITFIELD, WILLIAM T., Private
Born in Martin County where he resided as a farmer prior to enlisting at age 37, March 3, 1862. Reported present in November-December, 1862. Transferred to 2nd Company D, 15th Regiment N.C. Troops (5th Regiment N.C. Volunteers), January 9, 1863.

WICKS, JAMES A., Private
Born in Orange or Chatham County and resided in Chatham County where he was by occupation a farmer prior to enlisting at age 25, March 1, 1862. Captured at Frederick, Maryland, September 12, 1862. Confined at Fort Delaware, Delaware. Paroled and transferred to Aiken's Landing, James River, Virginia, October 2, 1862, for exchange. Declared exchanged at Aiken's Landing on November 10, 1862. Reported absent without leave in November-December, 1862. Transferred to 2nd Company D, 15th Regiment N.C. Troops (5th Regiment N.C. Volunteers), January 9, 1863.

WILLIAMS, ADDISON J., Private
Born in Chatham County where he resided as a farmer prior to enlisting at age 19, March 19, 1862. Captured by the enemy on an unspecified date. Paroled at Leesburg, Virginia, October 2, 1862. Reported present in November-December, 1862. Transferred to 2nd Company D, 15th Regiment N.C. Troops (5th Regiment N.C. Volunteers), January 9, 1863.

WORKMAN, ADDISON F., Private
Born in Chatham County and resided in Orange County where he was by occupation a farmer prior to enlisting in Chatham County at age 16, March 18, 1862. Discharged at Lynchburg, Virginia, on or about December 2, 1862, by reason of "pulmonary tuberculosis with tender years."

2ND COMPANY B

This company was raised in Cleveland County and was known as the "Cleveland Mountain Boys." It served initially as Company D of the 15th Regiment N.C. Troops (5th Regiment N.C. Volunteers) but was transferred to the 49th Regiment on January 9, 1863, in exchange for Company B of the 49th. When the company joined the 49th Regiment it was designated 2nd Company B. After joining the regiment the company functioned as a part of the regiment, and its history for the remainder of the war is reported as a part of the regimental history.

The information contained in the following roster was compiled primarily from company muster rolls for January 9-December 31, 1863, and May 1-August 31, 1864. No company muster rolls were found for January 1-April 30, 1864, or for the period after August 31, 1864. Valuable information was obtained from primary records such as the North Carolina adjutant general's *Roll of Honor*, discharge certificates, medical records, prisoner of war records, *The War of the Rebellion: A Compilation of the Official Records of the Union and Confederate Armies*, militia records, newspaper casualty lists and obituaries, Confederate pension applications filed with the state of North Carolina, and the 1860 federal census of North Carolina. Secondary sources such as postwar rosters and histories, cemetery records, the *Confederate Veteran*, published genealogies, and records of the United Daughters of the Confederacy also provided useful information.

The following roster covers only the period from the date of the company's transfer to the end of the war. All service record information prior to January 9, 1863, has been recorded in the roster of 1st Company D, 15th Regiment N.C. Troops (5th Regiment N.C. Volunteers), in Volume V of this series.

OFFICERS

CAPTAINS

CORBETT, WILLIAM S.
Previously served as Captain of 1st Company D, 15th Regiment N.C. Troops (5th Regiment N.C. Volunteers). Transferred to this company on January 9, 1863. Injured in a railroad accident near Cherryville on March 28, 1863, while on his way home on furlough. Reported absent by reason of injuries until January 13, 1865, when he was retired from service.

MAGNESS, JUDSON JORDAN
Previously served as 1st Lieutenant of 1st Company D, 15th Regiment N.C. Troops (5th Regiment N.C. Volunteers). Transferred to this company on January 9, 1863. Mustered in as 1st Lieutenant. Reported present in January-December, 1863, and May-August, 1864. Promoted to Captain on January 13, 1865. Surrendered at Appomattox Court House, Virginia, April 9, 1865.

LIEUTENANTS

HICKS, FRANCIS Y., 3rd Lieutenant

Previously served as 3rd Lieutenant of 1st Company D, 15th Regiment N.C. Troops (5th Regiment N.C. Volunteers). Transferred to this company on January 9, 1863. Captured at Sandy Ridge (Lenoir County) on April 20, 1863. Confined at Fort Monroe, Virginia. Transferred to Fort Delaware, Delaware, on or about June 10, 1863. Transferred to Johnson's Island, Ohio, where he arrived on July 20, 1863. Paroled at Johnson's Island and transferred to Point Lookout, Maryland, February 20, 1865. No further records.

HORDE, RICHARD M., 2nd Lieutenant

Previously served as Musician in 1st Company D, 15th Regiment N.C. Troops (5th Regiment N.C. Volunteers). Transferred to this company on January 9, 1863. Mustered in as Musician. Reported present in January-December, 1863, and May-August, 1864. Appointed 2nd Lieutenant on September 1, 1864. Resigned on or about January 30, 1865, while under charges of absence without leave. Apparently his resignation was not accepted pending the resolution of the charges against him. Captured by the enemy at Fort Stedman, Virginia, March 25, 1865. Confined at Old Capitol Prison, Washington, D.C. Transferred to Fort Delaware, Delaware, March 30, 1865. Released at Fort Delaware on June 17, 1865, after taking the Oath of Allegiance.

LATTIMORE, DANIEL D., 2nd Lieutenant

Previously served as 2nd Lieutenant of 1st Company D, 15th Regiment N.C. Troops (5th Regiment N.C. Volunteers). Transferred to this company on January 9, 1863. Reported present in January-December, 1863. Wounded at Drewry's Bluff, Virginia, May 16, 1864. Returned to duty prior to July 1, 1864. Killed "by a minnie ball" at or near Petersburg, Virginia, on or about August 24, 1864.

NONCOMMISSIONED OFFICERS AND PRIVATES

ANTHONY, J. DAVID, Musician

Previously served as Musician in 1st Company D, 15th Regiment N.C. Troops (5th Regiment N.C. Volunteers). Transferred to this company on January 9, 1863. Reported present in January-December, 1863, and May-August, 1864.

BERRIER, ANDREW, Private

Previously served as Private in 1st Company D, 15th Regiment N.C. Troops (5th Regiment N.C. Volunteers). Transferred to this company on January 9, 1863, while listed as a deserter. Reported for duty on February 28, 1863. Captured at Sandy Ridge (Lenoir County) on April 20, 1863. Sent to Fort Monroe, Virginia. Paroled and transferred to City Point, Virginia, where he was received on May 28, 1863, for exchange. Deserted from camp on May 28, 1863. Arrested and "lodged in the guardhouse"

at Weldon on December 23, 1863. Roll of Honor indicates that he was discharged from service on October 16, 1863, "under writ of habeus corpus." No further records.

BOGGS, NOAH ELIAS, Sergeant

Previously served as Corporal in 1st Company D, 15th Regiment N.C. Troops (5th Regiment N.C. Volunteers). Transferred to this company on January 9, 1863. Mustered in as Corporal. Reported present in January-December, 1863. Wounded near Petersburg, Virginia, June 16-18, 1864. Returned to duty prior to July 1, 1864. Promoted to Sergeant subsequent to August 31, 1864. Captured at Fort Stedman, Virginia, March 25, 1865. Confined at Point Lookout, Maryland, March 28, 1865. Released at Point Lookout on June 23, 1865, after taking the Oath of Allegiance.

BRACKET, JOSEPH, Corporal

Previously served as Corporal in 1st Company D, 15th Regiment N.C. Troops (5th Regiment N.C. Volunteers). Transferred to this company on January 9, 1863. Reported present in January-December, 1863, and May-August, 1864. Captured at Five Forks, Virginia, April 1, 1865. Confined at Point Lookout, Maryland, April 5, 1865. Released at Point Lookout on June 23, 1865, after taking the Oath of Allegiance.

BRACKET, ROBERT, Private

Previously served as Private in 1st Company D, 15th Regiment N.C. Troops (5th Regiment N.C. Volunteers). Transferred to this company on January 9, 1863. Transferred to Company C, 15th Regiment N.C. Troops (5th Regiment N.C. Volunteers), January 15, 1863, in exchange for Private William A. Putnam.

BRINKLEY, D., Private

Previously served as Private in 1st Company D, 15th Regiment N.C. Troops (5th Regiment N.C. Volunteers). Transferred to this company on January 9, 1863, while listed as a deserter. Reported for duty on February 12, 1863. Reported present or accounted for in March-December, 1863, and May-August, 1864. Paroled at Greensboro on May 8, 1865.

BRINKLEY, HARRISON, Private

Previously served as Private in 1st Company D, 15th Regiment N.C. Troops (5th Regiment N.C. Volunteers). Transferred to this company on January 9, 1863, while listed as a deserter. Arrested and "lodged in guardhouse" at Weldon on December 23, 1863. Company records do not indicate whether he returned to duty. Paroled at Greensboro on or about May 8, 1865.

BRINKLEY, JOHN HAMILTON, Private

Previously served as Private in 1st Company D, 15th Regiment N.C. Troops (5th Regiment N.C. Volunteers). Transferred to this company on January 9, 1863. Reported present in January-December, 1863. Deserted on April 1, 1864. Arrested and was brought back to the company on August 31, 1864. Court-martialed on or about October 22, 1864. No further records.

BYERLY, GEORGE LINDSAY, Private

Previously served as Private in 1st Company D, 15th

Regiment N.C. Troops (5th Regiment N.C. Volunteers). Transferred to this company on January 9, 1863. Reported present or accounted for in January-December, 1863, and May-August, 1864. Hospitalized at Raleigh on August 22, 1864, with diarrhoea and anasarca. Returned to duty on December 6, 1864. Surrendered at Appomattox Court House, Virginia, April 9, 1865.

CABANISS, F. W., Private
Previously served as Private in 1st Company D, 15th Regiment N.C. Troops (5th Regiment N.C. Volunteers). Transferred to this company on January 9, 1863. Wounded at Sandy Ridge (Lenoir County) on April 20, 1863. Died at Goldsboro on April 28, 1863, of wounds.

CABANISS, HARVEY D., Private
Previously served as Assistant Quartermaster of the 15th Regiment N.C. Troops (5th Regiment N.C. Volunteers). Enlisted in this company with the rank of Private on July 27, 1863. Reported present or accounted for in August-December, 1863, and May-August, 1864. Survived the war.

CARTER, JAMES C., Private
Previously served as Private in 1st Company D, 15th Regiment N.C. Troops (5th Regiment N.C. Volunteers). Transferred to this company on January 9, 1863. Captured at Sandy Ridge (Lenoir County) on April 20, 1863. Sent to New Bern. Paroled and transferred to City Point, Virginia, where he was received on May 28, 1863, for exchange. "Ran away" but was apprehended and brought back to camp on June 12, 1863. Reported present in July-December, 1863. "Killed instantly" at Drewry's Bluff, Virginia, May 16, 1864.

CHARLES, N. L., Private
Resided in Davidson County and enlisted in Wake County at age 18, October 22, 1863, for the war. Reported present in November-December, 1863, and May-June, 1864. Wounded at Globe Tavern, Virginia, August 21, 1864. Survived the war.

CHARLES, R. FULTON, Private
Previously served as Private in 1st Company D, 15th Regiment N.C. Troops (5th Regiment N.C. Volunteers). Transferred to this company on January 9, 1863, while listed as a deserter. Reported for duty on February 28, 1863. Captured at Sandy Ridge (Lenoir County) on April 20, 1863. Sent to New Bern. Paroled on May 23, 1863, and transferred to City Point, Virginia, where he was received on May 28, 1863, for exchange. "Ran away" but was apprehended. Returned to duty on June 12, 1863. Reported present in July-December, 1863. Deserted at Goldsboro on January 24, 1864. Paroled at Greensboro on or about May 9, 1865.

CLARK, M. Y., Private
Enlisted in Cleveland County on August 24, 1864, for the war. Hospitalized at Richmond, Virginia, December 10, 1864, with an unspecified complaint. Returned to duty on or about January 11, 1865. Surrendered at Appomattox Court House, Virginia, April 9, 1865.

CLARK, R. F., Private
Enlisted in Cleveland County on April 7, 1864, for the war. Reported present in May-August, 1864. Wounded in the left thigh at Fort Stedman, Virginia, March 25, 1865. Left leg amputated. Captured in hospital at Petersburg, Virginia, April 3, 1865. Took the Oath of Allegiance at Petersburg on July 12, 1865. Released from hospital on July 13, 1865.

CLODFELTER, GEORGE R., Private
Previously served as Private in 1st Company D, 15th Regiment N.C. Troops (5th Regiment N.C. Volunteers). Transferred to this company on January 9, 1863, while listed as a deserter. Reported for duty on February 12, 1863. Captured at Sandy Ridge (Lenoir County) on April 20, 1863. Sent to New Bern. Paroled and transferred to City Point, Virginia, where he was received on May 28, 1863, for exchange. "Ran away" but was apprehended and brought back to camp on June 12, 1863. Deserted on August 16, 1863. Returned to duty on an unspecified date (probably subsequent to August 31, 1864). Deserted to the enemy on October 13, 1864. Confined at Washington, D.C., on or about October 15, 1864. Released on an unspecified date after taking the Oath of Allegiance.

CLODFELTER, J., Private
Previously served as Private in 1st Company D, 15th Regiment N.C. Troops (5th Regiment N.C. Volunteers). Transferred to this company on January 9, 1863. Captured at Sandy Ridge (Lenoir County) on April 20, 1863. Sent to New Bern. Paroled and transferred to City Point, Virginia, where he was received on May 28, 1863, for exchange. "Ran away" but was apprehended and brought back to camp on June 12, 1863. Reported present in July-December, 1863, and May-August, 1864. Captured at Hatcher's Run, Virginia, March 31, 1865. Confined at Point Lookout, Maryland, April 2, 1865. Released at Point Lookout on June 26, 1865, after taking the Oath of Allegiance.

COLLINS, J. WILLIAM, Private
Resided in Cleveland County and was by occupation a farmer prior to enlisting in Cleveland County at age 35, October 31, 1863, for the war. Reported present in November-December, 1863, and May-August, 1864. Captured near Petersburg, Virginia, February 6, 1865. Confined at Point Lookout, Maryland, February 9, 1865. Released at Point Lookout on May 15, 1865, after taking the Oath of Allegiance.

CONRAD, LINDSEY LEMUEL, Private
Previously served as Private in 1st Company D, 15th Regiment N.C. Troops (5th Regiment N.C. Volunteers). Transferred to this company on January 9, 1863; however, he was at that time absent by reason of having had his "left foot cut off" in an accident on the Raleigh and Gaston Railroad on October 28, 1862. Reported absent wounded through August, 1864. Survived the war.

COOK, JAMES MADISON, Private
Previously served as Private in 1st Company D, 15th Regiment N.C. Troops (5th Regiment N.C. Volunteers). Transferred to this company on January 9, 1863, while

absent by reason of wounds received at Sharpsburg, Maryland, September 17, 1862. Discharged on May 11, 1863, probably by reason of wounds received at Sharpsburg.

CORNISH, JACOB, Private
Previously served as Private in 1st Company D, 15th Regiment N.C. Troops (5th Regiment N.C. Volunteers). Transferred to this company on January 9, 1863. Captured at Sandy Ridge (Lenoir County) on April 20, 1863. Sent to New Bern. Paroled and transferred to City Point, Virginia, where he was received on May 28, 1863, for exchange. "Ran away" but was apprehended and brought back to camp on June 12, 1863. Reported present in July-December, 1863. Deserted at Goldsboro on January 28, 1864. Returned to duty on an unspecified date (probably subsequent to August 31, 1864). Captured at Fort Stedman, Virginia, March 25, 1865. Confined at Point Lookout, Maryland, March 28, 1865. Released at Point Lookout on June 24, 1865, after taking the Oath of Allegiance.

CRAVER, F., Private
Previously served as Private in 1st Company D, 15th Regiment N.C. Troops (5th Regiment N.C. Volunteers). Transferred to this company on January 9, 1863, while listed as a deserter. Reported for duty on February 15, 1863. Reported present in March-June, 1863. Deserted at Rocky Mount on August 16, 1863. Arrested and "lodged in guardhouse" at Weldon on December 23, 1863. No further records.

CRAVER, G. N., Private
Previously served as Private in 1st Company D, 15th Regiment N.C. Troops (5th Regiment N.C. Volunteers). Transferred to this company on January 9, 1863, while listed as a deserter. Reported for duty on February 15, 1863. Reported present in March-June, 1863. Deserted at Rocky Mount on August 16, 1863. Arrested and was "lodged in guardhouse" at Weldon on December 23, 1863. Returned to duty on an unspecified date. Captured at Globe Tavern, Virginia, August 21, 1864. Confined at Washington, D.C. Released on or about August 31, 1864, after taking the Oath of Allegiance.

CROUCH, JACOB, Private
Previously served as Private in 1st Company D, 15th Regiment N.C. Troops (5th Regiment N.C. Volunteers). Transferred to this company on January 9, 1863. Died in hospital at Wilson on February 21-23, 1863, of disease.

CROWDER, J. W., Private
Previously served as Private in Company D, 2nd Regiment N.C. Junior Reserves. Transferred to this company on August 31, 1864. Hospitalized at Richmond, Virginia, February 28, 1865, with chronic diarrhoea. Furloughed for sixty days on March 31, 1865.

DELLINGER, NOAH H., Private
Previously served as Private in 1st Company D, 15th Regiment N.C. Troops (5th Regiment N.C. Volunteers). Transferred to this company on January 9, 1863. Reported present in January-December, 1863. Killed at Drewry's Bluff, Virginia, May 16, 1864.

DEVINEY, J. G., Private
Resided in Cleveland County and enlisted at Drewry's Bluff, Virginia, at age 18, June 20, 1863, for the war. Reported present through December, 1863. Wounded in the left arm at Drewry's Bluff on May 16, 1864. Reported absent wounded through August, 1864. Returned to duty on an unspecified date. Wounded in the abdomen and captured at Five Forks, Virginia, April 1, 1865. Confined at Point Lookout, Maryland, April 5, 1865. No further records.

DISHER, H., Private
Previously served as Private in 1st Company D, 15th Regiment N.C. Troops (5th Regiment N.C. Volunteers). Transferred to this company on January 9, 1863. Reported absent sick for most of the period from January 9 through September 30, 1863. Discharged on October 16, 1863, under a writ of habeas corpus.

DISHER, THOMAS, Private
Previously served as Private in 1st Company D, 15th Regiment N.C. Troops (5th Regiment N.C. Volunteers). Transferred to this company on January 9, 1863. Captured at Sandy Ridge (Lenoir County) on April 20, 1863. Sent to New Bern. Paroled and transferred to City Point, Virginia, where he was received on May 28, 1863, for exchange. Reported present in July-December, 1863. Wounded in the left hand at Drewry's Bluff, Virginia, May 16, 1864. Hospitalized at Richmond, Virginia. Returned to duty prior to July 1, 1864. Captured at Five Forks, Virginia, April 1, 1865. Confined at Hart's Island, New York Harbor, April 7, 1865. Released at Hart's Island on June 18, 1865, after taking the Oath of Allegiance.

DIVINNY, WILLIAM G., Private
Previously served as Private in 1st Company D, 15th Regiment N.C. Troops (5th Regiment N.C. Volunteers). Transferred to this company on January 9, 1863, while reported absent without leave. Failed to report for duty. Listed as a deserter and dropped from the rolls of the company on or about March 1, 1863.

ELLER, SAMUEL F., Private
Previously served as Private in 1st Company D, 15th Regiment N.C. Troops (5th Regiment N.C. Volunteers). Transferred to this company on January 9, 1863. Reported present in January-December, 1863. Captured near Drewry's Bluff, Virginia, May 16, 1864. Confined at Point Lookout, Maryland, May 19, 1864. Transferred to Elmira, New York, August 16, 1864. Released at Elmira on June 16, 1865, after taking the Oath of Allegiance.

ELLIOCUTT, T. C., Private
Place and date of enlistment not reported; however, he probably enlisted subsequent to August 31, 1864. Paroled at Greensboro on or about May 9, 1865.

ELLIOTT, SAMUEL C., Private
Resided in Davidson County and enlisted in Wake County at age 25, October 22, 1863, for the war. Reported present through December, 1863. Deserted at Goldsboro on January 28, 1864.

ELLIS, WILLIAM H., Private

Previously served as Private in 1st Company D, 15th Regiment N.C. Troops (5th Regiment N.C. Volunteers). Transferred to this company on January 9, 1863. Reported present in January-December, 1863. Captured near Drewry's Bluff, Virginia, May 16, 1864. Confined at Point Lookout, Maryland, May 19, 1864. Transferred to Elmira, New York, August 16, 1864. Released at Elmira on or about June 16, 1865, after taking the Oath of Allegiance.

ESSICK, RANSOM, Private

Previously served as Private in 1st Company D, 15th Regiment N.C. Troops (5th Regiment N.C. Volunteers). Transferred to this company on January 9, 1863, while listed as a deserter. Reported for duty on January 28, 1863. Captured at Sandy Ridge (Lenoir County) on April 20, 1863. Sent to New Bern. Paroled and transferred to City Point, Virginia, where he was received on May 28, 1863, for exchange. "Ran away" but was apprehended and brought back to camp on June 12, 1863. Was apparently not present for duty with the company in July-December, 1863. Reported present in May-June, 1864. Captured at Globe Tavern, Virginia, August 21, 1864. Released on an unspecified date. [North Carolina pension records indicate that he was wounded in the right arm by a shell on an unspecified date.]

ESSICK, THOMAS, Private

Previously served as Private in 1st Company D, 15th Regiment N.C. Troops (5th Regiment N.C. Volunteers). Transferred to this company on January 9, 1863, while listed as a deserter. Reported for duty on February 15, 1863. Reported present or accounted for in March-December, 1863, and May-August, 1864. Captured at Fort Stedman, Virginia, March 25, 1865. Confined at Point Lookout, Maryland, March 28, 1865. Released at Point Lookout on June 12, 1865, after taking the Oath of Allegiance.

EVERHART, A., Private

Previously served as Private in 1st Company D, 15th Regiment N.C. Troops (5th Regiment N.C. Volunteers). Transferred to this company on January 9, 1863. Died in hospital at Goldsboro on May 10, 1863, of disease and/or a gunshot wound.

EVERHART, BRITTON, Private

Previously served as Private in 1st Company D, 15th Regiment N.C. Troops (5th Regiment N.C. Volunteers). Transferred to this company on January 9, 1863. Captured at Sandy Ridge (Lenoir County) on April 20, 1863. Sent to New Bern. Paroled and transferred to City Point, Virginia, where he was received on May 28, 1863, for exchange. "Ran away" but was apprehended and returned to camp on June 12, 1863. Reported present in July-December, 1863, and May-August, 1864. Captured at or near Five Forks, Virginia, on or about April 1, 1865. Confined at Hart's Island, New York Harbor, April 7, 1865. Released at Hart's Island on June 18, 1865, after taking the Oath of Allegiance.

EVERHART, C., Private

Previously served as Private in 1st Company D, 15th Regiment N.C. Troops (5th Regiment N.C. Volunteers).

Transferred to this company on January 9, 1863, while absent wounded. Reported for duty in March-April, 1863. Reported present or accounted for in May-December, 1863. Wounded near Petersburg, Virginia, June 16-18, 1864. Returned to duty prior to July 1, 1864. Captured at Five Forks, Virginia, April 1, 1865. Confined at Hart's Island, New York Harbor, April 7, 1865. Released at Hart's Island on June 18, 1865, after taking the Oath of Allegiance.

EVERHART, HAMILTON, Private

Previously served as Private in 1st Company D, 15th Regiment N.C. Troops (5th Regiment N.C. Volunteers). Transferred to this company on January 9, 1863, while listed as a deserter. Arrested and brought in for duty with this company on August 31, 1864. Deserted to the enemy on or about November 4, 1864. Confined at Camp Hamilton, Virginia. Released at Camp Hamilton on November 14, 1864, after taking the Oath of Allegiance.

EVERHART, MICHAEL, Private

Previously served as Private in 1st Company D, 15th Regiment N.C. Troops (5th Regiment N.C. Volunteers). Transferred to this company on January 9, 1863. Reported present in January-December, 1863, and May-August, 1864. Surrendered at Appomattox Court House, Virginia, April 9, 1865.

EVERHART, WILLIAM, Private

Previously served as Private in 1st Company D, 15th Regiment N.C. Troops (5th Regiment N.C. Volunteers). Transferred to this company on January 9, 1863, while listed as a deserter. Reported for duty on or about February 20, 1864. Sent to hospital on or about the same date. Hospitalized at Charlotte on May 15, 1864, with chronic rheumatism. Furloughed on August 5, 1864. No further records.

FORBES, JOSEPH T., Private

Previously served as Private in 1st Company D, 15th Regiment N.C. Troops (5th Regiment N.C. Volunteers). Transferred to this company on January 9, 1863. Reported present in January-December, 1863, and May-June, 1864. Transferred to Company K of this regiment on July 1, 1864.

FOUTS, A., Private

Previously served as Private in 1st Company D, 15th Regiment N.C. Troops (5th Regiment N.C. Volunteers). Transferred to this company on January 9, 1863. Reported present in January-December, 1863. Wounded at Bermuda Hundred, Virginia, May 20, 1864. Returned to duty on an unspecified date. Wounded in the face near Petersburg, Virginia, June 21-July 1, 1864. Died in hospital at Richmond, Virginia, September 1, 1864, of wounds.

FREELAND, CHARLES, Private

Place and date of enlistment not reported; however, he probably enlisted subsequent to August 31, 1864. Deserted to the enemy on or about March 7, 1865. Confined at Washington, D.C., March 10, 1865. Released on an unspecified date after taking the Oath of Allegiance.

FRITTS, HENDERSON, Private

Previously served as Private in 1st Company D, 15th Regiment N.C. Troops (5th Regiment N.C. Volunteers). Transferred to this company on January 9, 1863. Captured at Sandy Ridge (Lenoir County) on April 20, 1863. Sent to New Bern. Paroled and transferred to City Point, Virginia, where he was received on May 28, 1863, for exchange. Reported present in July-December, 1863. Captured near Drewry's Bluff, Virginia, May 16, 1864. Confined at Point Lookout, Maryland, May 19, 1864. Transferred to Elmira, New York, August 16, 1864. Died at Elmira on August 22, 1864. Cause of death not reported.

FULTZ, A., Private

Previously served as Private in 1st Company D, 15th Regiment N.C. Troops (5th Regiment N.C. Volunteers). Transferred to this company on January 9, 1863. Reported present in January-December, 1863, and May-August, 1864. Captured at Five Forks, Virginia, April 1, 1865. Confined at Hart's Island, New York Harbor, April 7, 1865. Released at Hart's Island on June 18, 1865, after taking the Oath of Allegiance.

FULTZ, FRANCIS, Private

Previously served as Private in 1st Company D, 15th Regiment N.C. Troops (5th Regiment N.C. Volunteers). Transferred to this company on January 9, 1863, while reported absent wounded. Failed to report for duty when his furlough expired on February 1, 1863. Reported "in the woods" in July-August, 1863. Dropped from the rolls of the company in September-October, 1863.

GIBSON, OLIVER P., Private

Previously served as Private in Company F, 56th Regiment N.C. Troops. Transferred to this company on March 25, 1864. Wounded in the breast and right thigh at Drewry's Bluff, Virginia, May 16, 1864. Reported absent wounded through August, 1864. Hospitalized at Charlotte on January 20, 1865, apparently still suffering from wounds received at Drewry's Bluff. Left the hospital without permission on May 1, 1865.

GLADDEN, JAMES A., Private

Resided in Cleveland County where he enlisted at age 38, September 20, 1863, for the war. Reported present or accounted for in October-December, 1863, and May-August, 1864. Wounded in the left leg at or near Petersburg, Virginia, November 9, 1864. Left leg amputated. Hospitalized at Richmond, Virginia. Furloughed on or about January 10, 1865.

GLADDEN, W. H., Private

Previously served as Private in 1st Company D, 15th Regiment N.C. Troops (5th Regiment N.C. Volunteers). Transferred to this company on January 9, 1863. Captured at Sandy Ridge (Lenoir County) on April 20, 1863. Sent to New Bern. Paroled and transferred to City Point, Virginia, where he was received on May 28, 1863, for exchange. "Ran away" but was apprehended and brought back to camp on June 12, 1863. Reported present through December, 1863. Killed at Drewry's Bluff, Virginia, May 16, 1864.

GOINS, MICHAEL H., Private

Previously served as Private in 1st Company D, 15th Regiment N.C. Troops (5th Regiment N.C. Volunteers). Transferred to this company on January 9, 1863. Captured at Sandy Ridge (Lenoir County) on April 20, 1863. Sent to New Bern. Paroled and transferred to City Point, Virginia, where he was received on May 28, 1863, for exchange. Reported present in June-December, 1863, and May-August, 1864.

GREEN, G. M., Private

Resided in Cleveland County and was by occupation county sheriff prior to enlisting in Cleveland County at age 44, November 15, 1863, for the war. Shot through the breast and killed in a skirmish with black Federal cavalrymen at Suffolk, Virginia, March 9, 1864. [May have served previously as Private in Company I, 38th Regiment N.C. Troops.]

GRUBB, R., Private

Previously served as Private in 1st Company D, 15th Regiment N.C. Troops (5th Regiment N.C. Volunteers). Transferred to this company on January 9, 1863, while absent wounded. Reported for duty in March-April, 1863. Reported present or accounted for in May-December, 1863, and May-August, 1864.

HARTMAN, JOHN A., Private

Previously served as Private in 1st Company D, 15th Regiment N.C. Troops (5th Regiment N.C. Volunteers). Transferred to this company on January 9, 1863. Reported present in January-December, 1863, and May-August, 1864. Captured at Fort Stedman, Virginia, March 25, 1865. Confined at Point Lookout, Maryland, March 28, 1865. Released at Point Lookout on June 27, 1865, after taking the Oath of Allegiance.

HOYLE, DANIEL A., Corporal

Previously served as Private in 1st Company D, 15th Regiment N.C. Troops (5th Regiment N.C. Volunteers). Transferred to this company on January 9, 1863, while reported absent without leave. Mustered in as Private. Reported for duty prior to March 1, 1863. Reported present in March-December, 1863, and May-June, 1864. Wounded at Globe Tavern, Virginia, August 21, 1864. Returned to duty prior to August 31, 1864. Promoted to Corporal subsequent to August 31, 1864. Captured at Five Forks, Virginia, April 1, 1865. Confined at Point Lookout, Maryland, April 5, 1865. Released at Point Lookout on June 27, 1865, after taking the Oath of Allegiance.

HUNT, L., Private

Place and date of enlistment not reported; however, he probably enlisted subsequent to August 31, 1864. Deserted to the enemy on or about February 15, 1865. Confined at Washington, D.C., February 21, 1865. Released on an unspecified date after taking the Oath of Allegiance.

HUNT, THOMAS C., Private

Born in Cleveland County where he resided as a farmer prior to enlisting in Cleveland County at age 17,

September 20, 1863, for the war. Reported present in October-December, 1863. Wounded near Petersburg, Virginia, June 16, 1864. Reported absent wounded through August, 1864. Hospitalized at Charlotte on November 7, 1864, with anasarca. Furloughed on January 3, 1865.

HUNT, WILLIAM H., Corporal

Previously served as Corporal in 1st Company D, 15th Regiment N.C. Troops (5th Regiment N.C. Volunteers). Transferred to this company on January 9, 1863, while absent wounded. Reported for duty prior to March 1, 1863. Reported present in March-December, 1863, and May-August, 1864. Hospitalized at Richmond, Virginia, on or about January 12, 1865, with a gunshot wound of the right thigh. Place and date wounded not reported. Furloughed for sixty days on January 28, 1865.

IRBY, J. R., JR., Private

Resided in Cleveland County and was by occupation a master mason prior to enlisting in Cleveland County at age 27, July 27, 1863, for the war. Reported present in August-December, 1863, and May-August, 1864. Deserted to the enemy on or about March 4, 1865. Confined at Washington, D.C., March 8, 1865. Released on an unspecified date after taking the Oath of Allegiance.

IRVIN, A. H., Private

Previously served as Private in 1st Company D, 15th Regiment N.C. Troops (5th Regiment N.C. Volunteers). Transferred to this company on January 9, 1863. Reported present or accounted for through December, 1863. Wounded in the right shoulder at or near Drewry's Bluff, Virginia, on or about May 13, 1864. Hospitalized at Richmond, Virginia. Furloughed for thirty days on June 9, 1864. Returned to duty on or about July 9, 1864. Reported present through August, 1864.

IRVIN, J. J., Private

Resided in Cleveland County where he enlisted at age 18, February 20, 1863, for the war. Reported present through December, 1863. Killed in the trenches near Petersburg, Virginia, June 30, 1864.

LATTIMORE, JOHN L., Sergeant

Previously served as Corporal in 1st Company D, 15th Regiment N.C. Troops (5th Regiment N.C. Volunteers). Transferred to this company on January 9, 1863. Mustered in as Corporal. Reported present in January-December, 1863. Wounded in the left hand at Drewry's Bluff, Virginia, May 16, 1864. Returned to duty in July-August, 1864. Promoted to Sergeant on July 18, 1864. Surrendered at Appomattox Court House, Virginia, April 9, 1865.

LEDFORD, WILLIAM, Private

Previously served as Private in 1st Company D, 15th Regiment N.C. Troops (5th Regiment N.C. Volunteers). Transferred to this company on January 9, 1863, while absent without leave. Reported for duty prior to March 1, 1863. Reported present in March-December, 1863, and May-August, 1864. Hospitalized at Richmond, Virginia, February 10, 1865, with chronic diarrhoea. Furloughed for thirty days on or about February 21, 1865.

LEONARD, FELIX W., Private

Previously served as Private in 1st Company D, 15th Regiment N.C. Troops (5th Regiment N.C. Volunteers). Transferred to this company on January 9, 1863, while absent without leave. Reported for duty in September-October, 1863. Reported present in November-December, 1863, and May-August, 1864. Captured at Fort Stedman, Virginia, March 25, 1865. Confined at Point Lookout, Maryland, March 28, 1865. Released at Point Lookout on June 28, 1865, after taking the Oath of Allegiance.

LONDON, JOHN R., Sergeant

Previously served as Sergeant in 1st Company D, 15th Regiment N.C. Troops (5th Regiment N.C. Volunteers). Transferred to this company on January 9, 1863. Reported present in January-December, 1863. Wounded near Petersburg, Virginia, June 16-18, 1864. Returned to duty prior to July 1, 1864. Appointed Ensign (1st Lieutenant) on July 18, 1864, and transferred to the Field and Staff of this regiment.

McENTIRE, R. M., Private

Resided in Cleveland County where he enlisted at age 42, August 31, 1863, for the war. Reported present in November-December, 1863, and May-August, 1864.

MAGNESS, S. P., Sergeant

Previously served as Sergeant in 1st Company D, 15th Regiment N.C. Troops (5th Regiment N.C. Volunteers). Transferred to this company on January 9, 1863. Reported present in January-December, 1863, and May-August, 1864. Surrendered at Appomattox Court House, Virginia, April 9, 1865.

MARTIN, BRYAN, Private

Resided in Franklin County. Place and date of enlistment not reported; however, he probably enlisted subsequent to August 31, 1864. Captured at Sutherland's Station, Virginia, April 2, 1865. Confined at Hart's Island, New York Harbor, April 7, 1865. Released at Hart's Island on June 17, 1865, after taking the Oath of Allegiance.

MASSIE, R. B., Private

Enlistment date not reported; however, he probably enlisted subsequent to August 31, 1864. Captured at Hatcher's Run, Virginia, April 2, 1865. Confined at Hart's Island, New York Harbor, April 7, 1865. Died at Hart's Island on or about May 25, 1865, of "chronic diarrhoea."

MODE, A. F., Private

Previously served as Private in 1st Company D, 15th Regiment N.C. Troops (5th Regiment N.C. Volunteers). Transferred to this company on January 9, 1863. Reported present in January-December, 1863, and May-August, 1864. Deserted to the enemy on or about February 26, 1865. Confined at Washington, D.C., March 1, 1865. Released on an unspecified date after taking the Oath of Allegiance.

MODE, DEVANEY, Private

Previously served as Private in Company I, 38th Regiment N.C. Troops. Enlisted in this company in Cleveland County on April 4, 1864, for the war. Wounded in the left thigh at Drewry's Bluff, Virginia, on or about May 16, 1864. Hospitalized at Richmond, Virginia. Returned to duty prior to July 1, 1864. Reported present in July-August, 1864. Deserted to the enemy on or about February 15, 1865. Confined at Washington, D.C., February 21, 1865. Released on an unspecified date after taking the Oath of Allegiance.

MODE, JAMES C., Private
Previously served as Private in 1st Company D, 15th Regiment N.C. Troops (5th Regiment N.C. Volunteers). Transferred to this company on January 9, 1863. Reported present in January-December, 1863, and May-August, 1864. Deserted to the enemy on or about February 24, 1865. Confined at Washington, D.C., February 27, 1865. Released on an unspecified date after taking the Oath of Allegiance. [His service record while a member of the 15th Regiment appears under the name of J. Mode in Volume V, page 541, of this series.]

MODE, JOSEPH T., Private
Previously served as Private in Company I, 38th Regiment N.C. Troops. Enlisted in this company in Cleveland County on October 18, 1863, for the war. Reported present in November-December, 1863. Captured at or near Fort Darling, Virginia, May 14, 1864. Confined at Point Lookout, Maryland, May 18, 1864. Transferred to Elmira, New York, August 15, 1864. Released at Elmira on June 19, 1865, after taking the Oath of Allegiance.

MORTON, JOHN, Private
Place and date of enlistment not reported; however, he probably enlisted subsequent to August 31, 1864. Deserted to the enemy on or about February 14, 1865. Confined at Washington, D.C., February 20, 1865. Released on an unspecified date after taking the Oath of Allegiance.

PARKER, A. J., Private
Resided in Cleveland County where he enlisted at age 36, February 20, 1863, for the war. Reported present in March-July, 1863. Died in hospital at Wilson on August 7, 1863, of "febris typhoid."

PARKER, JOSEPH, Private
Previously served as Private in 1st Company D, 15th Regiment N.C. Troops (5th Regiment N.C. Volunteers). Transferred to this company on January 9, 1863. Captured at Sandy Ridge (Lenoir County) on April 20, 1863. Sent to New Bern. Paroled and transferred to City Point, Virginia, where he was received on May 28, 1863, for exchange. Returned to duty prior to July 1, 1863. Reported present in July-December, 1863, and May-June, 1864. Killed at or near Petersburg, Virginia, on or about July 23, 1864.

PENNY, JOHN G., Private
Resided in Cleveland County. Place and date of enlistment not reported; however, he probably enlisted subsequent to August 31, 1864. Captured at Five Forks, Virginia, April 1, 1865. Confined at Point Lookout, Maryland, April 6, 1865. Released at Point Lookout on June 17, 1865, after taking the Oath of Allegiance.

PETTY, JAMES F., Private
Previously served as Private in 1st Company D, 15th Regiment N.C. Troops (5th Regiment N.C. Volunteers). Transferred to this company on January 9, 1863. Reported present or accounted for in January-December, 1863, and May-August, 1864.

PHILBECK, AMOS H., Private
Previously served as Private in 1st Company D, 15th Regiment N.C. Troops (5th Regiment N.C. Volunteers). Transferred to this company on January 9, 1863. Captured at Sandy Ridge (Lenoir County) on April 20, 1863. Sent to New Bern. Paroled and transferred to City Point, Virginia, where he was received on May 28, 1863, for exchange. Returned to duty prior to July 1, 1863. Reported present in July-December, 1863. Wounded at Drewry's Bluff, Virginia, May 16, 1864. Returned to duty in July-August, 1864. Captured at Five Forks, Virginia, April 1, 1865. Confined at Point Lookout, Maryland, April 5, 1865. Released at Point Lookout on June 17, 1865, after taking the Oath of Allegiance.

PHILBECK, P. H., Private
Previously served as Private in 1st Company D, 15th Regiment N.C. Troops (5th Regiment N.C. Volunteers). Transferred to this company on January 9, 1863. Reported present through December, 1863. Wounded in the hand at Drewry's Bluff, Virginia, May 16, 1864. Returned to duty in July-August, 1864. Apparently deserted to the enemy prior to October 8, 1864, when he took the Oath of Allegiance at City Point, Virginia.

PHILBECK, T. G., Private
Resided in Cleveland County where he enlisted at age 18, February 18, 1864, for the war. Reported present in May-July, 1864. Hospitalized at Richmond, Virginia, August 17, 1864, with chronic diarrhoea. Furloughed for thirty days on August 27, 1864. Deserted to the enemy on or about February 24, 1865. Confined at Washington, D.C., February 27, 1865. Released on an unspecified date after taking the Oath of Allegiance. [North Carolina pension records indicate that he was wounded in the arm at Drewry's Bluff, Virginia, May 10, 1864.]

PRICE, WILLIAM P., Sergeant
Previously served as Private in 1st Company D, 15th Regiment N.C. Troops (5th Regiment N.C. Volunteers). Transferred to this company on January 9, 1863, while absent without leave. Reported for duty on August 16, 1863, and brought a certificate proving that "he had not been able to return until he did." Mustered in as Private. Reported present in September-December, 1863, and May-August, 1864. Promoted to Sergeant on July 1, 1864. Captured at Five Forks, Virginia, April 1, 1865. Confined at Point Lookout, Maryland, April 5, 1865. Released at Point Lookout on June 17, 1865, after taking the Oath of Allegiance.

PUTNAM, E. L., Private
Previously served as Private in Company C, 15th Regiment N.C. Troops (5th Regiment N.C. Volunteers). Transferred to this company on January 15, 1863, in exchange for Private John A. Waters. Reported present

in January-December, 1863, and May-August, 1864. Deserted to the enemy on or about February 15, 1865. Confined at Washington, D.C., February 21, 1865. Released on an unspecified date after taking the Oath of Allegiance.

PUTNAM, MARTIN, Private
Previously served as Private in 1st Company D, 15th Regiment N.C. Troops (5th Regiment N.C. Volunteers). Transferred to this company on January 9, 1863, while listed as a deserter. Reported for duty on an unspecified date (probably subsequent to August 31, 1864). Deserted to the enemy on or about February 15, 1865. Confined at Washington, D.C., February 21, 1865. Released on an unspecified date after taking the Oath of Allegiance.

PUTNAM, SAMUEL, Private
Previously served as Private in 1st Company D, 15th Regiment N.C. Troops (5th Regiment N.C. Volunteers). Transferred to this company on January 9, 1863. Reported present or accounted for in January-December, 1863. Wounded in the left arm (possibly also in the head and left thigh) at Drewry's Bluff, Virginia, May 16, 1864. Left arm amputated. Hospitalized at Richmond, Virginia. Furloughed for sixty days on June 12, 1864. No further records. Survived the war.

PUTNAM, WILLIAM A., Private
Previously served as Private in Company C, 15th Regiment N.C. Troops (5th Regiment N.C. Volunteers). Transferred to this company on January 15, 1863, in exchange for Private Robert Brackett. Reported present or accounted for in January-December, 1863, and May-June, 1864. Wounded in the right leg at Globe Tavern, Virginia, August 21, 1864. Right leg amputated. Retired from service on January 28, 1865. Captured in hospital at Richmond, Virginia, April 3, 1865. Took the Oath of Allegiance at Richmond on May 28, 1865.

ROLLINS, S. R., Private
Enlisted in Cleveland County on April 4, 1864, for the war. Wounded in the head and captured at Drewry's Bluff, Virginia, May 16, 1864. Sent to Fort Monroe, Virginia. No further records.

SHERRILL, ADAM T., Private
Previously served as Private in Company E, 3rd Regiment N.C. Junior Reserves. Transferred to this company on an unspecified date (probably in March, 1865). Survived the war.

SHIELDS, R. D., Sergeant
Previously served as Sergeant in 1st Company D, 15th Regiment N.C. Troops (5th Regiment N.C. Volunteers). Transferred to this company on January 9, 1863. Reported present in January-December, 1863. Wounded in the right foot at Drewry's Bluff, Virginia, May 16, 1864. Hospitalized at Richmond, Virginia. Furloughed on May 22, 1864. Died on June 8, 1864, presumably of wounds. Place of death not reported.

SHORT, JAMES, Private
Resided in Rutherford County and enlisted in Wayne

County at age 47, April 1, 1863, for the war as a substitute for Robert W. Hunt. Died on or about April 29, 1863, of "febris typhoides." Place of death not reported. [Robert W. Hunt served as 3rd Lieutenant of 1st Company D, 15th Regiment N.C. Troops (5th Regiment N.C. Volunteers), until May 2, 1862, when he was defeated for reelection. Apparently Hunt was conscripted into 2nd Company B, 49th Regiment, in March, 1863, and chose to hire Private Short as a substitute rather than serve in the ranks.]

SHORT, WADE H., Private
Previously served as Private in 1st Company D, 15th Regiment N.C. Troops (5th Regiment N.C. Volunteers). Enlisted in this company on February 20, 1863. Reported present in March-December, 1863. Deserted "on the march" near Drewry's Bluff, Virginia, June 16, 1864.

SPECK, J. P., Private
Previously served as Private in 1st Company D, 15th Regiment N.C. Troops (5th Regiment N.C. Volunteers). Transferred to this company on January 9, 1863. Deserted from hospital on February 23, 1863. Returned from desertion on an unspecified date. Reported in prison at Salisbury from December, 1863, through August, 1864, for desertion. Hospitalized at Richmond, Virginia, on or about December 15, 1864, with "large abscess of neck scrofulas." Furloughed for sixty days on or about February 21, 1865.

THOMASON, JOHN, Private
Previously served as Private in 1st Company D, 15th Regiment N.C. Troops (5th Regiment N.C. Volunteers). Transferred to this company on January 9, 1863, while listed as a deserter. Reported for duty on or about February 7, 1863. Deserted at Rocky Mount on August 16, 1863. Returned to duty on an unspecified date. Reported present in May-June, 1864. Wounded in the left knee (fracture) at or near Petersburg, Virginia, July 14-15, 1864. Hospitalized at Petersburg where he died on July 20, 1864, of "gangrene." [His service record while a member of the 15th Regiment appears under the name of J. Thompson in Volume V, page 542, of this series.]

TOWRY, R. P., Private
Previously served as Private in 1st Company D, 15th Regiment N.C. Troops (5th Regiment N.C. Volunteers). Transferred to this company on January 9, 1863. Reported present or accounted for in January-December, 1863. Reported "missing on the march" on June 16, 1864. Reported under arrest for desertion in July-August, 1864. Returned to duty prior to October 30, 1864, when he was wounded in the right arm at or near Petersburg, Virginia. Hospitalized at Richmond, Virginia. Furloughed for sixty days on or about November 24, 1864.

WATERS, JOHN A., Private
Previously served as Private in 1st Company D, 15th Regiment N.C. Troops (5th Regiment N.C. Volunteers). Transferred to this company on January 9, 1863. Transferred to Company C, 15th Regiment N.C. Troops (5th Regiment N.C. Volunteers), January 15, 1863, in exchange for Private E. L. Putnam.

WATERS, JONATHAN, Private
Previously served as Private in 1st Company D, 15th Regiment N.C. Troops (5th Regiment N.C. Volunteers). Transferred to this company on January 9, 1863. Reported present in January-December, 1863, and May-August, 1864. Captured at Five Forks, Virginia, April 1, 1865. Confined at Point Lookout, Maryland, April 5, 1865. Released at Point Lookout on June 21, 1865, after taking the Oath of Allegiance.

WHITE, THOMAS, Private
Previously served as Private in 1st Company D, 15th Regiment N.C. Troops (5th Regiment N.C. Volunteers). Transferred to this company on January 9, 1863. Reported present or accounted for in January-December, 1863, and May-August, 1864. Surrendered at Appomattox Court House, Virginia, April 9, 1865.

WIGGINS, R. M., Private
Previously served as Private in 1st Company D, 15th Regiment N.C. Troops (5th Regiment N.C. Volunteers). Transferred to this company on January 9, 1863, while absent without leave. Reported for duty prior to March 1, 1863. Reported absent sick (apparently suffering from an ankle injury) through October, 1863. Reported on detail as a guard and shoemaker at Charlotte from December 29, 1863, through August 31, 1864. Hospitalized at Charlotte on November 3, 1864, with tonsillitis. Returned to duty on November 30, 1864. No further records. Survived the war.

WIGGINS, WILLIAM M., Private
Resided in Cleveland County where he enlisted at age 42, December 16, 1863, for the war. Wounded at Drewry's Bluff, Virginia, May 16, 1864. Returned to duty in July-August, 1864. No further records. Survived the war.

WILLIAMS, SANDY, _____
North Carolina pension records indicate that he served in this company.

WITHROW, J. C., Private
Previously served as Private in 1st Company D, 15th Regiment N.C. Troops (5th Regiment N.C. Volunteers). Transferred to this company on January 9, 1863. Reported present in January-December, 1863, and May-June, 1864. Wounded at Globe Tavern, Virginia, August 21, 1864. Hospitalized at Richmond, Virginia. Furloughed for thirty days on August 31, 1864. No further records.

WITHROW, THOMAS J., Sergeant
Previously served as Sergeant in 1st Company D, 15th Regiment N.C. Troops (5th Regiment N.C. Volunteers). Transferred to this company on January 9, 1863, while absent wounded. Reported absent wounded through December, 1863. Briefly returned to duty in January-February, 1864. Reported absent on furlough from February 25 through August 31, 1864. No further records. Survived the war.

WITHROW, WILLIAM P., 1st Sergeant
Previously served as 1st Sergeant of 1st Company D, 15th Regiment N.C. Troops (5th Regiment N.C. Volunteers).

Transferred to this company on January 9, 1863, while absent wounded. Reported for duty in March-April, 1863. Reported present in May-December, 1863, and May-August, 1864. Captured at Five Forks, Virginia, April 1, 1865. Confined at Point Lookout, Maryland, April 5, 1865. Released at Point Lookout on June 21, 1865, after taking the Oath of Allegiance. [The Oath of Allegiance that he signed at Point Lookout indicates that he was blind in the left eye.]

WRIGHT, BRYSON P., Private
Place and date of enlistment not reported; however, he probably enlisted subsequent to August 31, 1864. Captured at Fort Stedman, Virginia, March 25, 1865. Confined at Point Lookout, Maryland, March 28, 1865. Released at Point Lookout on June 21, 1865, after taking the Oath of Allegiance.

COMPANY C

This company was raised in Rowan County and enlisted in Rowan County in February-March, 1862. It was mustered into state service at Camp Mangum, near Raleigh, on April 21, 1862, and assigned to the 49th Regiment N.C. Troops as Company C. After joining the regiment the company functioned as part of the regiment, and its history for the remainder of the war is reported as a part of the regimental history.

The information contained in the following roster was compiled primarily from a company muster-in and descriptive roll dated April 21, 1862, and from company muster rolls for November 1, 1862-December 31, 1863, and May 1-August 31, 1864. No company muster rolls were located for May 1-October 31, 1862; January 1-April 30, 1864; or for the period after August 31, 1864. Valuable information was obtained from primary records such as the North Carolina adjutant general's *Roll of Honor*, discharge certificates, medical records, prisoner of war records, *The War of the Rebellion: A Compilation of the Official Records of the Union and Confederate Armies*, militia records, newspaper casualty lists and obituaries, Confederate pension applications filed with the state of North Carolina, and the 1860 federal census of North Carolina. Secondary sources such as postwar rosters and histories, cemetery records, the *Confederate Veteran*, published genealogies, and records of the United Daughters of the Confederacy also provided useful information.

OFFICERS

CAPTAINS

CHAMBERS, PINCKNEY BROWN
Born in Iredell County where he resided as a farmer prior to enlisting in Iredell County at age 41. Elected Captain on February 25, 1862. Appointed Major on November 1,

1862, and transferred to the Field and Staff of this regiment.

CHAMBERS, HENRY ALEXANDER

Previously served as Private in Company C, 4th Regiment N.C. State Troops. Appointed Captain of this company on December 3, 1862. Reported present or accounted for in January-December, 1863, and May-August, 1864. Wounded in the scalp at Five Forks, Virginia, April 1, 1865. Surrendered at Appomattox Court House, Virginia, April 9, 1865. He was "youthful in age, but clear-minded, steadfast and useful in all emergencies, ripe in judgment beyond his years, and as fearless as a lion."

LIEUTENANTS

BOWERS, GILES, 1st Lieutenant

Born in Stanly County* and resided in Rowan County where he was by occupation a miner prior to enlisting in Rowan County at age 27. Appointed 1st Lieutenant on March 13, 1862. Placed under arrest by order of General D. H. Hill in July, 1862. Reason he was arrested not reported. Returned to duty on May 29, 1863. Arrested again on June 2, 1863. Returned to duty on June 8, 1863. Reported present or accounted for in July-December, 1863, and May-August, 1864. Captured at Five Forks, Virginia, April 1, 1865. Confined at Johnson's Island, Ohio, April 11, 1865. Released at Johnson's Island on June 18, 1865, after taking the Oath of Allegiance.

KRIDER, CHARLES CORNELIUS, 2nd Lieutenant

Born in Rowan County where he resided as a farmer prior to enlisting in Rowan County at age 35. Appointed 2nd Lieutenant on April 9, 1862. Reported present from November, 1862, through December, 1863, and in May-June, 1864. Wounded in the right shoulder by a piece of shell near Petersburg, Virginia, July 8, 1864. Returned to duty prior to September 1, 1864. Wounded in the left leg at Fort Stedman, Virginia, March 25, 1865. Left leg amputated. Hospitalized at Petersburg where he was captured on April 3, 1865. Hospitalized at Alexandria, Virginia, April 6, 1865. Transferred to hospital at Washington, D.C., June 13, 1865. Released at Washington on June 15, 1865, after taking the Oath of Allegiance.

THOMPSON, JOHN NELSON, SR., 3rd Lieutenant

Born in Mecklenburg County and resided in Rowan County where he was by occupation a farmer prior to enlisting in Rowan County at age 26, March 19, 1862. Mustered in as Private. Promoted to 1st Sergeant in October, 1862. Elected 3rd Lieutenant on December 29, 1862. Reported present or accounted for from November, 1862, through December, 1863, and in May-August, 1864. Captured at Sayler's Creek, Virginia, April 6, 1865. Confined at Old Capitol Prison, Washington, D.C., April 14, 1865. Transferred to Johnson's Island, Ohio, April 21, 1865. Released at Johnson's Island on June 20, 1865, after taking the Oath of Allegiance.

NONCOMMISSIONED OFFICERS AND PRIVATES

ALBRIGHT, GEORGE, Private

Resided in Rowan County and was by occupation a farmer prior to enlisting in Rowan County at age 40, September 23, 1863, for the war. Reported present or accounted for in October-December, 1863, and May-August, 1864. Captured at or near Five Forks, Virginia, April 1, 1865. Confined at Point Lookout, Maryland, April 3, 1865. Released at Point Lookout on June 6, 1865, after taking the Oath of Allegiance.

ALBRIGHT, MICHAEL, Private

Resided in Rowan County and was by occupation a farmer prior to enlisting in Rowan County at age 40, November 12, 1863, for the war. Reported present or accounted for in December, 1863, and May-August, 1864. Wounded in the back at Five Forks, Virginia, April 1, 1865. Hospitalized at Petersburg, Virginia, where he was captured on April 3, 1865. Transferred to a Federal hospital at Point of Rocks, Virginia, on or about April 17, 1865. Hospitalized at Fort Monroe, Virginia, May 17, 1865. Transferred to Camp Hamilton, Virginia, May 25, 1865. Released at Camp Hamilton on May 31, 1865, after taking the Oath of Allegiance.

BAILEY, DANIEL, Private

Born in Davidson County and resided in Rowan County where he was by occupation a farmer prior to enlisting in Rowan County at age 37, March 18, 1862, as a substitute. Reported present in November-December, 1862. Deserted on an unspecified date. Court-martialed on an unspecified date and confined at Petersburg, Virginia. Returned to duty on February 16, 1863. Reported present or accounted for through December, 1863. Wounded at Drewry's Bluff, Virginia, May 16, 1864. Reported absent wounded through August, 1864. Paroled at Salisbury on June 12 or June 17, 1865.

BARBER, JOHN R., Private

Born in Rowan County where he resided as a farmer prior to enlisting in Rowan County at age 24, March 19, 1862. Reported present from November, 1862, through December, 1863, and in May-August, 1864.

BARGER, JACOB A., Private

Born in Rowan County where he resided as a farmer prior to enlisting in Rowan County at age 26, March 19, 1862. Sent to hospital sick on August 25, 1862. Released from hospital on an unspecified date. Failed to return to duty. Listed as a deserter and was dropped from the rolls of the company on February 10, 1863. Returned to duty in March-April, 1863. Reported present or accounted for in May-December, 1863. Reported absent without leave from May 1 through August 31, 1864. Returned to duty on an unspecified date. Captured at Five Forks, Virginia, April 1, 1865. Confined at Point Lookout, Maryland, April 5, 1865. Released at Point Lookout on June 23, 1865, after taking the Oath of Allegiance. [North Carolina pension records indicate that he was wounded near Petersburg, Virginia, March 25, 1865, when he was "struck in lower belly by a sharp pole."]

BARGER, MONROE, Sergeant
Resided in Rowan County where he enlisted at age 33, March 19, 1862. Mustered in as Sergeant. Reported present or accounted for from November, 1862, through December, 1863, and in May-August, 1864. Captured at Five Forks, Virginia, April 1, 1865. Confined at Point Lookout, Maryland, April 5, 1865. Released at Point Lookout on June 23, 1865, after taking the Oath of Allegiance.

BEEKER, PHILIP S., Private
Born in Davidson County and resided in Rowan County where he was by occupation a farmer prior to enlisting in Rowan County at age 32, March 19, 1862. Died in hospital at Front Royal, Virginia, November 20, 1862, of disease.

BENSON, ROBERT L., Private
Enlisted in Rowan County on June 3, 1864, for the war. Reported present in July-August, 1864. Surrendered at Appomattox Court House, Virginia, April 9, 1865.

BENSON, SAMUEL S., Private
Born in Rowan County where he resided as a farmer prior to enlisting in Rowan County at age 25, March 19, 1862. Reported present from November, 1862, through December, 1863. Wounded in the head at Bermuda Hundred, Virginia, May 20, 1864. Reported absent wounded through August, 1864. Returned to duty on an unspecified date. Captured at Five Forks, Virginia, April 1, 1865. Confined at Point Lookout, Maryland, April 5, 1865. Released at Point Lookout on June 23, 1865, after taking the Oath of Allegiance.

BUNN, JAMES CAID, Private
Born in Franklin County and resided in Rowan County where he was by occupation a carpenter prior to enlisting in Rowan County at age 31, March 18, 1862. Wounded at Malvern Hill, Virginia, July 1, 1862. Reported absent without leave on August 4, 1862. Returned to duty in January-February, 1863. Reported present or accounted for in March-December, 1863, and May-June, 1864. Reported absent without leave on August 11, 1864. Took the Oath of Allegiance at Salisbury on June 15, 1865.

CARPENTER, JOHN N., Private
Resided in Wake County and enlisted at Camp Holmes, near Raleigh, July 28, 1864, for the war. Hospitalized at Richmond, Virginia, December 8, 1864, with chronic rheumatism or intermittent fever. Returned to duty on March 25, 1865. Captured at Five Forks, Virginia, April 1, 1865. Confined at Point Lookout, Maryland, April 5, 1865. Released at Point Lookout on June 26, 1865, after taking the Oath of Allegiance.

CHAMBERS, RICHARD M., Private
Born in Rowan County where he resided as a farmer prior to enlisting in Rowan County at age 22, March 19, 1862. Died on April 23, 1862, of disease. Place of death not reported.

COLE, JAMES BRANDON, Private
Born in Rowan County where he resided as a farmer prior to enlisting in Rowan County at age 19, March 24, 1862.

Reported present or accounted for from November, 1862, through December, 1863. "Wounded in the head by stray ball" near Petersburg, Virginia, June 27, 1864. Hospitalized at Richmond, Virginia. Furloughed for fifty days on July 26, 1864. Captured at Five Forks, Virginia, April 1, 1865. Confined at Point Lookout, Maryland, April 5, 1865. Released at Point Lookout on June 24, 1865, after taking the Oath of Allegiance.

COOK, THOMAS M., Private
Born in Rowan County where he resided as a farmer prior to enlisting in Rowan County at age 34, March 19, 1862. Captured at Frederick, Maryland, on or about September 12, 1862. Confined at Fort Delaware, Delaware. Paroled and transferred to Aiken's Landing, James River, Virginia, October 2, 1862, for exchange. Declared exchanged at Aiken's Landing on November 10, 1862. Reported absent without leave through December, 1862. Returned to duty in January-February, 1863. Reported present or accounted for in March-December, 1863, and May-August, 1864. Wounded by a shell in the trenches near Petersburg, Virginia, on or about November 9, 1864. Died on November 10, 1864, of wounds.

CRESS, LAWSON, Private
Born in Cabarrus County and resided in Rowan County where he was by occupation a farmer prior to enlisting in Rowan County at age 21, September 23, 1863, for the war. Wounded in both hips at Drewry's Bluff, Virginia, May 16, 1864. Hospitalized at Richmond, Virginia, where he died on May 21, 1864, of wounds.

DANIEL, WYLIE B., Private
Born in Davie County and resided in Rowan County where he was by occupation a miner prior to enlisting in Rowan County at age 24, March 18, 1862. Wounded at Malvern Hill, Virginia, July 1, 1862. Returned to duty on an unspecified date. Reported present from November, 1862, through December, 1863. Killed at Drewry's Bluff, Virginia, May 16, 1864.

DINGLE, WILLIAM, Private
Born in England and resided in Rowan County where he was by occupation a miner prior to enlisting in Rowan County at age 34, March 17, 1862. Captured at or near Sharpsburg, Maryland, on or about September 17, 1862. Requested that he not be paroled and exchanged. That request was granted, and he was released on or about October 3, 1862. Listed as a deserter and dropped from the rolls of the company in February, 1863.

EARNHARDT, MOSES G., Private
Born in Rowan County where he resided as a miner or farmer prior to enlisting in Rowan County at age 26, March 19, 1862. Reported present or accounted for from November, 1862, through December, 1863, and in May-August, 1864. Furloughed from hospital at Richmond, Virginia, February 25, 1865.

ELLIOTT, JULIUS A., Private
Born in Rowan County where he resided as a farmer prior to enlisting in Rowan County at age 23, March 19, 1862. Mustered in as Private. Appointed Musician on December

17, 1862. Reported present from November, 1862, through December, 1863. Captured at Drewry's Bluff, Virginia, May 13, 1864. Confined at Point Lookout, Maryland, May 18, 1864. Transferred to Elmira, New York, August 15, 1864. Arrived at Elmira on August 17, 1864. Reduced to ranks on an unspecified date subsequent to August 31, 1864. Paroled at Elmira on February 9, 1865. Received at Boulware's Wharf, James River, Virginia, on or about February 20, 1865, for exchange. Paroled at Salisbury on May 18, 1865. Took the Oath of Allegiance at Salisbury on June 10, 1865.

FELKER, WILLIAM, Private

Born in Rowan County where he resided as a farmer prior to enlisting in Rowan County at age 18, October 17, 1863, for the war. Reported present in November-December, 1863, and May-August, 1864. Hospitalized at Richmond, Virginia, February 23, 1865, with pneumonia. Furloughed for sixty days on March 24, 1865. Paroled at Salisbury on May 16, 1865. Took the Oath of Allegiance at Salisbury on June 10, 1865.

FINCH, WILLIAM H., Private

Born in Granville County and was by occupation a farmer prior to enlisting in Rowan County at age 42, October 17, 1863, for the war. Reported present in November-December, 1863. Reported absent sick from March 3 through July 31, 1864. Reported in hospital at Wilson in August-December, 1864. Survived the war.

FREEZE, JACOB, Private

Born in Rowan County where he resided as a farmer prior to enlisting in Rowan County at age 24, March 19, 1862. Reported present from November, 1862, through December, 1863. Stunned by a shell at Drewry's Bluff, Virginia, May 16, 1864. Returned to duty in a few hours. Wounded in the head by a shell fragment at or near Petersburg, Virginia, on or about August 24, 1864. Hospitalized at Petersburg. "A large piece of skull bone was taken out but the piece of shell could not be found." Died at Petersburg on August 27, 1864, of wounds.

GALLIMORE, W. B., Private

Place and date of enlistment not reported. Wounded at Sharpsburg, Maryland, September 17, 1862. Died on September 18, 1862, of wounds. Place of death not reported.

GALLIMORE, WILLIAM F., Private

Resided in Davidson County. Place and date of enlistment not reported; however, he probably enlisted subsequent to August 31, 1864. Captured at Five Forks, Virginia, April 1, 1865. Confined at Point Lookout, Maryland, April 4, 1865. Released at Point Lookout on June 27, 1865, after taking the Oath of Allegiance.

GEARY, SAMPSON, Private

Born in England and resided in Union County where he was by occupation a miner prior to enlisting in Rowan County at age 35, March 17, 1862. Deserted on July 28, 1862.

GEISLER, JOHN, Sergeant

Born in Tirol, Empire of Austria, and resided in Rowan

County where he was by occupation a miner prior to enlisting in Rowan County at age 40, March 15, 1862. Mustered in as Private. Promoted to Sergeant on July 1, 1862. Wounded at Sharpsburg, Maryland, September 17, 1862. Returned to duty on an unspecified date. Reported present from November, 1862, through December, 1863, and in May-June, 1864. Wounded at Globe Tavern, Virginia, August 21, 1864. Hospitalized at Richmond, Virginia, where he died on November 6, 1864, of wounds.

GILLEAN, HEZEKIAH C., Private

Resided in Rowan County. Place and date of enlistment not reported; however, he probably enlisted subsequent to August 31, 1864. Captured at Five Forks, Virginia, April 1, 1865. Confined at Point Lookout, Maryland, April 4, 1865. Released at Point Lookout on June 27, 1865, after taking the Oath of Allegiance. [Records of the United Daughters of the Confederacy give his birth date as April 15, 1837.]

GILLEAN, JOHN N., Private

Resided in Rowan County where he enlisted at age 29, July 7, 1862, for the war. Died at Montgomery White Sulphur Springs, Virginia, December 5, 1862, of "ty[phoid] pneu[monia]."

GRAHAM, HENRY CLAY, Private

Born in Rowan County where he resided as a farmer prior to enlisting in Rowan County at age 18, April 12, 1862. Died at Winchester, Virginia, October 11, 1862, of "ty[phoid] fever."

GRAHAM, JOSEPH, Private

Born in Rowan County where he resided as a farmer prior to enlisting in Rowan County at age 52, March 21, 1862, as a substitute for Charles Waggoner. Deserted on August 12, 1862. Returned to duty on November 28, 1862. Reported absent sick from January 8 through December 31, 1863. Reported absent without leave from May 1 through August 31, 1864. Hospitalized at Richmond, Virginia, February 24, 1865, with intermittent fever. Furloughed for sixty days on March 16, 1865. Took the Oath of Allegiance at Salisbury on June 2, 1865.

GRAHAM, JOSEPH C., Private

Born in Rowan County where he resided as a farmer prior to enlisting in Rowan County at age 40, September 23, 1863, for the war. Reported present in November-December, 1863, and May-August, 1864. Surrendered at Appomattox Court House, Virginia, April 9, 1865.

GRAHAM, RICHARD S., Private

Born in Rowan County where he resided as a farmer prior to enlisting in Rowan County at age 25, March 19, 1862. Died in hospital at Petersburg, Virginia, August 10, 1862, of "ty[phoid] fever."

GRIFFIN, THOMAS J., Private

Enlisted in Rowan County on February 24, 1864, for the war. Reported present in May-June, 1864. Company records indicate that he was captured at Globe Tavern, Virginia, August 21, 1864; however, records of the Federal Provost Marshal do not substantiate that report. No further records.

HALL, JOHN A., Private

Resided in Rowan County where he enlisted on April 9, 1864, for the war. Wounded at Drewry's Bluff, Virginia, May 16, 1864. Returned to duty on or about August 3, 1864. "Painfully wounded in the [left] leg by a piece of shell as he was coming out of the trenches" near Petersburg, Virginia, October 21, 1864. Hospitalized at Richmond, Virginia. Furloughed for sixty days on November 11, 1864. Paroled at Salisbury on May 3, 1865. Took the Oath of Allegiance at Salisbury on June 26, 1865.

HALL, THOMAS F., Private

Born in Rowan County where he resided as a farmer prior to enlisting in Rowan County at age 30, April 29, 1862, for the war. Reported absent sick in hospital at Richmond, Virginia, from December 5, 1862, through December 31, 1863. Detailed at Harrell's Mills on April 29, 1864. Reported absent on detached service with the assistant commissary of subsistence of this regiment in July-August, 1864. Captured at Fort Stedman, Virginia, March 25, 1865. Confined at Point Lookout, Maryland, until released on June 27, 1865, after taking the Oath of Allegiance.

HARKEY, MILAS, Private

Born in Rowan County where he resided as a farmer prior to enlisting in Rowan County at age 21, March 24, 1862. Reported present from November, 1862, through December, 1863, and in May-August, 1864. "Shot through the mouth by a Yankee Sharpshooter" on December 1, 1864, "while on inspection in the trenches. . . ." Hospitalized at Richmond, Virginia. Furloughed for sixty days on December 19, 1864. Returned to duty prior to March 25, 1865, when he was captured at Fort Stedman, Virginia. Confined at Point Lookout, Maryland, until released on June 27, 1865, after taking the Oath of Allegiance.

HARRISON, BENNETT A., Private

Born in Rowan County where he resided as a farmer prior to enlisting in Rowan County at age 39, March 21, 1862, as a substitute. Discharged on May 30, 1862, by reason of disability.

HARTMAN, JOHN B., Private

Born in Rowan County where he resided as a farmer prior to enlisting in Rowan County at age 21, March 22, 1862. Hospitalized at Richmond, Virginia, July 8, 1862, with "finger shot off." Place and date wounded not reported. Reported absent wounded or absent without leave through December, 1862. Returned to duty on February 14, 1863. Sent to hospital at Petersburg, Virginia, June 20, 1863. Reported absent sick in July-December, 1863, and May-June, 1864. Reported absent without leave on August 23, 1864. Hospitalized at Raleigh on February 6, 1865, with "anurisma aorta." Furloughed for sixty days on March 23, 1865. Paroled at Salisbury on May 11, 1865. Took the Oath of Allegiance at Salisbury on June 3, 1865.

HATLEY, SIMEON W., Corporal

Born in Stanly County* and resided in Rowan County where he was by occupation a miner prior to enlisting in Rowan County at age 26, March 18, 1862. Mustered in as Corporal. Died in hospital at Goldsboro on July 2, 1862, of disease.

HENLEY, JOHN D., Private

Born in Rowan County where he resided as a carpenter prior to enlisting in Rowan County at age 49, April 4, 1862. Sent to hospital on August 25, 1862. Reported absent without leave in November-December, 1862. Returned to duty in January-February, 1863. Reported absent sick in March-December, 1863, and May-August, 1864. Paroled at Salisbury on June 10, 1865.

HILL, WILLIAM J., Private

Born in Rowan County where he resided as a farmer prior to enlisting in Rowan County at age 45, March 19, 1862. Reported present from November, 1862, through December, 1863, and in May-June, 1864. Died in hospital at Richmond, Virginia, July 25, 1864, of "hepatitis chronica."

HOFFNER, ATLAS, Private

Born in Rowan County where he resided as a farmer prior to enlisting in Rowan County at age 22, March 19, 1862. Died at Goldsboro on or about May 23, 1862, of "measles."

HOLDSHOUSER, JOHN, Private

Born in Rowan County where he resided as a farmer prior to enlisting in Rowan County at age 19, March 19, 1862. Died on May 10, 1862, of disease. Place of death not reported.

JOHNSTON, GEORGE W., Private

Resided in Rowan County and enlisted on March 18, 1865, for the war. Captured at hospital at Richmond, Virginia, April 3, 1865. Reported in hospital at Petersburg, Virginia, May 25, 1865. Released on an unspecified date. Took the Oath of Allegiance at Salisbury on June 12, 1865.

JOHNSTON, WILLIAM, Private

Born in Davidson County and resided in Rowan County where he was by occupation a farmer prior to enlisting in Rowan County at age 21, March 19, 1862. Reported present from November, 1862, through December, 1863, and in May-August, 1864. Surrendered at Appomattox Court House, Virginia, April 9, 1865. Took the Oath of Allegiance at Salisbury on June 10, 1865. [North Carolina pension records indicate that he was wounded at the Chickahominy River, Virginia, in 1864.]

JORDAN, JAMES S., Private

Enlisted in Rowan County on April 23, 1864, for the war. Wounded in the back at Bermuda Hundred, Virginia, May 20, 1864. Returned to duty prior to July 1, 1864. Wounded in the right foot at Petersburg, Virginia, August 13, 1864. Furloughed from hospital at Richmond, Virginia, September 3, 1864. Survived the war.

KERN, DANIEL, JR., Private

Born in Rowan County where he resided as a farmer prior to enlisting in Rowan County at age 21, March 21, 1862. Detailed for duty as a gunsmith on May 31, 1862. Served as a gunsmith at Richmond, Virginia, through August, 1864.

KETCHIE, NOAH, Private

Born in Rowan County and resided in Iredell County where he was by occupation a farmer prior to enlisting in Rowan County at age 22, March 19, 1862. Reported present from November, 1862, through December, 1863. Wounded in the hip and/or buttocks at Drewry's Bluff, Virginia, on or about May 16, 1864. Hospitalized at Richmond, Virginia. Furloughed for sixty days on or about May 31, 1864. Reported absent on furlough through August, 1864. Returned to duty on an unspecified date. Captured at Fort Stedman, Virginia, March 25, 1865. Confined at Point Lookout, Maryland, until released on June 28, 1865, after taking the Oath of Allegiance.

LENTZ, CALEB A., Private

Born in Rowan County where he resided as a farmer prior to enlisting in Rowan County at age 18, October 17, 1863, for the war. Reported present or accounted for in November-December, 1863, and May-August, 1864. Captured at Five Forks, Virginia, April 1, 1865. Confined at Point Lookout, Maryland, April 5, 1865. Released at Point Lookout on June 28, 1865, after taking the Oath of Allegiance.

LENTZ, ELI CRAWFORD, Corporal

Born in Rowan County and resided in Rowan or Stanly County where he was by occupation a farmer prior to enlisting in Rowan County at age 25, March 22, 1862. Mustered in as Private. Appointed Musician (Drum Major) prior to January 1, 1863. Reported present from November, 1862, through December, 1863. Reduced to ranks in November-December, 1863. Wounded at Drewry's Bluff, Virginia, May 16, 1864. Returned to duty prior to July 1, 1864. Reported present in July-August, 1864. Promoted to Corporal on August 22, 1864. Captured at Fort Stedman, Virginia, March 25, 1865. Confined at Point Lookout, Maryland, until released on May 15, 1865, after taking the Oath of Allegiance.

LINK, JAMES M., Private

Born in Rowan County where he resided as a blacksmith prior to enlisting in Rowan County at age 28, March 22, 1862. "On the 19th day of June 1862 . . . [he] fell exhausted in the road while on a march between Richmond and Malvern Hill. . . ." Reported absent sick until October 20, 1863, when he was discharged by reason of "partial hemiplegia and complete aphonia the result of sunstroke." "He is and for over twelve months has been entirely dumb."

LUDWICK, ALFRED F., Sergeant

Born in Cabarrus County and resided in Rowan County where he was by occupation a blacksmith prior to enlisting in Rowan County at age 32, March 18, 1862. Mustered in as Sergeant. Died at Gold Hill (Rowan County) on May 14, 1862, of "measles."

LYERLY, ISAAC, Corporal

Resided in Rowan County and was by occupation a farmer prior to enlisting in Rowan County at age 24, July 7, 1862, for the war. Mustered in as Private. Reported present from November, 1862, through December, 1863, and in May-August, 1864. Promoted to Corporal subsequent to August 31, 1864. Surrendered at Appomattox Court House, Virginia, April 9, 1865.

LYERLY, JULIUS A., Corporal

Born in Rowan County where he resided as a farmer prior to enlisting in Rowan County at age 18, March 19, 1862. Mustered in as Corporal. Reported present from November, 1862, through December, 1863, and in May-June, 1864. Wounded by Federal artillery fire at Globe Tavern, Virginia, August 21, 1864. Hospitalized at Richmond, Virginia. Furloughed for thirty days on August 27, 1864. Returned to duty on an unspecified date. Captured at Five Forks, Virginia, April 1, 1865. Confined at Hart's Island, New York Harbor, April 7, 1865. Released at Hart's Island on June 19, 1865, after taking the Oath of Allegiance.

McCANLESS, DAVID A., Private

Resided in Rowan County where he enlisted at age 18, September 9, 1863, for the war. Reported present in October-December, 1863. Wounded in the right elbow near Petersburg, Virginia, June 17, 1864. Hospitalized at Richmond, Virginia. Furloughed for forty days on or about October 20, 1864. Company records do not indicate whether he returned to duty. Took the Oath of Allegiance at Salisbury on July 8, 1865.

McCANLESS, JOHN D., Private

Resided in McDowell County and enlisted in Rowan County at age 17, September 21, 1863, for the war. Reported present in October-December, 1863. Hospitalized at Raleigh on June 20, 1864, with acute diarrhoea. Furloughed for sixty days on August 29, 1864. Returned to duty on an unspecified date. Hospitalized at Richmond, Virginia, March 27, 1865, with a gunshot wound of the hip. Place and date wounded not reported. Captured in hospital at Richmond on April 3, 1865. Transferred to the Federal Provost Marshal on April 22, 1865. Released on or about May 25, 1865, after taking the Oath of Allegiance.

McCARN, GEORGE W., Private

Born in Davidson County and resided in Rowan County where he was by occupation a teamster prior to enlisting in Rowan County at age 20, March 18, 1862. Wounded in the left hand at Malvern Hill, Virginia, July 1, 1862. Returned to duty on an unspecified date. Reported present from November, 1862, through December, 1863, and in May-June, 1864. Reported absent sick in July-August, 1864. Hospitalized at Richmond, Virginia, September 2, 1864, with conjunctivitis. Transferred to Farmville, Virginia, April 1, 1865. Took the Oath of Allegiance at Salisbury on June 19, 1865. "While retreating from the enemy [near Kinston in 186(4)] he became overheated, and to revive him cold water was thrown on him," causing him to catch a "severe cold which settled in his eyes and [eventually] injured his sight so as to render him unable at times to see sufficiently to attend to any work or business."

McCLELLAN, E. T., Private

Resided in Iredell County. Place and date of enlistment not reported; however, he probably enlisted subsequent to August 31, 1864. Wounded in the head (saber cut) and captured near Petersburg, Virginia, March 25 or April 1, 1865. Hospitalized at City Point, Virginia. Confined at Old Capitol Prison, Washington, D.C., April 17, 1865.

Transferred to Elmira, New York, May 1, 1865. Released at Elmira on July 11, 1865, after taking the Oath of Allegiance. [Federal medical records dated April, 1865, give his age as 25.]

McDANIEL, JOHN W., Private
Enlisted at Petersburg, Virginia, on or about August 25, 1864, for the war. "Volunteered with the consent of the enrolling officer; not of conscript age." Deserted on January 27, 1865. Took the Oath of Allegiance at Gordonsville, Virginia, June 13, 1865.

MASK, MARION, Private
Born in Richmond County and resided in Rowan County where he was by occupation a miner prior to enlisting in Rowan County at age 27, March 19, 1862. Reported present from November, 1862, through December, 1863. Wounded in the right shoulder at Drewry's Bluff, Virginia, May 16, 1864, but remained on duty. Reported present in May-August, 1864. Wounded in the right thigh at Fort Stedman, Virginia, March 25, 1865. Hospitalized at Petersburg, Virginia. Leg amputated. Captured in hospital at Petersburg on April 3, 1865. Died in hospital at Petersburg on June 14, 1865, of wounds.

MAUNEY, FRANKLIN H., Corporal
Born in Cabarrus County and resided in Rowan County where he was by occupation a farmer prior to enlisting in Rowan County at age 16, April 9, 1862. Mustered in as Corporal. Reported present or accounted for from November, 1862, through December, 1863, and in May-June, 1864. Wounded by Federal artillery fire at Globe Tavern, Virginia, August 21, 1864. No further records.

MENIS, ANDREW, Private
Born in Rowan County where he resided as a farmer prior to enlisting in Rowan County at age 44, October 17, 1863, for the war. Reported present in November-December, 1863. Died in hospital at Wilson on April 20, 1864, of "chronic diarrhoea."

MENIS, JAMES F., Private
Born in Rowan County where he resided as a farmer prior to enlisting in Rowan County at age 22, March 19, 1862. Died in hospital at Richmond, Virginia, December 22, 1862, of "pneumonia."

MESSEMORE, GEORGE W., Private
Born in Rowan County where he resided as a miller prior to enlisting in Rowan County at age 19, March 20, 1862. Detailed as a blacksmith at Richmond, Virginia, on or about January 1, 1863. Reported absent on detail at Richmond through August, 1864. Captured at Fort Stedman, Virginia, March 25, 1865. Confined at Point Lookout, Maryland, March 31, 1865. Released at Point Lookout on or about May 13, 1865, after taking the Oath of Allegiance. [Served in 1st Company C, 2nd Battalion Virginia Infantry (Local Defense), while on detail at Richmond.]

MILLER, ALEXANDER M., Private
Born in Rowan County where he resided as a farmer prior to enlisting in Rowan County at age 33, March 19, 1862.

Hospitalized at Petersburg, Virginia, on or about August 25, 1862, with bronchitis. Returned to duty on or about April 27, 1863. Hospitalized at Richmond, Virginia, June 26, 1863. Returned to duty prior to September 1, 1863. Reported present in September-December, 1863, and May-August, 1864. Captured at Fort Stedman, Virginia, March 25, 1865. Confined at Point Lookout, Maryland, until released on June 29, 1865, after taking the Oath of Allegiance.

MILLER, GEORGE W., Private
Born in Cabarrus County and resided in Rowan County where he was by occupation a miner prior to enlisting in Rowan County at age 28, March 19, 1862. Reported present from November, 1862, through December, 1863, and in May-August, 1864. Hospitalized at Richmond, Virginia, October 12, 1864, with an unspecified complaint. Furloughed for sixty days on November 22, 1864.

MILLER, JAMES, Private
Born in Rowan County where he resided as a farmer prior to enlisting in Rowan County at age 36, September 23, 1863, for the war. Reported present in October-December, 1863. Died in hospital at Richmond, Virginia, June 25, 1864, of "febris typh[oid]."

MOYLE, WILLIAM, Private
Born in England and resided in Rowan County where he was by occupation a miner prior to enlisting in Rowan County at age 37, March 18, 1862. Deserted on August 12, 1862. Returned from desertion on August 15, 1862. Hospitalized at Petersburg, Virginia, August 28, 1862, with acute bronchitis. Released from hospital on November 14, 1862. Reported in confinement at Richmond, Virginia, through December, 1862. "Started to [the] company" in January-February, 1863, but failed to report for duty. Listed as a deserter and dropped from the rolls of the company on March 1, 1863. Took the Oath of Allegiance at City Point, Virginia, December 23, 1864.

NASH, ABRAHAM, Private
Born in Davie County* and resided in Rowan County where he was by occupation a farmer prior to enlisting in Rowan County at age 34, March 19, 1862. Reported present from November, 1862, through December, 1863, and in May-August, 1864. Captured at Fort Stedman, Virginia, March 25, 1865. Confined at Point Lookout, Maryland, until released on June 29, 1865, after taking the Oath of Allegiance.

NASH, WYLIE A., Private
Resided in Rowan County where he enlisted at age 32, April 11, 1862. Reported present from November, 1862, through December, 1863, and in May-August, 1864. Captured at Five Forks, Virginia, April 1, 1865. Confined at Point Lookout, Maryland, April 5, 1865. Released at Point Lookout on June 29, 1865, after taking the Oath of Allegiance.

NIFONG, WYLIE, Private
Resided in Davidson County and was by occupation a farmer prior to enlisting at age 19, March 18, 1865, for the war. Hospitalized at Danville, Virginia, April 3, 1865,

with a gunshot wound of the left shoulder. Place and date wounded not reported. Furloughed for thirty days on April 8, 1865.

NOAH, MILUS A., Sergeant

Born in Stanly County* and resided in Rowan County where he was by occupation a shoemaker prior to enlisting in Rowan County at age 23, March 24, 1862, as a substitute. Mustered in as Sergeant. Killed at Malvern Hill, Virginia, July 1, 1862.

PLUMMER, MATTHEW, Private

Born in Rowan County where he resided as a farmer prior to enlisting in Rowan County at age 24, March 19, 1862. Reported present from November, 1862, through December, 1863. Wounded at Drewry's Bluff, Virginia, May 16, 1864. Returned to duty prior to July 1, 1864. Reported present in July-August, 1864. Captured at Fort Stedman, Virginia, March 25, 1865. Confined at Point Lookout, Maryland, until released on June 16, 1865, after taking the Oath of Allegiance.

POWLAS, ELI, Private

Resided in Rowan County and was by occupation a farmer. Place and date of enlistment not reported; however, he probably enlisted subsequent to August 31, 1864. Was about 42 years of age at time of enlistment. Captured at Five Forks, Virginia, April 1, 1865. Confined at Point Lookout, Maryland, April 5, 1865. Released at Point Lookout on June 16, 1865, after taking the Oath of Allegiance.

POWLAS, JESSE, Private

Resided in Rowan County and was by occupation a farmer. Place and date of enlistment not reported; however, he probably enlisted subsequent to August 31, 1864. Was about 37 years of age at time of enlistment. Captured at Five Forks, Virginia, April 1, 1865. Confined at Point Lookout, Maryland, April 5, 1865. Released at Point Lookout on June 30, 1865, after taking the Oath of Allegiance.

RATTS, BURRELL R., Private

Born in Davidson County* and resided in Rowan County where he was by occupation a farmer prior to enlisting in Rowan County at age 44, September 23, 1863, for the war. Reported present or accounted for in October-December, 1863, and May-August, 1864. Took the Oath of Allegiance at Salisbury on June 9, 1865.

RAY, JAMES T., 1st Sergeant

Born in Pittsylvania County, Virginia, and resided in Rowan County where he was by occupation a farmer prior to enlisting in Rowan County at age 26, March 19, 1862. Mustered in as 1st Sergeant. Reduced to ranks on October 1, 1862. Reappointed 1st Sergeant on or about December 29, 1862. Reported present from November, 1862, through December, 1863, and in May-August, 1864. Captured at Fort Stedman, Virginia, March 25, 1865. Confined at Point Lookout, Maryland, until released on June 17, 1865, after taking the Oath of Allegiance.

REEVES, JOEL P., Private

Resided in Rowan County. Place and date of enlistment

not reported; however, he probably enlisted subsequent to August 31, 1864. Captured at Five Forks, Virginia, April 1, 1865. Confined at Point Lookout, Maryland, April 5, 1865. Released at Point Lookout on June 17, 1865, after taking the Oath of Allegiance. [North Carolina pension records indicate that he was wounded at Petersburg, Virginia, March 25, 186(5).]

RICE, JOSEPH A., Private

Resided in Rowan County where he enlisted at age 22, April 18, 1863, for the war. Reported present in May-December, 1863, and May-June, 1864. Reported absent on sick leave of sixty days on July 7, 1864. Wounded in the left leg at Fort Stedman, Virginia, March 25, 1865. Hospitalized at Petersburg, Virginia. Captured in hospital at Petersburg on April 3, 1865. Transferred to a Federal hospital at Point of Rocks, Virginia, April 9, 1865. Hospitalized at Fort Monroe, Virginia, April 13, 1865. Died at Fort Monroe on June 23, 1865, of "chronic diarrhoea."

RICE, WILLIAM G., Private

Resided in Rowan County where he enlisted at age 18, September 16, 1863, for the war. Reported present in October-December, 1863, and May-August, 1864. Captured at Five Forks, Virginia, April 1, 1865. Confined at Point Lookout, Maryland, April 5, 1865. Released at Point Lookout on June 17, 1865, after taking the Oath of Allegiance.

RITCHIE, GEORGE M., Private

Born in Rowan County where he resided as a farmer prior to enlisting in Rowan County at age 32, March 19, 1862. Reported present from November, 1862, through December, 1863. Wounded in the head in the trenches near Petersburg, Virginia, June 22, 1864, by a Federal sharpshooter. Hospitalized at Petersburg where he died on July 2, 1864, of wounds.

ROBISON, JAMES H., Private

Born in Rowan County where he resided as a farmer prior to enlisting in Rowan County at age 28, March 19, 1862. Reported present from November, 1862, through December, 1863, and in May-June, 1864. Wounded in the head near Petersburg, Virginia, August 24, 1864. "He . . . was some distance to the rear when a minie ball struck him above the left eye." Hospitalized at Petersburg on August 26, 1864. Furloughed for sixty days on or about September 1, 1864. Returned to duty on an unspecified date. Surrendered at Appomattox Court House, Virginia, April 9, 1865. Took the Oath of Allegiance at Salisbury on June 10, 1865.

ROBISON, THOMAS T., Sergeant

Born in Rowan County where he resided as a farmer prior to enlisting in Rowan County at age 31, March 19, 1862. Mustered in as Sergeant. Reported present or accounted for from November, 1862, through December, 1863, and in May-August, 1864. Captured at Five Forks, Virginia, April 1, 1865. Confined at Point Lookout, Maryland, April 5, 1865. Released at Point Lookout on June 19, 1865, after taking the Oath of Allegiance.

RODGERS, HENRY H., Private
Born in Rowan County where he resided as a farmer prior to enlisting in Rowan County at age 18, September 23, 1863, for the war. Reported present in October-December, 1863, and May-August, 1864. Hospitalized at Richmond, Virginia, February 28, 1865, with pneumonia. Furloughed for thirty days on March 28, 1865. Paroled at Salisbury on May 13, 1865.

SAFRIET, JAMES A., Private
Born in Rowan County and was by occupation a farmer prior to enlisting in Rowan County at age 18, October 17, 1863, for the war. Killed at Drewry's Bluff, Virginia, May 16, 1864.

SHAVER, ALVIN W., Corporal
Born in Iredell County where he resided as a farmer prior to enlisting in Rowan County at age 19, March 19, 1862. Mustered in as Private. Promoted to Corporal on December 25, 1862. Reported present from November, 1862, through December, 1863, and in May-August, 1864. Captured at Fort Stedman, Virginia, March 25, 1865. Confined at Point Lookout, Maryland, until released on June 20, 1865, after taking the Oath of Allegiance.

SHAVER, M. A., Private
Place and date of enlistment not reported; however, he probably enlisted subsequent to August 31, 1864. Hospitalized at Richmond, Virginia, March 3, 1865, with "pneumonia" and died on March 13, 1865.

SHUPING, ANDREW, Private
Born in Rowan County where he resided as a farmer prior to enlisting in Rowan County at age 41, October 17, 1863, for the war. Reported present or accounted for in November-December, 1863, and May-August, 1864. Captured at Five Forks, Virginia, April 1, 1865. Confined at Point Lookout, Maryland, April 5, 1865. Released at Point Lookout on June 20, 1865, after taking the Oath of Allegiance.

SIDES, RANSOM, Private
Born in Stanly County* and resided in Rowan County where he was by occupation a farmer prior to enlisting in Rowan County at age 31, March 18, 1862. Reported present from November, 1862, through December, 1863. Wounded in the head by a shell fragment at Drewry's Bluff, Virginia, May 15, 1864. Reported absent wounded through June, 1864. Detailed for light duty in hospital at Kittrell's Spring on July 12, 1864. Returned to duty subsequent to August 31, 1864. Killed in the trenches near Petersburg, Virginia, December 14, 1864, during a severe mortar shelling.

SKEEN, JESSE, Private
Born in Davidson County and resided in Rowan County where he was by occupation a blacksmith prior to enlisting in Rowan County at age 29, March 18, 1862. Reported on detached service as brigade blacksmith for most of the period from November, 1862, through August, 1864. Surrendered at Appomattox Court House, Virginia, April 9, 1865.

SMITH, JOHN C., Private
Born in Rowan County where he resided prior to enlisting at age 18, May 11, 1862, for the war. Died at Goldsboro on May 26, 1862, of "typhoid fever."

SPANG, WILEY, Private
Place and date of enlistment not reported; however, he probably enlisted subsequent to August 31, 1864. Paroled at Greensboro on May 8, 1865.

STIKELEATHER, JOHN McK., Private
Born in Rowan County where he resided as a farmer prior to enlisting in Rowan County at age 22, September 23, 1863, for the war. Reported present in October-December, 1863. Wounded in the right shoulder at Drewry's Bluff, Virginia, May 16, 1864. Returned to duty prior to July 1, 1864. Reported present in July-August, 1864. Wounded in the hand and/or left knee at Fort Stedman, Virginia, March 25, 1865. Hospitalized at Richmond, Virginia. Paroled at Statesville or Morganton on May 20, 1865.

STONE, RICHARD A., Sergeant
Born in Stanly County* and resided in Rowan County where he was by occupation a carpenter prior to enlisting in Rowan County at age 24, March 24, 1862. Mustered in as Private. Promoted to Sergeant prior to January 1, 1863. Reported present from November, 1862, through December, 1863. Wounded at Drewry's Bluff, Virginia, May 16, 1864. Returned to duty prior to July 1, 1864. Reported present in July-August, 1864. Captured at Five Forks, Virginia, April 1, 1865. Confined at Point Lookout, Maryland, April 5, 1865. Released at Point Lookout on June 3, 1865, after taking the Oath of Allegiance.

STONE, ROBERT J., Private
Place and date of enlistment not reported; however, he probably enlisted subsequent to August 31, 1864. Captured at Five Forks, Virginia, April 1, 1865. Confined at Point Lookout, Maryland, April 5, 1865. Released at Point Lookout on June 3, 1865, after taking the Oath of Allegiance.

STYERS, WILLIAM O., Private
Born in Davidson County and resided in Rowan County where he was by occupation a farmer prior to enlisting in Rowan County at age 16, April 5, 1862, as a substitute. Reported absent without leave on August 22, 1862. Returned to duty on February 7, 1863. Reported present in November-December, 1863. Wounded in the finger at Drewry's Bluff, Virginia, May 16, 1864. Finger amputated. Returned to duty prior to July 1, 1864. Reported present in July-August, 1864. Deserted to the enemy on the morning of January 22, 1865. Confined at Washington, D.C., January 30, 1865. Released on an unspecified date after taking the Oath of Allegiance.

SUMMERS, JOHN N., Private
Resided in Rowan County. Place and date of enlistment not reported; however, he probably enlisted subsequent to August 31, 1864. Captured at Five Forks, Virginia, April 1, 1865. Confined at Point Lookout, Maryland, April 5, 1865. Released at Point Lookout on June 20, 1865, after taking the Oath of Allegiance.

TERRELL, JOHN, Private
Born in England and resided in Rowan County where he was by occupation a miner prior to enlisting in Rowan County at age 27, March 19, 1862. Reported absent sick in hospital from June 29 through December 31, 1862. Returned to camp on February 14, 1863. Reported present or accounted for in March-December, 1863, and May-August, 1864. Surrendered at Appomattox Court House, Virginia, April 9, 1865. Took the Oath of Allegiance at Salisbury on June 9, 1865.

THOMAS, JAMES, Private
Born in England and resided in Rowan County where he was by occupation a miner prior to enlisting in Rowan County at age 32, March 19, 1862. Deserted on August 12, 1862. "Retaken" on August 15, 1862. Held in confinement until November 5, 1862, when he rejoined the company. Reported present or accounted for in January-December, 1863. "Struck in the back by a gun which was violently thrown against him by a shell hitting it" at Drewry's Bluff, Virginia, May 15, 1864. "Shot in the head and instantly killed" while sharpshooting in the trenches near Petersburg, Virginia, June 24, 1864.

THOMASON, TURNER P., Private
Previously served as 2nd Lieutenant of Company B, 2nd Regiment N.C. Junior Reserves. Transferred to this company on July 28, 1864. Mustered in as Private. Captured at Five Forks, Virginia, April 1, 1865. Confined at Point Lookout, Maryland, April 5, 1865. Released at Point Lookout on June 20, 1865, after taking the Oath of Allegiance.

THOMASON, WILLIAM A., Private
Resided in Rowan County where he enlisted at age 31, April 18, 1863, for the war. Reported present or accounted for in May-December, 1863, and May-August, 1864. Paroled at Salisbury on May 3, 1865.

THOMPSON, BENJAMIN TURNER, Private
Resided in Rowan County where he enlisted at age 20, July 7, 1862, for the war. Hospitalized at Charlottesville, Virginia, November 6, 1862, with an unspecified complaint. Returned to duty on February 14, 1863. Reported present in March-December, 1863, and May-August, 1864. Surrendered at Appomattox Court House, Virginia, April 9, 1865.

THOMPSON, JOHN N., JR., Private
Born in Rowan County where he resided as a farmer prior to enlisting in Rowan County at age 18, March 19, 1862. Killed at Malvern Hill, Virginia, July 1, 1862.

THOMPSON, THOMAS L., Private
Born in Rowan County where he resided as a farmer prior to enlisting in Rowan County at age 26, March 19, 1862. Reported present from November, 1862, through December, 1863, and in March-August, 1864. Surrendered at Appomattox Court House, Virginia, April 9, 1865.

THOMPSON, WILLIAM A., Private
Born in Rowan County where he resided as a farmer prior to enlisting in Rowan County at age 30, March 19, 1862.

Reported present or accounted for from November, 1862, through December, 1863. Wounded at Drewry's Bluff, Virginia, May 16, 1864. Returned to duty prior to July 1, 1864. Died in hospital at Richmond, Virginia, October 17, 1864, of "colitis acuta."

THOMPSON, WILLIAM HENRY, Corporal
Born in Rowan County where he resided as a farmer prior to enlisting in Rowan County at age 22, March 18, 1862. Mustered in as Private. Promoted to Corporal on December 25, 1862. Reported present from November, 1862, through December, 1863. Wounded at Drewry's Bluff, Virginia, May 16, 1864. Returned to duty on an unspecified date. Wounded ("both knees broken by a shell") at Globe Tavern, Virginia, August 21, 1864. Died on the same date of wounds.

TROUTMAN, TRAVIS, Private
Born in Rowan County where he resided as a farmer prior to enlisting in Rowan County at age 25, March 28, 1862. Reported present or accounted for from September, 1862, through December, 1863, and in May-August, 1864; however, he was absent sick during much of that period. Captured at Fort Stedman, Virginia, March 25, 1865. Confined at Point Lookout, Maryland, until released on June 21, 1865, after taking the Oath of Allegiance.

VANDERBURG, FRANCIS, Private
Born in Cabarrus County and resided in Rowan County where he was by occupation a farmer prior to enlisting in Rowan County at age 20, March 18, 1862. Reported absent without leave on September 18, 1862. Captured by the enemy on or about the same date. Paroled on October 3, 1862. Failed to rejoin the company and was dropped from the rolls as a deserter on February 10, 1863.

WATSON, DAVID F., Private
Resided in Rowan County and was by occupation a farmer. Place and date of enlistment not reported; however, he probably enlisted subsequent to August 31, 1864. Was about 30 years of age at time of enlistment. Captured at Fort Stedman, Virginia, March 25, 1865. Confined at Point Lookout, Maryland, until released on May 15, 1865, after taking the Oath of Allegiance.

WATSON, JAMES F., Corporal
Born in Rowan County where he resided as a teacher prior to enlisting in Rowan County at age 22, March 19, 1862. Mustered in as Corporal. Died in hospital at Richmond, Virginia, on or about July 24, 1862, of "typhoid fever."

WATSON, JOHN B., Private
Born in Rowan County where he resided as a farmer prior to enlisting in Rowan County at age 20, March 19, 1862. Killed at Malvern Hill, Virginia, July 1, 1862.

WATSON, THOMAS T., Private
Born in Rowan County where he resided as a farmer prior to enlisting in Rowan County at age 18, March 19, 1862, as a substitute. Killed at Malvern Hill, Virginia, July 1, 1862.

WILLIAMS, JOHN G., Private
Born in England and resided in Rowan County where he was by occupation a miner prior to enlisting in Rowan County at age 21, March 18, 1862. Wounded at Malvern Hill, Virginia, July 1, 1862. Died at Richmond, Virginia, July 17, 1862, of wounds.

WISE, ALEXANDER, Private
Resided in Rowan County where he enlisted on April 19, 1864, for the war. Reported present in May-August, 1864. Captured at Five Forks, Virginia, April 1, 1865. Confined at Point Lookout, Maryland, April 5, 1865. Released on June 22, 1865, after taking the Oath of Allegiance.

WISE, EDWARD, Private
Born in Rowan County where he resided as a farmer prior to enlisting in Rowan County at age 32, March 19, 1862. Wounded in the right arm at Malvern Hill, Virginia, July 1, 1862. Hospitalized at Richmond, Virginia. Furloughed for thirty days on July 21, 1862. Returned to duty on an unspecified date. Reported present in January-December, 1863. Wounded at Drewry's Bluff, Virginia, May 16, 1864. Hospitalized at Richmond. Furloughed for sixty days on June 2, 1864. Returned to duty on August 25, 1864. Hospitalized at Farmville, Virginia, April 7, 1865, with a gunshot wound. Place and date wounded not reported. Paroled at Farmville prior to April 22, 1865. Took the Oath of Allegiance at Salisbury on June 3, 1865.

YOUNTS, JULIUS L., Private
Resided in Davidson County and enlisted in October, 1864, for the war. Captured at Fort Stedman, Virginia, March 25, 1865. Confined at Point Lookout, Maryland, until released on June 22, 1865, after taking the Oath of Allegiance.

COMPANY D

This company was raised in Moore County and enlisted at Carthage in March, 1862. It was mustered into state service at Camp Mangum, near Raleigh, on April 23, 1862, and assigned to the 49th Regiment N.C. Troops as Company D. After joining the regiment the company functioned as a part of the regiment, and its history for the remainder of the war is reported as a part of the regimental history.

The information contained in the following roster was compiled primarily from a company muster-in and descriptive roll dated April 23, 1862, and from company muster rolls for November 1, 1862-December 31, 1863, and May 1-August 31, 1864. No company muster rolls were located for May 1-October 31, 1862; January 1-April 30, 1864; or for the period after August 31, 1864. Valuable information was obtained from primary records such as the North Carolina adjutant general's *Roll of Honor*, discharge certificates, medical records, prisoner of war records, *The War of the Rebellion: The Official Records of the Union and Confederate Armies*, militia records, newspaper casualty lists and obituaries, Confederate pension applications filed with the state of North Carolina, and the 1860 federal census of North Carolina. Secondary sources such as postwar rosters and histories, cemetery records, the *Confederate Veteran*, published genealogies, and records of the United Daughters of the Confederacy also provided useful information.

OFFICERS

CAPTAINS

BLACK, WILLIAM MARTIN
Previously served as Assistant Quartermaster of the 35th Regiment N.C. Troops. Appointed Captain of this company to rank from March 3, 1862. Reported present from November, 1862, through October, 1863. Resigned on November 23, 1863, after he was declared incompetent by a board of examination. Resignation accepted on December 7, 1863. [Prior to his service in the 35th Regiment N.C. Troops he served as 2nd Lieutenant in the 51st Regiment N.C. Militia.]

BARRETT, DAVID SAMUEL
Born in Moore County where he resided as a farmer prior to enlisting in Moore County at age 21. Elected 1st Lieutenant on March 3, 1862. Reported present or accounted for from November, 1862, through December, 1863. Promoted to Captain on December 7, 1863. Reported present in May-August, 1864. Survived the war. [Previously served as 2nd Lieutenant in the 51st Regiment N.C. Militia.]

LIEUTENANTS

BARRETT, ALEXANDER, 2nd Lieutenant
Resided in Moore County where he enlisted at age 35, January 27, 1863, for the war. Mustered in as Private. Appointed 2nd Lieutenant on June 9, 1863. Reported present in January-December, 1863, and May-August, 1864. Surrendered at Appomattox Court House, Virginia, April 9, 1865.

BARRETT, WILLIAM A., 2nd Lieutenant
Born in Moore County where he resided as a farmer prior to enlisting in Moore County at age 22. Elected 2nd Lieutenant on March 3, 1862. Resigned on July 13, 1862, to accept a position as a colporteur. Resignation accepted on July 18, 1862.

BLUE, NEILL C., 3rd Lieutenant
Born in Moore County where he resided as a farmer prior to enlisting in Moore County at age 23, March 13, 1862. Mustered in as 1st Sergeant. Elected 3rd Lieutenant on June 15, 1862. Reported present or accounted for from November, 1862, through December, 1863, and in May-August, 1864. Wounded at or near Petersburg, Virginia, November 9, 1864. Hospitalized at Richmond, Virginia. Furloughed on or about January 19, 1865. Dropped from the rolls of the company on April 1, 1865.

FRY, NEILL A., 2nd Lieutenant
Born in Moore County where he resided as a farmer prior to enlisting in Moore County at age 24. Elected 2nd Lieutenant on March 3, 1862. Died in hospital in Virginia on June 20, 1862, of "cerebritis."

ROULHAC, THOMAS R., 1st Lieutenant
Previously served as Sergeant Major of this regiment. Appointed 1st Lieutenant on June 15, 1864, and transferred to this company. Captured at Five Forks, Virginia, April 1, 1865. Confined at Old Capitol Prison, Washington, D.C., April 5, 1865. Transferred to Johnson's Island, Ohio, April 9, 1865. Released at Johnson's Island on June 19, 1865, after taking the Oath of Allegiance.

NONCOMMISSIONED OFFICERS AND PRIVATES

BARRETT, WILLIAM R., Private
Resided in Moore County and was by occupation a farmer prior to enlisting in Moore County at age 32, January 27, 1863, for the war. Reported present through July, 1863. Deserted on August 5, 1863. Returned from desertion on December 15, 1863. Captured by the enemy at Bermuda Hundred, Virginia, June 2, 1864. Confined at Point Lookout, Maryland, June 12, 1864. Transferred to Elmira, New York, July 9, 1864. Paroled at Elmira on October 11, 1864. Received at Venus Point, Savannah River, Georgia, November 15, 1864, for exchange.

BEAN, ELI C., Private
Born in Davidson County and resided in Moore County where he was by occupation a farmer prior to enlisting in Moore County at age 40, March 13, 1862. Reported present in November-December, 1862. Deserted on or about April 3, 1863. Dropped from the rolls of the company. Went over to the enemy on or about December 26, 1864. Confined at Washington, D.C., December 30, 1864. Released on an unspecified date after taking the Oath of Allegiance.

BENNETT, GARDNER, Private
Enlisted in Moore County on March 16, 1863, for the war. Deserted on August 5, 1863.

BLACK, ARCHIBALD, Private
Born in Moore County where he resided as a farmer prior to enlisting in Moore County at age 27, March 13, 1862. Died at Goldsboro on or about June 3, 1862, of disease.

BLACK, ARCHIBALD M., Private
Resided in Moore County where he enlisted at age 20, May 12, 1862, for the war. Wounded at Malvern Hill, Virginia, July 1, 1862. Returned to duty on an unspecified date. Reported present in November-December, 1862. Reported absent sick in January-October, 1863. Returned to duty in November-December, 1863. Reported present in May-August, 1864.

BLACK, DUNCAN, Private
Born in Moore County where he resided as a farmer prior to enlisting in Moore County at age 50, March 12, 1862.

Mustered in as Corporal. Reduced to ranks on June 20, 1862. Reported in hospital with ascites and debility from December 6, 1862, through January 16, 1863. Returned to duty on January 17, 1863. Reported at home on sick furlough in March-December, 1863, and May-August, 1864.

BRITT, ANDREW J., Private
Born in Moore County where he resided prior to enlisting in Moore County at age 17, March 12, 1862. Reported present from November, 1862, through December, 1863. Reported absent with leave in May-June, 1864. Deserted in July-August, 1864.

BROWN, WILLIAM A., Private
Born in Moore County where he resided as a farmer prior to enlisting in Moore County at age 26, March 12, 1862. Died in hospital at Petersburg, Virginia, July 26, 1862, of "meningitis."

BROWN, WILLIAM P., Private
Born in Moore County where he resided prior to enlisting in Moore County at age 22, March 13, 1862. Reported absent sick in November-December, 1862. Deserted on February 14, 1863.

BURROUGHS, ELIJAH B., Private
Born in Chatham County and resided in Moore County where he was by occupation a cabinetmaker prior to enlisting in Moore County at age 34, March 14, 1862. Deserted at Petersburg, Virginia, in November-December, 1862. Reported present in January-February, 1863. Deserted at Kinston on April 3, 1863.

CADDELL, ARCHIBALD B., Private
Born in Moore County where he resided prior to enlisting in Moore County at age 26, March 13, 1862. Died in hospital at Petersburg, Virginia, July 17, 1862, of "typhoid febris."

CADDELL, NEILL B., Private
Born in Moore County where he resided as a farmer prior to enlisting in Moore County at age 20, March 13, 1862. Reported present from November, 1862, through December, 1863. Wounded in the left thigh near Drewry's Bluff, Virginia, May 16, 1864. Hospitalized at Richmond, Virginia. Furloughed for sixty days on June 2, 1864. Returned to duty subsequent to August 31, 1864. Surrendered at Appomattox Court House, Virginia, April 9, 1865.

CAMPBELL, ANGUS, Private
Born in Moore County where he resided as a farmer prior to enlisting in Moore County at age 34, March 14, 1862. Died in hospital at Petersburg, Virginia, September 23, 1862, of "diptheria" and/or "feb[ris] typhoides."

CAMPBELL, DANIEL, Private.
Resided in Moore County and was by occupation a miller prior to enlisting in Moore County at age 57, April 3, 1863, for the war as a substitute. Reported present in May-December, 1863, and May-August, 1864.

CLARK, JOHN B., Corporal

Born in Moore County where he resided as a farmer prior to enlisting in Moore County at age 29, March 14, 1862. Mustered in as Private. Promoted to Corporal on or about June 15, 1863. Reported present from November, 1862, through December, 1863. Captured at Bermuda Hundred, Virginia, June 2, 1864. Confined at Point Lookout, Maryland, June 12, 1864. Transferred to Elmira, New York, July 8, 1864. Released at Elmira on July 3, 1865, after taking the Oath of Allegiance. [Previously served as 3rd Lieutenant in the 51st Regiment N.C. Militia.]

COLE, DUNCAN, Private

Born in Moore County where he resided as a farmer prior to enlisting in Moore County at age 21, March 13, 1862. Reported present from November, 1862, through December, 1863. Hospitalized at Richmond, Virginia, May 18, 1864, with a gunshot wound. Place and date wounded not reported. Furloughed for sixty days on June 4, 1864. No further records.

COLE, MALCOLM, Private

Born in Moore County where he resided prior to enlisting in Moore County at age 21, March 14, 1862. Discharged on October 6, 1862, by reason of "derangement of several months standing & believed to be permanent & incurable." Enlisted in Company A, 27th Regiment N.C. Troops, April 1, 1864. Transferred to this company on January 7, 1865. Captured at Five Forks, Virginia, April 1, 1865. Confined at Point Lookout, Maryland, April 5, 1865. Released at Point Lookout on June 24, 1865, after taking the Oath of Allegiance.

COPELAND, JOHN N., Private

Born in Moore County where he resided as a shoemaker prior to enlisting in Moore County at age 29, March 13, 1862. Wounded at Malvern Hill, Virginia, July 1, 1862. Returned to duty on an unspecified date. Reported present from November, 1862, through December, 1863. Wounded near Petersburg, Virginia, June 18, 1864. Died (probably at Petersburg) on the same date of wounds.

COX, JOHN A., Private

Born in Moore County where he resided as a farmer prior to enlisting in Moore County at age 23, March 14, 1862. Wounded at Fredericksburg, Virginia, December 13, 1862. Hospitalized at Richmond, Virginia. Returned to duty on or about February 8, 1863. Reported present in March-December, 1863, and May-August, 1864. Hospitalized at Richmond on January 3, 1865, with intermittent fever. Captured in hospital at Richmond on April 3, 1865. Transferred to Newport News, Virginia, April 23, 1865. Released at Newport News on June 30, 1865, after taking the Oath of Allegiance.

COX, McDONALD, Private

Born in Moore County where he resided as a farmer prior to enlisting in Moore County at age 20, March 13, 1862. Reported present from November, 1862, through December, 1863, and in May-August, 1864. Captured at Fort Stedman, Virginia, March 25, 1865. Confined at Point Lookout, Maryland, March 31, 1865. Released at Point Lookout on May 13, 1865, after taking the Oath of Allegiance.

CROOK, SILAS D., Private

Born in Montgomery County and resided in Moore County where he was by occupation a cabinetmaker prior to enlisting in Moore County at age 24, March 13, 1862. Died in hospital near Drewry's Bluff, Virginia, July 7, 1862, of "typhoid fever."

CURRIE, ARCHIBALD, Private

Born in Moore County where he resided as a farmer prior to enlisting in Moore County at age 20, March 13, 1862. Reported present or accounted for from November, 1862, through December, 1863, and in May-August, 1864. Captured at Five Forks, Virginia, April 1, 1865. Confined at Point Lookout, Maryland, April 5, 1865. Released at Point Lookout on June 24, 1865, after taking the Oath of Allegiance.

DAVIDSON, JOHN, Private

Born in Moore County where he resided as a farmer prior to enlisting in Moore County at age 25, March 15, 1862. Hospitalized at Richmond, Virginia, December 24, 1862, with diarrhoea. Transferred to Danville, Virginia, January 8, 1863. Died in hospital at Danville on March 4, 1863, of "variola."

DAVIS, STEPHEN D., Private

Resided in Moore County. Place and date of enlistment not reported; however, he probably enlisted subsequent to August 31, 1864. Captured at Five Forks, Virginia, April 1, 1865. Confined at Point Lookout, Maryland, April 5, 1865. Released at Point Lookout on June 12, 1865, after taking the Oath of Allegiance.

FRY, ALEXANDER M., 1st Sergeant

Resided in Moore County where he enlisted at age 32, May 10, 1862, for the war. Mustered in as Private. Promoted to 1st Sergeant on July 15, 1862. Wounded at Sharpsburg, Maryland, September 17, 1862. Reported present from November, 1862, through December, 1863, and in May-August, 1864.

FRY, GRAFTON R., Private

Born in Moore County where he resided as a farmer prior to enlisting in Moore County at age 18, March 15, 1862. Reported absent without leave in November-December, 1862. Returned to duty in January-February, 1863. Reported present in March-December, 1863. Captured at Bermuda Hundred, Virginia, June 2, 1864. Confined at Point Lookout, Maryland, June 12, 1864. Transferred to Elmira, New York, July 9, 1864. Paroled at Elmira on March 14, 1865. Received at Boulware's Wharf, James River, Virginia, on or about March 18, 1865, for exchange. Captured in Chatham County on an unspecified date. Paroled at Avin's Ferry on April 25, 1865.

FRY, JACOB B., Private

Resided in Moore County where he enlisted at age 19, March 17, 1863, for the war. Reported present or accounted for in April-December, 1863, and May-August, 1864. Survived the war. [North Carolina pension records indicate that he became deaf as a result of the explosion of an artillery shell.]

FRY, JOSEPH, Sergeant
Born in Moore County where he resided as a farmer prior to enlisting in Moore County at age 19, March 13, 1862. Mustered in as Sergeant. Died in hospital at Petersburg, Virginia, July 7, 1862, of "febris typhoides."

FRY, MURDOCH P., Private
Born in Moore County where he resided as a farmer prior to enlisting in Moore County at age 18, March 28, 1862. Reported present or accounted for from November, 1862, through December, 1863, and in May-August, 1864.

FRY, THOMAS M., Private
Born in Moore County where he resided as a farmer prior to enlisting in Moore County at age 22, March 13, 1862. Mustered in as Corporal. Reduced to ranks prior to May 1, 1863. Reported present or accounted for in April-October, 1863. Reported on detail as a hospital nurse at Wilson in November-December, 1863. Reported absent on detached service in May-August, 1864. Survived the war. [North Carolina pension records indicate that he was wounded on June 2, 1863.]

GRAHAM, GEORGE, Private
Born in Moore County where he enlisted on March 13, 1862. Reported absent without leave on or about April 23, 1862.

HARPER, JOHN, Private
Born in Chatham County and resided in Moore County where he was by occupation a gunsmith prior to enlisting in Moore County at age 49, March 15, 1862. No further records.

HUNSUCKER, WILLIAM W., Sergeant
Born in Moore County where he resided as a shoemaker prior to enlisting in Moore County at age 31, March 14, 1862. Mustered in as Corporal. Promoted to Sergeant on July 15, 1862. Reported present or accounted for from November, 1862, through December, 1863, and in May-August, 1864. Captured at Five Forks, Virginia, April 1, 1865. Confined at Point Lookout, Maryland, April 5, 1865. Released at Point Lookout on June 27, 1865, after taking the Oath of Allegiance.

JOHNSON, ALEXANDER, JR., Private
Born in Moore County where he resided as a farmer prior to enlisting in Moore County at age 17, March 13, 1862. Wounded at Malvern Hill, Virginia, July 1, 1862. Returned to duty on an unspecified date. Reported present from November, 1862, through December, 1863. Reported absent wounded in May-August, 1864. Place and date wounded not reported. Died in hospital at Richmond, Virginia, October 19, 1864, of "pneumonia."

JOHNSON, ALEXANDER, SR., Private
Born in Moore County where he resided as a farmer prior to enlisting in Moore County at age 43, March 13, 1862. Reported present or accounted for from November, 1862, through December, 1863, and in May-August, 1864. Furloughed for sixty days from hospital at Richmond, Virginia, December 29, 1864. No further records.

JOHNSON, SANDY, Private
Place and date of enlistment not reported; however, he probably enlisted subsequent to August 31, 1864. Paroled at Raleigh on or about May 6, 1865.

JONES, ELKIN D., Private
Born in Moore County where he resided as a farmer prior to enlisting in Moore County at age 22, March 13, 1862. Wounded in the forearm at Malvern Hill, Virginia, July 1, 1862. Hospitalized at Richmond, Virginia. Furloughed on July 11, 1862. Reported absent without leave in November-December, 1862. Returned to duty in January-February, 1863. Reported absent on furlough in March-November, 1863. Reported absent without leave on December 28, 1863. Captured at Fort Stedman, Virginia, March 25, 1865. Confined at Washington, D.C. Transferred to Point Lookout, Maryland, March 30, 1865. Released at Point Lookout on May 13, 1865, after taking the Oath of Allegiance.

KELLY, ARCHIBALD C., Private
Born in Moore County where he resided as a farmer prior to enlisting in Moore County at age 42, March 13, 1862. Discharged on December 26, 1862, by reason of "blindness from opacity of cornea." [According to a pension application filed by his widow in 1885, Private Kelly's blindness resulted from "hard labor in the service and exposure."]

KELLY, H. B., _____
Place and date of enlistment not reported; however, he probably enlisted subsequent to August 31, 1864. Surrendered at Appomattox Court House, Virginia, April 9, 1865.

KENNEDY, JOHN A., Private
Enlisted in Moore County on May 20, 1864, for the war. Reported absent sick in hospital in June-August, 1864. No further records.

KENNEDY, NEILL, Private
Enlisted in Moore County on April 15, 1864, for the war. Reported absent sick in hospital in May-August, 1864. Hospitalized at Richmond, Virginia, March 8, 1865, with a gunshot wound of the head. Place and date wounded not reported. Died in hospital at Richmond on March 12, 1865, of wounds. [Company muster roll dated July-August, 1864, states that he was under 18 years of age.]

LAMBERT, ELI, Private
Enlisted in Moore County on February 1, 1864, for the war. Reported present in May-June, 1864. Deserted on August 10, 1864.

LONG, I. I., Private
Enlisted at Garysburg. Date of enlistment not reported; however, he probably enlisted subsequent to June 30, 1864. Surrendered at Appomattox Court House, Virginia, April 9, 1865.

LOVE, EDMOND, Private
Born in Moore County where he resided as a farmer prior to enlisting in Moore County at age 22, March 13, 1862.

Reported absent sick in hospital from November, 1862, through June, 1863. Reported present in July-December, 1863. Hospitalized at Raleigh on August 3, 1864, with a gunshot wound of the left leg. Place and date wounded not reported. Returned to duty on March 6, 1865. Captured in hospital at Raleigh on April 13, 1865.

LOVE, RICHARD A., Private
Born in Cumberland County and resided in Moore County where he was by occupation a farmer prior to enlisting in Moore County at age 23, March 13, 1862. Reported present from November, 1862, through December, 1863, and in May-August, 1864. Surrendered at Appomattox Court House, Virginia, April 9, 1865.

McCALLUM, ANGUS, Private
Resided in Moore County where he enlisted at age 30, March 13, 1863, for the war. Reported present in April-December, 1863. Captured at Bermuda Hundred, Virginia, June 2, 1864. Confined at Point Lookout, Maryland, June 12, 1864. Transferred to Elmira, New York, July 9, 1864. Died at Elmira on August 14, 1864, of "jaundice."

McCASKILL, MALCOLM, Private
Resided in Moore County where he enlisted at age 25, May 12, 1862, for the war. Reported present or accounted for from November, 1862, through December, 1863, and in May-August, 1864.

McDONALD, JOHN T., Sergeant
Resided in Moore County where he enlisted at age 23, May 12, 1862, for the war. Mustered in as Private. Promoted to Sergeant in March-April, 1863. Reported present from November, 1862, through December, 1863. Killed at Drewry's Bluff, Virginia, May 16, 1864.

McDONALD, KENNETH M., Private
Born in Moore County where he resided as a farmer prior to enlisting in Moore County at age 18, March 20, 1862. Mustered in as Private. Promoted to Sergeant on an unspecified date. Wounded in the breast at Sharpsburg, Maryland, September 17, 1862. Reduced to ranks in March-April, 1863. Reported absent by reason of wounds received at Sharpsburg from November, 1862, through December, 1863, and in May-August, 1864. Paroled at Avin's Ferry on April 23, 1865.

McDONALD, MURDOCH SWEEN, Private
Born in Moore County where he resided as a farmer prior to enlisting in Moore County at age 18, March 20, 1862. Reported present from November, 1862, through February, 1863. Hospitalized at Wilmington on April 30, 1863, with morbi verii. Furloughed from hospital on July 3, 1863. Reported absent on furlough through December, 1863. Returned to duty on an unspecified date. Reported present in May-August, 1864. Surrendered at Appomattox Court House, Virginia, April 9, 1865.

McDONALD, RANDOLPH J., Private
Born in Moore County where he resided as a farmer prior to enlisting in Moore County at age 46, March 15, 1862. Wounded at Sharpsburg, Maryland, September 17, 1862.

Died at Winchester, Virginia, October 4, 1862, of wounds.

McFARLAND, DUGALD, Private
Born in Moore County where he resided prior to enlisting in Moore County at age 24, March 13, 1862. Died on or about August 7, 1862, of disease. Place of death not reported.

McILWINNIN, JAMES, Private
Resided in Moore County and was by occupation a farmer prior to enlisting in Moore County at age 41, March 13, 1862. Reported absent without leave on April 23, 1862.

McINNIS, DUNCAN, Private
Born in Moore County where he resided as a farmer prior to enlisting in Moore County at age 24, March 14, 1862. Reported absent sick in November-December, 1862. Deserted on February 14, 1863. Returned from desertion on or about June 1, 1864, and was placed under arrest. Returned to duty in July-August, 1864. Captured at Fort Stedman, Virginia, March 25, 1865. Confined at Point Lookout, Maryland, until released on or about May 13, 1865, after taking the Oath of Allegiance.

McINNIS, JOHN, _____
Born in Moore County and enlisted at age 44, October 15, 1864, for the war. Wounded near Petersburg, Virginia, November 23, 1864. Died in a field hospital near Petersburg on November 24, 1864, of wounds.

McINTOSH, ASA S., Sergeant
Born in Moore County where he resided as a farmer prior to enlisting in Moore County at age 19, March 13, 1862. Mustered in as Sergeant. Reported present from November, 1862, through December, 1863, and in May-August, 1864.

McKENNIS, A., Private
Place and date of enlistment not reported; however, he probably enlisted subsequent to August 31, 1864. Captured at Fort Stedman, Virginia, March 25, 1865. Confined at Point Lookout, Maryland, March 31, 1865. Released at Point Lookout on May 14, 1865, after taking the Oath of Allegiance.

McKINNON, JOHN A., Corporal
Born in Moore County where he resided as a farmer prior to enlisting in Moore County at age 34, March 13, 1862. Mustered in as Sergeant. Reduced to the rank of Corporal prior to January 1, 1863. Reported present from November, 1862, through December, 1863, and in May-August, 1864. Hospitalized at Petersburg, Virginia, September 13, 1864, with a gunshot wound of the head. Place and date wounded not reported. Died in hospital at Petersburg on September 15, 1864, of wounds.

McLEAN, KENNETH, Private
Resided in Moore County where he enlisted at age 28, May 12, 1862, for the war. Reported present or accounted for from November, 1862, through December, 1863, and in May-August, 1864. Hospitalized at Fayetteville on December 27, 1864, with an unspecified complaint.

Reported still in hospital at Fayetteville on February 28, 1865.

McMILLIAN, ARCHIBALD, Private
Born in Moore County where he resided as a farmer prior to enlisting in Moore County at age 29, March 13, 1862. Died in hospital at Petersburg, Virginia, on or about August 9, 1862, of "febris typhoideș."

McNATT, EDWARD, Private
Resided in Moore County where he enlisted at age 38, July 18, 1863, for the war. Reported present in August-December, 1863. Wounded near Petersburg, Virginia, June 16-18, 1864. Returned to duty prior to July 1, 1864. Hospitalized at Richmond, Virginia, January 13, 1865, with an unspecified complaint. No further records.

MANESS, BARTIMEUS, Private
Resided in Moore County where he enlisted at age 22, January 27, 1863, for the war. Deserted at Kinston on April 3, 1863. Returned to duty subsequent to December 31, 1863. Reported present or accounted for in May-August, 1864. Survived the war.

MANESS, JOHN W., Private
Resided in Moore County where he enlisted at age 19, January 27, 1863, for the war. Reported present or accounted for through December, 1863. Wounded in the nose near Petersburg, · Virginia, June 18, 1864. Hospitalized at Petersburg. Transferred to hospital at Farmville, Virginia, on or about June 25, 1864. Furloughed for sixty days on July 8, 1864. Hospitalized at Richmond, Virginia, on or about November 16, 1864, with catarrhus. Furloughed for sixty days on December 8, 1864. [May have served previously as Private in Company H, 26th Regiment N.C. Troops.]

MANESS, SHADRACK, Private
Resided in Moore County where he enlisted at age 16, January 27, 1863, for the war. Reported absent sick in March-October, 1863. Reported absent without leave on December 28, 1863. Returned to duty on an unspecified date. Killed near Petersburg, Virginia, June 21, 1864.

MATHESON, CORNELIUS, Private
Born in Montgomery County and resided in Moore County where he was by occupation a farmer prior to enlisting in Moore County at age 20, March 13, 1862. Reported present from November, 1862, through August, 1863. Reported on detached service at Weldon in September-October, 1863. Reported on detached service at Garysburg in November-December, 1863. Killed near Petersburg, Virginia, June 21, 1864.

MAULDIN, JAMES, Private
Enlisted in Moore County on March 20, 1862. Reported absent without leave on April 23, 1862.

MEDLIN, BENJAMIN J., Private
Resided in Moore County where he enlisted at age 17, March 20, 1863, for the war as a substitute. Reported present or accounted for in April-December, 1863, and May-August, 1864. Captured at Five Forks, Virginia,

April 1, 1865. Confined at Point Lookout, Maryland, April 5, 1865. Released at Point Lookout on June 15, 1865, after taking the Oath of Allegiance.

MONROE, BENJAMIN F., Corporal
Born in Moore County where he resided as a farmer prior to enlisting in Moore County at age 25, March 13, 1862. Mustered in as Private. Promoted to Corporal on July 15, 1862. Reported present or accounted for from November, 1862, through December, 1863, and in May-August, 1864. Captured at Five Forks, Virginia, April 1, 1865. Confined at Point Lookout, Maryland, April 5, 1865. Released at Point Lookout on June 6, 1865, after taking the Oath of Allegiance.

MONROE, HUGH B., Private
Born in Moore County where he resided as a farmer prior to enlisting in Moore County at age 23, March 13, 1862. Reported present from November, 1862, through December, 1863. Wounded in the right ankle and captured at Bermuda Hundred, Virginia, June 2, 1864. Right foot amputated. No further records.

MONROE, JAMES C., Private
Born in Moore County where he resided as a farmer prior to enlisting in Moore County at age 18, March 13, 1862. Reported present or accounted for from November, 1862, through December, 1863. Killed near Petersburg, Virginia, June 18, 1864.

MONROE, LEVI D., Private
Born in Moore County where he resided as a farmer prior to enlisting in Moore County at age 21, March 13, 1862. Reported present from November, 1862, through December, 1863, and in May-August, 1864.

MONROE, WILLIAM J., Private
Resided in Moore County where he enlisted at age 20, April 1, 1863, for the war. Reported present or accounted for in April-December, 1863, and May-June, 1864. Killed near Petersburg, Virginia, August 4, 1864.

MOORE, BRIANT, Private
Born in Moore County where he resided prior to enlisting in Moore County at age 27, March 15, 1862. Died at Goldsboro on July 5, 1862, of disease.

MOORE, WILLIAM S., Private
Resided in Moore County where he enlisted at age 18, January 27, 1863, for the war. Deserted at Kinston on April 3, 1863. Dropped from the rolls of the company on or about July 1, 1863. Apprehended on an unspecified date. Reported under arrest for desertion in May-June, 1864. No further records.

MUSE, JOHN B., Private
Born in Moore County where he resided as a farmer prior to enlisting in Moore County at age 22, March 13, 1862. Deserted in October, 1862. Returned to duty on an unspecified date (probably in January, 1863). Deserted on February 14, 1863.

MUSE, KINDRED, Private

Resided in Moore County where he enlisted at age 27, May 10, 1862, for the war. Hospitalized on July 13, 1862, with rubeola. Returned to duty on September 18, 1862. Reported present from November, 1862, through December, 1863, and in May-August, 1864.

MUSE, WESLEY B., Private

Previously served as Private in Company E, 63rd Regiment N.C. Troops (5th Regiment N.C. Cavalry). Transferred to this company on February 16, 1865. Hospitalized at Petersburg, Virginia, March 17, 1865. Transferred to another hospital on April 2, 1865. No further records.

PARISH, DAVID, Private

Resided in Moore County where he enlisted at age 17, April 3, 1863, for the war as a substitute. Reported present in May-December, 1863, and May-August, 1864. Hospitalized at Richmond, Virginia, on or about October 17, 1864, with acute colitis. Returned to duty on March 4, 1865. Captured at Fort Stedman, Virginia, March 25, 1865. Confined at Point Lookout, Maryland, March 31, 1865. Released at Point Lookout on May 13, 1865, after taking the Oath of Allegiance.

PARISH, J. B., Private

Resided in Moore County and was by occupation a farmer. Place and date of enlistment not reported; however, he probably enlisted subsequent to August 31, 1864. Captured at Fort Stedman, Virginia, March 25, 1865. Confined at Point Lookout, Maryland, March 31, 1865. Released at Point Lookout on May 14, 1865, after taking the Oath of Allegiance.

PATTERSON, JOHN A., Private

Resided in Moore County where he enlisted at age 30, May 12, 1862, for the war. Reported present or accounted for from November, 1862, through December, 1863. Wounded in the hand near Petersburg, Virginia, June 18, 1864. Hospitalized at Petersburg. Returned to duty in July-August, 1864. Died in hospital at Richmond, Virginia, on or about September 27, 1864, of "pneumonia."

PATTERSON, SAMUEL D., Private

Born in Moore County where he resided as a farmer prior to enlisting in Moore County at age 20, March 13, 1862. Died in hospital at Staunton, Virginia, December 25, 1862, of "phthisis pulmonalis."

RAY, WILLIAM A., Corporal

Born in Moore County where he resided as a farmer prior to enlisting in Moore County at age 20, March 13, 1862. Mustered in as Corporal. Reported present in November-December, 1862. Died in hospital at Goldsboro on February 22, 1863, of "typhoid fever."

REDDEN, THOMAS CALVIN, Private

Resided in Moore County where he enlisted at age 21, March 13, 1862. Reported present from November, 1862, through December, 1863, and in May-August, 1864. Surrendered at Appomattox Court House, Virginia, April 9, 1865.

SMITH, ANDERSON H., Private

Born in Moore County where he resided as a farmer prior to enlisting in Moore County at age 25, March 13, 1862. Hospitalized at Petersburg, Virginia, July 28, 1862, with chronic diarrhoea. Returned to duty on August 16, 1862. Wounded in the groin at Fredericksburg, Virginia, December 13, 1862. Returned to duty on January 26, 1863. Reported present in February-December, 1863, and May-June, 1864. Deserted on August 4, 1864.

SMITH, HENRY C., Private

Resided in Moore County and was by occupation a farmer prior to enlisting in Moore County at age 17, September 9, 1863, for the war. Mustered in as Private. Reported present in October-December, 1863, and May-August, 1864. Promoted to Corporal on July 23, 1864. Reduced to ranks prior to March 25, 1865, when he was captured at Fort Stedman, Virginia. Confined at Point Lookout, Maryland, March 31, 1865. Released at Point Lookout on May 14, 1865, after taking the Oath of Allegiance.

SMITH, WILLIS H., Private

Born in Moore County where he resided as a farmer prior to enlisting in Moore County at age 18, March 13, 1862. Captured at Frederick, Maryland, September 12, 1862. Sent to Fort Delaware, Delaware. Paroled and transferred to Aiken's Landing, James River, Virginia, October 2, 1862, for exchange. Declared exchanged at Aiken's Landing on November 10, 1862. Reported present from November, 1862, through December, 1863, and in May-August, 1864. Transferred to Company A, 27th Regiment N.C. Troops, January 7, 1865.

STUART, ENOCH, Private

Enlisted in Moore County on January 1, 1864, for the war. Wounded severely in the back near Petersburg, Virginia, June 23, 1864. Reported absent wounded through August, 1864. No further records.

STUART, JOHN L., Private

Resided in Moore County where he enlisted at age 20, March 15, 1862. Reported present or accounted for from November, 1862, through December, 1863, and in May-August, 1864. Wounded in the left ankle (fracture) and captured at Five Forks, Virginia, April 1, 1865. Hospitalized at Washington, D.C., April 10, 1865. Released from hospital on August 1, 1865, after taking the Oath of Allegiance. [His left leg was amputated on an unspecified date, possibly after August 1, 1865.]

TAYLOR, NAPOLEON B., Private

Previously served as Private in Company H, 26th Regiment N.C. Troops. Enlisted in this company in Moore County on February 23, 1864, for the war. Reported present in May-August, 1864. Deserted to the enemy on or about February 12, 1865. Confined at Washington, D.C. Hospitalized at Washington on or about February 20, 1865, with pneumonia. Was probably released on or about March 31, 1865, after taking the Oath of Allegiance.

THOMAS, JESSE, Private

Born in Moore County where he resided as a farmer prior to enlisting in Moore County at age 40, March 13, 1862.

Died at home in Moore County on October 30, 1862, of "diphtheria."

THOMAS, JOHN C., Private

Enlisted at Camp Holmes, near Raleigh, December 16, 1863, for the war. Reported present in May-June, 1864. Died in hospital at Richmond, Virginia, August 4, 1864, of disease.

THOMAS, JOSEPH P., Private

Born in Moore County where he resided as a farmer prior to enlisting in Moore County at age 20, March 13, 1862. Died near Petersburg, Virginia, on or about August 9, 1862, of "typhoid fever."

THOMAS, WILEY F., Private

Enlisted at Camp Holmes, near Raleigh, December 16, 1863, for the war. Reported present in May-June, 1864. Died in hospital at Richmond, Virginia, August 12, 1864, of disease.

THROWER, JOHN T., Sergeant

Born in Moore County where he resided as a farmer prior to enlisting in Moore County at age 26, March 13, 1862. Mustered in as Private. Promoted to Corporal on June 10, 1862. Reported present or accounted for from November, 1862, through December, 1863, and in May-August, 1864. Promoted to Sergeant on May 20, 1864. Captured at Five Forks, Virginia, April 1, 1865. Confined at Point Lookout, Maryland, April 5, 1865. Released at Point Lookout on June 21, 1865, after taking the Oath of Allegiance.

WALLIS, HIRAM, Private

Born in Moore County where he resided as a farmer prior to enlisting in Moore County at age 24, March 13, 1862. Killed at Sharpsburg, Maryland, September 17, 1862.

WALLIS, ISHAM, Private

Born in Moore County where he resided as a farmer prior to enlisting in Moore County at age 21, March 13, 1862. Failed to report for duty. Listed as a deserter and dropped from the rolls of the company on February 14, 1863.

WARNER, EDWARD, Sergeant

Born in Moore County where he resided as a farmer prior to enlisting in Moore County at age 23, March 13, 1862. Mustered in as Sergeant. Reported present from November, 1862, through December, 1863, and in May-August, 1864. Wounded in the left knee and/or left thigh at Five Forks, Virginia, April 1, 1865. Hospitalized at Petersburg, Virginia, where he was captured on April 3, 1865. Confined in a Federal hospital at Point of Rocks, Virginia, April 15, 1865. Transferred to hospital at Fort Monroe, Virginia, where he arrived on May 17, 1865. Confined at Camp Hamilton, Virginia, May 25, 1865. Released at Camp Hamilton on May 31, 1865, after taking the Oath of Allegiance.

WARNER, NEILL R., Private

Enlisted in Moore County on January 27, 1863, for the war. Deserted at Petersburg, Virginia, June 1, 1863.

WARNER, SWAIN, Private

Resided in Moore County and was by occupation a farmer prior to enlisting in Moore County at age 34, January 27, 1863, for the war. Reported present in February-December, 1863, and May-August, 1864. Hospitalized at Richmond, Virginia, October 5, 1864, with chronic colitis and returned to duty on November 25, 1864.

WILFONG, J. H., Private

Place and date of enlistment not reported; however, he probably enlisted subsequent to August 31, 1864. Wounded in the left foot at Five Forks, Virginia, April 1, 1865. Captured by the enemy on an unspecified date. Confined in a Federal hospital at Point of Rocks, Virginia, April 17, 1865. Hospitalized at Fort Monroe, Virginia, May 17, 1865. Confined at Camp Hamilton, Virginia, May 28, 1865. Released at Camp Hamilton on May 31, 1865, after taking the Oath of Allegiance. [Federal medical records dated May, 1865, give his age as 23.]

WILLIAMS, MARSHAL, _____

North Carolina pension records indicate that he served in this company.

WILLIAMSON, MATTHEW, Private

Born in Moore County where he resided as a farmer prior to enlisting in Moore County at age 24, March 14, 1862. Reported present from November, 1862, through June, 1863. Deserted on or about August 10, 1863. Went over to the enemy on or about October 8, 1864. Confined at Washington, D.C., October 12, 1864. Released at Washington on an unspecified date after taking the Oath of Allegiance.

WILLIAMSON, PATRICK, _____

Enlisted in Moore County on March 12, 1863, for the war. Deserted at Kinston on April 3, 1863.

WILLIAMSON, WYATT, Private

Resided in Moore County and was by occupation a farmer prior to enlisting in Moore County at age 40, March 12, 1863, for the war. Deserted at Kinston on April 3, 1863. Dropped from the rolls of the company prior to May 1, 1863. Reported sick in hospital in November-December, 1863. Returned to duty on an unspecified date. Reported present in May-June, 1864. Reported absent sick in July-August, 1864. Died in hospital at Richmond, Virginia, September 14, 1864, of "dysenteria chron[ic]."

WOOD, WESLEY W., Private

Born in Moore County where he resided as a farmer prior to enlisting in Moore County at age 30, March 13, 1862. Reported present or accounted for from November, 1862, through December, 1863, and in May-August, 1864. Captured at Fort Stedman, Virginia, March 25, 1865. Confined at Point Lookout, Maryland, March 31, 1865. Released at Point Lookout on May 14, 1865, after taking the Oath of Allegiance.

COMPANY E

This company was raised in Iredell County and enlisted at Statesville in February-March, 1862. It was mustered into state service at Camp Mangum, near Raleigh, on April 21, 1862, and assigned to the 49th Regiment N.C. Troops as Company E. After joining the regiment the company functioned as a part of the regiment, and its history for the remainder of the war is reported as a part of the regimental history.

The information contained in the following roster was compiled primarily from a company muster-in and descriptive roll dated April 21, 1862, and from company muster rolls for November 1, 1862-December 31, 1863, and May 1-August 31, 1864. No company muster rolls were located for May 1-October 31, 1862; January 1-April 30, 1864; or for the period after August 31, 1864. Valuable information was obtained from primary records such as the North Carolina adjutant general's *Roll of Honor*, discharge certificates, medical records, prisoner of war records, *The War of the Rebellion: A Compilation of the Official Records of the Union and Confederate Armies*, militia records, newspaper casualty lists and obituaries, Confederate pension applications filed with the state of North Carolina, and the 1860 federal census of North Carolina. Secondary sources such as postwar rosters and histories, cemetery records, the *Confederate Veteran*, published genealogies, and records of the United Daughters of the Confederacy also provided useful information.

OFFICERS

CAPTAINS

MOORE, ALEXANDER DAVIS

Born in Iredell County where he resided as a merchant prior to enlisting in Iredell County at age 32. Elected Captain on March 8, 1862. Wounded at Sharpsburg, Maryland, September 17, 1862. Reported absent sick without leave in November-December, 1862. Returned to duty in January-February, 1863. Arrested on October 27, 1863. Reason he was arrested not reported. Reported absent sick in November-December, 1863. Resigned on March 5, 1864, because of "my own private interests as well as the 'good of the service.'" Resignation accepted on March 22, 1864. [Previously served as Captain in the 79th Regiment N.C. Militia.]

HARRIS, EDWIN VICTOR

Previously served as Private in Company A, 4th Regiment N.C. State Troops. Transferred to this company upon appointment as 1st Lieutenant on or about December 25, 1862. Reported present or accounted for in January-December, 1863, and May-June, 1864. Promoted to Captain on March 22, 1864. Shot in the neck and killed by a "stray minie [ball]" while returning to his position on July 30, 1864, after the Battle of the Crater. The ball "struck poor Ed, passing through his neck cutting the great artery."

CRAWFORD, JOHN THOMAS

Born in Iredell County where he resided as a farmer prior to enlisting in Iredell County at age 25, April 1, 1862. Mustered in as Sergeant. Elected 3rd Lieutenant on December 29, 1862. Reported present or accounted for from November, 1862, through December, 1863, and in May-August, 1864. Promoted to 1st Lieutenant on or about June 15, 1864. Promoted to Captain on July 30, 1864. Captured at Five Forks, Virginia, April 1, 1865. Confined at Old Capitol Prison, Washington, D.C. Transferred to Johnson's Island, Ohio, April 9, 1865. Released at Johnson's Island on June 18, 1865, after taking the Oath of Allegiance. [Previously served as Captain in the 79th Regiment N.C. Militia.]

LIEUTENANTS

BAILEY, RICHARD A., 1st Lieutenant

Born in Iredell County where he resided as a farmer prior to enlisting in Iredell County at age 23, March 17, 1862. Mustered in as Sergeant. Promoted to 1st Sergeant on December 22, 1862. Reported present from November, 1862, through December, 1863. Elected 2nd Lieutenant on or about June 3, 1864. Wounded in the arm at the Battle of the Crater, near Petersburg, Virginia, July 30, 1864. Promoted to 1st Lieutenant on the same date. Returned to duty on an unspecified date. Captured at Five Forks, Virginia, April 1, 1865. Confined at Old Capitol Prison, Washington, D.C., April 5, 1865. Transferred to Johnson's Island, Ohio, April 9, 1865. Released at Johnson's Island on June 18, 1865, after taking the Oath of Allegiance.

JAMES, THOMAS A., 1st Lieutenant

Born in Iredell County where he resided as a farmer prior to enlisting in Iredell County at age 47. Elected 1st Lieutenant on or about April 11, 1862. Resigned on or about July 27, 1862, by reason of "chronic rheumatic affection of the muscles of the back and legs. His constitution is also somewhat enfeebled by advancing age and exposure in the field." Resignation accepted on August 6, 1862.

SHARPE, ABNER CLAYTON, 2nd Lieutenant

Born in Iredell County where he resided as a farmer prior to enlisting in Iredell County at age 21, February 26, 1862. Mustered in as Private. Hospitalized at Richmond, Virginia, August 22, 1862, with an unspecified wound. Place and date wounded not reported. Returned to duty on January 10, 1863. Reported present in February-December, 1863, and May-August, 1864. Was reported on duty as a courier during much of that period. Elected 2nd Lieutenant on August 31, 1864. Captured at Five Forks, Virginia, April 1, 1865. Confined at Old Capitol Prison, Washington, D.C., April 5, 1865. Transferred to Johnson's Island, Ohio, April 9, 1865. Released at Johnson's Island on June 20, 1865, after taking the Oath of Allegiance.

STONE, RUFUS A., 2nd Lieutenant

Born in Iredell County where he resided as a farmer prior to enlisting in Iredell County at age 26, March 1, 1862. Mustered in as Private. Promoted to Corporal prior to

January 1, 1863. Reported present or accounted for from November, 1862, through December, 1863, and in May-August, 1864; however, he was reported absent sick during much of that period. Promoted to Sergeant on May 27, 1864. Elected 2nd Lieutenant on or about September 17, 1864. Captured at Five Forks, Virginia, April 1, 1865. Confined at Old Capitol Prison, Washington, D.C., April 5, 1865. Transferred to Johnson's Island, Ohio, April 9, 1865. Released at Johnson's Island on June 20, 1865, after taking the Oath of Allegiance.

SUMMERS, JOHN STEPHENSON, 1st Lieutenant
Previously served as Corporal in Company A, 7th Regiment N.C. State Troops. Transferred to this company upon appointment as 2nd Lieutenant on December 22, 1862. Reported present or accounted for in January-December, 1863. Promoted to 1st Lieutenant on March 22, 1864. Killed near Petersburg, Virginia, on or about June 24, 1864. [Previously served as 2nd Lieutenant in the 79th Regiment N.C. Militia.]

NONCOMMISSIONED OFFICERS AND PRIVATES

ALBRIGHT, R. H., Private
Enlisted at Petersburg, Virginia, June 13, 1864, for the war. Mustered in as Private. Appointed Musician on July 20, 1864. Reported present in July-August, 1864. Reduced to ranks subsequent to August 31, 1864. Surrendered at Appomattox Court House, Virginia, April 9, 1865.

ALEXANDER, CHARLES, Sergeant
Born in Cabarrus County and resided in Mecklenburg County where he was by occupation a merchant prior to enlisting in Iredell County at age 28, March 1, 1862. Mustered in as Sergeant. Reported present or accounted for from November, 1862, through December, 1863. Reduced to ranks on July 15, 1863, "for improper conduct." Reported present in May-August, 1864. Promoted to Sergeant on August 31, 1864. Captured at Fort Stedman, Virginia, March 25, 1865. Confined at Point Lookout, Maryland, March 28, 1865. Released at Point Lookout on June 22, 1865, after taking the Oath of Allegiance.

BAILEY, MILAS ALEXANDER, Musician
Resided in Iredell County where he enlisted at age 18, July 7, 1863, for the war. Mustered in as Private. Appointed Musician in September-October, 1863. Reported present or accounted for in August-December, 1863, and May-June, 1864. Died in hospital at Richmond, Virginia, July 30, 1864, of "pneumonia."

BARRETT, JOHN F., Private
Resided in Iredell County where he enlisted at age 18, August 21, 1863, for the war. Reported present in September-December, 1863. Hospitalized at Petersburg, Virginia, June 17, 1864, with a gunshot wound. Place and date wounded not reported. Reported absent wounded through August, 1864. Company records do not indicate whether he returned to duty. Wounded in the right thigh at or near Five Forks, Virginia, on or about April 1, 1865.

Hospitalized at Farmville, Virginia. Captured at or near Farmville on or about April 7, 1865. Paroled at Farmville prior to April 22, 1865.

BELL, THOMAS L., 1st Sergeant
Born in Iredell County where he resided as a merchant prior to enlisting in Iredell County at age 23, March 28, 1862. Mustered in as 1st Sergeant. Wounded in the left arm at Malvern Hill, Virginia, July 1, 1862. Discharged on December 22, 1862, by reason of "anchylosis of the elbow" resulting from the wound he received at Malvern Hill.

BOST, LAWSON O., Private
Born in Rowan County and resided in Iredell County where he was by occupation a carpenter prior to enlisting in Iredell County at age 22, March 1, 1862. Reported absent without leave in November-December, 1862. Returned to duty in January-February, 1863. Reported present in March-December, 1863, and May-August, 1864. Hospitalized at Richmond, Virginia, March 13, 1865, with chronic diarrhoea. Captured in hospital at Richmond on April 3, 1865. Transferred to Newport News, Virginia, April 23, 1865. Released at Newport News on June 16, 1865, after taking the Oath of Allegiance.

BOST, MANUEL, Private
Resided in Iredell County where he enlisted at age 18, August 15, 1863, for the war. Reported present in September-December, 1863, and May-August, 1864. Deserted to the enemy on or about March 14, 1865.

BRADFORD, DAVID L., Private
Born in Cabarrus County and resided in Iredell County where he was by occupation a farmer or carpenter prior to enlisting in Iredell County at age 23, March 1, 1862. Reported absent sick from November, 1862, through October, 1863. Discharged on December 28, 1863, by reason of "phthisis left lung."

BRADFORD, JAMES S., Private
Born in Cabarrus or Iredell County and resided in Iredell County where he was by occupation a farmer prior to enlisting in Iredell County at age 21, March 1, 1862. Died in hospital at Petersburg, Virginia, August 30, 1862, of "diarrhoea chronica."

BRADY, JOSEPH M., Sergeant
Born in Iredell County where he resided as a farmer prior to enlisting in Iredell County at age 30, February 26, 1862. Mustered in as Corporal. Reported present or accounted for from November, 1862, through February, 1863. Promoted to Sergeant in January-February, 1863. Wounded at Sandy Ridge (Lenoir County) on April 20, 1863. Reported absent on furlough through October, 1863. Returned to duty in November-December, 1863. Reported present in May-August, 1864. Hospitalized at Richmond, Virginia, October 25, 1864, with an unspecified complaint. Returned to duty on December 8, 1864. Captured at Fort Stedman, Virginia, March 25, 1865. Confined at Point Lookout, Maryland, until released on June 21, 1865, after taking the Oath of Allegiance.

BYERS, WILLIAM M., Private

Born in Iredell County where he resided as a farmer prior to enlisting in Iredell County at age 22, March 17, 1862. Captured at Malvern Hill, Virginia, July 1, 1862. Confined at Fort Columbus, New York Harbor. Transferred to Fort Delaware, Delaware, July 9, 1862. Paroled on an unspecified date. Exchanged at Aiken's Landing, James River, Virginia, August 5, 1862. Returned to duty on an unspecified date. Reported present from November, 1862, through December, 1863. Died in hospital at Richmond, Virginia, October 11, 1864, of "typhoid fever."

CAMPBELL, GEORGE P., Private

Born in Iredell County where he resided as a farmer prior to enlisting in Iredell County at age 41, March 1, 1862. Reported absent without leave in November-December, 1862. Returned to duty in January-February, 1863. Reported present in March-December, 1863, and May-August, 1864. Captured at Five Forks, Virginia, April 1, 1865. Confined at Point Lookout, Maryland, April 5, 1865. Released at Point Lookout on June 24, 1865, after taking the Oath of Allegiance.

CARRIGAN, ROBERT A., Private

Born in Iredell County where he resided as a farmer prior to enlisting in Iredell County at age 17, March 22, 1862. Reported present from November, 1862, through February, 1863. Wounded at Sandy Ridge (Lenoir County) on April 20, 1863. Reported absent wounded through December, 1863. Returned to duty on an unspecified date. Captured at Drewry's Bluff, Virginia, May 16, 1864. Confined at Point Lookout, Maryland, May 21, 1864. Paroled at Point Lookout on February 10, 1865. Received at Cox's Wharf, James River, Virginia, on or about February 14, 1865, for exchange. Hospitalized at Richmond, Virginia, February 15, 1865, with chronic diarrhoea. Furloughed for forty days on February 18, 1865. Paroled at Statesville on May 26, 1865.

CLARK, JAMES MEL, Private

Born in Iredell County where he resided as a farmer prior to enlisting in Iredell County at age 18, March 22, 1862. Mustered in as Corporal. Reported present from November, 1862, through December, 1863. Appointed Musician prior to January 1, 1863. Reduced to ranks on August 26, 1863. Reported present in May-August, 1864. Captured at Five Forks, Virginia, April 1, 1865. Confined at Point Lookout, Maryland, April 5, 1865. Released at Point Lookout on June 21, 1865, after taking the Oath of Allegiance.

CLAYWELL, JOHN H., Private

Born in Iredell County where he resided as a farmer prior to enlisting in Iredell County at age 27, May 7, 1862, for the war. Reported present or accounted for from November, 1862, through December, 1863; however, he was reported absent sick during much of that period. Reported absent sick in May-August, 1864. Hospitalized at Richmond, Virginia, November 19, 1864, with phthisis pulmonalis. Furloughed for sixty days on December 1, 1864. Took the Oath of Allegiance at Salisbury on May 30, 1865.

CLOAR, WILLIAM F., Private

Born in Iredell County where he resided as a farmer prior to enlisting in Iredell County at age 22, February 26, 1862. Reported present from November, 1862, through December, 1863, and in May-August, 1864. Surrendered at Appomattox Court House, Virginia, April 9, 1865.

CRAWFORD, ABRAM L., Private

Born in Iredell County where he resided as a farmer prior to enlisting in Iredell County at age 34, March 23, 1862. Reported absent without leave in November-December, 1862. Returned to duty in January-February, 1863. Reported present in March-December, 1863. Wounded in the breast near Petersburg, Virginia, June 24, 1864. Died on or about July 7, 1864, of wounds. Buried in Blandford Cemetery, Petersburg.

CRAWFORD, JAMES M., Corporal

Born in Iredell County where he resided as a farmer prior to enlisting in Iredell County at age 22, February 26, 1862. Mustered in as Private. Reported present from November, 1862, through December, 1863, and in May-August, 1864. Promoted to Corporal on June 1, 1864. Wounded in the right lung (possibly also in the throat) and captured at Five Forks, Virginia, April 1, 1865. Confined in a Federal field hospital until May 7, 1865, when he was hospitalized at Washington, D.C. Released at Washington on or about June 14, 1865, after taking the Oath of Allegiance.

CREWS, ROBERT MARTIN, Private

Born in Iredell County where he resided as a mechanic prior to enlisting in Iredell County at age 19, March 4, 1862. Reported present or accounted for from November, 1862, through December, 1863, and in May-August, 1864. Captured at Five Forks, Virginia, April 1, 1865. Confined at Point Lookout, Maryland, April 5, 1865. Released at Point Lookout on June 21, 1865, after taking the Oath of Allegiance. [North Carolina pension records indicate that he was wounded in the left thigh on an unspecified date and was also injured (sight in right eye damaged) by the explosion of a shell.]

CRUISE, JOHN W., Private

Born in Iredell County where he resided as a farmer prior to enlisting in Iredell County at age 20, March 8, 1862. Reported present or accounted for from November, 1862, through December, 1863, and in May-August, 1864. Captured at Fort Stedman, Virginia, March 25, 1865. Confined at Point Lookout, Maryland, until released on June 24, 1865, after taking the Oath of Allegiance.

DAY, GEORGE W., Corporal

Born in Iredell County where he resided as a farmer prior to enlisting in Iredell County at age 21, March 1, 1862. Mustered in as Private. Reported present or accounted for from November, 1862, through December, 1863. Promoted to Corporal on July 15, 1863. Reported present in May-August, 1864. Captured at Five Forks, Virginia, April 1, 1865. Confined at Point Lookout, Maryland, April 5, 1865. Released at Point Lookout on June 26, 1865, after taking the Oath of Allegiance.

DAY, ROBERT O., Private
Born in Iredell County where he resided as a farmer prior to enlisting in Iredell County at age 26, March 7, 1862. Died in hospital at Petersburg, Virginia, August 1, 1862, of "febris typhoides."

FARRIS, JOHN T., Private
Enlisted in Rowan County on April 19, 1864, for the war. Mustered in as Musician. Reported present in May-August, 1864. Reduced to ranks subsequent to August 31, 1864. Surrendered at Appomattox Court House, Virginia, April 9, 1865.

FREELAND, SILAS A., Private
Born in Iredell County where he resided as a mechanic prior to enlisting in Iredell County at age 23, March 31, 1862. Reported present from November, 1862, through December, 1863, and in May-August, 1864. Survived the war.

FREEZE, EDWARD L., Private
Born in Iredell County where he resided as a farmer prior to enlisting in Iredell County at age 26, March 8, 1862. Reported present from November, 1862, through December, 1863, and in May-August, 1864. Deserted to the enemy on or about March 14, 1865. Confined at Washington, D.C., March 18, 1865. Released on an unspecified date after taking the Oath of Allegiance.

FREEZE, JOHN F., Private
Born in Rowan County and resided in Iredell County where he was by occupation a farmer prior to enlisting in Iredell County at age 29, March 1, 1862. Reported present from November, 1862, through December, 1863. Killed near Petersburg, Virginia, June 18, 1864.

FREEZE, PETER, Private
Enlisted in Iredell County on October 16, 1863, for the war. Reported present or accounted for in November-December, 1863, and May-August, 1864. Hospitalized at Richmond, Virginia, on or about March 13, 1865, with chronic diarrhoea and/or debilitas. Furloughed for sixty days on March 31, 1865.

FREEZE, S. ANDREW, Private
Born in Iredell County where he resided as a farmer prior to enlisting in Iredell County at age 18, March 31, 1862. Reported present from November, 1862, through December, 1863. Wounded in the left hand at Drewry's Bluff, Virginia, on or about May 16, 1864. Hospitalized at Richmond, Virginia. Furloughed for sixty days on June 3, 1864. Returned to duty prior to September 1, 1864. Captured at Farmville, Virginia, April 6, 1865. Confined at Newport News, Virginia, April 14, 1865. Released at Newport News on June 27, 1865, after taking the Oath of Allegiance.

FREEZE, WILLIAM, Corporal
Born in Iredell County where he resided as a farmer prior to enlisting in Iredell County at age 18, March 1, 1862. Mustered in as Private. Reported present or accounted for from November, 1862, through December, 1863, and in May-August, 1864. Promoted to Corporal on June 1, 1864.

Captured at or near Five Forks, Virginia, on or about April 2, 1865. Confined at Point Lookout, Maryland, April 5, 1865. Released at Point Lookout on June 26, 1865, after taking the Oath of Allegiance.

GARRISON, WILLIAM N., Private
Resided in Iredell County and was by occupation a buggymaker. Place and date of enlistment not reported; however, he probably enlisted subsequent to August 31, 1864. Was about 36 years of age at time of enlistment. Hospitalized at Richmond, Virginia, December 8, 1864, with a gunshot wound of the left hand. Place and date wounded not reported. Furloughed for sixty days on December 16, 1864. Returned to duty on an unspecified date. Captured at Five Forks, Virginia, April 1, 1865. Confined at Point Lookout, Maryland, April 5, 1865. Released at Point Lookout on June 21, 1865, after taking the Oath of Allegiance.

GIBSON, HUGH S., Private
Born in Iredell or Rowan County and resided in Iredell County where he was by occupation a farmer prior to enlisting in Iredell County at age 25, February 26, 1862. Died at Winchester, Virginia, October 6, 1862. Cause of death not reported.

GIBSON, WILLIAM N., Private
Born in Iredell County where he resided as a farmer prior to enlisting in Iredell County at age 21, February 26, 1862. Reported absent without leave in November-December, 1862. Reported present in January-December, 1863, and May-August, 1864. Hospitalized at Richmond, Virginia, February 23, 1865, with chronic diarrhoea. Returned to duty on March 24, 1865. Captured at Five Forks, Virginia, April 1, 1865. Confined at Point Lookout, Maryland, April 5, 1865. Released at Point Lookout on June 3, 1865, after taking the Oath of Allegiance.

GOODNIGHT, PETER A., Private
Born in Cabarrus County and resided in Iredell County where he was by occupation a farmer prior to enlisting in Iredell County at age 29, February 26, 1862. Reported present or accounted for from November, 1862, through December, 1863. Killed at Drewry's Bluff, Virginia, May 16, 1864.

HAM, W. N., Private
Previously served as Private in Company D, Mallett's N.C. Battalion (Camp Guard). Transferred to this company on June 12, 1864. Killed by a sharpshooter near Petersburg, Virginia, July 22, 1864.

HOLLAND, JOHN F., Private
Previously served as Private in Company B, Mallett's N.C. Battalion (Camp Guard). Transferred to this company on June 16, 1864. Captured at Five Forks, Virginia, April 1, 1865. Confined at Point Lookout, Maryland, April 5, 1865. Released at Point Lookout on June 27, 1865, after taking the Oath of Allegiance.

HOLLAND, REMUS W., Private
Born in Iredell County where he resided as a farmer prior to enlisting in Iredell County at age 20, March 17, 1862.

Reported present or accounted for from November, 1862, through December, 1863, and in May-August, 1864. Captured at Five Forks, Virginia, April 1, 1865. Confined at Point Lookout, Maryland, April 5, 1865. Released at Point Lookout on June 27, 1865, after taking the Oath of Allegiance.

HUNNICUTT, RICHARD N., Private
Resided in Alexander County. Place and date of enlistment not reported; however, he probably enlisted subsequent to August 31, 1864. Captured at Fort Stedman, Virginia, March 25, 1865. Confined at Point Lookout, Maryland, until released on June 27, 1865, after taking the Oath of Allegiance.

JAMES, ELISHA, Private
Born in Union County* and resided in Iredell County where he was by occupation a farmer prior to enlisting in Iredell County at age 28, March 17, 1862. Died in hospital at Petersburg, Virginia, September 13, 1862, of "febris typhoides."

JAMES, GODFREY, Private
Born in Union County* and resided in Iredell County where he was by occupation a farmer prior to enlisting in Iredell County at age 23, March 17, 1862. Reported present or accounted for from November, 1862, through December, 1863, and in May-August, 1864; however, he was reported absent sick during much of that period. Captured at Five Forks, Virginia, April 1, 1865. Confined at Point Lookout, Maryland, April 5, 1865. Released at Point Lookout on June 28, 1865, after taking the Oath of Allegiance.

JENKINS, ALFRED L., Private
Born in Guilford County and resided in Iredell County where he was by occupation a farmer prior to enlisting in Iredell County at age 25, March 1, 1862. Hospitalized at Richmond, Virginia, September 25, 1862, with a gunshot wound and typhoid fever. Furloughed on October 2, 1862. Returned to duty prior to January 1, 1863. Detailed for duty as a sawyer on March 9, 1863. Reported on duty as a sawyer at Wilmington through December, 1863. Rejoined the company on an unspecified date. Hospitalized at Petersburg, Virginia, June 17, 1864, with a gunshot wound of the right hand. Place and date wounded not reported. Returned to duty prior to July 1, 1864. Hospitalized at Richmond on January 28, 1865, with an unspecified complaint. Furloughed for sixty days on January 29, 1865.

JORDAN, P. C., Private
Born in Iredell County where he resided as a mechanic prior to enlisting in Iredell County at age 31, March 5, 1862. Reported absent without leave in November-December, 1862. Reported absent sick in March-December, 1863, and May-August, 1864. Survived the war.

KENNERLY, E. WILLIAM, Private
Resided in Iredell County and was by occupation a farmer prior to enlisting in Mecklenburg County at age 40, February 14, 1864, for the war. Reported present in May-August, 1864.

LECKIE, JOHN H., 1st Sergeant
Born in Iredell County where he resided as a tinner prior to enlisting in Iredell County at age 25, March 31, 1862. Mustered in as Corporal. Promoted to Sergeant on July 15, 1863. Reported present or accounted for from November, 1862, through December, 1863, and in May-August, 1864. Promoted to 1st Sergeant on May 27, 1864. Died in hospital at Salisbury on December 24, 1864, of "diarrhoea ch[ronic]."

LEWIS, NELSON L., Private
Born in Iredell County where he resided as a farmer prior to enlisting in Iredell County at age 22, February 26, 1862. Reported present or accounted for from November, 1862, through December, 1863, and in May-August, 1864. Surrendered at Appomattox Court House, Virginia, April 9, 1865. Served as a teamster during much of the war.

LUCKEY, JOHN A., Private
Born in Rowan County and resided in Iredell County where he was by occupation a farmer prior to enlisting in Iredell County at age 26, March 12, 1862. Died at Winchester, Virginia, October 6, 1862, of disease.

McCLELLAND, THOMAS, Private
Previously served as Private in Company D, Mallett's N.C. Battalion (Camp Guard). Transferred to this company on June 1, 1864. Wounded in the right hip and/or right thigh and captured at Five Forks, Virginia, April 1, 1865. Hospitalized at Washington, D.C., April 10, 1865. Transferred to Old Capitol Prison, Washington, D.C., April 17, 1865. No further records.

McCLELLAND, WILLIAM AUGUSTUS, Private
Born in Iredell County where he resided as a farmer prior to enlisting in Iredell County at age 32, March 1, 1862. Died at Goldsboro on June 12, 1862, of disease.

McGOWAN, GEORGE M., Private
Born in Burke County and was by occupation a farmer prior to enlisting in Iredell County at age 27, March 4, 1862. Discharged prior to April 22, 1862. Reason discharged not reported.

MASON, E., Private
Place and date of enlistment not reported; however, he probably enlisted subsequent to August 31, 1864. Captured in hospital at Richmond, Virginia, April 3, 1865. Reported still in hospital at Richmond on May 28, 1865. No further records.

MASSEY, EMMIT S., Private
Born in Iredell County where he resided as a mechanic prior to enlisting in Iredell County at age 29, March 1, 1862. Mustered in as Private. Reported present from November, 1862, through December, 1863. Promoted to Corporal in January-February, 1863. Reduced to ranks on July 15, 1863. Reported present or accounted for in May-August, 1864. Captured at Five Forks, Virginia, April 1, 1865. Confined at Point Lookout, Maryland, April 5, 1865. Released at Point Lookout on June 21, 1865, after taking the Oath of Allegiance. [North Carolina pension

indicate that he was wounded at Petersburg, Virginia, and at Drewry's Bluff, Virginia.]

MILLER, ISAIAH, Private
Born in Catawba County* and resided in Iredell County where he was by occupation a farmer prior to enlisting in Rowan County at age 25, April 4, 1862. Discharged on October 17, 1862, by reason of disability.

MILLER, LEVAN M., Private
Born in Catawba County* and resided in Iredell County where he was by occupation a farmer prior to enlisting in Iredell County at age 22, March 22, 1862. Wounded in the right leg at Fredericksburg, Virginia, December 13, 1862. Returned to duty prior to January 1, 1863. Reported absent sick in March-December, 1863, and May-August, 1864. Survived the war.

MILLS, JOHN, Private
Resided in Iredell County where he enlisted at age 18, August 21, 1863, for the war. Reported present or accounted for in September-December, 1863, and May-August, 1864. Paroled at Richmond, Virginia, May 3, 1865.

MOOSE, DANIEL P., Private
Born in Iredell County where he resided as a farmer prior to enlisting in Iredell County at age 32, February 26, 1862. Reported absent without leave in November-December, 1862. Returned to duty in January-February, 1863. Reported present in March-June, 1863. Deserted on July 16, 1863. Returned from desertion on August 10, 1863. Reported in confinement at Weldon through December, 1863. Confined at Castle Thunder Prison, Richmond, Virginia, on an unspecified date. Escaped from Castle Thunder Prison on May 18, 1864. Went over to the enemy on or about January 24, 1865. Confined at Washington, D.C., January 30, 1865. Released on an unspecified date after taking the Oath of Allegiance.

MOOSE, GEORGE H., Private
Born in Catawba County and resided in Iredell County where he was by occupation a farmer prior to enlisting in Iredell County at age 18, March 1, 1862. Reported present or accounted for from November, 1862, through December, 1863, and in May-August, 1864. Captured at Five Forks, Virginia, April 1, 1865. Confined at Point Lookout, Maryland, April 5, 1865. Released at Point Lookout on June 29, 1865, after taking the Oath of Allegiance.

MORRISON, EPHRAIM, Private
Previously served as Corporal in Company D, Mallett's N.C. Battalion (Camp Guard). Transferred to this company on June 12, 1864. Reported present in July-August, 1864. Hospitalized at Richmond, Virginia, February 24, 1865, with acute bronchitis. Captured in hospital at Richmond on April 3, 1865. Transferred to Newport News, Virginia, April 23, 1865. Released at Newport News on June 30, 1865, after taking the Oath of Allegiance.

MORRISON, WILLIAM C., Private
Born in Iredell County where he resided as a farmer prior to enlisting in Iredell County at age 42, February 26, 1862. Reported present or accounted for from November, 1862, through December, 1863. Wounded at Drewry's Bluff, Virginia, on or about May 16, 1864. Hospitalized at Richmond, Virginia. Furloughed for thirty days on October 6, 1864. Returned to duty on an unspecified date. Captured at Five Forks, Virginia, April 1, 1865. Confined at Point Lookout, Maryland, April 5, 1865. Released at Point Lookout on June 21, 1865, after taking the Oath of Allegiance.

MORROW, HUGH M., Private
Born in Mecklenburg County and resided in Iredell County where he was by occupation a farmer prior to enlisting in Iredell County at age 22, March 1, 1862. Reported absent without leave in November-December, 1862. Returned to duty in January-February, 1863. Reported absent sick in March-December, 1863, and May-August, 1864. Hospitalized at Richmond, Virginia, November 19, 1864, with ulcers. Furloughed for sixty days on December 16, 1864. Paroled at Statesville on May 28, 1865.

NORTON, NICHOLAS A., Private
Born in Granville County and resided in Iredell County where he was by occupation a farmer prior to enlisting in Iredell County at age 22, April 4, 1862. Reported absent sick in November-December, 1862. Returned to duty in January-February, 1863. Captured at Sandy Ridge (Lenoir County) on April 20, 1863. Sent to Fort Monroe, Virginia. Paroled and transferred to City Point, Virginia, where he was received on May 28, 1863, for exchange. Returned to duty prior to July 1, 1863. Reported present in July-December, 1863, and May-August, 1864. Deserted to the enemy on or about March 9, 1865. Confined at Washington, D.C., March 13, 1865. Released on an unspecified date after taking the Oath of Allegiance.

OWEN, THOMAS B., Private
Resided in Iredell County and was by occupation a farmer. Place and date of enlistment not reported; however, he probably enlisted subsequent to August 31, 1864. Was about 37 years of age at time of enlistment. Hospitalized at Richmond, Virginia, February 23, 1865, with chronic hepatitis. Captured in hospital at Richmond on April 3, 1865. Paroled on April 23, 1865.

PATTERSON, JOSEPH ROBERT GRIER, Corporal
Born in Alexander County* and resided in Iredell County where he was by occupation a farmer prior to enlisting in Iredell County at age 19, March 10, 1862. Mustered in as Private. Reported present from November, 1862, through December, 1863. Promoted to Corporal on July 15, 1863. Reported present in May-August, 1864. Killed at Petersburg, Virginia, January 12, 1865.

REID, ALFRED L., Sergeant
Born in Caswell County and resided in Iredell County where he was by occupation a farmer prior to enlisting in Iredell County at age 27, March 17, 1862. Mustered in as Sergeant. Reported present from November, 1862, through December, 1863, and in May-August, 1864.

Wounded in the neck and captured at Five Forks, Virginia, April 1, 1865. Hospitalized at Washington, D.C., April 8, 1865. Confined at Old Capitol Prison, Washington, April 24, 1865. Transferred to Elmira, New York, May 1, 1865. Released at Elmira on July 7, 1865, after taking the Oath of Allegiance.

ROSEMAN, CYRUS P., Private
Enlisted in this company on May 7, 1862, after deserting from Company F, 38th Regiment N.C. Troops, April 28, 1862. Reported present from November, 1862, through December, 1863, and in May-August, 1864. Hospitalized at Richmond, Virginia, February 13, 1865, with chronic diarrhoea. Returned to duty on March 4, 1865. Deserted to the enemy on or about March 14, 1865. Confined at Washington, D.C., March 18, 1865. Released at Washington on an unspecified date after taking the Oath of Allegiance.

ROSEMAN, THEODORE A., Private
Resided in Rowan County. Place and date of enlistment not reported; however, he probably enlisted subsequent to August 31, 1864. Was about 19 years of age at time of enlistment. Deserted to the enemy on or about March 8, 1865. Confined at Washington, D.C., March 10, 1865. Released on an unspecified date after taking the Oath of Allegiance.

SHARPE, FRANCIS M., Private
Born in Iredell County where he resided as a farmer prior to enlisting in Iredell County at age 22, March 1, 1862. Reported on detail as a nurse from November, 1862, through February, 1863. Reported absent on sick furlough in March-June, 1863. Returned to duty in September-October, 1863. Reported present in November-December, 1863, and May-August, 1864. Captured at Five Forks, Virginia, April 1, 1865. Confined at Point Lookout, Maryland, April 5, 1865. Released at Point Lookout on June 19, 1865, after taking the Oath of Allegiance.

SHARPE, LEANDER DAVIDSON, Private
Born in Iredell County where he resided as a farmer prior to enlisting in Iredell County at age 23, February 26, 1862. Reported present from November, 1862, through December, 1863, and in May-June, 1864. Wounded at the Battle of the Crater, near Petersburg, Virginia, July 30, 1864. Hospitalized at Richmond, Virginia, where he died on or about August 18, 1864, of wounds.

SHARPE, WILLIAM P., Private
Born in Iredell County where he resided as a farmer prior to enlisting in Iredell County at age 21, February 26, 1862. Wounded at Malvern Hill, Virginia, July 1, 1862. Returned to duty on an unspecified date. Reported present from November, 1862, through June, 1863. Deserted on or about July 19, 1863. Returned from desertion on or about October 22, 1863. Reported absent in confinement through December, 1863. Returned to duty on an unspecified date. Reported present in May-August, 1864. Deserted to the enemy on or about January 27, 1865. Confined at Washington, D.C., February 1, 1865. Released on an unspecified date after taking the Oath of Allegiance.

SHERRELL, LELAND, Private
Born in Rowan County and resided in Iredell County where he was by occupation a farmer prior to enlisting in Rowan County at age 18, April 4, 1862. Reported missing at Malvern Hill, Virginia, July 1, 1862. Returned to duty on an unspecified date. Reported present from November, 1862, through December, 1863, and in May-August, 1864. Deserted to the enemy on or about March 14, 1865. Confined at Washington, D.C., March 18, 1865. Released on an unspecified date after taking the Oath of Allegiance.

SHUPPING, JEREMIAH A., Private
Born in Rowan County and resided in Iredell County where he was by occupation a farmer prior to enlisting in Iredell County at age 18, March 1, 1862. Captured at Frederick, Maryland, September 12, 1862. Confined at Fort Delaware, Delaware. Transferred to Aiken's Landing, James River, Virginia, October 2, 1862, for exchange. Received at Aiken's Landing on October 6, 1862. Hospitalized at Richmond, Virginia, October 13, 1862, with hepatitis. Furloughed for thirty days on November 8, 1862. Reported absent without leave prior to January 1, 1863. Returned to duty in January-February, 1863. Reported present in March-December, 1863, and May-August, 1864. [May have been wounded by a mortar shell fragment in the trenches near Petersburg, Virginia, December 15, 1864.]

SHUPPING, SMITH A., Private
Resided in Iredell or Orange County and enlisted in Iredell County at age 17, August 10, 1863, for the war. Reported present in September-December, 1863, and May-August, 1864. Captured at Five Forks, Virginia, April 1, 1865. Confined at Point Lookout, Maryland, April 5, 1865. Released at Point Lookout on June 20, 1865, after taking the Oath of Allegiance. [May have been wounded by a mortar shell fragment in the trenches near Petersburg, Virginia, December 15, 1864.]

STAMPER, GEORGE W., Private
Born in Iredell County where he resided as a farmer prior to enlisting in Iredell County at age 20, March 1, 1862. Discharged on June 8, 1862, by reason of "consumption."

STAMPER, L. FRANKLIN, Private
Born in Iredell County where he resided as a farmer prior to enlisting in Iredell County at age 21, March 1, 1862. Reported present or accounted for from November, 1862, through August, 1863. Reported absent sick at home in September-December, 1863. Died in Iredell County on February 23, 1864, of disease.

TAYS, SAMUEL L., Sergeant
Born in Iredell County where he resided as a tanner prior to enlisting in Iredell County at age 33, March 17, 1862. Mustered in as Private. Promoted to Sergeant in January-February, 1863. Reported present from November, 1862, through December, 1863, and in May-June, 1864. Wounded in the right leg by a shell near Petersburg, Virginia, July 9, 1864. Right leg amputated. Retired on February 21, 1865. [Was elected 2nd Lieutenant of the company on October 7, 1862, but was "rejected by board."]

WATT, WILLIAM T., Private

Previously served as Private in Company D, Mallett's N.C. Battalion (Camp Guard). Transferred to this company on June 12, 1864. Reported present in July-August, 1864. Wounded in the side (possibly also in the left arm and right thigh) at Fort Stedman, Virginia, March 25, 1865. Hospitalized at Petersburg, Virginia, where he was captured on April 3, 1865. Transferred to a Federal hospital at Point of Rocks, Virginia, where he was admitted on April 9, 1865. Transferred to hospital at Fort Monroe, Virginia, May 17, 1865. Released at Fort Monroe on or about June 21, 1865, after taking the Oath of Allegiance. [Records of the Federal Provost Marshal dated May-June, 1865, give his age as 21.]

WAUGH, SIMEON A., Private

Born in Iredell County where he resided as a farmer prior to enlisting in Iredell County at age 26, March 7, 1862. Reported present from November, 1862, through February, 1863. Wounded in the right lung and captured at Sandy Ridge (Lenoir County) on April 20, 1863. Hospitalized at New Bern. Transferred to Fort Monroe, Virginia, on or about July 18, 1863. Paroled at Fort Monroe on August 4, 1863. Returned to duty subsequent to December 31, 1863. Reported present in May-June, 1864. Reported absent wounded in July-August, 1864. Place and date wounded not reported. Wounded in the right lung while on picket near Petersburg, Virginia, December 15, 1864. Hospitalized at Petersburg where he died on December 23, 1864, of wounds.

WEBER, G. W., Private

Previously served as Private in Company D, Mallett's N.C. Battalion (Camp Guard). Transferred to this company on June 12, 1864. Reported present in July-August, 1864. Captured at Five Forks, Virginia, April 1, 1865. Confined at Point Lookout, Maryland, April 5, 1865. Released at Point Lookout on June 21, 1865, after taking the Oath of Allegiance.

WOODS, JAMES R., Private

Born in Iredell County where he resided as a farmer prior to enlisting in Iredell County at age 30, March 4, 1862. Reported present from November, 1862, through December, 1863. Wounded in the shoulder at Drewry's Bluff, Virginia, May 16, 1864. Hospitalized at Richmond, Virginia, where he died on or about May 24, 1864, of wounds.

WOODSIDES, JOHN FRUNO, Private

Born in Iredell County where he resided as a farmer prior to enlisting in Iredell County at age 24, February 26, 1862. Mustered in as Corporal. Reported absent without leave in November-December, 1862. Returned to duty in January-February, 1863. Reported present in March-August, 1863. Reported present but under arrest in September-December, 1863. Reason he was arrested not reported. Reduced to ranks in January-June, 1864. Returned to duty on an unspecified date. Reported present in May-August, 1864. Captured at or near Five Forks, Virginia, on or about April 2, 1865. Confined at Point Lookout, Maryland, April 5, 1865. Released at Point Lookout on June 16, 1865, after taking the Oath of Allegiance. [Previously served as 3rd Lieutenant in the 79th Regiment N.C. Militia.]

COMPANY F

This company, known as the "Mecklenburg Guards," was raised in Mecklenburg County and enlisted at Charlotte in March-April, 1862. It was mustered into state service at Camp Mangum, near Raleigh, on April 21, 1862, and assigned to the 49th Regiment N.C. Troops as Company F. After joining the regiment the company functioned as a part of the regiment, and its history for the remainder of the war is reported as a part of the regimental history.

The information contained in the following roster was compiled primarily from a company muster-in and descriptive roll dated April 21, 1862, and from company muster rolls for November 1, 1862-December 31, 1863, and July 1-October 31, 1864. No company muster rolls were located for May 1-October 31, 1862; January 1-June 30, 1864; or for the period after October 31, 1864. Valuable information was obtained from primary records such as the North Carolina adjutant general's *Roll of Honor*, discharge certificates, medical records, prisoner of war records, *The War of the Rebellion: A Compilation of the Official Records of the Union and Confederate Armies*, militia records, newspaper casualty lists and obituaries, Confederate pension applications filed with the state of North Carolina, and the 1860 federal census of North Carolina. Secondary sources such as postwar rosters and histories, cemetery records, the *Confederate Veteran*, published genealogies, and records of the United Daughters of the Confederacy also provided useful information.

OFFICERS

CAPTAINS

DAVIS, JAMES TAYLOR

Previously served as Private in Company B, 1st Regiment N.C. Infantry (6 months, 1861). Elected Captain of this company on April 21, 1862. Reported present or accounted for from November, 1862, through August, 1863. Appointed Major on September 16, 1863, and transferred to the Field and Staff of this regiment.

ARDREY, JAMES P.

Born in Mecklenburg County where he resided as a farmer prior to enlisting at age 24. Elected 3rd Lieutenant on or about April 12, 1862. Promoted to 1st Lieutenant on July 1, 1862. Reported present from November, 1862, through December, 1863. Promoted to Captain on September 16, 1863. Wounded at Drewry's Bluff, Virginia, May 14, 1864, while attempting to dislodge a nest of Federal sharpshooters. Fell near the enemy lines and could not be recovered. Died on the battlefield of wounds. Body recovered and brought into camp on May 16, 1864.

GRIER, JOHN C.

Born in Mecklenburg County where he resided prior to enlisting in Mecklenburg County at age 22, March 14,

1862. Mustered in as Sergeant. Elected 3rd Lieutenant on October 7, 1862. Reported present or accounted for from November, 1862, through December, 1863. Promoted to 2nd Lieutenant on July 16, 1863. Promoted to 1st Lieutenant on September 16, 1863. Promoted to Captain on May 14, 1864. Wounded in the arm and thigh by a mortar shell near Petersburg, Virginia, July 23, 1864. Reported absent wounded or absent sick through November, 1864. Returned to duty on an unspecified date. Captured at Five Forks, Virginia, April 1, 1865. Confined at Old Capitol Prison, Washington, D.C., April 5, 1865. Transferred to Johnson's Island, Ohio, April 9, 1865. Released at Johnson's Island on June 18, 1865, after taking the Oath of Allegiance.

LIEUTENANTS

BARNETT, JOHN W., 1st Lieutenant
Born in Mecklenburg County where he resided as a farmer prior to enlisting at age 33. Elected 1st Lieutenant on April 21, 1862. Killed at Malvern Hill, Virginia, July 1, 1862.

BARNETT, WILLIAM P., 1st Lieutenant
Resided in Mecklenburg County where he enlisted at age 26, May 5, 1862, for the war. Mustered in as Private. Reported present or accounted for from November, 1862, through December, 1863. Elected 3rd Lieutenant on July 16, 1863. Promoted to 2nd Lieutenant on September 16, 1863. Promoted to 1st Lieutenant on May 4, 1864. Killed at Drewry's Bluff, Virginia, May 16, 1864.

ELLIOTT, SAMUEL H., 1st Lieutenant
Born in Mecklenburg County where he resided as a student prior to enlisting in Mecklenburg County at age 23, March 14, 1862. Mustered in as Private. Wounded at Malvern Hill, Virginia, July 1, 1862. Returned to duty on an unspecified date. Wounded at Sharpsburg, Maryland, September 17, 1862. Promoted to Sergeant on October 7, 1862. Furloughed for sixty days on November 16, 1862. Returned to duty prior to March 1, 1863. Reported present in March-December, 1863. Elected 2nd Lieutenant in January, 1864. Promoted to 1st Lieutenant on or about May 14, 1864. Wounded in the buttocks and/or hip at Drewry's Bluff, Virginia, May 14, 1864. Returned to duty in July-August, 1864. Surrendered at Appomattox Court House, Virginia, April 9, 1865.

ELMS, JAMES H., 2nd Lieutenant
Resided in Mecklenburg County where he enlisted at age 29, May 5, 1862, for the war. Mustered in as Private. Promoted to Corporal on October 7, 1862. Reported present from November, 1862, through December, 1863. Elected 2nd Lieutenant on May 16, 1864. Wounded in the arm at Bermuda Hundred, Virginia, June 2, 1864. Returned to duty in July-August, 1864. Captured at Five Forks, Virginia, April 2, 1865. Confined at Old Capitol Prison, Washington, D.C., April 5, 1865. Transferred to Johnson's Island, Ohio, April 9, 1865. Released at Johnson's Island on June 19, 1865, after taking the Oath of Allegiance.

GRIER, ROBERT H., 2nd Lieutenant
Born in Mecklenburg County where he resided as a student prior to enlisting at age 20. Elected 3rd Lieutenant on April 21, 1862. Wounded at King's School House, Virginia, June 25, 1862. Promoted to 2nd Lieutenant on July 1, 1862. Died in hospital at Richmond, Virginia, July 17, 1862, of wounds.

NEEL, SAMUEL R., 3rd Lieutenant
Previously served as Private in Company C, 1st Regiment N.C. Infantry (6 months, 1861). Enlisted in this company in Mecklenburg County at age 21, March 30, 1862. Mustered in as Private. Promoted to Corporal in November, 1862. Wounded at Malvern Hill, Virginia, July 1, 1862. Returned to duty on an unspecified date. Reported present from November, 1862, through December, 1863. Promoted to Sergeant prior to May 14, 1864, when he was wounded at Drewry's Bluff, Virginia. Returned to duty in July-August, 1864. Appointed 3rd Lieutenant on July 18, 1864. Surrendered at Appomattox Court House, Virginia, April 9, 1865. [His surname is spelled Neil in Volume III of this series, but the correct spelling is Neel.]

POTTS, JOHN G., 2nd Lieutenant
Born in Mecklenburg County where he resided as a student prior to enlisting in Mecklenburg County at age 21, March 14, 1862. Mustered in as 1st Sergeant. Elected 2nd Lieutenant on July 15, 1862. Wounded in the left elbow (fracture) at Sharpsburg, Maryland, September 17, 1862. Reported absent wounded until he resigned on May 26, 1863, by reason of "anchylosis of the left elbow" resulting from wounds received at Sharpsburg. "The forearm is bent upon the arm at right angles. There is still a considerable ulcer near the fracture through which several splinters of bone have been discharged. There is also a considerable discharge of pus, indicating the probable presence of necrosed bone." Resignation accepted on July 16, 1863.

NONCOMMISSIONED OFFICERS AND PRIVATES

ALEXANDER, ENOCH E., Private
Born in Mecklenburg County where he resided as a farmer prior to enlisting in Mecklenburg County at age 23, March 24, 1862. Reported present or accounted for from November, 1862, through December, 1863, and in May-August, 1864. Captured at Fort Stedman, Virginia, March 25, 1865. Confined at Point Lookout, Maryland, until released on June 22, 1865, after taking the Oath of Allegiance.

ALEXANDER, JOHN J., Private
Born in Mecklenburg County where he resided as a farmer prior to enlisting in Mecklenburg County at age 29, April 16, 1862, for the war. Wounded at Malvern Hill, Virginia, July 1, 1862. Died on July 2, 1862, of wounds. Place of death not reported.

ALEXANDER, ROBERT N., Private
Born in Mecklenburg County where he resided as a

mechanic prior to enlisting in Mecklenburg County at age 20, March 14, 1862. Mustered in as Corporal. Deserted at Shepherdstown, [West] Virginia, September 16, 1862. Reduced to ranks prior to January 1, 1863. Dropped from the rolls of the company in March-April, 1863. Returned to duty on an unspecified date. Reported present in July-August, 1864. Killed near Petersburg, Virginia, December 11, 1864.

ALEXANDER, THEOPHILUS B., Private
Born in Mecklenburg County where he resided as a farmer prior to enlisting in Mecklenburg County at age 20, March 25, 1862. Died in hospital at Staunton, Virginia, October 29, 1862, of "diarrhoea chronica."

ALEXANDER, WILLIAM P., Private
Born in Mecklenburg County where he resided as a farmer prior to enlisting in Mecklenburg County at age 26, March 14, 1862. Wounded in the right hand at Sharpsburg, Maryland, September 17, 1862. Returned to duty on or about January 24, 1863. Reported present in February-December, 1863, and July-August, 1864. Captured at Fort Stedman, Virginia, March 25, 1865. Confined at Point Lookout, Maryland, until released on June 22, 1865, after taking the Oath of Allegiance.

ALLEN, AMZI W., Private
Resided in Mecklenburg County and was by occupation a master carpenter prior to enlisting in Mecklenburg County at age 36, August 10, 1863, for the war. Reported present in September-December, 1863. Wounded in the left thigh at Globe Tavern, Virginia, August 21, 1864. Hospitalized at Richmond, Virginia. Transferred to hospital at Charlotte where he arrived on or about October 28, 1864. Furloughed on March 24, 1865.

ASHLEY, WILLIAM A., Private
Resided in Mecklenburg County where he enlisted at age 30, April 25, 1862, for the war. Deserted at Shepherdstown, [West] Virginia, September 16, 1862. Returned from desertion on January 6, 1863. Reported present in March-December, 1863, and May-August, 1864. Hospitalized at Richmond, Virginia, December 10, 1864, with chronic diarrhoea. Reported in hospital at Richmond through April 1, 1865. Paroled at Charlotte on May 17, 1865.

BELL, ROBERT C., Sergeant
Born in Lincoln County and resided in Mecklenburg County or in York District, South Carolina, where he was by occupation a farmer prior to enlisting in Mecklenburg County at age 35, March 20, 1862. Mustered in as Private. Promoted to Sergeant prior to January 1, 1863. Reported present in November-December, 1862. Reported on duty as a clerk and laborer at Magnolia from January, 1863, through June, 1864. Rejoined the company on an unspecified date. Captured near Petersburg, Virginia, April 2, 1865. Confined at Point Lookout, Maryland, April 5, 1865. Released at Point Lookout on June 23, 1865, after taking the Oath of Allegiance.

BENNETT, DOCTOR G., Private
Born in York District, South Carolina, and resided in South Carolina where he was by occupation a farmer prior to enlisting in Mecklenburg County at age 32, April 1, 1862. Wounded at Malvern Hill, Virginia, July 1, 1862. Returned to duty prior to September 17, 1862, when he was wounded in the arm at Sharpsburg, Maryland. Arm amputated. Reported absent wounded through August, 1864.

BLACK, WILLIAM, Private
Place and date of enlistment not reported; however, he probably enlisted subsequent to August 31, 1864. Surrendered at Appomattox Court House, Virginia, April 9, 1865.

BOLICK, NOAH, Private
Resided in Mecklenburg County and was by occupation a blacksmith. Place and date of enlistment not reported; however, he probably enlisted subsequent to August 31, 1864. Was about 35 years of age at time of enlistment. Surrendered at Appomattox Court House, Virginia, April 9, 1865.

BROWN, JAMES G., Private
Resided in Mecklenburg County and was by occupation a farmer prior to enlisting in Mecklenburg County at age 26, April 29, 1862, for the war. Reported present from November, 1862, through December, 1863, and in May-August, 1864. Captured at Five Forks, Virginia, April 1, 1865. Confined at Point Lookout, Maryland, April 5, 1865. Released at Point Lookout on June 23, 1865, after taking the Oath of Allegiance.

BROWN, WARREN H., Private
Resided in Mecklenburg County and was by occupation a farm laborer prior to enlisting in Mecklenburg County at age 24, May 5, 1862, for the war. Reported present or accounted for from November, 1862, through December, 1863, and in May-August, 1864. Died at Petersburg, Virginia, December 20, 1864. Cause of death not reported.

CALDWELL, THOMAS C., _____
North Carolina pension records indicate that he served in this company.

CAROTHERS, THOMAS M., Private
Resided in York District, South Carolina, and enlisted in Mecklenburg County at age 31, May 12, 1862, for the war. Mustered in as Private. Hospitalized on July 18, 1862, with typhoid fever. Returned to duty on November 6, 1862. Reported present or accounted for from December, 1862, through December, 1863. Appointed Musician on July 1, 1863. Reduced to ranks subsequent to December 31, 1863. Reported absent sick in May-August, 1864. Transferred to Company E, 17th Regiment South Carolina Infantry, December 6, 1864.

CHAPEL, DANIEL, _____
North Carolina pension records indicate that he served in this company.

COFFEY, BENJAMIN L., Private
Born in Mecklenburg County where he resided prior to enlisting in Mecklenburg County at age 17, December 13,

1863, for the war. Killed at Bermuda Hundred, Virginia, June 2, 1864.

CRANE, JOB S., Private
Born in New York and resided in Union County where he was by occupation a cabinetmaker prior to enlisting in Mecklenburg County at age 41, July 30, 1863, for the war. Reported present in August-December, 1863. Wounded in the hand at Bermuda Hundred, Virginia, June 2, 1864. Detailed at Charlotte on an unspecified date. No further records.

CRENSHAW, JOHN, Private
Born in Mecklenburg County where he resided as a farmer prior to enlisting in Mecklenburg County at age 17, April 1, 1862. Wounded at Sharpsburg, Maryland, September 17, 1862. Returned to duty prior to January 1, 1863. Reported present or accounted for in January-December, 1863. Wounded in the shoulder at Bermuda Hundred, Virginia, June 2, 1864. Reported absent wounded through August, 1864. Retired to the Invalid Corps on February 3, 1865. Returned to duty with the company on an unspecified date. Surrendered at Appomattox Court House, Virginia, April 9, 1865.

CULP, JOHN, Private
Born in Lancaster District, South Carolina, and resided in Mecklenburg County where he was by occupation a farmer prior to enlisting in Mecklenburg County at age 31, March 14, 1862. Reported present from November, 1862, through December, 1863. Served as a teamster during most of that period. Wounded in the right knee and/or right thigh near Drewry's Bluff, Virginia, May 14, 1864. Reported absent wounded through August, 1864. Paroled at Charlotte on May 18, 1865.

DAVIS, H. H., Private
Place and date of enlistment not reported; however, he probably enlisted subsequent to August 31, 1864. Surrendered at Appomattox Court House, Virginia, April 9, 1865.

DeARMOND, JAMES BOYCE, Private
Resided in Mecklenburg County where he enlisted at age 42, October 10, 1863, for the war. Reported present in November-December, 1863. Wounded in the left foot near Petersburg, Virginia, August 10, 1864. Left foot amputated. Furloughed for sixty days from hospital at Petersburg on September 22, 1864. Survived the war.

DUNN, JAMES R., Corporal
Resided in Mecklenburg County and was by occupation a farmer prior to enlisting in Mecklenburg County at age 29, April 1, 1862. Mustered in as Color Sergeant. Wounded at Malvern Hill, Virginia, July 1, 1862. "Complimented by Col. [Stephen D.] Ramseur for gallant conduct" at Malvern Hill. Returned to duty on an unspecified date. Reported present from November, 1862, through December, 1863. Reduced to ranks in March-April, 1863. Promoted to Corporal in January-August, 1864. Reported present in May-August, 1864. Surrendered at Appomattox Court House, Virginia, April 9, 1865.

ELLIOTT, JAMES A., Sergeant
Born in Mecklenburg County where he resided as a student prior to enlisting in Mecklenburg County at age 19, March 14, 1862. Mustered in as Sergeant. Wounded at Malvern Hill, Virginia, July 1, 1862. Discharged on October 12, 1862, by reason of "rheumatism & valvular disease of the heart. . . ."

EZZELL, JAMES A., Sergeant
Born in Mecklenburg County where he resided as a farmer prior to enlisting in Mecklenburg County at age 22, March 21, 1862. Mustered in as Corporal. Promoted to Sergeant on October 7, 1862. Reported present or accounted for from November, 1862, through December, 1863, and in May-August, 1864. Surrendered at Appomattox Court House, Virginia, April 9, 1865.

FARIS, JOHN A., Private
Born in York District, South Carolina, where he resided as a farmer prior to enlisting in Mecklenburg County at age 35, March 24, 1862. Reported present or accounted for from November, 1862, through December, 1863. Hospitalized at Richmond, Virginia, June 5, 1864, with a gunshot wound. Place and date not reported. Furloughed for forty days on July 23, 1864. Hospitalized at Richmond on December 8, 1864. Furloughed on or about January 12, 1865.

FIELDS, MINOS A., Private
Resided in Mecklenburg County where he enlisted at age 38, August 20, 1863, for the war. Reported present or accounted for in September-December, 1863, and May-August, 1864. Captured at or near Five Forks, Virginia, on or about April 1, 1865. Confined at Point Lookout, Maryland, April 13, 1865. No further records.

FINCHER, JOHN E., Private
Born in Union County and resided in Mecklenburg County where he enlisted at age 18, March 21, 1863, for the war. Reported present in April-December, 1863. Died in hospital at Richmond, Virginia, July 5-6, 1864, of disease.

FINCHER, OSBORNE, Private
Born in Union County and resided in Mecklenburg County where he was by occupation a farmer prior to enlisting in Mecklenburg County at age 19, March 19, 1862. Deserted at Petersburg, Virginia, August 18, 1862. Returned from desertion on January 15, 1863. Transferred to Company B, 52nd Regiment N.C. Troops, on or about February 4, 1863, in exchange for Private Marion L. Harkey.

FLANNAGAN, LEE B., Private
Born in Mecklenburg County where he resided prior to enlisting in Mecklenburg County at age 42, August 20, 1863, for the war. Reported present or accounted for in September-December, 1863, and May-August, 1864. Killed near Petersburg, Virginia, November 10, 1864.

FRENCH, WILLIAM, Private
Resided in Mecklenburg County and was by occupation a farmer prior to enlisting in Mecklenburg County at age

36, March 14, 1862. Deserted on August 19, 1862. Returned from desertion on November 12, 1862. Reported present or accounted for in January-December, 1863, and May-August, 1864. Captured at Five Forks, Virginia, April 1, 1865. Confined at Point Lookout, Maryland, April 5, 1865. Released at Point Lookout on June 26, 1865, after taking the Oath of Allegiance.

GARRISON, AARON, Private
Resided in York District, South Carolina, and enlisted at age 44, May 10, 1862, for the war as a substitute. Died in hospital at Petersburg, Virginia, June 21, 1862, of "pneumonia."

GORDON, ADAM E., Private
Resided in South Carolina and enlisted at Charlotte at age 32, April 21, 1862, for the war. Reported present from November, 1862, through December, 1863. Reported absent without leave in July-August, 1864. Transferred to Company I, 17th Regiment South Carolina Infantry, December 9, 1864.

GOUGER, JAMES H., Private
Previously served as Ordnance Sergeant of this regiment. Reduced to ranks and transferred to this company in January-August, 1864. Reported on detached service at China Grove in July-August, 1864. Paroled at Salisbury on May 19, 1865. Took the Oath of Allegiance at Salisbury on June 14, 1865.

GRIER, LAWRENCE, Private
Enlisted in Mecklenburg County on April 15, 1864, for the war. Reported present in May-August, 1864. Captured at Five Forks, Virginia, April 1, 1865. Confined at Point Lookout, Maryland, April 4, 1865. Died at Point Lookout on May 31, 1865, of "gen[era]l debility."

GRIFFIN, EGBERT, Private
Was by occupation a farmer prior to enlisting in Mecklenburg County at age 42, March 14, 1862. Reported absent on expired furlough in November-December, 1862. Reported present or accounted for in January-December, 1863, and May-August, 1864. Hospitalized at Richmond, Virginia, February 24, 1865, with intermittent fever. Transferred to Farmville, Virginia, April 1, 1865. No further records.

GRIFFIN, ISAAC G., Private
Born in Mecklenburg County where he resided as a farmer prior to enlisting in Mecklenburg County at age 23, March 14, 1862. Reported present from November, 1862, through December, 1863, and in May-August, 1864.

GRIFFITH, JONATHAN WALLACE, Private
Born in Mecklenburg County where he resided as a farmer prior to enlisting in Mecklenburg County at age 31, March 14, 1862. Reported present or accounted for from November, 1862, through December, 1863. Wounded in the left hip at Drewry's Bluff, Virginia, May 14, 1864. Hospitalized at Richmond, Virginia. Furloughed for sixty days on June 6, 1864. Declared physically unfit for field duty on or about August 20, 1864; however, he rejoined the company on an unspecified date. Captured at Five

Forks, Virginia, April 1, 1865. Confined at Point Lookout, Maryland, April 4, 1865. Released at Point Lookout on June 27, 1865, after taking the Oath of Allegiance.

GRIFFITH, THOMAS D., Private
Born in Mecklenburg County where he resided as a farm laborer prior to enlisting in Mecklenburg County at age 44, September 7, 1863, for the war. Reported present in October-December, 1863. Wounded in the chest near Drewry's Bluff, Virginia, on or about May 13, 1864. Hospitalized at Richmond, Virginia, where he died on or about May 15, 1864, of wounds.

HALL, N. C., _____
North Carolina pension records indicate that he served in this company.

HANNON, JAMES J., Sergeant
Born in Mecklenburg County where he resided as a farmer prior to enlisting in Mecklenburg County at age 28, March 21, 1862. Mustered in as Private. Reported present or accounted for from November, 1862, through December, 1863, and in May-June, 1864. Hospitalized at Richmond, Virginia, July 29, 1864, with debilitas and chronic diarrhoea. Returned to duty on September 17, 1864. Promoted to Sergeant subsequent to September 17, 1864. Retired to the Invalid Corps on March 21, 1865. Reason he was retired not reported. Captured in hospital at Richmond on April 3, 1865. Transferred to Newport News, Virginia, April 23, 1865. Released at Newport News on June 30, 1865, after taking the Oath of Allegiance.

HARKEY, DAVID E., Private
Born in Mecklenburg County where he resided as a farmer prior to enlisting in Mecklenburg County at age 28, March 14, 1862. Reported present or accounted for from November, 1862, through December, 1863, and in May-August, 1864. Surrendered at Appomattox Court House, Virginia, April 9, 1865.

HARKEY, JAMES J., Corporal
Born in Mecklenburg County and resided in Union County where he was by occupation a farmer prior to enlisting in Mecklenburg County at age 25, March 12, 1862. Mustered in as Private. Wounded at Fredericksburg, Virginia, December 13, 1862. Returned to duty prior to January 1, 1863. Reported present in January-December, 1863. Hospitalized at Richmond, Virginia, June 4, 1864, with a gunshot wound. Place and date wounded not reported. Returned to duty on July 31, 1864. Promoted to Corporal on August 5, 1864. Surrendered at Appomattox Court House, Virginia, April 9, 1865.

HARKEY, MARION L., Private
Previously served as Private in Company B, 52nd Regiment N.C. Troops. Transferred to this company on or about February 4, 1863, in exchange for Private Osborne Fincher. Reported present in March-December, 1863, and May-August, 1864. Captured at Five Forks, Virginia, April 1, 1865. Confined at Point Lookout, Maryland,

April 5, 1865. Released at Point Lookout on June 27, 1865, after taking the Oath of Allegiance.

HARKEY, WASHINGTON, Private

Previously served as Private in Company C, 9th Regiment N.C. State Troops (1st Regiment N.C. Cavalry). Enlisted in this company in Mecklenburg County at age 28, May 20, 1862, for the war. Reported present from November, 1862, through December, 1863, and in May-August, 1864. Hospitalized at Richmond, Virginia, February 24, 1865, with syphilis. Captured in hospital at Richmond on April 3, 1865. Transferred to Newport News, Virginia, April 23, 1865. Released at Newport News on June 16, 1865, after taking the Oath of Allegiance.

HARTIS, JAMES L., Private

Born in Mecklenburg County and resided in Union County where he was by occupation a farmer prior to enlisting in Mecklenburg County at age 47, March 19, 1862. Wounded at Sharpsburg, Maryland, September 17, 1862. Returned to duty in January-February, 1863. Reported present in March-December, 1863, and July-August, 1864. Hospitalized at Richmond, Virginia, February 28, 1865, with acute diarrhoea. Furloughed for sixty days on March 29, 1865.

HARTIS, JOHN S., Private

Born in Mecklenburg County and resided in Mecklenburg or Union County where he was by occupation a farmer prior to enlisting in Mecklenburg County at age 16, April 1, 1862. Reported present from November, 1862, through December, 1863, and in May-August, 1864. Wounded and captured at Five Forks, Virginia, April 1, 1865. Confined at Point Lookout, Maryland, April 5, 1865. Released at Point Lookout on June 13, 1865, after taking the Oath of Allegiance.

HAWFIELD, JAMES W., Private

Resided in Mecklenburg County and was by occupation a farmer prior to enlisting in Mecklenburg County at age 27, May 5, 1862, for the war. Hospitalized at Richmond, Virginia, December 8, 1862, with pleurisy. Returned to duty in January-February, 1863. Reported present in March-December, 1863, and May-August, 1864. Surrendered at Appomattox Court House, Virginia, April 9, 1865.

HENNIGAN, JAMES E., Corporal

Resided in Mecklenburg County where he enlisted at age 18, May 5, 1862, for the war. Mustered in as Private. Hospitalized at Petersburg, Virginia, July 28, 1862, with pneumonia. Returned to duty on September 1, 1862. Reported present from November, 1862, through December, 1863. Wounded at Bermuda Hundred, Virginia, May 20, 1864. Promoted to Corporal in May-August, 1864. Returned to duty prior to July 1, 1864. Surrendered at Appomattox Court House, Virginia, April 9, 1865.

HOWARD, JONATHAN M., Private

Born in Union County* where he resided prior to enlisting in Mecklenburg County at age 21, March 26, 1862. Reported present from November, 1862, through December, 1863. Wounded in the right leg at Drewry's

Bluff, Virginia, May 14, 1864. Reported absent wounded through August 31, 1864. Survived the war.

HUDSON, WILSON M., Private

Previously served as Private in Company I, 48th Regiment N.C. Troops. Transferred to this company on or about March 19, 1862. Reported present from November, 1862, through December, 1863. Wounded in the leg, both arms, and left hand (middle finger shot off) at Drewry's Bluff, Virginia, May 14, 1864. Hospitalized at Richmond, Virginia. Furloughed for sixty days on May 31, 1864. Returned to duty on an unspecified date. Captured at Fort Stedman, Virginia, March 25, 1865. Confined at Point Lookout, Maryland, March 31, 1865. Released at Point Lookout on May 13, 1865, after taking the Oath of Allegiance.

JAMISON, EMORY, Private

Born in Mecklenburg County where he resided as a farmer prior to enlisting in Mecklenburg County at age 20, March 14, 1862. Captured at Frederick, Maryland, September 12, 1862. Confined at Fort Delaware, Delaware. Transferred to Aiken's Landing, James River, Virginia, October 2, 1862, for exchange. Declared exchanged at Aiken's Landing on November 10, 1862. Died at home in Mecklenburg County on November 18 or November 28, 1862, of disease.

JOHNSON, DANIEL J., Private

Previously served as Private in Company F, 35th Regiment N.C. Troops. Transferred to this company on May 29, 1863, in exchange for Private William A. Newell. Reported present in June-December, 1863. Killed at Bermuda Hundred, Virginia, May 20, 1864.

JOHNSON, JAMES A., Private

Born in Mecklenburg County where he resided prior to enlisting in Mecklenburg County at age 50, July 27, 1862, for the war as a substitute for Private Green C. Morris. Reported present or accounted for from November, 1862, through December, 1863, and in May-August, 1864. Killed (probably near Petersburg, Virginia) October 10, 1864.

KEENAN, DAVID G., Private

Born in Mecklenburg County where he resided as a farmer prior to enlisting in Mecklenburg County at age 22, March 14, 1862. Wounded in the leg at Malvern Hill, Virginia, July 1, 1862. Leg amputated. Died in hospital at Richmond, Virginia, July 2, 1862, of wounds.

KENIER, JOHN RIGHT, Private

Born in Mecklenburg County where he resided as a farmer prior to enlisting in Mecklenburg County at age 31, March 14, 1862. Reported present or accounted for from November, 1862, through December, 1863. Wounded at Drewry's Bluff, Virginia, May 16, 1864. Returned to duty prior to July 1, 1864. Captured at Five Forks, Virginia, April 1, 1865. Confined at Point Lookout, Maryland, April 5, 1865. Released at Point Lookout on June 28, 1865, after taking the Oath of Allegiance.

KENIER, WILLIAM, Private

Place and date of enlistment not reported; however, he probably enlisted subsequent to August 31, 1864.

Captured by the enemy on April 1-9, 1865. Hospitalized at Newport News, Virginia, May 8, 1865, with "debilitas & diarrhoea." Died in hospital at Newport News on May 24, 1865.

KERR, J. A., Private

Enlisted in Mecklenburg County on December 11, 1863, for the war as a substitute for Private James Kerr (his father). Wounded at Drewry's Bluff, Virginia, May 16, 1864. Returned to duty prior to July 1, 1864. Reported present in July-August, 1864. Hospitalized at Richmond, Virginia, December 20, 1864, with a gunshot wound of the buttocks. Place and date wounded not reported. Furloughed on February 11, 1865. Returned to duty on an unspecified date and was wounded in the right hip. Captured in hospital at Richmond on April 3, 1865. Died in hospital at Richmond on May 14, 1865, of wounds.

KERR, JAMES, Private

Resided in Mecklenburg County and was by occupation a farmer prior to enlisting in Mecklenburg County at age 44, August 16, 1863, for the war. Discharged on or about December 11, 1863, after providing Private J. A. Kerr (his son) as a substitute. Paroled at Charlotte on May 3, 1865.

KERR, SAMUEL, Private

Born in Mecklenburg County where he resided as a farmer prior to enlisting in Mecklenburg County at age 31, March 14, 1862. Hospitalized at Petersburg, Virginia, August 19, 1862, with acute diarrhoea. Returned to duty on October 20, 1862. Reported present from November, 1862, through December, 1863. Wounded in the groin at Bermuda Hundred, Virginia, June 2, 1864. Died in hospital at Petersburg on or about June 4, 1864, of wounds.

KIRKPATRICK, SILAS A., Private

Resided in Mecklenburg County and was by occupation a farmer prior to enlisting in Mecklenburg County at age 33, March 22, 1863, for the war. Reported present in April-December, 1863, and May-August, 1864. Hospitalized at Richmond, Virginia, December 18, 1864, with pneumonia. Captured in hospital at Richmond on April 3, 1865. Transferred to Newport News, Virginia, April 23, 1865. Released at Newport News on June 16, 1865, after taking the Oath of Allegiance. [North Carolina pension records indicate that he was wounded at Petersburg, Virginia, in March, 1864.]

LASSITER, H. C., ⸻

North Carolina pension records indicate that he served in this company. [May have served previously as Private in Company L, 22nd Regiment N.C. Troops (12th Regiment N.C. Volunteers).]

McALLISTER, HENRY B., Musician

Resided in Mecklenburg County and was by occupation a "laborer in [a] wool factory" prior to enlisting in Mecklenburg County at age 22, March 23, 1862. Mustered in as Private. Reported present from November, 1862, through June, 1863. Appointed Musician on July 1, 1863. Reported absent taking music lessons at Richmond, Virginia, in July-August, 1863. Rejoined the company in

September-October, 1863. Reported present in November-December, 1863, and May-August, 1864. Reduced to ranks subsequent to August 31, 1864. Surrendered at Appomattox Court House, Virginia, April 9, 1865.

McRAINY, SAMUEL, Private

Born in Mecklenburg County where he resided as a farmer prior to enlisting in Mecklenburg County at age 21, March 30, 1862. Died in hospital at Petersburg, Virginia, August 17, 1862, of "febris remittens."

MANSON, WILLIAM L., 1st Sergeant

Born in Mecklenburg County where he resided as a farmer prior to enlisting in Mecklenburg County at age 29, March 14, 1862. Mustered in as Corporal. Wounded at Malvern Hill, Virginia, July 1, 1862. Returned to duty on an unspecified date. Promoted to 1st Sergeant on October 7, 1862. Reported present from November, 1862, through December, 1863, and in May-August, 1864. Captured at or near Five Forks, Virginia, on or about April 1, 1865. Confined at Point Lookout, Maryland, April 5, 1865. Released at Point Lookout on June 29, 1865, after taking the Oath of Allegiance.

MILLER, WILLIAM T., Sergeant

Resided in South Carolina and enlisted in Mecklenburg County at age 24, May 25, 1862, for the war. Mustered in as Private. Promoted to Corporal in November, 1862. Promoted to Sergeant prior to November 26, 1862, when he died in hospital at Richmond, Virginia, of "typhoid fever."

MOORE, WILLIAM W., Private

Resided in Mecklenburg County where he enlisted at age 31, May 20, 1862, for the war. Reported present from November, 1862, through December, 1863, and in May-August, 1864. Deserted to the enemy on or about November 22, 1864. Confined at Washington, D.C., November 25, 1864. Released at Washington on an unspecified date after taking the Oath of Allegiance.

MORRIS, GREEN C., Private

Resided in Mecklenburg County and enlisted at age 24, May 20, 1862, for the war. Discharged on July 27, 1862, after providing Private James A. Johnson as a substitute.

MORRIS, JOHN W., Private

Born in Mecklenburg County and resided in Union County where he was by occupation a farmer prior to enlisting in Mecklenburg County at age 33, March 13, 1862. Reported present from November, 1862, through December, 1863, and in May-August, 1864. Survived the war. [North Carolina pension records indicate that he was wounded in the hand at Petersburg, Virginia, in June, 1864.]

MORRIS, WILLIAM, Private

Born in Mecklenburg County and resided in Union County where he was by occupation a farmer prior to enlisting in Mecklenburg County at age 44, March 13, 1862. Deserted at Petersburg, Virginia, on or about August 19, 1862. Returned to duty on December 10, 1862.

Reported absent on detached service at Magnolia through June, 1863. Rejoined the company in July-August, 1863. Reported present or accounted for in September-December, 1863, and May-August, 1864. Reported missing in Virginia in early April, 1865. Survived the war. [North Carolina pension records indicate that he suffered a broken arm at Magnolia in August, 1863.]

NANNY, MARTIN, _____
North Carolina pension records indicate that he served in this company.

NEAL, LARKIN M., Sergeant
Born in Mecklenburg County where he resided as a student prior to enlisting in Mecklenburg County at age 19, April 1, 1862. Mustered in as Sergeant. Killed at Sharpsburg, Maryland, September 17, 1862.

NEEL, THOMAS W., Private
Resided in Mecklenburg County where he enlisted on May 16, 1864, for the war. Reported present in June-August, 1864. Captured at Petersburg, Virginia, April 3, 1865. Confined at Point Lookout, Maryland, April 5, 1865. Released at Point Lookout on June 15, 1865, after taking the Oath of Allegiance.

NEEL, WILLIAM B., Private
Born in Mecklenburg County where he resided as a farmer prior to enlisting in Mecklenburg County at age 28, March 30, 1862. Discharged on November 28, 1862, after providing Private William T. A. Tidwell as a substitute.

NEELY, WILLIAM AMZIE, Private
Resided in Mecklenburg County where he enlisted at age 18, August 15, 1863, for the war. Reported present in September-December, 1863. Wounded at Bermuda Hundred, Virginia, May 20, 1864. Returned to duty prior to July 1, 1864. Surrendered at Appomattox Court House, Virginia, April 9, 1865.

NEWELL, WILLIAM A., Private
Born in Lancaster District, South Carolina, and resided in Union County, North Carolina, where he was by occupation a farmer prior to enlisting in Mecklenburg County at age 31, March 12, 1862. Wounded at Malvern Hill, Virginia, July 1, 1862. Reported absent wounded through December, 1862. Returned to duty in January-February, 1863. Transferred to Company F, 35th Regiment N.C. Troops, May 29, 1863, in exchange for Private Daniel J. Johnson.

OSBORNE, JONATHAN HUDSON, Private
Born in Union County* and resided in Mecklenburg County where he was by occupation a farmer prior to enlisting in Mecklenburg County at age 37, March 14, 1862. Reported present or accounted for from November, 1862, through December, 1863. Wounded in the "lower extremities left" at Drewry's Bluff, Virginia, on or about May 13, 1864. Reported absent wounded through August, 1864. Furloughed from hospital on February 19, 1865.

PALMER, JAMES B., Private
Enlisted in Mecklenburg County on April 16, 1862, for

the war. Failed to report for duty and was dropped from the rolls of the company on or about March 1, 1863.

PAXTON, SAMUEL L., Private
Born in Union County and resided in Mecklenburg County where he was by occupation a farmer prior to enlisting in Mecklenburg County at age 17, March 19, 1862. Reported present or accounted for from November, 1862, through December, 1863. Captured (or deserted to the enemy) at Bottom's Bridge, Virginia, June 6-7, 1864. Confined at Point Lookout, Maryland, June 15, 1864. Released at Point Lookout on June 27, 1864, after taking the Oath of Allegiance and joining the U.S. Army. Assigned to Company K, 1st Regiment U.S. Volunteer Infantry.

PERRY, JACOB B., _____
North Carolina pension records indicate that he served in this company.

PHIFER, ELIJAH M., Private
Born in Mecklenburg County where he resided as a farmer prior to enlisting in Mecklenburg County at age 44, March 14, 1862. Shot in the back at Malvern Hill, Virginia, July 1, 1862. Died in hospital at Richmond, Virginia, July 25 or July 28, 1862, of wounds.

PIERCE, JOHN, Private
Born in Mecklenburg County and resided in Union County where he was by occupation a farmer prior to enlisting in Mecklenburg County at age 28, March 14, 1862. Killed at Malvern Hill, Virginia, July 1, 1862.

PIERCE, LEONIDAS M., Private
Resided in Union County and enlisted in Mecklenburg County at age 18, November 17, 1862, for the war. Reported present from November, 1862, through December, 1863. Wounded at Globe Tavern, Virginia, August 21, 1864. Hospitalized at Richmond, Virginia. Furloughed on or about August 29, 1864. Returned to duty on an unspecified date. Surrendered at Appomattox Court House, Virginia, April 9, 1865.

PORTER, ROBERT A., Private
Born in Mecklenburg County where he resided as a farmer prior to enlisting in Mecklenburg County at age 21, March 14, 1862. Wounded at Sharpsburg, Maryland, September 17, 1862. Returned to duty on an unspecified date. Reported present from November, 1862, through December, 1863. Wounded in the arm at Drewry's Bluff, Virginia, May 14, 1864. Returned to duty prior to July 1, 1864. Hospitalized at Charlotte on January 2, 1865, with chronic diarrhoea. Returned to duty on February 28, 1865. Hospitalized at Charlotte on March 3, 1865, with intermittent fever. Furloughed on April 18, 1865. Paroled at Charlotte on May 15, 1865.

PORTER, SAMUEL L., Private
Born in Mecklenburg County where he resided as a farmer prior to enlisting in Mecklenburg County at age 36, April 18, 1863, for the war. Reported present in May-December, 1863. Wounded at Drewry's Bluff, Virginia, on or about May 14, 1864. Died in hospital at Richmond,

Virginia, on or about September 14, 1864, of "diarrhoea ac[ute]."

PORTER, ZENAS, Private

Born in Mecklenburg County where he resided as a farmer prior to enlisting in Mecklenburg County at age 33, March 14, 1862. Reported present or accounted for from November, 1862, through December, 1863. Wounded at Drewry's Bluff, Virginia, May 16, 1864. Returned to duty prior to July 1, 1864. Captured at Five Forks, Virginia, April 1, 1865. Confined at Point Lookout, Maryland, April 5, 1865. Released at Point Lookout on June 16, 1865, after taking the Oath of Allegiance.

PRATHER, AUGUSTUS R., Private

Born in Mecklenburg County where he resided as a farmer prior to enlisting in Mecklenburg County at age 25, March 30, 1862. Captured at or near Sharpsburg, Maryland, on or about September 17, 1862. Paroled on or about October 4, 1862. Died in hospital at Richmond, Virginia, November 20 or November 30, 1862, of disease.

PRATHER, SILAS F., Sergeant

Born in Mecklenburg County where he resided as a merchant prior to enlisting in Mecklenburg County at age 30, March 14, 1862. Mustered in as Private. Promoted to Corporal in November, 1862. Reported present or accounted for from November, 1862, through December, 1863, and in May-August, 1864. Promoted to Sergeant on August 5, 1864. Captured at or near Five Forks, Virginia, on or about April 1, 1865. Confined at Point Lookout, Maryland, April 5, 1865. Released at Point Lookout on June 16, 1865, after taking the Oath of Allegiance.

PREVITT, ALLEN, Private

Born in Robeson County and resided in Mecklenburg County where he was by occupation a farmer prior to enlisting in Mecklenburg County at age 50, March 16, 1862. Deserted at Petersburg, Virginia, August 20, 1862. Returned from desertion on February 26, 1863. Reported present or accounted for in March-August, 1863. Discharged on October 20, 1863, by reason of "general debility and old age."

RATTERREE, WILLIAM L., Private

Resided in Mecklenburg County where he enlisted at age 39, September 7, 1863, for the war. Reported present in October-December, 1863. Wounded in the stomach at Bermuda Hundred, Virginia, June 2, 1864. Hospitalized at Petersburg, Virginia, where he died on June 6, 1864, of wounds.

REA, DAVID J., Private

Born in Mecklenburg County where he resided as a farmer prior to enlisting in Mecklenburg County at age 27, April 15, 1862. Hospitalized at Richmond, Virginia, December 6, 1862, with pneumonia. Transferred to another hospital on February 17, 1863. Returned to duty on or about March 1, 1863. Reported present in March-December, 1863. Wounded near Drewry's Bluff, Virginia, May 16, 1864. Reported absent wounded through August, 1864. No further records.

REID, WILLIAM N., Private

Resided in Mecklenburg County and enlisted at age 22, March 23, 1862. Wounded at Malvern Hill, Virginia, July 1, 1862. Died at or near Richmond, Virginia, on or about July 19, 1862, of wounds.

RICHARDSON, JAMES HIRAM, Private

Born in Mecklenburg County where he resided as a farmer prior to enlisting in Mecklenburg County at age 29, March 14, 1862. Reported present from November, 1862, through December, 1863, and in May-August, 1864. Captured at Five Forks, Virginia, April 1, 1865. Confined at Point Lookout, Maryland, April 5, 1865. Released at Point Lookout on June 19, 1865, after taking the Oath of Allegiance.

ROSS, WILLIAM A., Private

Born in Cabarrus County and resided in Mecklenburg County where he was by occupation a blacksmith prior to enlisting in Mecklenburg County at age 25, March 14, 1862. Reported present or accounted for from November, 1862, through December, 1863, and in May-August, 1864. Served as regimental blacksmith during much of the war. Survived the war.

SHAW, JONES NEWTON, Private

Born in Mecklenburg County where he resided as a farmer prior to enlisting in Mecklenburg County at age 36, March 13, 1862. Reported present or accounted for from November, 1862, through December, 1863. Hospitalized at Charlotte on May 15, 1864, with chronic pleuritis. Returned to duty on July 19, 1864. Paroled at Charlotte on May 12, 1865.

SHAW, LOCK W. A., Private

Previously served as Private in Company B, 1st Regiment N.C. Infantry (6 months, 1861). Enlisted in this company on July 19, 1864, for the war. Deserted to the enemy on or about October 26, 1864. Confined at Camp Hamilton, Virginia, November 1, 1864. Released on an unspecified date after taking the Oath of Allegiance.

SMITH, ELLISON, Private

Born in Union County* and resided in Mecklenburg County where he was by occupation a farmer prior to enlisting in Mecklenburg County at age 32, March 19, 1862. Wounded in the foot at or near Malvern Hill, Virginia, on or about July 1, 1862. Hospitalized at Richmond, Virginia. Returned to duty on an unspecified date. Wounded and captured at or near Sharpsburg, Maryland, on or about September 17, 1862. Hospitalized at Baltimore, Maryland. Confined at Fort McHenry, Maryland, February 14, 1863. Paroled and transferred to City Point, Virginia, where he was received on February 18, 1863, for exchange. Reported absent on sick furlough through October, 1863. Reported on detached service at Charlotte from November, 1863, through June, 1864. Rejoined the company in July-August, 1864. Hospitalized at Richmond on February 21, 1865, with rheumatism. Captured in hospital at Richmond on April 3, 1865. Transferred to Newport News, Virginia, April 23, 1865. Released at Newport News on June 30, 1865, after taking the Oath of Allegiance.

SMITH, WILLIAM J. B., Corporal
Born in Mecklenburg County where he resided as a
farmer prior to enlisting in Mecklenburg County at age
25, March 3, 1862. Mustered in as Private. Promoted to
Corporal on October 7, 1862. Reported present from
November, 1862, through December, 1863. Killed near
Drewry's Bluff, Virginia, May 14, 1864.

SPRATT, ANDREW PINKNEY, Private
Resided in South Carolina and enlisted in Mecklenburg
County at age 26, May 12, 1862, for the war. Captured
at Frederick, Maryland, September 12, 1862. Confined
at Fort Delaware, Delaware. Paroled and transferred to
Aiken's Landing, James River, Virginia, October 2, 1862,
for exchange. Hospitalized at Richmond, Virginia,
October 8, 1862, with carditis. Returned to duty on or
about January 26, 1863. Reported present through
December, 1863. Wounded in the right elbow at or near
Bermuda Hundred, Virginia, on or about May 19, 1864.
Hospitalized at Richmond. Detailed for duty as a hospital
nurse at Charlotte on or about October 7, 1864. Reported
on detail at Charlotte through February 7, 1865. Paroled
at Charlotte on May 3, 1865.

SQUIRES, MARCUS D., Corporal
Born in Mecklenburg County where he resided as a
farmer prior to enlisting in Mecklenburg County at age
20, March 14, 1862. Mustered in as Private. Wounded at
Malvern Hill, Virginia, July 1, 1862. Returned to duty on
an unspecified date. Reported present from November,
1862, through December, 1863, and in May-August, 1864.
Promoted to Corporal on August 5, 1864. Surrendered at
Appomattox Court House, Virginia, April 9, 1865.

STANFORD, CHARLES L., Private
Born in Mecklenburg County where he resided as a
farmer prior to enlisting in Mecklenburg County at age
37, March 4, 1862. Reported present from November,
1862, through December, 1863, and in May-August, 1864.
Survived the war.

STEPHENSON, WILLIAM J., Private
Resided in Union County and enlisted in Mecklenburg
County at age 27, April 2, 1862. Wounded at Malvern
Hill, Virginia, July 1, 1862. Reported absent wounded
through December, 1862. Reported on duty as a wagon
guard in January-February and May-June, 1863. Reported
present in July-December, 1863, and May-August, 1864.
Hospitalized at Richmond, Virginia, December 13, 1864,
with dysentery. Furloughed for sixty days on January 28,
1865.

STITT, JAMES MORRISON, Private
Resided in Union County and enlisted in Mecklenburg
County at age 27, April 19, 1862, for the war. Captured
at Frederick, Maryland, September 12, 1862. Confined
at Fort Delaware, Delaware. Paroled and transferred to
Aiken's Landing, James River, Virginia, October 2, 1862,
for exchange. Declared exchanged at Aiken's Landing on
November 10, 1862. Reported present from December,
1862, through December, 1863. Wounded in the left thigh
(fracture) at Bermuda Hundred, Virginia, June 2, 1864.
Hospitalized at Petersburg, Virginia, where he died on or
about June 5, 1864, of wounds.

SWANN, JOHN B., Private
Resided in Mecklenburg County where he enlisted on
April 15, 1864, for the war. Hospitalized at Petersburg,
Virginia, May 30, 1864, with rubeola. Transferred to
another hospital on June 18, 1864. Reported present in
July-August, 1864. Captured at Fort Stedman, Virginia,
March 25, 1865. Confined at Point Lookout, Maryland,
until released on June 20, 1865, after taking the Oath of
Allegiance.

TAYLOR, EDWARD S., Private
Resided in Mecklenburg County where he enlisted at age
44, August 13, 1863, for the war. Reported present in
September-December, 1863. Wounded accidentally on
June 4, 1864. Reported absent wounded through August,
1864. No further records.

TAYLOR, JAMES P., Private
Born in Mecklenburg County where he resided prior to
enlisting in Mecklenburg County at age 19, May 6, 1864,
for the war. Reported present in June-August, 1864.
Wounded in the breast by a shell fragment near
Petersburg, Virginia, December 19, 1864. Returned to
duty on or about February 1, 1865. Captured at Five
Forks, Virginia, April 1, 1865. Confined at Point
Lookout, Maryland, April 5, 1865. Released at Point
Lookout on June 21, 1865, after taking the Oath of
Allegiance.

TAYLOR, JOHN ARCHIBALD R., Private
Born in Mecklenburg County where he resided as a
farmer prior to enlisting in Mecklenburg County at age
27, March 30, 1862. Reported present or accounted for
from November, 1862, through February, 1863. Reported
in hospital at Charlotte in March-August, 1863. Reported
on detached service at Raleigh in September-October,
1863. Reported on detached service at Weldon in
November-December, 1863, and in May, 1864.
Hospitalized at Charlotte on June 19, 1864, with an
unspecified complaint. Furloughed on August 2, 1864.
Survived the war. [North Carolina pension records
indicate that he injured his foot in May, 1864.]

TEVEPAUGH, J. L., _____
North Carolina pension records indicate that he served
in this company.

TEVEPAUGH, WILLIAM A., Private
Born in Mecklenburg County where he resided as a
farmer prior to enlisting in Mecklenburg County at age
20, March 14, 1862. Captured at or near Sharpsburg,
Maryland, on or about September 17, 1862. Paroled on
or about October 4, 1862. Reported present from
November, 1862, through December, 1863. Killed near
Drewry's Bluff, Virginia, May 14, 1864.

TIDWELL, F. A., _____
North Carolina pension records indicate that he served
in this company.

TIDWELL, WILLIAM T. A., Private
Previously served as Private in Company E, 12th
Regiment N.C. Troops (2nd Regiment N.C. Volunteers).

Enlisted in this company in Mecklenburg County on November 28, 1862, for the war as a substitute for Private William B. Neel. Reported present from December, 1862, through December, 1863, and in May-August, 1864. Wounded ("right arm shattered") at or near Five Forks, Virginia, on or about April 1, 1865. Hospitalized at Danville, Virginia, April 3, 1865. No further records.

TURNER, FRANCIS M., Private
Resided in Mecklenburg County where he enlisted at age 25, April 16, 1862, for the war. Reported present or accounted for from November, 1862, through December, 1863, and in May-August, 1864. No further records.

WALKER, ELIJAH M., Private
Resided in Union County and enlisted in Mecklenburg County at age 22, April 29, 1862, for the war. Wounded at Sharpsburg, Maryland, September 17, 1862. Returned to duty in January-February, 1863. Reported present in March-December, 1863. Reported absent without leave in May-August, 1864.

WARWICK, JAMES MORRISON, Private
Previously served as Private in Company B, 1st Regiment N.C. Infantry (6 months, 1861). Enlisted in this company in Mecklenburg County at age 26, April 10, 1862. Wounded at Malvern Hill, Virginia, July 1, 1862. Reported absent wounded through October, 1863. Reported absent disabled by gunshot wounds in November-December, 1863, and May-August, 1864. Paroled at Charlotte on May 18, 1865.

WATSON, JAMES ADOLPHUS, Private
Born in Chester District, South Carolina, and resided in South Carolina where he was by occupation a farmer prior to enlisting in Mecklenburg County at age 30, March 28, 1862. Died at Goldsboro on May 23, 1862, of disease.

WATSON, JOHN B., Private
Born in Mecklenburg County and resided in South Carolina where he was by occupation a farmer prior to enlisting in Mecklenburg County at age 37, March 28, 1862. Wounded at Malvern Hill, Virginia, July 1, 1862. Reported in hospital at Raleigh in November-December, 1862. Returned to duty in January-February, 1863. Reported present in March-April, 1863. Reported in hospital in May-December, 1863. Transferred to 2nd Company H, 6th Regiment South Carolina Infantry, in January-June, 1864.

WATTS, J. SILAS, Private
Born in Iredell County and resided in Mecklenburg County where he was by occupation a farmer prior to enlisting in Mecklenburg County at age 26, March 14, 1862. Reported present or accounted for from November, 1862, through December, 1863. Wounded in the arm at Drewry's Bluff, Virginia, May 16, 1864. Hospitalized at Richmond, Virginia. Furloughed for sixty days on June 7, 1864. Returned to duty prior to September 1, 1864. Wounded in the right arm at Fort Stedman, Virginia, March 25, 1865. Hospitalized at Richmond. Survived the war.

WEEKS, JOSEPH L., Sergeant
Resided in Mecklenburg County where he enlisted at age 22, May 5, 1862, for the war. Mustered in as Sergeant. Wounded at Sharpsburg, Maryland, September 17, 1862. Returned to duty in January-February, 1863. Reported present in March-December, 1863. Wounded at Drewry's Bluff, Virginia, May 14, 1864. Returned to duty prior to September 1, 1864. Captured at Five Forks, Virginia, April 1, 1865. Confined at Point Lookout, Maryland, April 5, 1865. Released at Point Lookout on June 21, 1865, after taking the Oath of Allegiance.

WHITESIDES, WILLIAM H., Private
Resided in York District, South Carolina, and enlisted in Mecklenburg County at age 18, May 12, 1862, for the war. Wounded at Sharpsburg, Maryland, September 17, 1862. Reported present from November, 1862, through December, 1863, and in May-August, 1864. Wounded at or near Five Forks, Virginia, on or about April 1, 1865. No further records.

WINGATE, JOHN PLANNER, Private
Born in York District, South Carolina, and resided in Mecklenburg County where he was by occupation a farmer prior to enlisting in Mecklenburg County at age 25, March 12, 1862. Wounded at Sharpsburg, Maryland, September 17, 1862. Returned to duty on an unspecified date. Reported present from November, 1862, through December, 1863, and in May-August, 1864. Wounded at or near Petersburg, Virginia, October 13, 1864. Reported in hospital at Danville, Virginia, April 4, 1865, with pneumonia. No further records.

WINGATE, WILLIAM C., Private
Resided in Mecklenburg County and was by occupation a farmer prior to enlisting in Mecklenburg County at age 35, May 5, 1862, for the war. Hospitalized at Danville, Virginia, December 28, 1862, with debilitas. Returned to duty on February 20, 1863. Reported present through April, 1863. Reported absent in hospital in May-August, 1863. Returned to duty in September-October, 1863. Reported present in November-December, 1863. Hospitalized at Richmond, Virginia, June 5, 1864, with a gunshot wound. Place and date wounded not reported. Returned to duty on August 3, 1864. Wounded at Globe Tavern, Virginia, August 21, 1864. Returned to duty on an unspecified date. Captured at Fort Stedman, Virginia, March 25, 1865. Confined at Point Lookout, Maryland, until released on June 21, 1865, after taking the Oath of Allegiance. [North Carolina pension records indicate that he was wounded in the right hand at Petersburg, Virginia, on an unspecified date.]

WOLFE, JOHN W., Private
Born in Mecklenburg County where he resided as a farmer prior to enlisting in Mecklenburg County at age 32, March 14, 1862. Mustered in as Corporal. "Voluntarily" reduced to ranks on July 15, 1862. Reported present from November, 1862, through December, 1863, and in May-August, 1864. Hospitalized at Richmond, Virginia, October 5, 1864, with chronic colitis. Returned to duty on November 25, 1864. Surrendered at Appomattox Court House, Virginia, April 9, 1865. Served as an ambulance driver during most of the war.

COMPANY G

This company, known as the "Kings Mountain Tigers," was raised in Cleveland County and enlisted at Shelby on March 18, 1862. It was mustered into state service at Camp Mangum, near Raleigh, on April 17, 1862, and assigned to the 49th Regiment N.C. Troops as Company G. After joining the regiment the company functioned as a part of the regiment, and its history for the war period is reported as a part of the regimental history.

The information contained in the following roster was compiled primarily from a company muster-in and descriptive roll dated April 17, 1862, and from company muster rolls for November 1, 1862-December 31, 1863, and May 1-August 31, 1864. No company muster rolls were located for May 1-October 31, 1862; January 1-April 30, 1864; or for the period after August 31, 1864. Valuable information was obtained from primary records such as the North Carolina adjutant general's *Roll of Honor*, discharge certificates, medical records, prisoner of war records, *The War of the Rebellion: A Compilation of the Official Records of the Union and Confederate Armies*, militia records, newspaper casualty lists and obituaries, Confederate pension applications filed with the state of North Carolina, and the 1860 federal census of North Carolina. Secondary sources such as postwar rosters and histories, cemetery records, the *Confederate Veteran*, published genealogies, and records of the United Daughters of the Confederacy also provided useful information.

OFFICERS

CAPTAINS

ROBERTS, RUFUS
Born in Rutherford County and resided in Cleveland County where he was by occupation a farmer prior to enlisting in Cleveland County at age 33. Elected Captain on March 18, 1862. Resigned on November 17, 1862, by reason of ill health. According to one of his commanding officers, he was "wanting in discipline and capacity. . . ."

DIXON, COLUMBUS H.
Born in Lincoln County and resided in Cleveland County where he was by occupation a farmer prior to enlisting in Cleveland County at age 26. Elected 1st Lieutenant on March 18, 1862. Promoted to Captain on November 17, 1862. Reported present or accounted for from November, 1862, through December, 1863. Wounded in the arm at the Battle of the Crater, near Petersburg, Virginia, July 30, 1864. Returned to duty on an unspecified date. Killed at the Weldon Railroad, near Petersburg, December 14, 1864, "during a fierce mortar shelling."

DIXON, BENJAMIN F.
Resided in Cleveland County where he enlisted at age 18, February 25, 1863, for the war. Mustered in as Private. Reported present from November, 1862, through

December, 1863. Appointed 3rd Lieutenant on June 9, 1863. Promoted to 2nd Lieutenant on February 29, 1864. Wounded in the left forearm at Drewry's Bluff, Virginia, May 16, 1864. Reported absent wounded through August, 1864. Promoted to Captain on or about January 1, 1865. Captured at Five Forks, Virginia, April 1, 1865. Confined at Old Capitol Prison, Washington, D.C., April 5, 1865. Transferred to Johnson's Island, Ohio, April 9, 1865. Released at Johnson's Island on June 18, 1865, after taking the Oath of Allegiance.

LIEUTENANTS

COVINGTON, JOHN T., 3rd Lieutenant
Born in Rutherford County and resided in Cleveland County where he was by occupation a farmer prior to enlisting in Cleveland County at age 27, March 18, 1862. Mustered in as Private. Promoted to Corporal on May 15, 1862. Promoted to Sergeant prior to January 1, 1863. Promoted to 1st Sergeant on January 1, 1863. Reported present from November, 1862, through December, 1863, and in May-August, 1864. Appointed 3rd Lieutenant on July 18, 1864. Captured at Fort Stedman, Virginia, March 25, 1865. Confined at Old Capitol Prison, Washington, D.C. Transferred to Fort Delaware, Delaware, March 30, 1865. Released at Fort Delaware on June 17, 1865, after taking the Oath of Allegiance. [May have been wounded in Virginia in May-October, 1864.]

FALLS, ALFRED V., 2nd Lieutenant
Born in Lincoln County and resided in Cleveland County where he was by occupation a farmer prior to enlisting in Cleveland County at age 43. Elected 2nd Lieutenant on March 18, 1862. Resigned on an unspecified date. Reason he resigned not reported. Resignation accepted on May 15, 1862.

FULTON, JAMES PRESTON, 2nd Lieutenant
Born in York District, South Carolina, and resided in Cleveland County, North Carolina, where he was by occupation a farmer prior to enlisting in Cleveland County at age 27. Elected 2nd Lieutenant on March 18, 1862. Killed at Sharpsburg, Maryland, September 17, 1862.

HERRINGTON, LEONARD A., 2nd Lieutenant
Born in Williamsburg District, South Carolina, and resided in Cleveland County, North Carolina, where he was by occupation a merchant prior to enlisting in Cleveland County at age 21, March 18, 1862. Mustered in as 1st Sergeant. Elected 2nd Lieutenant on or about May 12, 1862. Killed at Sharpsburg, Maryland, September 17, 1862.

HORAN, GEORGE P., 1st Lieutenant
Previously served as 3rd Lieutenant of 1st Company D, 15th Regiment N.C. Troops (5th Regiment N.C. Volunteers). Enlisted in this company in Cleveland County on March 18, 1862. Mustered in as Corporal. Elected 2nd Lieutenant on October 7, 1862. Promoted to 1st Lieutenant on November 17, 1862. Reported present or accounted for from December, 1862, through

December, 1863. Resigned on February 16, 1864. Reason he resigned not reported; however, in a notation on his letter of resignation Colonel L. M. McAfee of the 49th Regiment stated that "the service will be benefited by the acceptance of this resignation." Resignation accepted on February 29, 1864.

WEAVER, SYLVESTER J., 1st Lieutenant
Born in Rutherford County and resided in Cleveland County where he was by occupation a farmer prior to enlisting in Cleveland County at age 22, March 18, 1862. Mustered in as Corporal. Promoted to 1st Sergeant on an unspecified date. Appointed 3rd Lieutenant on December 29, 1862. Promoted to 2nd Lieutenant on or about February 25, 1863. Reported present from November, 1862, through December, 1863. Promoted to 1st Lieutenant on February 29, 1864. Reported present in May-August, 1864. Captured at Five Forks, Virginia, April 1, 1865. Confined at Old Capitol Prison, Washington, D.C., April 5, 1865. Transferred to Johnson's Island, Ohio, April 9, 1865. Released at Johnson's Island on June 20, 1865, after taking the Oath of Allegiance.

NONCOMMISSIONED OFFICERS AND PRIVATES

ADAMS, N. H., Private
Born in Lincoln County and resided in Cleveland County where he was by occupation a carpenter prior to enlisting in Cleveland County at age 33, March 18, 1862. Deserted at Drewry's Bluff, Virginia, on or about July 25, 1862.

ALEXANDER, T. P., Private
Born in Cleveland County where he resided as a farmer prior to enlisting in Cleveland County at age 18, March 18, 1862. Reported present or accounted for from November, 1862, through December, 1863, and in May-August, 1864. Detailed for duty as a hospital nurse at Richmond, Virginia, November 14, 1864. Captured in hospital at Richmond on April 3, 1865. Paroled on or about April 18, 1865.

ALLEN, DAVID, JR., Private
Resided in Cleveland County and was by occupation a farm laborer. Place and date of enlistment not reported; however, he probably enlisted subsequent to August 31, 1864. Was about 35 years of age at time of enlistment. Captured at Fort Stedman, Virginia, March 25, 1865. Confined at Point Lookout, Maryland, until released on June 22, 1865, after taking the Oath of Allegiance.

ALLEN, LARKIN, Private
Resided in Cleveland County and was by occupation a farm laborer prior to enlisting in Cleveland County at age 42, August 13, 1863, for the war. Reported present in September-December, 1863, and May-June, 1864. Reported absent wounded in July-August, 1864. Place and date wounded not reported. Hospitalized at Richmond, Virginia, October 28, 1864, with an unspecified complaint (probably intermittent fever). Returned to duty on December 29, 1864. No further records.

ALLEN, M. A., Private
Born in Cleveland County where he resided as a farmer prior to enlisting in Cleveland County at age 18, March 18, 1862. Wounded at Sharpsburg, Maryland, September 17, 1862. Reported absent without leave in November-December, 1862. Reported absent sick in January-June, 1863. Returned to duty in July-August, 1863. Reported present in September-December, 1863, and May-August, 1864. Hospitalized at Petersburg, Virginia, December 15, 1864, with a gunshot wound of the left femur. Place and date wounded not reported. Died in hospital at Petersburg on December 27, 1864, presumably of wounds.

ALLEN, WILLIAM S., Private
Born in Cleveland County where he resided as a farmer prior to enlisting in Cleveland County at age 17, March 18, 1862, as a substitute. Reported absent without leave on September 5, 1862. Returned to duty on February 10, 1863. Deserted on June 12, 1863. Arrested on June 17, 1863, and was confined at Castle Thunder Prison, Richmond, Virginia. Reported in confinement at Richmond through December, 1863. Returned to duty on an unspecified date. Reported present in May-August, 1864. Paroled at Farmville, Virginia, April 11-21, 1865.

BARBER, W. G., Private
Enlisted in Cleveland County on March 1, 1864, for the war. Reported present in May-August, 1864. Died in hospital at Richmond, Virginia, on or about September 12, 1864, of "colitis chron[ic]."

BARNES, HARVEY A., Private
Resided in Cleveland County where he enlisted on February 25, 1864, for the war. Reported present in May-August, 1864. Captured at Fort Stedman, Virginia, March 25, 1865. Confined at Point Lookout, Maryland, until released on June 23, 1865, after taking the Oath of Allegiance.

BARRETT, PERRY, Private
Resided in Cleveland County where he enlisted at age 16, November 10, 1862, as a substitute for Private John Edmond Roberts of this company. Reported present or accounted for from November, 1862, through December, 1863, and in May-August, 1864. Wounded in the head near Petersburg, Virginia, in September-October, 1864. Returned to duty on an unspecified date. Captured at or near Five Forks, Virginia, on or about April 1, 1865. Confined at Point Lookout, Maryland, April 5, 1865. Released at Point Lookout on June 23, 1865, after taking the Oath of Allegiance.

BEACH, THOMAS E., _____
North Carolina pension records indicate that he served in this company.

BEASON, ARCHIBALD, Private
Previously served as Private in Company K of this regiment. Transferred to this company on or about October 1, 1862. Reported present from November, 1862, through December, 1863, and in May-August, 1864.

BIRD, WILLIAM H., Private
Resided in Cleveland County where he enlisted at age 30,

August 13, 1863, for the war. Reported present in September-December, 1863. Reported absent wounded in May-August, 1864. Place and date wounded not reported. Hospitalized at Richmond, Virginia, February 28, 1865, with a gunshot wound of the right lung. Place and date wounded not reported. Captured in hospital at Richmond on April 3, 1865. Died in hospital at Richmond on May 11, 1865, of "chronic diarrhoea."

BLACK, SAMUEL A., Private
Born in York District, South Carolina, and resided in Cleveland County, North Carolina, where he was by occupation a farmer prior to enlisting in Cleveland County at age 38, March 18, 1862. Wounded at Fredericksburg, Virginia, December 13, 1862. Returned to duty prior to January 1, 1863. Reported present or accounted for in January-December, 1863, and May-August, 1864. Surrendered at Appomattox Court House, Virginia, April 9, 1865.

BRIDGES, JOHN L., 1st Sergeant
Born in York District, South Carolina, and resided in Cleveland County, North Carolina, where he was by occupation a farmer prior to enlisting in Cleveland County at age 30, March 18, 1862. Mustered in as Sergeant. Reported present from November, 1862, through December, 1863, and in May-August, 1864. Promoted to 1st Sergeant on July 18, 1864. Captured at Fort Stedman, Virginia, March 25, 1865. Confined at Point Lookout, Maryland, until released on June 23, 1865, after taking the Oath of Allegiance.

CALK, FATE, Private
Place and date of enlistment not reported; however, he probably enlisted subsequent to August 31, 1864. Captured at Five Forks, Virginia, April 1, 1865. Confined at Point Lookout, Maryland, April 5, 1865. Died at Point Lookout on or about June 13, 1865. Cause of death not reported.

CAMP, L. A., Private
Born in Lincoln County and resided in Cleveland County where he was by occupation a shoemaker prior to enlisting in Cleveland County at age 32, March 18, 1862. Reported present or accounted for from November, 1862, through December, 1863, and in May-August, 1864. Surrendered at Appomattox Court House, Virginia, April 9, 1865. Served as a harnessmaker, shoemaker, and teamster at various times during the war.

CARPENTER, WILLIAM A. J., Sergeant
Born in Lincoln County and resided in Cleveland County where he was by occupation a farmer prior to enlisting in Cleveland County at age 40, March 18, 1862. Mustered in as Private. Reported present or accounted for from November, 1862, through December, 1863, and in May-August, 1864. Promoted to Sergeant subsequent to August 31, 1864. Captured at Five Forks, Virginia, April 1, 1865. Confined at Point Lookout, Maryland, April 5, 1865. Released at Point Lookout on June 24, 1865, after taking the Oath of Allegiance. Served in the ambulance corps during much of the war.

COBB, JOHN H., Private
Resided in Cleveland County where he enlisted at age 26, February 25, 1863, for the war. Reported present or accounted for in March-December, 1863, and May-August, 1864. Captured at Five Forks, Virginia, April 1, 1865. Confined at Point Lookout, Maryland, April 5, 1865. Released at Point Lookout on June 24, 1865, after taking the Oath of Allegiance.

COBB, R. J., Private
Resided in Cleveland County where he enlisted at age 18, February 25, 1863, for the war. Reported present in March-December, 1863, and May-August, 1864. Deserted to the enemy on or about February 21, 1865. Confined at Washington, D.C., February 24, 1865. Released on an unspecified date after taking the Oath of Allegiance.

COBB, WILLIAM WESLEY, JR., Private
Born in Lincoln County and resided in Cleveland County where he enlisted at age 15, March 18, 1862. Wounded at Sharpsburg, Maryland, September 17, 1862. Returned to duty on an unspecified date. Reported present from November, 1862, through December, 1863, and in May-August, 1864. Captured at Fort Stedman, Virginia, March 25, 1865. Confined at Point Lookout, Maryland, until released on June 26, 1865, after taking the Oath of Allegiance.

COLLINS, JOHN S., Private
Born in Cleveland County where he resided as a farmer prior to enlisting in Cleveland County at age 20, March 18, 1862. Reported present or accounted for from November, 1862, through December, 1863, and in May-August, 1864. Hospitalized at Richmond, Virginia, on or about August 29, 1864, with chronic diarrhoea. Returned to duty on October 1, 1864. Captured at Fort Stedman, Virginia, March 25, 1865. Confined at Point Lookout, Maryland, March 29, 1865. Released at Point Lookout on June 26, 1865, after taking the Oath of Allegiance.

COLLINS, MARTIN, Private
Resided in Cleveland County and was by occupation a farmer prior to enlisting in Cleveland County at age 27, March 18, 1862. Died in hospital at Petersburg, Virginia, June 28, 1862, of "febris remittens."

COSTNER, A. W., Private
Born in Lincoln County and resided in Cleveland County where he was by occupation a farmer prior to enlisting in Cleveland County at age 29, March 18, 1862. Reported present from November, 1862, through December, 1863, and in May-August, 1864. Deserted to the enemy on or about February 21, 1865. Confined at Washington, D.C., February 24, 1865. Released on an unspecified date after taking the Oath of Allegiance.

CRAWFORD, R. N., Private
Enlisted in Cleveland County on June 4, 1864, for the war. Killed "in Virginia" on July 8, 1864.

CULP, JOHN H., Private
Born in Chester District, South Carolina, and was by occupation a schoolteacher prior to enlisting in Cleveland

County, North Carolina, at age 33, March 18, 1862. Rejected for service. Reason he was rejected not reported.

CULP, L. A., Private
Resided in Cleveland County where he enlisted at age 18, August 6, 1863, for the war. Reported present in September-December, 1863, and May-August, 1864. Hospitalized at Richmond, Virginia, December 8, 1864, with acute bronchitis. Returned to duty on December 13, 1864. No further records.

DAVIS, DRURY DOBBINS, Private
Born in Cleveland County* where he resided as a farmer prior to enlisting in Cleveland County at age 25, March 18, 1862. Reported missing at Malvern Hill, Virginia, July 1, 1862. Returned to duty on an unspecified date. Reported present from November, 1862, through December, 1863, and in May-June, 1864. Deserted to the enemy while on picket duty on or about July 10, 1864. Confined at Old Capitol Prison, Washington, D.C. Transferred to Elmira, New York, July 23, 1864. Died at Elmira on February 7, 1865, of "variola."

DAVIS, JOHN B., Corporal
Born in Lincoln County and resided in Cleveland County where he was by occupation a farmer prior to enlisting in Cleveland County at age 41, March 18, 1862. Mustered in as Corporal. Wounded at Sharpsburg, Maryland, September 17, 1862. Reported absent without leave in November-December, 1862. Reported sick in hospital at Goldsboro in January-February, 1863. Died in hospital at Goldsboro on May 2, 1863, of "smallpox."

DEAL, DANIEL, Private
Place and date of enlistment not reported; however, he probably enlisted subsequent to August 31, 1864. Paroled at Salisbury on May 22, 1865.

DICKSON, JAMES A., Private
Resided in Cleveland County and was by occupation a wagonmaker. Place and date of enlistment not reported; however, he probably enlisted subsequent to August 31, 1864. Was about 29 years of age at time of enlistment. Captured at Five Forks, Virginia, April 1, 1865. Confined at Point Lookout, Maryland, April 5, 1865. Released at Point Lookout on June 26, 1865, after taking the Oath of Allegiance.

DILLINGER, J. D., Private
Resided in Cleveland County where he enlisted on November 20, 1863, for the war. Wounded in the leg at the Battle of the Crater, near Petersburg, Virginia, July 30, 1864. Returned to duty prior to September 1, 1864. Captured at Five Forks, Virginia, April 1, 1865. Confined at Point Lookout, Maryland, April 5, 1865. Released at Point Lookout on June 26, 1865, after taking the Oath of Allegiance.

DILLINGHAM, A. G., Private
Born in Lincoln County and resided in Cleveland County where he was by occupation a farmer prior to enlisting in Cleveland County at age 31, March 18, 1862. Died at Raleigh on June 18, 1862, of disease.

DIXON, WILLIAM, JR., Private
Resided in Cleveland County where he enlisted at age 37, May 5, 1862, for the war. Hospitalized at Petersburg, Virginia, August 19, 1862, with acute rheumatism. Returned to duty on November 14, 1862. Reported absent sick from December, 1862, through October, 1863. Returned to duty in November-December, 1863. Reported present in May-August, 1864. Captured at or near Five Forks, Virginia, on or about April 1, 1865. Confined at Point Lookout, Maryland, April 13, 1865. Released at Point Lookout on June 26, 1865, after taking the Oath of Allegiance.

DIXON, WILLIAM W., Private
Resided in Cleveland County and was by occupation a farmer prior to enlisting in Cleveland County at age 39, February 25, 1863, for the war. Reported present in March-December, 1863, and May-August, 1864. Deserted to the enemy on or about February 21, 1865. Confined at Washington, D.C., February 24, 1865. Released on an unspecified date after taking the Oath of Allegiance.

EARL, B. G., Private
Born in Lincoln County and resided in Cleveland County where he was by occupation a farmer prior to enlisting in Cleveland County at age 27, March 18, 1862. Died at Raleigh on June 15, 1862, of disease.

EARL, L. G., Private
Born in Lincoln County and resided in Cleveland County where he was by occupation a farmer prior to enlisting in Cleveland County at age 20, March 18, 1862. Reported present or accounted for from November, 1862, through December, 1863, and in May-August, 1864. Deserted to the enemy on or about February 21, 1865. Confined at Washington, D.C., February 24, 1865. Released on an unspecified date after taking the Oath of Allegiance.

EARLES, JOHN, Private
Resided in Cleveland County and enlisted at age 21, May 5, 1862, for the war. Died at Goldsboro on June 18, 1862. Cause of death not reported.

EARLS, ISAAC H., Private
Resided in Cleveland County where he enlisted at age 18, February 25, 1863, for the war. Reported present in March-December, 1863, and May-August, 1864. Surrendered at Appomattox Court House, Virginia, April 9, 1865.

ETTERS, HENRY, Private
Resided in Cleveland County and was by occupation a farmer prior to enlisting in Cleveland County at age 36, February 25, 1863, for the war. Reported present in March-December, 1863, and May-August, 1864. Wounded in the left arm by a shell near Petersburg, Virginia, October 25, 1864. Left arm amputated. Retired from service on February 21, 1865.

FALLS, FRANCIS M., Private
Resided in Cleveland County where he enlisted at age 16, March 1, 1864, for the war. Reported present in May-August, 1864. Captured at Fort Stedman, Virginia, March

25, 1865. Confined at Point Lookout, Maryland, until released on June 26, 1865, after taking the Oath of Allegiance.

FALLS, J. C., Private

Resided in Cleveland County where he enlisted at age 18, August 13, 1863, for the war. Reported present in September-December, 1863, and May-August, 1864.

FALLS, JAMES F., Corporal

Born in Lincoln County and resided in Cleveland County where he was by occupation a farmer prior to enlisting in Cleveland County at age 26, March 18, 1862. Mustered in as Sergeant. Reduced to ranks on October 1, 1862. Reported absent without leave in November-December, 1862. Reported present in January-December, 1863, and May-August, 1864. Promoted to Corporal prior to April 1, 1865, when he was captured at Five Forks, Virginia. Confined at Point Lookout, Maryland, until released on June 26, 1865, after taking the Oath of Allegiance.

FALLS, JAMES H., Private

Resided in Cleveland County where he enlisted at age 32, May 5, 1862, for the war. Reported present from November, 1862, through December, 1863. Hospitalized at Richmond, Virginia, March 9, 1864, with "consolidation l[eft] lung." Furloughed for sixty days on March 29, 1865. Wounded in the head at the Battle of the Crater, near Petersburg, Virginia, July 30, 1864. Returned to duty prior to September 1, 1864. Captured at Fort Stedman, Virginia, March 25, 1865. Confined at Point Lookout, Maryland, until released on June 26, 1865, after taking the Oath of Allegiance. [North Carolina pension records indicate that he was wounded near Petersburg on September 1, 1863.]

FORTENBERRY, WILLIAM, Private

Born in Cleveland County where he resided as a farmer prior to enlisting in Cleveland County at age 19, March 18, 1862. Discharged on October 5, 1862, by reason of "chronic disease of the spleen & stomach, and a state of general anemia. . . ." Reenlisted in the company on an unspecified date (probably subsequent to August 31, 1864). Captured at Fort Stedman, Virginia, March 25, 1865. Confined at Point Lookout, Maryland, until released on June 26, 1865, after taking the Oath of Allegiance.

FRANCIS, T. A., Private

Resided in Cleveland County and was by occupation a master carpenter prior to enlisting in Cleveland County at age 37, May 5, 1862, for the war. Hospitalized at Petersburg, Virginia, July 22, 1862, with typhoid fever. Returned to duty on November 16, 1862. Reported present or accounted for from December, 1862, through December, 1863, and in May-August, 1864. Reported on duty as a wheelwright in October-December, 1864. Surrendered at Appomattox Court House, Virginia, April 9, 1865.

FULTON, HORATIO D., Sergeant

Born in York District, South Carolina, and resided in Cleveland County, North Carolina, where he was by occupation a farmer prior to enlisting in Cleveland

County at age 24, March 18, 1862. Mustered in as Sergeant. Reported absent sick from November, 1862, through April, 1863. Returned to duty in May-June, 1863. Reported present or accounted for in July-December, 1863, and May-June, 1864. Reported absent wounded in July-August, 1864. Survived the war.

GAMBLE, W. F., Corporal

Born in Cleveland County where he resided as a farmer prior to enlisting in Cleveland County at age 17, March 18, 1862. Mustered in as Private. Reported present from November, 1862, through December, 1863. Promoted to Corporal on January 1, 1864. Reported present in May-August, 1864. Deserted to the enemy on or about February 21, 1865. Confined at Washington, D.C., February 24, 1865. Released on an unspecified date after taking the Oath of Allegiance.

GARDNER, DANIEL, Private

Born in Union County* and resided in Cleveland County where he was by occupation a farmer prior to enlisting in Cleveland County at age 46, March 18, 1862. Deserted on September 17, 1862. Returned from desertion on or about November 12, 1862. Court-martialed on December 28, 1862, and sentenced to be shot. Sentence remitted. Reported sick in hospital at Richmond, Virginia, in January-February, 1863. Returned to duty in March-April, 1863. Reported present or accounted for in May-December, 1863, and May-August, 1864. Captured at Five Forks, Virginia, April 1, 1865. Confined at Point Lookout, Maryland, April 5, 1865. Died at Point Lookout on June 21, 1865, of "chronic diarrh[oea]."

GARDNER, JAMES L., Private

Born in Cleveland County* where he resided as a schoolteacher prior to enlisting in Cleveland County at age 45, March 18, 1862. Died in hospital at Raleigh on July 31, 1862, of disease.

GARDNER, R. M., _____

North Carolina pension records indicate that he served in this company.

GIBBONS, A. I., Private

Place and date of enlistment not reported; however, he probably enlisted subsequent to August 31, 1864. Surrendered at Appomattox Court House, Virginia, April 9, 1865.

GIBBONS, JOHN H., Private

Born in Cleveland County where he resided as a farmer prior to enlisting in Cleveland County at age 16, March 18, 1862, as a substitute for his father. Reported present from November, 1862, through December, 1863, and in May-August, 1864. Died in Virginia on October 20, 1864, of disease.

GILL, G. R., Private

Resided in Cleveland County and was by occupation a farm laborer prior to enlisting in Cleveland County at age 37, February 25, 1863, for the war. Reported present in March-December, 1863. Wounded in the head near Petersburg, Virginia, June 21-27, 1864. Died in hospital at Petersburg on June 27, 1864, of wounds.

GLADDEN, HENRY J., Private
Born in Lincoln County and resided in Cleveland County where he was by occupation a farm laborer prior to enlisting in Cleveland County at age 41, March 18, 1862. Died in hospital at Richmond, Virginia, on or about January 5, 1863, of "pneumonia."

GLADDEN, RUFUS C., Private
Resided in Cleveland County where he enlisted at age 31, May 5, 1862, for the war. Reported absent sick from November, 1862, through December, 1863. Reported absent without leave in April-June, 1864. Reported absent sick in July-August, 1864. Survived the war.

GOFORTH, A. J., Private
Born in Cleveland County where he resided as a farmer prior to enlisting in Cleveland County at age 19, March 18, 1862. Reported present from November, 1862, through December, 1863, and in May-August, 1864. Deserted to the enemy on or about March 6, 1865. Confined at Washington, D.C., March 10, 1865. Released on an unspecified date after taking the Oath of Allegiance.

GOFORTH, G. W., Musician
Born in Cleveland County where he resided as a farmer prior to enlisting in Cleveland County at age 18, March 18, 1862. Mustered in as Private. Appointed Musician prior to March 1, 1863. Reported present or accounted for from November, 1862, through December, 1863, and in May-June, 1864. Died in hospital at Richmond, Virginia, August 7, 1864, of disease.

GOFORTH, HENRY P., Private
Previously served as Private in 2nd Company K, 5th Regiment South Carolina Infantry. Transferred to this company on August 8, 1864. Reported present in July-August, 1864. Deserted to the enemy on or about February 21, 1865. Confined at Washington, D.C., February 24, 1865. Released on an unspecified date after taking the Oath of Allegiance.

GOFORTH, ISAAC W., Sergeant
Born in Lincoln County and resided in Cleveland County where he was by occupation a farmer prior to enlisting in Cleveland County at age 27, March 18, 1862. Mustered in as Sergeant. Killed at Sharpsburg, Maryland, September 17, 1862.

GOFORTH, JOHN WESLEY, Corporal
Born in Cleveland County* where he resided as a farmer prior to enlisting in Cleveland County at age 22, March 18, 1862. Mustered in as Private. Promoted to Corporal on January 1, 1863. Reported present from November, 1862, through December, 1863, and in May-August, 1864. Captured at Fort Stedman, Virginia, March 25, 1865. Confined at Point Lookout, Maryland, until released on June 27, 1865, after taking the Oath of Allegiance.

GOFORTH, SAMUEL, Private
Resided in Cleveland County and was by occupation a miller. Place and date of enlistment not reported; however, he probably enlisted subsequent to August 31, 1864. Was about 43 years of age at time of enlistment.

Captured at Five Forks, Virginia, April 1, 1865. Confined at Point Lookout, Maryland, April 5, 1865. Released at Point Lookout on June 27, 1865, after taking the Oath of Allegiance.

GOFORTH, WASH LaFAYETTE, Private
Resided in Cleveland County where he enlisted at age 18, February 25, 1863, for the war. Reported present from November, 1862, through December, 1863, and in May-August, 1864. Captured at Fort Stedman, Virginia, March 25, 1865. Confined at Point Lookout, Maryland, until released on June 27, 1865, after taking the Oath of Allegiance.

GOFORTH, WILLIAM C., Private
Resided in Cleveland County and was by occupation a farmer prior to enlisting in Cleveland County at age 28, March 18, 1862. Wounded in the right lung and captured at Sharpsburg, Maryland, September 17, 1862. Received for exchange at Aiken's Landing, James River, Virginia, November 2, 1862. Hospitalized at Richmond, Virginia, where he died on November 16, 1862, of wounds.

HANCE, THOMAS W., Private
Resided in Cleveland County where he enlisted at age 18, August 13, 1863, for the war. Reported present in September-December, 1863, and May-August, 1864. Captured at Fort Stedman, Virginia, March 25, 1865. Confined at Point Lookout, Maryland, until released on June 4, 1865, after taking the Oath of Allegiance.

HARDIN, R. H., Private
Resided in Cleveland County where he enlisted at age 23, March 18, 1862. Reported present in November-December, 1862. Died in hospital at Wilmington on March 6, 1863. Cause of death not reported.

HARDIN, THOMAS C., Private
Resided in Cleveland County where he enlisted at age 19, May 5, 1862, for the war. Reported present or accounted for from November, 1862, through December, 1863, and in May-August, 1864. Surrendered at Appomattox Court House, Virginia, April 9, 1865. Served as a teamster and wagon guard during much of the war.

HARMON, JOHN G., Private
Born in Lincoln County and resided in Cleveland County where he was by occupation a blacksmith prior to enlisting in Cleveland County at age 46, March 18, 1862. Reported absent sick in November-December, 1862. Hospitalized at Richmond, Virginia, January 7, 1863, with typhoid pneumonia. Transferred to Huguenot Springs, Virginia, January 16, 1863. Returned to duty subsequent to August 31, 1864. Captured at Fort Stedman, Virginia, March 25, 1865. Confined at Point Lookout, Maryland, where he died on April 11, 1865, of "inflammation of lungs."

HARMON, SAMUEL, Private
Resided in Cleveland County and was by occupation a farmer prior to enlisting in Cleveland County at age 38, February 25, 1863, for the war. Reported present in March-December, 1863, and May-August, 1864. Captured

at Fort Stedman, Virginia, March 25, 1865. Confined at Point Lookout, Maryland, until released on June 27, 1865, after taking the Oath of Allegiance.

HARMON, T. W., Corporal
Born in Lincoln County and resided in Cleveland County where he was by occupation a farmer prior to enlisting in Cleveland County at age 29, March 18, 1862. Mustered in as Musician (Drummer). Reduced to ranks prior to March 1, 1863. Promoted to Corporal on or about March 1, 1863. Reported present or accounted for from November, 1862, through December, 1863. Wounded in the right leg at Drewry's Bluff, Virginia, on or about May 16, 1864. Hospitalized at Richmond, Virginia. Furloughed for sixty days on May 27, 1864. Detailed as a hospital attendant at Raleigh on July 27, 1864. Captured in hospital at Raleigh on April 13, 1865. Paroled on an unspecified date.

HARMON, W. W., Private
Resided in Cleveland County where he enlisted at age 22, March 18, 1862. Reported present from November, 1862, through December, 1863, and in May-June, 1864. Killed at Globe Tavern, Virginia, August 21, 1864.

HARMON, WILLIAM HENRY, Private
Born in Cleveland or Gaston* County and resided in Cleveland County where he was by occupation a farmer prior to enlisting in Cleveland County at age 20, March 18, 1862. Reported present from November, 1862, through December, 1863, and in May-August, 1864. Deserted to the enemy on or about February 21, 1865. Confined at Washington, D.C., February 24, 1865. Released on an unspecified date after taking the Oath of Allegiance.

HARRIS, ROBERT W., Private
Resided in Cleveland County and was by occupation a master mechanic prior to enlisting in Cleveland County at age 52, May 5, 1862, for the war as a substitute. Reported present or accounted for from November, 1862, through December, 1863, and in May-August, 1864. Hospitalized at Richmond, Virginia, March 15, 1865, with debilitas. Transferred to Farmville, Virginia, April 1, 1865. Paroled at Lynchburg, Virginia, April 15, 1865.

HAYES, JONATHAN J., Private
Resided in Cleveland County where he enlisted at age 28, on or about February 25, 1863, for the war. Reported present in July-December, 1863. Reported sick in hospital in May-August, 1864. Died in hospital at Richmond, Virginia, on or about September 10, 1864, of "colitis chronic."

HAYS, JAMES J., Private
Born in Lincoln County and resided in Cleveland County where he was by occupation a shoemaker prior to enlisting in Cleveland County at age 30, March 18, 1862. Reported absent without leave in November-December, 1862. Reported present in January-December, 1863. Reported sick in hospital at Charlotte in May-June, 1864. Reported on duty as a hospital attendant at Charlotte in July-August, 1864.

HAYS, W. D., Private
Born in York District, South Carolina, and resided in Cleveland County, North Carolina, where he was by occupation a farmer prior to enlisting in Cleveland County at age 21, March 18, 1862. Hospitalized at Richmond, Virginia, December 10, 1862. Died in hospital at Richmond on February 21, 1863, of "chr[onic] diarrhoea."

HOPPER, CLAYTON C., Private
Resided in Cleveland County. Place and date of enlistment not reported; however, he probably enlisted subsequent to August 31, 1864. Captured at Fort Stedman, Virginia, March 25, 1865. Confined at Point Lookout, Maryland, until released on June 13, 1865, after taking the Oath of Allegiance.

HOWELL, JOHN J., Private
Resided in Cleveland County where he enlisted at age 18, May 5, 1862, for the war. Reported present or accounted for from November, 1862, through December, 1863, and in May-August, 1864. Captured at Five Forks, Virginia, April 1, 1865. Confined at Point Lookout, Maryland, April 5, 1865. Released at Point Lookout on June 27, 1865, after taking the Oath of Allegiance.

HOWELL, S. H., Private
Resided in Cleveland County where he enlisted at age 24, May 5, 1862, for the war. Reported present from November, 1862, through December, 1863, and in May-August, 1864. Wounded in the right lung at Fort Stedman, Virginia, March 25, 1865. Hospitalized at Petersburg, Virginia. Died in hospital at Petersburg on April 9-10, 1865, of wounds.

HOWELL, THOMAS, Private
Born in Cleveland County* where he resided as a farmer prior to enlisting in Cleveland County at age 27, March 18, 1862. Wounded at Sharpsburg, Maryland, September 17, 1862. Hospitalized at Richmond, Virginia. Furloughed on September 30, 1862. Reported absent without leave in November-December, 1862. Returned to duty in January-February, 1863. Reported present in March-December, 1863, and May-June, 1864. Wounded in the arm at the Battle of the Crater, near Petersburg, Virginia, July 30, 1864. Died on August 22, 1864, of wounds. Place of death not reported.

HOWELL, W. E., Private
Enlisted in Cleveland County on April 1, 1864, for the war. Reported present in May-June, 1864. Died in hospital at Richmond, Virginia, on or about August 2, 1864, of disease.

HOWSER, D. R., Private
Born in York District, South Carolina, and resided in South Carolina where he was by occupation a farmer prior to enlisting in Cleveland County, North Carolina, at age 23, March 18, 1862. Reported present or accounted for from November, 1862, through December, 1863, and in May-June, 1864. Died on August 4, 1864, of disease. Place of death not reported.

HUFFSTETLER, ALEXANDER CALEB, Private
Resided in Cleveland County and was by occupation a farmer prior to enlisting in Cleveland County at age 34, May 5, 1862, for the war. Captured at Malvern Hill, Virginia, July 1, 1862. Confined at Fort Columbus, New York Harbor, July 6, 1862. Transferred to Fort Delaware, Delaware, July 9, 1862. Paroled and transferred to Aiken's Landing, James River, Virginia, where he was received on July 12, 1862, for exchange. Declared exchanged at Aiken's Landing on August 5, 1862. Returned to duty on an unspecified date. Reported present from November, 1862, through December, 1863, and in May-August, 1864. Deserted to the enemy on or about February 24, 1865. Confined at Washington, D.C., February 27, 1865. Released on an unspecified date after taking the Oath of Allegiance.

HUFFSTETLER, EPHRAIM C., Private
Resided in Gaston County and enlisted at age 17 in the autumn of 1864 for the war. Captured at Five Forks, Virginia, April 1, 1865. Confined at Point Lookout, Maryland, April 5, 1865. Released at Point Lookout on June 13, 1865, after taking the Oath of Allegiance.

KANIPE, JOHN, Private
Born in Lincoln County and resided in Cleveland County where he was by occupation a glazier prior to enlisting in Cleveland County at age 38, March 18, 1862. Reported present or accounted for from November, 1862, through December, 1863, and in May-July, 1864. Killed (probably near Petersburg, Virginia) on August 3, 1864.

LACKEY, J. A., Private
Born in Cleveland County where he resided as a farmer prior to enlisting in Cleveland County at age 17, March 18, 1862. Wounded at Malvern Hill, Virginia, July 1, 1862. Detailed as a hospital nurse at Winchester, Virginia, September 10, 1862. Died at Richmond, Virginia, prior to March 1, 1863, of wounds received at Malvern Hill.

LONG, R. J., Private
Resided in Cleveland County where he enlisted at age 21, May 5, 1862, for the war. Reported absent sick from November, 1862, through October, 1863. Died in hospital at Wilson on November 20, 1863, of "febris typhoides."

LOWERY, WILLIAM, Private
Resided in Cleveland County and was by occupation a farmer. Place and date of enlistment not reported; however, he probably enlisted subsequent to August 31, 1864. Was about 42 years of age at time of enlistment. Captured at Fort Stedman, Virginia, March 25, 1865. Confined at Point Lookout, Maryland, until released on or about June 29, 1865, after taking the Oath of Allegiance.

LYNN, S. M., Private
Enlisted in Cleveland County on March 1, 1864, for the war. Reported present in May-August, 1864. Deserted to the enemy on or about February 21, 1865. Confined at Washington, D.C., February 24, 1865. Released on an unspecified date after taking the Oath of Allegiance.

McAFEE, AUGUST A., Private
Enlisted as Private in Company E, 12th Regiment N.C. Troops (2nd Regiment N.C. Volunteers), April 22, 1861; however, he was rejected for service with that unit because of general disability. Enlisted in this company at age 21, August 13, 1863, for the war. Reported present or accounted for in September-December, 1863, and May-August, 1864. Assigned to light duty as a clerk during much of the war.

McDANIEL, DAVID, Private
Born in York District, South Carolina, and resided in Cleveland County, North Carolina, where he was by occupation a farmer prior to enlisting in Cleveland County at age 45, March 18, 1862. Deserted on September 16, 1862. Brought back to camp under guard on November 15, 1862. Court-martialed and sentenced to be shot; however, his sentence was remitted and he was "confined to hard labor with ball and chain." Released on August 22, 1863. Returned to duty in September-October, 1863. Died in hospital at Wilson on February 23, 1864, of "diphtheria."

McDONALD, ALFRED M., Private
Previously served as Private in Company K, Palmetto Sharpshooters (Jenkins's Regiment). Transferred to this company on June 9, 1864. Company records indicate that he was taken prisoner before he could report for duty; however, records of the Federal Provost Marshal do not substantiate that report. No further records.

McGILL, ALEXANDER D., Private
Resided in Gaston County where he enlisted at age 39, February 25, 1863, for the war. Reported present in March-December, 1863, and May-August, 1864. Furloughed on September 24, 1864. No further records.

McGILL, T. J., Sergeant
Born in Lincoln County and resided in Gaston County where he was by occupation a farmer prior to enlisting in Cleveland County at age 26, March 18, 1862. Mustered in as Private. Promoted to Corporal on June 1, 1862. Wounded at Sharpsburg, Maryland, September 17, 1862. Hospitalized at Richmond, Virginia. Furloughed on September 30, 1862. Reported absent without leave in November-December, 1862. Reported sick in hospital at Goldsboro in January-April, 1863. Returned to duty in May-June, 1863. Reported present in July-December, 1863, and May-August, 1864. Promoted to Sergeant on July 18, 1864. Captured at Fort Stedman, Virginia, March 25, 1865. Confined at Point Lookout, Maryland, March 31, 1865. Released at Point Lookout on June 29, 1865, after taking the Oath of Allegiance.

McGILL, WILLIAM O., Private
Resided in Cleveland County and was by occupation a farmer prior to enlisting in Cleveland County at age 28, May 5, 1862, for the war. Reported present from November, 1862, through December, 1863, and in May-August, 1864. Captured at Five Forks, Virginia, April 1, 1865. Confined at Point Lookout, Maryland, April 5, 1865. Released at Point Lookout on June 29, 1865, after taking the Oath of Allegiance.

McSWAIN, SAMUEL O., Private

Resided in Cleveland County and was by occupation a farmer prior to enlisting in Cleveland County at age 24, March 18, 1862. Reported absent without leave in November-December, 1862. Returned to duty in January-February, 1863. Reported absent sick or absent on furlough in March-December, 1863. No further records.

MAYFIELD, JOHN M., Private

Resided in Cleveland County where he enlisted at age 44, March 1, 1864, for the war. Reported present in May-August, 1864. Captured at Fort Stedman, Virginia, March 25, 1865. Confined at Point Lookout, Maryland, until released on June 29, 1865, after taking the Oath of Allegiance.

MAYHEW, DAVID, Private

Resided in Cleveland County. Place and date of enlistment not reported; however, he probably enlisted subsequent to August 31, 1864. Captured at Five Forks, Virginia, April 1, 1865. Confined at Point Lookout, Maryland, April 5, 1865. Released at Point Lookout on June 29, 1865, after taking the Oath of Allegiance.

MITCHAM, R. J., Private

Born in Lincoln County and resided in Cleveland County where he was by occupation a farmer prior to enlisting in Cleveland County at age 27, March 18, 1862. Reported absent without leave in November-December, 1862. Returned to duty in January-February, 1863. Reported present in March-December, 1863. Wounded in the right thigh at Drewry's Bluff, Virginia, on or about May 16, 1864. Hospitalized at Richmond, Virginia. Returned to duty on or about July 13, 1864. Deserted to the enemy on or about February 24, 1865. Confined at Washington, D.C., February 27, 1865. Released on an unspecified date after taking the Oath of Allegiance.

MORROW, W. B., Private

Born in York District, South Carolina, and resided in Cleveland County, North Carolina, where he was by occupation a farmer prior to enlisting in Cleveland County at age 25, March 18, 1862. Died in hospital at Richmond, Virginia, December 14, 1862, of "variola confluent."

MULLINAUX, JOHN W., Private

Resided in Cleveland County where he enlisted at age 18, March 1, 1864, for the war. Reported absent sick in May-August, 1864. Wounded in the head and captured at Fort Stedman, Virginia, March 25, 1865. Hospitalized at Washington, D.C., March 28, 1865. Transferred to Old Capitol Prison, Washington, April 17, 1865. Transferred to Elmira, New York, May 11, 1865. Died at Elmira on May 24, 1865, of "erysipelas."

NANCE, VINSEN, Private

Born in Wilkes County and resided in Cleveland County where he was by occupation a farmer prior to enlisting in Cleveland County at age 25, March 18, 1862. Reported present from November, 1862, through December, 1863, and in May-August, 1864. [North Carolina pension records indicate that he was wounded in the right hip by a piece of shell on an unspecified date.]

NEAL, J. C., Private

Born in Gaston County* and resided in Cleveland County where he was by occupation a farmer or mechanic prior to enlisting in Cleveland County at age 20, March 18, 1862. Mustered in as Private. Reported present or accounted for from November, 1862, through December, 1863. Promoted to Color Corporal on May 2, 1863. Reduced to ranks on December 31, 1863. Wounded in the left thigh (fracture) at Drewry's Bluff, Virginia, on or about May 16, 1864. Hospitalized at Richmond, Virginia. Furloughed for sixty days on September 24, 1864. Retired from service on February 15, 1865, by reason of necrosis of left thigh.

NEAL, J. W., Private

Born in Cleveland* or Lincoln County and resided in Cleveland County where he was by occupation a millwright prior to enlisting in Cleveland County at age 53, March 18, 1862. Discharged on July 15, 1862, by reason of "inguinal hernia on the right side. . . . The injury is of recent occurrence, is very painful, and is the result of overexertion in the service."

NOGGLE, SYLVANUS J., Private

Resided in Cleveland County where he enlisted at age 26, May 5, 1862, for the war. Wounded in the left leg at Sharpsburg, Maryland, September 17, 1862. Returned to duty on an unspecified date. Reported present from November, 1862, through December, 1863, and in May-June, 1864. Transferred to Company H, 2nd Regiment Confederate Engineer Troops, June 1, 1864.

OATES, WILLIAM S. A., Private

Resided in Cleveland County and was by occupation a farmer. Place and date of enlistment not reported; however, he probably enlisted subsequent to August 31, 1864. Was about 39 years of age at time of enlistment. Captured at Five Forks, Virginia, April 1, 1865. Confined at Point Lookout, Maryland, April 5, 1865. Released at Point Lookout on June 29, 1865, after taking the Oath of Allegiance.

OWENSBY, FRANCIS M., Private

Resided in Cleveland or Gaston County and enlisted in Cleveland County at age 18, August 13, 1863, for the war. Reported present in September-December, 1863, and May-August, 1864. Captured at Fort Stedman, Virginia, March 25, 1865. Confined at Point Lookout, Maryland, until released on June 29, 1865, after taking the Oath of Allegiance.

PATTERSON, D. C., Private

Resided in Cleveland County and was by occupation a farmer prior to enlisting in Cleveland County at age 29, February 25, 1863, for the war. Reported present in March-December, 1863, and May-June, 1864. Reported absent wounded in July-August, 1864. Place and date wounded not reported. No further records.

PATTERSON, MILEN M., Private

Born in Lincoln County and resided in Cleveland County where he was by occupation a farmer prior to enlisting in Cleveland County at age 28, March 18, 1862. Reported present from November, 1862, through December, 1863, and in May-June, 1864. Killed at the Battle of the Crater, near Petersburg, Virginia, July 30, 1864.

PATTERSON, PINKNEY D., Private
Born in Lincoln County and resided in Cleveland County where he was by occupation a carpenter prior to enlisting in Cleveland County at age 29, March 18, 1862. Mustered in as Musician (Drummer). Reduced to ranks prior to January 1, 1863. Reported present from November, 1862, through December, 1863, and in May-August, 1864. Deserted to the enemy on or about February 24, 1865. Confined at Washington, D.C., February 27, 1865. Released on an unspecified date after taking the Oath of Allegiance.

PATTERSON, S. CROWDER, Private
Born in Cleveland County where he resided as a farmer prior to enlisting in Cleveland County at age 16, March 18, 1862. Reported present or accounted for from November, 1862, through December, 1863, and in May-August, 1864. Killed at Globe Tavern, Virginia, August 21, 1864.

PATTERSON, W. W., Private
Resided in Cleveland County where he enlisted at age 20, March 18, 1862. Died in hospital at Danville, Virginia, on or about January 4, 1863, of "pneumonia."

PORTER, JOSEPH M., Private
Resided in Cleveland County and enlisted at age 20, May 5, 1862, for the war. Died on September 8, 1862, of disease. Place of death not reported.

PRUIT, P. H., Private
Resided in Cleveland County and was by occupation a farmer prior to enlisting in Cleveland County at age 34, May 5, 1862, for the war. Reported present from November, 1862, through December, 1863. Reported sick in hospital in May-June, 1864. Died prior to November 1, 1864, of disease. Place of death not reported.

PUTNAM, A. C., Private
Born in Cleveland County where he resided as a farmer prior to enlisting at age 21, May 5, 1862. Transferred to Company K of this regiment prior to September 17, 1862.

PUTNAM, D. C., Private
Resided in Cleveland County and was by occupation a farmer prior to enlisting in Cleveland County at age 28, May 5, 1862, for the war. Reported present or accounted for from November, 1862, through December, 1863. Wounded in the shoulder near Petersburg, Virginia, June 21-22, 1864. Hospitalized at Petersburg. Transferred to hospital at Richmond, Virginia, June 24, 1864. Returned to duty on or about August 21, 1864. Wounded in the right leg at Fort Stedman, Virginia, March 25, 1865. Hospitalized at Richmond where he was captured on April 3, 1865. Released on an unspecified date.

PUTNAM, ELIAS W., Sergeant
Born in Lincoln County and resided in Cleveland or Iredell County where he was by occupation a carpenter prior to enlisting in Cleveland County at age 29, March

18, 1862. Mustered in as Private. Promoted to Sergeant on October 1, 1862. Reported present from November, 1862, through December, 1863, and in May-August, 1864. Captured near Petersburg, Virginia, March 22, 1865. Confined at Point Lookout, Maryland, March 27, 1865. Released at Point Lookout on June 16, 1865, after taking the Oath of Allegiance.

PUTNAM, J. H., Private
Born in Cleveland County where he resided as a farmer prior to enlisting in Cleveland County at age 18, March 18, 1862. Killed at Fredericksburg, Virginia, December 13, 1862.

PUTNAM, JOHN BERRY, Private
Born in Cleveland County where he resided as a farmer prior to enlisting in Cleveland County at age 20, March 18, 1862. Died in hospital at Richmond, Virginia, July 18, 1862, of "typhoid fever."

PUTNAM, L. D., Private
Enlisted in Cleveland County at age 19, April 1, 1864, for the war. Reported present in May-August, 1864. Survived the war.

PUTNAM, P. G., Private
Resided in Cleveland County where he enlisted at age 19, May 5, 1862, for the war. Reported present from November, 1862, through December, 1863. Died on May 19, 1864, of disease. Place of death not reported.

PUTNAM, W. H., Private
Resided in Cleveland County where he enlisted at age 24, May 5, 1862, for the war. Reported present from November, 1862, through December, 1863. Wounded in the head at Drewry's Bluff, Virginia, May 13, 1864. Reported absent wounded through August, 1864. Reported on detail as a provost guard at Raleigh in December, 1864. Survived the war.

PUTNAM, WILLIAM ROSWELL, Private
Resided in Cleveland County where he enlisted at age 27, May 5, 1862, for the war. Reported present from November, 1862, through December, 1863, and in May-August, 1864. Deserted to the enemy on or about February 21, 1865. Confined at Washington, D.C., February 24, 1865. Released on an unspecified date after taking the Oath of Allegiance.

REID, J. B., Private
Born in Cleveland County where he resided as a farmer prior to enlisting in Cleveland County at age 18, March 18, 1862. Wounded at Malvern Hill, Virginia, July 1, 1862. Returned to duty on an unspecified date. Reported present from November, 1862, through December, 1863. Wounded in the right hip at Drewry's Bluff, Virginia, on or about May 16, 1864. Hospitalized at Richmond, Virginia. Returned to duty on July 8, 1864. Deserted on August 20, 1864.

REID, MARTEN, Private
Born in Cleveland County where he resided as a farmer prior to enlisting in Cleveland County at age 16, March

18, 1862, as a substitute. Hospitalized at Richmond, Virginia, December 9, 1862, with chronic diarrhoea. Reported absent sick through June, 1863. Returned to duty in July-August, 1863. Reported present in September-December, 1863. Wounded in the head at the Battle of the Crater, near Petersburg, Virginia, July 30, 1864. Returned to duty prior to September 1, 1864. Hospitalized at Richmond on February 9, 1865, with chronic diarrhoea. Furloughed for sixty days on March 2, 1865.

RIDDLE, J. L., Private
Born in Wilkes County and resided in Cleveland County where he was by occupation a farmer prior to enlisting in Cleveland County at age 24, March 18, 1862. Wounded at Sharpsburg, Maryland, September 17, 1862. Reported absent without leave in November-December, 1862. Returned to duty in January-February, 1863. Reported present in March-December, 1863, and May-June, 1864. Furloughed from hospital at Richmond, Virginia, August 15, 1864. Wounded prior to November 1, 1864. No further records.

ROBERTS, JOHN EDMOND, Private
Resided in Cleveland County and enlisted at age 20, March 18, 1862. Discharged on November 1, 1862, after providing Private Perry Barrett as a substitute.

RUNYAN, J. P., Private
Resided in Cleveland County where he enlisted at age 23, May 5, 1862, for the war. Reported present from November, 1862, through December, 1863, and in May-August, 1864. Captured at Five Forks, Virginia, April 1, 1865. Confined at Point Lookout, Maryland, April 5, 1865. Died at Point Lookout on June 22, 1865, of "feb[ris] int[ermittent]."

SANDERS, D. C., Private
Born in Rutherford County and resided in Cleveland County where he was by occupation a farmer prior to enlisting in Cleveland County at age 46, March 18, 1862. Deserted on October 22, 1862. Returned from desertion on February 11, 1863. Reported absent sick in March-August, 1863. Returned to duty in September-October, 1863. Reported present or accounted for in November-December, 1863, and May-August, 1864. Surrendered at Appomattox Court House, Virginia, April 9, 1865.

SARVIS, ALEXANDER, Private
Resided in Cleveland County where he enlisted at age 18, March 1, 1864, for the war. Reported present in May-August, 1864. Furloughed for sixty days on November 8, 1864. Captured at Fort Stedman, Virginia, March 25, 1865. Confined at Point Lookout, Maryland, until released on June 20, 1865, after taking the Oath of Allegiance.

SARVIS, THOMAS, Private
Born in Lincoln County and resided in Cleveland County where he was by occupation a farmer prior to enlisting in Cleveland County at age 45, March 18, 1862. Wounded in the back and captured at Sharpsburg, Maryland, September 17, 1862. Sent to Fort McHenry, Maryland. Transferred to Fort Monroe, Virginia, October 27, 1862.

Paroled and transferred to Aiken's Landing, James River, Virginia, where he was received on November 2, 1862, for exchange. Declared exchanged at Aiken's Landing on November 10, 1862. Reported absent without leave through December, 1862. Reported absent wounded or absent sick in January-December, 1863. Returned to duty on an unspecified date. Reported present in May-August, 1864. Captured at Fort Stedman, Virginia, March 25, 1865. Confined at Point Lookout, Maryland, until released on June 20, 1865, after taking the Oath of Allegiance.

SHIELDS, ALEXANDER M., Private
Previously served as Private in Company H, 34th Regiment N.C. Troops. Transferred to this company in March-June, 1864. Deserted to the enemy on or about March 6, 1865. Confined at Washington, D.C., March 10, 1865. Released on an unspecified date after taking the Oath of Allegiance.

SPARKS, A. CRIGHTON, Private
Resided in Cleveland County and was by occupation a farmer prior to enlisting in Cleveland County at age 27, May 5, 1862, for the war. Died at or near Fredericksburg, Virginia, December 2, 1862, of "ty[phoid] fever."

SPARROW, WILLIAM H., Private
Resided in Cleveland County. Place and date of enlistment not reported; however, he probably enlisted subsequent to August 31, 1864. Captured at Five Forks, Virginia, April 1, 1865. Confined at Point Lookout, Maryland, April 5, 1865. Released at Point Lookout on June 20, 1865, after taking the Oath of Allegiance.

STARNES, RUFUS P., Private
Born in York District, South Carolina, and resided in Cleveland County, North Carolina, where he was by occupation a farmer prior to enlisting in Cleveland County at age 16, March 18, 1862. Reported present or accounted for from November, 1862, through December, 1863. Wounded in the left hand near Petersburg, Virginia, on or about June 17, 1864. Returned to duty in July-August, 1864. Captured at Five Forks, Virginia, April 1, 1865. Confined at Point Lookout, Maryland, April 5, 1865. Released at Point Lookout on June 30, 1865, after taking the Oath of Allegiance.

WARE, J. F., Private
Resided in Cleveland County where he enlisted at age 18, August 13, 1863, for the war. Reported present in September-December, 1863, and May-August, 1864. Deserted to the enemy on or about February 20, 1865. Confined at Washington, D.C., February 24, 1865. Released on an unspecified date after taking the Oath of Allegiance.

WARE, JAMES A., Private
Enlisted in Cleveland County on March 1, 1864, for the war. Reported present in May-October, 1864. Deserted to the enemy on or about February 21, 1865. Confined at Washington, D.C., February 24, 1865. Released on an unspecified date after taking the Oath of Allegiance.

WARE, JAMES G., Private
Born in Lincoln County and resided in Cleveland County where he was by occupation a farmer prior to enlisting in Cleveland County at age 33, March 18, 1862. Wounded in the right breast at Sharpsburg, Maryland, September 17, 1862. Hospitalized at Richmond, Virginia. Furloughed for thirty days on October 15, 1862. Reported absent wounded through October, 1863. Reported on detached service at Salisbury in November-December, 1863. Returned to duty on an unspecified date. Reported present in May-August, 1864. Captured in hospital at Richmond on April 3, 1865. Transferred to Newport News, Virginia, April 23, 1865. Released at Newport News on June 30, 1865, after taking the Oath of Allegiance.

WARE, JAMES W., Sergeant
Born in Cleveland County where he resided as a farmer prior to enlisting at age 21, March 18, 1862. Mustered in as Corporal. Promoted to Sergeant on March 1, 1863. Reported present or accounted for from November, 1862, through December, 1863, and in May-August, 1864. Captured at Fort Stedman, Virginia, March 25, 1865. Confined at Point Lookout, Maryland, until released on June 22, 1865, after taking the Oath of Allegiance.

WARE, JOHN C., Private
Resided in Cleveland County where he enlisted at age 18, August 13, 1863, for the war. Reported present in September-December, 1863, and May-August, 1864. Captured at Fort Stedman, Virginia, March 25, 1865. Confined at Point Lookout, Maryland, until released on June 22, 1865, after taking the Oath of Allegiance.

WARE, M. L., Corporal
Born in Cleveland County where he resided as a farmer prior to enlisting in Cleveland County at age 18, March 18, 1862. Mustered in as Private. Reported present or accounted for from November, 1862, through December, 1863, and in May-August, 1864. Promoted to Corporal on July 18, 1864. Furloughed on September 26, 1864. Deserted to the enemy on or about March 6, 1865. Confined at Washington, D.C., March 10, 1865. Released on an unspecified date after taking the Oath of Allegiance.

WARE, MARTIN S., Private
Born in Lincoln County and resided in Cleveland County where he was by occupation a farmer prior to enlisting in Cleveland County at age 19, March 18, 1862. Reported missing at Malvern Hill, Virginia, July 1, 1862. Returned to duty on an unspecified date. Reported present from November, 1862, through December, 1863, and in May-August, 1864. Captured at Five Forks, Virginia, April 1, 1865. Confined at Point Lookout, Maryland, April 5, 1865. Released at Point Lookout on June 22, 1865, after taking the Oath of Allegiance.

WARE, RUFUS A., Private
Enlisted in Cleveland County on May 1, 1864, for the war. Wounded in the head near Petersburg, Virginia, June 21-July 1, 1864. Returned to duty on or about July 1, 1864. Captured at Fort Stedman, Virginia, March 25, 1865.

Confined at Point Lookout, Maryland, until released on June 6, 1865, after taking the Oath of Allegiance.

WARE, WILLIAM O., Private
Born in Cleveland County where he resided as a farmer prior to enlisting in Cleveland County at age 18, March 18, 1862. Died in hospital at Petersburg, Virginia, on or about August 7, 1862, of "febris typhoides."

WATERS, JOHN M., Private
Resided in Cleveland County and was by occupation a blacksmith prior to enlisting in Cleveland County at age 51, March 18, 1862. Captured at Malvern Hill, Virginia, July 1, 1862. Confined at Fort Columbus, New York Harbor, July 6, 1862. Transferred to Fort Delaware, Delaware, July 9, 1862. Paroled and transferred to Aiken's Landing, James River, Virginia, where he was received on July 12, 1862. Declared exchanged at Aiken's Landing on August 5, 1862. Returned to duty on an unspecified date. Reported present from November, 1862, through December, 1863, and in May-June, 1864. Killed (probably near Petersburg, Virginia) on July 8, 1864.

WATERS, W. P., Private
Born in Lincoln County and resided in Cleveland County where he was by occupation a blacksmith prior to enlisting in Cleveland County at age 16, March 18, 1862. Killed at Sharpsburg, Maryland, September 17, 1862.

WATTERSON, JOHN, Private
Resided in Cleveland County and was by occupation a farmer prior to enlisting in Cleveland County at age 42, February 25, 1863, for the war. Reported present in March-December, 1863, and May-August, 1864. Captured at Fort Stedman, Virginia, March 25, 1865. Confined at Point Lookout, Maryland, until released on June 22, 1865, after taking the Oath of Allegiance. [May have been wounded in May-October, 1864.]

WATTERSON, P. H., Corporal
Born in Lincoln County and resided in Cleveland County where he was by occupation a farmer prior to enlisting in Cleveland County at age 25, March 18, 1862. Mustered in as Private. Wounded at Malvern Hill, Virginia, July 1, 1862. Returned to duty on an unspecified date. Reported present or accounted for from November, 1862, through December, 1863, and in May-August, 1864. Promoted to Corporal subsequent to August 31, 1864. Captured at Five Forks, Virginia, April 1, 1865. Confined at Point Lookout, Maryland, April 5, 1865. Released at Point Lookout on June 22, 1865, after taking the Oath of Allegiance.

WATTERSON, ROBERT N., Private
Resided in Cleveland County and was by occupation a farmer prior to enlisting in Cleveland County at age 32, May 5, 1862, for the war. Reported present or accounted for from November, 1862, through December, 1863, and in May-August, 1864. Captured at Fort Stedman, Virginia, March 25, 1865. Confined at Point Lookout, Maryland, until released on June 21, 1865, after taking the Oath of Allegiance.

WEBB, JAMES, _____
North Carolina pension records indicate that he served in this company.

WEBB, SYLVESTER, _____
North Carolina pension records indicate that he served in this company.

WEIR, J. W., _____
North Carolina pension records indicate that he served in this company.

WHETSTINE, W. F., Private
Born in Lincoln County and resided in Cleveland County where he was by occupation a farmer prior to enlisting in Cleveland County at age 24, March 18, 1862. Reported absent without leave in November-December, 1862. Returned to duty in January-February, 1863. Reported present in March-December, 1863, and May-June, 1864. Captured at Globe Tavern, Virginia, August 21, 1864. Confined at Point Lookout, Maryland, August 24, 1864. Paroled at Point Lookout on or about February 10, 1865. Received at Cox's Wharf, James River, Virginia, on or about February 14, 1865, for exchange. Hospitalized at Richmond, Virginia, February 15, 1865, with an unspecified complaint. Transferred to another hospital on February 16, 1865. No further records.

WHITE, HENRY P., Private
Born in York District, South Carolina, and resided in York District or in Cleveland County, North Carolina, where he was by occupation a farmer prior to enlisting in Cleveland County at age 45, March 18, 1862. Reported present from November, 1862, through December, 1863, and in May-August, 1864. Captured at Fort Stedman, Virginia, March 25, 1865. Confined at Point Lookout, Maryland, until released on June 22, 1865, after taking the Oath of Allegiance.

WILLIAMS, B. B., Private
Born in Rutherford County and resided in Cleveland County where he was by occupation a farmer prior to enlisting in Cleveland County at age 26, March 18, 1862. Reported absent without leave in November-December, 1862. Reported absent sick in January-October, 1863. Reported absent without leave in November-December, 1863. Reported absent sick in May-August, 1864. Hospitalized at Charlotte on January 6, 1865, with dyspepsia. Furloughed on January 24, 1865.

WILLIAMS, J. E., Private
Place and date of enlistment not reported; however, he probably enlisted subsequent to August 31, 1864. Died prior to November 29, 1864. Place, date, and cause of death not reported.

WINTERS, JOHN A., Private
Born in Lincoln County and resided in Cleveland County where he was by occupation a farmer prior to enlisting in Cleveland County at age 36, March 18, 1862. Reported present or accounted for from November, 1862, through December, 1863, and in May-August, 1864. Captured at Five Forks, Virginia, April 1, 1865. Confined at Point Lookout, Maryland, April 5, 1865. Released at Point Lookout on June 22, 1865, after taking the Oath of Allegiance.

WRAY, WILLIAM ARTHUR, Private
Resided in Cleveland County and was by occupation a farm laborer prior to enlisting in Cleveland County at age 23, May 5, 1862, for the war. Reported present or accounted for from November, 1862, through December, 1863, and in May-August, 1864. Surrendered at Appomattox Court House, Virginia, April 9, 1865. Served as a teamster during much of the war.

COMPANY H

This company, known as the "Gaston Rangers," was raised in Gaston County and enlisted at Dallas in March, 1862. It was mustered into state service at Camp Mangum, near Raleigh, on April 21, 1862, and assigned to the 49th Regiment N.C. Troops as Company H. After joining the regiment the company functioned as a part of the regiment, and its history for the remainder of the war is reported as a part of the regimental history.

The information contained in the following roster was compiled primarily from a company muster-in and descriptive roll dated April 21, 1862, and from company muster rolls for November 1, 1862-December 31, 1863, and May 1-August 31, 1864. No company muster rolls were located for May 1-October 31, 1862; January 1-April 30, 1864; or for the period after August 31, 1864. Valuable information was obtained from primary records such as the North Carolina adjutant general's Roll of Honor, discharge certificates, medical records, prisoner of war records, The War of the Rebellion: A Compilation of the Official Records of the Union and Confederate Armies, militia records, newspaper casualty lists and obituaries, Confederate pension applications filed with the state of North Carolina, and the 1860 federal census of North Carolina. Secondary sources such as postwar rosters and histories, cemetery records, the Confederate Veteran, published genealogies, and records of the United Daughters of the Confederacy also provided useful information.

OFFICERS

CAPTAINS

PETTY, CHARLES Q.
Born in Spartanburg District, South Carolina, and resided in Gaston County where he was by occupation a farmer prior to enlisting in Gaston County at age 31. Elected Captain on March 22, 1862. Reported present or accounted for from November, 1862, through December, 1863. Wounded in the shoulder at Drewry's Bluff, Virginia, in May, 1864. Returned to duty prior to July 1, 1864. Appointed Major on August 5, 1864, and transferred to the Field and Staff of this regiment.

TORRENCE, JOHN N.

Born in Lincoln County and resided in Gaston County where he was by occupation a farmer prior to enlisting in Gaston County at age 19, March 22, 1862. Mustered in as Sergeant. Promoted to 1st Sergeant on an unspecified date. Elected 3rd Lieutenant on January 1, 1863. Reported present or accounted for from November, 1862, through December, 1863. Promoted to 2nd Lieutenant on May 17, 1864. Promoted to 1st Lieutenant on or about June 23, 1864. Reported present in May-August, 1864. Promoted to Captain on August 5, 1864. Wounded at Fort Stedman, Virginia, March 25, 1865. Returned to duty on an unspecified date. Surrendered at Appomattox Court House, Virginia, April 9, 1865.

LIEUTENANTS

LINEBERGER, JAMES WELLINGTON, 2nd Lieutenant

Resided in Gaston County and enlisted at age 28. Elected 3rd Lieutenant on March 22, 1862. Promoted to 2nd Lieutenant on June 28, 1862. Reported present from November, 1862, through December, 1863. Wounded in the right breast at Drewry's Bluff, Virginia, May 14, 1864. Hospitalized at Richmond, Virginia. Died in hospital at Richmond on or about May 23, 1864, of wounds.

LINEBERGER, JOHN F., 1st Lieutenant

Born in Lincoln County and resided in Gaston County where he was by occupation a farmer prior to enlisting in Gaston County at age 23. Elected 1st Lieutenant on March 22, 1862. Resigned on June 1, 1862, by reason of sickness. Resignation accepted on June 28, 1862. Later served as Private in Company I, 34th Regiment N.C. Troops.

LOVE, ANDREW J., 1st Lieutenant

Born in Lincoln County and resided in Gaston County where he was by occupation a merchant prior to enlisting in Gaston County at age 26, May 13, 1862, for the war. Mustered in as Private. Reported present from November, 1862, through December, 1863. Promoted to Corporal in July-August, 1863. Reported present in May-August, 1864. Appointed 3rd Lieutenant on June 15, 1864. Promoted to 2nd Lieutenant on June 23, 1864. Promoted to 1st Lieutenant on August 5, 1864. No further records.

MENDENHALL, CYRUS ERASTUS, 2nd Lieutenant

Born in Lincoln County and resided in Gaston County where he was by occupation a divinity student prior to enlisting in Mecklenburg County at age 24, March 14, 1863, for the war. Mustered in as Private. Appointed Chaplain of this regiment on June 26, 1863, but declined the appointment. Reported present in March-December, 1863, and May-August, 1864. Reported on duty as acting regimental Ordnance Sergeant in May-June, 1864. Promoted to 1st Sergeant on July 1, 1864. Appointed 2nd Lieutenant on September 26, 1864. Hospitalized at Richmond, Virginia, January 25, 1865, with "febris catarrh typh[oid]" and died on or about February 10,

1865. ["He had about completed his theological course when the emergency of the war called loudly for his services. He cheerfully responded to this demand. He was prematurely licensed by the Independent Church at this time, in order to preach to his fellow soldiers. . . . His fellow soldiers speak and write of his high military qualifications and Christian deportment." (Charlotte *Western Democrat*, April 11, 1865.)]

NEAGLE, J. E., 3rd Lieutenant

Born in Lincoln County and resided in Gaston County where he was by occupation a physician prior to enlisting in Gaston County at age 29, March 22, 1862. Mustered in as Private. Promoted to Sergeant on an unspecified date. Elected 3rd Lieutenant on or about June 15, 1862. Resigned on an unspecified date for reasons relating to the management of his plantation. Resignation accepted on or about January 1, 1863.

RANKIN, LAWSON LAFAYETTE, 2nd Lieutenant

Born in Lincoln County and resided in Gaston County where he was by occupation a farmer prior to enlisting in Gaston County at age 19, March 22, 1862. Mustered in as Private. Wounded at Malvern Hill, Virginia, July 1, 1862. Returned to duty on an unspecified date. Promoted to Sergeant prior to January 1, 1863. Reported present from November, 1862, through December, 1863, and in May-August, 1864. Appointed 3rd Lieutenant on July 6, 1864. Promoted to 2nd Lieutenant on August 5, 1864. Wounded in the left leg at Fort Stedman, Virginia, March 25, 1865. Left leg amputated. Hospitalized at Petersburg, Virginia, where he "bled to death" on March 31, 1865. [For additional information see the service record of Corporal Edward W. Carson of this company.]

RANKIN, WALLACE A., 1st Lieutenant

Born in Lincoln County and resided in Gaston County where he was by occupation a farmer prior to enlisting in Gaston County at age 18. Elected 2nd Lieutenant on March 22, 1862. Promoted to 1st Lieutenant on June 28, 1862. Reported present from November, 1862, through December, 1863. "Mortally wounded through the head by sharp shooters, in the breastworks, in front of Petersburg," Virginia, June 22, 1864. "He survived ten hours after receiving the fatal blow, but never spake." Died on June 23, 1864. "Greatly beloved by his company."

WILSON, ROBERT NEWTON, 2nd Lieutenant

Resided in Gaston County where he enlisted at age 23, May 13, 1862, for the war. Mustered in as Private. Reported present or accounted for from November, 1862, through December, 1863, and in May-August, 1864. Elected 2nd Lieutenant on September 1, 1864. Captured at Five Forks, Virginia, April 1, 1865. Confined at Old Capitol Prison, Washington, D.C., April 5, 1865. Transferred to Johnson's Island, Ohio, April 9, 1865. Released at Johnson's Island on June 20, 1865, after taking the Oath of Allegiance. [May have been wounded slightly at Malvern Hill, Petersburg, and Fort Stedman, Virginia.]

NONCOMMISSIONED OFFICERS AND PRIVATES

ADAMS, E. W., Private
Born in Lincoln County and resided in Gaston County where he was by occupation a farmer or mason prior to enlisting in Gaston County at age 36, March 22, 1862. Wounded in the leg at Malvern Hill, Virginia, July 1, 1862. Died on August 10, 1862, of wounds. Place of death not reported.

ANDERS, E. M., _____
North Carolina pension records indicate that he served in this company.

ANDERS, L. CLARK, Private
Born in Gaston County* where he enlisted at age 29, May 13, 1862, for the war. Hospitalized on August 20, 1862, with typhoid fever. Returned to duty on October 8, 1862. Died "at home" on November 25, 1862, of disease.

ANTHONY, JAMES CARSON, Private
Resided in Gaston County where he enlisted at age 30, May 10, 1862, for the war. Wounded by a shell at Fredericksburg, Virginia, December 13, 1862. Detailed for duty as a blacksmith at Magnolia on February 21, 1863. Transferred for duty as a blacksmith at Wilmington in the spring of 1863. Reported absent on duty at Wilmington through December, 1863, and in May-August, 1864. Survived the war.

BALDWIN, CEPHAS, Private
Born in Lincoln County and resided in Gaston County where he was by occupation a farmer prior to enlisting in Gaston County at age 18, March 22, 1862. Wounded at Malvern Hill, Virginia, July 1, 1862. Returned to duty on an unspecified date. Reported present or accounted for from November, 1862, through December, 1863. Wounded in the right hand at Drewry's Bluff, Virginia, in May, 1864. Returned to duty on or about June 14, 1864. Killed in the trenches near Petersburg, Virginia, June 23, 1864.

BEATIE, WILLIAM C., Private
Born in Lincoln County and resided in Gaston County where he was by occupation a mason prior to enlisting in Gaston County at age 28, March 22, 1862. Wounded in the left arm at Sharpsburg, Maryland, September 17, 1862. Discharged on March 10 or April 10, 1863, by reason of disability from wounds.

BELL, MARTIN, Private
Previously served as Private in Company I, 11th Regiment N.C. Troops (1st Regiment N.C. Volunteers). Transferred to this company on May 1, 1862. Died at Hillsboro, Virginia, September 18-20, 1862, of disease.

BERRY, ENOS M., Private
Born in Lincoln County and resided in Gaston County where he was by occupation a farmer prior to enlisting in Gaston County at age 20, March 22, 1862. Disabled while tearing up railroad track near Winchester, Virginia, in 1862. Reported absent sick from November, 1862,
through December, 1863, and in May-August, 1864. Survived the war.

BLACKWOOD, JOSEPH, Private
Born in Burke County and resided in Gaston County where he was by occupation a farmer prior to enlisting in Gaston County at age 42, March 22, 1862. Wounded at Malvern Hill, Virginia, July 1, 1862. Returned to duty on an unspecified date. Reported present in January-December, 1863, and May-June, 1864. Hospitalized at Petersburg, Virginia, August 10, 1864, with a gunshot wound of the left leg. Place and date wounded not reported. Left leg amputated. Died in hospital at Petersburg on September 14, 1864, of wounds.

BOYD, ROBERT FRANKLIN, Private
Born in South Carolina and resided in Gaston County where he enlisted at age 22, May 15, 1862, for the war. Captured at or near Malvern Hill, Virginia, July 1, 1862. Confined at Fort Columbus, New York Harbor, July 6, 1862. Transferred to Fort Delaware, Delaware, July 9, 1862. Exchanged at Aiken's Landing, James River, Virginia, August 5, 1862. Returned to duty on an unspecified date. Reported present from November, 1862, through December, 1863. Wounded in the arm and/or hand at Drewry's Bluff, Virginia, on or about May 15, 1864. Returned to duty in July-August, 1864. Captured at Five Forks, Virginia, April 1, 1865. Confined at Point Lookout, Maryland, April 5, 1865. Released at Point Lookout on June 23, 1865, after taking the Oath of Allegiance.

BRIMER, ANDREW T., Private
Resided in Gaston County where he enlisted at age 17, March 22, 1862. Reported present from November, 1862, through February, 1863. Transferred to Company K, 10th Regiment N.C. State Troops (1st Regiment N.C. Artillery), March 20, 1863, in exchange for Sergeant Harrison Hall. [Private Brimer's name is erroneously listed as Anthony T. Brimer in Volume I, page 159, of this series.]

BRISON, H. B., Private
Born in Lincoln County and resided in Gaston County where he was by occupation a carpenter prior to enlisting in Gaston County at age 46, March 22, 1862. Reported present or accounted for from November, 1862, through December, 1863, and in May-August, 1864. Died in hospital at Richmond, Virginia, on or about September 1, 1864, of "dysenteria ac[ute]."

BRISON, J. B. P., Private
Resided in Gaston County where he enlisted at age 25, March 22, 1862. Wounded in the jaw at Malvern Hill, Virginia, July 1, 1862. Reported absent without leave in August-December, 1862. Returned to duty in January-February, 1863. Reported present or accounted for in March-December, 1863. Reported absent on detached service at Weldon in May-August, 1864. Paroled at Chester, South Carolina, May 5, 1865.

BRISON, JOSEPH W., Private
Born in Lincoln County and resided in Gaston County where he was by occupation a carpenter prior to enlisting

in Gaston County at age 22, March 22, 1862. Mustered in as Corporal. Promoted to Sergeant prior to January 1, 1863. Reported present from November, 1862, through December, 1863. Appointed Musician in July-August, 1863. Reduced to ranks on May 1, 1864. Wounded in the lung, left side, and right arm at Drewry's Bluff, Virginia, May 16, 1864. Died in hospital at Richmond, Virginia, on or about June 10, 1864, of wounds.

BRISON, S. B. A., Private
Born in Lincoln County and resided in Gaston County where he was by occupation a farmer prior to enlisting in Gaston County at age 20, March 22, 1862. Killed at Malvern Hill, Virginia, July 1, 1862.

BRISON, T. L., Private
Resided in Gaston County and enlisted at age 18, May 16, 1862, for the war. Killed at Sharpsburg, Maryland, September 17, 1862, while "bearing the colors."

BROWN, MONROE, Private
Born in Lincoln County and resided in Gaston County where he was by occupation a farmer prior to enlisting in Gaston County at age 23, March 22, 1862. Hospitalized at Petersburg, Virginia, August 9, 1862, with typhoid fever. Furloughed for thirty days on September 26, 1862. Reported absent without leave in November-December, 1862. Returned to duty in January-February, 1863. Reported present or accounted for in March-December, 1863, and May-August, 1864. Wounded in the back and captured at Fort Stedman, Virginia, March 25, 1865. Confined at Point Lookout, Maryland, until released on June 23, 1865, after taking the Oath of Allegiance.

CARSON, EDWARD W., Corporal
Born in Gaston* or Lincoln County and resided in Gaston County where he was by occupation a farmer prior to enlisting in Gaston County at age 24, March 22, 1862. Mustered in as Private. Wounded in the arm "by a spent ball and disabled for a few days" at Sharpsburg, Maryland, September 17, 1862. Reported absent sick from November, 1862, through February, 1863. Returned to duty in March-April, 1863. Reported present in May-December, 1863, and May-August, 1864. Promoted to Corporal subsequent to August 31, 1864. Surrendered at Appomattox Court House, Virginia, April 9, 1865. ["On the retreat (from Fort Stedman, Virginia, March 25, 1865) . . . he carried back Lieutenant (Lawson L.) Rankin (of this company), who had been severely wounded and who soon afterward died in hospital."]

CHERRY, ALBERT, Private
Born in Lincoln County and resided in Gaston County where he was by occupation a farmer prior to enlisting in Gaston County at age 23, March 22, 1862. Captured at or near Sharpsburg, Maryland, on or about September 17, 1862. Paroled on October 4, 1862. Reported absent without leave in November-December, 1862. Listed as a deserter on February 14, 1863. Reported present or accounted for in March-December, 1863. Wounded in the abdomen (contusion) at Drewry's Bluff, Virginia, May 14, 1864. Hospitalized at Farmville, Virginia, June 26, 1864, with chronic diarrhoea. Furloughed for fifty days on July 20, 1864. Hospitalized at Petersburg, Virginia,

December 22, 1864, with hysteria. Returned to duty on January 6, 1865. Paroled at Burkeville, Virginia, April 14-17, 1865.

CHERRY, WORKMAN H., Private
Resided in Gaston County and was by occupation a farmer prior to enlisting in Gaston County at age 30, August 20, 186[3], for the war. Reported present in September-December, 1863. Wounded in the foot at Drewry's Bluff, Virginia, May 16, 1864. Hospitalized at Richmond, Virginia, July 14, 1864, with remittent fever. Furloughed for thirty days on August 12, 1864. Paroled at or near Burkeville, Virginia, April 14-17, 1865.

CLEMMER, GEORGE P., Private
Born in Lincoln County and resided in Gaston County where he was by occupation a farmer prior to enlisting in Gaston County at age 26, March 22, 1862. Reported present or accounted for from November, 1862, through December, 1863, and in May-August, 1864. Reported on duty as a teamster during most of the war. Survived the war.

CLEMMER, J. L., Private
Born in Lincoln County and resided in Gaston County where he was by occupation a farmer prior to enlisting in Gaston County at age 30, March 22, 1862. Reported present from November, 1862, through December, 1863. Killed at Drewry's Bluff, Virginia, May 15, 1864.

COMBEST, WILLIAM, Private
Resided in Gaston County and was by occupation a cooper prior to enlisting in Gaston County at age 22, May 3, 1862, for the war. Hospitalized at Richmond, Virginia, January 19, 1863, with "typhoid pneumonia" and died on January 26, 1863.

COOK, JAMES MADISON, Private
Born near Crowders Mountain, in present-day Gaston County, August 16, 1840, and resided in Gaston County where he enlisted on May 13, 1862, for the war. Reported present or accounted for from November, 1862, through December, 1863, and in May-August, 1864. Wounded in the side and right arm (possibly also in the breast) while on picket duty near Petersburg, Virginia, December 17, 1864. Hospitalized at Richmond, Virginia. Furloughed for sixty days on January 26, 1865. Survived the war.

COOK, JOHN B., Private
Resided in Gaston County and was by occupation a farm laborer prior to enlisting in Gaston County at age 28, May 13, 1862, for the war. Died in hospital at Richmond, Virginia, December 7 or December 31, 1862, of "smallpox."

COOK, MADISON, Private
Born in South Carolina and resided in Gaston County where he was by occupation a ditcher prior to enlisting in Gaston County at age 48, August 16, 1862, for the war as a substitute. Wounded in the heel at Sharpsburg, Maryland, September 17, 1862. Reported absent wounded or absent sick from November, 1862, through December, 1863, and in May-August, 1864. Hospitalized at

Richmond, Virginia, December 8, 1864, with a gunshot wound of the right knee. Place and date wounded not reported. Retired to the Invalid Corps on December 30, 1864.

COSTNER, AARON C., Private
Born in Lincoln County and resided in Gaston County where he was by occupation a farmer prior to enlisting in Gaston County at age 19, March 22, 1862. Deserted on September 20, 1862. Returned from desertion on January 6, 1863. Reported present in March-December, 1863, and May-August, 1864. Captured at Fort Stedman, Virginia, March 25, 1865. Confined at Point Lookout, Maryland, until released on June 24, 1865, after taking the Oath of Allegiance.

COSTNER, E. S., Private
Born in Gaston County where he resided as a farmer prior to enlisting in Gaston County at age 16, March 22, 1862. Reported present or accounted for from November, 1862, through December, 1863, and in May-August, 1864. Surrendered at Appomattox Court House, Virginia, April 9, 1865. Served as a teamster during much of the war.

COSTNER, JOSEPH M., Private
Resided in Gaston County where he enlisted at age 18, August 10, 1863, for the war. Reported present in September-December, 1863, and May-August, 1864. Wounded in the face near Petersburg, Virginia, December 1, 1864. Furloughed from hospital at Richmond, Virginia, December 22, 1864. Returned to duty on an unspecified date. Captured at Five Forks, Virginia, April 1, 1865. Confined at Point Lookout, Maryland, April 5, 1865. Released at Point Lookout on June 24, 1865, after taking the Oath of Allegiance.

COSTNER, JOSEPH W., Private
Born in Lincoln County and resided in Gaston County where he was by occupation a carpenter or millwright prior to enlisting in Gaston County at age 24, March 22, 1862. Reported present or accounted for from November, 1862, through December, 1863. Deserted on an unspecified date. Returned to duty on June 20, 1864. "Shocked" (presumably stunned by a shell) at or near Globe Tavern, Virginia, on or about August 21, 1864. Returned to duty on an unspecified date. Captured at Fort Stedman, Virginia, March 25, 1865. Confined at Point Lookout, Maryland, March 31, 1865. Released at Point Lookout on May 13, 1865, after taking the Oath of Allegiance.

COSTNER, M. S. P., Private
Born in Gaston County* where he resided as a farmer prior to enlisting in Gaston County at age 18, March 22, 1862. Reported present from November, 1862, through December, 1863, and in May-August, 1864. Survived the war.

COSTNER, W. F., Private
Resided in Gaston County where he enlisted at age 18, September 4, 1863, for the war. Reported present through December, 1863. Wounded in the jaw at Drewry's Bluff, Virginia, May 16, 1864. Died on or about the same date of wounds.

COSTNER, ZIMRI, Private
Born in Lincoln County and resided in Gaston County where he was by occupation a farmer prior to enlisting in Gaston County at age 25, March 22, 1862. Deserted on September 20, 1862. Apprehended on an unspecified date (probably in September, 1863). Court-martialed on October 6, 1863, and sentenced to be shot. Shot for desertion on the morning of May 2, 1864.

CRAWFORD, JAMES, Private
Born in South Carolina and resided in Gaston County where he was by occupation a farmer prior to enlisting in Gaston County at age 44, September 4, 1863, for the war. Reported present through December, 1863. Died at Chaffin's Bluff, Virginia, May 16 or June 16, 1864, of disease.

CRAWFORD, JAMES ALEXANDER, Private
Resided in Gaston County and enlisted at age 17. Place and date of enlistment not reported; however, he probably enlisted subsequent to August 31, 1864. Captured at Five Forks, Virginia, April 1, 1865. Confined at Point Lookout, Maryland, April 5, 1865. Released at Point Lookout on June 24, 1865, after taking the Oath of Allegiance.

CRAWFORD, THOMAS O., Private
Born in York District, South Carolina, and resided in Gaston County where he was by occupation a farmer prior to enlisting in Gaston County at age 38, March 22, 1862. Wounded in the heel at Malvern Hill, Virginia, July 1, 1862. Hospitalized at Richmond, Virginia, where he died on July 26, 1862, of wounds.

DAVIS, J. C., Private
Previously served as Private in Company G, 18th Regiment South Carolina Infantry. Transferred to this company on August 9, 1864. Reported absent sick through August, 1864. Captured at Fort Stedman, Virginia, March 25, 1865. Confined at Point Lookout, Maryland, March 31, 1865. Released at Point Lookout on May 13, 1865, after taking the Oath of Allegiance.

DAVIS, JAMES, Private
Born in Iredell County and resided in Gaston County where he was by occupation a farmer prior to enlisting in Gaston County at age 40, March 22, 1862. Mustered in as Corporal. Wounded in the head and captured at Malvern Hill, Virginia, July 1, 1862. Confined at Fort Columbus, New York Harbor, July 6, 1862. Transferred to Fort Delaware, Delaware, July 9, 1862. Paroled and transferred to Aiken's Landing, James River, Virginia, where he was received on July 12, 1862. Declared exchanged at Aiken's Landing on August 5, 1862. Returned to duty on an unspecified date. Reduced to ranks prior to January 1, 1863. Reported present from November, 1862, through December, 1863, and in May-August, 1864. Paroled on April 18, 1865.

DAVIS, T. L., Private
Previously served as Private in Company G, 18th Regiment South Carolina Infantry. Transferred to this company in January-June, 1864. Killed by a sharpshooter in the trenches near Petersburg, Virginia, July 21, 1864.

DECK, EUSEBIUS, Corporal
Born in Lincoln County and resided in Gaston County where he was by occupation a farmer prior to enlisting in Gaston County at age 20, March 22, 1862. Mustered in as Private. Reported present or accounted for from November, 1862, through December, 1863, and in May-August, 1864. Promoted to Corporal on July 6, 1864. Captured at Five Forks, Virginia, April 1, 1865. Confined at Point Lookout, Maryland, April 5, 1865. Released at Point Lookout on June 26, 1865, after taking the Oath of Allegiance.

DILLING, FRENO, Corporal
Born in Lincoln County and resided in Gaston County where he was by occupation a farmer prior to enlisting in Gaston County at age 23, March 22, 1862. Mustered in as Corporal. Reduced to ranks prior to January 1, 1863. Promoted to Corporal on May 1, 1863. Reported present or accounted for from November, 1862, through December, 1863, and in May-August, 1864. Survived the war.

FAIRES, JESSE A., Private
Born in York District, South Carolina, and resided in Gaston County where he was by occupation a farmer prior to enlisting at age 17, May 13, 1862, for the war. Wounded at Malvern Hill, Virginia, July 1, 1862. Discharged on September 27, 1862, by reason of being underage. Reenlisted in the company on September 4, 1863. Reported present in September-December, 1863, and May-August, 1864. Captured at Five Forks, Virginia, April 1, 1865. Confined at Point Lookout, Maryland, April 5, 1865. Released at Point Lookout on June 26, 1865, after taking the Oath of Allegiance.

FALLS, WILLIAM, Private
Resided in Gaston County where he enlisted at age 18, May 10, 1862, for the war. Reported present or accounted for from November, 1862, through December, 1863. Wounded in the breast and hands and captured at Drewry's Bluff, Virginia, May 14, 1864. Died of wounds. Place and date of death not reported.

FERGUSON, ALFRED, Private
Resided in Gaston County where he enlisted at age 24, May 13, 1862, for the war. Reported present or accounted for from November, 1862, through December, 1863, and in May-August, 1864. Captured at Five Forks, Virginia, April 1, 1865. Confined at Point Lookout, Maryland, April 5, 1865. Released at Point Lookout on June 26, 1865, after taking the Oath of Allegiance.

FERGUSON, COLUMBUS, Private
Resided in Gaston County and enlisted at age 26, May 13, 1862, for the war. Died in hospital at Petersburg, Virginia, September 16, 1862, of "febris remittens."

FERGUSON, JAMES, Private
Resided in Gaston County and was by occupation a farmer prior to enlisting in Gaston County at age 40, September 4, 1863, for the war. Reported present or accounted for in September-December, 1863, and May-August, 1864. Paroled at Farmville, Virginia, April 11-21, 1865.

FERGUSON, L. B., Private
Resided in Gaston County and enlisted in Mecklenburg County at age 18, March 14, 1863, for the war. Reported present in April-December, 1863, and May-August, 1864. Paroled at Farmville, Virginia, April 11-21, 1865.

FERGUSON, THOMAS W., Private
Born in Lincoln County and resided in Gaston County where he was by occupation a farmer prior to enlisting in Gaston County at age 33, March 22, 1862. Died at Raleigh on May 7-9, 1862, of disease.

FLOWERS, ROBERT G., Private
Resided in Gaston County where he enlisted at age 18, May 10, 1862, for the war. Reported present from November, 1862, through December, 1863. Wounded in the arm at Drewry's Bluff, Virginia, May 14, 1864. Returned to duty in July-August, 1864. Hospitalized at Farmville, Virginia, April 6, 1865, with furunculus. Paroled at Farmville prior to April 22, 1865.

FORD, A. P., Private
Resided in Gaston County where he enlisted at age 34, May 10, 1862, for the war. Reported present or accounted for from November, 1862, through December, 1863, and in May-August, 1864. Surrendered at Appomattox Court House, Virginia, April 9, 1865.

FORD, JAMES H., Private
Resided in Gaston County and was by occupation a farmer prior to enlisting in Gaston County at age 39, March 1, 1863, for the war. Reported present or accounted for in March-December, 1863, and May-August, 1864. Wounded in the hand at Five Forks, Virginia, April 1, 1865. Surrendered at Appomattox Court House, Virginia, April 9, 1865.

FORD, JOHN M., Sergeant
Born in Lincoln County and resided in Gaston County where he was by occupation a farmer prior to enlisting in Gaston County at age 18, March 22, 1862. Mustered in as Private. Promoted to Corporal prior to January 1, 1863. Promoted to Sergeant in July-August, 1863. Reported present or accounted for from November, 1862, through December, 1863, and in May-August, 1864. Hospitalized at Richmond, Virginia, December 10, 1864, with an unspecified complaint. Furloughed for sixty days on December 29, 1864. Wounded in the side at Fort Stedman, Virginia, March 25, 1865. Captured at Five Forks, Virginia, April 1, 1865. Confined at Point Lookout, Maryland, April 5, 1865. Released at Point Lookout on June 26, 1865, after taking the Oath of Allegiance.

FOY, JAMES L., Private
Resided in Gaston County where he enlisted at age 18, August 10, 1863, for the war. Reported present in September-December, 1863, and May-August, 1864. Deserted to the enemy on or about February 25, 1865. Confined at Washington, D.C., March 1, 1865. Released on an unspecified date after taking the Oath of Allegiance.

FOY, JOHN F., Private

Born in Lincoln County and resided in Gaston County where he was by occupation a farmer prior to enlisting in Gaston County at age 26, March 22, 1862. Reported present from November, 1862, through December, 1863. Wounded in the breast and/or hand at Drewry's Bluff, Virginia, May 16, 1864. Returned to duty prior to July 1, 1864. Reported present in July-August, 1864. Paroled at Farmville, Virginia, April 11-21, 1865.

FOY, SOLOMON E., Private

Born in Lincoln or Cleveland* County and resided in Gaston County where he was by occupation a farmer prior to enlisting in Gaston County at age 23, March 22, 1862. Wounded in the right arm in the charge at Malvern Hill, Virginia, July 1, 1862. Right arm amputated. Reported absent wounded through August, 1864. Survived the war.

FRONEBERGER, LEWIS, Private

Born in Lincoln County and resided in Gaston County where he was by occupation a farmer prior to enlisting in Gaston County at age 38, March 22, 1862. Mustered in as Sergeant. Reduced to ranks prior to January 1, 1863. Reported present from November, 1862, through December, 1863. Reported absent on detached service with the Engineer Corps in May-June, 1864. Transferred to the Engineer Corps on July 1, 1864.

GAMBLE, A. J., Private

Born in Lincoln County and resided in Gaston County where he was by occupation a farmer prior to enlisting in Gaston County at age 30, March 22, 1862. Mustered in as Corporal. Reduced to ranks prior to January 1, 1863. Reported present or accounted for from November, 1862, through December, 1863, and in May-August, 1864. Surrendered at Appomattox Court House, Virginia, April 9, 1865.

GAMBLE, ROBERT F., Private

Resided in Gaston County where he enlisted at age 44, September 4, 1863, for the war. Reported present in September-December, 1863. Wounded in the shoulder at Petersburg, Virginia, June 16-18, 1864. Returned to duty prior to July 1, 1864. Captured at Five Forks, Virginia, April 1, 1865. Confined at Point Lookout, Maryland, April 5, 1865. Released at Point Lookout on June 27, 1865, after taking the Oath of Allegiance.

GLEMMER, G. P., Private

Place and date of enlistment not reported. Surrendered at Appomattox Court House, Virginia, April 9, 1865.

HALL, HARRISON, Private

Previously served as Sergeant in Company K, 10th Regiment N.C. State Troops (1st Regiment N.C. Artillery). Transferred to this company with the rank of Private on March 10, 1863, in exchange for Private Andrew T. Brimer. Appointed acting Hospital Steward and transferred for temporary duty with the Field and Staff of this regiment on or about the same date. Promoted to the permanent rank of Hospital Steward on November 11, 1864, and assigned to permanent duty with the Field and Staff of this regiment.

HAMILTON, LARKIN H., Private

Born in Lincoln County and resided in Gaston County where he was by occupation a farmer prior to enlisting in Gaston County at age 33, March 22, 1862. Died in hospital at Petersburg, Virginia, August 7, 1862, of "febris typhoides."

HANNA, WILLIAM DIXON, Private

Born in Lincoln County and resided in Gaston County where he was by occupation a farmer prior to enlisting in Gaston County at age 21, March 22, 1862. Reported present or accounted for from November, 1862, through December, 1863, and in May-August, 1864. Survived the war.

HAVNER, DANIEL, Private

Resided in Gaston County and was by occupation a farm laborer prior to enlisting in Gaston County at age 21, March 13, 1862. Failed to report for duty. Listed as a deserter on February 14, 1863.

HAYES, J. H., Private

Resided in Gaston County where he enlisted at age 36, May 13, 1862, for the war. Reported absent sick on September 3, 1862. Returned to duty on or about January 17, 1863. Reported present in February-December, 1863. Wounded in the heel and right thigh (possibly also in the side) at Drewry's Bluff, Virginia, May 16, 1864. Hospitalized at Richmond, Virginia. Furloughed for sixty days on June 4, 1864. Survived the war.

HAYES, J. J., Private

Resided in Gaston County and enlisted in Mecklenburg County at age 37, March 14, 1863, for the war. Reported present in April-December, 1863. Wounded in the hand at Drewry's Bluff, Virginia, in May, 1864. Returned to duty prior to July 1, 1864. Reported present in July-August, 1864. Wounded in the right breast at Fort Stedman, Virginia, March 25, 1865. Hospitalized at Petersburg, Virginia. Captured in hospital at Richmond, Virginia, April 3, 1865. Paroled on April 25, 1865.

HELMS, J. T., Private

Born in Lincoln County and resided in Gaston County where he was by occupation a farmer prior to enlisting in Gaston County at age 20, March 22, 1862. Died at Raleigh on May 27, 1862, of disease.

HELTON, MILTON B., Private

Resided in Gaston County where he enlisted at age 48, October 3, 1862, for the war as a substitute. Reported present from November, 1862, through December, 1863. Wounded in the side at Drewry's Bluff, Virginia, May 16, 1864. Returned to duty prior to July 1, 1864. Reported present in July-August, 1864. Captured at Five Forks, Virginia, April 1, 1865. Confined at Point Lookout, Maryland, April 5, 1865. Released at Point Lookout on June 27, 1865, after taking the Oath of Allegiance.

HENDERSON, J. W., Private

Born in York District, South Carolina, and resided in Gaston County where he was by occupation a farmer prior to enlisting in Gaston County at age 38, March 22, 1862.

Reported absent sick from November, 1862, through August, 1863. Returned to duty in September-October, 1863. Reported present in November-December, 1863, and May-August, 1864. Hospitalized at Richmond, Virginia, December 8, 1864, with a gunshot wound of the right thigh. Place and date wounded not reported. Furloughed for sixty days on January 28, 1865. Surrendered at Appomattox Court House, Virginia, April 9, 1865.

HENDERSON, JONATHAN, Private
Enlisted at age 45. Place and date of enlistment not reported; however, he probably enlisted subsequent to August 31, 1864. Killed at Five Forks, Virginia, April 1, 1865.

HENDERSON, ROBERT F., Sergeant
Resided in Gaston County where he enlisted at age 37, March 22, 1862. Mustered in as Private. Promoted to Sergeant prior to January 1, 1863. Reported present or accounted for from November, 1862, through December, 1863, and in May-June, 1864. Wounded in the arm at the Battle of the Crater, near Petersburg, Virginia, July 30, 1864. Reported absent wounded through August, 1864. Reported on detail at Raleigh in December, 1864, by reason of disability from wounds. Survived the war.

HENDERSON, W. J., Private
Born in Gaston County* where he resided as a farmer prior to enlisting in Gaston County at age 17, March 22, 1862. Reported present from November, 1862, through December, 1863. Wounded in the left thigh at Drewry's Bluff, Virginia, in May, 1864. Hospitalized at Richmond, Virginia. Reported absent wounded through August, 1864. Returned to duty on an unspecified date. Surrendered at Appomattox Court House, Virginia, April 9, 1865.

HOFFMAN, R. W., Private
Resided in Gaston County where he enlisted at age 33, May 13, 1862, for the war. Reported absent without leave on October 17, 1862. Listed as a deserter on February 14, 1863. Returned to duty in March-April, 1863. Reported present or accounted for in May-December, 1863, and May-August, 1864. Furloughed for sixty days on November 1, 1864. Survived the war.

HOLLAND, FRANKLIN, Private
Born in Gaston County* where he resided as a farmer prior to enlisting in Gaston County at age 29, May 1, 1862, for the war. Discharged on September 1, 1862, by reason of "disease of the heart" and "chronic bronchitis." Reenlisted in the company on March 14, 1863. Reported present in April-December, 1863. Wounded in the hand at Drewry's Bluff, Virginia, in May, 1864. Returned to duty in July-August, 1864. Captured at Five Forks, Virginia, April 1, 1865. Confined at Point Lookout, Maryland, April 5, 1865. Released at Point Lookout on June 27, 1865, after taking the Oath of Allegiance.

HOLLAND, JAMES R., Private
Born in Gaston County* where he resided as a farmer prior to enlisting in Gaston County at age 17, March 22,

1862. Reported present or accounted for from November, 1862, through February, 1863. Appointed Quartermaster Sergeant on March 1, 1863, and transferred to the Field and Staff of this regiment.

HOLLAND, JESSE, Private
Born in Lincoln County and resided in Gaston County where he was by occupation a blacksmith prior to enlisting in Gaston County at age 26, March 22, 1862. Reported absent without leave from August 5, 1862, through December, 1862. Returned to duty in January-February, 1863. Reported present or accounted for in March-December, 1863, and May-June, 1864. Killed in the trenches near Petersburg, Virginia, August 18, 1864.

HOLLAND, JULIUS A., Private
Resided in Gaston County and was by occupation a blacksmith. Place and date of enlistment not reported; however, he probably enlisted subsequent to August 31, 1864. Was about 52 years of age at time of enlistment. Captured at Five Forks, Virginia, April 1, 1865. Confined at Point Lookout, Maryland, April 5, 1865. Released at Point Lookout on June 13, 1865, after taking the Oath of Allegiance.

HOPE, JAMES, Private
Resided in Gaston County and enlisted at Ivor Station, Virginia, at age 39, June 11, 1863, for the war. Reported present or accounted for until December 25, 1863, when he was reported absent without leave. Returned to duty on an unspecified date. Wounded in the hand at Drewry's Bluff, Virginia, in May, 1864. One finger amputated. Furloughed for sixty days on June 7, 1864. Returned to duty prior to September 1, 1864. Wounded in the finger (probably near Petersburg, Virginia) on December 14, 1864. Survived the war.

HOVIS, JACOB J., Private
Resided in Gaston County and was by occupation a farmer prior to enlisting at age 26, May 13, 1862, for the war. Killed at Sharpsburg, Maryland, September 17, 1862.

HUFFSTETLER, ELI, Private
Born in Lincoln County and resided in Gaston County where he was by occupation a farmer prior to enlisting in Gaston County at age 45, March 22, 1862. Reported present from November, 1862, through February, 1863. Deserted on or about April 11, 1863. "Taken" on May 29, 1863, and brought back to the company. Returned to duty on June 3, 1863. Reported present in July-December, 1863, and May-June, 1864. Killed at Globe Tavern, Virginia, August 21, 1864.

HUFFSTETLER, JACOB, Private
Born in Lincoln County and resided in Gaston County where he was by occupation a farmer prior to enlisting in Gaston County at age 19, March 22, 1862. Captured at or near Malvern Hill, Virginia, on or about July 1, 1862. Confined at Fort Columbus, New York Harbor, July 6, 1862. Transferred to Fort Delaware, Delaware, July 9, 1862. Received at Aiken's Landing, James River, Virginia, July 12, 1862. Declared exchanged at Aiken's Landing on August 5, 1862. Returned to duty on an

unspecified date. Reported present or accounted for from November, 1862, through December, 1863. Wounded in the head at Drewry's Bluff, Virginia, May 16, 1864. Returned to duty in July-August, 1864. Captured at Five Forks, Virginia, April 1, 1865. Confined at Point Lookout, Maryland, April 5, 1865. Released at Point Lookout on June 27, 1865, after taking the Oath of Allegiance.

JENKINS, JOHN T., Private

Born in Lincoln County and resided in Gaston County where he was by occupation a farmer prior to enlisting in Gaston County at age 27, March 22, 1862. Reported present from November, 1862, through February, 1863. Died in hospital at Goldsboro on or about June 8, 1863, of "pneumonia."

KISER, WILLIAM H., Private

Resided in Gaston County where he enlisted on April 10, 1864, for the war. Reported present or accounted for in May-August, 1864. Captured at Five Forks, Virginia, April 1, 1865. Confined at Point Lookout, Maryland, April 5, 1865. Released at Point Lookout on June 28, 1865, after taking the Oath of Allegiance.

KNIGHT, CLEVELAND, Private

Born in Spartanburg District, South Carolina, and resided in Gaston County where he was by occupation a farmer prior to enlisting in Gaston County at age 18, March 22, 1862. Reported present or accounted for from November, 1862, through December, 1863. Wounded in the forehead at Drewry's Bluff, Virginia, May 16, 1864. Hospitalized at Richmond, Virginia, where he died on or about May 20, 1864, of wounds.

KNOWLES, MARION, Private

Resided in Gaston County and enlisted at age 20, May 3, 1862, for the war. Died at Petersburg, Virginia, on or about June 27, 1862, of "pneumonia."

LAWRENCE, JOHN A., Private

Born in Gaston County* where he resided as a farmer prior to enlisting in Gaston County at age 18, March 22, 1862. Killed at Malvern Hill, Virginia, July 1, 1862.

LAY, A. S., Private

Resided in Gaston County where he enlisted at age 25, March 22, 1862. Reported absent without leave on May 1, 1862. Listed as a deserter on February 14, 1863. Returned from desertion on August 20, 1864. Hospitalized at Farmville, Virginia, April 6, 1865, with diarrhoea. Captured in hospital at Farmville. Paroled at Farmville on April 11-21, 1865.

LAY, JOHN C., Private

Born in Lincoln or Gaston* County and resided in Gaston County where he was by occupation a farmer prior to enlisting in Gaston County at age 20, March 22, 1862. Died at Goldsboro on May 29, 1862, of disease.

LAY, W. J., Private

Born in Lincoln County and resided in Gaston County where he was by occupation a farmer prior to enlisting in Gaston County at age 23, March 22, 1862. Wounded

in the thigh and captured at Malvern Hill, Virginia, July 1, 1862. Confined at Fort Columbus, New York Harbor. Transferred to Fort Delaware, Delaware, July 9, 1862. Received at Aiken's Landing, James River, Virginia, July 12, 1862, for exchange. Declared exchanged at Aiken's Landing on August 5, 1862. Deserted on August 22, 1862. Returned from desertion on August 20, 1864. Hospitalized at Farmville, Virginia, April 6, 1865, with diarrhoea. Captured at Farmville. Paroled at Farmville on April 11-21, 1865.

LEEPER, ANDREW, Private

Born in Lincoln County and resided in Gaston County where he was by occupation a farmer prior to enlisting in Gaston County at age 21, March 22, 1862. Captured at Malvern Hill, Virginia, July 1, 1862. Confined at Fort Columbus, New York Harbor. Transferred to Fort Delaware, Delaware, July 9, 1862. Transferred to Aiken's Landing, James River, Virginia, July 12, 1862. Declared exchanged at Aiken's Landing on August 5, 1862. Returned to duty on an unspecified date. Reported present or accounted for from November, 1862, through December, 1863, and in May-August, 1864. Captured at Five Forks, Virginia, April 1, 1865. Confined at Point Lookout, Maryland, April 5, 1865. Released at Point Lookout on June 28, 1865, after taking the Oath of Allegiance.

LENHARDT, LAWRENCE K., Private

Born in Lincoln County and resided in Gaston County where he was by occupation a carpenter prior to enlisting in Gaston County at age 41, March 22, 1862. Reported present from November, 1862, through December, 1863. Wounded in the thigh at Drewry's Bluff, Virginia, on or about May 16, 1864. Hospitalized at Richmond, Virginia. Furloughed for sixty days on June 7, 1864. Returned to duty prior to September 1, 1864. Wounded in the abdomen by sharpshooters while on picket in the trenches near Petersburg, Virginia, December 16, 1864. Hospitalized at Petersburg where he died on December 22, 1864, of wounds.

LINEBERGER, LEWIS M., Private

Born in Lincoln County and resided in Gaston County where he was by occupation a farmer prior to enlisting in Gaston County at age 32, March 22, 1862. Reported present or accounted for from November, 1862, through December, 1863, and in May-June, 1864. Wounded in the side at or near the Weldon Railroad, near Petersburg, Virginia, on or about July 1, 1864. Returned to duty prior to September 1, 1864. Wounded in the head, breast, and right arm (possibly also in the hand) at Fort Stedman, Virginia, March 25, 1865. Captured in hospital at Richmond, Virginia, April 3, 1865. Transferred to Newport News, Virginia, where he was received on April 24, 1865. Released at Newport News on June 30, 1865, after taking the Oath of Allegiance.

LINEBERGER, R. A., Private

Born in Lincoln County and resided in Gaston County where he was by occupation a farmer prior to enlisting in Gaston County at age 22, March 22, 1862. Wounded at Sharpsburg, Maryland, September 17, 1862. Died at

Winchester, Virginia, October 22 or November 22, 1862, of wounds and/or "ty[phoid] fever."

LINEBERGER, W. C., Private
Resided in Gaston County where he enlisted at age 18, September 4, 1863, for the war. Reported present through December, 1863. Wounded in both thighs (possibly also in the foot) at Drewry's Bluff, Virginia, on or about May 16, 1864. Hospitalized at Richmond, Virginia. Furloughed on June 5, 1864. Returned to duty prior to September 1, 1864. Hospitalized at Richmond on November 23, 1864, with an unspecified complaint. Furloughed for sixty days on December 29, 1864. Survived the war.

LINEBERGER, W. V., Private
Enlisted in Halifax County at age 18, January 26, 1864, for the war. Reported present in May-August, 1864. Furloughed on September 2, 1864. Survived the war.

LONERGAN, PATRICK, Private
Enlisted in Halifax County at age 17, May 5, 1864, for the war. Hospitalized at Petersburg, Virginia, July 27, 1864, with "ch[ronic] diarrhoea." Died on July 29, 1864.

LOVE, JOHN A., Private
Enlisted in Halifax County on March 23, 1864, for the war. Died in hospital at Richmond, Virginia, June 18, 1864, of "febris typhoid."

McALLISTER, A. M., Private
Resided in Gaston County and enlisted in Mecklenburg County at age 31, March 14, 1863, for the war. Reported present through December, 1863. Wounded in the thigh and captured at Drewry's Bluff, Virginia, on or about May 14, 1864. Hospitalized at Point Lookout, Maryland. Died at Point Lookout on July 10 or July 13, 1864, of wounds.

McARTHUR, ANDREW L., Private
Born in Gaston County* where he resided as a farmer prior to enlisting in Gaston County at age 18, March 22, 1862. Hospitalized at Danville, Virginia, September 7, 1862, with diarrhoea. Returned to duty on October 10, 1862. Reported present from November, 1862, through December, 1863. Wounded in the breast and finger at Drewry's Bluff, Virginia, May 16, 1864. Finger amputated. Hospitalized at Richmond, Virginia, where he died on or about June 4, 1864, of wounds.

McARTHUR, J. A., Private
Resided in Gaston County where he enlisted at age 18, August 10, 1863, for the war. Reported present in September-December, 1863. Wounded in the hand at Drewry's Bluff, Virginia, in May, 1864. Reported absent wounded or absent on furlough through August, 1864. Returned to duty on an unspecified date. Wounded in the chest (possibly also in the jaw and abdomen) and captured at Fort Stedman, Virginia, March 25, 1865. Died in a Federal field hospital on April 1, 1865, of wounds.

McCARVER, HARVEY P., Private
Resided in Gaston County and was by occupation a farmer

prior to enlisting in Gaston County at age 22, May 5, 1862, for the war. Reported present or accounted for from November, 1862, through December, 1863, and in May-August, 1864. Surrendered at Appomattox Court House, Virginia, April 9, 1865.

McCARVER, J. E., Private
Resided in Gaston County where he enlisted at age 29, May 5, 1862, for the war. Reported present or accounted for from November, 1862, through December, 1863. "Finger shot off" at Drewry's Bluff, Virginia, May 16, 1864. Returned to duty in July-August, 1864. Surrendered at Appomattox Court House, Virginia, April 9, 1865.

McCULLOUGH, VINCENT A., Private
Resided in Gaston County and was by occupation a farmer. Place and date of enlistment not reported; however, he probably enlisted subsequent to August 31, 1864. Was about 38 years of age at time of enlistment. Died at Richmond, Virginia, February 3, 1865, of disease.

McKEE, AUGUSTUS A., Private
Born in Lincoln County and resided in Gaston County where he was by occupation a farmer prior to enlisting in Gaston County at age 38, March 22, 1862. Died in hospital at Goldsboro on or about June 20, 1862, of disease.

McLEAN, E. C., Private
Resided in Gaston County where he enlisted at age 18, August 10, 1863, for the war. Reported present through December, 1863. Wounded at Drewry's Bluff, Virginia, May 16, 1864. Died the same date of wounds.

McLEAN, JOHN CRAIG, Private
Resided in Gaston County where he enlisted at age 19, May 6, 1862, for the war. Mustered in as Private. Appointed acting Musician (Drummer) in March-April, 1863. Reported present or accounted for from November, 1862, through December, 1863. Promoted to the permanent rank of Musician (Drummer) in September-October, 1863. Reported present in May-August, 1864. Reduced to ranks subsequent to August 31, 1864. Paroled at Burkeville, Virginia, April 14-17, 1865.

McNAIR, E. A., Private
Resided in Gaston County where he enlisted at age 18, August 10, 1863, for the war. Reported present through December, 1863. Wounded in the thigh at Drewry's Bluff, Virginia, in May, 1864. Returned to duty prior to July 1, 1864. Reported present in July-August, 1864. Killed at Fort Stedman, Virginia, March 25, 1865.

MARTIN, WILLIAM D., Private
Born in Lincoln County and resided in Gaston County where he was by occupation a farmer prior to enlisting in Gaston County at age 19, March 22, 1862. Reported absent without leave from September 20 through December 31, 1862. Returned to duty in January-February, 1863. Reported present or accounted for in March-December, 1863. Wounded in the hips at Drewry's Bluff, Virginia, May 16, 1864. Reported absent wounded through August, 1864. Returned to duty on an unspecified

date. Surrendered at Appomattox Court House, Virginia, April 9, 1865.

MASSEY, W. G., Private

Resided in Gaston County where he enlisted at age 28, May 10, 1862, for the war. Deserted on September 20, 1862.

MOTON, R. ANDY, Private

Born in Lincoln County and resided in Gaston County where he was by occupation a farmer prior to enlisting in Gaston County at age 20, March 22, 1862. Deserted on September 20, 1862. Returned from desertion on February 25, 1863. Returned to duty prior to September 1, 1863. Reported present in September-December, 1863, and May-August, 1864. Captured at Fort Stedman, Virginia, March 25, 1865. Confined at Point Lookout, Maryland, March 31, 1865. Released at Point Lookout on May 14, 1865, after taking the Oath of Allegiance.

NEAGLE, JOHN L., Private

Resided in Gaston County and enlisted at Petersburg, Virginia, at age 21, May 8, 1862, for the war. Appointed Hospital Steward and transferred to the Field and Staff of this regiment prior to January 1, 1863.

OATES, THOMAS M., Private

Resided in Gaston County and was by occupation a farmer prior to enlisting in Mecklenburg County at age 36, March 14, 1863, for the war. Reported present in April-December, 1863, and May-August, 1864. Captured at Five Forks, Virginia, April 1, 1865. Confined at Point Lookout, Maryland, April 5, 1865. Released at Point Lookout on June 29, 1865, after taking the Oath of Allegiance.

O'DANIEL, CORNELIUS M., Private

Born in Lincoln County and resided in Gaston County where he was by occupation a farmer prior to enlisting in Gaston County at age 19, March 22, 1862. Died at Front Royal, Virginia, October 26, 1862, of "apoplexy."

PASOUR, ADAM M., Private

Born in Lincoln County and resided in Gaston County where he was by occupation a farmer prior to enlisting in Gaston County at age 28, March 22, 1862. Reported present from November, 1862, through December, 1863, and in May-August, 1864. Captured at Five Forks, Virginia, April 1, 1865. Confined at Point Lookout, Maryland, April 5, 1865. Released at Point Lookout on June 16, 1865, after taking the Oath of Allegiance.

PASOUR, ANDREW, Private

Resided in Gaston County and enlisted at age 20, May 13, 1862, for the war. Captured at Malvern Hill, Virginia, July 1, 1862. Confined at Fort Columbus, New York Harbor. Transferred to Fort Delaware, Delaware, July 9, 1862. Transferred to Aiken's Landing, James River, Virginia, where he was received on July 12, 1862. Declared exchanged at Aiken's Landing on August 5, 1862. Died in hospital at Petersburg, Virginia, August 25, 1862, of "cont[inue]d fever."

PASOUR, F. M., Private

Born in Lincoln County and resided in Gaston County where he was by occupation a farmer prior to enlisting in Gaston County at age 19, March 22, 1862. Wounded at Malvern Hill, Virginia, July 1, 1862. Died at Richmond, Virginia, July 13, 1862, of wounds.

PASOUR, JOHN P., Private

Resided in Gaston County and was by occupation a farmer prior to enlisting in Gaston County at age 29, May 13, 1862, for the war. Died at Winchester, Virginia, or at Petersburg, Virginia, November 23-25, 1862, of disease.

PASOUR, JOSEPH A., Private

Resided in Gaston County where he enlisted at age 19, March 22, 1862. Reported present from November, 1862, through December, 1863, and in May-August, 1864. Hospitalized at Richmond, Virginia, October 5, 1864, with typhoid fever. Returned to duty on October 17, 1864. Survived the war.

PASOUR, MOSES ELI, Private

Born in Lincoln County and resided in Gaston County where he was by occupation a farmer prior to enlisting in Gaston County at age 20, March 22, 1862. Reported absent without leave on July 1, 1862. Returned to duty on or about November 1, 1863. Wounded and captured at Drewry's Bluff, Virginia, May 16, 1864. Confined at Point Lookout, Maryland, May 19, 1864. Transferred to Elmira, New York, August 16, 1864. Paroled at Elmira on March 14, 1865. Received at Boulware's Wharf, James River, Virginia, on or about March 18, 1865, for exchange.

PAYNE, JOSEPH D., Private

Enlisted in Halifax County at age 17, April 25, 1864, for the war. Reported present through August, 1864. Captured at Five Forks, Virginia, April 1, 1865. Confined at Point Lookout, Maryland, April 5, 1865. Released at Point Lookout on June 8, 1865, after taking the Oath of Allegiance.

PAYNE, THOMAS L., Private

Born in Lincoln County and resided in Gaston County where he was by occupation a farmer prior to enlisting in Gaston County at age 17, March 22, 1862. Wounded at Malvern Hill, Virginia, July 1, 1862. Returned to duty on an unspecified date. Reported present from November, 1862, through December, 1863. Wounded in the left arm at Drewry's Bluff, Virginia, May 16, 1864. Reported absent wounded through August, 1864. Returned to duty on an unspecified date. Surrendered at Appomattox Court House, Virginia, April 9, 1865.

PEARSON, J. J., Private

Born in Gaston County* where he resided as a farmer prior to enlisting in Gaston County at age 18, March 22, 1862. Killed at Sharpsburg, Maryland, September 17, 1862.

PEARSON, W. A., Corporal

Resided in Gaston County where he enlisted at age 21, May 10, 1862, for the war. Mustered in as Private. Reported present from November, 1862, through

December, 1863, and in May-June, 1864. Promoted to Corporal on July 6, 1864. Wounded in the knee at Globe Tavern, Virginia, August 21, 1864. Furloughed on September 17, 1864. Returned to duty on an unspecified date. Paroled at Farmville, Virginia, April 11-21, 1865.

PIERCE, JOHN A., Private
Resided in Gaston County where he enlisted at age 24, May 5, 1862, for the war. Reported present or accounted for from November, 1862, through December, 1863. Killed at Drewry's Bluff, Virginia, May 16, 1864.

QUINN, THOMAS F., Private
Born in South Carolina and enlisted at age 35, May 13, 1862, for the war. Died in hospital at Petersburg, Virginia, July 18, 1862, of "ty[phoid] febris."

QUINN, W. F., Private
Resided in Gaston County and enlisted in Wayne County at age 19, May 22, 1862, for the war. Died in hospital at Front Royal, Virginia, on or about November 10, 1862, of disease.

RANKIN, EPHRAIM L., 1st Sergeant
Born in Lincoln County and resided in Gaston County where he was by occupation a farmer prior to enlisting in Gaston County at age 20, March 22, 1862. Mustered in as 1st Sergeant. Hospitalized at Danville, Virginia, September 7, 1862, with debilitas. Returned to duty on January 17, 1863. Reported present or accounted for through December, 1863. Killed at Drewry's Bluff, Virginia, May 16, 1864.

RANKIN, WADE D., Sergeant
Born in Lincoln County and resided in Gaston County where he was by occupation a farmer prior to enlisting in Gaston County at age 19, March 22, 1862. Mustered in as Private. Promoted to Sergeant prior to January 1, 1863. Reported present from November, 1862, through December, 1863, and in May-August, 1864. Survived the war.

RATCHFORD, W. A., Private
Born in Lincoln County and resided in Gaston County where he was by occupation a farmer prior to enlisting in Gaston County at age 20, March 22, 1862. Killed at Sharpsburg, Maryland, September 17, 1862.

RHODES, DANIEL, Private
Resided in Gaston County where he enlisted at age 48, March 22, 1862. Died in hospital at Front Royal, Virginia, November 5, 1862, of disease.

RHYNE, ABEL BROWN, Private
Resided in Gaston County where he enlisted at age 22, March 22, 1862. Reported present from November, 1862, through December, 1863, and in May-August, 1864. Survived the war.

RHYNE, ABEL PETERSON, Corporal
Born in Lincoln County and resided in Gaston County where he was by occupation a farmer prior to enlisting in Gaston County at age 18, March 22, 1862. Mustered in as Private. Promoted to Corporal prior to January 1, 1863. Reported present or accounted for from November, 1862, through December, 1863, and in May-August, 1864. Paroled at Dallas in May, 1865.

RHYNE, ELI S., Private
Resided in Gaston County where he enlisted at age 23, May 10, 1862, for the war. Wounded at Sharpsburg, Maryland, September 17, 1862. Died in hospital at Front Royal, Virginia, November 7, 1862, of wounds.

RHYNE, JACOB E., Sergeant
Resided in Gaston County where he enlisted at age 19, March 22, 1862. Mustered in as Sergeant. Reduced to ranks prior to January 1, 1863. Reported present from November, 1862, through December, 1863. Wounded near Petersburg, Virginia, June 16-18, 1864. Returned to duty prior to July 1, 1864. Promoted to Sergeant subsequent to August 31, 1864. Wounded in the left leg at Fort Stedman, Virginia, March 25, 1865. Hospitalized at Richmond, Virginia. Captured in hospital at Richmond on April 3, 1865. Transferred to Point Lookout, Maryland, May 2, 1865. Released on or about June 26, 1865, after taking the Oath of Allegiance.

RHYNE, JOHN BUNYAN, Private
Resided in Gaston County where he enlisted at age 18, September 4, 1863, for the war. Reported present or accounted for in September-December, 1863, and May-August, 1864. Hospitalized at Richmond, Virginia, December 5, 1864, with an unspecified complaint. Furloughed for sixty days on December 19, 1864. Returned to duty on an unspecified date. Surrendered at Appomattox Court House, Virginia, April 9, 1865.

RHYNE, JOHN LeROY, Sergeant
Born in Lincoln County and resided in Gaston County where he was by occupation a farmer prior to enlisting in Gaston County at age 22, March 22, 1862. Mustered in as Private. Promoted to Corporal prior to January 1, 1863. Reported present from November, 1862, through December, 1863, and in May-August, 1864. Promoted to Sergeant on July 6, 1864. Survived the war. [May have been wounded in Virginia in May-October, 1864.]

RHYNE, M. H., Sergeant
Born in Lincoln County and resided in Gaston County where he was by occupation a farmer prior to enlisting in Gaston County at age 19, March 22, 1862. Mustered in as Private. Reported present or accounted for from November, 1862, through December, 1863, and in May-August, 1864. Promoted to Sergeant subsequent to August 31, 1864. Captured at the Appomattox River, Virginia, April 3, 1865. Confined at Hart's Island, New York Harbor, April 11, 1865. Released at Hart's Island on June 19, 1865, after taking the Oath of Allegiance.

RHYNE, M. S., Private
Born in Lincoln County and resided in Gaston County where he was by occupation a farmer prior to enlisting in Gaston County at age 20, March 22, 1862. Died on August 28, 1862, of "sunstroke." Place of death not reported.

ROBINSON, S. M., Private

Place and date of enlistment not reported; however, he probably enlisted subsequent to August 31, 1864. Surrendered at Appomattox Court House, Virginia, April 9, 1865.

ROBINSON, WILLIAM E., Private

Born in Lincoln County and resided in Gaston County where he was by occupation a farmer prior to enlisting in Gaston County at age 20, March 22, 1862. Reported present from November, 1862, through December, 1863, and in May-August, 1864. Captured at Five Forks, Virginia, April 1, 1865. Confined at Point Lookout, Maryland, April 5, 1865. Released at Point Lookout on June 19, 1865, after taking the Oath of Allegiance. [May have been wounded in action on an unspecified date.]

RUMFELT, JOHN L., Private

Born in Lincoln County and resided in Gaston County where he was by occupation a farmer prior to enlisting in Gaston County at age 21, March 22, 1862. Hospitalized at Richmond, Virginia, December 4, 1862, with debilitas. Returned to duty on or about April 24, 1863. Reported present during May-December, 1863, and May-August, 1864. Captured at Five Forks, Virginia, April 1, 1865. Confined at Point Lookout, Maryland, April 5, 1865. Released at Point Lookout on June 19, 1865, after taking the Oath of Allegiance.

SMITH, ELI, Private

Resided in Gaston County and was by occupation a farmer prior to enlisting in Gaston County at age 41, September 4, 1863, for the war. Reported present in September-December, 1863, and May-June, 1864. Deserted on July 20, 1864. Drowned (possibly in the Appomattox River) on August 21, 1864. Place of death not reported.

SMITH, JAMES W., Private

Resided in Gaston County. Place and date of enlistment not reported; however, he probably enlisted subsequent to August 31, 1864. Captured at Five Forks, Virginia, April 1, 1865. Confined at Point Lookout, Maryland, April 5, 1865. Released at Point Lookout on June 20, 1865, after taking the Oath of Allegiance.

SMITH, JOHN L., Private

Born in Lincoln County and resided in Gaston County where he was by occupation a miller prior to enlisting in Gaston County at age 30, March 22, 1862. Reported absent sick from August 25, 1862, through June, 1863. Returned to duty in July-August, 1863. Reported present in September-December, 1863, and May-June, 1864. Deserted on July 20, 1864. Returned from desertion on August 20, 1864. Reported in confinement on September 30, 1864. Hospitalized at Richmond, Virginia, November 9, 1864, with an unspecified complaint. Furloughed for sixty days on November 29, 1864. Returned to duty on an unspecified date. Paroled at Farmville, Virginia, April 11-21, 1865.

STOWE, GREEN P., Private

Resided in Gaston County and enlisted at age 19, March 22, 1862. Died at Goldsboro on May 31, 1862, of disease.

STOWE, J. GREEN, Private

Resided in Gaston County and was by occupation a farmer prior to enlisting in Gaston County at age 26, May 3, 1862, for the war. Reported present from November, 1862, through December, 1863. Wounded in the left leg at Drewry's Bluff, Virginia, on or about May 16, 1864. Left leg amputated. Hospitalized at Richmond, Virginia. Furloughed for sixty days on July 22, 1864.

STOWE, WILLIAM I., Private

Resided in Gaston County and enlisted at age 22, May 13, 1862, for the war. Discharged prior to January 1, 1863, by reason of ill health. [May have served later in another regiment.]

STROUP, JOHANN H., Private

Born in Lincoln County and resided in Gaston County where he was by occupation a carpenter prior to enlisting in Gaston County at age 26, March 22, 1862. Died at Drewry's Bluff, Virginia, July 10, 1862, of disease. "Fell dead in physician's arms [while on sick call]."

STROUP, W. W., Private

Resided in Gaston County where he enlisted at age 32, May 10, 1862, for the war. Reported present from November, 1862, through December, 1863, and in May-August, 1864. No further records. [May have been wounded in Virginia in May-October, 1864.]

TEAGUE, BALDIN T. KIRBY, Private

Resided in Gaston County and enlisted in Mecklenburg County at age 39, March 14, 1863, for the war. Reported present in April-December, 1863, and May-August, 1864. Surrendered at Appomattox Court House, Virginia, April 9, 1865.

THOMAS, JOHN G., Private

Born in Lincoln County and resided in Gaston County where he was by occupation a farmer prior to enlisting in Gaston County at age 22, March 22, 1862. Wounded at Malvern Hill, Virginia, July 1, 1862. Died at Richmond, Virginia, July 24 or August 19, 1862, of wounds.

THORNE, J. F., Private

Born in Mecklenburg County and resided in Gaston County where he was by occupation a farmer prior to enlisting in Gaston County at age 19, March 22, 1862. Wounded at Fredericksburg, Virginia, December 13, 1862. Returned to duty prior to January 1, 1863. Reported present in January-December, 1863. Transferred to Company H, 18th Regiment South Carolina Infantry, in January-June, 1864, in exchange for Private J. C. Davis.

TORRENCE, WILLIAM MARCUS, Private

Born in Lincoln County and resided in Gaston County where he was by occupation a farmer prior to enlisting in Gaston County at age 20, March 22, 1862. Killed at Malvern Hill, Virginia, July 1, 1862.

TURNER, G. R., Private

Born in York District, South Carolina, and resided in Gaston County where he was by occupation a farmer prior to enlisting in Gaston County at age 19, March 22, 1862. Died in hospital at Richmond, Virginia, January 5 or February 10, 1863, of disease.

VICKERS, WILLIAM A., Private
Born in Lincoln County and resided in Gaston County where he was by occupation a farmer prior to enlisting in Gaston County at age 23, March 22, 1862. Died in hospital at Petersburg, Virginia, on or about July 28, 1862, of "febris typhoides."

WALLACE, DAVID H., Private
Born in York District, South Carolina, and resided in Gaston County where he was by occupation a farmer prior to enlisting in Gaston County at age 46, March 22, 1862. Died in hospital at Richmond, Virginia, December 4 or December 25, 1862, of disease.

WALLACE, MONROE, Private
Resided in Gaston County where he enlisted at age 20, May 13, 186[2], for the war. Died in hospital at Culpeper Court House, Virginia, September 24, 1862, of a gunshot wound. Place and date wounded not reported.

WARREN, W. C. P., Private
Resided in Gaston County where he enlisted at age 21, May 13, 1862, for the war. Reported present or accounted for from November, 1862, through December, 1863. Wounded in the hand at Drewry's Bluff, Virginia, on or about May 16, 1864. Hospitalized at Richmond, Virginia. Furloughed for sixty days on June 7, 1864. Returned to duty on or about August 6, 1864. Surrendered at Appomattox Court House, Virginia, April 9, 1865.

WHITE, JOHN B., Private
Born in Lincoln County and resided in Gaston County where he was by occupation a farmer prior to enlisting in Gaston County at age 22, March 22, 1862. Mustered in as Sergeant. Appointed Commissary Sergeant prior to August 2, 1862, and transferred to the Field and Staff of this regiment. Reduced to ranks and transferred back to this company prior to January 1, 1863. Appointed acting Commissary Sergeant in May-June, 1863, and transferred for temporary duty with the Field and Staff. Appointed to the permanent rank of Commissary Sergeant in July-August, 1864, and assigned to permanent duty with the Field and Staff.

WHITE, L. S., Private
Born in Lincoln County and resided in Gaston County where he was by occupation a farmer prior to enlisting in Gaston County at age 18, March 22, 1862. Died in hospital at Petersburg, Virginia, July 25, 1862, of "typhoid febris."

WHITESIDES, EDWARD W., Private
Resided in Gaston County where he enlisted at age 18, August 10, 1863, for the war. Reported present in September-December, 1863, and May-August, 1864. Hospitalized at Farmville, Virginia, April 2, 1865, with a gunshot wound of the right elbow. Place and date wounded not reported (probably wounded at Five Forks, Virginia, April 1, 1865). Transferred to hospital at

Danville, Virginia, April 8, 1865. Released from hospital on April 11, 1865. [May have been wounded in Virginia in May-October, 1864.]

WHITESIDES, J. F., Private
Resided in Gaston County where he enlisted at age 18, August 10, 1863, for the war. Reported present in September-December, 1863. Killed at Drewry's Bluff, Virginia, May 16, 1864.

WHITESIDES, JOHN GAMBLE, Private
Born in Lincoln County and resided in Gaston County where he was by occupation a farmer prior to enlisting in Gaston County at age 18, March 22, 1862. Reported present or accounted for from November, 1862, through December, 1863, and in May-June, 1864. Wounded in the chest and lung at the Battle of the Crater, near Petersburg, Virginia, July 30, 1864. Hospitalized at Petersburg where he died on August 6, 1864, of wounds.

WHITESIDES, ROBERT G., Private
Born in Lincoln County and resided in Gaston County where he was by occupation a farmer prior to enlisting in Gaston County at age 18, March 22, 1862. Died in hospital at Petersburg, Virginia, August 9, 1862, of "bilious fever."

WILSON, JERRY, _____
Negro. Servant of 2nd Lieutenant Robert N. Wilson of this company.

WILSON, JOSIAH J., Private
Resided in Gaston County where he enlisted at age 25, March 27, 1863, for the war. Mustered in as Private. Appointed Musician in July-August, 1863. Reported present in April-December, 1863, and May-August, 1864. Reduced to ranks subsequent to August 31, 1864. Surrendered at Appomattox Court House, Virginia, April 9, 1865.

WILSON, SAMUEL M., Private
Resided in Gaston County where he enlisted at age 28, May 13, 1862, for the war. Mustered in as Private. Promoted to Corporal in January-February, 1863. Appointed Musician in July-August, 1863. Reported present from November, 1862, through December, 1863, and in May-August, 1864. Reduced to ranks subsequent to August 31, 1864. Surrendered at Appomattox Court House, Virginia, April 9, 1865.

WILSON, WILLIAM, Private
Resided in Gaston County where he enlisted at age 41, September 4, 1863, for the war. Reported present in September-December, 1863, and May-August, 1864. Surrendered at Appomattox Court House, Virginia, April 9, 1865.

WORKMAN, E. J., Private
Resided in Gaston County where he enlisted at age 23, May 3, 1862, for the war. Wounded at Malvern Hill, Virginia, July 1, 1862. Hospitalized at Richmond, Virginia, where he died on July 8, 1862, of wounds.

COMPANY I

This company, known as the "Catawba Marksmen," was raised in Catawba County and enlisted in Catawba County on March 19, 1862. It was mustered into state service at Camp Mangum, near Raleigh, on April 16, 1862, and assigned to the 49th Regiment N.C. Troops as Company I. After joining the regiment the company functioned as a part of the regiment, and its history for the remainder of the war is reported as a part of the regimental history.

The information contained in the following roster was compiled primarily from a company muster-in and descriptive roll dated April 16, 1862, and from company muster rolls for November 1, 1862-December 31, 1863, and March 1-August 31, 1864. No company muster rolls were located for May 1-October 31, 1862; January 1-February 29, 1864; or for the period after August 31, 1864. Valuable information was obtained from primary records such as the North Carolina adjutant general's *Roll of Honor*, discharge certificates, medical records, prisoner of war records, *The War of the Rebellion: A Compilation of the Official Records of the Union and Confederate Armies*, militia records, newspaper casualty lists and obituaries, Confederate pension applications filed with the state of North Carolina, and the 1860 federal census of North Carolina. Secondary sources such as postwar rosters and histories, cemetery records, the *Confederate Veteran*, published genealogies, and records of the United Daughters of the Confederacy also provided useful information.

OFFICERS

CAPTAINS

CHENAULT, WILLIAM W.
Born in Catawba County* where he resided as a physician prior to enlisting in Catawba County at age 25. Elected Captain on March 22, 1862. Reported present in November-December, 1862. Died at Petersburg, Virginia, February 1, 1863, of "typhoid fever."

CONNOR, CHARLES FULTON
Born in Catawba County* where he resided as a merchant prior to enlisting in Catawba County at age 31. Elected 2nd Lieutenant on March 22, 1862. Promoted to 1st Lieutenant on or about July 24, 1862. Promoted to Captain on February 1, 1863. Reported present or accounted for from November, 1862, through December, 1863, and in March-August, 1864. Captured at Five Forks, Virginia, April 1, 1865. Sent to Washington, D.C. Transferred to Johnson's Island, Ohio, April 9, 1865. Released at Johnson's Island on June 18, 1865, after taking the Oath of Allegiance.

LIEUTENANTS

CONNOR, CASWELL AUGUSTUS, 2nd Lieutenant
Previously served as Corporal in Company D, 6th Regiment N.C. State Troops. Transferred to this company on October 1, 1862. Mustered in as Corporal. Promoted to Sergeant on October 15, 1862. Elected 3rd Lieutenant on March 16, 1863. Reported present or accounted for from November, 1862, through December, 1863. Promoted to 2nd Lieutenant on or about February 23, 1864. Reported present in March-August, 1864. Captured at Five Forks, Virginia, April 1, 1865. Sent to Washington, D.C. Transferred to Johnson's Island, Ohio, where he arrived on April 11, 1865. Released at Johnson's Island on June 18, 1865, after taking the Oath of Allegiance.

SHERRILL, JACOB W., 1st Lieutenant
Born in Catawba County* where he resided as a farmer prior to enlisting in Catawba County at age 29. Elected 3rd Lieutenant on March 22, 1862. Wounded in the right foot at Sharpsburg, Maryland, September 17, 1862. Hospitalized at Richmond, Virginia. Furloughed on October 22, 1862. Promoted to 1st Lieutenant on February 1, 1863. Returned to duty in March-April, 1863. Furloughed for thirty days on July 25, 1863, by reason of disability from wounds received at Sharpsburg. Returned to duty in November-December, 1863. Resigned on February 15, 1864, by reason of disability from wounds. Resignation accepted on February 23, 1864.

SHERRILL, JAMES H., 1st Lieutenant
Born in Iredell or Catawba County and resided in Catawba County where he was by occupation a farmer prior to enlisting in Catawba County at age 17, March 19, 1862. Mustered in as Sergeant. Promoted to 1st Sergeant on June 20, 1862. Elected 3rd Lieutenant on December 27, 1862. Promoted to 2nd Lieutenant on March 16, 1863. Reported present from November, 1862, through December, 1863. Promoted to 1st Lieutenant on February 23, 1864. Reported present in March-August, 1864. Promoted to Captain on March 1, 1865, and transferred to Company A of this regiment.

SHERRILL, JEPTHA, 1st Lieutenant
Born in Catawba County* where he resided as a farmer prior to enlisting in Catawba County at age 33. Elected 1st Lieutenant on March 22, 1862. Became sick and "had to stop on the road unable to march" on or about July 10, 1862. Hospitalized at Petersburg, Virginia, July 11, 1862, with "ty[phoid] febris" and died on July 23, 1862.

WITHERINGTON, STEPHEN, 2nd Lieutenant
Born in Catawba County* where he resided as a farmer prior to enlisting in Catawba County at age 23, March 19, 1862. Mustered in as 1st Sergeant. Reduced to the rank of Sergeant on June 20, 1862. Wounded at Fredericksburg, Virginia, on or about December 13, 1862. Returned to duty prior to January 1, 1863. Reported present in January-December, 1863, and March-August, 1864. Elected Brevet 2nd Lieutenant on July 6, 1864. Wounded in the face at Fort Stedman, Virginia, March 25,

1865. Hospitalized at Richmond, Virginia. Returned to duty on April 2, 1865. Hospitalized at Danville, Virginia, April 9, 1865, with a gunshot wound of the left thigh. Place and date wounded not reported. Survived the war.

NONCOMMISSIONED OFFICERS AND PRIVATES

ABERNATHY, MILTON A., Sergeant
Born in Catawba County* where he resided as a mechanic prior to enlisting in Catawba County at age 27, March 19, 1862. Mustered in as Private. Promoted to Corporal on June 20, 1862. Promoted to Sergeant on March 16, 1863. Reported present from November, 1862, through December, 1863, and in March-August, 1864. Captured at Five Forks, Virginia, April 1, 1865. Confined at Point Lookout, Maryland, April 5, 1865. Released at Point Lookout on June 22, 1865, after taking the Oath of Allegiance.

BENFIELD, WESLEY P., Private
Born in Catawba County* where he resided as a farmer prior to enlisting in Catawba County at age 32, March 19, 1862. Reported present from November, 1862, through December, 1863, and in March-August, 1864. Captured at Fort Stedman, Virginia, March 25, 1865. Confined at Point Lookout, Maryland, until released on June 23, 1865, after taking the Oath of Allegiance.

BLECKLEY, J. M., Private
Born in Catawba County* where he resided as a farmer prior to enlisting in Catawba County at age 27, March 19, 1862. Died in hospital at Richmond, Virginia, December 20, 1862, of "pneumonia."

BLECKLEY, WILLIAM L., Private
Born in Catawba County* where he resided as a farmer prior to enlisting in Catawba County at age 35, March 19, 1862. Reported present or accounted for from November, 1862, through December, 1863, and in March-August, 1864. Hospitalized at Richmond, Virginia, October 7, 1864, with chronic diarrhoea. Returned to duty on November 3, 1864. Captured at Fort Stedman, Virginia, March 25, 1865. Confined at Point Lookout, Maryland, until released on June 23, 1865, after taking the Oath of Allegiance.

BRADY, GEORGE A., Private
Born in Catawba County where he resided as a farmer prior to enlisting in Catawba County at age 18, March 19, 1862. Reported present from November, 1862, through December, 1863, and in March-August, 1864. Captured at Fort Stedman, Virginia, March 25, 1865. Confined at Point Lookout, Maryland, until released on June 23, 1865, after taking the Oath of Allegiance.

BRADY, JOHN F., Private
Resided in Catawba County where he enlisted at age 18, April 10, 1864, for the war. Reported present or accounted for in May-August, 1864. Captured at Five Forks,

Virginia, April 1, 1865. Confined at Point Lookout, Maryland, April 5, 1865. Released at Point Lookout on June 23, 1865, after taking the Oath of Allegiance.

BRAWLEY, PETER W., Private
Resided in Iredell County and enlisted in Halifax County at age 17, August 28, 1863, for the war. Reported present or accounted for in September-December, 1863. Wounded in the hip at Drewry's Bluff, Virginia, May 16, 1864. Hospitalized at Richmond, Virginia. Returned to duty on June 14, 1864. Transferred to Company A, 18th Regiment N.C. Troops (8th Regiment N.C. Volunteers), November 10, 1864.

BROTHERTON, HUGH, Private
Resided in Catawba County and enlisted in Iredell County. Enlistment date reported as August 26, 1862; however, he was not listed in the records of this company until May-June, 1864. Reported present in July-August, 1864. Wounded in the right thigh and knee at Fort Stedman, Virginia, March 25, 1865. Right leg amputated. Hospitalized at Petersburg, Virginia, where he was captured on April 3, 1865. Hospitalized at Fort Monroe, Virginia, April 15, 1865. Confined at Newport News, Virginia, May 9, 1865. Released at Newport News on June 15, 1865, after taking the Oath of Allegiance. [Federal hospital records dated April-May, 1865, give his age as 35.]

BROWN, ANDREW ELBERT, 1st Sergeant
Resided in Catawba County where he enlisted at age 19, May 3, 1862, for the war. Mustered in as Private. Appointed Musician on an unspecified date. Promoted to 1st Sergeant on January 1, 1863. Reported present from November, 1862, through December, 1863, and in March-August, 1864. Captured at Fort Stedman, Virginia, March 25, 1865. Confined at Point Lookout, Maryland, until released on June 23, 1865, after taking the Oath of Allegiance.

BROWN, HOSEA, Private
Born in Catawba County* where he resided as a farmer prior to enlisting in Catawba County at age 24, March 19, 1862. Mustered in as Corporal. Reported present from November, 1862, through December, 1863, and in March-August, 1864. Reduced to ranks in May-June, 1864. Wounded in the abdomen near Petersburg, Virginia, September 29, 1864. Hospitalized at Petersburg where he died on September 30, 1864, of wounds. [According to another report, he was killed by a minie ball about two o'clock on the morning of September 25, 1864.]

BROWN, JACOB, Private
Born in Catawba County* where he resided as a farmer prior to enlisting in Catawba County at age 34, March 19, 1862. Reported present from November, 1862, through December, 1863, and in March-April, 1864. Captured at Drewry's Bluff, Virginia, May 16, 1864. Confined at Point Lookout, Maryland, May 19, 1864. Paroled at Point Lookout on September 18, 1864. Received at Varina, Virginia, September 22, 1864, for exchange. Hospitalized at Richmond, Virginia, September 23, 1864, with chronic rheumatism. Furloughed for sixty days on October 4, 1864. Returned to duty on an unspecified date. Captured

at Five Forks, Virginia, April 1, 1865. Confined at Point Lookout on April 5, 1865. Released at Point Lookout on June 6, 1865, after taking the Oath of Allegiance.

BROWN, THOMPSON, Private
Born in Catawba County* where he resided as a mechanic prior to enlisting in Catawba County at age 37, March 19, 1862. Reported present or accounted for from November, 1862, through December, 1863, and in March-April, 1864. Killed at Drewry's Bluff, Virginia, May 16, 1864.

BROWN, WILLIAM J., Private
Resided in Catawba County. Place and date of enlistment not reported; however, he probably enlisted subsequent to August 31, 1864. Captured at Five Forks, Virginia, April 1, 1865. Confined at Point Lookout, Maryland, April 5, 1865. Released at Point Lookout on June 16, 1865, after taking the Oath of Allegiance.

BUMGARNER, JAMES M., Private
Born in Catawba County* where he resided as a farmer prior to enlisting in Catawba County at age 26, March 19, 1862. Wounded in the breast at Malvern Hill, Virginia, July 1, 1862. Reported absent on expired furlough in November-December, 1862. Returned to duty in January-February, 1863. Reported present in March-December, 1863, and March-August, 1864. Captured at Fort Stedman, Virginia, March 25, 1865. Confined at Point Lookout, Maryland, until released on June 23, 1865, after taking the Oath of Allegiance.

CALDWELL, ABEL, Private
Born in Catawba County where he resided as a farmer prior to enlisting in Catawba County at age 20, March 19, 1862. Reported present from November, 1862, through December, 1863, and in March-April, 1864. Wounded in the hand at Drewry's Bluff, Virginia, May 16, 1864. Returned to duty prior to July 1, 1864. Reported present in July-August, 1864. Captured at Fort Stedman, Virginia, March 25, 1865. Confined at Point Lookout, Maryland, until released on June 24, 1865, after taking the Oath of Allegiance.

CALDWELL, JAMES, Private
Resided in Catawba County. Place and date of enlistment not reported; however, he probably enlisted subsequent to August 31, 1864. Was about 43 years of age at time of enlistment. Captured at Fort Stedman, Virginia, March 25, 1865. Confined at Point Lookout, Maryland, until released on June 24, 1865, after taking the Oath of Allegiance.

CALDWELL, JAMES C., Private
Born in Catawba County where he resided as a farmer prior to enlisting in Catawba County at age 20, March 19, 1862. Reported present or accounted for from November, 1862, through December, 1863, and in March-August, 1864. Captured at Fort Stedman, Virginia, March 25, 1865. Confined at Point Lookout, Maryland, until released on June 24, 1865, after taking the Oath of Allegiance. [North Carolina pension records indicate that he was wounded in 1864.]

CALDWELL, LAWSON, Private
Born in Catawba County* where he resided as a farmer prior to enlisting in Catawba County at age 22, March 19, 1862. Died in hospital near Drewry's Bluff, Virginia, August 21, 1862, of disease.

CALDWELL, WILLIAM J., Sergeant
Resided in Catawba County where he enlisted at age 27, May 3, 1862, for the war. Mustered in as Private. Reported present from November, 1862, through December, 1863, and in March-April, 1864. Wounded in the arm at Drewry's Bluff, Virginia, May 16, 1864. Returned to duty prior to July 1, 1864. Promoted to Sergeant on July 6, 1864. Reported present in July-August, 1864. Captured at Five Forks, Virginia, April 1, 1865. Confined at Point Lookout, Maryland, April 5, 1865. Released at Point Lookout on June 24, 1865, after taking the Oath of Allegiance.

CLARK, DAVID J., Private
Resided in Catawba County and enlisted on November 16, 1864, for the war. Captured at Five Forks, Virginia, April 1, 1865. Confined at Point Lookout, Maryland, April 5, 1865. Released at Point Lookout on June 24, 1865, after taking the Oath of Allegiance.

COLLINS, HENRY, Private
Born in Catawba County where he resided as a farmer prior to enlisting in Catawba County at age 18, March 19, 1862. Reported present or accounted for from November, 1862, through December, 1863, and in March-May, 1864. Wounded "through body" by a sharpshooter in the trenches near Petersburg, Virginia, June 22, 1864. Hospitalized at Petersburg where he died on or about June 24, 1864, of wounds.

COLLINS, JAMES PINK, Private
Resided in Catawba County and enlisted in New Hanover County at age 17, March 3, 1863, for the war. Reported present in March-December, 1863, and March-April, 1864. Wounded in the shoulder at Drewry's Bluff, Virginia, May 16, 1864. Returned to duty prior to July 1, 1864. Wounded at Globe Tavern, Virginia, August 21, 1864. Returned to duty prior to September 1, 1864. Captured at Five Forks, Virginia, April 1, 1865. Confined at Point Lookout, Maryland, April 5, 1865. Released at Point Lookout on June 24, 1865, after taking the Oath of Allegiance.

CONELY, D. G., Private
Place and date of enlistment not reported; however, he probably enlisted subsequent to August 31, 1864. Paroled at Lynchburg, Virginia, April 15, 1865.

DANNER, JAMES MONROE, Private
Born in Catawba County* where he resided as a farmer prior to enlisting in Catawba County at age 21, March 19, 1862. Reported present or accounted for from November, 1862, through December, 1863, and in March-April, 1864. Killed in the trenches near Petersburg, Virginia, July 3, 1864.

DANNER, JOHN LEMUEL FRANKLIN, Private
Resided in Catawba County and enlisted in New Hanover

County at age 18, March 15, 1863, for the war. Reported present in April-December, 1863, and March-July, 1864. Wounded at Globe Tavern, Virginia, August 21, 1864. Returned to duty prior to September 1, 1864. Captured at Fort Stedman, Virginia, March 25, 1865. Confined at Point Lookout, Maryland, until released on June 11, 1865, after taking the Oath of Allegiance.

DAVIS, ANDREW L., Private
Born in Catawba County and enlisted at Petersburg, Virginia, June 3, 1863, for the war. Reported present in July-December, 1863, and March-April, 1864. Captured at Drewry's Bluff, Virginia, May 16, 1864. Confined at Point Lookout, Maryland, May 19, 1864. Exchanged on September 18, 1864. Hospitalized at Richmond, Virginia, September 22, 1864, with chronic diarrhoea. Furloughed on October 6, 1864. No further records.

DAVIS, JAMES, Private
Born in Catawba County* where he resided as a farmer prior to enlisting in Catawba County at age 29, March 19, 1862. Hospitalized at Richmond, Virginia, December 10, 1862, with an unspecified complaint. Furloughed for thirty days on January 10, 1863. Listed as a deserter on February 10, 1863. Reported absent on sick furlough in May-October, 1863. Returned to duty in November-December, 1863. Reported present or accounted for in March-August, 1864. Surrendered at Appomattox Court House, Virginia, April 9, 1865.

DAY, WILLIAM ALBERTUS, Private
Born in Catawba County where he resided as a farmer prior to enlisting in Catawba County at age 18, March 19, 1862. Reported present from November, 1862, through December, 1863, and in March-August, 1864. Captured at Five Forks, Virginia, April 1, 1865. Confined at Point Lookout, Maryland, April 5, 1865. Released at Point Lookout on June 11, 1865, after taking the Oath of Allegiance.

DOUGLAS, ELAM L., Private
Born in Catawba County where he resided as a farmer prior to enlisting in Catawba County at age 18, March 19, 1862. Transferred to Company D, 6th Regiment N.C. State Troops, October 1, 1862.

DRUM, J. PHILIP, Private
Resided in Catawba County where he enlisted at age 27, May 3, 1862, for the war. Reported present or accounted for from November, 1862, through December, 1863, and in May-August, 1864. Surrendered at Appomattox Court House, Virginia, April 9, 1865.

DRUM, JOHN W., Private
Resided in Catawba County and enlisted in Lenoir County at age 18, April 8, 1863, for the war. Killed in a skirmish near Boone's Mill on July 28, 1863.

DRUM, PETER MONROE, Private
Resided in Catawba County and enlisted in Lenoir County at age 39, April 8, 1863, for the war. Reported present or accounted for in May-December, 1863, and March-August, 1864. Wounded in the arm near Petersburg,

Virginia, on the night of October 4, 1864. Reported in hospital at Danville, Virginia, April 3, 1865, with a gunshot wound of the right arm (possibly the same wound received in October, 1864). Furloughed for thirty days on April 9, 1865.

DRUM, RUFUS L., Private
Enlisted at age 38 in November, 1864, for the war. Surrendered at Appomattox Court House, Virginia, April 9, 1865.

DRUM, THOMAS F., Private
Resided in Catawba County and was by occupation a farmer prior to enlisting at age 30, May 3, 1862, for the war. Wounded in the leg and/or knee at Malvern Hill, Virginia, July 1, 1862. Reported absent wounded through October, 1863. Returned to duty in November-December, 1863. Retired to the Invalid Corps on July 20, 1864; however, his retirement was apparently revoked and he returned to duty prior to September 1, 1864. Surrendered at Appomattox Court House, Virginia, April 9, 1865.

EDWARDS, WHEELER SIMEON, Private
Born in Catawba County* where he resided as a farmer prior to enlisting in Catawba County at age 24, March 19, 1862. Died in hospital at Petersburg, Virginia, on or about July 25, 1862, of "typhoid febris."

ELLER, ALEXANDER, Private
Born in Catawba County* where he resided as a miller prior to enlisting in Catawba County at age 21, March 19, 1862. Died in hospital at Petersburg, Virginia, July 26, 1862, of "typhoid febris."

ELLIOTT, JOHN L., Private
Born in Catawba County* where he resided as a farmer prior to enlisting in Catawba County at age 35, March 19, 1862. Reported present or accounted for from November, 1862, through December, 1863, and in March-August, 1864. Captured at Five Forks, Virginia, April 1, 1865. Confined at Point Lookout, Maryland, April 5, 1865. Released at Point Lookout on June 11, 1865, after taking the Oath of Allegiance.

FISH, ELCANAH, Corporal
Born in Catawba County where he resided as a farmer prior to enlisting in Catawba County at age 19, March 19, 1862. Mustered in as Private. Promoted to Corporal on March 16, 1863. Reported present from November, 1862, through December, 1863, and in March-June, 1864. Wounded near Petersburg, Virginia, July 13, 1864. Returned to duty prior to September 1, 1864. Captured at Fort Stedman, Virginia, March 25, 1865. Confined at Point Lookout, Maryland, until released on June 26, 1865, after taking the Oath of Allegiance.

FISHER, ELCANY, Private
Born in Catawba County* where he resided as a farmer prior to enlisting in Catawba County at age 27, March 19, 1862. Reported present or accounted for from November, 1862, through December, 1863, and in March-August, 1864. Captured at Fort Stedman, Virginia, March 25, 1865. Confined at Point Lookout, Maryland, until

released on June 26, 1865, after taking the Oath of Allegiance. [Was probably wounded near Petersburg, Virginia, in 1864.]

FISHER, JOSEPH, Private

Resided in Catawba County and was by occupation a house carpenter prior to enlisting in Catawba County at age 28, May 3, 1862, for the war. Reported present or accounted for from November, 1862, through December, 1863, and in March-August, 1864. Killed near Petersburg, Virginia, on the morning of November 6, 1864, "by a sixty-four pound shell falling on him and bursting—he was torn all to pieces."

FISHER, REUBEN, Private

Born in Lincoln County and resided in Catawba County where he was by occupation a farmer prior to enlisting in Catawba County at age 19, March 19, 1862. Wounded at Malvern Hill, Virginia, July 1, 1862. Died on July 6, 1862, of wounds. Place of death not reported.

FISHER, THOMAS M., Private

Born in Catawba County* where he resided as a farmer prior to enlisting in Catawba County at age 21, March 19, 1862. Reported present from November, 1862, through December, 1863, and in March-August, 1864. Captured at Fort Stedman, Virginia, March 25, 1865. Confined at Point Lookout, Maryland. Released at Point Lookout on June 26, 1865, after taking the Oath of Allegiance.

FISHER, WILLIAM J., Private

Resided in Catawba County where he enlisted at age 18, March 30, 1864, for the war. Reported present or accounted for in April-August, 1864. Captured at Fort Stedman, Virginia, March 25, 1865. Confined at Point Lookout, Maryland, until released on June 26, 1865, after taking the Oath of Allegiance.

FOX, LEE ALLISON, Private

Born in Catawba County* where he resided as a farmer prior to enlisting in Catawba County at age 44, March 19, 1862. Reported present or accounted for from November, 1862, through December, 1863, and in March-June, 1864. Wounded in the arm at the Battle of the Crater, near Petersburg, Virginia, July 30, 1864. Hospitalized at Richmond, Virginia. Furloughed on August 27, 1864. Died at home on an unspecified date. Cause of death not reported.

FREEMAN, JOHN C., Private

Born in Catawba County* where he resided as a farmer prior to enlisting in Catawba County at age 48, March 19, 1862. Hospitalized at Richmond, Virginia, September 26, 1862, with an unspecified complaint. Returned to duty in January-February, 1863. Discharged on or about March 27, 1863, by reason of disability.

GERMAN, JOHN H., Private

Born in Catawba County* and resided in Catawba or Lincoln County where he was by occupation a farmer prior to enlisting in Catawba County at age 47, March 19, 1862. Deserted on November 19, 1862. Returned from desertion on or about January 7, 1863. Reported present

in February-December, 1863, and March-August, 1864. Captured at or near Five Forks, Virginia, on or about April 1, 1865. Confined at Point Lookout, Maryland, on or about April 9, 1865. Released at Point Lookout on June 27, 1865, after taking the Oath of Allegiance. [May have been wounded near Petersburg, Virginia, on an unspecified date.]

GILLELAND, HENDERSON ALBERT, Private

Resided in Catawba County where he enlisted at age 18, October 9, 1863, for the war. Reported present or accounted for in November-December, 1863, and March-August, 1864. Captured at Fort Stedman, Virginia, March 25, 1865. Confined at Point Lookout, Maryland, until released on June 27, 1865, after taking the Oath of Allegiance.

GILLILAND, MARCUS, Private

Born in Catawba County where he resided as a farmer prior to enlisting in Catawba County at age 20, March 19, 1862. Reported present from November, 1862, through December, 1863, and in March-August, 1864. Wounded in the right lung at Fort Stedman, Virginia, March 25, 1865. Hospitalized at Petersburg, Virginia, where he died on March 29, 1865, of wounds.

GILLILAND, REUBEN, Private

Born in Catawba County where he resided as a farmer prior to enlisting in Catawba County at age 19, March 19, 1862. Died in hospital at Raleigh on or about April 21, 1862, of "pneumonia."

GILLILAND, THOMAS, Private

Place and date of enlistment not reported; however, he probably enlisted subsequent to August 31, 1864. Captured at Five Forks, Virginia, April 1, 1865. Confined at Point Lookout, Maryland, where he died on May 20, 1865, of "paralysis."

GOBLE, LAWSON, Private

Resided in Iredell County and was by occupation a farmer prior to enlisting in Iredell County at age 43, October 13, 1863, for the war. Reported present in November-December, 1863, and March-April, 1864. Deserted from camp near Petersburg, Virginia, on or about July 15, 1864. Returned from desertion on August 6, 1864, and was placed under arrest. Returned to duty on an unspecified date. Killed near Petersburg on or about November 15, 1864.

GOBLE, WILLIAM DAVIDSON F., Private

Resided in Iredell County where he enlisted at age 25, October 13, 1863, for the war. Reported present in November-December, 1863, and March-April, 1864. Wounded in the hand at Drewry's Bluff, Virginia, May 16, 1864. Deserted near Petersburg, Virginia, on or about July 15, 1864. Returned from desertion on August 6, 1864, and was placed under arrest. Returned to duty on an unspecified date. Captured at Five Forks, Virginia, April 1, 1865. Confined at Point Lookout, Maryland, April 5, 1865. Released at Point Lookout on June 27, 1865, after taking the Oath of Allegiance.

GOODMAN, ROBERT FRANKLIN, Private
Born in Catawba County* where he resided as a farmer
prior to enlisting in Catawba County at age 46, March 19,
1862. "Became sick on a forced march" and was
hospitalized at Petersburg, Virginia. Died in hospital at
Petersburg on July 21, 1862, of "febris typhoides" and/or
"pneumonia."

HAGER, JAMES, Private
Born in Catawba County* where he resided as a farmer
prior to enlisting in Catawba County at age 22, March 19,
1862. Died at Goldsboro on June 4 or August 18, 1862,
of disease.

HAGER, JOHN C., Private
Born in Catawba County* where he resided as a farmer
prior to enlisting in Catawba County at age 33, March 19,
1862. Reported present from November, 1862, through
August, 1863. Died in hospital at Weldon on September
1, 1863, of "febris typhoides."

HAGER, THOMAS O., Private
Born in Catawba County* where he resided as a farmer
prior to enlisting in Catawba County at age 28, March 19,
1862. Wounded in the leg at Malvern Hill, Virginia, July
1, 1862. Reported absent wounded through February,
1863. Returned to duty in March-April, 1863. Reported
absent on furlough in May-December, 1863, and March-
August, 1864, by reason of disability from wounds.

HAGER, WILLIAM H., Private
Born in Catawba County* where he resided as a farmer
prior to enlisting in Catawba County at age 31, March 19,
1862. Reported present or accounted for from November,
1862, through December, 1863, and in March-April, 1864.
Wounded in the trenches near Petersburg, Virginia, July
13, 1864. Died in hospital at Petersburg on July 22, 1864,
of wounds.

HAMILTON, LEONIDAS D., Private
Born in Catawba County where he resided as a farmer
prior to enlisting in Catawba County at age 19, March 19,
1862. Discharged on October 12, 1862, by reason of
"phthisis pulmonalis."

HARWELL, ELBERT, Private
Resided in Catawba County and was by occupation a
house carpenter prior to enlisting in Catawba County at
age 34, May 3, 1862, for the war. Reported present or
accounted for from November, 1862, through December,
1863, and in May-August, 1864. Surrendered at
Appomattox Court House, Virginia, April 9, 1865.

HARWELL, JAMES T., Private
Born in Catawba County where he resided as a farmer
prior to enlisting in Catawba County at age 19, March 19,
1862. Wounded at Sharpsburg, Maryland, September 17,
1862. Returned to duty in March-April, 1863. Reported
present in May-December, 1863, and March-August,
1864. Wounded near Petersburg, Virginia, October 14,
1864. Returned to duty on an unspecified date. Wounded
in the neck and toes while on picket duty at or near
Petersburg on December 3, 1864. Hospitalized at

Richmond, Virginia. Furloughed for sixty days on
December 16, 1864. Returned to duty on an unspecified
date. Captured at Five Forks, Virginia, April 1, 1865.
Confined at Point Lookout, Maryland, April 5, 1865.
Released at Point Lookout on June 27, 1865, after taking
the Oath of Allegiance.

HARWELL, JOHN, Private
Born in Catawba County* where he resided as a farmer
prior to enlisting in Catawba County at age 38, March 19,
1862. Wounded at Sharpsburg, Maryland, September 17,
1862. Returned to duty prior to January 1, 1863. Reported
present in January-December, 1863, and March-August,
1864. Surrendered at Appomattox Court House, Virginia,
April 9, 1865.

HARWELL, N. A., Private
Resided in Catawba County where he enlisted at age 27,
May 3, 1862, for the war. Died at Winchester, Virginia,
November 2, 1862. Cause of death not reported.

HILL, ISAAC L., Private
Born in Catawba County* where he resided as a mechanic
prior to enlisting in Catawba County at age 24, March 19,
1862. Detailed for duty as a shoemaker at Richmond,
Virginia, November 15, 1862. Reported absent on detail
at Richmond through August, 1864. Assigned to duty with
the 2nd Regiment Virginia Infantry (Local Defense) while
on duty at Richmond. Survived the war.

HILL, JOHN C., Private
Born in Catawba County where he resided as a farmer
prior to enlisting in Catawba County at age 19, March 19,
1862. Wounded at Malvern Hill, Virginia, July 1, 1862.
Returned to duty on an unspecified date. Reported present
from November, 1862, through December, 1863, and in
March-April, 1864. Wounded in the back at Drewry's
Bluff, Virginia, May 16, 1864. Hospitalized at Richmond,
Virginia, where he died on or about June 6, 1864, of
wounds.

HOLDSCLAW, WILLIAM J., Private
Born in Catawba County* where he resided as a mechanic
prior to enlisting in Catawba County at age 26, March 19,
1862. Reported present or accounted for from November,
1862, through December, 1863, and in March-August,
1864. Surrendered at Appomattox Court House, Virginia,
April 9, 1865.

HUNSUCKER, CALVIN A., Private
Previously served as Private in Company D, Mallett's
N.C. Battalion (Camp Guard). Enlisted in this company
in Iredell County on an unspecified date (probably in
May-June, 1864). Was about 26 years of age at time of
enlistment. Reported present in May-August, 1864.
Captured at Five Forks, Virginia, April 1, 1865. Confined
at Point Lookout, Maryland, April 5, 1865. Released at
Point Lookout on June 14, 1865, after taking the Oath of
Allegiance.

JENKINS, WILLIAM M., Private
Born in Catawba County* where he resided as a farmer
prior to enlisting in Catawba County at age 25, March 19,

1862. Wounded at Malvern Hill, Virginia, July 1, 1862. Returned to duty on an unspecified date. Reported present or accounted for from November, 1862, through December, 1863, and in March-August, 1864. Hospitalized at Richmond, Virginia, January 2, 1865, with ambustio. Furloughed for sixty days on January 28, 1865. Returned to duty prior to April 1, 1865, when he was captured at Five Forks, Virginia. Confined at Point Lookout, Maryland, April 5, 1865. Released at Point Lookout on June 14, 1865, after taking the Oath of Allegiance.

JONES, BEDFORD, Private
Resided in Iredell County where he enlisted at age 30, May 3, 1862, for the war. Died in hospital at Charlottesville, Virginia, on or about November 6, 1862, of "pneumonia."

JONES, ELBERT, Private
Resided in Catawba County where he enlisted at age 18, July 24, 1863, for the war. Reported present or accounted for in August-December, 1863, and March-August, 1864. Captured at Fort Stedman, Virginia, March 25, 1865. Confined at Point Lookout, Maryland, March 28, 1865. Released at Point Lookout on June 28, 1865, after taking the Oath of Allegiance. [North Carolina pension records indicate that he was wounded near Petersburg, Virginia, March 1, 1865.]

JONES, EVLIN H., Private
Resided in Catawba County. Place and date of enlistment not reported; however, he probably enlisted subsequent to August 31, 1864. Captured at Fort Stedman, Virginia, March 25, 1865. Confined at Point Lookout, Maryland, until released on June 28, 1865, after taking the Oath of Allegiance.

JONES, G. W., Private
Born in Catawba County* where he resided as a farmer prior to enlisting in Catawba County at age 31, March 19, 1862. Died at home in Catawba County on July 10, 1862, of "a relapse of the fever."

JONES, JEPTHA A., Private
Resided in Iredell County where he enlisted at age 22, May 3, 1862, for the war. Hospitalized at Richmond, Virginia, October 18, 1862, with debilitas. Returned to duty on or about December 28, 1862. Reported present or accounted for in January-December, 1863, and March-August, 1864. Reported in hospital at Danville, Virginia, March 30, 1865, with debilitas. Paroled at Salisbury on May 26, 1865.

JONES, JOSIAH F., Private
Born in Catawba County* where he resided as a farmer prior to enlisting in Catawba County at age 26, March 19, 1862. Mustered in as Sergeant. Reduced to ranks on June 20, 1862. Reported present or accounted for from November, 1862, through December, 1863, and in March-April, 1864. Wounded in the hand at Drewry's Bluff, Virginia, May 16, 1864. Hospitalized at Farmville, Virginia, June 20, 1864, with chronic diarrhoea. Furloughed for sixty days on or about August 9, 1864.

Returned to duty on an unspecified date. Captured at Five Forks, Virginia, April 1, 1865. Confined at Point Lookout, Maryland, April 5, 1865. Released at Point Lookout on June 28, 1865, after taking the Oath of Allegiance.

JONES, JULIUS T., Private
Resided in Catawba County and enlisted at age 20, May 3, 1862, for the war. Died at Goldsboro on June 1, 1862, of disease.

JONES, MILTON H., Private
Resided in Catawba County where he enlisted at age 27, May 3, 1862, for the war. Died in hospital at Petersburg, Virginia, on or about June 10, 1862, of "pneumonia."

JONES, PINKNEY LAFAYETTE, Private
Born in Catawba County* where he resided as a farmer prior to enlisting in Catawba County at age 23, March 19, 1862. Wounded at Malvern Hill, Virginia, July 1, 1862. Returned to duty on an unspecified date. Reported present from November, 1862, through December, 1863, and in March-August, 1864. Captured at Fort Stedman, Virginia, March 25, 1865. Confined at Point Lookout, Maryland, until released on June 21, 1865, after taking the Oath of Allegiance.

JONES, WILLIAM, Private
Born in Catawba County* where he resided as a farmer prior to enlisting in Catawba County at age 26, March 19, 1862. Wounded at Sharpsburg, Maryland, September 17, 1862. Returned to duty on an unspecified date. Reported present or accounted for from November, 1862, through December, 1863, and in March-April, 1864. Wounded in the left hand near Petersburg, Virginia, June 18, 1864. Furloughed for sixty days on or about July 19, 1864. Reported on duty as a hospital nurse at Charlotte from October 7 through December 31, 1864. Paroled at Charlotte on May 3, 1865.

JONES, WILSON, Private
Resided in Catawba County and was by occupation a farmer prior to enlisting at age 37, March 19, 1862. Died at home in Catawba County on July 10, 1862, of "pneumonia."

KALE, EPHRAIM, Private
Born in Catawba County where he resided as a farmer prior to enlisting in Catawba County at age 15, March 19, 1862. Discharged on or about September 27, 1862, by reason of being underage.

KALE, SIDNEY, Private
Resided in Catawba County where he enlisted at age 33, May 3, 1862, for the war. Reported present from November, 1862, through December, 1863, and in March-August, 1864. Captured at Fort Stedman, Virginia, March 25, 1865. Confined at Point Lookout, Maryland, until released on June 28, 1865, after taking the Oath of Allegiance.

KALE, THOMAS J., Private
Born in Catawba County where he resided as a farmer

prior to enlisting in Catawba County at age 18, March 19, 1862. Reported present from November, 1862, through December, 1863, and in March-April, 1864. Wounded in the face near Petersburg, Virginia, June 17, 1864. Reported absent wounded through August, 1864.

KEEVER, ANDREW, Private
Born in Catawba County* where he resided as a farmer prior to enlisting in Catawba County at age 31, March 19, 1862. Died in hospital at Petersburg, Virginia, July 29, 1862, of "febris typhoides."

KENNEDY, J. W., Private
Place and date of enlistment not reported; however, he probably enlisted subsequent to August 31, 1864. Deserted to the enemy on or about February 24, 1865. Confined at Washington, D.C., February 27, 1865. Released on an unspecified date after taking the Oath of Allegiance.

KIRKSEY, JACKSON W., Private
Resided in Catawba County where he enlisted at age 22, May 3, 1862, for the war. Reported absent sick for virtually the entire war. Suffered primarily from rheumatism but also from functional derangement of the heart, debility, and anemia. Captured in hospital at Richmond, Virginia, April 3, 1865. Released by Federal authorities on an unspecified date.

KIRKSEY, WILLIAM F., Private
Resided in Catawba County where he enlisted at age 24, May 3, 1862, for the war. Reported present or accounted for from November, 1862, through December, 1863, and in May-August, 1864; however, he was absent sick during much of that period. Hospitalized at Richmond, Virginia, on or about October 4, 1864, with debilitas. Captured in hospital at Richmond on April 3, 1865. Paroled on April 23, 1865.

LEE, JAMES S., Corporal
Born in Catawba County* where he resided as a blacksmith prior to enlisting in Catawba County at age 27, March 19, 1862. Mustered in as Corporal. Wounded at Malvern Hill, Virginia, July 1, 1862. Returned to duty on an unspecified date. Reported present from November, 1862, through December, 1863, and in March-April, 1864. Killed at Drewry's Bluff, Virginia, May 16, 1864.

LEE, ROBERT G., Private
Born in Catawba County* where he resided as a farmer prior to enlisting in Catawba County at age 23, March 19, 1862. Hospitalized at Richmond, Virginia, September 1, 1862, with neuralgia of the eyes. Furloughed for thirty days on October 22, 1862. Reported present in January-December, 1863, and May-August, 1864. Surrendered at Appomattox Court House, Virginia, April 9, 1865.

LITTON, A. JACKSON, Private
Resided in Iredell County where he enlisted at age 42, October 13, 1863, for the war. Reported present in November-December, 1863, and March-April, 1864. Wounded in the finger at Drewry's Bluff, Virginia, May 16, 1864. Returned to duty prior to July 1, 1864. Wounded

at Globe Tavern, Virginia, August 21, 1864. Returned to duty prior to September 1, 1864. Captured at Farmville, Virginia, April 6, 1865. Confined at Newport News, Virginia, April 14, 1865. Released at Newport News on June 27, 1865, after taking the Oath of Allegiance.

LITTON, ELCANAH C., Private
Resided in Catawba County and was by occupation a day laborer prior to enlisting in Catawba County at age 26, May 3, 1862, for the war. Died in hospital at Gordonsville, Virginia, December 7, 1862, of "pneumonia."

LITTON, ELIJAH, Private
Born in Catawba County where he resided as a farmer prior to enlisting in Catawba County at age 19, March 19, 1862. Died in a field hospital near Drewry's Bluff, Virginia, July 31, 1862, of "typhoid fever."

LOFTON, JAMES FRANKLIN, Private
Resided in Catawba County and was by occupation a farmer prior to enlisting in New Hanover County at age 36, March 3, 1863, for the war. Reported present in March-December, 1863, and March-April, 1864. Killed at Drewry's Bluff, Virginia, May 16, 1864.

LONG, WILLIAM T., Sergeant
Born in Catawba County* where he resided as a farmer prior to enlisting in Catawba County at age 24, March 19, 1862. Mustered in as Corporal. Promoted to Sergeant on June 20, 1862. Wounded at Malvern Hill, Virginia, July 1, 1862. Returned to duty on an unspecified date. Wounded at Sharpsburg, Maryland, September 17, 1862. Returned to duty on an unspecified date. Reported present or accounted for from November, 1862, through December, 1863, and in March-April, 1864. Wounded in the hand at Drewry's Bluff, Virginia, May 16, 1864. Reported absent wounded through August, 1864. Survived the war.

LOWRANCE, NERIUS CLINTON, Private
Born in Catawba County* where he resided as a farmer prior to enlisting in Catawba County at age 38, March 19, 1862. Wounded at Malvern Hill, Virginia, July 1, 1862. Returned to duty on an unspecified date. Reported present from November, 1862, through December, 1863, and in March-April, 1864. Killed in the trenches near Petersburg, Virginia, on or about July 13, 1864.

LOWRANCE, SIDNEY NELSON, Private
Born in Catawba County* where he resided as a farmer prior to enlisting in Catawba County at age 46, March 19, 1862. Wounded at Sharpsburg, Maryland, September 17, 1862. Returned to duty on an unspecified date. Reported present from November, 1862, through December, 1863, and in March-August, 1864. Surrendered at Appomattox Court House, Virginia, April 9, 1865.

McCOY, JAMES A., Private
Resided in Catawba County. Place and date of enlistment not reported; however, he probably enlisted subsequent to August 31, 1864. Captured at Fort Stedman, Virginia, March 25, 1865. Confined at Point Lookout, Maryland,

until released on June 29, 1865, after taking the Oath of Allegiance.

McLELLAND, ISAAC, _____

Negro. Served in an unspecified capacity with this company. Injured near Wilmington on an unspecified date by a falling limb or tree. Survived the war.

MARSHALL, W. CLARK, Private

Resided in Catawba County where he enlisted at age 18, October 11, 1863, for the war. Reported present or accounted for in November-December, 1863, and March-August, 1864. Captured at Five Forks, Virginia, April 1, 1865. Confined at Point Lookout, Maryland, April 5, 1865. Released at Point Lookout on June 29, 1865, after taking the Oath of Allegiance.

MITCHELL, CHRISTOPHER, _____

North Carolina pension records indicate that he served in this company.

MOODY, B. FRANK, Sergeant

Born in Catawba County* where he resided as a painter prior to enlisting in Catawba County at age 28, March 19, 1862. Mustered in as Sergeant. "Fell down by the roadside" on or about July 10, 1862, and was hospitalized at Richmond, Virginia. Died in hospital at Richmond on July 24, 1862, of "typhoid fever."

MOSS, G. W., Corporal

Born in Catawba County* where he resided prior to enlisting in Catawba County at age 22, March 19, 1862. Mustered in as Corporal. Wounded in the leg at Sharpsburg, Maryland, September 17, 1862. Reported absent wounded through February, 1863. Returned to duty in March-April, 1863. Reported present in May-December, 1863, and March-August, 1864. Captured at Fort Stedman, Virginia, March 25, 1865. Confined at Point Lookout, Maryland, until released on June 29, 1865, after taking the Oath of Allegiance.

NULL, GEORGE, Private

Born in Catawba County* where he resided as a farmer prior to enlisting in Catawba County at age 22, March 19, 1862. Wounded and captured at Malvern Hill, Virginia, July 1, 1862. Confined at Fort Delaware, Delaware, where he died (presumably of wounds). Date of death not reported.

POOL, WILLIAM S., Corporal

Born in Catawba County where he resided as a farmer prior to enlisting in Catawba County at age 18, March 19, 1862. Mustered in as Private. Wounded in the left ankle at Sharpsburg, Maryland, September 17, 1862. Returned to duty on an unspecified date. Reported present from November, 1862, through December, 1863, and in March-August, 1864. Promoted to Corporal in May-June, 1864. Captured at Fort Stedman, Virginia, March 25, 1865. Confined at Point Lookout, Maryland, until released on June 16, 1865, after taking the Oath of Allegiance.

POPE, DAVID, Private

Born in Catawba County* where he resided as a farmer

prior to enlisting in Catawba County at age 44, March 19, 1862. Died in hospital at Richmond, Virginia, on or about July 10, 1862, of "typhoid fever."

POPE, SILAS, Private

Born in Catawba County* where he resided as a farmer prior to enlisting in Catawba County at age 42, March 19, 1862. Wounded at Malvern Hill, Virginia, July 1, 1862. Returned to duty on an unspecified date. Reported present from November, 1862, through December, 1863, and in March-July, 1864. Wounded at Globe Tavern, Virginia, August 21, 1864. Returned to duty prior to September 1, 1864. Captured at Five Forks, Virginia, April 1, 1865. Confined at Point Lookout, Maryland, April 5, 1865. Released at Point Lookout on June 16, 1865, after taking the Oath of Allegiance.

POPE, WILLIAM FRANK, Private

Previously served as Private in Company A, 18th Regiment N.C. Troops (8th Regiment N.C. Volunteers). Transferred to this company on November 10, 1864. Captured at Five Forks, Virginia, April 1, 1865. Confined at Point Lookout, Maryland, April 5, 1865. Released at Point Lookout on June 16, 1865, after taking the Oath of Allegiance.

POWELL, ANDREW B., Private

Enlisted in Catawba County on February 13, 1864, for the war. Reported present in March-June, 1864. Wounded at Globe Tavern, Virginia, August 21, 1864. Returned to duty on an unspecified date. Surrendered at Appomattox Court House, Virginia, April 9, 1865.

POWELL, GEORGE TATE, Private

Born in Catawba County where he resided as a farmer prior to enlisting in Catawba County at age 17, March 19, 1862. Discharged on or about November 14, 1862, by reason of being underage. Reenlisted in the company in Catawba County on January 15, 1864. Reported present in March-April, 1864. Wounded in the neck at Drewry's Bluff, Virginia, May 16, 1864. Hospitalized at Richmond, Virginia. Furloughed for sixty days on May 21, 1864. Returned to duty in July-August, 1864. Surrendered at Appomattox Court House, Virginia, April 9, 1865.

REYNOLDS, WILLIAM T., Private

Born in Catawba County* where he resided as a farmer prior to enlisting in Catawba County at age 27, March 19, 1862. Wounded at Sharpsburg, Maryland, September 17, 1862. Returned to duty on an unspecified date. Reported present from November, 1862, through December, 1863, and in March-April, 1864. Wounded in the right thumb near Petersburg, Virginia, June 17, 1864. Hospitalized at Richmond, Virginia. Returned to duty on an unspecified date. Killed in the trenches near Petersburg on July 13, 1864.

RICHARDSON, JOHN H., Private

Born in Catawba County* where he resided as a farmer prior to enlisting in Catawba County at age 40, March 19, 1862. Deserted from camp near Petersburg, Virginia, on or about August 19, 1862.

ROBINSON, JAMES M., Private
Enlisted on or about March 19, 1862. Discharged on an unspecified date (probably prior to November 1, 1862). Reason discharged not reported.

RUFTY, MICHAEL, Private
Resided in Alexander County and was by occupation a merchant. Place and date of enlistment not reported; however, he probably enlisted subsequent to August 31, 1864. Was about 39 years of age at time of enlistment. Captured at Fort Stedman, Virginia, March 25, 1865. Confined at Point Lookout, Maryland, until released on June 17, 1865, after taking the Oath of Allegiance.

SETZER, JAMES PINK, Private
Born in Catawba County where he resided as a farmer prior to enlisting in Catawba County at age 17, March 19, 1862. Wounded at Malvern Hill, Virginia, July 1, 1862. Returned to duty on an unspecified date. Wounded at Sharpsburg, Maryland, September 17, 1862. Returned to duty on an unspecified date. Reported present from November, 1862, through December, 1863, and in March-April, 1864. Wounded in the hand at Drewry's Bluff, Virginia, May 16, 1864. Reported absent without leave on June 16, 1864. Listed as a deserter in July-August, 1864. Returned to duty on an unspecified date. Surrendered at Appomattox Court House, Virginia, April 9, 1865.

SHELTON, MEACON J., Musician
Resided in Catawba County and was by occupation a farmer prior to enlisting in Catawba County at age 25, March 19, 1862. Mustered in as Musician. Reported present or accounted for from November, 1862, through December, 1863, and in March-August, 1864. Paroled at Burkeville, Virginia, April 14-17, 1865. [Elected 2nd Lieutenant of this company on October 7, 1862, but was "rejected by (the examining) Board."]

SHERRILL, ADAM ELLIOTT, Private
Born in Catawba County where he resided as a farmer prior to enlisting in Catawba County at age 16, March 19, 1862. Reported present or accounted for from November, 1862, through December, 1863, and in March-August, 1864. Captured at Five Forks, Virginia, April 1, 1865. Confined at Point Lookout, Maryland, April 5, 1865. Released at Point Lookout on June 3, 1865, after taking the Oath of Allegiance. [Served as courier and orderly on the staff of General Matt Ransom during much of the war.]

SHERRILL, DAVID J., Private
Born in Catawba County* where he resided as a farmer prior to enlisting in Catawba County at age 45, March 19, 1862. Reported absent sick on an expired furlough in November-December, 1862. Listed as a deserter on February 10, 1863. Returned to duty on May 21, 1863. Reported present or accounted for in June-December, 1863, and March-April, 1864. Discharged on July 20, 1864, by reason of "general debility."

SHERRILL, SILAS WODFORD, Private
Born in Catawba County* where he resided as a farmer prior to enlisting in Catawba County at age 24, March 19,

1862. Wounded at Malvern Hill, Virginia, July 1, 1862. Returned to duty on an unspecified date. Reported present from November, 1862, through December, 1863, and in March-August, 1864. Captured at Five Forks, Virginia, April 1, 1865. Confined at Point Lookout, Maryland, April 5, 1865. Released at Point Lookout on June 20, 1865, after taking the Oath of Allegiance.

SIGMON, HENRY, Private
Born in Catawba County* where he resided as a farmer prior to enlisting in Catawba County at age 43, March 19, 1862. Killed at Malvern Hill, Virginia, July 1, 1862.

SIGMON, JAMES WASHINGTON, Sergeant
Born in Catawba County* where he resided as a farmer prior to enlisting in Catawba County at age 30, March 19, 1862. Mustered in as Sergeant. Reported present from November, 1862, through December, 1863, and in March-August, 1864. Captured at Five Forks, Virginia, April 1, 1865. Confined at Point Lookout, Maryland, April 5, 1865. Released at Point Lookout on June 20, 1865, after taking the Oath of Allegiance. [North Carolina pension records indicate that he suffered broken ribs from a shell wound received near Petersburg, Virginia, August 20, 1864.]

SIGMON, JULIUS A., Private
Resided in Catawba County where he enlisted at age 18, October 9, 1863, for the war. Reported present in November-December, 1863, and March-April, 1864. Wounded in the left hand (one finger amputated) near Petersburg, Virginia, on or about June 17, 1864. Hospitalized at Richmond, Virginia. Returned to duty on or about September 3, 1864. Hospitalized at Richmond on November 2, 1864, with pneumonia. Returned to duty on December 31, 1864. Captured at Five Forks, Virginia, April 1, 1865. Confined at Point Lookout, Maryland, April 5, 1865. Released at Point Lookout on June 30, 1865, after taking the Oath of Allegiance.

SIGMON, MARTIN A., Private
Resided in Catawba County where he enlisted at age 28, May 3, 1862, for the war. Reported present or accounted for from November, 1862, through December, 1863, and in March-June, 1864. Transferred to the Mining Corps in July-August, 1864.

STEWART, J. FRANKLIN, Private
Born in Iredell County where he resided as a farmer prior to enlisting in Catawba County at age 21, March 19, 1862. Reported present or accounted for from November, 1862, through December, 1863, and in March-April, 1864. Captured at Drewry's Bluff, Virginia, May 16, 1864. Confined at Point Lookout, Maryland, May 19, 1864. Transferred to Elmira, New York, August 16, 1864. Paroled at Elmira on October 11, 1864. Received at Venus Point, Savannah River, Georgia, November 15, 1864, for exchange. No further records.

STEWART, JEPTHA P., Corporal
Born in Catawba County* where he resided as a farmer prior to enlisting in Catawba County at age 25, March 19,

1862. Wounded at Malvern Hill, Virginia, July 1, 1862. Returned to duty on an unspecified date. Reported present from November, 1862, through December, 1863, and in March-April, 1864. Wounded in the leg near Petersburg, Virginia, June 16, 1864. Reported absent wounded through August, 1864. Returned to duty on an unspecified date. Captured at Five Forks, Virginia, April 1, 1865. Confined at Point Lookout, Maryland, April 5, 1865. Released at Point Lookout on June 20, 1865, after taking the Oath of Allegiance.

STILES, JOHN H., Private
Born in Catawba County* where he resided as a farmer prior to enlisting in Catawba County at age 23, March 19, 1862. Wounded at Malvern Hill, Virginia, July 1, 1862. Hospitalized at Richmond, Virginia, where he died on July 16 or July 22, 1862, of wounds.

STILES, MARCUS, Private
Born in Catawba County* where he resided as a farmer prior to enlisting in Catawba County at age 23, March 19, 1862. Sent to hospital sick from Shepherdstown, [West] Virginia, September 20, 1862. Died on an unspecified date. Place and cause of death not reported.

TRAFFENSTEDT, ABSALOM, Private
Born in Alexander County* where he resided as a farmer prior to enlisting in Catawba County at age 41, March 19, 1862. Deserted from camp near Petersburg, Virginia, August 19, 1862. Returned from desertion on February 22, 1863. Reported present in March-December, 1863, and March-August, 1864. Captured at Five Forks, Virginia, April 1, 1865. Confined at Point Lookout, Maryland, April 5, 1865. Released at Point Lookout on June 20, 1865, after taking the Oath of Allegiance.

TRAFFENSTEDT, DANIEL, Private
Resided in Catawba County where he enlisted at age 41, January 28, 1864, for the war. Reported present in March-April, 1864. Deserted near Petersburg, Virginia, on or about July 15, 1864. Returned from desertion on August 6, 1864. Reported under arrest through August 31, 1864. Died in hospital at Petersburg on September 22, 1864, of "colitis ch[ronic]."

TRAFFENSTEDT, NOAH, Private
Born in Catawba County* where he resided as a farmer prior to enlisting in Catawba County at age 34, March 19, 1862. Wounded at Malvern Hill, Virginia, July 1, 1862. Died at home in Catawba County on July 16, 1862, of wounds.

TURBYFIELD, JACKSON, Private
Born in Catawba County where he resided as a farmer prior to enlisting in Catawba County at age 17, March 19, 1862. Died in a field hospital near Drewry's Bluff, Virginia, August 2, 1862, of disease.

TURNER, JAMES, Private
Born in Catawba County* where he resided as a farmer prior to enlisting in Catawba County at age 57, March 19, 1862. Died in hospital at Raleigh on May 1 or May 4, 1862, of disease.

WEBB, NOEL, Private
Resided in Catawba County and enlisted at age 31 on or about January 1, 1865, for the war. Captured at Fort Stedman, Virginia, March 25, 1865. Confined at Point Lookout, Maryland, until released on June 22, 1865, after taking the Oath of Allegiance.

WILFONG, JOHN W., Private
Born in Catawba County where he resided as a farmer prior to enlisting in Catawba County at age 20, March 19, 1862. Wounded at Sharpsburg, Maryland, September 17, 1862. Returned to duty on an unspecified date. Reported present from November, 1862, through December, 1863, and in March-June, 1864. Wounded (probably in the left foot) at the Battle of the Crater, near Petersburg, Virginia, July 30, 1864. Captured in hospital at Petersburg on April 3, 1865. Transferred to a Federal hospital at Point of Rocks, Virginia, April 17, 1865. Reported still in hospital at Point of Rocks on May 19, 1865. Released on an unspecified date.

WYCKOFF, JOHN WESLEY, Private
Born in Catawba County* where he resided as a farmer prior to enlisting in Catawba County at age 34, March 19, 1862. Wounded at Malvern Hill, Virginia, July 1, 1862. Detailed as a factory superintendent on August 20, 1862. Reported absent on detail through April, 1864. Hospitalized at Richmond, Virginia, May 19, 1864, with an unspecified complaint. Transferred to hospital at Salisbury on or about May 29, 1864, but "instead of stopping in Salisbury [he] went on home. Was taken up [captured] at home & started back to his command and made his escape from the guard and [has] not [been] heard of since. . . ." Listed as a deserter on or about September 1, 1864.

WYCOFF, ANDREW A., Private
Born in Catawba County* where he resided as a farmer prior to enlisting in Catawba County at age 38, March 19, 1862. Listed as a deserter on September 20, 1862. Returned from desertion on February 9, 1863. Reported present in March-December, 1863, and March-April, 1864. "Accidentally shot himself in the hand" at Drewry's Bluff, Virginia, May 16, 1864. Returned to duty prior to July 1, 1864. Captured at Five Forks, Virginia, April 1, 1865. Confined at Point Lookout, Maryland, April 5, 1865. Released at Point Lookout on June 22, 1865, after taking the Oath of Allegiance.

COMPANY K

This company, known as the "Pleasant Home Guards," was raised in Lincoln and Gaston counties and enlisted in Lincoln County on March 15, 1862. It was mustered into state service at Camp Mangum, near Raleigh, on April 21, 1862, and assigned to the 49th Regiment N.C. Troops as Company K. After joining the regiment the company functioned as a part of the regiment, and its history for the remainder of the war is reported as a part of the regimental history.

The information contained in the following roster was

compiled primarily from a company muster-in and descriptive roll dated April 21, 1862, and from company muster rolls for November 1, 1862-December 31, 1863, and May 1-August 31, 1864. No company muster rolls were located for May 1-October 31, 1862; January 1-April 30, 1864; or for the period after August 31, 1864. Valuable information was obtained from primary records such as the North Carolina adjutant general's *Roll of Honor*, discharge certificates, medical records, prisoner of war records, *The War of the Rebellion: A Compilation of the Official Records of the Union and Confederate Armies*, militia records, newspaper casualty lists and obituaries, Confederate pension applications filed with the state of North Carolina, and the 1860 federal census of North Carolina. Secondary sources such as postwar rosters and histories, cemetery records, the *Confederate Veteran*, published genealogies, and records of the United Daughters of the Confederacy also provided useful information.

OFFICERS

CAPTAINS

BAXTER, PETER Z.
Born in Lincoln County where he resided as a farmer prior to enlisting in Lincoln County at age 40. Elected Captain on March 23, 1862. Reported present or accounted for from November, 1862, through May, 1863. Resigned on June 9, 1863, because "I do not wish to serve in my present position any longer. . . ." Resignation accepted on July 24, 1863.

PHIFER, GEORGE L.
Previously served as Sergeant Major of this regiment. Appointed 1st Lieutenant on December 22, 1862, and transferred to this company. Promoted to Captain on July 24, 1863. Reported present or accounted for in January-December, 1863. Wounded at Bermuda Hundred, Virginia, June 2, 1864. Appointed Aide-de-Camp on or about August 3, 1864, and transferred to the staff of General Robert F. Hoke.

ADAMS, JAMES T.
Born in Chester District, South Carolina, and resided in Lincoln County where he was by occupation a clerk prior to enlisting in Lincoln County at age 17, March 15, 1862. Mustered in as Private. Elected 3rd Lieutenant on February 1, 1863. Reported present from November, 1862, through December, 1863. Promoted to 1st Lieutenant on June 18, 1864. Reported present in May-June, 1864. Wounded in the leg in the trenches near Petersburg, Virginia, July 6, 1864. Promoted to Captain on August 3, 1864. Leg amputated on an unspecified date. Retired to the Invalid Corps on March 8, 1865.

LINDSAY, THOMAS WATKIN
Resided in Lincoln County where he enlisted at age 34, February 11, 1863, for the war. Mustered in as Private. Promoted to 1st Sergeant in March-April, 1863. Reported present or accounted for from November, 1862, through

December, 1863. Appointed 3rd Lieutenant on November 15, 1863. Reported present in May-August, 1864. Promoted to Captain on or about March 8, 1865. Reported in hospital at Danville, Virginia, March 13, 1865, suffering from chronic diarrhoea. No further records.

LIEUTENANTS

BEAM, GEORGE W., 2nd Lieutenant
Born in Lincoln County where he resided as a "manufacturer of lumber" prior to enlisting in Lincoln County at age 24, March 15, 1862. Mustered in as 1st Sergeant. Appointed 2nd Lieutenant on May 20, 1862. Resigned on or about October 13, 1862. Resignation accepted on November 8, 1862. [A notation on the back of his letter of resignation indicates that he resigned after failing to pass an examination for promotion to the rank of 1st Lieutenant.]

BRIGGS, WILLIAM B., 2nd Lieutenant
Born in York District, South Carolina, and resided in Gaston County prior to enlisting in Lincoln County at age 21. Elected 2nd Lieutenant on March 23, 1862. Resigned on or about June 5, 1862. Reason he resigned not reported.

DAMRON, JOHN D., 2nd Lieutenant
Born in Smith County, Virginia, and resided in Cleveland County where he was by occupation a farmer prior to enlisting in Lincoln County at age 30, March 15, 1862. Appointed 2nd Lieutenant on or about July 10, 1862. Resigned on December 22, 1862, because "another man has been made 1st Lt over me and I have not had a chance to be promoted by seniority and have not been examined to test my competency." Resignation accepted on or about January 6, 1863. [Other records in Lieutenant Damron's file indicate that he was "a good officer in every respect except that he will whenever he can get it drink liquor to excess." May have served later as Private in Company C, 59th Regiment N.C. Troops (4th Regiment N.C. Cavalry).]

FALLS, ROBERT W., 1st Lieutenant
Born in Lincoln County where he resided as a farmer prior to enlisting in Lincoln County at age 25. Elected 1st Lieutenant on March 23, 1862. Resigned on July 21, 1862, by reason of ill health resulting in part from an attack of continued fever and "a naturally feeble constitution." Resignation accepted on August 15, 1862.

MAUNEY, LAWSON, 2nd Lieutenant
Previously served as Sergeant in Company D, 24th Regiment N.C. Troops (14th Regiment N.C. Volunteers). Appointed 2nd Lieutenant and transferred to this company on August 1, 1864. Captured at Five Forks, Virginia, April 1, 1865. Confined at Washington, D.C., April 5, 1865. Transferred to Johnson's Island, Ohio, April 9, 1865. Released at Johnson's Island on June 19, 1865, after taking the Oath of Allegiance.

PHIFER, EDWARD X., 1st Lieutenant

Resided in Lincoln County and enlisted at Drewry's Bluff, Virginia, at age 17, July 12, 1862, for the war. Mustered in as Private. Promoted to 1st Sergeant prior to November 1, 1862. Elected 2nd Lieutenant on November 1, 1862. Reported present or accounted for from November, 1862, through December, 1863. Promoted to 1st Lieutenant on July 24, 1863. "Received his death wound through the lungs" near Petersburg, Virginia, June 18, 1864. Hospitalized at Petersburg where he died on July 18, 1864. "A bright, noble boy and faithful, light-hearted soldier."

WARLICK, RUFUS M., 2nd Lieutenant

Previously served as Private in Company K, 1st Regiment N.C. Infantry (6 months, 1861). Appointed 2nd Lieutenant of this company on March 23, 1862. Died in hospital at Petersburg, Virginia, on or about July 3, 1862, of "pneumonia."

NONCOMMISSIONED OFFICERS AND PRIVATES

ALEXANDER, DAVID M., Private

Born in Lincoln County where he resided as a farmer prior to enlisting in Lincoln County at age 32, March 15, 1862. Reported present from November, 1862, through June, 1863. Deserted on August 2, 1863. Arrested on August 17, 1863. Returned to duty on August 31, 1863. Reported present in September-December, 1863, and May-August, 1864. Captured at Fort Stedman, Virginia, March 25, 1865. Confined at Point Lookout, Maryland, until released on June 22, 1865, after taking the Oath of Allegiance.

ALEXANDER, JOHN F., Corporal

Born in Iredell County and resided in Lincoln County where he was by occupation a tailor prior to enlisting in Lincoln County at age 39, March 15, 1862. Mustered in as Private. Reported present from November, 1862, through December, 1863. Promoted to Corporal on November 15, 1863. Reported present in May-June, 1864. Reported absent wounded in July-August, 1864. Place and date wounded not reported. Died at or near Richmond, Virginia, on or about August 27, 1864, presumably of wounds.

ANTHONY, E., Private

Enlisted in Lincoln County on April 1, 1864, for the war. Wounded in the groin at the Battle of the Crater, near Petersburg, Virginia, July 30, 1864. Died of wounds. Place and date of death not reported.

ANTHONY, GIDEON C., Private

Born in Lincoln County where he resided as a farmer prior to enlisting in Lincoln County at age 22, March 15, 1862. Reported present or accounted for from November, 1862, through December, 1863, and in May-June, 1864. Wounded in the thigh at the Battle of the Crater, near Petersburg, Virginia, July 30, 1864. Returned to duty prior to September 1, 1864. Captured at Five Forks,

Virginia, April 1, 1865. Confined at Point Lookout, Maryland, April 5, 1865. Released at Point Lookout on June 22, 1865, after taking the Oath of Allegiance. "He was of cheery disposition, companionable, and treasured the memories of those eventful years, with the scenes around the camp fire, on the march, and in the smoke of battle."

ANTHONY, VARDREY, Private

Resided in Lincoln County where he enlisted at age 18, February 11, 1863, for the war. Reported present or accounted for in March-December, 1863. Killed at Drewry's Bluff, Virginia, May 16, 1864.

BAKER, BENNETT A., Private

Resided in Johnston County where he enlisted at age 17, June 1, 1863, for the war. Reported present in June-December, 1863, and May-August, 1864. Captured at Fort Stedman, Virginia, March 25, 1865. Confined at Point Lookout, Maryland, until released on June 23, 1865, after taking the Oath of Allegiance.

BAKER, JOHN H., Sergeant

Born in Cabarrus County and resided in Gaston County where he was by occupation an engineer prior to enlisting in Lincoln County at age 35, March 15, 1862. Mustered in as Corporal. Promoted to Sergeant on May 20, 1862. Reported present or accounted for from November, 1862, through December, 1863. Wounded at Drewry's Bluff, Virginia, May 16, 1864. Returned to duty in July-August, 1864. Captured at Fort Stedman, Virginia, March 25, 1865. Confined at Point Lookout, Maryland, until released on June 23, 1865, after taking the Oath of Allegiance.

BAXTER, THOMAS H., Private

Previously served as Private in Company E, 34th Regiment N.C. Troops. Transferred to this company on October 6, 1862, in exchange for Private Samuel J. Hoyle. Reported present until May 1, 1863, when he was discharged after providing a substitute.

BEAM, DAVID C., Private

Born in Lincoln County where he resided as a farmer prior to enlisting in Lincoln County at age 30, March 15, 1862. Mustered in as Corporal. Hospitalized at Richmond, Virginia, September 26, 1862, with a gunshot wound of the thumb or finger. Place and date wounded not reported. Furloughed for thirty days on January 12, 1863. Returned to duty prior to March 1, 1863. Promoted to Sergeant on October 10, 1863. Reported present in March-December, 1863, and May-June, 1864. Reported absent wounded in July-August, 1864. Place and date wounded not reported. Reduced to ranks on August 21, 1864. Returned to duty on an unspecified date. Captured at Five Forks, Virginia, April 1, 1865. Confined at Point Lookout, Maryland, April 5, 1865. Released at Point Lookout on June 23, 1865, after taking the Oath of Allegiance.

BEASON, ARCHIBALD, Private

Born in Lincoln County and resided in Gaston County where he was by occupation a miner prior to enlisting in

Lincoln County at age 35, March 15, 1862. Transferred to Company G of this regiment on or about October 1, 1862.

BENNETT, JOHN, Private
Born in Cleveland County and resided in Gaston County where he was by occupation a miner prior to enlisting in Lincoln County at age 18, March 15, 1862. Reported present from November, 1862, through December, 1863. Wounded at Bermuda Hundred, Virginia, May 20, 1864. Returned to duty on an unspecified date. Deserted to the enemy on or about July 10, 1864. Confined at Old Capitol Prison, Washington, D.C., July 19, 1864. Transferred to Elmira, New York, July 23, 1864. Released at Elmira on May 15, 1865, after taking the Oath of Allegiance.

BENNETT, ROBERT F., Corporal
Born in Lincoln County and resided in Gaston County where he was by occupation a miner prior to enlisting in Lincoln County at age 32, March 15, 1862. Mustered in as Private. Promoted to Corporal on July 21, 1862. Reported absent without leave in November-December, 1862. Returned to duty in January-February, 1863. Reduced to ranks on February 1, 1863. Reported present in March-December, 1863. Promoted to Corporal in September-October, 1863. Reported present in May-August, 1864. Transferred to Company A, 1st Regiment Confederate Engineer Troops, October 10, 1864.

BERRYHILL, PINKNEY L., Private
Born in Mecklenburg County where he resided as a miner prior to enlisting in Lincoln County at age 23, March 15, 1862. Reported present from November, 1862, through December, 1863, and in May-June, 1864. Deserted to the enemy on or about July 10, 1864. Confined at Old Capitol Prison, Washington, D.C., July 19, 1864. Transferred to Elmira, New York, July 23, 1864. Released at Elmira on May 29, 1865, after taking the Oath of Allegiance. [North Carolina pension records indicate that he was injured (stunned) in Virginia in September-November, 1864, by the explosion of a shell.]

BESS, THOMAS, Private
Born in Lincoln County where he resided as a farmer prior to enlisting in Lincoln County at age 38, March 15, 1862. Reported present or accounted for from November, 1862, through December, 1863, and in May-August, 1864. Surrendered at Appomattox Court House, Virginia, April 9, 1865.

BLACKBURN, DANIEL, Private
Enlisted in Lincoln County on April 1, 1864, for the war. Shot through the breast and killed at Drewry's Bluff, Virginia, May 16, 1864.

BLACKBURN, DAVID A., Private
Born in Lincoln County where he resided as a farmer prior to enlisting in Lincoln County at age 23, March 15, 1862. Wounded at Sharpsburg, Maryland, September 17, 1862. Returned to duty on an unspecified date. Reported present from November, 1862, through December, 1863. Wounded in the face (and possibly also in the shoulder) and captured at Drewry's Bluff, Virginia, May 16, 1864,

while attempting to rescue his mortally wounded brother Daniel (see preceding service record). Hospitalized at Point Lookout, Maryland. Released from hospital and was confined in the prison at Point Lookout on May 30, 1865. Released at Point Lookout on June 6, 1865, after taking the Oath of Allegiance.

BLUNT, GEORGE W., Private
Born in Mecklenburg County where he resided as a miner prior to enlisting in Lincoln County at age 35, March 15, 1862. Reported absent without leave in November-December, 1862. Returned to duty in January-February, 1863. Reported present in March-December, 1863. Reported absent on detached service with Company H, 2nd Regiment Confederate Engineer Troops, from May, 1864, through the end of the war.

BRACKETT, GEORGE W., Private
Born in Lincoln County and resided in Gaston County where he was by occupation a farmer prior to enlisting in Lincoln County at age 21, March 15, 1862. Died on May 10 or June 10, 1862, of disease. Place of death not reported.

BREWER, ELI H., Private
Resided in Wilkes County and was by occupation a farmer prior to enlisting in Wilkes County at age 28, October 19, 1863, for the war. Reported present or accounted for in November-December, 1863, and May-August, 1864. Paroled at Greensboro on May 1, 1865. [Was probably wounded slightly at or near Petersburg, Virginia, in May-August, 1864.]

BREWER, H. L., Private
Resided in Wilkes County and enlisted in Wake County at age 42, October 19, 1863, for the war. Reported absent sick in November-December, 1863. Hospitalized at Petersburg, Virginia, June 18, 1864, with a gunshot wound of the hand. Place and date wounded not reported. Reported absent wounded through August, 1864.

BREWER, NATHANIEL M., Private
Resided in Wilkes County and was by occupation a farmer prior to enlisting in Wake County at age 26, October 19, 1863, for the war. Reported present or accounted for in November-December, 1863. Deserted from hospital at Raleigh on May 24, 1864. Reported absent sick in July-August, 1864.

BRIGGS, JOHN W., Corporal
Born in Davidson County and resided in Gaston County where he was by occupation a miner prior to enlisting in Gaston County at age 23, March 15, 1862. Mustered in as Private. Captured in Maryland on September 11, 1862. Confined at Fort Delaware, Delaware. Paroled and transferred to Aiken's Landing, James River, Virginia, October 2, 1862. Declared exchanged at Aiken's Landing on November 10, 1862. Reported present or accounted for in January-December, 1863. Promoted to Corporal on November 15, 1863. Deserted to the enemy on or about June 11, 1864. Confined at Old Capitol Prison, Washington, D.C., June 14, 1864. Transferred to Elmira, New York, July 23, 1864. Released at Elmira

on September 19, 1864, after taking the Oath of Allegiance.

BRIGGS, THOMAS W., Private

Enlisted in Gaston County on March 15, 1862. Reported absent without leave in November-December, 1862.

BUMGARNER, ANDREW, Private

Resided in Cleveland County and was by occupation a farmer prior to enlisting in Lincoln County at age 40, February 11, 1863, for the war. Reported present or accounted for in March-December, 1863. Wounded in the left hand at Bermuda Hundred, Virginia, May 20, 1864. Deserted to the enemy on or about [March 14, 1865]. Confined at Washington, D.C., March 18, 1865. Released on an unspecified date after taking the Oath of Allegiance.

COMBS, CALVIN, _____

North Carolina pension records indicate that he served in this company.

CONNOR, JAMES P., Private

Resided in Cleveland County and enlisted in Lincoln County on April 1, 1864, for the war. Reported present in May-August, 1864. Captured at Five Forks, Virginia, April 1, 1865. Confined at Point Lookout, Maryland, April 5, 1865. Released at Point Lookout on June 24, 1865, after taking the Oath of Allegiance.

COSTNER, CHRISTOPHER, Private

Born in Lincoln County and resided in Cleveland County where he was by occupation a farmer prior to enlisting in Lincoln County at age 35, March 15, 1862. Died in hospital at Petersburg, Virginia, on or about July 16, 1862, of "typhoid febris."

DANCEY, CALVIN, Private

Previously served as Private in Company C, 26th Regiment N.C. Troops. Enlisted in this company on October 19, 186[3], for the war. Reported absent sick in November-December, 1863. Died in hospital at Weldon on January 18, 1864, of "variola."

DAUGHERTY, WILLIAM A., Private

Born in Cleveland County where he resided as a farmer prior to enlisting in Lincoln County at age 21, March 15, 1862. Reported present from November, 1862, through December, 1863, and in May-August, 1864. Surrendered at Appomattox Court House, Virginia, April 9, 1865.

DAVIS, ISAIAH I., Private

Born in Cleveland County where he resided as a blacksmith prior to enlisting in Lincoln County at age 18, March 15, 1862. Mustered in as Private. Promoted to Corporal prior to January 1, 1863. Reported present from November, 1862, through December, 1863. Promoted to Sergeant in September, 1863. Appointed Musician on October 10, 1863. Reported present in May-August, 1864. Reduced to ranks on an unspecified date. Surrendered at Appomattox Court House, Virginia, April 9, 1865.

DELLINGER, ADAM, Private

Born in Lincoln County where he resided prior to enlisting in Lincoln County at age 42, March 15, 1862. Reported present or accounted for from November, 1862, through December, 1863, and in May-August, 1864. Hospitalized at Richmond, Virginia, December 9, 1864, with chronic diarrhoea. Furloughed for sixty days on December 31, 1864. [Was probably wounded slightly at or near Petersburg, Virginia, in May-August, 1864.]

DELLINGER, PHILIP F., Private

Born in Lincoln County where he resided as a farmer prior to enlisting in Lincoln County at age 45, March 15, 1862. Reported present from November, 1862, through December, 1863, and in May-August, 1864. Captured at Five Forks, Virginia, April 1, 1865. Confined at Point Lookout, Maryland, April 5, 1865. Released at Point Lookout on June 21, 1865, after taking the Oath of Allegiance.

DIXON, JOHN, Private

Resided in Gaston County where he enlisted at age 30, February 11, 1863, for the war. Reported present in March-December, 1863. Wounded in the left side at Drewry's Bluff, Virginia, May 16, 1864. Returned to duty in July-August, 1864. Killed at Globe Tavern, Virginia, August 21, 1864.

DIXON, ROBERT W., Private

Born in Cleveland County* and resided in Gaston County where he was by occupation a farmer prior to enlisting in Lincoln County at age 26, March 15, 1862. Wounded at Malvern Hill, Virginia, July 1, 1862. Died on July 7, 1862, of wounds. Place of death not reported.

DORETY, JOHN HENRY, _____

North Carolina pension records indicate that he served in this company.

ELLIOTT, JOHN A., Private

Born in Mecklenburg County and resided in Gaston County where he was by occupation a miner prior to enlisting in Lincoln County at age 23, March 15, 1862. Died in hospital at Raleigh on or about May 18, 1862, of disease.

ELMORE, ELI A., Private

Born in Cleveland County* where he resided as a miner prior to enlisting in Lincoln County at age 26, March 15, 1862. Died on or about September 19, 1862, of disease. Place of death not reported.

ELMORE, EPHRAIM A., Private

Born in Lincoln County where he resided as a farmer prior to enlisting in Lincoln County at age 34, March 15, 1862. Reported present or accounted for from November, 1862, through June, 1863. Deserted on August 2, 1863. Arrested on August 17, 1863. Returned to duty on August 31, 1863. Reported present in September-December, 1863, and May-August, 1864. Wounded in the left thigh at Fort Stedman, Virginia, March 25, 1865. Hospitalized at Richmond, Virginia. Captured in hospital at Richmond on April 3, 1865. Transferred to Point Lookout, Maryland, May 2, 1865. Released at Point Lookout on or about June 28, 1865, after taking the Oath of Allegiance.

FISHER, LAWSON, Private
Born in Lincoln County where he resided as a farmer prior to enlisting in Lincoln County at age 34, March 15, 1862. Wounded at Malvern Hill, Virginia, July 1, 1862. Died in hospital at Mount Jackson, Virginia, on or about December 2, 1862, of "pneumonia."

FORBES, JOSEPH T., Private
Previously served as Private in 2nd Company B of this regiment. Transferred to this company on July 1, 1864. No further records.

FORD, BELTON, Private
Born in Chester District, South Carolina, and resided in Gaston County where he was by occupation a farmer prior to enlisting at age 36, March 15, 1862. Died in hospital at Raleigh on May 15, 1862, of "measles."

FORD, JOHN WESLEY, Sergeant
Born in Chester District, South Carolina, and resided in Gaston County where he was by occupation a farmer prior to enlisting in Lincoln County at age 22, March 15, 1862. Mustered in as Private. Promoted to Corporal on February 1, 1863. Reported present or accounted for from November, 1862, through December, 1863. Promoted to Sergeant on November 15, 1863. Wounded near Petersburg, Virginia, June 18, 1864. Reported absent wounded through August, 1864. Survived the war.

FREEMAN, RILEY W., Private
Born in Union County* and resided in Gaston County where he was by occupation a miner prior to enlisting in Lincoln County at age 24, March 15, 1862. Reported absent without leave in November-December, 1862. Returned to duty in January-February, 1863. Reported present in March-December, 1863. Wounded in the right thigh at Drewry's Bluff, Virginia, May 16, 1864. Hospitalized at Richmond, Virginia. Furloughed for sixty days on or about May 27, 1864. Reported absent wounded through August, 1864. Hospitalized at Charlotte on January 27, 1865, with a gunshot wound of the "lower left extremities." Place and date wounded not reported. Transferred to another hospital on April 14, 1865.

GRIGG, ABNER M., Private
Born in Lincoln County where he resided as a farmer prior to enlisting in Lincoln County at age 25, March 15, 1862. Mustered in as Sergeant. Wounded at Malvern Hill, Virginia, July 1, 1862. Reduced to ranks on July 2, 1862. Reported absent wounded from November, 1862, through August, 1863. Returned to duty in September-October, 1863. Reported absent wounded in November-December, 1863, and May-June, 1864. Reported absent on detached service at Charlotte in July-August, 1864. Hospitalized at Charlotte on December 20, 1864, with an ulcer of the left ankle and was furloughed on December 30, 1864.

GRIGG, ELI C., Private
Previously served as Private in Company C, 15th Regiment N.C. Troops (5th Regiment N.C. Volunteers). Transferred to this company on or about September 1, 1862. Wounded in the left arm at Fredericksburg, Virginia, December 13, 1862. Left arm amputated. Retired to the Invalid Corps on December 15, 1864.

GRIGG, WILLIAM D., Private
Born in Illinois and resided in Cleveland County where he was by occupation a farmer prior to enlisting in Cleveland or Lincoln County at age 28, March 15, 1862. Mustered in as Private. Promoted to Sergeant on February 1, 1863. Reported present from November, 1862, through December, 1863. Reduced to ranks in September-October, 1863. Reported present in May-August, 1864. Captured by the enemy on an unspecified date. Confined at Point Lookout, Maryland. Released at Point Lookout on June 27, 1865, after taking the Oath of Allegiance. [Was probably wounded slightly at or near Petersburg, Virginia, in May-August, 1864.]

GUFFEY, WILLIAM T., Private
Born in Rutherford County and resided in Gaston County where he was by occupation a farmer prior to enlisting in Gaston County at age 23, March 15, 1862. Reported present from November, 1862, through December, 1863, and in May-August, 1864. [During the siege of Petersburg "Private William Guffey . . . while rubbing up his field piece, as he was pleased to call his rifle, had the misfortune to have it smashed by a mortar shell. Seeing the shell, with the fuse burning rapidly and almost ready to explode, he cried out, 'Why, there is the darned old thing frying now,' and grabbing it up, threw it over the breastworks." Clark's *Regiments*, Volume V, page 15.]

HAFNER, GEORGE W., Private
Born in Lincoln County where he resided as a farmer prior to enlisting in Lincoln County at age 29, March 15, 1862. Mustered in as Sergeant. Reduced to ranks on February 13, 1863. Reported present from November, 1862, through June, 1863. Deserted on August 2, 1863. Reported under arrest in September-December, 1863. Returned to duty on an unspecified date. Reported present in May-August, 1864. Surrendered at Appomattox Court House, Virginia, April 9, 1865.

HAFNER, LAWSON, Private
Resided in Lincoln County where he enlisted at age 36, February 11, 1863, for the war. Reported present in March-December, 1863. Killed at Drewry's Bluff, Virginia, on or about May 16, 1864.

HAGANS, WARREN S., Private
Born in Lincoln County and resided in Gaston County where he was by occupation a farmer prior to enlisting in Lincoln County at age 22, March 15, 1862. Captured at Malvern Hill, Virginia, July 1, 1862. Confined at Fort Columbus, New York Harbor, July 6, 1862. Transferred to Fort Delaware, Delaware, July 9, 1862. Paroled and transferred to Aiken's Landing, James River, Virginia, where he was received on July 12, 1862, for exchange. Declared exchanged at Aiken's Landing on August 5, 1862. Died in hospital at Petersburg, Virginia, November 14, 1862, of "typhoid fever."

HANNA, Q. T., Private
Resided in Davidson County where he enlisted on January 1, 1864, for the war. Deserted to the enemy on or about June 11, 1864. Confined at Old Capitol Prison, Washington, D.C. Transferred to Elmira, New York, July 23, 1864. Released at Elmira on or about September 19, 1864, after taking the Oath of Allegiance.

HARMON, JACOB H., Private

Born in Cleveland County and resided in Gaston County where he was by occupation a farmer prior to enlisting in Lincoln County at age 18, March 15, 1862. Reported present or accounted for from November, 1862, through December, 1863. Deserted to the enemy on or about June 11, 1864. Confined at Old Capitol Prison, Washington, D.C. Transferred to Elmira, New York, July 23, 1864. Released at Elmira on September 19, 1864, after taking the Oath of Allegiance.

HARMON, JOHN L., Private

Resided in Gaston County where he enlisted at age 29, February 11, 1863, for the war. Reported present or accounted for in March-December, 1863, and May-August, 1864. Captured at Fort Stedman, Virginia, March 25, 1865. Confined at Point Lookout, Maryland, until released on June 27, 1865, after taking the Oath of Allegiance.

HARTMAN, NATHAN C., Private

Born in Lincoln County where he resided as a farmer prior to enlisting in Lincoln County at age 24, March 15, 1862. Wounded at Malvern Hill, Virginia, July 1, 1862. Reported absent without leave in November-December, 1862. Died on March 4 or March 8, 1863, of "excess of morphia."

HELMS, WILLIAM, Private

Born in Lincoln County where he resided as a farmer prior to enlisting in Lincoln County at age 37, March 15, 1862. Reported absent without leave in November-December, 1862. Reported absent sick in January-June, 1863. Hospitalized on August 28, 1863, with a gunshot wound of the left thigh. Place and date wounded not reported. Furloughed on October 5, 1863. Reported absent sick in November-December, 1863, and May-August, 1864.

HINMAN, SAMUEL, Private

Resided in Lincoln County where he enlisted at age 32, February 15, 1863, for the war. Reported present in March-December, 1863, and May-August, 1864. Captured at Five Forks, Virginia, April 1, 1865. Confined at Point Lookout, Maryland, April 5, 1865. Released at Point Lookout on June 27, 1865, after taking the Oath of Allegiance.

HOGAN, WARREN, _____

North Carolina pension records indicate that he served in this company.

HOUSER, DANIEL R., Corporal

Born in Lincoln County where he resided as a farmer prior to enlisting in Lincoln County at age 22, March 15, 1862. Mustered in as Private. Hospitalized on July 19, 1862, with diarrhoea. Returned to duty on September 2, 1862. Reported present from November, 1862, through December, 1863. Promoted to Corporal on October 10, 1863. Wounded at Bermuda Hundred, Virginia, June 2, 1864. Reported absent wounded through July, 1864. His transfer to Company F, 17th Regiment South Carolina Infantry, was approved on August 8, 1864; however, he

died at home in Lincoln County on August 1, 1864, of disease.

HOUSER, EMANUEL, Private

Enlisted at Camp Stokes at age 38, October 27, 1864, for the war. Detailed as a blacksmith on January 11, 1865. Surrendered at Appomattox Court House, Virginia, April 9, 1865.

HOUSER, FRANKLIN A., Private

Resided in Lincoln County where he enlisted at age 37, February 11, 1863, for the war. Reported present in March-December, 1863, and May-August, 1864. Wounded in the scalp at or near Fort Stedman, Virginia, on or about March 25, 1865. Hospitalized at Richmond, Virginia. Captured in hospital at Richmond on April 3, 1865. Transferred to Newport News, Virginia, April 23, 1865. Released at Newport News on June 30, 1865, after taking the Oath of Allegiance.

HOUSER, JACOB, Private

Resided in Lincoln County where he enlisted on April 1, 1864, for the war. Reported present or accounted for in May-August, 1864. Captured at Five Forks, Virginia, April 1, 1865. Confined at Point Lookout, Maryland, April 5, 1865. Released at Point Lookout on June 27, 1865, after taking the Oath of Allegiance.

HOUSER, JOSEPH, Corporal

Resided in Lincoln County where he enlisted at age 18, March 15, 1862. Mustered in as Private. Reported present from November, 1862, through December, 1863, and in May-August, 1864. Promoted to Corporal subsequent to August 31, 1864. Captured at Five Forks, Virginia, April 1, 1865. Confined at Point Lookout, Maryland, April 5, 1865. Released at Point Lookout on June 27, 1865, after taking the Oath of Allegiance.

HOUSER, LAWSON, Private

Resided in Lincoln County where he enlisted at age 18, February 11, 1863, for the war. Reported present from November, 1862, through December, 1863, and in May-August, 1864. Captured at or near Five Forks, Virginia, on or about April 1, 1865. Confined at Point Lookout, Maryland, April 5, 1865. Released at Point Lookout on June 27, 1865, after taking the Oath of Allegiance. "His comrades name him among the bravest of the brave. He was of sunny disposition, true to conviction and loyal to duty."

HOUSER, THOMAS, Private

Resided in Lincoln County where he enlisted at age 17, February 11, 1863, for the war. Reported present from November, 1862, through December, 1863, and in May-August, 1864. Surrendered at Appomattox Court House, Virginia, April 9, 1865.

HOYLE, B. W., Private

Resided in Lincoln County and was by occupation a farmer prior to enlisting in Lincoln County at age 37, February 11, 1863, for the war. Reported present or accounted for in March-December, 1863, and May-August, 1864. Reported in hospital at Danville, Virginia, April 5, 1865, with debilitas. No further records.

HOYLE, JOHN S., Private
Born in Lincoln County and was by occupation a farmer prior to enlisting in Lincoln County at age 23, March 15, 1862. No further records.

HOYLE, PETER C., Private
Born in Lincoln County where he resided as a farmer prior to enlisting in Lincoln County at age 49, March 15, 1862. Wounded at Sharpsburg, Maryland, September 17, 1862. Hospitalized at Richmond, Virginia, where he died on September 30, 1862, of wounds.

HOYLE, SAMUEL J., Private
Resided in Lincoln County and enlisted at age 21, March 15, 1862. Transferred to Company E, 34th Regiment N.C. Troops, on or about October 6, 1862, in exchange for Private Thomas H. Baxter.

HUFFSTETLER, HENRY C., Private
Born in Lincoln County and resided in Gaston County where he was by occupation a blacksmith prior to enlisting in Lincoln County at age 20, March 15, 1862. Reported present from November, 1862, through December, 1863. Deserted to the enemy on or about June 11, 1864. Confined at Old Capitol Prison, Washington, D.C. Transferred to Elmira, New York, July 23, 1864. Released at Elmira on September 19, 1864, after taking the Oath of Allegiance.

HULL, WILLIAM, Private
Resided in Catawba County where he enlisted at age 37, June 1, 1863, for the war. Reported present in July-December, 1863. Killed at Drewry's Bluff, Virginia, May 16, 1864.

HUSS, JACOB, Private
Place and date of enlistment not reported; however, he probably enlisted subsequent to August 31, 1864. Captured at Five Forks, Virginia, April 1, 1865. Confined at Point Lookout, Maryland, April 5, 1865. Released at Point Lookout on June 4, 1865, after taking the Oath of Allegiance.

HUTCHINSON, DAVID W., Private
Born in Mecklenburg County and resided in Gaston County prior to enlisting in Lincoln County at age 40, March 15, 1862. Reported absent without leave in November-December, 1862. Reported absent sick in January-October, 1863. Reported present in November-December, 1863. Deserted to the enemy on or about June 9, 1864. Confined at Old Capitol Prison, Washington, D.C. Transferred to Elmira, New York, July 23, 1864. Released at Elmira on September 19, 1864, after taking the Oath of Allegiance.

JACKSON, ANDREW, _____
North Carolina pension records indicate that he served in this company.

JACKSON, DRURY S., Private
Born in Spartanburg District, South Carolina, and resided in Gaston County where he was by occupation a farmer prior to enlisting in Lincoln County at age 22, March 15, 1862. Wounded in the neck at Fredericksburg, Virginia, December 13, 1862. Reported absent wounded through February, 1863. Returned to duty in March-April, 1863. Reported present in May-December, 1863, and May-August, 1864. Hospitalized at Richmond, Virginia, March 13, 1865, with an unspecified complaint. Transferred to Danville, Virginia, April 1, 1865. Paroled at Lynchburg, Virginia, on or about April 15, 1865.

JACKSON, SOLOMON L., Private
Born in Spartanburg District or York District, South Carolina, and resided in Gaston County where he was by occupation a farmer prior to enlisting in Lincoln County at age 24, March 15, 1862. Died in hospital at Raleigh on or about June 8, 1862, of "pneumonia."

JETTON, CHARLES P., Private
Born in Lincoln County where he resided as a student prior to enlisting in Lincoln County at age 16, March 15, 1862. Wounded at King's School House, Virginia, June 25, 1862. Returned to duty on an unspecified date. Reported present from November, 1862, through December, 1863, and in May-August, 1864. Survived the war.

JETTON, GEORGE M., Private
Resided in Lincoln County. Place and date of enlistment not reported; however, he probably enlisted subsequent to August 31, 1864. Captured at Five Forks, Virginia, April 1, 1865. Confined at Point Lookout, Maryland, April 5, 1865. Released at Point Lookout on June 14, 1865, after taking the Oath of Allegiance.

JOHNSON, A. T., Private
Resided in Johnston County where he enlisted at age 30, June 1, 1863, for the war. Deserted on or about August 20, 1863.

JOHNSON, C., Private
Resided in Johnston County and enlisted at age 32, June 1, 1863, for the war. Discharged on July 1, 1863. Reason discharged not reported.

JOHNSON, J. J., Private
Resided in Johnston County and enlisted in Wake County at age 27, June 1, 1863, for the war. Reported present or accounted for in July-December, 1863, and May-August, 1864. Was absent sick during most of that period. No further records.

JOHNSON, JOHN A., Private
Resided in Johnston County where he enlisted at age 19, June 1, 1863, for the war. Reported present in July-December, 1863, and May-August, 1864. Hospitalized at Richmond, Virginia, in November, 1864, with chronic diarrhoea. "Caught gambling" while a hospital patient in Richmond and was placed under arrest. Returned to duty on or about December 7, 1864. Captured at Five Forks, Virginia, April 1, 1865. Confined at Point Lookout, Maryland, April 5, 1865. Released at Point Lookout on June 28, 1865, after taking the Oath of Allegiance. [North Carolina pension records indicate that he was wounded near Petersburg, Virginia, in January, 1865.]

KANIPE, HENRY, Private
Born in Lincoln County where he resided as a farmer prior to enlisting in Lincoln County at age 28, March 15, 1862. Reported present from November, 1862, through December, 1863, and in May-August, 1864. Surrendered at Appomattox Court House, Virginia, April 9, 1865.

LACKEY, DAVID, Private
Resided in Lincoln County where he enlisted at age 31, March 15, 1862. Discharged on November 2, 1862. Reason discharged not reported.

LANGDON, ZACHARIAH, Private
Resided in Johnston County and was by occupation a farmer prior to enlisting in Johnston County at age 38, June 1, 1863, for the war. Reported present in June-December, 1863. Wounded at Drewry's Bluff, Virginia, on or about May 16, 1864. Returned to duty prior to July 1, 1864. Deserted on August 11, 1864.

LEDFORD, JAMES E., Private
Born in Lincoln County where he resided as a farmer prior to enlisting in Lincoln County at age 23, March 15, 1862. Reported present or accounted for from November, 1862, through December, 1863, and in May-August, 1864. Surrendered at Appomattox Court House, Virginia, April 9, 1865. Served as a teamster during much of the war.

LEDFORD, JEFF C., Private
Resided in Lincoln County where he enlisted at age 22, March 15, 1862. Reported present or accounted for from November, 1862, through December, 1863, and in May-June, 1864. Killed at or near Petersburg, Virginia, July 10, 1864.

LENHARDT, JACOB N., Private
Born in Lincoln County where he resided as a farmer prior to enlisting in Lincoln County at age 30, March 15, 1862. Captured at Frederick, Maryland, September 12, 1862. Confined at Fort Delaware, Delaware. Paroled and transferred to Aiken's Landing, James River, Virginia, October 2, 1862, for exchange. Declared exchanged at Aiken's Landing on November 10, 1862. Reported present from November, 1862, through June, 1863. Deserted on August 2, 1863. Arrested on August 17, 1863. Returned to duty on August 31, 1863. Reported present in September-December, 1863, and May-June, 1864. Killed at or near Globe Tavern, Virginia, on or about August 21, 1864.

LENHARDT, JOHN W., Private
Born in Lincoln County where he resided as a farmer prior to enlisting in Lincoln County at age 35, March 15, 1862. Wounded in the right hip at Fredericksburg, Virginia, December 13, 1862. Returned to duty in January-February, 1863. Deserted on August 2, 1863. Arrested on August 17, 1863. Returned to duty on August 31, 1863. Reported present in September-December, 1863, and May-August, 1864. Died in hospital at Richmond, Virginia, October 14, 1864, of "dysenteria (acuta)."

LENHARDT, JOSEPH, Private
Enlisted in Lincoln County on April 1, 1864, for the war.

Reported present through August, 1864. [Was probably wounded slightly at or near Petersburg, Virginia, in May-August, 1864.]

LEONARD, FRANKLIN J., Private
Resided in Lincoln County and was by occupation a farmer prior to enlisting in Lincoln County at age 40, February 11, 1863, for the war. Reported present in March-December, 1863. Wounded severely in the hip near Petersburg, Virginia, on or about June 21, 1864. Reported absent wounded through August, 1864. No further records.

LEONHARDT, CALVIN, Private
Resided in Lincoln County where he enlisted at age 16, February 11, 1863, for the war. Reported present in March-December, 1863, and May-August, 1864.

LITTON, ISAAC, Private
Resided in Lincoln County where he enlisted at age 43, September 1, 1863, for the war. Reported present in September-December, 1863, and May-June, 1864. Killed at the Battle of the Crater, near Petersburg, Virginia, July 30, 1864.

LOWE, JOHN, Private
Resided in Gaston County and enlisted in Lincoln County on April 1, 1864, for the war. Wounded in the finger prior to July 1, 1864. Place and date wounded not reported. Returned to duty in July-August, 1864. Captured at Fort Stedman, Virginia, March 25, 1865. Confined at Point Lookout, Maryland, until released on June 28, 1865, after taking the Oath of Allegiance.

LOWE, JOHN A., 1st Sergeant
Born in Lincoln County where he resided as a farmer prior to enlisting in Lincoln County at age 25, March 15, 1862. Mustered in as Sergeant. Reported present from November, 1862, through December, 1863. Promoted to 1st Sergeant on November 15, 1863. Reported present or accounted for in May-August, 1864. Hospitalized at Richmond, Virginia, December 8, 1864, with acute rheumatism. Returned to duty on December 13, 1864. Captured at Fort Stedman, Virginia, March 25, 1865. Confined at Point Lookout, Maryland, until released on June 28, 1865, after taking the Oath of Allegiance.

LOWE, MARCUS, Private
Born in Lincoln County and resided in Gaston County where he was by occupation a farmer prior to enlisting in Lincoln County at age 23, March 15, 1862. Reported present or accounted for from November, 1862, through December, 1863, and in May-August, 1864. Hospitalized at Richmond, Virginia, October 2, 1864, with an unspecified complaint. Transferred to another hospital on October 3, 1864. No further records.

MABURY, JOHN T., Private
Born in Gaston County* and was by occupation a miner prior to enlisting in Lincoln County at age 19, March 15, 1862. Died in hospital at Petersburg, Virginia, July 29, 1862, of "ty[phoid] febris."

McDONALD, STEPHEN J., Private
Resided in Lincoln or Cherokee County and enlisted in Lincoln County at age 23, February 11, 1863, for the war. Reported present or accounted for in March-December, 1863, and May-August, 1864. Deserted to the enemy on or about September 17, 1864. Confined at Washington, D.C., September 22, 1864. Released on an unspecified date after taking the Oath of Allegiance. [Probably served for a time as drillmaster of this company or regiment.]

MASSAGEE, ABNER, Private
Resided in Lincoln County and was by occupation a farmer prior to enlisting in Lincoln County at age 38, February 11, 1863, for the war. Deserted on or about April 10, 1863. Apprehended on an unspecified date. Reported in confinement until July 17, 1863, when he was hospitalized at Richmond, Virginia, with scorbutus. Reported absent sick through October, 1863. Returned to duty in November-December, 1863. Killed while on picket duty near Drewry's Bluff, Virginia, May 16 or June 20, 1864.

MAUNEY, NOAH H., Corporal
Born in Lincoln County where he resided as a farmer prior to enlisting in Lincoln County at age 29, March 15, 1862. Mustered in as Corporal. Reduced to ranks on July 1, 1862. Reported present from November, 1862, through December, 1863, and in May-August, 1864. Promoted to Corporal subsequent to August 31, 1864. Captured at Fort Stedman, Virginia, March 25, 1865. Confined at Point Lookout, Maryland, until released on June 29, 1865, after taking the Oath of Allegiance.

MAYFIELD, ROBERT N., Private
Born in Rutherford County and resided in Gaston County where he was by occupation a miner prior to enlisting in Lincoln County at age 58, March 15, 1862. Reported absent without leave in November-December, 1862. Returned to duty in January-February, 1863. Reported present or accounted for in March-August, 1863. Discharged on October 20, 1863, by reason of "general debility and old age."

MAYFIELD, THOMAS, Private
Resided in Gaston County and enlisted at age 20, March 15, 1862. Died in hospital at Petersburg, Virginia, June 27, 1862, of "pneumonia."

MAYFIELD, WILLIAM N., Private
Born in Rutherford County and resided in Gaston County where he was by occupation a miner prior to enlisting in Lincoln County at age 18, March 15, 1862. Died on July 11, 1862, of disease. Place of death not reported.

MICHAEL, JOHN M., Sergeant
Resided in Lincoln County where he enlisted at age 38, February 11, 1863, for the war. Mustered in as Private. Reported present in March-December, 1863, and May-August, 1864. Promoted to Sergeant subsequent to August 31, 1864. Captured at Five Forks, Virginia, April 1, 1865. Confined at Point Lookout, Maryland, April 5, 1865. Released at Point Lookout on June 15, 1865, after taking the Oath of Allegiance. [North Carolina pension records

indicate that he was wounded in the abdomen by a piece of shell at Petersburg, Virginia, on an unspecified date.]

MOORE, JOHN, Private
Resided in Johnston County where he enlisted at age 19, June 1, 1863, for the war. Died in hospital at Richmond, Virginia, August 9, 1863, of "diarrhoea chro[nic]."

OVERCASH, CALEB, Private
Enlisted in Lincoln County on April 1, 1864, for the war. Wounded near Petersburg, Virginia, June 16-18, 1864. Returned to duty prior to July 1, 1864. Reported absent sick in July-August, 1864. Hospitalized at Richmond, Virginia, February 24, 1865, with an unspecified complaint. Transferred to another hospital on February 25, 1865. No further records.

OWENS, ANDREW, Private
Enlisted in Lincoln County on November 1, 1863, for the war. Killed at Drewry's Bluff, Virginia, May 16, 1864.

PAGE, ELIAS, Private
Enlisted in Lincoln County on November 1, 1863, for the war. Reported present in November-December, 1863, and May-August, 1864. [Was probably wounded slightly at or near Petersburg, Virginia, in May-August, 1864.]

PARDEW, ELBERT M., Private
Resided in Wilkes County and enlisted in Wake County at age 19, October 19, 1863, for the war. Reported absent sick in November-December, 1863, and May-August, 1864. [North Carolina pension records indicate that he was wounded in the right leg and right arm at or near Drewry's Bluff, Virginia, in June, 186(4).]

PARKER, JACKSON, Private
Born in Cleveland County* and resided in Gaston County where he was by occupation a farmer prior to enlisting in Lincoln County at age 22, March 15, 1862. Died on May 15, 1862, of disease. Place of death not reported.

PUTNAM, A. C., Private
Previously served as Private in Company G of this regiment. Transferred to this company prior to September 17, 1862, when he was transferred to Company C, 15th Regiment N.C. Troops (5th Regiment N.C. Volunteers).

RABB, WILLIAM M., Private
Born in Lincoln County where he resided as a farmer or blacksmith prior to enlisting in Lincoln County at age 26, March 15, 1862. Wounded in the left hand at Malvern Hill, Virginia, July 1, 1862. Middle finger amputated. Discharged on November 7, 1862, by reason of disability from wounds. "The flexor muscles of the ring and index fingers are so rigidly contracted as to almost destroy the functions of [the] hand." [May have served later as Private in Company E, 34th Regiment N.C. Troops.]

REEP, GEORGE, Private
Resided in Lincoln County. Place and date of enlistment not reported; however, he probably enlisted subsequent to August 31, 1864. Captured at Fort Stedman, Virginia, March 25, 1865. Confined at Point Lookout, Maryland,

until released on June 17, 1865, after taking the Oath of Allegiance.

SELTON, C. P., Private
Place and date of enlistment not reported; however, he probably enlisted subsequent to August 31, 1864. Paroled at Burkeville, Virginia, April 14-17, 1865.

SHELL, WILLIAM HENRY, Sergeant
Born in Lincoln County where he resided as a farmer prior to enlisting in Lincoln County at age 22, March 15, 1862. Mustered in as Corporal. Captured at Sharpsburg, Maryland, September 17, 1862. Paroled on September 30, 1862. Returned to duty on an unspecified date. Promoted to Sergeant on February 1, 1863. Reported present or accounted for from November, 1862, through December, 1863, and in May-June, 1864. Wounded in the breast at the Battle of the Crater, near Petersburg, Virginia, July 30, 1864. Returned to duty prior to September 1, 1864. Hospitalized at Richmond, Virginia, October 7, 1864, with acute colitis. Furloughed for sixty days on December 16, 1864. Hospitalized at Richmond on March 16, 1865, with remittent fever. Captured in hospital at Richmond on April 3, 1865. Transferred to Newport News, Virginia, April 23, 1865. Released at Newport News on June 30, 1865, after taking the Oath of Allegiance.

SHEPHERD, WILLIAM R., Private
Born in Rockingham County and resided in Gaston County where he was by occupation a farmer prior to enlisting in Lincoln County at age 16, March 15, 1862. Discharged on or about July 10, 1862, by reason of being underage.

SHERRILL, GABRIEL POWELL, Corporal
Previously served as Private in Company K, 1st Regiment N.C. Infantry (6 months, 1861). Enlisted in this company in Catawba County on February 11, 1863, for the war. Mustered in as Private. Reported present in March-December, 1863, and May-August, 1864. Promoted to Corporal on June 11, 1864. Captured at Five Forks, Virginia, April 1, 1865. Confined at Point Lookout, Maryland, April 5, 1865. Released at Point Lookout on June 30, 1865, after taking the Oath of Allegiance.

SHERRILL, JOHN NELSON, Private
Enlisted on or about September 15, 1864, for the war. Captured at Five Forks, Virginia, April 1, 1865. Confined at Point Lookout, Maryland, April 5, 1865. Died at Point Lookout on May 3, 1865, of "int[ermittent] fever."

SHULL, CHARLES W., Private
Born in Lincoln County where he resided as a farmer prior to enlisting in Lincoln County at age 28, March 15, 1862. Reported absent without leave in November-December, 1862. Reported absent sick in January-February, 1863. Returned to duty prior to May 1, 1863. Deserted in May or early June, 1863. Court-martialed on June 10, 1863, for desertion and sentenced to be shot. Reported in confinement in September-December, 1863, and May-June, 1864. Apparently remained under sentence of death during that period. Sentence remitted on July 20, 1864, for volunteer service in the defense of Richmond

against the Sheridan raid the previous May. Returned to duty on an unspecified date. Reported absent wounded in August, 1864. Place and date wounded not reported. Returned to duty on an unspecified date. Captured at Fort Stedman, Virginia, March 25, 1865. Confined at Point Lookout, Maryland, until released on June 20, 1865, after taking the Oath of Allegiance. [North Carolina pension records indicate that he was wounded in the right leg near Petersburg, Virginia, in 186(4).]

SHULL, MOSES, Private
Resided in Lincoln County and was by occupation a farmer. Place and date of enlistment not reported; however, he probably enlisted subsequent to August 31, 1864. Was about 40 years of age at time of enlistment. Wounded in the neck and/or right hip and captured at Fort Stedman, Virginia, March 25, 1865. Hospitalized at Washington, D.C., March 30, 1865. Confined at Old Capitol Prison, Washington, April 17, 1865. Transferred to Elmira, New York, May 1, 1865. Released at Elmira on July 7, 1865, after taking the Oath of Allegiance.

SHULL, PEARSON, Private
Previously served as Private in Company E, 34th Regiment N.C. Troops. Enlisted in this company in Lincoln County on March 15, 1862. Captured at Frederick, Maryland, September 12, 1862. Confined at Fort Delaware, Delaware. Paroled and transferred to Aiken's Landing, James River, Virginia, October 2, 1862, for exchange. Declared exchanged at Aiken's Landing on November 10, 1862. Discharged on November 12, 1862, by reason of "physical disability."

SIMPSON, EVEN, Private
Resided in Gaston County and enlisted at age 30, March 15, 1862. Killed at Sharpsburg, Maryland, September 17, 1862.

SNOWDEN, W. G., Private
Enlisted in Lincoln County on November 1, 1863, for the war. Reported present in November-December, 1863. Wounded at Drewry's Bluff, Virginia, May 16, 1864. Reported absent wounded through August, 1864. Hospitalized at Richmond, Virginia, March 4, 1865, with pneumonia. Furloughed for sixty days on March 31, 1865.

SPRATT, JOSEPH L., Private
Born in Lincoln County where he resided as a farmer prior to enlisting in Lincoln County at age 17, March 15, 1862. Reported present from November, 1862, through June, 1863. Deserted on August 2, 1863. Arrested on August 17, 1863. Returned to duty on August 31, 1863. Reported present in September-December, 1863, and May-August, 1864. Captured at Fort Stedman, Virginia, March 25, 1865. Confined at Washington, D.C. Transferred to Point Lookout, Maryland, where he arrived on March 31, 1865. Released at Point Lookout on May 14, 1865, after taking the Oath of Allegiance.

STOGNER, HOLDEN, Private
Born in Stanly County* and resided in Gaston County where he was by occupation an engineer prior to enlisting in Lincoln County at age 38, March 15, 1862. Wounded

at Sharpsburg, Maryland, September 17, 1862. Died in hospital near Sharpsburg on or about the same date of wounds.

TAYLOR, A. JACKSON, Private
Resided in Lincoln County where he enlisted at age 40, February 11, 1863, for the war. Reported present or accounted for in March-December, 1863, and May-August, 1864. Wounded in the left hip and/or back at or near Fort Stedman, Virginia, on or about March 25, 1865. Hospitalized at Richmond, Virginia. Captured in hospital at Richmond on April 3, 1865. Transferred to Point Lookout, Maryland, May 2, 1865. Released at Point Lookout on June 26, 1865, after taking the Oath of Allegiance.

TIMMS, BENJAMIN, Private
Born in Chester District, South Carolina, and resided in Gaston County where he was by occupation a farmer prior to enlisting in Lincoln County at age 20, March 15, 1862. Mustered in as Private. Promoted to Corporal on February 1, 1863. Reported present or accounted for from November, 1862, through December, 1863. Reduced to ranks in January-June, 1864. Reported present in May-August, 1864.

TIMMS, JOHN, Private
Resided in Gaston County where he enlisted at age 38, June 1, 1863, for the war. Reported present or accounted for in June-December, 1863, and May-June, 1864. Died in hospital at Richmond, Virginia, July 21 or August 1, 1864, of disease.

TOWERY, GEORGE W., Private
Born in Lincoln County where he resided as a farmer prior to enlisting in Lincoln County at age 27, March 15, 1862. Captured at Malvern Hill, Virginia, July 1, 1862. Confined at Fort Columbus, New York Harbor, July 6, 1862. Transferred to Fort Delaware, Delaware, July 9, 1862. Exchanged at Aiken's Landing, James River, Virginia, August 5, 1862. Returned to duty on an unspecified date. Reported present from November, 1862, through December, 1863. Wounded slightly at or near Drewry's Bluff, Virginia, on or about May 16, 1864. Returned to duty prior to July 1, 1864. Reported present in July-August, 1864.

TOWERY, JOSEPH, Private
Born in Lincoln County where he resided as a farmer prior to enlisting in Lincoln County at age 23, March 15, 1862. Reported present or accounted for from November, 1862, through April, 1863. Died in hospital at Goldsboro on June 15, 1863, of "febris typhoides."

TRAMMEL, JAMES, Private
Resided in Lincoln County where he enlisted at age 17, March 15, 1863, for the war. Reported present in April-December, 1863, and May-August, 1864. Captured at Fort Stedman, Virginia, March 25, 1865. Confined at Point Lookout, Maryland, until released on June 21, 1865, after taking the Oath of Allegiance.

TRAMMEL, SAMUEL, Private
Born in Union District, South Carolina, and resided in

Lincoln County where he was by occupation a farmer prior to enlisting in Lincoln County at age 21, March 15, 1862. Killed at Malvern Hill, Virginia, July 1, 1862.

TRAMMEL, THOMAS, Private
Born in Union District, South Carolina, and resided in Lincoln County where he was by occupation a farmer prior to enlisting in Lincoln County at age 54, March 15, 1862. Reported present or accounted for from November, 1862, through December, 1863, and in May-August, 1864. Surrendered at Appomattox Court House, Virginia, April 9, 1865.

USERY, HAMPTON, Private
Born in Anson County and resided in Cleveland or Gaston County where he was by occupation a farmer prior to enlisting at age 38, March 15, 1862. Reported present from November, 1862, through December, 1863, and in May-August, 1864. Captured at Five Forks, Virginia, April 1, 1865. Confined at Point Lookout, Maryland, April 5, 1865. Released at Point Lookout on June 21, 1865, after taking the Oath of Allegiance.

WARD, MILES A., Private
Born in Lincoln County and was by occupation a farmer prior to enlisting in Lincoln County at age 54, March 15, 1862. Captured at Malvern Hill, Virginia, July 1, 1862. Confined at Fort Columbus, New York Harbor, July 6, 1862. Transferred to Fort Delaware, Delaware, July 9, 1862. Paroled and transferred to Aiken's Landing, James River, Virginia, where he was received on July 12, 1862. Declared exchanged at Aiken's Landing on August 5, 1862. Died in hospital at Petersburg, Virginia, on or about October 9, 1862, of "scarlatina" or "dropsy."

WEHUNT, CALEB, Private
Born in Lincoln County where he resided as a farmer prior to enlisting in Lincoln County at age 23, March 15, 1862. Reported present or accounted for from November, 1862, through December, 1863, and in May-June, 1864. Killed at or near Petersburg, Virginia, August 10, 1864.

WHETSTINE, GEORGE W., Private
Born in Lincoln County where he resided as a farmer prior to enlisting in Lincoln County at age 25, March 15, 1862. Discharged from service on September 1, 1862, by reason of "ch[ronic] diarrhoea" and/or "chronic enteritis" with "very great" emaciation.

WHITE, CALVIN, Private
Resided in Cleveland County and enlisted in Lincoln County at age 18, September 1, 1863, for the war. Reported present in September-December, 1863. Wounded at or near Petersburg, Virginia, June 16-18, 1864. Returned to duty prior to July 1, 1864. Reported present in July-August, 1864.

WHITE, DAVID, Private
Born in Rutherford County and resided in Cleveland or Lincoln County where he was by occupation a wagoner prior to enlisting in Lincoln County at age 42, March 15, 1862. Reported present or accounted for from November, 1862, through December, 1863, and in May-August, 1864.

Captured at Five Forks, Virginia, April 1, 1865. Confined at Point Lookout, Maryland, April 5, 1865. Released at Point Lookout on June 21, 1865, after taking the Oath of Allegiance.

WILLIS, W. J., Private
Enlisted in Lincoln County on November 1, 1863, for the war. Reported present through December, 1863. No further records.

WILSON, ALEXANDER H., Private
Born in Lincoln County where he resided as a farmer prior to enlisting in Lincoln County at age 35, March 15, 1862. Killed at Malvern Hill, Virginia, July 1, 1862.

WILSON, MAXWELL, Private
Born in Lincoln County where he resided as a farmer prior to enlisting in Lincoln County at age 44, March 15, 1862. Mustered in as Sergeant. Reduced to ranks on February 1, 1863. Reported present from November, 1862, through February, 1863. Discharged on May 1, 1863, after providing a substitute.

WILSON, N. B., Private
Resided in Lincoln County where he enlisted at age 16, March 15, 1863, for the war as a substitute. Reported present or accounted for in April-December, 1863. Died in hospital at Richmond, Virginia, June 24, 1864, of "febris typh[oid]."

WINECOFF, DANIEL, Private
Resided in Cabarrus County and was by occupation a farm laborer. Place and date of enlistment not reported; however, he probably enlisted subsequent to August 31, 1864. Was about 48 years of age at time of enlistment. Captured at Five Forks, Virginia, April 1, 1865. Confined at Point Lookout, Maryland, April 5, 1865. Released at Point Lookout on June 21, 1865, after taking the Oath of Allegiance.

WINTERS, JOHN W., Private
Born in Gaston County where he resided as a farmer prior to enlisting in Lincoln County at age 16, March 15, 1862. Reported present from November, 1862, through December, 1863. Killed at Drewry's Bluff, Virginia, May 16, 1864.

WRAY, JAMES CALVIN, Private
Born in York District, South Carolina, and resided in Gaston County prior to enlisting in Lincoln County at age 16, March 15, 1862. Hospitalized at Richmond, Virginia, September 27, 1862, with a gunshot wound. Place and date wounded not reported. Furloughed for thirty days on October 10, 1862. Reported absent without leave on or about November 10, 1862. Returned to duty in January-February, 1863. Reported present in March-December, 1863, and May-August, 1864. Deserted to the enemy on or about February 14, 1865. Confined at Washington, D.C., February 20, 1865. Released on an unspecified date after taking the Oath of Allegiance.

WRIGHT, HENRY, Private
Born in York District, South Carolina, and resided in

Lincoln County where he was by occupation a farmer prior to enlisting in Lincoln County at age 50, March 15, 1862. Died on June 15, 1862, of disease. Place of death not reported.

MISCELLANEOUS

Civil War records indicate that the following soldiers served in the 49th Regiment N.C. Troops; however, the companies in which these soldiers served are not reported.

BECK, ALEXANDER, Private
Place and date of enlistment not reported; however, he probably enlisted subsequent to August 31, 1864. Deserted to the enemy on or about November 22, 1864. Confined at Washington, D.C., November 25, 1864. Released on an unspecified date after taking the Oath of Allegiance.

BECK, PHILIP, Private
Place and date of enlistment not reported; however, he probably enlisted subsequent to August 31, 1864. Deserted to the enemy on or about October 6, 1864. Confined at Washington, D.C., October 10, 1864. Released on an unspecified date after taking the Oath of Allegiance.

BIRKSLEY, I. M., Private
Place and date of enlistment not reported; however, he probably enlisted subsequent to August 31, 1864. Paroled at or near Richmond, Virginia, on or about April 24, 1865.

COUNCIL, D. A., Private
Place and date of enlistment not reported; however, he probably enlisted subsequent to August 31, 1864. Deserted to the enemy on an unspecified date. Confined at Washington, D.C., April 11, 1865. Released on an unspecified date after taking the Oath of Allegiance.

EDDINS, C., _____
Place and date of enlistment not reported. Died at Salisbury on February 1, 1864, of "s[?]."

ELLIOTT, THOMAS WILLIAM, Private
Place and date of enlistment not reported; however, he probably enlisted subsequent to August 31, 1864. Deserted to the enemy on or about November 22, 1864. Confined at Washington, D.C., November 25, 1864. Released on an unspecified date after taking the Oath of Allegiance.

HALL, HENRY, Private
Resided in Duplin County. Place and date of enlistment not reported; however, he probably enlisted subsequent to August 31, 1864. Paroled at New Bern on April 17, 1865.

LAY, N. J., _____
Place and date of enlistment not reported; however, he

probably enlisted subsequent to August 31, 1864. Paroled at Farmville, Virginia, April 11-21, 1865.

LEONARD, RANSOM, Private

Resided in Davidson County. Place and date of enlistment not reported; however, he probably enlisted subsequent to August 31, 1864. Deserted to the enemy on or about December 18, 1864. Confined at Washington, D.C., December 21, 1864. Released on an unspecified date after taking the Oath of Allegiance.

McDONALD, J. W., Private

Resided in Rowan County. Place and date of enlistment not reported; however, he probably enlisted subsequent to August 31, 1864. Deserted to the enemy on or about January 26, 1865. Confined at Washington, D.C., February 1, 1865. Released on an unspecified date after taking the Oath of Allegiance.

McQUAIG, W. D., Private

Place and date of enlistment not reported; however, he probably enlisted subsequent to August 31, 1864. Deserted to the enemy on or about November 22, 1864. Confined at Washington, D.C., November 25, 1864. Released on an unspecified date after taking the Oath of Allegiance.

MOILE, MATTHEW, Private

Resided in Rowan County. Place and date of enlistment not reported; however, he probably enlisted subsequent to August 31, 1864. Deserted to the enemy on or about December 21, 1864. Confined at Washington, D.C., December 27, 1864. Released on an unspecified date after taking the Oath of Allegiance.

NEIL, CHARLES, _____

Place and date of enlistment not reported; however, he probably enlisted subsequent to August 31, 1864. Paroled at or near Richmond, Virginia, April 23, 1865.

ROST, M., Private

Place and date of enlistment not reported; however, he probably enlisted subsequent to August 31, 1864. Deserted to the enemy on an unspecified date. Confined at Washington, D.C., March 18, 1865. Released on an unspecified date after taking the Oath of Allegiance.

WINFIELD, MINOS A., Private

Resided in Mecklenburg County. Place and date of enlistment not reported; however, he probably enlisted subsequent to August 31, 1864. Took the Oath of Allegiance at Point Lookout, Maryland, June 21, 1865.

Private Kinchen Jahu Carpenter appears younger than his twenty-year-old enlistment age. His heavy wool coat is open to show his shirt and cravat. The black forage cap was specified in North Carolina regulations. Private Carpenter's "War Diary" is a major source of information concerning his regiment, the 50th North Carolina Troops. His service record appears on page 237 of this volume. Image furnished by Mrs. D. C. Ward, Lake Lure, North Carolina.

Prior to his enlistment this formidable looking officer, Albert O'Briant, of Company A, 50th Regiment, was a Person County farmer. The robust outdoor life he led seems apparent in this image taken after his election as 3rd Lieutenant on May 30, 1862. He survived the war by almost fifty years and sired ten children, the youngest of whom lived until 1975. Lieutenant O'Briant's service record appears on page 153 of this volume. Image furnished by William Hovatter, Roxboro, North Carolina.

50TH REGIMENT N.C. TROOPS

The 50th Regiment N.C. Troops was organized at Camp Mangum, near Raleigh, on or about April 15, 1862, and was composed of men recruited primarily in the counties of Harnett, Johnston, Moore, Person, Robeson, Rutherford, and Wayne. Its first colonel was Marshall D. Craton, a Wayne County physician who had served previously as lieutenant colonel of the 35th Regiment N.C. Troops. At Camp Mangum the men were issued "Confederate Pikes"[1] and spent the next six weeks, according to Lieutenant G. W. Watson of Company C, performing "drill—drill—drill—Squad drill—Officer's drill—Company drill—[and] Battalion drill. . . ."[2] On May 31 the regiment departed by rail for Weldon, in Halifax County near the Virginia border, where it arrived the next morning. It then crossed the Roanoke River to Garysburg, three miles beyond. There it was issued muskets and assigned, along with the 43rd and 45th Regiments N.C. Troops, to a brigade commanded by Colonel Junius Daniel of the 45th Regiment.

The 50th remained at Garysburg for almost three weeks, "drilling hard" and standing guard over the Roanoke River railroad bridge.[3] On June 19 the brigade departed for Petersburg, Virginia, where it was assigned to the division of Major General Theophilus H. Holmes. It was then moved to a defensive position just north of the city at Drewry's Bluff, on the south bank of the James River.

During the Seven Days' battles east of Richmond, June 25-July 1, 1862, Daniel's brigade was stationed on the extreme right flank of the Confederate army and saw relatively little action. On June 29 the brigade crossed over to the north bank of the James on a pontoon bridge. After spending a rainy night without tents the men were subjected the next day, in the words of Lieutenant Watson, to a "most terrifick" fire from Federal batteries and gunboats, which rained shells down "like hail" upon the untried Confederates.[4] According to Colonel Daniel's report, a "stampede" of the cavalry and artillery ensued during which the 50th and 43rd regiments became "slightly confused."[5] That incident, which was not without humorous overtones, was reported by Lieutenant J. C. Ellington of Company C as follows:

The scene was awe-inspiring, especially to raw troops who were under fire for the first time. Such a baptism of fire . . . has very rarely been experienced in the history of war. There was a slight depression in the road-way, and across the open space occupied by the Fiftieth Regiment was a plank fence. We were ordered to lie down behind this for such protection as it and the embankment on the road side might afford. About this time a squadron of cavalry . . . was stampeded by the explosion of a shell in their ranks, and in their wild flight rushed their horses against the plank fence which, like a dead-fall, caught many of our men who were held down . . . until we could throw down the rail fence on the opposite side of the road and allow them to

---

[1]"Confederate Pikes," as described by Private Kinchen Jahu Carpenter of Company I, 50th Regiment N.C. Troops, "consisted of a wooden handle about 10 feet long, at one end of which a dirk-shaped spear was securely fastened[,] and attached to this spear; at the shank or socket, was another steel blade in the form of a brier-hook, in order, as the boys said, that they could get them 'a going and a coming.' " Julie Carpenter Williams (ed.), *War Diary of Kinchen Jahu Carpenter* (Rutherfordton, North Carolina: privately published, 1955), 5, hereinafter cited as Williams, *War Diary.*

[2]G. W. Watson to "My dear Fannie," May 20, 1862, Mary A. Lyndall Papers, Manuscript Department, Duke University Library, Durham, hereinafter cited as Lyndall Papers.

[3]Williams, *War Diary*, 6.

[4]Watson to "My dear Fannie," July 10, 1862, Lyndall Papers.

[5]R. N. Scott and others (eds.), *The War of the Rebellion: A Compilation of the Official Records of the Union and Confederate Armies* (Washington: Government Printing Office, 70 volumes, 1880-1901), Series I, XI, Part II, 914, hereinafter cited as *Official Records (Army).*

escape, which they were not slow to do. In the confusion incident to this affair . . . the color-bearer of the Fiftieth Regiment escaped to the open field to the right of the road and planted the colors in full view of the fleet on the river, thereby concentrating their fire on our part of the line. It was some time before he was noticed standing solitary and alone in the open field, grasping his flag staff, which was firmly planted in the ground, as if bidding defiance to the whole Union army and navy, and the rest of mankind.[6]

For the shaken novices of the 50th Regiment, the day's misadventures were unfortunately not yet at an end. Shortly after "order had been restored," Captain T. H. Brem's battery was sent forward to reinforce a group of beleaguered Confederate artillerymen who were attempting to suppress the Federal cannoneers.[7] A few moments later the 50th Regiment was ordered to the support of the artillery but was promptly run down by Brem's Battery "in wild flight . . . knocking down and running over many of our men with their horses and guns."[8] When a succession of thunderous explosions nearby announced that a Federal battery was on their flank and had opened fire at short range, the men of the 50th retreated, apparently with noticeable enthusiasm, to the cover of a woods. Somewhat later they returned to their original position in the road, where they "remained steady" for the balance of the evening. Considering that the men of his brigade were "all new," Daniel thought that they had "behaved well."[9] Seven members of the 50th were wounded, two of them mortally.

During the evening of July 1 the regiment returned to its campground of the night of June 29. There it remained in line of battle for "12 to 15 hours in a drenching rain."[10] On July 3 the frazzled men, suffering severely from hunger, thirst, and fatigue, slogged their way through "very, very deep" mud to their former position at Drewry's Bluff.[11]

Daniel's men remained at Drewry's Bluff constructing entrenchments and fortifications for most of the next two months. During that time the Army of Northern Virginia was reorganized, and two new regiments—the 32nd and 53rd North Carolina Troops—were assigned to Daniel's brigade. On July 31 and August 1 the brigade took part in a movement to Merchant's Hope Church to support a forty-cannon bombardment of the Federal base at Harrison's Landing, on the James River. The Confederate artillerists, under orders to fire the twenty or thirty rounds with which they were supplied "as rapidly as possible, hitch up and retire," created an "indescribable . . . consternation" among the Federals and caused some damage to their shipping but inflicted few casualties.[12] The men then returned to Drewry's Bluff.

On August 29 Daniel's brigade was ordered to Richmond. Several days later it moved to Proctor's Creek, three miles down the James from Drewry's Bluff. There the men resumed "throwing up fortifications. . . . We have the Country fortified for some miles around Drewry's Bluff [Lieutenant Watson wrote]—so that, when Mr. Lincoln's men endeavor to get to Richmond by this route—they will have a hard road to travel."[13]

[6]Walter Clark (ed.), *Histories of the Several Regiments and Battalions from North Carolina in the Great War, 1861-'65* (Raleigh and Goldsboro: State of North Carolina, 5 volumes, 1901), III, 164, hereinafter cited as Clark, *Histories of the North Carolina Regiments.*
[7]Clark, *Histories of the North Carolina Regiments*, III, 164. Captain Brem commanded Company C, 10th Regiment N.C. State Troops (1st Regiment N.C. Artillery).
[8]Clark, *Histories of the North Carolina Regiments*, III, 165.
[9]*Official Records (Army)*, Series I, XI, Part II, 914. See also General Holmes's report on pages 906-908 of the same volume.
[10]Williams, *War Diary*, 8.
[11]Williams, *War Diary*, 8.
[12]Clark, *Histories of the North Carolina Regiments*, III, 168-169.
[13]Watson to "My dear Fannie," September 25, 1862, Lyndall Papers.

The 50th Regiment remained in the vicinity of Drewry's Bluff during the Sharpsburg campaign and for the remainder of 1862. Colonel Craton resigned on November 25 because of a physical disability and was replaced by James A. Washington, a Goldsboro merchant who was serving at the time as lieutenant colonel of the regiment. "In December [reported Lieutenant Ellington] we constructed comfortable log cabins in which to spend the winter. We completed them in time to move in just a few days before Christmas. We enjoyed a jolly Christmas and congratulated ourselves on being comfortably housed for the winter, but on the last day of December the brigade received 'marching orders,' and on 1 January, 1863, we started [by rail] for North Carolina. . . ."[14] The regiment arrived at Goldsboro on January 3. On February 3 it departed in a heavy snowstorm for Kinston, which it reached on February 7.

In March, 1863, the 50th Regiment, along with the rest of Daniel's brigade, took part in Major General D. H. Hill's attempt to recapture New Bern and Washington, North Carolina. Hill planned a three-column attack on New Bern in which one column, under Daniel, was to move directly against the town along the north side of the Trent River while two flanking columns, commanded by Brigadier Generals James J. Pettigrew and Beverly H. Robertson, advanced respectively down the north bank of the Neuse River and the south bank of the Trent. Pettigrew's orders were to bombard Fort Anderson and shell Federal gunboats on the Neuse, and Robertson's cavalrymen were to tear up the track of the Atlantic and North Carolina Railroad.

On March 13 Daniel's force encountered Federal pickets about ten miles southeast of New Bern. Driving the pickets before them, the Confederates soon came upon a lightly defended enemy line at Deep Gully, a small stream that flowed into the Trent. An artillery bombardment and an attack by four companies of the 50th Regiment speedily drove the Federals from their works, which the Confederates occupied for the night. New fighting broke out the next morning as the reinforced Federal defenders attempted unsuccessfully to recapture their position at Deep Gully. The Federals then retired to their main defenses at New Bern. Pettigrew, in the meantime, had been thwarted in his assignment by enemy gunboats, swampy terrain, and the inadequacy of his artillery. Unable to shell Fort Anderson into submission and unwilling to risk a problematical and costly infantry assault on a narrow front, he withdrew.

Hill then abandoned his campaign against New Bern and, after returning briefly to Kinston, marched with his reunited force against "Little Washington."[15] Hoping to prevent the arrival of Federal reinforcements by the Pamlico River, Hill positioned batteries at key points around the town and attempted to block the river with sunken hulks and pilings cut off below the waterline. Daniel's and Pettigrew's brigades were stationed east of the town to engage any Federal relief force that might advance from New Bern. Limited by an inadequate supply of artillery ammunition and prohibited by orders from attempting to capture Washington by storm, Hill began a sporadic shelling and settled down to starve the Unionists into submission. For its part the Federal garrison, which possessed adequate numbers, weapons, and munitions but was already on short rations, returned the Confederate battery fire and prepared for what it hoped would be a brief siege. One unlettered North Carolina soldier described the situation as follows:

We are heare in thre miles of Washington. We exspect to march evrry day on the enemy. We have bin a canonading evry day fore the last weak[.] [T]hey try to run up the river with their gun

---

[14]Clark, *Histories of the North Carolina Regiments*, III, 170.
[15]During the advance against Washington the 50th Regiment was temporarily attached to the Virginia brigade of Brigadier General Richard B. Garnett but quickly rejoined Daniel's brigade for the sixteen-day siege that began on March 30.

boats[,] but we beat them back[.] [W]e have got the river Blockadded[.] [W]e have got the sity serrounded so they can't reinforce. . . . [O]ur army is in site of the sitty[.] [O]ur Picket guard is in fifty yards of none another[.] But they ar not aloud to shoot at none another[.] [T]he citisson has ris white flags all in the sity and evy house.[16]

On April 9 the 50th Regiment, temporarily attached to Pettigrew's brigade, took part in the bloodless repulse of a Federal relief column at Blount's Creek, downstream from Washington on the Pamlico River. That small victory was negated on the evening of April 13 when the Federal steamer *Escort*, her decks piled with hay bales to protect her from artillery fire, ran the Confederate gauntlet, bringing supplies and the 5th Regiment Rhode Island Infantry. Two days later the *Escort* sailed blithely past the Confederate batteries on her return trip, this time in broad daylight. General Hill, convinced that Washington could not be taken, raised the siege on April 16 and retired to Greenville. After an all-night march on the 17th over roads described by one officer of the 50th Regiment as "the worst I ever saw," the weary Confederates reached Greenville the next day.[17]

Daniel's brigade remained at Greenville until May 1, when it was ordered to Kinston. On May 7 the brigade was sent to Core Creek, on the Atlantic and North Carolina Railroad a few miles southeast of Kinston, where it tore up several miles of track. When the other four regiments of Daniel's brigade were transferred to Virginia on or about May 17, 1863, the 50th Regiment remained behind at Kinston. The regiment was transferred shortly thereafter to the brigade of Brigadier General James G. Martin. Although theoretically composed of three regiments—the others being the 17th Regiment N.C. Troops (2nd Organization) and the 42nd Regiment N.C. Troops—Martin's brigade was in fact an administrative unit, and the three regiments continued to operate independently in North Carolina. During the remainder of May, all of June, and the first half of July, the 50th Regiment made repeated incursions into enemy territory around New Bern, capturing "a number" of pickets and scouts.[18]

On July 17 Brigadier General Edward E. Potter led a large force of Federal cavalrymen out of New Bern on a six-day raid that resulted in the destruction of the Wilmington and Weldon Railroad bridge over the Tar River at Rocky Mount and the burning of bridges at Greenville and Tarboro. Two steamboats and an ironclad were also destroyed along with hundreds of thousands of dollars worth of military supplies and other property. The 50th Regiment, operating out of Kinston, made a valiant effort to intercept the raiders and succeeded in delaying their retreat on July 20 and 21. Utilizing their mobility to good effect, the main body of Federals eluded the North Carolina infantrymen on the morning of July 22 and, hotly pursued by such cavalry as the Confederates had in hand, made their escape to New Bern. However, the rear guard of the Federal column, composed of Negro cavalrymen and contrabands (liberated slaves) traveling "in every conceivable style," was intercepted by the 50th Regiment at a bridge over a creek near the "Burney Place," in Craven County.

[W]e opened fire on the column with a small brass cannon [Lieutenant Ellington reported]. . . . This utterly demoralized the "contrabands" who, in their mad rush to keep pace with their erstwhile deliverers . . . who were now fleeing for their lives, failed to discover [see] us. The shock was so sudden and unexpected that the effect was indescribable. The great cavalcade,

[16]Quoted in John G. Barrett, *The Civil War in North Carolina* (Chapel Hill: The University of North Carolina Press, 1963), 159, hereinafter cited as Barrett, *The Civil War in North Carolina*.

[17]J. O. A. Kelly to his wife, April 19, 1863, Roster Document File Number 0426.

[18]Clark, *Histories of the North Carolina Regiments*, III, 173. During an engagement that probably occurred in mid-June, 1863, the 50th Regiment or some part thereof was "surprised" in an encounter with the Federals that cannot be identified. No significant casualties or consequences resulted. *Official Records (Army)*, Series I, XXVII, Part III, 936.

composed of men, women and children, perched on wagons, carts, buggies, carriages, and mounted on horses and mules, whipping, slashing and yelling like wild Indians, was suddenly halted by our fire upon the bridge. . . . One negro Captain, who was driving a pair of spirited iron-gray horses, attempted to rush past three of our men who were lying in the yard and was shot dead as he stood up in the buggy firing at them. . . . Many others were either killed or wounded in attempting to escape through the woods near by. In the excitement and confusion which ensued many of the vehicles were upset . . . and many others wrecked by the frightened horses. . . . We scoured the woods and gathered up several hundred negroes[,] among the number several infants and a number of small children. . . .[19]

At about 8 o'clock the 50th Regiment set off in pursuit of Potter.

For miles [Lieutenant Ellington's report continued] the road and woods on either side were strewn with all kinds of wearing apparel, table ware, such as fine china and silver ware, blankets, fine bed quilts and all sorts of ladies' wearing apparel. . . . [T]he few men of Colonel [J. T.] Kennedy's Cavalry and such as we were able to mount from time to time with the abandoned horses, kept up a running fight with the rear of the retreating column from the "Burney Place" to Street's Ferry. . . .[20]

Colonel Washington was censured for his conduct during the Potter raid and shortly thereafter submitted his resignation. Lieutenant Colonel George Wortham, a Granville County lawyer in civilian life, was promoted to colonel and placed in command of the regiment.

On August 9, 1863, the 50th Regiment was ordered to Wilmington, where it went into camp at Virginia Creek. The regiment remained in and around Wilmington until the spring of 1864 constructing fortifications, doing picket duty along the coast, and performing provost duties. Except for an occasional shelling by enemy warships, the regiment enjoyed a quiet period. One of the more interesting diversions occurred on March 24 when "a lieutenant of energy & determination" and "twenty picked men" were sent up the railroad to Bladenboro to "suppress" a "mob of low women" and deserters who were "attempting to plunder Gov[ernmen]t fr[eigh]t trains. . . ."[21] The outcome of the expedition is not known.

On April 27, 1864, the 50th Regiment was ordered to Rocky Mount. From there it moved to Tarboro and, on April 29, to Plymouth, which had just been recaptured, along with "Little Washington," by Confederate forces. Five companies of the regiment were stationed as a garrison at Plymouth and the other five at Washington. For the next six months the regiment performed garrison duty and was sent on raids into coastal counties between New Bern and the Virginia line to collect provisions for the Army of Northern Virginia.[22] Those raids, generally undertaken by small detachments, resulted in the seizure of valuable supplies and the capture of a considerable number of prisoners. Skirmishes occurred frequently but with few casualties on either side. On September 1 six companies of the regiment were reported at Plymouth and four at Wilmington. On October 23 the entire regiment was sent to Tarboro; it remained at Tarboro and its vicinity for the next month.

On November 24, 1864, about a week after the start of General Sherman's march from Atlanta to the sea, the 50th Regiment was transferred by rail to Augusta, Georgia. Upon arriving there three days later the regiment was ordered to Savannah; however, it was halted

[19]Clark, *Histories of the North Carolina Regiments*, III, 174-175.

[20]Clark, *Histories of the North Carolina Regiments*, III, 175.

[21]C. J. Elliott to Colonel Wortham, March 23, 1864, Confederate Papers (Miscellaneous), Number 172, Southern Historical Collection, University of North Carolina Library at Chapel Hill.

[22]Clark, *Histories of the North Carolina Regiments*, III, 177.

near Grahamville, South Carolina, about twenty-seven miles north of Savannah, where an enemy force was advancing against the Charleston and Savannah Railroad. A Federal lodgment on the railroad would make it virtually impossible for the Confederates to hold Savannah and would make evacuation of the city more difficult. After arriving at Honey Hill too late to take part in the successful defense of the railroad, the 50th Regiment resumed its journey to Savannah, which it reached on December 2. It was then assigned, along with the 10th Battalion N.C. Heavy Artillery, to Brigadier General Laurence S. Baker's brigade of Major General Lafayette McLaws's division and was ordered to Forty-five Mile Station on the Georgia Central Railroad. There it fought a delaying action against Sherman's advancing vanguard at the Ogeechee River bridge on December 9 and fell back to Savannah.

Although protected by a gauntlet of rivers, swamps, rice fields, and fortifications, Savannah's defenders, variously estimated between 10,000 and 18,000 men, were hopelessly outnumbered by Sherman's 62,000-man army. On December 20 the Confederate commander, Lieutenant General William J. Hardee, perceiving that he was about to be inextricably trapped, ordered the ships and docks in the harbor blown up and the city evacuated. Lit by the stygian glare of large waterfront fires, "an immense funeral procession" of soldiers and civilians escaped that night over a hastily improvised pontoon bridge.[23]

The Confederates fell back initially to Hardeeville, about fourteen miles north of Savannah on the Charleston and Savannah Railroad. General Baker was relieved from duty about this time because of disability from wounds and was replaced as brigade commander by Colonel Washington M. Hardy of the 60th Regiment N.C. Troops. A new regiment, the 77th Regiment N.C. Troops (7th Regiment N.C. Senior Reserves), was also assigned to the brigade. On December 26 the retreat resumed, and the 50th Regiment moved up the railroad another thirty miles to Pocotaligo.[24] There, on January 14, 1865, a sudden advance by the Federals nearly cut off the regiment from its only line of retreat. A fighting withdrawal ensued, and the regiment succeeded with difficulty in extricating itself. It then fell back with the rest of McLaws's division to the Salkehatchie River, where a new defensive line was established. On January 20, near Rivers' Bridge, Company I of the 50th and a Georgia unit, which were on independent scouting missions, exchanged gunfire after blundering into each other along the foggy, flooded banks of the Salkehatchie and suffered moderate casualties.

Two weeks later, on February 3, the Salkehatchie line was broken by the Federals. The 50th Regiment, after another narrow escape through the swamps at Buford's Bridge, withdrew about forty miles north to Branchville, where it rejoined McLaws's force. A new line at the Edisto River was turned by the Federals a few weeks later. The 50th Regiment then retreated to Florence, which it reached on February 25. The regiment and its sister units in Hardy's brigade, still moving north, crossed the Pee Dee River near Cheraw on March 3 and withdrew to Fayetteville, which fell in its turn before the relentless Federal juggernaut on March 11.

Sherman's army advanced northeast from Fayetteville on March 14 in two columns commanded respectively by Major General Henry W. Slocum, who feinted in the direction of Raleigh, and Major General Oliver O. Howard, who moved against Goldsboro to link up with the victorious Federal forces marching westward from the North Carolina coast. Hoping to draw Sherman's two columns farther apart and defeat them separately, Lieutenant General Joseph E. Johnston ordered Hardee to fight a delaying action against Slocum. By March 16

---

[23]Shelby Foote, *The Civil War, A Narrative*, III, *Red River to Appomattox* (New York: Random House, 1974), 712.

[24]On December 28, 1864, the effective strength of the 50th Regiment was officially reported to be 550 men. *Official Records (Army)*, Series I, XLIV, 999.

Hardee's meager, tatterdemalion force of 6,000 men, nearing the end of its rope after retreating, in the words of a South Carolina soldier, for "hundreds of miles, mainly on foot and in haste, through rain, mud, and water, without tents and on scant rations," was in line on a ridge near the Harnett County town of Averasboro.[25]

Although Hardee was in a strong position with his flanks somewhat protected by a swamp and a small river, Slocum enjoyed a numerical advantage of four or five to one. A frontal attack in combination with a move to turn the Confederate right flank drove Hardee's men from two defensive lines before the Federals were precariously halted at a third line until dark. During the night the men received orders to build fires as if going into camp and then "get down, stooping, or on 'all fours,' to withdraw, not speaking above a whisper."[26] While the bullets of Federal sharpshooters plinked bark and needles from the pine trees, Hardee's troops fell back.

> [W]e plodded all night March 16 (Thursday) [the South Carolinian continued], all day on Friday, camped on Friday night in the piney woods, [and] then went on to a place called Elevation [in Johnston County] by noon on Saturday. There we remained until early on Sunday, March 19, when we were moved by rapid tramping on to Bentonville. . . . From Thursday till midday Saturday, we were without any rations save a very small slice of raw bacon to each man. Our entire march from Charleston, S. C., to Greensboro, N. C., was hard; but the tramp from Averasboro to Elevation was about the worst we had in the whole stretch. . . .[27]

During the Battle of Averasboro, Hardee lost approximately 500 men killed, wounded, captured, and missing. Losses in the 50th Regiment were not reported.

Having marshaled most of his available forces and accomplished his goal of increasing the distance between Slocum and Howard, Johnston laid an ambush for Slocum at Bentonville on March 19. Cleverly deploying his 19,000 men in a woods behind a screen of cavalry, Johnston awaited the arrival of the strung-out, 26,000-man Federal column. Slocum, thinking he was confronted by the usual token cavalry opposition, saw no reason to wait for his entire command to come up and ordered a division forward to clear his front. That unsuspecting unit received "an awful volly [sic]" from massed Confederate infantry at a distance of about fifty feet.[28] A savage, hand-to-hand fight with clubbed muskets and ramrods ensued, and the Federals fell back in disarray. Rebounding quickly, Slocum's men came on again, concentrating their attack on troops under Lieutenant General Braxton Bragg on the Confederate left. Confederate infantry under Hardee and Lieutenant General A. P. Stewart then charged out of the brush and blackjack thickets in a devastating assault that crushed the undermanned and disorganized Federal left and precipitated, in the words of one candid Federal, "some of the best running ever did."[29] The Federal right wing then came under attack from the rear by Hardee and Stewart; shortly thereafter, units under the command of Bragg pitched into the beleaguered Federals from the front. Battling desperately amid a "continuous and remorseless roar of musketry," the Federal defenders narrowly succeeded in holding their position until reinforcements arrived to beat back the Confederate assault.[30] The

[25]Robert W. Sanders, "The Battle of Averasboro, N.C.," *Confederate Veteran*, XXXIV (June, 1926), 215, hereinafter cited as Sanders, "Averasboro."
[26]Sanders, "Averasboro," 216.
[27]Sanders, "Averasboro," 216.
[28]Charles S. Brown to "Mother & Etta," April 18, 1865, Charles S. Brown Papers, Duke Manuscript Department.
[29]Quoted in Barrett, *The Civil War in North Carolina*, 333.
[30]Benson J. Lossing, *Pictorial History of the Civil War in the United States of America* (Hartford: Thomas Belknap, 3 volumes, 1877), III, 501.

fighting then shifted again to the re-formed and reinforced Federal left, where five successive Confederate attacks were smashed by a "raging leaden hailstorm of grape and canister."[31]

McLaws's division, of which the 50th Regiment was still a part, arrived late on the battlefield and, instead of taking part in the assault of Hardee and Stewart as planned, was diverted unnecessarily to the Confederate left at the request of Bragg. Having received "no particular instructions," it remained in reserve during Bragg's attack.[32] That evening Hardy's men, thinking they were going to the relief of another unit, were double-quicked to the Confederate right. There, according to Lieutenant John G. Albright of the 77th North Carolina, they were mistakenly "rushed . . . up within twenty feet of the enemy's breastworks," where they received "a terrible volley."

We took shelter the best we could behind the pine trees [Albright continued], except some of us who were in a pond about sixty or seventy yards wide. These retreated across the pond, the officers shouting all the time, "You are shooting your own men."[33]

After a Confederate officer who was sent forward to investigate was captured by Federal vedettes, thereby firmly establishing the identity and hostile intentions of the soldiers manning the entrenchments, Hardy's men opened fire and, Albright improbably claimed, drove the enemy from their works. Losses in the 77th Regiment, according to Albright, were "fifty-one men in about half a minute."[34] The 50th Regiment's losses were calculated by Lieutenant Ellington to be "about one-third" of the men engaged.[35] Although that figure may well be exaggerated, the probability that the regiment suffered heavily during the "close" and "bloody" fighting on the evening of March 19 seems high.[36]

During the night Sherman, who was with Howard's wing of the Federal army, belatedly learned of the fighting at Bentonville. Preparations to go to the aid of Slocum began immediately, and by the afternoon of the 20th the army was reunited on the battlefield. Johnston, realizing that his gambit had failed, reluctantly remained at Bentonville in order to cover the evacuation of his wounded, an undertaking that, because of poor roads and a shortage of wagons, would require two days. Confronted now by a force twice the size of the one he had faced on the previous day, Johnston realigned his units in a configuration similar to a spraddled horseshoe. While ambulances rumbled over the Mill Creek bridge, in Johnston's immediate rear and his only line of retreat, the Confederate general resupplied his men as best he could and awaited developments. McLaws's division, including the 50th Regiment, was moved once again, this time to the extreme left of the Confederate line, where it faced some of Howard's newly arrived units.

General Sherman, for his part, had no more interest than Johnston in renewing the contest. Rarely inclined to expend lives in costly attacks if maneuver would accomplish his object, his primary concern for the moment was to reach the Goldsboro railhead. There he would be reinforced by powerful Federal units from the North Carolina coast and would obtain much needed supplies and equipment. Except for a sharp skirmish on the Confederate left involving units under the command of Major General Robert F. Hoke, the day passed without serious fighting.

[31]Samuel W. Ravenel, "Ask the Survivors of Bentonville," *Confederate Veteran*, XVIII (March, 1910), 124.
[32]*Official Records (Army)*, Series I, XLVII, Part I, 1091.
[33]Clark, *Histories of the North Carolina Regiments*, IV, 104.
[34]Clark, *Histories of the North Carolina Regiments*, IV, 104.
[35]Clark, *Histories of the North Carolina Regiments*, III, 198.
[36]Clarence C. Buel and Robert U. Johnson (eds.), *Battles and Leaders of the Civil War*, 4 volumes (New York: The Century Company, 1884), IV, 704.

The next day, March 21, Johnston continued to evacuate his wounded and remained in his works. Heavy skirmishing took place all along the line, but the only action of consequence was an unauthorized Federal attack by Major General Joseph A. Mower that broke through on the Confederate left and threatened to capture the vital bridge over Mill Creek. Against that penetration Johnston mustered just enough resistance to force the impetuous Federal general to pause and call for reinforcements, whereupon he was ordered by Sherman to withdraw.

Johnston fell back in the direction of Smithfield that night. Casualties sustained by the 50th Regiment in the three-day Battle of Bentonville were not officially reported but were probably heavy. McLaws's division as a whole lost 28 men killed, 153 wounded, and 22 missing.[37]

At Smithfield the Confederates enjoyed a brief respite. Johnston's army was reorganized, and the 50th Regiment and 10th Battalion were assigned to Brigadier General William W. Kirkland's brigade of Hoke's division. Other units in the brigade were the 17th Regiment N.C. Troops (2nd Organization) and the 42nd and 66th Regiments N.C. Troops.

On April 10 Sherman's inexorable advance resumed. Smithfield was captured on April 11, and Raleigh was occupied two days later. Johnston retreated with his small and, particularly after the surrender of Lee on April 9, rapidly shrinking army to the vicinity of Durham Station. There, with the authorization of President Jefferson Davis, a fugitive from the fallen Confederate capital, he opened negotiations with Sherman on April 17. Johnston surrendered at the Bennitt house, three miles west of Durham Station, on April 26, 1865. A week later, at Greensboro, the army was paroled. The number of members of the 50th Regiment who were present was not reported.

---

[37]*Official Records (Army)*, Series I, XLVII, Part I, 1060. Another report, which is unofficial and probably unreliable, states that the regiment, after being recruited in November to the improbable strength of "something over 900," mustered "less than half" of that number after Bentonville. Clark, *Histories of the North Carolina Regiments*, III, 199. (However, see footnote 24 above.) Whatever the exact figures, it is certain that casualty sources for this eve-of-surrender engagement are hard to come by and that those available for the 50th Regiment plainly do not reflect the losses the unit sustained there. The following rosters list 3 men killed, 2 wounded, and 1 captured at Bentonville. See also Jay Luvaas, *The Battle of Bentonville: March 19-20-21, 1865* (Smithfield, North Carolina: Medlin Printing Company, n.d.), unpaginated; John G. Barrett, *Sherman's March Through the Carolinas* (Chapel Hill: The University of North Carolina Press, 1956), 184; William B. Herring, III, "The Battle of Bentonville: March 19-21, 1865" (unpublished master's thesis, East Carolina University, 1982); Weymouth T. Jordan, Jr., *The Battle of Bentonville* (Wilmington: Broadfoot Publishing Company, 1990).

FIELD AND STAFF

COLONELS

CRATON, MARSHALL D.
Previously served as Lieutenant Colonel of the 35th Regiment N.C. Troops. Appointed Colonel on April 15, 1862, and transferred to this regiment. Resigned on November 25, 1862, by reason of "fistula in ano, the sequence of chronic diarrhoea and dyspepsia. . . ." Resignation accepted on December 1, 1862.

WASHINGTON, JAMES A.
Previously served as Captain of Company H, 2nd Regiment N.C. State Troops. Appointed Lieutenant Colonel on April 15, 1862, and transferred to this regiment. Promoted to Colonel on December 1, 1862. Resigned on October 30, 1863, after being "censured . . . [for his] conduct in the late Yankee raid upon Tarboro. . . ." [It appears that the censure of Colonel Washington was directly related to the events of July 22, 1863 (see regimental history).] Resignation accepted on November 9, 1863.

WORTHAM, GEORGE
Previously served as Captain of 2nd Company D, 12th Regiment N.C. Troops (2nd Regiment N.C. Volunteers). Appointed Major and transferred to this regiment on April 15, 1862. Promoted to Lieutenant Colonel on December 1, 1862. Reported present in September-October, 1863. Promoted to Colonel on November 10, 1863. Reported present in November-December, 1863. Reported present but in command of the brigade in November-December, 1864. Paroled at Greensboro on May 1, 1865.

LIEUTENANT COLONEL

VAN HOOK, JOHN C.
Previously served as Captain of Company A of this regiment. Appointed Major on December 1, 1862, and transferred to the Field and Staff. Reported present in September-October, 1863. Promoted to Lieutenant Colonel on November 10, 1863. Reported absent commanding an outpost at Virginia Creek, Topsail Sound, in January-February, 1864. Reported on duty as acting commander of the regiment in November-December, 1864.

MAJORS

WRIGHT, C. G.
Date of appointment as Major not reported. Reported on duty as Major of this regiment in January-February, 1864. No further records.

RYALS, HENRY J.
Previously served as Captain of Company D of this regiment. Appointed Major on April 11, 1864, and transferred to the Field and Staff. Reported absent on detail "to procure conscripts" in October, 1864. Reported present in November-December, 1864. Hospitalized at Greensboro on February 20, 1865, with catarrhus. Returned to duty on March 9, 1865.

ADJUTANTS

BORDEN, WILLIAM H.
Served as 1st Lieutenant of Company E of this regiment. May have served briefly in 1862 as acting Adjutant of this regiment.

WATSON, GEORGE WASHINGTON
Served as 3rd Lieutenant of Company C of this regiment. Served for a time in 1862 as acting Adjutant of this regiment.

EDMUNDSON, JESSE W.
Previously served as Sergeant Major of this regiment. [See Sergeants Major's section below.] Appointed Adjutant (1st Lieutenant) on October 29, 1862, to rank from October 21, 1862. Reported present in September-October, 1863, and January-February, 1864. Paroled at Greensboro on May 1, 1865.

ASSISTANT QUARTERMASTERS

BORDEN, EDWIN B.
Resided in Wayne County. Appointed Assistant Quartermaster (1st Lieutenant) on April 15, 1862. Resigned in May, 1862. Reason he resigned not reported.

DALRYMPLE, JAMES
Served as 3rd Lieutenant of Company F of this regiment. Reported on detail as Assistant Quartermaster and Assistant Commissary of Subsistence in November-December, 1862.

ADAMS, EDWARD W.
Resided in Wayne County. Appointed Assistant Quartermaster (Captain) on July 1, 1862, to rank from June 1, 1862 (confirmed on September 30, 1862). Apparently served as Assistant Quartermaster of this regiment until December 20, 1864, when he was transferred to the 67th Regiment N.C. Troops.

ASSISTANT COMMISSARIES OF SUBSISTENCE

PARKER, EDWARD SANDERS
Previously served as Corporal in Company H, 2nd Regiment N.C. State Troops. Appointed Assistant

Commissary of Subsistence (Captain) on July 1, 1862, to rank from June 1, 1862, and transferred to this regiment. Captured at Rodman's Point, Beaufort County, April 16, 1863. Sent to New Bern. Transferred to Fort Monroe, Virginia. Transferred to Fort Delaware, Delaware; however, on June 10, 1863, while en route to Fort Delaware on the steamer *Maple Leaf* he "rose on the guard [with a group of approximately seventy-six other Confederate officers], overpowered it and made [his] escape." Dropped from the rolls of the regiment on or about July 31, 1863, after his office was abolished by an act of the Confederate Congress.

DALRYMPLE, JAMES
Served as 3rd Lieutenant of Company F of this regiment. Reported on detail as Assistant Commissary of Subsistence and Assistant Quartermaster in November-December, 1862.

SURGEONS

DUFFY, WALTER
Resided in Rutherford County. Appointed Surgeon on April 30, 1862. Reported present in September-December, 1862. Resigned on May 21, 1863, because "I am fifty years of age, my health [is] feeble, and my family, who are exiles from New Bern, N.C. (leaving all my property behind them in the hands of the enemy) require my attention." Resignation accepted on May 28, 1863.

POTTER, FRANCIS W.
Previously served as Captain of 3rd Company G, 36th Regiment N.C. Troops (2nd Regiment N.C. Artillery). Appointed Assistant Surgeon on February 27, 1863. Assigned to duty with this regiment on or about November 23, 1863. Reported present in January-February, 1864. Promoted to Surgeon on or about April 20, 1864. Resigned on August 2, 1864. Reason he resigned not reported.

PATTON, JOHN D.
Resided in South Carolina. Appointed Assistant Surgeon of this regiment on an unspecified date. First listed in the records of this company on December 24, 1863. Reported present in January-February, 1864. Promoted to Surgeon on or about August 21, 1864. Reported present in November-December, 1864. Paroled at Greensboro on May 1, 1865.

ASSISTANT SURGEONS

EAVES, SPENCER
Previously served as Private in Company G, 16th Regiment N.C. Troops (6th Regiment N.C. Volunteers). Appointed Assistant Surgeon on April 26, 1862, and transferred to this regiment. Reported present in December, 1862, and in September-October, 1863. No further records.

NORMAN, I. F.
Place and date of enlistment not reported. Was probably appointed Assistant Surgeon subsequent to December 31, 1864. Paroled at Greensboro on May 1, 1865.

CHAPLAINS

MORAN, ROBERT S.
Methodist. Appointed Chaplain on July 1, 1862, to rank from June 1, 1862. Resigned on November 18, 1862, by reason of a "malignant and protracted attack of typhoid fever." Resignation accepted on November 22, 1862.

HAUGHTON, THOMAS BENBURY
Episcopalian. Resided in Washington County. Appointed Chaplain on July 28, 1863, to rank from January 26, 1863. Reported present in September, 1863-February, 1864. Furloughed on or about January 26, 1865. Paroled at Greensboro on May 1, 1865.

ENSIGN

YELVINGTON, RANSOM H.
Previously served as Sergeant in Company C of this regiment. Appointed Ensign (2nd Lieutenant) in March, 1864, and transferred to the Field and Staff. No further records.

SERGEANTS MAJOR

EDMUNDSON, JESSE W.
Previously served as Sergeant in Company E of this regiment. Promoted to Sergeant Major on May 1, 1862, and transferred to the Field and Staff. Appointed Adjutant (1st Lieutenant) on October 29, 1862, to rank from October 21, 1862. [See Adjutant's section above.]

GREEN, JOHN A.
Previously served as 1st Sergeant of Company E of this regiment. Promoted to Sergeant Major on December 21, 1862, and transferred to the Field and Staff. Reported present in September-October, 1863, and January-February, 1864. Discharged on an unspecified date (possibly on or about May 1, 1864) by reason of an unspecified illness. Died in hospital at Goldsboro on December 30, 1864, of "pneumonia."

WRIGHT, COUNCIL B.
Previously served as Private in Company E of this regiment. Promoted to Sergeant Major on May 1, 1864, and transferred to the Field and Staff. Reported present in November-December, 1864.

CHAMBERLAIN, S. W.
Resided in Wayne County. Place and date of enlistment not reported. Promotion record not reported. Paroled at Goldsboro in 1865.

QUARTERMASTER SERGEANTS

DALRYMPLE, JAMES
Served as Private in Company F of this regiment. Detailed as Quartermaster Sergeant on June 23, 1862, and transferred to the Field and Staff. Elected 3rd Lieutenant on July 15, 1862, and transferred back to Company F.

KELLY, WILLIAM JOSEPH
Previously served as Corporal in Company F of this regiment. Appointed Quartermaster Sergeant on July 15, 1862, and transferred to the Field and Staff. Reported present in September, 1863-February, 1864. Reduced to ranks on November 29, 1864, and transferred back to Company F.

COMMISSARY SERGEANTS

MASSEY, JOHN D.
Served as Private in Company C of this regiment. Appointed acting Commissary Sergeant on April 5, 1862, and transferred for temporary duty with the Field and Staff. Reported on duty as acting Commissary Sergeant until June 15, 1864, when he was elected 2nd Lieutenant and transferred to Company D of this regiment.

WIGGS, ARTHUR T.
Served as Private in Company C of this regiment. Appointed acting Commissary Sergeant on June 15, 1864, and transferred to the Field and Staff. Reported on detail as acting Commissary Sergeant through December, 1864. Paroled at Goldsboro on May 8, 1865.

ORDNANCE SERGEANTS

ATKINSON, BRIGHT
Previously served as Sergeant in Company B of this regiment. Appointed Ordnance Sergeant in September-December, 1862, and transferred to the Field and Staff. Reported present in September-October, 1863, and January-February, 1864. Reduced to ranks in March-December, 1864, and transferred back to Company B.

O'BRIANT, ALEXANDER
Previously served as Private in Company A of this regiment. Appointed Ordnance Sergeant in March-December, 1864, and transferred to the Field and Staff. Reported present in November-December, 1864. Paroled at Greensboro on May 9, 1865.

HOSPITAL STEWARDS

SMITH, THOMAS C.
Previously served as Private in Company I of this regiment. Appointed Hospital Steward on or about May 1, 1862; however, he apparently continued to serve with Company I. Transferred to the Field and Staff in January-October, 1863. Last reported in the records of the regiment on November 21, 1864.

SHEPPARD, JAMES L.
Previously served as Private in Company F of this regiment. Appointed Hospital Steward on December 1, 1863, and transferred to the Field and Staff. Reported present in January-February and November-December, 1864.

BAND

BROOKS, C. C., Musician
Born in Union County and was by occupation a farmer prior to enlisting in New Hanover County at age 17, February 20, 1864. Promotion record not reported. Reported present in November-December, 1864.

COX, ALEXANDER H., Chief Musician
Previously served as Sergeant in Company F of this regiment. Appointed Chief Musician in March-December, 1864, and transferred to the regimental band. Reported present in November-December, 1864. Captured in Chatham County on an unspecified date. Paroled at Avin's Ferry on April 26, 1865.

COX, HENRY A., Musician
Previously served as Corporal in Company F of this regiment. Appointed Musician in March-December, 1864, and transferred to the regimental band. Reported present in November-December, 1864. Captured in Chatham County on an unspecified date. Paroled at Avin's Ferry on April 26, 1865.

COX, WILLIAM J., Musician
Previously served as Private in Company F of this regiment. Appointed Musician in March-December, 1864, and transferred to the regimental band. Reported present in November-December, 1864. Captured in Chatham County on an unspecified date. Paroled at Avin's Ferry on April 26, 1865.

GREEN, C. P., Musician
Previously served as Private in Company I of this regiment. Appointed Musician in January-February, 1864, and transferred to the regimental band. Reduced to ranks on an unspecified date (probably prior to November 1, 1864) and transferred back to Company I.

KELLY, JOSEPH D., Musician
Previously served as Musician in Company F of this regiment. Transferred to the regimental band in March-December, 1864. Sent to hospital from Savannah, Georgia, in November-December, 1864. Survived the war.

KELLY, THOMAS M., Musician
Previously served as Private in Company F of this

regiment. Appointed Musician in March-December, 1864, and transferred to the regimental band. Reported present in November-December, 1864.

MADDOX, JAMES T., Musician

Previously served as Private in Company F of this regiment. Appointed Musician in March-December, 1864, and transferred to the regimental band. Reported sick in hospital at Goldsboro in November-December, 1864.

NUTT, WILLIAM HENRY, Drum Major

Previously served as Musician in Company B of this regiment. Appointed Drum Major and transferred to the regimental band in January-March, 1863. Complimented for bravery after he undertook a dangerous scouting mission at Deep Gully on March 13, 1863. Captured at Rodman's Point, Beaufort County, April 16, 1863. Sent to New Bern. Transferred to Fort Monroe, Virginia, on an unspecified date. Paroled at Fort Monroe and transferred to City Point, Virginia, where he was received on May 28, 1863, for exchange. Returned to duty on an unspecified date. Reported present in September-October, 1863. Reduced to ranks and transferred to Company A of this regiment in November-December, 1863.

POOLE, PERRIN P., Drum Major

Previously served as Private in Company C, 24th Regiment N.C. Troops (14th Regiment N.C. Volunteers). Was reportedly transferred to Company C of this regiment on or about May 18, 1862; however, records of Company C do not indicate that he served therein. Appointed Drum Major of this regiment on December 27, 1863. Reported present in November-December, 1864. Survived the war.

SIMPSON, H. W., Musician

Born in Union County and was by occupation a farmer prior to enlisting in New Hanover County at age 17, February 20, 1864, for the war. Was apparently mustered in with the rank of Musician. Reported present in November-December, 1864.

SLOAN, DAVID M., Musician

Previously served as Private in Company F of this regiment. Appointed Musician in March-December, 1864, and transferred to the regimental band. Reported sick in hospital at Goldsboro in November-December, 1864. Captured in Chatham County on an unspecified date. Paroled at Avin's Ferry on April 24, 1865.

SMITH, MARTIN ALEXANDER, Musician

Previously served as Private in Company F of this regiment. Appointed Musician in March-December, 1864, and transferred to the regimental band. Reported present in November-December, 1864.

STEPHENS, J. MARSHALL, Musician

Previously served as Private in Company F of this regiment. Appointed Musician in March-December, 1864, and transferred to the regimental band. Reported present in November-December, 1864. Captured in Chatham County on an unspecified date. Paroled at Avin's Ferry on April 27, 1865.

STEWART, J. F., Musician

Previously served as Private in Company F of this regiment. Appointed Musician in March-December, 1864, and transferred to the regimental band. Reported present in November-December, 1864. Survived the war.

TURNER, GEORGE W., Musician

Previously served as Private in Company F of this regiment. Appointed Musician in March-December, 1864, and transferred to the regimental band. Reported present in November-December, 1864.

TURNER, H. C., Musician

Previously served as Private in Company F of this regiment. Appointed Musician in May-December, 1864, and transferred to the regimental band. Reported present in November-December, 1864. Reduced to ranks in January-April, 1865, and transferred back to Company F.

COMPANY A

This company was raised in Person County and enlisted in Person County in March, 1862. It was mustered into state service at Camp Mangum, near Raleigh, on April 21, 1862, and assigned to the 50th Regiment N.C. Troops as Company A. After joining the regiment the company functioned as a part of the regiment, and its history for the remainder of the war is reported as a part of the regimental history.

The information contained in the following roster was compiled primarily from a company muster-in and descriptive roll dated April 21, 1862, and from company muster rolls for May 1-December 31, 1862, and September 1, 1863-February 29, 1864. No company muster rolls were located for January 1-August 31, 1863, or for the period after February 29, 1864. Valuable information was obtained from primary records such as the North Carolina adjutant general's *Roll of Honor*, discharge certificates, medical records, prisoner of war records, *The War of the Rebellion: A Compilation of the Official Records of the Union and Confederate Armies*, militia records, newspaper casualty lists and obituaries, Confederate pension applications filed with the state of North Carolina, and the 1860 federal census of North Carolina. Secondary sources such as postwar rosters and histories, cemetery records, the *Confederate Veteran*, published genealogies, and records of the United Daughters of the Confederacy also provided useful information.

OFFICERS

CAPTAINS

VAN HOOK, JOHN C.

Born in Caswell County and resided in Person County where he was by occupation a farmer prior to enlisting at age 31. Appointed Captain on April 21, 1862. Present or accounted for until he was appointed Major on

December 1, 1862, and transferred to the Field and Staff of this regiment. [Previously served as 1st Lieutenant in the 44th Regiment N.C. Militia.]

BURCH, JAMES A.
Born in Person County where he resided as a farmer prior to enlisting in Person County at age 32. Appointed 1st Lieutenant on April 21, 1862. Promoted to Captain on December 1, 1862. Reported present from September, 1863, through February, 1864. Hospitalized at Raleigh on March 6, 1865, with intermittent fever. Returned to duty on March 13, 1865. Paroled at Greensboro on May 11, 1865.

LIEUTENANTS

BLALOCK, WILLIAM A., 1st Lieutenant
Born in Person County where he resided as a farmer prior to enlisting at age 21. Appointed 2nd Lieutenant on April 21, 1862. Reported present but under arrest on August 31, 1862. Reason he was arrested not reported. Reported present in September-December, 1862. Promoted to 1st Lieutenant on December 1, 1862. Reported on detached service on October 28, 1863. Reported present in November-December, 1863. "Detailed to procure conscripts" on January 24, 1864. "Detailed to take ch[ar]g[e] of a Guard at Wrightsville" on February 24, 1864. Paroled at Greensboro on May 11, 1865.

LUNSFORD, ALLEN H., 3rd Lieutenant
Born in Person County where he resided as a farmer prior to enlisting in Person County at age 38. Appointed 3rd Lieutenant on April 21, 1862. Resigned on May 30, 1862. Reason he resigned not reported.

O'BRIANT, ALBERT, 2nd Lieutenant
Born in Person County where he resided as a farmer prior to enlisting in Person County at age 28, March 10, 1862. Mustered in as 1st Sergeant. Elected 3rd Lieutenant on May 30, 1862. Reported present in July-December, 1862. Promoted to 2nd Lieutenant on December 1, 1862. Reported present from September, 1863, through February, 1864. Paroled at Greensboro on May 9, 1865.

RAMSEY, ROBERT D., 3rd Lieutenant
Born in Person County where he resided as a farmer prior to enlisting in Person County at age 30, March 6, 1862. Mustered in as Private. Reported present in July-December, 1862. Appointed 3rd Lieutenant on January 13, 1863. Reported present or accounted for from September, 1863, through February, 1864.

NONCOMMISSIONED OFFICERS AND PRIVATES

ALLEN, MONROE S., Private
Born in Person County where he resided as a farmer prior to enlisting in Person County at age 20, March 1, 1862.

Reported present from June 30 through December 31, 1862. Transferred to Company G, 15th Regiment N.C. Troops (5th Regiment N.C. Volunteers), May 19, 1863, in exchange for Private Ephraim Wheeley.

ASHLEY, JAMES W., Private
Resided in Person County and was by occupation a farmer prior to enlisting in Person County at age 37, March 20, 1863, for the war. Reported present or accounted for from September, 1863, through February, 1864. Paroled at Greensboro on May 22, 1865.

BELL, JAMES H., _____
North Carolina pension records indicate that he served in this company.

BLACKARD, LAWRENCE H., Private
Born in Person County where he resided as a farmer prior to enlisting in Person County at age 26, March 13, 1862. Reported present or accounted for from March 13 through December 31, 1862, and from September 1 through December 11, 1863. Hospitalized at Wilmington on December 12, 1863, with pleuritis. Furloughed for thirty days on December 29, 1863. Returned to duty prior to March 1, 1864. Hospitalized at Wilmington on April 26, 1864, with chronic dysentery. Paroled at Greensboro on May 9, 1865.

BLACKARD, THOMAS W., Corporal
Resided in Person County and was by occupation a farmer prior to enlisting in Person County at age 32, May 1, 1862, for the war. Mustered in as Private. Reported present in May-December, 1862. Promoted to Corporal in January-October, 1863. Reported present from September, 1863, through February, 1864. Paroled at Greensboro on May 9, 1865.

BLALOCK, C., Private
Enlisted in Person County at age 38, June 27, 1863, for the war. Reported sick in hospital at Goldsboro from August 9, 1863, through April 12, 1864. Returned to duty on or about April 13, 1864. Paroled at Greensboro on May 11, 1865. [North Carolina pension records indicate that he received a slight wound in the leg on an unspecified date.]

BLALOCK, COLUMBUS C., Private
Born in Person County and was by occupation a farmer prior to enlisting in Person County at age 26, March 1, 1862. Reported present in March-December, 1862, and from September, 1863, through February, 1864. Last reported in the records of this company in July-September, 1864.

BLALOCK, GREEN W., Sergeant
Born in Person County where he resided as a farmer prior to enlisting in Person County at age 44, March 1, 1862. Mustered in as Sergeant. No further records.

BLALOCK, HASTEN, Private
Born in Person County and was by occupation a farmer prior to enlisting in Person County at age 23, March 1, 1862. Reported present in March-December, 1862, and

and from September, 1863, through February, 1864. Paroled at Greensboro on May 11, 1865.

BLALOCK, THOMAS, Private

Born in Person County and was by occupation a farmer prior to enlisting in Person County at age 25, March 1, 1862. Reported present in March-December, 1862. Died in hospital in North Carolina on May 26, 1863, of "pneumonia" and/or "bronchitis."

BLALOCK, WELDON DEWITT, _____

North Carolina pension records indicate that he served in this company.

BLALOCK, WILLIAM A., Private

Resided in Person County and was by occupation a farmer prior to enlisting in Person County at age 18, May 1, 1862, for the war. Hospitalized at Petersburg, Virginia, July 20, 1862, with typhoid fever. Returned to duty on August 29, 1862. Reported present but sick in September-December, 1862. Hospitalized at Wilmington on August 28, 1863, with debility. Returned to duty on September 4, 1863. Hospitalized at Wilmington on November 28, 1863, with debility. Returned to duty on December 11, 1863. Reported absent on sick furlough from December 20, 1863, through February 29, 1864. Last reported in the records of this company in July-September, 1864. Survived the war.

BLALOCK, WILLIAM P., Private

Born in Person County and was by occupation a farmer prior to enlisting in Person County at age 31, March 6, 1862. Reported present from March 6 through October 9, 1862. Reported in hospital at Petersburg, Virginia, from October 10, 1862, through December 31, 1862. Reported on detail as a butcher from June 20 through December 31, 1863. Reported present in January-February, 1864. Paroled at Greensboro on May 19, 1865.

BOOLS, BARTLETT, Private

Born in Person County and was by occupation a farmer prior to enlisting in Person County at age 24, March 13, 1862. Reported absent without leave on or about the same date.

BOWDEN, MADISON, Private

Resided in Person County and was by occupation a farmer prior to enlisting in Person County at age 44, September 18, 1863, for the war. Reported present or accounted for through February 29, 1864. Last reported in the records of this company in July-September, 1864.

BOWES, J. SAMUEL, Private

Born in Person County and was by occupation a farmer prior to enlisting in Person County at age 22, March 1, 1862. Present or accounted for through December, 1862, and in September-October, 1863. Detailed as a teamster on October 28, 1863. Hospitalized at Wilmington on or about February 12, 1864, with scabies. Returned to duty on March 7, 1864. Paroled at Greensboro on May 18, 1865.

BRADLEY, E., _____

Place and date of enlistment not reported. Reported in

hospital at Wilmington on April 30, 1863, with typhoid fever. No further records.

BRADSHER, JAMES M., Private

Born in Person County and was by occupation a farmer prior to enlisting in Person County at age 18, March 1, 1862. Discharged on an unspecified date by reason of "a great deficiency of the muscles of the right arm & chest."

BRADSHER, JOHN W., Private

Born in Person County and was by occupation a farmer prior to enlisting in Person County at age 32, March 1, 1862. Reported present through December, 1862, and from September, 1863, through February, 1864. Last reported in the records of this company in July-September, 1864.

BRIGHTWELL, JOHN J., Private

Born in Virginia and resided in Person County where he was by occupation a shoemaker prior to enlisting in Person County at age 37, March 1, 1862. No further records.

BROACH, JOHN H., Private

Born in Person County where he resided as a farmer prior to enlisting in Person County at age 24, March 1, 1862. Died in hospital at Petersburg, Virginia, July 28, 1862, of "febris typhoides."

BROACH, PLEASANT, Private

Born in Person County where he resided as a farmhand prior to enlisting in Person County at age 31, March 1, 1862. Reported present or accounted for through December, 1862. Reported absent sick from August 9 through October 31, 1863. Reported present from November, 1863, through February, 1864. No further records.

BROACH, RICHARD H., Private

Born in Person County where he resided as a farmer prior to enlisting in Person County at age 34, March 4, 1862. No further records.

BROOKS, A. W., Private

Place and date of enlistment not reported. Captured at Savannah, Georgia, December 21, 1864. Sent to Hilton Head, South Carolina. Confined at Fort Delaware, Delaware, March 12, 1865. Died at Fort Delaware on or about April 10, 1865, of "debility." [Federal hospital records dated January, 1865, give his age as 30.]

BROOKS, JAMES J., Private

Enlisted in Person County on September 26, 1862, for the war. Reported present in October-December, 1862, and September-December, 1863. Reported on detail as a coastguardsman at Wrightsville Sound in January-February, 1864. Paroled at Greensboro on or about May 10, 1865. [Previously served as 3rd Lieutenant in the 44th Regiment N.C. Militia.]

BROOKS, JOHN W. T., Private

Born in Person County and was by occupation a farmer prior to enlisting in Person County at age 20, March 13,

1862. Died "at home" on June 19, 1862. Cause of death not reported.

BROOKS, WYATT H., Private
Born in Person County and was by occupation a farmer prior to enlisting in Person County at age 19, March 13, 1862. Reported present in March-December, 1862, and September-December, 1863. Reported absent on detail as a coastguardsman at Wrightsville Sound in January-February, 1864. Paroled at Greensboro on May 9, 1865.

BROWN, BRANTLY, Private
Born in Orange County where he resided as a farmer prior to enlisting in Person County at age 32, March 1, 1862. Reported present or accounted for in March-December, 1862, and from November, 1863, through February, 1864. Paroled at Greensboro on May 19, 1865.

BROWN, CALVIN, Private
Born in Person County where he resided as a farmer prior to enlisting in Person County at age 37, March 6, 1862. Reported present in March-December, 1862, and September-December, 1863. Reported on detail as a coastguardsman at Wrightsville Sound in January-February, 1864. Hospitalized at Raleigh on March 20, 1865, with acute rheumatism. Transferred to another hospital on March 26, 1865.

BROWN, GREEN DANIEL, Private
Enlisted in Person County at age 19, September 18, 1863, for the war. Reported present through February, 1864. Paroled at Greensboro on May 16, 1865. [North Carolina pension records indicate that he was wounded severely in the left foot at or near Sumter, South Carolina, in 1864.]

BROWN, W. H., Private
Place and date of enlistment not reported. Reported on duty as a coastguardsman in January, 1864. No further records.

BURCH, THOMAS B., Private
Place and date of enlistment not reported. First listed in the records of this company in January-March, 1864. Paroled at Greensboro on May 11, 1865.

BURTON, DUDLEY, Private
Born in Person County where he resided as a farmer prior to enlisting in Person County at age 34, March 13, 1862. Reported present until July 15, 1862, when he was detailed as an ambulance driver. Reported on detail as an ambulance driver through March, 1864. Paroled at Greensboro on May 17, 1865.

CARVER, REUBEN C., Private
Born in Person County and was by occupation a farmer prior to enlisting in Person County at age 22, March 5, 1862. Reported present in March-December, 1862, and from September, 1863, through February, 1864. Hospitalized at Raleigh on November 6, 1864, with acute diarrhoea. Returned to duty on November 30, 1864. No further records.

CASH, PRESTON, Private
Enlisted on or about May 1, 1863, for the war. Hospitalized at Wilmington on October 16, 1863, with pleuritis. Returned to duty on October 31, 1863. Captured at River's Bridge, Salkehatchie River, South Carolina, February 3, 1865, when he was "found sick in house with arms [sic]." No further records.

CATES, COLUMBUS C., Private
Born in Person County and was by occupation a farmer prior to enlisting in Person County at age 26, March 1, 1862. Reported present or accounted for until October 25, 1862, when he was detailed to work at a sawmill. Returned to duty in November-December, 1863. Reported on detail as a coastguardsman at Wrightsville Sound in January-February, 1864. Paroled at Greensboro on May 17, 1865.

CATES, EPHRAIM, Private
Resided in Person County and was by occupation a farmhand prior to enlisting in Person County at age 32, September 18, 1863, for the war. Reported present through February, 1864. "Received in moribund condition" in hospital at Raleigh on March 18, 1865, and died on or about the same date of "colitis acute."

CATES, JOHN D., Private
Born in Person County where he resided as a farmer prior to enlisting in Person County at age 22, March 1, 1862. Discharged on July 19, 1862, by reason of "his general debility and liability to disease when exposed to the influence of sunshine or night air. He is constitutionally unfitted to endure fatigue and is evidently hereditarily predisposed to pulmonary disease."

CATES, RICHARD H., Private
Born in Person County where he resided as a farmer prior to enlisting in Person County at age 28, March 1, 1862. Discharged on July 20, 1862. Reason discharged not reported.

CATES, SAMUEL H., Private
Born in Person County and was by occupation a farmer prior to enlisting in Person County at age 19, March 1, 1862. Reported present until October 28, 1862, when he was detailed to work in a sawmill. Returned to duty in November-December, 1863. Reported on detail as a coastguardsman at Wrightsville Sound in January-February, 1864. Paroled at Greensboro on May 9, 1865.

CHANDLER, JESSE, _____
North Carolina pension records indicate that he served in this company.

CHANDLER, STEPHEN D., Private
Born in Person County and was by occupation a farmer prior to enlisting in Person County at age 37, March 13, 1862. Discharged on July 10, 1863[?]. Reason discharged not reported.

CHILDRESS, WILLIAM B., Private
Resided in Caswell County and was by occupation a

farmer prior to enlisting in Person County at age 25, April 15, 1862. Reported present in April-December, 1862, and from September, 1863, through February, 1864. Last reported in the records of this company in July-September, 1864.

CLAYTON, HENDERSON, Private
Born in Person County where he resided as a farmer prior to enlisting in Person County at age 26, March 6, 1862. Mustered in as Sergeant. Reported present through December, 1862. Promoted to 1st Sergeant on December 20, 1862. Reported present from September, 1863, through February, 1864. Reduced to ranks subsequent to February 29, 1864. Hospitalized at Raleigh on February 13, 1865, with intermittent fever. Returned to duty on March 13, 1865. Paroled at Greensboro in [May] 1865.

CLAYTON, J. B., Private
Enlisted in Person County on March 20, 1863, for the war. Reported present from September, 1863, through February, 1864. Last reported in the records of this company in July-September, 1864.

CLAYTON, JAMES H., Private
Born in Person County and was by occupation a farmer prior to enlisting in Person County at age 19, April 1, 1862. Hospitalized on July 22, 1862, with typhoid fever. Returned to duty on September 10, 1862. Reported present in November-December, 1862. Hospitalized at Wilmington on or about February 25, 1863, with dysentery. Returned to duty on March 7, 1863. Reported present or accounted for from September, 1863, through February, 1864. Paroled at Greensboro on May 9, 1865.

CLAYTON, JOHN D., Private
Resided in Person County and was by occupation a farmer prior to enlisting in Person County at age 26, May 1, 1862, for the war. Mustered in as Private. Promoted to Corporal prior to September 1, 1862. Reported present in May-December, 1862. Promoted to Sergeant in January-October, 1863. Reported present or accounted for from September, 1863, through February, 1864. Reduced to ranks subsequent to February 29, 1864. Paroled at Greensboro on May 9, 1865.

CLAYTON, L. G., Private
Resided in Person County and was by occupation a farmer prior to enlisting in Person County at age 39, September 18, 1863, for the war. Reported present until November 13, 1863, when he was detailed as a clerk in the quartermaster department. Reported absent on detail as a clerk or absent on furlough through February, 1864. Last reported in the records of this company in July-September, 1864.

CLAYTON, SOLOMON C., Private
Enlisted in Person County on May 1, 1862, for the war. Reported present in May-December, 1862, and from September, 1863, through February, 1864. Paroled at Greensboro on May 11, 1865.

CLAYTON, WILLIAM D., Private
Born in Person County and was by occupation a carpenter

prior to enlisting in Person County at age 23, March 1, 1862. Reported present in March-December, 1862, and from September, 1863, through February, 1864. Paroled at Greensboro on May 11, 1865.

COMPTON, W., Private
Enlisted in Person County on or about March 15, 186[3]. Died in hospital at Wilson on or about September 27, 1863, of "diarrhoea chronica."

DANIEL, CALVIN, Private
Born in Person County and was by occupation a farmer prior to enlisting in Person County at age 33, March 10, 1862. Reported present in March-December, 1862, and from September, 1863, through February, 1864. Last reported in the records of this company in July-September, 1864.

DANIEL, F. M., Private
Enlisted in Person County at age 17, February 12, 1864, for the war. Hospitalized at Raleigh on March 6, 1865, with catarrhus. Returned to duty on March 16, 1865. Hospitalized at Raleigh on April 8, 1865. Captured at Raleigh on April 13, 1865.

DAVENPORT, JAMES D., Private
Born in Halifax County, Virginia, and resided in Person County where he was by occupation a carpenter prior to enlisting in Person County at age 28, March 1, 1862. Died in hospital at Petersburg, Virginia, August 1, 1862, of "febris typhoides."

DENNY, NATHANIEL A., Private
Born in Person County and was by occupation a farmer prior to enlisting in Person County at age 28, March 10, 1862. Reported present in March-December, 1862. Died in hospital at Goldsboro on February 8, 1863, of "pneumonia."

DRAKE, SILAS A., Private
Resided in Person County and was by occupation a day laborer prior to enlisting in Person County at age 18, March 20, 1863, for the war. Reported present in September-December, 1863. Hospitalized at Wilmington on January 8, 1864, with acute rheumatism. Furloughed for thirty days on or about February 18, 1864. Hospitalized at Charlotte on January 19, 1865, with intermittent fever. Transferred to another hospital on January 24, 1865. Hospitalized at Raleigh on April 8, 1865. No further records.

DUNCAN, ISAIAH T., Private
Born in Person County and was by occupation a farmer prior to enlisting in Person County at age 38, March 15, 1862. No further records.

DUNCAN, JAMES W., Private
Born in Person County and was by occupation a farmer prior to enlisting in Person County at age 20, March 13, 1862. Reported present in March-December, 1862, and from September, 1863, through February, 1864. Survived the war.

EDMONDSON, J. N., Private

Enlisted in Person County on September 18, 1863, for the war. Reported present or accounted for through January, 1864. Hospitalized at Wilmington on February 23, 1864, with intermittent fever. Returned to duty on March 31, 1864. Paroled at Greensboro on May 11, 1865.

ELLISON, E. BYRD, Private

Born in Orange County and was by occupation a farmer prior to enlisting in Person County at age 26, March 1, 1862. Reported present or accounted for in March-December, 1862, and from September, 1863, through January, 1864. Reported on detail as a coastguardsman at Wrightsville Sound in February, 1864. Paroled at Greensboro on May 11, 1865.

ENNIS, JAMES, _____

North Carolina pension records indicate that he served in this company.

FERRELL, JOHN A., Private

North Carolina pension records indicate that he served in this company.

FERRELL, JOHN W., _____

North Carolina pension records indicate that he served in this company.

FREDERICK, ERASMUS D., Sergeant

Born in Person County and was by occupation a farmer prior to enlisting in Person County at age 20, March 1, 1862. Mustered in as Private. Reported present in March-December, 1862. Promoted to Corporal on May 30, 1862. Promoted to Sergeant in January-October, 1863. Reported present from September, 1863, through February, 1864. Paroled at Greensboro on May 9, 1865.

FREEMAN, GEORGE H., Musician

Born at Norfolk, Virginia, and resided in Person County where he was by occupation a tobacconist prior to enlisting in Person County at age 62, April 1, 1862. Mustered in as Musician. Reported present in March-December, 1862, and September-October, 1863. Hospitalized at Wilmington on November 28, 1863, with debilitas. Returned to duty on February 1, 1864. Discharged on March 13, 1864, by reason of "old age" and "debility."

GRAY, AUGUSTUS M., Private

Born in Greene County, Alabama, and was by occupation a farmer prior to enlisting in Person County at age 21, March 1, 1862. Reported present or accounted for in March-December, 1862, and from September, 1863, through January, 1864. Reported on detail as a coastguardsman at Wrightsville Sound in February, 1864. Last reported in the records of this company in July-September, 1864.

GRAY, GEORGE THOMAS, Sergeant

Born in Person County where he resided as a shoemaker prior to enlisting in Person County at age 27, March 1, 1862. Mustered in as Private. Reported present in March-December, 1862. Promoted to Sergeant in January-

October, 1863. Reported present or accounted for from September, 1863, through January, 1864. Reported on detail as a coastguardsman at Wrightsville Sound in February, 1864. Paroled at Greensboro on May 9, 1865.

HAMLIN, J. D., Private

Enlisted in Person County at age 20, February 1, 1863, for the war. Reported present from September, 1863, through February, 1864. Paroled at Greensboro on May 19, 1865.

HAMLIN, WILLIAM P., Private

Born in Person County and was by occupation a farmer prior to enlisting in Person County at age 22, March 1, 1862. Hospitalized at Petersburg, Virginia, July 20, 1862. Died in hospital at Petersburg on August 27, 1862, of "feb[ris] typhoid."

HARGIS, R., Private

Enlisted in Person County on September 18, 1863, for the war. Reported present through February, 1864. Last reported in the records of this company in July-September, 1864.

HARMON, FREDERICK, Private

Enlisted in Person County on May 1, 1862, for the war. Died in camp near Petersburg, Virginia, July 24, 1862. Cause of death not reported.

HARRIS, ALEXANDER B., Musician

Born in Halifax County, Virginia, and was by occupation a farmer prior to enlisting in Person County at age 18, March 1, 1862. Mustered in as Private. Reported present in March-December, 1862, and from September, 1863, through February, 1864. Appointed Musician in January-February, 1864. Last reported in the records of this company in July-September, 1864.

HARRIS, J. D., Private

Enlisted in Person County on March 20, 1863, for the war. Reported present from September, 1863, through February, 1864. Last reported in the records of this company in July-September, 1864.

HARRIS, JOHN E., Private

Enlisted in Person County on May 1, 1862, for the war. Hospitalized at Petersburg, Virginia, July 20, 1862, with typhoid fever. Returned to duty on September 1, 1862. Reported present or accounted for in September-December, 1862, and from September, 1863, through February, 1864. Paroled at Greensboro on May 9, 1865.

HARRIS, WILLIAM A., Private

Born in Campbell County, Virginia, and was by occupation a farmer prior to enlisting in Person County at age 29, March 1, 1862. Mustered in as Corporal. Promoted to Sergeant on May 30, 1862. Reported present in March-December, 1862. Reduced to ranks in January-October, 1863. Reported present from September, 1863, through February, 1864. Was still alive as of March 26, 1865.

HAWKINS, CALVIN, Private

Resided in Person County and was by occupation a farmer

prior to enlisting in Person County at age 35, May 1, 1862, for the war. Mustered in with an unspecified rank. Promoted to 1st Sergeant on May 30, 1862. Was apparently absent sick for much of the period from May 1 through December 31, 1862. Reduced to the rank of Sergeant on December 20, 1862. Reduced to the rank of Private prior to November 1, 1863. Reported present from September, 1863, through February, 1864. Paroled at Greensboro on May 11, 1865. [Previously served as 1st Lieutenant in the 44th Regiment N.C. Militia.]

HICKS, DAVID A., Private
Born in Person County and was by occupation a farmer prior to enlisting in Person County at age 21, March 1, 1862. Reported present in March-December, 1862, and from September, 1863, through February, 1864. Last reported in the records of this company in July-September, 1864. Survived the war.

HICKS, DAVID W., Private
Born in Person County and was by occupation a farmer prior to enlisting in Person County at age 18, March 1, 1862. Wounded at Malvern Cliffs, Virginia, June 30, 1862. Hospitalized at Richmond, Virginia, where he died on or about August 3, 1862, presumably of wounds.

HICKS, JAMES WASHINGTON, Private
Enlisted at age 17 on or about March 1, 186[4], for the war. Paroled at Greensboro on May 19, 1865.

HICKS, SOLOMON D., Private
Enlisted in Person County on April 8, 1862. Reported present or accounted for in April-December, 1862, and from September, 1863, through February, 1864. Last reported in the records of this company in July-September, 1864.

HICKS, T. W., Private
Enlisted in Person County on March 20, 1863, for the war. Reported present from September, 1863, through February, 1864. Paroled at Greensboro on May 19, 1865.

HOLSOMBACK, GEORGE W., Private
Born in Person County and was by occupation a farmer prior to enlisting in Person County at age 21, March 13, 1862. Reported absent sick for most of the period through December, 1862. Reported present or accounted for from September, 1863, through February, 1864. Last reported in the records of this company in July-September, 1864. Survived the war.

HOLSOMBACK, WILLIAM T., Private
Born in Person County or in Halifax County, Virginia, and was by occupation a farmer prior to enlisting in Person County at age 36, March 1, 1862. Reported absent with leave on April 21, 1862. Discharged on July 9, 1863, by reason of being over age.

HORTON, ELIJAH M., Private
Enlisted in Person County on May 1, 1862, for the war. Hospitalized on July 22, 1862, with diarrhoea and bronchitis. Returned to duty on October 21, 1862. Reported present or accounted for in November-

December, 1862, and from September, 1863, through February, 1864. Last reported in the records of this company in July-September, 1864.

HORTON, WILLIAM M., Private
Born in Person County and was by occupation a farmer prior to enlisting in Person County at age 18, March 1, 1862. Reported present in March-December, 1862, and from September, 1863, through February, 1864. Last reported in the records of this company in July-September, 1864.

HUDGINS, WILLIAM B., Private
Resided in Person County and was by occupation a day laborer prior to enlisting in Person County at age 37, March 20, 1863, for the war. Reported in confinement at Wilmington on October 19, 1863. Reason he was confined not reported. Reported present from November, 1863, through February, 1864. Reported in hospital at Raleigh on or about February 24, 1865. Furloughed for sixty days from hospital at Wake Forest on March 13, 1865. Paroled at Greensboro on May 9, 1865.

HYDER, WILLIAM H., _____
North Carolina pension records indicate that he served in this company.

JONES, BEDFORD, Private
Born in Person County and was by occupation a farmer prior to enlisting in Person County at age 19, March 1, 1862. Reported present or accounted for in March-December, 1862, and from September, 1863, through January, 1864. Reported on detail as a coastguardsman at Wrightsville Sound in February, 1864. Paroled at Greensboro on May 11, 1865.

JONES, CALVIN, Private
Born in Person County and was by occupation a farmer prior to enlisting in Person County at age 23, March 1, 1862. Reported present in March-December, 1862, and from September, 1863, through February, 1864. Hospitalized at Richmond, Virginia, May 23, 1864. Transferred to another hospital on May 24, 1864. Paroled at Greensboro on May 19, 1865.

JONES, JAMES T., Sergeant
Enlisted in Person County on May 1, 1862, for the war. Mustered in as Private. Promoted to Corporal prior to September 1, 1862. Reported present or accounted for in May-December, 1862, and from September, 1863, through January, 1864. Promoted to Sergeant in November-December, 1864. Reported on detail as a coastguardsman at Wrightsville Sound in February, 1864. Last reported in the records of this company in July-August, 1864.

JONES, ROBERT, Private
Born in Person County and was by occupation a farmer prior to enlisting in Person County at age 30, March 10, 1862. Detailed as a hospital nurse at Raleigh on or about May 15, 1862. Rejoined the company on or about October 22, 1862. Reported present in November-December, 1862. Reported on detail as a baker in August-October, 1863. Furloughed on December 20, 1863. Reported

present in January, 1864. Reported on detail as a coastguardsman at Wrightsville Sound in February, 1864. Last reported in the records of this company in July-September, 1864.

JORDAN, WILLIAM W., Private
Born in Orange County and was by occupation a farmer prior to enlisting in Person County at age 39, March 1, 1862. Was apparently discharged a few weeks after his enlistment. Reenlisted in the company on or about October 1, 1863, for the war. Reported present in January-February, 1864. Hospitalized at Raleigh on January 26, 1865, with chronic diarrhoea. Transferred to another hospital on March 19, 1865. Paroled at Greensboro on May 9, 1865.

LEA, ADDISEN, Sergeant
Born in Person County and was by occupation a farmer prior to enlisting in Person County at age 23, March 1, 1862. Mustered in as Private. Promoted to Sergeant prior to July 1, 1862. Died in hospital at Petersburg, Virginia, on or about August 5, 1862, of "continued fever."

LEA, CALVIN, Private
Enlisted in Person County at age 26, May 1, 1862, for the war. Reported present in May-December, 1862, and from September, 1863, through February, 1864. Paroled at Greensboro on May 11, 1865.

LEA, JAMES H., Private
Born in Person County and was by occupation a carpenter prior to enlisting in Person County at age 33, March 10, 1862. Was apparently rejected for service.

LEA, JOHN B., Private
Enlisted in Person County on September 18, 1863, for the war. Reported present or accounted for from September, 1863, through February, 1864. Paroled at Greensboro on May 9, 1865.

LEA, S. M., Private
Enlisted in Person County at age 31, August 4, 1863, for the war. Reported present until December 21, 1863, when he was hospitalized at Wilmington with intermittent fever. Returned to duty on February 22, 1864. Hospitalized at Charlotte on February 13, 1865, with rubeola. Furloughed on February 19, 1865. [North Carolina pension records indicate that he was wounded at or near Savannah, Georgia, in January, 1865.]

LEA, W. F., Private
Born in Person County where he enlisted on September 18, 1863, for the war. Reported present through February, 1864. Died on July 8, 1864, of disease. Place of death not reported.

LEA, WILLIAM A., Private
Enlisted in Person County on May 1, 1862, for the war. Reported present or accounted for in May-December, 1862, and from September, 1863, through February, 1864. Last reported in the records of this company in July-September, 1864.

LOFTIS, JOHN B., Private
Born in Person County and was by occupation a farmer prior to enlisting in Person County at age 21, March 1, 1862. Reported present or accounted for in March-December, 1862, and from September, 1863, through February, 1864. Hospitalized at Raleigh on November 6, 1864, with intermittent fever. Returned to duty on December 18, 1864. Survived the war.

LOFTIS, W. M., _____
North Carolina pension records indicate that he served in this company.

LONG, JOHN J., Private
Enlisted in Person County at age 18 on or about February 6, 1863, for the war. Reported present from September, 1863, through February, 1864. Paroled at Greensboro on May 9, 1865.

LONG, STEPHEN M., Private
Born in Person County and was by occupation a farmer prior to enlisting in Person County at age 20, March 1, 1862. Reported present until October 28, 1862, when he was detailed to work at a sawmill. Reported absent on detail through December, 1862. Reported present or accounted for from September, 1863, through February, 1864. Paroled at Greensboro on May 9, 1865.

LONG, WILLIAM M., Private
Born in Person County and was by occupation a tobacconist prior to enlisting in Person County at age 23, March 1, 1862. Reported present in March-September, 1862. Reported on detail as a teamster from October 1, 1862, through March 31, 1864. Paroled at Greensboro on May 10, 1865.

LONG, Z. T., _____
Previously served as Private in Company C, 3rd Regiment N.C. Junior Reserves. Transferred to this company on or about March 1, 186[5]. No further records.

LOY, WILLIAM M., Private
Born in Person County and was by occupation a farmer prior to enlisting in Person County at age 22, March 1, 1862. No further records.

MALONE, JOHN P., Private
Enlisted in Person County on February 10, 1863, for the war. Reported present from September, 1863, through February, 1864. Died at Washington, North Carolina, July 3, 1864, of disease.

MARSHALL, JAMES A., Private
Born in Person County and was by occupation a farmer prior to enlisting in Person County at age 18, March 1, 1862. Reported present or accounted for in March-December, 1862, and from September, 1863, through February, 1864. Paroled at Greensboro on May 11, 1865.

MITCHELL, R. S., Private
Enlisted in Person County at age 17, February 15, 1864, for the war. Paroled at Greensboro on May 17, 1865.

MITCHELL, WILLIAM E., Private
Born in Person County and was by occupation a farmer prior to enlisting in Person County at age 20, March 1, 1862. Reported present or accounted for in March-December, 1862, and from September, 1863, through February, 1864. Paroled at Greensboro on May 9, 1865.

MONEY, J. L., Private
Enlisted in Person County on March 20, 1863, for the war. Reported present from September, 1863, through February, 1864. Last reported in the records of this company in July-September, 1864.

MONEY, JOSEPH, Private
Born in Person County and was by occupation a farmer prior to enlisting in Person County at age 31, March 1, 1862. Reported present in March-December, 1862. Died in hospital at Raleigh on March 13, 1863, of "smallpox."

MOORE, GEORGE W., Private
Born in Person County and was by occupation a farmer prior to enlisting in Person County at age 21, March 1, 1862. Mustered in as Corporal. Promoted to Sergeant on August 17, 1862. Reported present in March-December, 1862. Reduced to ranks in January-October, 1863. Reported present from September, 1863, through February, 1864. Paroled at Greensboro on May 9, 1865.

MOORE, JOHN, Corporal
Born in Person County and was by occupation a farmer prior to enlisting in Person County at age 32, March 1, 1862. Mustered in as Corporal. Discharged on July 19, 1862, by reason of "an injury of the spine of long standing, which from present indications must have been fractured, as it is in a state of considerable constricture and protuberance on the left side which incapacitates him from carrying weight upon the back or enduring bodily fatigue." [Previously served as 3rd Lieutenant in the 44th Regiment N.C. Militia.]

MOORE, WILLIAM, Private
Born in Person County and was by occupation a farmer prior to enlisting in Person County at age 35, March 1, 1862. Reported present or accounted for in January-December, 1862. Reported on detail as a teamster from June 14 through December 31, 1863. Reported present in January-February, 1864. Last reported in the records of this company in July-September, 1864.

NORRIS, ELIJAH, Private
Born in Person County and was by occupation a farmer prior to enlisting in Person County at age 25, March 1, 1862. Died in hospital at Petersburg, Virginia, on or about August 7, 1862, of "continued fever."

NORRIS, EPHRAIM, Private
Born in Person County where he resided as a farmer prior to enlisting in Person County at age 32, March 1, 1862. Reported present in March-December, 1862, and from September, 1863, through January, 1864. Reported on detail as a coastguardsman at Fair Bluff in February, 1864. Paroled at Greensboro on May 11, 1865.

NORRIS, JOHN S., Private
Enlisted in Person County on May 1, 1862, for the war. Reported present until August 17, 1862, when he was detailed as a teamster. Reported on detail as a teamster through March, 1864. Paroled at Greensboro on May 19, 1865.

NORRIS, WILLIAM, Corporal
Born in Person County and was by occupation a farmer prior to enlisting in Person County at age 25, March 1, 1862. Mustered in as Private. Reported present in March-December, 1862. Promoted to Corporal in January-October, 1863. Reported present from September, 1863, through February, 1864. Paroled at Greensboro on May 19, 1865.

NUTT, WILLIAM HENRY, Private
Previously served as Drum Major of the regimental band. Reduced to ranks and transferred to this company in November-December, 1863. Appointed Musician and transferred to Company H of this regiment in January-February, 1864.

O'BRIANT, ALEXANDER, Private
Enlisted in Person County on May 1, 1862, for the war. Reported present in May-December, 1862, and from September, 1863, through February, 1864. Appointed Ordnance Sergeant in March-December, 1864, and transferred to the Field and Staff of this regiment.

O'BRIANT, HENRY, Private
Born in Person County and was by occupation a farmer prior to enlisting in Person County at age 20, March 1, 1862. Reported present or accounted for in March-December, 1862, and from September, 1863, through February, 1864. Hospitalized at Raleigh on February 17, 1865, with intermittent fever. Hospitalized at Raleigh on March 6, 1865, with debilitas. Returned to duty on March 13, 1865. Paroled at Greensboro on May 9, 1865.

O'BRIANT, JOHN, Private
Enlisted in Person County on May 1, 1862, for the war. Reported present or accounted for in March-December, 1862, and from September, 1863, through February, 1864. Hospitalized at Raleigh on March 6, 1865, with intermittent fever. Returned to duty on March 13, 1865. Paroled at Greensboro on May 9, 1865.

O'BRIANT, WILLIAM, Private
Born in Person County and was by occupation a farmer prior to enlisting in Person County at age 22, March 1, 1862. Reported present or accounted for in March-December, 1862, and from September, 1863, through February, 1864. Paroled at Greensboro on May 9, 1865.

PANTER, WYATT, Private
Born in Person County and was by occupation a farmer prior to enlisting in Person County at age 28, March 1, 1862. Reported present until September 10, 1862, when he was detailed as a nurse at the regimental hospital. Returned from detail on December 24, 1862. Died in hospital at Raleigh on February 11, 1863, of "pneumonia."

PORTERFIELD, DAVID R., Private
Resided in Person County and was by occupation a farmhand prior to enlisting in Person County at age 42, September 18, 1863, for the war. Reported present through February, 1864. Paroled at Greensboro on May 11, 1865.

RAY, NELSON, Private
Enlisted in Person County on April 20, 1863, for the war. Reported present from September, 1863, through February, 1864. Paroled at Greensboro on May 9, 1865.

RHEW, J. T., Private
Enlisted in Person County on November 15, 1862, for the war. Reported present in December, 1862, and from September, 1863, through February, 1864. Last reported in the records of this company in July-September, 1864.

RIMMER, ADDERSON, Private
Resided in Person County and was by occupation a farmer prior to enlisting in Person County at age 41, September 18, 1863, for the war. Reported present through February, 1864. Paroled at Greensboro on May 11, 1865.

RIMMER, HASTEN, Private
Resided in Person County and was by occupation a farmer prior to enlisting in Person County at age 36, March 15, 1863, for the war. Reported absent on sick furlough from October 5 through December 31, 1863. Reported present in January-February, 1864. Paroled at Greensboro on May 11, 1865.

RIMMER, SAMUEL R., Corporal
Resided in Person County and was by occupation a farmer prior to enlisting in Person County at age 27, May 1, 1862, for the war. Mustered in as Private. Reported present in May-December, 1862. Promoted to Corporal in January-October, 1863. Reported present or accounted for from September, 1863, through January, 1864. Reported on detail as a coastguardsman at Wrightsville Sound in February, 1864. Paroled at Greensboro on May 11, 1865.

RIMMER, WILLIAM, Private
Born in Person County and was by occupation a farmer prior to enlisting in Person County at age 21, March 1, 1862. Was apparently rejected for service. Reenlisted in the company on March 20, 1863. Reported absent on sick furlough from September 20 through October 31, 1863. Reported present from November, 1863, through February, 1864. Paroled at Greensboro on May 11, 1865.

ROGERS, SIMEON A., Private
Born in Person County and was by occupation a farmer prior to enlisting in Person County at age 22, March 10, 1862. Was apparently rejected for service.

ROYSTER, SOLOMON, Private
Enlisted in Person County on August 7, 1863, for the war. Reported absent sick with acute bronchitis and diarrhoea for much of the period from September, 1863, through February, 1864. Died in South Carolina on January 27, 1865. Cause of death not reported.

SATTERFIELD, WILLIAM D., _____
North Carolina pension records indicate that he served in this company.

SCOGGINS, J. J. W., Private
Enlisted in Person County on February 1, 1863, for the war. Reported present from September, 1863, through February, 1864. Hospitalized at Raleigh on February 17, 1865, with intermittent fever. No further records.

STANFIELD, WILLIAM A., Private
Born in Tennessee and resided in Caswell County where he was by occupation a clerk prior to enlisting in Person County at age 32, May 1, 1862, for the war. Hospitalized on July 22, 1862, with diarrhoea. Returned to duty on September 6, 1862. Reported present in September-December, 1862. Last reported in the records of this company on March 6, 1863.

SUIT, JOHN S., Private
Born in Person County and was by occupation a farmer prior to enlisting in Person County at age 35, March 13, 1862. Deserted on May 10, 1862. Company records do not indicate whether he returned to duty. Transferred to Company G, 15th Regiment N.C. Troops (5th Regiment N.C. Volunteers), December 10, 1863.

TRIMM, ROBERT B., Private
Born in Person County where he resided as a blacksmith prior to enlisting in Person County at age 29, March 1, 1862. Mustered in as Sergeant. Reported present in March-December, 1862. Reduced to ranks in January-October, 1863. Reported absent on detached service as a blacksmith in Person County from October 30, 1863, through April 15, 1864. Paroled at Greensboro on May 9, 1865.

VAUGHN, JOHN W., Private
Born in Person County and was by occupation a farmer prior to enlisting in Person County at age 18, March 10, 1862. Hospitalized on July 22, 1862, with typhoid fever. Returned to duty on September 2, 1862. Reported present in September-December, 1862, and from September, 1863, through February, 1864. Paroled at Greensboro on May 9, 1865.

WALKER, MOSES, _____
North Carolina pension records indicate that he served in this company.

WARREN, JOHN Q., Corporal
Born in Caswell County and resided in Person County where he was by occupation a farmer prior to enlisting in Person County at age 34, March 1, 1862. Mustered in as Corporal. Hospitalized at or near Petersburg, Virginia, July 22, 1862, with diarrhoea. Returned to duty on September 6, 1862. Reported present in September-December, 1862. Hospitalized at Wilmington on April 30, 1863, with gonorrhea. Returned to duty on an unspecified date. Reported present from September, 1863, through February, 1864. Paroled at Greensboro on May 19, 1865.

WATSON, RICHARD E., Private

Born in Person County where he resided as a farmer prior to enlisting in Person County at age 32, March 1, 1862. Reported present or accounted for in March-December, 1862. Hospitalized at Wilmington on September 9, 1863, with intermittent fever. Returned to duty on an unspecified date. Hospitalized at Wilmington on November 28, 1863, with debilitas. Reported in hospital at Wilmington until April 28, 1864, when he was furloughed. Last reported in the records of this company in July-September, 1864.

WATSON, WILLIAM ANDREW, Private

Born in Person County and was by occupation a shoemaker prior to enlisting in Person County at age 35, March 1, 1862. Died at Camp Mangum, near Raleigh, on or about May 24, 1862, of disease.

WESTBROOKS, JOHN, Private

Born in Person County and was by occupation a farmer prior to enlisting in Person County at age 19, March 1, 1862. Died in hospital at Petersburg, Virginia, July 17, 1862, of wounds. Place and date wounded not reported; however, he was probably wounded at Malvern Cliffs, Virginia, June 30, 1862.

WESTBROOKS, WILLIAM A., Private

Born in Person County and was by occupation a farmer prior to enlisting in Person County at age 24, March 1, 1862. Died on June 5, 1862. Place and cause of death not reported.

WHEELEY, EPHRAIM, Private

Previously served as Private in Company G, 15th Regiment N.C. Troops (5th Regiment N.C. Volunteers). Transferred to this company on May 19, 1863, in exchange for Private Monroe S. Allen. Reported present from September, 1863, through February, 1864. Paroled at Greensboro on May 11, 1865.

WHEELEY, OBADIAH, Private

Born in Person County where he resided as a farmer prior to enlisting in Person County at age 20, March 1, 1862. Reported present in March-December, 1862, and from September, 1863, through January, 1864. Reported on detail as a coastguardsman at Wrightsville Sound in February, 1864. Paroled at Greensboro on May 11, 1865.

WHEELEY, SAMUEL, Private

Born in Person County and was by occupation a farmer prior to enlisting in Person County at age 18, March 25, 1862. Reported present or accounted for in April-December, 1862, and from September, 1863, through January, 1864. Reported on detail as a coastguardsman at Wrightsville Sound in February, 1864. Last reported in the records of this company in July-September, 1864.

WHITEFIELD, ALEXANDER, Private

Enlisted on or about October 1, 186[4], for the war. Paroled at Greensboro on May 11, 1865.

WHITEFIELD, E., Private

Place and date of enlistment not reported; however, he probably enlisted subsequent to February 29, 1864. Paroled at Greensboro on May 9, 1865.

WHITEFIELD, THOMAS LIVINGSTON, Private

Enlisted in Person County on May 1, 1862, for the war. Reported present or accounted for through December, 1862; however, he was reported absent sick during much of that period. Died in hospital at Petersburg, Virginia, February 8, 1863, of "diarrhoea chron[ic]."

WHITEFIELD, YANCY W., Private

Born in Person County and was by occupation a farmer prior to enlisting in Person County at age 16, March 1, 1862. Reported present or accounted for in March-December, 1862, and from September, 1863, through February, 1864. Paroled at Greensboro on May 19, 1865.

WHITFIELD, D. F., Private

Place and date of enlistment not reported; however, he probably enlisted subsequent to February 29, 1864. Paroled at Greensboro on May 15, 1865.

WHITFIELD, J. W., Private

Enlisted in Person County on December 8, 1862, for the war. Died in hospital at Raleigh on April 19, 1863, of "fever."

WILKINS, RICHARD, _____

Resided in Orange County. Place and date of enlistment not reported; however, he probably enlisted subsequent to February 29, 1864. Took the Oath of Allegiance at Raleigh on June 2, 1865.

WILLIAMS, SMITH W., Private

Resided in Person County and was by occupation a farmhand prior to enlisting in Person County at age 26, May 1, 1862, for the war. Reported present or accounted for in May-December, 1862, and from September, 1863, through February, 1864. Captured in hospital at Savannah, Georgia, December 21, 1864. Sent to Fort Pulaski, Georgia. Transferred to Hilton Head, South Carolina, March 4, 1865. Transferred to Fort Delaware, Delaware, on an unspecified date. Died at Fort Delaware on or about March 29, 1865, of "ch[ronic] diarrhoea."

WRENN, GEORGE WARREN, Private

Born on November 22, 1845, and was by occupation a farmer. Enlisted in Person County on February 1, 1863, for the war. Reported present in September-October, 1863. Hospitalized at Wilmington on or about December 9, 1863, with pneumonia. Returned to duty on January 5, 1864. Reported on detail as a coastguardsman at Wrightsville Sound in February, 1864. Hospitalized at Raleigh on November 6, 1864, with intermittent fever. Returned to duty on November 29, 1864. Paroled at Greensboro on May 15, 1865.

WRIGHT, J. B., Private

Enlisted in Person County at age 19, August 20, 1863, for the war. Reported present through February, 1864. Last reported in the records of this company in July-September, 1864. Survived the war.

YARBROUGH, DAVID, Private
Born in Person County where he resided as a farmer prior to enlisting in Person County at age 37, March 13, 1862. No further records.

YARBROUGH, HENDERSON, Private
Resided in Person County and was by occupation a farmhand prior to enlisting in Person County at age 31, May 1, 1862, for the war. Reported present or accounted for in May-December, 1862, and from September, 1863, through February, 1864. Last reported in the records of this company in July-September, 1864.

YARBROUGH, JORDAN W., Private
Born in Person County where he resided as a farmer prior to enlisting in Person County at age 38, March 13, 1862. Enlisted in Company D, 13th Regiment N.C. Troops (3rd Regiment N.C. Volunteers), March 10, 1863.

COMPANY B

This company was raised in Robeson County and enlisted at Lumberton in February-March, 1862. It was mustered into state service at Camp Mangum, near Raleigh, on April 21, 1862, and assigned to the 50th Regiment N.C. Troops as Company B. After joining the regiment the company functioned as a part of the regiment, and its history for the remainder of the war is reported as a part of the regimental history.

The information contained in the following roster was compiled primarily from a company muster-in and descriptive roll dated April 21, 1862, and from company muster rolls for May 1-August 31, 1862; November 1-December 31, 1862; and September 1, 1863-February 29, 1864. No company muster rolls were found for September 1-October 31, 1862; January 1-August 31, 1863; or for the period after February 29, 1864. Valuable information was obtained from primary records such as the North Carolina adjutant general's *Roll of Honor*, discharge certificates, medical records, prisoner of war records, *The War of the Rebellion: A Compilation of the Official Records of the Union and Confederate Armies*, militia records, newspaper casualty lists and obituaries, Confederate pension applications filed with the state of North Carolina, and the 1860 federal census of North Carolina. Secondary sources such as postwar rosters and histories, cemetery records, the *Confederate Veteran*, published genealogies, and records of the United Daughters of the Confederacy also provided useful information.

OFFICERS

CAPTAIN

ATKINSON, E. C.
Previously served as Sergeant in 1st Company D, 12th Regiment N.C. Troops (2nd Regiment N.C. Volunteers).

Appointed Captain of this company on February 25, 1862. Reported present in March-December, 1862, and September-December, 1863. Reported present but under arrest in January-February, 1864. Reason he was arrested not reported. Returned to duty on an unspecified date. Captured at or near Fayetteville on or about March 11, 1865. Sent to New Bern. Transferred to Point Lookout, Maryland, where he arrived on April 3, 1865. Transferred to Washington, D.C., where he arrived on April 4, 1865. Transferred to Johnson's Island, Ohio, April 9, 1865. Arrived at Johnson's Island on April 11, 1865. Released at Johnson's Island on June 17, 1865, after taking the Oath of Allegiance.

LIEUTENANTS

ATKINSON, ATLAS, 1st Lieutenant
Previously served as Corporal in 1st Company D, 12th Regiment N.C. Troops (2nd Regiment N.C. Volunteers). Appointed 1st Lieutenant of this company on February 25, 1862. Reported present or accounted for in March-December, 1862, and from November, 1863, through February, 1864. Captured at or near Fayetteville on or about March 11, 1865. Sent to New Bern. Confined at Point Lookout, Maryland, April 3, 1865. Transferred to Washington, D.C., where he arrived on April 4, 1865. Hospitalized at Washington on April 4, 1865, with pneumonia. Released from hospital on May 5, 1865, and was transferred to Johnson's Island, Ohio. Arrived at Johnson's Island on May 13, 1865. Released at Johnson's Island on June 17, 1865, after taking the Oath of Allegiance.

COLLINS, RANDALL P., 2nd Lieutenant
Previously served as Sergeant in 1st Company D, 12th Regiment N.C. Troops (2nd Regiment N.C. Volunteers). Appointed 2nd Lieutenant of this company on February 25, 1862. Reported present or accounted for in March-December, 1862, and from September, 1863, through February, 1864. Hospitalized at Wilmington on May 5, 1864, with syphilis. Returned to duty on May 18 or June 15, 1864. Captured at or near Fayetteville on or about March 11, 1865. Sent to New Bern. Confined at Point Lookout, Maryland, April 3, 1865. Transferred to Washington, D.C., where he arrived on April 4, 1865. Transferred to Johnson's Island, Ohio, April 9, 1865. Arrived at Johnson's Island on April 11, 1865. Released at Johnson's Island on June 18, 1865, after taking the Oath of Allegiance.

JENKINS, WILLIAM B., 3rd Lieutenant
Born in Robeson County where he resided as a farmer prior to enlisting in Robeson County at age 27, February 28, 1862. Mustered in as Sergeant. Elected 3rd Lieutenant on December 20, 1862. Reported present or accounted for in March-December, 1862, and from September, 1863, through February, 1864. No further records.

WALTERS, WILLIAM P., 3rd Lieutenant
Born in Robeson County. Appointed 3rd Lieutenant on February 25, 1862. Resigned on December 8, 1862, by

reason of "marked symptoms of typhoid pneumonia. . . ." Resignation accepted on or about December 13, 1862. [Previously served as Captain in the 58th Regiment N.C. Militia.]

NONCOMMISSIONED OFFICERS AND PRIVATES

ABSHER, JOHN, Private
Born in Robeson County where he resided as a farmer prior to enlisting in Robeson County at age 35, February 28, 1862. Hospitalized at Petersburg, Virginia, July 20, 1862, with chronic diarrhoea. Returned to duty on August 29, 1862. Deserted on an unspecified date. Apprehended on or about October 26, 1862. Reported under arrest through December, 1862. Court-martialed on or about February 5, 1863. Returned to duty on an unspecified date. Reported present from September, 1863, through February, 1864. Hospitalized at Wilmington on April 18, 1864, with acute bronchitis. Transferred to Goldsboro on May 22, 1864. Last reported in the records of this company on June 7, 1864.

AMMON, A. J., _____
North Carolina pension records indicate that he served in this company.

ANDREWS, WILLIAM, Private
Enlisted at Lumberton on September 7, 1863, for the war. Reported present through February, 1864. Last reported in the records of this company in July-September, 1864.

ARNETT, FREDERICK, Private
Born in Robeson County and was by occupation a farmer prior to enlisting in Robeson County at age 30, February 28, 1862. Reported present in March-August, 1862, and from September, 1863, through February, 1864. Last reported in the records of this company in July-September, 1864.

ARNETT, WARREN C., Private
Enlisted in Robeson County on or about March 28, 1862. Reported present from September, 1863, through February, 1864. Last reported in the records of this company in July-September, 1864.

ASHLEY, STEPHEN W., Private
Born in Alabama and resided in Robeson County where he was by occupation a farmer prior to enlisting in Robeson County at age 37, September 3, 1863, for the war. Reported present through February, 1864. Last reported in the records of this company in July-September, 1864.

ATKINSON, BRIGHT, Sergeant
Previously served as Corporal in 1st Company D, 12th Regiment N.C. Troops (2nd Regiment N.C. Volunteers). Enlisted in this company in Robeson County on May 5, 1862, for the war. Mustered in as Private. Promoted to Sergeant on June 1, 1862. Reported present or accounted for until September-December, 1862, when he was

appointed Ordnance Sergeant and transferred to the Field and Staff of this regiment. Reduced to ranks in March-December, 1864, and transferred back to this company. Paroled at Greensboro on May 1, 1865.

ATKINSON, JOHN C., Private
Born in Robeson County where he resided as a farmer prior to enlisting in Robeson County at age 18, February 15, 1862. Mustered in as Private. Hospitalized at Petersburg, Virginia, July 21, 1862, with typhoid fever. Furloughed for thirty days on August 31, 1862. Returned to duty prior to December 31, 1862. Promoted to Sergeant on December 20, 1862. Reduced to ranks on August 24, 1863. Hospitalized at Wilmington on August 26, 1863, with debilitas. Furloughed for thirty days on or about September 25, 1863. Returned to duty prior to November 1, 1863. Reported present through February, 1864. Paroled at Greensboro on May 1, 1865.

BALDWIN, JOHN, _____
North Carolina pension records indicate that he served in this company.

BARFIELD, GOOLSBURY, Private
Born in Robeson County where he resided as a farmer prior to enlisting in Robeson County at age 52, February 26, 1862. Reported absent without leave prior to July 1, 1862. Returned to duty prior to September 1, 1862. Deserted on November 19, 1862. Discharged on June 8, 1863, by reason of "old age, feeble constitution and affection of the face."

BARFIELD, WILLIS A., Private
Resided in Robeson County where he enlisted on August 24, 1863, for the war. Reported present through February, 1864. Captured at Savannah, Georgia, December 21, 1864. Sent to Hilton Head, South Carolina. Transferred to Fort Delaware, Delaware, where he arrived on March 12, 1865. Released at Fort Delaware on June 19, 1865, after taking the Oath of Allegiance.

BARNES, CANADA, Private
Born in Robeson County and was by occupation a farmer prior to enlisting in Robeson County at age 19, February 28, 1862. Reported present or accounted for in March-August, 1862. Court-martialed on June 17, 1863, and sentenced to be shot. Reason he was court-martialed not reported. Sentence remitted on or about July 30, 1863. Returned to duty on an unspecified date. Reported present from September, 1863, through February, 1864. Last reported in the records of this company in July-September, 1864.

BARNES, E. P. D., Private
Enlisted in Robeson County on May 5, 1862, for the war. Reported sick in hospital in May-June, 1862. Reported absent without leave in July-August, 1862. Reported under arrest by sentence of court-martial in September-December, 1862. Returned to duty on an unspecified date. Reported absent on furlough in September-October, 1863. Hospitalized at Wilmington on November 28, 1863, with acute bronchitis. Reported absent sick through February, 1864. Hospitalized at Greensboro on February 23, 1865, with intermittent fever. Returned to duty the same date.

BARNES, H. H., Private
Enlisted in Robeson County on February 28, 1863, for the war. Reported present from September, 1863, through February, 1864. Last reported in the records of this company in July-September, 1864.

BARNES, JETHRO, Private
Born in Robeson County and was by occupation a farmer prior to enlisting in Robeson County at age 25, February 28, 1862. Reported present in March-December, 1862, and from September, 1863-February, 1864. Died in hospital at Raleigh on June 12, 1864, of "bronchitis chron[ic]."

BARNES, JOHN F., Private
Born in Robeson County and was by occupation a farmer prior to enlisting in Robeson County at age 24, February 22, 1862. Reported present or accounted for through December, 1862. Last reported in the records of this company in July-September, 1864.

BARNES, JOSEPH P., Private
Transferred to this company from an unspecified unit on October 27, 1864. No further records.

BARNES, MOORE, _____
North Carolina pension records indicate that he served in this company.

BARNES, OLIVER M., Private
Enlisted in Robeson County on May 5, 1862, for the war. Reported present in May-December, 1862. Hospitalized at Wilmington on September 19, 1863, with intermittent fever. Returned to duty on November 17, 1863. Reported present through February, 1864. Hospitalized at Wilmington on April 18, 1864, with acute bronchitis. Returned to duty on May 18, 1864. Hospitalized at Charlotte on February 6, 1865, with intermittent fever. Transferred to another hospital on February 19, 1865. Hospitalized at Raleigh on February 20, 1865, with catarrh. Furloughed on February 24, 1865.

BARNES, RICHARD RHODES, Corporal
Born in Robeson County where he resided as a farmer prior to enlisting in Robeson County at age 30, February 28, 1862. Mustered in as Private. Reported present in March-December, 1862. Promoted to Corporal in January-October, 1863. Reported present from September, 1863, through February, 1864. Captured at Fayetteville on March 12, 1865. Confined at Point Lookout, Maryland, April 3, 1865. Released at Point Lookout on June 24, 1865, after taking the Oath of Allegiance.

BARNES, TIMOTHY, Private
Born in Robeson County and was by occupation a farmer prior to enlisting in Robeson County at age 24, February 26, 1862. Reported present in March-August, 1862. Hospitalized at Petersburg, Virginia, October 22, 1862, with diarrhoea. Died in hospital at Petersburg on February 26, 1863, of "pneumonia" and "pleuritis."

BARNES, W. H., Private
Enlisted in Robeson County on May 5, 1862, for the war.

Reported present or accounted for in May-December, 1862. Deserted prior to February 5, 1864. "Many efforts [have been made by] the Home Guard to have him arrested but being in a section of country where there are many hiding places and most of the inhabitants favorable to desertion, every effort has proved of no avail." Survived the war.

BARNES, WILLIS P., Private
Resided in Robeson County and was by occupation a farmer prior to enlisting in Robeson County at age 30, May 5, 1862, for the war. Mustered in as Private. Promoted to 1st Sergeant on July 11, 1862. Reported present in May-December, 1862. Reduced to ranks in January-October, 1863. Court-martialed on June 15, 1863, and sentenced to be shot. Reason he was court-martialed not reported. Sentence remitted by Lieutenant General D. H. Hill on an unspecified date. Hospitalized at Wilmington on September 9, 1863, with chills and intermittent fever. Returned to duty on September 19, 1863. Reported present in November-December, 1863. Reported present but sick in January-February, 1864. No further records. [Previously served as 2nd Lieutenant in the 58th Regiment N.C. Militia.]

BASS, LEMON, Private
Born in Robeson County where he resided as a day laborer prior to enlisting in Robeson County at age 27, February 22, 1862. Died at Petersburg, Virginia, July 21, 1862. Cause of death not reported.

BASS, WILLIAM, Private
Born in Robeson County where he resided as a day laborer prior to enlisting in Robeson County at age 24, February 26, 1862. Hospitalized at Petersburg, Virginia, July 20, 1862, with typhoid fever and acute dysentery. Furloughed for thirty days on August 31, 1862. Reported absent without leave in December, 1862. Returned to duty on an unspecified date. Reported present from September, 1863, through February, 1864. Last reported in the records of this company in July-September, 1864. Survived the war.

BAXLEY, SAMUEL W., Private
Born in Robeson County where he resided as a farmer prior to enlisting in Robeson County at age 37, February 28, 1862. Was apparently rejected for service. Reason he was rejected not reported.

BAXLEY, WILLIAM H., Private
Born in Robeson County where he resided as a farmer prior to enlisting in Robeson County at age 27, February 28, 1862. Died in hospital at Raleigh on or about June 12, 1862, of "pneumonia."

BLACKBURN, JAMES, Private
Born in Robeson County and was by occupation a farmer prior to enlisting in Robeson County at age 39, February 28, 1862. Reported on leave of absence on April 21, 1862. No further records.

BRANCH, ALDEN, Private
Born in Robeson County and was by occupation a farmer prior to enlisting in Robeson County at age 35, February

28, 1862. Reported present or accounted for through December, 1862. Hospitalized at Wilmington on or about August 10, 1863, with pneumonia. Returned to duty on August 20, 1863. Reported present from September, 1863, through February, 1864. Last reported in the records of this company in July-September, 1864.

BRITT, A. A., Private
Enlisted on March 25, 1864, for the war. No further records.

BRITT, ALEXANDER, JR., Private
Previously served as Private in 1st Company D, 12th Regiment N.C. Troops (2nd Regiment N.C. Volunteers). Enlisted in this company on February 28, 1862. Hospitalized at Petersburg, Virginia, July 20, 1862, with remittent fever. Returned to duty on August 8, 1862. Deserted while on the march on August 19, 1862. Returned to duty on an unspecified date. Reported present in September-October, 1863. Reported absent without leave on December 22, 1863. Reported present in January-February, 1864. Last reported in the records of this company in July-September, 1864.

BRITT, ALEXANDER C., SR., Private
Previously served as Private in 1st Company D, 12th Regiment N.C. Troops (2nd Regiment N.C. Volunteers). Enlisted in this company in Robeson County on February 28, 1862. Reported present through December, 1862. Hospitalized at Wilmington on or about September 15, 1863, with debility and/or fever. Returned to duty on November 7, 1863. Reported present from November, 1863, through February, 1864. Hospitalized at Raleigh on November 6, 1864, with intermittent fever. Returned to duty on November 20, 1864.

BRITT, ALFRED, Private
Enlisted in Robeson County on October 7, 1863, for the war. Reported present through February, 1864. No further records.

BRITT, ALVA G., Musician
Previously served as Private in 1st Company D, 12th Regiment N.C. Troops (2nd Regiment N.C. Volunteers). Enlisted in this company in Robeson County on February 28, 1862. Mustered in as Private. Appointed Musician (Drum Major) prior to July 1, 1862. Reduced to the rank of Musician (Drummer) prior to September 1, 1862. Reported present or accounted for in March-December, 1862, and from September, 1863, through February, 1864. Last reported in the records of this company in July-September, 1864.

BRITT, C. C., Private
Enlisted in Robeson County on March 25, 1864, for the war. Reported absent on sick furlough on an unspecified date. No further records.

BRITT, COLEN L., Private
Born in Robeson County where he resided as a farmer prior to enlisting in Robeson County at age 18, February 26, 1862. Reported present or accounted for in March-December, 1862, and from September, 1863, through

February, 1864. Captured at Fayetteville on March 12, 1865. Confined at Point Lookout, Maryland, April 3, 1865. Released at Point Lookout on June 24, 1865, after taking the Oath of Allegiance.

BRITT, EDMUND, Private
Born in Robeson County where he resided prior to enlisting in Robeson County at age 18, October 9, 1863, for the war. Deserted on December 10, 1863.

BRITT, ENOCH W., Private
Resided in Robeson County and was by occupation a farm laborer prior to enlisting in Robeson County at age 22, May 5, 1862, for the war. Present or accounted for until he deserted on October 28, 1862. Rejoined the company on November 26, 1862, and was court-martialed. Reported present from September, 1863, through February, 1864. Last reported in the records of this company in July-September, 1864. Survived the war.

BRITT, HENRY L., Private
Previously served as Private in 1st Company D, 12th Regiment N.C. Troops (2nd Regiment N.C. Volunteers). Enlisted in this company in Robeson County on February 28, 1862. Mustered in as Sergeant. Reduced to ranks prior to June 1, 1862. Reported present until December 26, 1863, when he was reported absent without leave. Returned to duty on an unspecified date. Reported present in January-February, 1864. Last reported in the records of this company in July-September, 1864.

BRITT, HENRY P., Private
Born in Robeson County where he resided as a farmer prior to enlisting in Robeson County at age 40, February 28, 1862. Was apparently rejected for service. May have reenlisted in the company at a later date. No further records.

BRITT, JAMES E., Private
Previously served as Private in 1st Company D, 12th Regiment N.C. Troops (2nd Regiment N.C. Volunteers). Enlisted in this company in Robeson County on February 28, 1862. Mustered in as Sergeant. Reported present or accounted for through December, 1862. Reduced to ranks in January-October, 1863. Hospitalized at Wilmington on August 29, 1863, with intermittent fever. Returned to duty on September 7, 1863. Reported present from September, 1863, through February, 1864. Hospitalized at Charlotte on February 13, 1865, with intermittent fever. Hospitalized at Raleigh on February 20, 1865, with intermittent fever. Transferred to another hospital on February 24, 1865.

BRITT, JOHN W., Private
Born in Robeson County where he resided as a farm laborer prior to enlisting in Robeson County at age 21, February 28, 1862. Reported absent without leave in July-August, 1862. Returned to duty prior to December 31, 1862. Deserted on or about September 5, 1863. Returned to duty in January, 1864. Hospitalized at Wilmington on April 25, 1864. Transferred to hospital at Goldsboro on or about May 22, 1864. Discharged from hospital on July 7, 1864. Survived the war.

BRITT, JOSEPH, JR., Private
Enlisted on March 25, 1864, for the war. No further records.

BRITT, JOSEPH B., Private
Resided in Robeson County where he enlisted at age 15, February 28, 1863, for the war. Reported present or accounted for from September, 1863, through February, 1864. Captured at Fayetteville on March 12, 1865. Sent to New Bern. Confined at Point Lookout, Maryland, April 3, 1865. Released at Point Lookout on June 24, 1865, after taking the Oath of Allegiance.

BRITT, OLIVER P., Private
Resided in Robeson County where he enlisted at age 18, March 22, 1864, for the war. Died in Raleigh on or about November 26, 1864. Cause of death not reported.

BULLARD, JAMES THOMAS, Private
Resided in Robeson County and was by occupation a farmer prior to enlisting in Robeson County at age 25, May 5, 1862, for the war. Present or accounted for until he deserted near Drewry's Bluff, Virginia, December 3, 1862. Returned from desertion on January 1, 1863. Deserted on September 3, 1863. Returned to duty in January, 1864. Reported present through February, 1864. Survived the war.

BULLARD, JOSEPH, Private
Enlisted in Robeson County on May 5, 1862, for the war. Reported present or accounted for through December, 1862. Deserted on September 3, 1863. Rejoined the company in January, 1864. Last reported in the records of this company in July-September, 1864.

CALDER, PETER, Private
Born in Robeson County and was by occupation a farmer prior to enlisting in Robeson County at age 27, February 28, 1862. Was apparently rejected for service. Reenlisted in the company on August 24, 1863, for the war. Reported present through February, 1864. Last reported in the records of this company in July-September, 1864.

CALDER, W. C., _____
North Carolina pension records indicate that he served in this company.

CALDER, WILLIAM H., Musician
Enlisted in Robeson County at age 19, September 20, 1863, for the war. Reported present through December, 1863. Appointed Musician in January-February, 1864. Reported present but under arrest in January-February, 1864. Reason he was arrested not reported. Last reported in the records of this company in July-September, 1864. Survived the war.

CARTER, ALEXANDER, Private
Born in Robeson County and was by occupation a farmer prior to enlisting in Robeson County at age 19, February 28, 1862. Was apparently rejected for service.

COLLINS, F. W., Private
Enlisted in Robeson County on December 1, 1862, for the war. No further records.

COLLINS, G. R., Private
Enlisted in Robeson County on or about March 1, 1862. No further records.

COLLINS, JOHN H., 1st Sergeant
Previously served as Private in Company A, 31st Regiment N.C. Troops. Transferred to this company on or about January 16, 1863. Was presumably mustered in with the rank of 1st Sergeant. Reported present from September, 1863, through February, 1864. Last reported in the records of this company in July-September, 1864.

COLLINS, SAMUEL S., Private
Born in Robeson County where he resided as a farmer prior to enlisting in Robeson County at age 33, February 15, 1862. Reported present or accounted for in March-December, 1862, and from September, 1863, through February, 1864. Reported in hospital at Goldsboro in September-November, 1864. Captured at Fayetteville on March 12, 1865. Sent to New Bern. Transferred to Point Lookout, Maryland, where he arrived on April 30, 1865. Released at Point Lookout on June 26, 1865, after taking the Oath of Allegiance.

COLLINS, THOMAS D., Private
Born in Robeson County where he enlisted at age 18, February 15, 1862. Reported present through December, 1862. Detailed in the quartermaster department at Wilmington (probably as a carpenter) on September 18, 1863. Reported absent on detail through February, 1864. Last reported in the records of this company in July-September, 1864.

COLLINS, WILLIAM T., Musician
Resided in Robeson County where he enlisted at age 16, January 25, 1864, for the war. Mustered in as Musician. Last reported in the records of this company in July-September, 1864.

COOK, H., Private
Enlisted on February 21, 1864, for the war. Reported absent sick on an unspecified date. No further records.

COX, ELI, Private
Born in Robeson County and was by occupation a farmer prior to enlisting in Robeson County at age 19, February 28, 1862. Reported present or accounted for in March-December, 1862, and September-October, 1863. Hospitalized at Wilmington on December 21, 1863, with acute dysentery. Returned to duty on January 15, 1864. Reported present through February, 1864. Hospitalized at Wilmington on March 16, 1864, with acute rheumatism and was transferred on May 22, 1864. Hospitalized at Raleigh on September 16, 1864, with chronic rheumatism. Furloughed for sixty days on November 10, 1864. Hospitalized at Raleigh on January 17, 1865, with chronic rheumatism and was furloughed for sixty days on January 26, 1865.

COX, WILLIAM P., Private
Born in Robeson County where he resided as a farmer prior to enlisting in Robeson County at age 22, February 22, 1862. Reported present through August, 1862.

Deserted from camp near Drewry's Bluff, Virginia, on or about December 4, 1862. Returned to duty on an unspecified date. Reported present from September, 1863, through February, 1864. Captured at Fayetteville on March 12, 1865. Sent to New Bern. Confined at Point Lookout, Maryland, where he arrived on April 3, 1865. Released at Point Lookout on June 26, 1865, after taking the Oath of Allegiance.

DAVIS, ELIAS P., Private
Born in Robeson County where he resided as a farmer prior to enlisting in Robeson County at age 24, February 28, 1862. Reported present or accounted for in March-December, 1862, and from September, 1863, through February, 1864. Last reported in the records of this company in July-September, 1864. [May have served previously as Private in Company D, 18th Regiment N.C. Troops (8th Regiment N.C. Volunteers).]

DAVIS, HENRY P., Private
Born in Robeson County and was by occupation a farmer prior to enlisting in Robeson County at age 30, February 28, 1862. Reported present in March-December, 1862, and from September, 1863, through February, 1864. Last reported in the records of this company in July-September, 1864.

DAVIS, R. H., Private
Enlisted in Robeson County on April 14, 1864, for the war. Reported absent sick in 1864. No further records.

EDWARDS, ALEXANDER, Private
Born in Robeson County and was by occupation a farmer prior to enlisting in Robeson County at age 40, February 21, 1862. Reported present or accounted for in March-December, 1862, and from September, 1863, through February, 1864. Last reported in the records of this company in July-September, 1864.

FAIRCLOTH, DANIEL, _____
North Carolina pension records indicate that he served in this company.

FLACK, W. G., _____
North Carolina pension records indicate that he served in this company.

FREEMAN, EVAN, Private
Enlisted in Robeson County on February 9, 1863, for the war. Reported present from September, 1863, through February, 1864. Last reported in the records of this company in July-September, 1864.

FREEMAN, JOHN C., Private
Resided in Robeson County and was by occupation a farmer prior to enlisting in Robeson County at age 30, September 20, 1863, for the war. Reported present through February, 1864. Last reported in the records of this company in July-September, 1864.

GRAHAM, CALVIN, Private
Born in Robeson County and was by occupation a farmer prior to enlisting in Robeson County at age 21, February

28, 1862. Reported absent without leave prior to July 1, 1862. Returned to duty prior to September 1, 1862. Deserted from camp near Drewry's Bluff, Virginia, November 18, 1862.

GRAHAM, THOMAS, Private
Born in Robeson County and was by occupation a farmer prior to enlisting in Robeson County at age 22, February 26, 1862. Reported present or accounted for in March-December, 1862, and from September, 1863, through February, 1864. Last reported in the records of this company in July-September, 1864.

GRIMSLEY, TRAVIS L., Private
Previously served as Private in 1st Company D, 12th Regiment N.C. Troops (2nd Regiment N.C. Volunteers). Enlisted in this company in Robeson County on March 8, 1862. Mustered in as 1st Sergeant. Reduced to ranks on July 11, 1862. Reported present or accounted for in March-December, 1862, and from September, 1863, through February, 1864. Last reported in the records of this company in July-September, 1864.

HARDEN, JESSE, Private
Enlisted in Robeson County at age 21, February 1, 1864, for the war. Reported present in February, 1864. Survived the war. [North Carolina pension records indicate that he was wounded at Petersburg, Virginia, in 1864.]

HAYES, JOHN W., Private
Born in Robeson County and was by occupation a farmer prior to enlisting in Robeson County at age 19, February 28, 1862. Reported present in March-October, 1862, and from September, 1863, through February, 1864. Hospitalized at Fayetteville on September 23, 1864, with an unspecified complaint. Reported in hospital at Fayetteville through February 28, 1865. Survived the war.

HAYNES, FRANCIS MARION, _____
Records of the United Daughters of the Confederacy indicate that he served in this company.

HEDGEPETH, ARCH B., Private
Enlisted in Robeson County on May 5, 1862, for the war. Reported present or accounted for in May-December, 1862, and from September, 1863, through February, 1864. Captured at Fayetteville on March 12, 1865. Sent to New Bern. Confined at Point Lookout, Maryland, April 3, 1865. Died at Point Lookout on April 27, 1865, of "chronic diarrhoea."

HEDGEPETH, DANIEL, Private
Born in Robeson County where he resided as a farmer prior to enlisting in Robeson County at age 35, February 28, 1863, for the war. Hospitalized at Wilmington on October 5, 1863. Died in hospital at Wilmington on October 11, 1863, of "febris typhoides."

HEDGEPETH, JOEL D., Corporal
Born in Robeson County and was by occupation a farmer prior to enlisting in Robeson County at age 35, February 28, 1862. Mustered in as Private. Reported present until August 25, 1862, when he was hospitalized with remittent

fever. Returned to duty on October 16, 1862. Reported present through December, 1862. Promoted to Corporal in January-October, 1863. Reported present from September, 1863, through February, 1864. Captured at Fayetteville on March 12, 1865. Transferred to New Bern where he arrived on March 26, 1865. No further records.

HEDGEPETH, JOSEPH H., Private
Resided in Robeson County and was by occupation a farmer prior to enlisting in Robeson County at age 29, May 5, 1862, for the war. Reported present in May-December, 1862, and from September, 1863, through February, 1864. No further records.

HEDGEPETH, STEPHEN W., Private
Born in Robeson County where he resided as a farmer prior to enlisting in Robeson County at age 28, February 28, 1863, for the war. Hospitalized at Wilmington on October 5, 1863. Died in hospital at Wilmington on October 13, 1863, of "febris typhoides."

HERRING, JACK G., Private
Enlisted in Robeson County on September 7, 1863, for the war. Reported present or accounted for through February, 1864. Last reported in the records of this company in July-September, 1864.

HERRING, JOEL, Private
Enlisted at Lumberton on February 28, 1863, for the war. Reported present from September, 1863, through February, 1864. Last reported in the records of this company in July-September, 1864.

HERRING, LEWIS, Private
Enlisted in Robeson County on February 28, 1863, for the war. Reported present from September, 1863, through February, 1864. Last reported in the records of this company in July-September, 1864.

HERRING, MICHAEL B., Private
Born in Robeson County and was by occupation a blacksmith prior to enlisting in Robeson County at age 34, February 28, 1862. Reported sick in hospital at Raleigh on or about July 1, 1862. Returned to duty on an unspecified date. Reported present but on extra duty in December, 1862. Reported present from September, 1863, through February, 1864. Died in hospital at Columbia, South Carolina, on or about January 31, 1865, of disease.

HILL, WILLIAM M., Private
Previously served as Private in 1st Company D, 12th Regiment N.C. Troops (2nd Regiment N.C. Volunteers). Enlisted in this company in Robeson County on March 8, 1862. Mustered in as Corporal. Reported present in March-October, 1862. Reduced to ranks on November 18, 1862. Reported present from September, 1863, through February, 1864. Last reported in the records of this company in July-September, 1864.

IVEY, ARCHIBALD, Sergeant
Born in Robeson County and was by occupation a farmer prior to enlisting in Robeson County at age 21, February 28, 1862. Mustered in as Private. Reported absent sick

for much of the period from March through December, 1862. Promoted to Sergeant in September-December, 1862. Reported present from September, 1863, through February, 1864. Last reported in the records of this company in July-September, 1864.

IVEY, ARREN, Private
Born in Robeson County and was by occupation a farmer prior to enlisting in Robeson County at age 23, February 26, 1862. Hospitalized at Petersburg, Virginia, July 26, 1862, with typhoid fever and dysentery. Returned to duty on August 12, 1862. Reported present through December, 1862, and from September, 1863, through February, 1864. Last reported in the records of this company in July-September, 1864.

IVEY, ENOCH, Private
Resided in Robeson County and was by occupation a farmer prior to enlisting in Robeson County. Enlistment date reported as May 5, 1862. Was about 27 years of age at time of enlistment. Listed as a deserter in 1864. No further records.

IVEY, HENRY, Private
Born in Robeson County where he resided as a farmer prior to enlisting in Robeson County at age 26, February 26, 1862. Reported present or accounted for in March-November, 1862, and from September, 1863, through February, 1864. Last reported in the records of this company in July-September, 1864. Survived the war. [North Carolina pension records indicate that he was wounded at New Bern on November 10, 1863.]

IVEY, KADER, Private
Enlistment date reported as February 28, 1862. Listed as a deserter in 1864. No further records.

IVEY, KIBBEN, Private
Born in Robeson County and was by occupation a farmer prior to enlisting in Robeson County at age 18, February 26, 1862. Reported present in March-December, 1862, and from September, 1863, through February, 1864. No further records.

IVEY, OLIVER McKAY, Private
Previously served as Private in 1st Company D, 12th Regiment N.C. Troops (2nd Regiment N.C. Volunteers). Enlisted in this company in Robeson County on February 28, 1862. Mustered in as Sergeant. Reduced to ranks on June 1, 1862. Hospitalized at Petersburg, Virginia, July 20, 1862, with chronic bronchitis. Returned to duty on September 8, 1862. Reported present or accounted for in October-December, 1862, and from September, 1863, through February, 1864. Last reported in the records of this company in July-September, 1864. Survived the war.

IVEY, WILLIAM BERRY, Private
Born in Robeson County and resided in Columbus County where he was by occupation a farmer prior to enlisting in Robeson County at age 21, February 28, 1862. Reported present in March-December, 1862, and from September, 1863, through February, 1864. Last reported in the records of this company in July-September, 1864. Survived the war.

IVEY, ZEPHANIAS, Private
Resided in Robeson County and was by occupation a farmer prior to enlisting in Robeson County at age 37, October 6, 1863, for the war. Reported present or accounted for through February, 1864. Last reported in the records of this company in July-September, 1864.

JENKINS, ELIAS, Corporal
Resided in Robeson County where he enlisted on May 5, 1862, for the war. Mustered in as Private. Reported present or accounted for through December, 1862. Promoted to Corporal in January-October, 1863. Reported present from September, 1863, through February, 1864. Captured at Fayetteville on March 12, 1865. Confined at Point Lookout, Maryland, April 3, 1865. Released at Point Lookout on June 28, 1865, after taking the Oath of Allegiance.

JENKINS, HENRY P., Private
Resided in Robeson County and was by occupation a farmer prior to enlisting in Robeson County at age 31, September 3, 1863, for the war. Reported present or accounted for through February, 1864. Last reported in the records of this company in July-September, 1864.

JENKINS, IRVIN, Sergeant
Born in Robeson County and was by occupation a farmer prior to enlisting in Robeson County at age 24, February 28, 1862. Mustered in as Private. Promoted to Corporal on November 18, 1862. Reported present in March-December, 1862. Promoted to Sergeant in January-October, 1863. Reported present from September, 1863, through February, 1864. Last reported in the records of this company in July-September, 1864.

JENKINS, JOHN W., Private
Enlisted in Robeson County on May 5, 1862, for the war. Present or accounted for until he deserted from camp near Drewry's Bluff, Virginia, December 21, 1862. Returned to duty on an unspecified date. Reported present from September, 1863, through February, 1864. Last reported in the records of this company in July-September, 1864.

JENKINS, LEWIS, Sergeant
Born in Robeson County and was by occupation a farmer prior to enlisting in Robeson County at age 24, February 28, 1862. Mustered in as Corporal. Reported present in March-December, 1862. Promoted to Sergeant in January-October, 1863. Reported present from September, 1863, through February, 1864. Last reported in the records of this company in July-September, 1864.

JONES, JESSE, Private
Born in Robeson County and was by occupation a farmer prior to enlisting in Robeson County at age 29, February 28, 1862. Reported present or accounted for through December, 1862. Discharged on October 7, 1863. Reason discharged not reported.

JONES, NEHEMIAH H., Private
Born in Virginia and resided in Robeson County where he enlisted at age 23, May 5, 1862, for the war. Reported absent without leave prior to July 1, 1862. Returned to duty prior to September 1, 1862. Present or accounted for in September-December, 1862. Hospitalized at Wilmington on September 15, 1863, with chills and fever. Hospitalized at Wilmington on November 28, 1863, with ulcus. Returned to duty on December 28, 1863. Reported present in January-February, 1864. Last reported in the records of this company in July-September, 1864. Survived the war.

LAMB, ALEXANDER, Private
Previously served as Private in 1st Company D, 12th Regiment N.C. Troops (2nd Regiment N.C. Volunteers). Enlisted in this company in Robeson County on February 15, 1862. Reported present in March-December, 1862, and from September, 1863, through February, 1864. Last reported in the records of this company in July-September, 1864. Survived the war.

LAMB, BARNABAS, Private
Previously served as Private in 1st Company D, 12th Regiment N.C. Troops (2nd Regiment N.C. Volunteers). Enlisted in this company at Lumberton on February 15, 1862. Reported present or accounted for through December, 1862. Died in hospital at Petersburg, Virginia, on or about January 24, 1863, of "pneumonia typhoid."

LAMB, HUGH, Private
Born in Robeson County where he resided as a farmer prior to enlisting in Robeson County at age 22, February 28, 1862. Reported present or accounted for in March-December, 1862, and from September, 1863, through February, 1864. Hospitalized at Charlotte on February 6, 1865, with intermittent fever. Hospitalized at Greensboro on February 15, 1865, with a gunshot wound. Place and date wounded not reported. Transferred to another hospital on March 11, 1865. Survived the war.

LAMB, ISHAM, Private
Resided in Robeson County where he enlisted at age 18, September 1, 1864, for the war. No further records. Survived the war.

LAMB, McINTYRE, Private
Born in Robeson County where he enlisted at age 19, March 28, 1862. Died at Camp Mangum, near Raleigh, April 25, 1862, of "measles."

LAMB, MICHAEL, Private
Born in Robeson County where he resided as a mechanic prior to enlisting in Robeson County at age 32, February 15, 1862. Reported present or accounted for in March-December, 1862. Reported on detail (probably as a carpenter) in the quartermaster department at Wilmington from September 18, 1863, through February 29, 1864. Captured at Fayetteville on March 12, 1865. Sent to New Bern. Confined at Point Lookout, Maryland, April 3, 1865. Released at Point Lookout on June 29, 1865, after taking the Oath of Allegiance.

LAWSON, W. D., Private
Enlisted in Robeson County on March 15, 1864, for the war. "Died at home while absent without leave." Date and cause of death not reported.

LEE, JAMES, Private
Born in Robeson County and was by occupation a farmer prior to enlisting in Robeson County at age 17, February 26, 1862. Was apparently rejected for service. Reenlisted in the company on February 28, 1863. Hospitalized at Wilmington on July 26, 1863 (probably with intermittent fever). Returned to duty on October 12, 1863. Reported present through February, 1864. Last reported in the records of this company in July-September, 1864.

LEGGETT, ROBERT, Private
Resided in Robeson County and was by occupation a farm laborer prior to enlisting in Robeson County at age 26, May 5, 1862, for the war. Reported present or accounted for in May-December, 1862, and from September, 1863, through February, 1864. Last reported in the records of this company in July-September, 1864. Served as a teamster during part of the war.

LEGGETT, WILLIAM, Private
Resided in Robeson County and was by occupation a farm laborer prior to enlisting in Robeson County at age 23, May 5, 1862, for the war. Reported present in May-August, 1862. Court-martialed on June 24, 1863, and sentenced to be shot. Reason he was court-martialed not reported. Sentence remitted on an unspecified date. Reported present from September, 1863, through February, 1864. Last reported in the records of this company in July-September, 1864.

LEGGETT, WRIGHT, Private
Enlisted in Robeson County on September 7, 1863, for the war. Reported present or accounted for through February, 1864. Last reported in the records of this company in July-September, 1864.

LEWIS, DAWSON, Private
Resided in Robeson County and was by occupation a farmer prior to enlisting in Robeson County at age 47, February 28, 1863, for the war. Reported present or accounted for from September, 1863, through February, 1864. Last reported in the records of this company in July-September, 1864.

LEWIS, DWIGHT W., Private
Born in Robeson County where he resided as a farm laborer prior to enlisting in Robeson County at age 22, February 28, 1862. Reported present or accounted for in March-December, 1862, and from September, 1863, through February, 1864. Last reported in the records of this company in July-September, 1864.

LEWIS, HENRY P., Private
Born in Robeson County where he resided as a farmer prior to enlisting in Robeson County at age 28, February 28, 1862. Hospitalized at Petersburg, Virginia, July 20, 1862, with typhoid fever. Deserted on August 25, 1862. Apprehended on or about October 26, 1862, and was court-martialed. Returned to duty on an unspecified date. Reported present but sick in September-October, 1863. Reported present from November, 1863, through February, 1864. Died in North Carolina on January 3, 1865, of disease.

LEWIS, JOHN H., Private
Born in Robeson County and was by occupation a farmer prior to enlisting in Robeson County at age 18, March 28, 1862. Reported present in April-August, 1862, and from September, 1863, through February, 1864. Last reported in the records of this company in July-September, 1864.

LEWIS, JOHN P., Private
Enlisted in Robeson County at age 19, February 12, 1864, for the war. No further records. Survived the war.

LEWIS, WARREN A., Sergeant
Previously served as Private in 1st Company D, 12th Regiment N.C. Troops (2nd Regiment N.C. Volunteers). Enlisted in this company in Robeson County on May 5, 1862, for the war. Mustered in as Private. Promoted to Sergeant on June 1, 1862. Present or accounted for in May-December, 1862, and from September, 1863, through February, 1864. Captured at Fayetteville on March 12, 1865. Confined at Point Lookout, Maryland, April 3, 1865. Released at Point Lookout on June 29, 1865, after taking the Oath of Allegiance.

LOVITT, ALDRIDGE, Private
Resided in Robeson County and was by occupation a farm laborer prior to enlisting in Wayne County at age 21, January 10, 1863, for the war. Reported present from September, 1863, through February, 1864. Last reported in the records of this company in July-September, 1864.

LOVITT, BENJAMIN, Private
Resided in Robeson County where he enlisted at age 18, March 1, 1864, for the war. Died in October, 1864, while at home on furlough. Cause of death not reported.

LOVITT, DOSON, Private
Enlisted in Robeson County on February 28, 1863, for the war. Reported present from September, 1863, through February, 1864. No further records.

LOVITT, JOEL, Private
Born in Robeson County where he resided as a farmer prior to enlisting in Robeson County at age 40, February 28, 1862. Reported present in March-December, 1862, and from September, 1863, through February, 1864. Captured by the enemy on an unspecified date. Died at Fort Delaware, Delaware, March 16, 1865. Cause of death not reported.

LOVITT, JOHN, Private
Enlisted in Robeson County on August 24, 1863, for the war. Reported present from September, 1863, through February, 1864. Captured at Savannah, Georgia, December 21, 1864. Sent to Hilton Head, South Carolina. Confined at Fort Delaware, Delaware, March 12, 1865. Died at Fort Delaware on March 16, 1865, of "consumption."

LOVITT, MIZEL, Private
Born in Robeson County where he resided as a farmer prior to enlisting in Robeson County at age 27, February 28, 1862. Reported present in March-August, 1862, and from September, 1863, through February, 1864. Last

reported in the records of this company in July-September, 1864.

LOVITT, WILLIAM, Private
Resided in Robeson County and was by occupation a farmer prior to enlisting in Robeson County at age 27, May 5, 1862, for the war. Reported present in May-December, 1862. Hospitalized at Wilmington on or about October 2, 1863, with remittent fever. Returned to duty on November 5, 1863. Reported present through February, 1864. Last reported in the records of this company in July-September, 1864.

McPHATTER, ALEXANDER S., Private
Born in Robeson County where he resided as a farmer prior to enlisting in Robeson County at age 22, March 25, 1862. Reported present in April-August, 1862. Hospitalized at Wilmington on September 15, 1863, with colica. Returned to duty on September 23, 1863. Reported present or accounted for through February, 1864. Last reported in the records of this company in July-September, 1864.

MULDOON, JOHN, _____
Records of the 1st Regiment Connecticut Cavalry indicate that he was a Confederate prisoner who served in Company B, 50th Regiment N.C. Troops, and who enlisted in Company G, 1st Regiment Connecticut Cavalry, at Baltimore, Maryland, October 1, 1863. No further records.

NORTON, AUGUSTUS, Private
Resided in Robeson County and was by occupation a day laborer prior to enlisting in Robeson County at age 29, May 5, 1862, for the war. Reported present or accounted for through August, 1862. Reported absent without leave in September-December, 1862. Reported present but sick in September-October, 1863. Deserted on an unspecified date. Returned from desertion on December 22, 1863. Died on December 23, 1863. Place and cause of death not reported. [May have enlisted previously as Private in Company D, 18th Regiment N.C. Troops (8th Regiment N.C. Volunteers).]

NORTON, JOSHUA, Private
Resided in Robeson County and was by occupation a day laborer prior to enlisting in Robeson County at age 34, October 1, 1864, for the war. No further records.

NUTT, WILLIAM HENRY, Musician
Enlisted in Person County at age 15, May 5, 1862, for the war. Mustered in with the rank of Drum Major. Reduced to the rank of Musician prior to September 1, 1862. Appointed Drum Major and transferred to the regimental band in January-March, 1863.

PARKER, RICHARD, Private
Born in Columbus County and enlisted in Robeson County on May 5, 1862, for the war. Died in hospital at Raleigh on June 28, 1862, of "measles and typhoid fever."

PERRELL, C. S., Private
Resided in Johnston County. Place and date of enlistment not reported. Paroled at Goldsboro in 1865.

PITMAN, JOHN, Private
Resided in Robeson County where he enlisted on August 24, 1863, for the war. Reported present through February, 1864. Captured in Robeson County on March 4, 1865. Sent to New Bern. Confined at Point Lookout, Maryland, March 30, 1865. Released at Point Lookout on June 16, 1865, after taking the Oath of Allegiance.

PITMAN, LEWIS, Private
Born in Robeson County where he resided as a farmer prior to enlisting in Robeson County at age 24, February 28, 1862. Reported present in March-August, 1862, and from September, 1863, through February, 1864. Last reported in the records of this company in July-September, 1864.

POWELL, O. D., Private
Enlisted on April 22, 1864, for the war. Captured at Fayetteville on March 12, 1865. Sent to New Bern where he arrived on or about March 26, 1865. Admitted to a Federal hospital at New Bern on March 28, 1865, with chronic diarrhoea and inflammation of the lungs. Died on or about May 6, 1865.

PREVATT, CHARLES, Private
Born in Robeson County where he resided as a farmer prior to enlisting in Robeson County at age 25, February 28, 1862. Reported present or accounted for through July, 1862. Hospitalized at Richmond, Virginia, August 22, 1862, with chronic rheumatism. Returned to duty on September 15, 1862. Reported present or accounted for in October-December, 1862. Hospitalized at Wilmington on September 6, 1863, with continued fever. Returned to duty on September 7, 1863. Detailed as a carpenter at Wilmington on or about November 18, 1863. Reported on detached service through February, 1864. Last reported in the records of this company in July-September, 1864. Survived the war.

PURVIS, JOHN, Private
Born in Robeson County and was by occupation a farmer prior to enlisting in Robeson County at age 25, February 28, 1862. Mustered in as Corporal. Reported present in March-June, 1862. Hospitalized at Petersburg, Virginia, July 21, 1862, with typhoid fever. Returned to duty on September 8, 1862. Reported present or accounted for through December, 1862. Reduced to ranks in January-October, 1863. Reported present from September, 1863, through February, 1864. Last reported in the records of this company in July-September, 1864.

RHODES, HEZEKIAH, Private
Born in Robeson County where he resided as a farmer prior to enlisting in Robeson County at age 26, March 28, 1862. Reported present through December, 1862. Hospitalized at Wilmington on October 26, 1863, with remittent fever. Returned to duty on December 5, 1863. Reported present through February, 1864. Last reported in the records of this company in July-September, 1864. Served as a teamster during most of the war.

SEALY, EMCOIN, Private
Born in Robeson County and was by occupation a farmer

prior to enlisting in Robeson County at age 27, February 28, 1862. No further records.

SEALY, ISHAM, Private
Resided in Robeson County where he enlisted at age 18, February 28, 1864, for the war. Last reported in the records of this company in July-September, 1864.

SEALY, JACKSON, Private
Born in Robeson County where he resided as a farmer prior to enlisting in Robeson County at age 24, February 28, 1862. Reported present or accounted for in March-December, 1862, and from September, 1863, through February, 1864. Last reported in the records of this company in July-September, 1864.

SEALY, JOHN R., Private
Born in Robeson County where he resided as a farmer prior to enlisting in Robeson County at age 25, February 28, 1862. Reported present until October 28, 1862, when he was listed as a deserter. Returned from desertion on November 26, 1862, and was court-martialed. Returned to duty on an unspecified date. Reported present in September-November, 1863. Reported absent without leave on December 28, 1863. Returned from desertion on January 14, 1864, and was placed under arrest. No further records.

SEALY, MELVIN, Private
Resided in Robeson County where he enlisted at age 17, February 28, 1863, for the war. Reported present but sick in September-October, 1863. Hospitalized at Wilmington on November 28, 1863, with debilitas. Returned to duty on December 3, 1863. Furloughed for thirty days on January 16, 1864. Last reported in the records of this company in July-September, 1864.

SMALL, ALFRED B., Private
Enlisted in Robeson County at age 19, May 5, 1862, for the war. Reported present or accounted for in May-December, 1862. Reported in hospital at Wilmington on April 30, 1863, and August 26, 1863, with catarrhus. Reported present with the company from September, 1863, through February, 1864. Last reported in the records of this company in July-September, 1864. Survived the war.

SMALL, WILLIAM S., Private
Resided in Robeson County and was by occupation a farmer prior to enlisting in Robeson County at age 40, August 19, 1863, for the war. Reported present or accounted for through February, 1864. Last reported in the records of this company in July-September, 1864.

SNEED, W. B., Private
Enlisted in Robeson County on May 1, 1864, for the war. Last reported in the records of this company in July-September, 1864.

SPIVEY, CHARLES, Private
Born in Robeson County and was by occupation a farmer prior to enlisting in Robeson County at age 25, February 27, 1862. Reported present until August 10, 1862, when

he deserted. Returned from desertion on December 10, 1862, and was court-martialed. No further records.

SPIVEY, JOHN, Private
Born in Robeson County where he resided as a farmer prior to enlisting in Robeson County at age 23, February 27, 1862. Reported present until August 19, 1862, when he deserted while on the march. Returned from desertion on or about October 26, 1862, and was court-martialed. Returned to duty on an unspecified date (probably subsequent to March 31, 1864). Last reported in the records of this company in July-September, 1864.

STANLEY, WILLIAM B., Private
Born in Robeson County where he resided as a farmer prior to enlisting in Robeson County at age 35, February 28, 1862. Died in hospital at Petersburg, Virginia, July 22, 1862, of "typhoid fever."

STEPHENS, ANCEL, Private
Born in Robeson County where he resided as a tanner or farmer prior to enlisting in Robeson County at age 28, February 28, 1862. Reported present or accounted for through December, 1862. No further records.

STONE, BENJAMIN E., Private
Resided in Robeson County and was by occupation a farm laborer prior to enlisting in Robeson County at age 20, May 5, 1862, for the war. Reported present or accounted for through December, 1862. Last reported in the records of this company in July-September, 1864. Survived the war.

STONE, ELIAS B., Private
Resided in Robeson County and was by occupation a farm laborer prior to enlisting in Robeson County at age 22, May 5, 1862, for the war. Reported present through December, 1862. Deserted prior to May 4, 1864, when he was reported to be "still in the woods. Although repeated efforts have been made for his arrest by the Home Guard . . . owing to the nature of the county and the disposition of its inhabitants every effort has failed of success. It is believed he is harbored by disloyal citizens."

STONE, HARDY J., Private
Enlisted in Robeson County at age 20, May 5, 1862, for the war. Hospitalized at Petersburg, Virginia, July 29, 1862, with chronic bronchitis. Returned to duty on or about October 20, 1862. Reported absent on sick furlough on an unspecified date in 1864. Last reported in the records of this company in July-September, 1864. Survived the war.

STONE, ISHAM, Private
Resided in Robeson County and was by occupation a farmer prior to enlisting in Robeson County at age 24, May 5, 1862, for the war. Reported present until November 18, 1862, when he deserted from hospital at Petersburg, Virginia. Returned to duty on an unspecified date. Reported present from September, 1863, through February, 1864. Captured (or deserted to the enemy) at or near Savannah, Georgia, on an unspecified date (probably in December, 1864, or January, 1865).

Admitted to hospital at Savannah on January 19, 1865, with gonorrhea. Took the Oath of Allegiance on January 27, 1865.

STONE, JACOB, _____

North Carolina pension records indicate that he served in this company.

STONE, JAMES P., Private

Resided in Robeson County and was by occupation a day laborer prior to enlisting in Robeson County at age 24, May 5, 1862, for the war. Deserted on or about May 28, 1862. "This party is said to be . . . among the first that deserted in the county [of Robeson]. He is still lurking in the swamps in the lower part of the county. I have made every possible effort through the Home Guard to have him arrested, but because of traitors every effort has proved of no avail."

STONE, JOEL, Private

Born in Robeson County and was by occupation a farmer prior to enlisting in Robeson County at age 20, February 28, 1862. Reported present until October 22, 1862, when he was hospitalized with jaundice. Returned to duty on November 21, 1862. Hospitalized at Wilmington on September 19, 1863, with remittent fever. Returned to duty on October 12, 1863. Reported present from November, 1863, through February, 1864. Company records indicate that he was captured in hospital at Savannah, Georgia, on or about December 21, 1864; however, records of the Federal Provost Marshal do not substantiate that report. No further records.

STONE, JOSHUA, Private

Enlisted in Robeson County on or about February 28, 1862. Deserted on an unspecified date.

STONE, WILLIAM A., Private

Enlisted in Robeson County on May 5, 1862, for the war. Hospitalized at Petersburg, Virginia, July 20, 1862, with typhoid fever. Returned to duty on November 14, 1862. Hospitalized at Charlotte on February 13, 1865, with intermittent fever and was transferred on February 18, 1865.

THORNTON, RICHARD, Private

Records of the United Daughters of the Confederacy indicate that he served in this company.

TYLER, JOHN, Private

Born in Robeson County and was by occupation a farmer prior to enlisting in Robeson County at age 40, February 28, 1862. Reported absent without leave prior to July 1, 1862. Returned to duty prior to September 1, 1862. Deserted from camp near Drewry's Bluff, Virginia, November 18, 1862. Returned to duty on December 3, 1862. Reported present or accounted for from September, 1863, through February, 1864. Last reported in the records of this company in July-September, 1864.

WALTERS, ISAAC, Private

Born in Robeson County and was by occupation a farmer prior to enlisting in Robeson County at age 22, February 28, 1862. Reported present in March-December, 1862, and from September, 1863, through February, 1864. Last reported in the records of this company in July-September, 1864.

WALTERS, PHILIP, Private

Born in Robeson County and was by occupation a farmer prior to enlisting in Robeson County at age 24, February 15, 1862. Reported present or accounted for in March-December, 1862, and from September, 1863, through February, 1864. Last reported in the records of this company in July-September, 1864. Survived the war.

WALTERS, THOMAS F., Private

Enlisted in Robeson County at age 37, February 28, 186[4], for the war. Court-martialed on an unspecified date. Reason he was court-martialed not reported. No further records. Survived the war.

WALTERS, WILLIAM, Private

Born in Robeson County where he resided as a farmer prior to enlisting in Robeson County at age 20, February 28, 1862. Reported present or accounted for in March-December, 1862, and September-October, 1863. Hospitalized at Wilmington on November 28, 1863, with debilitas. Returned to duty on December 2, 1863. Reported present in January-February, 1864. Hospitalized at Raleigh on November 6, 1864, with intermittent fever. Returned to duty on November 17, 1864. Captured at Fayetteville on March 12, 1865. Sent to New Bern. Confined at Point Lookout, Maryland, April 3, 1865. Released at Point Lookout on June 21, 1865, after taking the Oath of Allegiance.

WALTERS, ZEB, Private

Enlisted in Robeson County on February 28, 1864, for the war. Last reported in the records of this company in July-September, 1864.

WATSON, Z., Private

Enlisted near Wilmington on February 1, 1864, for the war. No further records.

WATTS, ALVA, Private

Enlisted in Robeson County on October 20, 1863, for the war. Deserted on an unspecified date. Returned from desertion on December 22, 1863, and was placed under arrest. Reported "absent sick or present" in January-February, 1864. Hospitalized at Wilmington on November 25, 1864, with remittent fever. Transferred to Raleigh on December 26, 1864. Hospitalized at Raleigh on December 27, 1864, with chronic diarrhoea. Furloughed for sixty days on January 26, 1865.

WILLIAMS, HARLLEE, Corporal

Born in Robeson County and was by occupation a farmer prior to enlisting in Robeson County at age 22, February 28, 1862. Mustered in as Corporal. Reported present in March-August, 1862. Reported present but under arrest in September-December, 1862. Reason he was arrested not reported. Reported present from September, 1863, through February, 1864. Last reported in the records of this company in July-September, 1864.

COMPANY C

This company was raised in Johnston County and enlisted at Smithfield in February-March, 1862. It was mustered into state service at Camp Mangum, near Raleigh, on April 21, 1862, and assigned to the 50th Regiment N.C. Troops as Company C. After joining the regiment the company functioned as a part of the regiment, and its history for the remainder of the war is reported as a part of the regimental history.

The information contained in the following roster was compiled primarily from a company muster-in and descriptive roll dated April 21, 1862, and from company muster rolls for May 1-August 31, 1862; November 1-December 31, 1862; September 1, 1863-February 29, 1864; July 1 August 31, 1864; and October 31-December 31, 1864. No company muster rolls were located for September 1-October 31, 1862; January 1-August 31, 1863; March 1-June 30, 1864; September 1-October 30, 1864; or for the period after December 31, 1864. Valuable information was obtained from primary records such as the North Carolina adjutant general's *Roll of Honor*, discharge certificates, medical records, prisoner of war records, *The War of the Rebellion: A Compilation of the Official Records of the Union and Confederate Armies*, militia records, newspaper casualty lists and obituaries, Confederate pension applications filed with the state of North Carolina, and the 1860 federal census of North Carolina. Secondary sources such as postwar rosters and histories, cemetery records, the *Confederate Veteran*, published genealogies, and records of the United Daughters of the Confederacy also provided useful information.

OFFICERS

CAPTAINS

LUNCEFORD, ROBERT DARIUS
Born in Johnston County where he resided as a farmer prior to enlisting in Johnston County at age 29. Appointed Captain on February 25, 1862. Wounded by shell fragments at Malvern Cliffs, Virginia, June 30, 1862. Resigned on an unspecified date (probably in October, 1862) because "the circumstances of my family are such as absolutely to demand my presence with them." A notation on the back of his letter of resignation states that his resignation should be accepted because he had "made but little progress in drill[,] and the discipline of his company is not good. He has been at home nearly all the time since the battles around Richmond on sick furlough." Resignation accepted on December 15, 1862.

YOUNGBLOOD, THOMAS RICE
Resided in Johnston County and enlisted at age 35. Appointed 1st Lieutenant on April 21, 1862. Promoted to Captain on December 15, 1862. Reported present through December, 1862. Reported absent on sick furlough in September-October, 1863. Returned to duty in November-

December, 1863. Reported present or accounted for in January-February and July-August, 1864. Paroled at Goldsboro on May 13, 1865. [Previously served as 1st Lieutenant in the 41st Regiment N.C. Militia.]

LIEUTENANTS

ELLINGTON, JESSE THOMPSON, 1st Lieutenant
Born in Johnston County where he resided. Was by occupation a student at Wake Forest College prior to enlisting in Johnston County at age 20, February 25, 1862. Mustered in as Private. Elected 1st Lieutenant on December 20, 1862. Reported present or accounted for through December, 1862. Reported absent on sick furlough in September-October, 1863. Returned to duty in November-December, 1863. Reported on picket duty at Virginia Creek on Topsail Sound in February, 1864. Reported present or accounted for in July-August and November-December, 1864. Survived the war.

ELLINGTON, JOSEPH CRITTENDEN, 3rd Lieutenant
Born in Johnston County where he resided as a student prior to enlisting in Johnston County at age 18, February 17, 1862. Mustered in as 1st Sergeant. Appointed 3rd Lieutenant on October 20, 1862. Reported present or accounted for through December, 1862. Reported absent on sick furlough from October 1, 1863, through August 31, 1864. Returned to duty prior to January 1, 1865. Survived the war.

LANE, WILLIAM, 2nd Lieutenant
Born in Johnston County where he resided as a farmer prior to enlisting at age 37. Appointed 2nd Lieutenant on February 25, 1862. Reported present through December, 1862, and in September, 1863-January, 1864. Reported on picket duty at Virginia Creek on Topsail Sound in February, 1864. Reported present in July-August and November-December, 1864. [Previously served as 2nd Lieutenant in the 41st Regiment N.C. Militia.]

WATSON, GEORGE WASHINGTON, 3rd Lieutenant
Born in Lawrence County, Alabama, and resided in Johnston County where he was by occupation a farmer prior to enlisting at age 36. Appointed 3rd Lieutenant on February 25, 1862. Reported present through December, 1862. Resigned on September 8, 1863, by reason of "chronic rheumatism of eight months' standing" and "frequent attacks of remittent fever." Resignation accepted on September 26, 1863. [Served for a time in 1862 as acting Adjutant of the regiment.]

NONCOMMISSIONED OFFICERS AND PRIVATES

ADAMS, D. H., Private
Resided in Johnston County where he enlisted at age 22, June 15, 1863, for the war. Reported sick in hospital at Wilmington in September-October, 1863. Furloughed

from hospital for forty days on November 13, 1863. Returned to duty in January-February, 1864. Reported present in July-August and November-December, 1864.

ADAMS, DAVID H., Corporal

Born in Johnston County where he resided as a farmer prior to enlisting in Johnston County at age 20, April 12, 1862. Mustered in as Private. Reported present through October, 1862. Promoted to Corporal on January 10, 1863. Reported present but sick in camp in September-October, 1863. Reported present for duty in November, 1863-February, 1864. Also reported present in July-August and November-December, 1864.

ALLEN, JOSIAH G., Private

Born in Johnston County where he resided as a farmer prior to enlisting at age 28, March 12, 1862. Reported present through August, 1862. Deserted on December 4, 1862. Reported present but sick in camp in September-October, 1863. Returned to duty in November-December, 1863. Reported present through February, 1864. Deserted on August 8, 1864.

ALTMAN, JOHN J., Private

Born in Johnston County where he resided as a farmer prior to enlisting in Johnston County at age 19, March 31, 1862. Reported absent without leave on or about the same date. Transferred to Company E, 24th Regiment N.C. Troops (14th Regiment N.C. Volunteers), in April, 1862.

ATKINSON, W. H., Private

Enlisted in Johnston County on April 13, 1864, for the war. Reported present in July-August, 1864. Reported in hospital at Goldsboro in November-December, 1864. Paroled at Raleigh on May 8, 1865.

AUSTIN, ELBERT, Private

Resided in Johnston County and was by occupation a farmer prior to enlisting in Johnston County at age 39, February 24, 1863, for the war. Reported present but sick in September-October, 1863. Returned to duty in November-December, 1863. Reported present in January-February, July-August, and November-December, 1864.

AUSTIN, JAMES, Private

Born in Johnston County where he resided as a farmer prior to enlisting in Johnston County at age 36, February 24, 1863, for the war. Reported present but sick in camp in September-October, 1863. Returned to duty in November-December, 1863. Reported present in January-February, 1864. Died at Clayton on March 26, 1864. Cause of death not reported.

AUSTIN, JAMES E., Private

Resided in Johnston County and enlisted at age 16, October 13, 1864, for the war. Reported present through December, 1864.

AUSTIN, JOSEPH, Private

Previously served as Private in Mallett's N.C. Battalion (Camp Guard). Transferred to this company on an unspecified date (probably in March-August, 1864). Reported present in November-December, 1864.

AVERY, JOHN T., Private

Resided in Johnston County and enlisted at Camp Mangum, near Raleigh, at age 18, May 14, 1862, for the war. Reported present through August, 1862. Reported present but sick in camp in September-October, 1863. Returned to duty in November-December, 1863. Reported present in January-February, July-August, and November-December, 1864. Survived the war.

AYCOCK, LAWRENCE A., Private

Previously served as Private in Company C, Mallett's N.C. Battalion (Camp Guard). Transferred to this company on an unspecified date (probably in March-August, 1864). Reported present but sick in camp on or about August 31, 1864. Reported present in November-December, 1864.

BALLANCE, AARON, Private

Previously served as Private in Company E, Mallett's N.C. Battalion (Camp Guard). Transferred to this company on an unspecified date (probably in March-August, 1864). Reported present but sick in camp on or about August 31, 1864. Reported present in November-December, 1864. Hospitalized at Raleigh on February 18, 1865, with "pneumonia" and died on or about February 21, 1865.

BARBER, ERVIN G., _____

North Carolina pension records indicate that he served in this company.

BARBER, G. I., Private

Enlisted in Johnston County on or about March 14, 1864, for the war. Reported present in July-August and November-December, 1864.

BARBER, PULIA P., Private

Born in Johnston County where he resided as a farmer prior to enlisting in Johnston County at age 20, February 20, 1862. Reported absent without leave on or about April 21, 1862. Returned to duty prior to July 1, 1862. Reported present in July-August, 1862. Deserted at Drewry's Bluff, Virginia, December 14, 1862. Reported to be "still in the woods" on February 6, 1864. "This man has been hunted frequently but [we] have never been able to come up with him." Took the Oath of Allegiance at Raleigh on May 2, 1865. [May have served also in Company I, 24th Regiment N.C. Troops (14th Regiment N.C. Volunteers).]

BARBER, R. A., Private

Resided in Johnston County where he enlisted at age 18, April 26, 1862, for the war. Reported present through June, 1862. Reported absent in hospital in July-August, 1862. Reported at home on sick furlough in November-December, 1862. Reported in hospital at Wilmington in September-October, 1863. Returned to duty in November-December, 1863. Reported present in January-February, 1864. Reported present but sick in camp in July-August, 1864. Reported present in November-December, 1864.

BARBER, WILLIAM R. A., Private

Born in Johnston County where he resided as a farmer prior to enlisting in Johnston County at age 18, February

26, 1862. Reported absent without leave on or about April 21, 1862. Returned to duty prior to September 1, 1862. Deserted on December 14, 1862. Reported under arrest and in the military prison at Wilmington from September 25 through December 31, 1863. Rejoined the company in January-February, 1864. Reported present but sick in camp in July-August, 1864. Reported absent without leave in November-December, 1864.

BARNES, E. H., Private
Previously served as Private in Mallett's N.C. Battalion (Camp Guard). Transferred to this company on an unspecified date (probably in March-August, 1864). Reported present in November-December, 1864. Paroled at Goldsboro on May 15, 1865.

BATTON, HARDY, Private
Born in Johnston County where he resided as a farmer prior to enlisting in Johnston County at age 27, March 4, 1862. Died at Raleigh on April 26, 1862, of disease.

BATTON, WILLIAM H., Private
Resided in Johnston County and was by occupation a farmer prior to enlisting in Lenoir County at age 36, March 2, 1863, for the war. Reported present from September, 1863, through February, 1864. Reported present but sick in camp in July-August, 1864. Reported present in November-December, 1864. Hospitalized at Charlotte on February 13, 1865, with anasarca. Furloughed on February 19, 1865. Hospitalized at Raleigh on February 20, 1865, with "nostalgia." Returned to duty on March 6, 1865. Paroled at Goldsboro on May 4, 1865.

BOON, HENRY J., Private
Born in Johnston County where he resided as a farmer prior to enlisting in Johnston County at age 38, February 28, 1862. Discharged on May 26, 1862, probably because he was overage.

BOYKIN, HILLORY, Private
Resided in Johnston County and enlisted at Drewry's Bluff, Virginia, at age 21, September 5, 1862, for the war. Reported present in September, 1863-February, 1864. Also reported present in July-August and November-December, 1864. Survived the war.

BOYKIN, JOHN M., Private
Resided in Johnston County and enlisted at Drewry's Bluff, Virginia, at age 18, September 5, 1862, for the war. Reported present in September, 1863-February, 1864. Reported present but sick in camp in July-August, 1864. Reported present in November-December, 1864. Survived the war.

BOYKIN, JONATHAN, Private
Born in Johnston County where he resided as a farmer prior to enlisting in Johnston County at age 48, February 28, 1862. Reported absent without leave in July-August, 1862. Hospitalized on November 15, 1862, with debility. Returned to duty on December 4, 1862. Reported absent in hospital at Wilson from April 15, 1863, through December 31, 1864. Paroled at Goldsboro in 1865.

BRASWELL, LEWIS, Private
Enlisted in Johnston County at age 18, April 27, 1864, for the war. Reported present in July-August, 1864. Reported in hospital at Goldsboro in November-December, 1864. Survived the war.

BRICE, CHARLES, Private
Resided in Johnston County. Place and date of enlistment not reported. Paroled at Goldsboro on May 4, 1865.

BROADWELL, J. H., Private
Born in Johnston County where he resided as a farmer prior to enlisting in Johnston County at age 18, September 1, 1863, for the war. Reported present but sick in camp in September-October, 1863. Returned to duty in November-December, 1863. Reported present in January-February and July-August, 1864. Reported absent in hospital at Augusta, Georgia, in November-December, 1864. Discharged on April 6, 1865, by reason of "paralysis of lower extremities of a permanent character. . . ." [North Carolina pension records indicate that he was wounded at or near Augusta on January 11, 186(5).]

BROUGHTON, JOHN W., Private
Previously served as Private in Company C, Mallett's N.C. Battalion (Camp Guard). Transferred to this company in March-August, 1864. Reported present in November-December, 1864.

BUNN, A. G., Private
Resided in Johnston County and was by occupation a farmer prior to enlisting in Lenoir County at age 36, March 2, 1863, for the war. Reported sick in hospital at Wilson from April 1, 1863, through August 31, 1864. Reported present for duty in November-December, 1864.

CARTER, MOSES, Private
Resided in Johnston County and was by occupation a brickmason prior to enlisting in Johnston County at age 53, February 28, 1862. Reported absent without leave through August, 1862. Reported present but sick in camp in September-October, 1863. Hospitalized at Wilmington on November 9, 1863, with chronic diarrhoea. Returned to duty on December 2, 1863. Reported present through February, 1864. Also reported present in July-August and November-December, 1864. Deserted at Goldsboro on March 24, 1865. Sent to New Bern. Confined at Hart's Island, New York Harbor, on or about April 10, 1865. Released at Hart's Island on June 18, 1865, after taking the Oath of Allegiance.

COLYER, T. E., Private
Previously served as Private in Mallett's N.C. Battalion (Camp Guard). Transferred to this company on an unspecified date (probably in March-August, 1864). Reported present but sick in camp on or about August 31, 1864. Reported present for duty in November-December, 1864. Died in hospital at Charleston, South Carolina, January 29, 1865, of "typhoid fever."

COX, W. W., Private
Enlisted in Pitt County on April 26, 1863, for the war. Appears to have been detailed for light duty during most

or all of his military service. Reported on duty as an ordnance guard at Goldsboro on October 31, 1864. No further records

CREECH, LEVI P., Private
Born in Johnston County where he resided as a farmer prior to enlisting in Johnston County at age 21, March 26, 1862. Reported on duty as a teamster from October 1, 1862, through November 30, 1863. Hospitalized at Wilmington on December 10, 1863, with intermittent fever. Returned to duty on February 19, 1864. Reported on duty as a teamster in July-August and November-December, 1864.

CROCKER, BARDEN, Private
Born in Johnston County where he resided as a carpenter prior to enlisting in Johnston County at age 40, February 27, 1862. Discharged on May 26, 1862, probably because he was overage.

CROCKER, JAMES W., Private
Resided in Johnston County and enlisted at Camp Mangum, near Raleigh, at age 18, May 11, 1862, for the war. Reported present through August, 1862. Reported sick in camp in September-October, 1863. Hospitalized at Wilmington on November 28, 1863, with intermittent fever. Returned to duty on February 27, 1864. Reported present in July-August and November-December, 1864.

CROCKER, WILLIAM H., Private
Born in Johnston County where he resided as a farmer prior to enlisting in Johnston County at age 17, March 31, 1862. Died at Raleigh on May 21, 1862, of disease.

DAUGHTREY, JOHN, Private
Born in Sampson County and resided in Johnston County where he was by occupation a farmer prior to enlisting in Johnston County at age 47, February 28, 1862. Discharged on May 26, 1862, probably because he was overage.

DAUGHTRY, GEORGE WILLIAM, Private
Born in Sampson County and resided in Johnston County where he was by occupation a farmer prior to enlisting in Johnston County at age 30, March 8, 1862. Died at Pickett's Factory, Virginia, on or about July 10, 1862, of disease.

DAVIS, J. T., Private
Enlisted in Johnston County on April 11, 1864, for the war. Reported present in July-August, 1864. Hospitalized at Wilmington on December 30, 1864. Died in hospital at Wilmington on or about January 20, 1865, of "pneumonia."

DAVIS, JOSIAH, Private
Born in Johnston County where he resided as a farmer prior to enlisting in Johnston County at age 19, February 25, 1862. Died on May 28, 1862, of disease. Place of death not reported.

DAVIS, WILLIAM H., Private
Born in Edgecombe County and resided in Johnston County where he was by occupation a student prior to enlisting in Johnston County at age 18, March 8, 1862. Reported present through August, 1862. Transferred to the 4th Regiment South Carolina Cavalry on March 3, 1863.

DODD, H. L., Private
Enlisted in Johnston County at age 18, April 2, 1864, for the war. Reported present in July-August, 1864. Survived the war.

DODD, I. B., Private
Place and date of enlistment not reported; however, he probably enlisted in September-December, 1864. Reported present on or about December 31, 1864.

DODD, JAMES M., Private
Born in Johnston County where he resided as a farmer prior to enlisting in Johnston County at age 18, February 25, 1862. Reported present through August, 1862. Reported present but sick in camp in September-October, 1863. Hospitalized at Wilmington on November 28, 1863, with debilitas. Returned to duty on December 1, 1863. Reported present through February, 1864. Also reported present in July-August and November-December, 1864.

DODD, JOHN W., Private
Born in Johnston County where he resided as a farmer prior to enlisting in Johnston County at age 26, March 31, 1862. Reported present or accounted for through August, 1862. Reported present but sick in camp in September-October, 1863. Returned to duty in November-December, 1863. Reported present in January-February, July-August, and November-December, 1864.

DODD, Q. B., Private
Previously served as Private in Mallett's N.C. Battalion (Camp Guard). Transferred to this company on or about August 1, 1864. Reported present through August, 1864.

DUNCAN, A. R., Private
Previously served as Private in Company A, Mallett's N.C. Battalion (Camp Guard). Transferred to this company on an unspecified date (probably in September-December, 1864). Paroled at Raleigh on April 22, 1865.

DUNCAN, JAMES HENRY, Private
Born in Johnston County where he resided as a farmer prior to enlisting in Johnston County at age 22, February 25, 1862. Reported present through August, 1862. Reported absent on detached service in September-October, 1863. Rejoined the company in November-December, 1863, and was reported present through February, 1864. Reported present but sick in camp in July-August, 1864. Reported present in November-December, 1864. Survived the war.

DUNCAN, RANSOM H., Private
Born in Johnston County where he resided as a farmer prior to enlisting in Craven County at age 28, March 14, 1862. Reported absent in hospital on or about July 1, 1862. Returned to duty prior to September 1, 1862. Hospitalized at Wilmington on August 30, 1863, with continued fever. Returned to duty on October 6, 1863.

Hospitalized at Wilmington on November 28, 1863, with intermittent fever. Returned to duty on January 2, 1864. Reported present in July-August, 1864. Reported on duty as a teamster in November-December, 1864.

DUNCAN, W. S., Private
Born in Johnston County where he resided prior to enlisting at age 18, February 24, 1863, for the war. Died on June 30, 1863, of disease. Place of death not reported.

DUNCAN, WILLIAM HENRY, Private
Place and date of enlistment not reported. Paroled at Greensboro on May 1, 1865.

EARP, JAMES HENDERSON, Private
Born in Johnston County where he resided as a farmer prior to enlisting in Johnston County at age 34, February 28, 1862. Reported present through August, 1862. Reported present but sick in camp in September-October, 1863. Returned to duty in November-December, 1863. Reported present in January-February, July-August, and November-December, 1864. Paroled at Raleigh on May 11, 1865.

EARP, JOHN E., Private
Born in Johnston County where he resided as a farmer prior to enlisting in Johnston County at age 38, February 25, 1862. Discharged on May 26, 1862, probably because he was overage. Reenlisted in the company on April 1, 1863, for the war. Reported present in September, 1863-February, 1864, and July-August, 1864. Hospitalized at Raleigh on November 6, 1864, with intermittent fever. Returned to duty on November 9, 1864. Reported present through December, 1864.

EASON, JOHN WILLIAM, Private
Born in Johnston County where he resided as a farmer prior to enlisting in Johnston County at age 18, April 9, 1862. Reported present through August, 1862. Reported in hospital at Raleigh in September-October, 1863. Returned to duty in November-December, 1863. Reported present in January-February and July-August, 1864. Hospitalized at Raleigh on November 6, 1864, with intermittent fever. Returned to duty on November 30, 1864. Hospitalized at Charlotte on February 13, 1865, with typhoid pneumonia. Transferred to another hospital on February 18, 1865. Survived the war.

EATMAN, HARRIS H., Private
Born in Johnston County where he resided as a farmer prior to enlisting in Johnston County at age 18, February 28, 1862. Reported present through August, 1862. Reported absent in hospital in September-October, 1863. Hospitalized at Wilmington on November 28, 1863, with debilitas. Returned to duty on or about December 3, 1863. Reported present in January-February, July-August, and November-December, 1864. Paroled at Goldsboro on May 16, 1865.

EATMON, W. H., Private
Resided in Johnston County and enlisted in New Hanover County at age 17, February 20, 1864, for the war. Reported present but sick in camp in July-August, 1864. Reported present for duty in November-December, 1864. Paroled at Goldsboro on May 16, 1865.

EDWARDS, BRYANT, Private
Born in Johnston County where he resided as a farmer prior to enlisting in Johnston County at age 23, March 31, 1862. Hospitalized at Petersburg, Virginia, July 20, 1862. Died in hospital at Petersburg on or about October 18, 1862, of "feb[ris] typh[oid]."

EDWARDS, LEVI, Private
Born in Johnston County where he resided as a farmer prior to enlisting in Johnston County at age 19, March 26, 1862. Discharged on April 12, 1862, by reason of disability.

ELLIS, DON JUAN, Sergeant
Born in Johnston County where he resided as a farmer prior to enlisting in Johnston County at age 16, February 25, 1862. Mustered in as Sergeant. Reported present through August, 1862. Reported present but sick in camp in September-October, 1863. Returned to duty in November-December, 1863. Reported present in January-February, July-August, and November-December, 1864. Hospitalized at Greensboro on February 20, 1865, with catarrhus. Transferred to another hospital on February 23, 1865.

ELLIS, GEORGE WASHINGTON, Private
Enlisted in Johnston County at age 18, April 14, 1864, for the war. Reported present but sick in camp in July-August, 1864. Reported in hospital at Raleigh in November-December, 1864. Survived the war.

ELLIS, JACOB, Private
Resided in Johnston County and enlisted at Camp Mangum, near Raleigh, at age 18, May 11, 1862, for the war. Reported present through August, 1862. Reported sick in camp in November-December, 1862. Died in hospital at Raleigh on March 16, 1863, of "smallpox."

ELLIS, JOHN C., Private
Enlisted in Johnston County on or about April 14, 1864, for the war. Reported present but sick in camp in July-August, 1864. Reported present for duty in November-December, 1864.

FERRELL, J. D., Private
Previously served as Private in Company C, Mallett's N.C. Battalion (Camp Guard). Transferred to this company on an unspecified date (probably in September-December, 1864). Reported present on or about December 31, 1864. Hospitalized at Charlotte on February 6, 1865, with intermittent fever. No further records.

FURLEY, J. B., Corporal
Enlistment date reported as February 25, 1862; however, he was not listed on the rolls of this company until November-December, 1864, when he was reported present. Promotion record not reported. No further records.

GODWIN, AVERA E., Private
Resided in Johnston County where he enlisted at age 21, May 2, 1862, for the war. Reported present through August, 1862. Reported in hospital at Raleigh in September-October, 1863. Returned to duty in November-December, 1863. Reported on detail as a coastguardsman at Wrightsville Sound in February, 1864. Reported present in July-August and November-December, 1864. Paroled at Goldsboro on May 2, 1865.

GODWIN, JACOB H., Private
Resided in Johnston County and enlisted at Camp Holmes, near Raleigh, at age 31, October 16, 1862, for the war. Reported sick in hospital at Petersburg, Virginia, in November-December, 1862. Died in camp near Wilmington on October 16, 1863, of disease.

GODWIN, JAMES A., Private
Born in Johnston County where he resided prior to enlisting at Camp Mangum, near Raleigh, at age 27, May 11, 1862, for the war. Reported present through August, 1862. Reported sick in hospital at Goldsboro in November-December, 1862. Died at Goldsboro on February 28, 1863, of disease.

GODWIN, WILLIAM B., Private
Born in Johnston County where he resided as a farmer prior to enlisting in Johnston County at age 18, March 15, 1862. Reported present through August, 1862. Also reported present in September-December, 1863. Reported on detail as a coastguardsman at Wrightsville Sound in February, 1864. Reported present in July-August and November-December, 1864. Survived the war.

GREEN, NATHAN G., Private
Born in Johnston County where he resided as a farmer prior to enlisting in Johnston County at age 27, May 14, 1862, for the war. Reported absent in hospital in July-August, 1862. Reported on duty as a courier for Brigadier General James G. Martin from June 7, 1863, through August 31, 1864. Probably continued to serve as a courier for General Martin through December, 1864. Survived the war. [Previously served as Captain in the 41st Regiment N.C. Militia.]

GWINN, WILLIAM, Private
Resided in Johnston County where he enlisted at age 27, May 11, 1862, for the war. Reported present through August, 1862. Reported sick in camp in November-December, 1862. Reported present in September, 1863-February, 1864, and July-August, 1864. Captured near Plymouth on October 31, 1864. Sent to Fort Monroe, Virginia. Transferred to Point Lookout, Maryland, November 24, 1864. Died at Point Lookout on June 13, 1865, of "scurvy."

HARE, H. H., Private
Previously served as Private in Company A, Mallett's N.C. Battalion (Camp Guard). Transferred to this company on an unspecified date (probably in March-August, 1864). Reported present in November-December, 1864. Paroled at Goldsboro on May 3, 1865.

HARPER, JOHN R., Private
Resided in Johnston County where he enlisted at age 37, February 24, 1863, for the war. Reported present but sick in camp in September-October, 1863. Hospitalized at Wilmington on November 28, 1863, with intermittent fever. Returned to duty on December 2, 1863. Reported present or accounted for through February, 1864. Also reported present in July-August, 1864. Paroled at Raleigh on May 15, 1865.

HAYLES, JOHN, Private
Resided in Johnston County and was by occupation a ditcher prior to enlisting in Wake County at age 48, October 19, 1863, for the war. Reported present but sick in camp in July-August, 1864. Paroled at Goldsboro on May 3, 1865.

HERRING, JOHN, Private
Born in Duplin County and resided in Johnston County where he was by occupation a farmer prior to enlisting in Johnston County at age 39, March 3, 1862. Reported under arrest on June 30, 1862. Listed as a deserter on or about August 31, 1862. Reported in confinement at Castle Thunder Prison, Richmond, Virginia, in November-December, 1862. Deserted again on March 10, 1863.

HILL, MOSES, Private
Born in Johnston County where he resided as a farmer prior to enlisting in Johnston County at age 38, February 28, 1862. Reported present or accounted for through August, 1862. Reported sick in camp in November-December, 1862. Reported absent on detached service in September-October, 1863. Rejoined the company in November-December, 1863. Reported absent on detached service from January 20 through February 29, 1864. Reported present with the company in July-August and November-December, 1864.

HINTON, JESSE W., Private
Born in Johnston County where he resided as a farmer prior to enlisting in Johnston County at age 28, March 27, 1862. Reported absent without leave on June 30 and August 31, 1862. Returned to duty on an unspecified date. Reported present in September-December, 1863. Reported on detail as a coastguardsman at Wrightsville Sound in February, 1864. Reported present with the company in July-August, 1864. Captured near Plymouth on October 31, 1864. Confined at Fort Monroe, Virginia. Transferred to Point Lookout, Maryland, November 24, 1864. Released at Point Lookout on June 27, 1865, after taking the Oath of Allegiance.

HOCUT, JAMES A., Sergeant
Born in Johnston County where he resided as a farmer prior to enlisting in Johnston County at age 18, February 28, 1862. Mustered in as Private. Reported present through August, 1862. Promoted to Sergeant on January 1, 1863. Reported present but sick in camp in September-October, 1863. Returned to duty in November-December, 1863. Reported present in January-February, July-August, and November-December, 1864.

HOCUT, WILLIAM B., Private
Enlisted in Johnston County on August 25, 1864, for the war. Reported present in November-December, 1864.

HODGE, WILLIAM, Private
Resided in Johnston County where he enlisted at age 18. Enlistment date reported as May 1, 1862; however, he was not listed on the rolls of this company until September-October, 1863, when he was reported present. Reported present through February, 1864. Also reported present in July-August and November-December, 1864. Paroled at Goldsboro on May 3, 1865. [May have served previously in Mallett's N.C. Battalion (Camp Guard).]

HOLDER, MALIKIAH, Private
Enlisted in Johnston County on August 25, 1864, for the war. Reported present in November-December, 1864.

HOLLIMAN, C. M., Private
Previously served as Private in Company A, Mallett's N.C. Battalion (Camp Guard). Transferred to this company on an unspecified date (probably in March-August, 1864). Reported present on or about August 31, 1864. Also reported present in November-December, 1864. Paroled at Goldsboro on May 3, 1865.

HORNE, ASHLEY, Private
Resided in Johnston County and enlisted at Camp Mangum, near Raleigh, at age 18, May 27, 1862, for the war. Reported present through June, 1862. Reported absent in hospital in July-August, 1862. Transferred to Company C, 53rd Regiment N.C. Troops, October 7, 1863.

HORNE, SAMUEL R., Private
Resided in Johnston County and enlisted at Camp Mangum, near Raleigh, at age 26, May 16, 1862, for the war. Appointed 2nd Lieutenant and transferred to Company C, 53rd Regiment N.C. Troops, July 23, 1862.

HOWARD, EDMOND, Private
Resided in Johnston County where he enlisted at age 36, February 24, 1863, for the war. Reported present in September, 1863-February, 1864. Also reported present in July-August and November-December, 1864. Paroled at Goldsboro in 1865.

HOYLES, JOHN, Private
Enlisted in Wake County on October 18, 186[4], for the war. Reported present through December, 1864.

HUGHES, BRASWELL, Private
Born in Johnston County where he resided as a farmer prior to enlisting in Johnston County at age 23, February 27, 1862. Hospitalized on August 25, 1862, with typhoid fever. Returned to duty on October 14, 1862. Hospitalized at Wilmington on September 10, 1863, with intermittent fever. Returned to duty on September 29, 1863. Hospitalized at Wilmington on October 26, 1863. Furloughed for thirty days on December 1, 1863. Returned to duty on or about December 31, 1863. Reported present in January-February, July-August, and November-December, 1864.

JERNIGAN, KEDER, Private
Born in Johnston County where he resided as a farmer prior to enlisting in Johnston County at age 32, February 25, 1862. Died at Petersburg, Virginia, July 21, 1862, of disease.

JILLWAN, W., Private
Resided in Johnston County. Place and date of enlistment not reported (probably enlisted in January-April, 1865). Paroled at Goldsboro on May 2, 1865.

JOHNSON, CURTIS, Private
Born in Johnston County where he resided as a farmer prior to enlisting in Johnston County at age 28, March 14, 1862. Reported present through August, 1862. Reported on detail as a carpenter from September 23, 1863, through February 29, 1864. Reported present with the company in July-August, 1864. Reported on detail with the quartermaster department at Wilmington in November-December, 1864. Survived the war.

JOHNSON, HAYWOOD H., Private
Previously served as Private in Company E, Mallett's N.C. Battalion (Camp Guard). Transferred to this company on an unspecified date (probably in September-October, 1864). Captured near Plymouth on October 31, 1864. Confined at Fort Monroe, Virginia, on or about November 10, 1864. Transferred to Point Lookout, Maryland, November 24, 1864. Released at Point Lookout on June 28, 1865, after taking the Oath of Allegiance.

JOHNSON, M. B., Private
Born in Johnston County where he resided prior to enlisting at Drewry's Bluff, Virginia, at age 22, September 5, 1862, for the war. Hospitalized on December 1, 1862, with bronchitis. Returned to duty on December 14, 1862. Died at Drewry's Bluff, Virginia, on or about January 1, 1863, of disease.

JOHNSON, MARION, Private
Resided in Johnston County and was by occupation a farm laborer prior to enlisting at Drewry's Bluff, Virginia, at age 27, September 5, 1862, for the war. Reported sick in hospital at Petersburg, Virginia, in November-December, 1862. Hospitalized at Wilmington on September 10, 1863. Deserted from hospital on September 27, 1863. Rejoined the company on an unspecified date. Reported present in November, 1863-February, 1864. Also reported present in July-August and November-December, 1864.

JOHNSON, NATHAN, Private
Resided in Johnston County and was by occupation a farmer prior to enlisting at Drewry's Bluff, Virginia, at age 25, September 25, 1862, for the war. Reported sick in hospital at Goldsboro (and possibly also for a time at Raleigh) from January 10, 1863, through December, 1864.

JONES, CLAUDIUS B., Private
Enlisted in Johnston County at age 22, April 2, 1864, for the war. Reported present but sick in camp in July-August, 1864. Reported absent on sick furlough of sixty days in November-December, 1864. Survived the war.

JONES, JOHN CALVIN, Private

Born in Johnston County where he resided as a farmer prior to enlisting in Johnston County at age 21, March 20, 1862. Reported present through August, 1862. Reported present but sick in camp in September-October, 1863. Reported absent in hospital at Wilmington from November 27 through December 31, 1863. Returned to duty in January-February, 1864. Reported present in July-August and November-December, 1864. Survived the war.

JONES, JOHN TROY, Private

Born in Johnston County where he resided as a farmer prior to enlisting in Johnston County at age 22, February 25, 1862. Reported present through August, 1862. Reported absent on detached service in September-October, 1863. Rejoined the company in November-December, 1863. Reported on detail as a coastguardsman at Wrightsville Sound in February, 1864. Reported present with the company in July-August and November-December, 1864.

JONES, WILLIAM BENTON, Private

Resided in Johnston County where he enlisted at age 22, May 14, 1862, for the war. Reported present through August, 1862. Reported present but sick in camp in September-October, 1863. Hospitalized at Wilmington on November 9, 1863, with acute bronchitis. Returned to duty on December 19, 1863. Reported present in January-February, July-August, and November-December, 1864. Survived the war.

JONES, WILLIAM H., Private

Born in Johnston County where he resided as a farmer prior to enlisting in Johnston County at age 22, March 14, 1862. Reported absent without leave on or about July 1 and September 1, 1862. Returned to duty on an unspecified date. Reported present but sick in camp in September-October, 1863. Reported present in November-December, 1863. Reported on detached service on January 25, 1864. Reported present in July-August and November-December, 1864.

KENNEDY, JAMES H., Private

Resided in Johnston County where he enlisted at age 30, April 28, 1862, for the war. Reported present through June, 1862. Reported absent on detached service in September-October, 1863. Rejoined the company in November-December, 1863. Reported present in January-February, 1864. Reported on duty as a teamster in July-August, 1864. Reported present with the company in November-December, 1864. Paroled at Goldsboro on May 15, 1865.

KENNEDY, JOHN BUNYAN, Corporal

Born in Johnston County where he resided as a farmer prior to enlisting in Johnston County at age 20, February 5, 1862. Mustered in as Corporal. Reported present on surviving company muster rolls through December, 1864.

KING, WARREN D., Private

Born in Wake County where he resided as a farmer prior to enlisting in Halifax County at age 39, March 14, 1862. Discharged on May 26, 1862, probably because he was overage.

LEE, J. T., Private

Born in Johnston County where he resided prior to enlisting at age 31, March 12, 1862. Died in Johnston County on May 10, 1862, of disease.

LEE, JOHN I., Private

Born in Johnston County and was by occupation a farmer prior to enlisting in Craven County at age 31, March 12, 1862. Died on May 10, 1862. Place and cause of death not reported.

LEE, MARION WASHINGTON, Private

Born in Johnston County where he resided as a farmer prior to enlisting in Johnston County at age 27, February 19, 1862. Reported present through August, 1862. Hospitalized at Petersburg, Virginia, November 11, 1862, with chronic rheumatism. Returned to duty on February 8, 1863. Discharged from service on June 17, 1863, by reason of disability.

LYNCH, WILLIAM A., Private

Born in Johnston County where he resided as a farmer prior to enlisting in Johnston County at age 22, February 25, 1862. Reported present through August, 1862. Reported present but sick in camp in September-October, 1863. Hospitalized at Wilmington on November 28, 1863, with debilitas. Returned to duty on December 2, 1863. Reported present through February, 1864. Reported present but sick in camp in July-August, 1864. Reported in hospital at Columbia, South Carolina, in November-December, 1864. Died in South Carolina on February 1, 1865, of disease.

MASSEY, JOHN D., Private

Born in Johnston County where he resided as a farmer prior to enlisting in Johnston County at age 23, April 4, 1862. Appointed acting Commissary Sergeant on April 5, 1862, and assigned to temporary duty with the Field and Staff of this regiment. Reported on duty as acting Commissary Sergeant until June 15, 1864, when he was elected 2nd Lieutenant and transferred to Company D of this regiment.

MASSEY, P. T., Private

Resided in Johnston County and enlisted at age 25, May 28, 1862, for the war. Discharged on an unspecified date (probably prior to July 1, 1862) after being appointed tax collector of Johnston County.

MATTHEWS, THOMAS, Private

Resided in Wake County. Place and date of enlistment not reported; however, he probably enlisted on or about April 21, 1862. Discharged on May 26, 1862. Reason discharged not reported.

MAYNARD, WILLIAM HENRY, Private

Born in Wake County and resided in Johnston County where he was by occupation a farmer prior to enlisting in Johnston County at age 23, February 27, 1862. Reported in hospital on or about June 30, 1862. Returned to duty prior to September 1, 1862. Discharged on September 30, 1862. Reason discharged not reported. Reenlisted in the company on March 25, 1864. Reported present in July-August, 1864. Captured near Plymouth on October 31, 1864. Confined at Fort Monroe, Virginia, November 16, 1864. Transferred to Point Lookout, Maryland, November 25, 1864. Released at Point Lookout on June 29, 1865, after taking the Oath of Allegiance.

MUNNS, SAMUEL, Private
Born in Cumberland County and resided in Johnston County where he was by occupation a farmer prior to enlisting in Johnston County at age 28, February 22, 1862. Reported present through August, 1862. Died in hospital at Raleigh on March 15, 1863, of "smallpox."

NOWELL, JAMES A., Private
Born in Johnston County and resided in Wake County where he was by occupation a farmer prior to enlisting in Halifax County at age 40, March 15, 1862. Discharged on May 26, 1862, probably because he was overage.

OLIVER, E. M., Private
Resided in Johnston County where he enlisted at age 38, September 22, 1863, for the war. Reported present through February, 1864. Also reported present in July-August, 1864. Died at or near Savannah, Georgia, December 9, 1864. Cause of death not reported.

PARRISH, JUSTICE, Private
Resided in Johnston County and was by occupation a shoemaker prior to enlisting in Johnston County at age 27, May 11, 1862, for the war. Reported absent without leave through December, 1862. Hospitalized at Wilmington on or about February 18, 1863, with chronic rheumatism. Reported in hospital at Wilmington through August, 1864. Reported on light duty at Wilmington in November-December, 1864.

PARRISH, RICHARD, Private
Resided in Johnston County and enlisted at Drewry's Bluff, Virginia, at age 23, September 5, 1862, for the war. Hospitalized at Wilmington on September 10, 1863, with intermittent fever. Deserted from hospital on September 27, 1863. Apparently returned to the hospital prior to November 1, 1863. Reported sick in hospital at Wilmington through February, 1864. Returned to duty on an unspecified date. Reported present in November-December, 1864.

PEACOCK, JOHN, Private
Resided in Johnston County. Place and date of enlistment not reported; however, he probably enlisted in January-April, 1865. Paroled at Goldsboro on May 1, 1865.

PEARSON, B. B., Private
Resided in Nash County. Place and date of enlistment not reported; however, he probably enlisted in January-April, 1865. Paroled at Goldsboro on May 13, 1865.

PEEDIN, HILBERT F., Private
Enlisted in Johnston County at age 18, February 24, 1863, for the war. Hospitalized at Wilmington on August 30, 1863, with continued fever. Returned to duty on September 10, 1863. Hospitalized at Wilmington on October 26, 1863, with intermittent fever. Returned to

duty on December 8, 1863. Reported on detail as a coastguardsman at Wrightsville Sound in February, 1864. Rejoined the company on an unspecified date. Reported sick in hospital on August 5, 1864. Reported present with the company in November-December, 1864. Survived the war.

POLLARD, JOHN W., Private
Born in Wake County and resided in Johnston County where he was by occupation a farmer prior to enlisting in Johnston County at age 27, March 4, 1862. Reported present through August, 1862. Deserted on December 14, 1862. Returned to duty on an unspecified date. Hospitalized at Wilmington on September 7, 1863, with intermittent fever. Returned to duty on September 21, 1863. Reported present during January-February and July-August, 1864. Served as Musician of the garrison at Washington, North Carolina, from May 10 through August 31, 1864.

POOL, WILLIAM H., Private
Resided in Johnston County where he enlisted at age 28, May 11, 1862, for the war. Reported present in May-August, 1862, and September, 1863-February, 1864. Also reported present in July-August and November-December, 1864. Survived the war.

POOLE, A. S., Private
Previously served as Private in Company C, Mallett's N.C. Battalion (Camp Guard). Transferred to this company on an unspecified date (probably in March-August, 1864). Reported present but sick in camp on or about August 31, 1864. Reported present in November-December, 1864.

POOLE, PERRIN P., Private
Previously served as Private in Company C, 24th Regiment N.C. Troops (14th Regiment N.C. Volunteers). Was reportedly transferred to this company on or about May 18, 1862; however, records of this company do not indicate that he served herein. Later served as Drum Major of this regiment. [See regimental band.]

POOLE, S. C., Private
Resided in Johnston County and enlisted at Drewry's Bluff, Virginia, at age 18, November 28, 1862, for the war. Reported present but sick in camp in September-October, 1863. Hospitalized at Wilmington on November 3, 1863, with intermittent fever. Returned to duty on December 19, 1863. Reported present in January-February and July-August, 1864. May have served as acting Musician during those periods. Reported on duty as Musician in the hospital at Columbia, South Carolina, in November-December, 1864.

POOLE, W. C., Private
Previously served as Private in Company C, Mallett's N.C. Battalion (Camp Guard). Transferred to this company on an unspecified date (probably in March-August, 1864). Reported present but sick in camp on or about August 31, 1864. Died on December 5, 1864. Place and cause of death not reported.

POPE, JAMES K., Private
Previously served as Private in Mallett's N.C. Battalion (Camp Guard). Transferred to this company on an unspecified date (probably in March-August, 1864). Reported present but sick in camp on or about August 31, 1864. Reported present with the company in November-December, 1864. Hospitalized at Raleigh on February 18, 1865, with intermittent fever and diarrhoea. Furloughed for sixty days on February 23, 1865. Paroled at Goldsboro on May 15, 1865.

PRICE, GEORGE L., Private
Born in Johnston County where he resided as a farmer prior to enlisting in Johnston County at age 25, April 9, 1862. Reported present through August, 1862. Died on February 8, 1863, of disease. Place of death not reported.

PRICE, GIDEON, Private
Enlisted in Wake County on October 1, 1863, for the war. Reported present but sick in camp in July-August, 1864. Reported present with the company in November-December, 1864. Captured by the enemy on an unspecified date. Paroled at Cheraw, South Carolina, March 5, 1865.

PRICE, H. G., Private
Resided in Johnston County and was by occupation a farmer prior to enlisting in Johnston County at age 38, February 21, 1863, for the war. Reported present from September, 1863, through February, 1864. Also reported present in July-August and November-December, 1864.

PRICE, N. G., Private
Previously served as Private in Mallett's N.C. Battalion (Camp Guard). Transferred to this company on an unspecified date (probably in March-August, 1864). Reported present on or about August 31, 1864, and in November-December, 1864. Survived the war.

PRICE, QUILLA, Private
Previously served as Private in Mallett's N.C. Battalion (Camp Guard). Transferred to this company on an unspecified date (probably in March-August, 1864). Reported present but sick in camp on or about August 31, 1864. Reported absent on sick furlough of sixty days in November-December, 1864. Survived the war. [North Carolina pension records indicate that he became blind in his right eye and partially blind in his left eye after the war. He attributed the loss of his eyesight to "smoke during his service."]

RAINS, JOHN T., Private
Resided in Johnston County where he enlisted at age 18, February 24, 1863, for the war. Reported present in September, 1863-February, 1864. Also reported present in July-August and November-December, 1864. Survived the war.

RENFROW, WILLIAM CARY, 1st Sergeant
Born in Johnston County where he resided as a student prior to enlisting in Johnston County at age 17, February 25, 1862. Mustered in as Sergeant. Reported present or accounted for through August, 1862. Promoted to 1st

Sergeant in September-December, 1862. Reported present in September, 1863-February, 1864. Also reported present in July-August and November-December, 1864. Survived the war. [Later became governor of the Oklahoma Territory.]

ROSE, ELIAS, Private
Previously served as Private in Mallett's N.C. Battalion (Camp Guard). Transferred to this company on an unspecified date (probably in March-August, 1864). Reported present on or about August 31, 1864. Reported in hospital at Augusta, Georgia, in November-December, 1864.

ROSE, H. C., Private
Enlisted in Wake County on October 6, 1863, for the war. Reported present in July-August, 1864. Reported in hospital at Augusta, Georgia, in November-December, 1864.

ROSE, J. C., Private
Previously served as Private in Mallett's N.C. Battalion (Camp Guard). Transferred to this company on an unspecified date (probably in March-August, 1864). Reported present on or about August 31, 1864, and in November-December, 1864.

SMITH, JOSEPH B., Private
Born in Johnston County where he resided as a farmer prior to enlisting in Johnston County at age 18, February 25, 1862. Reported present through August, 1862. Reported present but sick in camp in September-October, 1863. Returned to duty in November-December, 1863. Reported present in January-February, July-August, and November-December, 1864. Survived the war.

SMITH, WILLIAM T., Corporal
Born in Wake County and resided in Johnston County where he was by occupation a farmer prior to enlisting in Johnston County at age 30, February 25, 1862. Mustered in as Corporal. Reported present through August, 1862. Reported present but sick in camp in September-October, 1863. Returned to duty in November-December, 1863. Reported present in January-February and July-August, 1864. Captured near Plymouth on or about October 31, 1864. Confined at Fort Monroe, Virginia. Transferred to Point Lookout, Maryland, where he arrived on November 25, 1864. Records of the Federal Provost Marshal indicate that he was released at Point Lookout on June 6, 1865, after taking the Oath of Allegiance; however, a North Carolina pension application filed by his widow in 1902 states that Corporal Smith died at Point Lookout in January, 1865.

SPENCER, J. RUFUS, Private
Resided in Johnston County and enlisted in New Hanover County at age 38, January 27, 1864, for the war. Reported present in July-August, 1864. Reported in hospital at Augusta, Georgia, in November-December, 1864. Paroled at Goldsboro on May 3, 1865.

STALLINGS, JAMES B., Private
Resided in Johnston County and was by occupation a

farmer prior to enlisting in Johnston County at age 40, September 12, 1863, for the war. Reported present through February, 1864. Also reported present in July-August and November-December, 1864.

STANLY, JACOB H., Private
Previously served as Private in Company C, 53rd Regiment N.C. Troops. Transferred to this company on October 7, 1863. Reported present but sick in camp in September-October, 1863. Returned to duty in November-December, 1863. Reported present in January-February, 1864. Reported present but sick in camp in July-August, 1864. Reported present in November-December, 1864.

STEPHENS, DAVID S., Private
Resided in Johnston County where he enlisted at age 18, July 20, 1862, for the war. Reported sick in hospital at Wilmington from September 21, 1863, through February 29, 1864. Returned to duty on an unspecified date. Reported present with the company in July-August and November-December, 1864. Survived the war.

STEVENS, JOHN C., Private
Enlisted at age 18 on September 25, 1864, for the war. Reported present in November-December, 1864. Survived the war. [North Carolina pension records indicate that he was wounded in the left arm at Savannah, Georgia, in the winter of 1864.]

STRICKLAND, WASHINGTON, Private
Born in Johnston County where he resided as a farmer prior to enlisting in Johnston County at age 17, March 24, 1862. Died on May 25, 1862, of disease. Place of death not reported.

SULLIVAN, HENRY, Private
Resided in Johnston County where he enlisted at age 38, May 27, 186[3], for the war. Reported present in September-December, 1863. Reported on detail as a coastguardsman at Wrightsville Sound in February, 1864. Reported present with the company in July-August and November-December, 1864.

SULLIVAN, JOHN HAYWOOD, Private
Resided in Johnston County and was by occupation a farmer prior to enlisting at age 18, February 24, 1863, for the war. Reported present in September-December, 1863. Reported on detail as a coastguardsman at Wrightsville Sound in February, 1864. Reported present with the company in July-August, 1864. Captured near Plymouth on or about October 31, 1864. Sent to Fort Monroe, Virginia. Transferred to Point Lookout, Maryland, November 24, 1864. Released at Point Lookout on May 15, 1865, after taking the Oath of Allegiance.

SULLIVAN, WILEY, Private
Born in Johnston County where he resided as a farmer prior to enlisting in Johnston County at age 26, February 24, 1862. Reported present through August, 1862. Reported absent on detached service in September-October, 1863. Rejoined the company in November-December, 1863. Reported on detail as a coastguardsman at Wrightsville Sound in February, 1864. Reported present

with the company in July-August, 1864. Reported in hospital at Charleston, South Carolina, in November-December, 1864.

SULLIVAN, WILLIAM, Private
Previously served as Private in Company A, Mallett's N.C. Battalion (Camp Guard). Transferred to this company on an unspecified date (probably in March-August, 1864). Reported present but sick in camp on or about August 31, 1864. Reported present in November-December, 1864.

TALTON, JAMES D., Private
Born in Johnston County where he resided as a farmer prior to enlisting in Johnston County at age 40, March 31, 1862. Discharged on May 26, 1862, probably by reason of being overage.

TALTON, JAMES T., Private
Born in Johnston County where he resided prior to enlisting at Camp Mangum, near Raleigh, at age 27, May 14, 1862, for the war. Died at Drewry's Bluff, Virginia, November 2, 1862, of "pneu[monia]."

TALTON, LEWIS, JR., Private
Born in Johnston County where he resided as a farmer prior to enlisting in Johnston County at age 23, February 20, 1862. Mustered in as Corporal. Reported absent on detached service through August, 1862. Hospitalized on November 5, 1862, with typhoid fever. Returned to duty on December 25, 1862. Reduced to ranks on January 10, 1863. Reported present but sick in camp in September-October, 1863. Hospitalized at Wilmington on November 28, 1863, with debilitas. Returned to duty on March 24, 1864. Reported present with the company in July-August and November-December, 1864. Paroled at Goldsboro in May, 1865.

TALTON, WILLIAM J., Private
Resided in Johnston County and was by occupation a farmer prior to enlisting in Johnston County at age 25, May 14, 1862, for the war. Reported present through August, 1862, and in September, 1863-February, 1864. Also reported present in July-August, 1864. Reported in hospital at Summerville, South Carolina, in November-December, 1864.

TINER, BYTHAN, Private
Born in Johnston County where he resided as a farmer prior to enlisting in Johnston County at age 20, March 31, 1862. Died on May 16, 1862, of disease. Place of death not reported.

TOMLINSON, NATHANIEL M., Private
Born in Johnston County where he resided as a farmer prior to enlisting in Johnston County at age 18, February 25, 1862. Reported present through August, 1862, and in September, 1863-February, 1864. Also reported present in July-August, 1864. Hospitalized at Wilmington on November 25, 1864, with remittent fever. Returned to duty on December 20, 1864. Survived the war.

TRULEY, JOEL BENTON, Corporal
Born in Johnston County where he resided as a farmer

prior to enlisting in Johnston County at age 20, February 25, 1862. Mustered in as Corporal. Reported absent in hospital through August, 1862. Reported sick in camp in November-December, 1862, and September-October, 1863. Hospitalized at Wilmington on November 28, 1863, with debilitas. Returned to duty on December 2, 1863. Reported present in January-February and July-August, 1864.

WALL, GEORGE G., Private
Born in Johnston County where he resided as a farmer prior to enlisting in Johnston County at age 19, February 24, 1862. Reported present through August, 1862. Hospitalized at Wilmington on September 7, 1863, with anemia. Returned to duty on September 24, 1863. Reported present through February, 1864. Also reported present in July-August and November-December, 1864. Survived the war.

WATSON, GILES, _____
North Carolina pension records indicate that he served in this company.

WATSON, JOHN H., Private
Resided in Johnston County where he enlisted at age 18, May 11, 1862, for the war. Reported present through August, 1862. Reported present but sick in camp in September-October, 1863. Hospitalized at Wilmington on November 28, 1863, with intermittent fever. Returned to duty on December 2, 1863. Reported present through February, 1864. Also reported present in July-August and November-December, 1864.

WATSON, QUINCY, Private
Resided in Johnston County and was by occupation a farmer prior to enlisting in Johnston County at age 45, July 20, 186[3], for the war. Hospitalized at Wilmington on October 21, 1863, with chronic diarrhoea. Furloughed for thirty days on November 17, 1863. Reported present in January-February, 1864. Reported present but sick in camp in July-August, 1864. Wounded in the throat and/or neck near Savannah, Georgia, December 10, 1864. Captured in hospital at Savannah on December 21, 1864. Sent to Hilton Head, South Carolina. Transferred to Fort Delaware, Delaware, where he arrived on March 12, 1865. Died at Fort Delaware on or about March 30, 1865, of "consumption."

WEBB, JOHN, Private
Born in Johnston County where he resided as a farmer prior to enlisting in Johnston County at age 45, March 3, 1862. Discharged on May 26, 1862, probably because he was overage.

WHEELER, JACOB, Private
Born in Johnston County where he resided as a farmer prior to enlisting in Johnston County at age 29, March 3, 1862. Reported present through August, 1862. Reported absent on sick furlough in November-December, 1862. Reported present but sick in camp in September-October, 1863. Returned to duty in November-December, 1863. Reported present in January-February, July-August, and November-December, 1864. Survived the war.

WHEELER, JOHN H., Private
Resided in Johnston County and enlisted at Camp Mangum, near Raleigh, at age 32, May 14, 1862, for the war. Reported present through August, 1862. Reported absent on detached service in September-October, 1863. Rejoined the company in November-December, 1863. Reported present or accounted for in January-February, July-August, and November-December, 1864.

WHITLEY, JESSE PHILLIP, Sergeant
Born in Johnston County where he resided as a farmer prior to enlisting in Craven County at age 18, March 12, 1862. Mustered in as Sergeant. Reported present through August, 1862. Reported present but sick in camp in September-October, 1863. Returned to duty in November-December, 1863. Reported present in January-February, July-August, and November-December, 1864. Survived the war.

WIGGS, ARTHUR T., Private
Born in Wayne County and resided in Johnston County where he was by occupation a farmer prior to enlisting in Johnston County at age 22, February 28, 1862. Reported present through August, 1862, and from September, 1863, through February, 1864. Appointed acting Commissary Sergeant on June 15, 1864, and transferred to the Field and Staff of this regiment. Reported on detail as acting Commissary Sergeant through December, 1864. Paroled at Goldsboro on May 8, 1865.

WIGGS, JOHN, Private
Born in Sampson County and resided in Johnston County where he was by occupation a farmer prior to enlisting in Johnston County at age 32, February 24, 1862. Reported present or accounted for through August, 1862. Died on July 20, 1863, of disease. Place of death not reported.

WIGGS, NEEDHAM M., Private
Born in Wayne County and resided in Johnston County where he was by occupation a farmer prior to enlisting in Johnston County at age 20, February 28, 1862. Reported present through August, 1862. Furloughed for forty days on November 27, 1863. Reported present in January-February and July-August, 1864. Died in hospital at Wilson on or about November 27, 1864, of "pneumonia."

WILDER, JOSEPH H., Private
Previously served as Private in Company F, Mallett's N.C. Battalion (Camp Guard). Transferred to this company on an unspecified date (probably in March-August, 1864). Reported present in November-December, 1864.

WILKINS, PHILLIP, Private
Born in Robeson County and was by occupation a farmer prior to enlisting in Johnston County at age 29, March 26, 1862. Reported present through August, 1862. Hospitalized at Wilmington on October 7, 1863, with intermittent fever. Returned to duty on October 16, 1863. Reported present from November, 1863, through February, 1864. Also reported present in July-August and November-December, 1864. Survived the war.

WILLIAMS, BENAJAH B., Private
Born in Johnston County where he resided as a farmer prior to enlisting in Johnston County at age 18, March 31, 1862. Discharged on May 5, 1862, by reason of disability.

WILLIAMS, CICERO, Private
Born in Wake County where he resided as a farmer prior to enlisting in Halifax County at age 29, March 15, 1862. Reported absent without leave through August 31, 1862. Reported present but sick in camp in September-October, 1863. Hospitalized at Wilmington on November 28, 1863, with icterus. Returned to duty on December 19, 1863. Reported present in January-February and July-August, 1864. Captured near Plymouth on or about October 31, 1864. Confined at Fort Monroe, Virginia. Transferred to Point Lookout, Maryland, November 24, 1864. Released at Point Lookout on May 14, 1865, after taking the Oath of Allegiance.

WILSON, ALLEN, Private
Born in Sampson County and resided in Johnston County where he was by occupation a farmer prior to enlisting in Johnston County at age 28, February 28, 1862. Died near Raleigh on May 6, 1862, of disease.

WOODALL, JAMES D., Private
Born in Johnston County where he resided as a farmer prior to enlisting in Johnston County at age 31, March 14, 1862. Reported present through August, 1862. Deserted on December 14, 1862, but was apprehended the next day. Reported present but sick in camp in September-October, 1863. Returned to duty in November-December, 1863. Reported absent sick in January-February, 1864. Reported in hospital at Raleigh in July-August, 1864. Hospitalized at Raleigh on November 6, 1864, with intermittent fever. Returned to duty on December 16, 1864. Survived the war.

YELVINGTON, BENNETT, Private
Born in Johnston County where he resided as a farmer prior to enlisting in Johnston County at age 44, February 27, 1862. Reported absent without leave through August, 1862. Returned to duty on an unspecified date. Reported present from September, 1863, through February, 1864. Also reported present in July-August and November-December, 1864.

YELVINGTON, RANSOM H., Sergeant
Born in Johnston County where he resided as a farmer prior to enlisting in Johnston County at age 26, February 25, 1862. Mustered in as Sergeant. Reported absent in hospital on or about June 30, 1862. Returned to duty prior to September 1, 1862. Reported present but sick in camp in September-October, 1863. Hospitalized at Wilmington on November 9, 1863, with acute diarrhoea. Returned to duty on November 28, 1863. Reported present in January-February, 1864. Appointed Ensign (2nd Lieutenant) in March, 1864, and transferred to the Field and Staff of this regiment.

YOUNGBLOOD, D. H., Private
Previously served in an unspecified unit. First listed in the records of this company in July-August, 1864, when he was reported present. Also reported present in November-December, 1864.

COMPANY D

This company was raised in Johnston County and enlisted in Johnston County in March-April, 1862. It was mustered into state service at Camp Mangum, near Raleigh, on April 21, 1862, and assigned to the 50th Regiment N.C. Troops as Company D. After joining the regiment the company functioned as a part of the regiment, and its history for the remainder of the war is reported as a part of the regimental history.

The information contained in the following roster was compiled primarily from a company muster-in and descriptive roll dated April 21, 1862, and from company muster rolls for May 1-August 31, 1862; November 1-December 31, 1862; September 1, 1863-February 29, 1864; July 1-August 31, 1864; and October 31-December 31, 1864. No company muster rolls were located for September 1-October 31, 1862; January 1-August 31, 1863; March 1-June 30, 1864; September 1-October 30, 1864; or for the period after December 31, 1864. Valuable information was obtained from primary records such as the North Carolina adjutant general's *Roll of Honor*, discharge certificates, medical records, prisoner of war records, *The War of the Rebellion: A Compilation of the Official Records of the Union and Confederate Armies*, militia records, newspaper casualty lists and obituaries, Confederate pension applications filed with the state of North Carolina, and the 1860 federal census of North Carolina. Secondary sources such as postwar rosters and histories, cemetery records, the *Confederate Veteran*, published genealogies, and records of the United Daughters of the Confederacy also provided useful information.

OFFICERS

CAPTAINS

RYALS, HENRY J.
Born in Johnston County where he resided as a farmer prior to enlisting at age 28. Appointed Captain on March 4, 1862. Reported present or accounted for through August, 1862. Reported present in December, 1862, and September, 1863-January, 1864. Reported on picket duty at Virginia Creek on Topsail Sound in February, 1864. Appointed Major on April 11, 1864, and transferred to the Field and Staff of this regiment.

BEST, WILLIAM BRIGHT
Previously served as Sergeant in Company H, 2nd Regiment N.C. State Troops. Transferred to this company upon appointment as 2nd Lieutenant on June 6, 1862. Reported present through August, 1862. Promoted to 1st Lieutenant on October 15, 1862. Reported present in November-December, 1862. Reported in hospital at Wilmington on April 30, 1863, with catarrh. Returned to duty on an unspecified date. Reported present in September-December, 1863. Placed under arrest on February 28, 1864. Reason he was arrested not reported.

Released from confinement on an unspecified date. Promoted to Captain on April 11, 1864. Reported present in July-August, 1864. Hospitalized at Charlotte on February 14, 1865. Transferred to hospital at Raleigh on February 15, 1865. Admitted to hospital at Greensboro on February 18, 1865. Paroled at Salisbury on May 16, 1865.

LIEUTENANTS

ADAMS, WILLIAM M., 3rd Lieutenant
Born in Johnston County where he resided as a farmer prior to enlisting in Johnston County at age 40, March 22, 1862. Mustered in as Corporal. Reduced to ranks prior to July 1, 1862. Promoted to Corporal on July 11, 1862. Reported present through August, 1862. Elected 3rd Lieutenant on December 20, 1862. Reported present in November, 1863-February, 1864, and July-August, 1864. Was granted a sick furlough of thirty days on September 30, 1864. No further records.

LEE, YOUNG J., 2nd Lieutenant
Born in Johnston County where he resided as a farmer. Appointed 2nd Lieutenant on March 4, 1862. Resigned on May 24, 1862. Resignation accepted on May 26, 1862. Reason he resigned not reported.

MASSEY, JOHN D., 2nd Lieutenant
Previously served as Private in Company C of this regiment. Also served for a time as acting Commissary Sergeant of this regiment. Elected 2nd Lieutenant and transferred to this company on June 15, 1864. Reported present in November-December, 1864. Paroled at Goldsboro on May 8, 1865.

PENNY, JOSEPH JAMES, 1st Lieutenant
Resided in Johnston County where he enlisted at age 19, May 5, 1862, for the war. Mustered in as Private. Promoted to Sergeant on May 15, 1862. Reduced to ranks on June 30, 1862. Promoted to Sergeant on August 14, 1862. Reported present in November-December, 1862. Appointed 2nd Lieutenant on October 20, 1863. Reported present in September, 1863-February, 1864. Promoted to 1st Lieutenant on May 13, 1864. Reported present in July-August and November-December, 1864. Last reported present in February, 1865.

NONCOMMISSIONED OFFICERS AND PRIVATES

ADAMS, ALSEY, Private
Resided in Johnston County and enlisted at age 38, February 25, 1863, for the war. Reported present in September, 1863-February, 1864. Also reported present in July-August and November-December, 1864. [May have served previously as Private in Company K, 27th Regiment N.C. Troops.]

ADAMS, HINTON C., Private
Resided in Johnston County where he enlisted at age 18, February 25, 1863, for the war. Reported present in September, 1863-February, 1864, and July-August, 1864. Reported absent sick in November-December, 1864. Hospitalized at Charlotte on January 15, 1865, with debilitas. Furloughed on January 17, 1865.

ADAMS, JAMES E., Private
Born in Harnett County* where he resided prior to enlisting in Wake County at age 20, May 14, 1862, for the war. Died in hospital at Raleigh on June 11, 1862, of "congestion of lungs."

ADAMS, JOSEPH E., Sergeant
Resided in Harnett County and enlisted in Johnston County at age 28, April 14, 1862. Mustered in as Private. Promoted to Sergeant on May 15, 1862. Reported present on surviving company muster rolls from May, 1862, through December, 1864. Survived the war.

ADAMS, WILLIAM HENRY, Private
Resided in Harnett County and enlisted in Wake County at age 20, May 14, 1862, for the war. Reported present or accounted for on surviving company muster rolls from May, 1862, through December, 1864. Survived the war.

ALLEN, JULIUS, Private
Resided in Johnston County where he enlisted at age 17, January 15, 1863, for the war as a substitute. Reported present in September, 1863-February, 1864. Also reported present in July-August and November-December, 1864.

ALLEN, LOVIT GREEN, Musician
Resided in Johnston County where he enlisted at age 18, January 15, 1863, for the war. Mustered in as Private. Appointed Musician in November-December, 1863. Reported present in September, 1863-February, 1864. Also reported present in July-August and November-December, 1864. Survived the war.

ALLEN, RANSOM G., Private
Resided in Johnston County and was by occupation a farmer prior to enlisting in Johnston County at age 38, February 25, 1863, for the war. Reported present in September, 1863-February, 1864, and July-August, 1864. Captured at Savannah, Georgia, December 21, 1864. Sent to Hilton Head, South Carolina. Transferred to Fort Delaware, Delaware, where he arrived on March 12, 1865. Released at Fort Delaware on June 19, 1865, after taking the Oath of Allegiance. Hospitalized at City Point, Virginia, June 23, 1865, with "chron[ic] diarrhoea." Died at City Point on July 4, 1865.

ALLEN, SIR WILLIAM, Private
Born in Johnston County where he resided as a farmer prior to enlisting in Johnston County at age 42, March 4, 1862. Mustered in as Sergeant. Reduced to ranks on July 16, 1862. Reported present through August, 1862. Also reported present in November-December, 1862. Discharged on or about February 15, 1863, after providing a substitute.

ALLEN, W. H., Corporal
Resided in Johnston County where he enlisted at age 29, January 18, 1863, for the war. Mustered in as Private. Promoted to Corporal in June, 1863. Reported present in September, 1863-February, 1864. Also reported present in July-August and November-December, 1864.

BAKER, ALLEN R., Private
Born in Johnston County where he resided as a farmer prior to enlisting in Johnston County at age 31, March 24, 1862. Reported absent without leave through August, 1862. Reported for duty on an unspecified date but deserted at Drewry's Bluff, Virginia, December 13, 1862. Returned to duty on an unspecified date. Reported present in September, 1863-February, 1864. Also reported present in July-August and November-December, 1864. Survived the war.

BAKER, JONATHAN, Private
Born in Johnston County where he resided as a farmer prior to enlisting in Johnston County at age 33, May 5, 1862, for the war. Reported present through August, 1862. Deserted from camp near Drewry's Bluff, Virginia, December 13, 1862. Returned to duty on an unspecified date. Reported present in September, 1863-February, 1864. Also reported present in July-August and November-December, 1864. Survived the war.

BAKER, MATTHEW M., Private
Born in Johnston County where he resided as a farmer prior to enlisting in Johnston County at age 25, April 1, 1862. Reported absent without leave through June, 1862. Reported for duty prior to September 1, 1862. Deserted at camp near Drewry's Bluff, Virginia, December 13, 1862. Returned to duty on an unspecified date. Reported present in September, 1863-February, 1864. Also reported present in July-August and November-December, 1864.

BARBER, JESSE M., Corporal
Born in Johnston County where he resided prior to enlisting in Johnston County at age 18, April 27, 1862, for the war. Mustered in as Private. Promoted to Corporal on June 10 or July 10, 1862. Reported present on surviving company muster rolls from May, 1862, through December, 1864.

BARBER, W. G., Private
Resided in Johnston County where he enlisted at age 44, August 20, 1863, for the war. Reported present in September, 1863-February, 1864. Also reported present in July-August and November-December, 1864.

BAREFOOT, BYTHAN B., Private
Born in Johnston County where he resided as a farmer prior to enlisting in Craven County at age 31, March 8, 1862. Enlisted in Company E, 24th Regiment N.C. Troops (14th Regiment N.C. Volunteers), March 18, 1862.

BEASLEY, EPHRAIM OXFORD, Private
Born in Johnston County where he resided as a farmer prior to enlisting in Johnston County at age 35, March 4, 1862. Mustered in as Sergeant. Reduced to ranks prior to July 1, 1862. Reported present through August, 1862.

Deserted from camp at Drewry's Bluff, Virginia, December 13, 1862. Court-martialed on June 18, 1863, for desertion and sentenced to be shot. Sentence remitted. Returned to duty on an unspecified date. Reported present in September, 1863-February, 1864. Also reported present in July-August and November-December, 1864. Survived the war.

BENSON, JOHN U., Private
Resided in Johnston County where he enlisted at age 22, October 3, 1862, for the war. Reported present in November-December, 1862, and September, 1863-February, 1864. Also reported present in July-August and November-December, 1864. Survived the war.

BLACKMAN, H. S., Private
Place and date of enlistment not reported; however, he probably enlisted in September-October, 1864. Captured near Plymouth on October 31, 1864. Confined at Fort Monroe, Virginia. Transferred to Point Lookout, Maryland, November 24, 1864. Paroled at Point Lookout on February 10, 1865. Received at Cox's Wharf, James River, Virginia, on or about February 14, 1865, for exchange.

BLACKMON, ASHLEY, Private
Born in Johnston County where he resided as a farmer prior to enlisting in Wake County at age 34, March 17, 1862. Present or accounted for through August, 1862. Deserted at camp near Drewry's Bluff, Virginia, November 18, 1862. Court-martialed on June 22, 1863, for desertion and sentenced to be shot. Sentence remitted. Returned to duty on an unspecified date. Reported present in September, 1863-February, 1864. Also reported present in July-August and November-December, 1864.

BLACKMON, RICHARD J., Private
Resided in Johnston County where he enlisted at age 17, April 27, 1862, for the war. Reported absent on detached service at Petersburg, Virginia, on or about August 31, 1862. Hospitalized at Petersburg on December 20, 1862, with an unspecified complaint. Returned to duty on an unspecified date. Reported present in September-October, 1863. Hospitalized at Wilmington on November 28, 1863, with acute rheumatism. Furloughed for sixty days on January 4, 1864. Hospitalized at Goldsboro on an unspecified date. Returned to duty on June 14, 1864. Reported present in July-August, 1864. Captured in Tyrrell County on September 29, 1864. Confined at Fort Monroe, Virginia. Transferred to Point Lookout, Maryland, November 24, 1864. Paroled on an unspecified date. Reported at Camp Lee, near Richmond, Virginia, on or about February 20, 1865.

BLEVINS, HARRISON, _____
North Carolina pension records indicate that he served in this company.

BRYANT, MAJOR, Private
Born in Harnett County* and resided in Johnston County where he was by occupation a farmer prior to enlisting in Wake County at age 21, March 13, 1862. Hospitalized at or near Petersburg, Virginia, July 26, 1862, with

debility. Returned to duty on September 1, 1862. Reported sick at home in November-December, 1862. Returned to duty on an unspecified date. Reported present in September, 1863-February, 1864. Also reported present in July-August and November-December, 1864.

BYRD, NEEDHAM T., Private
Born in Johnston County where he resided as a farmer prior to enlisting in Johnston County at age 22, March 14, 1862. Discharged on May 12, 1862, by reason of "inability."

CALLAWAY, JAMES M., _____
North Carolina pension records indicate that he served in this company.

CLIFTON, G. W., Private
Enlisted at Camp Holmes, near Raleigh, November 29, 1863, for the war. Reported present in July-August and November-December, 1864.

CLIFTON, GEORGE B., Private
Resided in Johnston County where he enlisted at age 18, February 25, 1863, for the war. Reported present in September, 1863-February, 1864. Also reported present in July-August and November-December, 1864. Survived the war.

CLIFTON, JAMES H., Private
Resided in Johnston County where he enlisted at age 30, October 9, 1862, for the war. Hospitalized at or near Petersburg, Virginia, November 5, 1862, with rheumatism. Transferred to hospital at Farmville, Virginia, on or about April 11, 1863. Returned to duty on April 22, 1863. Reported present in September, 1863-February, 1864. Also reported present in July-August and November-December, 1864. Paroled at Raleigh on May 18, 1865.

CLIFTON, JOEL R., Private
Resided in Johnston County where he enlisted at age 23, May 5, 1862, for the war. Reported present through June 30, 1862. Furloughed from hospital at Petersburg, Virginia, July 6, 1862. Reported absent sick at Petersburg on or about August 31, 1862. Reported at home on sick furlough in November-December, 1862. Reported present in September, 1863-February, 1864. Reported on detail as a teamster at Wilmington in July-August, 1864. Reported sick in hospital in November-December, 1864.

COATS, D. A., Private
Enlisted in Washington County on June 19, 1864, for the war. Reported present in July-August and November-December, 1864. Hospitalized at Charlotte on February 13, 1865, with chronic diarrhoea. Transferred to another hospital on February 18, 1865.

COATS, P. P., Private
Previously served as Private in Mallett's N.C. Battalion (Camp Guard). Transferred to this company on an unspecified date (probably in March-August, 1864). Reported present on or about August 31, 1864. Reported sick in hospital in November-December, 1864.

CRAWFORD, W. H., Private
Enlisted in Johnston County on January 1, 1864, for the war. Reported present through February, 1864. Died on June 21, 1864, of disease. Place of death not reported.

CREECH, EZEKIEL, Private
Born in Johnston County where he resided as a farmer prior to enlisting in Johnston County at age 20, March 4, 1862. Enlisted in Company I, 24th Regiment N.C. Troops (14th Regiment N.C. Volunteers), May 4, 1862.

CREECH, JAMES W., Corporal
Born in Johnston County where he resided as a farmer prior to enlisting in Johnston County at age 18, March 4, 1862. Mustered in as Corporal. Reported present through August 31, 1862. Also reported present in November-December, 1862, and September, 1863-February, 1864. Reported on detail to escort prisoners to Goldsboro in July-August, 1864. Reported present in November-December, 1864. Hospitalized at Greensboro on February 20, 1865, with catarrh. Transferred to another hospital on February 23, 1865.

CREECH, ROBERT G., Private
Born in Johnston County where he resided as a farmer prior to enlisting at age 25, March 4, 1862. Mustered in as Sergeant. Promoted to 1st Sergeant prior to July 1, 1862. Reduced to ranks on July 11, 1862. Reported present through August, 1862. Also reported present in November-December, 1862. Discharged on February 12, 1863, after providing a substitute.

CREECH, ROMULUS H., Private
Born in Johnston County where he resided as a farmer prior to enlisting in Wake County at age 16, April 16, 1862, for the war. Discharged on May 12, 1862, by reason of "inability."

DAVIS, ELISHA, _____
North Carolina pension records indicate that he served in this company.

DICKENS, J. K., Private
Enlisted at Camp Holmes, near Raleigh, at age 20, August 27, 1863, for the war. Reported present in July-August and November-December, 1864. Survived the war.

DOWDEN, EZEKIEL, Private
Born in Johnston County where he resided as a farmer prior to enlisting in Johnston County at age 24, April 8, 1862. Died at Raleigh on or about May 28, 1862. Cause of death not reported.

DUNN, SAMPSON, Private
Born in Johnston County where he resided as a farmer prior to enlisting in Johnston County at age 19, March 4, 1862. Reported present through August, 1862. Discharged on October 14, 1862, by reason of "phthisis pulmonalis in its incipient stage. . . ."

DUNN, SIR WILLIAM, Private
Born in Johnston County where he resided as a farmer prior to enlisting at age 24, March 17, 1862. Died in

hospital at Petersburg, Virginia, July 31, 1862, of "febris typhoides."

EDWARDS, JESSE, Private
Born in Johnston County where he resided as a farmer prior to enlisting in Johnston County at age 20, March 4, 1862. Reported present on surviving company muster rolls from May, 1862, through December, 1864. Survived the war.

EDWARDS, NICHOLAS, Private
Born in Johnston County where he resided as a farmer prior to enlisting in Johnston County at age 21, March 4, 1862. Reported present through August, 1862, and in November-December, 1862. Hospitalized at Wilmington on September 2, 1863, with continued fever. Returned to duty on September 9, 1863. Reported present through February, 1864. Also reported present in July-August, 1864. Reported sick in hospital in November-December, 1864. Survived the war.

ENNIS, JOHN ALLEN, Private
Resided in Johnston County and was by occupation a farmer prior to enlisting in Johnston County at age 42, September 4, 1863, for the war. Reported present through February, 1864. Also reported present in July-August, 1864. Reported sick in hospital in November-December, 1864.

ENNIS, LEVI, Private
Previously served as Private in Mallett's N.C. Battalion (Camp Guard). Transferred to this company on an unspecified date (probably in March-August, 1864). Reported present on or about August 31, 1864. Also reported present in November-December, 1864.

GUIN, JOHN, Private
Born in Johnston County where he resided as a farmer prior to enlisting in Johnston County at age 21, March 4, 1862. Reported absent without leave through June 30, 1862. Reported for duty prior to September 1, 1862. Reported present in November-December, 1862, and September, 1863-February, 1864. Also reported present in July-August and November-December, 1864. Survived the war.

HAYS, JOHN H., Private
Enlisted in Johnston County on March 26, 1864, for the war. Reported on picket duty in July-August, 1864. Died on September 21, 1864. Place and cause of death not reported.

HOLLY, DAVID, Private
Born in Sampson or Johnston County and resided in Johnston County where he was by occupation a farmer prior to enlisting in Johnston County at age 28, March 4, 1862. Deserted on May 20, 1862. Apprehended on September 5, 1862. Court-martialed and sentenced "to receive fifty lashes on his bare back, and to be branded in the left hand with the letter 'D' in presence of the Brigade to which he belongs and to be in close confinement for thirty days, the first and last ten days on bread and water. . . ." Died in North Carolina on or about August 9, 1863, of "febris typhoid."

HOLLY, JOHN C., Private
Born in Sampson County and resided in Johnston County where he was by occupation a farmer prior to enlisting in Johnston County at age 38, March 4, 1862. Discharged on May 2, 1862, by reason of "inability."

HOLMES, BRAZIL, Private
Enlisted in Washington County on August 3, 1864, for the war. Reported present on or about August 31, 1864. Reported absent without leave in November-December, 1864. Survived the war.

HOLMES, FREDERICK, Private
Born in Johnston County where he resided as a farmer prior to enlisting in Craven County at age 52, March 8, 1862. Reported present through August, 1862. Also reported present in November-December, 1862, and September-December, 1863. Reported absent on sick furlough in January-February, 1864. Reported absent without leave on July 2, 1864. Discharged on September 30, 1864, by reason of "chronic rheumatism, old age & general debility."

HOLMES, JAMES W., Private
Born in Johnston County where he resided as a farmer prior to enlisting in Johnston County at age 18, March 14, 1862. Reported present in May-August and November-December, 1862. Also reported present in September, 1863-February, 1864, and July-August, 1864. Reported absent without leave in November-December, 1864.

HOLMES, JOHN, SR., Private
Resided in Johnston County where he enlisted at age 43, September 4, 1863, for the war. Reported present through February, 1864. Also reported present in July-August, 1864. Reported absent sick with leave in November-December, 1864.

HOLMES, JOHN H., JR., Private
Born in Johnston County where he resided as a farmer prior to enlisting in Johnston County at age 20, March 12, 1862. Reported present through August, 1862. Deserted at camp near Drewry's Bluff, Virginia, December 13, 1862. Returned to duty on an unspecified date. Reported present in September, 1863-February, 1864. Deserted at Plymouth on August 18, 1864.

HOLMES, JOHN W., Private
Born in Johnston County where he resided as a farmer prior to enlisting in Craven County at age 22, March 8, 1862. Reported absent without leave through June, 1862. Reported for duty prior to September 1, 1862. Deserted from camp near Drewry's Bluff, Virginia, December 13, 1862. Returned to duty on an unspecified date. Reported present in September-December, 1863, and January-February, 1864. Detailed "to boat corn" in Hyde County in July-August, 1864. Survived the war.

INGRAM, ISAAC, Private
Born in Johnston County where he resided as a farmer prior to enlisting in Johnston County at age 38, April 8, 1862. Reported absent without leave through June, 1862. Reported for duty prior to September 1, 1862. Deserted

at camp near Drewry's Bluff, Virginia, November 18, 1862. Returned to duty on an unspecified date. Reported present in September, 1863-February, 1864, and July-August, 1864. Hospitalized at Raleigh on November 6, 1864, with chronic rheumatism. Transferred to another hospital on January 1, 1865.

INGRAM, NATHAN, Private
Resided in Johnston County and enlisted in Wake County at age 19, March 13, 1862. Reported present through June, 1862. Hospitalized at or near Petersburg, Virginia, July 26, 1862, with bronchitis. Returned to duty on September 17, 1862. Reported present in November-December, 1862, and September, 1863-February, 1864. Also reported present in July-August and November-December, 1864. Hospitalized at Raleigh on February 18, 1865, with general debility. Transferred to another hospital on February 24, 1865. Paroled at Greensboro on May 2, 1865.

JERNIGAN, JESSE L., Private
Resided in Johnston County and was by occupation a farmer prior to enlisting in Johnston County at age 33, October 9, 1862, for the war. Reported present in November-December, 1862, and September, 1863-February, 1864. Furloughed for ten days on July 17, 1864. Reported present in November-December, 1864.

JERNIGAN, L. M., Private
Enlisted in Johnston County on March 18, 1864, for the war. Reported present in July-August, 1864. Reported absent without leave in November-December, 1864.

JOHNSON, A. L., Private
Enlisted in Johnston County on March 26, 1864, for the war. Reported present in July-August, 1864. Reported sick in hospital in November-December, 1864.

JOHNSON, THOMAS, Private
Resided in Johnston County and enlisted at age 18, February 25, 1863, for the war. Reported present in September, 1863-February, 1864. Reported on picket duty in July-August, 1864. Died prior to December 20, 1864. Place, date, and cause of death not reported.

JONES, DAVID H., Private
Resided in Johnston County where he enlisted at age 25, May 5, 1862, for the war. Reported present through June, 1862. Reported absent sick at Petersburg, Virginia, on or about August 31, 1862. Reported at home on sick furlough in November-December, 1862. Returned to duty on an unspecified date. Reported present in September, 1863-February, 1864, and July-August, 1864. Reported sick in hospital in November-December, 1864.

JONES, GEORGE W., _____
North Carolina pension records indicate that he served in this company.

JONES, JASON, Private
Born in Johnston County where he resided as a farmer prior to enlisting in Johnston County at age 17, April 5, 1862. Reported present on August 31, 1862, and in

November-December, 1862. Died in hospital at Wilson on April 24, 1863, of "ty[phoid] fever."

KING, D. C., Private
Enlisted at Camp Holmes, near Raleigh, October 12, 1863, for the war. Reported present in July-August, 1864. Reported absent sick in November-December, 1864.

KING, GEORGE G., Private
Resided in Johnston County where he enlisted at age 40, February 25, 1863, for the war. Reported present in September, 1863-February, 1864, and July-August, 1864. Captured at or near Savannah, Georgia, December 10, 1864. Sent to Hilton Head, South Carolina. Confined at Point Lookout, Maryland, February 1, 1865. Released at Point Lookout on June 28, 1865, after taking the Oath of Allegiance.

LANGDON, E. H., Private
Previously served as Private in Company F, Mallett's N.C. Battalion (Camp Guard). Transferred to this company on an unspecified date (probably in March-August, 1864). Reported sick in hospital in November-December, 1864. Died at or near Charleston, South Carolina, February 9, 1865. Cause of death not reported.

LANGDON, J. H., Private
Previously served as Private in Company F, Mallett's N.C. Battalion (Camp Guard). Transferred to this company on an unspecified date (probably in March-August, 1864). Reported present on or about August 31, 1864. Reported sick in hospital in November-December, 1864. Survived the war.

LANDGON, JACOB M., Private
Previously served as Private in Company F, Mallett's N.C. Battalion (Camp Guard). Transferred to this company on an unspecified date (probably in March-August, 1864). Reported present in November-December, 1864. Survived the war.

LEE, B. R., Private
Resided in Johnston County where he enlisted at age 38, February 25, 1863, for the war. Reported present in September, 1863-February, 1864, and July-August, 1864. Hospitalized at Raleigh on November 6, 1864, with remittent fever and diarrhoea. Transferred to another hospital on January 1, 1865.

LEE, EDWARD, Sergeant
Resided in Johnston County and was by occupation a farm laborer prior to enlisting in Johnston County at age 25, April 19, 1862, for the war. Mustered in as Private. Promoted to Corporal prior to July 1, 1862. Reduced to ranks on July 11, 1862. Promoted to Corporal on August 14, 1862. Present or accounted for through August, 1862. Also reported present in November-December, 1862. Promoted to Sergeant on October 20, 1863. Reported present in September, 1863-February, 1864, and July-August, 1864. Hospitalized at Wilmington on November 25, 1864, with pneumonia. Returned to duty on December 2, 1864. Survived the war.

LEE, J. W., _____
North Carolina pension records indicate that he served in this company.

LEE, JAMES, Private
Resided in Johnston County where he enlisted at age 17, February 12, 1863, for the war as a substitute. Reported present in September, 1863-February, 1864. Deserted at Plymouth on or about August 18, 1864. Rejoined the company on September 26, 1864. Reported present in November-December, 1864.

LEE, JERRY A., Private
Born in Johnston County where he resided as a farmer prior to enlisting in Johnston County at age 28, March 4, 1862. Reported present through August, 1862. Deserted from camp near Drewry's Bluff, Virginia, November 18, 1862. Returned to duty on an unspecified date. Reported present in September, 1863-February, 1864. Deserted at Plymouth on August 7, 1864.

LEE, JOHN, JR., Private
Enlisted in Johnston County on February 2, 1864, for the war. Reported present in July-August, 1864. Reported sick in hospital at Wilson in November-December, 1864.

LEE, JOHN J., Private
Enlisted in Johnston County at age 19, February 2, 1864, for the war. Reported present in July-August and November-December, 1864. Survived the war.

LEE, WILLIAM H., Private
Born in Cumberland County and resided in Johnston County where he was by occupation a farmer prior to enlisting in Johnston County at age 18, March 24, 1862. Reported present through August, 1862. Deserted from camp near Drewry's Bluff, Virginia, December 13, 1862. Returned to duty on an unspecified date. Reported present in September, 1863-February, 1864. Deserted at Plymouth on August 18, 1864. Returned to duty on September 26, 1864. Reported present in November-December, 1864. Hospitalized at Greensboro on February 20, 1865, with catarrhus. Transferred to another hospital on February 22, 1865.

LUCAS, WILLIAM, Private
Resided in Johnston County where he enlisted at age 42, September 4, 1863, for the war. Reported present in September-October, 1863. Hospitalized at Wilmington on December 21, 1863, with irritatis spinalis. Returned to duty on January 19, 1864. Hospitalized at Wilmington on January 29, 1864, with debilitas. Returned to duty on February 24, 1864. Sent home on sick furlough on March 8, 1864. Reported absent on sick furlough through August, 1864. Reported absent without leave in November-December, 1864.

MASSENGILL, JOEL HENRY, Sergeant
Born in Johnston County where he resided as a farmer prior to enlisting in Johnston County at age 30, March 8, 1862. Mustered in as Corporal. Promoted to Sergeant on July 11, 1862. Reported present or accounted for through August, 1862. Also reported present in

November-December, 1862. Reported absent on sick furlough in September, 1863-February, 1864. Returned to duty on an unspecified date. Reported present in July-August, 1864. Hospitalized at Raleigh on November 6, 1864, with chronic diarrhoea. Returned to duty on November 22, 1864. Reported absent without leave in December, 1864. Survived the war. [Previously served as 1st Lieutenant in the 41st Regiment N.C. Militia.]

MASSINGILL, HENRY, Private
Enlisted in Johnston County at age 19, March 16, 1864, for the war. Reported present in July-August, 1864. Reported sick in hospital in November-December, 1864. Hospitalized at Greensboro on February 20, 1865, with phthisis pulmonalis. Transferred to another hospital on February 22, 1865. Survived the war.

MASSINGILL, NEEDHAM G., 1st Sergeant
Born in Johnston County where he resided as a farmer prior to enlisting in Johnston County at age 36, March 8, 1862. Mustered in as Sergeant. Promoted to 1st Sergeant on July 11, 1862. Reported present through June, 1862. Reported absent sick at Petersburg, Virginia, on or about August 31, 1862. Returned to duty on an unspecified date. Reported present in November-December, 1862, and September, 1863-February, 1864. Also reported present in July-August and November-December, 1864.

MASSINGILL, WILLIAM R., Private
Born in Johnston County where he resided as a farmer prior to enlisting at age 18, March 13, 1862. Enlisted as Private in Company E, 24th Regiment N.C. Troops (14th Regiment N.C. Volunteers), March 18, 1862.

MOORE, HAYWOOD, Private
Born in Johnston County where he resided as a farmer prior to enlisting in Johnston County at age 26, March 4, 1862. Reported absent without leave through June, 1862. Returned to duty prior to September 1, 1862. Deserted from camp near Drewry's Bluff, Virginia, December 13, 1862. Returned to duty on an unspecified date. Reported present in September, 1863-February, 1864, and July-August, 1864. Also reported present in November-December, 1864. Paroled at Raleigh on May 11, 1865.

MOORE, JOHN, Private
Born in Harnett County* and resided in Johnston County where he was by occupation a farmer prior to enlisting in Johnston County at age 28, March 4, 1862. Discharged on April 12, 1862, by reason of "inability."

MOORE, LEVI, Private
Born in Johnston County where he resided as a farmer prior to enlisting in Johnston County at age 21, March 8, 1862. Died at home in Johnston County on or about May 24, 1862, of disease.

MOORE, WALTER R., Private
Born in Johnston County where he resided as a farmer prior to enlisting in Johnston County at age 24, March 8, 1862. Reported present through August, 1862. Deserted from camp near Drewry's Bluff, Virginia,

December 13, 1862. Company records do not indicate that he returned to duty. Paroled at Raleigh on May 11, 1865.

MORGAN, JACKSON, Private
Born in Johnston County where he resided as a farmer prior to enlisting in Johnston County at age 20, March 14, 1862. Reported present through August, 1862. Died in hospital at Petersburg, Virginia, January 12, 1863, of "bronchitis chronica."

NORRIS, AMOS, _____
North Carolina pension records indicate that he served in this company.

PARKER, REDMOND, Private
Born in Edgecombe County and resided in Johnston County where he was by occupation a farmer prior to enlisting in Johnston County at age 28, April 8, 1862. Hospitalized at Richmond, Virginia, August 22, 1862, with chronic diarrhoea. Returned to duty on August 26, 1862. Reported present in November-December, 1862. Detailed as a teamster on October 17, 1862. Reported present with the company in November, 1863-February, 1864. Also reported present in July-August and November-December, 1864.

PARKER, YOUNG E., Private
Enlisted in Johnston County on March 19, 1864, for the war. Deserted at Plymouth on August 18, 1864. Returned from desertion on November 28, 1864. Survived the war.

PARRISH, JAMES, Private
Resided in Johnston County and was by occupation a farmer prior to enlisting at Camp Holmes, near Raleigh, at age 40, September 12, 1863, for the war. Reported present in July-August and November-December, 1864.

PARRISH, RANSOM, Private
Resided in Johnston County and was by occupation a farmer prior to enlisting at Camp Holmes, near Raleigh, at age 42, October 12, 1863, for the war. Reported present in July-August, 1864. Reported sick in hospital in November-December, 1864.

POLLARD, BENJAMIN J., Private
Born in Johnston County where he resided as a farmer prior to enlisting in Johnston County at age 19, March 14, 1862. Hospitalized at or near Petersburg, Virginia, July 26, 1862, with debility. Returned to duty on August 18, 1862. Reported present in November-December, 1862, and September, 1863-February, 1864. Also reported present in July-August, 1864. Hospitalized at Raleigh on November 6, 1864, with intermittent fever. Furloughed for sixty days on November 14, 1864. Survived the war.

POLLARD, SAMUEL J., Musician
Born in Wake County and resided in Johnston County where he was by occupation a farmer prior to enlisting in Johnston County at age 32, March 4, 1862. Mustered in as Sergeant. Reduced to ranks on an unspecified date. Appointed Musician on July 30, 1862. Reported present through August, 1862. Deserted from camp near Drewry's Bluff, Virginia, December 13, 1862. Returned to duty on

an unspecified date. Reported present in September-October, 1863. Reported sick at home in November, 1863-February, 1864. Reported present in July-August, 1864. Reported sick in hospital in November-December, 1864. Survived the war.

POLLARD, W. H., _____
North Carolina pension records indicate that he served in this company.

POPE, JERRY, Private
Born in Johnston County where he resided as a farmer prior to enlisting in Johnston County at age 24, March 14, 1862. Reported present through August, 1862. Reported sick in hospital at Petersburg, Virginia, in November-December, 1862. Returned to duty on an unspecified date. Reported present in September, 1863-February, 1864. Also reported present in July-August and November-December, 1864. Survived the war.

PULLIAM, JAMES, _____
North Carolina pension records indicate that he served in this company.

ROOPE, KING M., _____
North Carolina pension records indicate that he served in this company.

RYALS, JOHN W., Private
Resided in Johnston County and was by occupation a cooper prior to enlisting in Johnston County on February 2, 1864, for the war. Reported present in July-August, 1864. Reported sick in hospital in November-December, 1864. Survived the war.

RYALS, RICHARD B., Private
Born in Johnston County where he resided as a farmer prior to enlisting in Craven County at age 36, March 8, 1862. Mustered in as Corporal. Reduced to ranks on June 10, 1862. Reported present through August, 1862. Reported absent sick in hospital in November-December, 1862. Reported absent on sick furlough in September-December, 1863. Returned to duty in January-February, 1864. Reported present in July-August and November-December, 1864. Hospitalized at Charlotte on February 6, 1865, with chronic diarrhoea. Transferred to another hospital the same date. Paroled at Raleigh on May 22, 1865.

RYALS, WILLIAM M., Private
Resided in Johnston County and was by occupation a farmer prior to enlisting in Johnston County at age 32, September 4, 1863, for the war. Reported present through February, 1864. Also reported present in July-August, 1864. Hospitalized at Raleigh on November 6, 1864, with intermittent fever and acute diarrhoea. Furloughed for sixty days on December 22, 1864.

SANDERS, ASHLEY S., Private
Born in Johnston County where he resided as a farmer prior to enlisting in Johnston County at age 25, March 8, 1862. Died in Johnston County on or about June 6, 1862, of disease.

STANLY, ELIJAH, Private

Resided in Johnston County and enlisted in Wake County at age 23, May 15, 1862, for the war. Reported present through August, 1862. Deserted from camp near Drewry's Bluff, Virginia, November 18, 1862. Returned to duty on an unspecified date. Reported present in September, 1863-February, 1864. Also reported present in July-August and November-December, 1864. Paroled at Raleigh on May 15, 1865. Survived the war.

STANLY, GIDEON, Private

Previously served as Private in Company D, 31st Regiment N.C. Troops. Enlisted in this company in Johnston County on February 25, 1863, for the war. Reported present in September, 1863-February, 1864. Also reported present in July-August and November-December, 1864. Survived the war.

STANLY, NICHOLAS, Private

Previously served as Private in Company D, 31st Regiment N.C. Troops. Enlisted in this company in Johnston County February 10, 1863, for the war. Hospitalized at Wilmington on August 29, 1863, with typhoid fever. Returned to duty on September 2, 1863. Hospitalized at Wilmington on November 27, 1863, with ascites. Returned to duty on December 1, 1863. Reported sick at home in January-February, 1864. Discharged from service on July 30, 1864. Reason discharged not reported. Paroled at Raleigh on May 15, 1865.

STEPHENSON, J. E., Private

Previously served as Private in Mallett's N.C. Battalion (Camp Guard). Transferred to this company on an unspecified date (probably in March-August, 1864). Hospitalized at Raleigh on November 6, 1864, with intermittent fever. Returned to duty on November 22, 1864. Reported absent without leave on or about December 31, 1864. Took the Oath of Allegiance at Raleigh on June 2, 1865.

STEPHENSON, JONATHAN, Private

Resided in Johnston County where he enlisted at age 38, February 13, 1863, for the war. Reported present in September, 1863-February, 1864. Also reported present in July-August, 1864. Reported sick in hospital in November-December, 1864. [North Carolina pension records indicate that he died at Columbia, South Carolina, in the spring of 1865.]

STEPHENSON, MANLY, Private

Resided in Johnston County and was by occupation a farmer prior to enlisting in Johnston County at age 28, October 3, 1862, for the war. Reported present in November-December, 1862, and September, 1863-February, 1864. Also reported present in July-August and November-December, 1864. Survived the war.

STEVENS, JAMES WILLIAM, Private

Born in Johnston County where he resided as a farmer prior to enlisting in Johnston County at age 20, March 15, 1862. Mustered in as Private. Appointed Musician on August 18, 1862. Reported present in November-December, 1862, and September, 1863-February, 1864.

Reduced to ranks in November-December, 1863. Reported present in July-August, 1864. Reported absent sick in November-December, 1864.

STRICKLAND, JULIUS W., Sergeant

Born in Johnston County where he resided as a farmer prior to enlisting in Johnston County at age 19, March 8, 1862. Mustered in as Corporal. Appointed Musician prior to July 1, 1862. Promoted to Sergeant on August 14, 1862. Hospitalized at or near Petersburg, Virginia, October 22, 1862, with pneumonia. Returned to duty on March 18, 1863. Hospitalized at Farmville, Virginia, March 19, 1863, with pneumonia. Returned to duty on March 31, 1863. Reported present in September, 1863-February, 1864, and July-August, 1864. Reported sick in hospital in November-December, 1864. Survived the war.

STRICKLAND, WILEY, Private

Born in Sampson County and resided in Johnston County where he was by occupation a farmer prior to enlisting in Johnston County at age 47, March 8, 1862. Reported present or accounted for through August, 1862. Deserted from camp near Drewry's Bluff, Virginia, November 18, 1862. Court-martialed on June 20, 1863, for desertion and sentenced to be shot. Sentence remitted. Returned to duty on an unspecified date. Reported present in September, 1863-February, 1864. Also reported present in July-August and November-December, 1864. Hospitalized at Greensboro on February 20, 1865, with catarrhus. Transferred to another hospital on February 23, 1865.

STRICKLAND, WILLIAM H., Private

Born in Johnston or Cumberland County and resided in Johnston County where he was by occupation a farmer prior to enlisting in Johnston County at age 20, March 4, 1862. Reported present through August, 1862. Died at Drewry's Bluff, Virginia, on or about October 18, 1862, of "cerebritis."

SUGG, AQUILLA, Private

Resided in Johnston County where he enlisted at age 43, September 4, 1863, for the war. Reported present through February, 1864. Also reported present in July-August and November-December, 1864. Hospitalized at Greensboro on February 20, 1865, with pneumonia. Transferred to another hospital on February 23, 1865. Survived the war. [North Carolina pension records indicate that his left jaw was injured on an unspecified date.]

SURLS, D. H., Private

Enlisted in Washington County on July 13, 1864, for the war. Reported present in July-August, 1864. Reported sick in hospital in November-December, 1864.

TEMPLE, CASWELL, Private

Resided in Johnston County where he enlisted at age 29, February 8, 1863, for the war. Reported present in September, 1863-February, 1864. Also reported present in July-August and November-December, 1864. Survived the war.

THORNTON, WILLIAM E., Private

Born in Sampson County and resided in Johnston County

where he was by occupation a farmer prior to enlisting in Johnston County at age 36, March 4, 1862. Discharged on May 26, 1862, by reason of being overage.

TOOLE, BITHAN L., Corporal
Resided in Johnston County where he enlisted at age 18, July 4, 1863, for the war. Mustered in as Private. Promoted to Corporal on October 31, 1863. Reported present in September, 1863-February, 1864, and July-August, 1864. Reported absent sick in November-December, 1864. Died at or near Augusta, Georgia, on or about February 10, 1865. Cause of death not reported.

WATKINS, COMMODORE, Private
Born in Johnston County where he resided prior to enlisting at age 43, February 25, 1863, for the war. Died at Tarboro on or about April 23, 1863, of disease.

WHEELER, HENRY, Private
Enlisted in Washington County on June 13, 1864, for the war. Reported present in July-August, 1864. Reported absent on sick furlough in November-December, 1864.

WIGGS, JOHN T., Private
Resided in Wake County where he enlisted at age 30, May 12, 1862, for the war. Reported sick in hospital at Wilson on or about June 30, 1862. Returned to duty prior to September 1, 1862. Reported present in November-December, 1862, and September, 1863-February, 1864. Also reported present in July-August and November-December, 1864. Paroled at Raleigh on May 11, 1865.

WOODALL, WILLIAM H., Private
Resided in Johnston County where he enlisted at age 19, October 9, 1862, for the war. Hospitalized at Petersburg, Virginia, November 2, 1862, with intermittent fever. Returned to duty on November 14, 1862. Reported present in September, 1863-February, 1864. Also reported present in July-August and November-December, 1864.

COMPANY E

This company was raised in Wayne County and enlisted at Goldsboro in January-March, 1862. It was mustered into state service at Camp Mangum, near Raleigh, on April 29, 1862, and assigned to the 50th Regiment N.C. Troops as Company E. After joining the regiment the company functioned as a part of the regiment, and its history for the remainder of the war is reported as a part of the regimental history.

The information contained in the following roster was compiled primarily from a company muster-in and descriptive roll dated April 29, 1862, and from company muster rolls for May 1-August 31, 1862; November 1-December 31, 1862; and September 1, 1863-February 29, 1864. No company muster rolls were located for September 1-October 31, 1862; January 1-October 31, 1863; or for the period after February 29, 1864. Valuable information was obtained from primary records such as the North Carolina adjutant general's *Roll of Honor*, discharge certificates, medical records, prisoner of war records, *The War of the*

Rebellion: A Compilation of the Official Records of the Union and Confederate Armies, militia records, newspaper casualty lists and obituaries, Confederate pension applications filed with the state of North Carolina, and the 1860 federal census of North Carolina. Secondary sources such as postwar rosters and histories, cemetery records, the *Confederate Veteran*, published genealogies, and records of the United Daughters of the Confederacy also provided useful information.

OFFICERS

CAPTAINS

GRISWOLD, JOHN B.
Born in Wayne County where he resided as a bookkeeper prior to enlisting at age 36. Appointed Captain on April 29, 1862. Reported present through June, 1862. Reported present but sick in July-August, 1862. Reported present in November-December, 1862. No further records.

BURWELL, PHILIP L.
Date of appointment as Captain not reported. First listed in the records of this company in September-October, 1863, when he was reported present but sick. Hospitalized at Wilson on December 24, 1863, with an unspecified complaint. Returned to duty in January-February, 1864. Resigned on March 16, 1864. Reason he resigned not reported. Resignation accepted on March 24, 1864.

GARDNER, WILLIAM T.
Born in Wayne County where he resided as a farmer prior to enlisting at age 35. Appointed 1st Lieutenant on April 29, 1862. Reported present in May-August and November-December, 1862. Also reported present in September, 1863-February, 1864. Appointed Captain on March 24, 1864. Last reported in the records of this company on July 10, 1864. Survived the war.

LIEUTENANTS

BORDEN, WILLIAM H., 1st Lieutenant
Previously served as 2nd Lieutenant of Company A, 27th Regiment N.C. Troops. Transferred to this company on or about March 7, 1862. Mustered in as 2nd Lieutenant. Reported present in May-August and November-December, 1862. Reported absent on furlough in September-October, 1863. Reported present or accounted for in November, 1863-February, 1864. Promoted to 1st Lieutenant on March 24, 1864. Paroled at Greensboro on May 1, 1865. [May have served briefly in 1862 as acting Adjutant of this regiment.]

EDWARDS, WILLIAM L., 2nd Lieutenant
Born in Greene County and resided in Wayne County where he was by occupation a butcher prior to enlisting

at age 35. Appointed 2nd Lieutenant on April 29, 1862. Reported present in May-June, 1862. Reported absent on detached service in July-August, 1862. Resigned on October 20, 1862, by reason of "bad health." Resignation accepted on November 19, 1862.

GRISWOLD, GEORGE C., 2nd Lieutenant
Resided in Wayne County and enlisted at Petersburg, Virginia, at age 21, June 22, 1862, for the war. Mustered in as Private. Promoted to Sergeant on or about the same date he enlisted. Reported present in May-August and November-December, 1862. Elected 2nd Lieutenant on November 24, 1862. Reported present in September-December, 1863. Hospitalized at Wilmington on January 25, 1864, with syphilis. Furloughed for thirty days on February 10, 1864. Paroled at Greensboro on May 1, 1865.

JONES, GEORGE T., 2nd Lieutenant
Previously served as Private in Captain John B. Griswold's Company (Provost Guard), N.C. Local Defense Troops. Transferred to this company on October 20, 1863. Reported present in November-December, 1863. Reported on detail as an adjutant's clerk in January-February, 1864. Appointed 2nd Lieutenant on April 25, 1864. Hospitalized at Greensboro on January 9, 1865, with fever. Returned to duty on February 11, 1865. Paroled at Raleigh on April 14, 1865.

NONCOMMISSIONED OFFICERS AND PRIVATES

ANDERSON, RICHARD, Private
Born in Wayne County where he enlisted on March 17, 1862. Reported present in May-August, 1862. Reported present but sick in November-December, 1862. Died prior to January 20, 1864. Place, date, and cause of death not reported.

BARFIELD, JEREMIAH, Private
Born in Greene County where he resided as a farmer prior to enlisting in Wayne County at age 18, January 13, 1862. Reported present in May-August and November-December, 1862. Hospitalized at Wilmington on August 10, 1863, with otitis. Returned to duty on August 18, 1863. Reported present in September, 1863-February, 1864. Paroled at Goldsboro on May 3, 1865.

BASS, JACOB, Corporal
Born in Wayne County and was by occupation a cooper prior to enlisting in Wayne County at age 33, April 3, 1862. Mustered in as Private. Reported present in May-August and November-December, 1862. Promoted to Corporal in January-October, 1863. Reported present in September, 1863-February, 1864. Paroled at Greensboro on April 28, 1865.

BASS, JESSE, Private
Previously served as Private in Captain John B. Griswold's Company (Provost Guard), N.C. Local Defense Troops. Transferred to this company on or about October 20, 1863. Reported present in November,

1863-February, 1864. Captured near Savannah, Georgia, December 15, 1864. Sent to Hilton Head, South Carolina. Transferred to Point Lookout, Maryland, where he arrived on February 1, 1865. Released at Point Lookout on June 23, 1865, after taking the Oath of Allegiance.

BASS, WILLIAM, Private
Born in Johnston County and was by occupation a farmer prior to enlisting in Craven County at age 20, March 7, 1862. Reported present in May-August and November-December, 1862. Also reported present in September, 1863-February, 1864. Survived the war.

BATTON, JAMES C., Private
Enlisted at Petersburg, Virginia, July 25, 1862, for the war. Reported present but sick in November-December, 1862. Reported present in September, 1863-February, 1864. Hospitalized at or near Petersburg on May 22, 1864, with a gunshot wound. Place and date wounded not reported. Last reported in the records of this company in July-September, 1864.

BENFREM, T. N., Private
Resided in Johnston County. Place and date of enlistment not reported; however, he probably enlisted subsequent to February 29, 1864. Paroled at Goldsboro on May 3, 1865.

BEVENER, J., Private
Resided in Johnston County. Place and date of enlistment not reported; however, he probably enlisted subsequent to February 29, 1864. Paroled at Goldsboro on May 3, 1865.

BOYKIN, ELLINGTON B., Private
Born in Johnston County and was by occupation a farmer prior to enlisting in Wayne County at age 24, March 17, 1862. Reported absent without leave on May 10, 1862. Returned to duty on September 5, 1862. Hospitalized at Petersburg, Virginia, November 5, 1862, with an unspecified complaint. Furloughed for thirty days on December 18, 1862. Reported present in September, 1863-February, 1864. Last reported in the records of this company in July-September, 1864. Survived the war.

BOYKIN, JACOB, Private
Resided in Johnston County and enlisted at Camp Burgwyn, near Wilmington, January 5, 1864, for the war. Paroled at Goldsboro in 1865. Survived the war.

BREWER, JESSE J., Private
Born in Johnston County where he resided as a farmer prior to enlisting in Johnston County at age 25, March 12, 1862. Reported present in May-August and November-December, 1862. Deserted on an unspecified date. Returned to duty on January 5, 1864. Reported present through February, 1864. Hospitalized at Charlotte on February 13, 1865, with remittent fever. Transferred to another hospital on February 18, 1865. Paroled at Goldsboro on May 3, 1865. [North Carolina pension records indicate that he was wounded in the right hand at Fort Moultrie, South Carolina, in 1863.]

BREWER, SOLOMON, Private
Enlisted on October 17, 1862, for the war. Deserted at Drewry's Bluff, Virginia, December 10, 1862.

BROWN, BARDEN, _____
North Carolina pension records indicate that he served in this company.

BROWN, JOHN, Private
Born in Chatham County and was by occupation a farmer prior to enlisting in Wayne County at age 35, January 13, 1862. No further records.

BURNS, DUNCAN, Private
Born in Wayne County and was by occupation a farmer prior to enlisting in Wayne County at age 16, March 1, 1862. Reported absent without leave on or about April 29, 1862.

BUTTS, SAMUEL, Private
Born in Greene County and was by occupation a farmer prior to enlisting in Wayne County at age 18, January 20, 1862. Reported present in May-August, 1862. Reported absent sick in November-December, 1862. Reported present in September, 1863-February, 1864. Last reported in the records of this company in July-September, 1864.

CROCKER, BERRY F., Sergeant
Born in Johnston County and was by occupation a carpenter prior to enlisting in Wayne County at age 30, January 13, 1862. Mustered in as Sergeant. Reported present in May-June, 1862. Reported present but sick in July-August, 1862. Reported present in November-December, 1862, and September, 1863-February, 1864. Last reported in the records of this company in July-September, 1864.

CROCKER, BRIDGERS, Private
Born in Johnston County and was by occupation a farmer prior to enlisting in Johnston County at age 18, February 28, 1862. Reported present in May-August and November-December, 1862. Also reported present in September, 1863-February, 1864. Hospitalized at Charlotte on February 6, 1865, with rheumatism. Transferred to another hospital the same date. Survived the war.

CROCKER, JOSEPH, _____
North Carolina pension records indicate that he served in this company.

CRUMPLER, R. W., _____
North Carolina pension records indicate that he served in this company.

DANIEL, JOHN R., Private
Born in Wayne County where he resided as a farmer prior to enlisting in Craven County at age 39, January 28, 1862. No further records.

DANIEL, NEEDHAM, Private
Born in Wayne County and was by occupation a farmer prior to enlisting in Wayne County at age 20, March 11, 1862. Reported present in May-June, 1862. Hospitalized

at Petersburg, Virginia, July 18, 1862. Returned to duty subsequent to August 31, 1862. Reported present in November-December, 1862, and September, 1863-February, 1864. Last reported in the records of this company in July-September, 1864.

DANIEL, WILLIAM H., Corporal
Born in Wayne County and was by occupation a farmer prior to enlisting in Wayne County at age 35, January 13, 1862. Mustered in as Corporal. No further records.

DAVIS, BARTLETT, Sergeant
Born in Wayne County where he resided as a farmer prior to enlisting in Wayne County at age 34, January 13, 1862. Mustered in as Private. Reported present in May-August and November-December, 1862. Promoted to Corporal on November 24, 1862. Promoted to Sergeant in January-October, 1863. Reported present in September, 1863-February, 1864. Last reported in the records of this company in July-September, 1864. Survived the war.

DEANS, JESSE, Private
Born in Harnett County* and enlisted at Camp Mangum, near Raleigh, May 15, 1862, for the war. Reported absent without leave on May 29, 1862. Returned to duty on an unspecified date. Died in hospital at Petersburg, Virginia, July 21, 1862, of "continued fever." [He was 23 years of age at the time of his death.]

DICKINSON, JAMES, Sergeant
Born in Wayne County where he resided as a farmer prior to enlisting in Wayne County at age 43, January 22, 1862. Mustered in as Private. Reported present in May-June, 1862. Promoted to Corporal prior to July 1, 1862. Reported present but sick in July-August, 1862. Promoted to Sergeant on November 24, 1862. Reported present in November-December, 1862, and September, 1863-February, 1864. Paroled at Goldsboro on May 13, 1865.

DONALDSON, A. J., Private
Place and date of enlistment not reported. Records of the Federal Provost Marshal indicate that he was in confinement at Old Capitol Prison, Washington, D.C., in October, 1862, after being captured on an unspecified date. Paroled and transferred to Aiken's Landing, James River, Virginia, where he was received on November 2, 1862, for exchange. Declared exchanged at Aiken's Landing on November 10, 1862. No further records.

EDMUNDSON, JESSE W., Sergeant
Enlisted at Camp Mangum, near Raleigh, April 29, 1862, for the war. Mustered in as Sergeant. Promoted to Sergeant Major on May 1, 1862, and transferred to the Field and Staff of this regiment.

EDWARDS, BENJAMIN, Private
Enlisted at Camp Mangum, near Raleigh, at age 27, April 29, 1862, for the war. Reported absent sick in May-August and November-December, 1862. Sent home on "unlimited furlough" on February 20, 1863. Reported absent sick in September, 1863-February, 1864. Last reported in the records of this company in July-September, 1864. Survived the war.

EDWARDS, ERASTUS, Private
Previously served as Private in Captain John B. Griswold's Company (Provost Guard), N.C. Local Defense Troops. Transferred to this company on or about October 20, 1863. Reported present in November, 1863-February, 1864. Last reported in the records of this company in July-September, 1864.

EDWARDS, HENRY T., Private
Born in Johnston County and enlisted in Wayne County at age 35, March 12, 1862. Reported present in May-August and November-December, 1862. Furloughed for seven days on June 30, 1863. Reported present in September, 1863-February, 1864. Last reported in the records of this company in July-September, 1864.

EVERITT, D. E., Private
Resided in Wilson County. Place and date of enlistment not reported; however, he probably enlisted in March-September, 1864. Paroled at Goldsboro in 1865.

EXUM, WILLIAM D., Private
Born in Wayne County and was by occupation a farmer prior to enlisting in Wayne or Craven County at age 31, February 12, 1862. Reported present in May-August, 1862. Deserted at Drewry's Bluff, Virginia, December 10, 1862. Was apparently apprehended on or about December 31, 1862. Returned to duty on an unspecified date. Reported present in September, 1863-February, 1864. Captured by the enemy at or near Goldsboro on March 23, 1865. Took the Oath of Allegiance the same date. [North Carolina pension records indicate that he was wounded in the Seven Days' battles near Richmond, Virginia, in June-July, (1862).]

FLOWERS, EXUM, Corporal
Born in Nash County and was by occupation a cooper prior to enlisting in Wayne County at age 36, January 13, 1862. Mustered in as Private. Reported present in May-August and November-December, 1862. Promoted to Corporal in January-October, 1863. Reported present in September, 1863-February, 1864. Last reported in the records of this company in July-September, 1864.

GARDNER, JAMES, Private
Born in Wayne County and was by occupation a farmer prior to enlisting in Wayne County at age 22, January 13, 1862. Reported present in May-June, 1862. Reported present but sick in July-August, 1862. Reported present in November-December, 1862, and September, 1863-February, 1864. Last reported in the records of this company in July-September, 1864.

GARDNER, W. J., Private
Resided in Wayne County. Place and date of enlistment not reported; however, he probably enlisted subsequent to February 29, 1864. Paroled at Goldsboro in 1865.

GARRIS, JONATHAN G., Corporal
Born in Wayne County where he resided as a farmer prior to enlisting in Wayne County at age 28, January 24, 1862. Mustered in as Corporal. Reported present in July-August and November-December, 1862. Hospitalized at

Wilmington on August 10, 1863, with intermittent fever. Returned to duty on August 28, 1863. Reported present in September, 1863-February, 1864. Captured at or near Goldsboro on April 3, 1865. Sent to New Bern. Confined at Fort Monroe, Virginia, April 25, 1865. Transferred to Newport News, Virginia, where he arrived on May 1, 1865. Released at Newport News on June 30, 1865, after taking the Oath of Allegiance.

GHOLSON, DURELL B., Private
Born in Mecklenburg County, Virginia, and was by occupation an overseer or farmer prior to enlisting in Wayne or Craven County at age 24, February 12, 1862. Reported sick in hospital at Petersburg, Virginia, June 26, 1862. Returned to duty subsequent to August 31, 1862. Reported present in November-December, 1862. Reported absent sick in September-October, 1863. Reported present in November, 1863-February, 1864. Paroled at Greensboro on May 1, 1865. [Was a resident of Warren County in 1860.]

GODDIN, STEPHEN, Private
Born in Johnston County and was by occupation a farmer prior to enlisting in Johnston County at age 27, March 10, 1862. Mustered in as Corporal. Reported sick in hospital at Petersburg, Virginia, June 23, 1862. Reported present but sick in July-August, 1862. Reported present in November-December, 1862. Reduced to ranks in January-October, 1863. Reported present in September, 1863-February, 1864. Hospitalized at Charlotte on February 6, 1865, with phthisis. Furloughed on February 14, 1865.

GODDIN, THEOPHILUS, Private
Born in Johnston County and was by occupation a farmer prior to enlisting in Wayne County at age 23, March 31, 1862. Reported sick in hospital at Wilson on June 19, 1862. Returned to duty subsequent to August 31, 1862. Reported present in November-December, 1862, and September, 1863-February, 1864. Last reported in the records of this company in July-September, 1864.

GOODMAN, JAMES, Private
Resided in Wayne County. Place and date of enlistment not reported; however, he probably enlisted subsequent to February 29, 1864. Paroled at Goldsboro on May 3, 1865.

GOODWIN, GEORGE, Private
Place and date of enlistment not reported; however, he probably enlisted subsequent to February 29, 1864. Deserted to the enemy at or near Goldsboro on March 24, 1865. Sent to New Bern. Transferred to Hart's Island, New York Harbor, April 10, 1865. Escaped from the guardhouse at Hart's Island on or about July 6, 1865.

GREEN, JOHN A., 1st Sergeant
Born in Wayne County and was by occupation a student prior to enlisting at Goldsboro at age 17, March 16, 1862. Mustered in as 1st Sergeant. Reported present in May-August, 1862. Promoted to Sergeant Major on December 21, 1862, and transferred to the Field and Staff of this regiment.

GRICE, JAMES, Private
Born in Johnston County and resided in Wayne County where he was by occupation a farmer prior to enlisting in Wayne County at age 22, April 12, 1862. Reported sick in hospital at Petersburg, Virginia, June 28, 1862. Reported present in July-August and November-December, 1862. Also reported present in September, 1863-February, 1864. Last reported in the records of this company in July-September, 1864. Survived the war. [North Carolina pension records indicate that he was wounded near Richmond, Virginia, on an unspecified date.]

GRICE, WILLIAM H., Private
Born in Johnston County and was by occupation a farmer prior to enlisting in Wayne County at age 17, March 11, 1862. Reported present in May-August, 1862. Reported present but sick in November-December, 1862. Reported present in September, 1863-February, 1864. Last reported in the records of this company in July-September, 1864. Survived the war.

HAM, RICHARD, Private
Born in Wayne County where he resided as a blacksmith prior to enlisting in Wayne County at age 44, February 8, 1862. No further records.

HAM, WILLIAM, Musician
Born in Wayne County and was by occupation a laborer prior to enlisting in Wayne County at age 18, March 4, 1862. Mustered in as Private. Appointed Musician prior to July 1, 1862. Reported present in May-August and November-December, 1862. Also reported present in September-December, 1863. No further records.

HEAD, THOMAS W., Private
Born in Wayne County and was by occupation a farmer prior to enlisting in Wayne County at age 17, February 7, 1862. Reported present in May-August and November-December, 1862. Reported absent without leave on October 22, 1863. Returned to duty prior to January 1, 1864. Reported present in January-February, 1864. Last reported in the records of this company in July-September, 1864. Survived the war.

HILL, WILLIAM G., Private
Born in Wayne County and was by occupation a farmer prior to enlisting in Wayne County at age 21, January 13, 1862. Died in hospital at Petersburg, Virginia, July 7, 1862, of "typhoid fever."

HINTON, FRANCIS M., Private
Born in Johnston County where he resided as a farmer prior to enlisting in Wayne County at age 21, March 30, 1862. Reported present in May-August and November-December, 1862. Deserted on an unspecified date. Returned to duty on February 8, 1864. Reported present through February, 1864. Paroled in 1865.

HOOD, B., Private
Resided in Wayne County. Place and date of enlistment not reported; however, he probably enlisted subsequent to February 29, 1864. Paroled at Goldsboro on May 3, 1865.

HOOKS, ALBERT, Private
Born in Wayne County where he resided as a farmer prior to enlisting in Wayne County at age 26, February 10, 1862. Died at Camp Mangum, near Raleigh, on or about April 19, 1862. Cause of death not reported.

HORN, JAMES H., Private
Born in Wayne County and was by occupation a farmer prior to enlisting in Wayne County on January 13, 1862. Reported present in May-August, 1862. Reported present but sick in November-December, 1862. Reported present in September, 1863-February, 1864. Paroled at Goldsboro on May 8, 1865.

HOWARD, JOHN, Private
Born in Beaufort County and was by occupation a laborer prior to enlisting in Wayne County at age 56, March 5, 1862. No further records.

HOWELL, JOHN W., Private
Born in Wayne County where he enlisted on February 1, 1862. Reported absent without leave on or about April 29, 1862.

HOWELL, WILLIAM H., Private
Born in Wayne County and was by occupation a ditcher prior to enlisting in Wayne County at age 50, March 13, 1862. Reported present in May-August and November-December, 1862. Also reported present in September-October, 1863. Hospitalized at Wilmington on December 19, 1863, with acute dysentery. Returned to duty on December 28, 1863. Reported present in January-February, 1864. Last reported in the records of this company in July-September, 1864.

HUGHES, WILLIAM, Private
Born in Wayne County where he enlisted on January 13, 1862. Reported absent without leave on May 24, 1862. Failed to return to duty and was listed as a deserter prior to March 1, 1864.

JASSER, D., Private
Resided in Wayne County. Place and date of enlistment not reported; however, he probably enlisted subsequent to February 29, 1864. Paroled at Goldsboro on May 3, 1865.

JOHNSON, WILLIS, Private
Born in Johnston County where he resided as a farmer prior to enlisting in Wayne County at age 24, March 17, 1862. Died in hospital at Petersburg, Virginia, on or about July 9, 1862, of "typhoid fever."

JONES, JAMES, Private
Born in Johnston County and was by occupation a farmer prior to enlisting in Wayne County at age 19, March 31, 1862. Reported sick in hospital at Petersburg, Virginia, June 23, 1862. Returned to duty subsequent to December 31, 1862. Reported present in September, 1863-February, 1864. Last reported in the records of this company in July-September, 1864.

JONES, LEVI, Private
Born in Wayne County and was by occupation a farmer prior to enlisting in Wayne County at age 18, March 24, 1862. No further records.

KEEN, WILEY, Private
Born in Johnston County and enlisted in Wayne County on March 7, 1862. Died in Johnston County prior to September 1, 1862, of disease.

KENNEDY, BRIGHT, Private
Born in Johnston County and was by occupation a shoemaker prior to enlisting in Wayne County at age 50, January 13, 1862. Reported present in May-August and November-December, 1862. Also reported present in September, 1863-February, 1864. Hospitalized at Charlotte on February 6, 1865, with hemerotophia. Furloughed on February 21, 1865.

LANGLY, NATHAN, Private
Enlisted at Camp Mangum, near Raleigh, April 29, 1862, for the war. Reported sick in hospital at Petersburg, Virginia, in May-June, 1862. Reported present in July-August and November-December, 1862. Also reported present in September, 1863-February, 1864. Last reported in the records of this company in July-September, 1864.

LANGSTON, DAVID, Private
Born in Wayne County and was by occupation a farmer prior to enlisting in Wayne County at age 17, March 2, 1862. Reported present in May-August and November-December, 1862. Sent to hospital at Greenville on June 30, 1863. Died on August 26, 1863, of disease. Place of death not reported.

LATHAM, NORFLEET FRANKLIN, Private
Born in Wayne County where he resided as a farmer prior to enlisting in Wayne County at age 32, January 13, 1862. Mustered in as Sergeant. Reported absent without leave in May-June, 1862. Reported present in July-August and November-December, 1862. Promoted to 1st Sergeant on December 21, 1862. Reported present in September, 1863-February, 1864. Reduced to ranks subsequent to February 29, 1864. Paroled at Goldsboro on May 3, 1865.

LEWIS, WILLIAM E., Private
Born in Wayne County and was by occupation a farmer prior to enlisting in Wayne County at age 18, April 1, 1862. No further records.

LONDON, WILLIAM T., _____
Place and date of enlistment not reported. Furloughed for fourteen days on January 25, 1864. No further records.

MOYE, WILLIAM E., Private
Born in Pitt County and was by occupation a farmer prior to enlisting in Wayne County at age 40, January 13, 1862. No further records.

MOZINGO, CALVIN, Private
Born in Wayne County and was by occupation a farmer prior to enlisting in Wayne County at age 30, January 13, 1862. Reported present in May-August, 1862. Reported

present but sick in November-December, 1862. Died in hospital at Goldsboro on January 17, 1863, of "typhoid fever."

MOZINGO, MARK, Private
Born in Wayne County where he resided as a farmer prior to enlisting in Wayne County at age 34, January 13, 1862. Reported absent without leave in May-June, 1862. Returned to duty in July-August, 1862. Reported present but sick in November-December, 1862. Reported present in September, 1863-February, 1864. Last reported in the records of this company in July-September, 1864.

OLIVER, FESTUS, Private
Born in Johnston County where he resided as a farmer prior to enlisting in Wayne County at age 18, February 28, 1862. Reported present in May-August, 1862. Deserted on December 10, 1862. Returned to duty on an unspecified date. Reported present in September, 1863-February, 1864. Last reported in the records of this company in July-September, 1864.

OVERMAN, JOHN, Private
Born in Wayne County where he enlisted. Date of enlistment not reported. Reported absent without leave on or about April 29, 1862.

OWENS, WILLIAM H., Private
Previously served in Captain J. B. Griswold's Independent Company, Goldsboro Provost Guard. Transferred to this company on January 31, 1864. Hospitalized at Wilmington on February 23, 1864, with syphilis. Returned to duty on March 21, 1864. Hospitalized at Goldsboro on or about August 27, 1864, with an unspecified complaint. Discharged from hospital the same date. Captured at Bamburg[?] on February 7, 1865. Sent to New Bern. Confined at Hart's Island, New York Harbor, April 10, 1865. Died at Hart's Island on May 12, 1865, of "pneumonia."

PEEL, WILLIAM, Private
Born in Nash County and resided in Wilson County where he was by occupation a farmer prior to enlisting in Wayne County on January 13, 1862. Reported present in May-June, 1862. Hospitalized at Petersburg, Virginia, July 20, 1862, with remittent fever. Returned to duty on August 8, 1862. Hospitalized at or near Petersburg on December 1, 1862, with debility. Returned to duty on December 14, 1862. Reported present in September, 1863-February, 1864. Paroled at Goldsboro on May 9, 1865.

PENNINGTON, WILLIAM, Private
Place and date of enlistment not reported. Paroled at Goldsboro in 1865.

PERSON, BENJAMIN T., Private
Born in Wayne County and was by occupation a laborer prior to enlisting in Wayne County at age 18, March 31, 1862. Reported present in May-August and November-December, 1862. Also reported present in September, 1863-February, 1864. Paroled at Greensboro in 1865.

RADFORD, GEORGE W., Private
Born in Johnston County and was by occupation a farmer

prior to enlisting in Wayne County on February 28, 1862. Reported absent without leave through December, 1862. Returned to duty on an unspecified date. Reported present in September, 1863-February, 1864. Last reported in the records of this company in July-September, 1864.

RADFORD, RUFUS W., Private
Born in Johnston County where he resided as a farmer prior to enlisting in Wayne County at age 21, February 28, 1862. Reported present in May-June, 1862. Reported present but sick in July-August, 1862. Reported present in November-December, 1862, and September, 1863-February, 1864. Paroled at Goldsboro on May 3, 1865.

RADFORD, STEPHEN, Private
Enlisted on October 15, 1863, for the war. Reported present in November, 1863-February, 1864. Died in hospital at Wilson on December 6, 1864, of "feb[ris] remit[tent]."

RAPER, ROBINSON, Private
Born in Johnston County and was by occupation a farmer prior to enlisting in Johnston County at age 28, March 12, 1862. Died in hospital at Raleigh on or about April 21, 1862, of "rubeola."

RENTFRO, JAMES I., Private
Born in Johnston County and was by occupation a farmer prior to enlisting in Wayne County at age 19, March 17, 1862. Reported present in May-June, 1862. Reported present but sick in July-August and November-December, 1862. Reported present in September, 1863-February, 1864. Last reported in the records of this company in July-September, 1864.

ROBERTS, ELCANA, Private
Born in Wayne County and was by occupation a farmer prior to enlisting in Wayne County at age 21, January 17, 1862. Reported present in May-June, 1862. Hospitalized at Petersburg, Virginia, July 20, 1862, with chronic diarrhoea. Returned to duty on August 8, 1862. Furloughed for forty days on December 6, 1862. Hospitalized at Goldsboro in July, 1863. Reported absent sick in September-October, 1863. Reported on duty as a hospital guard at Goldsboro in November-December, 1863. Discharged from hospital at Goldsboro and ordered to report to his company on June 15, 1864. Last reported in the records of this company in July-September, 1864. Survived the war. [North Carolina pension records indicate that he suffered a broken arm at Greenville in 1863.]

ROBINSON, JAMES P., Private
Born in Wayne County where he resided as a farmer prior to enlisting in Wayne County at age 21, February 10, 1862. Reported present in May-August and November-December, 1862. Also reported present in September, 1863-February, 1864. Captured near Savannah, Georgia, on or about December 8, 1864. Sent to Hilton Head, South Carolina. Confined at Point Lookout, Maryland, February 1, 1865. Released at Point Lookout on June 17, 1865, after taking the Oath of Allegiance.

ROBINSON, JOHN, Private
Born in Wayne County and was by occupation a farmer prior to enlisting in Wayne County at age 22, February 10, 1862. Died in hospital at Raleigh on or about April 17, 1862, of "enteric fever."

SASSER, HILLIARD, Private
Born in Wayne County and was by occupation a farmer prior to enlisting in Wayne County at age 30, January 28, 1862. Reported present in May-August and November-December, 1862. Also reported present in September, 1863-February, 1864. Last reported in the records of this company in July-September, 1864.

SASSER, WILEY, Musician
Place and date of enlistment not reported; however, he probably enlisted in November-December, 1863. Promotion record not reported. Reported present in January-February, 1864. Last reported in the records of this company in July-September, 1864.

SELLERS, RICHARD, Private
Born in Johnston County and was by occupation a trader prior to enlisting in Wayne County at age 30, February 28, 1862. Mustered in as Sergeant. Reported absent without leave on May 15, 1862. Reduced to ranks prior to July 1, 1862. Listed as a deserter on an unspecified date. Returned from desertion on October 15, 1863. Reported present in November, 1863-February, 1864. Last reported in the records of this company in July-September, 1864.

SEYMOUR, LEONIDAS B., Private
Born in Wayne County where he enlisted on March 4, 1862. Reported absent without leave on May 23, 1862. Apprehended on or about September 5, 1862. Court-martialed for desertion on or about January 13, 1863. Found guilty and sentenced "to receive thirty-nine lashes on his bare back, every three months, for the period of the war, to be branded in the left hand with the letter 'D,' and to be put to hard labor in Richmond, with ball and chain, weighing twelve pounds, attached to left leg, for the balance of the War." Returned to duty with the company prior to November 1, 1863. Hospitalized at Wilmington on November 27, 1863, with debilitas. Returned to duty on December 14, 1863. Reported present in January-February, 1864. Last reported in the records of this company in July-September, 1864.

SILLIVENT, LEMUEL, Private
Born in Wayne County and was by occupation a farmer prior to enlisting in Wayne County at age 34, March 13, 1862. Reported absent without leave from May 20 through August 31, 1862. Returned to duty on an unspecified date. Deserted at Drewry's Bluff, Virginia, December 10, 1862. Returned to duty on an unspecified date. Reported present in September, 1863-February, 1864. Last reported in the records of this company in July-September, 1864.

SMITH, HENRY E., Private
Born in Wayne County where he resided as a farmer prior to enlisting in Wayne County at age 40, January 13, 1862. Reported present in May-June, 1862. Hospitalized at

Richmond, Virginia, August 21, 1862. Returned to duty prior to January 1, 1863. Reported present in September, 1863-February, 1864. Paroled at Goldsboro on May 3, 1865.

SMITH, JOSIAH, Private
Born in Wayne County where he resided prior to enlisting in Wayne County on January 13, 1862. Reported present in May-August and November-December, 1862. Furloughed for five days on June 30, 1863. Reported present in September-November, 1863. Hospitalized at Wilmington on December 19, 1863, with acute rheumatism. Returned to duty on January 15, 1864. Paroled at Goldsboro on May 3, 1865.

SMITH, THOMAS, Private
Born in Wayne County where he resided as a farmer prior to enlisting in Wayne County at age 30, January 13, 1862. Mustered in as Corporal. Reported present in May-August and November-December, 1862. Also reported present in September, 1863-February, 1864. Reduced to ranks subsequent to February 29, 1864. Captured at or near Goldsboro on March 24, 1865. Sent to New Bern. Confined at Point Lookout, Maryland, April 3, 1865. Released at Point Lookout on June 20, 1865, after taking the Oath of Allegiance.

STARLING, DANIEL A., Private
Born in Johnston County and was by occupation a farmer prior to enlisting in Wayne County at age 22, March 8, 1862. Reported present in May-June, 1862. Hospitalized at Petersburg, Virginia, August 3, 1862. Reported absent in hospital through December, 1862. Deserted on an unspecified date. Returned to duty on October 15, 1863. Reported present through February 29, 1864. Last reported in the records of this company in July-September, 1864. Survived the war.

STARLING, JOHN, Private
Enlisted at Camp Burgwyn, near Raleigh, in February, 1864, for the war. Last reported in the records of this company in July-September, 1864.

STRICKLAND, HENRY J., Sergeant
Born in Nash County and was by occupation a farmer prior to enlisting in Craven County at age 24, March 7, 1862. Mustered in as Sergeant. Reported present in May-August and November-December, 1862. Sent to hospital at Raleigh on May 20, 1863. Reported present in September, 1863-February, 1864. Paroled at Goldsboro on May 15, 1865.

THOMAS, JONATHAN, Private
Born in Wayne County where he enlisted on February 13, 1862. Reported present in May-August and November-December, 1862. Also reported present in September, 1863-February, 1864. Last reported in the records of this company in July-September, 1864.

TRIPP, BENJAMIN F., Private
Born in Pitt County and was by occupation a cooper or shoemaker prior to enlisting in Wayne County on March 11, 1862. Discharged on February 22, 1863, by reason of being overage. Discharge certificate gives his age as 37.

TRIPP, WILLIAM, Private
Born in Pitt County and resided in Wayne County where he was by occupation a farmer prior to enlisting in Wayne County at age 45, January 13, 1862. Discharged on February 10, 1863, by reason of being overage.

VICK, JOHN A., Private
Born in Wayne County and was by occupation a clerk prior to enlisting in Wayne County at age 22, February 18, 1862. Discharged on or about April 29, 1862. Reason discharged not reported.

WATSON, ROBERT R., Private
Enlisted in Lenoir County on March 4, 1863, for the war. Reported in hospital at Wilmington on April 30, 1863, with neuralgia. Returned to duty on an unspecified date. Reported present in September, 1863-February, 1864. Last reported in the records of this company in July-September, 1864.

WATSON, WILLIAM H., Private
Born in Johnston County and was by occupation a farmer prior to enlisting in Wayne County at age 18, March 12, 1862. Reported present in May-August and November-December, 1862. Also reported present in September-October, 1863. Hospitalized at Wilmington on November 28, 1863, with acute bronchitis. Transferred to another hospital on March 24, 1864. Hospitalized at Charlotte on May 15, 1864, with "ulcus" and died on July 9, 1864.

WILLIAMS, BENJAMIN B., Private
Born in Wayne County and was by occupation a farmer prior to enlisting in Wayne County on March 10, 1862. Reported absent without leave on or about April 29, 1862.

WILLIAMS, WILLIAM T., Private
Born in Wayne County and was by occupation a farmer prior to enlisting in Wayne County at age 44, January 13, 1862. Reported present in May-August and November-December, 1862. Also reported present in September, 1863-February, 1864. Hospitalized at Charlotte on February 6, 1865, with rheumatism. Returned to duty on February 9, 1865.

WINN, DAVID, Private
Born in Martin County and was by occupation a farmer prior to enlisting in Wayne County at age 18, February 8, 1862. Reported present in May-June, 1862. Reported present but sick in July-August, 1862. Reported present in November-December, 1862, and September, 1863-February, 1864. Last reported in the records of this company in July-September, 1864.

WRIGHT, COUNCIL B., Private
Previously served in Captain J. B. Griswold's Independent Company, Goldsboro Provost Guard. Transferred to this company on January 31, 1864. Was about 17 years of age in 1864. Reported on detail in the quartermaster's department in January-February, 1864. Promoted to Sergeant Major on May 1, 1864, and transferred to the Field and Staff of this regiment.

COMPANY F

This company, known as the "Moore Sharpshooters," was raised in Moore County and enlisted in Moore County on March 14, 1862. It was mustered into state service at Camp Mangum, near Raleigh, on April 21, 1862, and assigned to the 50th Regiment N.C. Troops as Company F. After joining the regiment the company functioned as a part of the regiment, and its history for the remainder of the war is reported as a part of the regimental history.

The information contained in the following roster was compiled primarily from a company muster-in and descriptive roll dated April 21, 1862, and from company muster rolls for May 1-June 30, 1862; September 1 December 31, 1862; September 1, 1863-February 29, 1864; and October 31-December 31, 1864. No company muster rolls were located for July 1-August 31, 1862; January 1-August 31, 1863; March 1-October 30, 1864; or for the period after December 31, 1864. Valuable information was obtained from primary records such as the North Carolina adjutant general's *Roll of Honor*, discharge certificates, medical records, prisoner of war records, *The War of the Rebellion: The Official Records of the Union and Confederate Armies*, militia records, newspaper casualty lists and obituaries, Confederate pension applications filed with the state of North Carolina, and the 1860 federal census of North Carolina. Secondary sources such as postwar rosters and histories, cemetery records, the *Confederate Veteran*, published genealogies, and records of the United Daughters of the Confederacy also provided useful information.

OFFICERS

CAPTAIN

KELLY, JAMES OSCAR ABNER
Born on July 28, 1833. Resided in Moore County. Appointed Captain on March 14, 1862. Reported present or accounted for in May-June and September-December, 1862. Also reported present in September-December, 1863. Detailed for fourteen days to procure instruments for the regimental band on February 5, 1864. Sent to hospital sick on December 3, 1864. Survived the war.

LIEUTENANTS

BOLIN, ALEXANDER, 1st Lieutenant
Resided in Moore County. Appointed 2nd Lieutenant on March 14, 1862. Promoted to 1st Lieutenant on May 27, 1862. Reported present in May-June and September-December, 1862. Reported absent with leave in September-October, 1863. Reported present in November, 1863-February, 1864. Wounded (probably near Savannah, Georgia) on or about December 10, 1864. Returned to duty prior to January 1, 1865. Survived the war.

DALRYMPLE, JAMES, 3rd Lieutenant
Born in Moore County and was by occupation a schoolteacher prior to enlisting in Moore County at age 26, March 14, 1862. Mustered in as Private. Detailed as Quartermaster Sergeant on June 23, 1862. Elected 3rd Lieutenant on July 15, 1862. Reported present in September-October, 1862. Reported on detail as regimental Assistant Commissary of Subsistence and Assistant Quartermaster in November-December, 1862. Rejoined the company on an unspecified date. Reported present in September, 1863-February, 1864, and November-December, 1864. Survived the war.

DOUGLAS, NATHAN, 1st Lieutenant
Appointed 1st Lieutenant on March 14, 1862. Resigned on May 27, 1862. Reason he resigned not reported.

WATSON, MALCOLM McFARLAND, 2nd Lieutenant
Resided in Moore County and enlisted at age 29. Appointed 3rd Lieutenant on March 14, 1862. Promoted to 2nd Lieutenant on April 21, 1862. Reported present in May-June and September-December, 1862. Also reported present in September, 1863-February, 1864, and November-December, 1864. Survived the war.

NONCOMMISSIONED OFFICERS AND PRIVATES

ALLEN, ADOLPHUS, Private
Place and date of enlistment not reported. Sent to hospital on November 25, 1864. No further records.

ALLEN, CHARLES G., Private
Born in Moore County and was by occupation a farmer prior to enlisting in Moore County at age 27, March 14, 1862. Reported present in May-June and September-December, 1862. Also reported present in September, 1863-February, 1864, and November-December, 1864.

ALLEN, FORNEY, Private
Born in Taliaferro County, Georgia, and was by occupation a farmer prior to enlisting in Moore County at age 20, March 14, 1862. Reported present in May-June and September-December, 1862. Also reported present in September, 1863-February, 1864. Hospitalized at Wilmington on November 25, 1864, with herpes. Transferred to Wilson on December 26, 1864. Hospitalized at Charlotte on February 13, 1865, with ulcus. Returned to duty on February 17, 1865. Survived the war.

ALLEN, JAMES, Private
Born in Taliaferro County, Georgia, and was by occupation a carpenter prior to enlisting in Moore County at age 24, March 14, 1862. Reported present in May-June and September-December, 1862. Also reported present in September-October, 1863. Detailed as a carpenter at Wilmington on November 14, 1863. Reported absent on detail at Wilmington through February 29, 1864. Reported present in November-December, 1864. Captured in

Chatham County on an unspecified date. Paroled at Avin's Ferry on April 24, 1865.

ALLEN, THOMAS, Private
Born in Moore County and was by occupation a farmer prior to enlisting in Moore County at age 31, March 14, 1862. Died in hospital at Raleigh on June 18, 1862, of disease.

ANNIER, JOHN, Private
Born in Guinup, England, and was by occupation a miner prior to enlisting in Moore County at age 35, March 14, 1862. Reported present in May-June and September-December, 1862. Reported on detail as a bridge guard from June 18, 1863, until January 13, 1864, when he was detailed as a hospital nurse at Goldsboro. Reported on duty as a nurse at Goldsboro through November, 1864.

BAKER, NEILL A., Sergeant
Previously served as Private in Company G, 17th Regiment Mississippi Infantry. Transferred to this company on or about May 27, 1862. Mustered in as Private. Reported present in September-October, 1862. Reported on detail as regimental Commissary Sergeant and Quartermaster Sergeant in November-December, 1862. Rejoined the company on an unspecified date. Promoted to Sergeant in January-October, 1863. Reported present in September, 1863-February, 1864. Wounded in the head at the Ogeechee River bridge, near Savannah, Georgia, on or about December 9, 1864. Died at or near Savannah on December 16, 1864, of wounds.

BLACKMAN, JESSE FORDHAM, Private
Enlisted in Moore County at age 28, May 7, 1862, for the war. Reported present in May-June and September-December, 1862. Reported under arrest on October 18, 1863. Reason he was arrested not reported. Returned to duty in November-December, 1863. Reported present in January-February and November-December, 1864.

BOBBITT, RICHARD M., Private
Born in Moore County where he resided as a carpenter prior to enlisting in Moore County at age 28. Enlistment date reported as March 6, 1862; however, he was not listed in the records of this company until June 17, 1863. Detailed as a carpenter at Wilmington on October 14, 1863. Reported absent on detail at Wilmington through February 29, 1864. Sent to hospital sick on December 19, 1864. Survived the war.

BROOKS, JOB TERRELL, Private
Enlisted in Chatham County at age 18, December 17, 1862, for the war. Reported present in September, 1863-February, 1864. Sent to hospital at Raleigh on October 25, 1864. Furloughed on an unspecified date. Was granted a furlough extension on February 24, 1865. Survived the war.

BROOKS, WILLIAM MARSH, Sergeant
Born in Chatham County and enlisted in Moore County at age 25, March 14, 1862. Mustered in as Sergeant. Reported present in May-June, 1862. Reported present but sick in camp in September-December, 1862. Reported

present in September-December, 1863. Reported absent on detached duty from January 27 through February 29, 1864. Reported present in November-December, 1864.

BROWN, G. W., _____
North Carolina pension records indicate that he served in this company.

BRYAN, REDIN, Private
Resided in Moore County where he enlisted on May 1, 1862, for the war. Reported present in May-June and September-October, 1862. Transferred to Company A, 63rd Regiment N.C. Troops (5th Regiment N.C. Cavalry), November 26, 1862.

BUCHANAN, A. J., Private
Enlisted in Moore County on March 13, 1863, for the war. Sent to hospital at Greenville on June 16, 1863. Reported present in September, 1863-February, 1864, and November-December, 1864.

BUCHANAN, CERNEY, Private
Born in Chatham County and was by occupation a farmer prior to enlisting in Moore County at age 35, March 14, 1862. Discharged (probably because he was overage) prior to July 1, 1862.

BUCHANAN, ELBERT, Private
Resided in Chatham County and was by occupation a farmer prior to enlisting in Moore County at age 43, November 5, 1863, for the war. Present or accounted for through February, 1864. Also reported present in November-December, 1864.

BUCHANAN, HILLIARD S., Private
Resided in Chatham County and enlisted in Moore County on August 1, 1863, for the war. Reported present in September, 1863-February, 1864. Captured at or near Plymouth on or about September 29, 1864. Confined at Fort Monroe, Virginia, on or about November 16, 1864. Transferred to Point Lookout, Maryland, where he arrived on November 25, 1864. Released at Point Lookout on June 23, 1865, after taking the Oath of Allegiance.

BUCHANAN, J. RUFFE, Private
Enlisted in Moore County on July 24, 1863, for the war. Reported present in September, 1863-February, 1864. Captured at or near Plymouth on or about October 31, 1864. Confined at Fort Monroe, Virginia, November 16, 1864. Transferred to Point Lookout, Maryland, November 24, 1864. Paroled and exchanged on an unspecified date. Captured by the enemy in Chatham County on an unspecified date. Paroled at Avin's Ferry on April 25, 1865.

BUCHANAN, J. W., Private
Enlisted in Moore County at age 25, March 13, 1863, for the war. Reported present in September, 1863-February, 1864. Hospitalized at Raleigh on February 18, 1865, with intermittent fever. Returned to duty on March 1, 1865. Captured in Chatham County on an unspecified date. Paroled on April 25, 1865.

BUCHANAN, JOSEPH, Corporal
Enlisted at age 27, March 14, 1862. No further records.

BUCHANAN, RILEY, Private
Born in Moore County and was by occupation a farmer prior to enlisting in Moore County at age 27, March 14, 1862. Reported present but sick in May-June, 1862. Hospitalized at Petersburg, Virginia, July 23, 1862, with typhoid fever. Furloughed for thirty days on September 26, 1862. Reported present in November-December, 1862, and September, 1863-February, 1864. Also reported present in November-December, 1864.

BUCHANAN, RUFFIN, Private
Enlisted in Moore County on May 5, 1862, for the war. Reported present but sick in May-June, 1862. Reported sick in camp in September-October, 1862. Reported present in November-December, 1862, and September, 1863-February, 1864. Also reported present in November-December, 1864.

BUCHANAN, SAMUEL R. B., Private
Enlisted in Moore County at age 23, August 1, 1863, for the war. Reported present in September, 1863-February, 1864, and November-December, 1864. Survived the war.

CAMERON, DUGALD C., Private
Enlisted at age 23, March 14, 1862. No further records.

CATES, THOMAS, Private
Enlisted in Orange County on August 1, 1862, for the war. Reported present in September, 1863-February, 1864. No further records.

CHAPEL, M. C., _____
North Carolina pension records indicate that he served in this company.

CHRISTIAN, GEORGE W., Private
Previously served as Private in Company I, 31st Regiment N.C. Troops. Enlisted in this company on March 21, 1862. Reported present in May-June and September-December, 1862. Also reported present in September, 1863-February, 1864. Last reported in the records of this company on June 14, 1864.

COX, ALEXANDER H., Sergeant
Born in Moore County and was by occupation a farmer prior to enlisting in Moore County at age 18, March 14, 1862. Mustered in as Sergeant. Reported present in May-June and September-December, 1862. Also reported present in September, 1863-February, 1864. Appointed Chief Musician in March-December, 1864, and transferred to the regimental band.

COX, BENTON PETTY, Private
Resided in Moore County and was by occupation a farmer prior to enlisting in Moore County at age 43, August 1, 1863, for the war. Reported present in September, 1863-February, 1864, and November-December, 1864.

COX, HENRY A., Corporal
Resided in Moore County and was by occupation a farmer prior to enlisting in Moore County at age 32, May 1, 1862, for the war. Mustered in as Private. Reported present in May-June and September-December, 1862. Promoted to Corporal in January-October, 1863. Reported present in September, 1863-February, 1864. Appointed Musician in March-December, 1864, and transferred to the regimental band. [Previously served as Captain in the 51st Regiment N.C. Militia.]

COX, SANDY, _____
North Carolina pension records indicate that he served in this company.

COX, THOMAS C., Private
Resided in Moore County and was by occupation a farmer prior to enlisting in Moore County at age 24, May 1, 1862, for the war. Died in hospital at Petersburg, Virginia, on or about August 7, 1862, of "continued fever."

COX, WILLIAM J., Private
Enlisted in Moore County on May 1, 1862, for the war. Reported present in May-June and September-December, 1862. Also reported present in September, 1863-February, 1864. Appointed Musician in March-December, 1864, and transferred to the regimental band.

DALRYMPLE, MALCOLM, Private
Born in Moore County and was by occupation a farmer prior to enlisting in Moore County at age 24, March 14, 1862. Reported absent without leave in May-June, 1862. Detailed to work at a sawmill on October 28, 1862. Reported absent on detail through December, 1862. Rejoined the company on an unspecified date. Reported present in September-December, 1863. Reported absent on detached service from January 27 through February 29, 1864. Reported present in November-December, 1864. Survived the war.

DALRYMPLE, WILLIAM M., Private
Resided in Moore County and was by occupation a farmer prior to enlisting in Moore County at age 24, May 1, 1862, for the war. Reported present but sick in May-June, 1862. Reported present in September-December, 1862, and September-December, 1863. Reported absent on detached service from January 27 through February 29, 1864. Reported present in November-December, 1864.

DICKEN, JAMES T., Private
Enlisted in Moore County on November 6, 1863, for the war. Reported present through February, 1864. Captured at Savannah, Georgia, December 21, 1864. Hospitalized at Savannah on January 19, 1865, with chronic diarrhoea. Sent to Hilton Head, South Carolina, on an unspecified date. Transferred to Fort Delaware, Delaware, where he arrived on March 12, 1865. Released at Fort Delaware on June 19, 1865, after taking the Oath of Allegiance. [Federal hospital records dated December, 1864, give his age as 46.]

DICKEN, THOMAS, Private
Enlisted in Moore County on March 15, 1863, for the war. Furloughed for twenty-five days on April 4, 1863. Reported present in September-December, 1863. Sent to

hospital at Wilmington on February 21, 1864. Died (presumably at Wilmington) on March 7, 1864, of disease.

DICKENS, JOHN T., _____
North Carolina pension records indicate that he served in this company.

DOUGLAS, R. B., Private
Enlisted at age 17, January 23, 1864, for the war. Reported present in November-December, 1864. Hospitalized at Charlotte on February 13, 1865, with intermittent fever. Transferred to another hospital on February 18, 1865. Survived the war.

FUQUAY, JOHN, Private
Resided in Chatham County and enlisted in Moore County at age 19, January 20, 1863, for the war. Reported present in September, 1863-February, 1864. Captured at or near Plymouth on or about September 29, 1864. Confined at Fort Monroe, Virginia. Transferred to Point Lookout, Maryland, where he arrived on November 25, 1864. Released at Point Lookout on June 26, 1865, after taking the Oath of Allegiance.

GILCHREST, CHARLES A., Private
Born in Moore County and was by occupation a farmer prior to enlisting in Moore County at age 19, March 14, 1862. Reported present in May-June and September-December, 1862. Reported present but sick in camp in September-October, 1863. Reported present in November, 1863-February, 1864, and November-December, 1864. Survived the war. [North Carolina pension records indicate that he was wounded at Bentonville in (March) 1865.]

GILMORE, JASPER H., Sergeant
Born in Chatham County where he resided as a farmer prior to enlisting in Moore County at age 25, March 14, 1862. Mustered in as Sergeant. Reported absent sick in May-June, 1862. Reported present in September-December, 1862. Died in hospital at Wilson on March 20, 1863, of "febris typhoides," "pneumonia," and/or "consumption."

GODFREY, HENRY A., Private
Born in Moore County where he resided as a farmer prior to enlisting in Moore County at age 35, March 14, 1862. Discharged (probably because he was overage) prior to July 1, 1862.

GODFREY, JOHN, Sergeant
Born in Moore County where he resided as a farmer prior to enlisting in Moore County at age 27, March 14, 1862. Mustered in as Sergeant. Reported present in May-June, 1862. Reported present but sick in camp in September-October, 1862. Reported present in November-December, 1862. Reported present or accounted for in September, 1863-February, 1864. Hospitalized at Raleigh on November 6, 1864, with debilitas. Returned to duty on December 12, 1864. Survived the war.

GUNTER, AMBROSE A., Private
Resided in Chatham County and was by occupation a

farmer prior to enlisting in Moore County at age 28, July 24, 1863, for the war. Hospitalized at Wilmington on September 1, 1863. Returned to duty on October 28, 1863. Reported present in November, 1863-February, 1864, and November-December, 1864. Survived the war.

HANLEY, D. M., Private
Resided in Moore County. Place and date of enlistment not reported; however, he probably enlisted subsequent to February 29, 1864. Paroled at Greensboro on May 1, 1865.

HARRINGTON, A. M., Private
Resided in Moore County where he enlisted at age 47, July 24, 1863, for the war. Reported present in September-December, 1863. Reported absent on detached service from January 27 through February 29, 1864. Reported present in November-December, 1864.

HARRIS, WILLIAM, Private
Enlisted on October 6, 1863, for the war. Transferred to Company K of this regiment in November-December, 1863.

HAWLEY, JOHN ALLEN, Private
Born in Sampson County and was by occupation a farmer prior to enlisting in Moore County at age 27, May 5, 1862, for the war. Reported present but sick in camp in September-October, 1862. Reported present in November-December, 1862. Sent to hospital at Goldsboro on February 6, 1863. Reported present in September, 1863-February, 1864, and November-December, 1864. Survived the war. [Previously served as 2nd Lieutenant in the 51st Regiment N.C. Militia.]

HERRING, LOUIS, Private
Born in Alamance County* and enlisted in Moore County on May 1, 1862, for the war. Reported present but sick in May-June, 1862. Reported present in September-December, 1862. Died in North Carolina on or about February 6, 1863, of "pneumonia."

HICKS, DANIEL M., _____
North Carolina pension records indicate that he served in this company.

HIGHT, JAMES H., Private
Enlisted on January 20, 1863, for the war. Reported present in September, 1863-February, 1864. Hospitalized at Wilmington on November 25, 1864, with chronic diarrhoea and/or a hernia. Furloughed for sixty days on December 21, 1864.

HUGHES, ORIN TURNER, Private
Born in Chatham County and was by occupation a farmer prior to enlisting in Chatham County at age 21, March 14, 1862. Reported present in May-June and September-December, 1862. Also reported present in September, 1863-February, 1864, and November-December, 1864.

HUGHES, SPENCER, Private
Born in Moore County and was by occupation a farmer prior to enlisting in Moore County at age 27, March 14,

1862. Reported absent without leave in May-June, 1862. Returned to duty on or about July 1, 1862. Detailed as an ambulance driver on October 18, 1862. Rejoined the company in November-December, 1862. Reported present in September-October, 1863. Reported absent on sick leave of thirty days on December 30, 1863. Returned to duty prior to March 1, 1864. Reported present in November-December, 1864. Survived the war.

HUGHES, WILLIAM, Private
Enlisted in Moore County at age 25, January 20, 1863, for the war. Reported present in September, 1863-February, 1864, and November-December, 1864. Captured in Chatham County on an unspecified date. Paroled at Avin's Ferry on April 24, 1865.

HUNTER, BENJAMIN W., 1st Sergeant
Born in Moore County where he resided as a millwright prior to enlisting in Moore County at age 25, March 14, 1862. Mustered in as 1st Sergeant. Reported present in May-June and September-December, 1862. Also reported present in September, 1863-February, 1864. Sent to hospital sick on December 25, 1864. Captured in Chatham County on an unspecified date. Paroled at Avin's Ferry on April 24, 1865.

HUNTER, JOHN G., Corporal
Born in Johnston County and was by occupation a farmer prior to enlisting in Moore County at age 42, March 14, 1862. Mustered in as Corporal. Discharged (probably by reason of being over 35 years of age) prior to July 1, 1862.

HUNTER, JOHN M., Private
Born in Cumberland County and resided in Harnett County where he was by occupation a blacksmith prior to enlisting in Moore County at age 36, March 14, 1862. Reported present in May-June, 1862. Reported present but sick in camp in September-October, 1862. Reported present in November-December, 1862. Hospitalized at Wilmington on September 11, 1863, with intermittent fever. Furloughed for thirty days on or about September 25, 1863. Returned to duty in November-December, 1863. Reported present in January-February, 1864. Sent to hospital sick on October 25, 1864. Captured in Chatham County on an unspecified date. Paroled at Avin's Ferry on April 24, 1865.

JOHNSTON, DAVID, Private
Enlisted in Moore County at age 32, May 2, 1862, for the war. Mustered in as Musician. Reported present in May-June and September-December, 1862. Reduced to ranks in January-October, 1863. Reported present in September, 1863-February, 1864, and November-December, 1864. Captured in Chatham County on an unspecified date. Paroled at Avin's Ferry on April 27, 1865.

KELLY, ARCHIBALD A., Private
Born in Chatham County where he resided as a farmer prior to enlisting in Moore County at age 20, March 14, 1862. Reported present in May-June and September-December, 1862. Furloughed on or about October 28, 1863. Returned to duty in November-December, 1863. Reported present in January-February and November-December, 1864. Survived the war.

KELLY, BENJAMIN, Private
Born in Moore County and resided in Chatham County where he was by occupation a farmer prior to enlisting in Moore County at age 46, March 14, 1862. Reported present in May-June and September-December, 1862. No further records.

KELLY, H. M., _____
North Carolina pension records indicate that he served in this company.

KELLY, HENRY, Private
Born in Moore County and was by occupation a farmer prior to enlisting in Chatham County at age 33, March 14, 1862. Reported present in May-June and September-December, 1862. Also reported present in September, 1863-February, 1864, and November-December, 1864.

KELLY, HUGH, Private
Born in Moore County and was by occupation a farmer prior to enlisting in Moore County at age 18, March 14, 1862. Reported present in May-June and September-December, 1862. Also reported present in September, 1863-February, 1864, and November-December, 1864.

KELLY, J. DAVID, Private
Enlisted in Moore County on May 1, 1862, for the war. Reported absent sick in May-June, 1862. Returned to duty on or about July 1, 1862. Reported present in September-December, 1862, and September, 1863-February, 1864. Also reported present in November-December, 1864.

KELLY, JOHN B., Private
Born in Chatham County and was by occupation a millwright prior to enlisting in Chatham or Moore County at age 25, March 14, 1862. Reported present in May-June and September-October, 1862. Reported present but sick in camp in November-December, 1862. Hospitalized at Wilmington on August 16, 1863. Returned to duty on November 5, 1863. Furloughed for sixty days on November 18, 1863. Returned to duty prior to March 1, 1864. Reported present in November-December, 1864. Captured in Chatham County on an unspecified date. Paroled at Avin's Ferry on April 24, 1865.

KELLY, JOSEPH D., Musician
Enlisted at age 22, May 15, 1862, for the war. Mustered in as Musician. Reported present in September, 1863-February, 1864. Transferred to the regimental band in March-December, 1864.

KELLY, O. W., Private
Enlisted at age 27, March 14, 1862. No further records.

KELLY, RODERICK, Private
Born in Moore County where he resided as a shoemaker prior to enlisting in Moore County at age 43, March 15, 1862. Discharged (probably because he was over 35 years of age) prior to July 1, 1862.

KELLY, SPENCER, Private
Enlisted in Moore County at age 21, March 14, 1863, for the war. Reported present in September, 1863-February, 1864, and November-December, 1864. Survived the war.

KELLY, STEPHEN, Private
Born in Moore County and was by occupation a farmer prior to enlisting in Chatham County at age 37, March 14, 1862. Reported present in May-June, 1862. Reported present but sick in camp in September-October, 1862. Reported present in November-December, 1862, and September-October, 1863. Detailed as a carpenter at Wilmington on November 14, 1863. Reported on detail at Wilmington through February 27, 1864. Reported present in November-December, 1864.

KELLY, THOMAS M., Private
Born in Moore County and was by occupation a shoemaker prior to enlisting in Moore County at age 22, March 14, 1862. Reported present in May-June and September-December, 1862. Also reported present in September, 1863-February, 1864. Appointed Musician in March-December, 1864, and transferred to the regimental band.

KELLY, WILLIAM JOSEPH, Private
Enlisted in Moore County on May 5, 1862, for the war. Mustered in as Corporal. Appointed Quartermaster Sergeant on July 15, 1862, and transferred to the Field and Staff of this regiment. Reduced to ranks on November 29, 1864, and transferred back to this company. No further records.

KNIGHT, JAMES L., Private
Born in Moore County and was by occupation a farmer prior to enlisting in Moore County at age 25, March 14, 1862. Reported present but sick in May-June, 1862. Reported present in September-December, 1862, and September, 1863-February, 1864. Captured at or near Plymouth on or about September 29, 1864. Sent to Roanoke Island. Confined at Fort Monroe, Virginia, November 16, 1864. Transferred to Point Lookout, Maryland, where he arrived on November 25, 1864. Paroled at Point Lookout on March 28, 1865. Received at Boulware's Wharf, James River, Virginia, March 30, 1865, for exchange.

KNIGHT, JOHN L., Private
Born in Moore County and was by occupation a farmer prior to enlisting in Moore County at age 27, March 14, 1862. Reported present in May-June and September-December, 1862. Also reported present in September, 1863-February, 1864, and November-December, 1864. Survived the war.

LASHLEY, JOHN L., Private
Born in Moore County and was by occupation a farmer prior to enlisting in Moore County at age 30, April 30, 1862, for the war. Reported present in May-June, 1862. Died at Petersburg, Virginia, on or about August 9, 1862, of disease.

LAURENCE, JOSEPH T., Corporal
Born in Chatham County and was by occupation a farmer prior to enlisting in Moore County at age 26, March 14, 1862. Mustered in as Corporal. Reported present but sick in May-June, 1862. Reported present in September-October, 1862. Reported present but sick in camp in November-December, 1862. Reported present in September, 1863-February, 1864, and November-December, 1864.

LAWRENCE, D. K., Corporal
Place and date of enlistment not reported. Furloughed for fourteen days on April 22, 1863. No further records.

LETT, WILLIAM D., Private
Born in Moore County where he resided as a silversmith prior to enlisting in Moore County at age 24, March 14, 1862. Reported on detail to repair guns from April 28 through July 1, 1862. Reported absent without leave ("said to be sick") on or about July 1, 1862. Reported present but sick in camp in September-December, 1862. No further records.

LUTHER, GEORGE W., Private
Enlisted on March 13, 1863, for the war. Reported present in November-December, 1864.

McAULEY, JAMES D., Private
Resided in Moore County and was by occupation a farmer prior to enlisting in Moore County at age 38, January 20, 1863, for the war. Reported present in September, 1863-February, 1864, and November-December, 1864. Captured in Chatham County on an unspecified date. Paroled at Avin's Ferry on April 25, 1865.

McBRYDE, THOMAS, Private
Born in Moore County and was by occupation a farmer prior to enlisting in Moore County at age 40, March 31, 1862. Discharged (probably because he was over 35 years of age) prior to July 1, 1862.

McDONALD, JOHN A., Private
Born in Harnett County* and was by occupation a farmer prior to enlisting in Moore County at age 26, March 14, 1862. Reported present but sick in May-June, 1862. Reported present in September-October, 1862. Detailed as an ambulance driver on December 2, 1862. Rejoined the company subsequent to December 31, 1862. Detailed as brigade butcher on or about June 20, 1863. Reported absent on detail in September, 1863-February, 1864, and November-December, 1864.

McFARLAND, JOHN B., Private
Born in Moore County where he resided as a gunsmith prior to enlisting in Moore County at age 30, March 14, 1862. Reported on detail to repair guns from April 28 through July 1, 1862. Detailed to work in a sawmill on October 28, 1862. Reported on detail (apparently as an armorer) in the repair shop at Goldsboro from July 3, 1863, through December 31, 1864.

McFARLAND, WILLIAM M., Private
Born in Moore County where he resided as a farmer prior to enlisting in Moore County at age 18, March 14, 1862. Reported present in May-June and September-December, 1862. Reported on detail as a carpenter at Wilmington from October 14, 1863, through February 29, 1864. Reported present in November-December, 1864.

McINTYRE, S., _____
Place and date of enlistment not reported. Confederate gravestone records indicate that he died (probably at or near Raleigh) on December 17, 1864.

McLEAN, HUGH, Private
Born in Harnett County* and was by occupation a gunsmith prior to enlisting in Moore County at age 25, March 14, 1862. Reported on detail to repair guns from April 28 through July 1, 1862. Hospitalized at Petersburg, Virginia, August 13, 1862. Died in hospital at Petersburg on September 8, 1862, of "feb[ris] typhoides."

McNEILL, ALEXANDER, Private
Enlisted in Moore County at age 28, May 14, 1862, for the war. Reported present in September-December, 1862, and September, 1863-February, 1864. Also reported present in November-December, 1864. Captured in Chatham County on an unspecified date. Paroled at Avin's Ferry on April 26, 1865.

McNEILL, ANDREW J., Private
Born in Moore County where he resided as a farmer prior to enlisting in Moore County at age 38, March 14, 1862. Reported present in May-June, 1862. Died in hospital at Petersburg, Virginia, August 10, 1862, of "typhoid fever."

McNEILL, JOHN, JR., Private
Enlisted in Moore County on May 14, 1862, for the war. Reported present in September-December, 1862, and September, 1863-February, 1864. Sent to hospital sick on October 23, 1864. No further records.

McNEILL, JOHN, SR., Private
Enlisted in Moore County on May 14, 1862, for the war. Reported present in September-December, 1862. Reported absent with leave on or about October 26, 1863. Reported present in November, 1863-February, 1864. Captured in Chatham County on an unspecified date. Paroled at Avin's Ferry on April 24, 1865.

McNEILL, JOHN A., Private
Enlisted in Moore County on March 13, 1863, for the war. Reported present in September, 1863-February, 1864. Hospitalized at Raleigh on November 6, 1864, with intermittent fever. Returned to duty on November 23, 1864. Present or accounted for through December, 1864.

McNEILL, NEILL, Private
Enlisted in Moore County on March 13, 1863, for the war. Reported present in September, 1863-February, 1864. Hospitalized at Raleigh on November 9, 1864, with debilitas. Returned to duty on November 23, 1864. Survived the war.

McNEILL, NEILL A., Private
Enlisted in Moore County on May 14, 1862, for the war. Died at Petersburg, Virginia, July 16, 1862, of disease.

McNEILL, TORQUILL, Private
Enlisted in Moore County on May 14, 1862, for the war. Reported present in September-December, 1862, and

September, 1863-February, 1864. Also reported present in November-December, 1864.

MADDOX, JAMES T., Private
Born in Moore County and was by occupation a farmer prior to enlisting in Moore County at age 18, March 14, 1862. Reported present in May-June, 1862. Reported present but sick in camp in September-October, 1862. Hospitalized at Petersburg, Virginia, on or about November 2, 1862, with abscesses. Transferred to another hospital on November 16, 1862. Returned to duty on an unspecified date. Reported present in September, 1863-February, 1864. Appointed Musician in March-December, 1864, and transferred to the regimental band.

MARSHBURN, J. S., Private
Born in Moore County and was by occupation a farmer prior to enlisting in Moore County at age 32. Enlistment date reported as March 14, 1862; however, he is not listed on any of the surviving muster rolls of the regiment. Presumably reported for duty after February 29, 1864. Paroled at Greensboro on May 11, 1865.

MUCKLE, BENJAMIN, Private
Born in Moore County and was by occupation a farmer prior to enlisting in Moore County at age 37, March 14, 1862. Reported absent sick in May-June, 1862. Reported present but sick in camp in September-December, 1862. Sent to hospital at Raleigh on March 15, 1863. Reported present in September, 1863-February, 1864. Hospitalized at Wilmington on November 25, 1864, with remittent fever. Returned to duty on December 3, 1864. Sent to hospital sick on December 19, 1864. No further records.

NIVEN, DAVID, Private
Enlisted in Moore County on August 13, 1863, for the war. Reported present in September, 1863-February, 1864, and November-December, 1864.

OLIVER, ALFRED C., Private
Born in Moore County and was by occupation a farmer prior to enlisting in Moore County at age 20, March 14, 1862. Reported present in May-June and September-December, 1862. Also reported present in September-October, 1863. Detailed as a carpenter at Wilmington on November 14, 1863. Reported on detail at Wilmington through February, 1864. Died in hospital at Raleigh on or about December 8, 1864, of "feb[ris] congestiva."

OLIVER, JOHN, Private
Enlisted in Moore County at age 33, May 5, 1862, for the war. Reported present but sick in May-June, 1862. Reported present in September-December, 1862. Detailed as a carpenter at Wilmington on September 16, 1863. Reported absent on detail through February 29, 1864. Reported present in November-December, 1864. Survived the war.

OLIVER, M. T., Private
Resided in Moore County and was by occupation a farmer prior to enlisting in Chatham County at age 32, July 7, 1862, for the war. Detailed as a carpenter at Wilmington on September 16, 1863. Reported absent on detail through

February, 1864. Hospitalized at Raleigh on November 6, 1864, with intermittent fever. Returned to duty on December 2, 1864. Survived the war.

OLIVER, MOSES H., Private

Born in Moore County where he resided as a farmer prior to enlisting in Moore County at age 38, March 14, 1862. Reported present in May-June and September-October, 1862. Reported present but sick in camp in November-December, 1862. Reported present in September, 1863-February, 1864, and November-December, 1864. Captured in Chatham County on an unspecified date. Paroled at Avin's Ferry on April 24, 1865.

OLIVER, WILLIS M., Private

Enlisted in Moore County on March 20, 1863, for the war. Sent to hospital at Greenville on June 15, 1863. Detailed as a carpenter at Wilmington on October 14, 1863. Reported absent on detail through February 29, 1864. Hospitalized at Raleigh on November 6, 1864, with remittent fever. Returned to duty on December 2, 1864.

PIPKIN, JOHN E. J., Corporal

Born in Moore County and was by occupation a carpenter prior to enlisting in Moore County at age 28, March 14, 1862. Mustered in as Corporal. Reported present but sick in May-June, 1862. Reported present in September-December, 1862, and September, 1863-February, 1864. Captured at or near Plymouth on or about September 29, 1864. Confined at Fort Monroe, Virginia, on or about November 16, 1864. Transferred to Point Lookout, Maryland, November 24, 1864. Paroled and exchanged on an unspecified date. Hospitalized at Richmond, Virginia, February 15, 1865, with chronic diarrhoea. Furloughed for sixty days on March 6, 1865.

PIPKIN, WILLIAM, Private

Born in Moore County and was by occupation a farmer prior to enlisting in Moore County at age 40, March 14, 1862. Died in hospital at Petersburg, Virginia, July 24, 1862, of "feb[ris] typh[oides]."

REED, HENRY S., Private

Enlisted in Moore County on May 1, 1862, for the war. Reported present but sick in May-June and September-October, 1862. Reported present in November-December, 1862, and September-October, 1863. Reported on detail as a blacksmith at Fayetteville from December 12, 1863, through December, 1864. Attached to Company A and later to Company G, 2nd Battalion N.C. Local Defense Troops, while on detail at Fayetteville.

SCARBROUGH, JAMES C., Private

Born in Randolph County and resided in Moore County where he was by occupation a farmer prior to enlisting in Moore County at age 24, March 14, 1862. Reported on detail as an ambulance driver from June 16, 1862, through February, 1864. Reported present in November-December, 1864. Survived the war.

SHEPPARD, JAMES L., Private

Born in Moore County and was by occupation a physician prior to enlisting in Moore County at age 29, March 14,

1862. Reported present in May-June and September-December, 1862. Reported on detail to attend the sick of the regiment from July 4 through October 31, 1863. Appointed Hospital Steward on December 1, 1863, and transferred to the Field and Staff of this regiment.

SHEPPARD, JOHN A., Private

Enlisted in Moore County on March 14, 1863, for the war. Reported present in September, 1863-February, 1864, and November-December, 1864.

SLOAN, DAVID M., Private

Born in Moore County and was by occupation a farmer prior to enlisting in Moore County at age 18, May 3, 1862, for the war. Reported absent sick in May-June, 1862. Reported present but sick in camp in September-October, 1862. Reported present in November-December, 1862, and September, 1863-February, 1864. Appointed Musician in March-December, 1864, and transferred to the regimental band.

SMITH, MARTIN ALEXANDER, Private

Born in Chatham County and was by occupation a farmer prior to enlisting in Moore County at age 24, March 14, 1862. Reported present but sick in May-June, 1862. Hospitalized at Petersburg, Virginia, July 20, 1862, with typhoid fever. Returned to duty on August 25, 1862. Reported present in September-December, 1862. Reported present but sick in camp in September-October, 1863. Reported present in November, 1863-February, 1864. Appointed Musician in March-December, 1864, and transferred to the regimental band.

SPIVEY, JORDAN, Private

Enlisted at age 49, March 14, 1862. No further records.

STEPHENS, J. MARSHALL, Private

Enlisted in Moore County on May 5, 1862, for the war. Reported present in May-June and September-December, 1862. Also reported present in September, 1863-February, 1864. Appointed Musician in March-December, 1864, and transferred to the regimental band.

STEWART, ANDREW JACKSON, Private

Born in Moore or Harnett* County and was by occupation a farmer prior to enlisting in Moore County at age 26, March 14, 1862. Reported absent sick in May-June, 1862. Reported present in September-December, 1862. Died in hospital at Wilmington on September 4, 1863, of "febris remittens."

STEWART, C. E., Private

Enlisted in Moore County on May 1, 1862, for the war. Reported present in May-June, 1862. Hospitalized at Petersburg, Virginia, July 20, 1862, with typhoid fever. Returned to duty on November 16, 1862. Died at Goldsboro on February 3, 1863, of disease.

STEWART, DREWRY, Private

Born in Harnett County* where he resided as a farmer prior to enlisting in Moore County at age 43, March 14, 1862. Reported on detail as a teamster from June 1 through December 31, 1862. Discharged on January 2, 1863, possibly after providing a substitute.

STEWART, J. F., Private

Born in Harnett County* and was by occupation a farmer prior to enlisting at Drewry's Bluff, Virginia, at age 16, January 2, 1863, for the war. Reported present in September-December, 1863. Reported absent on detached duty from January 27 through February 29, 1864. Appointed Musician in March-December, 1864, and transferred to the regimental band.

STEWART, JOHN A., Private

Born in Harnett County* where he resided as a blacksmith prior to enlisting in Moore County at age 31, March 14, 1862. Reported absent without leave in May-June, 1862. Hospitalized at Petersburg, Virginia, August 8, 1862, with an unspecified complaint. Returned to duty in November-December, 1862. Reported on detail as a blacksmith from June 10, 1863, through December 31, 1864.

STEWART, WILLIAM H., Private

Born in Harnett County* where he resided as a carpenter prior to enlisting in Moore County at age 26, March 14, 1862. Mustered in as Private. Promoted to Corporal on July 20, 1862. Reported on detail as a sawmill worker from October 28 through December 31, 1862. Reduced to ranks in January-October, 1863. Reported on detail as regimental blacksmith from May 18, 1863, through February 29, 1864. Reported on detail at Tarboro from November 19 through December 31, 1864.

STONE, ARCHIBALD, Private

Enlisted on January 20, 1863, for the war. Reported present in September-December, 1863. Reported absent on detached service from January 27 through February 29, 1864. Hospitalized at Wilmington on December 29, 1864, with chronic rheumatism. Hospitalized at Greensboro on February 23, 1865, with catarrhus. Returned to duty the same date. Hospitalized at Charlotte on March 4, 1865, with intermittent fever. Returned to duty on March 10, 1865.

THOMAS, BENJAMIN W., Private

Enlisted on October 10, 1862, for the war. Hospitalized at or near Petersburg, Virginia, October 22, 1862, with rheumatism. Returned to duty on November 10, 1862. Reported on detail as a carpenter at Wilmington from September 16, 1863, through February 29, 1864. Hospitalized at Goldsboro on an unspecified date. Returned to duty on May 29, 1864. Sent to hospital sick on December 1, 1864. Hospitalized at Charlotte on February 13, 1865, with neuralgia. Transferred to another hospital on or about February 15, 1865. Hospitalized at Charlotte on April 28, 1865, with typhoid fever. Paroled in May, 1865.

THOMAS, DAVID A., Private

Born in Moore County and was by occupation a farmer prior to enlisting in Moore County at age 23, March 14, 1862. Reported present in May-June, 1862. Hospitalized at Petersburg, Virginia, August 6, 1862. Returned to duty in November-December, 1862. Sent to hospital at Goldsboro on March 15, 1863. Reported present in September, 1863-February, 1864, and November-December, 1864. Paroled at Charlotte on May 4, 1865.

THOMAS, HENRY PEYTON, Private

Born in Moore County and was by occupation a farmer prior to enlisting in Moore County at age 23, March 14, 1862. Reported present in May-June and September-October, 1862. Hospitalized at Petersburg, Virginia, November 11, 1862, with chronic bronchitis. Transferred to another hospital on November 14, 1862. Returned to duty prior to January 1, 1863. Furloughed on or about October 28, 1863. Hospitalized at Wilmington on November 28, 1863, with orchitis. Returned to duty on December 19, 1863. Reported present in January-February and November-December, 1864.

THOMAS, J. W., SR., Private

Enlisted in Moore County on February 9, 1863, for the war. Hospitalized at Wilmington on August 28, 1863, with intermittent fever. Returned to duty on September 21, 1863. Reported present in October, 1863-February, 1864. Reported on detail with the subsistence department at Tarboro from October 15 through December 31, 1864.

THOMAS, JACKSON J., Private

Born in Moore County and was by occupation a farmer prior to enlisting in Moore County at age 32, March 14, 1862. Reported present in May-June, 1862. Reported sick in camp in September-October, 1862. Reported present in November-December, 1862, and September, 1863-February, 1864. Reported at home on sick furlough from September 4 through December 31, 1864. Survived the war. [North Carolina pension records indicate that he was wounded in the right foot in Bertie County on an unspecified date.]

THOMAS, JASPER, Private

Born in Moore County and was by occupation a farmer prior to enlisting in Moore County at age 26, March 14, 1862. Deserted on May 10, 1862. Apprehended in October, 1862. Court-martialed and sentenced "to receive thirty-nine lashes on his bare back, to be branded in the left hand with the letter 'D,' and to be put to hard labor for six months on Government work, with ball and chain weighing twelve pounds, attached to his left leg." Returned to duty subsequent to December 31, 1862. Reported present in September, 1863-February, 1864, and November-December, 1864. Hospitalized at Raleigh on February 17, 1865, with intermittent fever. Was issued clothing at the hospital on February 20, 1865. No further records.

THOMAS, JOHN L., Private

Enlisted in Moore County on August 13, 1863, for the war. Reported present in September, 1863-February, 1864. Sent to hospital sick on November 29, 1864. Died at or near Augusta, Georgia, on or about January 25, 1865. Cause of death not reported.

THOMAS, JOHN M. B., Private

Born in Moore County and was by occupation a farmer prior to enlisting in Moore County at age 21, March 14, 1862. Reported present in May-June and September-December, 1862. Also reported present in September, 1863-February, 1864, and November-December, 1864. Survived the war. [North Carolina pension records indicate that he was wounded in the foot near Charleston,

South Carolina, February 14, 1865. "All of the anterior part of foot was shot away—leaving only the heel. . . ."]

THOMAS, JOHN P., Private
Born in Moore County and was by occupation a farmer prior to enlisting in Moore County at age 29, March 14, 1862. Reported present but sick in May-June and September-October, 1862. Reported present in November-December, 1862, and September-October, 1863. Reported on detail as a carpenter at Wilmington from November 14, 1863, through February 29, 1864. Reported present in November-December, 1864.

THOMAS, JOHN W., JR., Private
Born in Moore County and was by occupation a farmer prior to enlisting in Moore County at age 21, March 14, 1862. Reported present in May-June and September-December, 1862. Also reported present in September, 1863-February, 1864, and November-December, 1864. Captured in Chatham County on an unspecified date. Paroled at Avin's Ferry on April 24, 1865.

THOMAS, JOSEPH H., Private
Born in Moore County and was by occupation a blacksmith prior to enlisting in Moore County at age 48, March 14, 1862. Reported present in May-June and September-December, 1862. Also reported present in September-October, 1863. Reported on detail as a blacksmith at the Fayetteville arsenal from December 12, 1863, through December 31, 1864. Attached to Company A and later to Company G, 2nd Battalion N.C. Local Defense Troops, while on detail at Fayetteville.

THOMAS, LUTHER R., Private
Born in Moore County and was by occupation a farmer prior to enlisting in Moore County at age 18, March 14, 1862. Reported present in May-June and September-October, 1862. Reported present but sick in camp in November-December, 1862. Reported present in September, 1863-February, 1864. Hospitalized at Raleigh on November 6, 1864, with intermittent fever. Returned to duty on November 28, 1864. Hospitalized at Fayetteville on December 8, 1864, with an unspecified complaint. Reported in hospital at Fayetteville through February 28, 1865. Captured in Chatham County on an unspecified date. Paroled at Avin's Ferry on April 24, 1865.

THOMAS, ROBERT B., Private
Born in Moore County and was by occupation a farmer prior to enlisting in Moore County at age 24, March 14, 1862. Reported present in May-June, 1862. Hospitalized at or near Petersburg, Virginia, August 25, 1862, with remittent fever. Returned to duty on October 26, 1862. Reported present in November-December, 1862, and September, 1863-February, 1864. Sent to hospital sick on October 24, 1864. Reported absent sick through December, 1864. Survived the war. [North Carolina pension records indicate that he was wounded in North Carolina, South Carolina, Georgia, and Virginia.]

TURNER, GEORGE W., Private
Enlisted in Moore County on May 10, 1862, for the war. Reported present in May-June, 1862. Hospitalized at

Petersburg, Virginia, July 20, 1862, with remittent fever. Transferred to another hospital on November 14, 1862. Returned to duty on December 3, 1862. Transferred "to government workshops" prior to January 1, 1863, by reason of deafness. Rejoined the company on an unspecified date. Reported present in September, 1863-February, 1864. Appointed Musician in March-December, 1864, and transferred to the regimental band.

TURNER, H. C., Private
Enlisted on April 29, 186[4], for the war. Appointed Musician on an unspecified date and transferred to the regimental band. Reported on duty with the regimental band in November-December, 1864. Reduced to ranks in January-April, 1865, and transferred back to this company. Surrendered at Augusta, Georgia, May 26, 1865. Hospitalized at Augusta on June 7, 1865, with abscesses. No further records.

TURNER, THOMAS J., Private
Enlisted at Camp Holmes, near Raleigh, May 7, 1863, for the war. Reported present in September, 1863-February, 1864. Hospitalized at Raleigh on November 6, 1864, with intermittent fever. Transferred to another hospital on January 1, 1865.

WATSON, ALEXANDER, Private
Born in Moore County and was by occupation a farmer prior to enlisting in Moore County at age 23, March 14, 1862. Reported present in May-June and September-December, 1862. Also reported present in September, 1863-February, 1864, and November-December, 1864.

WATSON, GARNER, Private
Enlisted in Moore County at age 20, May 5, 1862, for the war. Reported present but sick in May-June, 1862. Reported present in September-December, 1862. Reported present but sick in camp in September-October, 1863. Reported present in November, 1863-February, 1864, and November-December, 1864. Survived the war.

WATSON, M. K., Private
Place and date of enlistment not reported. Reported present in November-December, 1864.

WATSON, NEILL T., Private
Born in Moore County and was by occupation a farmer prior to enlisting in Moore County at age 30, March 14, 1862. Reported present in May-June, 1862. Reported on detail as a sawmill worker from October 28 through December 31, 1862. Reported present but sick in camp in September-October, 1863. Reported present in November, 1863-February, 1864, and November-December, 1864.

WELDON, JOHN J., Private
Born in Moore County and was by occupation a farmer prior to enlisting in Moore County at age 23, March 14, 1862. Reported present in May-June, 1862. Reported present but sick in camp in September-October, 1862. Reported present in November-December, 1862, and September, 1863-February, 1864. Also reported present in November-December, 1864. Captured in Chatham County on an unspecified date. Paroled at Avin's Ferry on April 24, 1865.

WICKER, BENJAMIN PARKER, Private
Born in Moore County where he resided as a farmer prior
to enlisting in Moore County at age 19, May 1, 1862, for
the war. Sent to hospital at Raleigh on April 19, 1863.
Reported present in May-June and September-December,
1862. Died in Moore County on September 9, 1863, of
disease.

WICKER, DAVID WARREN, Private
Resided in Moore County and was by occupation a farmer
prior to enlisting in Moore County at age 27, May 1, 1862,
for the war. Reported present in May-June and September-
December, 1862. Reported present but sick in camp in
September-October, 1863. Reported present in November,
1863-February, 1864, and November-December, 1864.

WICKER, ELIJAH M., Private
Born in Moore County and was by occupation a farmer
prior to enlisting in Moore County at age 27, March 14,
1862. Wounded in the back by a shell fragment at Malvern
Cliffs, Virginia, June 30, 1862. Returned to duty on or
about the same date. Reported present in September-
December, 1862, and September, 1863-February, 1864.
Also reported present in November-December, 1864.
Survived the war.

WICKER, ELISHA, Private
Resided in Moore County and was by occupation a farmer
prior to enlisting in Moore County at age 48, August 15,
1863, for the war. Reported present in September,
1863-February, 1864, and November-December, 1864.

WICKER, GREEN B., Private
Born in Moore County and was by occupation a farmer
prior to enlisting in Moore County at age 20, March 14,
1862. Reported present in May-June, 1862. Hospitalized
at Petersburg, Virginia, July 20, 1862, with acute
dysentery. Returned to duty on August 25, 1862. Reported
present in September-October, 1862. Reported present
but sick in camp in November-December, 1862. Reported
present in September, 1863-February, 1864, and
November-December, 1864. Survived the war.

WICKER, J. A., Private
Enlisted in Moore County on January 25, 186[4], for the
war. Reported present in February, 1864, and November-
December, 1864.

WICKER, THOMAS R., Private
Born in Moore County and was by occupation a farmer
prior to enlisting in Moore County at age 29, March 14,
1862. Reported absent without leave in May-June, 1862.
Returned to duty on an unspecified date. Reported present
in September-December, 1862, and September,
1863-February, 1864. Also reported present in November-
December, 1864. Survived the war.

WICKER, WILLIAM W., Private
Enlisted in Moore County on May 5, 1862, for the war.
Reported present in May-June and September-December,
1862. Also reported present in September-October, 1863.

Reported on detail as a teamster from November 28, 1863,
through May 19, 1864. Reported present in November-
December, 1864.

WILLIAMS, J. H., Private
Born in Moore County and was by occupation a farmer
prior to enlisting in Moore County at age 23, March 14,
1862. Reported present in May-June and September-
December, 1862. Furloughed for ten days from hospital
at Goldsboro on August 27, 1863. Reported absent sick on
or about October 31, 1863. Reported present in November,
1863-February, 1864. Hospitalized at Raleigh on
November 6, 1864, with intermittent fever. Returned to
duty on February 6, 1865. Survived the war.

WILLIAMS, THOMAS, Private
Previously served as Private in Company A, 63rd
Regiment N.C. Troops (5th Regiment N.C. Cavalry).
Transferred to this company on November 26, 1862.
Reported present in September, 1863-February, 1864.
Hospitalized at Raleigh on November 6, 1864, with
intermittent fever. Furloughed for sixty days on
November 14, 1864. Hospitalized at Fayetteville on
December 23, 1864. Reported still in hospital at
Fayetteville on February 28, 1865.

WOMACK, JOHN B., Private
Enlisted in Moore County at age 17, June 20, 1863, for
the war. Reported present in September, 1863-February,
1864. Sent to hospital sick on October 9, 1864. Survived
the war.

WOOD, ARCHIBALD, Private
Born in Harnett County* and was by occupation a farmer
prior to enlisting in Moore County at age 18, March 14,
1862. Discharged on July 1, 1862. Reason discharged not
reported. Reenlisted in the company on March 15, 1863.
Reported present in September, 1863-February, 1864, and
November-December, 1864. Survived the war.

YARBROUGH, ELIAS G., Private
Born in Harnett County* and was by occupation a farmer
prior to enlisting in Moore County at age 18, March 14,
1862. Reported present in May-June and September-
December, 1862. Also reported present in September,
1863-February, 1864. Hospitalized in Raleigh on
November 6, 1864, with intermittent fever. Returned to
duty on December 2, 1864. Survived the war.

YARBROUGH, JAMES, Private
Place and date of enlistment not reported. Sent to hospital
on October 19, 1864. No further records.

YARBROUGH, WILLIAM T., Corporal
Born in Chatham County and was by occupation a
millwright prior to enlisting in Moore County at age 22,
March 14, 1862. Mustered in as Corporal. Reported
present in May-June and September-December, 1862.
Reported absent on furlough on or about October 28,
1863. Reported present in November, 1863-February,
1864. Died of disease at the Scuppernong River on
September 25, 1864.

COMPANY G

This company, known as "Rutherford Farmers," was raised in Rutherford County and enlisted in Rutherford County in March, 1862. It was mustered into state service at Camp Mangum, near Raleigh, on April 21, 1862, and assigned to the 50th Regiment N.C. Troops as Company G. After joining the regiment the company functioned as a part of the regiment, and its history for the remainder of the war is reported as a part of the regimental history.

The information contained in the following roster was compiled primarily from a company muster-in and descriptive roll dated April 21, 1862, and from company muster rolls for May 31-July 31, 1862; November 1-December 31, 1862; and September 1, 1863-February 29, 1864. No company muster rolls were located for May 1-30, 1862; August 1-October 31, 1862; January 1-August 31, 1863; or for the period after February 29, 1864. Valuable information was obtained from primary records such as the North Carolina adjutant general's *Roll of Honor*, discharge certificates, medical records, prisoner of war records, *The War of the Rebellion: A Compilation of the Official Records of the Union and Confederate Armies*, militia records, newspaper casualty lists and obituaries, Confederate pension applications filed with the state of North Carolina, and the 1860 federal census of North Carolina. Secondary sources such as postwar rosters and histories, cemetery records, the *Confederate Veteran*, published genealogies, and records of the United Daughters of the Confederacy also provided useful information.

OFFICERS

CAPTAIN

ANDREWS, GEORGE W.

Born in Rutherford County where he resided prior to enlisting at age 24. Appointed Captain on March 24, 1862. Reported present in July, 1862. Reported present but sick in camp in November-December, 1862. Reported present in September-December, 1863. Furloughed for twenty days on January 16, 1864. Paroled at Greensboro on May 1, 1865.

LIEUTENANTS

FLACK, JOHN P., 2nd Lieutenant

Born in Rutherford County where he resided as a farmer prior to enlisting in Rutherford County at age 24, March 24, 1862. Mustered in as Corporal. Reported present in June-July, 1862. Reported on detail as a sawmill worker from October 28 through December 31, 1862. Promoted to Sergeant in January-October, 1863. Reduced to ranks

on December 12, 1863. Reported present in September, 1863-February, 1864. Hospitalized at Wilmington on November 25, 1864, with pneumonia. Returned to duty on December 12, 1864. Appointed 2nd Lieutenant on February 26, 1865. Survived the war.

HAMPTON, SAMUEL D., 3rd Lieutenant

Born in Rutherford County where he resided as a farmer prior to enlisting in Rutherford County at age 35, March 24, 1862. Mustered in as Sergeant. Reported present in June-July, 1862. Appointed 3rd Lieutenant on July 17, 1862. Reported present in November-December, 1862. Reported absent sick from October 2 through December 31, 1863. Reported present but sick in camp in January-February, 1864. Resigned on November 4, 1864, by reason of "chronic inflammation of the liver. . . ." Resignation accepted on January 7, 1865.

LOGAN, REUBEN F., 2nd Lieutenant

Born in Rutherford County and was by occupation a farmer prior to enlisting in Rutherford County at age 27, March 24, 1862. Mustered in as Sergeant. Reported present in June-July, 1862. Appointed 2nd Lieutenant on July 15, 1862. Reported present in November-December, 1862, and September, 1863-February, 1864. Last reported in the records of this company on January 19, 1865, when he was granted a leave of absence.

LONG, THOMAS J., 3rd Lieutenant

Born in Rutherford County and was by occupation a farmer prior to enlisting at age 32. Appointed 3rd Lieutenant on April 21, 1862. Resigned on June 11, 1862, because "my health is such [that] I am wholly incapable of discharging the duties of my office." Resignation accepted on July 16, 1862.

MORRISON, JOHN A., 1st Lieutenant

Born in Rutherford County and enlisted at age 23. Appointed 2nd Lieutenant on March 24, 1862. Promoted to 1st Lieutenant on June 24, 1862. Reported present in June-July, 1862. Reported present or accounted for in November-December, 1862. Captured at Rodman's Point (Beaufort County) on April 16, 1863. Sent to New Bern. Transferred to Fort Monroe, Virginia, May 23, 1863. Transferred from Fort Monroe to Fort Delaware, Delaware, on the steamer *Maple Leaf* but was "one of the prisoners . . . who, on June 10, 1863 . . . rose on the guard, overpowered it and made their escape." Rejoined the company on an unspecified date. Reported present in September-December, 1863. Reported absent with leave "to get married" on February 15, 1864. Last reported in the records of this company on July 10, 1864.

NABORS, ASBURY H., 1st Lieutenant

Born in Laurens District, South Carolina, and was by occupation a physician prior to enlisting at age 24. Appointed 1st Lieutenant on March 24, 1862. Resigned on June 16, 1862, by reason of "stricture of urethra and disease of the prostate gland. . . ." Resignation accepted on June 24, 1862.

NONCOMMISSIONED OFFICERS AND PRIVATES

ADAIR, COLUMBUS C., Private

Resided in Rutherford County and was by occupation a farmer prior to enlisting in Rutherford County at age 21, March 24, 1862. Reported present in June-July, 1862. Reported absent on furlough from October 30 until November 30, 1862. Reported absent without leave from November 30 through December 31, 1862. Hospitalized at Wilmington on October 29, 1863, with intermittent fever. Returned to duty on November 7, 1863. Deserted from camp near Wilmington on November 28, 1863.

ADAIR, GOVAN, Private

Resided in Rutherford County where he enlisted at age 21, July 8, 1863, for the war. Reported present in September-October, 1863. Deserted from camp near Wilmington on November 28, 1863.

ADAIR, J. W., Private

Place and date of enlistment not reported; however, he probably enlisted in January-August, 1863. Deserted on August 30, 1863.

ANDREWS, DeWITT QUINCEY, 1st Sergeant

Born in Rutherford County and was by occupation a farmer prior to enlisting in Rutherford County at age 22, March 24, 1862. Mustered in as Sergeant. Reported present in June-July, 1862. Hospitalized at or near Petersburg, Virginia, August 4, 1862, with a gunshot wound. Place and date wounded not reported. Returned to duty on September 6, 1862. Reported present in November-December, 1862. Promoted to 1st Sergeant in January-October, 1863. Furloughed for fourteen days on June 10, 1863. Reported absent sick on October 19, 1863. Returned to duty in November-December, 1863. Reported present in January-February, 1864. Hospitalized at Charlotte on February 6, 1865, with intermittent fever. Transferred to another hospital on April 26, 1865.

BECKERSTAFF, A., Private

Place and date of enlistment not reported (probably enlisted subsequent to February 29, 1864). Paroled at Cheraw, South Carolina, March 5, 1865.

BIGGERSTAFF, BARUCH, Sergeant

Born in Rutherford County on July 13, 1842. Resided in Rutherford County and was by occupation a farmer prior to enlisting in Rutherford County on March 24, 1862. Mustered in as Private. Reported present in June-July, 1862. Reported on detail as a sawmill worker from October 28 through December 31, 1862. Rejoined the company on an unspecified date. Hospitalized at Wilmington on October 2, 1863, with continued fever. Returned to duty on October 10, 1863. Reported present in November, 1863-February, 1864. Promoted to Sergeant subsequent to February 29, 1864. Paroled at Greensboro on May 1, 1865.

BIGGERSTAFF, BENJAMIN FRANKLIN, Sergeant

Resided in Rutherford County where he enlisted at age 22, March 24, 1862. Mustered in as Private. Reported present in June-July, 1862. Reported on detail as a sawmill worker from October 28 through December 31, 1862. Promoted to Sergeant in January-October, 1863. Reported present in September, 1863-February, 1864. Hospitalized at Charlotte on February 13, 1865, with chronic diarrhoea. Furloughed on February 19, 1865.

BIGGERSTAFF, ELIJAH, JR., Private

Born in Rutherford County where he resided as a farmer prior to enlisting in Rutherford County age 28, March 24, 1862. Reported present in June-July and November-December, 1862. Furloughed for fourteen days on June 30, 1863. Reported present in September, 1863-February, 1864. Hospitalized at Greensboro on March 19, 1865, with an unspecified complaint. Paroled at Greensboro on May 1, 1865.

BIGGERSTAFF, ELIJAH, SR., Private

Resided in Rutherford County where he enlisted on October 8, 1862, for the war. Reported present but sick in camp in November-December, 1862, and September-October, 1863. Returned to duty in November-December, 1863. Reported present in January-February, 1864. Last reported in the records of this company in July-September, 1864.

BIGGERSTAFF, JACOB, Private

Enlisted in Rutherford County on October 8, 1862, for the war. Reported present in November-December, 1862, and September, 1863-February, 1864. Last reported in the records of this company in July-September, 1864.

BIGGERSTAFF, THOMAS, Private

Born in Rutherford County and was by occupation a farmer prior to enlisting in Rutherford County at age 18, March 24, 1862. Reported present in June-July and November-December, 1862. Hospitalized at Wilmington on September 9, 1863, with intermittent fever. Returned to duty on October 5, 1863. Reported present in November, 1863-February, 1864. Last reported in the records of this company in July-September, 1864. Survived the war. [A Confederate pension application filed with the state of Florida indicates that both of his legs were broken when he was run over by a wagon during the war.]

BLACK, G. L., Private

Enlisted in Rutherford County on October 8, 1862, for the war. Reported present in November-December, 1862, and September, 1863-February, 1864. Hospitalized at Raleigh on November 6, 1864, with intermittent fever and was treated "by the external application of turpentine as a substitute for . . . quinine." Returned to duty on December 26, 1864.

BLACK, JAMES H., Private

Born in Rutherford County and was by occupation a farmer prior to enlisting in Rutherford County at age 27, March 24, 1862. Reported present in June-July, 1862. Reported present but sick in camp in November-December, 1862. Reported present in September, 1863-February, 1864. Last reported in the records of this company in July-September, 1864. Survived the war.

BLACK, WILLIAM W., Private
Born in Rutherford County and was by occupation a farmer prior to enlisting in Rutherford County at age 29, March 24, 1862. Dropped from the rolls of the company prior to July 1, 1862. Reason he was dropped not reported.

BLANKENSHIP, HEZEKIAH, Corporal
Born in Rutherford County and was by occupation a farmer prior to enlisting in Rutherford County at age 27, March 24, 1862. Mustered in as Corporal. Died in hospital at Petersburg, Virginia, August 5, 1862, of "diarrhoea."

BLANKINSHIP, WILLIAM W., Private
Born in Rutherford County and was by occupation a farmer prior to enlisting in Rutherford County at age 35, March 24, 1862. Deserted at Camp Mangum, near Raleigh, May 2, 1862.

BOONE, ANDREW C., Private
Born in Rutherford County and was by occupation a farmer prior to enlisting in Rutherford County at age 19, March 24, 1862. Reported present in June-July and November-December, 1862. Hospitalized at Wilmington on September 26, 1863, with intermittent fever. Returned to duty on October 5, 1863. Reported present in October-December, 1863. Furloughed on February 17, 1864. Hospitalized at Wilmington on November 25, 1864, with remittent fever. Returned to duty on December 23, 1864. Admitted to hospital at Greensboro on March 19, 1865. Survived the war.

BOONE, LAFAYETTE, _____
Was reported to be serving in this company on an unspecified date in 1864.

BOONE, THOMAS, Private
Born in Burke County and resided in Rutherford County where he was by occupation a farmer prior to enlisting in Rutherford County on March 24, 1862. Reported absent without leave in July, 1862. Reported on extra duty as a butcher in December, 1862. Hospitalized at Wilmington on August 28, 1863, with anemia. Returned to duty on September 4, 1863. Reported absent on sick furlough from September 18 through December 31, 1863. Discharged on February 15, 1864, by reason of "large inguinal hernia, chronic rheumatism, & old age. . . ." Discharge certificate gives his age as 61.

BRANDLE, NOAH R., Private
Born in Rutherford County and was by occupation a farmer prior to enlisting in Rutherford County at age 21, March 24, 1862. Reported absent without leave in June-July, 1862. Reported present in November-December, 1862. Sent to hospital at Goldsboro on March 25, 1863. Reported present in September, 1863-February, 1864. Paroled at Greensboro on May 1, 1865. [North Carolina pension records indicate that he was wounded and lost his eyesight while in the service and was also ruptured while carrying a log.]

CALLOWAY, JAMES, Private
Born in Buncombe County and was by occupation a

farmer prior to enlisting in Rutherford County at age 49, March 24, 1862. Dropped from the rolls of the company prior to July 1, 1862. Reason he was dropped not reported.

CAMPBELL, WILLIAM, _____
North Carolina pension records indicate that he served in this company.

CARSON, JOHN C., Private
Born in Rutherford County where he resided as a farmer prior to enlisting in Rutherford County at age 31, March 24, 1862. Reported present in June, 1862. Hospitalized at Petersburg, Virginia, August 13, 1862, with acute rheumatism. Returned to duty on August 16, 1862. Reported present but sick in camp in November-December, 1862. Reported present in September, 1863-February, 1864. Last reported in the records of this company in July-September, 1864.

CHURCH, CHARLES F., Private
Born in Rutherford County and was by occupation a farmer prior to enlisting in Rutherford County at age 19, March 24, 1862. Died in hospital at Petersburg, Virginia, July 26, 1862, of "debilitas."

CLEMENTS, JOHN A., Private
Born in Rutherford County and was by occupation a farmer prior to enlisting in Rutherford County at age 26, March 24, 1862. Died at Camp Mangum, near Raleigh, May 29, 1862. Cause of death not reported.

COCHRAN, JAMES REID, Private
Enlisted in Rutherford County at age 22, March 24, 1862. Mustered in as Corporal. Reported absent without leave in June, 1862. Hospitalized at or near Petersburg, Virginia, August 4, 1862, with typhoid fever. Returned to duty on October 1, 1862. Reported present in November-December, 1862. Reduced to ranks prior to January 1, 1863. Hospitalized at Wilmington on September 15, 1863, with dysentery. Rejoined the company prior to November 1, 1863. Reported present in November, 1863-February, 1864. Hospitalized at Wilmington on November 25, 1864, with remittent fever. Returned to duty on December 2, 1864.

COCHRAN, JOHN R., Musician
Born in Rutherford County and was by occupation a farmer prior to enlisting in Rutherford County at age 26, March 24, 1862. Mustered in as Private. Reported present in June-July and November-December, 1862. Hospitalized at Wilmington on August 28, 1863, with debility. Returned to duty on September 16, 1863. Reported present but sick in camp on or about October 31, 1863. Reported present in January, 1863-February, 1864. Appointed Musician on January 14, 1864. Last reported in the records of this company in July-September, 1864.

COCHRAN, WILLIAM C., Private
Born in Rutherford County where he resided as a trader prior to enlisting in Rutherford County at age 32, April 11, 1862. Reported present or accounted for in June-July,

1862. Hospitalized at or near Petersburg, Virginia, August 25, 1862, with icterus. Returned to duty on September 4, 1862. Reported present in November-December, 1862. Detailed for duty as a carpenter at Wilmington on September 17, 1863. Hospitalized at Wilmington on October 15, 1863, with diarrhoea. Returned to duty on October 22, 1863. Reported present in November-December, 1863. Reported present but sick in camp in January-February, 1864. Deserted to the enemy at Roanoke Island on an unspecified date. Sent to New Bern. Transferred to Fort Monroe, Virginia, where he arrived on November 16, 1864. Released at Fort Monroe on December 30, 1864, after taking the Oath of Allegiance.

COLES, W., Private
Enlisted in New Hanover County on January 17, 1864, for the war. No further records.

COXEY, RICHARD, Private
Enlisted in Rutherford County on January 22, 1863, for the war. Reported present in September-October, 1863. Hospitalized at Wilmington on November 28, 1863, with icterus. Returned to duty on January 11, 1864. Reported present but sick in camp through February, 1864. Hospitalized at Wilmington on March 25, 1864, with anasarca. Returned to duty on May 23, 1864. Paroled at Greensboro on May 1, 1865.

CURRY, DAVID H., Private
Enlisted in Rutherford County at age 24, January 22, 1863, for the war. Reported present in September-December, 1863. Reported present but sick in camp in January-February, 1864. Last reported in the records of this company in July-September, 1864. Survived the war.

DAVES, WILLIAM S., Private
Born in Rutherford County where he resided as a farmer prior to enlisting in Rutherford County at age 26, March 24, 1862. Reported present in June-July and November-December, 1862. Also reported present in September-December, 1863. Reported absent on detached service as a guard at Fair Bluff (Columbus County) in January-February, 1864. Hospitalized at Raleigh on November 9, 1864, with intermittent fever. Returned to duty on November 30, 1864. Survived the war.

EARLES, JOHN W., Private
Born in Rutherford County and was by occupation a farmer prior to enlisting in Rutherford County at age 19, March 24, 1862. Deserted at Camp Mangum, near Raleigh, April 16, 1862. Arrested on October 16, 1862. Court-martialed and sentenced "to receive twenty lashes on his bare back, to be branded in the left hand with the letter 'D,' and to be in solitary confinement on bread and water for fourteen days." No further records.

EARLES, MARTIN L., Private
Born in Cleveland County and was by occupation a farmer prior to enlisting in Rutherford County at age 15, March 24, 1862. Hospitalized at Raleigh prior to July 1, 1862, with an unspecified complaint. Reported absent on sick furlough from July 14 through December 31, 1862. No further records.

EARLY, WILLIAM, Private
Enlisted in Rutherford County on December 5, 1863, for the war. Reported present in January-February, 1864. Last reported in the records of this company in July-September, 1864.

ERWIN, WILLIAM M., Corporal
Born in Rutherford County and was by occupation a farmer prior to enlisting in Rutherford County at age 26, March 24, 1862. Mustered in as Private. Promoted to Corporal prior to July 1, 1862. Died near Petersburg, Virginia, August 16, 1862, of disease.

FLACK, C. J., Private
Enlisted in Rutherford County at age 19, July 8, 1863, for the war. Reported present in September-October, 1863. Hospitalized at Wilmington on December 28, 1863, with typhoid fever. Furloughed for thirty days on February 9, 1864. Last reported in the records of this company in July-September, 1864. Survived the war.

FLACK, LEWIS B., Private
Enlisted in Rutherford County on May 10, 1862, for the war. Reported present or accounted for in June-July and November-December, 1862. Also reported present in September, 1863-February, 1864. Hospitalized at Charlotte on February 6, 1865, with intermittent fever. Reported in hospitals at Charlotte and Raleigh until he returned to duty on March 11, 1865. Killed at Bentonville on March 19-21, 1865.

FORTUNE, WILLIAM PINCKNEY, Sergeant
Born in Rutherford County where he resided as a merchant prior to enlisting in Rutherford County at age 22, March 24, 1862. Mustered in as Private. Reported absent without leave in July, 1862. Returned to duty on an unspecified date. Reported present in November-December, 1862. Promoted to Corporal prior to January 1, 1863. Reported present in September, 1863-February, 1864. Promoted to Sergeant subsequent to February 29, 1864. Paroled at Greensboro on May 1, 1865.

FORTUNE, WILLIAMSON M., Private
Born in Rutherford County where he resided as a farmer prior to enlisting in Rutherford County at age 26, March 24, 1862. Mustered in as Sergeant. Reported absent without leave in July, 1862. Returned to duty on an unspecified date. Reported present in November-December, 1862. Reduced to ranks prior to January 1, 1863. Hospitalized at Wilmington on or about August 22, 1863, with anasarca. Reported present in September, 1863-February, 1864. Last reported in the records of this company in July-September, 1864.

GOWENS, MARTIN, Private
Born in Rutherford County where he enlisted on October 8, 1862, for the war. Reported present but sick in camp in November-December, 1862. Died in hospital at Wilson on or about February 21, 1863, of "pneumonia."

GRAYSON, WILLIAM G., Private
Born in Burke County and resided in Rutherford County where he was by occupation a farmer prior to enlisting

in Rutherford County at age 21, March 24, 1862. Reported absent without leave in July, 1862. Returned to duty on an unspecified date. Reported present in November-December, 1862, and September, 1863-February, 1864. Survived the war.

GUFFEY, SAMUEL R., Private
Born in Rutherford County and was by occupation a farmer prior to enlisting in Rutherford County at age 19, March 24, 1862. Reported present in June-July and November-December, 1862. Also reported present in September-December, 1863. Reported on detail as a guard at Fair Bluff (Columbus County) in January-February, 1864. Paroled at Greensboro on May 1, 1865.

GUFFEY, THOMAS A., Private
Born in Rutherford County and was by occupation a farmer prior to enlisting in Rutherford County at age 19, March 24, 1862. Reported present in June-July, 1862. Reported present but sick in camp in November-December, 1862. Sent to hospital at Greenville on June 30, 1863. Reported present in September-December, 1863. Reported absent on detail as a guard at Fair Bluff (Columbus County) in January-February, 1864. Last reported in the records of this company in July-September, 1864.

GUFFY, JOHN, Private
Born in Rutherford County and was by occupation a farmer prior to enlisting in Rutherford County at age 26, March 31, 1862. Died in hospital at Petersburg, Virginia, August 1, 1862, of "continued fever."

HAWKINS, HAMPTON P., Private
Place and date of enlistment not reported; however, he probably enlisted subsequent to February 29, 1864. Hospitalized at Wilmington on November 25, 1864, with remittent fever. Returned to duty on December 20, 1864. Paroled at Greensboro on May 1, 1865.

HAWKINS, WILLIAM L., Private
Born in Rutherford County and was by occupation a farmer prior to enlisting in Rutherford County at age 19, March 24, 1862. Hospitalized at Petersburg, Virginia, July 20, 1862. Died in hospital at Petersburg on July 23, 1862, of "feb[ris] typh[oides]."

HEDALSTON, JOHN H., Private
Enlisted in Rutherford County on January 28, 1864, for the war. Reported present through February, 1864. Hospitalized at Wilson on an unspecified date with splenitis. No further records.

HEMPHILL, THOMAS POSEY, Private
Enlisted in Rutherford County on May 10, 1862, for the war. Reported present in June-July, 1862. Discharged on September 27, 1862. Reason discharged not reported. Later served as Corporal in Company I of this regiment.

HENSLEY, W. M., Private
Enlisted in Rutherford County at age 19, December 17, 1863, for the war. Reported present in January-February, 1864. Last reported in the records of this company in July-September, 1864. Survived the war.

HICKS, WILLIAM G., Private
Enlisted in Rutherford County at age 34, October 8, 1862, for the war. Hospitalized at or near Petersburg, Virginia, December 3, 1862, with catarrh. Returned to duty on December 25, 1862. Reported present in September-October, 1863. Hospitalized at Wilmington on November 28, 1863, with debilitas. Returned to duty on December 10, 1863. Reported present in January-February, 1864. Hospitalized at Wilmington on November 25, 1864, with remittent fever. Returned to duty on December 17, 1864. Survived the war.

HIGGINS, WILLIAM L., Private
Born in Burke County and resided in Rutherford County where he was by occupation a farmer prior to enlisting in Rutherford County at age 29, March 29, 1862. Reported present in June-July, 1862. Reported present but sick in camp in November-December, 1862. Hospitalized at Wilmington on August 26, 1863, with colica. Returned to duty on September 6, 1863. Reported present through February, 1864. Last reported in the records of this company in July-September, 1864. Survived the war.

HILL, A. C., Private
Enlisted in Rutherford County on January 6, 1864, for the war. Reported present through February, 1864. Hospitalized at Wilmington on November 25, 1864, with remittent fever. Returned to duty on December 2, 1864.

HILL, C. J., Private
Enlisted in Rutherford County at age 18, December 29, 1863, for the war. Reported present in January-February, 1864. Last reported in the records of this company in July-September, 1864. Survived the war.

HILL, W. S., Private
Resided at "Pattonshouse." Place and date of enlistment not reported; however, he probably enlisted subsequent to February 29, 1864. Paroled at Salisbury on May 2, 1865.

HOWSER, WILLIAM H. C., Private
Enlisted in August, 1864, for the war. Paroled at Greensboro on May 1, 1865.

HUDDLESTON, J. H., Private
Enlisted in New Hanover County on February 2, 1864, for the war. No further records.

HUNT, ABSALOM, Private
Enlisted in Rutherford County on February 21, 1863, for the war. Reported absent without leave from April 22 through October 22, 1863. Reported present in November, 1863-February, 1864. No further records.

HUNT, ALFRED W., Private
Resided in Rutherford County and was by occupation a farmer prior to enlisting in Rutherford County on or about October 8, 186[3], for the war. Was about 30 years of age at time of enlistment. Reported present in October, 1863-February, 1864. No further records.

HUTCHENS, JOHN C., Private
Enlisted in Rutherford County at age 20, October 8, 1862, for the war. Reported present but sick in camp in November-December, 1862. Reported present in September, 1863-February, 1864. Hospitalized at Raleigh on November 6, 1864, with intermittent fever. Returned to duty on December 26, 1864. Survived the war.

JARRELL, ADAM, Private
Born in Rutherford County where he resided as a farmer prior to enlisting in Rutherford County at age 45, March 22, 1862. Was apparently rejected for service (probably by reason of being over 35 years of age).

JARRELL, DOCK J., Private
Born in Rutherford County where he enlisted on October 8, 1862, for the war. Reported present but sick in camp in November-December, 1862. Died in hospital at Raleigh on May 9, 1863, of "epilepsy."

JOHNSON, AARON, Private
Resided in Rutherford County and was by occupation a day laborer prior to enlisting in Rutherford County at age 32, October 8, 1862, for the war. Hospitalized at or near Petersburg, Virginia, December 3, 1862, with rubeola. Returned to duty on December 25, 1862. Reported present in September-October, 1863. Hospitalized at Wilmington on November 28, 1863, with debilitas. Returned to duty on December 2, 1863. Reported present in January-February, 1864. Hospitalized at Wilmington on March 25, 1864, with remittent fever. Transferred to Goldsboro on May 22, 1864. Last reported in the records of this company in July-September, 1864.

JOHNSON, HEZEKIAH W., Private
Born in Surry County and was by occupation a farmer prior to enlisting in Rutherford County at age 35, March 24, 1862. Died at Camp Mangum, near Raleigh, May 30, 1862. Cause of death not reported.

JOHNSON, R., Private
Place and date of enlistment not reported; however, he probably enlisted subsequent to February 29, 1864. Hospitalized at Wilmington on November 25, 1864, with remittent fever. Returned to duty on November 30, 1864. Hospitalized at Charlotte on February 17, 1865, with chronic diarrhoea. Transferred to another hospital on February 18, 1865. Captured at Athens, Georgia, May 8, 1865, and was paroled the same date.

JONES, WILLIAM, Private
Enlisted in Rutherford County on October 8, 1862, for the war. Reported present in November-December, 1862, and September, 1863-February, 1864. Last reported in the records of this company in July-September, 1864.

KEETER, JAMES A., _____
North Carolina pension records indicate that he served in this company.

KEETER, WILLIAM H., Private
Enlisted in Rutherford County on May 10, 1862, for the war. Reported present in May-July, 1862. Reported

present but sick in November-December, 1862. Reported present in September, 1863-February, 1864. Hospitalized at Charlotte on February 13, 1865, with rubeola and/or intermittent fever. Returned to duty on March 5, 1865.

KING, WILLIAM, _____
Place and date of enlistment not reported; however, he probably enlisted subsequent to February 29, 1864. Died at or near Hopewell, Virginia, March 25, 1865. Cause of death not reported.

KOON, L., _____
Place and date of enlistment not reported; however, he probably enlisted subsequent to February 29, 1864. Died at or near Charleston, South Carolina, January 20, 1865. Cause of death not reported.

KOONE, CALVIN, Private
Born in Rutherford County and was by occupation a farmer prior to enlisting in Rutherford County at age 27, March 24, 1862. Mustered in as Private. Reported present in June-July and November-December, 1862. Promoted to Corporal in July-December, 1862. Reported present in September, 1863-February, 1864. Reduced to ranks on December 12, 1863. Died in hospital at Plymouth on September 1 or October 11, 1864, of disease.

KOONE, DEWALT, Private
Born in Rutherford County and was by occupation a mechanic prior to enlisting in Rutherford County at age 39, April 18, 1862, for the war. Deserted near Petersburg, Virginia, August 24, 1862. Returned to duty on an unspecified date. Sent to hospital at Wilson on May 19, 1863. Reported absent on detached service as a carpenter or blacksmith at Wilmington from September 17, 1863, through February 29, 1864. Last reported in the records of this company in July-September, 1864.

KOONE, ELISHA, Private
Born in Rutherford County and was by occupation a farmer prior to enlisting in Rutherford County at age 19, March 24, 1862. Reported present or accounted for in June-July, 1862. Granted a sick furlough of sixty days on November 2, 1862. Reported present in September, 1863-February, 1864. Hospitalized at Wilmington on November 25, 1864, with scabies. Returned to duty on November 30, 1864. Hospitalized at Charlotte on February 17, 1865, with remittent fever. Transferred to another hospital on February 18, 1865. Survived the war.

KOONE, JAMES, Private
Born in Rutherford County and was by occupation a farmer prior to enlisting in Rutherford County at age 21, March 24, 1862. Died at Camp Mangum, near Raleigh, May 8, 1862, of disease.

LARGIN, JOSEPH A., Private
Born in Rutherford County where he enlisted on May 10, 1862, for the war. Died at Mechanicsville, Virginia, July 18, 1862, of disease.

LONG, FRANCIS M., Private
Born in Rutherford County and was by occupation a

farmer prior to enlisting in Rutherford County at age 23, March 24, 1862. Died in hospital at Petersburg, Virginia, July 11, 1862, of "remit[tent] fever."

LONG, WILLIAM L., Corporal
Born in Rutherford County and was by occupation a farmer prior to enlisting in Rutherford County at age 20, March 24, 1862. Mustered in as Private. Reported present in June-July and November-December, 1862. Promoted to Corporal in January-October, 1863. Reported present in September-December, 1863. Reported absent on detail as a guard at Fair Bluff (Columbus County) in January-February, 1864. Last reported in the records of this company in July-September, 1864. Survived the war.

McFARLAND, JAMES S., Private
Born in Rutherford County and was by occupation a farmer prior to enlisting in Rutherford County at age 20, March 24, 1862. Reported present in June-July and November-December, 1862. Also reported present in September, 1863-February, 1864. Last reported in the records of this company in July-September, 1864.

MASHBURN, J. H., Private
Enlisted in Rutherford County on January 8, 1864, for the war. Reported present through February, 1864. Paroled at Greensboro on May 12, 1865.

MELTON, DAVID H., Private
Born in Rutherford County and was by occupation a farmer prior to enlisting in Rutherford County at age 25, March 22, 1862. Dropped from the rolls of the company prior to July 1, 1862. Reason he was dropped not reported.

MELTON, ELIJAH D., Private
Born in Rutherford County and was by occupation a farmer prior to enlisting in Rutherford County at age 32, March 24, 1862. Mustered in as Corporal. Reported present in June-July, 1862. Reported sick in camp in November-December, 1862. Promoted to Sergeant in July-December, 1862. Reduced to ranks in January-October, 1863. Reported present in September, 1863-February, 1864. Hospitalized at Wilmington on November 25, 1864, with remittent fever. Returned to duty on December 2, 1864. Hospitalized at Charlotte on February 6, 1865, with intermittent fever. Hospitalized at Raleigh on February 18, 1865, with intermittent fever and acute diarrhoea. Transferred to another hospital on March 19, 1865. Survived the war.

MELTON, JESSE G., Private
Born in Rutherford County and was by occupation a farmer prior to enlisting in Rutherford County at age 18, March 24, 1862. Reported present in June-July and November-December, 1862. Also reported present in September, 1863-February, 1864. Last reported in the records of this company in July-September, 1864. Survived the war.

MELTON, JOHN M., Private
Born in Rutherford County and was by occupation a farmer prior to enlisting in Rutherford County at age 44,

March 24, 1862. Deserted at Camp Mangum, near Raleigh, May 2, 1862.

MELTON, JOSEPH G., Private
Born in Rutherford County and was by occupation a farmer prior to enlisting in Rutherford County at age 35, March 24, 1862. Deserted on May 20, 1862. Apprehended on November 24, 1862, and was placed under arrest. Court-martialed on an unspecified date. Returned to duty on an unspecified date. Reported present in September, 1863-February, 1864. [May have served later as Private in Company C, 34th Regiment N.C. Troops.]

MELTON, JOSHUA S., Private
Born in Rutherford County and was by occupation a farmer prior to enlisting in Rutherford County at age 22, March 24, 1862. Died in hospital at Petersburg, Virginia, August 10, 1862, of "meningitis."

MELTON, JOSIAH S., Private
Born in Rutherford County and was by occupation a farmer prior to enlisting in Rutherford County at age 23, March 24, 1862. Reported present in June-July and November-December, 1862. Also reported present in September, 1863-February, 1864. No further records.

MELTON, PHILIP H., Private
Born in Rutherford County and was by occupation a farmer prior to enlisting in Rutherford County at age 28, March 24, 1862. Died at Camp Mangum, near Raleigh, May 19, 1862. Cause of death not reported.

MELTON, WILLIAM, Private
Born in Rutherford County where he resided as a farmer prior to enlisting in Rutherford County at age 19, March 24, 1862. Died in hospital at Raleigh on or about May 31, 1862. Cause of death not reported.

MONTEITH, G. W., Private
Enlisted in Rutherford County at age 20, October 19, 1863, for the war. Reported present in November, 1863-February, 1864. Last reported in the records of this company in July-September, 1864. Survived the war.

MONTEITH, JOHN C., Private
Born in Rutherford County and was by occupation a farmer prior to enlisting in Rutherford County at age 22, March 24, 1862. Reported present in June-July and November-December, 1862. Also reported present in September, 1863-February, 1864. Last reported in the records of this company in July-September, 1864. Survived the war.

MOONEY, JAMES M., Private
Enlisted in Rutherford County at age 19, October 8, 1862, for the war. Reported present but sick in camp in November-December, 1862. Sent to hospital at Tarboro on April 23, 1863. Reported present in September, 1863-February, 1864. Paroled at Greensboro on May 1, 1865.

MORGAN, HUMPHREY P., Private
Born in Burke County and was by occupation a farmer

prior to enlisting in Rutherford County at age 28, March 24, 1862. Died in camp near Petersburg, Virginia, August 2, 1862, of disease.

MORGAN, J. F., _____
North Carolina pension records indicate that he served in this company.

MORGAN, JAMES, Private
Born in Rutherford County and was by occupation a farmer prior to enlisting in Rutherford County at age 19, March 24, 1862. Hospitalized at Petersburg, Virginia, July 20, 1862, with chronic bronchitis. Returned to duty on August 16, 1862. Reported present in November-December, 1862, and September, 1863-February, 1864. Hospitalized at Greensboro in March, 1865, with an unspecified complaint. Paroled at Charlotte on or about May 1, 1865.

MORGAN, JETHRO, Private
Enlisted in Rutherford County on July 8, 1863, for the war. Reported present in September, 1863-February, 1864. Hospitalized at Wilmington on November 25, 1864, with an unspecified complaint. Returned to duty on November 30, 1864.

MORGAN, PORTER O., Private
Born in Rutherford County where he resided as a farmer prior to enlisting in Rutherford County at age 31, March 24, 1862. Reported present in June-July and November-December, 1862. Also reported present in September, 1863-February, 1864. Captured (probably in hospital) at Savannah, Georgia, December 21, 1864. Sent to Hilton Head, South Carolina. Confined at Fort Delaware, Delaware, March 12, 1865. Died at Fort Delaware on or about June 4, 1865, of "int[ermittent] fever."

MORRISON, PERRY M., Sergeant
Born in Rutherford County where he resided as a farmer prior to enlisting in Rutherford County at age 20, March 24, 1862. Mustered in as Private. Appointed Musician prior to July 1, 1862. Promoted to Sergeant in July-December, 1862. Reported present in June-July and November-December, 1862. Also reported present in September, 1863-February, 1864. Hospitalized at Charlotte on February 6, 1865, with intermittent fever. Furloughed on February 19, 1865. Survived the war.

MORRISON, ROBERT P., Private
Resided in Rutherford County and was by occupation a farmer prior to enlisting in Rutherford County at age 54, January 22, 1863, for the war. Reported present in September, 1863-February, 1864. Last reported in the records of this company in July-September, 1864.

NANNEY, AMOS, Private
Born in Rutherford County and was by occupation a farmer prior to enlisting in Rutherford County at age 34, March 24, 1862. Mustered in as 1st Sergeant. Reported sick in hospital at Wilson in June-July, 1862. Reported present in November-December, 1862. Reduced to ranks in January-October, 1863. Furloughed for fourteen days on June 21, 1863. Hospitalized at Wilmington on August

26, 1863, with syphilis. Returned to duty on October 8, 1863. Reported present in September, 1863-February, 1864. Hospitalized at Wilmington on November 25, 1864, with pneumonia. Returned to duty on December 20, 1864.

NANNEY, COBURN, Private
Born in Rutherford County and was by occupation a farmer prior to enlisting in Rutherford County at age 31, March 24, 1862. Died in hospital at Petersburg, Virginia, August 17, 1862, of "febris typhoides."

NANNEY, WILLIAM, Private
Born in Rutherford County where he resided as a mechanic prior to enlisting in Rutherford County at age 28, March 24, 1862. Died in hospital at Petersburg, Virginia, August 8, 1862, of disease.

NIX, ENOCH P., Private
Born in Rutherford County and was by occupation a farmer prior to enlisting in Rutherford County at age 23, March 24, 1862. Reported present in June-July and November-December, 1862. Sent to hospital at Raleigh on April 29, 1863. Reported present in September, 1863-February, 1864. Hospitalized at Greensboro in March, 1865, with an unspecified complaint.

NIX, WILLIAM F., Corporal
Born in Rutherford County and was by occupation a farmer prior to enlisting in Rutherford County at age 24, March 24, 1862. Mustered in as Private. Reported present in June-July and November-December, 1862. Promoted to Corporal in January-October, 1863. Reported present in September-December, 1863. Reported present but sick in camp in January-February, 1864. Hospitalized at Wilmington on November 25, 1864, with pneumonia. Returned to duty on December 12, 1864.

NOLEN, JOHN, Private
Enlisted in Rutherford County on October 8, 1862, for the war. Reported sick in hospital at Petersburg, Virginia, from November 15 through December 31, 1862. Hospitalized at Wilmington on August 10, 1863, with pneumonia. Returned to duty on August 18, 1863. Reported present but sick in camp in September-October, 1863. Reported present in November, 1863-February, 1864. Hospitalized at Raleigh on November 6, 1864, with intermittent fever. Returned to duty on November 23, 1864.

PARTON, JOHN, Private
Resided in Rutherford County and was by occupation a day laborer prior to enlisting in Rutherford County at age 24, January 22, 1863, for the war. Mustered in as Private. Reported present in September-October, 1863. Hospitalized at Wilmington on November 28, 1863, with debilitas. Returned to duty on or about December 2, 1863. Appointed Musician (Drummer) on December 5, 1863. Reported present in December, 1863-February, 1864. Reduced to ranks on an unspecified date. Last reported in the records of this company in July-September, 1864. Survived the war.

POPE, J. S., _____
North Carolina pension records indicate that he served in this company.

QUEEN, WILLIAM N., Private
Resided in Rutherford County and was by occupation a farmer prior to enlisting in Rutherford County at age 51, February 24, 1863, for the war. Reported present in September-October, 1863. Hospitalized at Wilmington on November 28, 1863, with debilitas. Returned to duty on December 2, 1863. Reported present in December, 1863-February, 1864. Hospitalized at Charlotte on February 6, 1865, with intermittent fever. Furloughed on February 19, 1865.

SIMS, JOSEPH P., Private
Born in Rutherford County and was by occupation a farmer prior to enlisting in Rutherford County at age 24, March 24, 1862. Reported present in June-July and November-December, 1862. Hospitalized at Wilmington on September 14, 1863, with dysentery. Returned to duty prior to November 1, 1863. Reported present in November, 1863-February, 1864. Hospitalized at Wilmington on November 25, 1864, with remittent fever. Returned to duty on November 30, 1864. Hospitalized at Raleigh on March 15, 1865, with intermittent fever. Returned to duty on March 24, 1865.

SISK, A. J., Private
Enlisted in Rutherford County at age 29, October 8, 1862, for the war. Reported present in November-December, 1862, and September-December, 1863. Reported absent on detail as a guard at Fair Bluff (Columbus County) in January-February, 1864. Hospitalized at Raleigh on November 9, 1864, with intermittent fever. Returned to duty on November 30, 1864. Survived the war.

SMART, HENRY KERR, Private
Born in Rutherford County where he resided as a farmer prior to enlisting in Rutherford County at age 36, March 24, 1862. Reported present in June-July, 1862. Reported present but sick in November-December, 1862, and September-October, 1863. Reported present in November, 1863-February, 1864. Captured at Bentonville on March 22, 1865. Sent to New Bern. Confined at Hart's Island, New York Harbor, April 10, 1865. Released at Hart's Island on June 19, 1865, after taking the Oath of Allegiance.

SMILEY, M., Corporal
Place and date of enlistment not reported; however, he probably enlisted subsequent to February 29, 1864. Promotion record not reported. Reported in hospital at Madison, Georgia, March 4, 1865.

SMITH, C. A. D., _____
North Carolina pension records indicate that he served in this company.

SORRELLS, ISRAEL P., Private
Born in Rutherford County and was by occupation a farmer prior to enlisting in Rutherford County at age 27, March 24, 1862. Reported present in June-July and

November-December, 1862. Also reported present in September-December, 1863. Reported absent on detail as a guard at Fair Bluff (Columbus County) in January-February, 1864. Last reported in the records of this company in July-September, 1864. Survived the war.

SORRELS, JESSE C., Private
Enlisted in Rutherford County on May 10, 1862, for the war. Reported present in June-July and November-December, 1862. Also reported present in September, 1863-February, 1864. Hospitalized at Charlotte on February 6, 1865, with intermittent fever. Furloughed on February 19, 1865.

SPRATT, SAMUEL L., Private
Born in Rutherford County and was by occupation a farmer prior to enlisting in Rutherford County at age 23, March 24, 1862. Reported on duty as a teamster from May 27, 1862, through March 31, 1864. Last reported in the records of this company in July-September, 1864. Survived the war.

STEWART, JOHN H., Private
Born in Rutherford County where he resided as a mechanic prior to enlisting in Rutherford County at age 45, March 22, 1862. No further records.

STREET, ANTHONY, Private
Born in Rutherford County and was by occupation a farmer prior to enlisting in Rutherford County at age 27, March 28, 1862. Died at Camp Mangum, near Raleigh, May 17, 1862, of disease.

SUTTLE, JOHN H., Private
Born in Pickens District, South Carolina, and was by occupation a farmer prior to enlisting in Rutherford County at age 18, March 24, 1862. Reported present in June-July, 1862. Reported present but sick in camp in November-December, 1862. Hospitalized at Wilmington on August 29, 1863, with intermittent fever. Returned to duty on September 21, 1863. Reported present in November, 1863-February, 1864. No further records.

SUTTLE, WILLIAM, Private
Born in Warren County, Tennessee, and was by occupation a farmer or harness maker prior to enlisting in Rutherford County at age 48, March 24, 1862. Hospitalized at Petersburg, Virginia, July 28, 1862, with chronic rheumatism, enteritis, and typhoid fever. Returned to duty on August 8, 1862. Hospitalized at or near Petersburg on December 3, 1862, with rheumatism. Returned to duty on December 25, 1862. Reported sick in hospital at Wilson from March 8, 1863, through February 29, 1864. Discharged at Plymouth on July 30, 1864, by reason of "general debility, decrepitude and old age."

TOMBERLIN, JOHN H., Private
Born in Rutherford County and was by occupation a farmer prior to enlisting in Rutherford County at age 26, March 24, 1862. Hospitalized at or near Petersburg, Virginia, August 18, 1862, with intermittent fever. Returned to duty on September 5, 1862. Reported present

in November-December, 1862, and September, 1863-February, 1864. Survived the war.

TOMBERLIN, V. B., Private
Enlisted in Rutherford County on October 9, 1863, for the war. Reported present in September, 1863-February, 1864. Hospitalized at Charlotte on February 6, 1865, and died on February 26, 1865, of "pneumonia."

TONEY, JOHN, Private
Enlisted in Rutherford County at age 25, October 8, 1862, for the war. Reported present but sick in camp in November-December, 1862. Reported present in September, 1863-February, 1864. Last reported in the records of this company in July-September, 1864. Survived the war.

UNGER, LAWRENCE, Private
Born in France and was by occupation a mechanic prior to enlisting in Rutherford County at age 38, March 21, 1862. No further records. Survived the war.

UPTON, BENJAMIN B., Private
Born in Burke County and was by occupation a farmer prior to enlisting in Rutherford County at age 35, March 24, 1862. Reported present in June-July, 1862. Reported present but sick in camp in November-December, 1862. Sent to hospital at Greenville on June 19, 1863. Reported present in September, 1863-February, 1864. Captured (probably in hospital) at Savannah, Georgia, December 21, 1864. Hospitalized at Savannah on December 31, 1864, with chronic diarrhoea. Reported in hospital at Savannah on January 19, 1865, with intermittent fever. Sent to Hilton Head, South Carolina, on an unspecified date. Transferred to Fort Delaware, Delaware, where he arrived on March 12, 1865. Died at Fort Delaware on or about April 17, 1865, of "ch[ronic] diarrhoea."

UPTON, EDWARD, Private
Born in Rutherford County and was by occupation a farmer prior to enlisting in Rutherford County at age 28, March 24, 1862. Reported present in June-July and November-December, 1862. Also reported present in September, 1863-February, 1864. Deserted to the enemy at Roanoke Island on an unspecified date. Confined at Fort Monroe, Virginia, November 16, 1864. Released at Fort Monroe on or about December 30, 1864, after taking the Oath of Allegiance.

VICKERS, ALEXANDER R., Private
Born in Rutherford County and was by occupation a farmer prior to enlisting in Rutherford County at age 21, March 24, 1862. Reported present in June-July and November-December, 1862. Reported present but sick in camp in September-October, 1863. Reported present in November, 1863-February, 1864. Hospitalized at Charlotte on April 26, 1865, with diarrhoea. Paroled on May 10, 1865.

VICKERS, J. N., Private
Enlisted in Rutherford County on October 8, 1862, for the war. Reported present in November-December, 1862, and September, 1863-February, 1864. Hospitalized at

Charlotte on April 26, 1865, with diarrhoea. Transferred to another hospital on April 27, 1865.

VICKERS, J. W., Private
Enlisted in Rutherford County on October 8, 1862, for the war. Reported present in November-December, 1862, and September, 1863-February, 1864. Last reported in the records of this company in July-September, 1864.

VICKERS, THOMAS J., Private
Born in Rutherford County and was by occupation a farmer prior to enlisting in Rutherford County at age 24, March 24, 1862. Reported present in June-July and November-December, 1862. Furloughed for fourteen days on June 10, 1863. Reported present in September, 1863-February, 1864. Last reported in the records of this company in July-September, 1864. Survived the war.

VICKERS, W. B., Private
Enlisted in Rutherford County on October 8, 1862, for the war. Reported present but sick in camp in November-December, 1862. Sent to hospital at Raleigh on March 25, 1863. Reported in hospital at Wilmington on or about April 30, 1863, with abscesses. Reported present with the company in September, 1863-February, 1864. Hospitalized at Charlotte on February 6, 1865, with intermittent fever. Returned to duty on February 19, 1865.

WALKER, A. R., Private
Enlisted in Rutherford County on March 21, 1863, for the war. Reported present in September, 1863-February, 1864. Last reported in the records of this company in July-September, 1864.

WALKER, ELIAS, Private
Born in Rutherford County where he resided as a farmer prior to enlisting in Rutherford County at age 36, March 29, 1862. Hospitalized at Wilmington on September 14, 1863, with dysentery. Returned to duty on October 15, 1863. Reported present in November, 1863-February, 1864. Last reported in the records of this company in July-September, 1864. Survived the war.

WALKER, JAMES W., Private
Place and date of enlistment not reported; however, he probably enlisted subsequent to February 29, 1864. Paroled at Goldsboro on May 1, 1865.

WALKER, JEREMIAH S., Private
Born in Rutherford County and was by occupation a farmer prior to enlisting in Rutherford County at age 47, March 24, 1862. Reported present in September, 1863-February, 1864. Last reported in the records of this company in July-September, 1864.

WALKER, RICHARD ALLEN, _____
North Carolina pension records indicate that he served in this company.

WALLACE, A. K., Private
Resided in Rutherford County and was by occupation a blacksmith prior to enlisting in Rutherford County at age 44, January 6, 1864, for the war. Reported present through

February, 1864. Last reported in the records of this company in July-September, 1864.

WALLACE, FRANCIS L., Sergeant
Born in Rutherford County where he resided as a farmer prior to enlisting in Rutherford County at age 21, March 24, 1862. Mustered in as Private. Promoted to Corporal prior to July 1, 1862. Reported present in June-July and November-December, 1862. Promoted to Sergeant in January-October, 1863. Reported present in September, 1863-February, 1864. Last reported in the records of this company in July-September, 1864.

WALLACE, JOHN D., Private
Resided in Rutherford County where he enlisted at age 18, December 3, 1863, for the war. Reported present in January-February, 1864. Last reported in the records of this company in July-September, 1864.

WALLACE, JOSEPH L., Private
Born in Rutherford County where he resided as a farmer prior to enlisting in Rutherford County at age 27, March 24, 1862. Reported present in June-July and November-December, 1862. Reported on duty as a teamster at Weldon and Petersburg, Virginia, in June, 1863. Reported on detail as a carpenter at Wilmington from September 17, 1863, through February 29, 1864. Last reported in the records of this company in July-September, 1864.

WALLACE, LAWSON A., Sergeant
Born in Rutherford County and was by occupation a farmer prior to enlisting in Rutherford County at age 28, March 24, 1862. Mustered in as Private. Reported present in July-December, 1862. Reported present but sick in camp in November-December, 1862. Reported present in September, 1863-February, 1864. Promoted to Sergeant on February 15, 1864. Died at Summerville, South Carolina, January 27, 1865, of disease.

WALTERS, WILLIAM, Private
Born in Rutherford County and was by occupation a farmer prior to enlisting in Rutherford County at age 42, March 24, 1862. Deserted on June 4, 1862. Apprehended on October 16, 1862, and was placed under arrest. Court-martialed and sentenced "to hard labor for six months with ball and chain weighing twelve pounds attached to his left leg, to be bucked every Sunday during this time in presence of the Regiment, either at inspection or dress parade." Deserted again on April 20, 1863. Arrested in Rutherford County on August 29, 1864. Court-martialed and sentenced to be shot. No further records.

WATERS, JONATHAN, Private
Born in Rutherford County and was by occupation a farmer prior to enlisting in Rutherford County at age 39, March 24, 1862. Deserted on June 4, 1862. Apprehended on October 16, 1862, and placed under arrest. Returned to duty on an unspecified date. Hospitalized at Wilmington on September 4, 1863, with intermittent fever. Returned to duty on September 18, 1863. Reported present in October, 1863-February, 1864. Hospitalized at Wilmington on November 25, 1864, with gastralgia. Returned to duty on December 20, 1864. Paroled at Cheraw, South Carolina, March 5, 1865.

WATSON, DANIEL W., Private
Resided in Rutherford County. Place and date of enlistment not reported; however, he probably enlisted subsequent to February 29, 1864. Was about 19 years of age at time of enlistment. Captured by the enemy on an unspecified date. Hospitalized at New Bern on March 30, 1865. Died in hospital at New Bern on April 3, 1865, of "chronic diarrhoea."

WATSON, JAMES WINFIELD, Private
Born in Rutherford County and was by occupation a farmer prior to enlisting in Rutherford County at age 19, March 24, 1862. Reported present in June-July and November-December, 1862. Also reported present in September, 1863-February, 1864. Last reported in the records of this company in July-September, 1864. Survived the war.

WATSON, SAMUEL ALLISON, Private
Born in Rutherford County on August 28, 1844. Enlisted in Rutherford County on December 24, 1862, for the war. Reported present in November-December, 1862, and September-October, 1863. Reported present but sick in camp in November-December, 1863. Reported present in January-February, 1864. Hospitalized at Wilmington on November 25, 1864, with remittent fever. Returned to duty on December 5, 1864. Survived the war.

YELTON, W. J., Private
Enlisted in Rutherford County on October 8, 1862, for the war. Died at or near Point of Rocks, Virginia, December 2, 1862, of "febris typhoides."

COMPANY H

•

This company was raised in Harnett County and enlisted at Lillington in March-April, 1862. It was mustered into state service at Camp Mangum, near Raleigh, on April 21, 1862, and assigned to the 50th Regiment N.C. Troops as Company H. After joining the regiment the company functioned as a part of the regiment, and its history for the remainder of the war is reported as a part of the regimental history.

The information contained in the following roster was compiled primarily from a company muster-in and descriptive roll dated April 21, 1862, and from company muster rolls for May 1-June 30, 1862; November 1-December 31, 1862; September 1, 1863-February 29, 1864; July 1-August 31, 1864; and October 31-December 31, 1864. No company muster rolls were located for July 1-October 31, 1862; January 1-August 31, 1863; March 1-June 30, 1864; September 1-October 30, 1864; or for the period after December 31, 1864. Valuable information was obtained from primary records such as the North Carolina adjutant general's *Roll of Honor*, discharge certificates, medical records, prisoner of war records, *The War of the Rebellion: A Compilation of the Official Records of the Union and Confederate Armies*, militia records, newspaper casualty lists and obituaries, Confederate pension applications filed with the state of North Carolina, and the 1860 federal census of North Carolina. Secondary sources such as postwar rosters and histories, cemetery records, the *Confederate Veteran*, published genealogies, and records of the United Daughters of the Confederacy also provided useful information.

OFFICERS

CAPTAIN

ATKINSON, JOSEPH HENRY

Born in Harnett County* where he resided as a merchant prior to enlisting at age 33. Appointed Captain on March 24, 1862. Reported present in June and November-December, 1862. Also reported present in September-December, 1863. Reported present but on court-martial duty in January-February, 1864. Reported present but sick in July-August, 1864. Discharged from hospital at Thomasville on April 7, 1865. Reason he was hospitalized not reported. Paroled at Greensboro on May 1, 1865.

LIEUTENANTS

BRANTLY, BENJAMIN F., 1st Lieutenant

Enlisted at Camp Mangum, near Raleigh, May 18, 1862, for the war. Mustered in as Sergeant. Reported present in May-June and November-December, 1862. Appointed 2nd Lieutenant on December 17, 1862. Reported present in September, 1863-February, 1864. Reported present but sick in July-August, 1864. Promoted to 1st Lieutenant on November 23, 1864.

BRANTLY, JOHN, 2nd Lieutenant

Resided in Harnett County. Appointed 2nd Lieutenant on March 24, 1862. Reported present in May-June and November-December, 1862. Also reported present in September, 1863 February, 1864, and July-August, 1864.

BYRD, DAVID S., 3rd Lieutenant

Born in Harnett County.* Appointed 3rd Lieutenant on March 24, 1862. Reported sick at home in May-June, 1862. Resigned on December 4, 1862, by reason of "physical disability." Resignation accepted on December 10, 1862, but he continued to serve in the company with the rank of Private. [See Noncommissioned Officers and Privates section below.]

McLEAN, JOHN PEABODY, 1st Lieutenant

Previously served as Private in Company H, 1st Regiment N.C. Infantry (6 months, 1861). Appointed 1st Lieutenant of this company on March 24, 1862. Reported present in May-June and November-December, 1862. Also reported present in September-October, 1863. Reported absent with leave in November-December, 1863. Reported present in January-February, 1864. Resigned on August 18, 1864, by reason of "debility consequent upon a broken constitution which renders him entirely unfit for the

service. . . ." Resignation accepted on August 30, 1864. [North Carolina pension records indicate that he died in hospital at Charleston, South Carolina, January 6, 1865, of disease.]

PARKER, ANTHONY L., 2nd Lieutenant

Resided in Harnett County and enlisted at Camp Davis, near Wilmington, at age 17, September 18, 1863, for the war. Mustered in as Private. Reported present in September-December, 1863. Reported present but on picket duty in January-February, 1864. Reported present in July-August, 1864. Appointed 2nd Lieutenant on November 23, 1864.

ROBERTS, FRANKLIN N., 2nd Lieutenant

Previously served as Captain of Company F, 1st Regiment N.C. Infantry (6 months, 1861). Appointed 2nd Lieutenant on an unspecified date. Apparently declined the appointment. Later served as Private in 2nd Company B, 36th Regiment N.C. Troops (2nd Regiment N.C. Artillery).

NONCOMMISSIONED OFFICERS AND PRIVATES

AUTRY, JOHN H., Private

Enlisted in Harnett County at age 29, April 29, 1862, for the war. Reported present in May-June and November-December, 1862. Also reported present in September-December, 1863. Reported at home on sick furlough of thirty days in January-February, 1864. Reported present in July-August, 1864. Sent to hospital at Summerville, South Carolina, in November-December, 1864. Survived the war.

AUTRY, WILEY, Private

Born in Harnett County* where he resided as a farmer prior to enlisting in Harnett County at age 35, March 24, 1862. Reported absent sick in May-June, 1862. Reported present in November-December, 1862, and September, 1863-February, 1864. Also reported present in July-August and November-December, 1864. Hospitalized at Charlotte on February 13, 1865, with debilitas. Furloughed on February 14, 1865.

BAIN, HUGH, Private

Enlisted in Cumberland County at age 16, April 29, 1862[?], for the war; however, he was not listed in the records of this company until April-June, 1864. Reported present in July-August and November-December, 1864. Survived the war.

BAIN, WILLIAM A., Private

Enlisted at age 17, April 1, 1864, for the war. Paroled at Thomasville on May 1, 1865. Survived the war.

BAKER, JOSEPH, Private

Born in Harnett County* and was by occupation a farmer prior to enlisting in Harnett County on March 11, 1862. Dropped from the rolls of the company prior to July 1, 1862. Reason he was dropped not reported.

BALES, WILLIAM B., Private
Born in Harnett County* and was by occupation a farmer prior to enlisting in Harnett County on March 24, 1862. Reported present in May-June and November-December, 1862. Also reported present in September, 1863-February, 1864. Reported absent on detail boating corn at Gum Neck (Tyrrell County) in July-August, 1864. Reported present in November-December, 1864.

BISHOP, ASA, Private
Born in Harnett County* and was by occupation a farmer prior to enlisting in New Hanover County on November 18, 1863, for the war. Reported present in November-December, 1863. Reported at home on sick furlough of thirty days in January-February, 1864. Discharged on April 2, 1864, by reason of "valvular disease of the heart. . . ." Discharge certificate gives his age as 42.

BISHOP, NATHAN M., Private
Previously served as Private in Company I, 31st Regiment N.C. Troops. Enlisted in this company on March 24, 1862. Reported present but sick in May-June, 1862. Reported present in November-December, 1862. Reported on duty as a blacksmith at Kinston July 9-September 19 and October 1-10, 1863. Reported present in November, 1863-February, 1864, and July-August, 1864. Hospitalized at Wilmington on November 25, 1864, with remittent fever. Returned to duty on December 2, 1864.

BLACK, DUNCAN, Private
Born in Harnett County* where he resided as a shopkeeper prior to enlisting in Harnett County at age 24, March 24, 1862. Reported present in May-June and November-December, 1862. Transferred to Company F, 15th Regiment N.C. Troops (5th Regiment N.C. Volunteers), May 20, 1863, in exchange for Private James R. Hobbs.

BOYLES, WILLIAM B., _____
North Carolina pension records indicate that he served in this company.

BRITT, KENNETH, Private
Enlisted in New Hanover County on March 12, 1864, for the war. Reported present in July-August, 1864.

BROOKS, ROBERT W., _____
North Carolina pension records indicate that he served in this company.

BYRD, AQUILLA, SR., Private
Resided in Harnett County and was by occupation a farmer prior to enlisting in Harnett County at age 28, April 29, 1862, for the war. Reported present in May-June and November-December, 1862. Also reported present in September-December, 1863. Reported present on duty as a "town guard" (possibly at Wilmington) in January-February, 1864. Reported present in July-August and November-December, 1864. Hospitalized at Charlotte on February 18, 1865, with intermittent fever. Transferred to another hospital the same date.

BYRD, BRIGHT D., Private
Born in Harnett County* where he enlisted on April 29, 1862, for the war. Reported present in November-December, 1862, and September-December, 1863. Hospitalized at Wilmington on February 22, 1864, after he fell under a railroad car while boarding a train and severely injured one of his feet. Foot amputated. Died in hospital at Wilmington on or about March 25, 1864, of injuries and/or "febris typhoides."

BYRD, DAVID S., Private
Previously served as 3rd Lieutenant of this company. Resignation accepted on December 10, 1862; however, he continued to serve in the company with rank of Private. Furloughed from hospital at Goldsboro on May 17, 1863. Reported absent sick in September-October, 1863. Reported present in November, 1863-February, 1864. Reported in hospital at Tarboro in July-August, 1864. Reported present in November-December, 1864.

BYRD, EDWARD D., 1st Sergeant
Born in Harnett County* and was by occupation a farmer prior to enlisting in Harnett County on March 24, 1862. Mustered in as 1st Sergeant. Reported present in November-December, 1862, and September, 1863-February, 1864. Also reported present in July-August, 1864. Hospitalized at Fayetteville on December 2, 1864, with an unspecified complaint. Reported still in hospital on or about February 28, 1865.

BYRD, JAMES L., Private
Born in Harnett County* where he resided as a farmer prior to enlisting in Harnett County at age 21, March 24, 1862. Reported present in September, 1863-February, 1864, and July-August, 1864. Hospitalized at Raleigh on November 6, 1864, with remittent fever. Returned to duty on November 16, 1864. Survived the war.

BYRD, JOHN H., Private
Born in Harnett County* and was by occupation a farmer prior to enlisting in Harnett County on March 24, 1862. Reported present in May-June and November-December, 1862. Also reported present in September, 1863-February, 1864; July-August, 1864; and November-December, 1864. Survived the war.

BYRD, LEMUEL W., Private
Born in Harnett County* and was by occupation a farmer prior to enlisting in Harnett County on March 24, 1862. Reported present but sick in May-June, 1862. Hospitalized at Petersburg, Virginia, July 28, 1862, with typhoid fever. Transferred on August 25, 1862. Reported on detail as a shoemaker at Raleigh and later at Salisbury from December 5, 1862, through December 31, 1863. Reported present in January-February and July-August, 1864. Hospitalized at Wilmington on December 29, 1864, with acute diarrhoea. Transferred to Raleigh on January 15, 1865. Reported in hospital at Raleigh through March 13, 1865. [He was reportedly discharged on June 8, 1863, by reason of "his liability to epilepsy which is a frequent occurrence in his case"; however, it appears that his

discharge was cancelled. Discharge certificate gives his age as 39.]

BYRD, REDDIN, Sergeant

Resided in Harnett County and was by occupation a farmer prior to enlisting in Harnett County at age 35, April 29, 1862, for the war. Promotion record not reported. Reported absent sick in November-December, 1862. Reported present in September, 1863-February, 1864; July-August, 1864; and November-December, 1864.

CARPENTER, ROBERT, Private

Born in Harnett County* where he resided as a farmer prior to enlisting in Harnett County at age 32, March 24, 1862. Reported present but sick in May-June, 1862. Reported present in November-December, 1862. Furloughed for seven days on July 30, 1863. Reported present in September, 1863-February, 1864. Also reported present in July-August and November-December, 1864. Survived the war.

CHAMPION, JAMES, Private

Born in Harnett County* where he resided as a farmer prior to enlisting in Harnett County at age 45, March 11, 1862. Was apparently discharged (probably by reason of being over 35 years of age) prior to July 1, 1862. Survived the war.

COX, ISHAM, Private

Enlisted in New Hanover County on March 5, 1864, for the war. Deserted at Plymouth on August 13, 1864. Rejoined the company on an unspecified date. Court-martialed on or about October 21, 1864. Returned to duty on an unspecified date. Paroled at Greensboro on May 1, 1865.

COX, JOSEPH W., Private

Enlisted in New Hanover County on March 5, 1864, for the war. Deserted from camp at Plymouth on August 13, 1864. Discharged from hospital at Goldsboro on October 19, 1864. Reason he was hospitalized not reported. Court-martialed on or about October 31, 1864. No further records.

COX, STEPHEN D., Private

Born in Harnett County* and was by occupation a farmer prior to enlisting in Harnett County on March 24, 1862. Reported present in May-June and November-December, 1862. Also reported present in September, 1863-February, 1864; July-August, 1864; and November-December, 1864. Paroled at Greensboro on May 1, 1865.

CUMMINGS, JOHN, Private

Enlisted in Cumberland County at age 20, June 1, 1864, for the war. Reported present in July-August, 1864. Reported in hospital at Tarboro in November-December, 1864. Survived the war.

DARROCH, J. L., _____

North Carolina pension records indicate that he served in this company.

DARROCH, MALCOLM, JR., Private

Born in Harnett County* and was by occupation a farmer prior to enlisting in Harnett County on or about March 24, 1862. Died at Camp Mangum, near Raleigh, May 24, 1862, of "pneumonia." Was 17 years of age at the time of his death.

DARROCH, MALCOLM, SR., Private

Born in Jura, Scotland, and resided in Harnett County where he was by occupation a farmer prior to enlisting in Harnett County at age 34, March 24, 1862. Reported present in May-June, 1862. Hospitalized at Petersburg, Virginia, July 23, 1862, with acute diarrhoea. Returned to duty on September 8, 1862. Reported present in November-December, 1862. Detailed to guard baggage on May 21, 1863. Reported on detail as a guard at Goldsboro in September, 1863-February, 1864; July-August, 1864; and November-December, 1864.

DARROCH, NEILL, Private

Born in Harnett County* and was by occupation a farmer prior to enlisting in Harnett County on March 24, 1862. Died in hospital at Petersburg, Virginia, on or about July 15, 1862, of "pneumonia." Was 27 years of age at the time of his death.

DEAN, GREEN L., Private

Enlisted in Harnett County on April 29, 1862, for the war. Hospitalized at Richmond, Virginia, August 22, 1862, with debility. Returned to duty on September 25, 1862. Died at Drewry's Bluff, Virginia, October 22, 1862, of "febris typhoides."

DEAN, J. A., Private

Enlisted in Harnett County on April 29, 1862, for the war. Reported absent sick in May-June, 1862. No further records.

DEAN, WILLIAM P., Private

Enlisted in Harnett County at age 21, April 29, 1862, for the war. Reported absent sick in May-June, 1862. Reported present in November-December, 1862, and September, 1863-February, 1864. Also reported present in July-August and November-December, 1864. Survived the war.

DEAN, WILLIAM R., Corporal

Enlisted in Harnett County at age 28, April 29, 1862, for the war. Mustered in as Private. Reported absent sick in May-June, 1862. Reported present in November-December, 1862. Promoted to Corporal on December 17, 1862. Furloughed for fourteen days on June 17, 1863. Reported present in September, 1863-February, 1864; July-August, 1864; and November-December, 1864. Survived the war.

DORMAN, CALVIN L., Private

Enlisted at Camp Davis, near Wilmington, at age 18, September 5, 1863, for the war. Reported present in September, 1863-February, 1864; July-August, 1864; and November-December, 1864. Survived the war.

DORMAN, ISAAC B., Private

Born in Harnett County* where he enlisted on April 29, 1862, for the war. Reported present in June, 1862. Died in camp near Drewry's Bluff, Virginia, on or about November 29, 1862, of "cerebritis."

DORMAN, JOHN T., Private

Previously served as Sergeant in Company B, 10th Battalion N.C. Heavy Artillery. Transferred to this company with the rank of Private on August 23, 1863. Reported present in September-December, 1863. Reported on detail as a guard at Fair Bluff (Columbus County) in January-February, 1864. Reported on detail to haul corn in July-August, 1864. Reported present in November-December, 1864. Survived the war. [North Carolina pension records indicate that he was wounded on January 1, 1865.]

DOUVET, JOHN L., _____

North Carolina pension records indicate that he served in this company.

DRAUGHON, GEORGE THEOPHILUS, Private

Previously served as Private in Company F, 1st Regiment N.C. Infantry (6 months, 1861). Enlisted in this company in Lenoir County on February 22, 1863, for the war. Reported present in September-October, 1863. Reported on duty as regimental hospital nurse from December 2, 1863, through December 31, 1864. Paroled at Greensboro on May 1, 1865.

DRAUGHON, WILLIAM G., Private

Enlisted in Harnett County on April 29, 1862, for the war. Reported present in May-June and November-December, 1862. Also reported present in September, 1863-February, 1864, and July-August, 1864. Paroled at Greensboro on May 1, 1865.

DRIVER, WESLEY, Private

Born in Harnett County* where he resided as a farmer prior to enlisting in Harnett County at age 39, March 3, 1862. Dropped from the rolls of the company prior to July 1, 1862. Reason he was dropped not reported.

FAUCETTE, THOMAS B., Private

Enlisted at Camp Davis, near Wilmington, October 6, 1863, for the war. Detailed as a carpenter at Wilmington on or about November 18, 1863. Reported on detail as a mechanic at Wilmington in January-February, 1864. Reported present with the company in July-August, 1864. Hospitalized at Raleigh on November 6, 1864, with intermittent fever. Returned to duty on December 13, 1864.

FUQUAY, GEORGE W., _____

North Carolina pension records indicate that he served in this company.

FUQUAY, JOHN A., Private

Born in Harnett County* where he resided as a farmer prior to enlisting in Harnett County at age 25, March 24, 1862. Reported absent sick in May-June, 1862. Reported present in September-October, 1863. Captured (probably in eastern North Carolina) on November 13, 1863. Confined at Fort Monroe, Virginia, November 18, 1863. Transferred to Fort Norfolk, Virginia, on an unspecified date. Transferred to Point Lookout, Maryland, where he arrived on December 29, 1863. Died at Point Lookout on or about March 1, 1865, of "chronic dysentery."

FUQUAY, STEPHEN W., Private

Born in Harnett County* and was by occupation a farmer prior to enlisting in Harnett County on or about March 24, 1862. Dropped from the rolls of the company prior to July 1, 1862. Reason he was dropped not reported.

GEARMAN, GABRIEL, Private

Born in Harnett County* and was by occupation a farmer prior to enlisting in Harnett County on March 24, 1862. Reported present in May-June and November-December, 1862. Also reported present in September, 1863-February, 1864, and July-August, 1864. Died in hospital at Charleston, South Carolina, December 27, 1864, of disease.

GILBERT, HENRY T., Private

Born in Harnett County* and was by occupation a farmer prior to enlisting in Harnett County at age 27, March 24, 1862. Reported present but sick in May-June, 1862. Reported present in November-December, 1862, and September, 1863-February, 1864. Also reported present in July-August, 1864. Hospitalized at Goldsboro on an unspecified date. Reason he was hospitalized not reported. Discharged from hospital on October 10, 1864. Reported at home sick in November-December, 1864. Survived the war.

GILBERT, WILLIAM D., Private

Born in Harnett County* where he resided as a farmer prior to enlisting in Harnett County at age 42, March 24, 1862. Hospitalized at Petersburg, Virginia, November 4, 1862, with chronic rheumatism. Returned to duty on or about November 23, 1862. Reported present in December, 1862. Also reported present in September, 1863-February, 1864, and July-August, 1864. Died in hospital at Raleigh on November 28, 1864, of "peritonitis."

GREGORY, ALEXANDER D., Private

Resided in Harnett County and was by occupation a farmer prior to enlisting in Harnett County at age 29, April 29, 1862, for the war. Reported in hospital at Wilson in May-June, 1862. Reported present in November-December, 1862, and September, 1863-February, 1864. Also reported present in July-August and November-December, 1864.

GREGORY, MATTHEW W., Private

Resided in Harnett County and was by occupation a laborer prior to enlisting in Harnett County at age 30, April 29, 1862, for the war. Reported present in May-June and November-December, 1862. Also reported present in September, 1863-February, 1864, and July-August, 1864. Reported sick at home in November-December, 1864.

HAHN, FRANCIS, Private
Enlisted in New Hanover County on February 16, 1864, for the war. Deserted near Wilmington on February 26, 1864.

HAIGWOOD, KENNETH, Private
Born in Harnett County* and was by occupation a farmer prior to enlisting in Harnett County on March 24, 1862. Reported sick at home in May-June, 1862. Reported present in November-December, 1862. Reported in hospital at Wilmington on August 10, 1863, with pneumonia. Reported at home on sick furlough in September-October, 1863. Reported sick at home in November, 1863-February, 1864. Reported present in July-August, 1864. Discharged at Plymouth on September 30, 1864, by reason of "kidney disease, old age & general debility." Discharge certificate gives his age as 51.

HAIR, D. J., Private
Enlisted in New Hanover County on January 1, 1864, for the war. Dropped from the rolls of the company on February 15, 1864. Reason he was dropped not reported. [May have served later as Private in Company F, 51st Regiment N.C. Troops.]

HILLIARD, DAVID, Private
Born in Harnett County* where he resided as a farmer prior to enlisting in Harnett County at age 50 on or about March 24, 1862. Was apparently discharged (presumably by reason of being over 35 years of age) prior to July 1, 1862.

HOBBS, JAMES R., Musician
Previously served as Private in Company F, 15th Regiment N.C. Troops (5th Regiment N.C. Volunteers). Transferred to this company on May 20, 1863, in exchange for Private Duncan Black. Mustered in as Private. Reported present in September, 1863-February, 1864. Appointed Musician in January-February, 1864. Reported present in July-August and November-December, 1864.

HOBBS, JOHN W., Private
Born in Harnett County* and was by occupation a farmer prior to enlisting in Harnett County on March 24, 1862. Reported absent sick in May-June, 1862. Reported present in November-December, 1862. Hospitalized at Wilmington on October 13, 1863, with chronic bronchitis. Furloughed for forty days on November 3, 1863. Reported present in January-February, July-August, and November-December, 1864.

HOBBS, LEWIS, Private
Enlisted in New Hanover County on April 20, 1864, for the war. Reported present in July-August, 1864. Hospitalized at Wilmington on November 25, 1864, with remittent fever. Furloughed for sixty days on December 9, 1864. Hospitalized at Fayetteville on February 10, 1865. Reason he was hospitalized not reported. Reported in hospital at Fayetteville through February 28, 1865.

HOBBY, JAMES I., Private
Born in Harnett County* and was by occupation a farmer prior to enlisting in Harnett County on March 24, 1862.

Reported in hospital at Wilson in May-June, 1862. Discharged from service on December 3, 1862, by reason of "paralysis."

HOBSON, LEWIS H., Private
Resided in Cumberland County and was by occupation a farm laborer prior to enlisting in Harnett County at age 25, April 29, 1862, for the war. Reported present in November-December, 1862. No further records. Survived the war.

HOLDER, ITHRA, Private
Resided in Harnett County and was by occupation a farmer prior to enlisting in Harnett County at age 45, October 6, 1863, for the war. Reported present in October, 1863-February, 1864. Reported present but sick in July-August, 1864. Reported in hospital at Summerville, South Carolina, in November-December, 1864.

HOLDER, JACOB, Private
Enlisted at Camp Davis, near Wilmington, at age 42, October 6, 1863, for the war. Reported present in November-December, 1863. Reported at home on sick furlough of thirty days in January-February, 1864. Reported present in July-August and November-December, 1864. Survived the war.

HOLDER, RILEY, Private
Born in Harnett County* and was by occupation a farmer prior to enlisting in Harnett County at age 17, March 24, 1862. Reported absent sick in May-June, 1862. Reported present in November-December, 1862, and September, 1863-February, 1864. Also reported present in July-August and November-December, 1864. Survived the war.

HOLDER, THOMAS, Private
Enlisted in Lenoir County at age 22, March 18, 1863, for the war. Reported present in September, 1863-February, 1864, and July-August, 1864. Hospitalized at Wilmington on November 25, 1864, with remittent fever. Returned to duty on December 2, 1864. Survived the war.

HOLDER, WILLIAM, Private
Born in Harnett County* and was by occupation a farmer prior to enlisting in Harnett County on March 24, 1862. Reported sick in hospital at Petersburg, Virginia, in May-June, 1862. Reported present in November-December, 1862, and September, 1863-February, 1864. Also reported present in July-August, 1864. Reported absent sick in November-December, 1864.

HOLDER, WILLIAM H., Private
Born in Harnett County* and was by occupation a farmer prior to enlisting in Harnett County on March 24, 1862. Reported present in May-June and November-December, 1862. Detailed as a teamster on February 1, 1863. Reported on detail as a teamster in September, 1863-February, 1864. Reported absent on detail boating corn at Gum Neck (Tyrrell County) in July-August, 1864. Reported present in November-December, 1864.

JERNIGAN, JOSEPH MARTIN, Private
Enlisted at Tarboro at age 21, April 29, 1864, for the war.

Reported present in July-August and November-December, 1864. Survived the war.

JOHNSON, E. A., Private
Enlisted on or about May 3, 186[4], for the war. Reported in hospital in November-December, 1864.

JONES, DOCTOR T., Private
Resided in Harnett County and was by occupation a farmer prior to enlisting in Harnett County at age 30, April 29, 1862, for the war. Reported present in May-June and November-December, 1862. Also reported present in September, 1863-February, 1864; July-August, 1864; and November-December, 1864. Captured at or near Fayetteville on or about March 8, 1865. Sent to New Bern. Confined at Fort Monroe, Virginia, April 25, 1865. Transferred to Newport News, Virginia, May 1, 1865. Released at Newport News on June 30, 1865, after taking the Oath of Allegiance.

KENNEDY, JOHN R., Private
Enlisted at Camp Davis, near Wilmington, October 20, 1863, for the war. Reported present in November, 1863-February, 1864, and July-August, 1864.

McKINNIE, JOHN L., Private
Born in Harnett County* where he enlisted on March 24, 1862. Reported present but sick in May-June, 1862. Reported present in November-December, 1862, and September, 1863-February, 1864. Also reported present in July-August and November-December, 1864.

McLEAN, JOHN, Sergeant
Enlisted in Harnett County on April 29, 1862, for the war. Mustered in as Sergeant. Reported present in May-June and November-December, 1862. Also reported present in September, 1863-February, 1864, and July-August, 1864. Died at or near Charleston, South Carolina, January 3, 1865. Cause of death not reported.

McPHAIL, DOUGLE A., Private
Born in Harnett County* and was by occupation a farmer prior to enlisting in Harnett County on March 24, 1862. Reported present in May-June, 1862. Wounded in the left forearm at Malvern Cliffs, Virginia, June 30, 1862. Left forearm amputated. Discharged on October 13, 1862, by reason of disability. Discharge certificate gives his age as 23.

McPHAIL, GEORGE VINCENT, Private
Enlisted at Camp Davis, near Wilmington, at age 19, October 6, 1863, for the war. Reported present in November, 1863-February, 1864, and July-August, 1864. Reported in hospital at Charleston, South Carolina, in November-December, 1864. Survived the war.

McPHAIL, JOHN L., Private
Born in Harnett County* and was by occupation a farmer prior to enlisting in Harnett County at age 20, March 24, 1862. Reported present in May-June and November-December, 1862. Furloughed for fourteen days on June 17, 1863. Reported present in September-December, 1863. Reported on duty as a camp guard in January-February,

1864. Reported present in July-August, 1864. Reported in hospital at Augusta, Georgia, in November-December, 1864. Paroled at Salisbury on May 2, 1865. Survived the war.

McRAE, JOHN S., _____
North Carolina pension records indicate that he served in this company.

MASON, DANIEL A., Private
Enlisted in New Hanover County on February 26, 1864, for the war. Reported present in July-August, 1864. Hospitalized at Wilmington on November 25, 1864, with remittent fever. Returned to duty on December 26, 1864. Hospitalized at Charlotte on February 18, 1865, with intermittent fever. Returned to duty the same date.

MESSER, DUSHIA A., Private
Born in Harnett* or Johnston County and was by occupation a farmer prior to enlisting in Harnett County on March 24, 1862. Reported present in May-June and November-December, 1862. Discharged at Goldsboro on January 22, 1863, by reason of "chronic articular rheumatism, dysentery of long-standing, loss of appetite, flesh and strength. . . ." Discharge certificate gives his age as 24.

MESSER, WHITLEY, Private
Resided in Harnett County and was by occupation a farmer prior to enlisting in Harnett County at age 52, April 29, 1862, for the war. Reported present but sick in May-June, 1862. Reported on detail as a carpenter in December, 1862, and September-December, 1863. Reported on detail as a mechanic at Wilmington in January-February, 1864. Reported present in July-August and November-December, 1864.

NUTT, WILLIAM HENRY, Musician
Previously served as Private in Company A of this regiment. Appointed Musician and transferred to this company in January-February, 1864. No further records.

O'QUINN, ALEXANDER, Private
Born in Harnett County* and was by occupation a farmer prior to enlisting in Harnett County on March 24, 1862. Died in North Carolina on June 27, 1862, of "pneumonia" and "typhoid fever."

O'QUINN, BURREL B., Corporal
Born in Harnett County* and was by occupation a farmer prior to enlisting in Harnett County at age 34, March 24, 1862. Mustered in as Private. Reported present but sick in May-June, 1862. Reported present in November-December, 1862, and September, 1863-February, 1864. Also reported present in July-August, 1864. Promoted to Corporal in September-December, 1864. Reported present in November-December, 1864. Survived the war. [North Carolina pension records indicate that he was wounded in the foot at Cone Creek on March 24, 1864.]

PARKER, B. F., Private
Place and date of enlistment not reported; however, he probably enlisted subsequent to August 31, 1864.

Wounded in the left side and captured at or near Savannah, Georgia, on or about December 24, 1864. Hospitalized at Savannah where he died on January 1, 1865, of wounds.

PARKER, DUNCAN H., Corporal
Born in Harnett County* and was by occupation a farmer prior to enlisting in Harnett County on March 24, 1862. Mustered in as Private. Promoted to Corporal prior to July 1, 1862. Reported present in May-June and November-December, 1862. Also reported present in September, 1863-February, 1864; July-August, 1864; and November-December, 1864.

PARKER, JAMES, Private
Enlisted in Washington County on October 7, 1864, for the war. Reported present in November-December, 1864.

PARKER, JOSEPH W., Private
Enlisted in New Hanover County at age 23, January 20, 1864, for the war. Reported present in January-February and July-August, 1864. Reported in hospital at Summerville, South Carolina, in November-December, 1864. Hospitalized at Charlotte on February 6, 1865, with intermittent fever. Transferred to another hospital on February 18, 1865. Hospitalized at Richmond on March 6, 1865, with debilitas. Furloughed for thirty days on March 8, 1865. Paroled at Greensboro on or about April 29, 1865.

PARKER, SAMUEL N., Corporal
Born in Harnett County* and was by occupation a farmer prior to enlisting in Harnett County at age 18, March 24, 1862. Mustered in as Private. Reported present in May-June and November-December, 1862. Promoted to Corporal on or about November 17, 1862. Reported present in September, 1863-February, 1864. Reported absent on detail boating corn at Gum Neck (Tyrrell County) in July-August, 1864. Reported present in November-December, 1864. Survived the war.

PARKER, WILLIAM J., Private
Enlisted in New Hanover County on December 8, 1863, for the war. Reported present in December, 1863-February, 1864; July-August, 1864; and November-December, 1864.

PATTERSON, ARCHIBALD B., Private
Enlisted in Cumberland County at age 18, April 27, 1864, for the war. Reported present in July-August and November-December, 1864. Survived the war.

PATTERSON, JOHN W., Private
Enlisted in Harnett County at age 29, April 29, 1862, for the war. Reported absent sick in May-June, 1862. Reported present in November-December, 1862, and September, 1863-February, 1864. Also reported present in July-August, 1864. Reported in hospital at Charleston, South Carolina, in November-December, 1864. Survived the war.

PATTERSON, ROBERT J., Private
Born in Harnett County* and was by occupation a farmer

prior to enlisting in Harnett County at age 26, March 24, 1862. Reported present in May-June and November-December, 1862. Also reported present in September, 1863-February, 1864; July-August, 1864; and November-December, 1864. Survived the war. [North Carolina pension records indicate that he was wounded in the head near Savannah, Georgia, in January, 1865.]

PEARSON, WILLIAM H., Sergeant
Born in Harnett County* and was by occupation a farmer prior to enlisting in Harnett County on March 24, 1862. Mustered in as Private. Promoted to Corporal prior to July 1, 1862. Reported present in May-June and November-December, 1862. Promoted to Sergeant on December 17, 1862. Furloughed for seven days on July 30, 1863. Reported present or accounted for in September, 1863-February, 1864. Sent to Goldsboro with prisoners in July-August, 1864. Reported on detail at Fort Branch in November-December, 1864.

RAY, CORNELIUS, Private
Born in Harnett County* and was by occupation a farmer prior to enlisting in Harnett County on March 24, 1862. Died on June 30, 1862. Place and cause of death not reported.

RAY, DAVID, Private
Born in Harnett County* and was by occupation a farmer prior to enlisting in Harnett County at age 36, March 24, 1862. Reported present but sick in May-June, 1862. Hospitalized at Petersburg, Virginia, August 13, 1862, with typhoid fever. Returned to duty on September 15, 1862. Reported present in November-December, 1862, and September, 1863-February, 1864. Also reported present in July-August, 1864. Reported sick at home in November-December, 1864. Survived the war.

RAY, JOHN, Private
Born in Harnett County* and was by occupation a farmer prior to enlisting in Harnett County on March 24, 1862. Reported present but sick in May-June, 1862. Reported present in November-December, 1862, and September-December, 1863. Reported present or accounted for in January-February and July-August, 1864. Reported sick at home in November-December, 1864.

RAY, NIVIN, Private
Resided in Harnett County and was by occupation a laborer prior to enlisting in New Hanover County at age 38, November 3, 1863, for the war. Reported present in November, 1863-February, 1864; July-August, 1864; and November-December, 1864.

REAVES, ROBERT D., Sergeant
Resided in Harnett County and was by occupation a farmer prior to enlisting in Harnett County at age 26, April 29, 1862, for the war. Mustered in as Sergeant. Reported absent sick in May-June, 1862. Reported present in November-December, 1862, and September, 1863-February, 1864. Also reported present in July-August, 1864. Captured (probably in hospital) at or near Savannah, Georgia, December 21, 1864. Reported in a Federal hospital on December 22, 1864, with intermittent fever. Sent to Hilton Head, South Carolina. Transferred to

Point Lookout, Maryland, where he arrived on February 1, 1865. Released at Point Lookout on June 19, 1865, after taking the Oath of Allegiance.

SALMON, EDWARD A., Private

Enlisted in Lenoir County on May 2, 1863, for the war. Reported present in September-October, 1863. Hospitalized at Wilmington on November 28, 1863, with ulcus. Returned to duty on December 2, 1863. Reported absent on furlough in January-February, 1864. Reported present in July-August, 1864.

SALMON, JAMES P., Private

Resided in Harnett County and was by occupation a turpentine laborer prior to enlisting in Lenoir County at age 23, May 2, 1863, for the war. Reported absent sick in September-October, 1863. Reported present in November, 1863-February, 1864. Hospitalized at Wilmington on March 23, 1864, with rubeola. Returned to duty on April 5, 1864. Reported present in July-August and November-December, 1864. Captured near Fayetteville on March 8, 1865. Sent to New Bern. Confined at Point Lookout, Maryland, March 30, 1865. Released at Point Lookout on June 20, 1865, after taking the Oath of Allegiance. [North Carolina pension records indicate that he was wounded at Plymouth in July or August, 1864.]

SENTER, JOHN W., Private

Enlisted in Lenoir County on May 2, 1863, for the war. Reported absent sick at home in September-October, 1863. No further records.

SMITH, JOHN G., Private

Born in Harnett County* and resided in Johnston County where he was by occupation a farmer prior to enlisting in Harnett County on or about March 24, 1862. Died at Camp Mangum, near Raleigh, on or about May 20, 1862, of "pneumonia." He was 19 years of age at the time of his death.

SPENCE, NEILL A., Private

Enlisted in Lenoir County on May 2, 1863, for the war. Reported in hospital at Wilson in September-October, 1863. No further records.

STEPHENS, BENJAMIN F., Private

Enlisted in Harnett County at age 19, April 21, 1864, for the war. Reported present in July-August and November-December, 1864. Survived the war. [North Carolina pension records indicate that he was injured "by falling timbers while constructing breastworks" near Savannah, Georgia, January 5, 1865.]

STEPHENS, JOHN L., Private

Enlisted in New Hanover County on November 21, 1863, for the war. Reported present in December, 1863-February, 1864, and July-August, 1864. Hospitalized at Raleigh on January 16, 1865, with a gunshot wound of the left arm. Returned to duty on February 6, 1865.

STEPHENS, JOSEPH S., Private

Enlisted in Harnett County at age 18, April 21, 1864, for

the war. Reported on picket duty at Cross Landing (Tyrrell County) in July-August, 1864. Reported present in November-December, 1864. Survived the war.

STEPHENS, KELLY, Private

Born in Harnett County* and was by occupation a farmer prior to enlisting in Harnett County on March 24, 1862. Reported present in May-June, 1862. Hospitalized at Richmond, Virginia, August 22, 1862, with catarrh. Returned to duty on September 1, 1862. Reported present in November-December, 1862, and September, 1863-February, 1864. Also reported present in July-August, 1864. Reported sick in hospital in November-December, 1864.

STEWART, ALEXANDER, Private

Enlisted in Cumberland County on June 1, 1864, for the war. Reported present in July-August and November-December, 1864.

STEWART, DANIEL R., Private

Born in Harnett County* and was by occupation a farmer prior to enlisting in Harnett County on March 24, 1862. Reported present but sick in May-June, 1862. Died in hospital at Petersburg, Virginia, July 28, 1862, of "febris typhoides."

STEWART, G. A., Sergeant

Place and date of enlistment not reported; however, he probably enlisted subsequent to August 31, 1864. Promotion record not reported. Paroled at Greensboro on or about April 28, 1865.

STEWART, JOHN A., Private

Enlisted in New Hanover County on March 6, 1864, for the war. Reported present in July-August and November-December, 1864.

STEWART, NEILL A., Private

Enlisted in New Hanover County at age 19, March 6, 1864, for the war. Hospitalized at Wilmington on April 27, 1864, with remittent fever. Returned to duty on May 19, 1864. Reported on picket at Cross Landing (Tyrrell County) in July-August, 1864. Survived the war.

STONE, J. S., _____

North Carolina pension records indicate that he served in this company.

STONE, JOHN S., Private

Born in Harnett County* and was by occupation a farmer prior to enlisting in Harnett County on or about March 24, 1862. Died in North Carolina on or about April 15, 1862, of disease.

STRICKLAND, JOHN, Private

Enlisted in New Hanover County on December 19, 1863, for the war. Reported present in January-February and July-August, 1864. Captured at or near Plymouth on or about October 31, 1864. Confined at Fort Monroe, Virginia, on or about November 16, 1864. Transferred to Point Lookout, Maryland, November 24, 1864. Paroled at Point Lookout on February 18, 1865. Received at

Boulware's and Cox's Wharfs, James River, Virginia, on or about February 21, 1865, for exchange. Hospitalized at Richmond, Virginia, February 22, 1865, with pneumonia. Furloughed on March 9, 1865.

TART, WILLIAM T., Private
Enlisted in Harnett County on April 29, 1862, for the war. Reported present in May-June and November-December, 1862. Also reported present in September, 1863-February, 1864; July-August, 1864; and November-December, 1864.

THOMAS, JAMES A., Private
Born in Harnett County* where he enlisted on March 24, 1862. Reported present but sick in May-June, 1862. Hospitalized at Petersburg, Virginia, November 5, 1862. Died in hospital at Petersburg on November 18, 1862, of "congestive fever."

THOMAS, LUTHER, Private
Born in Harnett County* where he resided as a farmer prior to enlisting in Harnett County at age 45, February 25, 1862. Was apparently discharged (probably by reason of being over 35 years of age) prior to July 1, 1862. Survived the war.

TRUELOVE, TIMOTHY, Private
Born in Harnett County* where he resided as a farmer prior to enlisting in Harnett County at age 38, March 24, 1862. Reported sick in hospital at Wilson in May-June, 1862. Discharged on or about August 2, 1862, by reason of "general bad health and evident predisposition to white swelling [cancer] which has already seriously impaired the movement of his left hip joint."

WARWICK, GEORGE, Private
Born in Harnett County* and was by occupation a farmer prior to enlisting in Harnett County at age 27, March 24, 1862. Reported present in May-June and November-December, 1862. Reported present or accounted for in September, 1863-February, 1864, and July-August, 1864. Reported in hospital at Summerville, South Carolina, in November-December, 1864. Survived the war.

WARWICK, JOHN J., Private
Born in Harnett County* and was by occupation a farmer prior to enlisting in Lenoir County on March 18, 1863, for the war. Sent to hospital at Goldsboro on July 16, 1863. Reported present in September, 1863-February, 1864; July-August, 1864; and November-December, 1864. Captured near Fayetteville on March 8, 1865. Sent to New Bern. Confined at Point Lookout, Maryland, March 30, 1865. Died at Point Lookout on April 10, 1865, of "inflammation of the lungs."

WATKINS, JOHN W., Corporal
Born in Harnett County* where he enlisted on April 29, 1862, for the war. Mustered in as Corporal. Reported present in May-June, 1862. Died in camp at Drewry's Bluff, Virginia, on or about November 17, 1862, of "typhoid pneumonia."

WATSON, HENRY, Private
Born in Harnett County* and was by occupation a farmer prior to enlisting in Harnett County on or about March 24, 1862. Dropped from the rolls of the company prior to July 1, 1862. Reason he was dropped not reported.

WHITE, WESTON, Private
Born in Harnett County* where he resided as a farmer prior to enlisting in Harnett County at age 34, March 24, 1862. Reported sick at home in May-June, 1862. Died in hospital at or near Petersburg, Virginia, September 5, 1862, of "febris typhoides."

WILSON, ANDERSON, Private
Born in Harnett County* where he resided as a mechanic prior to enlisting in Harnett County at age 42, March 3, 1862. Dropped from the rolls of the company prior to July 1, 1862. Reason he was dropped not reported.

WILSON, JOHN TYLER MONROE, Private
Born in Harnett County* and was by occupation a mechanic prior to enlisting in Harnett County at age 18, March 24, 1862. Reported present in May-June and November-December, 1862. Also reported present in September-October, 1863. Reported absent on detail as a carpenter at Wilmington in November, 1863-February, 1864. Reported absent on furlough of eighteen days in July-August, 1864. Hospitalized at Raleigh on October 4, 1864, with intermittent fever. Returned to duty on October 20, 1864. Reported present in November-December, 1864. Survived the war.

WILSON, MONROE A., _____
Place and date of enlistment not reported. Detailed for duty at Wilmington in the quartermaster's department on November 19, 1863. No further records.

WILSON, NEILL A., Private
Resided in Harnett County and enlisted in Cumberland County on June 1, 1864, for the war. Reported present in July-August and November-December, 1864. Paroled at Greensboro on May 1, 1865.

WOOD, CALVIN, Private
Born in Harnett County* and was by occupation a farmer prior to enlisting in Harnett County at age 35, March 24, 1862. Reported present but sick in May-June, 1862. Reported present in November-December, 1862. Sent to hospital at Goldsboro on January 25, 1863. Reported present in September-October, 1863. Died in hospital at Wilmington on or about December 21, 1863, of "rheum[atism] of heart."

WOOD, HENRY H., Private
Enlisted in New Hanover County at age 42, March 12, 1864, for the war. Reported present in July-August, 1864. Survived the war.

WOOD, JAMES, Private
Born in Harnett County* and was by occupation a farmer prior to enlisting in Harnett County at age 18, March 24, 1862. Reported present but sick in May-June, 1862. Reported present in November-December, 1862, and

September, 1863-February, 1864. Reported on picket duty at Cross Landing (Tyrrell County) in July-August, 1864. Reported present in November-December, 1864.

WOOD, T. F., _____
North Carolina pension records indicate that he served in this company.

WOODELL, TROY, Private
Enlisted in New Hanover County on March 5, 1864, for the war. Deserted from camp near Plymouth on August 13, 1864. Apprehended on an unspecified date and was court-martialed. Confined at Salisbury. Hospitalized at Salisbury on November 23, 1864. Died in hospital at Salisbury on January 5, 1865, of "diarrhoea."

WOODELL, ZACHARIAH, Private
Born in Robeson County and enlisted in New Hanover County on March 5, 1864, for the war. Deserted from camp at Plymouth on August 13, 1864. Apprehended on an unspecified date and was court-martialed. Confined at Salisbury. Hospitalized at Salisbury on March 4, 1865. Died in hospital at Salisbury on March 10, 1865, of "pneumonia."

COMPANY I

This company, known as the "Rutherford Regulars" and "Rutherford Regulators," was raised in Rutherford County and enlisted in Rutherford County in March, 1862. It was mustered into state service at Camp Mangum, near Raleigh, on April 29, 1862, and assigned to the 50th Regiment N.C. Troops as Company I. After joining the regiment the company functioned as a part of the regiment, and its history for the remainder of the war is reported as a part of the regimental history.

The information contained in the following roster was compiled primarily from a company muster-in and descriptive roll dated April 29, 1862, and from company muster rolls for May 1-December 31, 1862; September 1, 1863-February 29, 1864; and April 30-December 31, 1864. No company muster rolls were located for January 1-August 31, 1863; March 1-April 29, 1864; or for the period after December 31, 1864. Valuable information was obtained from primary records such as the North Carolina adjutant general's *Roll of Honor*, discharge certificates, medical records, prisoner of war records, *The War of the Rebellion: A Compilation of the Official Records of the Union and Confederate Armies*, militia records, newspaper casualty lists and obituaries, Confederate pension applications filed with the state of North Carolina, and the 1860 federal census of North Carolina. Secondary sources such as postwar rosters and histories, cemetery records, the *Confederate Veteran*, published genealogies, and records of the United Daughters of the Confederacy also provided useful information.

OFFICERS

CAPTAIN

EAVES, JOHN B.
Resided in Rutherford County and was by occupation a merchant prior to enlisting at age 24. Appointed Captain on March 25, 1862. Reported present through December, 1862. Also reported present in September, 1863-February, 1864. Reported absent sick in May-December, 1864. Hospitalized at Greensboro on March 19, 1865, with an unspecified complaint. No further records.

LIEUTENANTS

BOSTICK, SAMUEL E., 1st Lieutenant
Born in Cherokee County, Georgia, and resided in Rutherford County where he was by occupation a farmer prior to enlisting in Rutherford County at age 32, March 19, 1862. Mustered in as Sergeant. Hospitalized at or near Petersburg, Virginia, July 4, 1862, with colic. Returned to duty on July 17, 1862. Appointed 2nd Lieutenant on July 17, 1862. Reported present or accounted for through December, 1862. Also reported present or accounted for in September, 1863-February, 1864, and May-December, 1864. Promoted to 1st Lieutenant on January 20, 1865. Hospitalized at Raleigh on April 10, 1865, with an unspecified complaint. Transferred to another hospital on April 12, 1865.

BURNETT, CARTER, 2nd Lieutenant
Born in South Carolina and resided in Rutherford County where he was by occupation a landlord prior to enlisting at age 48. Appointed 2nd Lieutenant on April 29, 1862. Resigned on June 11, 1862, because "my health forbids my remaining longer in service. . . ." Resignation accepted on July 17, 1862.

CORBETT, WILLIAM M., 1st Lieutenant
Resided in Rutherford County and enlisted at age 31. Appointed 1st Lieutenant on April 29, 1862. Reported present through December, 1862. Reported present or accounted for in September, 1863-February, 1864, and May-December, 1864. Accidentally killed in a skirmish with another Confederate unit at the Salkehatchie River, South Carolina, January 20, 1865. [See regimental history.] "He was a brave young man and greatly beloved by all his company."

EAVES, ANDREW J., 2nd Lieutenant
Resided in Rutherford County and was by occupation a druggist prior to enlisting at age 26. Appointed 2nd Lieutenant on April 29, 1862. Reported present or accounted for through August, 1862. Resigned on or about July 18, 1862, by reason of "not being capable of performing the duties of a soldier." His letter of resignation is annotated by the colonel of the regiment as

follows: "Lt. Eaves is a very timid young man, and not in my judgement mentally qualified to discharge the duties of his office. I therefore recommend the acceptance of his resignation without further investigation into his conduct the 30 June 1862. He is wholly unfit for his present position as lieutenant in his company." Other records indicate that he was "suffering from mental aberration." Resignation accepted on or about September 6, 1862. [For information concerning the events of June 30, 1862, see regimental history.]

HILLARD, JESSE, 2nd Lieutenant
Born in Rowan County and resided in Rutherford County where he enlisted on March 17, 1862. Mustered in as Sergeant. Promoted to 1st Sergeant on July 1, 1862. Elected 2nd Lieutenant on September 24, 1862. Reported present through December, 1862. Also reported present in September, 1863-February, 1864, and May-December, 1864. Reported in hospital at Greensboro in March, 1865.

MOORE, FRANCIS, 2nd Lieutenant
Born in Rutherford County where he resided as a farmer prior to enlisting in Rutherford County at age 30, March 17, 1862. Mustered in as Sergeant. Hospitalized at or near Petersburg, Virginia, July 22, 1862, with remittent fever. Returned to duty on September 9, 1862. Reported present but sick in camp in September-October, 1862. Reported present in November-December, 1862, and September, 1863-February, 1864. Reduced to ranks on November 30, 1863. Reported present in May-December, 1864. Appointed 2nd Lieutenant on February 26, 1865.

NONCOMMISSIONED OFFICERS AND PRIVATES

ALLEN, ELIJAH P., Private
Enlisted in Wake County on October 10, 186[2], for the war. Hospitalized at Petersburg, Virginia, December 4, 1862, with typhoid fever. Furloughed on March 11, 1863. Returned from sick furlough on September 6, 1863. Reported present in November-December, 1863. Reported present but sick in camp in January-February, 1864. Reported present in May-December, 1864.

ALLEN, JAMES W., Private
Born in Rutherford County where he enlisted at age 28, March 27, 1862. Reported present through December, 1862. Also reported present in September-December, 1863. Reported on detached service at Fair Bluff (Columbus County) in January-February, 1864. Reported present in May-December, 1864.

ARWOOD, B. F., Private
Enlisted in Wake County. Date of enlistment not reported; however, he probably enlisted subsequent to February 29, 1864. Captured by the enemy on an unspecified date. Admitted to a Federal hospital at Savannah, Georgia, December 26, 1864, with debility. Died in hospital at Savannah on March 10, 1865, of "chronic diarrhoea."

BABER, CAMPBELL S., Private
Born in Rutherford County and was by occupation a farmer prior to enlisting in Rutherford County at age 21, March 17, 1862. Reported present through December, 1862. Reported present or accounted for in September, 1863-February, 1864, and May-December, 1864. Hospitalized at Raleigh on April 10, 1865. Transferred to another hospital on April 12, 1865.

BENNICK, GEORGE, Corporal
Born in Catawba County* and was by occupation a farmer prior to enlisting in Rutherford County at age 22, March 17, 1862. Mustered in as Private. Reported absent sick in May-June, 1862. Returned to duty in July-August, 1862. Promoted to Corporal on September 24, 1862. Reported present in November-December, 1862. No further records.

BENNICK, HENRY J., Private
Enlisted in Rutherford County at age 21, May 17, 1862, for the war. Hospitalized at Petersburg, Virginia, July 20, 1862, with parotitis. Returned to duty on November 14, 1862. Reported present in September, 1863-February, 1864, and May-December, 1864. Hospitalized at Raleigh on March 25, 1865, with intermittent fever. Returned to duty on March 29, 1865. Survived the war.

BENNICK, J. S., Private
Previously served in the 2nd Regiment Virginia Infantry. Transferred to this company on an unspecified date. Paroled at Salisbury on May 12, 1865.

BIGHAM, WILLIAM W., Private
Born in Rutherford County and was by occupation a farmer prior to enlisting in Rutherford County at age 22, March 17, 1862. Reported present in May-June, 1862. Died in hospital at Petersburg, Virginia, on or about August 13, 1862, of "continued fever."

BLAND, JACOB C., Private
Enlisted in Wake County on or about September 1, 1863, for the war. Reported present in May-December, 1864. No further records.

BLAND, THOMAS R., Private
Enlisted in Rutherford County at age 33, May 12, 1862, for the war. Reported present but sick through June, 1862. Reported present in July-December, 1862. Hospitalized at Wilmington on August 28, 1863, with dysentery. Returned to duty on September 7, 1863. Reported present in October, 1863-February, 1864, and May-December, 1864. Survived the war.

BLANKENSHIP, JAMES, Corporal
Place and date of enlistment not reported; however, he probably enlisted subsequent to February 29, 1864. No further records.

BLANKENSHIP, JOSEPH B., Private
Resided in Rutherford County and was by occupation a farmer prior to enlisting in Wake County at age 26, October 10, 1862, for the war. Reported present but sick in camp in October-December, 1862. Reported present in

September-October, 1863. Hospitalized at Wilmington on
or about November 28, 1863, with chronic rheumatism.
Returned to duty on December 12, 1863. Hospitalized at
Wilmington on December 21, 1863, with acute diarrhoea.
Returned to duty on January 15, 1864. Reported present
but sick in camp through February 29, 1864. Reported on
duty as a teamster in August, 1864. Survived the war.

BOLTON, JACKSON, Private
Born in Rutherford County where he resided as a farmer
prior to enlisting in Rutherford County at age 28, April
13, 1862. Reported absent without leave in May-June,
1862. Reported in hospital at Petersburg, Virginia, in
July-August, 1862. Reported absent sick or absent on
furlough in September-December, 1862. Transferred to
Company I, 56th Regiment N.C. Troops, January 1, 1863.

BOSTICK, GEORGE, Private
Born in Cherokee County, Georgia, and resided in
Rutherford County where he was by occupation a farmer
prior to enlisting in Rutherford County at age 28, March
21, 1862. Reported absent sick from June 1 through
October, 1862. Recommended for discharge on November
11, 1862, by reason of "disease of the upper part of the
windpipe (chronic laryngitis) attended with severe cough,
derangement of his digestive organs, and loss of
strength." Discharged on or about March 21, 1863, after
providing W. L. Padgett as a substitute. "Released his
substitute" on December 14, 1863, and returned to duty
with the company. Reported sick but on detached service
at Camp Burgwyn, near Wilmington, in January-
February, 1864. Reported present in May-December,
1864. Hospitalized at Greensboro on May 19, 1865.

BRACKET, WILLIAM, Private
Born in Rutherford County and was by occupation a
farmer prior to enlisting in Rutherford County at age 17,
April 7, 1862. Reported present in May-September, 1862.
Discharged on or about October 19, 1862, by reason of
"epilepsy."

BRADLEY, A. HAMPTON, Sergeant
Born in Rutherford County and was by occupation a
farmer prior to enlisting in Rutherford County at age 19,
March 17, 1862. Mustered in as Corporal. Reported
present in May-June, 1862. Promoted to Sergeant on July
18, 1862. Reported present but sick in camp in September-
October, 1862. Hospitalized at Wilmington on or about
September 4, 1863, with intermittent fever. Returned to
duty on September 12, 1863. Reported present in
November, 1863-February, 1864, and May-December,
1864.

BRADLEY, JAMES, Private
Born in Rutherford County where he resided as a farmer
prior to enlisting in Rutherford County at age 25, April
5, 1862. Reported absent without leave in May-June,
1862. Hospitalized at Petersburg, Virginia, August 9,
1862, with acute diarrhoea. Returned to duty on
September 25, 1862. Reported present in November-
December, 1862, and September, 1863-February, 1864.
Also reported present in May-December, 1864.

BRADLEY, THOMAS D., _____
Place and date of enlistment not reported. Listed in the
records of this company in April-June, 1864. No further
records.

BRADLEY, WILSON, Private
Born in Rutherford County and was by occupation a
farmer prior to enlisting in Rutherford County at age 20,
April 5, 1862. Reported absent without leave in May-June,
1862. Reported present in July-September, 1862, and
September, 1863-February, 1864. Also reported present in
May-December, 1864. Hospitalized at Wilmington on
November 25, 1864, with remittent fever. Returned to
duty on December 2, 1864. Survived the war.

BURNETT, LANDRUM, Private
Enlisted in Rutherford County on March 17, 186[3], for
the war. Hospitalized at Wilmington on September 12,
1863, with continued fever. Returned to duty on October
16, 1863. Reported present in November, 1863-February,
1864, and May-December, 1864.

BUTLER, OTHIEL, Private
Born in Rutherford County and was by occupation a
farmer prior to enlisting in Rutherford County at age 23,
March 21, 1862. Reported absent without leave in May-
June, 1862. Died at home in Rutherford County on July
5, 1862. Cause of death not reported.

BUTLER, STEVEN R., Private
Born in Rutherford County where he enlisted on June 5,
1863, for the war. Hospitalized at Wilmington on
September 1, 1863, with remittent fever. Returned to duty
on September 7, 1863. Reported present in October,
1863-February, 1864. Hospitalized at Wilmington on
April 18, 1864, with pneumonia. Transferred to
Goldsboro on May 22, 1864. Died at Washington, North
Carolina, August 9, 1864. Cause of death not reported.

CARPENTER, JOHN CHRISTENBURY, Musician
Enlisted in Rutherford County at age 18, February 2,
1863, for the war. Mustered in as Private. Reported
present but sick in camp in September-October, 1863.
Reported present in November, 1863-February, 1864.
Appointed Musician in January-February, 1864. Reported
present in May-August, 1864. Survived the war.

CARPENTER, KINCHEN JAHU, Private
Born in Rutherford County where he resided prior to
enlisting in Rutherford County at age 20, May 8, 1862,
for the war. Hospitalized at Petersburg, Virginia, July 20,
1862, with acute diarrhoea. Returned to duty on
November 14, 1862. Reported present in September,
1863-February, 1864, and May-August, 1864. Served with
the company until the end of the war.

CHURCH, WILLIAM B., Private
Previously served as Private in Company G, 16th
Regiment N.C. Troops (6th Regiment N.C. Volunteers).
Enlisted in this company in Rutherford County on July
1, 1863, for the war. Reported present in September,
1863-February, 1864, and May-December, 1864.

COLE, JASON, Private
Enlisted in Wake County on or about September 1, 1863, for the war. Reported present in May-December, 1864.

COOK, W. D., Private
Enlisted on September 1, 186[4], for the war. Reported present in May-October, 1864. Paroled at Cheraw, South Carolina, March 5, 1865.

COOPER, JOHN O., 1st Sergeant
Born in Rutherford County where he resided as a mechanic prior to enlisting in Rutherford County at age 30, March 19, 1862. Mustered in as Private. Promoted to Sergeant prior to July 1, 1862. Promoted to 1st Sergeant on September 24, 1862. Reported present in May-September, 1862. Reported on detail as foreman at a sawmill from October 28, 1862, through January 3, 1863. Reported present in September, 1863-February, 1864, and May-December, 1864.

CULBREATH, WILLIAM M., Private
Born in Rutherford County where he resided as a farmer prior to enlisting in Rutherford County at age 32, May 3, 1862, for the war. Died at Petersburg, Virginia, July 16, 1862. Cause of death not reported.

DAVIS, BARNEY W., Private
Enlisted in Wake County. Date of enlistment was probably subsequent to February 29, 1864. Reported present in May-December, 1864.

DAVIS, JACOB L., Private
Enlisted in Rutherford County on May 4, 1862, for the war. Reported present in May-June, 1862. Hospitalized at Petersburg, Virginia, August 9, 1862, with intermittent fever. Returned to duty on August 25, 1862, but deserted the same date. Reported present but under arrest in November-December, 1862. Court-martialed on an unspecified date. Furloughed for twenty-five days on April 20, 1863, by reason of sickness. Hospitalized at Wilmington on September 12, 1863, with continued fever. Returned to duty on December 16, 1863. Reported present in January-February and May-December, 1864. Hospitalized at Charlotte on February 13, 1865, with intermittent fever. Returned to duty on March 12, 1865. Paroled at Charlotte on May 6, 1865.

DePRIEST, J. G., Private
Enlisted in Wake County on or about September 29, 1863, for the war. Reported present in May-December, 1864.

DePRIEST, THOMAS BAXTER, Private
Enlisted on August 1, 1864, for the war. Reported present in August-December, 1864.

DOBBINS, CHRISTOPHER C., Private
Enlisted in Rutherford County at age 19, May 3, 1862, for the war. Reported present in May-December, 1862. Confined in the guard house at Goldsboro on or about June 20, 1863. Reason he was confined not reported. Reported present in September-December, 1863. Reported present but sick in camp in January-February, 1864. Sent to hospital on December 20, 1864. Survived the war.

DOBBINS, GEORGE R., Private
Born in Rutherford County and was by occupation a mechanic prior to enlisting in Rutherford County at age 31, March 17, 1862. Reported present but sick in May-June, 1862. Reported present in July-December, 1862, and September, 1863-February, 1864. Also reported present in May-December, 1864.

DOBBINS, JEFF J., Private
Resided in Rutherford County and was by occupation a day laborer prior to enlisting in Rutherford County. Date of enlistment not reported. Deserted on an unspecified date. Returned to duty on February 7, 1864. Reported present in May-December, 1864.

DOBBINS, WILLIAM BALLARD, Private
Born in Rutherford County where he enlisted at age 20, March 17, 1862. Sent to hospital at Richmond, Virginia, on or about June 30, 1862, after he was "ran [sic] over by [a] horseman." Returned to duty prior to September 1, 1862. Reported present but sick in September-December, 1862. Hospitalized at Wilmington on August 10, 1863, with rheumatism. Returned to duty prior to November 1, 1863. Reported present in November, 1863-February, 1864. Hospitalized at Wilmington on April 27, 1864, with remittent fever. Returned to duty on May 23, 1864. Sent to hospital at Washington, North Carolina, October 1, 1864. No further records.

DOGGETT, JAMES G., Private
Born in Rutherford County and was by occupation a farmer prior to enlisting in Rutherford County at age 28, March 21, 1862. Reported present but sick in May-June, 1862. Reported present in July-December, 1862. Furloughed for fourteen days on July 30, 1863. Reported present in September-October, 1863. Hospitalized at Wilmington on December 6, 1863, with a gunshot wound. Place and date wounded not reported. Returned to duty on March 24, 1864. Hospitalized at Raleigh on November 6, 1864, with intermittent fever. Died in hospital at Raleigh on December 9, 1864, of "pneumonia typh[oid]."

DOGGETT, JAMES LEWIS, Corporal
Enlisted in Rutherford County at age 32, May 8, 1862, for the war. Mustered in as Private. Reported present in July-December, 1862. Promoted to Corporal prior to November 1, 1862. Reported present in September, 1863-February, 1864, and May-December, 1864.

DOGGETT, JOHN HUGH, Private
Enlisted in Rutherford County on May 16, 1862, for the war. Sent to hospital at Petersburg, Virginia, June 25, 1862. Reported absent in hospital or absent on furlough until he rejoined the company on November 3, 1862. Reported present in November-December, 1862, and September, 1863-February, 1864. Also reported present in May-December, 1864.

DOGGETT, WILLIAM D., Private
Born in Rutherford County where he resided as a farmer prior to enlisting in Rutherford County at age 26, March 21, 1862. Reported present in May-December, 1862, and September-October, 1863. Sent to hospital at Wilmington on December 16, 1863. Reported absent in hospital

through February, 1864. Reported present in May-December, 1864. Survived the war.

DOWNEY, THOMAS J., Private
Born in Rutherford County and was by occupation a farmer prior to enlisting in Rutherford County at age 30, March 17, 1862. Hospitalized at Petersburg, Virginia, July 20, 1862, with acute bronchitis. Returned to duty on August 11, 1862. Reported present but sick in camp in September-October, 1862. Reported present in November-December, 1862, and September-December, 1863. Furloughed for thirty days on February 23, 1864. Reported present in May-December, 1864. Survived the war.

DUNDEN, _____, _____
Place and date of enlistment not reported. Died on May 29, 1862 (probably at or near Raleigh). Cause of death not reported.

EARLEY, JOHN, Private
Born in Rutherford County where he resided as a farmer prior to enlisting in Rutherford County at age 21, April 18, 1862, for the war. Reported present in May-December, 1862. Furloughed for twenty-five days on June 28, 1863. Reported present in September, 1863-February, 1864, and May-December, 1864.

FLINN, JOHN, Private
Enlisted in Rutherford County on May 16, 1862, for the war as a substitute for Private W. G. Minler. Reported absent without leave through June, 1862. Reported present in July-October, 1862. Reported on detail as a butcher in November-December, 1862. No further records.

FLYNN, THOMAS J., Private
Born in Rutherford County and was by occupation a farmer prior to enlisting in Rutherford County at age 18, April 13, 1862. Reported present in May-August, 1862. Reported present but sick in camp in September-October, 1862. Reported present in November-December, 1862. Returned from "desertion" on October 20, 1863. Court-martialed but was apparently found innocent. Reported present but sick in camp in January-February, 1864. Reported present in May-December, 1864.

FORBUSH, DAVID R., Private
Born in Rutherford County and was by occupation a farmer prior to enlisting in Rutherford County at age 27, March 17, 1862. Reported present in May-September, 1862. Reported on detail as a sawmill worker from October 28, 1862, through January 3, 1863. Reported present in September, 1863-February, 1864, and May-December, 1864. Survived the war.

FORBUSH, FRANKLIN, Private
Born in Rutherford County and was by occupation a farmer prior to enlisting in Rutherford County at age 21, March 24, 1862. Reported absent sick or absent without leave from June 15 through December 31, 1862. Sent to hospital at Raleigh on June 1, 1863. Returned to duty on October 30, 1863. No further records. [May have served later as Private in Company C, 34th Regiment N.C. Troops.]

FRANCIS, JOHN M., Private
Born in Lincoln County and was by occupation a farmer prior to enlisting in Rutherford County at age 33, March 21, 1862. Detailed as a teamster on or about May 25, 1862. Hospitalized at Petersburg, Virginia, August 11, 1862, with debilitas. Returned to duty on November 14, 1862. Reported on detail as a teamster through February, 1864. Reported absent with General James G. Martin at Asheville in May-December, 1864.

GOODE, FRANK M., Private
Enlisted in Wake County on or about July 1, 186[4], for the war. Reported present in July-December, 1864. No further records.

GOODE, JAMES MILTON WEBB, Private
Resided in Rutherford County and was by occupation a farmer prior to enlisting in Wake County on January 1, 1864, for the war. Was about 19 years of age at time of enlistment. Survived the war.

GREEN, ALBERT, Private
Born in Rutherford County and was by occupation a farmer prior to enlisting in Rutherford County at age 22, April 13, 1862. Reported present in May-December, 1862, and September, 1863-February, 1864. Also reported present in May-December, 1864. Survived the war.

GREEN, ANDREW J., Sergeant
Born in Rutherford County and was by occupation a farmer prior to enlisting in Rutherford County at age 25, March 22, 1862. Mustered in as Private. Reported present in May-December, 1862, and September, 1863-February, 1864. Promoted to Corporal on December 1, 1863. Promoted to Sergeant on November 1, 1864. Reported present in May-December, 1864.

GREEN, C. P., Private
Enlisted in Rutherford County on May 30, 1863, for the war. Mustered in as Private. Reported present in September-December, 1863. Appointed Musician in January-February, 1864, and transferred to the regimental band. Reduced to ranks on an unspecified date and transferred back to this company. Reported present in May-December, 1864. Hospitalized at Charlotte on February 6, 1865, with otorrhea. Furloughed on February 14, 1865.

GREEN, J. G., Private
Place and date of enlistment not reported; however, he probably enlisted subsequent to February 29, 1864. Captured by the enemy at or near Savannah, Georgia, on an unspecified date (probably in December, 1864). Hospitalized at Savannah on December 24, 1864, with intermittent fever. Hospital records give his age as 18. No further records.

GREEN, OLIVER, Private
Born in Rutherford County and enlisted on April 30, 1862, for the war. Died in hospital at Petersburg, Virginia, August 31, 1862, of "diarrhoea." Was 28 years of age at the time of his death.

GREEN, SANDERS DONEHEW, Private
Born in Rutherford County and was by occupation a farmer prior to enlisting in Rutherford County at age 21, March 22, 1862. Reported present but sick in May-June, 1862. Reported present in July-August, 1862. Reported present but sick in camp in September-October, 1862. Reported present or accounted for in November-December, 1862, and September, 1863-February, 1864. Also reported present in May-December, 1864. Survived the war.

GREENWAY, JOHN W., Private
North Carolina pension records indicate that he served in this company.

GREENWAY, L. E., Private
Enlisted in Wake County on October 10, 1862, for the war. Reported present in September-December, 1862, and September, 1863-February, 1864. Also reported present in May-December, 1864.

GROVES, J. B., Private
Enlisted in Wake County on October 10, 1862, for the war. Reported present in September-December, 1862, and September, 1863-February, 1864. Also reported present in May-December, 1864. Hospitalized at Raleigh on February 17, 1865, with intermittent fever. Returned to duty on February 22, 1865.

HALL, GEORGE W., Private
Born in Rutherford County and was by occupation a farmer prior to enlisting at age 19, March 19, 1862. Reported absent sick or absent without leave until he rejoined the company on December 11, 1862. Was again reported absent sick on an unspecified date. Rejoined the company on October 14, 1863. Reported present in November-December, 1863. Hospitalized at Wilmington on January 27, 1864, with chronic diarrhoea. Returned to duty on April 21, 1864. Last reported in the records of this company in July-September, 1864.

HAMPTON, A. S., Private
Enlisted in Wake County. Date of enlistment not reported; however, he probably enlisted subsequent to February 29, 1864. Reported present in May-December, 1864. Died in hospital at Columbia, South Carolina, February 22, 1865, of "pneumonia."

HAMPTON, B. F. C., Private
Enlisted in Wake County. Date of enlistment not reported; however, he probably enlisted subsequent to February 29, 1864. Reported present in May-December, 1864. Died in hospital at Columbia, South Carolina, February 27, 1865, of "typhoid fever." [May have served previously as Private in Company G, 16th Regiment N.C. Troops (6th Regiment N.C. Volunteers).]

HAMRICK, ELIAS, Private
Born in Rutherford County where he enlisted at age 19, November 9, 1863, for the war. Reported present in November, 1863-February, 1864, and May-December, 1864. Survived the war.

HARDIN, BERRY P., Private
Born in Rutherford County where he resided as a farmer prior to enlisting in Rutherford County at age 33, March 29, 1862. Reported absent without leave in May-August, 1862. Reported present but under arrest in September-December, 1862. Court-martialed on an unspecified date and was sentenced "to fourteen days solitary confinement on bread and water." Returned to duty on an unspecified date. Hospitalized at Wilmington on August 28, 1863, with rheumatism. Returned to duty on September 7, 1863. Reported present in September, 1863-February, 1864. Died in hospital at Wilmington on or about March 15, 1864, of "pneumonia."

HARDIN, JAMES B., Private
Born in Rutherford County where he resided as a brickmason prior to enlisting in Rutherford County at age 38, March 21, 1862. Mustered in as Sergeant. Reduced to ranks in September-October, 1862. Reported present in May-December, 1862, and September-December, 1863. Reported present but sick in camp in January-February, 1864. Reported present in May-December, 1864. Survived the war.

HARDIN, JESSE N., Private
Born in Rutherford County where he resided as a farmer prior to enlisting in Rutherford County at age 24, March 21, 1862. Reported present in May-August, 1862. Reported on detail as a sawmill worker from October 28, 1862, through January 3, 1863. Reported present in September, 1863-February, 1864, and May-December, 1864. Survived the war.

HARDIN, JOHN E., Private
Born in Rutherford County where he resided as a farmer prior to enlisting in Rutherford County at age 18, March 21, 1862. Reported present but sick in May-June, 1862. Reported present in September-December, 1862, and September, 1863-February, 1864. Captured at Savannah, Georgia, on or about December 21, 1864. Hospitalized at Savannah on January 19, 1865, with chronic diarrhoea. Sent to Hilton Head, South Carolina, on an unspecified date. Transferred to Fort Delaware, Delaware, where he arrived on March 12, 1865. Released at Fort Delaware on or about June 19, 1865, after taking the Oath of Allegiance.

HARDIN, LaFAYETTE C., Private
Enlisted at age 17, October 25, 1864, for the war. Reported present in November-December, 1864. Survived the war.

HARMON, ALFRED, Private
Born in Rutherford County where he enlisted at age 22, March 21, 1862. Dropped from the rolls of the company prior to July 1, 1862. Reason he was dropped not reported.

HARMON, ANDREW, Private
Born in Rutherford County where he resided as a blacksmith prior to enlisting in Rutherford County at age 31, March 21, 1862. Sent to hospital on June 25, 1862. Reported absent in hospital or absent on furlough through October, 1862. Died in Rutherford County on or about December 23, 1864, of "dropsy."

HARMON, JOSEPH, Private
Enlisted in Rutherford County prior to April 29, 1862. Reported absent without leave on April 29, 1862. No further records.

HARREL, DAVID, Private
Born in Rutherford County and was by occupation a farmer prior to enlisting in Rutherford County at age 29, March 21, 1862. Reported present in May-December, 1862, and September, 1863-February, 1864. Also reported present in May-December, 1864. Hospitalized at Charlotte on February 18, 1865, with chronic diarrhoea. Transferred to another hospital on the same date.

HARRELL, ALFRED W., 1st Sergeant
Born in Rutherford County and was by occupation a farmer prior to enlisting in Rutherford County at age 40, March 19, 1862. Mustered in as 1st Sergeant. Dropped from the rolls of the company (probably because he was over 35 years of age) prior to July 1, 1862.

HARRIS, ANDERSON, Private
Enlisted in Wake County. Date of enlistment not reported; however, he probably enlisted subsequent to February 29, 1864. Reported present in May-December, 1864.

HARVEY, ALLEN, Private
Born in Spartanburg District, South Carolina, and was by occupation a farmer prior to enlisting in Rutherford County at age 48, March 19, 1862. Reported present in May-August, 1862. Reported present but sick in camp in September-December, 1862, and September-October, 1863. Hospitalized at Wilmington on November 27, 1863, with debilitas. Returned to duty on December 4, 1863. Reported sick in camp in January-February, 1864. Reported present in May-December, 1864.

HEMPHILL, THOMAS POSEY, Corporal
Previously served as Private in Company G of this regiment. Enlisted in this company on or about September 1, 1863, for the war. Died in hospital at Wilson on November 26, 1864. Cause of death not reported.

HOLLAND, WILLIAM C., Private
Resided in Rutherford County and was by occupation a farmer prior to enlisting in Rutherford County at age 31, May 12, 1862, for the war. Reported present or accounted for in May-December, 1862, and September, 1863-February, 1864. Reported present in May-December, 1864. Survived the war.

HOLLIFIELD, JAMES, Musician
Born in Rutherford County and was by occupation a farmer prior to enlisting in Rutherford County at age 20, March 19, 1862. Mustered in as Private. Reported present in May-December, 1862. Appointed Musician in July-August, 1862. Reported present or accounted for in September, 1863-February, 1864, and May-December, 1864. Hospitalized at Charlotte on February 6, 1865, with debilitas. Returned to duty on March 3, 1865. Survived the war.

HUNT, JOHN, Private
Born in Cleveland County* and was by occupation a

mechanic prior to enlisting in Rutherford County at age 22, March 27, 1862. Reported present in May-June, 1862. Reported in hospital at Petersburg, Virginia, in July-August, 1862. Reported present but sick in camp in September-December, 1862. Reported present in September, 1863-February, 1864, and May-December, 1864.

HUNTER, JOHN E., Private
Born in Rutherford County and was by occupation a farmer prior to enlisting in Rutherford County at age 18, March 22, 1862. Died near Petersburg, Virginia, July 18, 1862, of disease.

HUNTSINGER, WILLIAM, Private
Previously served as Private in Company I, 56th Regiment N.C. Troops. Transferred to this company on January 1, 1863. Reported under arrest at Wilmington in November-December, 1863. Reason he was arrested not reported. Reported present in January-February, 1864. Hospitalized at Raleigh on November 6, 1864, with intermittent fever. Returned to duty on November 27, 1864. Hospitalized at Raleigh on February 17, 1865, with intermittent fever. Returned to duty on February 22, 1865.

HYDEN, W. H., Private
Enlisted in Wake County. Date of enlistment not reported; however, he probably enlisted subsequent to February 29, 1864. Sent to hospital at Tarboro on November 1, 1864. No further records.

JARVIS, MARTIN, Private
Enlisted in Wake County. Date of enlistment not reported; however, he probably enlisted subsequent to February 29, 1864. Sent to hospital at Augusta, Georgia, November 30, 1864. No further records.

JONES, ROBERT Y., Private
Born in Rutherford County where he enlisted on May 12, 1862, for the war. Died (probably at Richmond, Virginia) on July 26, 1862, of "typhoid fever."

KENNEDY, C. A., Private
Enlisted in Rutherford County. Enlistment date not reported; however, he probably enlisted subsequent to February 29, 1864. Reported present in May-December, 1864.

LEE, JOHN WALKER, Private
Born in Rutherford County and was by occupation a mechanic prior to enlisting in Rutherford County at age 24, April 13, 1862. Reported present in May-June, 1862. Hospitalized at Petersburg, Virginia, August 9, 1862, with intermittent fever. Returned to duty on November 3, 1862. Reported present through December, 1862. Listed as a deserter on an unspecified date. Rejoined the company on October 20, 1863. Reported on duty as a teamster from January 2 through March 1, 1864. Reported present in May-December, 1864. Survived the war.

LEWIS, CHARLES RUFUS, Sergeant
Born in Rutherford County and was by occupation a farmer prior to enlisting in Rutherford County at age 21,

March 17, 1862. Mustered in as Corporal. Reported present but sick in May-June, 1862. Reported present in July-August, 1862. Promoted to Sergeant on September 24, 1862. Reported present in September-December, 1862. Hospitalized at Wilmington on or about August 29, 1863, with intermittent fever. Furloughed for thirty days on or about September 25, 1863. Reported present in November-December, 1863. Reported absent on detached service at Camp Burgwyn, near Wilmington, in January-February, 1864. Reported present in May-December, 1864.

LOGAN, JOSEPH C., Private
Born in Rutherford County and was by occupation a farmer prior to enlisting in Rutherford County at age 19, March 17, 1862. Mustered in as Corporal. Reported present in May-December, 1862. Furloughed for fourteen days on July 30, 1863. Promoted to Sergeant on December 1, 1863. Reported present in September, 1863-February, 1864. Reduced to ranks on October 31, 1864. Reported present in May-December, 1864. Hospitalized at Charlotte on February 13, 1865, with intermittent fever. Returned to duty on March 1, 1865. Survived the war.

LONG, WATSON, Private
Enlisted in Wake County on October 10, 1862, for the war. Reported present but sick in camp in November-December, 1862. Reported absent under arrest at Wilmington in November-December, 1863. Reported present in January-February and May-December, 1864.

LOVELACE, J. L., Private
Enlisted in Wake County. Date of enlistment not reported; however, he probably enlisted subsequent to February 29, 1864. Reported present in May-December, 1864.

McCURRIE, H. C., Private
Place and date of enlistment not reported; however, he probably enlisted subsequent to February 29, 1864. Reported present in May-December, 1864.

McDANIEL, ANDREW HUDLOW, Private
Born in Rutherford County and was by occupation a farmer prior to enlisting in Rutherford County at age 17, March 27, 1862. Reported absent sick in May-June, 1862. Reported present in July-December, 1862, and September-December, 1863. Reported absent on detached service at Fair Bluff (Columbus County) in January-February, 1864. Reported present in May-December, 1864. Survived the war.

McDANIEL, G. E., Private
Place and date of enlistment not reported; however, he probably enlisted subsequent to February 29, 1864. Reported present but sick in camp in May-December, 1864.

McDANIEL, LEWIS, Private
Born in Rutherford County where he resided as a farmer prior to enlisting in Rutherford County at age 29, July 2, 1863, for the war. Reported present but sick in camp in September-October, 1863. Reported present in November, 1863-February, 1864. Died at Washington, North Carolina, July 23, 1864, of "fever."

McDANIEL, MATTHEW McBEE, Private
Enlisted in Rutherford County. Date of enlistment not reported; however, he probably enlisted subsequent to February 29, 1864. Hospitalized at Wilmington on April 24, 1864, with remittent fever. Returned to duty on July 2, 1864. Reported present in July-December, 1864.

McDANIEL, REUBEN, Private
Born in Rutherford County and enlisted on May 4, 1862, for the war. Reported absent sick in May-June, 1862. Died at home in Rutherford County on July 7, 1862. Cause of death not reported.

McEACHIN, S. M., Private
Enlisted in Rutherford County. Probably enlisted subsequent to February 29, 1864. Died at Raleigh on December 19, 1864. Cause of death not reported.

MARVIN, JAMES, Private
Place and date of enlistment not reported; however, he probably enlisted subsequent to February 29, 1864. No further records.

MILLER, ASPASIA EARL, Private
Enlisted in Wake County. Date of enlistment not reported; however, he probably enlisted subsequent to February 29, 1864. Reported present in May-December, 1864.

MILLER, DANIEL FRANKLIN, Corporal
Enlisted in Rutherford County at age 33, May 10, 1862, for the war. Mustered in as Private. Reported present in May-December, 1862. Hospitalized at Wilmington on August 25, 1863, with anemia. Returned to duty on September 7, 1863. Furloughed for fourteen days on October 21, 1863. Returned to duty prior to January 1, 1864. Reported on detail as a mechanic at Wilmington in January-February, 1864. Promoted to Corporal on November 1, 1864. Reported present in May-December, 1864. Survived the war.

MINLER, W. G., _____
Place and date of enlistment not reported. Discharged prior to July 1, 1862, after providing Private John Flinn as a substitute.

MORGAN, A. F., Private
Enlisted in Rutherford County at age 18, July 1, 1863, for the war. Reported present in September-December, 1863. Reported present but sick in camp in January-February, 1864. Hospitalized at Wilmington on March 29, 1864, with rubeola. Transferred to another hospital on May 22, 1864. Reported present in May-December, 1864. Survived the war.

MORGAN, ELIJAH MERRIMON, Private
Resided in Rutherford County where he enlisted at age 17, March 20, 1864, for the war. No further records.

MORRIS, GEORGE W., Sergeant
Born in Rutherford County and was by occupation a farmer prior to enlisting in Rutherford County at age 24, March 17, 1862. Mustered in as Corporal. Hospitalized at Petersburg, Virginia, July 20, 1862, with remittent

fever. Returned to duty on August 11, 1862. Reported present in September-December, 1862, and September-December, 1863. Reported on detached service at Fair Bluff (Columbus County) in January-February, 1864. Promoted to Sergeant on November 1, 1864. Reported present in May-December, 1864. Furloughed on an unspecified date because he was suffering from intermittent fever. Furlough extended on March 25, 1865.

MORRIS, JAMES, Corporal
Enlisted in Rutherford County at age 18, May 12, 1862, for the war. Mustered in as Private. Hospitalized at or near Petersburg, Virginia, July 26, 1862, with catarrh febris. Returned to duty on August 2, 1862. Reported present in September-December, 1862, and September-December, 1863. Reported on detached service at Fair Bluff (Columbus County) in January-February, 1864. Promoted to Corporal on November 1, 1864. Reported present in May-December, 1864. Survived the war.

MORRIS, JOSEPH B., _____
Enlisted in Rutherford County. Date of enlistment not reported; however, he probably enlisted subsequent to February 29, 1864. Reported present in May-December, 1864.

MORROW, ALFRED, Private
Enlisted in Rutherford County. Date of enlistment not reported; however, he probably enlisted subsequent to February 29, 1864. Reported present in May-December, 1864.

MORROW, DAVID, _____
North Carolina pension records indicate that he served in this company.

MORROW, ELBERT G., Private
Born in Rutherford County where he resided prior to enlisting in Rutherford County on June 1, 1863, for the war. Reported present in September, 1863-February, 1864. Deserted to the enemy at or near Savannah, Georgia, December 21, 1864. Hospitalized at Savannah on December 24, 1864, with intermittent fever. Sent to Hilton Head, South Carolina, on an unspecified date. Reported at Hilton Head on January 25, 1865. No further records. [May have served previously as Private in Company I, 34th Regiment N.C. Troops.]

MORROW, JAMES, Private
Place and date of enlistment not reported; however, he probably enlisted subsequent to February 29, 1864. No further records.

NANNEY, GEORGE WASHINGTON, Private
Enlisted in Rutherford County at age 18, July 1, 1863, for the war. Reported present in September-October, 1863. Hospitalized at Wilmington on November 19, 1863, with catarrh. Returned to duty on December 2, 1863. Reported present in January-February and May-December, 1864. Survived the war.

NORVILLE, SAMUEL, Private
Enlisted in Rutherford County on May 8, 1862, for the

war. Sent to hospital at Wilson prior to July 1, 1862. Reported present in July-August, 1862. Deserted at Point of Rocks, Virginia, October 30, 1862. Returned to duty on an unspecified date. Reported present in September, 1863-February, 1864. Sent to hospital at Augusta, Georgia, December 1, 1864.

NORVILLE, WILLIAM A., Private
Enlisted in Wake County on October 10, 1862, for the war. Reported present in September-December, 1862. Deserted on an unspecified date. Returned from desertion on February 13, 1864. [A North Carolina pension application filed by his widow in 1909 states that Private Norville was transferred from the 50th Regiment "to a Confederate gunboat." The pension application also states that he was wounded at Fort Fisher on December 5, 1864, and died on December 12, 1864.]

PADGETT, BARNEY, Private
Place and date of enlistment not reported; however, he probably enlisted subsequent to February 29, 1864. No further records.

PADGETT, HIX, Corporal
Born in Rutherford County and was by occupation a farmer prior to enlisting in Rutherford County at age 23, March 21, 1862. Mustered in as Private. Reported present in May-August, 1862. Reported present but sick in camp in September-October, 1862. Reported present in November-December, 1862, and September, 1863-February, 1864. Promoted to Corporal on November 1, 1864. Reported present in May-December, 1864.

PADGETT, J. C., Private
Enlisted in Rutherford County on April 1, 1864, for the war. Sent to hospital at Charleston, South Carolina, December 1, 1864. No further records.

PADGETT, LEANDER, Private
Enlisted in Wake County on or about September 7, 1863, for the war. Sent to hospital at Goldsboro on November 1, 1864. No further records.

PADGETT, MANSEL, Private
Enlisted in Wake County on or about September 1, 1863, for the war. Reported present in May-December, 1864.

PADGETT, MORRIS, Private
Enlisted in Rutherford County on April 1, 1864, for the war. Died at Washington, North Carolina, July 20, 1864. Cause of death not reported.

PADGETT, NOAH, Private
Born in Rutherford County where he resided as a farmer prior to enlisting in Rutherford County at age 38, March 19, 1862. Reported present but sick in May-June, 1862. Reported present in July-October, 1862. Reported present but sick in camp in November-December, 1862. Reported present in September, 1863-February, 1864. Reported present but sick in camp in May-December, 1864. Hospitalized at Charlotte on February 13, 1865, with intermittent fever. Furloughed on February 21, 1865.

PADGETT, TIRREL, Private
Enlisted in Wake County on or about September 7, 1863, for the war. Sent to hospital at Goldsboro on November 1, 1864. No further records.

PADGETT, W. L., Private
Enlisted at age 17, March 21, 1863, for the war as a substitute for Private George Bostick of this company. Reported present in September-October, 1863. Was apparently discharged on December 14, 1863, after Private Bostick returned to duty.

PAGE, TRUSCAN CHEVES, _____
Enlisted in Wake County on or about October 14, 1863, for the war. Reported present in May-December, 1864.

PANNEL, J. M., Private
Enlisted in Wake County on or about September 7, 1863, for the war. Reported present in May-December, 1864.

PINTUFF, BARNEY B., Private
Born in Rutherford County where he resided as a farmer prior to enlisting in Rutherford County at age 24, March 21, 1862. Reported present in May-August, 1862. Deserted at Point of Rocks, Virginia, October 30, 1862. Returned to duty subsequent to January 1, 1863. Hospitalized at Wilmington on August 28, 1863, with pneumonia. Returned to duty on November 14, 1863. Furloughed for thirty days on November 28, 1863. Returned to duty on February 28, 1864. Reported present but sick in camp in May-December, 1864.

PINTUFF, MICHAEL P., Private
Born in Rutherford County where he resided as a farmer prior to enlisting in Rutherford County at age 22, March 22, 1862. Hospitalized at Petersburg, Virginia, July 20, 1862, with chronic rheumatism. Returned to duty on August 11, 1862. Reported present in September-December, 1862. Reported present or accounted for in September-December, 1863. Reported on detached service at Wrightsville Sound in January-February, 1864. Reported present in May-December, 1864. Survived the war.

POPE, I. S., Private
Place and date of enlistment not reported; however, he probably enlisted subsequent to February 29, 1864. Hospitalized at Wilmington on November 25, 1864, with remittent fever. Returned to duty on December 5, 1864. Paroled at Greensboro on or about April 28, 1865.

QUESENBERRY, D., Private
Place and date of enlistment not reported; however, he probably enlisted subsequent to February 29, 1864. Captured in hospital at Richmond, Virginia, April 3, 1865. Died in hospital at Richmond on April 13, 1865, of "remittent fever."

ROBERSON, SMITH, Private
Born in Georgia and was by occupation a mechanic prior to enlisting in Rutherford County at age 34, March 21, 1862. Dropped from the rolls of the company prior to July 1, 1862. Reason he was dropped not reported.

ROGERS, WILLIAM, Private
Born in Rutherford County and was by occupation a farmer prior to enlisting in Rutherford County at age 30, March 19, 1862. Reported present in May-August, 1862. Reported present but sick in camp in September-December, 1862. Reported present in September-December, 1863. Reported present but sick in camp in January-February, 1864. Reported present in May-December, 1864.

SCOGGINS, JOSEPH, _____
Previously served as Sergeant in Company B, Mallett's N.C. Battalion (Camp Guard). Transferred to this company on an unspecified date (probably subsequent to February 29, 1864). Reported present in May-December, 1864.

SCRUGGS, ROBERT, Private
Enlisted in Rutherford County on March 21, 1862. Reported present in May-December, 1862, and September-December, 1863. Reported on detached service at Fair Bluff (Columbus County) in January-February, 1864. Reported present in May-December, 1864.

SHEHAN, EDWARD, Private
Enlisted in Rutherford County at age 24, January 19, 1863, for the war. Reported absent under arrest at Wilmington in November-December, 1863. Reason he was arrested not reported. Reported present for duty in January-February and May-December, 1864. Survived the war.

SHEHAN, JACKSON, Private
Born in Burke County and was by occupation a farmer prior to enlisting in Rutherford County at age 24, April 13, 1862. Reported present in May-December, 1862. Reported absent under arrest at Wilmington in November-December, 1863. Reason he was arrested not reported. Reported present for duty in January-February and May-December, 1864.

SHEHAN, JAMES, Private
Born in Rutherford County and was by occupation a farmer prior to enlisting in Rutherford County at age 24, March 22, 1862. Reported present in May-December, 1862, and September, 1863-February, 1864. Also reported present in May-December, 1864. Survived the war.

SMITH, DOC MILLER, _____
North Carolina pension records indicate that he served in this company.

SMITH, EDLEY MARTIN, Private
Born in Rutherford County and was by occupation a farmer prior to enlisting in Rutherford County at age 20, March 19, 1862. Mustered in as Private. Appointed Musician in July-August, 1862. Hospitalized at Petersburg, Virginia, July 20, 1862, with intermittent fever. Reduced to ranks on September 30, 1862. Returned to duty on November 14, 1862. Reported present in September-October, 1863. Furloughed for thirty days on November 10, 1863. Reported present in January-February and May-December, 1864. Survived the war.

SMITH, GEORGE W., Private

Enlisted in Rutherford County on May 12, 1862, for the war. Reported present in May-December, 1862, and September-December, 1863. Reported on detached service at Fair Bluff (Columbus County) in January-February, 1864. Reported present in May-December, 1864. Hospitalized at Charlotte on March 5, 1865, with remittent fever. Returned to duty on March 12, 1865.

SMITH, M. L., Private

Enlisted in Rutherford County on January 27, 1863, for the war. Sent to hospital at Wilson on July 2, 1863. Reported on detail as a hospital nurse at Wilson from October 1, 1863, through December 31, 1864.

SMITH, THOMAS C., Private

Resided in Rutherford County and was by occupation a druggist or farmer prior to enlisting in Rutherford County at age 24, March 17, 1862. Mustered in as Private. Appointed Hospital Steward on or about May 1, 1862; however, he apparently continued to serve with this company. Reported absent sick in May-June, 1862. Reported present in July-December, 1862. Transferred to the Field and Staff of this regiment prior to November 1, 1863.

SORRELLS, CHARLES H., Private

Born in Rutherford County and was by occupation a farmer prior to enlisting in Rutherford County at age 20, March 27, 1862. Reported present in May-August, 1862. Reported present but sick in camp in September-October, 1862. Reported present in November-December, 1862, and September, 1863-February, 1864. Also reported present in May-December, 1864. Survived the war.

SPARKS, MERIT R., Private

Born in Rutherford County and was by occupation a farmer prior to enlisting in Rutherford County at age 17, March 28, 1862. Deserted from Camp Mangum, near Raleigh, May 5, 1862.

TATE, ALBERT, Private

Place of enlistment not reported. Probably enlisted subsequent to February 29, 1864. Sent to hospital at Goldsboro on November 10, 1864. No further records.

TAYLOR, ROBERT C., Private

Born in Rutherford County and was by occupation a farmer prior to enlisting in Rutherford County at age 18, March 17, 1862. Died at Camp Mangum, near Raleigh, May 22, 1862. Cause of death not reported.

THOMPSON, HOSEA H., Private

Born in Rutherford County and was by occupation a farmer prior to enlisting in Rutherford County at age 40, April 1, 1862. Reported present but sick in May-June, 1862. Reported present in July-October, 1862. Reported present but sick in camp in November-December, 1862. Reported absent on sick furlough from May 12 through December 31, 1863. Reported at home "confined to bed with rheumatism" in January-February, 1864. Last reported in the records of this company in July-September, 1864.

TROUT, WILLIAM GAITHER, Private

Resided in Rutherford County where he enlisted at age 18, February 2, 1863, for the war. Reported present in September, 1863-February, 1864, and May-December, 1864.

UPCHURCH, WILLIAM, Private

Resided in Rutherford County and was by occupation a day laborer prior to enlisting in Rutherford County at age 26, April 30, 1862, for the war. Reported absent in hospital at Petersburg, Virginia, in May-June, 1862. Reported present in July-December, 1862, and September, 1863-February, 1864. Also reported present in May-December, 1864.

WALKER, ELIJAH, Private

Born in Rutherford County and was by occupation a farmer prior to enlisting in Rutherford County at age 25, March 19, 1862. Reported present but sick in May-June, 1862. Hospitalized at Petersburg, Virginia, August 6, 1862, with acute diarrhoea. Furloughed for thirty days on September 24, 1862. Reported absent on furlough in November-December, 1862. Reported present in September-December, 1863. Reported on detached service at Wilmington in January-February, 1864. Reported present in May-December, 1864. Survived the war. [North Carolina pension records indicate that he was wounded in the finger near Washington, North Carolina, in February, 1864.]

WALKER, JESSE R., Private

Born in Rutherford County and was by occupation a farmer prior to enlisting in Rutherford County at age 28, March 21, 1862. Reported present but sick in May-June, 1862. Hospitalized at Petersburg, Virginia, August 6, 1862, with acute diarrhoea. Returned to duty on August 25, 1862. Reported on detail as a sawmill worker from October 28, 1862, through January 3, 1863. Hospitalized at Wilmington on August 29, 1863, with dysentery. Returned to duty on September 7, 1863. Reported present in September, 1863-February, 1864, and May-December, 1864. Survived the war.

WALKER, WILLIAM, Private

Enlisted in Wake County. Probably enlisted subsequent to February 29, 1864. Reported present in May-December, 1864. Hospitalized at Greensboro on January 31, 1865, with catarrhus. Transferred on March 3, 1865. Paroled at Greensboro on May 1, 1865. Was apparently serving as a teamster at the time of his parole.

WALL, A. C., Private

Enlisted in Wake County on or about September 1, 1863, for the war. Mustered in as Sergeant. Reduced to ranks on June 1, 1864. Sent to hospital on November 1, 1864. No further records.

WALL, J. N., Private

Enlisted in Wake County on or about September 1, 1863, for the war. Sent to hospital on November 1, 1864. No further records.

WALL, M. W., _____
Enlisted in Wake County on or about September 1, 1863, for the war. Reported present in May-December, 1864. Wounded at Averasboro on March 16, 1865. Survived the war.

WEATHERS, MARTIN A., _____
North Carolina pension records indicate that he served in this company.

WEBB, PATILLO P., Private
Previously served as Private in Company C, 34th Regiment N.C. Troops. Enlisted in this company in Rutherford County on June 2, 1863, for the war. Reported on duty as a teamster from June 10, 1863, through March 31, 1864. Reported present in May-December, 1864. Hospitalized at Charlotte on April 26, 1865, with rubeola. Transferred to another hospital on April 27, 1865.

WILKIE, WASHINGTON J., Private
Enlisted in Wake County at age 29, October 10, 1862, for the war. Reported present in November-December, 1862, and September-October, 1863. Reported on detail as a mechanic at Wilmington in November, 1863-February, 1864. Reported present in May-December, 1864. Survived the war.

WILKINS, JOHN, Sergeant
Born in Rutherford County and was by occupation a farmer prior to enlisting in Rutherford County at age 18, March 19, 1862. Mustered in as Private. Reported present in May-December, 1862. Promoted to Corporal in November, 1862-October, 1863. Reported present in September, 1863-February, 1864. Promoted to Sergeant on November 1, 1864. Reported present in May-December, 1864.

WILKINS, M. A., Private
Enlisted in Wake County on or about September 1, 1863, for the war. Sent to hospital on or about November 1, 1864. No further records.

WILKINS, WILLIAM I., Private
Enlisted in Rutherford County on December 1, 1863, for the war. Reported present in December, 1863-February, 1864, and May-December, 1864. Hospitalized at Greensboro in March, 1865. No further records.

WILLIAMS, HARVEY C., Private
Born in Rutherford County and was by occupation a farmer prior to enlisting in Rutherford County at age 18, March 19, 1862. Reported present in May-December, 1862. Reported absent on furlough of fourteen days on October 21, 1862. Reported present in November-December, 1863. Reported absent on detached service at Fair Bluff (Columbus County) in January-February, 1864. Reported present in May-December, 1864. Survived the war.

WILSON, ATHEN E., Private
Born in Rutherford County where he enlisted at age 24, March 19, 1862. Mustered in as Private. Promoted to Sergeant on July 18, 1862. Reported present in

May-August, 1862. Reported present but sick in camp in September-October, 1862. Furloughed for twenty-five days on November 8, 1862. Reported present in September, 1863-February, 1864. Reduced to ranks on October 31, 1864. Reported present in May-December, 1864.

WILSON, JOSEPH G., Private
Born in Rutherford County and was by occupation a farmer prior to enlisting in Rutherford County at age 18, March 22, 1862. Reported present in May-August, 1862. Reported on detail as a hospital nurse in October, 1862. Hospitalized at or near Petersburg, Virginia, December 7, 1862, with debility. Returned to duty on December 18, 1862. Reported present in September, 1863-February, 1864. Captured in hospital at Savannah, Georgia, December 21, 1864. Sent to Fort Pulaski, Georgia. Transferred to Hilton Head, South Carolina, March 4, 1865. No further records.

WOMACK, LANDRUN, Private
Born in Rutherford County where he enlisted on July 1, 1863, for the war. Hospitalized at Wilmington on September 1, 1863, with continued fever. Returned to duty on September 6, 1863. Reported present in September-December, 1863. Reported present but sick in camp in January-February, 1864. Died near Wilmington on March 7, 1864. Cause of death not reported.

WOMACK, NOAH W., Private
Born in Rutherford County where he enlisted at age 20, March 21, 1862. Reported absent sick in May-June, 1862. Reported present in July-August, 1862. Reported present but sick in camp in September-December, 1862. Reported present in September-December, 1863. Reported on detached service as a nurse at Camp Burgwyn, near Wilmington, in January-February, 1864. Reported present in May-December, 1864. Survived the war.

WOMICK, THOMAS, Private
Born in Rutherford County where he enlisted at age 24, March 21, 1862. Discharged on May 8, 1862, by reason of "inability." [May have served later as Private in Company D, 16th Regiment N.C. Troops (6th Regiment N.C. Volunteers).]

YARBROUGH, G., _____
Place and date of enlistment not reported; however, he probably enlisted subsequent to February 29, 1864. Died at or near Augusta, Georgia, April 15, 1865. Cause of death not reported.

COMPANY K

This company, known as the "Green River Rifles," was raised in Rutherford County and enlisted in Rutherford County on March 27, 1862. It was mustered into state service at Camp Mangum, near Raleigh, on April 29, 1862, and assigned to the 50th Regiment N.C. Troops as Company K. After joining the regiment the company functioned as a part of the regiment, and its history for the remainder of the war is reported as a part of the regimental history.

The information contained in the following roster was compiled primarily from a company muster-in and descriptive roll dated April 29, 1862, and from company muster rolls for May 1-August 31, 1862; November 1-December 31, 1862; and September 1, 1863-February 29, 1864. No company muster rolls were located for September 1-October 31, 1862; January 1-August 31, 1863; or for the period after February 29, 1864. Valuable information was obtained from primary records such as the North Carolina adjutant general's *Roll of Honor*, discharge certificates, medical records, prisoner of war records, *The War of the Rebellion: A Compilation of the Official Records of the Union and Confederate Armies*, militia records, newspaper casualty lists and obituaries, Confederate pension applications filed with the state of North Carolina, and the 1860 federal census of North Carolina. Secondary sources such as postwar rosters and histories, cemetery records, the *Confederate Veteran*, published genealogies, and records of the United Daughters of the Confederacy also provided useful information.

OFFICERS

CAPTAINS

WILKINS, SAMUEL
Born in Polk County* and resided in Rutherford County where he was by occupation a hotelkeeper prior to enlisting in Rutherford County at age 43. Appointed Captain on March 27, 1862. Reported present or accounted for in May-August, 1862. Resigned on November 27, 1862, because of "my age . . ., my property, [which is] under execution and very shortly to be sold at great sacrifice unless I can . . . attend to this matter, and the very feeble health of my wife." Resignation accepted on December 7, 1862.

FORD, GEORGE B.
Born in Rutherford County where he resided prior to enlisting at age 34. Appointed 1st Lieutenant on or about March 27, 1862. Reported present or accounted for in May-August and November-December, 1862. Promoted to Captain on December 7, 1862. Reported present in September-October, 1863. Reported absent without leave in November-December, 1863. Reported present in January-February, 1864. No further records.

LIEUTENANTS

FORD, PINKNEY B., 3rd Lieutenant
Born in Rutherford County where he resided as a farmer prior to enlisting in Rutherford County at age 26, March 27, 1862. Mustered in as 1st Sergeant. Reported present in May-June, 1862. Appointed 3rd Lieutenant on July 17, 1862. Reported present in July-August and November-December, 1862. Also reported present in September-

October, 1863. Reported under arrest in November-December, 1863. Reason he was arrested not reported. Reported present in January-February, 1864. Died in hospital at Charleston, South Carolina, February 21, 1865. Cause of death not reported.

HAMPTON, JOSEPH L., 3rd Lieutenant
Born in Rutherford County and enlisted at age 36. Appointed 3rd Lieutenant on March 27, 1862. Resigned on June 11, 1862, by reason of "disease of the liver attended by dysenteric symptoms with occasional hemorrhages from the bowels." Resignation accepted on July 15, 1862.

HARRIS, JOSEPH H., 2nd Lieutenant
Born in Rutherford County where he resided prior to enlisting in Rutherford County on March 27, 1862. Mustered in as Sergeant. Reported present in May-August, 1862. Reduced to ranks on July 7, 1862. Promoted to Sergeant on September 1, 1862. Hospitalized at or near Petersburg, Virginia, December 12, 1862, with a hernia. Returned to duty on December 18, 1862. Furloughed for fourteen days on July 19, 1863. Reduced to ranks in January-October, 1863. Reported present or accounted for in September, 1863-February, 1864. Appointed 2nd Lieutenant on June 7, 1864. Hospitalized at Wilmington on November 25, 1864, with remittent fever. Returned to duty on December 22, 1864.

MILLER, JAMES A., 1st Lieutenant
Previously served as Private in Company C, 34th Regiment N.C. Troops. Appointed 2nd Lieutenant on March 27, 1862, and transferred to this company. Reported present in May-August and November-December, 1862. Promoted to 1st Lieutenant on December 7, 1862. Reported present or accounted for in September, 1863-February, 1864. Paroled at Greensboro on May 1, 1865. [The date cited in Volume IX, page 281, of this series relative to his transfer from the 34th Regiment N.C. Troops is erroneous.]

MITCHELL, HIRAM J., 2nd Lieutenant
Born in Lincoln County and was by occupation a brickmason prior to enlisting in Rutherford County at age 47, March 27, 1862. Mustered in as Sergeant. Reported present in May-August and November-December, 1862. Appointed 2nd Lieutenant on December 17, 1862. Resigned on May 19, 1863, by reason of "lumbago and articular rheumatism. . . ." Resignation accepted on June 23, 1863.

WILKINS, LEWIS, 2nd Lieutenant
Born in Polk County* and resided in Rutherford County where he was by occupation a farmer prior to enlisting in Rutherford County at age 19, March 27, 1862. Mustered in as Corporal. Reported present or accounted for in May-August, 1862. Promoted to Sergeant on September 1, 1862. Reported present in November-December, 1862. Appointed 2nd Lieutenant on June 29, 1863. Reported present in September, 1863-February, 1864. Resigned on April 7, 1864, because he wished to serve in a cavalry unit. His letter of resignation is annotated by the colonel of the 50th Regiment as follows: "Lieutenant Wilkins will never make an officer. He is ignorant of the duties of his

station and makes no effort to inform himself. . . . The good of the service requires that he should not remain in his present position." Resignation accepted on April 21, 1864.

NONCOMMISSIONED OFFICERS AND PRIVATES

ABRAMS, H. P., _____
Place and date of enlistment not reported; however, he probably enlisted subsequent to February 29, 1864. First listed in the records of this company in July-September, 1864. No further records.

ADCOCK, J. W., _____
North Carolina pension records indicate that he served in this company.

ALBRIGHT, ELIAS, Corporal
Resided in Rutherford County and was by occupation a carpenter prior to enlisting at Camp Holmes, near Raleigh, at age 22, October 10, 1862, for the war. Mustered in as Private. Reported present in November-December, 1862. Promoted to Corporal in January-October, 1863. Reported present in September-December, 1863. Reported on detail as a carpenter on February 18, 1864. Last reported in the records of this company in July-September, 1864.

ALEXANDER, ELIAS A., Private
Born in Rutherford County where he resided as a farmer prior to enlisting in Rutherford County at age 40, April 19, 1862, for the war. Was apparently discharged (probably because he was over 35 years of age) prior to July 1, 1862. [May have served later as Private in Company I, 34th Regiment N.C. Troops.]

ALEXANDER, MAJOR R., Sergeant
Born in Rutherford County and was by occupation a carpenter prior to enlisting in Rutherford County at age 48, March 27, 1862. Mustered in as Sergeant. Was apparently discharged (probably because he was over 35 years of age) prior to July 1, 1862.

BABER, JAMES L., Private
Enlisted in Rutherford County on March 27, 1862. Reported present in May-August, 1862. Sent to hospital at Petersburg, Virginia, January 8, 1863. Reason he was hospitalized not reported. Hospitalized at Wilmington on or about April 30, 1863, with debility. Returned to duty on June 1, 1863. Reported present in September, 1863-February, 1864. Hospitalized at Charlotte on February 6, 1865, with "chron[ic] rheumatism." Transferred to another hospital on February 14, 1865.

BALLARD, SOLOMON, Private
Enlisted in Rutherford County on March 27, 1862. Reported present but sick in May-June, 1862. Reported present in July-August and November-December, 1862. Deserted near Kinston on May 12, 1863. Returned from

desertion and was pardoned on or about February 18, 1864. Last reported in the records of this company in July-September, 1864.

BANTER, JOEL F., Private
Born in Rutherford County and enlisted at Camp Holmes, near Raleigh, October 5, 1862, for the war. Reported present in November-December, 1862, and September, 1863-February, 1864. Hospitalized at Wilmington on March 9, 1864. Died in hospital at Wilmington on March 26, 1864, of "febris congestiva."

BARLOW, ELIPHET, Private
Place and date of enlistment not reported; however, he probably enlisted subsequent to February 29, 1864. Hospitalized at Raleigh on November 6, 1864, with intermittent fever. Furloughed for sixty days to King's Creek (Caldwell County), November 14, 1864. Paroled at Greensboro on May 1, 1865.

BERRY, WILLIAM, Private
Enlisted at Camp Burgwyn, near Wilmington, February 19, 1864, for the war. No further records.

BLACKWELL, CALVIN, Private
Place and date of enlistment not reported; however, he probably enlisted subsequent to February 29, 1864. First listed in the records of this company in April-June, 1864. Died in hospital at Columbia, South Carolina, February 23, 1865, of "pneumonia."

BLACKWELL, JAMES WILLIAM, Corporal
Born in Spartanburg District, South Carolina, and was by occupation a shoemaker prior to enlisting in Rutherford County at age 53, March 27, 1862. Mustered in as Private. Reported present in May-August and November-December, 1862. Promoted to Corporal in January-October, 1863. Reported present in September, 1863-February, 1864. Hospitalized at Wilmington on November 25, 1864, with remittent fever. Returned to duty on December 2, 1864. Hospitalized at Charlotte on March 5, 1865, with intermittent fever. Returned to duty on March 12, 1865.

BLACKWELL, MARION, Musician
Previously served as Private in Company D, 16th Regiment N.C. Troops (6th Regiment N.C. Volunteers). Enlisted in this company in Rutherford County on March 27, 1862. Mustered in as Private. Reported present in May-August, 1862. Hospitalized at or near Petersburg, Virginia, December 12, 1862, with dysentery. Returned to duty on December 28, 1862. Reported present or accounted for in September, 1863-February, 1864. Appointed Musician in January-February, 1864. Last reported in the records of this company in July-September, 1864.

BOLICK, A. P., _____
North Carolina pension records indicate that he served in this company.

BRACK, ROBERT F., Private
Born in Buncombe County and resided in Rutherford

County where he was by occupation a shoemaker prior to enlisting in Rutherford County at age 26, March 27, 1862. Reported present in May-August and November-December, 1862. Reported on duty as a teamster from January 1, 1863, through March 31, 1864. Last reported in the records of this company in July-September, 1864.

BRADLEY, ABSALOM B., Private
Resided in Rutherford County and was by occupation a laborer prior to enlisting in Rutherford County at age 48, March 27, 1862. Failed to report for duty. Listed as a deserter and dropped from the rolls of the company on or about January 1, 1863.

BRADLEY, AUGUSTUS, Private
Enlisted in Rutherford County on March 27, 1862. Reported absent without leave in May-June, 1862. Reported present in July-August, 1862. Deserted at Drewry's Bluff, Virginia, December 14, 1862. Returned to duty on an unspecified date. Reported present in September, 1863-February, 1864. Last reported in the records of this company in July-September, 1864.

BRADLEY, B. F., Private
Enlisted in Rutherford County on March 27, 1862. Dropped from the rolls of the company prior to July 1, 1862. Reason he was dropped not reported.

BRADY, ALFRED, Private
Enlisted at Camp Holmes, near Raleigh, October 5, 1862, for the war. Hospitalized at Petersburg, Virginia, December 4, 1862. Returned to duty on an unspecified date. Reported present in September, 1863-February, 1864. Captured at or near Savannah, Georgia, on or about December 22, 1864. Hospitalized at Savannah on December 22, 1864. Died in hospital at Savannah on January 3, 1865, of "typhoid pneumonia." [Federal hospital records dated December, 1864-January, 1865, give his age as 21.]

BROOKSHIRE, JOHN, Private
Place and date of enlistment not reported; however, he probably enlisted subsequent to February 29, 1864. Paroled at Greensboro on May 1, 1865.

BRYAN, A. H., ———
Place and date of enlistment not reported; however, he probably enlisted subsequent to February 29, 1864. Died (probably at or near Raleigh) on December 15, 1864. Cause of death not reported.

BURGIN, R. L., Private
Place and date of enlistment not reported. Deserted at Drewry's Bluff, Virginia, December 1, 1862.

BURNEY, W. A., Private
Place and date of enlistment not reported; however, he probably enlisted subsequent to February 29, 1864. Hospitalized at Charlotte on January 15, 1865, with intermittent fever. Returned to duty on February 25, 1865. Paroled at Greensboro on May 17, 1865.

BYAS, VEDO, Private
Born in Greenville District, South Carolina, and resided in Rutherford County where he was by occupation a day laborer prior to enlisting in Rutherford County at age 29, March 27, 1862. Hospitalized at Petersburg, Virginia, July 20, 1862, with chronic bronchitis. Returned to duty on August 8, 1862. Died in hospital at Petersburg on November 22, 1862, of "typhoid fever."

BYAS, WILLIAM, Private
Born in Greenville District, South Carolina, and resided in Rutherford County where he was by occupation a day laborer prior to enlisting in Rutherford County at age 24, March 27, 1862. Reported present but sick in May-June, 1862. Reported present in July-August, 1862. Died near Drewry's Bluff, Virginia, November 1, 1862, of "febris typhoides."

CANADA, THOMAS, Private
Born in Rutherford County and was by occupation a farmer prior to enlisting in Rutherford County at age 35, March 27, 1862. Furloughed for fifteen days on May 20, 1862. Failed to return from furlough and was reported absent without leave through December, 1862. Dropped from the rolls of the company on or about January 1, 1863.

CANTRELL, GEORGE, Private
Enlisted in Rutherford County on March 27, 1862. Furloughed for fifteen days on May 20, 1862. Failed to return from furlough and was reported absent without leave through December, 1862. Later listed as a deserter. Returned from desertion on February 13, 1864, and was pardoned. Hospitalized at Richmond, Virginia, June 20, 1864, with catarrhus. Transferred to another hospital on June 21, 1864. Hospitalized at Richmond on July 15, 1864, with dyspepsia. Furloughed on August 29, 1864. No further records.

CLIFTON, SAMUEL, ———
North Carolina pension records indicate that he served in this company.

COLE, DAVID, Private
Enlisted in the spring of 1864 for the war. Place of enlistment not reported. Paroled at Greensboro on May 1, 1865.

COOLY, J. C., Private
Resided in Johnston County. Place and date of enlistment not reported; however, he probably enlisted subsequent to February 29, 1864. Paroled at Goldsboro on May 2, 1865.

CORN, NOAH W., Private
Enlisted in Rutherford County at age 20, March 27, 1862. Reported present but sick in May-June, 1862. Reported present in July-August and November-December, 1862. Also reported present in September-October, 1863. Hospitalized at Wilmington on December 2, 1863. Returned to duty on December 12, 1863. Reported present in January-February, 1864. Hospitalized at Wilmington on

April 27, 1864, with gonorrhea. Transferred to another hospital on May 22, 1864. Hospitalized at Raleigh on November 9, 1864, with intermittent fever. Returned to duty on November 22, 1864. Survived the war.

CRANE, MARK W., Private
Born in Pickens District, South Carolina, and resided in Rutherford County where he was by occupation a farmer prior to enlisting in Rutherford County at age 52, March 27, 1862. Reported present in May-August and November-December, 1862. Sent to hospital at Goldsboro on July 17, 1863. Reported present in September-December, 1863. Discharged on February 19, 1864, by reason of "old age . . . general debility and decrepitude."

CROCKER, MADISON, Private
Enlisted in Rutherford County on March 27, 1862. Reported sick in hospital at Petersburg, Virginia, in May-June, 1862. Reported present in July-August and November-December, 1862. Hospitalized at Wilmington on September 1, 1863, with remittent fever. Returned to duty on September 7, 1863. Reported present in November, 1863-February, 1864. Paroled at Greensboro on May 1, 1865.

DANIEL, FRANCIS L., Private
Born in Rutherford County and was by occupation a farmer prior to enlisting in Rutherford County at age 36, March 27, 1862. Was apparently discharged (probably because he was over 35 years of age) prior to July 1, 1862. Reenlisted in the company on November 11, 1863. Reported present through February, 1864. Paroled on March 5, 1865.

DANIEL, JOSEPH C., Corporal
Born in Rutherford County and was by occupation a farmer prior to enlisting in Rutherford County at age 39, March 27, 1862. Mustered in as Corporal. Was apparently discharged (probably because he was over 35 years of age) prior to July 1, 1862.

DePRIEST, JAMES BYNUM, Sergeant
Resided in Rutherford County and was by occupation a farmer prior to enlisting at Camp Holmes, near Raleigh, at age 32, October 7, 1862, for the war. Mustered in as Private. Reported present in November-December, 1862. Hospitalized at Wilmington on September 2, 1863, with intermittent fever. Returned to duty on September 16, 1863. Reported present in October, 1863-February, 1864. Promoted to Sergeant subsequent to February 29, 1864. Deserted to the enemy at Roanoke Island on an unspecified date. Sent to New Bern. Confined at Fort Monroe, Virginia, November 16, 1864. Released at Fort Monroe on December 30, 1864, after taking the Oath of Allegiance.

DUNAHOE, CRUCK, Private
Enlisted in Rutherford County on March 27, 1862. Reported present or accounted for in May-June, 1862. Sent to hospital at Petersburg, Virginia, July 29, 1862. Died at or near Petersburg on January 24, 1863. Cause of death not reported.

DUNN, JOHN B., Private
Born in Anson County and resided in Rutherford County where he was by occupation a day laborer prior to enlisting in Rutherford County at age 38, March 27, 1862. Reported present in May-August and November-December, 1862. Also reported present in September, 1863-February, 1864. Captured at Plymouth on October 31, 1864. Confined at Fort Monroe, Virginia. Transferred to Point Lookout, Maryland, where he arrived on November 25, 1864. Died at Point Lookout on March 30, 1865, of "congest[ion] brain."

DYER, ELISHA, Private
Born in Rutherford County and was by occupation a farmer prior to enlisting in Rutherford County at age 20, March 27, 1862. Reported present in May-August and November-December, 1862. Also reported present in September, 1863-February, 1864. Last reported in the records of this company in July-September, 1864. Survived the war.

FOWLER, A. BENJAMIN, Private
Enlisted in Rutherford County on March 27, 1862. Reported absent without leave from May 31 through August 31, 1862. Reported under arrest in November-December, 1862. Court-martialed on an unspecified date. Returned to duty on an unspecified date. Reported present in September, 1863-February, 1864. Hospitalized at Charlotte on February 18, 1865, with intermittent fever. Transferred to another hospital the same date. Paroled at Greensboro on May 1, 1865.

FOWLER, ZACHARIAH, Private
Resided in Polk County and was by occupation a farmer prior to enlisting in Polk County at age 48, April 12, 1862. Dropped from the rolls of the company (probably because he was over 35 years of age) prior to July 1, 1862.

FRASIER, DAVID, Private
Enlisted at Camp Holmes, near Raleigh, October 12, 1863, for the war. Hospitalized at Wilmington on October 22, 1863, with acute diarrhoea. Returned to duty on October 28, 1863. Reported present in November, 1863-February, 1864. Last reported in the records of this company in July-September, 1864.

GATTIS, WILLIAM, Private
Born in Rutherford County and was by occupation a farmer prior to enlisting in Rutherford County at age 22, March 27, 1862. Died in hospital at Wilson on June 26, 1862, of "typhoid fever."

GRAY, DAVID JASPER, Private
Born in Rutherford County and was by occupation a farmer prior to enlisting at age 42, March 27, 1862. Was apparently discharged (probably because he was over 35 years of age) prior to July 1, 1862.

GREEN, ELIAS G., Private
Enlisted in Rutherford County on March 27, 1862. Reported present but sick in May-June, 1862. Reported absent on detached service in July-August, 1862. Hospitalized at or near Petersburg, Virginia, December

12, 1862, with diarrhoea. Returned to duty on December 25, 1862. Reported present in September, 1863-February, 1864. Hospitalized at Wilmington on December 29, 1864, with acute diarrhoea. Returned to duty on January 13, 1865.

GREENLEE, DAVID W., Private
Resided in McDowell County and was by occupation a college student prior to enlisting in Rutherford County at age 21, March 27, 1862. Reported present in May-June, 1862. Reported in hospital at Petersburg, Virginia, from July 20 through December 31, 1862. Rejoined the company on an unspecified date. Furloughed for fourteen days on July 19, 1863. Reported present in September-October, 1863. Hospitalized at Wilmington on November 28, 1863, with pneumonia. Returned to duty on February 22, 1864. Hospitalized at Raleigh on November 6, 1864, with intermittent fever. Returned to duty on November 27, 1864. Paroled at Charlotte on or about May 18, 1865.

GREENLEE, TILMAN, _____
North Carolina pension records indicate that he served in this company.

HAMILTON, STEPHEN J., Private
Born in York District, South Carolina, and was by occupation a farmer prior to enlisting in Rutherford County at age 17, March 27, 1862. Reported present or accounted for in May-August and November-December, 1862. Also reported present or accounted for in September, 1863-February, 1864. Last reported in the records of this company in July-September, 1864.

HAMILTON, THOMAS S., Private
Born in Mecklenburg County and resided in Rutherford County where he was by occupation a farmer prior to enlisting in Rutherford County at age 50, March 27, 1862. Reported present but sick in May-June, 1862. Reported present in July-August and November-December, 1862. Discharged on June 8, 1863, by reason of "chronic rheumatism and general bad health."

HAMPTON, THOMAS J., Private
Born in Rutherford County and was by occupation a farmer prior to enlisting in Rutherford County at age 27, March 27, 1862. Mustered in as Corporal. Reduced to ranks prior to September 1, 1862. Reported on duty as a wagon master, forage master, or teamster from October 1, 1862, through March 1, 1864. Killed at Bentonville on March 19-21, 1865.

HAMRICK, A. B., Private
Enlisted at Camp Holmes, near Raleigh, October 7, 1862, for the war. Reported present in November-December, 1862. No further records.

HAMRICK, ROBERT B., Private
Resided in Rutherford County and was by occupation a day laborer prior to enlisting at Camp Holmes, near Raleigh, at age 32, in October, 1862, for the war. Reported present in September, 1863-February, 1864. Survived the war. [North Carolina pension records indicate that he was wounded at Bentonville in March, 1865.]

HARRIS, CALVIN B., _____
North Carolina pension records indicate that he served in this company.

HARRIS, COLEMAN B., Private
Enlisted at Camp Holmes, near Raleigh, October 5, 1862, for the war. Reported present in November-December, 1862. Hospitalized at Wilmington on September 4, 1863, with intermittent fever. Reported absent in hospital or absent on furlough through February, 1864. Hospitalized at Wilmington on December 29, 1864, with remittent fever. Returned to duty on January 14, 1865.

HARRIS, ELIAS, Private
Enlisted in Rutherford County in October, 1863, for the war. Hospitalized at Wilmington on January 21, 1864. Died in hospital at Wilmington on February 2, 1864, of "febris typhoides."

HARRIS, G. B., Private
Enlisted at Camp Holmes, near Raleigh, October 5, 1862, for the war. Reported present (possibly under arrest) in November-December, 1862. No further records.

HARRIS, G. W., Sergeant
Enlisted at Camp Holmes, near Raleigh, October 27, 1862, for the war. Mustered in as Sergeant. Reported present in September, 1863-February, 1864. Hospitalized at Wilmington on April 23, 1864, with remittent fever. Transferred to another hospital on May 22, 1864. Last reported in the records of this company in July-September, 1864.

HARRIS, HERBERT, Private
Born in McDowell County and enlisted at Camp Holmes, near Raleigh, October 5, 1862, for the war. Hospitalized at Petersburg, Virginia, November 4, 1862, with remittent fever. Returned to duty on November 20, 1862. Died near Kinston on March 4, 1863. Cause of death not reported.

HARRIS, KELSEY, Private
Enlisted in Rutherford County in October, 1863, for the war. Reported present in November-December, 1863. Last reported in the records of this company in July-September, 1864.

HARRIS, WILLIAM, Private
Previously served as Private in Company F of this regiment. Transferred to this company in November-December, 1863. Reported present in January-February, 1864. Died at or near Wilson on November 9, 1864, of "fever."

HAYNES, BENJAMIN G., Sergeant
Enlisted in Rutherford County on March 27, 1862. Mustered in as Private. Reported present or accounted for in May-August, 1862. Promoted to Corporal on September 1, 1862. Reported present in November-December, 1862. Promoted to Sergeant in January-October, 1863. Reported present in September, 1863-February, 1864. Last reported in the records of this company in July-September, 1864.

HEAD, PHILIP, Private
Resided in Rutherford County and was by occupation a day laborer prior to enlisting in Rutherford County at age 30, March 27, 1862. Reported present or accounted for in May-August, 1862. Deserted on December 1, 1862. Returned to duty on an unspecified date. Reported present in September-December, 1863. Furloughed for seven days on February 22, 1864. Last reported in the records of this company in July-September, 1864.

HESTER, JAMES M., Private
Resided in Polk County and was by occupation a farmer prior to enlisting in Rutherford County at age 37, August 12, 1863, for the war. Reported present in September, 1863-February, 1864. Hospitalized at Charlotte on February 13, 1865, with pneumonia. Returned to duty on March 7, 1865. [May have served previously as Private in Company I, 34th Regiment N.C. Troops.]

HIPPS, JAMES G., Private
Enlisted in July, 1864, for the war. Paroled at Greensboro on May 1, 1865.

HUDGINS, JAMES W., Private
Enlisted in Rutherford County on March 27, 1862. Reported present but sick in May-June, 1862. Reported present in July-August and November-December, 1862. Reported present or accounted for in September, 1863-February, 1864. Last reported in the records of this company in July-September, 1864.

HUDGINS, WILLIAM D., Private
Born in Newberry District, South Carolina, and was by occupation a farmer prior to enlisting in Rutherford County at age 43, March 27, 1862. Reported present in May-June, 1862. Hospitalized at or near Petersburg, Virginia, August 4, 1862, with diarrhoea. Returned to duty on September 6, 1862. Reported present in November-December, 1862. Reported in hospital at Kinston from March 28 through October 31, 1863. Reported present with the company in January-February, 1864. Hospitalized at Raleigh on February 18, 1865, with chronic diarrhoea. Transferred to another hospital on February 24, 1865.

HUNTSINGER, NOAH, Private
Resided in Polk County and was by occupation a farmer. Place and date of enlistment not reported; however, he probably enlisted subsequent to February 29, 1864. Was about 44 years of age at time of enlistment. Paroled at Greensboro on May 1, 1865.

HUNTSINGER, TOLIVER, Private
Resided in Polk County and was by occupation a farmer prior to enlisting at Camp Holmes, near Raleigh, at age 26, in October, 1862, for the war. Deserted at Drewry's Bluff, Virginia, December 1, 1862. Returned to duty on an unspecified date. Reported present in September-October, 1863. Reported absent on sick furlough from December 20, 1863, through February, 1864. Paroled at Greensboro on May 1, 1865.

HUSKINS, ALEX, _____
North Carolina pension records indicate that he served in this company.

JENKINS, JOHN, Private
Born in Rutherford County and resided in Johnston County where he was by occupation a farmer prior to enlisting in Rutherford County at age 21, March 27, 1862. Reported present in July-August and November-December, 1862. Also reported present in September, 1863-February, 1864. Paroled at Goldsboro on May 13, 1865.

JENKINS, LEVI, Private
Enlisted in Rutherford County in February, 1863, for the war. Reported present in September, 1863-February, 1864. Last reported in the records of this company in July-September, 1864.

JENKINS, WILLIAM, Private
Born in Rutherford County and was by occupation a farmer prior to enlisting in Rutherford County at age 31, March 27, 1862. Reported present but sick in May-June, 1862. Reported present in July-August, 1862. Deserted at Drewry's Bluff, Virginia, December 1, 1862.

JOHNSON, ANDY J., Private
Enlisted in Rutherford County at age 27, August 18, 1863, for the war. Reported present in September, 1863-February, 1864. Last reported in the records of this company in July-September, 1864. Survived the war.

JONES, SAMUEL J., Corporal
Born in Polk County* and was by occupation a farmer prior to enlisting in Rutherford County at age 19, March 27, 1862. Mustered in as Private. Reported present in May-August and November-December, 1862. Promoted to Corporal in September-December, 1862. Died on May 12, 1863. Place and cause of death not reported.

JUSTICE, T. L., Private
Enlisted at Camp Holmes, near Raleigh, in October, 1862, for the war. Deserted at Drewry's Bluff, Virginia, December 1, 1862. Hospitalized at Wilmington on August 28, 1863, with intermittent fever. Returned to duty on September 28, 1863. Reported present in October, 1863-February, 1864. Last reported in the records of this company in July-September, 1864.

LEDBETTER, A. B., Corporal
Born in McDowell County* and enlisted at Camp Holmes, near Raleigh, at age 26, October 5, 1862, for the war. Mustered in as Private. Hospitalized at or near Petersburg, Virginia, December 1, 1862, with typhoid fever. Returned to duty on December 7, 1862. Promoted to Corporal in January-October, 1863. Reported present in September, 1863-February, 1864. Last reported in the records of this company in July-September, 1864. Survived the war.

LEDBETTER, ANDREW, _____
Enlisted on or about August 20, 1863, for the war. Died at Plymouth on August 14, 1864, of disease.

LEDBETTER, JONATHAN, Private
Enlisted at Camp Holmes, near Raleigh, October 12, 1863, for the war. Reported present or accounted for in October, 1863-February, 1864. Last reported in the records of this company in July-September, 1864.

LEDFORD, DANIEL H., Private
Born in Cleveland County* and was by occupation a farmer prior to enlisting in Rutherford County at age 24, March 27, 1862. Dropped from the rolls of the company prior to July 1, 1862. Reason he was dropped not reported.

LEDFORD, FREDERICK, Private
Born in Cleveland County* and resided in Polk County where he was by occupation a farmer prior to enlisting in Rutherford County at age 29, March 27, 1862. Reported in hospital at Wilson in May-August, 1862. Detailed for duty as a hospital nurse at Wilson on October 1, 1862. Rejoined the company in December, 1862. Reported present in September, 1863-February, 1864. Paroled at Cheraw, South Carolina, March 5, 1865.

LEDFORD, J. A., Private
Enlisted in Rutherford County on March 27, 1862. Reported absent without leave from May 31 through August 31, 1862. Dropped from the rolls of the company prior to January 1, 1863. Reason he was dropped not reported.

LITTLEJOHN, FRANCIS F., Private
Born in Polk County* and enlisted in Polk or Rutherford County on March 27, 1862. Died in hospital at Petersburg, Virginia, July 10, 1862, of "pneumonia" or "relapse measles."

LOLLAR, THOMAS D., Sergeant
Born in Rutherford County and was by occupation a farmer prior to enlisting in Rutherford County at age 21, March 27, 1862. Mustered in as Corporal. Promoted to Sergeant on May 31, 1862. Died in hospital at Petersburg, Virginia, August 7, 1862, of "typhoid fever."

LONG, JOHN A., Private
Born in Rutherford County and was by occupation a farmer prior to enlisting in Rutherford County at age 27, March 27, 1862. Reported present or accounted for in May-August and November-December, 1862. Detailed as a courier on May 24, 1863. Reported on duty as a courier in September-October, 1863. Reported present in November, 1863-February, 1864. Killed at Bentonville on March 19-21, 1865.

LOVELACE, CICERO, Private
Born in Cleveland County and was by occupation a farmer prior to enlisting in Rutherford County at age 17, March 27, 1862. Reported sick in hospital at Petersburg, Virginia, in May-June, 1862. Reported present in July-August, 1862. Deserted at Drewry's Bluff, Virginia, December 1, 1862.

McBRIER, JOHN, Private
Enlisted in Rutherford County in February, 1863, for the war. Reported present in September-October, 1863. No further records.

McCANNON, HARVEY, Private
Born in Chester District, South Carolina, and was by occupation a farmer prior to enlisting in Rutherford County at age 47, March 27, 1862. Reported absent without leave from May 1 through August 31, 1862. Dropped from the rolls of the company prior to January 1, 1863.

McCRAW, JAMES ASBERRY, Private
Resided in Rutherford County and was by occupation a laborer prior to enlisting at Camp Holmes, near Raleigh, at age 25, October 5, 1862, for the war. Reported present in November-December, 1862, and September, 1863-February, 1864. Last reported in the records of this company in July-September, 1864.

McDADE, FRANKLIN G., Sergeant
Born in Polk County* and was by occupation a farmer prior to enlisting in Polk or Rutherford County at age 23, March 27, 1862. Mustered in as Private. Promoted to Corporal on July 7, 1862. Reported present in May-August and November-December, 1862. Furloughed for fourteen days on June 28, 1863. Promoted to Sergeant in January-October, 1863. Reported present in September, 1863-February, 1864. Paroled at Greensboro on May 1, 1865.

McDADE, SPARTAN, Private
Born in Greenville District, South Carolina, and resided in Polk County where he was by occupation a farmer prior to enlisting in Rutherford County at age 27, March 27, 1862. Mustered in as Sergeant. Reported present but sick in May-June, 1862. Reported present in July-August, 1862. Reported absent with leave on December 10, 1862. Reduced to ranks in January-October, 1863. Deserted near Kinston on May 12, 186[3]. Returned from desertion on October 22, 1863, and was pardoned. Reported present in November-December, 1863. Hospitalized at Wilmington on January 27, 1864, with gonorrhea. Returned to duty on February 17, 1864. Last reported in the records of this company in July-September, 1864.

MILLARD, JOSEPH, Sergeant
Place and date of enlistment not reported; however, he probably enlisted subsequent to February 29, 1864. Promotion record not reported. First listed in the records of this company in July-September, 1864. Reported absent on furlough on March 28, 1865.

MILLER, KERR BOYCE, Private
Previously served as Private in Company E, McRae's Battalion N.C. Cavalry. Transferred to this company subsequent to December 5, 1863. First reported in the records of this company in July-September, 1864. Reported absent on furlough in March-April, 1865.

MILWOOD, JOHN, Private
Born in Union District, South Carolina, and was by occupation a farmer prior to enlisting in Rutherford County at age 34, March 27, 1862. Reported present but

sick in May-June, 1862. Reported present in July-August and November-December, 1862. Also reported present in September-December, 1863. Died near Wilmington on February 19, 1864. Cause of death not reported.

MOORE, ANDREW J., Private
Born in Rutherford County and was by occupation a farmer prior to enlisting in Rutherford County at age 47, March 27, 1862. Was apparently discharged (probably because he was over 35 years of age) prior to July 1, 1862.

MOORE, JOHN TERRELL, Private
Born in Polk County* and was by occupation a farmer prior to enlisting in Rutherford County at age 23, March 27, 1862. Died at or near Petersburg, Virginia, July 10, 1862, of "typhoid fever."

MULL, SAMUEL, Private
Resided in Burke County. Place and date of enlistment not reported; however, he probably enlisted subsequent to February 29, 1864. First listed in the records of this company in July-September, 1864. Paroled at Salisbury on May 2, 1865.

NODINE, CHARLES C., Private
Born in Polk County* where he resided prior to enlisting in Rutherford County on March 27, 1862. Died at or near Petersburg, Virginia, July 9, 1862, of "brain fever."

NODINE, THOMAS, Private
Enlisted in Rutherford County on March 27, 1862. Dropped from the rolls of the company prior to July 1, 1862. Reason he was dropped not reported.

OWENS, RICHARD, Private
Born in Polk County* where he resided as a farmer prior to enlisting in Polk or Rutherford County at age 19, March 27, 1862. Reported present but sick in May-June, 1862. Reported present in July-August and November-December, 1862. Also reported present in September, 1863-February, 1864. Paroled at Greensboro on May 1, 1865.

OWENS, THOMAS, Private
Born in Polk County* and was by occupation a farmer prior to enlisting in Rutherford County at age 23, March 27, 1862. Reported present but sick in May-June, 1862. Reported present in July-August, 1862. Died in hospital at Petersburg, Virginia, November 21, 1862, of "typhoid fever."

PAGE, STEPHEN, Private
Born in Polk County* and was by occupation a farmer prior to enlisting in Polk or Rutherford County at age 18, March 27, 1862. Reported present in May-August, 1862. Discharged on or about November 14, 1862, by reason of "phthisis pulmonalis."

PANTHER, GEORGE W., _____
North Carolina pension records indicate that he served in this company.

PANTHER, JOSEPH, _____
North Carolina pension records indicate that he served in this company.

PROCTER, RUFUS, Private
Place and date of enlistment not reported; however, he probably enlisted subsequent to February 29, 1864. Paroled at Greensboro on May 1, 1865.

QUEEN, RICHARD, Private
Born in Rutherford County where he enlisted at age 29, March 27, 1862. Reported absent without leave in May-August, 1862. Dropped from the rolls of the company prior to January 1, 1863.

RAINS, WILLIAM, Private
Born in Buncombe County and resided in Polk County where he was by occupation a farmer prior to enlisting in Polk or Rutherford County at age 24, March 27, 1862. Reported present in May-August and November-December, 1862. Also reported present in September, 1863-February, 1864. Hospitalized at Wilmington on March 8, 1864, with chronic rheumatism. Returned to duty on March 21, 1864. Hospitalized at Charlotte on February 6, 1865, with ulcus. Returned to duty on February 9, 1865. Paroled at Greensboro on May 1, 1865.

ROBERTS, ABEL H., Private
Born in Burke County and resided in Rutherford County where he was by occupation a hatter prior to enlisting in Rutherford County at age 45, March 27, 1862. Was apparently discharged (probably because he was over 35 years of age) prior to July 1, 1862.

ROBERTS, HARVEY C., Private
Born in Rutherford County where he enlisted on March 27, 1862. Failed to report for duty and was dropped from the rolls of the company on or about January 1, 1863.

ROBERTS, W. A. E., 1st Sergeant
Previously served as Private in Company G, 16th Regiment N.C. Troops (6th Regiment N.C. Volunteers). Enlisted in this company in Rutherford County on March 27, 1862. Mustered in as Private. Reported present in May-June, 1862. Promoted to Sergeant prior to July 1, 1862. Promoted to 1st Sergeant on July 17, 1862. Reported present in November-December, 1862, and September-December, 1863. Hospitalized at Wilmington on January 27, 1864, with syphilis. Returned to duty on February 17, 1864. Hospitalized at Wilmington on March 8, 1864, with syphilis. Returned to duty on May 18, 1864. No further records.

SHEHAN, EDWARD, Private
Born in Polk County* and was by occupation a farmer prior to enlisting in Rutherford County at age 21, March 27, 1862. Reported present in May-June, 1862. Died in hospital at Petersburg, Virginia, August 5, 1862, of "febris typhoides."

SHEHAN, HENRY, Private
Born in Rutherford County and was by occupation a farmer prior to enlisting in Rutherford or Polk County at

age 34, March 27, 1862. Reported present in May-August and November-December, 1862. Also reported present in September, 1863-February, 1864. Last reported in the records of this company in July-September, 1864.

SHEHAN, JOHN, JR., Private
Born in Polk County* and was by occupation a farmer prior to enlisting in Polk County at age 17, April 12, 1862. Was apparently discharged (probably because he was under 18 years of age) prior to July 1, 1862.

SMITH, HENRY, Private
Born in Rutherford County and was by occupation a farmer prior to enlisting in Rutherford County at age 23, March 27, 1862. Reported present in May-August, 1862. Reported under arrest in November-December, 1862. Reason he was arrested not reported. Court-martialed on or about March 5, 1863. Returned to duty on an unspecified date. Sent to hospital at Wilson on July 3, 1863. Reported present in September, 1863-February, 1864. Last reported in the records of this company in July-September, 1864.

SMITH, HUEY, Private
Born in Burke County and was by occupation a farmer prior to enlisting in Rutherford County at age 44, March 27, 1862. Reported absent without leave from May 1 through August 31, 1862. Dropped from the rolls of the company prior to January 1, 1863.

SMITH, WILLIAM D., Private
Enlisted in Rutherford County at age 29, March 27, 1862. Reported present or accounted for in May-August and November-December, 1862. Sent to hospital at Goldsboro on January 4, 1863. Rejoined the company on September 3, 1863. Reported present in November, 1863-February, 1864. Hospitalized at Raleigh on November 6, 1864, with intermittent fever. Returned to duty on November 23, 1864. Hospitalized at Charlotte on February 13, 1865, with intermittent fever. Furloughed on February 14, 1865.

SNOWDEN, THOMAS F., Private
Resided in Polk County and was by occupation a day laborer prior to enlisting in Polk County at age 35, March 27, 1862. Reported present in May-August and November-December, 1862. Hospitalized at Wilmington on September 1, 1863, with debility. Returned to duty on September 7, 1863. Reported present in October, 1863-February, 1864. Hospitalized at Charlotte on May 15, 1864, with chronic rheumatism. Returned to duty on June 4, 1864. Last reported in the records of this company in July-September, 1864.

STEDMAN, JASON, Private
Born in Rutherford County and was by occupation a farmer prior to enlisting in Rutherford or Polk County at age 23, March 27, 1862. Reported present in May-August, 1862. Deserted at Drewry's Bluff, Virginia, December 1, 1862. Hospitalized at Wilmington on August 26, 1863, with typhoid fever. Returned to duty prior to November 1, 1863. Reported present in November, 1863-February, 1864. Last reported in the records of this company in July-September, 1864.

STEWART, JOHN, Private
Place and date of enlistment not reported; however, he probably enlisted subsequent to February 29, 1864. Paroled at Greensboro on May 1, 1865.

SUTTLES, JOSEPH, Private
Born in Rutherford County and was by occupation a farmer prior to enlisting in Rutherford County at age 27, March 27, 1862. Reported present in May-August and November-December, 1862. Also reported present in September, 1863-February, 1864. Last reported in the records of this company in July-September, 1864. Survived the war.

SUTTLES, ROBERT, Private
Born in Rutherford County and was by occupation a farmer prior to enlisting in Rutherford County at age 37, March 27, 1862. Furloughed in May, 1862. Failed to return to duty. Dropped from the rolls of the company on or about January 1, 1863.

SUTTLES, WILLIAM, Private
Was by occupation a farmer prior to enlisting in Rutherford County on March 27, 1862. Furloughed on June 3, 1862. Reported absent without leave in July-August, 1862. Reported present in November-December, 1862, and September, 1863-February, 1864. Last reported in the records of this company in July-September, 1864.

TERRELL, JOEL L., Private
Born in Rutherford County and was by occupation a carpenter prior to enlisting in Rutherford County at age 52, March 27, 1862. Reported absent without leave in May-June, 1862. Reported present in July-August, 1862. Discharged at Drewry's Bluff, Virginia, October 6, 1862, by reason of "broken down constitution, feeble health, physical inability and advanced age."

TOMBERLIN, JOHN H., Corporal
Enlisted in Rutherford County on March 27, 1862. Mustered in as Private. Reported present in May-June, 1862. Reported in hospital at Richmond, Virginia, in July-August, 1862. Reported present in November-December, 1862, and September, 1863-February, 1864. Promoted to Corporal on December 31, 1863. Last reported in the records of this company in July-September, 1864.

WARREN, ACHILLES, Private
Enlisted in Rutherford County on March 27, 1862. Reported present in November-December, 1862, and September, 1863-February, 1864. Last reported in the records of this company in July-September, 1864.

WARREN, ARCHIBALD, Private
Born in Rutherford County and was by occupation a farmer prior to enlisting in Rutherford County at age 19, March 27, 1862. Hospitalized at Petersburg, Virginia, July 20, 1862, with typhoid fever. Returned to duty on July 28, 1862. Hospitalized at Richmond, Virginia, August 22, 1862, with acute diarrhoea. Returned to duty on August 26, 1862. Reported present in November-December, 1862. Sent to hospital at Goldsboro on July 3,

1863. Reported present in September-October, 1863. Hospitalized at Wilmington on December 12, 1863, with debilitas. Returned to duty on February 22, 1864. No further records.

WARREN, KILLIS B., Private
Born in Rutherford County and was by occupation a farmer prior to enlisting in Rutherford County at age 22, March 27, 1862. Reported present in May-August, 1862. No further records.

WATKINS, PHILIP, Sergeant
Enlisted in Rutherford County on March 27, 1862. Mustered in as Private. Reported present but sick in May-June, 1862. Reported present in July-August and November-December, 1862. Promoted to Corporal in January-October, 1863. Reported present in September, 1863-February, 1864. Promoted to Sergeant on December 31, 1863. Hospitalized at Wilmington on November 25, 1864, with remittent fever. Returned to duty on December 3, 1864. Paroled at Greensboro on May 1, 1865.

WHEELING, CARSON, _____
Place and date of enlistment not reported. Died at or near Raleigh in June, 1862. Cause of death not reported.

WHISNANT, ARCHIBAL, Private
Born in Lincoln County and resided in Polk County where he was by occupation a farmer prior to enlisting in Rutherford County at age 30, March 27, 1862. Mustered in as Private. Reported present in May-August, 1862. Promoted to Corporal on September 1, 1862. Sent to hospital at Petersburg, Virginia, November 4, 1862. Reduced to ranks prior to January 1, 1863. Returned to duty on an unspecified date. Reported present in September, 1863-February, 1864. Last reported in the records of this company in July-September, 1864.

WILKIE, OLIVER J., Private
Born in Rutherford County and was by occupation a farmer prior to enlisting in Rutherford County at age 24, March 27, 1862. Reported present in May-August and November-December, 1862. Also reported present in September, 1863-February, 1864. Hospitalized at Charlotte on March 5, 1865, with intermittent fever. Returned to duty on March 12, 1865. Survived the war.

WILKINSON, JOHN V., Private
Born in Greenville District, South Carolina, and resided in Rutherford County where he was by occupation a blacksmith prior to enlisting in Rutherford County at age 38, March 27, 1862. Was apparently discharged (probably because he was over 35 years of age) prior to July 1, 1862.

WILLIAMS, O. P., Private
Resided in McDowell County and was by occupation a farmer. Place and date of enlistment not reported; however, he probably enlisted subsequent to February 29, 1864. Was about 36 years of age at time of enlistment. First listed in the records of this company in April-June, 1864. Captured at Athens, Georgia, May 8, 1865. Paroled at Athens on or about the same date.

WILSON, JOSEPH, Private
Enlisted in Rutherford County on August 18, 1863, for the war. Reported present in September-October, 1863. Hospitalized at Wilmington on November 28, 1863, with debilitas. Returned to duty on January 9, 1864. Reported present in February, 1864. Last reported in the records of this company in July-September, 1864.

WOOD, ANDES, Private
Resided in Rutherford County and was by occupation a laborer prior to enlisting in Rutherford County at age 27, March 27, 1862. Mustered in as Private. Reported present in May-August and November-December, 1862. Promoted to Sergeant in January-October, 1863. Reported present in September, 1863-February, 1864. Reduced to ranks on December 31, 1863. Last reported in the records of this company in July-September, 1864.

WOOD, AUGUSTUS, Private
Born in Union District, South Carolina, and was by occupation a farmer prior to enlisting in Rutherford County at age 22, March 27, 1862. Reported present but sick in May-June, 1862. Reported present in July-August, 1862. Deserted at Drewry's Bluff, Virginia, December 1, 1862. Returned to duty on an unspecified date. Reported present or accounted for in September, 1863-February, 1864. Paroled at Newton on or about April 19, 1865.

WOOD, JOHN, Private
Born in Union District, South Carolina, and was by occupation a farmer prior to enlisting in Rutherford County at age 18, March 27, 1862. Reported present in May-August and November-December, 1862. Also reported present in September, 1863-February, 1864. Discharged at Plymouth on October 6, 1864, by reason of "epilepsy; he has 'fits' so often as to wholly disqualify him for service."

MISCELLANEOUS

Civil War records indicate that the following soldiers served in the 50th Regiment N.C. Troops; however, the companies in which these soldiers served are not reported.

ADAMS, JAMES, _____
Place and date of enlistment not reported. Died at or near Raleigh in 1862. Cause of death not reported.

ALLGARD, THOMAS, Private
Resided in Wilson County. Place and date of enlistment not reported. Paroled at Goldsboro on May 2, 1865.

BAILEY, W. H., _____
Place and date of enlistment not reported. Died at or near Raleigh on June 15, 1862. Cause of death not reported.

BALDWIN, R. W., _____
Place and date of enlistment not reported. Died at or near Raleigh on June 19, 1862. Cause of death not reported.

BARTON, J., Private
Place and date of enlistment not reported. Captured at Athens, Georgia, May 8, 1865. Paroled on or about the same date.

CLARK, WILLIAM, Private
Resided at Baltimore, Maryland. Place and date of enlistment not reported. Paroled at Greensboro on May 1, 1865.

DODGE, M., Private
Place and date of enlistment not reported. Captured at Athens, Georgia, May 8, 1865.

HEDES, W. H., Private
Place and date of enlistment not reported. Captured at Athens, Georgia, May 8, 1865.

JAMMER, G., _____
Place and date of enlistment not reported. Died at or near Charleston, South Carolina, January 1, 1865. Cause of death not reported.

McCOLLINS, S., Private
Place and date of enlistment not reported. Captured at Athens, Georgia, May 8, 1865. Paroled on or about the same date.

McCURRY, J. C., _____
Place and date of enlistment not reported. First listed in the records of this regiment in January-March, 1864. Reported on furlough in Rutherford County on March 27, 1865.

OVERBY, JAMES T., Private
Previously served as Private in Company B, 12th Regiment N.C. Troops (2nd Regiment N.C. Volunteers). Was reportedly transferred to this regiment in May, 1862. No further records.

POUCH, JOHN, Private
Resided in Madison County. Place and date of enlistment not reported. Captured by the enemy on an unspecified date. Confined at Fort Delaware, Delaware. Released at Fort Delaware on June 19, 1865, after taking the Oath of Allegiance.

SALLY, JAMES R., _____
North Carolina pension records indicate that he served in this regiment.

SEAMS, JOHN, Private
Place and date of enlistment not reported. Name appears on a List of Prisoners paroled at Leesburg, Virginia, October 2, 1862. No further records.

SHELLA, T. H., _____
Place and date of enlistment not reported. Died at or near Raleigh on an unspecified date (probably in 1862). No further records.

SMITH, O. P., Private
Place and date of enlistment not reported. Captured at Athens, Georgia, May 8, 1865. Paroled on or about the same date.

SMITH, W. M., Private
Place and date of enlistment not reported. Captured at Athens, Georgia, May 8, 1865. Paroled on or about the same date.

TOWNSEND, JACOB, Private
Resided in Watauga County. Place and date of enlistment not reported. Deserted to the enemy on an unspecified date. Sent to Louisville, Kentucky. Released at Louisville on or about October 22, 1864, after taking the Oath of Allegiance.

WEST, E. P., Private
Place and date of enlistment not reported. Captured at Athens, Georgia, May 8, 1865. Paroled on or about the same date.

WILLOUGHBY, SOLOMON, _____
North Carolina pension records indicate that he served in this regiment.

Andrew Jackson Ashley, as he looked as a Lieutenant in Company E, 51st Regiment. He wears an officer's double-breasted frock coat with large bellows-sleeves gathered at the shoulders. His U.S. M 1833 Dragoon saber is suspended from a belt with a two-piece sword beltplate or buckle. Ashley was appointed Captain of his company in May, 1864. On July 1, 1864, he sustained a fatal head wound near Petersburg, Virginia. His service record appears on page 320 of this volume. Image furnished by Wiley R. Taylor, Fairmont, North Carolina.

Captain Samuel White Maultsby, Sr., Company H, 51st Regiment, as he appeared early in the war. He wears a regulation double-breasted frock coat with officer's sleeve braid. His sword and revolver holster are suspended from a belt with a two-piece interlocking buckle. The black forage cap and trouser stripes denote infantry. Captain Maultsby was wounded severely in the right thigh at Drewry's Bluff, Virginia, in May, 1864, but returned to duty and survived the war. His service record appears on page 354 of this volume. Image furnished by Frank E. Galloway, Bolivia, North Carolina.

51st REGIMENT N.C. TROOPS

The 51st Regiment N.C. Troops was organized at Wilmington in April, 1862, and was composed of men recruited primarily in the counties of Brunswick, Columbus, Cumberland, Duplin, New Hanover, Robeson, and Sampson. Field officers were elected on April 30. John Lucas Cantwell, a Wilmington cotton broker who had previously served as captain of Company D, 13th Battalion N.C. Infantry, was elected colonel. Private W. J. Burney of Company G, whose experiences during the next few months probably typified those of the regiment, wrote home in early May that he had "drawed" a coat, a pair of pants, and two shirts and, though unable to get anything to eat except "Bacon and salt Beef," he was "very well satafide" and "living easy." "We dont drill any worth while to mention," Burney continued with evident gratification, and "only stand guard some times." Writing on May 7 from Camp Holmes, near Wilmington, Burney reported that the regiment was in a "very prety place" with "good water," a "high hill," and "a plenty of good shades to drill in."[1]

This agreeable period was temporarily interrupted on May 30 when Burney and other members of his company were ordered to report to a nearby outpost for ten days of guard duty. "We come down with only one days rations," Burney complained, and "it was Two or three days before they sent us any thing to eat." The new camp was also "very sick[ly]," and several members of the company became ill. The arrival by rail of scores of soldiers who had been wounded on May 27 at Hanover Court House, Virginia, further deepened Burney's gloom. "I never saw the like of wounded men in my life as have pass[ed] throug[h] here for the last week," he wrote on June 5. "Some of the wounded was welling [wailing] to go to the hospitle. . . . [E]very time the train come in there was [an] operation[?] to cary [them] of[f]."[2]

The regiment remained in the vicinity of Wilmington (at various times it was at Camps Morgan, Holmes, Davis, French, Lamb, and Leventhorpe) until June 26, when eight of its ten companies were sent to Fort Johnston, near Smithville (present-day Southport), on the west bank of the Cape Fear River.[3] After arriving that evening in time to see a blockade-runner that had been mistaken for a Federal warship take a shell through its "engine ho[u]se" and run aground, Burney and his comrades settled into their new quarters. "We are very well fixt here," Burney reported. "We are station[ed] in the garison and have house[s] to stay in and good water too. . . . I think that I would like to Stay here all the time."[4]

A tranquil period of about ten weeks followed during which the 51st Regiment's major activity consisted of a series of moves back and forth between Wilmington and Fort Johnston. In early September the regiment was ordered to Kinston, about thirty miles northwest of Federal-occupied New Bern, where it arrived on September 12. Writing to his sister two days later from Camp Campbell, near Kinston, Private Burney reported that he was again in a "verry prety place" with good water but was forced to drill four times daily, including once before breakfast.[5] On October 1 or thereabout the regiment was assigned to the brigade of

---

[1]William J. Burney to his father, May 1 and May 7, 1862, Roster Document File Number 0473, Civil War Roster Project, Division of Archives and History, Raleigh, hereinafter cited as Burney Letters, RDF 0473. In his May 1 letter Burney also reported that he had been detailed for a day to help unload the steamer *Nashville*, which had arrived "one day last week" bringing gun powder, 18,000 rifles, and a "large cargo" of miscellaneous items such as blankets, "peper," and cloth.

[2]William J. Burney to his father, June 5, 1862, Burney Letters, RDF 0473.

[3]Companies D and K remained behind to fortify batteries on the Cape Fear.

[4]William J. Burney to his father, June 29, 1862, Burney Letters, RDF 0473. "I can see the old blockad at any time that I will look for them," Burney wrote. "I saw six [Federal ships] yesterday."

[5]William J. Burney to his sister, September 14, 1862, Burney Letters, RDF 0473.

Brigadier General Thomas L. Clingman, which was composed of the 8th, 31st, 51st, and 61st Regiments N.C. Troops.[6]

In late October Burney's company was involved in a skirmish with the enemy east of Kinston and captured eighty stands of arms. According to Burney, there was "but little loss on either side."[7] On the night of the 22nd the regiment was ordered to march in the direction of Kinston in response to a report of a Federal force advancing against the town.

> [It] was nine or ten miles to go in night [Burney wrote.] And some of the men was as bare footed as they was the day they come into this world[.] And there was right smart frost that morning. . .
> You had aught to have . . . seen dan Haddock[.] [H]e was one of the bear footted one[s]. . . . I am nearly naked . . . but if I cant get off [to bring clothes from home] . . . you may keep them for [now]. . . . I hope I will get off before long as there is men going home after clothing and ther things. . . .[8]

The 51st Regiment remained in the Kinston area on picket and scout duty for almost two months. This period was an active and difficult one for the regiment with long marches and frequent contact with the enemy. Private Burney reported an early November march near Trenton through snow, water that was sometimes "up to our knese," and mud "over our ankles."[9] Federal pickets were driven in near New Bern during a night attack, and other skirmishes were fought near New Bern on November 4, November 9, and again on about the 12th. In the latter engagement the regiment lost, according to Private David Gurganious of Company A, one man killed, one missing and presumed captured, and one who had "shot his hand off."[10]

On November 17 the regiment, including a "badly weared" Private Burney, returned to Wilmington, where it went into camp at Camp Mears, on Wrightsville Sound.[11] From there it moved to Camps Clingman (November 21) and Whiting (November 27), both near Wilmington.[12]

On December 16 the regiment departed by rail for Goldsboro to protect the important railroad bridge there from an enemy force advancing from New Bern under Brigadier General John G. Foster. When Foster arrived at Goldsboro the next day the 51st Regiment was in a position equidistant between the railroad bridge and a "country [road]" bridge a half mile upstream. The railroad bridge and road bridge were covered respectively by the 52nd Regiment N.C. Troops, of Brigadier General James J. Pettigrew's brigade, and the 8th Regiment N.C. State Troops, of Clingman's brigade. The Confederate force of perhaps 2,000 men, commanded by Clingman, found itself confronted by a small army five times its size that promptly opened fire on the 52nd Regiment. The 51st was sent to the support of its sister unit, but the two overmatched regiments were quickly "broken" by heavy volleys of musketry

---

[6]The precise dates on which the constituent units of Clingman's brigade were assigned are uncertain; however, it appears probable that the 51st and 61st regiments were placed under Clingman on or about October 1, 1861, and the 8th and 31st regiments were assigned to his command in late November.

[7]William J. Burney to his father, October 26, 1862, Burney Letters, RDF 0473.

[8]William J. Burney to his father, October 26, 1862, Burney Letters, RDF 0473.

[9]William J. Burney to his father, November 20, 1862, Burney Letters, RDF 0473. Colonel Cantwell resigned as colonel of the 51st Regiment on October 19, 1862. Lieutenant Colonel Hector McKethan, a Fayetteville resident and former lieutenant in Company H, 1st Regiment N.C. Infantry, was promoted in his place.

[10]David Gurganious to his wife, November 14, 1862, John Henry Murphy Papers, Southern Historical Collection, University of North Carolina Library at Chapel Hill.

[11]William J. Burney to his father, November 20, 1862, Burney Letters, RDF 0473.

[12]At least part of the regiment appears to have been at Camp Hedrick, in the Wilmington area, on November 20. See William J. Burney to his father, November 20, 1862, Burney Letters, RDF 0473.

and a barrage of Federal shells.[13] After rallying and returning to their line, the men gave way again. The Federals then fired the bridge and, to prevent any Confederate effort to save it, opened up on the structure with their field guns. Convinced that the flames were doing their work, Foster began withdrawing towards New Bern, leaving Colonel H. C. Lee's brigade to follow as rear guard.[14]

In the meantime the 51st and 52nd Regiments, bolstered by the arrival of reinforcements, maneuvered into a position from which to counterattack. Advancing across a 1,000-yard-wide field swept by heavy batteries supported by infantry, the two regiments reached a point 300 yards from the enemy position. There, raked by "showers" of grape and musketry and unable to endure the "fearful" losses they were sustaining, they fell back in disarray. Colonel Lee then withdrew toward New Bern. The 51st Regiment lost, according to General Clingman's report of December 21, 6 men killed, 43 wounded, and 8 missing. According to a report of the regimental adjutant dated January 15, 1863, the regiment lost 5 men killed and 55 wounded.[15]

On December 28 the 51st Regiment left Goldsboro on foot for Camp Whiting, Wilmington, which it reached on January 2, 1863. The arrivals and departures of blockade-runners and Federal attempts to intercept them occupied the men's attention and probably dominated their activities during the next six weeks. In a letter home on January 16 Private Burney reported that one of the Federal ships had run aground and was being shot to pieces by Confederate artillery. Its crew had been captured and jailed.[16] In early February Company D was sent to Robeson County under orders to "capture or, if necessary, destroy" a group of deserters and "freebooters" whose depredations had produced "deplorable" conditions. The outcome of the expedition is unknown.[17] Food shortages, which appear to have been frequent if not precisely chronic, continued to plague the regiment. In a letter dated February 13 an angry Private Burney told his father that he had

> not had any meat since last Wednesday diner [February 5] And I can not tell you when we will get any[.] [N]othing but bread and a little rice[.] [Y]ou may know there is some confusion [disgruntlement?] in camp this morning[.] [N]one here got any [meat?] to eat[.] I think of home at this time[.] I want them to give me some thing to eat if they are going to try to keep me here[.] [Y]ou can tell all the neighbors that they may look for me if they dont give me some meat[.] I will leave just as sure as god made me[.][18]

---

[13]R. N. Scott and others (eds.), *The War of the Rebellion: A Compilation of the Official Records of the Union and Confederate Armies* (Washington: Government Printing Office, 70 volumes, 1880-1901), Series I, XVIII, 118, hereinafter cited as *Official Records (Army)*.

[14]Walter Clark (ed.), *Histories of the Several Regiments and Battalions from North Carolina in the Great War, 1861-'65* (Raleigh and Goldsboro: State of North Carolina, 5 volumes, 1901), III, 230, hereinafter cited as Clark, *Histories of the North Carolina Regiments*; *Official Records (Army)*, Series I, XVIII, 118. Although Foster's claim that the bridge was fired by hand is confirmed by some Confederate witnesses and has been accepted by historians, at least one Confederate officer at the scene told a different story. Captain J. J. Bradbury of the Wilmington and Weldon Railroad Guards (an independent company) stated in a letter dated December 27, 1862, that the bridge was fired "on the top [roof] within 20 feet of the Southern end, by the bursting of a shell thereon by the enemy. . . . Three out of the six men who are said to have fired the bridge, fell by the fire of my men and none of them got within 50 yards. . . ." *Wilmington Journal* (Weekly), January 1, 1863. See also the *Wilmington Journal* (Weekly) of January 8, 1863, containing the observations of one "A. A. McB," who visited the battlefield on December 30, 1862.

[15]*Official Records (Army)*, Series I, XVIII, 58, 119; National Archives Record Group 109, War Department Collection of Compiled Confederate Records (North Carolina), Regimental Return for the 51st Regiment dated December, 1862, hereinafter cited as Record Group 109. An "official" casualty list published in the *Wilmington Journal* (Weekly) of January 8, 1863, indicates that 5 men were killed, 50 wounded, and 5 missing. The roster compiled for this volume lists 8 men killed or mortally wounded, 45 wounded, and 0 captured.

[16]William J. Burney to his father, January 16, 1863, Burney Letters, RDF 0473.

[17]*Official Records (Army)*, Series I, XVIII, 879.

[18]William J. Burney to his father, February 13, 1863, Burney Letters, RDF 0473.

During the early weeks of 1863 an increase in Federal naval activity along the coasts of South Carolina and Georgia, punctuated by attacks on Savannah's Fort McAllister, necessitated the sending of reinforcements to the area, and in mid-February Clingman's brigade was ordered to move by rail to Charleston. The 51st Regiment began its redeployment on the evening of February 17, and by the 19th the entire regiment was encamped near Charleston at Camp McKethan. On March 4 the 51st was sent by rail to Savannah, where an eight-hour bombardment of Fort McAllister by ships of the Federal navy had occurred the previous day. When the Federals failed to launch further attacks on the city and its defenses the 51st returned to Charleston on March 9. Three days later the men pitched their tents on James Island, in Charleston Harbor. In a letter to a neighbor Private Burney wrote that the weather was "plesent" but James Island was "very windy" and sometimes the "dust [sandstorms] is so bad that we can Scarsely see."[19] The health of the men also deteriorated, and malaria and other diseases caused "many" deaths.[20] To supplement the "scanty" and "unwholesome" rations they were issued the men hunted rabbits, which they killed in such numbers as to seemingly threaten the extinction of the island's entire colony.[21] Morale revived somewhat on March 28 when Clingman's brigade was reviewed by General P. G. T. Beauregard. Standing in line of battle with weapons at shoulder arms and bayonets "glittering," the men heard themselves pronounced "veteran[s]" and a "credit" to their "noble" state.[22] The 51st Regiment took no part in the repulse of a heavy attack by the Federal navy on April 7, being stationed some distance from the mouth of the harbor.

Convinced that Charleston could not be taken by naval assault alone, the Federals began formulating plans for a joint land-sea operation. No immediate threat being in evidence to the Confederate authorities, the 51st Regiment was pulled back from James Island to Charleston on the evening of May 1 and departed for Wilmington by rail the next morning. Exhausted after three consecutive sleepless nights and with a "great many" of its members sick, the regiment reached Wilmington after nightfall on May 2.[23] On May 5 it went into camp at Camp Florida, on Topsail Sound. The regiment moved to Camp Whiting on May 24 and to Camp Davis, on Middle Sound, on May 29. On June 6 four companies (B, D, E, and H) were detached and sent to Magnolia (Duplin County) on the Wilmington and Weldon Railroad. On July 1 the detachment intercepted a Federal raiding party in the vicinity of Warsaw. After a brief skirmish the raiders fell back toward New Bern, leaving some stragglers in the hands of the Confederates. The four companies rejoined the remainder of the regiment at Wilmington about a week later. On July 11 all four regiments of Clingman's brigade were ordered to return to Charleston, where the anticipated Federal assault by land and sea had begun the previous day.

The city of Charleston was well protected both by fortifications and natural endowments. Two rivers, the Ashley and Cooper, flanked it on either side, flowing into a broad harbor. Three miles across the water from Charleston, standing on an artificial island near the harbor's narrow mouth, stood Fort Sumter, a multitiered, pentagonal-shaped bastion of masonry construction. Two large, well-fortified islands, Sullivan's Island and Morris Island, lay across the channels to the north and south of Sumter. On Sullivan's Island, venerable Fort Moultrie and Batteries Bee and Beauregard constituted the major defenses; Morris Island's defenses included Battery Gregg and, about half a mile to the south, Fort Wagner, a moat-

[19]William J. Burney to David Perry, April 26, 1863, Burney Letters, RDF 0473.
[20]Clark, *Histories of the North Carolina Regiments*, IV, 484.
[21]Clark, *Histories of the North Carolina Regiments*, III, 206; *Wilmington Journal* (Weekly), April 2, 1863. See also *Wilmington Journal* (Weekly), April 30, 1863.
[22]*Wilmington Journal* (Weekly), April 2, 1863.
[23]William J. Burney to his father, May 3, 1863, Burney Letters, RDF 0473.

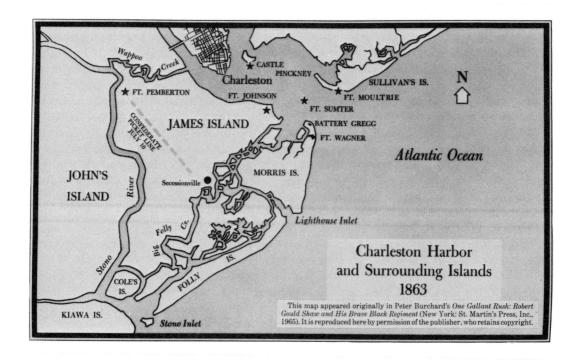

Charleston Harbor and Surrounding Islands 1863

This map appeared originally in Peter Burchard's *One Gallant Rush: Robert Gould Shaw and His Brave Black Regiment* (New York: St. Martin's Press, Inc., 1965). It is reproduced here by permission of the publisher, who retains copyright.

ringed field work of sand, turf, and palmetto logs. Folly Island, to the southeast of Morris Island, was already in Federal hands, but between the Federals and Charleston lay the expansive marshes and mud flats of James Island, defended by forts, rifle pits, and battery emplacements. Mines, underwater obstructions, and floating rope mats, together with treacherous currents and shoals, further complicated the Federal task. In command of the city's defenses and ample garrison was the flamboyant but redoubtable General Beauregard, whose achievements included the capture of Fort Sumter in April, 1861.

The Federal plan of attack called for the infantry force on Folly Island to cross the narrow inlet to Morris Island, capture Fort Wagner and Battery Gregg, establish a new artillery position in the vicinity of Battery Gregg, and then reduce Fort Sumter from the point-blank range of scarcely more than a mile. After clearing a channel through the harbor obstructions, the final advance on Charleston would be made.

On July 10 the assault was launched and, with the help of a supporting barrage from the fleet, moved rapidly forward against token Confederate opposition until it was brought up short by fire from Fort Wagner. An attack the next day, after the fort had been reinforced by newly arrived Georgia and South Carolina units, was repulsed with heavy losses. The Federal commander, Brigadier General Quincy A. Gillmore, then brought up 40 long-range cannon and siege mortars. By the evening of July 18, following a five-day bombardment, he was ready to test the fort's defenses again.

In the meantime Clingman's brigade arrived from Wilmington. The 31st and 51st Regiments, along with several South Carolina units, relieved the garrison at Fort Wagner on July 13 and were subjected for the next five days to a "terrible" shelling by Gillmore's guns and by ships of the Federal fleet.[24] Unable to reply effectively to the Federal fire, the

---

[24]According to Lieutenant A. A. McKethan of Company B, 51st North Carolina, the average volume of the Federal fire during this period was "twenty-eight shells per minute by actual count from sunrise to 7 p. m." Clark,

Confederate defenders, on short rations and suffering from a "great scarcity" of water, huddled miserably in the safety but 100-degree-plus heat of their expansive bombproof and submitted to the "hail of iron."[25]

On the morning of July 18 the Federals opened an intensified, land-and-sea bombardment of Fort Wagner, lambasting its defenders, in the words of Private Burney, with "Balls and shells till we was all nearly exhausted."[26] A pulverizing, 9,000-shell barrage rained down on the fort for eleven hours, gradually rising to crescendos, according to a dazed officer of the 51st Regiment, "not recorded in history."[27]

> Huge clouds of sand were blown into the air from the craters formed by the bursting shells [another Confederate officer wrote]; the water of the bay was lashed into foam and thrown high in jets of spray by the ricocheting shots from the ironclads bounding from the water over the parapets and bursting within the work, while a dense cloud of sulphurous smoke hung like a pall over the scene.[28]

A feeble attempt to reply to the Federals was quickly abandoned, and most of the men took shelter in the bombproof, allowing their comrades at Battery Gregg and Fort Sumter to deliver such response as was forthcoming. At about 7:45 p.m., by which time the night was, according to Private Burney, "dark as pitch," the Federals launched an infantry attack spearheaded by a black regiment, the 54th Massachusetts.[29] Forced by the narrowness of the hilly, shell-pitted beach to advance in company columns rather than line of battle, the gallant but inexperienced and tightly packed black soldiers were mowed down in droves by "terrible" fusillades of musketry that lit the Confederate parapet, according to one observer, with a shimmering "fringe of fire."[30]

Scrambling through the fort's protective moat, a few members of the 54th reached the ramparts. There, according to Private A. T. Jackson of the 51st North Carolina, they were "pull[ed] . . . over" and "knock[ed] . . . in the head" by Confederate defenders "maddened and infuriated at the sight of negro troops."[31] Three other Federal regiments, advancing

---

Histories of the North Carolina Regiments, III, 207. This figure, which would suggest a daily bombardment in excess of 18,000 shells, is clearly much too high as it exceeds by at least fifty percent the heavier bombardment to which the fort was subjected on July 18. Another estimate was made by Confederate Brigadier General W. B. Taliaferro, who reported that the "average number of projectiles thrown at the work" on the 15th, 16th, and 17th was "300 daily" from ten o'clock in the morning until five in the afternoon. *Official Records (Army)*, Series I, XXVIII, Part I, 417. This figure would indicate an average of less than one shell per minute and is probably too low. See also footnote 27 below.

[25]Clark, *Histories of the North Carolina Regiments*, III, 206-207.

[26]William J. Burney to his father, July 20, 1863, Burney Letters, RDF 0473.

[27]*Wilmington Journal* (Weekly), July 23, 1863. The average per-minute volume of the Federal fire on July 18 is not entirely certain. Most historians accept General Taliaferro's report that the bombardment lasted for eleven hours "without cessation or intermission" and consisted of "9,000 solid shot and shell of all sizes, from 15-inch down ward." *Official Records (Army)*, Series I, XXVIII, Part I, 417. There is also agreement that the intensity of the bombardment increased markedly as the day progressed and did not begin to reach full stride until noon. *Official Records (Army)*, Series I, XXVIII, Part I, 201. In any case, Taliaferro's 9,000-shell estimate, which he considered conservative, would indicate an average volume of almost fourteen shells per minute. No doubt the figure was considerably higher by the time of the Federal assault.

[28]Samuel Jones, *The Siege of Charleston* (New York: The Neale Publishing Company, 1911), 233.

[29]William J. Burney to his father, July 26, 1863, Burney Letters, RDF 0473.

[30]*Charleston Courier*, July 20, 1863. See also the *Charleston Mercury*, July 25, 1863.

[31]Unpublished "Personal Reminiscences of the Civil War," Private A. T. Jackson (Company I, 51st Regiment N.C. Troops), Civil War Collection, Box 71, Folder 1, page 2, Archives, Division of Archives and History, Raleigh, hereinafter cited as Jackson, "Personal Reminiscences"; S. J. Cobb, "Service of Tar Heels," *Confederate Veteran*, VIII (May, 1900), 216, hereinafter cited as Cobb, "Service of Tar Heels." According to a letter dated July 20, 1863, written by an unidentified officer of the 51st Regiment and published in the *Wilmington Journal* (Weekly) of July 23, 1863, ten black soldiers were taken prisoner by the regiment.

despite the disruption caused by portions of the 54th Massachusetts rushing through their ranks like "a crowd of maniacs," were similarly raked by the blistering Confederate musketry but succeeded in breaching the defenses and establishing a position atop the bombproof.[32] At that point another wave of Federal attackers arrived and, mistaking their comrades on the bombproof for Confederates in the darkness, opened a lethal fire from the rear. As night deepened over the "indescribable" scene of carnage the Federal survivors surrendered.[33]

Dawn revealed a charnel house of mangled and dismembered blue-clad bodies. In the grim words of historian Peter Burchard:

> The dead lay sprawled on Wagner's slopes, and at the bottom of the moat they lay in a pile like a swarm of insects struck by a pestilence. Negroes and whites were strewn together along the white sands for three quarters of a mile, some washed by the waves. . . .[34]

More than 1,500 Federals were dead, wounded, or prisoners. Casualties in the 51st Regiment were officially reported as 16 men killed, 52 wounded, and 6 missing—about one-third of the Confederate total. In his report describing the battle, General Beauregard praised the regiment for its "heroic conduct" and for "retriev[ing] the honor of the State," which had been sullied, in his opinion, by the "unworthy behavior" of its sister unit, the 31st North Carolina.[35]

The exhausted, shell-shocked men of the 51st were withdrawn from Fort Wagner the next morning but, after recuperative duty in less exposed positions, returned to the fort on July 29. In the meantime the Federals began siege operations, digging zigzag trenches and moving heavy artillery pieces closer and closer to the ramparts. That tactic, which would require almost two months to produce results, quickly reduced conditions in the fort to new levels of intolerability. "The men were at all times exposed to the enemy's fire, both from the land and from the sea," a member of the 8th North Carolina recalled. "An attack had to be prepared for any instant, either night or day. . . . All the rations had to be prepared elsewhere and carried there. The water too, was bad."[36] Depending on the circumstances of the moment, the fort's harried defenders rushed back and forth between the maddening noise, heat, and stench of the bombproof and the open areas of the fort, where enemy shells and sharpshooters were likely to bring sudden death. After firing for weeks at the same stationary target, the Federal artillerymen were able to sight their pieces with pinpoint accuracy, while the naval gunners became adept at ricocheting shells off the water so that they careened into the fort at low angles and exploded in its deepest recesses. The establishment of a hospital in the bombproof added a new dimension of horror as the groans and supplications of the maimed and dying mingled with the thunderous crashes of the shells.

---

[32]John Johnson, *The Defense of Charleston Harbor, Including Fort Sumter and the Adjacent Islands, 1863-1865* (Charleston: Walker, Evans, and Cogswell Company, 1890), 104.

[33]*Official Records (Army)*, Series I, XXVIII, Part I, 419, 524. See also Clark, *Histories of the North Carolina Regiments*, III, 208-209.

[34]Peter Burchard, *One Gallant Rush: Robert Gould Shaw and his Brave Black Regiment* (New York: St. Martin's Press, 1965), 142.

[35]*Wilmington Journal* (Weekly), July 23, 1863; *Official Records (Army)*, Series I, XXVIII, Part I, 77. Service records compiled for this volume indicate that the regiment lost 23 men killed or mortally wounded, 50 wounded, and 0 captured. See also *Official Records (Army)*, Series I, XXVIII, 524-526; National Archives, Confederate States Army Casualties: Lists and Narrative Reports, 1861-1865 (M836), Roll 3.

[36]Clark, *Histories of the North Carolina Regiments*, IV, 485.

The 51st Regiment was relieved again on August 3 but returned for another tour August 11-16. During its July 29-August 3 tour the regiment lost two men killed and seven wounded, a remarkably low figure considering the volume of Federal fire and one probably explained best by a North Carolina soldier's laconic observation that "one shell would fill up the hole made by the last."[37] In fact, one unidentified member of the 51st reported from Sullivan's Island on August 29, "to all appearance[s]" Wagner was "unharmed."[38]

Meanwhile, the Federal trenches continued to move inexorably forward. By August 29 the enemy sappers had captured the fort's forward rifle pits and were "uncomfortably near" the main works.[39] By September 6 they had reached the moat. Faced with the certainty of an overpowering assault, the garrison was quietly withdrawn that night. Fort Sumter, which had been under fire from Federal land batteries on Morris Island since August 17, had been reduced by the 23rd to a cratered and shapeless ruin. Its defenders, although without artillery, successfully repulsed a Federal attempt to storm the fort on September 8.

Unable to capture Charleston, "the cradle of rebellion," without suffering unacceptable casualties for a prize whose value was, in any case, largely symbolic, the Federals contented themselves with pounding Fort Sumter to rubble, and the contest settled into a stalemate. The 51st Regiment was stationed on Sullivan's Island, where it was subjected to a shelling on September 2 that resulted in the deaths of two men. On September 25 the regiment moved to Long Island, just north of Sullivan's Island. There, according to one unidentified member of the regiment in a letter dated October 15, the men recovered their health while feasting on "a number of fine venison" and "plenty of oysters." Morale improved as two men at a time from each company were granted ten-day furloughs. On November 2 the regiment returned to Sullivan's Island for what proved to be its last tour of duty at Charleston before heading home to North Carolina.[40]

On November 29 the 51st Regiment departed by rail for Camp Pender, near Hamilton (Martin County), North Carolina, in response to renewed Federal activity in the eastern part of the state. Three weeks later, on December 19, it moved to Camp Battle, near Tarboro, where the men gratefully received "liberal donations" of socks and other "necessaries of life" from citizens of the town.[41] Several companies were sent out on picket details. On January 6, 1864, the regiment was sent by rail to Petersburg, Virginia, where it arrived the next day. On the 29th the regiment, with the 8th Regiment N.C. State Troops, left its comfortable quarters at Petersburg and returned to North Carolina to take part in Major General George E. Pickett's campaign against New Bern.

The Confederate attempt to recapture the strategic city of New Bern, lying at the confluence of the Neuse and Trent rivers, was prompted largely by Federal raids and depredations in the eastern part of the state that had resulted in the destruction of large

---

[37]*Fayetteville Observer* (Weekly), August 17, 1863; Clark, *Histories of the North Carolina Regiments*, III, 208. Casualties during the regiment's August 11-16 tour are unknown but were probably light.

[38]*Fayetteville Observer* (Semiweekly), September 7, 1863. The same writer reported that there were "a good many sick" in the regiment but "the cases are mostly light and soon over—caused I suppose by the bad water (cistern) and exposure to the sun." See also *Official Records (Army)*, Series I, XXVIII, Part I, 93.

[39]*Fayetteville Observer* (Semiweekly), September 7, 1863. The letter writer quoted in the preceding footnote stated that the Federal lines were within 250 or 300 yards of the main Confederate works on August 29.

[40]*Fayetteville Observer* (Weekly), October 26, 1863. Additional accounts of the defense of Charleston, including one by General Beauregard, appear in Clarence C. Buel and Robert U. Johnson (eds.), *Battles and Leaders of the Civil War* (New York: The Century Company, 4 volumes, 1884), IV, 1-75. See also E. Milby Burton, *The Siege of Charleston, 1861-1865* (Columbia: University of South Carolina Press, 1970), 151-182; Rowena Reed, *Combined Operations in the Civil War* (Annapolis: Naval Institute Press, 1978), 295-320; T. Harry Williams, *P. G. T. Beauregard: Napoleon in Gray* (Baton Rouge: Louisiana State University Press, 1955), 185-196; and [author unidentified], "Life in Battery Wagner," *Land We Love*, Volume II, Number 5 (March, 1867), 351-355.

[41]*Fayetteville Observer* (Semiweekly), January 14 and January 25, 1864.

quantities of foodstuffs and other property and devastated civilian morale. Pickett, commanding a force of about 13,000 men concentrated at Kinston, planned a three-column attack. One column, under Brigadier General Robert F. Hoke, was to move directly against New Bern along the north bank of the Trent, "endeavor to surprise the troops on Batchelder's Creek, silence the guns in the Star fort and batteries near the Neuse, and penetrate the town in that direction."[42] A second column, commanded by Brigadier General Seth M. Barton, was to advance along the south bank of the Trent, capture the three forts defending New Bern's southern approaches, and foreclose any possibility of reinforcement by land or water from Beaufort or Morehead City. If practicable, Barton's column was to cross the Atlantic and North Carolina Railroad bridge into the town. The third column, under Colonel James Dearing, would move down the north bank of the Neuse, neutralize or capture Fort Anderson (across the Neuse from New Bern), and attempt to situate itself so as to open an enfilading fire on the works defending the town against Hoke. At the same time a naval force of fourteen cutters would descend the Neuse and attack any Federal gunboats that were encountered.

On the morning of January 30, 1864, Pickett's three columns set out toward their various objectives. Hoke's column, of which the 51st Regiment was a part, camped on the night of the 31st about two miles from the Batchelder's Creek bridge, which was defended by a Federal blockhouse and other works. A predawn attack by Hoke's men failed to achieve surprise and the bridge was destroyed, whereupon Hoke's men crossed the creek on logs and drove the Federals from their position. One member of the 51st Regiment, Private William E. Pugh of Company C, was killed. Hoke then moved on to New Bern, some ten miles from Batchelder's Creek, where he halted to await Barton's attack from the south. Barton, however, having arrived at his objective, found himself confronted by a seeming maze of breastworks, blockhouses, gun emplacements, forts, and felled trees set in terrain that was dangerously open in some places and impassably marshy in others. He therefore decided not to attack and sent a request to Pickett, who was with Hoke's column, for new instructions. Colonel Dearing, across the Neuse, likewise sent word to Pickett that Fort Anderson, his objective, was too powerful to attack. Following a desultory exchange of fire with the enemy during which the 51st Regiment, although somewhat protected by "thick trees," suffered several casualties, an angry and frustrated Pickett, calling for a court of inquiry into Barton's conduct, withdrew to Kinston.[43]

On February 8 the regiment departed by rail for Petersburg, where it occupied its previous quarters at Camp Hill. Except for a seven-day "reconnoissance [sic] in force" in the vicinity of Suffolk and Ivor Station during early May, the regiment remained at Camp Hill performing the "regular routine of Camp duty" for almost three months.[44]

On May 5, 1864, while a revitalized Army of the Potomac under the strategic direction of Lieutenant General Ulysses S. Grant marched into the Wilderness area near Chancellorsville and prepared to do battle with the Army of Northern Virginia, a Federal force of 30,000 men under the command of Major General Benjamin F. Butler began landing at City Point, Virginia, on the James River northeast of Petersburg. The 52nd Regiment skirmished with Federal pickets on the City Point road on May 9, and about 11:30 that evening—"a beautiful starlight night"—two companies of the regiment launched an assault against an isolated New Hampshire regiment. Surprised by the rare night attack the New Hampshire soldiers,

[42]*Official Records (Army)*, Series I, XXXIII, 1102.
[43]Jackson, "Personal Reminiscences," 4; *Official Records (Army)*, Series I, XXXIII, 94.
[44]*Wilmington Journal* (Weekly), June 2, 1864; Record Group 109, Company D, 51st Regiment N.C. Troops muster roll for March-April, 1864.

according to a highly colored (if not fanciful) account in the Petersburg *Express*, fell back in "wild confusion," presenting a "dark moving mass" from which a chorus of screams went up at every Confederate volley. After chasing the New Hampshiremen for "two miles or more" and arousing "the whole Yankee camp," the two companies returned to their lines "without the loss of a man."[45]

On May 10 Clingman's brigade, of which the 51st Regiment was still a part, was ordered to reinforce the Confederate defenders at Drewry's Bluff, a key fortification on the James whose loss would sever communications between Richmond and Petersburg and expose the Confederate capital to attack from the south. Clingman's brigade arrived during the night of May 10-11 and went into a reserve position behind the brigade of Brigadier General Bushrod Johnson. After seeing action as skirmishers on May 13, 14, and 15, the men of the 51st Regiment took part on May 16 in a costly assault that inflicted 4,000 casualties on the Federals and drove Butler back toward Bermuda Hundred, a neck of land between the James and Appomattox rivers. "About daybreak," wrote Captain W. H. S. Burgwyn, an officer on General Clingman's staff,

> General Robert Ransom, on our extreme left, opened the fight with his division, and succeeded in driving the enemy before him. . . . General Bushrod Johnson then engaged the enemy . . . [and was followed by General Hoke, who] attacked with our (Clingman's) and General Corse's Brigades at about 9 a. m. At the word "Charge," our two regiments, the Fifty-first and Thirty-first . . . in concert with Corse's Brigade . . . started for the enemy. . . . I sprang upon the parapet, waved my hat and yelled with all my might. As soon as I could cross the ditch in front I ran ahead of the [Fifty-first] regiment . . . call[ing] on the men to follow, and nobly did they come on, though the enemy's sharpshooters fired as fast as they could pull trigger. . . . Though the line was considerably disorganized . . . crossing the ditch and . . . going through the thick underbrush, not a man faltered. About three hundred yards from our works . . ., there appearing some hesitation in the advance, I seized the colors of the Fifty-first Regiment. . . . Running in advance about 200 yards, we came to the enemy's first line posted by squads in pits. . . . I rushed past the pits, and the Yankees surrendered in crowds. . . .[46]

Spotting a Federal artillery piece blazing away at a distance of about 250 yards, Burgwyn took off again.

> With a yell that must have caused the Yankees to quake, we started, passed by the gun and kept on at full speed to charge the enemy's main line of battle about 450 yards off, posted behind rifle pits. Giving the colors to the color-bearer, I ran in advance . . . cheering as loud as I could. . . . The first to reach the works[,] I fell down . . . exhausted, but rising up as the men commenced to mount the works, I climbed over and we started after the flying enemy. But now, not only in our immediate front, but on both flanks the enemy were in tremendous odds, and opened fire on us. With the enemy in front and on both flanks and no supports, we fell back. . . .
> About 5 p. m., we started in pursuit with General Bushrod Johnson's Brigade and halted for the night close up to the enemy. . . .[47]

According to statistics prepared by Colonel McKethan on the day after the battle, the 51st Regiment lost 25 men killed, 111 wounded, and 24 missing.[48] Skirmishing continued on May

---

[45]Quoted from the *Petersburg Express* in the Raleigh *Daily Confederate*, May 17, 1864.
[46]Clark, *Histories of the North Carolina Regiments*, IV, 491-492.
[47]Clark, *Histories of the North Carolina Regiments*, IV, 492.
[48]*Fayetteville Observer* (Semiweekly), May 23, 1864. Figures compiled for this volume indicate that the regiment lost 40 men killed or mortally wounded, 105 wounded, and 27 captured. For a brief contemporary account of the battle of May 16, see the Raleigh *Daily Confederate*, May 21, 1864.

17, 18, and 19 as Butler completed his withdrawal. On May 20 the Confederates attacked again, thereby "corking" Butler in the famous Bermuda Hundred "bottle." For the period May 17-26 the 51st Regiment lost, according to a letter written by regimental Adjutant John C. Latta on May 27, five men killed and twenty-two wounded.[49]

The 51st Regiment remained in the Bermuda Hundred line until the morning of May 31 when, in response to desperate calls from General Robert E. Lee for reinforcements in the face of an impending assault by the Army of the Potomac, it was dispatched by rail to Richmond with two other regiments of Clingman's brigade (the 8th and 31st). From there it marched eight miles northeast to the strategic crossroads at Cold Harbor, where dismounted and outnumbered cavalrymen under Major General Fitzhugh Lee were attempting to fend off a Federal assault.

> [As] soon as we got hear [wrote Private John G. Hall of Company G, 51st Regiment] they run us right in among the Yankees[.] [W]e had a very hot engagement for about an hour[.] [O]ur Regiment was sent to the left of the brigade[.] [T]here was nothing on our right but some dismounted cavelry[.] [T]hey shot a while and when they saw the enemy coming [in] pretty large force they all run away[.] [T]hat left our . . . right exposed to the enemy[.] [T]hey were a flanking us on the right and left so we were compelled to fall back and in falling back we lost a good many killed and wounded[.] [W]e fell back about too or three hundred yards and formed a line of battle and stayed until the next morning.[50]

As a result of this defeat Cold Harbor was occupied by Federal cavalry, who began entrenching in anticipation of a Confederate attack the next day. According to Adjutant Latta in a letter dated June 1 the regiment lost seven men killed and thirty-eight wounded on May 31.[51]

During the night the remainder of Hoke's division, of which Clingman's brigade was now a part, arrived on the field along with Major General Joseph B. Kershaw's division of Anderson's corps. Under orders from Lee to attempt to recapture the Cold Harbor crossroads, Kershaw's division, with an untried South Carolina regiment in the lead, launched an attack on the morning of June 1 and was met by a sheet of fire from the seven-shot Spencer carbines of the Federal cavalrymen and murderous blasts of grape and canister. Staggered, the South Carolinians fled for their lives, reducing Kershaw's attack to a shambles. Hoke, who had been under orders to join in the assault, did not move at all. Sensing that a Federal counterattack would follow shortly, the Confederates, working in many cases with nothing more than bayonets and their bare hands, hastily began throwing up breastworks.[52] In the afternoon Federal infantry units launched a "furious" attack and drove a wedge through a ravine where Hoke's left, held by Clingman, and Kershaw's right joined.[53] Clingman's men were hotly engaged in the fighting and suffered severe casualties before the arrival of reinforcements restored the situation. "The Yankees charged us about three or four oclock in the evening," Private Hall wrote,

> and we ran them back[.] [A]bout a half an hour [later] they flanked our men on the left and came up in our rear[.] [T]hey killed and took a good many of our men prisoners[.] [T]hey came up in

[49]*Wilmington Journal* (Weekly), June 2, 1864.
[50]John G. Hall to his father, June 3, 1864, Private Collections, W. P. Hall Collection, PC 551, Archives, Division of Archives and History, Raleigh, hereinafter cited as Hall Collection, PC 551.
[51]*Wilmington Journal* (Weekly), June 16, 1864.
[52]Hall Collection, PC 551, John G. Hall to his father, June 3, 1864.
[53]*Official Records (Army)*, Series I, XXXVI, Part I, 1059.

ten steps of us before we knew any thing about them[.] [T]hey ordered us to lay down our arms and some did but we dident[.] [T]he 61rst Regt [which had arrived from Petersburg] reinforced us and we charged them back[,] killing and wounding a great many. . . .[54]

Convinced that the Confederate infantry were too weakened and demoralized by the events of the last month to withstand another blow, Grant planned a massive assault on the Confederate line for the morning of June 2; however, one of his corps missed its way during the night and arrived in such a state of exhaustion that the attack had to be delayed. A Confederate probing attack further disrupted the timetable. In the late afternoon a heavy rain began to fall, causing the assault to be postponed until the next day. In the meantime Lee received reinforcements and his men perfected their defensive works, folding them into the landscape with such skill that the deadliness of their interlocking fields of fire was at least partially concealed.

Early on the cool, misty morning of June 3, 50,000 Federals, many of whom rightly sensed that they were being sent to their deaths, advanced through the mud into a curtain of fire whose thunderous roar was clearly audible in Richmond eight miles away. Smothered by the hail of musketry and storm of case shot and double-shotted canister that raked them from several angles, the Federals milled in confusion and agony, unable to advance or, because of their comrades charging up behind them, retreat. In a matter of minutes the attack was over, with at least 7,000 Federals dead or wounded. The 51st Regiment, after suffering very heavy casualties (34 killed, 58 wounded, and 128 captured) in hard fighting on May 31 and June 1, had been relieved on the morning of June 2 and sent "a little in the rear." The imperturbable Private Hall, writing to his father while stray minie balls flew over his head during the horrific battle of the 3rd, passed on a secondhand but accurate report that the Federal dead "are lying in files in front of our breast works."[55] Although the regiment's position was bracketed by heavy Federal attacks, the fighting ended so quickly that the 51st was not called to the front.

The two armies remained in their steaming, muddy, malodorous trenches for the next nine days. The 51st Regiment, according to a letter dated June 8 from an unidentified member to the *Fayetteville Observer*, was still "in good spirits and cheerful" although casualties had been "pretty heavy" since the regiment "left Petersburg with 800 men" in early May.

---

[54]Hall Collection, PC 551, John G. Hall to his father, June 3, 1864. Clingman's brigade was accused by Anderson of having "given way," thereby causing Brigadier General William T. Wofford's brigade, on Clingman's left, to be flanked and routed. Clingman, for his part, denounced the allegation within a week of the battle and went to his grave more than thirty years later still stoutly claiming that it was Wofford's brigade that had broken, with the result that Clingman's men were flanked and attacked from the rear. In a letter dated June 5, 1864, and quoted in the Raleigh *Daily Confederate* of June 8, 1864, Clingman stated that the Federal attack of June 1 "was repeatedly and signally repulsed with great loss to the enemy in my entire front. Near our left, where they came in columns, their dead were much thicker than I have ever seen them on any battle field. . . . There was, however, in the beginning of the engagement, a brigade from another State than my own, stationed on our left. This brigade did give way, and while the contest was going on in our front, the enemy, in large force, occupied the ground on our left flank and rear. After we had repelled the last attack in front, and the men were cheering along the line, the 8th regiment, which formed my left, was suddenly attacked on its left flank and rear. The woods there being thick, and the smoke dense, the enemy had approached within a few yards and opened a heavy fire on the rear of the 8th as well as its left. . . . [I]t, by facing in two directions, attempted to hold its position, and thus lost about two thirds [sic] of its numbers." The letter goes on to state that the 31st and 61st regiments came to the aid of the 8th, and the brigade, assisted by the 27th Georgia, drove back the Federal flank attack and reoccupied its original position. Clingman's account and the one that Private Hall wrote two days after the battle are remarkably similar, but Hall's also suggests the probability that the 51st Regiment, which was immediately to the right of the 8th, was struck from the rear by the same attack that flanked its sister unit. See also Clingman's postwar history of the same battle in Clark, *Histories of the North Carolina Regiments*, V, 197-205.
[55]Hall Collection, PC 551, John G. Hall to his father, June 3, 1864. Regimental casualty figures for May 31 and June 1 are based on information compiled for this volume.

"Plentiful" rations—"1/2 lb. bacon [daily] and plenty of bread" as well as such "extras" as coffee, sugar and onions—helped keep up morale, as did the "compliment[s]" of General Hoke for the regiment's conduct under the "trying circumstances" of June 1st.[56]

On the night of June 12 Grant quietly pulled his men back and began a long southward sidle to the east of Richmond. Aware of Grant's departure but forced to cover Richmond until he was certain that his opponent had crossed the James River, Lee moved slowly south. On June 14 Grant's army began crossing the James; in the meantime a Federal corps under Major General W. F. Smith arrived by water to reinforce Butler at Bermuda Hundred. With Lee still north of the James, a vigorous attack the next day on Beauregard's ragtag force of 3,000 men manning the Petersburg defenses would almost certainly have resulted in the capture of the city, isolating Richmond and changing the course of the war. However, the opportunity was bungled through delays, a reluctance to test the formidable Petersburg defenses after the butchery at Cold Harbor, and a series of tragicomic staff-work blunders involving faulty maps, contradictory orders, and failure to apprise key commanders and subordinates of plans. An attack late in the day, although desultory, easily drove the Confederate defenders from a mile-long segment of their outer works. During the night Beauregard ordered the division of the recently promoted Major General Bushrod Johnson, which was "corking" Butler at Bermuda Hundred, to march to the Petersburg lines. Hoke's division, including Clingman's brigade and the 51st Regiment, also arrived, bringing Beauregard's strength up to about 15,000 men. Major units of the Army of the Potomac also reached the field, and by sunrise on the 16th some 75,000 Federals were present.

Poised again for what might have been the climactic battle of the war, the Federals fumbled away their advantage. A series of disjointed attacks, delivered with minimal aggressiveness, resulted in the capture of several redans and some trenches. Those breakthroughs were not vigorously exploited, and Federal casualties were inordinately high. Expertly shifting his limited resources as the crisis of the moment dictated, Beauregard left whole segments of the ten-mile-long Petersburg fortifications virtually undefended, gambling that a coordinated assault would not be forthcoming. Clingman's brigade was involved in heavy fighting on the 16th, and on the 17th a potentially disastrous Federal penetration was sealed off by Clingman's and Brigadier General Matt Ransom's brigades after a bayonet charge and hand-to-hand fight with clubbed muskets. During the two-day battle at Petersburg the 51st Regiment lost 16 men killed, 25 wounded, and 26 captured.[57]

That night Beauregard ordered his exhausted troops to fall back to a shorter line closer to Petersburg, and major elements of the Army of Northern Virginia arrived. Renewed attacks the next day resulted in no significant gains for the Federals. After overrunning Beauregard's abandoned line and discovering, at the cost of severe casualties, that Lee's men were on the field, the Federal soldiers simply declined to repeat the bloody fiasco at Cold Harbor by attacking the Confederates in their earthworks. One of the few units to obey the orders of its officers, a green regiment from Maine, lost 632 men out of 850 in a matter of minutes— among the heaviest casualties suffered by a Federal regiment in a single battle during the war.

Frustrated in his attempt to seize Petersburg and end the war with a single stroke, Grant reviewed his options while his army set to work building fortifications. A westward thrust to cut the Petersburg and Weldon Railroad, one of the two remaining railroad supply routes to the south, was successfully parried by Lee on June 22-23, convincing Grant that a protracted

---

[56]*Fayetteville Observer* (Semiweekly), June 16, 1864.
[57]Casualty figures are based on data compiled for this volume. For Clingman's account of the fighting on June 17, see the Raleigh *Daily Confederate*, July 18, 1864. Clingman admits that he threatened at one moment of crisis to have an uncooperative captain from another brigade "bayoneted in the trenches."

siege was in the offing.[58] Accordingly, construction of extensive siege fortifications began in early July and continued throughout the month. On July 30 Grant made a bid to breach the Confederate defenses by tunneling beneath them and planting a large mine. The resulting spectacular explosion produced a hole 170 feet long, 60 to 80 feet wide, and 30 feet deep, but the stunned Confederates rallied and, with the help of reinforcements, including two regiments of Clingman's brigade (the 8th and the 61st), inflicted a bloody repulse on the charging Federals.

Grant then returned to his siege strategy and on August 18 made a new and this time successful lunge toward the Petersburg and Weldon Railroad, capturing Globe Tavern and then turning north in the direction of Petersburg. A Confederate counterattack that afternoon brought the advance to a halt and, with the aid of reinforcements, including Clingman's brigade, drove the Federals back in the direction of Globe Tavern the next day. One member of the 51st Regiment described the fight as "a regular woods scramble, it being impossible to preserve anything like a line of battle on account of the density of the woods[.] [T]he result was that we captured a large number of prisoners, and suffered considerable loss ourselves, some of our men being captured and recaptured several times."[59] Although the Confederates recovered some lost ground, they were unable to dislodge the tenacious Federals from Globe Tavern. A renewed effort on the 21st also failed, and the Petersburg and Weldon Railroad was permanently severed. During the fighting at Globe Tavern the 51st Regiment lost 4 men killed, 3 wounded, and 25 captured.[60]

Clingman's brigade remained in the Petersburg trenches until September 30 when it was moved north of the James to the vicinity of Fort Harrison, an important link in the Richmond defenses that had been seized by the Federals in a surprise attack on the previous day. Three ill-coordinated attempts to recapture the fort, in which Clingman's men played a leading role, were repulsed with heavy casualties. "At the command the Fifty-first rushed forward with the other regiments of the brigade," Lieutenant A. A. McKethan of Company B reported,

preserving their alignment until the stockade [abatis] was reached, which they found impossible to pass. To retreat was death, so the only chance was to throw down their guns and pull up these obstructions, which the men at once attempted, but a double line armed with repeating rifles posted in front of the works, and a deadly fire from the garrison in the fort . . . and the concentration of all the artillery upon them, made the position untenable and the task impossible, so that the few left were forced to seek shelter offered by two old buildings near the works.[61]

Writing with unconcealed bitterness of the same attack, which was undertaken on Lee's orders over General Hoke's protests, staff officer Burgwyn recounted the battle as follows:

The troops were formed for the assault in a ravine some two hundred yards from the fort. The enemy had diligently strengthened its defenses since the day before and, in anticipation of the

[58]Adjutant John W. Latta, in a letter dated June 23, 1864, states that since June 2 the regiment had lost 9 men killed, 40 wounded, and 26 missing. *Wilmington Journal* (Weekly), July 21, 1864. According to an article appearing in the Raleigh *Daily Confederate*, June 27, 1864, the 51st lost, in battles from May 12 through June 17, 60 men killed, 225 wounded, and 148 captured, not counting 22 officers who were also casualties of unspecified descriptions.

[59]Clark, *Histories of the North Carolina Regiments*, III, 213.

[60]Casualty figures are based on information compiled for this volume. Supplies continued to reach the Army of Northern Virginia over the Petersburg and Weldon Railroad via a wagon detour around Globe Tavern.

[61]Clark, *Histories of the North Carolina Regiments*, III, 213-214.

attack, had massed his troops in several ranks deep [*sic*], and they were armed with Spencer repeating rifles. Realizing how great would be the loss of his men in such a charge, General Hoke importuned General Lee, who was directing the movement in person, not to order it to be made; but to select a new line of defence [*sic*]. . . . General Lee's reply was that he would first reduce the enemy's works by his artillery before the assault should be made, and create a diversion by an attack on the enemy's flank simultaneously with Hoke's advance.[62]

After an argument between Hoke and the artillery commander in which the latter refused to risk his horses to position his guns as Hoke wished, the preliminary bombardment began:

[T]he ground shook with the mighty concussion [Burgwyn continued]; the smoke enveloped the field, the enemy retreated under the protection of his earth works. At the given signal, Clingman's Brigade rushed for the works. As one man the enemy flashed his defiance from a thousand guns; the flank attack miscarried; the supports failed to come up; the charging line melted away; the fort was reached but no farther. As many as were able, in the darkness of the night got back to our lines. The wounded and captured were taken to northern hospitals and northern prisons. The dead were buried under the flag of truce, but the artillery horses were saved. . . .[63]

According to Burgwyn, about one-third of the men who took part in the charge were killed, wounded, or captured. Captain Edward White, assistant adjutant general of Clingman's brigade, stated in a report filed a few days after the battle that the brigade had suffered 528 casualties of whom 104 were members of the 51st Regiment. Of the latter number, 5 men were killed, 45 wounded, 2 wounded and captured, 51 missing, and 1 not otherwise accounted for.[64] Whatever the exact figures, losses in the 51st Regiment were clearly severe at Fort Harrison and staggering for the period from May 1 through September 30. During those five months the strength of the regiment declined, according to one estimate, from approximately 800 men to 145.[65]

After the calamitous failure to recapture Fort Harrison, Hoke's division remained in the lines north of the James River. "We have to ly in our trenches day and knight Rain or Shine Hot or Coald," wrote one of "Lee's miserables." "[T]hair is some killed or wounded moar or less evry day by morter shells or Sharp Shooters[.] [T]he men have become so carless they don car much for any thing."[66]

---

[62]Clark, *Histories of the North Carolina Regiments*, IV, 495-496.

[63]Clark, *Histories of the North Carolina Regiments*, IV, 496.

[64]Clark, *Histories of the North Carolina Regiments*, IV, 496; Raleigh *Daily Confederate*, October 11 and October 12, 1864. According to another report, the brigade went into the fight at Fort Harrison with 857 guns and "in ten or fifteen minutes" lost 587. Clark, *Histories of the North Carolina Regiments*, III, 214. Information compiled for this volume indicates that the 51st Regiment lost 19 men killed or missing and presumed killed, 43 wounded, and 41 captured. Of the 41 captured, at least 16 were wounded.

[65]Clark, *Histories of the North Carolina Regiments*, III, 214. Another estimate for the same period, which is almost certainly too high at one extreme and too low at the other, indicates that the regiment was reduced from "about nine hundred . . . to forty-five guns and eight officers." Cobb, "Service of Tar Heels," 216. In a letter dated November 1, 1864, 2nd Lieutenant C. L. Cowles of Company B stated that between May 13 and September 30, 1864, the company lost 10 men killed or mortally wounded, 4 dead of disease, 27 wounded, and 23 captured. Cowles reported that 2 officers and 15 men were absent sick, 1 officer and 15 men were present for duty, and 11 men were present but sick. *Wilmington Journal* (Weekly), November 10, 1864. In a letter dated September 20, 1864, 2nd Lieutenant C. T. Guy of Company I reported that the company had lost 15 men killed, 27 wounded, and 47 captured during the period from May 10 through August 19. "We have now present with the Company only twenty-nine," Guy continued, "twenty of which are reported for duty." *Fayetteville Observer* (Weekly), October 24, 1864.

[66][Signature missing] to John A. Ray, July 29, 1864, Nevin Ray Papers, Duke Manuscript Department.

On December 22 Hoke's division was ordered to move by rail to Wilmington to assist in defending Fort Fisher against an anticipated amphibious assault commanded by the ubiquitous Butler. Proceeding circuitously via Danville and Greensboro, advance elements of the division reached Wilmington on the afternoon of the 24th "after a long and fatiguing ride on the cars in extremely cold weather."[67] Finding that a preliminary naval bombardment was already in progress, the men marched immediately to Sugar Loaf Hill, just north of Fort Fisher. The next day Federal infantry landed but, after skirmishing briefly, withdrew ingloriously to their ships and sailed away. Butler having been promptly replaced by a more competent officer, Brigadier General Alfred H. Terry, the Federal fleet returned on January 12, and the next day an assault force landed unopposed.

The 51st Regiment, which returned to Wilmington on or about December 28, was dispatched again to Fort Fisher with the rest of Hoke's division. In the meantime Terry's men constructed between the hours of 2:00 and 8:00 a.m. on the morning of the 14th "a good breast-work, reaching from the river to the sea," whose purposes were to prevent an attack on the Federal rear while Fort Fisher was being stormed and to cut off the fort from reinforcements.[68] Fearing the wrath of the Federal fleet, which was pulverizing the fort with an even more awesome barrage than the one delivered against Fort Wagner, General Braxton Bragg, Hoke's superior, ignored the desperate calls for help of the beleaguered defenders, and on January 15 the fort was stormed and captured.

Hoke's division held the line below Wilmington until February 19, when it was pulled back in the face of a Federal advance up the west bank of the Cape Fear River. The division then withdrew to Wilmington, crossed the Northeast Cape Fear River, and, in an effort to slow the Federal advance, burned the bridges. After Wilmington fell on February 22, Hoke's troops were ordered to Kinston to oppose a Federal column advancing on Goldsboro from New Bern.

The Battle of Kinston (also known as Wise's Forks and Southwest Creek) was fought on March 7-10 in an effort by the Confederates to prevent or at least delay the junction of Federal forces in eastern North Carolina with the oncoming army of Major General William T. Sherman. Mustering about 6,500 men (with an additional 2,000 en route), Bragg confronted a Federal army of perhaps 10,000 that would increase to around 15,000 before the end of the battle. After bringing the Federal advance to a halt with artillery fire on March 7, Hoke's division and a smaller force under Lieutenant General D. H. Hill attacked the Federal left and right respectively on the morning of March 8. Two isolated Federal regiments were overrun and captured by Hoke, and Hill also made good progress on the right. However, a major tactical error by Bragg at that critical juncture sent Hill marching away from the fighting, and the Confederate advantage was lost. Following a day of "warm skirmish[ing]" highlighted by a feeble probe by Hoke against the Federal lines, Bragg attempted another double envelopment with Hoke and Hill on the 10th.[69] After marching through "swamps and pocosons and dense pine forests" in an unsuccessful attempt to get in the enemy's rear, Hoke's men delivered a "resolute and determined" assault that was smashed by cannon fire and a flank attack by Federal infantry.[70] Hill's "less vigorous" and slightly mistimed assault was called off by Bragg after the repulse of Hoke.[71] Bragg then fell back through Goldsboro to Smithfield, where his force was united with that of General Joseph E. Johnston on March 17.[72]

[67]Charles G. Elliott, "Kirkland's Brigade, Hoke's Division, 1864-65," Southern Historical Society Papers, XXIII (1895), 166, hereinafter cited as Elliott, "Kirkland's Brigade."

[68]Official Records (Army), Series I, XLVI, Part I, 397.

[69]Official Records (Army), Series I, XLVII, Part I, 978.

[70]Elliott, "Kirkland's Brigade," 170; Official Records (Army), Series I, XLVII, Part I, 978.

[71]Official Records (Army), Series I, XLVII, Part I, 978.

[72]Information compiled for this volume indicates that the 51st Regiment lost 1 man killed, 2 wounded, and 3 captured at Kinston; however, these figures are almost certainly too low.

In the meantime Sherman's relentless army, after its destructive sweep through South Carolina, captured Fayetteville on March 11. On the 14th it resumed its march, advancing to the northeast in two columns commanded respectively by Major General Henry W. Slocum, who feinted in the direction of Raleigh, and Major General Oliver O. Howard, who moved against Goldsboro to link up with the victorious Federal force advancing westward from Kinston. Hoping to draw Sherman's two columns further apart and defeat them separately, Johnston ordered Lieutenant General William J. Hardee to fight a delaying action against Slocum. At Averasboro on March 16 Hardee, outnumbered on the order of four or five to one, fought a careful defensive battle, precariously holding off Slocum's attacking army and then quietly slipping away during the night to join forces with Johnston at Smithfield.

Having marshaled most of his available forces and succeeded in increasing the distance between Slocum and Howard, Johnston laid an ambush for Slocum at Bentonville on March 19. Cleverly deploying his 20,000 men in a woods behind a screen of cavalry, Johnston awaited the arrival of the strung-out, 30,000-man Federal column. Slocum, thinking that he was confronted by the usual token cavalry opposition, saw no reason to wait for his entire command to come up and ordered a division forward to clear his front. That unsuspecting unit received "an awful volly [sic]" from massed Confederate infantry at a distance of about fifty feet.[73] A savage, hand-to-hand fight with clubbed muskets and ramrods ensued, and the Federals fell back in disarray. Rebounding quickly, Slocum's men came on again, concentrating their "vigorous" attack on Hoke's division on the Confederate left and causing Bragg to issue an unnecessary call for reinforcements that deprived Johnston of an essential division at a critical moment.[74] Shortly thereafter Confederate infantry under Hardee and Lieutenant General A. P. Stewart stormed out of the brush and blackjack thickets in a devastating assault that crushed the undermanned and disorganized Federal left wing and precipitated, in the words of one candid Federal, "some of the best running ever did."[75] The Federal right wing then came under attack from the rear by Hardee and Stewart; shortly thereafter, units under the command of Bragg pitched into the beleaguered Federals from the front. Battling desperately amid a "continuous and remorseless roar of musketry," the Federal defenders narrowly succeeded in holding their position until reinforcements arrived to beat back the Confederate attack.[76] The fighting then shifted again to the re-formed and reinforced Federal left, where five successive Confederate assaults were smashed by a "raging leaden hailstorm of grape and canister."[77]

During the night of March 19 Sherman, who was with Howard's wing of the Federal army, belatedly learned of the fighting at Bentonville. Preparations to go to the aid of Slocum began immediately, and by the afternoon of the 20th the army was reunited on the battlefield. Johnston, realizing that his gambit had failed, remained at Bentonville to cover the evacuation of his wounded, an undertaking that, because of poor roads and a shortage of wagons, would require two days. Confronted now by a force twice the size of the one he had faced on the previous day, Johnston realigned his units in a configuration similar to a spraddled horseshoe to cover the longer Federal line. While ambulances rumbled over the Mill Creek bridge, in Johnston's immediate rear and his only line of retreat, the Confederate general resupplied his men as best he could and anxiously awaited developments.

---

[73]Charles S. Brown to "Mother & Etta," April 18, 1865, Charles S. Brown Papers, Duke Manuscript Department.

[74]*Official Records (Army)*, Series I, XLVII, Part I, 1056.

[75]Quoted in John G. Barrett, *The Civil War in North Carolina* (Chapel Hill: The University of North Carolina Press, 1963), 333.

[76]Benson J. Lossing, *Pictorial History of the Civil War in the United States of America* (Hartford: Thomas Belknap, 3 volumes, 1877), III, 501.

[77]Samuel W. Ravenel, "Ask the Survivors of Bentonville," *Confederate Veteran*, XVIII (March, 1910), 124.

General Sherman, for his part, had no more interest than Johnston in renewing the contest. Rarely inclined to expend lives in costly attacks if maneuver would accomplish his object, his primary concern for the moment was to reach the Goldsboro railhead. There he would be reinforced by powerful Federal units from the North Carolina coast and would obtain much needed supplies and equipment. Except for several "brisk" but relatively minor attacks on Hoke's front, the day passed quietly.[78]

The next day, March 21, Johnston continued to evacuate his wounded and remained in his works. Heavy skirmishing took place all along the line, but the only action of consequence was an unauthorized attack by the Federal division of Major General Joseph A. Mower that broke through on the Confederate left and threatened to capture the vital bridge over Mill Creek. Against that penetration Johnston mustered just enough resistance to force the impetuous Federal commander to pause and call for reinforcements, whereupon Sherman ordered him to withdraw. Johnston fell back in the direction of Smithfield that night. Casualties sustained by the 51st Regiment in the Battle of Bentonville, although not officially reported, were probably heavy. Hoke's division as a whole lost, according to Johnston's report, 61 men killed, 471 wounded, and 202 missing.[79]

At Smithfield the Confederates enjoyed a brief respite while Johnston's army was reorganized. The egregious Bragg was removed from field command, and Hoke's division was placed under Hardee. Clingman's brigade, of which the 51st Regiment was still a part, remained under Hoke.[80]

On April 10 Sherman's inexorable advance resumed. Smithfield was captured on April 11, and Raleigh was occupied two days later. Johnston retreated with his small and, particularly after the surrender of Lee on April 9, rapidly shrinking army to the vicinity of Durham Station. There, with the authorization of President Jefferson Davis, a fugitive from the fallen Confederate capital, he opened negotiations with Sherman on April 17. On April 26, 1865, at the home of James Bennitt, three miles west of Durham Station, Johnston surrendered. A week later, when the army was paroled at Greensboro, thirty-six members of the 51st Regiment were present to receive their paroles.

---

[78]*Official Records (Army)*, Series I, XLVII, Part I, 1056.

[79]*Official Records (Army)*, Series I, XLVII, Part I, 1060. Information compiled for this volume indicates that the 51st Regiment lost 0 men killed, 5 wounded, and 3 captured. These figures, which are based on the few casualty sources that were located for this eve-of-surrender engagement, plainly do not reflect the true losses of the regiment.

[80]*Official Records (Army)*, Series I, XLVII, Part I, 1061-1062.

FIELD AND STAFF

COLONELS

CANTWELL, JOHN LUCAS

Previously served as Captain of Company D, 13th Battalion N.C. Infantry. Appointed Colonel to rank from April 30, 1862, and transferred to this regiment. Resigned on October 19, 1862, by reason of "circumstances of an imperative personal character. . . ." Later served as Captain of Company F, 3rd Regiment N.C. State Troops.

McKETHAN, HECTOR McALLESTER

Previously served as Captain of Company I of this regiment. Elected Major on April 30, 1862, and transferred to the Field and Staff. Promoted to Colonel on January 19, 1863. Wounded near Petersburg, Virginia, June 17, 1864. Returned to duty prior to September 1, 1864. Hospitalized at Wilmington on January 15, 1865, with melancholia. Transferred to another hospital on February 1, 1865. No further records.

LIEUTENANT COLONELS

ALLEN, WILLIAM A.

Previously served as Captain of Company C of this regiment. Appointed Lieutenant Colonel on April 30, 1862, and transferred to the Field and Staff. Present or accounted for until he resigned on January 5, 1863, "because of . . . imputation[s] against my character" and also because of "rheumatism." Lieutenant Colonel Allen was being court-martialed at the time for "com[ing] into the camp of his Regt at Rockfish Church intoxicated" on the night of December 30, 1862; for using "the most abusive and insulting language to Major Hector McKethan" on the same occasion; and for challenging Major McKethan "to fight him with pistols." Resignation accepted on January 19, 1863.

HOBSON, CALEB B.

Previously served as Captain of Company B of this regiment. Appointed Lieutenant Colonel on April 9, 1863, and transferred to the Field and Staff. Present or accounted for until killed at Fort Harrison, Virginia, September 30, 1864.

MAJOR

McDONALD, JAMES R.

Previously served as Captain of Company D of this regiment. Appointed Major on April 9, 1863, and transferred to the Field and Staff. Present or accounted for until captured at Cold Harbor, Virginia, on or about May 31, 1864. Confined at Point Lookout, Maryland, June 11, 1864. Transferred to Fort Delaware, Delaware, June 23, 1864. Transferred to Hilton Head, South Carolina, August 20, 1864. Transferred to Fort Pulaski, Georgia, on an unspecified date subsequent to October 20, 1864. Transferred back to Hilton Head on or about January 1, 1865. Transferred to Fort Delaware on March 12, 1865. Released at Fort Delaware on July 24, 1865, after taking the Oath of Allegiance.

ADJUTANTS

LATTA, JOHN R.

Previously served as a Drillmaster. Appointed Adjutant (1st Lieutenant) of this regiment on July 11, 1862, to rank from June 1, 1862. Present or accounted for until he resigned on September 3, 1864. Reason he resigned not reported. Resignation accepted on September 21, 1864.

TAYLOR, JAMES H.

Previously served as 3rd Lieutenant of Company I of this regiment. Appointed Adjutant (1st Lieutenant) on January 12, 1865, to rank from September 21, 1864, and transferred to the Field and Staff. Paroled at Greensboro on May 1, 1865.

ASSISTANT QUARTERMASTER

ROCKWELL, HENRY CLAY

Previously served as 2nd Lieutenant of Company H of this regiment. Appointed Assistant Quartermaster (Captain) on April 30, 1862, and transferred to the Field and Staff. Present or accounted for until appointed Assistant Quartermaster (Captain) of General T. L. Clingman's brigade on September 20, 1864, and transferred.

ASSISTANT COMMISSARY OF SUBSISTENCE

KETCHUM, DAVID W.

Previously served as 2nd Lieutenant of Company G of this regiment. Appointed Assistant Commissary of Subsistence (Captain) on April 30, 1862, and transferred to the Field and Staff. Was officially dropped from the rolls of the regiment on February 5, 1863, after "having failed to execute the Bonds required by law"; however, he continued to sign vouchers and to serve with the regiment through November 26, 1863.

SURGEON

MORRISEY, SAMUEL BUNTING

Born in Sampson County and was by occupation a physician prior to enlisting in Robeson County at age 32. Appointed Surgeon on July 11, 1862, to rank from May 1,

1862. Present or accounted for through February, 1865. Paroled at Greensboro on May 1, 1865.

ASSISTANT SURGEONS

STEPHENS, JAMES M.
Appointed Assistant Surgeon to rank from August 9, 1862. No further records.

McGEE, JAMES W.
Previously served as Private in Company C of this regiment. Appointed Assistant Surgeon on October 14, 1862, to rank from June 1, 1862, and transferred to the Field and Staff. Present or accounted for through February, 1865. Paroled at Greensboro on May 1, 1865.

CHAPLAINS

BROOKS, H. C.
Appointed Chaplain on June 2, 1862. Reported absent sick through July, 1862. Resigned prior to September 1, 1862.

SHAW, COLIN
Presbyterian. Previously served as Chaplain of the 18th Regiment N.C. Troops (8th Regiment N.C. Volunteers). Transferred to this regiment on or about January 1, 1863. Present or accounted for until he resigned on October 27, 1863, because "the condition of my family is such as to require by personal attention which cannot be longer delayed without serious loss. . . ." Resignation accepted on October 31, 1863.

ALFORD, JAMES B.
Methodist Episcopalian. Born in Wayne County in 1813 and resided in Randolph County. Appointed Chaplain on August 20, 1864, to rank from July 20, 1864. Present or accounted for through January 2, 1865. Paroled at Greensboro on May 1, 1865.

ENSIGNS

TURNER, DAVID W.
Previously served as Private in Company C of this regiment. Appointed Color Sergeant on May 9, 1862, and transferred to the Field and Staff. Reduced to ranks in January-February, 1863, and transferred back to Company C.

GUY, WILLIAM ANTHONY
Previously served as Private in Company I of this regiment. Appointed Ensign (1st Lieutenant) on July 7, 1864, and transferred to the Field and Staff. Captured near Globe Tavern, Virginia, August 19, 1864. Confined at Old Capitol Prison, Washington, D.C., August 22,

1864. Transferred to Fort Delaware, Delaware, August 27, 1864. Released at Fort Delaware on June 17, 1865, after taking the Oath of Allegiance.

DRILLMASTER

LYONS, W. D.
Appointed Drillmaster of this regiment on July 1, 1862. Reported present with the regiment through August 13, 1862. No further records.

SERGEANTS MAJOR

STANFORD, GEORGE W.
Previously served as Sergeant in Company C of this regiment. Promoted to Sergeant Major on April 30, 1862, and transferred to the Field and Staff. Resigned as Sergeant Major on August 8, 1862. Returned to duty with Company C with the rank of Sergeant.

ATWOOD, JOEL P.
Previously served as Sergeant in Company C of this regiment. Promoted to Sergeant Major on September 1, 1862, and transferred to the Field and Staff. Reduced to ranks and transferred back to Company C on February 20, 1863.

ELLIOTT, ALEXANDER, JR.
Previously served as Sergeant in Company K of this regiment. Promoted to Sergeant Major on April 23, 1863, and transferred to the Field and Staff. Appointed 3rd Lieutenant on October 1, 1863, and transferred back to Company K.

COWLES, CHARLES L.
Previously served as Private in Company B of this regiment. Promoted to Sergeant Major on November 1, 1863, and transferred to the Field and Staff. Appointed 2nd Lieutenant on July 26, 1864, and transferred back to Company B.

McMILLAN, WILLIAM DOUGALD
Previously served as Private in Company K of this regiment. Promoted to Sergeant Major on or about July 6, 1864, and transferred to the Field and Staff. Wounded in the shoulder at Fort Harrison, Virginia, September 30, 1864. Returned to duty in November-December, 1864. Paroled at Greensboro on May 1, 1865. [Was also wounded at Bermuda Hundred, Virginia (probably in May, 1864); at Cold Harbor, Virginia (probably on May 31, 1864); and at Petersburg, Virginia, on an unspecified date.]

QUARTERMASTER SERGEANTS

FRENCH, WILLIAM R.
Served as Private in Company E of this regiment. Reported on detail as acting regimental Quartermaster

Sergeant in June-October, 1862. Transferred back to Company E in November-December, 1862.

McKENZIE, WILLIAM M.

Previously served as Private in Company D of this regiment. Appointed Quartermaster Sergeant on November 27, 1862, and transferred to the Field and Staff. Present or accounted for through December, 1864. Paroled at Greensboro on May 1, 1865.

COMMISSARY SERGEANTS

PARKER, WILLIAM L.

Served as Corporal in Company B of this regiment. Appointed acting Commissary Sergeant on June 4, 1862, and transferred to the Field and Staff. Promoted to the permanent rank of Commissary Sergeant on June 23, 1862. Present or accounted for through August, 1863. Reported absent on detail with the brigade commissary department from September-October, 1863, through December, 1864. Hospitalized at Raleigh on March 20, 1865, with typhoid fever. No further records.

DAFFRON, GEORGE W.

Served as Private in Company E of this regiment. Reported on duty as acting Commissary Sergeant for an unspecified period in 1863.

ORDNANCE SERGEANTS

MURPHY, JOHN A.

Previously served as Private in Company K of this regiment. Appointed Ordnance Sergeant on May 2, 1862, and transferred to the Field and Staff. Present or accounted for until discharged on December 10, 1862, by reason of "bronchial inflammation which threatens to become consumption."

MOORE, THOMAS McGEE

Previously served as Private in Company C of this regiment. Appointed acting Ordnance Sergeant on December 10, 1862, and transferred to the Field and Staff. Promoted to the permanent rank of Ordnance Sergeant on an unspecified date and assigned to permanent duty with the Field and Staff. Present or accounted for through August, 1864.

HOSPITAL STEWARD

ROBESON, ALBERT T.

Enlisted in Sampson County on April 20, 1862, for the war. Mustered in as Hospital Steward. Present or accounted for through August, 1864. Paroled at Greensboro on May 1, 1865.

COMPANY A

This company was raised primarily in New Hanover County and enlisted in New Hanover County in February-March, 1862. It was mustered into state service at Wilmington on April 19, 1862, and assigned to the 51st Regiment N.C. Troops as Company A. After joining the regiment the company functioned as a part of the regiment, and its history for the remainder of the war is reported as a part of the regimental history.

The information contained in the following roster was compiled primarily from a company muster-in and descriptive roll dated April 19, 1862, and from company muster rolls for April 19, 1862-December 31, 1864. No company muster rolls were located for the period after December 31, 1864. Valuable information was obtained from primary records such as the North Carolina adjutant general's *Roll of Honor*, discharge certificates, medical records, prisoner of war records, *The War of the Rebellion: A Compilation of the Official Records of the Union and Confederate Armies*, militia records, newspaper casualty lists and obituaries, Confederate pension applications filed with the state of North Carolina, and the 1860 federal census of North Carolina. Secondary sources such as postwar rosters and histories, cemetery records, the *Confederate Veteran*, published genealogies, and records of the United Daughters of the Confederacy also provided useful information.

OFFICERS

CAPTAINS

WALKER, GEORGE F.

Born in New Hanover County where he resided as a farmer prior to enlisting in New Hanover County at age 29. Appointed Captain on February 6, 1862. Reported under arrest on July 8, 1862. Court-martialed on or about September 16, 1862. Reason he was court-martialed not reported. Returned to duty prior to November 1, 1862. Resigned on May 14, 1863. Reason he resigned not reported. Resignation accepted on May 20, 1863.

SOUTHERLAND, EDWARD

Previously served as 2nd Lieutenant of Company D, 13th Battalion N.C. Infantry. Promoted to 1st Lieutenant on April 15, 1862, and transferred to this company. Promoted to Captain on May 30, 1863. Present or accounted for until wounded in the right thigh at Fort Wagner, Charleston, South Carolina, July 18, 1863. Returned to duty in September-October, 1863. Present or accounted for through December, 1864.

LIEUTENANTS

HAWES, REUBEN J. T., 3rd Lieutenant

Previously served as Sergeant in Company D, 13th

Battalion N.C. Infantry. Transferred to this company on April 15, 1862, with the rank of Sergeant. Appointed 3rd Lieutenant on August 1, 1863. Present or accounted for until wounded in the back and both legs and captured at Fort Harrison, Virginia, September 30, 1864. Left foot amputated. Reported in hospital at Fort Monroe, Virginia, until May 1, 1865, when he was released and furnished transportation to his home in North Carolina.

LITTLEJOHN, WILLIAM HERBERT, 1st Lieutenant
Previously served as acting Adjutant of the 21st, 26th, and 53rd Regiments N.C. Troops. Appointed 3rd Lieutenant of this company on May 29, 1863. Wounded in the right knee and left thigh at Fort Wagner, Charleston, South Carolina, July 18, 1863. Promoted to 1st Lieutenant on August 24, 1863. Returned to duty in September-October, 1863. Reported absent on detached service at Petersburg, Virginia, from January 28 through April 30, 1864. Rejoined the company prior to September 1, 1864. Reported absent sick in September-October, 1864. Returned to duty in November-December, 1864. Hospitalized at Greensboro on February 22, 1865, with catarrhus. Transferred to another hospital on February 23, 1865. No further records. [For an account of the distinguished part he played in driving a nest of Federal sharpshooters from their position near Fort Wagner on July 14, 1863, see the *Wilmington Journal* (Weekly) of August 13, 1863.]

McALLISTER, JOHN W., 2nd Lieutenant
Born in New Hanover County where he resided as a farmer prior to enlisting at age 25. Appointed 2nd Lieutenant on February 8, 1862. Reported present or accounted for through April, 1863. Reported present but under arrest on May 26, 1863. Dismissed from the service on August 24, 1863. Reason he was dismissed not reported. [Previously served as Captain in the 23rd Regiment N.C. Militia.]

SOUTHERLAND, WILLIAM J., 3rd Lieutenant
Previously served as Sergeant in Company D, 13th Battalion N.C. Infantry. Transferred to this company on April 15, 1862. Mustered in as Corporal. Promoted to Sergeant in September-October, 1862. Appointed 3rd Lieutenant on July 30, 1863. Present or accounted for until wounded in the left thigh at Drewry's Bluff, Virginia, May 16, 1864. Reported absent wounded through December, 1864. Paroled at Greensboro on April 28, 1865.

WALKER, WASHINGTON H., 3rd Lieutenant
Appointed 3rd Lieutenant on or about May 10, 1862. No further records.

NONCOMMISSIONED OFFICERS AND PRIVATES

ACKLEY, J. R., _____
Resided in Sampson County. Place and date of enlistment not reported. Paroled at Goldsboro on May 12, 1865.

ADAMS, JOSEPH, Private
Born in Robeson County and enlisted at Camp Holmes, near Wilmington, May 23, 1863, for the war. Present or accounted for until he deserted at Sullivan's Island, Charleston, South Carolina, on or about July 22, 1863. Apprehended on an unspecified date (probably in early November, 1863). Court-martialed on or about November 29, 1863. Reported absent under arrest through April, 1864. Returned to duty prior to June 1, 1864, when he was captured at Cold Harbor, Virginia. Confined at Point Lookout, Maryland, June 11, 1864. Transferred to Elmira, New York, July 12, 1864. Killed in a railroad accident at Shohola, Pennsylvania, July 15, 1864, while en route to Elmira.

ASTON, LEANDER, Private
Resided in Guilford County and was by occupation a farmer prior to enlisting at Camp Holmes, near Wilmington, at age 25, May 23, 1863, for the war. Captured at Petersburg, Virginia, on or about June 16, 1864. Confined at Point Lookout, Maryland, June 19, 1864. Transferred to Elmira, New York, July 9, 1864. Died at Elmira on December 3, 1864, of "pneumonia."

ATKINSON, THOMAS, Corporal
Previously served as Private in Company D, 13th Battalion N.C. Infantry. Transferred to this company on April 15, 1862. Mustered in as Private. Wounded slightly at Fort Wagner, Charleston, South Carolina, July 18, 1863. Returned to duty prior to September 1, 1863. Promoted to Corporal on January 1, 1864. Present or accounted for until wounded in the shoulder and captured at Fort Harrison, Virginia, September 30, 1864. Confined at Point Lookout, Maryland, October 5, 1864. Paroled at Point Lookout and transferred to Boulware's Wharf, James River, Virginia, March 19, 1865, for exchange. Took the Oath of Allegiance at Raleigh on May 31, 1865.

BAKER, RANDAL J., Private
Enlisted in New Hanover County on February 8, 1864, for the war. Present or accounted for until wounded in the right arm at Drewry's Bluff, Virginia, May 16, 1864. Hospitalized at Richmond, Virginia. Furloughed for sixty days on June 5, 1864. Returned to duty on or about August 4, 1864. Wounded in the right leg and left arm at Fort Harrison, Virginia, September 30, 1864. Right leg amputated. Hospitalized at Richmond. Furloughed for sixty days on December 14, 1864. Survived the war.

BEDWELL, ALFRED, _____
North Carolina pension records indicate that he served in this company.

BLACKWELL, LEVI, Private
Born in Bladen County where he resided as a farmer prior to enlisting in New Hanover County at age 16, April 11, 1862. Discharged on or about April 17, 1862, presumably by reason of being underage.

BLAYLUFF, M. M., Private
Enlisted at Camp Holmes, near Wilmington, May 21, 1863, for the war. Deserted on May 28, 1863.

BRINSON, JOHN, Private
Previously served as Private in Company D, 13th Battalion N.C. Infantry. Transferred to this company on April 15, 1862. Present or accounted for until captured near Globe Tavern, Virginia, August 19, 1864. Confined at Point Lookout, Maryland. Paroled at Point Lookout on March 14, 1865. Received at Boulware's Wharf, James River, Virginia, March 16, 1865, for exchange.

BROADHURST, JOHN C., Private
Born in New Hanover County and resided in Duplin County where he was by occupation a physician prior to enlisting in New Hanover County at age 39, March 15, 1862. Mustered in as Sergeant. Reduced to ranks in September-October, 1863. Present or accounted for through December, 1864. Reported on duty as a hospital nurse during most of the war.

BROTHERS, JOHN R., Private
Born in New Hanover County and was by occupation a farmer prior to enlisting at Burgaw at age 16, February 11, 1862. Present or accounted for until wounded in the left hand near Petersburg, Virginia, June 17, 1864. Returned to duty on June 28, 1864. Wounded at Petersburg on September 22, 1864. Hospitalized at Richmond, Virginia, where he died on or about September 24, 1864, of wounds.

BROWNING, SAMUEL J., Private
Previously served as Private in Company D, 13th Battalion N.C. Infantry. Transferred to this company on or about May 26, 1862. Reported absent sick almost continuously through May, 1863. Discharged on June 13, 1863, by reason of "old age, piles, also his eyes are at times so much inflamed as to almost deprive him of his sight."

BULLARD, DOGET, Private
Previously served as Private in Company A, 31st Regiment N.C. Troops. Transferred to this company on or about May 26, 1862. Failed to report for duty and was dropped from the rolls. [Service record omitted in the roster for Company A, 31st Regiment N.C. Troops, in Volume VIII of this series.]

BULLARD, WILLIAM H., Private
Enlisted at Camp Holmes, near Wilmington, May 21, 1863, for the war. Reported sick in hospital at Charleston, South Carolina, August 8, 1863. Furloughed for thirty days on or about August 18, 1863. Reported absent without leave on or about September 18, 1863. Returned to duty in March-April, 1864. Wounded in the thigh at Drewry's Bluff, Virginia, on or about May 15, 1864. Returned to duty in June, 1864. Wounded in the left side at Fort Harrison, Virginia, September 30, 1864. Reported absent wounded through December, 1864. Survived the war.

BYRD, JAMES F., Corporal
Previously served as Private in Company D, 13th Battalion N.C. Infantry. Transferred to this company on April 15, 1862, with the rank of Private. Promoted to Corporal on September 1, 1862. Present or accounted for until wounded while on picket (probably at or near Charleston, South Carolina) on or about October 9, 1863.

Furloughed for thirty days on or about October 19, 1863. Died on October 25, 1863, of wounds. Place of death not reported (probably Duplin County).

BYRD, TIMOTHY S., Private
Enlisted in Duplin County on April 16, 1864, for the war. Reported present in November-December, 1864.

BYRD, WILLIAM BENJAMIN, Private
Previously served as Private in Company D, 13th Battalion N.C. Infantry. Transferred to this company on April 15, 1862. Reported absent sick in March-June, 1863. Returned to duty in July-August, 1863. Reported absent on detached service as a nurse in September-October, 1863. Reported present but sick in November-December, 1863. Reported absent without leave for an unspecified period during January-February, 1864. Returned to duty in March-April, 1864. Wounded at Drewry's Bluff, Virginia, May 16, 1864. Returned to duty prior to September 30, 1864, when he was captured at Fort Harrison, Virginia. Confined at Point Lookout, Maryland, October 5, 1864. Paroled at Point Lookout and transferred to Boulware's Wharf, James River, Virginia, where he was received on March 19, 1865, for exchange.

CALK, HENRY, Private
Enlisted at Camp Holmes, near Raleigh, in January-April, 1864, for the war. Deserted on an unspecified date. Returned from desertion on October 10, 1864. Company records indicate that he deserted to the enemy on October 20, 1864; however, records of the Federal Provost Marshal do not substantiate that report. No further records.

CANFEL, JOHN, Private
Previously served as Private in Company D, 13th Battalion N.C. Infantry. Transferred to this company on April 15, 1862. Wounded in the left side (burn) at Fort Wagner, Charleston, South Carolina, July 18, 1863. Returned to duty prior to September 1, 1863. Present or accounted for until captured near Richmond, Virginia, October 8, 1864. Sent to Bermuda Hundred, Virginia. Confined at Point Lookout, Maryland, November 24, 1864. Released at Point Lookout on May 13, 1865, after taking the Oath of Allegiance.

CARMACK, SAMUEL, Private
Previously served as Private in Company D, 13th Battalion N.C. Infantry. Transferred to this company on April 15, 1862. Deserted prior to July 1, 1862. Reported present but under arrest in July-August, 1862. Returned to duty in September-October, 1862. Reported present or accounted for until April 10, 1864, when he was reported sick in hospital at Petersburg, Virginia. Reported absent without leave on July 24, 1864. Returned to duty on October 17, 1864. Reported present in November-December, 1864.

CARRIGAN, THOMAS W., Private
Enlisted in Orange County on May 18, 1863, for the war. Reported sick in hospital at Charleston, South Carolina, on or about August 18, 1863. Furloughed for thirty days on an unspecified date. Reported absent without leave on October 5, 1863. Returned to duty on January 23, 1864.

Reported sick in hospital at Petersburg, Virginia, April 9, 1864. Returned to duty prior to September 1, 1864. Reported present in September-October, 1864. Transferred to Company L, 17th Regiment N.C. Troops (2nd Organization), November 5, 1864.

CAVANESS, THOMAS, Private
Born in Chatham County and enlisted at Camp Holmes, near Wilmington, May 25, 1863, for the war. Reported present but sick in July-August, 1863. Reported sick in hospital at Charleston, South Carolina, September 15, 1863. Died in hospital (presumably at Charleston) on November 1, 1863. Cause of death not reported. [May have been assigned previously to 2nd Company D, 15th Regiment N.C. Troops (5th Regiment N.C. Volunteers).]

COWAN, HUGH M., Private
Born in New Hanover County and was by occupation a farmer prior to enlisting at Burgaw at age 44, February 11, 1862. Mustered in as Private. Appointed Musician in July-October, 1862. Reported absent sick at Wilmington from February 16 through April 30, 1863. Reduced to ranks in March-April, 1863. Discharged from service on June 8, 1863, by reason of "hemorage [sic] of the lungs, fistulas, and general debility."

CROOM, JUDSON W., 1st Sergeant
Born in New Hanover County where he resided as a farmer prior to enlisting in New Hanover County at age 18, February 8, 1862. Mustered in as Sergeant. Promoted to 1st Sergeant on October 31, 1863. Present or accounted for until captured at New Bern on February 3, 1864. Confined at Point Lookout, Maryland, February 27, 1864. Transferred to Elmira, New York, July 12, 1864. Released at Elmira on May 21, 1865, after taking the Oath of Allegiance.

CULBRETH, MARSHALL B., Private
Born in Sampson County in 1822 and resided in Sampson County where he was by occupation a farmer prior to enlisting on May 14, 1862, for the war. Served as a guard at the Fayetteville Arsenal from July 14, 1862, through August 31, 1863. Discharged on December 31, 1863, by reason of "double reducible hernia of two years duration."

DICKSON, MAJOR EVERITT, Private
Previously served as Private in Captain G. W. Cox's Company, Atlantic and North Carolina Railroad Bridge Guard. Transferred to this company on February 12, 1864. Captured at Petersburg, Virginia, on or about June 16, 1864. Confined at Point Lookout, Maryland, June 19, 1864. Transferred to Elmira, New York, July 27, 1864. Paroled at Elmira on October 11, 1864, and transferred to Point Lookout. Transferred to Venus Point, Savannah River, Georgia, where he was received on November 15, 1864, for exchange.

DuBOSE, JACOB W., Private
Born in New Hanover County and was by occupation a farmer prior to enlisting in New Hanover County at age 32, February 8, 1862. Present or accounted for until captured near Globe Tavern, Virginia, August 19, 1864. Confined at Point Lookout, Maryland, August 22, 1864.

Paroled at Point Lookout on or about October 30, 1864. Transferred to Venus Point, Savannah River, Georgia, for exchange; however, he died on board the U.S. Hospital Steamer *Baltic* on November 14, 1864, of "ch[ronic] diarrhoea" and was buried at Hilton Head, South Carolina.

EDWARDS, LEVI, Private
Enlisted at Camp Holmes, near Wilmington, May 8, 1863, for the war. Present or accounted for until he was reported missing in action at Fort Harrison, Virginia, September 30, 1864.

EDWARDS, WASHINGTON, Private
Born in Bladen County and was by occupation a student prior to enlisting in New Hanover County at age 16, February 11, 1862. Discharged (presumably by reason of being underage) prior to April 20, 1862. Died prior to December 17, 1864. Place, date, and cause of death not reported.

ENNIS, JAMES F., Sergeant
Previously served as Private in Company D, 13th Battalion N.C. Infantry. Transferred to this company on April 15, 1862. Mustered in as Private. Promoted to Sergeant on October 31, 1863. Wounded in the arm at Drewry's Bluff, Virginia, on or about May 15, 1864. Hospitalized at Richmond, Virginia. Furloughed for sixty days on June 3, 1864. Returned to duty on an unspecified date. Captured at Fort Harrison, Virginia, September 30, 1864. Confined at Point Lookout, Maryland, October 5, 1864. Paroled at Point Lookout on March 17, 1865. Received at Boulware's Wharf, James River, Virginia, March 19, 1865, for exchange.

EVANS, WILLIAM C., Private
Born in New Hanover County and was by occupation a farmer prior to enlisting in New Hanover County at age 35, February 19, 1862. Present or accounted for until discharged on June 13, 1863, by reason of "mental imbecility & epilepsy. . . ." Other discharge records state that he was unfit for duty owing to "old age & he is also subject to fits having had several since he has been in the company."

FARMER, MOSES B., Private
Previously served as Private in Company K, 66th Regiment N.C. Troops. Transferred to this company on February 12, 1864. Wounded at Drewry's Bluff, Virginia, May 16, 1864. Returned to duty prior to September 1, 1864. Present or accounted for through December, 1864. Paroled at Greensboro on May 1, 1865.

FORREST, SIDNEY, Private
Enlisted in Orange County on May 18, 1863, for the war. Reported absent sick in hospital at Charleston, South Carolina, August 1, 1863. Furloughed for thirty days on an unspecified date. Reported absent without leave on October 1, 1863. Returned to duty on February 1, 1864. Present or accounted for until hospitalized at Danville, Virginia, on or about June 1, 1864, with intermittent fever. Left the hospital at Danville without permission on June 16, 1864. Reported absent without leave through December, 1864. Paroled at Greensboro on May 16, 1865.

FULGUM, ROBERT L., Private
Previously served as Private in Company D, 13th Battalion N.C. Infantry. Transferred to this company on April 15, 1862. Present or accounted for through December, 1864.

FUTCH, JACOB, Private
Born in New Hanover County and was by occupation a farmer prior to enlisting at Burgaw at age 21, April 11, 1862. Reported absent without leave on October 30, 1862. Returned to duty in November-December, 1862. Reported absent under arrest on July 23, 1863. Reason he was arrested not reported. Reported sick in hospital at Charleston, South Carolina, on or about September 1, 1863. Furloughed for thirty days on an unspecified date. Reported absent without leave on or about October 1, 1863. Reported absent on detached service at brigade headquarters on or about December 1, 1863. Rejoined the company in January-February, 1864. Wounded in the left hand at Cold Harbor, Virginia, June 1, 1864. Returned to duty on or about December 24, 1864.

GARRISS, GEORGE W., Private
Enlisted in New Hanover County on July 14, 1862, for the war. Present or accounted for until captured at Cold Harbor, Virginia, June 1, 1864. Confined at Point Lookout, Maryland. Transferred to Elmira, New York, July 12, 1864. Paroled at Elmira and transferred to the James River, Virginia, on or about February 20, 1865, for exchange. Hospitalized at Richmond, Virginia, on or about March 10, 1865, with an unspecified complaint. Furloughed for sixty days on March 22, 1865.

GURGANIOUS, DAVID, Sergeant
Born in New Hanover County and was by occupation a farmer prior to enlisting in New Hanover County at age 26, February 8, 1862. Mustered in as Sergeant. Present or accounted for through February, 1863. Hospitalized at Charleston, South Carolina, on or about April 23, 1863. Died at Charleston on May 1, 1863, of "pneumonia."

GURGANIOUS, JOHN D., Private
Born in New Hanover County and was by occupation a farmer prior to enlisting in New Hanover County at age 41, March 11, 1862. Present or accounted for until hospitalized at Wilmington on or about August 20, 1862. Died in hospital at Wilmington on September 6, 1862, of "typhoid fever."

GUY, JOHN J., Private
Previously served as Private in Company D, 13th Battalion N.C. Infantry. Transferred to this company on April 15, 1862. Mustered in as Corporal. Reduced to ranks in September-October, 1862. Present or accounted for until captured at Cold Harbor, Virginia, June 1, 1864. Confined at Point Lookout, Maryland, June 11, 1864. Transferred to Elmira, New York, July 12, 1864. Released at Elmira on June 21, 1865, after taking the Oath of Allegiance.

HALL, JEREMIAH P., 1st Sergeant
Previously served as 1st Sergeant of Company D, 13th Battalion N.C. Infantry. Transferred to this company on April 15, 1862. Reported at home on sick leave in June-July, 1862. Died at Hallsville on August 10, 1862, of "consumption."

HARRELL, JOHN W. U., Private
Previously served as Sergeant in Company D, 13th Battalion N.C. Infantry. Transferred to this company on April 15, 1862. Mustered in as Private. Reported on detached duty as a hostler in April-August, 1862. Reported absent sick from October 17 through December 31, 1862. Returned to duty in January-February, 1863. Reported sick in hospital at Charleston, South Carolina, from August 20 through October 31, 1863. Reported absent without leave on December 5, 1863. Returned to duty prior to January 14, 1864. Wounded in the left hand at Fort Harrison, Virginia, September 30, 1864. Died in hospital at Richmond, Virginia, November 3, 1864, of wounds.

HARRELSON, AARON B., Private
Born in Columbus County and was by occupation a farmer prior to enlisting in New Hanover County at age 22, March 4, 1862. Present or accounted for until wounded slightly in the knee at Goldsboro on December 17, 1862. Transferred to Company G of this regiment in January, 1863.

HARVEY, HENRY, Private
Enlisted under an assumed name in New Hanover County on August 2, 1862, for the war. Present or accounted for until January-February, 1863, when he was discovered to be a deserter from a South Carolina artillery company. He was then turned over to his original company at Charleston, South Carolina.

HARVEY, WILLIAM, Private
Enlisted under an assumed name in New Hanover County on August 2, 1862, for the war. Deserted on September 11, 1862. Was later discovered to have been a deserter from a South Carolina artillery company at the time of his enlistment.

HERRING, JAMES E., Private
Born in New Hanover County and was by occupation a farmer prior to enlisting in New Hanover County at age 48, March 13, 1862. Present or accounted for until wounded in the neck at Cold Harbor, Virginia, May 31, 1864. Hospitalized at Richmond, Virginia. Furloughed for thirty days on June 7, 1864. Reported absent without leave on or about July 7, 1864. Hospitalized at Wilmington on September 12, 1864, with ulcus. Returned to duty on October 10, 1864. Reported sick in hospital at Greensboro in November-December, 1864.

HIGHSMITH, SAMUEL L., Private
Enlisted in New Hanover County on May 16, 1862, for the war. Present or accounted for until wounded slightly in the hip at Goldsboro on December 17, 1862. Hospitalized at Wilson. Reported in hospital at Wilson through February, 1863. Detailed as a hospital nurse at Charleston, South Carolina, on or about April 28, 1863. Rejoined the company in May-June, 1863. Reported present but sick in July-August, 1863. Returned to duty in September-October, 1863. Present or accounted for until wounded near Petersburg, Virginia, June 28, 1864.

Hospitalized at Richmond, Virginia (he was also suffering from chronic diarrhoea). Furloughed for thirty days on July 30, 1864. Reported absent wounded or absent sick through October, 1864. Reported absent on detached service in November-December, 1864. Paroled at Greensboro on May 1, 1865.

HINSON, ELIJAH, Private
Previously served as Private in Company D, 13th Battalion N.C. Infantry. Transferred to this company on April 15, 1862. Died at Fort Johnston, near Smithville (present-day Southport), July 12, 1862. Cause of death not reported.

HOLMES, EDWARD, Private
Born in 1843 and enlisted at Camp Holmes, near Wilmington, May 12, 1862, for the war. Present or accounted for until wounded at Fort Wagner, Charleston, South Carolina, July 18, 1863. Returned to duty in January-February, 1864. Present or accounted for until captured at Fort Harrison, Virginia, September 30, 1864. Confined at Point Lookout, Maryland. Paroled at Point Lookout on March 17, 1865. Transferred to Boulware's Wharf, James River, Virginia, where he was received on March 19, 1865, for exchange.

HOMAN, JOHN, Private
Born in New Hanover County where he resided as a farmer prior to enlisting in New Hanover County at age 49, February 12, 1862. Died at home in New Hanover County on April 27, 1862, of "pneumonia."

HOWEL, AARON, JR., Private
Born in Robeson County. Enlisted originally in Company A, 31st Regiment N.C. Troops, at age 22, April 13, 1862, but failed to report for duty with that unit. Transferred to this company where he also failed to report. Dropped from the company rolls on an unspecified date. [He is not listed in the roster for Company A, 31st Regiment N.C. Troops, in Volume VIII of this series. He is probably the soldier listed as A. Howell in the miscellaneous section for the 31st Regiment, Volume VIII, page 531.]

HUNT, CALVIN, Private
Previously served as Private in Company D, 13th Battalion N.C. Infantry. Transferred to this company on April 15, 1862. Present or accounted for through August, 1864. Reported absent sick in hospital at Richmond, Virginia, in September-December, 1864.

JONES, CALVIN, Private
Resided in Edgecombe County and enlisted at Camp Holmes, near Raleigh, February 4, 1864, for the war. Reported sick in hospital at Petersburg, Virginia, in May-August, 1864. Reported on duty as a hospital nurse at Petersburg in September-October, 1864. Rejoined the company in November-December, 1864. Paroled at Goldsboro on May 23, 1865.

JONES, ROBERT, _____
North Carolina pension records indicate that he served in this company.

KELLAHAN, ORREN, Private
Enlisted at Camp Holmes, near Wilmington, May 25, 1863, for the war. Present or accounted for until transferred to Company H of this regiment on January 1, 1864.

KENNEDY, JESSE THOMAS, _____
North Carolina pension records indicate that he served in this company.

KERR, MILTON, Private
Born in New Hanover County where he resided as a farmer prior to enlisting in New Hanover County at age 45, March 1, 1862. Present or accounted for through April, 1864; however, he was reported absent sick during most of that period. Captured at Cold Harbor, Virginia, June 1, 1864. Confined at Point Lookout, Maryland, June 11, 1864. Transferred to Elmira, New York, July 12, 1864. Died at Elmira on February 13, 1865, of "chronic diarrhoea."

KERR, WILLIAM D., Sergeant
Born in New Hanover County and was by occupation a farmer prior to enlisting at Camp Morgan, near Wilmington, at age 23, May 2, 1862, for the war. Mustered in as Private. Promoted to Corporal in September-October, 1862. Promoted to Sergeant on October 31, 1863. Present or accounted for until captured at Cold Harbor, Virginia, June 1, 1864. Confined at Point Lookout, Maryland, June 11, 1864. Transferred to Elmira, New York, July 12, 1864. Arrived at Elmira on July 17, 1864. Paroled at Elmira on March 2, 1865, and transferred to the James River, Virginia, for exchange. Hospitalized at Richmond, Virginia, March 9, 1865. Died in hospital at Richmond on March 17, 1865, of "debilitas."

KINION, JACOB, Private
Born in New Hanover County where he resided as a farmer prior to enlisting in New Hanover County at age 34, March 1, 1862. Present or accounted for until he died at home in New Hanover County on March 11, 1864. Cause of death not reported.

KINLAW, OLIVER, Private
Enlisted at Camp Holmes, near Wilmington, May 18, 1863, for the war. Present or accounted for through November, 1863. Hospitalized at Wilmington on December 5, 1863, with acute rheumatism. Deserted on December 24, 1863. Reported absent sick in February-August, 1864. Reported absent without leave from hospital at Wilmington in September-December, 1864.

LAWHORN, JOHN H., Corporal
Born in Duplin County and was by occupation a farmer prior to enlisting in New Hanover County at age 32, March 1, 1862. Mustered in as Private. Appointed Musician (Fifer) in July-August, 1862. Reduced to ranks in March-April, 1863. Promoted to Corporal on October 31, 1863. Present or accounted for until wounded in the left wrist near Petersburg, Virginia, on or about September 23, 1864. Hospitalized at Richmond, Virginia. Furloughed for sixty days on December 7, 1864.

LEWIS, ALFRED, Private
Born in New Hanover County and was by occupation a
cooper prior to enlisting in New Hanover County at age
47, February 8, 1862. Present or accounted for through
December, 1864.

LEWIS, HILLSMAN, Private
Previously served as Private in Company D, 13th
Battalion N.C. Infantry. Transferred to this company on
April 15, 1862. Present or accounted for until killed at
Bermuda Hundred, Virginia, May 22, 1864.

LEWIS, McTHOMAS, Private
Enlisted in camp on March 1, 1863, for the war. Present
or accounted for through December, 1864.

McPHALTER, ALEX, Private
Previously enlisted in Company A, 31st Regiment N.C.
Troops. Failed to report for duty with that unit.
Transferred to this company on April 13, 1862. Failed to
report for duty and was dropped from the company rolls
prior to July 1, 1862.

MALPASS, HANSON, Sergeant
Born in New Hanover County and was by occupation a
farmer prior to enlisting in New Hanover County at age
15, March 14, 1862. Mustered in as Private. Promoted to
Sergeant on October 31, 1863. Present or accounted for
through December, 1864. Survived the war.

MALPASS, OWEN M., Private
Born in New Hanover County and was by occupation a
farmer prior to enlisting in New Hanover County at age
16, March 1, 1862. Reported present but under arrest in
July-August, 1862. Reason he was arrested not reported.
Returned to duty in September-October, 1862. Present or
accounted for until captured at Cold Harbor, Virginia,
June 1, 1864. Confined at Point Lookout, Maryland, June
11, 1864. Transferred to Elmira, New York, July 12, 1864.
Died at Elmira on September 29, 1864, of "chronic
diarrhoea."

MALPASS, RICHARD T., Private
Born in New Hanover County and was by occupation a
farmer prior to enlisting in New Hanover County at age
32, March 1, 1862. Listed as a deserter in April-June,
1862. Reported present but under arrest in July-August,
1862. Discharged on September 27, 1862, after being
court-martialed. Enlisted in Company L, 17th Regiment
N.C. Troops (2nd Organization), April 14, 1863.
Transferred back to this company on November 5, 1864.
Hospitalized at Richmond, Virginia, December 7, 1864,
with chronic diarrhoea. Furloughed for sixty days on or
about January 26, 1865.

MATHIS, LOUIS H., Private
Enlisted at Camp Whiting, near Wilmington, January 8,
1863, for the war. Present or accounted for until wounded
in the right foot at Fort Wagner, Charleston, South
Carolina, July 18, 1863. Returned to duty prior to
September 1, 1863. Present or accounted for through
December, 1864. Paroled at Greensboro on May 1, 1865.

MATHIS, RICHARD, Private
Previously served as Private in Company D, 13th
Battalion N.C. Infantry. Transferred to this company on
April 15, 1862. Present or accounted for until killed near
Petersburg, Virginia, July 14, 1864.

MOORE, AMERICUS V., Private
Born in New Hanover County where he resided as a
farmer prior to enlisting in Harnett County at age 20,
February 25, 1862. Discharged prior to April 20, 1862.
Reason discharged not reported.

MOORE, CHARLES H., Corporal
Born in New Hanover County and was by occupation a
farmer prior to enlisting in New Hanover County at age
20, February 8, 1862. Mustered in as Private. Promoted
to Corporal on October 31, 1863. Captured at Cold
Harbor, Virginia, June 1, 1864. Confined at Point
Lookout, Maryland, June 11, 1864. Transferred to Elmira,
New York, July 12, 1864. Paroled on March 2, 1865,
and transferred to the James River, Virginia, for
exchange. Hospitalized at Richmond, Virginia, March 10,
1865, with debilitas. Furloughed for sixty days on March
16, 1865.

MOORE, JAMES A., Sergeant
Enlisted at Camp Holmes, near Wilmington, May 12,
1862, for the war. Mustered in as Private. Promoted to
Sergeant on May 8, 1863. Present or accounted for until
captured at Cold Harbor, Virginia, June 1, 1864.
Confined at Point Lookout, Maryland, June 11, 1864.
Transferred to Elmira, New York, July 12, 1864. Paroled
at Elmira on October 11, 1864. Died at Fort Monroe,
Virginia, October 31, 1864, while being transferred for
exchange. Cause of death not reported.

MOORE, LUTHER W., Private
Born in New Hanover County where he enlisted on March
31, 1863, for the war. Present or accounted for until
wounded at Drewry's Bluff, Virginia, May 16, 1864. Died
at Drewry's Bluff on May 17, 1864, of wounds.

MURRAY, SAMUEL, Private
Enlisted at Camp Holmes, near Wilmington, May 21,
1863, for the war. Present or accounted for until captured
at Fort Harrison, Virginia, September 30, 1864. Confined
at Point Lookout, Maryland, October 5, 1864. Died at
Point Lookout on December 27, 1864, of "acute
diarrhoea."

ORR, TURLEY W., Private
Born in New Hanover County and was by occupation a
farmer prior to enlisting in New Hanover County at age
48, March 14, 1862. Present or accounted for until
wounded in the right hip at or near Drewry's Bluff,
Virginia, on or about May 15, 1864. Hospitalized at
Richmond, Virginia. Furloughed for thirty days on
October 6, 1864. Reported absent without leave on or
about November 5, 1864.

PAGE, JOHN, Private
Enlisted at Camp Holmes, near Raleigh, February 8,
1864, for the war. Present or accounted for until

hospitalized at Wilmington on December 30, 1864, with anasarca. Furloughed for sixty days on January 13, 1865.

PETERSON, HENRY S., Private
Born in Sampson County where he resided as a farmer prior to enlisting at age 30 on or about April 26, 1862, for the war. Died in hospital at Wilmington on or about May 26, 1862, of "febris typhoides."

PHILLIPS, THOMAS, Private
Enlisted at Camp Holmes, near Wilmington, at age 30, May 23, 1863, for the war. Present or accounted for until he deserted at Sullivan's Island, Charleston, South Carolina, July 23, 1863. Listed as a deserter through December, 1863. Hospitalized at or near Richmond, Virginia, May 4, 1864, with intermittent fever. Reported sick in hospital or absent on furlough through October, 1864. Reported absent on detached service in November-December, 1864. Survived the war.

POOL, THOMAS, Private
Enlisted at Camp Holmes, near Wilmington, May 23, 1863, for the war. Deserted at Sullivan's Island, Charleston, South Carolina, July 23, 1863. Captured in hospital at Raleigh on April 13, 1865, by Federal forces. No further records.

PORTER, JAMES A., Private
Resided in Wayne County and was by occupation an overseer prior to enlisting in Wayne County at age 33, April 16, 1863, for the war. Present or accounted for until July 10, 1863, when he was reported absent without leave. Returned to duty on August 19, 1863, but was again reported absent without leave from December 3 through December 9, 1863. Court-martialed on an unspecified date. Released from arrest and return to duty in March-April, 1864. Present or accounted for through December, 1864. Paroled at Goldsboro on May 6, 1865.

PORTER, JAMES H., Private
Born in Cumberland County and resided in Wayne County where he was by occupation a farmer prior to enlisting at Camp Morgan, near Wilmington, at age 18, April 30, 1862, for the war. Present or accounted for until he was reported absent without leave on or about December 4, 1863. Returned to duty in January-February, 1864. Wounded in the arm (flesh) at or near Drewry's Bluff, Virginia, on or about May 14, 1864. Hospitalized at Richmond, Virginia. Furloughed for sixty days on May 22, 1864. Returned to duty prior to September 1, 1864. Captured at Fort Harrison, Virginia, September 30, 1864. Confined at Point Lookout, Maryland, October 5, 1864. Paroled at Point Lookout on or about February 13, 1865. Received at Cox's Wharf, James River, Virginia, on or about February 15, 1865, for exchange. Paroled at Goldsboro on May 6, 1865.

PREVO, W. HENRY B., Private
Enlisted at Camp Holmes, near Wilmington, May 23, 1863, for the war. Deserted at Sullivan's Island, Charleston, South Carolina, July 23, 1863.

QUINN, THOMAS F., Private
Born in Lincoln County and enlisted at Camp Holmes,

near Wilmington, May 24, 1863, for the war. Present or accounted for until hospitalized at Richmond, Virginia, March 4, 1864, with a gunshot wound of the left hand. Place and date wounded not reported. Died in hospital at Richmond on or about May 24, 1864, of "variola."

RACKLEY, JOSEPH R., Private
Previously served as Private in Company D, 13th Battalion N.C. Infantry. Transferred to this company on April 15, 1862. Present or accounted for through December, 1864. Paroled at Goldsboro on May 12, 1865.

RACKLEY, JOSHUA A., Private
Previously served as Private in Company D, 13th Battalion N.C. Infantry. Transferred to this company on April 15, 1862. Reported absent sick from October 11 through December 31, 1862. Returned to duty in January-February, 1863. Present or accounted for until January 16, 1864, when he was reported absent without leave. Returned to duty on February 14, 1864. Wounded in the right hand at or near Drewry's Bluff, Virginia, on or about May 14, 1864. Hospitalized at Richmond, Virginia. Furloughed for sixty days on May 22, 1864. Returned to duty in September-October, 1864. Reported absent without leave in November-December, 1864. Survived the war. [North Carolina pension records indicate that his left arm was injured at Drewry's Bluff (presumably on the same date that he was wounded in the right arm) when he was run over by an ambulance.]

REGISTER, CULLEN, _____
North Carolina pension records indicate that he served in this company.

ROAN, WILEY M., Private
Enlisted at Camp Holmes, near Wilmington, at age 35, May 21, 1863, for the war. Deserted at Sullivan's Island, Charleston, South Carolina, August 11, 1863.

ROBERTS, JOHN R., Private
Previously served as Private in Company D, 13th Battalion N.C. Infantry. Transferred to this company on April 15, 1862. Mustered in as Private. Promoted to Corporal on September 1, 1862. Present or accounted for until wounded accidentally at Sullivan's Island, Charleston, South Carolina, September 2, 1863. Sent to regimental hospital. Furloughed for sixty days on December 29, 1863. Reduced to ranks on January 1, 1864. Reported absent wounded through December, 1864. No further records.

ROWE, WILLIAM F., Private
Born in New Hanover County and was by occupation a farmer prior to enlisting in New Hanover County at age 24, March 1, 1862. Present or accounted for until wounded in the knee at Charleston, South Carolina, July 30-August 3, 1863. Returned to duty prior to September 1, 1863. Hospitalized at Wilmington on December 5, 1863, with ascites. Died in hospital at Wilmington on March 31, 1864, of "febris typhoides."

ROZIER, N. RUSSEL, Private
Enlisted at Camp Holmes, near Wilmington, May 23,

1863, for the war. Deserted at Sullivan's Island, Charleston, South Carolina, August 9, 1863. Returned to duty on November 12, 1863. Present or accounted for until wounded in both hips and captured at Fort Harrison, Virginia, September 30, 1864. Presumably died of wounds.

ROZIER, OLIVER, Private
Born in Robeson County and enlisted at Camp Holmes, near Wilmington, May 23, 1863, for the war. Hospitalized at Charleston, South Carolina, August 5, 1863, with an unspecified complaint. Furloughed for thirty days on an unspecified date. Reported absent without leave on October 13, 1863. Returned to duty on January 13, 1864. Died in hospital at Petersburg, Virginia, March 8, 1864, of "pneumonia."

SELLERS, GEORGE L., Private
Enlisted at Camp Holmes, near Wilmington, May 24, 1863, for the war. Reported present but sick in June, 1863. Sent on sick leave on July 10, 1863. Discharged "by the civil authority" in August, 1863. Reason he was discharged not reported.

SEWELL, THOMAS, Private
Previously served as Private in Company D, 13th Battalion N.C. Infantry. Transferred to this company on April 15, 1862. Discharged on July 7, 1862, by reason of "very feeble constitution and general debility. . . ." Other medical records indicate that he was "totally unfit to perform the duties of a soldier."

SIMMONS, ISAAC, Private
Born in Columbus County and was by occupation a farmer prior to enlisting in New Hanover County at age 19, April 1, 1862. Discharged on July 1, 1862. Reason discharged not reported. Later served in Company G of this regiment.

SMITH, JOHN, Private
Previously enlisted in Company A, 31st Regiment N.C. Troops. Failed to report for duty and was transferred to this company prior to June 1, 1862. Also failed to report for duty with this company and was dropped from the rolls prior to July 1, 1862.

SNYDER, WILLIAM H., Private
Place and date of enlistment not reported. Records of the Federal Provost Marshal indicate that he was captured in an ambulance near Petersburg, Virginia, August 19, 1864, and was sent to City Point, Virginia, the next day. No further records.

SOUTHERLAND, HUGH, Private
Enlisted in Duplin County at age 17, October 20, 1863, for the war. Present or accounted for through December, 1864. Paroled at Greensboro on May 1, 1865.

STOKES, AARON, Private
Enlisted at Camp Holmes, near Wilmington, May 25, 1863, for the war. Deserted at Sullivan's Island, Charleston, South Carolina, July 23, 1863.

STONE, J., Private
Previously enlisted in Company A, 31st Regiment N.C.

Troops, but failed to report for duty with that unit. Transferred to this company on April 15, 1862. Failed to report for duty and was dropped from the company rolls prior to July 1, 1862.

STRICKLAND, ISAAC, Private
Enlisted at Camp Holmes, near Raleigh, February 8, 1864, for the war. Present or accounted for through December, 1864.

THOMAS, JAMES, Private
Previously enlisted in Company A, 31st Regiment N.C. Troops, but failed to report for duty with that unit. Transferred to this company on or about April 13, 1862. Failed to report for duty and was dropped from the company rolls prior to July 1, 1862.

TROY, EDMOND, Private
Enlisted at Camp Vance on February 23, 1864, for the war. Deserted on or about April 25, 1864.

TURNER, EDWARD W., Private
Previously served as Private in Company H of this regiment. Transferred to this company on January 1, 1864. Present or accounted for until captured at Cold Harbor, Virginia, June 1, 1864. Confined at Point Lookout, Maryland, June 11, 1864. Transferred to Elmira, New York, July 12, 1864. Paroled at Elmira on or about February 20, 1865, and transferred to the James River, Virginia, for exchange.

TURNER, JOHN W., Private
Previously served as Private in Company D, 13th Battalion N.C. Infantry. Transferred to this company on April 15, 1862. Reported present but sick in July-August, 1862. Reported absent sick from September 17 through December 31, 1862. Returned to duty in January-February, 1863. Present or accounted for until hospitalized at Wilmington on or about July 20, 1863, with typhoid fever. Furloughed for thirty days on or about August 21, 1863. Returned to duty in September-October, 1863. Present or accounted for until hospitalized at Richmond, Virginia, in May-August, 1864. Returned to duty in November-December, 1864.

VANCANNON, JOHN W., Private
Born in Moore County and enlisted at Camp Holmes, near Wilmington, May 23, 1863, for the war. Present or accounted for until wounded at Drewry's Bluff, Virginia, May 16, 1864. Died at Richmond, Virginia, May 19, 1864, of wounds.

VANN, JOHN R., Private
Enlisted in Duplin County on February 13, 1863, for the war. Reported present but sick in March-April, 1863. Hospitalized at Wilmington on or about June 29, 1863, with debility. Returned to duty on July 23, 1863. Hospitalized at Charleston, South Carolina, August 13, 1863, with an unspecified complaint. Returned to duty in September-October, 1863. Present or accounted for until wounded in the forearm by the accidental discharge of a rifle on or about January 29, 1864. Arm amputated. Hospitalized at Petersburg, Virginia. Furloughed on or

about February 28, 1864. Retired to the Invalid Corps on October 7, 1864.

VANN, WILLIAM T., Private

Born in Sampson County where he resided as a farmer prior to enlisting in Sampson County at age 33, March 28, 1862. Mustered in as Corporal. Promoted to 1st Sergeant in September-October, 1862. Present or accounted for until reported sick in hospital at Charleston, South Carolina, August 15, 1863. Furloughed from hospital in September-October, 1863. Reported absent without leave on October 19, 1863. Reduced to ranks on October 31, 1863. Returned to duty on December 1, 1863. Detailed for unspecified duty at Petersburg, Virginia, January 28, 1864. Reported absent sick in the division hospital in May-August, 1864. Returned to duty in September-October, 1864. Reported present in November-December, 1864.

VICK, SAMUEL, Private

Previously served as Private in Company D, 13th Battalion N.C. Infantry. Transferred to this company on April 15, 1862. Present or accounted for until hospitalized at Wilmington on or about August 20, 1862, with "continued fever." Died in hospital at Wilmington on September 1, 1862.

WALKER, EDWARD J., Private

Born in New Hanover County and was by occupation a farmer prior to enlisting in New Hanover County at age 17, February 8, 1862. Present or accounted for until July 8, 1863, when he was reported absent without leave. Reported absent without leave through December, 1863. Dropped from the company rolls in January-February, 1864.

WALKER, MOSES, Private

Born in New Hanover County and was by occupation a cooper prior to enlisting in New Hanover County at age 49, February 8, 1862. Reported absent on detail guarding government stores at Fayetteville from July 14, 1862, through August, 1863. Rejoined the company in September-October, 1863. Discharged on December 31, 1863, by reason of "double reducible hernia of 2 years duration. . . ."

WALKER, SAMUEL J., Corporal

Born in New Hanover County and was by occupation a farmer prior to enlisting in New Hanover County at age 19, February 8, 1862. Mustered in as Corporal. Present or accounted for until wounded in the hip and left hand at Cold Harbor, Virginia, June 1, 1864. Reported absent wounded until January 7, 1865, when he was retired from service by reason of permanent disability from wounds.

WALLACE, JOHN P., Private

Previously served as Private in Company D, 13th Battalion N.C. Infantry. Transferred to this company on April 15, 1862. Present or accounted for through December, 1862. Reported on detail as a nurse in the smallpox hospital at Wilmington from January 15 through December 31, 1863. Reported absent on detached duty at Petersburg, Virginia, in January-February, 1864. Rejoined the company on an unspecified date. Wounded

accidentally in the left arm at Petersburg on or about May 23, 1864. Reported absent wounded through August, 1864. Reported on duty with the quartermaster's office at Magnolia in September-October, 1864. Reported absent in November-December, 1864, by reason of the accidental wound he received at Petersburg. Retired to the Invalid Corps on January 5, 1865.

WALTERS, THOMAS F., Private

Enlisted at Camp Holmes, near Wilmington, May 25, 1863, for the war. Deserted at Sullivan's Island, Charleston, South Carolina, on or about July 22, 1863.

WARD, JOSEPH, Musician

Born in New Hanover County and was by occupation a laborer prior to enlisting in New Hanover County at age 16, March 7, 1862. Mustered in as Musician (Drummer). Present or accounted for until reported absent without leave on or about August 28, 1862. Returned to duty prior to November 1, 1862. Reported absent without leave in November-December, 1862. Reported absent sick at Wilmington from January 20 through February 28, 1863. Returned to duty in March-April, 1863. Present or accounted for through December, 1864.

WELLS, JAMES H., Private

Enlisted at Camp Holmes, near Wilmington, May 28, 1863, for the war. Deserted the same date.

WEST, DAVID JAMES, Private

Previously served as Private in Company D, 13th Battalion N.C. Infantry. Transferred to this company on April 15, 1862. Killed at Fort Wagner, Charleston, South Carolina, July 18, 1863.

WILLIAMSON, WILLIAM, Private

Enlisted at Camp Holmes, near Wilmington, May 23, 1863, for the war. Wounded in the side at Fort Wagner, Charleston, South Carolina, July 30-August 3, 1863. Furloughed on August 27, 1863. Reported absent without leave from October 21, 1863, through February 29, 1864. Dropped from the rolls of the company in May-August, 1864.

WILTON, WILLIAM R., Private

Born in New Hanover County and was by occupation a farmer prior to enlisting in New Hanover County at age 48, March 1, 1862. Present or accounted for through April, 1864; however, he was reported absent sick during much of that period. Died in hospital at Petersburg, Virginia, May 1, 1864. Cause of death not reported.

WOOD, WILLIAM THOMAS, Private

Previously served as Private in Company G of this regiment. Transferred to this company in January, 1863. Present or accounted for until he deserted from hospital at Mount Pleasant, South Carolina, on or about October 1, 1863. Returned to duty in March-April, 1864. Captured at Cold Harbor, Virginia, June 1, 1864. Confined at Point Lookout, Maryland, June 11, 1864. Transferred to Elmira, New York, July 12, 1864. Paroled at Elmira on October 11, 1864. Received at Venus Point, Savannah River, Georgia, November 15, 1864, for exchange.

WOODCOCK, HANSON M., Private
Born in New Hanover County and was by occupation a farmer prior to enlisting in New Hanover County at age 19, March 15, 1862. Present or accounted for through January, 1863; however, he was reported absent sick during most of that period. Discharged on February 6, 1863, by reason of "paralysis."

WOODCOCK, NELSON, Private
Born in New Hanover County and was by occupation a farmer prior to enlisting in New Hanover County at age 16, March 15, 1862. Discharged on or about April 19, 1862, presumably by reason of being underage.

WOODCOCK, WILLIAM L., Private
Born in New Hanover County and was by occupation a farmer prior to enlisting in New Hanover County at age 19, March 1, 1862. Present or accounted for until hospitalized at Charleston, South Carolina, April 23, 1863, with an unspecified complaint. Furloughed from hospital on August 18, 1863. Returned to duty in January-February, 1864. Wounded in the left hip at Drewry's Bluff, Virginia, on or about May 16, 1864. Reported absent wounded or absent sick through August, 1864. Returned to duty prior to September 30, 1864, when he was wounded in the right shoulder at Fort Harrison, Virginia. Hospitalized at Richmond, Virginia. Furloughed for thirty-five days on October 3, 1864. Reported absent without leave on or about November 9, 1864.

ZAY, JAMES, Private
Born in Onslow County and was by occupation a laborer prior to enlisting in New Hanover County at age 16, March 17, 1862. Discharged on or about April 19, 1862, presumably by reason of being underage.

COMPANY B

This company, known as the "Warsaw Sampsons," was raised in Duplin and Sampson counties and enlisted in those counties in February-March, 1862. It was mustered into state service at Wilmington on April 2, 1862, and assigned to the 51st Regiment N.C. Troops as Company B. After joining the regiment the company functioned as a part of the regiment, and its history for the remainder of the war is reported as a part of the regimental history.

The information contained in the following roster was compiled primarily from a company muster-in and descriptive roll dated April 2, 1862, and from company muster rolls for April 2, 1862-February 29, 1864, and April 30-December 31, 1864. No company muster rolls were located for March 1-April 29, 1864, or for the period after December 31, 1864. Valuable information was obtained from primary records such as the North Carolina adjutant general's *Roll of Honor*, discharge certificates, medical records, prisoner of war records, *The War of the Rebellion: A Compilation of the Official Records of the Union and Confederate Armies*, militia records, newspaper casualty lists and obituaries, Confederate pension applications filed with the state of North Carolina, and the 1860 federal census of North Carolina. Secondary sources such as postwar rosters and histories, cemetery records, the *Confederate Veteran*, published genealogies, and records of the United Daughters of the Confederacy also provided useful information.

OFFICERS

CAPTAINS

HOBSON, CALEB B.
Born in Yadkin County* and resided in Duplin County where he was by occupation a merchant prior to enlisting in Duplin County at age 31. Appointed Captain on February 10, 1862. Present or accounted for until he was appointed Lieutenant Colonel on April 9, 1863, and transferred to the Field and Staff of this regiment. [Previously served as 2nd Lieutenant in the 26th Regiment N.C. Militia.]

BELL, WALTER R.
Born in Duplin County where he resided as a merchant prior to enlisting in Duplin County at age 32. Appointed 1st Lieutenant on February 15, 1862. Promoted to Captain on April 9, 1863. Present or accounted for until wounded in the left arm at Cold Harbor, Virginia, May 31, 1864. Left arm amputated. Reported absent wounded until he was retired to the Invalid Corps on November 4, 1864. Paroled at Goldsboro on May 9, 1865.

HERRING, THOMAS JAMES
Born in Sampson County and was by occupation a farmer prior to enlisting in Duplin County at age 20. Appointed 3rd Lieutenant on March 8, 1862. Promoted to 2nd Lieutenant on April 9, 1863. Wounded at Fort Wagner, Charleston, South Carolina, July 18, 1863. Returned to duty in September-October, 1863. Present or accounted for until wounded in the head at Cold Harbor, Virginia, June 1, 1864. Promoted to 1st Lieutenant on July 9, 1864. Promoted to Captain on November 4, 1864. Returned to duty in November-December, 1864. Paroled at Greensboro on May 10, 1865.

LIEUTENANTS

COWLES, CHARLES L., 2nd Lieutenant
Born in Connecticut and was by occupation a tailor prior to enlisting in Duplin County at age 33, February 17, 1862. Mustered in as Private. Promoted to Corporal on October 4, 1862. Reduced to ranks on April 9, 1863. Present or accounted for through October, 1863. Served as a tailor and as a clerk to the regimental adjutant during much of that period. Promoted to Sergeant Major on November 1, 1863, and transferred to the Field and Staff of this regiment. Appointed 2nd Lieutenant on July 26, 1864, and transferred back to this company. Present or accounted for through December, 1864.

McKETHAN, AUGUSTUS A., JR., 3rd Lieutenant
Previously served as Private in Company K of this regiment. Appointed 3rd Lieutenant on November 4, 1864, and transferred to this company. Present or accounted for through December, 1864. Paroled at Greensboro on May 1, 1865.

SMITH, JESSE T., 1st Lieutenant
Born in Sampson County where he resided as a clerk prior to enlisting in Duplin County at age 24, March 8, 1862. Mustered in as Sergeant. Appointed 2nd Lieutenant on April 9, 1863. Present or accounted for until wounded at Fort Wagner, Charleston, South Carolina, July 18, 1863. Returned to duty prior to September 1, 1863. Present or accounted for until captured at Cold Harbor, Virginia, June 1, 1864. Confined at Point Lookout, Maryland, June 11, 1864. Transferred to Fort Delaware, Delaware, June 23, 1864. Promoted to 1st Lieutenant on November 4, 1864, while a prisoner of war. Released at Fort Delaware on June 6, 1865, after taking the Oath of Allegiance.

SWINSON, JOHN E., 1st Lieutenant
Born in Duplin County where he resided as a railroad agent prior to enlisting in Duplin County at age 28. Appointed 2nd Lieutenant on March 8, 1862. Present or accounted for until wounded slightly in the face at Goldsboro on December 17, 1862. Returned to duty in March-April, 1863. Promoted to 1st Lieutenant on April 9, 1863. Present or accounted for until he was reported absent sick in hospital at Columbia, South Carolina, August 11, 1863. Reported absent sick until June 6, 1864, when he was dropped from the rolls of the company. Resigned on July 9, 1864. [Previously served as 1st Lieutenant in the 26th Regiment N.C. Militia.]

NONCOMMISSIONED OFFICERS AND PRIVATES

ARMSTRONG, EDWARD, Private
Born in Sampson County in 1827 and resided in Sampson County where he was by occupation a farmer prior to enlisting in Sampson County on February 18, 1862. Present or accounted for through June, 1863. Deserted in July-August, 1863. Apprehended prior to September 1, 1863, and was placed under arrest at Charleston, South Carolina. Court-martialed on or about November 5, 1863. Reported under arrest through December, 1863. Returned to duty in January-February, 1864. Present or accounted for through December, 1864.

ARMSTRONG, JOHN, Private
Born in Sampson County and was by occupation a cooper prior to enlisting in Duplin County at age 42, February 19, 1862. Present or accounted for until wounded at Charleston, South Carolina, September 18, 1863. Returned to duty prior to November 1, 1863. Present or accounted for until captured at Fort Harrison, Virginia, September 30, 1864. Confined at Point Lookout,

Maryland, where he died on December 10, 1864, of "chronic diarrhoea."

BELL, ELIAS, Private
Enlisted in Lenoir County on October 6, 1862, for the war. Reported for duty in November-December, 1862. Present or accounted for through August, 1864. Served as orderly in charge of the horses of the regimental officers during much of that period. Captured near Richmond, Virginia, October 7, 1864. Confined at Point Lookout, Maryland, October 29, 1864. Paroled at Point Lookout on or about February 10, 1865. Received at Cox's Wharf, James River, Virginia, February 14, 1865, for exchange. Hospitalized at Richmond on February 14, 1865, with an unspecified complaint. Furloughed on February 23, 1865.

BELL, FELIX, Private
Born in Sampson County and resided in Duplin County where he was by occupation a farmer prior to enlisting at Camp Morgan, near Wilmington, at age 28, April 28, 1862, for the war. Reported absent without leave in November-December, 1862. Reported sick at Camp Whiting, near Wilmington, February 17, 1863. Returned to duty in March-April, 1863. Present or accounted for until he was reported sick in the regimental hospital at Tarboro in November-December, 1863. Transferred to Company A, 2nd Regiment Confederate Engineer Troops, in January-February, 1864.

BELL, THOMAS, Private
Born in Sampson County in 1825 and was by occupation a farmer prior to enlisting in Sampson County on February 11, 1863, for the war. Present or accounted for until wounded in the abdomen at Drewry's Bluff, Virginia, May 14, 1864. Furloughed for sixty days on July 19, 1864. Retired to the Invalid Corps on November 15, 1864.

BEST, BENJAMIN S., Private
Born in Duplin County where he enlisted on April 23, 1862, for the war. Present or accounted for until wounded at Cold Harbor, Virginia, June 1, 1864. Died of wounds the same date.

BEST, WILLIAM R., Private
Resided in Duplin County where he enlisted on February 13, 1863, for the war. Wounded in the leg at Fort Harrison, Virginia, September 30, 1864. Returned to duty prior to November 1, 1864. Present or accounted for through January 4, 1865. Paroled at Goldsboro on May 24, 1865.

BLANCHARD, DAVID J., Corporal
Born in Duplin County and was by occupation a farmer prior to enlisting in New Hanover County at age 46, March 7, 1862. Mustered in as Private. Promoted to Corporal on August 26, 1864. Present or accounted for through December, 1864. Survived the war.

BOON, JOHN H., Private
Born in Duplin County where he resided as a farmer prior to enlisting in Duplin County at age 28, March 1, 1862.

Present or accounted for until wounded in the right leg (possibly also in the back and abdomen) and captured near Globe Tavern, Virginia, August 19, 1864. Confined at various Federal hospitals until confined at Old Capitol Prison, Washington, D.C., November 23, 1864. Transferred to Elmira, New York, December 16, 1864. Paroled at Elmira on March 10, 1865. Received at Boulware's Wharf, James River, Virginia, March 15, 1865, for exchange.

BOON, JOSEPH F., Private
Born in Duplin County and was by occupation a farmer prior to enlisting in Duplin County at age 15, March 17, 1862. Present or accounted for through February, 1864. Reported absent on detail as a hospital nurse at Richmond, Virginia, in May-August, 1864. Returned to duty prior to September 30, 1864, when he was wounded at Fort Harrison, Virginia. Reported absent wounded or absent sick through December, 1864.

BOWEN, GEORGE W., Private
Enlisted at Camp Morgan, near Wilmington, May 2, 1862, for the war. Wounded slightly (not hospitalized) in May-July, 1864. Present or accounted for until captured near Globe Tavern, Virginia, August 19, 1864. Confined at Point Lookout, Maryland, August 22, 1864. Paroled at Point Lookout on or about March 14, 1865. Received at Boulware's Wharf, James River, Virginia, March 16, 1865, for exchange.

BOYETTE, JOHN ANKRUM, Private
Born in Duplin County where he resided as a student prior to enlisting in Duplin County at age 15, March 17, 1862. Present or accounted for through December, 1863. Reported on duty as a provost guard at Petersburg, Virginia, in January-February, 1864. Wounded in the hand at Cold Harbor, Virginia, June 1, 1864. Returned to duty in September-October, 1864. Present or accounted for through December, 1864. Paroled at Goldsboro on May 8, 1865.

BRADSHAW, DANIEL J., Private
Born in Sampson County where he resided as a farmer prior to enlisting in New Hanover County at age 24, March 26, 1862. Reported present during July, 1862-January, 1863. Reported on detached duty building signal houses near Charleston, South Carolina, from February 23 through June 30, 1863. Reported on detail under Lieutenant Young "in charge of torpedoes" at Mount Pleasant, South Carolina, in July-October, 1863. Rejoined the company in November-December, 1863. Reported on duty as a provost guard at Petersburg, Virginia, in January-February, 1864. Captured at Cold Harbor, Virginia, May 31, 1864. Confined at Point Lookout, Maryland, June 8, 1864. Transferred to Elmira, New York, August 16, 1864. Paroled at Elmira on October 11, 1864, and transferred for exchange. Died in hospital at Baltimore, Maryland, October 26, 1864, of "chronic diarrhoea" before he could be exchanged.

BROCK, G. T., _____
Resided in Sampson County. Place and date of enlistment not reported. Paroled at Goldsboro on May 22, 1865.

BROWN, GEORGE W., Private
Born in Duplin County and was by occupation a shoemaker prior to enlisting in Duplin County at age 28, February 24, 1862. Reported absent sick from October 9 through December 31, 1862. Returned to duty in January-February, 1863. Wounded slightly (not hospitalized) in May-July, 1864. Present or accounted for until December 28, 1864, when he was reported absent without leave.

BROWN, JAMES ARTHUR, Private
Born in Sampson County in 1838 and was by occupation a shoemaker prior to enlisting in Sampson County on February 15, 1862. Present or accounted for until wounded seriously by a shell at Goldsboro on December 17, 1862. Hospitalized at Wilson. Returned to duty prior to March 1, 1863. Present or accounted for until captured at Cold Harbor, Virginia, June 1, 1864. Confined at Point Lookout, Maryland, June 11, 1864. Transferred to Elmira, New York, July 12, 1864. Died at Elmira on November 29, 1864, of "pneumonia."

BROWN, OWEN T., Private
Born in Sampson County in 1845 and was by occupation a farm laborer prior to enlisting in Sampson County on February 11, 1863, for the war. Present or accounted for through June, 1863. Reported sick in hospital at Charleston, South Carolina, in July-August, 1863. Hospitalized at Wilmington on September 29, 1863, with intermittent fever. Deserted on October 2, 1863. Returned to duty prior to November 1, 1863. Wounded slightly (not hospitalized) in May-July, 1864. Present or accounted for through December, 1864. Survived the war.

BRYANT, NICHOLAS F., Private
Born in Sampson County and was by occupation a carpenter prior to enlisting in Duplin County at age 23, March 3, 1862. Mustered in as Private. Promoted to Corporal prior to July 1, 1862. Reduced to ranks on October 14, 1862. Hospitalized at Goldsboro on October 28, 1862, with an unspecified complaint. Detailed to work on gunboats on December 5, 1862. Dropped from the rolls of the company in January-February, 1863. Survived the war.

CARLTON, HENRY J., Private
Enlisted on April 25, 1862, for the war. Present or accounted for through February, 1864. Wounded in the hand near Petersburg, Virginia, June 17, 1864. Reported absent wounded through August, 1864. Reported absent without leave on September 15, 1864. Returned to duty in November-December, 1864. Survived the war.

CARPENTER, JOE, _____
North Carolina pension records indicate that he served in this company.

CARROLL, JOHN C., Private
Previously served as Private in Company D, 13th Battalion N.C. Infantry. Transferred to this company on April 15, 1862. Present or accounted for through December, 1862; however, he was reported absent sick during much of that period. Died near Magnolia on January 4, 1863, of disease.

CARROLL, WILLIAM D., Corporal
Resided in Duplin County and enlisted at Camp Allen (probably near Kinston) at age 17, November 13, 1862, for the war. Mustered in as Private. Present or accounted for through December, 1864. Promoted to Corporal on August 26, 1864. Paroled at Goldsboro on May 22, 1865.

CARROLL, WILLIAM S., Private
Born in Sampson County and enlisted in Duplin County on May 24, 1862, for the war. Mustered in as Musician. Reduced to ranks on September 1, 1862. Appointed Musician on May 1, 1863. Again reduced to ranks in January-February, 1864. Present or accounted for until he died in hospital at Richmond, Virginia, August 8, 1864, of "chronic diarrhoea."

CHASE, WILLIAM H., Private
Born in Duplin County and resided in Sampson County where he was by occupation a laborer prior to enlisting in Duplin County at age 23, March 21, 1862. Present or accounted for until he was detached to work on signal houses near Charleston, South Carolina, from February 23 through April 30, 1863. Rejoined the company in May-June, 1863. Detailed with "commissary stores" at Mount Pleasant, South Carolina, in July-August, 1863. Rejoined the company in September-October, 1863. Present or accounted for until wounded in the hand at Cold Harbor, Virginia, June 1, 1864. Furloughed on June 6, 1864. Returned to duty in September-October, 1864. Reported absent without leave on December 28, 1864.

CHESNUTT, DANIEL H., Corporal
Enlisted at Camp Morgan, near Wilmington, April 28, 1862, for the war. Mustered in as Private. Promoted to Corporal on August 26, 1864. Present or accounted for until December 28, 1864, when he was reported absent without leave.

CHESNUTT, JACOB L., Private
Born in Sampson County where he resided as a farmer prior to enlisting at age 23, March 7, 1862. Reported on detached duty as a wagon driver at Kinston in September-October, 1862. Reported absent without leave in November-December, 1862. Returned to duty in January-February, 1863. Present or accounted for until he died in hospital at Wilmington on May 28, 1863, of "pneumonia" and "diphtheria."

CHESTNUTT, WILLIAM N., _____
Born in Sampson County and was by occupation a farmer prior to enlisting in Duplin County on March 29, 1862. Reported absent with leave on April 2, 1862. No further records.

COBB, JAMES, Private
Born in Sampson County where he resided as a shoemaker prior to enlisting in Sampson County at age 55, February 22, 1862. Present or accounted for through August, 1862. Sent to hospital at Goldsboro on October 23, 1862, with an unspecified complaint. Returned to duty in November-December, 1862. Reported present but sick in camp in January-April, 1863. Discharged on or about May 9, 1863, by reason of "chronic rheumatism which has distorted one of his feet. He has also [a] cataract in the left eye.

Private Cobb has been unfit for active military duty since he joined the regt and has for the last three or four months been constantly on the sick list."

DICKSON, CALVIN L., Private
Born in Duplin County and was by occupation a laborer prior to enlisting at Sullivan's Island, Charleston, South Carolina, August 7, 1863, for the war. Discharged on September 18, 1863, by reason of "mental and physical inability" including a "predisposition to scrofula" and "inguinal hernia of the right side. . . ." Discharge certificate gives his age as 27. Reenlisted in the company on October 2, 1864. Present or accounted for through December, 1864.

EZZELL, CHESNUTT J., Corporal
Born in Duplin County and was by occupation a farmer prior to enlisting in Duplin County at age 18, February 20, 1862. Mustered in as Private. Promoted to Corporal in March-May, 1864. Present or accounted for until wounded in the leg near Drewry's Bluff, Virginia, May 13, 1864. Leg amputated. Hospitalized at Richmond, Virginia, where he died on June 5, 1864, of "tetanus."

EZZELL, CURTIS H., Private
Born in Duplin County and was by occupation a laborer prior to enlisting in Duplin County at age 18, February 24, 1862. Present or accounted for through February, 1864. Reported on detached service with the Pioneer Corps in May-August, 1864. Wounded slightly (not hospitalized) on May 31, 1864. Reported absent sick at division hospital in September-October, 1864. Reported absent without leave on December 28, 1864.

EZZELL, ELISHA HENRY, Private
Born in Duplin County and was by occupation a farmer prior to enlisting in Duplin County at age 35, March 1, 1862. Present or accounted for until discharged on September 1, 1862, after furnishing Harris Howard as a substitute.

EZZELL, JOSEPH C., Private
Born in Duplin County and was by occupation a laborer prior to enlisting in Duplin County at age 20, February 24, 1862. Present or accounted for until wounded in the left arm at Cold Harbor, Virginia, June 1, 1864. Left arm amputated. Retired to the Invalid Corps on October 20, 1864.

EZZELL, LEWIS T., Private
Enlisted at Camp French, near Wilmington, June 25, 1862, for the war. Present or accounted for until wounded at Fort Wagner, Charleston, South Carolina, July 18, 1863. Hospitalized at Charleston where he died on August 19, 1863, of wounds.

EZZELL, LEWIS W., Private
Born in Duplin County and was by occupation a laborer prior to enlisting in Duplin County at age 27, February 20, 1862. Present or accounted for through June, 1863. Reported under arrest at Charleston, South Carolina, in July-August, 1863, for desertion. Court-martialed on or about November 5, 1863. Returned to duty in January-

February, 1864. Present or accounted for through December, 1864.

EZZELL, RABON J., Private
Born in Sampson County and was by occupation a laborer prior to enlisting in Duplin County at age 27, February 21, 1862. Present or accounted for until killed at Fort Wagner, Charleston, South Carolina, July 18, 1863.

EZZELL, WILLIAM W., Private
Born in Duplin County and was by occupation a shoemaker prior to enlisting in Duplin County at age 33, February 23, 1862. Present or accounted for through December, 1863. Reported under arrest in camp in January-February, 1864. Reason he was arrested not reported. Detailed for light duty in hospital at Richmond, Virginia, on or about February 24, 1864, by reason of "deformity in the legs" which had made him "unfit for military service since his first enlistment. . . ." Reported absent without leave on or about September 13, 1864. Returned to duty on November 9, 1864, and was detached for service in the quartermaster's department.

EZZELL, ZACHARIAH, Private
Born in Duplin County where he resided as a laborer prior to enlisting in Duplin County at age 17, February 24, 1862. Wounded slightly (not hospitalized) at Cold Harbor, Virginia, May 31, 1864. Present or accounted for until December 28, 1864, when he was reported absent without leave. Paroled at Goldsboro on May 8, 1865.

FISHER, J. G., _____
North Carolina pension records indicate that he served in this company.

FREDERICK, SIMON P., Private
Previously served as Private in 1st Company C, 12th Regiment N.C. Troops (2nd Regiment N.C. Volunteers). Enlisted in this company in Duplin County on March 8, 1862. Detailed for "permanent detached duty with the Signal Corps" on July 26, 1862, and ordered to report to Smithville (present-day Southport). Dropped from the rolls of the company in January-February, 1864.

FURMAGE, JOHN J., Private
Born in Bladen County and resided in Duplin County where he was by occupation a farmer prior to enlisting in New Hanover County at age 35, March 26, 1862. Present or accounted for until he deserted on November 1, 1862. Returned from desertion on June 1, 1863, and was placed under arrest. Returned to duty in July-August, 1863. Present or accounted for through February, 1864. Reported present but sick in quarters in May-August, 1864. Hospitalized at Richmond, Virginia, October 17, 1864, with an unspecified complaint (probably ascites). Furloughed for sixty days on December 24, 1864.

GAVIN, WILLIAM A., Private
Born in Duplin County and was by occupation a laborer prior to enlisting in Duplin County at age 18, March 1, 1862. Present or accounted for until transferred to Company B, 1st Battalion N.C. Heavy Artillery, June 1, 1863, in exchange for Private Kenan Merritt.

GAYLOR, JOHN B., Private
Previously served as Private in Company I, 9th Regiment N.C. State Troops (1st Regiment N.C. Cavalry). Transferred to this company on August 3, 1864. Present or accounted for through December, 1864. Took the Oath of Allegiance on April 8, 1865.

GAYLOR, LEWIS, Private
Born in Duplin County where he resided as a carpenter prior to enlisting at Camp Mangum, near Raleigh, at age 24, April 25, 1862, for the war. Present or accounted for until detailed to work in the government shops at Wilmington on February 7, 1863. Rejoined the company in March-April, 1863. Reported on detail at Wilmington working on gunboats from June, 1863, through October, 1864. Rejoined the company in November-December, 1864. No further records.

GOODRICH, GEORGE W., Private
Born in Sampson County where he resided as a farm laborer prior to enlisting at Camp Holmes, near Wilmington, at age 26, May 12, 1862, for the war. Present or accounted for until he died in hospital at Wilmington on January 17 or January 27, 1863, of "febris typhoides."

GOORE, ISAAC, JR., Private
Born in Duplin County where he resided as a miller prior to enlisting in Duplin County at age 48, February 19, 1862. Present or accounted for until he was sent to hospital at Goldsboro on October 23, 1862. Reported absent sick in November-December, 1862. Discharged on January 22, 1863, by reason of "rheumatism, old age, and consequent debility. He has never been able to drill or perform any duty. . . ."

GUY, ALEXANDER, Private
Born in Columbia, South Carolina, and resided in Duplin County where he was by occupation a cooper prior to enlisting in Duplin County at age 38, March 4, 1862. Present or accounted for until wounded in the shoulder at Drewry's Bluff, Virginia, May 16, 1864. Hospitalized at Richmond, Virginia, May 18, 1864. Furloughed for sixty days on May 31, 1864. Returned to duty prior to September 1, 1864. Wounded in the right thigh (fracture) and captured at Fort Harrison, Virginia, September 30, 1864. Right leg amputated. Hospitalized at Fort Monroe, Virginia, where he died on October 11 or October 19, 1864, of "pyaemia."

GUY, DAVID T., _____
Enlisted on January 15, 1865, for the war. No further records.

HARGROVE, ALVIN, Private
Born in Sampson County in 1826 and resided in Sampson County where he was by occupation a brickmason prior to enlisting in Sampson County at age 34, March 5, 1862. Present or accounted for until he was detached to work on signal houses near Charleston, South Carolina, February 23, 1863. Rejoined the company in May-June, 1863, and was sent to Wilmington for provisions. Reported present from July, 1863, through February, 1864. Wounded in the left hand at or near Drewry's Bluff, Virginia, May 14, 1864. Hospitalized at Richmond,

Virginia. Furloughed for sixty days on June 3, 1864. Returned to duty prior to September 1, 1864, and was detailed as an ambulance driver. Reported absent sick in September-December, 1864. Hospitalized at Wilmington on January 27, 1865, with ulcus. Returned to duty on January 30, 1865. Survived the war.

HARGROVE, BENJAMIN, JR., Private
Born in Sampson County where he resided as a wheelwright prior to enlisting in Sampson County at age 35, March 20, 1862. Present or accounted for until he was sent to hospital at Raleigh on September 17, 1862. Reported absent sick at Goldsboro in November-December, 1862. Rejoined the company in January-February, 1863. Present or accounted for until December 4, 1863, when he was reported absent without leave. Reported sick in hospital in Goldsboro in January-February, 1864. Returned to duty on an unspecified date. Wounded slightly (not hospitalized) in May-July, 1864. Reported absent without leave on December 28, 1864. Paroled at Goldsboro on May 23, 1865.

HARRELL, WILLIAM T., Private
Born in Martin County and was by occupation a laborer prior to enlisting in Sampson County at age 36, March 3, 1862. Present or accounted for until he died at Smithville (present-day Southport) on July 28, 1862, of disease.

HERRING, ISAAC W., Private
Born in Sampson County and resided in Duplin County where he was by occupation a farmer prior to enlisting in Sampson County at age 18, March 3, 1862. Reported on detail as a shoemaker in October, 1862. Wounded slightly (not hospitalized) in May-July, 1864. Present or accounted for until captured at Fort Harrison, Virginia, September 30, 1864. Confined at Point Lookout, Maryland, October 5, 1864. Paroled at Point Lookout on October 30, 1864. Received at Venus Point, Savannah River, Georgia, November 15, 1864, for exchange. Rejoined the company prior to January 1, 1865. Paroled at Goldsboro on May 22, 1865.

HOLLINGSWORTH, LEONARD W., Private
Born in Duplin County and resided in Sampson County where he was by occupation a farmer prior to enlisting in Duplin County at age 35, March 4, 1862. Present or accounted for until wounded at Drewry's Bluff, Virginia, May 16, 1864. Returned to duty prior to June 21, 1864, when he was killed by a sharp shooter "on the line" near Petersburg, Virginia.

HOWARD, HARRIS, Private
Born in Wayne County and resided in Duplin County where he was by occupation a farmer prior to enlisting in New Hanover County at age 62, September 1, 1862, for the war as a substitute for Private Elisha Henry Ezzell. Reported absent without leave on October 6, 1862. Died in hospital at Wilmington on or about December 8, 1862, of disease.

HOWARD, JOHN T., Private
Born in Duplin County and was by occupation a farmer prior to enlisting on December 23, 1863, for the war.

Reported present but under arrest in January-February, 1864. Reason he was arrested not reported. Detailed for light duty as a hospital nurse at Richmond, Virginia, on or about March 25, 1864. Reported absent on detail at Richmond through December, 1864. [Other records indicate that he had been nearsighted "from infancy." He "cannot see at all in the dark and cannot see well in the daytime till the object comes in close proximity. . . ." Was about 24 years of age at time of enlistment.]

JACKSON, JOSEPH G., Private
Born in Wayne County and was by occupation a distiller prior to enlisting at Camp Davis, near Wilmington, May 17, 1862, for the war. Present or accounted for through October, 1864; however, he was reported absent sick during most of that period. Discharged on November 28, 1864, by reason of "chronic articular rheumatism . . . causing great debility and emaciation of the general system [and] rendering locomotion very difficult. . . . [He is] unable to carry himself in an erect posture." Discharge certificate gives his age as 33. [Previously served as 2nd Lieutenant in the 26th Regiment N.C. Militia.]

JOHNSON, MITCHELL, Private
Born in Sampson County and was by occupation a farmer prior to enlisting at Camp Holmes, near Wilmington, at age 18, May 6, 1862, for the war. Present or accounted for through August, 1864; however, he was reported absent sick during most of that period. Discharged on September 25, 1864, by reason of "general dropsy, more especially of the abdomen and chest, and effusion into the pericardial sac. . . ."

JONES, STEPHEN, Private
Born in Sampson County in 1815 and was by occupation a cooper prior to enlisting in Sampson County on February 24, 1862. Present or accounted for until he died at Camp Campbell, near Kinston, October 19, 1862, of "disease of the throat."

JONES, WILLIAM, Private
Born in Greene County and was by occupation a farmer prior to enlisting in Duplin County at age 50, March 4, 1862. Present or accounted for through August, 1864; however, he was reported absent sick during much of that period. Wounded in the right thigh at Fort Harrison, Virginia, September 30, 1864. Hospitalized at Richmond, Virginia. Furloughed for sixty days on October 21, 1864. Reported absent without leave on or about December 20, 1864.

LANIER, BRYANT, Private
Enlisted in Duplin County on April 13, 1863, for the war. Present or accounted for through December, 1864; however, he was reported absent sick during much of that period.

LANIER, DAVID, Private
Born in Duplin County where he enlisted on February 13, 1863, for the war. Present or accounted for until captured at Cold Harbor, Virginia, June 1, 1864. Confined at Point Lookout, Maryland, June 11, 1864. Transferred to Elmira, New York, July 12, 1864. Injured in a railroad accident at

Shohola, Pennsylvania, July 15, 1864. Died at Elmira on August 29, 1864, of "hospital gangrene."

LANIER, STEPHEN, Private
Enlisted in Duplin County on September 30, 1864, for the war. Hospitalized at Wilmington on December 30, 1864, with pneumonia. Returned to duty on January 14, 1865.

McARTHUR, JOHN T., Sergeant
Born in Sampson County where he resided as a farmer prior to enlisting in Duplin County at age 19, March 8, 1862. Mustered in as Sergeant. Present or accounted for until wounded slightly at Fort Wagner, Charleston, South Carolina, July 18, 1863. Returned to duty in September-October, 1863. Present or accounted for through December, 1864. Paroled at Goldsboro on May 23, 1865

McARTHUR, WILLIAM A., Private
Born in Sampson County in 1842 and was by occupation a farmer prior to enlisting in Sampson County on March 17, 1862. Present or accounted for until July-August, 1863, when he was reported sick in hospital at Charleston, South Carolina. Returned to duty in September-October, 1863. Present or accounted for until captured at Fort Harrison, Virginia, September 30, 1864. Confined at Point Lookout, Maryland, October 5, 1864. Paroled at Point Lookout and transferred to Boulware's Wharf, James River, Virginia, where he was received on March 19, 1865, for exchange.

MERRITT, FRANCIS M., Private
Born in Sampson County in 1845 and was by occupation a student prior to enlisting in Sampson County on June 30, 1863, for the war. Reported absent sick in September-December, 1863. Reported absent without leave from January 4 through January 17, 1864. Wounded in the arm at Drewry's Bluff, Virginia, May 14, 1864. Reported absent in hospital through October, 1864. Reported absent without leave on December 28, 1864.

MERRITT, GEORGE W., Sergeant
Born in Duplin County where he resided as a farmer prior to enlisting in Duplin County at age 18, February 23, 1862. Mustered in as Private. Promoted to Corporal prior to July 1, 1862. Promoted to Sergeant in March-August, 1864. Wounded at Cold Harbor, Virginia, May 31, 1864. Returned to duty prior to September 30, 1864, when he was wounded in the thigh at Fort Harrison, Virginia. Returned to duty prior to December 31, 1864. Paroled at Goldsboro on May 8, 1865.

MERRITT, ISAAC, Private
Born in Duplin County and was by occupation a carpenter prior to enlisting in Duplin County at age 43, March 11, 1862. Present or accounted for until he died in hospital at Richmond, Virginia, August 5, 1864, of "chronic diarrhoea."

MERRITT, JAMES THOMAS, _____
North Carolina pension records indicate that he served in this company.

MERRITT, KENAN, Private
Previously served as Private in Company B, 1st Battalion

N.C. Heavy Artillery. Transferred to this company on June 1, 1863, in exchange for Private William A. Gavin. Present or accounted for until transferred to Company A, 2nd Regiment Confederate Engineers, in January-February, 1864.

MERRITT, MORDECAI M., Private
Resided in Duplin County where he enlisted on February 14, 1863, for the war. Present or accounted for through November, 1864. Hospitalized at Wilmington on December 30, 1864, with remittent fever. Transferred to hospital at Greensboro on January 17, 1865. Returned to duty on January 25, 1865. Paroled at Goldsboro on May 8, 1865.

MERRITT, PAYTON, Private
Born in Sampson County in 1825 and was by occupation a farmer prior to enlisting in Duplin County on March 29, 1862. Wounded slightly at Goldsboro on December 17, 1862. Returned to duty in February, 1863. Present or accounted for until killed at Fort Wagner, Charleston, South Carolina, July 18, 1863.

MERRITT, RICHARD, Private
Born in Duplin County and was by occupation a ditcher prior to enlisting in Duplin County at age 43, February 17, 1862. Present or accounted for through October, 1862. Reported absent sick in November, 1862-April, 1863. Discharged on May 19, 1863, by reason of "rheumatismus."

MERRITT, THOMAS W., Private
Born in Sampson County and was by occupation a farmer prior to enlisting in Sampson County at age 36, March 5, 1862. Mustered in as Private. Appointed Musician prior to July 1, 1862. Reduced to ranks on September 1, 1862. Present or accounted for until wounded in the hand at Drewry's Bluff, Virginia, on or about May 14, 1864. Returned to duty prior to September 1, 1864. Present or accounted for through December, 1864.

MERRITT, WILLIAM JAMES, Private
Born in Sampson County and was by occupation a farmer prior to enlisting in Duplin County at age 21, February 18, 1862. Present or accounted for until December 4, 1863, when he was reported absent without leave. Returned to duty in January-February, 1864. Present or accounted for until wounded in the leg and captured at Cold Harbor, Virginia, June 1, 1864. Confined at Point Lookout, Maryland, June 11, 1864. Transferred to Elmira, New York, July 12, 1864. Paroled at Elmira on February 20, 1865, and transferred to the James River, Virginia, for exchange.

MILLER, ROBERT J., Private
Born in Duplin County where he resided as a farmer prior to enlisting in Duplin County at age 32, February 15, 1862. Present or accounted for until captured at Cold Harbor, Virginia, June 1, 1864. Confined at Point Lookout, Maryland, June 11, 1864. Transferred to Elmira, New York, July 12, 1864. Paroled at Elmira on October 11, 1864, and transferred to Point Lookout. Died at Point Lookout on October 22, 1864, of "chronic diarrhoea."

MOORE, J., Private
Resided in Duplin County. Place and date of enlistment not reported (probably enlisted in January-April, 1865). Paroled at Goldsboro on May 11, 1865.

MURPHY, WILLIAM F., Private
Previously served as 1st Sergeant of Company I, 20th Regiment N.C. Troops (10th Regiment N.C. Volunteers). Later served as a Drillmaster. Enlisted in this company in Sampson County on March 5, 1862. Appointed 1st Lieutenant and transferred to Company K of this regiment on March 17, 1862. Later served as Captain of Company K.

PAGE, W., Private
Place and date of enlistment not reported. Listed on a regimental record dated June, 1862. No further records.

PARKER, DANIEL W., Private
Resided in Sampson County and was by occupation a cooper prior to enlisting at age 39, October 20, 1864, for the war. Reported absent on detached service in the quartermaster's department in November-December, 1864. No further records.

PARKER, LARKIN NEWBY, Private
Born in Sampson County where he resided as a farmer prior to enlisting in Sampson County at age 32, March 3, 1862. Mustered in as Sergeant. Present or accounted for until captured near Globe Tavern, Virginia, August 19, 1864. Confined at Point Lookout, Maryland, August 22, 1864. Reduced to ranks on August 26, 1864, while a prisoner of war. Paroled at Point Lookout on February 13, 1865. Received at Cox's Wharf, James River, Virginia, on or about February 15, 1865, for exchange.

PARKER, NICHOLAS, Corporal
Born in Sampson County where he resided as a farmer prior to enlisting in Sampson County at age 38, March 5, 1862. Mustered in as Private. Promoted to Corporal on April 9, 1863. Present or accounted for until wounded in the leg at Drewry's Bluff, Virginia, May 16, 1864. Hospitalized at Richmond, Virginia, where he died on or about June 4, 1864, of wounds.

PARKER, WILLIAM L., Corporal
Born in Sampson County and resided in Duplin County where he was by occupation a farmer prior to enlisting in Duplin County at age 30, March 1, 1862. Mustered in as Corporal. Appointed acting Commissary Sergeant on June 4, 1862, and transferred to the Field and Staff of this regiment. Promoted to the permanent rank of Commissary Sergeant on June 23, 1862.

PATTERSON, JOHN O., Private
Resided in Duplin County and enlisted at Camp Holmes, near Wilmington, May 15, 1862, for the war. Wounded slightly (not hospitalized) at Cold Harbor, Virginia, June 5, 1864. Present or accounted for through December, 1864. Paroled at Hillsborough on May 8, 1865.

PATTERSON, WILLIAM J., _____
Resided in Duplin County and enlisted at Camp Holmes,

near Wilmington, May 12, 1862, for the war. Present or accounted for through December, 1864. Paroled at Goldsboro on May 8, 1865.

PEEL, MARK, Private
Resided in Wilson County. Place and date of enlistment not reported (probably enlisted in January-April, 1865). Paroled at Goldsboro on May 11, 1865.

PHILLIPS, ABSALOM, Private
Born in Duplin County where he resided as a farmer prior to enlisting at Camp Holmes, near Wilmington, at age 27, May 15, 1862, for the war. Present or accounted for until November-December, 1862, when he was reported absent without leave. Discharged on February 9, 1863, by reason of "phthisis."

PIPKIN, STEPHEN I., Private
Born in Sampson County where he resided as a farmer prior to enlisting in Sampson County at age 37, March 29, 1862. No further records.

POLLOCK, ALFRED C., Private
Born in Duplin County where he resided as a laborer prior to enlisting in Duplin County at age 18, March 13, 1862. Mustered in as Private. Appointed Musician on September 1, 1862. Reduced to ranks in March-April, 1863. Present or accounted for until captured near Globe Tavern, Virginia, August 19, 1864. Confined at Point Lookout, Maryland, August 24, 1864. Paroled at Point Lookout on October 11, 1864. Received at Cox's Wharf, James River, Virginia, October 15, 1864, for exchange. Reported absent without leave on November 28, 1864. Paroled at Goldsboro on May 12, 1865.

POLLOCK, LUKE, Private
Born in Duplin County and was by occupation a millwright prior to enlisting in Duplin County at age 57, March 19, 1862. Present or accounted for until discharged on April 13, 1864, by reason of disability.

POWELL, WILEY, Private
Born in Duplin County where he resided as a farmer prior to enlisting in Duplin County at age 28, March 2, 1862. Present or accounted for until wounded in the hip (flesh) at Drewry's Bluff, Virginia, May 16, 1864. Hospitalized at Richmond, Virginia. Furloughed for sixty days on May 22, 1864. Reported sick in hospital at Goldsboro in August-October, 1864. Returned to duty in November-December, 1864. Survived the war.

POWELL, WILLIAM, Private
Born in Sampson County and was by occupation a farmer prior to enlisting in Duplin County at age 40, March 4, 1862. Present or accounted for until he died in hospital at Petersburg, Virginia, June 30, 1864, of "pneumonia."

RACKLEY, SHERMAN, Private
Born in Sampson County where he resided as a laborer prior to enlisting in Sampson County at age 39, March 3, 1862. Present or accounted for until wounded in the hand at Drewry's Bluff, Virginia, May 16, 1864. Returned to duty prior to September 1, 1864. Present or accounted for through December, 1864.

RACKLEY, WILLIAM E., Private

Born in Sampson County on March 15, 1841, and was by occupation a mechanic prior to enlisting in Duplin County on March 13, 1862. Wounded slightly (not hospitalized) at Cold Harbor, Virginia, May 31, 1864. Present or accounted for through December, 1864. Survived the war. [North Carolina pension records indicate that he was wounded in the shoulder in Virginia in July, 1863.]

REGISTER, BURRELL M., Private

Enlisted in Duplin County on August 23, 1863, for the war. Present or accounted for until wounded in the right thigh and captured at Cold Harbor, Virginia, June 1, 1864. Right leg amputated. Hospitalized at Washington, D.C., where he died on June 15, 1864, of wounds. Federal medical records give his age as 18.

REGISTER, GEORGE R., Private

Born in Sampson County where he resided as a farm laborer prior to enlisting in Duplin County at age 34, March 3, 1862. Present or accounted for until detailed at Sullivan's Island, Charleston, South Carolina, "overseeing Negroes" from September 21 through November 30, 1863. Present or accounted for from December 1, 1863, until June 1, 1864, when he was captured at Cold Harbor, Virginia. Confined at Point Lookout, Maryland, June 16, 1864. Transferred to Elmira, New York, July 12, 1864. Paroled at Elmira on March 14, 1865. Received at Boulware's Wharf, James River, Virginia, on or about March 18, 1865, for exchange.

REGISTER, SAMUEL R., Private

Born in Sampson County and enlisted in New Hanover County at age 38, February 14, 1863, for the war. Present or accounted for until wounded by a shell in the trenches near Petersburg, Virginia, July 5, 1864. Died at the brigade hospital on July 6, 1864, of wounds.

RIVENBARK, DANIEL J., Private

North Carolina pension records indicate that he served in this company.

SANDERSON, ISAAC, Private

Resided in Duplin County and was by occupation a laborer prior to enlisting in Duplin County at age 30, April 24, 1862, for the war. Present or accounted for until captured at Petersburg, Virginia, June 16, 1864. Confined at Point Lookout, Maryland, June 19, 1864. Transferred to Elmira, New York, July 9, 1864. Released at Elmira on June 14, 1865, after taking the Oath of Allegiance.

SANDLIN, HIRAM L., Sergeant

Born in Duplin County and was by occupation a farmer prior to enlisting in Duplin County at age 23, March 21, 1862. Mustered in as Sergeant. Present or accounted for through February, 1864; however, he was reported sick in camp during much of that period. Transferred to 2nd Company I, 10th Regiment N.C. State Troops (1st Regiment N.C. Artillery), March 3, 1864, by reason of "diseased feet which make him incapable of marching. . . . [He] is a good [and] able soldier and willing to do his duty . . . but cannot do service in [the] infantry. . . ."

SELLERS, DAVID G., Private

Born in Sampson County and was by occupation a farmer prior to enlisting on December 23, 1863, for the war. Reported absent without leave from January 10 until January 22, 1864. Present or accounted for until discharged on February 23, 186[5], by reason of "chronic bronchitis." Discharge certificate gives his age as 35.

SMITH, ALBERT O., Private

Born in Sampson County and was by occupation a farmer prior to enlisting in Sampson County at age 20, March 8, 1862. Present or accounted for until wounded in the leg at Goldsboro on December 17, 1862. Leg amputated. Hospitalized at Goldsboro where he died on January 8, 1863, of wounds.

SMITH, AMOS J., Private

Born in Sampson County in 1847 and resided in Duplin County where he was by occupation a student prior to enlisting near Charleston, South Carolina, March 1, 1863, for the war. Present or accounted for until captured at Petersburg, Virginia, June 16, 1864. Confined at Point Lookout, Maryland, June 18, 1864. Transferred to Elmira, New York, July 9, 1864. Released at Elmira on July 3, 1865, after taking the Oath of Allegiance.

SMITH, DAVID J., Private

Previously served as Private in 1st Company C, 12th Regiment N.C. Troops (2nd Regiment N.C. Volunteers). Enlisted in this company in Sampson County on March 3, 1862. Mustered in as Corporal. Reduced to ranks on July 1, 1862. Present or accounted for until wounded slightly in the thigh at Drewry's Bluff, Virginia, May 14, 1864. Wounded at Cold Harbor, Virginia, May 31, 1864. Returned to duty prior to September 30, 1864, when he was wounded in the side at Fort Harrison, Virginia. Hospitalized at Richmond, Virginia. Returned to duty in November-December, 1864. Paroled at Greensboro on May 1, 1865.

SMITH, LEWIS H., Private

Born in Sampson County in 1844 and resided in Sampson County where he was by occupation a farmer prior to enlisting in Wayne County on January 21, 1864, for the war. Discharged on or about March 19, 1864, by reason of being "ill-grown and unhealthy." Paroled at Goldsboro on May 19, 1865.

SPRINGS, JACOB, Private

Born in Sampson County and was by occupation a farm hireling prior to enlisting in Sampson County at age 24, February 22, 1862. Present or accounted for through March, 1863; however, he was reported absent sick during most of that period. Discharged on April 22, 1863, by reason of "consumption" and "rheumatism." Other medical records indicate that he was "unable to walk without crutches, his limbs are wasting away, his appitite [sic] poor, his tongue red and shining, very anemic, and in short he shows all signs of a feeble [and] shattered constitution."

STRICKLAND, CALVIN M., Corporal

Enlisted at Camp Morgan, near Wilmington, at age 31, April 25, 1862, for the war. Mustered in as Private.

Wounded slightly (not hospitalized) in May-July, 1864. Promoted to Corporal on August 26, 1864. Present or accounted for until wounded in the right leg and captured at Fort Harrison, Virginia, September 30, 1864. Confined at Point Lookout, Maryland, October 5, 1864. Paroled at Point Lookout on March 17, 1865. Received at Boulware's Wharf, James River, Virginia, March 19, 1865, for exchange. Survived the war.

STRICKLAND, JEREMIAH, Private
Enlisted at Camp Davis, near Wilmington, May 29, 1862, for the war. Reported on duty as company cook in May-October, 1864. Present or accounted for through December, 1864.

STRICKLAND, JOSIAH, Private
Born in Duplin County and enlisted on December 23, 1863, for the war. Died in hospital at Petersburg, Virginia, March 27, 1864, of "pneumonia."

STRICKLAND, WILLIAM H., Private
Resided in Bladen County and enlisted in Duplin County on February 13, 1863, for the war. Present or accounted for through December, 1864. Paroled at Greensboro on May 1, 1865.

SUTTON, MICHAEL WESLEY, Private
Previously served as Private in Company A, 30th Regiment N.C. Troops. Enlisted in this company at Clinton on March 5, 1862. Present or accounted for until wounded in the back and side and captured at Cold Harbor, Virginia, June 1, 1864. Hospitalized at White House, Virginia. Transferred to hospital at Davids Island, New York Harbor, where he arrived on June 15, 1864. Transferred to Elmira, New York, October 9, 1864. Released at Elmira on June 19, 1865, after taking the Oath of Allegiance.

THEMEGLEY, T. F., Private
Resided in Wayne County. Place and date of enlistment not reported; however, he probably enlisted in January-April, 1865. Paroled at Goldsboro on an unspecified date in 1865.

THORNTON, THOMAS J., Sergeant
Enlisted in Duplin County on March 6, 1862. Mustered in as Private. Wounded slightly in the shoulder at Goldsboro on December 17, 1862. Returned to duty prior to January 1, 1863. Promoted to Corporal on May 17, 1863. Wounded at Fort Wagner, Charleston, South Carolina, July 18, 1863. Returned to duty in November-December, 1863. Promoted to Sergeant on August 26, 1864. Present or accounted for through December, 1864. Hospitalized at Raleigh on April 6, 1865. No further records.

TUCKER, A., _____
Place and date of enlistment not reported; however, he probably enlisted in January-April, 1865. Paroled at Petersburg, Virginia, July 29, 1865.

TUCKER, CALVIN, Sergeant
Born in Duplin County where he resided as a cooper prior to enlisting in Duplin County at age 25, March 8, 1862. Mustered in as Corporal. Promoted to Sergeant on May 17, 1863. Present or accounted for until wounded by "Yankee sharpshooters" near Petersburg, Virginia, July 11, 1864. Died at the brigade hospital on July 12, 1864, of wounds.

TUCKER, KILBY, Private
Born in Duplin County where he resided as a laborer prior to enlisting in Duplin County at age 28, February 15, 1862. Present or accounted for until captured at Petersburg, Virginia, June 16, 1864. Confined at Point Lookout, Maryland, June 19, 1864. Transferred to Elmira, New York, July 9, 1864. Released at Elmira on July 11, 1865, after taking the Oath of Allegiance.

TUCKER, WILLIAM, Private
Born in Duplin County and was by occupation a laborer prior to enlisting in Duplin County at age 44, February 15, 1862. Present or accounted for until he was killed by a shell on July 1, 1864, while serving in the trenches near Petersburg, Virginia.

TURNIDGE, JOHN JAMES, _____
North Carolina pension records indicate that he served in this company.

WADE, ARETOS I., Sergeant
Resided in Duplin County and was by occupation a farmer prior to enlisting in Duplin County at age 31, April 21, 1862, for the war. Mustered in as Private. Promoted to Corporal on April 9, 1863. Present or accounted for until wounded at Fort Wagner, Charleston, South Carolina, July 18, 1863. Returned to duty prior to September 1, 1863. Wounded slightly (not hospitalized) in May-July, 1864. Promoted to Sergeant on August 26, 1864. Present or accounted for through December, 1864. Survived the war.

WALL, T. J., _____
Enlisted in February, 1865, for the war. No further records.

WATERS, BENAJAH, Private
Born in Sampson County and was by occupation a farmer prior to enlisting in New Hanover County at age 32, March 7, 1862. Mustered in as Private. Appointed Musician on September 1, 1862. Reduced to ranks in March-April, 1863. Present or accounted for until wounded in the right shoulder at Drewry's Bluff, Virginia, May 14, 1864. Hospitalized at Richmond, Virginia. Furloughed for sixty days on May 23, 1864. Returned to duty in November-December, 1864. Survived the war.

WATERS, MATTHEW J., Private
Born in Sampson County and was by occupation a laborer prior to enlisting in Sampson County at age 27, March 3, 1862. Present or accounted for through May, 1863. Reported absent sick from June 29 through October 31, 1863. Returned to duty in November-December, 1863. Present or accounted for until wounded in the hand at Petersburg, Virginia, June 16, 1864. Reported absent without leave on September 22, 1864.

WATSON, BENJAMIN, Private

Enlisted on October 20, 1864, for the war. Present or accounted for through December, 1864. Captured at Kinston (may have been a deserter) on March 19, 1865. No further records.

WEST, THADDEUS L., Private

Born in Duplin County and was by occupation a laborer prior to enlisting in Duplin County at age 24, February 21, 1862. Present or accounted for until killed at Drewry's Bluff, Virginia, May 16, 1864.

WHITFIELD, GEORGE W., Private

Born in Sampson County and was by occupation a farmer prior to enlisting in New Hanover County at age 23, March 7, 1862. Deserted on November 1, 1862. Returned "of his own accord" and was imprisoned at Petersburg, Virginia, to await trial. Died in hospital at Petersburg on May 24, 1864, of "febris typhoides."

WILEY, JAMES, Private

Enlisted at Camp Holmes, near Wilmington, May 12, 1862, for the war. Reported on detached duty working on gunboats at Wilmington from June 27 through December, 1864.

WILLIAMS, ROBERT K., Private

Previously served as Private in 1st Company C, 12th Regiment N.C. Troops (2nd Regiment N.C. Volunteers). Enlisted in this company in Duplin County on March 6, 1862. Appointed 1st Lieutenant of Company A, Mallett's N.C. Battalion (Camp Guard), on or about November 1, 1862.

WILLIAMSON, JASPER B., Private

Born in Sampson County and resided in Wayne County where he was by occupation a farm laborer prior to enlisting in Duplin County at age 18, March 21, 1862. Present or accounted for until captured at Cold Harbor, Virginia, June 1, 1864. Confined at Point Lookout, Maryland, June 11, 1864. Transferred to Elmira, New York, July 12, 1864. Paroled at Elmira on January 17, 1865. Received at Boulware's Wharf, James River, Virginia, January 21, 1865, for exchange. Hospitalized at Richmond, Virginia, on January 21, 1865, with chronic diarrhoea and debility. Furloughed for sixty days on January 26, 1865. Survived the war.

WILLIAMSON, JESSE R., 1st Sergeant

Born in Sampson County and resided in Duplin County where he was by occupation a carpenter prior to enlisting in Duplin County at age 26, March 6, 1862. Mustered in as 1st Sergeant. Present or accounted for through October, 1862. Reported absent sick in November-December, 1862, and from February 15 through April 30, 1863. Returned to duty in May-June, 1863. Present or accounted for until captured at Fort Harrison, Virginia, September 30, 1864. Confined at Point Lookout, Maryland, October 5, 1864. Paroled at Point Lookout on February 18, 1865. Received at Boulware's Wharf, James River, Virginia, on or about February 20, 1865, for exchange. Survived the war.

WILLIAMSON, PAGE, Private

Resided in Sampson County and enlisted in Duplin County at age 19, May 21, 1862, for the war. Present or accounted for through August, 1863. Reported absent sick in September-December, 1863. Returned to duty in January-February, 1864. Present or accounted for through December, 1864. Paroled at Goldsboro on May 24, 1865.

WILSON, JOHN J., Private

Resided in Duplin County where he enlisted on April 29, 1862, for the war. Present or accounted for until he died at home in Duplin County on or about July 15, 1863, of "typhoid fever."

WOOD, FREDERICK A., Private

Born in Onslow or Duplin County and was by occupation a farmer prior to enlisting in Duplin County at age 31, February 23, 1862. Mustered in as Corporal. Wounded in the thigh by a shell at Goldsboro on December 17, 1862. Returned to duty in January-February, 1863. Reduced to ranks on April 9, 1863. Appointed Musician on May 1, 1863. Reduced to ranks in July-August, 1863. Present or accounted for until wounded at Cold Harbor, Virginia, June 1, 1864. Hospitalized at Richmond, Virginia. Furloughed for sixty days on June 17, 1864. Died "at home" on July 6, 1864, of wounds.

WOOD, WILLIAM M., Private

Enlisted at Camp Hill, near Petersburg, Virginia, May 1, 1864, for the war. Present or accounted for through December, 1864.

COMPANY C

This company, known as the "Duplin Stars," was raised in Duplin County and enlisted in Duplin County in February-March, 1862. It was mustered into state service at Wilmington on April 8, 1862, and assigned to the 51st Regiment N.C. Troops as Company C. After joining the regiment the company functioned as a part of the regiment, and its history for the remainder of the war is reported as a part of the regimental history.

The information contained in the following roster was compiled primarily from a company muster-in and descriptive roll dated April 8, 1862, and from company muster rolls for April 30, 1862-February 29, 1864, and April 30-December 31, 1864. No company muster rolls were located for April 9-29, 1862; March 1-April 29, 1864; or for the period after December 31, 1864. Valuable information was obtained from primary records such as the North Carolina adjutant general's *Roll of Honor*, discharge certificates, medical records, prisoner of war records, *The War of the Rebellion: A Compilation of the Official Records of the Union and Confederate Armies*, militia records, newspaper casualty lists and obituaries, Confederate pension applications filed with the state of North Carolina, and the 1860 federal census of North Carolina. Secondary sources such as postwar rosters and histories, cemetery records, the *Confederate Veteran*, published genealogies, and records of the United Daughters of the Confederacy also provided useful information.

OFFICERS

CAPTAINS

ALLEN, WILLIAM A.
Previously served as 2nd Lieutenant of 1st Company C, 12th Regiment N.C. Troops (2nd Regiment N.C. Volunteers). Appointed Captain of this company on February 11, 1862. Appointed Lieutenant Colonel on April 30, 1862, and transferred to the Field and Staff of this regiment.

STANFORD, SAMUEL M.
Born in Duplin County where he resided as a lawyer prior to enlisting in Duplin County at age 23. Appointed 1st Lieutenant on February 11, 1862. Promoted to Captain on April 30, 1862. Present or accounted for until September-October, 1863, when he was reported absent on sick furlough. Reported absent without leave from December 14 until December 27, 1863. Reported present in January-February, 1864. Reported absent sick in May-August, 1864. Resigned on September 19, 1864. Reason he resigned not reported; however, the colonel commanding the 51st Regiment commented on his resignation as follows: "This officer is totally inefficient as a company commander. The interest of his company & the good of the service will be materially promoted by accepting his resignation."

WATSON, EDWARD L.
Previously served as Private in 1st Company C, 12th Regiment N.C. Troops (2nd Regiment N.C. Volunteers). Enlisted in this company in Duplin County on February 14, 1862. Mustered in as Sergeant. Appointed 3rd Lieutenant on May 13, 1862. Present or accounted for until wounded at Drewry's Bluff, Virginia, May 16, 1864. Returned to duty prior to September 1, 1864. Promoted to Captain on September 19, 1864. Present or accounted for through December, 1864. Paroled at Greensboro on May 1, 1865.

LIEUTENANTS

BRANCH, JAMES G., 1st Lieutenant
Born in Duplin County where he resided as a farmer prior to enlisting in Duplin County at age 39. Elected 2nd Lieutenant on February 15, 1862. Promoted to 1st Lieutenant on April 30, 1862. Wounded slightly at Goldsboro on December 17, 1862. Reported absent on recruiting service in Duplin County on February 9, 1863. Returned to duty in March-April, 1863. Present or accounted for until he resigned on December 23, 1863, because "my personal attention is required at home on account of the very painfull [sic] affliction of my wife." He was also reported to be suffering from an "inguinal hernia of the left side and chronic nephritis. . . ." Resignation accepted on January 21, 1864.

HOUSTON, HIRAM V., 1st Lieutenant
Previously served as Private in 1st Company C, 12th Regiment N.C. Troops (2nd Regiment N.C. Volunteers). Enlisted in this company in Duplin County on February 14, 1862. Mustered in as 1st Sergeant. Reduced to the rank of Sergeant in May-June, 1863. Appointed 3rd Lieutenant on January 26, 1864. Reported on duty as acting commander of Company E of this regiment in September-October, 1864. Promoted to 1st Lieutenant on November 4, 1864. Present or accounted for through December, 1864. Paroled at Greensboro on May 1, 1865.

JAMES, ROBINSON C., 1st Lieutenant
Born in Sampson County where he resided as a teacher and farmer prior to enlisting at age 28. Appointed 3rd Lieutenant on February 15, 1862. Promoted to 1st Lieutenant on January 21, 1864. Present or accounted for until wounded in the right arm at Cold Harbor, Virginia, June 1, 1864. Right arm amputated. Retired to the Invalid Corps on November 4, 1864.

SULLIVAN, ANDREW McI., 2nd Lieutenant
Born in Duplin County and was by occupation a student prior to enlisting in Duplin County at age 17, March 7, 1862. Mustered in as Corporal. Promoted to Sergeant in January-February, 1863. Reduced to ranks in May-June, 1863. Reported on duty as General Thomas L. Clingman's orderly in July-December, 1863. Promoted to Sergeant on February 1, 1864. Appointed 2nd Lieutenant on September 30, 1864. Present or accounted for through December, 1864. Wounded at Kinston in March, 1865.

NONCOMMISSIONED OFFICERS AND PRIVATES

ALBERTSON, PETER H., Private
Born in Duplin County where he resided as a grocer prior to enlisting in Duplin County at age 49, March 3, 1862. Present or accounted for through January, 1863. Reported absent on sick furlough from February 12 through April 30, 1863. Reported on detail as a hospital nurse at Wilmington in May-August, 1863. Detailed as a hospital nurse at Charleston, South Carolina, in September-October, 1863. Reported absent sick from November, 1863, through August, 1864. Reported absent without leave in September-December, 1864.

ALPHIN, DANIEL J., Private
Born in Duplin County where he resided as a farmer prior to enlisting in Duplin County at age 36, March 19, 1862. Reported absent sick in July-October, 1862. Discharged on December 14, 1862. Reason discharged not reported. Reenlisted in the company on an unspecified date (probably in May-June, 1864). Wounded in the chest near Petersburg, Virginia, in June, 1864. Hospitalized at Petersburg where he died on June 24, 1864, of wounds.

ALPHIN, WILLIAM, Private
Born in Duplin County where he resided as a farmer prior to enlisting in Duplin County at age 60, March 3, 1862. Present or accounted for through June, 1862. Reported

absent sick in July-October, 1862. Granted a discharge on December 14, 1862, by reason of "rheumatismus chr[onic]"; however, he had died in Duplin County on November 3, 1862. Cause of death not reported.

ATWOOD, JOEL P., Private
Born at Hartford, Connecticut, and resided in Duplin County where he was by occupation a merchant prior to enlisting in Duplin County at age 17, February 26, 1862. Mustered in as Sergeant. Promoted to Sergeant Major on September 1, 1862, and transferred to the Field and Staff of this regiment. Reduced to ranks and transferred back to this company on February 20, 1863. Reported on detached service with General Thomas L. Clingman's staff in March-April, 1863. Rejoined the company in May-June, 1863. Present or accounted for until killed at Drewry's Bluff, Virginia, May 15, 1864.

BASS, E. C., _____
North Carolina pension records indicate that he served in this company.

BLANTON, MOSES, Private
Born in Sampson County where he resided as a farmer prior to enlisting in Duplin County at age 34, March 29, 1862. No further records.

BOSTICK, DANIEL, Private
Enlisted in Duplin County at age 17, April 21, 1862, for the war. Present or accounted for through December, 1864. Survived the war.

BOSTICK, DANIEL J., Private
Previously served as Private in Company D, 13th Battalion N.C. Infantry. Transferred to this company on April 15, 1862. Present or accounted for until captured at Cold Harbor, Virginia, June 1, 1864. Confined at Point Lookout, Maryland, June 11, 1864. Transferred to Elmira, New York, July 12, 1864. Released at Elmira on July 3, 1865, after taking the Oath of Allegiance.

BOSTICK, DAVID R., Private
Previously served as Private in Company D, 13th Battalion N.C. Infantry. Transferred to this company on April 15, 1862. Present or accounted for until wounded in the finger at Drewry's Bluff, Virginia, on or about May 16, 1864. Finger amputated. Hospitalized at Richmond, Virginia. Furloughed for sixty days on June 3, 1864. Returned to duty in September-October, 1864. Present or accounted for through December, 1864. Paroled at Greensboro on May 1, 1865.

BOSTICK, ELIJAH, Private
Enlisted in Duplin County on March 30, 1863, for the war. Killed at Fort Wagner, Charleston, South Carolina, July 18, 1863.

BOWDEN, WILLIAM B., Sergeant
Born in Duplin County where he resided as a farmer prior to enlisting in Duplin County at age 25, February 15, 1862. Mustered in as Private. Promoted to Sergeant on April 30, 1862. Present or accounted for until wounded slightly at Fort Wagner, Charleston, South Carolina, July

18, 1863. Returned to duty in September-October, 1863. Wounded at Cold Harbor, Virginia, May 31, 1864. Returned to duty prior to September 1, 1864. Present or accounted for through December, 1864. Paroled at Goldsboro on May 23, 1865.

BRANCH, THOMAS, Private
Born in New Hanover County and was by occupation a farmer prior to enlisting in Duplin County at age 42, February 15, 1862. Present or accounted for until he deserted on May 29, 1863.

CAISON, LEWIS, Private
Born in Sampson County and was by occupation a farmer prior to enlisting in New Hanover County at age 28, March 6, 1862. Present or accounted for through December, 1864.

CAISON, WILLIAM B., Private
Previously served as Private in Company C, 63rd Regiment N.C. Troops (5th Regiment N.C. Cavalry). Transferred to this company on November 25, 1863, in exchange for Private Thomas Ezzell. Reported absent without leave through December, 1863. Reported on guard duty at Petersburg, Virginia, in January-February, 1864. Reported present in April-December, 1864. Survived the war.

CARROLL, ROBERT J., Private
Enlisted in Duplin County on April 19, 1862, for the war. Present or accounted for until killed at Fort Wagner, Charleston, South Carolina, July 18, 1863.

CARTER, LEONARD H., Private
Born in Sampson County and was by occupation a farmer prior to enlisting in New Hanover County at age 20, March 10, 1862. Present or accounted for until he died on October 18, 1863. Place and cause of death not reported.

CHESNUTT, JOHN K., Private
Previously served as Private in Company D, 13th Battalion N.C. Infantry. Transferred to this company on April 15, 1862. Present or accounted for until killed at Sullivan's Island, Charleston, South Carolina, September 1, 1863.

CHESTNUTT, D. J., Private
Resided in Sampson County and enlisted in Wake County at age 44, October 16, 1864, for the war. Present or accounted for through December, 1864.

CHESTNUTT, G. FRANKLIN, Private
Born in Duplin County and was by occupation a farmer prior to enlisting in New Hanover County at age 17, March 10, 1862. Present or accounted for through December, 1864. Survived the war.

CHESTNUTT, NICHOLAS P., Private
Born in Sampson County in 1820 and resided in Sampson County where he was by occupation a farmer prior to enlisting in Wake County on October 16, 1864, for the war. Present or accounted for through December, 1864. Survived the war.

COTTLE, W. HENRY, Private
Enlisted at Camp Whiting, near Wilmington, at age 17, February 16, 1863, for the war. Present or accounted for until wounded in the thigh at Fort Harrison, Virginia, September 30, 1864. Hospitalized at Richmond, Virginia. Furloughed for sixty days on November 21, 1864. Survived the war.

CROSSLAND, SABASTIAN T., Private
Previously served as Sergeant in Company A, 35th Regiment N.C. Troops. Transferred to this company on January 17, 1864, in exchange for Corporal John E. Hussey. Mustered in as Private. Present or accounted for through October, 1864. Reported absent under arrest at Richmond, Virginia, in November-December, 1864. Reason he was arrested not reported. Hospitalized at Salisbury on January 11, 1865, with an unspecified complaint. Returned to duty on February 5, 1865. No further records.

CUMMINGS, JAMES M., Private
Born in Duplin County and was by occupation a farmer or mechanic prior to enlisting in Duplin County at age 49, February 24, 1862. Present or accounted for until hospitalized at Wilmington on May 4, 1863, with debilitas. Discharged from service on October 22, 1863, by reason of "chronic rheumatism producing permanent contraction of the muscles of the leg."

DAIL, JULIUS V., Private
Enlisted in New Hanover County on April 15, 1862. Hospitalized at Wilmington on July 31, 1862, with typhoid fever. Returned to duty on August 12, 1862. Present or accounted for through December, 1864. Paroled at Greensboro on May 1, 1865.

DAIL, LEMUEL L., Private
Resided in Duplin County and was by occupation a farmer and turpentine worker prior to enlisting in New Hanover County at age 37, April 15, 1862. Present or accounted for until hospitalized at Petersburg, Virginia, June 30, 1864, with debilitas. Transferred to hospital at Richmond, Virginia, on or about July 1, 1864. Died in hospital at Richmond on July 22, 1864, of "gastritis."

DAIL, THOMAS F., Private
Enlisted in New Hanover County on May 12, 1862, for the war. Present or accounted for until wounded at or near Petersburg, Virginia, on or about June 17, 1864. Reported absent wounded until December 19, 1864, when he was retired to the Invalid Corps.

DAIL, W. M., Private
Enlisted in Wayne County on April 13, 1864, for the war. Present or accounted for through December, 1864. Paroled at Greensboro on May 1, 1865.

EZZELL, THOMAS, Private
Born in Sampson County and was by occupation a farmer prior to enlisting in New Hanover County at age 25, March 5, 1862. Present or accounted for until transferred to Company C, 63rd Regiment N.C. Troops (5th Regiment N.C. Cavalry), November 25, 1863, in exchange for Private William B. Caison.

FEADWELL, W. C., Private
Enlisted on December 12, 186[4], for the war. Present or accounted for through December, 1864.

FIELDS, WILLIAM B., Private
Previously served as Private in Company D, 13th Battalion N.C. Infantry. Transferred to this company on April 15, 1862. Present or accounted for until captured near Globe Tavern, Virginia, August 19, 1864. Confined at Point Lookout, Maryland, August 22, 1864. Apparently he arrived at Point Lookout under an assumed name and was exchanged under that name on an unspecified date. Company records do not indicate whether he returned to duty; however, he was captured by the enemy at Goldsboro on March 22, 1865. Took the Oath of Allegiance at Goldsboro on March 23, 1865.

FUSSELL, WILLIAM H., Corporal
Born in Duplin County and was by occupation a farmer prior to enlisting in Duplin County at age 19, March 19, 1862. Mustered in as Private. Promoted to Corporal on February 1, 1864. Present or accounted for until captured near Globe Tavern, Virginia, August 19, 1864. Confined at Point Lookout, Maryland, August 24, 1864. Paroled at Point Lookout on February 13, 1865. Received at Cox's Wharf, James River, Virginia, on or about February 15, 1865, for exchange.

GARNER, FRANCIS M., Private
Born in Duplin County where he resided as a farmer prior to enlisting in Duplin County at age 20, February 15, 1862. Present or accounted for until wounded in the leg at Fort Wagner, Charleston, South Carolina, July 18, 1863. Leg amputated. Reported absent wounded through August, 1864.

GARNER, SIMEON, Private
Resided in Duplin County and was by occupation a farmer prior to enlisting in New Hanover County at age 32, April 15, 1862. Hospitalized at Wilmington on August 25, 1862, with typhoid fever. Returned to duty on September 5, 1862. Present or accounted for through October, 1864. Reported absent without leave in November-December, 1864. Paroled at Greensboro on May 1, 1865.

GAUM, DANIEL H., Private
Place and date of enlistment not reported (probably enlisted in January-April, 1865). Paroled at Greensboro on May 1, 1865.

GRADY, D., Private
Place and date of enlistment not reported (probably enlisted in January-April, 1865). Paroled at Greensboro on or about April 29, 1865.

GRADY, FREDERICK, Private
Enlisted in New Hanover County on April 15, 1862. Present or accounted for until discharged on October 10, 1862. Reason discharged not reported.

GRADY, WILLIAM HENRY, Sergeant
Born in Duplin County and was by occupation a student prior to enlisting in Duplin County at age 19, March 17,

1862. Mustered in as Corporal. Promoted to Sergeant in May-June, 1863. Present or accounted for until wounded at Drewry's Bluff, Virginia, May 14, 1864. Returned to duty in November-December, 1864. Hospitalized at Greensboro on March 9, 1865, with a gunshot wound. Place and date wounded not reported (probably wounded at Kinston, March 7-8, 1865). Paroled at Greensboro on April 29, 1865.

GROVES, GEORGE F., Private
Born in Sampson County and was by occupation a farmer prior to enlisting in New Hanover County at age 18, March 10, 1862. Present or accounted for until killed at Fort Wagner, Charleston, South Carolina, July 18, 1863.

HALL, EDWARD JAMES, Sergeant
Previously served as Corporal in Company D, 13th Battalion N.C. Infantry. Transferred to this company on April 15, 1862. Mustered in as Private. Promoted to Sergeant on May 13, 1862. Present or accounted for until wounded in the groin and buttocks at Drewry's Bluff, Virginia, May 14, 1864. Hospitalized at Richmond, Virginia. Furloughed for sixty days on or about August 4, 1864. Reported absent wounded through December, 1864. Survived the war.

HUNTER, HOGAN, Private
Born in Duplin County where he resided as a farmer prior to enlisting in Duplin County at age 30, March 3, 1862. Present or accounted for until wounded at Fort Wagner, Charleston, South Carolina, July 18, 1863. Reported absent wounded until January 16, 1864, when he was reported absent without leave.

HUSSEY, JOHN E., Corporal
Previously served as Sergeant in Company D, 13th Battalion N.C. Infantry. Transferred to this company on April 15, 1862. Mustered in as Sergeant. Reduced to the rank of Corporal in January-February, 1863. Present or accounted for until transferred to Company A, 35th Regiment N.C. Troops, January 17, 1864, in exchange for Sergeant Sabastian T. Crossland.

JAMES, DAVID HINTON, Corporal
Enlisted in New Hanover County on May 2, 1862, for the war. Mustered in as Private. Wounded slightly at Goldsboro on December 17, 1862. Returned to duty in January-February, 1863. Promoted to Corporal in November-December, 1864. Present or accounted for through December, 1864.

JAMES, JOHN J., Private
Enlisted in Lenoir County on October 1, 1862, for the war. Present or accounted for until wounded in the right arm at Drewry's Bluff, Virginia, May 14, 1864. Hospitalized at Richmond, Virginia, where he died on May 24, 1864, of wounds.

JAMES, KENNETH, Private
Enlisted in Duplin County on February 21, 1863, for the war. Present or accounted for until wounded at Fort Wagner, Charleston, South Carolina, July 18, 1863. Reported absent wounded until October 15, 1863, when he

was reported absent without leave. Returned to duty on or about February 25, 1864. Present or accounted for until he died in hospital at Goldsboro on February 8, 1865, of "febris typhoides."

JONES, JAMES, Private
Born in Duplin County and was by occupation a farmer prior to enlisting in Duplin County at age 18, March 19, 1862. Present or accounted for until wounded at Fort Wagner, Charleston, South Carolina, July 18, 1863. Reported absent wounded until October 21, 1863, when he was reported absent without leave. Returned to duty in November-December, 1863. Present or accounted for through February, 1864. Reported absent sick in April-October, 1864. Returned to duty in November-December, 1864. Paroled at Greensboro on May 1, 1865.

JONES, JONAS, Private
Enlisted at Camp Whiting, near Wilmington, January 3, 1863, for the war. Wounded slightly in the hand at Fort Wagner, Charleston, South Carolina, July 30-August 3, 1863. Present or accounted for through July, 1864. Company records indicate that he was captured near Globe Tavern, Virginia, August 19, 1864; however, records of the Federal Provost Marshal do not substantiate that report. Was probably killed near Globe Tavern.

JONES, LEWIS R., Private
Enlisted at Fort Johnston, near Smithville (present-day Southport), at age 17, July 3, 1862, for the war. Present or accounted for until wounded in the hand at Drewry's Bluff, Virginia, on or about May 13, 1864. Hospitalized at Richmond, Virginia. Reported absent wounded or absent sick through August, 1864. Returned to duty in September-October, 1864. Reported absent without leave in November-December, 1864. Survived the war.

JONES, NATHAN J., Private
Born in Duplin County and was by occupation a farmer prior to enlisting in Duplin County at age 27, March 3, 1862. Present or accounted for through May, 1862. Reported absent sick from June 7, 1862, until December 14, 1862, when he was discharged by reason of "paralysis."

JONES, WILLIAM, Private
Born in Duplin County and was by occupation a farmer prior to enlisting in Duplin County at age 46, March 3, 1862. Present or accounted for until captured at or near Petersburg, Virginia, on or about June 16, 1864. Confined at Fort Monroe, Virginia. Transferred to Elmira, New York, July 9, 1864. Arrived at Elmira on July 12, 1864. Died at Elmira on October 28, 1864, of "typhoid pneumonia."

KEATHLEY, ARCHELAUS, Private
Enlisted at Camp Holmes, near Wilmington, at age 16, May 9, 1862, for the war. Present or accounted for until captured at Fort Harrison, Virginia, September 30, 1864. Confined at Point Lookout, Maryland, October 5, 1864. Paroled at Point Lookout on March 17, 1865. Received at Boulware's Wharf, James River, Virginia, March 19, 1865, for exchange. Survived the war.

KEATHLEY, ELISHA HERRING, Private
Enlisted in New Hanover County on May 17, 1862, for the war. Present or accounted for until wounded in the arm and/or left foot at or near Drewry's Bluff, Virginia, on or about May 17, 1864. Hospitalized at Richmond, Virginia. Assigned to duty with the Ambulance Corps prior to September 1, 1864. Rejoined the company in September-October, 1864. Present or accounted for through December, 1864. Paroled at Greensboro on May 1, 1865.

KEATHLY, LEWIS, Private
Enlisted in New Hanover County on March 17, 1862. Present or accounted for until killed at Drewry's Bluff, Virginia, May 16, 1864.

KIMMY, JAMES M., Private
Born in Duplin County and was by occupation a farmer prior to enlisting in Duplin County at age 42, March 15, 1862. No further records.

LANIER, HOSEA F., Private
Enlisted at Fort Johnston, near Smithville (present-day Southport), July 12, 1862, for the war. Present or accounted for until wounded at or near Cold Harbor, Virginia, on or about July 3, 1864. Hospitalized at Richmond, Virginia. Furloughed for thirty days on July 23, 1864. Returned to duty in September-October, 1864. Present or accounted for through December, 1864.

LANIER, JOSEPH J., Private
Born in Duplin County where he resided as a farmer prior to enlisting in Duplin County at age 30, March 1, 1862. Present or accounted for until captured at or near Bentonville on or about March 21, 1865. Sent to New Bern. Confined at Hart's Island, New York Harbor, April 10, 1865. Released at Hart's Island on June 19, 1865, after taking the Oath of Allegiance.

LEE, WILLIAM BIZZELL, Private
Born in Screven County, Georgia, and was by occupation a farmer prior to enlisting in Sampson County at age 28, March 3, 1862. Present or accounted for until wounded in the left hand at Cold Harbor, Virginia, May 31, 1864. Three fingers amputated. Hospitalized at Richmond, Virginia. Reported absent wounded or absent sick through December, 1864. Survived the war.

McGEE, JAMES W., Private
Previously served as Private in 1st Company C, 12th Regiment N.C. Troops (2nd Regiment N.C. Volunteers). Enlisted in this company on May 14, 1862, for the war. Appointed Assistant Surgeon on October 14, 1862, to rank from June 1, 1862, and transferred to the Field and Staff of this regiment.

McLEAN, ELI, _____
North Carolina pension records indicate that he served in this company.

MATHIS, BENJAMIN D., Private
Born in Duplin County where he resided as a farmer prior to enlisting in Duplin County at age 19, March 1, 1862.

Present or accounted for through December, 1864. Paroled at Greensboro on May 1, 1865.

MATHIS, BRYAN, Private
Born in Duplin County and was by occupation a farmer prior to enlisting in Duplin County at age 45, February 22, 1862. Present or accounted for until September-October, 1863, when he was reported absent without leave. Returned to duty in November-December, 1863. Present or accounted for until November-December, 1864, when he was reported absent without leave.

MATHIS, FLEET C., Private
Born in Sampson County and resided in Duplin County where he was by occupation a farmer prior to enlisting in Duplin County at age 47, March 28, 1862. Reported at home sick on August 20, 1862. Reported absent without leave in September-December, 1862. Furloughed for thirty days on February 4, 1863. Reported absent without leave in May-June, 1863. Reported at home on sick furlough in July-August, 1863. Reported absent without leave in September-October, 1863. Reported sick in hospital at Charleston, South Carolina, in November, 1863-February, 1864. Hospitalized at Richmond, Virginia, June 3, 1864, with debility. Furloughed for thirty days on June 12, 1864. Reported absent without leave in September-December, 1864.

MATHIS, JACOB EDWARD, Private
Enlisted in New Hanover County on January 5, 1863, for the war. Present or accounted for until wounded at Cold Harbor, Virginia, May 31, 1864. Hospitalized at Richmond, Virginia. Returned to duty in September-October, 1864. Reported present in November-December, 1864. Paroled at Greensboro on May 1, 1865.

MATHIS, LUTHER R., Private
Born in Duplin County and was by occupation a farmer prior to enlisting in New Hanover County at age 28, March 6, 1862. Present or accounted for until captured at or near Petersburg, Virginia, on or about June 16, 1864. Confined at Point Lookout, Maryland, June 19, 1864. Transferred to Elmira, New York, July 9, 1864. Paroled at Elmira on February 9, 1865. Received at Boulware's Wharf, James River, Virginia, on or about February 20, 1865, for exchange. Survived the war.

MATHIS, PEYTON P., Private
Born in Sampson County and was by occupation a farmer prior to enlisting in Sampson County at age 18, March 28, 1862. Present or accounted for until wounded in the left hand at Cold Harbor, Virginia, May 31, 1864. Reported absent wounded through October, 1864. Hospitalized at Richmond, Virginia, November 28, 1864, with gonorrhoea. Survived the war. [North Carolina pension records indicate that he was wounded in the head at "Drewry's Bluff, Virginia, June, 1863."]

MATHIS, THOMAS B., Private
Enlisted in Wake County on October 16, 1864, for the war. Present or accounted for through December, 1864. Transferred to the 63rd Regiment N.C. Troops (5th Regiment N.C. Cavalry) on February 3, 1865.

MERRITT, ALSA, Private

Enlisted at Camp Holmes, near Raleigh, at age 19, January 1, 1864, for the war. Present or accounted for through December, 1864. Survived the war.

MERRITT, HIRAM, Private

Enlisted at Camp Battle, near Tarboro, December 24, 1863, for the war. Present or accounted for through December, 1864.

MERRITT, HUBBARD, Private

Born in Sampson County and was by occupation a farmer prior to enlisting in Sampson County at age 21, March 1, 1862. Present or accounted for until killed at Fort Wagner, Charleston, South Carolina, July 31, 1863.

MERRITT, LEVI, Private

Born in Sampson County where he resided as a farmer prior to enlisting in Duplin County at age 33, March 28, 1862. Present or accounted for until he deserted on September 11, 1862. Returned to duty on February 7, 1863. Present or accounted for until he deserted on August 21, 1863. Apprehended prior to November 1, 1863, and was imprisoned at Charleston, South Carolina. Reported under arrest in November-December, 1863. Returned to duty in January-February, 1864. Wounded slightly in the neck at Fort Harrison, Virginia, September 30, 1864. Present or accounted for through December, 1864. Survived the war.

MERRITT, LEWIS W., Private

Previously served as Private in Company E, Mallett's N.C. Battalion (Camp Guard). Transferred to this company on June 10, 1864. Present or accounted for through December, 1864. Survived the war.

MERRITT, ROBERT, Private

Born in Duplin County and was by occupation a farmer prior to enlisting in New Hanover County on April 15, 1862. Present or accounted for until July 12, 1863, when he was reported absent without leave. Reported absent without leave through October, 1863. Reported sick in hospital at Charleston, South Carolina, in November-December, 1863. Discharged on January 26, 1864, by reason of "inguinal hernia and rheumatism of many years standing." Discharge certificate gives his age as 47.

MERRITT, ROBERT HOOKS, Private

Previously served as Private in Company D, 13th Battalion N.C. Infantry. Transferred to this company on April 15, 1862. Present or accounted for until he deserted on September 11, 1862. Returned to duty on February 7, 1863. Hospitalized at Wilmington on or about July 12, 1863, with typhoid fever. Returned to duty in September-October, 1863. Wounded in Virginia in June, 1864. Returned to duty prior to September 1, 1864. Present or accounted for through December, 1864.

MILLER, WILLIAM H., Corporal

Born in Sampson County and was by occupation a farmer prior to enlisting in Duplin County at age 33, February 15, 1862. Mustered in as Private. Promoted to Corporal in September-October, 1863. Present or accounted for through December, 1864. Survived the war.

MILLIS, ALONZO, Musician

Born in New Hanover County where he enlisted at age 16, April 4, 1862. Mustered in as Musician (Drummer). Present or accounted for through December, 1864. Paroled at Greensboro on May 1, 1865.

MILLS, JOSEPH D., Private

Born in New Hanover County and was by occupation a farmer prior to enlisting in Duplin County at age 18, March 18, 1862. Present or accounted for until wounded in the head at Drewry's Bluff, Virginia, May 15, 1864. Hospitalized at Richmond, Virginia, where he died on May 22, 1864, of wounds.

MOORE, THOMAS McGEE, Private

Enlisted at Camp Holmes, near Wilmington, May 12, 1862, for the war. Present or accounted for until he was appointed acting Ordnance Sergeant on December 10, 1862, and transferred to the Field and Staff of this regiment. Appointed to the permanent rank of Ordnance Sergeant on an unspecified date and assigned to permanent duty with the Field and Staff.

OWENS, GABRIEL, Private

Previously served as Private in Company C, 63rd Regiment N.C. Troops (5th Regiment N.C. Cavalry). Transferred to this company on February 3, 1865.

PAGE, JOHN E., Private

Enlisted in Wake County on October 16, 1864, for the war. Present or accounted for through December, 1864.

PARNEL, ISAAC, Private

Born in Wayne County and was by occupation a farmer prior to enlisting in Duplin County at age 30, February 15, 1862. Died in hospital at Wilmington on April 19, 1862. Cause of death not reported.

PETERSON, W. S., Private

Enlisted in Wake County on October 16, 1864, for the war. Present or accounted for through December, 1864.

PICKETT, JOHN L., Private

Enlisted at Camp French, near Wilmington, June 25, 1862, for the war. Present or accounted for until wounded at Fort Wagner, Charleston, South Carolina, July 18, 1863. Returned to duty prior to September 1, 1863. Present or accounted for through December, 1864. Hospitalized at Wilmington on January 23, 1865, with dysentery. Returned to duty on February 8, 1865.

PRICE, EDEN, Private

Resided in Duplin County and was by occupation a farmer prior to enlisting in New Hanover County at age 42, April 15, 1862. Present or accounted for until wounded near Petersburg, Virginia, June 19, 1864. Died the same date.

PRICE, JOEL, Private

Born at Mount Olive and resided in Duplin County prior to enlisting in New Hanover County at age 19, April 15, 1862. Present or accounted for until wounded in the jaw (fracture) near Petersburg, Virginia, June 17, 1864. Hospitalized at Petersburg where he died on June 25, 1864, of wounds.

PUGH, WILLIAM E., Private
Born in Sampson County where he resided as a carpenter prior to enlisting in New Hanover County at age 43, March 6, 1862. Present or accounted for through August, 1863; however, he was reported absent on detail as a carpenter at Wilmington during most of that period. Reported absent sick at Mount Pleasant, South Carolina, in September-October, 1863. Returned to duty in November-December, 1863. Killed at Batchelder's Creek on February 1, 1864.

QUINN, ICHABOD, Private
Born in Duplin County where he resided as a farmer prior to enlisting in New Hanover County at age 37, March 6, 1862. Died in Duplin County on June 27, 1862, of "ty[phoid] pneumonia." [A tribute of respect appears in the *Wilmington Journal* (Weekly) of August 7, 1862.]

REAVES, TIMOTHY, Private
Enlisted in New Hanover County on April 15, 1862. Present or accounted for until November-December, 1862, when he was reported absent on sick leave. Returned to duty in January-February, 1863. Present or accounted for until July-August, 1863, when he was reported absent on sick furlough. Returned to duty in September-October, 1863. Present or accounted for through February, 1864. Reported absent sick in May-October, 1864. Returned to duty on November 5, 1864. Present or accounted for through December, 1864. Captured in hospital at Raleigh on April 13, 1865. No further records.

REGISTER, JAMES E., Private
Born in Duplin County and was by occupation a farmer prior to enlisting in Duplin County at age 30, March 3, 1862. Present or accounted for until wounded at Drewry's Bluff, Virginia, May 16, 1864. Returned to duty prior to September 1, 1864. Present or accounted for through December, 1864.

REGISTER, RICHARD J., Private
Born in Duplin County and resided in Sampson County where he was by occupation a farmer prior to enlisting in Duplin County at age 27, March 28, 1862. Present or accounted for until he deserted on August 21, 1863. Reported present but under arrest in September-December, 1863. Returned to duty in January-February, 1864. Present or accounted for through December, 1864. Survived the war.

REGISTER, ROBERT MARSHAL, Private
Born in Duplin County and was by occupation a farmer prior to enlisting in New Hanover County at age 24, March 7, 1862. Reported absent sick from July 7 through December 31, 1862. Returned to duty in January-February, 1863. Reported absent sick through August, 1863. Reported absent without leave in September, 1863-February, 1864. Reported on detail as a hospital nurse at Wilmington in May-October, 1864. Rejoined the company in November-December, 1864. Survived the war.

RIVENBARK, BENJAMIN R., Private
Born in Duplin County where he resided as a farmer prior

to enlisting in Duplin County at age 35, March 3, 1862. Present or accounted for through December, 1864.

ROBINSON, JOSIAH, Private
Born in Duplin County and resided in Sampson County where he was by occupation a farmer prior to enlisting in Duplin County at age 28, March 29, 1862. Present or accounted for until hospitalized at Wilmington on January 6, 1863, with smallpox. Reported absent sick until May-June, 1863, when he was detailed as a nurse in the smallpox hospital at Wilmington. Reported on duty as a nurse or guard through February, 1864. Rejoined the company prior to May 16, 1864, when he was wounded at Drewry's Bluff, Virginia. Hospitalized at Richmond, Virginia. Furloughed for sixty days on August 5, 1864. Reported absent wounded through December, 1864.

ROBINSON, WILLIAM E., Private
Born in Duplin County and was by occupation a farmer prior to enlisting in Sampson County at age 19, March 3, 1862. Wounded in the abdomen at Goldsboro on December 17, 1862. Hospitalized at Goldsboro where he died on December 31, 1862, of wounds.

RODGERS, J. E., Private
Enlisted in Wake County on October 16, 1864, for the war. Reported absent on detached service as a shoemaker in November-December, 1864.

SAULS, WILLIAM J., Private
Served as Private in Company G, 41st Regiment N.C. Troops (3rd Regiment N.C. Cavalry). An order transferring him to this company was issued on March 7, 1865, but it is doubtful that the transfer took place.

SIKES, CHARLES M., Private
Resided in Sampson County and was by occupation a farm laborer prior to enlisting in Wake County at age 39, October 16, 1864, for the war. Present or accounted for through December, 1864. Survived the war. [North Carolina pension records indicate that he was wounded in an unspecified battle.]

SOUTHERLAND, ABRAHAM, Private
Born in Duplin County and was by occupation a farmer prior to enlisting in Duplin County at age 22, February 24, 1862. Present or accounted for until wounded in the side at Goldsboro on December 17, 1862. Returned to duty in May-June, 1863. Present or accounted for through December, 1864.

SOUTHERLAND, BRYAN, Private
Resided in Duplin County and was by occupation a farmer prior to enlisting at the Wrightsville arsenal at age 40, November 20, 1862, for the war. Present or accounted for through June, 1863. Reported absent sick from July, 1863, through August, 1864. Reported absent without leave in September-December, 1864. Paroled at Charlotte on May 3, 1865.

SOUTHERLAND, GEORGE N., Private
Previously served as Private in Company B, 41st Regiment N.C. Troops (3rd Regiment N.C. Cavalry). Transferred to

this company on March 29, 1862. Mustered in as Corporal. Reported absent sick from September 11, 1862, through August, 1863. Reduced to ranks in January-February, 1863. Reported absent without leave on October 15, 1863. Died at home in Duplin County on January 13, 1864. Cause of death not reported.

SOUTHERLAND, JAMES, Private
Resided in Duplin County and enlisted in New Hanover County on December 18, 1862, for the war. Present or accounted for through December, 1864. Captured at or near Kinston on March 20-22, 1865. Confined at Hart's Island, New York Harbor, April 10, 1865. Released at Hart's Island on June 18, 1865, after taking the Oath of Allegiance.

SOUTHERLAND, THOMAS J., Private
Born in Duplin County and was by occupation a cooper prior to enlisting in Duplin County at age 47, March 1, 1862. Present or accounted for through December, 1864. Hospitalized at Greensboro on February 23, 1865, with intermittent fever. Transferred to another hospital the next day. Hospitalized again at Greensboro on March 10, 1865. Survived the war.

STANFORD, GEORGE W., 1st Sergeant
Born in Duplin County and was by occupation a student prior to enlisting in Duplin County at age 19, February 14, 1862. Mustered in as Sergeant. Promoted to Sergeant Major on April 30, 1862, and transferred to the Field and Staff of this regiment. Resigned as Sergeant Major on August 8, 1862, and returned to duty with this company with the rank of Sergeant. Promoted to 1st Sergeant in May-June, 1863. Present or accounted for until wounded in the left thigh (fracture) at Cold Harbor, Virginia, May 31, 1864. Hospitalized at Richmond, Virginia, where the doctors "pronounced the case hopeless and declined to operate." Was further weakened by diarrhoea and "symptoms of erysipelas." The wound was opened (apparently by the doctors for purposes of examining it) on June 26, 1864. Died in hospital at Richmond on August 7, 1864, of wounds.

STANFORD, HENRY C., Corporal
Enlisted in Duplin County at age 15, April 22, 1862, for the war. Mustered in as Private. Promoted to Corporal in January-February, 1863. Hospitalized at Wilmington on July 12, 1863, with dysentery. Returned to duty on August 11, 1863. Present or accounted for through December, 1864. Survived the war.

STANFORD, LEONIDAS, Private
Born in Duplin County where he resided as a student prior to enlisting in Duplin County at age 16, March 1, 1862. Mustered in as Corporal. Reduced to ranks in January-February, 1863. Present or accounted for through December, 1864. Paroled at Goldsboro on May 23, 1865.

STEVENS, JOHN T., Private
Born in Sampson County and was by occupation a mechanic prior to enlisting in New Hanover County at age 38, March 10, 1862. Present or accounted for through August, 1863. Reported absent sick in September, 1863-February, 1864. Returned to duty on an unspecified

date. Captured near Globe Tavern, Virginia, August 19, 1864. Confined at Point Lookout, Maryland, August 24, 1864. Paroled at Point Lookout on November 1, 1864. Received at Venus Point, Savannah River, Georgia, November 15, 1864, for exchange.

SULLIVAN, ADAM, Private
Enlisted in New Hanover County on April 15, 1862. Present or accounted for until captured at Cold Harbor, Virginia, June 1, 1864. Confined at Point Lookout, Maryland, June 11, 1864. Transferred to Elmira, New York, July 9, 1864. Died at Elmira on October 18, 1864, of "consumption."

SULLIVAN, ELIAS, Private
Enlisted on May 5, 1863, for the war. Present or accounted for through August, 1864. Stunned by a shell at Fort Harrison, Virginia, September 30, 1864. Reported sick in hospital at Richmond, Virginia, in October-December, 1864. Returned to duty on or about December 30, 1864. Paroled at Greensboro on May 1, 1865.

SULLIVAN, LEMUEL L., Private
Born in Duplin County where he resided as a farmer prior to enlisting in Duplin County at age 20, February 22, 1862. Reported absent sick in July-October, 1862. Returned to duty in November-December, 1862. Present or accounted for until wounded in the shoulder at Drewry's Bluff, Virginia, on or about May 14, 1864. Reported absent wounded through October, 1864. Reported on detached service "with wagon train" in November-December, 1864. Paroled at Greensboro on May 1, 1865.

SUMMERLIN, DAVID C., Private
Enlisted at Camp Holmes, near Wilmington, May 14, 1862, for the war. Present or accounted for until sent to hospital at Raleigh on September 19, 1862. Returned to duty in January-February, 1863. Company records indicate that he was captured at New Bern on February 3, 1864; however, records of the Federal Provost Marshal do not substantiate that report. No further records.

SUMMERLIN, JAMES LOUIS, Private
Enlisted in Duplin County on April 1, 1863, for the war. Present or accounted for through April, 1864. Company records indicate that he was wounded and captured at Cold Harbor, Virginia, May 31, 1864; however, records of the Federal Provost Marshal do not substantiate that report. No further records.

SUMMERLIN, JOHN D., Private
Resided in Duplin or Wilson County and enlisted at Camp Holmes, near Wilmington, May 14, 1862, for the war. Present or accounted for through October, 1862. Reported absent sick in November-December, 1862. Returned to duty in January-February, 1863. Reported absent sick in hospital at Columbia, South Carolina, in March-April, 1863. Returned to duty in May-June, 1863. Reported sick in hospital at Wilmington in July-August, 1863. Returned to duty in September-October, 1863. Present or accounted for through February, 1864. Reported absent sick in the brigade hospital in May-August, 1864. Reported present in September-December, 1864. Paroled at Goldsboro on

May 22, 1865. [North Carolina pension records indicate that he was wounded in the left arm at "Drewry's Bluff, Virginia, in 1863."]

SUMMERLIN, JOHN J., Private
Born in Duplin County where he resided as a farmer prior to enlisting in Duplin County at age 21, March 1, 1862. Hospitalized at Wilmington on July 28, 1862, with remittent fever. Returned to duty on August 21, 1862. Present or accounted for until killed at Cold Harbor, Virginia, May 31, 1864.

SUMMERLIN, LEVI, Private
Born in Duplin County where he resided as a farmer prior to enlisting in Duplin County at age 40, March 1, 1862. Present or accounted for until October 10, 1862, when he was sent to hospital at Goldsboro. Furloughed from hospital prior to November 1, 1862. Reported absent on furlough until September-October, 1863, when he was reported absent without leave. Reported absent without leave through August, 1864.

SUMMERLIN, THOMAS, Private
Born in Duplin County where he resided as a farmer prior to enlisting in Duplin County at age 42, March 1, 1862. Present or accounted for until hospitalized at Wilmington on or about July 28, 1862, with typhoid fever. Rejoined the company in September-October, 1862. Hospitalized at Wilmington on February 17, 1863, with diarrhoea. Returned to duty on or about March 16, 1863. Present or accounted for until May-August, 1864, when he was reported sick in hospital at Richmond, Virginia. Died in hospital at Richmond on September 10, 1864, of "diarrhoea chron[ic]."

TAYLOR, JOHN F., Private
Enlisted in Wake County on October 16, 1864, for the war. Present or accounted for through December, 1864.

TAYLOR, KENAN, Private
Born in Duplin County where he resided as a farmer prior to enlisting in Duplin County at age 17, February 15, 1862. Present or accounted for through December, 1864. Paroled at Greensboro on May 1, 1865.

TAYLOR, MITCHELL, Private
Born in Duplin County where he resided as a farmer prior to enlisting in Duplin County at age 48, February 15, 1862. Present or accounted for through December, 1862. Left sick at Wilmington in January-February, 1863. Returned to duty prior to March 1, 1863. Present or accounted for through December, 1864.

TAYLOR, PAUL, Private
Enlisted at Camp Holmes, near Wilmington, May 14, 1862, for the war. Present or accounted for until killed at Fort Harrison, Virginia, September 30, 1864. [Previously served as 1st Lieutenant in the 26th Regiment N.C. Militia.]

THOMAS, JOHN IVEY, Corporal
Born in Duplin County and was by occupation a farmer prior to enlisting in Duplin County at age 44, March 15,

1862. Mustered in as Private. Promoted to Corporal in May-June, 1863. Present or accounted for until killed at Cold Harbor, Virginia, May 31, 1864.

TURNER, DAVID W., Private
Born in Marengo County, Alabama, and was by occupation a farmer prior to enlisting in New Hanover County at age 24, March 29, 1862. Mustered in as Private. Appointed Color Sergeant on May 9, 1862, and transferred to the Field and Staff of this regiment. Reduced to ranks in January-February, 1863, and transferred back to this company. Present or accounted for until captured at Cold Harbor, Virginia, June 1, 1864. Confined at Point Lookout, Maryland, June 11, 1864. Transferred to Elmira, New York, July 12, 1864. Died at Elmira on January 12, 1865, of "pneumonia."

UMBERGER, C. W., _____
North Carolina pension records indicate that he served in this company.

WADE, CLARK M., Private
Born in Duplin County where he resided as a farmer prior to enlisting in Duplin County at age 32, March 3, 1862. Mustered in as Private. Promoted to Corporal in January-February, 1863. Present or accounted for until July-August, 1863, when he was reported sick in quarters. Reported at home on furlough in September-October, 1863. Reduced to ranks in September-October, 1863. Returned to duty in November-December, 1863. Wounded in Virginia in June, 1864. Returned to duty prior to September 1, 1864. Present or accounted for through December, 1864. Captured at or near Goldsboro on March 22, 1865. Sent to New Bern. Confined at Hart's Island, New York Harbor, April 10, 1865. Released at Hart's Island on June 19, 1865, after taking the Oath of Allegiance.

WATERS, J. E., Private
Enlisted in Wake County on October 16, 1864, for the war. Present or accounted for through December, 1864.

WATKINS, ROBERT R., Private
Resided in Edgecombe County and enlisted at Camp Battle, near Tarboro, December 28, 1863, for the war. Reported absent without leave on January 29, 1864. Returned to duty on February 7, 1864. Wounded slightly in the leg at Fort Harrison, Virginia, September 30, 1864. Present or accounted for until he was reported absent without leave in November-December, 1864. Paroled at Goldsboro on May 26, 1865.

WATSON, DAVID R., Sergeant
Born in Sampson County and was by occupation a carpenter prior to enlisting in Sampson County at age 19, February 15, 1862. Mustered in as Private. Present or accounted for until wounded in the side at Goldsboro on December 17, 1862. Reported absent wounded or absent sick with smallpox until July 1, 1863, when he returned to duty. Promoted to Sergeant in November-December, 1864. Present or accounted for through December, 1864. Paroled at Raleigh on May 23, 1865.

WHALEY, BRADDOCK, Private

Born in Duplin County where he resided as a farmer prior to enlisting in Duplin County at age 39, April 1, 1862. Present or accounted for until September-October, 1863, when he was reported sick in hospital at Charleston, South Carolina. Returned to duty in November-December, 1863. Present or accounted for until captured at Cold Harbor, Virginia, June 1, 1864. Confined at Point Lookout, Maryland, June 11, 1864. Transferred to Elmira, New York, July 12, 1864. Released at Elmira on July 3, 1865, after taking the Oath of Allegiance.

WHITFIELD, BENJAMIN H., Private

Born in Duplin County and was by occupation a farmer prior to enlisting at age 38, March 24, 1862. Present or accounted for through August, 1862. Reported present but sick in September-October, 1862. Reported at home on sick leave in November-December, 1862. Returned to duty prior to March 1, 1863. Present or accounted for until hospitalized at Wilmington on or about July 12, 1863, with bilious fever. Returned to duty on September 29, 1863. Present or accounted for until hospitalized at Richmond, Virginia, October 6, 1864, with an unspecified complaint. Returned to duty on November 26, 1864. Present or accounted for through December, 1864. Paroled at Greensboro on May 1, 1865.

WHITFIELD, J. T., Private

Born in Duplin County and was by occupation a farmer prior to enlisting in New Hanover County on April 15, 1862. Present or accounted for through October, 1862. Reported absent sick in November-December, 1862. Discharged on February 11, 1863, by reason of "cardiac [illegible]." Discharge certificate gives his age as 33.

WILSON, JAMES D., Private

Born in Sampson County where he resided as a farmer prior to enlisting at age 25, March 26, 1862. Present or accounted for until hospitalized at Wilmington on May 4, 1863, with pneumonia. Returned to duty on May 18, 1863. Present or accounted for through December, 1864. Survived the war.

COMPANY D

This company, known as the "Scotch Tigers," was raised in Robeson County and enlisted in Robeson County in March, 1862. It was mustered into state service at Camp Mangum, near Raleigh, on April 14, 1862, and assigned to the 51st Regiment N.C. Troops as Company D. After joining the regiment the company functioned as a part of the regiment, and its history for the remainder of the war is reported as a part of the regimental history.

The information contained in the following roster was compiled primarily from a company muster-in and descriptive roll dated April 14, 1862, and from company muster rolls for April 14, 1862-December 31, 1864. No company muster rolls were located for the period after December 31, 1864. Valuable information was obtained from primary records such as the North Carolina adjutant general's *Roll of Honor*, discharge certificates, medical records, prisoner of war records, *The War of the Rebellion: A Compilation of the Official Records of the Union and Confederate Armies*, militia records, newspaper casualty lists and obituaries, Confederate pension applications filed with the state of North Carolina, and the 1860 federal census of North Carolina. Secondary sources such as postwar rosters and histories, cemetery records, the *Confederate Veteran*, published genealogies, and records of the United Daughters of the Confederacy also provided useful information.

OFFICERS

CAPTAINS

McDONALD, JAMES R.

Previously served as Private in Company F, 1st Regiment N.C. Infantry (6 months, 1861). Appointed Captain of this company on February 22, 1862. Present or accounted for until he was appointed Major on April 9, 1863, and transferred to the Field and Staff of this regiment.

McEACHERN, ROBERT J.

Previously served as Private in Company F, 1st Regiment N.C. Infantry (6 months, 1861). Appointed 1st Lieutenant of this company on February 22, 1862. Promoted to Captain on April 9, 1863. Present or accounted for until wounded slightly at Fort Wagner, Charleston, South Carolina, July 18, 1863. Returned to duty prior to September 1, 1863. Present or accounted for until wounded at Cold Harbor, Virginia, May 31, 1864. Hospitalized at Petersburg, Virginia, where he died on June 21, 1864, of wounds.

MALLOY, JOHN DOUGLAS

Previously served as Private in Company F, 24th Regiment N.C. Troops (14th Regiment N.C. Volunteers). Appointed 2nd Lieutenant to rank from April 11, 1862, and transferred to this company. Promoted to 1st Lieutenant on April 30, 1863. Present or accounted for until wounded slightly in the neck at Fort Wagner, Charleston, South Carolina, July 18, 1863. Returned to duty in September-October, 1863. Present or accounted for until captured at Drewry's Bluff, Virginia, May 16, 1864. Confined at Point Lookout, Maryland, May 19, 1864. Promoted to Captain on June 18, 1864, while a prisoner of war. Transferred from Point Lookout to Fort Delaware, Delaware, June 23, 1864. Transferred to Hilton Head, South Carolina, August 20, 1864. Confined at Fort Pulaski, Georgia, October 20, 1864. Transferred back to Hilton Head where he was reported in confinement on January 1, 1865. Transferred to Fort Delaware where he arrived on March 12, 1865. Released at Fort Delaware on June 16, 1865, after taking the Oath of Allegiance.

LIEUTENANTS

BOON, WILLIAM R., 3rd Lieutenant
Previously served as Private in Company H, 1st Regiment N.C. Infantry (6 months, 1861). Enlisted in this company in Cumberland County on March 7, 1862. Mustered in as 1st Sergeant. Present or accounted for until hospitalized at Richmond, Virginia, June 6, 1864, with a gunshot wound. Place and date wounded not reported (probably wounded at Cold Harbor, Virginia, May 31-June 3, 1864). Appointed 3rd Lieutenant on July 25, 1864. Returned to duty prior to August 19, 1864, when he was captured near Globe Tavern, Virginia. Confined at Old Capitol Prison, Washington, D.C., August 22, 1864. Transferred to Fort Delaware, Delaware, August 27, 1864. Released at Fort Delaware on June 17, 1865, after taking the Oath of Allegiance.

CURRIE, FRANCIS S., 2nd Lieutenant
Previously served with an unknown rank (probably Private) in Company K, 38th Regiment N.C. Troops. Enlisted as Private in this company on April 5, 1862. Appointed 2nd Lieutenant on July 18, 1864. Present or accounted for until wounded in the right shoulder at Fort Harrison, Virginia, September 30, 1864. Returned to duty in November-December, 1864. Present or accounted for through December, 1864. [Prior to his service in Company K, 38th Regiment N.C. Troops, he served as Captain in the 59th Regiment N.C. Militia.]

McCALLUM, JAMES B., 2nd Lieutenant
Born in Robeson County where he resided as a farmer prior to enlisting at age 25. Appointed 3rd Lieutenant on March 11, 1862. Promoted to 2nd Lieutenant on or about April 14, 1862. Present or accounted for until wounded at Drewry's Bluff, Virginia, May 16, 1864. Died the same date of wounds.

McEACHERN, HECTOR, 1st Lieutenant
Enlisted at Camp Allen (probably near Kinston) on November 13, 1862, for the war. Mustered in as Private. Elected 3rd Lieutenant on April 23, 1863. Promoted to 1st Lieutenant on May 16, 1864. Present or accounted for until wounded in the right thigh and testicles and captured at Drewry's Bluff, Virginia, May 16, 1864. Confined at various Federal hospitals. Paroled at Fort Monroe, Virginia, August 18, 1864. Received at Aiken's Landing, James River, Virginia, August 22, 1864, for exchange. Reported absent on furlough through October, 1864. Returned to duty in November-December, 1864. Present or accounted for through December, 1864. [May have served previously as 2nd Lieutenant of Company G, 24th Regiment N.C. Troops (14th Regiment N.C. Volunteers). Medical records dated May-August, 1864, give his age as 22.]

NONCOMMISSIONED OFFICERS AND PRIVATES

BARKER, ANDERSON R., Private
Enlisted in Robeson County on April 26, 1862, for the war. Present or accounted for until he died at Camp Whiting, near Wilmington, December 11, 1862, of "diphtheria."

BAXLEY, ERVIN H., Private
Enlisted in Robeson County on April 26, 1862, for the war. Present or accounted for until January 28, 1863, when he was reported absent without leave. Returned to duty on March 6, 1863. Present or accounted for until he deserted at Sullivan's Island, Charleston, South Carolina, August 9, 1863.

BAXTER, MILTON, Private
Resided in Robeson County and enlisted at James Island, Charleston, South Carolina, at age 27, March 13, 1863, for the war. Present or accounted for through December, 1864. Survived the war.

BLANCHARD, HENRY, Private
Born in Harnett County* and was by occupation a laborer prior to enlisting in Cumberland County at age 30, March 17, 1862. Present or accounted for through December, 1864.

BRAMMER, T. P., _____
North Carolina pension records indicate that he served in this company.

BROWN, ARCHIBALD, Private
Born in Robeson County where he resided as a farmer prior to enlisting in Robeson County at age 34, April 26, 1862, for the war. Discharged on June 21, 1862, by reason of "phthisis & general debility. . . ." Reenlisted in the company on March 3, 1863. Reported present through April, 1863. Reported absent sick in May-October, 1863. Returned to duty in November-December, 1863. Present or accounted for through December, 1864.

BROWN, PETER B., Private
Resided in Robeson County and was by occupation a farmer prior to enlisting at Camp Holmes, near Raleigh, at age 42, October 29, 1864, for the war. Present or accounted for through December, 1864.

BURNEY, CHARLES H., Private
Born in Bladen County and was by occupation a farmer prior to enlisting in Cumberland County at age 18, March 17, 1862. Present or accounted for through December, 1864.

BURNEY, JAMES, Private
Born in Bladen County where he resided as a cooper or farmer prior to enlisting in Cumberland County at age 26, March 17, 1862. Present or accounted for until hospitalized at Wilmington on December 1, 1863, with "fever." Furloughed for thirty days on December 29, 1863. Returned to duty prior to March 1, 1864. Wounded in the left shoulder at Drewry's Bluff, Virginia, May 16, 1864. Hospitalized at Richmond, Virginia. Furloughed for sixty days on May 30, 1864. Reported absent wounded through December, 1864.

CAMERON, JAMES R., Private

Born in Moore County and was by occupation a blacksmith prior to enlisting at "Crossroads" at age 49, March 8, 1862. Present or accounted for until hospitalized at Wilmington on January 30, 1863, with "abcessus." Returned to duty on March 11, 1863. Hospitalized at Wilmington on May 29, 1863, with pneumonia. Furloughed for thirty days on June 11, 1863. Returned to duty in November-December, 1863. Present or accounted for until wounded in the right arm at or near Drewry's Bluff, Virginia, May 18, 1864. Hospitalized at Richmond, Virginia, where he died on May 24, 1864, of wounds.

CARLISLE, ATLAS, Private

Enlisted at James Island, Charleston, South Carolina, March 13, 1863, for the war. Present or accounted for until he died in hospital at Charleston on August 17, 1863. Cause of death not reported.

CARLISLE, DAVID BLOUNT, Private

Born in Robeson County and was by occupation a farmer prior to enlisting in Robeson County at age 23, March 6, 1862. Present or accounted for until he died at Charleston, South Carolina, May 2, 1863. Cause of death not reported.

CARLISLE, DENNIS L., Corporal

Born in Robeson County and was by occupation a farmer prior to enlisting in Cumberland County at age 39, April 7, 1862. Mustered in as Private. Promoted to Corporal in November-December, 1862. Present or accounted for until captured near Petersburg, Virginia, June 16, 1864. Confined at Point Lookout, Maryland, June 19, 1864. Transferred to Elmira, New York, July 9, 1864. Died at Elmira on September 29, 1864, of "chronic diarrhoea."

CARLISLE, ERVIN, Private

Born in Robeson County where he resided prior to enlisting in Robeson County at age 42, August 14, 1863, for the war. Present or accounted for through December, 1864. Paroled at Raleigh on April 19, 1865.

CARVER, JOSHUA, Private

Born in Cumberland County and was by occupation a farmer prior to enlisting in Cumberland County at age 37, February 24, 1862. Present or accounted for until wounded in the hand at Sullivan's Island, Charleston, South Carolina, in the summer of 1863. Reported absent wounded until December 1, 1863, when he was reported absent without leave. Returned to duty in March-April, 1864. Wounded and captured at Cold Harbor, Virginia, on or about June 1, 1864. Confined at Point Lookout, Maryland, June 11, 1864. Transferred to Elmira, New York, July 12, 1864. Paroled at Elmira on October 11, 1864. Received at Venus Point, Savannah River, Georgia, November 15, 1864, for exchange. Survived the war.

CLAPP, SIDNEY P., Private

Enlisted in Robeson County on April 26, 1862, for the war. Present or accounted for through December, 1864. Served for a time as a teamster.

COBB, STEPHEN J., JR., Private

Enlisted in Robeson County on April 26, 1862, for the war. Present or accounted for until hospitalized at Wilmington on or about January 30, 1863, with abscesses. Returned to duty on March 11, 1863. Present or accounted for until hospitalized at Wilmington on or about December 5, 1863, with debilitas. Returned to duty on March 31, 1864. Wounded at Cold Harbor, Virginia, May 31, 1864. Reported absent wounded through October, 1864. Returned to duty in November-December, 1864. Present or accounted for through December, 1864. Survived the war. [Previously served as 1st Lieutenant in the 59th Regiment N.C. Militia.]

CONLEY, JOHN A., Private

Resided in Robeson County where he enlisted on April 26, 1862, for the war. Reported absent sick in July-October, 1862. Returned to duty in November-December, 1862. Present or accounted for until October 21, 1863, when he was reported absent on sick furlough. Returned to duty in March-April, 1864. Present or accounted for through December, 1864. Survived the war.

CONLEY, JOHN C., Private

Born in Robeson County where he resided as a carpenter prior to enlisting at "Crossroads" at age 30, March 8, 1862. Present or accounted for until wounded at Drewry's Bluff, Virginia, May 16, 1864. Returned to duty prior to September 1, 1864. Present or accounted for through December, 1864. Survived the war.

CONLEY, THOMAS J., Private

Enlisted in New Hanover County on December 15, 1862, for the war. Present or accounted for until wounded in the right knee and captured at Drewry's Bluff, Virginia, May 16, 1864. Hospitalized at Fort Monroe, Virginia. Paroled and exchanged on an unspecified date. Admitted to hospital at Richmond, Virginia, March 16, 1865, and was transferred to another hospital the next day. No further records.

CONLEY, WILLIAM SCOTT, Private

Born in Robeson County and was by occupation a farmer prior to enlisting in Robeson County at age 24, March 5, 1862. Present or accounted for through December, 1864.

CONNELLY, FRANCIS H., Corporal

Born in Robeson County and was by occupation a farmer prior to enlisting at "Crossroads" at age 22, March 8, 1862. Mustered in as Private. Promoted to Corporal prior to July 1, 1862. Wounded in the right leg by a shell at Goldsboro on December 17, 1862. Reported absent wounded until January 5, 1864, when he was discharged by reason of "very great contraction" of the leg muscles as a result of wounds received at Goldsboro.

COUNCIL, JAMES, Private

Resided in Robeson County and was by occupation a farmer prior to enlisting in Robeson County at age 39, December 18, 1862, for the war. Present or accounted for until July-August, 1863, when he was reported absent sick. Returned to duty in September-October, 1863. Present or accounted for until May-August, 1864, when he was reported absent sick. Returned to duty in September-October, 1864. Present or accounted for through December, 1864. Hospitalized at Greensboro on February 23, 1865, with intermittent fever. Returned to duty on February 25, 1865. Survived the war.

COUNCIL, JOHN M., Private
Resided in Robeson County and was by occupation a farmer prior to enlisting in Robeson County at age 43, August 19, 1863, for the war. Present or accounted for until wounded at Drewry's Bluff, Virginia, May 18, 1864. Returned to duty in September-October, 1864. Present or accounted for through December, 1864.

COUNCIL, WILLIAM, Private
Resided in Robeson County and was by occupation a farmer prior to enlisting in Robeson County at age 36, December 18, 1862, for the war. Present or accounted for through December, 1864.

CURRIE, ARCHIBALD M., Private
Enlisted in Robeson County at age 21, April 26, 1862, for the war. Present or accounted for through December, 1864. "Won a name for fearlessness under fire." Survived the war.

CURRIE, DANIEL J., Private
Born in Robeson County where he resided as a farmer prior to enlisting at age 21, March 27, 1862. Present or accounted for until wounded in the left ankle at Drewry's Bluff, Virginia, May 16, 1864. Hospitalized at Richmond, Virginia. Leg amputated. Furloughed for sixty days on July 30, 1864. Reported absent wounded through October, 1864. Retired from service in November-December, 1864.

CURRIE, DANIEL McG., Private
Born in Robeson County and was by occupation a farmer prior to enlisting in Robeson County at age 19, March 28, 1862. Present or accounted for until wounded in the right thigh (flesh) and captured at Fort Harrison, Virginia, September 30, 1864. Hospitalized at Fort Monroe, Virginia, where he died on October 26, 1864, of wounds.

CURRIE, GILBERT G., Private
Resided in Robeson County and was by occupation a farmer prior to enlisting in Robeson County at age 26, April 26, 1862, for the war. Present or accounted for through December, 1864. Served for a time in 1864 as company cook.

CURRIE, RANDAL M., Corporal
Previously served with an unspecified rank (probably Private) in Company K, 38th Regiment N.C. Troops. Enlisted in this company on March 22, 1862. Mustered in as Private. Present or accounted for until wounded at Goldsboro on December 17, 1862. Returned to duty in July-August, 1863. Promoted to Corporal on September 21, 1864. Present or accounted for until killed at Fort Harrison, Virginia, September 30, 1864.

DALLAS, HUGH, Private
Born in Robeson County and was by occupation a farmer

prior to enlisting in Robeson County at age 26, March 5, 1862. Present or accounted for until wounded near Petersburg, Virginia, on or about June 16, 1864. Died near Petersburg on June 17, 1864, of wounds.

DAVIS, ELIAS S., Private
Resided in Robeson County and enlisted at "Crossroads" at age 21, April 26, 1862, for the war. Present or accounted for through December, 1864.

DAVIS, ERVIN Q., Private
Resided in Robeson County where he enlisted at age 22, April 26, 1862, for the war. Present or accounted for until captured at Cold Harbor, Virginia, June 1, 1864. Confined at Point Lookout, Maryland, June 11, 1864. Transferred to Elmira, New York, July 12, 1864. Died at Elmira on February 1, 1865, of "remittent fever."

DAVIS, HANSON, Private
Previously served as Private in Company D, 19th Regiment N.C. Troops (2nd Regiment N.C. Cavalry). Transferred to this company on January 13, 1865. No further records.

DAVIS, J. M., _____
North Carolina pension records indicate that he served in this company.

DAVIS, WILLIAM J., Private
Previously served as Private in Company D, 19th Regiment N.C. Troops (2nd Regiment N.C. Cavalry). Transferred to this company on January 13, 1865. No further records.

EDGE, SIMEON B., Private
Born in Bladen County and was by occupation a farmer prior to enlisting in Cumberland County at age 21, March 4, 1862. Present or accounted for until wounded ("crushed knee") at Fort Wagner, Charleston, South Carolina, July 30-August 3, 1863. Leg amputated. Hospitalized at Charleston where he died on September 27, 1863, of wounds.

EVANS, DUNCAN C., Private
Enlisted in Robeson County on April 26, 1862, for the war. Present or accounted for until he died in hospital at Wilmington on January 28, 1863, of "fever." Was 28 years of age at the time of his death.

EVANS, JAMES A., Private
Born in Robeson County and was by occupation a cooper prior to enlisting in Cumberland County at age 27, March 6, 1862. Present or accounted for until wounded slightly in the arm at Fort Wagner, Charleston, South Carolina, July 18, 1863. Reported absent wounded through December, 1864. Survived the war.

FOWLER, WILLIAM H., Private
Born in Robeson County and was by occupation a farmer prior to enlisting at age 28, March 7, 1862. Present or accounted for until discharged on December 11, 1862. Reason discharged not reported. Apparently returned to duty in January-April, 1865, as he was captured in hospital at Raleigh on April 13, 1865.

GALBREATH, MALCOLM, Private
Born in Robeson County where he resided as a farmer prior to enlisting at Camp Whiting, near Wilmington, at age 37, January 23, 1863, for the war. Wounded slightly in the hip and knee at Fort Wagner, Charleston, South Carolina, July 30-August 3, 1863. Present or accounted for until captured at Cold Harbor, Virginia, June 1, 1864. Confined at Point Lookout, Maryland, June 11, 1864. Transferred to Elmira, New York, July 12, 1864. Died at Elmira on September 2, 1864, of "chronic diarrhoea."

GODWIN, OLLIN, Private
Born in Sampson County and resided in Cumberland County where he was by occupation a laborer prior to enlisting in Cumberland County at age 49, March 17, 1862. Present or accounted for through June, 1862. Reported on detached duty guarding commissary stores at Fayetteville from July, 1862, through August, 1863. Rejoined the company in September-October, 1863. Hospitalized at Petersburg, Virginia, January 8, 1864, with chronic rheumatism. Furloughed for sixty days on January 14, 1864. Hospitalized at Fayetteville on March 10, 1864, with an unspecified complaint. Returned to duty in November-December, 1864. Present or accounted for through December, 1864.

GRAHAM, ARCHIBALD, Private
Born in Robeson County where he resided as a farmer prior to enlisting in Robeson County at age 35, March 16, 1862. Present or accounted for until wounded at Fort Wagner, Charleston, South Carolina, July 18, 1863. Reported absent wounded or absent sick until December 19, 1864, when he was retired to the Invalid Corps.

GRAHAM, DUNCAN J., Private
Enlisted at Petersburg, Virginia, February 11, 1864, for the war. Present or accounted for through December, 1864. Hospitalized at Raleigh on January 18, 1865, with rubeola. Returned to duty on February 2, 1865.

GRAHAM, GEORGE A., Private
Resided in Robeson County where he enlisted at age 26, April 26, 1862, for the war. Present or accounted for until wounded at or near Drewry's Bluff, Virginia, on or about May 16, 1864. Returned to duty on an unspecified date. Reported present in September-October, 1864. Present or accounted for through December, 1864. Survived the war.

GRAHAM, HECTOR R., Sergeant
Born in Robeson County where he resided as a farmer prior to enlisting in Robeson County at age 43, April 5, 1862. Mustered in as Private. Promoted to Sergeant prior to July 1, 1862. Present or accounted for through December, 1864. Hospitalized at Greensboro on February 22, 1865, with intermittent fever. Transferred to hospital at Raleigh on February 23, 1865. Captured in hospital at Raleigh on April 13, 1865. Paroled at Raleigh on April 23, 1865. Died in hospital at Raleigh on May 6, 1865. Cause of death not reported. [Previously served as 2nd Lieutenant in the 59th Regiment N.C. Militia.]

GRAHAM, JAMES CALVIN, Private
Resided in Robeson County and enlisted at Petersburg,

Virginia, at age 17, August 8, 1864, for the war. Wounded in the right leg near Globe Tavern, Virginia, August 19, 1864. Reported absent wounded through December, 1864. Survived the war.

GRAHAM, ROBERT, Private
Born in Robeson County where he resided as a farmer prior to enlisting in Cumberland County at age 30, March 5, 1862. Present or accounted for until wounded in the left side at Drewry's Bluff, Virginia, May 16, 1864. Returned to duty prior to June 16, 1864, when he was wounded at Petersburg, Virginia. Died on or about the same date.

GREEN, HENRY H., Private
Enlisted at Camp Whiting, near Wilmington, February 12, 1863, for the war. Present or accounted for until wounded in the face at Drewry's Bluff, Virginia, May 20, 1864. Hospitalized at Petersburg, Virginia, where he died on or about June 2, 1864, of wounds.

HAIR, WILLIAM JAMES, Private
Born in Cumberland County and was by occupation a farmer prior to enlisting in Cumberland County at age 30, March 5, 1862. Present or accounted for until wounded in the arm at Goldsboro on December 17, 1862. Returned to duty prior to January 1, 1863. Discharged on January 31, 1863, by reason of "an enlargement of the spermatic cords. . . ."

HARDIN, HUGH, Private
Born in Robeson County and was by occupation a laborer prior to enlisting in Cumberland County at age 18, March 12, 1862. Present or accounted for until he deserted at Sullivan's Island, Charleston, South Carolina, August 10, 1863. Returned to duty in September-October, 1863. Present or accounted for until wounded at Drewry's Bluff, Virginia, May 16, 1864. Returned to duty prior to October 7, 1864, when he was captured (probably deserted to the enemy) near Petersburg, Virginia. Took the Oath of Allegiance at Bermuda Hundred, Virginia, on or about October 21, 1864, and was released.

HARDIN, LOUIS, Private
Born in Sampson County and was by occupation a laborer prior to enlisting in Cumberland County at age 24, April 7, 1862. Present or accounted for until captured (probably deserted to the enemy) near Petersburg, Virginia, October 7, 1864. Took the Oath of Allegiance at Bermuda Hundred, Virginia, on or about October 21, 1864, and was released.

HARRELL, ELISHA, Private
Born in Robeson County and was by occupation a farmer prior to enlisting in Cumberland County at age 45, March 12, 1862. Present or accounted for until discharged at Wilmington on May 23, 1863, by reason of "debility from age."

HOWELL, AMOS, Private
Resided in Robeson County and was by occupation a farmer prior to enlisting in Robeson County at age 50, April 26, 1862, for the war. Present or accounted for until

December 1, 1863, when he was reported absent without leave. Returned to duty in January-February, 1864. Present or accounted for until August 19, 1864, when he was reported absent without leave. Returned to duty on September 23, 1864. Present or accounted for through December, 1864.

HUMPHREY, DUNCAN C., Private
Born in Robeson County where he resided as a farmer prior to enlisting in Robeson County at age 24, April 26, 1862, for the war. Discharged on July 4, 1862, by reason of "chronic rheumatism and dropsy."

HUMPHREY, LEWIS, Private
Resided in Robeson County and was by occupation a farmer prior to enlisting in Robeson County at age 28, April 26, 1862, for the war. Present or accounted for through December, 1864.

HUMPHREY, MATTHEW, Private
Resided in Robeson County and was by occupation a farmer prior to enlisting at James Island, Charleston, South Carolina, at age 29, March 13, 1863, for the war. Present or accounted for until September-October, 1863, when he was reported sick in hospital in Charleston. Returned to duty in January-February, 1864. Present or accounted for until wounded at Drewry's Bluff, Virginia, May 16, 1864. Returned to duty in November-December, 1864. Present or accounted for through December, 1864.

HUMPHREY, WILLIAM JAMES, Private
Resided in Robeson County and was by occupation a farmer prior to enlisting in Robeson County at age 25, April 26, 1862, for the war. Present or accounted for until wounded at Cold Harbor, Virginia, May 31, 1862. Returned to duty prior to June 17, 1864, when he was wounded in the head at Petersburg, Virginia. Blinded as a result of his wounds. Retired to the Invalid Corps on November 25, 1864.

JOHNSON, ARCHIBALD McGREGOR, 1st Sergeant
Resided in Robeson County and enlisted at "Crossroads" at age 19, April 26, 1862, for the war. Mustered in as Corporal. Promoted to 1st Sergeant on September 26, 1864. Present or accounted for until transferred to Company D, 19th Regiment N.C. Troops (2nd Regiment N.C. Cavalry), January 13, 1865.

KINLAW, PINKNEY G., Corporal
Previously served as Private in Company A, 31st Regiment N.C. Troops. Transferred to this company on or about March 20, 1862. Mustered in as Private. Promoted to Corporal prior to July 1, 1862. Present or accounted for until hospitalized at Wilmington on January 27, 1863, with intermittent fever. Returned to duty on March 2, 1863. Present or accounted for until wounded slightly at Drewry's Bluff, Virginia, May 16, 1864, when a ball was deflected by his belt buckle. Reported absent without leave on September 1, 1864. Survived the war. [Correct middle initial is G, as indicated above.]

LEGGETT, GEORGE W., Private
Born in Robeson County where he resided prior to

enlisting in Robeson County at age 18, April 26, 1862, for the war. Present or accounted for until he died in hospital at Charleston, South Carolina, March 20, 1863. Cause of death not reported.

LIEUPO, JOHN, Private
Enlisted in Robeson County on August 19, 1863, for the war. Present or accounted for through February, 1864; however, he was reported absent sick during most of that period. Returned to duty in March-April, 1864. Present or accounted for through December, 1864.

LINBACK, W. R., Private
Place and date of enlistment not reported. Died in hospital at Richmond, Virginia, February 2, 1865, of "pneumonia."

LITTLE, DUNCAN, Private
Enlisted at Camp Whiting, near Wilmington, December 19, 1862, for the war. Present or accounted for until captured near Globe Tavern, Virginia, August 19, 1864. Confined at Point Lookout, Maryland, August 22, 1864. Paroled at Point Lookout on or about October 20, 1864. Received at Venus Point, Savannah River, Georgia, November 15, 1864, for exchange.

LITTLE, GILBERT G., Private
Born in Robeson County and was by occupation a farmer prior to enlisting in Robeson County at age 28, March 5, 1862. Present or accounted for until wounded in the left thigh at Fort Harrison, Virginia, September 30, 1864. Hospitalized at Richmond, Virginia, where he died on October 3, 1864, of wounds.

LITTLE, JAMES A., Private
Enlisted in Robeson County at age 25, April 26, 1862, for the war. Present or accounted for until wounded at Drewry's Bluff, Virginia, May 16, 1864. Returned to duty prior to September 1, 1864. Present or accounted for through December, 1864. Survived the war.

LITTLE, ROBERT F., Private
Born in Robeson County and was by occupation a farmer prior to enlisting in Robeson County at age 19, March 5, 1862. Present or accounted for until wounded at Drewry's Bluff, Virginia, May 20, 1864. Hospitalized at Petersburg, Virginia, where he died on or about June 12, 1864, of wounds.

LIVINGSTON, PETER, Private
Enlisted in Robeson County on April 26, 1862, for the war. Present or accounted for until captured at Cold Harbor, Virginia, June 1, 1864. Confined at Point Lookout, Maryland, June 11, 1864. Transferred to Elmira, New York, July 12, 1864. Arrived at Elmira on July 17, 1864. Paroled at Elmira on March 10, 1865. Received at Boulware's Wharf, James River, Virginia, March 15, 1865, for exchange.

LUMSDEN, WILLIAM McK., Private
Enlisted in Lenoir County on September 17, 1862, for the

war as a substitute. Reported absent without leave in November-December, 1862. Returned to duty prior to January 1, 1863. Present or accounted for through December, 1863; however, he was reported absent sick or absent on duty as a commissary guard during most of that period. Returned to duty in January-February, 1864. Present or accounted for through April, 1864. Reported absent sick in May-August, 1864. Reported on light duty in the ordnance department at Petersburg, Virginia, in September-December, 1864. Hospitalized at Richmond, Virginia, January 30, 1865, with chronic diarrhoea. Furloughed for sixty days on February 20, 1865.

McCALLUM, HENRY H., Private
Resided in Robeson County and was by occupation a farm laborer prior to enlisting in Robeson County at age 21, April 26, 1862, for the war. Present or accounted for until captured at Fort Harrison, Virginia, September 30, 1864. Confined at Point Lookout, Maryland, October 5, 1864. Paroled at Point Lookout on or about March 17, 1865, and transferred to Boulware's Wharf, James River, Virginia, where he was received on March 19, 1865, for exchange.

McCORMICK, WILLIAM, Private
Born in Robeson County where he resided as a farmer prior to enlisting in Robeson County at age 40, March 1, 1862. Present or accounted for until he died in hospital at Richmond, Virginia, October 9, 1864, of "diarrhoea chron[ic]."

McDONALD, ARCHIBALD N., Private
Born in Robeson County and resided in Cumberland County where he was by occupation a farmer prior to enlisting in Robeson County at age 23, April 5, 1862. Present or accounted for until captured at Cold Harbor, Virginia, June 1, 1864. Confined at Point Lookout, Maryland, June 11, 1864. Transferred to Elmira, New York, July 12, 1864. Released at Elmira on July 3, 1865, after taking the Oath of Allegiance.

McDONALD, GEORGE P., Private
Enlisted in Robeson County on April 26, 1862, for the war. Present or accounted for until captured near Globe Tavern, Virginia, August 19, 1864. Confined at Point Lookout, Maryland, August 22, 1864. Paroled at Point Lookout on or about March 17, 1865, and transferred to Boulware's Wharf, James River, Virginia, where he was received on March 19, 1865, for exchange.

McDONALD, HENRY J., Private
Born in Robeson County and was by occupation a farmer prior to enlisting in Robeson County at age 25, March 1, 1862. Present or accounted for through December, 1863. Reported on duty as a wagoner during most of that period. Rejoined the company in January-February, 1864. Present or accounted for through April, 1864. Reported on duty as a hostler in May-August, 1864. Hospitalized at Richmond, Virginia, October 23, 1864, with anasarca. Returned to duty on December 28, 1864. Hospitalized at Wilmington on January 3, 1865, with pneumonia. Returned to duty on February 6, 1865. Hospitalized at Greensboro on February 23, 1865, with catarrhus. Returned to duty on February 25, 1865.

McDONALD, JAMES ALEXANDER, Private
Enlisted in Robeson County on April 26, 1862, for the war. Present or accounted for until wounded near Petersburg, Virginia, in June, 1864. Returned to duty on an unspecified date and was detailed as a teamster. Reported present in September-December, 1864. Hospitalized at Richmond, Virginia, March 20, 1865, with rheumatism. Furloughed for thirty days on March 24, 1865.

McDONALD, JOHN, Musician
Born in Robeson County and was by occupation a farmer prior to enlisting at age 26, March 5, 1862. Mustered in as Musician. No further records.

McDONALD, MALCOLM J., Private
Enlisted in Cumberland County on November 11, 1862, for the war. Present or accounted for until killed at Fort Wagner, Charleston, South Carolina, July 18, 1863.

McDOUGALD, MALCOLM A., Private
Enlisted in Robeson County on April 26, 1862, for the war. Present or accounted for through October, 1862. Reported absent without leave in November-December, 1862. Returned to duty prior to January 1, 1863. Reported sick in hospital at Summerville, South Carolina, in July-October, 1863. Returned to duty in November-December, 1863. Present or accounted for until detailed for service with the engineer department at Petersburg, Virginia, and transferred to the 2nd Regiment Confederate Engineer Troops in May-August, 1864. [Previously served as 2nd Lieutenant in the 59th Regiment N.C. Militia.]

McGEACHY, ALEXANDER CURRIE, Private
Enlisted at "Crossroads" at age 28, July 9, 1862, for the war. Present or accounted for until transferred to Company G, 24th Regiment N.C. Troops (14th Regiment N.C. Volunteers), October 15, 1863.

McGEACHY, JOHN DAVID, Private
Born in Robeson County where he resided as a farmer prior to enlisting in Robeson County at age 20, April 26, 1862, for the war. Present or accounted for through March 21, 1865.

McGOUGAN, DANIEL A., Private
Enlisted in Robeson County on December 24, 1862, for the war. Present or accounted for until hospitalized at Wilmington on January 18, 1863, with intermittent fever. Returned to duty on February 10, 1863. Present or accounted for until wounded near Petersburg, Virginia, in June, 1864. Returned to duty on an unspecified date. Reported present in September-December, 1864.

McGOUGAN, HUGH, Private
Born in Robeson County and was by occupation a farmer prior to enlisting in Robeson County at age 24, March 8, 1862. Present or accounted for through August, 1863. Reported absent sick in September-October, 1863. Returned to duty in November-December, 1863. Present or accounted for until wounded in the head at Fort Harrison, Virginia, September 30, 1864. Hospitalized at Richmond, Virginia, where he died on October 17, 1864, of wounds.

McINNIS, JOHN M., Private

Born in Robeson County where he resided as a farmer prior to enlisting in Robeson County at age 32, March 1, 1862. Died at Wilmington on June 5, 1862. Cause of death not reported.

McKAY, GEORGE A., Private

Enlisted at James Island, Charleston, South Carolina, March 13, 1863, for the war. Present or accounted for through April, 1863. No further records.

McKENZIE, WILLIAM M., Sergeant

Born in Argyleshire, Scotland, and was by occupation a distiller prior to enlisting in Robeson County at age 32, March 1, 1862. Mustered in as Private. Promoted to Sergeant prior to July 1, 1862. Present or accounted for until appointed Quartermaster Sergeant on November 27, 1862, and transferred to the Field and Staff of this regiment.

McLEAN, DANIEL, Private

Enlisted at age 20, in November, 1864, for the war. Wounded at Bentonville, March 19-21, 1865. Survived the war.

McLEAN, JOHN A., Private

Born in Robeson County and was by occupation a farmer prior to enlisting in Robeson County at age 24, March 1, 1862. Present or accounted for through December, 1864.

McLEAN, MARTIN, Private

Enlisted at James Island, Charleston, South Carolina, at age 22, March 13, 1863, for the war. Present or accounted for through December, 1864. Survived the war.

McMERCER, SAUL, Private

Enlisted at Petersburg, Virginia, January 15, 1864, for the war. Present or accounted for until captured at Cold Harbor, Virginia, June 1, 1864. Confined at Point Lookout, Maryland, June 11, 1864. Transferred to Elmira, New York, July 12, 1864. Died at Elmira on July 27, 1864, of "chronic diarrhoea."

McMILLAN, DANIEL J., Private

Born in Robeson County and was by occupation a farmer prior to enlisting in Cumberland County at age 20, March 18, 1862. Mustered in as Musician. Reduced to ranks prior to July 1, 1862. Present or accounted for through October, 1862. Reported absent without leave in November-December, 1862. Returned to duty prior to January 1, 1863. Present or accounted for until he deserted at Sullivan's Island, Charleston, South Carolina, August 23, 1863. Returned to duty on April 13, 1864. Captured at Cold Harbor, Virginia, June 1, 1864. Confined at Point Lookout, Maryland, June 11, 1864. Transferred to Elmira, New York, July 12, 1864. Died at Elmira on October 21, 1864, of "chronic diarrhoea."

McMILLAN, GEORGE DELANEY, Private

Born in Cumberland County and was by occupation a painter prior to enlisting in Cumberland County at age 18, March 26, 1862. Reported absent on detached service through June, 1862. Reported absent sick in July-October, 1862. Returned to duty in November-December, 1862. Present or accounted for until wounded in the foot at Fort Wagner, Charleston, South Carolina, July 30-August 3, 1863. Returned to duty prior to September 1, 1863. Reported absent sick in May-August, 1864. Returned to duty in September-October, 1864. Present or accounted for through December, 1864. Survived the war.

McMILLAN, HECTOR J., Private

Born in Robeson County and was by occupation a farmer prior to enlisting in Robeson County at age 19, March 1, 1862. Mustered in as Musician. Reduced to ranks prior to July 1, 1862. Present or accounted for until discharged on July 23, 1862, by reason of "threatened phthisis & general anemia."

McMILLAN, MALCOLM, Private

Enlisted in Robeson County on April 26, 1862, for the war. Present or accounted for until November-December, 1862, when he was reported absent without leave. Returned to duty in January-February, 1863. Present or accounted for through April, 1863. Reported absent sick in May-August, 1863. Returned to duty in September-October, 1863. Hospitalized at Petersburg, Virginia, January 12, 1864, with an unspecified complaint. Reported absent sick through August, 1864. Discharged on October 20, 1864, by reason of "general debility" and "lameness in the right leg caused by an abscess. . . ."

McMILLAN, NEILL A., Private

Born in Robeson County where he resided as a farmer prior to enlisting in Robeson County at age 23, March 1, 1862. Died at Camp Mangum, near Raleigh, April 21, 1862. Cause of death not reported.

McMILLAN, WILLIAM JAMES, Private

Previously served as Private in 1st Company D, 12th Regiment N.C. Troops (2nd Regiment N.C. Volunteers). Enlisted in this company on April 26, 1862, for the war. Present or accounted for until September-October, 1862, when he was reported absent sick. Returned to duty in November-December, 1862. Discharged on January 31, 1863. Reason discharged not reported.

McNEILL, JAMES A., Corporal

Resided in Robeson County where he enlisted on April 26, 1862, for the war. Mustered in as Private. Promoted to Corporal in January-February, 1864. Present or accounted for through December, 1864. Survived the war.

McPAUL, TIMOTHY D., Sergeant

Previously served as Private in Company A, 5th Regiment N.C. State Troops. Enlisted in this company in Robeson County on March 1, 1862. Mustered in as Private. Promoted to Corporal prior to July 1, 1862. Promoted to Sergeant in November-December, 1862. Present or accounted for until wounded and captured at Cold Harbor, Virginia, May 31, 1864. Confined at Point Lookout, Maryland, June 11, 1864. Transferred to Elmira, New York, July 12, 1864. Released at Elmira on June 14, 1865, after taking the Oath of Allegiance.

McRAE, MALCOLM L., Private
Born in Robeson County and was by occupation a farmer prior to enlisting in Robeson County at age 28, March 1, 1862. Present or accounted for through August, 1863. Reported absent sick in September-October, 1863. Returned to duty in November-December, 1863. Present or accounted for through December, 1864. Survived the war. [North Carolina pension records indicate that he was wounded in the right shoulder at Petersburg, Virginia, June 15, 186(4).]

McRAE, MALCOLM W., Private
Born in Robeson County where he resided as a farmer prior to enlisting in Robeson County at age 22, March 1, 1862. Present or accounted for until hospitalized at Wilmington on May 4, 1863, with debility. Furloughed for thirty days on June 27, 1863. Hospitalized at Wilmington on July 25, 1863, with debility and was furloughed for thirty days on or about the same date. Returned to duty prior to September 1, 1863. Present or accounted for until wounded and captured at Cold Harbor, Virginia, May 31, 1864. Confined at Point Lookout, Maryland, June 8, 1864. Exchanged on September 30, 1864. Returned to duty in November-December, 1864. Present or accounted for through December, 1864. Survived the war.

McRAE, PETER P., Sergeant
Born in Robeson County where he resided as a farmer prior to enlisting in Robeson County at age 34, March 1, 1862. Mustered in as Private. Promoted to Sergeant prior to July 1, 1862. Present or accounted for through December, 1864.

McRAE, RODERICK S., Private
Previously served as Private in Company G, 24th Regiment N.C. Troops (14th Regiment N.C. Volunteers). Transferred to this company on October 15, 1863. Present or accounted for until wounded at Drewry's Bluff, Virginia, May 16, 1864. Returned to duty prior to June 1, 1864, when he was wounded at Cold Harbor, Virginia. Died of wounds on or about the same date.

McRIMMON, MURDOCK, Sergeant
Born in Marion District, South Carolina, and was by occupation a farmer prior to enlisting at age 25, March 19, 1862. Mustered in as Private. Promoted to Sergeant prior to July 1, 1862. Present or accounted for through June, 1863. Reported absent sick in July-August, 1863. Returned to duty in September-October, 1863. Present or accounted for through December, 1864.

McRIMMON, NEILL, Private
Enlisted in Robeson County on April 26, 1862, for the war. Present or accounted for until he died in hospital at Charleston, South Carolina, August 13, 1863. Cause of death not reported.

MALONE, WILLIS, Private
Born in Moore County and was by occupation a farmer prior to enlisting in Cumberland County at age 24, March 18, 1862. Present or accounted for until January-February, 1863, when he was reported absent sick. Returned to duty in March-April, 1863. Present or accounted for until December 19, 1863, when he was reported absent without leave. Returned to duty in January-February, 1864. Present or accounted for until wounded in the right arm (fracture) near Petersburg, Virginia, June 17, 1864. Arm amputated. Hospitalized at Petersburg. Furloughed on August 26, 1864. Died in hospital at Fayetteville on October 10, 1864, of wounds.

MASON, LEVI, Private
Born in Cumberland County where he resided as a farmer prior to enlisting at age 47, March 3, 1862. Present or accounted for through June, 1862. Reported on detail as a commissary guard at Fayetteville from July-August, 1862, through October, 1864. Transferred to Company G, 2nd Battalion N.C. Local Defense Troops, in November-December, 1864.

MERCER, JOHN PICKET, Private
Previously served as Private in 1st Company D, 12th Regiment N.C. Troops (2nd Regiment N.C. Volunteers). Enlisted in this company in Cumberland County on March 20, 1862. Present or accounted for until wounded in the right leg and captured at Cold Harbor, Virginia, June 1, 1864. Confined at Point Lookout, Maryland, June 11, 1864. Transferred to Elmira, New York, July 12, 1864. Paroled at Elmira on March 10, 1865. Received at Boulware's Wharf, James River, Virginia, March 15, 1865, for exchange. Survived the war.

MERCER, MILES V., Private
Born in Robeson County where he resided prior to enlisting at "Crossroads" at age 23, April 26, 1862, for the war. Present or accounted for until wounded in the left elbow at Cold Harbor, Virginia, June 1, 1864. Left arm amputated. Hospitalized at Richmond, Virginia. Furloughed on July 15, 1864. Retired from service prior to January 1, 1865.

MORRISON, DANIEL A., Private
Born in Robeson County and was by occupation a farmer prior to enlisting at age 20, March 19, 1862. Present or accounted for until wounded near Petersburg, Virginia, June 19, 1864. Died on or about July 8, 1864, of wounds. Place of death not reported.

MUSSLEWHITE, ABEL, Private
Resided in Robeson County where he enlisted at age 26, April 26, 1862, for the war. Discharged on June 5, 1862, by reason of "dropsy."

MUSSLEWHITE, ARCHIBALD, Private
Previously served as Private in Company A, 31st Regiment N.C. Troops. Transferred to this company on or about March 7, 1862. Present or accounted for through June, 1863. Hospitalized at Wilmington on June 5, 1863, with remittent fever. Returned to duty on June 26, 1863. Furloughed on or about August 11, 1863. Returned to duty in November-December, 1863. Wounded in the left shoulder at Cold Harbor, Virginia, June 1, 1864. Returned to duty prior to July 1, 1864. Present or accounted for through December, 1864. Survived the war.

MUSSLEWHITE, AUGUSTUS, Private
Enlisted at "Crossroads" on April 26, 1862, for the war.

Present or accounted for until he was reported missing after the battle at Goldsboro on December 17, 1862. Returned to duty prior to January 1, 1863. Reported absent sick in January-February, 1863. Returned to duty in March-April, 1863. Present or accounted for until May-August, 1864, when he was reported in hospital at Raleigh. Reported sick in hospital at Wilmington in September-December, 1864.

MUSSLEWHITE, CALVIN, Private
Born in Robeson County and was by occupation a farmer prior to enlisting in Cumberland County at age 26, March 19, 1862. Present or accounted for until September-October, 1862, when he was reported sick in hospital. Returned to duty in November-December, 1862. Discharged on January 31, 1863, by reason of "chronic dysentery."

MUSSLEWHITE, JACOB, Private
Born in Robeson County and was by occupation a farmer prior to enlisting in Cumberland County at age 25, April 7, 1862. Present or accounted for until wounded at Fort Wagner, Charleston, South Carolina, July 18, 1863. Returned to duty prior to September 1, 1863. Present or accounted for until wounded slightly in the leg at Fort Harrison, Virginia, September 30, 1864. Returned to duty prior to November 1, 1864. Reported present in November-December, 1864.

MUSSLEWHITE, LEWIS, Private
Previously served as Private in Company A, 31st Regiment N.C. Troops. Transferred to this company on or about March 7, 1862. Present or accounted for until wounded in the arm and shoulder at Fort Wagner, Charleston, South Carolina, July 18, 1863. Reported absent wounded through February, 1864. Reported on detail for light duty at Charlotte in March-December, 1864.

MUSSLEWHITE, NATHAN, Private
Born in Robeson County where he resided as a farmer prior to enlisting in Robeson County at age 29, April 26, 1862, for the war. Present or accounted for until hospitalized at Wilmington on May 25, 1863, with chronic diarrhoea. Furloughed on June 2, 1863. Returned to duty in July-August, 1863. Present or accounted for until wounded in the lungs near Petersburg, Virginia, June 17, 1864. Hospitalized at Petersburg where he died on June 24, 1864, of wounds.

MUSSLEWHITE, RANDALL, Private
Resided in Robeson County and was by occupation a farmer prior to enlisting in Cumberland County at age 31, April 25, 1863, for the war. Reported on guard duty at Wilmington and Fayetteville in May-August, 1863. Reported absent sick in September-October, 1863. Returned to duty in November-December, 1863. Present or accounted for through April, 1864. Reported sick in hospital at Richmond, Virginia, in May-December, 1864.

NELSON, NEILL L. McF., Private
Born in Robeson County where he resided as a farmer prior to enlisting at "Crossroads" at age 34, March 8, 1862. Present or accounted for through June, 1862.

Reported absent sick in July-August, 1862. Returned to duty in September-October, 1862. Present or accounted for through April, 1863. Reported absent sick in May-October, 1863. Returned to duty in November-December, 1863. Present or accounted for until hospitalized at Petersburg, Virginia, March 29, 1864, with an unspecified complaint. Reported absent sick through December, 1864.

OVERTON, JACKSON, Private
Born in Cumberland County and was by occupation a laborer prior to enlisting in Cumberland County at age 23, February 24, 1862. Present or accounted for until hospitalized at Wilmington on June 8, 1863, with typhoid fever. Furloughed for thirty days on or about June 27, 1863. Returned to duty in September-October, 1863. Reported absent without leave on December 17, 1863. Returned to duty on or about January 5, 1864. Present or accounted for until wounded at Cold Harbor, Virginia, June 1, 1864. Returned to duty prior to September 30, 1864, when he was wounded in the right thigh at Fort Harrison, Virginia. Reported absent wounded through December, 1864.

PARHAM, WILLIAM H., Private
Born in Robeson County and was by occupation a laborer prior to enlisting in Cumberland County at age 22, March 7, 1862. Reported absent without leave on or about April 14, 1862.

PATTERSON, MALLOY, Private
Resided in Robeson County where he enlisted on April 26, 1862, for the war. Present or accounted for until appointed 2nd Lieutenant on or about February 20, 1863, and transferred to Company D, 46th Regiment N.C. Troops.

PATTERSON, ROBERT M., Private
Born in Pitt County and was by occupation a farmer prior to enlisting in Cumberland County at age 33, April 1, 1862. Present or accounted for until wounded in the face at Drewry's Bluff, Virginia, May 15, 1864. Blinded in the right eye as a result of his wounds. Hospitalized at Richmond, Virginia. Furloughed for sixty days on May 26, 1864. Retired from service prior to January 1, 1865.

PAUL, HECTOR C., _____
North Carolina pension records indicate that he served in this company.

POWERS, HENRY T., Private
Enlisted at James Island, Charleston, South Carolina, March 13, 1863, for the war. Present or accounted for until hospitalized at Petersburg, Virginia, January 12, 1864, with an unspecified complaint (probably scabies). Returned to duty on or about March 3, 1864. Present or accounted for through December, 1864.

POWERS, JAMES, Private
Enlisted at James Island, Charleston, South Carolina, March 13, 1863, for the war. Present or accounted for until he died at Wilmington on May 26, 1863, of "typh[oid] pneumon[ia]."

RALZAMON, MUSSLEWHITE, Private

Enlisted in Robeson County on April 26, 1862, for the war. Died on July 11, 1862. Place and cause of death not reported.

ROZIER, AMOS L., Private

Born in Robeson County and was by occupation a farmer prior to enlisting in Cumberland County at age 28, April 7, 1862. Present or accounted for until captured at Drewry's Bluff, Virginia, May 16, 1864. Confined at Point Lookout, Maryland, May 19, 1864. Transferred to Elmira, New York, August 16, 1864. Paroled at Elmira on March 2, 1865, and transferred to the James River, Virginia, for exchange. Hospitalized at Charlotte on March 21, 1865, with "ch[ronic] diarrhoea" and died on March 26, 1865.

ROZIER, EVANDER C., Private

Enlisted at "Howellsville" on December 1, 1862, for the war. Present or accounted for until captured at Cold Harbor, Virginia, June 1, 1864. Confined at Point Lookout, Maryland, June 11, 1864. Transferred to Elmira, New York, July 12, 1864. Died at Elmira on November 23, 1864, of "pneumonia."

ROZIER, ROBERT A., Private

Resided in Robeson County where he enlisted on April 26, 1862, for the war. Present or accounted for until captured at Petersburg, Virginia, June 16, 1864. Confined at Point Lookout, Maryland. Transferred to Elmira, New York, where he arrived on July 12, 1864. Released at Elmira on June 12, 1865, after taking the Oath of Allegiance.

RUSSELL, WESLEY SOULE, Private

Born in Robeson County and enlisted in Cumberland County at age 23, November 7, 1862, for the war. Present or accounted for through December, 1864. Served as a clerk in the quartermaster's department during most of the war. Survived the war.

SCOTT, WILLIAM H., Private

Born in Sampson County and was by occupation a laborer prior to enlisting in Cumberland County at age 22, March 7, 1862. Present or accounted for until captured at Petersburg, Virginia, June 16, 1864. Confined at Point Lookout, Maryland, June 19, 1864. Transferred to Elmira, New York, July 9, 1864. Died at Elmira on January 23, 1865, of "pneumonia."

SCRIVEN, THOMAS JAMES, Private

Born in Bladen County where he resided as a farmer prior to enlisting in Cumberland County at age 27, March 7, 1862. Present or accounted for until August 19, 1864, when he was reported absent without leave.

SHAW, ARCHIBALD JAMES, Private

Born in Robeson County where he resided as a farmer prior to enlisting in Robeson County at age 23, March 5, 1862. Present or accounted for until hospitalized at Wilmington on February 16, 1863, with continued fever. Returned to duty on March 11, 1863. Present or accounted for until captured at Petersburg, Virginia, June 16, 1864. Confined at Point Lookout, Maryland, June 19, 1864.

Transferred to Elmira, New York, July 9, 1864. Died at Elmira on March 24, 1865, of "pneumonia."

SHAW, DANIEL, Private

Born in Robeson County and enlisted at "Longbridge" at age 29, March 5, 1862. Present or accounted for until wounded in the mouth at Cold Harbor, Virginia, May 31, 1864. Hospitalized at Richmond, Virginia. Furloughed for thirty days on June 9, 1864. Returned to duty prior to September 1, 1864. Present or accounted for through December, 1864.

SHAW, JOHN A., Private

Born in Robeson County where he resided as a farmer prior to enlisting in Robeson County at age 33, March 5, 1862. Present or accounted for until October 16, 1863, when he was reported absent on sick furlough. Returned to duty in January-February, 1864. Present or accounted for until captured at Petersburg, Virginia, June 16, 1864. Confined at Point Lookout, Maryland, June 19, 1864. Transferred to Elmira, New York, July 9, 1864. Paroled at Elmira on October 11, 1864, and transferred for exchange. Died at or near Baltimore, Maryland, October 14, 1864. Cause of death not reported.

SHAW, MALCOLM, Private

Resided in Robeson County and enlisted at Camp Whiting, near Wilmington, at age 25, December 18, 1862, for the war. Present or accounted for until wounded in the right leg at Cold Harbor, Virginia, June 1, 1864. Hospitalized at Richmond, Virginia. Furloughed for sixty days on June 9, 1864. Reported absent wounded through December, 1864.

SHAW, NORMAN, Private

Resided in Robeson County and was by occupation a farmer prior to enlisting at Camp Whiting, near Wilmington, at age 35, December 18, 1862, for the war. Present or accounted for until captured near Globe Tavern, Virginia, August 19, 1864. Confined at Point Lookout, Maryland, August 22, 1864. Paroled at Point Lookout on March 14, 1865. Received at Boulware's Wharf, James River, Virginia, March 16, 1865, for exchange.

SMITH, JAMES A., Private

Born in Bladen County and enlisted in Cumberland County at age 27, March 7, 1862. Present or accounted for until wounded at Goldsboro on December 17, 1862. Died at Goldsboro on December 21, 1862, of wounds.

SPIDE, S. S., _____

Resided in Duplin County. Place and date of enlistment not reported. Paroled at Goldsboro on May 22, 1865.

STEWART, JAMES, Private

Resided in Robeson County and enlisted in Lenoir County on November 11, 1862, for the war. Hospitalized at Wilmington on or about June 5, 1863, with continued fever. Returned to duty on June 26, 1863. Died at home on July 30, 1863, of "bowel consumption." Was about 50 years of age at the time of his death.

STONE, ANDREW J., Private

Born in Robeson County where he resided as a farmer prior to enlisting in Cumberland County at age 32, February 26, 1862. Present or accounted for until discharged on September 2, 1862, by reason of a hernia.

TAYLOR, ISAAC, Private

Born in Brunswick County and was by occupation a farmer prior to enlisting in Robeson County at age 50, March 1, 1862. Present or accounted for until he deserted at Camp Whiting, near Wilmington, November 25, 1862.

TURNER, G. T., _____

North Carolina pension records indicate that he served in this company.

UNDERWOOD, ACY J., Private

Born in Wake County where he resided as a laborer prior to enlisting in Cumberland County at age 23, March 28, 1862. Reported absent without leave on or about April 14, 1862.

WALLACE, TRISTRAM L., Private

Resided in Robeson County and was by occupation a laborer prior to enlisting in Robeson County at age 23, April 26, 1862, for the war. Present or accounted for until November-December, 1862, when he was reported absent without leave. Returned to duty prior to January 1, 1863. Present or accounted for through December, 1864. Survived the war.

WEBB, JOHN E., Private

Born in Johnston County and resided in Robeson County where he enlisted on April 26, 1862, for the war. Present or accounted for until he died in hospital at Charleston, South Carolina, April 9, 1863. Cause of death not reported.

WEST, JAMES, Private

Born in Cumberland County and was by occupation a farmer prior to enlisting in Cumberland County at age 23, April 7, 1862. Present or accounted for until wounded slightly in the hand at Goldsboro on December 17, 1862. Returned to duty prior to January 1, 1863. Present or accounted for until he deserted at Sullivan's Island, Charleston, South Carolina, August 9, 1863. Deserted to the enemy at Fayetteville on or about March 11, 1865. Sent to Fort Monroe, Virginia. Transferred to Washington, D.C., April 2, 1865. No further records.

WHITE, DANIEL, Private

Enlisted at Camp Holmes, near Raleigh, October 29, 1864, for the war. Present or accounted for through December, 1864.

WHITE, LEWIS M., _____

North Carolina pension records indicate that he served in this company.

WHITE, NEILL D., Private

Resided in Robeson County and enlisted on July 9, 1862, for the war. Present or accounted for until November-December, 1862, when he was reported absent without leave. Returned to duty prior to January 1, 1863. Present or accounted for until wounded near Petersburg, Virginia, June 16, 1864. Reported absent wounded through December, 1864.

WHITE, R. M., Private

Resided in Robeson County. Place and date of enlistment not reported; however, he probably enlisted in January, 1865. Hospitalized at Richmond, Virginia, January 17, 1865, with chronic bronchitis. Captured in hospital at Richmond on April 3, 1865. Transferred to Newport News, Virginia, April 23, 1865. Released at Newport News on June 15, 1865, after taking the Oath of Allegiance.

WILKES, ANGUS J., Private

Born in Robeson County and was by occupation a farmer prior to enlisting at "Crossroads" at age 25, March 8, 1862. Present or accounted for until May-August, 1864, when he was reported absent sick at the division hospital. Reported on detail as an ambulance driver in September-October, 1864. Hospitalized at Richmond, Virginia, December 23, 1864, with chronic bronchitis. Furloughed for sixty days on January 26, 1865.

WILLIS, JOHN W., Private

Enlisted at Petersburg, Virginia, at age 18, February 11, 1864, for the war. Wounded in the right leg at Drewry's Bluff, Virginia, May 16, 1864. Returned to duty prior to May 31, 1864, when he was wounded at Cold Harbor, Virginia. Returned to duty in November-December, 1864. Hospitalized at Raleigh on January 18, 1865, with diarrhoea and rheumatism. Furloughed for sixty days on February 20, 1865.

WOOD, ALFRED B., Private

Born in Wake County and was by occupation a farmer prior to enlisting in Cumberland County at age 20, March 7, 1862. Present or accounted for through December, 1864.

WOOD, JOHN, Private

Born in Johnston County and was by occupation a farmer prior to enlisting in Cumberland County at age 29, March 7, 1862. Present or accounted for through December, 1864. Survived the war.

WOODELL, ANDREW JACKSON, Private

Born in Chatham County and was by occupation a farmer prior to enlisting in Cumberland County at age 25, March 7, 1862. Present or accounted for through December, 1864. Survived the war.

COMPANY E

This company, known as the "Clay Valley Rangers," was raised in Robeson County and enlisted at Lumberton on February 28, 1862. It was mustered into state service at Wilmington on April 10, 1862, and assigned to the 51st Regiment N.C. Troops as Company E. After joining the regiment the company functioned as a part of the regiment, and its history for the remainder of the war is reported as a part of the regimental history.

The information contained in the following roster was compiled primarily from a company muster-in and descriptive roll dated April 10, 1862, and from company muster rolls for February 28, 1862-December 31, 1864. No company muster rolls were located for the period after December 31, 1864. Valuable information was obtained from primary records such as the North Carolina adjutant general's *Roll of Honor*, discharge certificates, medical records, prisoner of war records, *The War of the Rebellion: A Compilation of the Official Records of the Union and Confederate Armies*, militia records, newspaper casualty lists and obituaries, Confederate pension applications filed with the state of North Carolina, and the 1860 federal census of North Carolina. Secondary sources such as postwar rosters and histories, cemetery records, the *Confederate Veteran*, published genealogies, and records of the United Daughters of the Confederacy also provided useful information.

OFFICERS

CAPTAINS

MOORE, WILLIS P.
Born in Robeson County where he resided as a farmer prior to enlisting in Robeson County at age 32. Appointed Captain on February 28, 1862. Present or accounted for until September-October, 1862, when he was reported absent sick. Resigned on November 24, 1862, because "I have been troubled with asthma for the last eight years"; also, "my wife has gone entirely blind and is in a helpless condition & during my absence my house has been entered and plundered by burglars." Resignation accepted on December 9, 1862.

POPE, WILLIS H.
Previously served as Private in Company A, 46th Regiment N.C. Troops. Appointed 1st Lieutenant on February 28, 1862, and transferred to this company. Promoted to Captain on December 11, 1862. Present or accounted for until wounded in the abdomen and legs at Drewry's Bluff, Virginia, May 16, 1864. Died in hospital at Richmond, Virginia, May 17, 1864, of wounds.

ASHLEY, ANDREW JACKSON
Born in Alabama and resided in Robeson County where he was by occupation a farmer prior to enlisting in Robeson County at age 28. Appointed 3rd Lieutenant on February 28, 1862. Promoted to 1st Lieutenant on December 11, 1862. Promoted to Captain on May 18, 1864. Present or accounted for until wounded in the head near Petersburg, Virginia, July 1, 1864. Hospitalized at Richmond, Virginia, where he died on August 30, 1864, of wounds.

HOUSTON, HIRAM V.
Was serving as 3rd Lieutenant of Company C, 51st Regiment N.C. Troops, when he was reported on duty as

acting commander of this company in September-October, 1864.

LIEUTENANTS

BULLOCK, WILLIAM A., 3rd Lieutenant
Previously served as Private in 1st Company D, 12th Regiment N.C. Troops (2nd Regiment N.C. Volunteers). Enlisted in this company at Camp Holmes, near Wilmington, May 12, 1862, for the war. Mustered in as Private. Elected 3rd Lieutenant on August 15, 1864. Present or accounted for until captured near Globe Tavern, Virginia, August 19, 1864. Confined at Washington, D.C., August 22, 1864. Transferred to Fort Delaware, Delaware, where he arrived on August 29, 1864. No further records.

FLOYD, FRANCIS FULTON, 3rd Lieutenant
Resided in Robeson County and was by occupation a farmer prior to enlisting at Camp Holmes, near Wilmington, at age 30, May 15, 1862, for the war. Mustered in as Private. Present or accounted for until November-December, 1862, when he was reported absent without leave. Returned to duty in January-February, 1863. Promoted to Corporal in September-October, 1863. Appointed 3rd Lieutenant prior to March 1, 1864. Present or accounted for until captured near Petersburg, Virginia, June 16, 1864. Confined at Point Lookout, Maryland, June 19, 1864. Transferred to Fort Delaware, Delaware, June 23, 1864. Transferred to Hilton Head, South Carolina, August 20, 1864. Reported in confinement at Fort Pulaski, Georgia, October 20, 1864. Transferred back to Hilton Head subsequent to December 26, 1864. Transferred to Fort Delaware where he arrived on March 12, 1865. Released at Fort Delaware on June 17, 1865, after taking the Oath of Allegiance. [Previously served as 2nd Lieutenant in the 58th Regiment N.C. Militia.]

PITMAN, JAMES P., 1st Lieutenant
Previously served as Corporal in 1st Company D, 12th Regiment N.C. Troops (2nd Regiment N.C. Volunteers). Enlisted in this company at Camp Holmes, near Wilmington, May 5, 1862, for the war. Mustered in as Private. Appointed 3rd Lieutenant on January 7, 1863. Hospitalized at Wilmington on or about May 13, 1863, with typhoid fever. Furloughed for thirty days on June 16, 1863. Returned to duty prior to September 1, 1863. Promoted to 1st Lieutenant on May 18, 1864. Wounded in Virginia in June, 1864. Returned to duty prior to September 1, 1864. Captured at Fort Harrison, Virginia, September 30, 1864. Confined at Old Capitol Prison, Washington, D.C. Transferred to Fort Delaware, Delaware, October 21, 1864. Released at Fort Delaware on June 17, 1865, after taking the Oath of Allegiance.

THOMPSON, GILES W., 1st Lieutenant
Previously served as Private in 1st Company D, 12th Regiment N.C. Troops (2nd Regiment N.C. Volunteers). Appointed 2nd Lieutenant of this company on February 28, 1862. Promoted to 1st Lieutenant on December 11,

1862. Present or accounted for until killed at Fort Wagner, Charleston, South Carolina, July 18, 1863.

NONCOMMISSIONED OFFICERS AND PRIVATES

AMMONS, CAMERON, Private
Enlisted in New Hanover County on May 5, 1862, for the war. Died in hospital at Wilmington on June 15, 1862. Cause of death not reported.

ASHLEY, JAMES ROBESON, Private
Born in Robeson County where he resided as a farmer prior to enlisting in Robeson County at age 32, February 28, 1862. Present or accounted for until wounded in the head at Drewry's Bluff, Virginia, on or about May 15, 1864. Hospitalized at Danville, Virginia, May 18, 1864. Transferred to hospital at Wilmington on an unspecified date. Returned to duty on August 6, 1864. Present or accounted for until December 28, 1864, when he was reported absent without leave.

BARKER, RILEY A., Private
Born in Robeson County where he resided as a farmer prior to enlisting in Robeson County at age 37, February 28, 1862. Present or accounted for until he died in hospital at Wilmington on June 1, 1862, of "continued fever" and/or "rubeola."

BARNES, ALDRED A., Private
Born in Robeson County and was by occupation a farmer prior to enlisting in Robeson County at age 38, February 28, 1862. Present or accounted for until wounded at Fort Wagner, Charleston, South Carolina, July 18, 1863. Returned to duty prior to September 1, 1863. Present or accounted for until captured at Cold Harbor, Virginia, June 1, 1864. Confined at Point Lookout, Maryland, June 11, 1864. Transferred to Elmira, New York, July 12, 1864. Died at Elmira on October 4, 1864, of "pneumonia."

BARNES, HENRY P., Private
Born in Robeson County and was by occupation a farmer prior to enlisting in Robeson County at age 20, February 28, 1862. Present or accounted for until he deserted on September 1, 1862. Reported under arrest at Petersburg, Virginia, in March-April, 1864. Returned to duty on an unspecified date. Deserted from the trenches near Petersburg on July 12, 1864.

BASS, GILSON, Private
Born in Robeson County where he resided as a laborer prior to enlisting in Robeson County at age 41, February 28, 1862. Present or accounted for until he died at Camp Davis, near Wilmington, June 2, 1862. Cause of death not reported.

BASS, NEVILL, Private
Born in Robeson County where he resided as a laborer prior to enlisting in Robeson County at age 43, February 28, 1862. Present or accounted for through December, 1864.

BASS, THOMAS, Private
Born in Robeson County where he resided as a laborer prior to enlisting in Robeson County at age 31, February 28, 1862. Present or accounted for through April, 1863. Reported absent on furlough in May-June, 1863. Reported absent sick in July-August, 1863. Returned to duty in September-October, 1863. Present or accounted for through December, 1864.

BIGGS, H. H., Private
Born in Robeson County where he resided as a farmer prior to enlisting in Robeson County at age 21, February 28, 1862. Present or accounted for until September-October, 1862, when he was reported absent without leave. Returned to duty in January-February, 1863. Present or accounted for through December, 1864; however, he was reported absent sick during most of that period. Survived the war.

BLACKMAN, DILLEN, Private
Born in Robeson County and was by occupation a laborer prior to enlisting in Robeson County at age 18, February 28, 1862. Present or accounted for until he was sent on a sick furlough of sixty days on April 16, 1864. Returned to duty on an unspecified date. Wounded in the right arm at Cold Harbor, Virginia, on or about June 1, 1864. Reported absent wounded through December, 1864.

BLACKMAN, JOHN C., Private
Born in Robeson County and was by occupation a laborer prior to enlisting in Robeson County at age 17, February 28, 1862. Present or accounted for until wounded in the hand at Cold Harbor, Virginia, May 31, 1864. Reported absent wounded through October, 1864. Returned to duty in November-December, 1864. Hospitalized at Raleigh on January 18, 1865, with a gunshot wound of the hand. Transferred to another hospital on March 8, 1865. Paroled at Thomasville on May 1, 1865.

BLACKMAN, WILLIAM, Private
Born in Robeson County and was by occupation a laborer prior to enlisting in Robeson County at age 48, February 28, 1862. Present or accounted for through April, 1863. Reported absent sick in May-August, 1863. Reported absent without leave in September-December, 1863. Discharged on or about February 29, 1864, by reason of "disability."

BOONE, JAMES W., Private
Resided in Robeson County where he enlisted at age 18, February 9, 1863, for the war. Present or accounted for until captured at Cold Harbor, Virginia, June 1, 1864. Confined at Point Lookout, Maryland, June 11, 1864. Transferred to Elmira, New York, July 12, 1864. Released at Elmira on June 16, 1865, after taking the Oath of Allegiance.

BOWMAN, HENRY, Private
Place and date of enlistment not reported. Deserted to the enemy on October 21, 1864. Released on October 22, 1864, after taking the Oath of Allegiance.

BRANCH, AMON J., Private
Resided in Robeson County and enlisted at Camp Holmes,

near Wilmington, at age 20, May 1, 1862, for the war. Present or accounted for until wounded in the right arm at Fort Wagner, Charleston, South Carolina, July 18, 1863. Returned to duty prior to September 1, 1863. Present or accounted for until captured at Cold Harbor, Virginia, June 1, 1864. Confined at Point Lookout, Maryland, June 11, 1864. Transferred to Elmira, New York, July 12, 1864. Released at Elmira on July 3, 1865, after taking the Oath of Allegiance.

BRANCH, ETHEMORE T. C., Private
Enlisted at Camp Holmes, near Wilmington, May 12, 1862, for the war. Present or accounted for until wounded at Fort Wagner, Charleston, South Carolina, July 18, 1863. Returned to duty prior to September 1, 1863. Present or accounted for through December, 1864.

BRANCH, TALTON D., Private
Enlisted at Camp Holmes, near Wilmington, May 12, 1862, for the war. Present or accounted for through October, 1862; however, he was reported absent sick during most of that period. Reported absent without leave on December 10, 1862. Returned to duty in March-April, 1863. Present or accounted for until November-December, 1864, when he was reported absent without leave.

BRITT, ARCHIBALD, Private
Enlisted at Charleston, South Carolina, March 9, 1863, for the war. Present or accounted for through December, 1864.

BRITT, CALVIN C., Private
Resided in Robeson County and was by occupation a farmer prior to enlisting at Charleston, South Carolina, at age 31, March 9, 1863, for the war. Present or accounted for until killed at Drewry's Bluff, Virginia, May 14, 1864.

BRITT, CASWELL, Private
Resided in Robeson County and enlisted at Charleston, South Carolina, March 9, 1863, for the war. Present or accounted for until captured at Cold Harbor, Virginia, June 1, 1864. Confined at Point Lookout, Maryland, June 11, 1864. Transferred to Elmira, New York, July 12, 1864. Arrived at Elmira on July 17, 1864. Released at Elmira on July 3, 1865, after taking the Oath of Allegiance.

BRITT, JOEL, Private
Enlisted at Camp Holmes, near Wilmington, May 12, 1862, for the war. Present or accounted for until he died in hospital at Richmond, Virginia, October 21, 1864, of "pneumonia."

BRITT, JOHN J., Private
Enlisted at Camp Holmes, near Wilmington, at age 27, May 12, 1862, for the war. Present or accounted for through December, 1864. Survived the war. [North Carolina pension records indicate that he was wounded at Drewry's Bluff, Virginia, May 14, 1864.]

BRITT, LABON, Private
Born in Bladen County and resided in Robeson County prior to enlisting at Wilmington at age 36, May 25, 1863,

for the war. Present or accounted for until he died at or near Charleston, South Carolina, August 29, 1863. Cause of death not reported.

BROGDEN, WILLIAM, Private
Born in Marion District, South Carolina, and was by occupation a farmer prior to enlisting in Robeson County at age 27, February 28, 1862. Present or accounted for until November 1, 1862, when he was reported absent without leave. Returned to duty in March-April, 1863. Present or accounted for until he deserted on August 21, 1863. Returned to duty in September-October, 1863. Present or accounted for until wounded at Cold Harbor, Virginia, May 31, 1864. Hospitalized at Richmond, Virginia, where he died on June 16, 1864, of wounds.

BULLARD, JOHN J., Private
Enlisted at Petersburg, Virginia, March 24, 1864, for the war. Present or accounted for through December, 1864.

BULLOCK, ATLAS, Private
Previously served as Private in 1st Company D, 12th Regiment N.C. Troops (2nd Regiment N.C. Volunteers). Enlisted in this company in New Hanover County on May 12, 1862, for the war. Present or accounted for through December, 1864.

BULLOCK, COLON E., Private
Enlisted at Camp Holmes, near Wilmington, May 12, 1862, for the war. Present or accounted for until wounded in the hand at Fort Harrison, Virginia, September 30, 1864. Reported absent wounded through October, 1864. Reported absent without leave in November-December, 1864.

BULLOCK, DAVIS, _____
North Carolina pension records indicate that he served in this company.

BULLOCK, JOHN, Private
Resided in Robeson County and enlisted in New Hanover County on May 12, 1862, for the war. Present or accounted for through August, 1864. Hospitalized at Wilmington on September 12, 1864, with debilitas. Returned to duty on December 9, 1864. Reported present through December, 1864.

BULLOCK, JOHN L., Private
Was by occupation a farmer prior to enlisting at Camp Holmes, near Wilmington, May 12, 1862, for the war. Present or accounted for through October 31, 1862. Discharged on an unspecified date. Reason discharged not reported. Reenlisted in the company on June 15, 1863. Present or accounted for until October 21, 1863, when he was reported absent without leave. Returned to duty in November-December, 1863. Present or accounted for until wounded in the hand at or near Petersburg, Virginia, on or about June 17, 1864. Returned to duty in November-December, 1864. Present or accounted for through December, 1864.

BULLOCK, JOSEPH H., Sergeant
Previously served as Private in 1st Company D, 12th

Regiment N.C. Troops (2nd Regiment N.C. Volunteers). Enlisted in this company at Camp Holmes, near Wilmington, May 12, 1862, for the war. Mustered in as Private. Present or accounted for until November-December, 1862, when he was reported absent without leave. Returned to duty in January-February, 1863. Promoted to Corporal on June 1, 1863. Promoted to Sergeant in March-August, 1864. Present or accounted for until wounded in the foot at Fort Harrison, Virginia, September 30, 1864. Returned to duty on November 8, 1864. Present or accounted for through December, 1864. Survived the war.

BULLOCK, MEREDITH, Private
Resided in Robeson County and was by occupation a farmer prior to enlisting in New Hanover County at age 37, September 12, 1863, for the war. Present or accounted for until wounded at Drewry's Bluff, Virginia, on or about May 13, 1864. Returned to duty prior to September 1, 1864. Present or accounted for through December, 1864. Survived the war.

BULLOCK, MICHAEL R., Private
Resided in Robeson County and was by occupation a farmer prior to enlisting at Camp Holmes, near Wilmington, at age 28, May 12, 1862, for the war. Present or accounted for until wounded in the hand at Drewry's Bluff, Virginia, on or about May 13, 1864. Hospitalized at Richmond, Virginia. Reported absent wounded until September-October, 1864, when he was reported absent without leave. Returned to duty in November-December, 1864. Present or accounted for through December, 1864. Survived the war.

BUTLER, ISHAM R., Private
Born in South Carolina and resided in Robeson County where he was by occupation a farmer prior to enlisting at Camp Holmes, near Wilmington, at age 29, May 12, 1862, for the war. Present or accounted for until November-December, 1862, when he was reported absent without leave. Returned to duty in January-February, 1863. Present or accounted for until September 22, 1863, when he was reported absent without leave. Returned to duty on October 25, 1863. Present or accounted for until wounded at Drewry's Bluff, Virginia, May 16, 1864. Reported absent wounded until November-December, 1864, when he was reported absent without leave.

BYRD, ISAAC, Private
Born in Robeson County and was by occupation a farmer prior to enlisting in Robeson County at age 23, February 28, 1862. Present or accounted for until he died in Robeson County on or about September 5, 1862, of "typhoid fever."

CARTER, NEILL, Private
Resided in Robeson County and enlisted in New Hanover County at age 18, April 28, 1862, for the war. Present or accounted for until wounded at Drewry's Bluff, Virginia, on or about May 13, 1864. Returned to duty prior to September 1, 1864. Wounded in the arm at Fort Harrison, Virginia, September 30, 1864. Reported absent without leave in November-December, 1864. Survived the war.

CARTER, ZACHARIAH, Private
Born in Robeson County where he resided as a farmer prior to enlisting in Robeson County at age 38, February 28, 1862. Present or accounted for until he was reported absent sick in July-October, 1863. Returned to duty in November-December, 1863. Present or accounted for through April, 1864. Reported absent sick in May-December, 1864.

DAFFRON, GEORGE W., Private
Born in Chatham County and resided in Robeson County where he was by occupation a farmer prior to enlisting in Robeson County at age 52, February 28, 1862. Mustered in as Corporal. Reduced to ranks in September-October, 1863. Present or accounted for until hospitalized at Richmond, Virginia, October 5, 1864, with chronic rheumatism. Returned to duty on February 24, 1865. Served for a time in 1863 as acting regimental Commissary Sergeant. No further records.

DAVIS, JAMES T., Private
Born in Robeson County and was by occupation a farmer prior to enlisting in Robeson County at age 17, February 28, 1862. Present or accounted for until November-December, 1862, when he was reported absent without leave. Returned to duty in January-February, 1863. Present or accounted for until "killed by sharpshooters" at or near Petersburg, Virginia, July 15, 1864.

DAVIS, JOHN L., Private
Enlisted in New Hanover County on June 2, 1863, for the war. Present or accounted for through December, 1864.

FLOYD, CHARLES JOHNSON, Private
Resided in Robeson County and was by occupation a farmer prior to enlisting at Camp Holmes, near Wilmington, at age 32, May 15, 1862, for the war. Present or accounted for until December 2, 1863, when he was reported absent without leave. Returned to duty on December 29, 1863. Present or accounted for until killed while on picket duty near Drewry's Bluff, Virginia, May 14, 1864.

FLOYD, WILLIAM PINKNEY, Private
Born in Robeson County where he resided prior to enlisting at Charleston, South Carolina, at age 17, March 9, 1863, for the war. Present or accounted for until he died in hospital at Petersburg, Virginia, on or about May 1, 1864, of "febris typhoides."

FRENCH, WILLIAM R., Private
Born in Perquimans County or in Mississippi and was by occupation a farmer prior to enlisting in Robeson County at age 18, February 28, 1862. Reported on detail as acting regimental Quartermaster Sergeant in June-October, 1862. Rejoined the company in November-December, 1862. Reported absent sick in November, 1862-February, 1863. Reported on detached service with the brigade and later with the division quartermaster's department from March, 1863, through December, 1864.

GIBSON, E., Private
Previously served in an unspecified cavalry unit

(probably Company F, 41st Regiment N.C. Troops [3rd Regiment N.C. Cavalry]). Transferred to this company on or about December 2, 1863, in exchange for Private William A. McLeod. Failed to report for duty and was dropped from the rolls of the company prior to March 1, 1864.

GRAHAM, JOSEPH C., Private

Born in Robeson County where he resided as a farmer prior to enlisting in Robeson County at age 26, February 28, 1862. Present or accounted for until he deserted on July 17, 1863.

GREGORY, MATTHEW, Private

Enlisted in New Hanover County at age 18, April 28, 1862, for the war. Present or accounted for until wounded in the head at or near Drewry's Bluff, Virginia, on or about May 14, 1864. Hospitalized at Richmond, Virginia. Transferred to Lynchburg, Virginia, July 8, 1864. Reported in hospital at Wilmington on November 29, 1864. Recommended for a furlough extension of thirty days on January 4, 1865. Survived the war.

GREGORY, WILLIAM, Private

Born in Robeson County and was by occupation a farmer prior to enlisting in Robeson County at age 19, February 28, 1862. Present or accounted for through November, 1862. Reported absent sick in Robeson County from December 21, 1862, through April 30, 1863. Returned to duty in May-June, 1863. Present or accounted for until captured near Petersburg, Virginia, on or about June 16, 1864. Confined at Point Lookout, Maryland, June 19, 1864. Transferred to Elmira, New York, July 9, 1864. Released at Elmira on July 19, 1865, after taking the Oath of Allegiance.

GRIMSLEY, ANDREW J., Private

Born in Robeson County where he resided as a farmer prior to enlisting in Robeson County at age 20, February 28, 1862. Present or accounted for until killed at Cold Harbor, Virginia, June 1, 1864.

GRIMSLEY, BRIGHT, Private

Born in Robeson County and resided in Columbus County where he was by occupation a farmer prior to enlisting in Robeson County at age 23, February 28, 1862. Present or accounted for until wounded in the head at Charleston, South Carolina, July 30-August 3, 1863. Returned to duty prior to September 1, 1863. Present or accounted for until captured near Petersburg, Virginia, June 16, 1864. Confined at Point Lookout, Maryland, June 19, 1864. Transferred to Elmira, New York, July 9, 1864. Released at Elmira on July 3, 1865, after taking the Oath of Allegiance.

GRIMSLEY, EVERETT, Private

Born in Robeson County and was by occupation a farmer prior to enlisting in Robeson County at age 17, February 28, 1862. Present or accounted for until he deserted on June 30, 1862. Returned to duty prior to September 1, 1862. Present or accounted for until wounded at Fort Wagner, Charleston, South Carolina, July 18, 1863. Returned to duty prior to September 1, 1863. Wounded at Cold Harbor, Virginia, May 31, 1864. Returned to duty

prior to September 1, 1864. Reported absent without leave in September-December, 1864.

GRIMSLEY, GEORGE, Private

Enlisted in New Hanover County on April 28, 1862, for the war. Deserted on June 30, 1862. Returned to duty prior to September 1, 1862. Present or accounted for until killed at Drewry's Bluff, Virginia, May 14, 1864.

GRIMSLEY, LEWIS, Private

Born in Robeson County and was by occupation a farmer prior to enlisting in Robeson County at age 20, February 28, 1862. Deserted on June 30, 1862. Returned to duty prior to September 1, 1862. Present or accounted for until wounded in the breast near Drewry's Bluff, Virginia, May 16, 1864. Returned to duty on May 21, 1864. Hospitalized at Richmond, Virginia, June 5, 1864, with a gunshot wound of the left hand. Place and date wounded not reported; however, he was probably wounded at Cold Harbor, Virginia, on or about June 1, 1864. Furloughed for sixty days on June 17, 1864. Returned to duty prior to September 1, 1864. Present or accounted for through December, 1864. Survived the war.

HAMMOND, JOHN, Private

Born in Robeson County where he resided as a farmer prior to enlisting in Robeson County at age 33, February 28, 1862. Present or accounted for until November-December, 1862, when he was reported absent sick. Returned to duty in January-February, 1863. Present or accounted for until he was reported sick in camp in May-June, 1863. Returned to duty in July-August, 1863. Present or accounted for until November-December, 1864, when he was reported absent sick at the division hospital.

HAMMOND, SIDNEY P., Sergeant

Born in Robeson County and was by occupation a farmer prior to enlisting in Robeson County at age 22, February 28, 1862. Mustered in as Private. Promoted to Corporal in January-February, 1863. Promoted to Sergeant on June 1, 1863. Present or accounted for until killed at Cold Harbor, Virginia, June 1, 1864.

HARRELL, WILLIAM H., Corporal

Born in Robeson County and was by occupation a farmer prior to enlisting in Robeson County at age 19, February 28, 1862. Mustered in as Corporal. Present or accounted for until November-December, 1862, when he was reported absent without leave. Returned to duty in January-February, 1863. Present or accounted for until captured at Cold Harbor, Virginia, June 1, 1864. Confined at Point Lookout, Maryland, June 11, 1864. Transferred to Elmira, New York, July 12, 1864. Released at Elmira on July 3, 1865, after taking the Oath of Allegiance.

HERRING, DAWSEY, Private

Enlisted in New Hanover County on April 28, 1862, for the war. Present or accounted for until discharged at Camp Whiting, near Wilmington, December 3, 1862. Reason discharged not reported.

HILLIARD, WILLIAM J., Private
Resided in Robeson County and enlisted at Camp Holmes, near Wilmington, May 15, 1862, for the war. Present or accounted for until hospitalized at Wilmington on July 11, 1863, with rheumatism. Furloughed for thirty days on July 22, 1863. Returned to duty in September-October, 1863. Present or accounted for until captured near Drewry's Bluff, Virginia, May 16, 1864. Confined at Point Lookout, Maryland, May 19, 1864. Transferred to Elmira, New York, where he arrived on August 18, 1864. Paroled at Elmira on October 11, 1864. Received at Venus Point, Savannah River, Georgia, November 15, 1864, for exchange.

HODGES, JOHN, Private
Enlisted in Robeson County. Date of enlistment not reported. A company record dated April 10, 1862, states that he was "absent, thigh broken." No further records.

HOLDEN, JOHN THOMAS, Musician
Enlisted in New Hanover County on December 1, 1862, for the war. Mustered in as Musician. Present or accounted for through December, 1864.

INMAN, FLOYD H., _____
Place and date of enlistment not reported. Reported absent sick in December, 1862. Dropped from the rolls of the company on or about January 1, 1863.

INMAN, HENRY W., Private
Born in Robeson County and was by occupation a farmer prior to enlisting in Robeson County at age 28, February 28, 1862. Present or accounted for until hospitalized at Wilmington on or about June 28, 1862, with typhoid fever. Returned to duty in July-August, 1862. Reported absent sick from September, 1862, through February, 1863. Returned to duty in March-April, 1863. Present or accounted for until killed at Cold Harbor, Virginia, June 1, 1864.

ISRAEL, JOHN, Private
Resided in Robeson County and was by occupation a farmer prior to enlisting in New Hanover County at age 31, June 2, 1863, for the war. Present or accounted for until he deserted on August 19, 1863. Reported under arrest in March-April, 1864. Returned to duty prior to June 1, 1864, when he was captured at Cold Harbor, Virginia. Confined at Point Lookout, Maryland, June 11, 1864. Transferred to Elmira, New York, July 12, 1864. Died at Elmira on September 6, 1864, of "dropsy from hepatic disease."

IVEY, HUGH R., Private
Born in Robeson County and was by occupation a farmer prior to enlisting in Robeson County at age 29, February 28, 1862. Present or accounted for until November-December, 1862, when he was reported absent sick. Returned to duty in January-February, 1863. Present or accounted for until July-August, 1863, when he was reported sick in hospital. Returned to duty on October 29, 1863. Present or accounted for through April, 1864. Wounded in the left shoulder at or near Drewry's Bluff, Virginia, on or about May 16, 1864. Hospitalized at Richmond, Virginia. Reported absent wounded or absent

sick through August, 1864. Returned to duty in September-October, 1864. Reported absent on detached service in November-December, 1864.

JOHNSON, JOHN M., Private
Enlisted in New Hanover County on May 5, 1862, for the war. Died in hospital at Wilmington on June 17, 1862, of "typhoid fever" and was "taken home by his father."

LAMB, PETER, Private
Resided in Robeson County and was by occupation a farmer prior to enlisting in New Hanover County at age 33, May 25, 1863, for the war. Present or accounted for until December 2, 1863, when he was reported absent without leave. Returned to duty in January-February, 1864. Present or accounted for until killed at or near Drewry's Bluff, Virginia, on or about May 16, 1864.

LANE, JOSEPH C., Private
Enlisted at Camp Holmes, near Wilmington, May 29, 1862, for the war. Present or accounted for until September-October, 1862, when he was reported absent sick. Returned to duty in November-December, 1862. Present or accounted for until May-August, 1864, when he was reported absent wounded. Place and date wounded not reported. Returned to duty in September-October, 1864. Present or accounted for through December, 1864.

LEE, ASA C., Private
Resided in Robeson County and was by occupation a farmer prior to enlisting at Camp Holmes, near Wilmington, at age 32, May 29, 1862, for the war. Present or accounted for until wounded at Fort Wagner, Charleston, South Carolina, July 18, 1863. Returned to duty prior to September 1, 1863. Present or accounted for through October, 1864. Reported absent without leave in November-December, 1864.

LEE, DAVID L., Private
Enlisted at Petersburg, Virginia, January 14, 1864, for the war. Present or accounted for until captured at Cold Harbor, Virginia, June 1, 1864. Confined at Point Lookout, Maryland, June 11, 1864. Transferred to Elmira, New York, July 12, 1864. Died at Elmira on September 20, 1864, of "chronic diarrhoea."

LEE, JAMES L., Private
Resided in Robeson County and was by occupation a farmer prior to enlisting at Camp Holmes, near Wilmington, at age 24, May 29, 1862, for the war. Present or accounted for until September-October, 1862, when he was reported absent sick. Returned to duty in November-December, 1862. Present or accounted for until November-December, 1864, when he was reported absent without leave. Survived the war.

LEE, JESSE, Private
Enlisted in New Hanover County on May 20, 1863, for the war. Present or accounted for through June, 1863. Reported sick in hospital in July-October, 1863. Deserted on or about December 2, 1863.

LEE, WILLIAM O., Private
Resided in Robeson County and was by occupation a

farmer prior to enlisting at Camp Holmes, near Wilmington, at age 28, May 29, 1862, for the war. Reported absent sick in June, 1862, and September-October, 1862. Returned to duty in November-December, 1862. Reported absent sick in January-February, 1863. Returned to duty in March-April, 1863. Reported sick in camp or absent sick in May-August, 1863. Reported absent without leave on August 21, 1863. Returned to duty on or about January 25, 1864. Present or accounted for until captured at Cold Harbor, Virginia, June 1, 1864. Confined at Point Lookout, Maryland, June 11, 1864. Transferred to Elmira, New York, July 12, 1864. Paroled at Elmira and transferred to the James River, Virginia, February 20, 1865, for exchange. Hospitalized at Richmond, Virginia, February 28, 1865, with an unspecified complaint. Furloughed for thirty days on March 6, 1865.

McCORMICK, PHILIP B., Private
Resided in Robeson County and enlisted in New Hanover County on May 5, 1862, for the war. Deserted at Camp Holmes, near Wilmington, May 30, 1862. Returned to duty in July-August, 1863. Present or accounted for through December, 1864.

McCORMICK, WESLEY, Private
Enlisted at Camp Holmes, near Wilmington, May 5, 1862, for the war. Present or accounted for until captured at Fort Harrison, Virginia, September 30, 1864. Confined at Point Lookout, Maryland, October 5, 1864. Paroled at Point Lookout and transferred to Boulware's Wharf, James River, Virginia, where he was received on March 19, 1865, for exchange.

McFARLAND, JAMES R., Private
Enlisted in New Hanover County on May 15, 1862, for the war. Died in hospital at Wilmington on or about June 3, 1862, of "typhoid fever."

McFARLAND, JOHN W., Private
Enlisted in New Hanover County on May 15, 1862, for the war. Died in hospital at Wilmington on or about June 6, 1862. Cause of death not reported.

McFARLAND, WILLIAM F., Private
Enlisted in New Hanover County on May 15, 1862, for the war. Present or accounted for until he died in hospital at Wilmington on June 6, 1862, of "continued fever."

McLEAN, ALEXANDER, Private
Born in Robeson County and was by occupation a farmer prior to enlisting in Robeson County at age 22, February 28, 1862. Present or accounted for until November-December, 1862, when he was reported absent sick without leave. Returned to duty in January-February, 1863. Present or accounted for until hospitalized at Wilmington on July 1, 1863, with dropsy. Furloughed for thirty days on July 25, 1863. Returned to duty in September-October, 1863. Present or accounted for until May-August, 1864, when he was reported absent sick at the brigade hospital. Returned to duty in September-October, 1864. Present or accounted for through December, 1864. Survived the war.

McLEAN, ARCHIBALD S., Private
Born in Robeson County and was by occupation a farmer prior to enlisting in Robeson County at age 19, February 28, 1862. Present or accounted for until November-December, 1862, when he was reported absent without leave. Returned to duty in January-February, 1863. Present or accounted for until he died in hospital at Wilmington on May 18, 1863, of "feb[ris] typh[oides]."

McLEAN, HECTOR R., Private
Born in Robeson County and was by occupation a farmer prior to enlisting in Robeson County at age 23, February 28, 1862. Present or accounted for through April, 1863; however, he was reported absent sick during most of that period. Discharged on or about May 23, 1863, by reason of "disability." Reenlisted in the company at Richmond, Virginia, December 3, 1864, for the war. Present or accounted for through December, 1864.

McLEAN, WESTON G., 1st Sergeant
Previously served as Private in 1st Company D, 12th Regiment N.C. Troops (2nd Regiment N.C. Volunteers). Enlisted in this company in Robeson County on February 28, 1862. Mustered in as Sergeant. Present or accounted for until November-December, 1862, when he was reported absent without leave. Returned to duty in January-February, 1863. Promoted to 1st Sergeant in March-April, 1863. Present or accounted for until captured at Cold Harbor, Virginia, June 1, 1864. Confined at Point Lookout, Maryland, June 11, 1864. Transferred to Elmira, New York, July 12, 1864. Paroled at Elmira on or about February 20, 1865, and transferred to the James River, Virginia, for exchange. Hospitalized at Richmond, Virginia, March 4, 1865, with "diarrhoea ch[ronic]" and died on March 12, 1865.

McLEOD, WILLIAM A., Private
Born in Marlboro District, South Carolina, and resided in Robeson County where he was by occupation a farmer prior to enlisting in Robeson County at age 40, February 28, 1862. Present or accounted for until November-December, 1862, when he was reported absent without leave. Returned to duty in January-February, 1863. Present or accounted for through October, 1863. Transferred to an unspecified cavalry unit (probably Company F, 41st Regiment N.C. Troops [3rd Regiment N.C. Cavalry]) on or about December 2, 1863, in exchange for Private E. Gibson. Failed to report for duty with his new unit.

McNEILL, EMORY D., Private
Enlisted at Petersburg, Virginia, March 24, 1864, for the war. Present or accounted for until wounded slightly in the head at Fort Harrison, Virginia, September 30, 1864. Returned to duty prior to November 1, 1864. Reported present through December, 1864.

McNEILL, JAMES S., Private
Enlisted in Robeson County on February 28, 1862. Present or accounted for through August, 1864; however, he was reported absent on detached service (probably as a teamster) during much of that period. Reported absent sick in September-October, 1864. Rejoined the company

in November-December, 1864. Present or accounted for through December, 1864.

MARTIN, ROBERT H., Private
Resided in Robeson County and was by occupation a farmer prior to enlisting at Camp Holmes, near Wilmington, at age 27, May 5, 1862, for the war. Present or accounted for until captured at Cold Harbor, Virginia, June 1, 1864. Confined at Point Lookout, Maryland, June 11, 1864. Transferred to Elmira, New York, July 12, 1864. Died at Elmira on August 25, 1864, of "chronic diarrhoea."

MILLER, ZACHARIAH H., Corporal
Enlisted in New Hanover County on April 21, 1862, for the war. Mustered in as Private. Deserted at Wilmington on June 26, 1862. Returned to duty prior to September 1, 1862. Promoted to Corporal in May-August, 1864. Present or accounted for until hospitalized at Richmond, Virginia, on or about August 8, 1864, with diarrhoea. Furloughed for thirty days on August 27, 1864. Reported absent without leave in October-December, 1864.

MITCHELL, HUGH G., Private
Enlisted at Camp Holmes, near Wilmington, May 15, 1862, for the war. Reported absent sick in September-October, 1862. Reported absent without leave in November-December, 1862. Returned to duty in January-February, 1863. Present or accounted for until transferred to Company A, 2nd Regiment Confederate Engineer Troops, August 3, 1863.

MOODY, RICHARD, _____
North Carolina pension records indicate that he served in this company.

MOORE, GREEN W., Sergeant
Born in Robeson County and was by occupation a farmer prior to enlisting in Robeson County at age 16, February 28, 1862. Mustered in as Private. Reported absent without leave in November-December, 1862. Returned to duty in January-February, 1863. Promoted to Sergeant on September 30, 1863. Present or accounted for until wounded in the left thigh (flesh) near Petersburg, Virginia, June 17, 1864. Hospitalized at Petersburg where he died on July 23, 1864, of wounds.

MOORE, RICHARD H., Sergeant
Born in Robeson County where he resided as a farmer prior to enlisting in Robeson County at age 27, February 28, 1862. Mustered in as Corporal. Promoted to Sergeant on September 16, 1862. Present or accounted for until captured near Petersburg, Virginia, June 15, 1864. Confined at Point Lookout, Maryland, June 19, 1864. Transferred to Elmira, New York, July 12, 1864. Paroled at Elmira on March 10, 1865. Received at Boulware's Wharf, James River, Virginia, March 15, 1865, for exchange. Died on or about May 3, 1865, of disease. Place of death not reported.

MORRIS, JOHN C., Private
Enlisted in New Hanover County on April 21, 1862, for the war. Present or accounted for through October, 1862.

Reported absent on detached service at Wilmington from November, 1862, through April, 1864. Reported present but sick in May-August, 1864. Wounded in the right arm at Fort Stedman, Virginia, September 30, 1864. Reported absent sick in November-December, 1864. Paroled at Greensboro on May 1, 1865.

PARKER, EVERETT, Private
Resided in Robeson County and was by occupation a farm laborer prior to enlisting in New Hanover County at age 28, June 2, 1863, for the war. Present or accounted for until March 17, 1864, when he was reported absent without leave. Returned to duty prior to June 1, 1864, when he was captured at Cold Harbor, Virginia. Confined at Point Lookout, Maryland, June 11, 1864. Transferred to Elmira, New York, July 12, 1864. Paroled at Elmira on October 11, 1864. Received at Venus Point, Savannah River, Georgia, November 15, 1864, for exchange. Survived the war.

PARKER, JOSEPH, Private
Born in Marion District, South Carolina, and was by occupation a farmer prior to enlisting in Robeson County at age 17, February 28, 1862. Reported present but under arrest in March-June, 1862. Reason he was arrested not reported. Returned to duty prior to September 1, 1862. Present or accounted for until killed at Fort Wagner, Charleston, South Carolina, July 18, 1863.

PAUL, ABRAHAM, Private
Enlisted in New Hanover County at age 22, April 30, 1862, for the war. Discharged prior to July 1, 1862, presumably by reason of injuries to his right foot received in an accident near Wilmington.

PETERSON, JOHN, Private
Previously served as Private in 1st Company D, 12th Regiment N.C. Troops (2nd Regiment N.C. Volunteers). Enlisted in this company in Robeson County on February 28, 1862. Present or accounted for until captured at Cold Harbor, Virginia, June 1, 1864. Confined at Point Lookout, Maryland, June 11, 1864. Transferred to Elmira, New York, July 12, 1864. Died at Elmira on February 14, 1865, of "chronic diarrhoea."

PITMAN, ISHAM, Private
Resided in Robeson County and was by occupation a farmer prior to enlisting at Camp Holmes, near Wilmington, at age 34, May 5, 1862, for the war. Present or accounted for until November-December, 1862, when he was reported absent without leave. Returned to duty in January-February, 1863. Furloughed for thirty days from hospital at Wilmington on June 16, 1863, by reason of debility resulting from typhoid fever. Returned to duty in July-August, 1863. Present or accounted for until captured at Cold Harbor, Virginia, June 1, 1864. Confined at Point Lookout, Maryland, June 11, 1864. Transferred to Elmira, New York, July 12, 1864. Paroled at Elmira on October 11, 1864. Died at Fort Monroe, Virginia, November 2, 1864, of "pneumonia" while being transferred for exchange. [Previously served as 1st Lieutenant in the 58th Regiment N.C. Militia.]

PITTMAN, RANDOLPH, Corporal

Previously served as Private in 1st Company D, 12th Regiment N.C. Troops (2nd Regiment N.C. Volunteers). Enlisted in this company in Robeson County on February 28, 1862. Mustered in as Corporal. Present or accounted for through April, 1863. Reported absent on detached service at Wilmington (probably with the C.S. Navy) from May, 1863, through February, 1864. Rejoined the company in March-April, 1864. Present or accounted for until wounded in the right leg at Drewry's Bluff, Virginia, May 16, 1864. Hospitalized at Richmond, Virginia. Furloughed for sixty days on June 8, 1864. Returned to duty in November-December, 1864. Present or accounted for through December, 1864.

POWELL, PATRICK M., Private

Born in Robeson County where he resided as a farmer prior to enlisting in Robeson County at age 46, February 28, 1862. Present or accounted for until killed at Cold Harbor, Virginia, May 31, 1864.

PREVATT, ALFRED R., Private

Born in Robeson County and was by occupation a farmer prior to enlisting in Robeson County at age 21, February 28, 1862. Deserted on or about June 15, 1862. Returned to duty in July-August, 1862. Reported absent without leave in September-October, 1862. Listed as a deserter in March-April, 1863, and dropped from the rolls of the company. Survived the war.

PREVATT, ANDREW J., Private

Resided in Robeson County and was by occupation a farmer prior to enlisting at Camp Holmes, near Wilmington, at age 23, May 10, 1862, for the war. Hospitalized at Wilmington on or about June 16, 1862, with orchitis. Deserted on July 27, 1862. Returned to duty prior to September 1, 1862. Present or accounted for through December, 1862. Reported absent sick in Robeson County from January 20 through June 30, 1863. Returned to duty in July-August, 1863. Present or accounted for through April, 1864. Died at home in Robeson County on August 5, 1864, of disease.

PREVATT, ELIAS, Private

Born in Robeson County where he resided prior to enlisting at age 19, February 28, 1862. Present or accounted for through October, 1862. Reported absent without leave in November-December, 1862. Returned to duty in January-February, 1863. Present or accounted for until captured at Cold Harbor, Virginia, June 1, 1864. Confined at Point Lookout, Maryland, June 11, 1864. Transferred to Elmira, New York, July 12, 1864. Died at Elmira on December 13, 1864, of "chronic diarrhoea."

PREVATT, HENRY C., Private

Enlisted at Camp Holmes, near Wilmington, May 10, 1862, for the war. Present or accounted for until October 4, 1863, when he was reported absent without leave. Returned to duty in January-February, 1864. Present or accounted for until wounded at Drewry's Bluff, Virginia, May 16, 1864. Returned to duty prior to June 1, 1864, when he was captured at Cold Harbor, Virginia. Confined at Point Lookout, Maryland, June 11, 1864. Transferred to Elmira, New York, July 12, 1864. Paroled at Elmira on

February 20, 1865, and transferred to the James River, Virginia, for exchange. Died in hospital at Richmond, Virginia, March 27, 1865. Cause of death not reported.

PREVATT, JAMES P., Private

Born in Robeson County where he resided as a farmer prior to enlisting in Robeson County at age 22, February 28, 1862. Present or accounted for until November-December, 1862, when he was reported absent without leave. Returned to duty in January-February, 1863. Present or accounted for until captured near Globe Tavern, Virginia, August 19, 1864. Confined at Point Lookout, Maryland, August 22, 1864. Paroled at Point Lookout on or about February 10, 1865. Received at Cox's Wharf, James River, Virginia, on or about February 15, 1865, for exchange. Hospitalized at Richmond, Virginia, February 16, 1865, with chronic diarrhoea. Furloughed for sixty days on March 7, 1865.

PREVATT, JORDAN, Private

Born in Robeson County and was by occupation a farmer prior to enlisting in Robeson County at age 26, February 28, 1862. Present or accounted for until November-December, 1862, when he was reported absent without leave. Reported absent sick in January-February, 1863. Returned to duty in March-April, 1863. Reported absent sick in May-August, 1863. Reported absent without leave on September 1, 1863. Returned to duty on or about December 20, 1863. Present or accounted for until captured at Fort Harrison, Virginia, September 30, 1864. Confined at Point Lookout, Maryland, October 5, 1864. Released at Point Lookout on June 3, 1865, after taking the Oath of Allegiance.

PREVATT, MICHAEL, Private

Born in Robeson County where he resided as a farmer prior to enlisting at Wilmington at age 32, May 25, 1863, for the war. Present or accounted for through June, 1863. Reported sick in hospital in July-October, 1863. Reported absent without leave for one month and twelve days in November-December, 1863. Present or accounted for until he died in hospital at Petersburg, Virginia, May 18, 1864, of "pneumonia."

PREVATT, PETER P., Private

Resided in Robeson County and was by occupation a farmer prior to enlisting in New Hanover County at age 28, May 25, 1863, for the war. Reported sick in hospital in July-August, 1863. Returned to duty in September-October, 1863. Present or accounted for until he was reported sick in hospital at Petersburg, Virginia, in March-April, 1864. Returned to duty in May-August, 1864. Present or accounted for through December, 1864.

PREVATT, WILLIAM W., Sergeant

Born in Robeson County where he resided as a farmer prior to enlisting in Robeson County at age 21, February 28, 1862. Mustered in as Private. Reported absent without leave in March-June, 1862. Returned to duty in July-August, 1862. Present or accounted for until November-December, 1862, when he was reported absent without leave. Reported absent sick in January-February, 1863. Returned to duty in March-April, 1863. Promoted to Corporal in May-August, 1864. Wounded in Virginia in

June, 1864. Returned to duty prior to September 1, 1864. Wounded slightly in the finger at Fort Harrison, Virginia, September 30, 1864. Returned to duty prior to November 1, 1864. Promoted to Sergeant in November-December, 1864. Present or accounted for through December, 1864.

PREVATT, WILLIS P., Private

Resided in Robeson County and was by occupation a farm laborer prior to enlisting in New Hanover County at age 19, May 25, 1863, for the war. Present or accounted for until he died in hospital at or near Charleston, South Carolina, August 27-29, 1863. Cause of death not reported.

RANSOM, ARTHUR, Private

Born in Bladen County and was by occupation a farmer prior to enlisting in Robeson County at age 22, February 28, 1862. Present or accounted for until August 10, 1862, when he was reported absent without leave. Returned to duty in March-April, 1863. Present or accounted for until wounded at Cold Harbor, Virginia, May 31, 1864. Reported absent wounded or absent sick through December, 1864.

RATLEY, RICHARD C., Private

Resided in Robeson County and was by occupation a farmer prior to enlisting at age 32, February 28, 1862. Dropped from the rolls of the company prior to July 1, 1862. Reason he was dropped not reported.

SEALEY, NICHOLAS T., Private

Resided in Robeson County and was by occupation a farmer prior to enlisting at Camp Holmes, near Wilmington, at age 30, May 5, 1862, for the war. Present or accounted for until he deserted in July, 1863.

SEALY, NEPHISON, Private

Enlisted on February 28, 1862. Dropped from the rolls of the company prior to July 1, 1862. Reason he was dropped not reported.

SMITH, GEORGE A., Sergeant

Previously served as Private in 1st Company D, 12th Regiment N.C. Troops (2nd Regiment N.C. Volunteers). Enlisted in this company in Robeson County on February 28, 1862. Mustered in as 1st Sergeant. Reduced to the rank of Sergeant in July-August, 1862. Present or accounted for until November-December, 1862, when he was reported absent without leave. Returned to duty in January-February, 1863. Present or accounted for until captured at Cold Harbor, Virginia, June 1, 1864. Confined at Point Lookout, Maryland, June 11, 1864. Transferred to Elmira, New York, July 9, 1864. Paroled at Elmira on March 2, 1865, and transferred to the James River, Virginia, for exchange. Hospitalized at Richmond, Virginia, March 7, 1865, with debilitas and was furloughed for thirty days on March 8, 1865.

SMITH, JAMES P., Sergeant

Previously served as Corporal in 1st Company D, 12th Regiment N.C. Troops (2nd Regiment N.C. Volunteers). Enlisted in this company in Robeson County on February 28, 1862. Mustered in as Sergeant. Promoted to 1st

Sergeant on September 16, 1862. Reduced to the rank of Sergeant in March-April, 1863. Present or accounted for until captured at Cold Harbor, Virginia, June 1, 1864. Confined at Point Lookout, Maryland, June 11, 1864. Transferred to Elmira, New York, July 9, 1864. Paroled at Elmira on March 14, 1865. Received at Boulware's Wharf, James River, Virginia, on or about March 18, 1865, for exchange. Survived the war.

SMITH, RICHARD R., Private

Enlisted in New Hanover County at age 18, May 20, 1863, for the war. Present or accounted for through December, 1864. Survived the war.

SNIPES, HUGH G., Private

Resided in Robeson County and enlisted in New Hanover County at age 19, June 2, 1863, for the war. Present or accounted for until wounded in the left shoulder at or near Globe Tavern, Virginia, on or about August 19, 1864. Reported absent wounded through October, 1864. Returned to duty in November-December, 1864. Paroled at Greensboro on May 1, 1865.

SNIPES, NELSON, Private

Born in Robeson County where he resided as a farmer prior to enlisting in Robeson County at age 46, February 28, 1862. Present or accounted for until wounded and captured at Drewry's Bluff, Virginia, on or about May 14, 1864. Hospitalized at Point Lookout, Maryland, where he died on May 28, 1864, of wounds.

STEPHENS, FRANCIS, Private

Enlisted at Camp Holmes, near Wilmington, at age 21, May 5, 1862, for the war. Present or accounted for through December, 1864. Survived the war.

TAYLOR, AMOS, Private

Born in Robeson County and was by occupation a laborer prior to enlisting in Robeson County at age 16, February 28, 1862. Present or accounted for until wounded in the left shoulder at or near Cold Harbor, Virginia, on or about June 1, 1864. Hospitalized at Richmond, Virginia. Furloughed for sixty days on June 17, 1864. Returned to duty prior to September 1, 1864. Captured at Fort Harrison, Virginia, September 30, 1864. Confined at Point Lookout, Maryland, October 5, 1864. Paroled at Point Lookout on November 1, 1864. Received at Venus Point, Savannah River, Georgia, November 15, 1864, for exchange.

TAYLOR, BENJAMIN, Private

Born in Robeson County and was by occupation a laborer prior to enlisting in Robeson County at age 19, February 28, 1862. Present or accounted for until he died in hospital at Petersburg, Virginia, April 1, 1864, of "pneumonia."

TAYLOR, WILLIS, Private

Resided in Robeson County and was by occupation a farmer prior to enlisting at Richmond, Virginia, at age 41, December 3, 1864, for the war. Present or accounted for through December, 1864.

THOMPSON, JAMES P., Sergeant

Born in Robeson County where he resided as a farmer prior to enlisting in Robeson County at age 22, February 28, 1862. Mustered in as Sergeant. Present or accounted for through October, 1862. Reported absent without leave in November-December, 1862. Reported absent sick in January-February, 1863. Returned to duty in March-April, 1863. Discharged on May 20, 1863, after providing a substitute.

THOMPSON, JOHN, Private

Resided in Robeson County where he enlisted on February 28, 1862. Died in Robeson County on June 20, 1862. Cause of death not reported.

THOMPSON, JOHN EASY, Private

Born in Robeson County and was by occupation a farmer prior to enlisting in Robeson County at age 30, February 28, 1862. Present or accounted for until captured at Cold Harbor, Virginia, June 1, 1864. Confined at Point Lookout, Maryland, June 11, 1864. Transferred to Elmira, New York, July 12, 1864. Released at Elmira on July 3, 1865, after taking the Oath of Allegiance.

THOMPSON, JOHN S., Private

Enlisted in New Hanover County on May 27, 1863, for the war. Present or accounted for through June, 1863. Reported absent sick in July-August, 1863. Returned to duty in September-October, 1863. Present or accounted for until he died in hospital at Petersburg, Virginia, on or about May 8, 1864, of "febris typhoides" and/or "pneumonia."

THOMPSON, OLIVER T., Corporal

Born in Robeson County and was by occupation a farmer prior to enlisting in Robeson County at age 17, February 28, 1862. Mustered in as Private. Promoted to Corporal on September 16, 1862. Present or accounted for until killed near Petersburg, Virginia, June 17, 1864.

THOMPSON, THEODORE ASHLEY, Private

Born in Robeson County and was by occupation a farmer prior to enlisting in Robeson County at age 16, February 28, 1862. Present or accounted for through August, 1862. Reported absent sick in September-October, 1862. Returned to duty in November-December, 1862. Present or accounted for until "killed by sharpshooters" at or near Petersburg, Virginia, August 2, 1864.

THOMPSON, WILLIAM A., Private

Resided in Robeson County and enlisted at Charleston, South Carolina, at age 18, March 9, 1863, for the war. Present or accounted for until killed near Petersburg, Virginia, June 17, 1864.

THOMSON, W., _____

Place and date of enlistment not reported. Name appears on a regimental record dated December, 1862, which states that he was absent sick. No further records.

TOWNSEND, CHARLES F., Private

Born in Robeson County where he resided as a farmer prior to enlisting in Robeson County at age 22, February 28, 1862. Present or accounted for until wounded in the right arm by a shell at Sullivan's Island, Charleston, South Carolina, in September, 1863. Right arm amputated. Reported absent wounded through October, 1864. Survived the war.

TOWNSEND, FULLER C., Private

Born in Robeson County where he resided as a farmer prior to enlisting in Robeson County at age 28, February 28, 1862. Present or accounted for until November-December, 1862, when he was reported absent without leave. Reported absent on detached service in January-April, 1863. Rejoined the company in May-June, 1863. Present or accounted for until "wounded by [a] sharpshooter" at or near Petersburg, Virginia, in the summer of 1864. Returned to duty in November-December, 1864. Present or accounted for through December, 1864.

TOWNSEND, JACKSON, Private

Born in Robeson County and was by occupation a farmer prior to enlisting in Robeson County at age 39, February 28, 1862. Present or accounted for through August, 1862. Reported absent sick in September-December, 1862. Reported absent on detached service in January-February, 1863. Rejoined the company in March-April, 1863. Reported absent sick and absent on detached service in May-October, 1863. Rejoined the company in November-December, 1863. Reported absent sick in January-April, 1864. Reported absent on detached service in May-October, 1864. Rejoined the company in November-December, 1864. Present or accounted for through December, 1864. Survived the war.

TYNER, WILEY J., Private

Born in Robeson County where he resided as a farm laborer prior to enlisting at age 24, February 28, 1862. Reported present but under arrest in March-June, 1862. Reason he was arrested not reported. Returned to duty in July-August, 1862. Present or accounted for until November-December, 1862, when he was reported absent without leave. Returned to duty in January-February, 1863. Present or accounted for until he deserted on or about May 28, 1864.

WARD, JOHN F., Private

Born in Robeson County where he resided as a farmer prior to enlisting in Robeson County at age 36, February 28, 1862. Mustered in as Sergeant. Reduced to ranks in July-October, 1862. Hospitalized at Wilmington on May 9, 1862, with orchitis. Returned to duty on June 12, 1862. Reported absent sick in September-October, 1862. Returned to duty in November-December, 1862. Present or accounted for until hospitalized at Wilmington on December 5, 1863, with icterus. Returned to duty on January 7, 1864. Reported sick in hospital at Richmond, Virginia, in May-August, 1864. Returned to duty in September-October, 1864. Present or accounted for through December, 1864.

WATSON, NOAH, Private

Born in Marion District, South Carolina, and was by occupation a farmer prior to enlisting in Robeson County at age 20, February 28, 1862. Died in hospital at

Wilmington on or about May 28, 1862, of "congestive chill."

WILCOX, REDDEN, Private
Born in Robeson County and was by occupation a farmer prior to enlisting in Robeson County at age 16, February 28, 1862. Present or accounted for until wounded at Fort Wagner, Charleston, South Carolina, July 18, 1863. Returned to duty prior to September 1, 1863. Present or accounted for until captured at Cold Harbor, Virginia, June 1, 1864. Confined at Point Lookout, Maryland, June 11, 1864. Transferred to Elmira, New York, July 12, 1864. Died at Elmira on November 28, 1864, of "pleuro pneumonia."

WILCOX, RICHARD B., Private
Resided in Robeson County and was by occupation a farmer prior to enlisting in New Hanover County at age 37, February 8, 1863, for the war. Present or accounted for until he died in hospital at Wilmington on or about June 12, 1863, of "febris typh[oi]d."

WILKINS, DANIEL, Private
Born in Robeson County and was by occupation a farmer prior to enlisting in Robeson County at age 18, February 28, 1862. Dropped from the rolls of the company on or about April 10, 1862. Reason he was dropped not reported.

WILKINS, JOHN M., Private
Born in Robeson County and was by occupation a farmer prior to enlisting in Robeson County at age 18, February 28, 1862. Present or accounted for until he died at Kinston on October 8, 1862, of "ty[phoid] fever."

WILKINSON, JAMES, Private
Born in Robeson County and was by occupation a farmer prior to enlisting in Robeson County at age 17, February 28, 1862. Reported absent sick from September, 1862, through May, 1863. Discharged on June 4, 1863, by reason of "a *very severe* attack of fever. . . ."

WILKINSON, MALCOLM, Private
Born in Robeson County where he resided as a farmer prior to enlisting in Robeson County at age 25, February 28, 1862. Present or accounted for until wounded in the left leg at Fort Wagner, Charleston, South Carolina, July 18, 1863. Left leg amputated. Reported absent wounded until September-October, 1864, when he was retired from service.

WILLIAMS, GILES B., Corporal
Resided in Columbus County and enlisted at Camp Holmes, near Wilmington, April 30, 1862, for the war. Mustered in as Private. Promoted to Corporal in March-April, 1864. Present or accounted for until captured at Cold Harbor, Virginia, June 1, 1864. Confined at Point Lookout, Maryland, June 11, 1864. Transferred to Elmira, New York, July 12, 1864. Released at Elmira on July 3, 1865, after taking the Oath of Allegiance.

WILLIAMS, JOHN HENRY, Private
Born in Robeson County and was by occupation a farmer

prior to enlisting in Robeson County at age 21, February 28, 1862. Present or accounted for through December, 1864.

WILLIAMS, ROWLAND F., Private
Born in Robeson County on October 15, 1843, and resided in Robeson County prior to enlisting at Camp Holmes, near Wilmington, April 30, 1862, for the war. Present or accounted for until wounded in the right forearm at Drewry's Bluff, Virginia, May 16, 1864. Hospitalized at Richmond, Virginia. Furloughed for sixty days on June 3, 1864. Returned to duty prior to September 1, 1864. Present or accounted for through December, 1864. Survived the war.

COMPANY F

This company, known as the "Ashpole True Boys," was raised in Robeson County and enlisted at Lumberton on March 10, 1862. It was mustered into state service at Wilmington on April 21, 1862, and assigned to the 51st Regiment N.C. Troops as Company F. After joining the regiment the company functioned as a part of the regiment, and its history for the remainder of the war is reported as a part of the regimental history.

The information contained in the following roster was compiled primarily from a company muster-in and descriptive roll dated April 21, 1862, and from company muster rolls dated March 10, 1862-December 31, 1864. No company muster rolls were located for the period after December 31, 1864. Valuable information was obtained from primary records such as the North Carolina adjutant general's *Roll of Honor*, discharge certificates, medical records, prisoner of war records, *The War of the Rebellion: A Compilation of the Official Records of the Union and Confederate Armies*, militia records, newspaper casualty lists and obituaries, Confederate pension applications filed with the state of North Carolina, and the 1860 federal census of North Carolina. Secondary sources such as postwar rosters and histories, cemetery records, the *Confederate Veteran*, published genealogies, and records of the United Daughters of the Confederacy also provided useful information.

OFFICERS

CAPTAINS

WALTER, ALFRED B.
Born in South Carolina and resided in Robeson County where he was by occupation a physician prior to enlisting in Robeson County at age 25. Appointed Captain on March 10, 1862. Resigned on August 18, 1862, by reason of "constitutional debility caused by chronic dysentery. . . ." Resignation accepted on August 23, 1862.

NORMENT, WILLIAM STOKES
Previously served as Captain of Company D, 18th
Regiment N.C. Troops (8th Regiment N.C. Volunteers).
Appointed Captain of this company on August 23, 1862.
Present or accounted for until wounded in the right leg
at Fort Harrison, Virginia, September 30, 1864. Reported
absent wounded through December, 1864.

LIEUTENANTS

FULMORE, ANDREW C., 1st Lieutenant
Previously served as Private in 1st Company D, 12th
Regiment N.C. Troops (2nd Regiment N.C. Volunteers).
Appointed 1st Lieutenant of this company on March 10,
1862. Present or accounted for until October 29, 1863,
when he was reported absent without leave. Returned to
duty in November-December, 1863. Present or accounted
for until hospitalized at Richmond, Virginia, June 16,
1864, with acute diarrhoea. Returned to duty on July 6,
1864. Hospitalized at Richmond on August 4, 1864, with
chronic diarrhoea. Furloughed on August 11, 1864.
Returned to duty in November-December, 1864, but was
reported absent on sick furlough on December 20, 1864.
Surrendered at Augusta, Georgia, May 25, 1865, and was
paroled the same date.

HARTMAN, JACOB W., 2nd Lieutenant
Previously served as Private in 1st Company D, 12th
Regiment N.C. Troops (2nd Regiment N.C. Volunteers).
Appointed 2nd Lieutenant of this company on March 10,
1862. Present or accounted for until May-August, 1864,
when he was reported absent wounded. Place and date
wounded not reported. Returned to duty in September-
October, 1864. Reported on duty as commander of the
company in September-December, 1864. Paroled at
Greensboro on May 1, 1865.

HIGLEY, GILBERT P., 2nd Lieutenant
Born at East Granby, Connecticut, and resided in Robeson
County where he was by occupation a carpenter prior to
enlisting at age 38. Appointed 2nd Lieutenant on March
10, 1862. Present or accounted for until wounded and
captured at Cold Harbor, Virginia, June 1, 1864.
Confined at Point Lookout, Maryland, June 11, 1864.
Transferred to Fort Delaware, Delaware, June 23, 1864.
Transferred to Hilton Head, South Carolina, August 20,
1864. Reported at Fort Pulaski, Georgia, on or about
October 20, 1864. Transferred back to Hilton Head on
November 19, 1864. Transferred to Fort Delaware where
he arrived on March 12, 1865. Released at Fort Delaware
on June 17, 1865, after taking the Oath of Allegiance.

NONCOMMISSIONED OFFICERS AND PRIVATES

ALFIN, D. J., Private
Enlisted at Camp Holmes, near Raleigh, March 10, 1864,
for the war. Present or accounted for until wounded near

Petersburg, Virginia, June 16, 1864. Hospitalized at
Richmond, Virginia, where he died of wounds. Date of
death not reported.

BAKER, JESSE E., Private
Enlisted at Nichols Depot, South Carolina, May 1, 1862,
for the war. Present or accounted for until captured at
Cold Harbor, Virginia, June 1, 1864. Confined at Point
Lookout, Maryland, June 11, 1864. Transferred to Elmira,
New York, July 12, 1864. Killed in a railroad accident at
Shohola, Pennsylvania, July 15, 1864, while en route to
Elmira.

BARBER, NOAH, Private
Born in Pitt County and was by occupation a farmer prior
to enlisting in Robeson County at age 33, March 10, 1862.
Present or accounted for until he deserted in September-
October, 1862. Returned to duty in November-December,
1862. Present or accounted for until wounded at Fort
Wagner, Charleston, South Carolina, July 18, 1863.
Reported absent wounded through December, 1863.
Listed as a deserter and dropped from the rolls of the
company in January-February, 1864.

BASS, FREDERICK, Private
Born in Robeson County where he resided as a farmer
prior to enlisting in Robeson County at age 25, March 10,
1862. Present or accounted for until November-
December, 1862, when he was reported absent without
leave. Returned to duty in January-February, 1863.
Present or accounted for until August 18, 1863, when he
was reported absent without leave. Returned to duty in
January-February, 1864. Reported under arrest at
Petersburg, Virginia, in March-April, 1864, for
desertion. Returned to duty in May-August, 1864. Present
or accounted for through December, 1864.

BAXLEY, ARCHIBALD C., Private
Born in Robeson County where he resided as a laborer
prior to enlisting in Robeson County at age 29, March 10,
1862. Present or accounted for through August, 1862.
Reported absent sick in September-December, 1862.
Returned to duty in January-February, 1863. Present or
accounted for until killed at Fort Wagner, Charleston,
South Carolina, July 18, 1863.

BAXLEY, HENRY J., Private
Resided in Robeson County and was by occupation a
laborer prior to enlisting in Robeson County at age 27,
March 10, 1862. Present or accounted for until July-
August, 1862, when he was reported absent sick.
Returned to duty in September-October, 1862. Present or
accounted for until hospitalized at Wilmington on or
about July 10, 1863, with typhoid fever. Returned to duty
in January-February, 1864. Present or accounted for until
August 12, 1864, when he was reported absent on sick
furlough. Returned to duty in November-December, 1864.
Present or accounted for through December, 1864.

BAXLEY, HENRY L., Private
Born in Robeson County where he resided as a farmer
prior to enlisting in Robeson County at age 24, March 10,
1862. Present or accounted for until captured near
Petersburg, Virginia, on or about June 16, 1864. Confined

at Point Lookout, Maryland, June 19, 1864. Transferred to Elmira, New York, July 9, 1864. Released at Elmira on July 11, 1865, after taking the Oath of Allegiance.

BAXLEY, MILES S., Private
Born in Robeson County and was by occupation a farmer prior to enlisting in Robeson County at age 24, March 10, 1862. Present or accounted for until wounded at Goldsboro on December 17, 1862. Returned to duty prior to January 1, 1863. Present or accounted for until August 8, 1863, when he was reported absent without leave. Hospitalized at Wilson on December 5, 1863, with an unspecified complaint. Returned to duty in January-February, 1864. Reported on detail as a hospital guard at Petersburg, Virginia, in March-April, 1864. Wounded in the hand at Drewry's Bluff, Virginia, May 16, 1864. Returned to duty prior to August 19, 1864, when he was captured near Globe Tavern, Virginia. Confined at Point Lookout, Maryland, August 24, 1864. Paroled at Point Lookout on or about March 14, 1865. Received at Boulware's Wharf, James River, Virginia, March 16, 1865, for exchange. Survived the war.

BAXLEY, PETER D., Private
Enlisted in Robeson County on March 10, 1862. Listed as a deserter on the same date. Company records dated November-December, 1862, indicate that he died in Robeson County on an unknown date. Cause of death not reported.

BAXLEY, WILLIAM H. R., Private
Born in Robeson County where he resided as a farmer prior to enlisting in Robeson County at age 23, March 10, 1862. Mustered in as Sergeant. Reduced to ranks prior to July 1, 1862. Present or accounted for until wounded seriously at Goldsboro on December 17, 1862. Reported absent wounded through April, 1863. Reported absent in prison at Wilmington "awaiting trial" (probably for absence without leave) in May-June, 1863. Reported in hospital at Augusta, Georgia, in July-August, 1863. Returned to duty in September-October, 1863. Present or accounted for until captured at Drewry's Bluff, Virginia, May 16, 1864. Confined at Point Lookout, Maryland, May 19, 1864. Transferred to Elmira, New York, in August, 1864. Released at Elmira on May 17, 1865, after taking the Oath of Allegiance.

BLANKS, JAMES W., Private
Born in Robeson County and was by occupation a farmer prior to enlisting in Robeson County at age 18, March 10, 1862. Present or accounted for until December 3, 1863, when he was reported absent without leave. Returned to duty in January-February, 1864. Present or accounted for until wounded in the shoulder at Drewry's Bluff, Virginia, May 16, 1864. Hospitalized at Richmond, Virginia. Returned to duty on June 23, 1864. Present or accounted for through December, 1864. Survived the war.

BLOUNT, JAMES W., Private
Enlisted in Robeson County on March 10, 1862. Reported absent without leave on or about April 21, 1862. May have enlisted previously in another company. No further records.

BOON, JACKSON, Private
Born in Nash County and resided in Robeson County where he was by occupation a laborer prior to enlisting in Robeson County at age 34, March 10, 1862. Present or accounted for until wounded slightly in the thigh at Fort Harrison, Virginia, September 30, 1864. Returned to duty prior to November 1, 1864. Reported present through December, 1864. Paroled at Goldsboro on May 9, 1865.

BOON, WILLIAM, Private
Born in Halifax County and was by occupation a laborer prior to enlisting in Robeson County at age 41, March 10, 1862. Present or accounted for until killed at Fort Wagner, Charleston, South Carolina, July 18, 1863.

BREWER, JESSE A., Private
Born in Robeson County and was by occupation a laborer prior to enlisting in Robeson County at age 18, March 10, 1862. Present or accounted for until wounded at Goldsboro on December 17, 1862. Returned to duty prior to January 1, 1863. Present or accounted for until captured at Cold Harbor, Virginia, June 1, 1864. Confined at Point Lookout, Maryland, June 11, 1864. Released at Point Lookout on or about June 20, 1864, after taking the Oath of Allegiance and joining the U.S. Army. Assigned to Company I, 1st Regiment U.S. Volunteer Infantry.

BREWER, JOHN C., Private
Born in Robeson County and was by occupation a laborer prior to enlisting in Robeson County at age 18, March 10, 1862. Discharged on April 10, 1862. Reason discharged not reported.

BREWER, RICHARD, Private
Born in Robeson County where he resided as a farmer prior to enlisting in Robeson County at age 24, March 10, 1862. Present or accounted for until August 3, 1863, when he was reported absent without leave. Listed as a deserter and dropped from the rolls of the company in January-February, 1864.

BREWER, WILLIAM, Private
Born in Robeson County and was by occupation a laborer prior to enlisting in Robeson County at age 25, March 10, 1862. Present or accounted for until wounded in the right shoulder at Drewry's Bluff, Virginia, on or about May 16, 1864. Hospitalized at Richmond, Virginia. Furloughed for forty days on June 6, 1864. Returned to duty in November-December, 1864. Present or accounted for through December, 1864. Survived the war.

BRIGMAN, ALEXANDER B., Private
Born in Marion District, South Carolina, and was by occupation a laborer prior to enlisting in Robeson County at age 23, March 10, 1862. Present or accounted for until August 7, 1863, when he was reported absent without leave. Listed as a deserter and dropped from the rolls of the company in January-February, 1864.

BRIGMAN, WELLINGTON, Private
Born in Marion District, South Carolina, and was by occupation a farmer prior to enlisting in Robeson County

at age 22, March 10, 1862. Present or accounted for until he deserted in September-October, 1862. Apprehended on December 12, 1862. Deserted again (or escaped) on December 15, 1862. Reported present in January-June, 1863. Reported absent without leave on August 7, 1863. Listed as a deserter in January-February, 1864. Hospitalized at Petersburg, Virginia, January 6, 1864, with pneumonia. Returned to duty on January 29, 1864. Deserted from hospital at Petersburg on or about April 20, 1864. Turned himself over to Federal authorities at Fayetteville on March 11, 1865. Sent to Fort Monroe, Virginia. Released at Fort Monroe on or about April 5, 1865, after taking the Oath of Allegiance.

BULLOCK, CHARLES BAKER, Private
Previously served as Private in 1st Company D, 12th Regiment N.C. Troops (2nd Regiment N.C. Volunteers). Enlisted in this company at Nichols Depot, South Carolina, May 1, 1862, for the war. Reported absent sick through August, 1862. Returned to duty in September-October, 1862. Present or accounted for until wounded in the thigh (flesh) at Drewry's Bluff, Virginia, May 16, 1864. Returned to duty prior to September 1, 1864. Reported absent wounded in September-October, 1864. Place and date wounded not reported. Returned to duty in November-December, 1864. Present or accounted for through December, 1864.

BULLOCK, HENRY JOHNSON, Private
Born in Robeson County where he resided as a farmer prior to enlisting in Robeson County at 31, March 10, 1862. Died at Camp Davis, near Wilmington, July 8, 1862, of "typhoid pneumonia."

BULLOCK, JESSE, Private
Born in Robeson County and was by occupation a farmer prior to enlisting in Robeson County at age 19, March 10, 1862. Present or accounted for until killed at Drewry's Bluff, Virginia, May 16, 1864.

BUTLER, WILLIAM, Private
Born in Robeson County and was by occupation a farmer prior to enlisting in Robeson County at age 21, March 10, 1862. Present or accounted for until August 3, 1863, when he was reported absent without leave. Returned to duty in September-October, 1863. Present or accounted for until wounded in the hip and back at Drewry's Bluff, Virginia, May 16, 1864. Hospitalized at Richmond, Virginia. Transferred to another hospital on July 20, 1864. Returned to duty prior to September 1, 1864. Present or accounted for through December, 1864.

BYRD, ELIJAH, Private
Born in Robeson County and was by occupation a farmer prior to enlisting in Robeson County at age 24, March 10, 1862. Deserted on January 4, 1863. Returned to duty prior to March 1, 1863. Present or accounted for until wounded at Drewry's Bluff, Virginia, May 16, 1864. Hospitalized at Richmond, Virginia, where he died on June 6, 1864, of wounds.

BYRD, JOSHUA, Private
Born in Robeson County and resided in Marion District, South Carolina, where he was by occupation a farmer

prior to enlisting in Robeson County at age 18, March 10, 1862. Present or accounted for until wounded at Drewry's Bluff, Virginia, May 16, 1864. Returned to duty prior to August 19, 1864, when he was wounded in the head and captured near Globe Tavern, Virginia. Blinded as a result of his wounds. Confined at various Federal hospitals until January 8, 1865, when he was confined at Point Lookout, Maryland. Released at Point Lookout on June 26, 1865, after taking the Oath of Allegiance.

CLEMENTS, SAMUEL, Private
Born in Wake County and was by occupation a farmer prior to enlisting in Robeson County at age 30, March 10, 1862. Present or accounted for until killed at Fort Wagner, Charleston, South Carolina, July 18, 1863.

DANIELS, LEROY R., Corporal
Enlisted at Nichols Depot, South Carolina, May 1, 1862, for the war. Mustered in as Private. Promoted to Corporal on February 29, 1864. Present and accounted for until captured at Cold Harbor, Virginia, June 1, 1864. Confined at Point Lookout, Maryland, June 11, 1864. Transferred to Elmira, New York, July 12, 1864. Paroled at Elmira on March 10, 1865. Received at Boulware's Wharf, James River, Virginia, March 15, 1865, for exchange.

DEES, ROBERT, Private
Born in Anson County and resided in Robeson County where he was by occupation a laborer prior to enlisting in Robeson County at age 30, March 10, 1862. Present or accounted for until captured at Cold Harbor, Virginia, June 1, 1864. Confined at Point Lookout, Maryland, June 11, 1864. Transferred to Elmira, New York, July 12, 1864. Paroled at Elmira on March 14, 1865. Received at Boulware's Wharf, James River, Virginia, March 18, 1865, for exchange.

DOUGLAS, GEORGE, Musician
North Carolina pension records indicate that he served in this company as a drummer boy.

DOUGLASS, JAMES E., Private
Born in Robeson County where he resided as a laborer prior to enlisting in Robeson County at age 18, March 10, 1862. Present or accounted for until captured at Cold Harbor, Virginia, June 1, 1864. Confined at Point Lookout, Maryland, June 11, 1864. Transferred to Elmira, New York, July 12, 1864. Released at Elmira on July 3, 1865, after taking the Oath of Allegiance.

EVANS, DAVIDSON, Private
Enlisted at Nichols Depot, South Carolina, May 1, 1862, for the war. Present or accounted for until he deserted on August 3, 1862. Reported in prison at Wilmington awaiting trial in May-June, 1863. Court-martialed and sentenced to death; however, he was released and returned to the company on August 10, 1863. Deserted on August 11, 1863.

EVANS, MICHAEL, Private
Enlisted at Nichols Depot, South Carolina, May 1, 1862, for the war. Present or accounted for until he deserted on

August 3, 1862. Apprehended on August 6, 1862. Deserted on September 18, 1862. Dropped from the rolls of the company in January-February, 1863.

FAULK, DANIEL ASHBURY, Sergeant
Resided in Robeson County and was by occupation a farmer prior to enlisting in Robeson County at age 28, May 1, 1862, for the war. Mustered in as Sergeant. Present or accounted for until May-August, 1864, when he was reported sick in hospital at Richmond, Virginia. Returned to duty in September-October, 1864. Present or accounted for through December, 1864.

FAULK, JAMES C., Sergeant
Born in Robeson County and was by occupation a farmer prior to enlisting in Robeson County at age 23, March 10, 1862. Mustered in as Sergeant. Present or accounted for until wounded slightly at Goldsboro on December 17, 1862. Returned to duty in January-February, 1863. Present or accounted for until wounded at Fort Wagner, Charleston, South Carolina, July 18, 1863. Returned to duty in September-October, 1863. Present or accounted for until wounded at Drewry's Bluff, Virginia, May 16, 1864. Hospitalized at Raleigh on August 28, 1864, with a gunshot wound of the left arm (possibly the same wound he received at Drewry's Bluff). Place and date wounded not reported. Reported on detail in hospital at Raleigh in September-December, 1864.

FLOYD, FAULKNER J., Sergeant
Previously served as Private in 1st Company D, 12th Regiment N.C. Troops (2nd Regiment N.C. Volunteers). Enlisted in this company in New Hanover County on May 1, 1862, for the war. Mustered in as Corporal. Present or accounted for until wounded at Drewry's Bluff, Virginia, May 16, 1864. Returned to duty prior to September 1, 1864. Present or accounted for through December, 1864. Promoted to Sergeant in January-April, 1865. Paroled at Greensboro on May 1, 1865.

FLOYD, MEMORY J., Private
Enlisted at Camp Hill, near Petersburg, Virginia, March 26, 1864, for the war. Reported sick in hospital at Petersburg in April, 1864. Reported absent on sick furlough from June 1 through December 31, 1864. No further records.

FORD, THOMAS P., Private
Born in Marion District, South Carolina, and was by occupation a farmer prior to enlisting in Robeson County at age 35, March 10, 1862. Mustered in as Corporal. Reduced to ranks prior to July 1, 1862. Appointed Musician in July-August, 1862. Reduced to ranks in January-February, 1863. Present or accounted for until August 3, 1863, when he was reported absent without leave. Returned to duty in September-October, 1863. Present or accounted for until captured at Drewry's Bluff, Virginia, May 16, 1864. Confined at Point Lookout, Maryland, on or about May 20, 1864. Paroled at Point Lookout and transferred to Boulware's Wharf, James River, Virginia, where he was received on March 19, 1865, for exchange. Hospitalized at Richmond, Virginia, March 19, 1865, with scorbutus. Transferred to hospital

at Charlotte where he arrived on April 1, 1865. Died in hospital on April 2, 1865, of "scorbutus."

GOODSON, ANDREW J., Private
Born in Horry District, South Carolina, and was by occupation a laborer prior to enlisting in Robeson County at age 18, March 10, 1862. Discharged on April 10, 1862. Reason discharged not reported.

GOODSON, CHARLES P., Private
Enlisted at Camp Holmes, near Raleigh, February 9, 1864, for the war. Present or accounted for through December, 1864.

GRANTHAM, STEPHEN, Private
Enlisted in Robeson County on March 10, 1862. Present or accounted for until wounded at Fort Wagner, Charleston, South Carolina, July 18, 1863. Died in hospital at Charleston on August 24, 1863, of wounds.

GRIMSLEY, JAMES, Private
Resided in Robeson County and was by occupation a farmer prior to enlisting in Robeson County at age 32, March 10, 1862. Reported absent sick in May-June, 1862. Returned to duty in July-August, 1862. Deserted on November 4, 1862. Returned to duty in January-February, 1863. Deserted on August 18, 1863.

HAIR, D. J., Private
Enlisted at Camp Holmes, near Raleigh, February 22, 1864, for the war. Present or accounted for until he deserted on May 1, 1864. [May have served previously as Private in Company H, 50th Regiment N.C. Troops.]

HAIR, HUGH, Private
Enlisted at Camp Holmes, near Raleigh, February 11, 1864, for the war. Present or accounted for until he deserted on May 1, 1864.

HAIR, ROBERT, Private
Enlisted at Camp Holmes, near Raleigh, February 11, 1864, for the war. Present or accounted for until he deserted on May 1, 1864.

HAMMONDS, DOUGALD, Private
Born in Robeson County and was by occupation a farmer prior to enlisting in Robeson County at age 18, March 10, 1862. Present or accounted for until December 3, 1863, when he was reported absent without leave. Returned to duty in January-February, 1864. Present or accounted for until captured at Drewry's Bluff, Virginia, May 16, 1864. Confined at Point Lookout, Maryland, May 21, 1864. Released at Point Lookout on June 7, 1864, after taking the Oath of Allegiance and joining the U.S. Army. Assigned to Company K, 1st Regiment U.S. Volunteer Infantry.

HARRINGTON, CHARLES TURNER, Sergeant
Born in Chatham County and was by occupation a farmer prior to enlisting in Robeson County at age 34, March 10, 1862. Mustered in as Sergeant. Present or accounted for until wounded at Fort Wagner, Charleston, South Carolina, July 18, 1863. Returned to duty in September-

October, 1863. Present or accounted for through December, 1864. Survived the war.

HARTMAN, JOHN E., Musician
Born in Cumberland County and was by occupation a student prior to enlisting in Robeson County at age 16, March 10, 1862. Mustered in as Musician (Drummer). Present or accounted for through December, 1864. Paroled at Greensboro on May 1, 1865.

HAYES, BENNET J., Corporal
Born in Marion District, South Carolina, and resided in Robeson County where he was by occupation a farmer prior to enlisting in Robeson County at age 28, March 10, 1862. Mustered in as Private. Promoted to Corporal prior to July 1, 1862. Present or accounted for until he was wounded in November-December, 1862, while attempting to capture deserters. Returned to duty in March-April, 1863. Present or accounted for until captured near Petersburg, Virginia, June 16, 1864. Confined at Point Lookout, Maryland, June 19, 1864. Transferred to Elmira, New York, July 9, 1864. Paroled at Elmira on October 11, 1864. Received at Venus Point, Savannah River, Georgia, November 15, 1864, for exchange.

HAYES, LEVI C., Private
Born in South Carolina and resided in Robeson County where he was by occupation a farmer prior to enlisting in Robeson County at age 29, March 10, 1862. Mustered in as Corporal. Discharged "by Surgeon" on or about April 28, 1862. Reenlisted in the company on February 1, 1863, with the rank of Private. Present or accounted for through December, 1864. Hospitalized at Greensboro on March 9, 1865. No further records.

HAZLEWOOD, HIRAM G., Private
North Carolina pension records indicate that he served in this company.

HENDERSON, JEPSEY, Private
Born in Marion District, South Carolina, and was by occupation a farmer prior to enlisting in Robeson County at age 36, March 10, 1862. Present or accounted for until killed at Fort Wagner, Charleston, South Carolina, July 18, 1863.

HERRING, OLIVER, Private
Enlisted at Camp Holmes, near Raleigh, March 10, 1864, for the war. Present or accounted for until captured at Drewry's Bluff, Virginia, May 16, 1864. Confined at Point Lookout, Maryland, May 18, 1864. Transferred to Elmira, New York, in August, 1864. Died at Elmira on October 3, 1864, of "chronic diarrhoea."

HODGE, BENJAMIN, Private
Born in Marion District, South Carolina, and resided in Robeson County where he was by occupation a farmer prior to enlisting in Robeson County at age 54, March 10, 1862. Reported absent without leave in March-June, 1862. Returned to duty in July-August, 1862. Deserted on October 20, 1862.

HODGE, MATHEW, Private
Born in Marion District, South Carolina, and was by

occupation a laborer prior to enlisting in Robeson County at age 40, March 10, 1862. Reported absent without leave in March-June, 1862. Returned to duty in July-August, 1862. Deserted on October 20, 1862.

HUGGINS, THOMAS, Private
Resided in Robeson County and enlisted on May 1, 1862, for the war. Present or accounted for through June, 1862. Reported absent sick in July-August, 1862. Deserted from hospital at Wilmington in September, 1862. Returned to duty on an unspecified date. Reported absent without leave on January 24, 1863. Returned to duty on June 13, 1863. Present or accounted for through October, 1863. Reported absent sick on November 29, 1863. Died at home in Robeson County prior to January 1, 1865, of "consumption."

HUMPHREY, WILLIAM P., Private
Born in Robeson County and was by occupation a farmer prior to enlisting in Robeson County at age 18, March 10, 1862. Present or accounted for through April, 1864. Wounded at Drewry's Bluff, Virginia, on or about May 15, 1864. Returned to duty prior to September 30, 1864, when he was wounded at Fort Harrison, Virginia. Returned to duty on November 22, 1864. Reported present through December, 1864.

ISRAEL, WRIGHT, _____
North Carolina pension records indicate that he served in this company.

JOLLY, HUGH J., Private
Was by occupation a farmer prior to enlisting at Nichols Depot, South Carolina, May 1, 1862, for the war. Present or accounted for through October, 1862. Discharged on December 1, 1862. Later served as Private in Company K, 26th Regiment South Carolina Infantry.

JONES, ALVI, Private
Born in Anson County and resided in Robeson County where he was by occupation a laborer prior to enlisting in Robeson County at age 45, March 10, 1862. Hospitalized at Wilmington on April 14, 1862, with gonorrhea. Returned to duty on April 18, 1862. Dropped from the rolls of the company prior to July 1, 1862. Reason he was dropped not reported.

JONES, JESSE B., Private
Enlisted at Camp Davis, near Wilmington, July 1, 1863, for the war. Present or accounted for until he was reportedly wounded and captured at Cold Harbor, Virginia, May 31, 1864. Was probably killed at Cold Harbor.

JOYNER, GEORGE W., Private
Born in Pitt County and was by occupation a cooper prior to enlisting in Robeson County at age 34, March 10, 1862. Present or accounted for until March-April, 1864, when he was reported absent sick. Returned to duty in May-August, 1864. Hospitalized at Richmond, Virginia, October 2, 1864, with intermittent fever. Furloughed for thirty days on October 21, 1864. Died at Nichols Depot, South Carolina, November 25, 1864. Cause of death not reported.

JOYNER, MEREDITH, Private
Born in Nash County and was by occupation a cooper prior to enlisting in Robeson County at age 35, March 10, 1862. Present or accounted for through December, 1864.

LOCK, STEPHEN, Private
Born in Robeson County and was by occupation a farmer prior to enlisting in Robeson County at age 23, March 10, 1862. Present or accounted for until wounded at Fort Wagner, Charleston, South Carolina, July 18, 1863. Hospitalized at Charleston where he died on August 21, 1863, of wounds.

LOCUSS, JAMES A., Cook
Enlisted at Richmond, Virginia, October 31, 1864, for the war. Present or accounted for through December, 1864.

McDONALD, FRANKLIN M., Private
Enlisted at Petersburg, Virginia, April 23, 1864, for the war. Present or accounted for until captured at Cold Harbor, Virginia, June 1, 1864. Confined at Point Lookout, Maryland, June 11, 1864. Transferred to Elmira, New York, July 12, 1864. Paroled at Elmira on October 11, 1864. Died at Point Lookout on October 28, 1864, of "chronic diarrhoea."

McLEAN, NEILL B., Private
Born in Robeson County and was by occupation a farmer prior to enlisting in Robeson County at age 24, March 10, 1862. Present or accounted for through October, 1862. Reported absent without leave in November-December, 1862. Returned to duty in January-February, 1863. No further records.

McLELLAN, DANIEL B., Private
Enlisted at Petersburg, Virginia, April 8, 1864, for the war. Present or accounted for until wounded in the right thigh at Drewry's Bluff, Virginia, May 16, 1864. Reported absent without leave on July 14, 1864. Returned to duty in September-October, 1864. Present or accounted for through December, 1864.

McLELLAN, WILLIAM B., Corporal
Born in Marion District, South Carolina, and was by occupation a farmer prior to enlisting in Robeson County at age 18, March 10, 1862. Mustered in as Private. Promoted to Corporal prior to July 1, 1862. Present or accounted for until wounded at Cold Harbor, Virginia, May 31, 1864. Hospitalized at Richmond, Virginia. Furloughed for sixty days on June 10, 1864. Returned to duty on an unspecified date. Wounded in the head at Fort Harrison, Virginia, September 30, 1864. Returned to duty prior to November 1, 1864. Present or accounted for through December, 1864.

MINCEY, GEORGE, Private
Was by occupation a student prior to enlisting in Robeson County on March 10, 1862. Discharged on June 9, 1862. Reason discharged not reported.

MORGAN, KENNETH T., Private
Born in Robeson County and was by occupation a farmer prior to enlisting in Robeson County at age 24, March 10, 1862. Present or accounted for through December, 1864.

MORRIS, ABRAHAM, Private
Born in Robeson County and was by occupation a farmer prior to enlisting in Robeson County at age 20, March 10, 1862. Reported absent sick through December, 1862. Returned to duty in January-February, 1863. Reported sick in hospital at Charleston, South Carolina, in March-April, 1863. No further records.

MORRIS, JAMES M., Private
Enlisted at Charleston, South Carolina, March 1, 1863, for the war. Present or accounted for until hospitalized at Richmond, Virginia, August 8, 1864, with diarrhoea. Furloughed for sixty days on August 27, 1864. Returned to duty in November-December, 1864. Present or accounted for through December, 1864.

MORRIS, ROBERT, Private
Enlisted in Robeson County on March 10, 1862. Discharged by the surgeon on April 28, 1862. Reason discharged not reported.

MUSSLEWHITE, JOHN R., Private
Born in Virginia and enlisted in Robeson County on March 10, 1862. Present or accounted for until wounded at or near Bermuda Hundred, Virginia, on or about May 25, 1864. Died at or near Petersburg, Virginia, May 25, 1864, of wounds. Death records give his age as 17.

MUSSLEWHITE, RHODES, Private
Enlisted at "Holmes Landing" on May 1, 1863, for the war. Hospitalized at Wilmington on or about May 29, 1863, with "intermittent fever." Died in hospital at Wilmington on September 13, 1863. Cause of death not reported.

MUSSLEWHITE, WILEY M., Private
Born in Robeson County where he enlisted at age 20, March 10, 1862. Reported absent sick through August, 1862. Returned to duty in September-October, 1862. Present or accounted for through December, 1862. Reported sick in hospital at Wilmington in May-June, 1863. No further records.

NORMAN, W. A., Private
Resided in Yadkin County and enlisted at Camp Holmes, near Raleigh, February 10, 1864, for the war. Deserted on April 18, 1864. Went over to the enemy on an unspecified date. Confined at Knoxville, Tennessee, June 11, 1864. Transferred to Louisville, Kentucky. Released after taking the Oath of Allegiance at Louisville on June 16, 1864.

NORMAN, WILLIS P., Private
Enlisted at Nichols Depot, South Carolina, May 1, 1862, for the war. "Dishonorably discharged" on July 6, 1862. Reason discharged not reported.

ODUM, JEREMIAH, Private
Born in Marion District, South Carolina, and was by occupation a farmer prior to enlisting in Robeson County

at age 37, March 10, 1862. Present or accounted for through April, 1864. Wounded at Drewry's Bluff, Virginia, May 16, 1864. Hospitalized at Richmond, Virginia. Furloughed for sixty days on June 2, 1864. Reported absent wounded through December, 1864.

OXENDINE, WILLIAM, Private
Enlisted at Camp Morgan, near Wilmington, May 1, 1862, for the war. Failed to reported for duty and was reported absent without leave. Listed as a deserter and dropped from the rolls of the company on April 30, 1863.

PAGE, DAVID, Private
Born in Marion District, South Carolina, and was by occupation a farmer prior to enlisting in Robeson County at age 51, March 10, 1862. Reported absent sick in March-June, 1862. Returned to duty in July-August, 1862. Died in hospital at Wilmington on October 18, 1862. Cause of death not reported.

PAGE, JOHN J., Private
Enlisted at Nichols Depot, South Carolina, May 1, 1862, for the war. Reported absent sick through August, 1862. Returned to duty in September-October, 1862. Present or accounted for until March-April, 1863, when he was reported absent sick. Returned to duty in May-June, 1863. Died in hospital at Columbia, South Carolina, August 27, 1863. Cause of death not reported.

PALMER, WILLIAM M., Private
Previously served as Private in Company H, 1st Regiment Georgia Volunteer Infantry (Ramsey's). Enlisted in this company at Dahlonega, Georgia, February 27, 1863, for the war. Present or accounted for until December 3, 1863, when he was reported absent without leave. Returned to duty in January-February, 1864. Present or accounted for through December, 1864.

PARHAM, WILLIAM H., Private
Born in Robeson County and was by occupation a farmer prior to enlisting in Robeson County at age 22, March 10, 1862. Present or accounted for until he deserted in September-October, 1862. Returned to duty in November-December, 1862. Present or accounted for until hospitalized at Danville, Virginia, on or about June 4, 1864, with a gunshot wound of the hand. Furloughed on June 6, 1864. Returned to duty in September-October, 1864. Present or accounted for through December, 1864.

PERNELL, ANSON B., Private
Born in Robeson County and was by occupation a farmer prior to enlisting in Robeson County at age 22, March 10, 1862. Mustered in as Corporal. Reduced to ranks prior to July 1, 1862. Present or accounted for until November-December, 1862, when he was reported sick in hospital at Goldsboro. Detailed as a hospital nurse at Goldsboro on December 20, 1862. Returned to duty in March-April, 1863. Present or accounted for until hospitalized at Augusta, Georgia, August 31, 1863, with an unspecified complaint. Returned to duty in January-February, 1864. Wounded slightly in the left arm at Fort Harrison, Virginia, September 30, 1864. Returned to duty prior to November 1, 1864. Reported present in November-December, 1864.

PITTMAN, JAMES B., Private
Born in Robeson County and was by occupation a student prior to enlisting in Robeson County at age 18, March 10, 1862. Dropped from the rolls of the company prior to July 1, 1862. Reason he was dropped not reported.

PRIDGEON, BRYANT, Private
Born in Moore County and resided in Robeson County where he was by occupation a laborer prior to enlisting in Robeson County at age 44, March 10, 1862. Present or accounted for through October, 1862. Reported sick in hospital at Wilmington in November-December, 1862. Hospitalized at Wilmington on February 16, 1863, with continued fever. Returned to duty on March 20, 1863. Hospitalized at Wilmington prior to May 1, 1863. No further records.

RATLEY, CALVIN, Private
Born in Robeson County and was by occupation a laborer prior to enlisting in Robeson County at age 18, March 10, 1862. No further records.

RATLEY, JOSEPH, Private
Born in Robeson County and was by occupation a laborer prior to enlisting in Robeson County at age 27, March 10, 1862. No further records.

REVELS, ELI, Private
Born in Robeson County and was by occupation a laborer prior to enlisting in Robeson County at age 18, March 10, 1862. No further records.

REVELS, HENRY, Private
Born in Robeson County and was by occupation a laborer prior to enlisting in Robeson County at age 35, March 10, 1862. "Discovered to be a Negro" and was discharged prior to July 1, 1862.

REVELS, HINSON, _____
North Carolina pension records indicate that he served in this company.

REVELS, JONATHAN, Private
Born in Robeson County and was by occupation a farmer prior to enlisting in Robeson County at age 40, March 10, 1862. "Discovered to be a Negro" and was discharged prior to July 1, 1862.

RODGERS, WILLIAM S., Private
Born in Marion District, South Carolina, and was by occupation a farmer prior to enlisting in Robeson County at age 23, March 10, 1862. Present or accounted for until captured at Cold Harbor, Virginia, June 1, 1864. Confined at Point Lookout, Maryland, on or about June 12, 1864. Released at Point Lookout on June 27, 1864, after taking the Oath of Allegiance and joining the U.S. Army. Assigned to Company K, 1st Regiment U.S. Volunteer Infantry.

SPARKMAN, GEORGE A., Private
Enlisted at Nichols Depot, South Carolina, May 1, 1862, for the war. Present or accounted for through May, 1864. Various records indicate that he was wounded and

captured at Cold Harbor, Virginia, May 31, 1864; however, records of the Federal Provost Marshal do not substantiate that report. Was probably killed at Cold Harbor.

SPARKMAN, WILLIAM P., Private
Born in Robeson County and was by occupation a farmer prior to enlisting in Robeson County at age 32, March 10, 1862. Present or accounted for until November-December, 1862, when he was reported absent sick. Returned to duty in January-February, 1863. Present or accounted for until captured at Cold Harbor, Virginia, June 1, 1864. Confined at Point Lookout, Maryland, June 11, 1864. Transferred to Elmira, New York, July 12, 1864. Died at Elmira on October 13, 1864, of "chro[nic] diarr[hoea]."

SPIVEY, AIKIN, Private
Enlisted at Camp Davis, near Wilmington, June 12, 1863, for the war. Wounded at Fort Wagner, Charleston, South Carolina, July 18, 1863. Died in hospital at Charleston on August 24, 1863, of wounds.

SPIVEY, HENRY, Private
Born in Marion District, South Carolina, and was by occupation a student prior to enlisting in Robeson County at age 21, March 10, 1862. Present or accounted for until wounded at Drewry's Bluff, Virginia, May 16, 1864. Returned to duty in November-December, 1864. Present or accounted for through December, 1864. Survived the war.

SPIVEY, JOHN Q., Private
Enlisted in Robeson County on December 1, 1864, for the war. Present or accounted for through December, 1864. Wounded in the shoulder at or near Bentonville on or about March 19-21, 1865. Reported in hospital at Raleigh on March 27, 1865.

SPIVEY, LEWIS J., Sergeant
Born in Robeson County and was by occupation a farmer prior to enlisting in Robeson County at age 29, March 10, 1862. Mustered in as Sergeant. Present or accounted for until wounded in the right leg at Drewry's Bluff, Virginia, May 16, 1864. Hospitalized at Richmond, Virginia, where his leg was amputated on June 17, 1864. Furloughed on or about July 18, 1864. Reported absent wounded until February 16, 1865, when he was retired to the Invalid Corps.

SPIVEY, SAMUEL, Corporal
Born in Horry District, South Carolina, and was by occupation a blacksmith prior to enlisting in Robeson County at age 41, March 10, 1862. Mustered in as Corporal. Present or accounted for until November-December, 1862, when he was reported absent without leave. Returned to duty in January-February, 1863. Present or accounted for until killed at Fort Wagner, Charleston, South Carolina, July 18, 1863.

SUGARD, D. J., Private
Enlisted at Camp Holmes, near Raleigh, January 25, 1864, for the war. Deserted on April 18, 1864.

TAYLOR, DAVID D., Private
Born in Nash County and was by occupation a farmer prior to enlisting in Robeson County at age 21, March 10, 1862. Present or accounted for until hospitalized at Wilson on December 5, 1863, with an unspecified complaint. Returned to duty in January-February, 1864. Present or accounted for until captured at Cold Harbor, Virginia, June 1, 1864. Confined at Point Lookout, Maryland, June 11, 1864. Transferred to Elmira, New York, July 12, 1864. Died at Elmira on March 4, 1865, of "febris typhoid."

TAYLOR, STEPHEN, Private
Born in Robeson County and was by occupation a farmer prior to enlisting in Robeson County at age 19, March 10, 1862. Present or accounted for through December, 1864. Survived the war.

TOWNSEND, FLOYD, Private
Was by occupation a farmer prior to enlisting in Robeson County at age 28, March 10, 1862. Present or accounted for until February 17, 1863, when he was left sick at Wilmington. Returned to duty in March-April, 1863. Present or accounted for until killed near Petersburg, Virginia, June 22, 1864.

TYNER, NICHOLAS, Private
Born in Robeson County and was by occupation a farmer prior to enlisting in Robeson County at age 46, March 10, 1862. Present or accounted for until July-August, 1862, when he was reported absent without leave. Listed as a deserter in September-October, 1862. Returned to duty on an unspecified date but deserted again on December 15, 1862. Returned to duty in January-February, 1863. Present or accounted for until September-October, 1864, when he was reported absent sick. Returned to duty in November-December, 1864.

TYNER, WILLIAM, Private
Born in Robeson County where he resided as a farmer prior to enlisting at age 39, March 10, 1862. Present or accounted for until November-December, 1862, when he was reported absent without leave. Returned to duty in January-February, 1863. Present or accounted for until captured at Cold Harbor, Virginia, June 1, 1864. Confined at Point Lookout, Maryland, June 11, 1864. Transferred to Elmira, New York, July 12, 1864. Died at Elmira on July 18, 1864, of a "contusion."

WALTERS, LUCUS, Private
Enlisted at Nichols Depot, South Carolina, May 1, 1862, for the war. Hospitalized at Wilmington on or about May 29, 1862, with anthrax. Returned to duty on June 2, 1862. Present or accounted for until September-October, 1862, when he was reported absent sick. Reported absent without leave in November, 1862-February, 1863. Reported absent sick or absent without leave from March, 1863, until September-October, 1863, when he returned to duty. Hospitalized at Charleston, South Carolina, November 21, 1863, with an unspecified complaint. Returned to duty in January-February, 1864. Present or accounted for until wounded accidentally in the left hand at or near Petersburg, Virginia, September 2, 1864. Hospitalized at Petersburg. Reported absent on sick

furlough in Robeson County in November-December, 1864.

WATSON, SAMUEL D., 1st Sergeant
Born in Robeson County and was by occupation a student prior to enlisting in Robeson County at age 20, March 10, 1862. Mustered in as 1st Sergeant. Present or accounted for until wounded in the arm at Drewry's Bluff, Virginia, on or about May 13, 1864. Returned to duty prior to June 1, 1864, when he was captured at Cold Harbor, Virginia. Confined at Point Lookout, Maryland, June 11, 1864. Transferred to Elmira, New York, July 12, 1864. Killed in a railroad accident at Shohola, Pennsylvania, July 15, 1864, while en route to Elmira.

WOODWARD, GEORGE W., Private
Born in Cumberland County and enlisted at Camp Holmes, near Raleigh, at age 18, March 14, 1864, for the war. Present or accounted for until wounded in the neck and/or right hand at or near Bermuda Hundred, Virginia, on or about May 20, 1864. Hospitalized at Petersburg, Virginia. Transferred to Raleigh on or about June 1, 1864. Returned to duty in September-October, 1864. Hospitalized at Wilmington on December 30, 1864, with a gunshot wound. Place and date wounded not reported. Returned to duty on January 5, 1865. Survived the war.

COMPANY G

This company was raised primarily in Columbus, Duplin, and Brunswick counties and enlisted at Wilmington in January-March, 1862. It was mustered into state service at Camp Holmes, near Wilmington, on April 1, 1862, and assigned to the 51st Regiment N.C. Troops as Company G. After joining the regiment the company functioned as a part of the regiment, and its history for the remainder of the war is reported as a part of the regimental history.

The information contained in the following roster was compiled primarily from a company muster-in and descriptive roll dated April 1, 1862, and from company muster rolls for April 1, 1862-February 29, 1864, and April 30-December 31, 1864. No company muster rolls were located for March 1-April 29, 1864, or for the period after December 31, 1864. Valuable information was obtained from primary records such as the North Carolina adjutant general's *Roll of Honor*, discharge certificates, medical records, prisoner of war records, *The War of the Rebellion: A Compilation of the Official Records of the Union and Confederate Armies*, militia records, newspaper casualty lists and obituaries, Confederate pension applications filed with the state of North Carolina, and the 1860 federal census of North Carolina. Secondary sources such as postwar rosters and histories, cemetery records, the *Confederate Veteran*, published genealogies, and records of the United Daughters of the Confederacy also provided useful information.

OFFICERS

CAPTAIN

LIPPITT, JAMES WRIGHT
Born in New Hanover County where he resided as a druggist prior to enlisting at age 26. Appointed Captain on March 14, 1862. Present or accounted for until July-August, 1863, when he was reported absent sick. Returned to duty in September-October, 1863. Present or accounted for through December, 1864. Paroled at Greensboro on May 1, 1865.

LIEUTENANTS

CHINNIS, SAMUEL R., 1st Lieutenant
Born in Brunswick County and resided in Columbus County where he was by occupation a farmer prior to enlisting at age 31. Appointed 1st Lieutenant on March 22, 1862. Present or accounted for until July-August, 1862, when he was reported absent sick. Rejoined the company in November-December, 1862. Present or accounted for until he resigned on September 15, 1863, in order to "join the Navy." Resignation accepted on October 1, 1863. [No evidence of service in the C.S. Navy was located for this officer.]

EVANS, JACOB A., 1st Lieutenant
Born in Brunswick County and was by occupation a farmer prior to enlisting in New Hanover County at age 34. Appointed 3rd Lieutenant on March 22, 1862. Present or accounted for until September-October, 1862, when he was reported absent sick. Reported present but sick in November-December, 1862. Returned to duty in January-February, 1863. Present or accounted for until August 14, 1863, when he was reported absent on sick furlough. Promoted to 1st Lieutenant on October 1, 1863. Returned to duty in November-December, 1863. Present or accounted for until wounded at Bermuda Hundred, Virginia, May 16, 1864. Reported absent wounded or absent sick through August, 1864. Hospitalized at Wilmington on September 20, 1864, with acute bronchitis. Returned to duty on November 5, 1864. Present or accounted for through December, 1864.

GOWAN, BENJAMIN A., 3rd Lieutenant
Born in Horry District, South Carolina, and resided in Columbus County where he was by occupation a farmer prior to enlisting in Columbus County at age 24, March 4, 1862. Mustered in as Sergeant. Present or accounted for until July-August, 1863, when he was reported sick in hospital at Charleston, South Carolina. Returned to duty in November-December, 1863. Reduced to ranks on December 26, 1863. Elected 3rd Lieutenant on January 15, 1864. Present or accounted for until captured near Petersburg, Virginia, June 16, 1864. Confined at Point Lookout, Maryland, June 18, 1864. Transferred to Fort Delaware, Delaware, June 23, 1864. Transferred to Hilton

Head, South Carolina, August 20, 1864. Confined at Fort Pulaski, Georgia, October 20, 1864. Transferred back to Hilton Head on an unspecified date subsequent to December 26, 1864. Transferred to Fort Delaware where he arrived on March 12, 1865. Died at Fort Delaware on March 22, 1865, of "dysentery."

KETCHUM, DAVID W., 2nd Lieutenant
Previously served as Private in Company F, 1st Regiment N.C. Infantry (6 months, 1861). Appointed 2nd Lieutenant of this company on March 22, 1862. Appointed Assistant Commissary of Subsistence (Captain) on April 30, 1862, and transferred to the Field and Staff of this regiment.

LIPPITT, THOMAS B., 2nd Lieutenant
Resided in New Hanover County. Elected 2nd Lieutenant on November 28, 1863. Present or accounted for through December, 1864. Paroled at Greensboro on May 1, 1865.

YOPP, FRANKLIN V. B., 3rd Lieutenant
Born in New Hanover County and was by occupation a brickmason prior to enlisting in New Hanover County at age 29, March 24, 1862. Mustered in as 1st Sergeant. Appointed 3rd Lieutenant on August 23, 1862. Present or accounted for through October, 1863; however, he was reported absent sick during most of that period. Resigned on November 13, 1863, by reason of "chronic hepatitis producing extreme emaciation from the effects of which he has suffered about three years." Resignation accepted on November 30, 1863.

NONCOMMISSIONED OFFICERS AND PRIVATES

ARNOLD, JOHN, Private
Born in Columbus County where he resided as a farmer prior to enlisting in Columbus County at age 45, March 4, 1862. Present or accounted for until wounded at Goldsboro on December 17, 1862. Returned to duty prior to January 1, 1863. Present or accounted for until wounded at Fort Wagner, Charleston, South Carolina, July 18, 1863. Returned to duty in January-February, 1864. Present or accounted for until wounded at Cold Harbor, Virginia, June 1, 1864. Returned to duty in September-October, 1864. Present or accounted for through December, 1864.

BACHELOR, JAMES M., _____
North Carolina pension records indicate that he served in this company.

BAKER, ARCHIBALD M., Private
Previously served as Private in Company E, 36th Regiment N.C. Troops (2nd Regiment N.C. Artillery). Transferred to this company on May 9, 1863. Present or accounted for through December, 1864. Survived the war.

BEASLEY, WILLIAM JACKSON, Private
Born in New Hanover County and was by occupation a farmer prior to enlisting in Brunswick County at age 30,

March 31, 1862. Present or accounted for until killed at Fort Harrison, Virginia, September 30, 1864.

BELL, OWEN, Private
Born in Onslow County and was by occupation a farmer prior to enlisting in New Hanover County at age 18, March 8, 1862. Present or accounted for until August 20, 1863, when he was reported absent sick. Hospitalized at Wilmington on December 5, 1863, with ulcus. Transferred to another hospital on March 24, 1864. Returned to duty prior to May 31, 1864, when he was wounded at Cold Harbor, Virginia. Died at or near Richmond, Virginia, on or about June 13, 1864, of wounds.

BENDER, JOHN L., Private
Born in Jones County and was by occupation a farmer prior to enlisting in New Hanover County at age 31, March 5, 1862. Present or accounted for until July-August, 1863, when he was reported absent without leave. Returned to duty in September-October, 1863. Present or accounted for until captured near Drewry's Bluff, Virginia, May 16, 1864. Confined at Point Lookout, Maryland, May 19, 1864. Released at Point Lookout on June 7, 1864, after taking the Oath of Allegiance and joining the U.S. Army. Assigned to Company K, 1st Regiment U.S. Volunteer Infantry.

BENTON, NELSON, Private
Born in Brunswick County where he resided as a farmer prior to enlisting in New Hanover County at age 40, January 15, 1862. Present or accounted for until wounded at or near Drewry's Bluff, Virginia, on or about May 13, 1864. Returned to duty in September, 1864. Wounded in the back and ankle and captured at Fort Harrison, Virginia, September 30, 1864. No further records.

BENTON, SIMEON, Private
Born in Columbus County and was by occupation a farmer prior to enlisting in New Hanover County at age 27, May 1, 1862, for the war. Present or accounted for until November-December, 1862, when he was reported absent without leave. Returned to duty in January-February, 1863. Reported absent sick and absent on guard duty in March-June, 1863. Rejoined the company in July-August, 1863. Present or accounted for until wounded at Drewry's Bluff, Virginia, May 16, 1864. Hospitalized at Richmond, Virginia, where he died on June 17, 1864, of wounds.

BESSENT, JAMES H., Corporal
Enlisted at James Island, Charleston, South Carolina, March 9, 1863, for the war. Mustered in as Private. Promoted to Corporal in March-May, 1864. Present or accounted for until captured at Cold Harbor, Virginia, on or about June 1, 1864. Confined at Point Lookout, Maryland, June 11, 1864. Transferred to Elmira, New York, July 12, 1864. Killed in a railroad accident at Shohola, Pennsylvania, July 15, 1864, while en route to Elmira.

BLACKMAN, JAMES B., Private
Born in Columbus County where he resided as a farmer prior to enlisting in New Hanover County at age 34, April 10, 1862. Present or accounted for until November-December, 1863, when he was reported absent sick.

Returned to duty in January-February, 1864. Reported on detached service as a hospital cook in May-December, 1864. Survived the war.

BLACKMAN, McDANIEL, Private
Born in Columbus County where he resided prior to enlisting at Petersburg, Virginia, at age 16, April 27, 1864, for the war. Wounded slightly at Cold Harbor, Virginia, May 31, 1864. Returned to duty prior to September 1, 1864. Wounded in the shoulder and/or chest at Fort Harrison, Virginia, September 30, 1864. Hospitalized at Richmond, Virginia. Captured in hospital at Richmond on April 3, 1865. Paroled on an unspecified date.

BLAKE, ALVA FRANKLIN, Private
Born in Columbus County where he resided as a farmer prior to enlisting in New Hanover County at age 25, April 25, 1862, for the war. Present or accounted for until wounded accidentally on July 12, 1863. Reported absent wounded through December, 1863. Reported on detached service as a provost guard at Petersburg, Virginia, in January-August, 1864. Rejoined the company prior to September 30, 1864, when he was captured at Fort Harrison, Virginia. Confined at Point Lookout, Maryland, October 5, 1864. Paroled at Point Lookout on March 17, 1865. Received at Boulware's Wharf, James River, Virginia, March 19, 1865, for exchange. Survived the war.

BLAKE, JOHN BEATY, Corporal
Born in Columbus County and was by occupation a farmer prior to enlisting at age 17, March 4, 1862. Mustered in as Private. Present or accounted for until November-December, 1862, when he was reported absent sick. Returned to duty in January-February, 1863. Reported absent sick in May-June, 1863. Reported absent without leave in July-August, 1863. Returned to duty in September-October, 1863. Promoted to Corporal in March-June, 1864. Present or accounted for until wounded at Cold Harbor, Virginia, on or about June 2, 1864. Reported absent wounded through August, 1864. Reported absent on detached service with the brigade quartermaster in September-October, 1864. Reported absent without leave on December 13, 1864. Survived the war.

BLALOCK, HARDY, Private
Born in Sampson County and resided in Cumberland County where he was by occupation a farmer prior to enlisting in New Hanover County at age 46, March 7, 1862. Present or accounted for through August, 1862. Reported absent sick in September-October, 1862. Returned to duty in November-December, 1862. Present or accounted for through April, 1863. Reported absent on furlough or absent sick in hospital in May-August, 1863. Returned to duty in September-October, 1863. Present or accounted for until hospitalized at Richmond, Virginia, August 16, 1864, with intermittent fever. Furloughed for thirty days on September 22, 1864. Reported absent without leave on November 20, 1864.

BLANTON, ENOCH, Private
Previously served as Private in Company D, 13th

Battalion N.C. Infantry. Transferred to this company on April 15, 1862. Present or accounted for until November-December, 1862, when he was reported absent without leave. Reported sick at home in January-February, 1863. Returned to duty in March-April, 1863. Present or accounted for until killed at Fort Wagner, Charleston, South Carolina, July 18, 1863.

BLANTON, JOHN W., Private
Born in Duplin County and was by occupation a farmer prior to enlisting in New Hanover County at age 18, March 6, 1862. Present or accounted for until he died in hospital at Richmond, Virginia, on or about July 13, 1864, of "fever."

BLANTON, JOSEPH J., Private
Previously served as Private in Company D, 13th Battalion N.C. Troops. Transferred to this company on April 15, 1862. Present or accounted for until wounded at Fort Wagner, Charleston, South Carolina, July 18, 1863. Returned to duty prior to September 1, 1863. Present or accounted for until captured at Cold Harbor, Virginia, on or about June 1, 1864. Confined at Point Lookout, Maryland, June 11, 1864. Transferred to Elmira, New York, July 12, 1864. Died at Elmira on January 18, 1865, of "variola."

BLANTON, MOSES, Private
Born in Sampson County where he resided as a farmer prior to enlisting in New Hanover County at age 39, April 15, 1862. Present or accounted for until wounded at Fort Wagner, Charleston, South Carolina, July 18, 1863. Returned to duty prior to September 1, 1863. Present or accounted for until wounded in Virginia in June, 1864. Returned to duty prior to September 1, 1864. Reported present in September-December, 1864.

BOONE, SAMPSON, 1st Sergeant
Born in Duplin County and was by occupation a farmer prior to enlisting in New Hanover County at age 24, March 10, 1862. Mustered in as Corporal. Promoted to Sergeant in September-October, 1862. Present or accounted for until July-August, 1863, when he was reported sick in hospital at Wilmington. Returned to duty in September-October, 1863. Promoted to 1st Sergeant in March-May, 1864. Present or accounted for until captured at Cold Harbor, Virginia, on or about June 1, 1864. Confined at Point Lookout, Maryland, June 11, 1864. Transferred to Elmira, New York, July 12, 1864. Died at Elmira on November 24, 1864, of "chronic diarrhoea."

BOSWELL, AMOS, Private
Born in Columbus County where he resided as a farmer prior to enlisting in New Hanover County at age 25, May 1, 1862, for the war. Present or accounted for until he was reported in jail at Wilmington in November-December, 1862. Reason he was jailed not reported. Returned to duty in January-February, 1863. Present or accounted for until he died at Mount Pleasant, South Carolina, September 17, 1863. Cause of death not reported.

BRINKLEY, J. B., _____
North Carolina pension records indicate that he served in this company.

BROWN, KILBY, Private
Born in Duplin County and was by occupation a farmer prior to enlisting in New Hanover County at age 34, March 3, 1862. Present or accounted for until November-December, 1862, when he was reported absent without leave. Returned to duty in January-February, 1863. Present or accounted for through February, 1864. Reported on duty as company cook in May-October, 1864. Reported on detached duty at General Robert F. Hoke's headquarters in November-December, 1864.

BUFFKIN, ELIAS J., Private
Born in Columbus County where he resided as a farmer prior to enlisting in New Hanover County at age 32, May 14, 1862, for the war. Present or accounted for until he died at home in Columbus County on April 23, 1863. Cause of death not reported.

BURNEY, WILLIAM JAMES, Private
Born in Bladen County where he resided as a farmer prior to enlisting in New Hanover County at age 23, March 5, 1862. Present or accounted for until wounded slightly in the head at Fort Wagner, Charleston, South Carolina, July 18, 1863. Transferred to 3rd Company B, 36th Regiment N.C. Troops (2nd Regiment N.C. Artillery), prior to September 1, 1863.

CANNON, ROBERT T., Private
Born in New Hanover County and was by occupation a laborer prior to enlisting in New Hanover County at age 19, March 5, 1862. Present or accounted for until he died in hospital at Wilmington on June 18, 1863, of "febris."

CARTWRIGHT, DAVID J., Private
Born in Columbus County and was by occupation a farmer prior to enlisting in Columbus County at age 18, March 4, 1862. Present or accounted for until November-December, 1862, when he was reported absent without leave. Returned to duty in January-February, 1863. Reported absent sick in March-April, 1863. Returned to duty in May-June, 1863. Reported absent sick in July-October, 1863. Returned to duty in November-December, 1863. Present or accounted for through December, 1864.

CARTWRIGHT, GEORGE W., Private
Born in Columbus County and was by occupation a laborer prior to enlisting in Columbus County at age 20, March 4, 1862. Present or accounted for until November-December, 1862, when he was reported absent without leave. Returned to duty in January-February, 1863. Reported absent sick in March-June, 1863. Returned to duty in July-August, 1863. Reported absent sick from September 13 through October 31, 1863. Returned to duty in November-December, 1863. Present or accounted for until wounded at or near Bermuda Hundred, Virginia, May 20, 1864. Reported absent wounded through October, 1864. Returned to duty in November-December, 1864. Present or accounted for through December, 1864.

CARTWRIGHT, JACOB, Private
Born in Columbus County where he resided as a farmer prior to enlisting at Camp Whiting, near Wilmington, at age 28, February 2, 1863, for the war. Present or accounted for until he died at Mount Pleasant, South Carolina, September 3, 1863. Cause of death not reported.

CHESTNUT, JAMES M., Private
Born in Duplin County and was by occupation a farmer prior to enlisting in New Hanover County at age 48, March 10, 1862. Present or accounted for until July-August, 1863, when he was reported sick in hospital in Charleston, South Carolina. Returned to duty in November-December, 1863. Present or accounted for until May-August, 1864, when he was reported absent on detached service near Petersburg, Virginia. Rejoined the company in September-October, 1864. Left sick at Greensboro in November-December, 1864.

COLEMAN, LOTT CASWELL, Private
Born in Columbus County where he resided as a farmer prior to enlisting in New Hanover County at age 28, May 15, 1862, for the war. Reported absent sick in July-December, 1862. Returned to duty in January-February, 1863. Present or accounted for until transferred to Company E, 36th Regiment N.C. Troops (2nd Regiment N.C. Artillery), May 9, 1863.

CONAWAY, WILLIAM H., Sergeant
Born in Onslow County and was by occupation a farmer prior to enlisting in New Hanover County at age 36, March 3, 1862. Mustered in as Sergeant. Present or accounted for until killed at Cold Harbor, Virginia, June 1, 1864.

COTTLE, NIXON, Private
Born in Duplin County and was by occupation a farmer prior to enlisting in New Hanover County at age 25, March 24, 1862. Present or accounted for until killed at Cold Harbor, Virginia, June 1, 1864.

CRAIG, CHARLES M., Private
Born in New Hanover County and was by occupation a laborer prior to enlisting in New Hanover County at age 18, February 10, 1862. Present or accounted for until May-June, 1863, when he was reported absent sick. Reported absent without leave from August 20 through October 31, 1863. Returned to duty in November-December, 1863. Present or accounted for until captured at Fort Harrison, Virginia, September 30, 1864. Confined at Point Lookout, Maryland, October 5, 1864. Paroled at Point Lookout on January 17, 1865. Received at Boulware's Wharf, James River, Virginia, January 21, 1865, for exchange.

CRAWFORD, JOHN B., Private
Born in Richmond County, Georgia, and was by occupation a farmer prior to enlisting in New Hanover County at age 23, March 29, 1862. Deserted on April 11, 1862.

DANIEL, JOHN W., Private
Born in Bladen County and was by occupation a schoolteacher prior to enlisting in New Hanover County at age 37, March 3, 1862. Present or accounted for until May-August, 1864, when he was reported sick in hospital at Richmond, Virginia. Reported absent on sick furlough in September-October, 1864. Returned to duty in

November-December, 1864. Present or accounted for through December, 1864.

DAVID, JAMES, Private
Born at Abbeville, South Carolina, and was by occupation a laborer prior to enlisting in New Hanover County at age 17, March 13, 1862. Reported absent without leave on or about April 1, 1862. Dropped from the rolls of the company prior to July 1, 1862. Reason he was dropped not reported.

DAWSON, AMOS, Private
Born in Onslow County and was by occupation a laborer prior to enlisting in New Hanover County at age 37, March 29, 1862. Present or accounted for until July-August, 1863, when he was reported absent without leave. Reported under arrest at Charleston, South Carolina, in September-December, 1863. Died in hospital at Petersburg, Virginia, February 18, 1864, of "pneumonia."

DYSON, JAMES T., Private
Born in Columbus County where he resided as a farmer prior to enlisting in New Hanover County at age 31, March 5, 1862. Discharged prior to July 1, 1862. Reason he was discharged not reported. Reenlisted in the company at Long Island, Charleston, South Carolina, October 10, 1863. Present or accounted for until discharged on January 19, 1864, by reason of "white swelling [cancer]."

DYSON, SOLOMON ASBERRY, Private
Born in Columbus County where he resided prior to enlisting in New Hanover County at age 17, February 2, 1863, for the war. Present or accounted for until May-June, 1863, when he was reported in jail at Wilmington. Reason he was jailed not reported. Died in hospital at Wilmington on July 5, 1863, of "febris typhoides."

EDWARDS, W. PINCKNEY, Private
Born in Columbus County where he resided prior to enlisting at Petersburg, Virginia, at age 17, April 27, 1864, for the war. Killed at Cold Harbor, Virginia, May 31, 1864.

ELLIS, JAMES, Musician
Born in Onslow County and was by occupation a laborer prior to enlisting in New Hanover County at age 16, March 24, 1862. Mustered in as Private. Appointed Musician in July-August, 1862. Present or accounted for until hospitalized at Wilmington on July 6, 1864, with a gunshot wound. Place and date wounded not reported. Returned to duty on August 16, 1864. Present or accounted for through December, 1864.

EVANS, ANCHRAM H., Private
Born in Brunswick County and was by occupation a farmer prior to enlisting in Brunswick County at age 24, January 25, 1862. Mustered in as Sergeant. Promoted to 1st Sergeant in September-October, 1862. Present or accounted for until July-August, 1863, when he was reported sick in hospital at Charleston, South Carolina. Returned to duty in September-October, 1863. Reduced to

ranks in March-August, 1864. Present or accounted for until September-October, 1864, when he was reported absent. Reported absent on detached service in November-December, 1864. Survived the war.

EVANS, JOHN B., Private
Enlisted at age 42, August 20, 1864, for the war. Reported sick in hospital at Richmond, Virginia, through December, 1864. Returned to duty on January 4, 1865. No further records. Survived the war.

EVANS, WILLIAM W., Private
Born in Brunswick County and was by occupation a farmer prior to enlisting in New Hanover County at age 19, March 8, 1862. Mustered in as Corporal. Reduced to ranks on February 9, 1863. Present or accounted for until he died in hospital at Wilmington on June 28, 1863, of "febris typhoides."

FAIRFAX, THOMAS A., Private
Resided in Columbus County and was by occupation a farmer prior to enlisting in New Hanover County at age 28, May 1, 1862, for the war. Wounded slightly at Goldsboro on December 17, 1862. Returned to duty prior to January 1, 1863. Present or accounted for until killed near Petersburg, Virginia, on or about July 2, 1864.

FOWLER, HARMON, Private
Born in Horry District, South Carolina, and resided in Columbus County where he was by occupation a farmer prior to enlisting in Columbus County at age 35, February 2, 1863, for the war. Present or accounted for through February, 1864. Reported absent on detached service with the Engineer Corps in May-December, 1864. Survived the war.

FOWLER, LABAN, Corporal
Previously served as Private in Company D, 20th Regiment N.C. Troops (10th Regiment N.C. Volunteers). Enlisted in this company in Columbus County on February 2, 1863, for the war. Mustered in as Private. Present or accounted for until January-February, 1864, when he was reported absent without leave. Returned to duty on an unspecified date. Wounded at Drewry's Bluff, Virginia, on or about May 16, 1864. Returned to duty prior to September 1, 1864. Reported absent sick in the brigade hospital in September-December, 1864. Returned to duty on March 16, 1865. Promoted to Corporal on an unspecified date. Paroled at Greensboro on or about May 1, 1865.

GAPPINS, JAMES J., Private
Previously served as Private in Company H of this regiment. Transferred to this company on March 1, 1863. Reported absent sick in March-April, 1863. Returned to duty in May-June, 1863. Present or accounted for until December 30, 1863, when he was reported absent without leave. Returned to duty on or about February 22, 1864, and was hospitalized at Petersburg, Virginia. Reported absent sick until November 30, 1864, when he was reported absent without leave.

GASKILL, FURNEY, Private
Born in Carteret County and was by occupation a laborer

prior to enlisting in New Hanover County at age 46, March 12, 1862. Present or accounted for until wounded in the left ankle near Petersburg, Virginia, June 17, 1864. Reported absent wounded until December 1, 1864, when he was reported absent without leave. Returned to duty on December 15, 1864. No further records.

GODWIN, GUY W., Private
Born in Columbus County where he resided as a farmer prior to enlisting in New Hanover County at age 42, April 4, 1862. Present or accounted for until he deserted on August 30, 1862. Returned to duty in March-April, 1863. Present or accounted for until he died in hospital at Florence, South Carolina, December 8, 1863, of wounds received "on the train" on an unspecified date.

GOWAN, JAMES T., Private
Resided in Columbus County and enlisted in New Hanover County at age 23, May 1, 1862, for the war. Present or accounted for until captured at Cold Harbor, Virginia, on or about June 1, 1864. Confined at Point Lookout, Maryland, June 11, 1864. Transferred to Elmira, New York, July 12, 1864. Released at Elmira on June 12, 1865, after taking the Oath of Allegiance.

GREEN, LEVI, Private
Born in Columbus County where he resided as a farmer prior to enlisting in New Hanover County at age 30, May 1, 1862, for the war. Present or accounted for until November-December, 1862, when he was reported absent without leave. Returned to duty in January-February, 1863. Present or accounted for until he died in hospital at Wilmington on July 24, 1863, of "febris typh[oi]d."

HADDOCK, DANIEL A., Private
Born in Bladen County where he resided as a farmer or laborer prior to enlisting in New Hanover County at age 27, March 5, 1862. Present or accounted for until July-August, 1863, when he was reported absent sick in hospital at Charleston, South Carolina. Reported absent without leave on October 13, 1863. Reported absent sick from November, 1863, through February, 1864. Reported absent without leave on August 1, 1864. Returned to duty on December 5, 1864. Present or accounted for through December, 1864.

HALL, JOHN G., Private
Previously served in an unspecified unit. Transferred to this company on May 31, 1864. Wounded near Petersburg, Virginia, June 17, 1864. Returned to duty on January 5, 1865.

HAMMONDS, WILEY F., Private
Born in Columbus County where he resided as a farmer prior to enlisting in Columbus County at age 33, February 2, 1863, for the war. Reported absent sick in March-April, 1863. Returned to duty in May-June, 1863. Reported absent without leave in July-August, 1863. Returned to duty in September-October, 1863. Reported absent without leave on December 1, 1863. Returned to duty on or about January 14, 1864. Hospitalized at Petersburg, Virginia, February 12, 1864. Died in hospital at Petersburg on March 4, 1864, of "pneumonia."

HANSLEY, JOHN D., Private
Born in New Hanover County where he resided as a farmer prior to enlisting in New Hanover County at age 46, February 12, 1862. Discharged "by the surgeon" on May 28, 1862. Reason discharged not reported.

HARDY, JOHN, Private
Born in Horry District, South Carolina, and was by occupation a farmer prior to enlisting in New Hanover County at age 47, March 15, 1862. Reported absent without leave through June, 1862. Reported for duty in July-August, 1862. Present or accounted for until November-December, 1862, when he was reported in jail under sentence of court-martial. No further records.

HARRELSON, AARON B., Private
Previously served as Private in Company A of this regiment. Transferred to this company in January, 1863. Present or accounted for until July-August, 1863, when he was reported absent without leave. Returned to duty in September-October, 1863. Present or accounted for until August 1, 1864, when he was reported absent without leave. Returned to duty prior to September 30, 1864, when he was captured at Fort Harrison, Virginia. Confined at Point Lookout, Maryland, October 5, 1864. Paroled at Point Lookout on or about February 10, 1865. Received at Cox's Wharf, James River, Virginia, on or about February 14, 1865, for exchange. Hospitalized at Richmond, Virginia, February 15, 1865, with an unspecified complaint. Transferred to another hospital on February 16, 1865. No further records.

HATCHER, HENRY C., Private
Born in Duplin County and was by occupation a farmer prior to enlisting in New Hanover County at age 16, March 18, 1862. Present or accounted for until he died in hospital at Charleston, South Carolina, August 15, 1863. Cause of death not reported.

HAWES, ASA W., Private
Born in Duplin County and was by occupation a farmer prior to enlisting in New Hanover County at age 22, March 6, 1862. Present or accounted for until transferred to Company A, 2nd Regiment Confederate Engineer Troops, January 23, 1864.

HIGGINS, JESSE B., Private
Enlisted in Edgecombe County on December 28, 1863, for the war. Transferred to Company C, 8th Regiment N.C. State Troops, February 19, 1864, in exchange for Private John P. Murrell.

HINSON, ASA KELLY, Private
Resided in Columbus County and was by occupation a farmer prior to enlisting in New Hanover County at age 18, July 12, 1863, for the war. Present or accounted for until reported absent sick at Charleston, South Carolina, September 27, 1863. Returned to duty in January-February, 1864. Present or accounted for until wounded at Drewry's Bluff, Virginia, May 16, 1864. Hospitalized at Richmond, Virginia, where he died on May 24, 1864, of wounds.

HINSON, EDWARD P., Corporal

Born in Columbus County where he resided as a farmer prior to enlisting in Columbus County at age 21, March 4, 1862. Mustered in as Private. Promoted to Corporal in March-April, 1863. Present or accounted for until killed near Petersburg, Virginia, June 17, 1864.

HINSON, JOHN L., Private

Born in Columbus County where he resided as a farmer prior to enlisting in Columbus County at age 19, March 4, 1862. Present or accounted for until wounded at Drewry's Bluff, Virginia, May 16, 1864. Returned to duty on May 31, 1864. Present or accounted for until captured at Fort Harrison, Virginia, September 30, 1864. Confined at Point Lookout, Maryland, October 5, 1864. Paroled at Point Lookout on February 13, 1865. Received at Cox's Wharf, James River, Virginia, February 15, 1865, for exchange.

HINSON, JOHN P., Private

Enlisted in New Hanover County at age 29, May 1, 1862, for the war. Present or accounted for until November-December, 1862, when he was reported absent without leave. Returned to duty in January-February, 1863. Present or accounted for until wounded at Fort Wagner, Charleston, South Carolina, July 18, 1863. Returned to duty in September-October, 1864. Present or accounted for through December, 1864. Survived the war.

HINSON, ROBERT R., Private

Born in Robeson County and resided in Columbus County where he was by occupation a farmer prior to enlisting in Columbus County at age 34, March 12, 1862. Mustered in as Corporal. Present or accounted for until September-October, 1862, when he was reported absent sick. Reported absent without leave in November-December, 1862. Returned to duty in January-February, 1863. Wounded at Fort Wagner, Charleston, South Carolina, July 18, 1863. Returned to duty prior to September 1, 1863. Reduced to ranks on December 26, 1863. Present or accounted for until wounded at Drewry's Bluff, Virginia, May 13, 1864. Reported absent wounded through August, 1864. Returned to duty in September-October, 1864. Present or accounted for through December, 1864. Survived the war.

HORNE, WILLIAM F., Private

Born in Onslow County and resided in Columbus County where he was by occupation a farmer prior to enlisting in Columbus County at age 26, March 4, 1862. Present or accounted for until November-December, 1862, when he was reported sick in hospital at Wilmington. Returned to duty in January-February, 1863. Present or accounted for until August 25, 1863, when he was reported absent without leave. Dropped from the rolls of the company in March-August, 1864.

HUMPHREY, JOHN, Private

Born in New Hanover County and was by occupation a farmer prior to enlisting in New Hanover County at age 19, March 3, 1862. Present or accounted for until captured at Drewry's Bluff, Virginia, May 16, 1864. Confined at Point Lookout, Maryland, May 21, 1864. Died at Point Lookout on March 5, 1865, of "chronic dysentery."

IKENER, WARD, Private

Previously served as Private in Company C, 18th Regiment N.C. Troops (8th Regiment N.C. Volunteers). Enlisted in this company at Camp Whiting, near Wilmington, February 2, 1863, for the war. Present or accounted for until captured at Cold Harbor, Virginia, June 1, 1864. Confined at Point Lookout, Maryland, June 11, 1864. Transferred to Elmira, New York, July 12, 1864. Died at Elmira on November 18, 1864, of "remittent fever."

INMAN, JESSE, Private

Resided in Columbus County and enlisted at Wilmington on May 15, 1862, for the war. Present or accounted for until September 27, 1863, when he was reported sick in hospital at Charleston, South Carolina. Reported absent sick through December, 1863. Died at home in Columbus County in January, 1864. Cause of death not reported.

JENRETTE, JOHN H., Private

Resided in Columbus County and was by occupation a farmer prior to enlisting in New Hanover County at age 18, February 2, 1863, for the war. Reported absent sick in May-June, 1863. Reported absent without leave on August 20, 1863. Died in Columbus County prior to January 1, 1864. Date and cause of death not reported.

JERNIGAN, WILLIS, Private

Resided in Columbus County and enlisted in New Hanover County at age 24, May 1, 1862, for the war. Present or accounted for until March-April, 1863, when he was reported absent sick. Returned to duty in May-June, 1863. Wounded at Fort Wagner, Charleston, South Carolina, July 18, 1863. Returned to duty in November-December, 1863. Present or accounted for until wounded in the left hand (finger amputated) at or near Bermuda Hundred, Virginia, on or about May 20, 1864. Hospitalized at Petersburg, Virginia. Furloughed for sixty days on May 25, 1864. Wounded in the foot at Fort Harrison, Virginia, September 30, 1864. Reported absent wounded through December, 1864.

JOLLY, DANIEL JASPER, Private

Resided in Columbus County and enlisted in New Hanover County at age 17, July 1, 1863, for the war. Present or accounted for until captured at Cold Harbor, Virginia, on or about June 1, 1864. Confined at Point Lookout, Maryland, June 11, 1864. Transferred to Elmira, New York, July 12, 1864. Released at Elmira on July 3, 1865, after taking the Oath of Allegiance. [Twin brother of Jesse R. Jolly.]

JOLLY, JESSE R., Private

Resided in Columbus County and enlisted in New Hanover County at age 16, May 14, 1862, for the war. Present or accounted for until wounded slightly at Goldsboro on December 17, 1862. Returned to duty prior to January 1, 1863. Present or accounted for until wounded at Cold Harbor, Virginia, May 31, 1864. Hospitalized at Petersburg, Virginia, where he died on June 19, 1864, of wounds. [Twin brother of Daniel Jasper Jolly.]

KENT, ROBERT, Private

Born in New Hanover County and was by occupation a laborer prior to enlisting in New Hanover County at age 18, February 10, 1862. Present or accounted for until he deserted on or about August 18, 1862. Returned to duty on July 15, 1863. Present or accounted for until he deserted to the enemy on or about September 4, 1864.

KETCHUM, JAMES F., Sergeant

Born in New Hanover County and was by occupation a student prior to enlisting in New Hanover County at age 18, March 15, 1862. Mustered in as Sergeant. Present or accounted for until captured at Fort Harrison, Virginia, September 30, 1864. Confined at Point Lookout, Maryland, October 5, 1864. Died at Point Lookout on March 19, 1865, of "pneumonia."

KING, CHRISTOPHER C., Private

Born in Onslow County and was by occupation a farmer prior to enlisting in New Hanover County at age 15, March 10, 1862. Present or accounted for through December, 1864. Survived the war.

KING, MARSDEN, Sergeant

Born in Bladen County where he resided as a farmer prior to enlisting in New Hanover County at age 32, March 10, 1862. Mustered in as Private. Promoted to Corporal in September-October, 1862. Promoted to Sergeant in March-August, 1864. Present or accounted for until wounded near Petersburg, Virginia, June 16, 1864. Reported absent wounded or absent sick through December, 1864.

KNOWLES, STEPHEN, Private

Previously served as Private in Company D, 13th Battalion N.C. Infantry. Transferred to this company on April 15, 1862. Present or accounted for until wounded near Petersburg, Virginia, June 17, 1864. Reported absent wounded until September-October, 1864, when he was reported absent without leave. Returned to duty in November-December, 1864. Present or accounted for through December, 1864. Survived the war.

LATTA, ADAM G., Private

Enlisted in New Hanover County on July 1, 1863, for the war. Reported absent on detached service as a clerk at General Thomas L. Clingman's headquarters through December, 1864. Paroled at Greensboro on May 1, 1865.

LAWRENCE, WILLIAM J. H., Private

Born in New Hanover County and was by occupation a farmer prior to enlisting in New Hanover County at age 36, March 10, 1862. No further records.

LAWSON, JESSE, Private

Born in Robeson County and resided in Columbus County where he was by occupation a farmer prior to enlisting in New Hanover County at age 50, May 15, 1862, for the war. Present or accounted for until July-August, 1863, when he was reported absent without leave. Reported absent under arrest at Charleston, South Carolina, in September-October, 1863. Died in hospital at Petersburg, Virginia, February 16, 1864, of "diarrhoea chronica."

LENNON, JOHN P., Private

Enlisted in March, 1862. Reported absent with leave on or about April 1, 1862. No further records.

LONG, DANIEL M., Private

Previously served as Private in Company C, 18th Regiment N.C. Troops (8th Regiment N.C. Volunteers). Enlisted in this company in New Hanover County on February 2, 1863, for the war. Present or accounted for until May-June, 1863, when he was reported absent without leave. Returned to duty in July-August, 1863. Present or accounted for until captured at Cold Harbor, Virginia, June 1, 1864. Confined at Point Lookout, Maryland, June 11, 1864. Transferred to Elmira, New York, July 12, 1864. Released at Elmira on June 21, 1865, after taking the Oath of Allegiance.

McPHERSON, JOHN A., Private

Resided in Columbus County and was by occupation a farmer prior to enlisting in Columbus County at age 18, February 2, 1863, for the war. Present or accounted for until July-August, 1863, when he was reported absent without leave. Returned to duty in September-October, 1863. Present or accounted for through February, 1864. Reported absent in hospital or absent sick in May-October, 1864. Reported absent without leave in November-December, 1864.

McPHERSON, JOSHUA, Private

Born in Columbus County where he resided as a farmer prior to enlisting in New Hanover County at age 18, January 31, 1863, for the war. Present or accounted for until May-June, 1863, when he was reported absent sick. Returned to duty in July-August, 1863. Present or accounted for until discharged on October 19, 1863. Reason discharged is illegible.

MERCER, JOHN Q., Private

Born in Columbus County where he resided as a farmer prior to enlisting in New Hanover County at age 33, February 11, 1863, for the war. Reported absent sick through June, 1863. Reported absent without leave from August 20 through October 31, 1863. Returned to duty in November-December, 1863. Present or accounted for until hospitalized at Winchester, Virginia, August 1, 1864, with a gunshot wound. Place and date wounded not reported. Reported absent on detached service on or about August 31, 1864. Hospitalized at Richmond, Virginia, November 26, 1864, with chronic diarrhoea. Returned to duty on December 28, 1864.

MERCER, WILLIAM, Private

Resided in Columbus County and was by occupation a farmer prior to enlisting at Camp Whiting, near Wilmington, at age 37, January 31, 1863, for the war. Died in hospital at Charleston, South Carolina, March 8, 1863. Cause of death not reported.

MERRITT, JAMES A., Private

Born in Sampson County and resided in Duplin County where he was by occupation a farmer prior to enlisting in New Hanover County at age 17, March 19, 1862. Present or accounted for through December, 1864. Paroled at Goldsboro on May 23, 1865.

MERRITT, MARLEY, Private

Previously enlisted as Private in Company K, 20th Regiment N.C. Troops (10th Regiment N.C. Volunteers). Enlisted in this company in Columbus County on March 5, 1862. Present or accounted for until wounded in the back and right hip at Goldsboro on December 17, 1862. Returned to duty prior to January 1, 1863. Present or accounted for through February, 1864; however, he was reported on detail with the quartermaster's department during much of that period. Reported on detached service with General Robert F. Hoke's ordnance train in May-August, 1864. Wounded slightly in Virginia in June, 1864. Reported on detached duty as an ambulance driver in September-October, 1864. Rejoined the company in November-December, 1864. Survived the war.

MERRITT, WILLIAM M., Private

Born in Sampson County and was by occupation a laborer prior to enlisting in New Hanover County at age 19, March 15, 1862. Present or accounted for until May-June, 1863, when he was reported absent sick. Returned to duty in July-August, 1863. Reported absent without leave on December 24, 1863. Rejoined the company on or about January 23, 1864, and was placed under arrest. Returned to duty prior to May 16, 1864, when he was wounded at Drewry's Bluff, Virginia. Returned to duty on an unspecified date. Killed near Petersburg, Virginia, August 24, 1864.

MILLICAN, SAUNDERS, Private

Born in Brunswick County and resided in Columbus County where he was by occupation a farmer prior to enlisting in Columbus County at age 35, February 2, 1863, for the war. Transferred to Company H of this regiment on March 1, 1863.

MOORE, CHARLES A., Private

Born in Craven County and was by occupation a laborer prior to enlisting in New Hanover County at age 17, February 10, 1862. Present or accounted for through June, 1862. Reported absent without leave in July-August, 1862. Returned to duty prior to September 1, 1862. Reported absent without leave in November-December, 1862. Returned to duty in January-February, 1863. Present or accounted for until May-June, 1863, when he was reported in confinement at the Wilmington jail. Reason he was jailed not reported. Returned to duty prior to July 18, 1863, when he was killed at Fort Wagner, Charleston, South Carolina.

MURRELL, JOHN P., Private

Previously served as Private in Company C, 8th Regiment N.C. State Troops. Transferred to this company on February 19, 1864, in exchange for Private Jesse B. Higgins. Present or accounted for until wounded at or near Petersburg, Virginia, July 28, 1864. Returned to duty in September-October, 1864. Present or accounted for through December, 1864.

NEALY, JOHN ALLEN, Private

Resided in Columbus County where he enlisted at age 17, February 2, 1863, for the war. Present or accounted for until May-August, 1864, when he was reported absent sick in Columbus County. Returned to duty in September-

October, 1864. Present or accounted for through December, 1864. Survived the war.

NELSON, WILLIAM A., Private

Resided in Brunswick County where he enlisted at age 26, July 7, 1862, for the war. Present or accounted for until wounded in the left thigh at Drewry's Bluff, Virginia, May 16, 1864. Returned to duty prior to September 1, 1864. Wounded in the left arm and/or right thigh at Fort Harrison, Virginia, September 30, 1864. Reported absent wounded through December, 1864. Survived the war.

NEWTON, WILLIAM B., Private

Previously served as Private in Company D, 13th Battalion N.C. Infantry. Transferred to this company on April 15, 1862. Present or accounted for until discharged on April 14, 1863. Reason discharged not reported.

NOBLES, AVERITT, Private

Born in Columbus County on March 15, 1828, and resided in Columbus County where he was by occupation a farmer prior to enlisting in New Hanover County on May 1, 1862, for the war. Present or accounted for through June, 1863. Reported absent without leave in July-August, 1863. Returned to duty in September-October, 1863. Present or accounted for until wounded in the left thigh at Drewry's Bluff, Virginia, May 16, 1864. Hospitalized at Richmond, Virginia. Furloughed for sixty days on May 31, 1864. Returned to duty prior to September 1, 1864. Wounded in the neck at Fort Harrison, Virginia, September 30, 1864. Returned to duty prior to November 1, 1864. Reported present in November-December, 1864. Survived the war.

NOBLES, EMANUEL, Private

Born in Columbus County where he resided as a farmer prior to enlisting in New Hanover County at age 22, May 5, 1862, for the war. Present or accounted for until November-December, 1862, when he was reported absent without leave. Returned to duty in January-February, 1863. Wounded at or near Fort Wagner, Charleston, South Carolina, on or about July 18, 1863. Returned to duty prior to September 1, 1863. Hospitalized at Mount Pleasant, South Carolina, October 22, 1863. Returned to duty in November-December, 1863. Present or accounted for until he died in hospital at Richmond, Virginia, September 3, 1864, of "diarrh[oea] chron[ic]."

NOBLES, JOHN CRAWFORD, Private

Previously served as Private in Company D, 20th Regiment N.C. Troops (10th Regiment N.C. Volunteers). Enlisted in this company at Camp Whiting, near Wilmington, January 31, 1863, for the war. Present or accounted for until captured at Cold Harbor, Virginia, on or about June 1, 1864. Confined at Point Lookout, Maryland, June 11, 1864. Transferred to Elmira, New York, July 12, 1864. Paroled at Elmira on October 11, 1864. Received at Venus Point, Savannah River, Georgia, November 15, 1864, for exchange.

NORRIS, ELCANEY, Private

Born in Columbus County where he resided as a farmer prior to enlisting in Columbus County at age 26, March 5, 1862. Reported absent without leave on an unspecified date. Returned to duty in July-August, 1862. Reported absent sick in September-October, 1862. Returned to duty in November-December, 1862. Present or accounted for until July-August, 1863, when he was reported absent without leave. Returned to duty in September-October, 1863. Reported absent without leave for approximately thirty-three days in November-December, 1863. Killed at Drewry's Bluff, Virginia, May 16, 1864.

NORRIS, SOLOMON, Private
Resided in Columbus County and enlisted in Brunswick County at age 17, July 15, 1862, for the war. Present or accounted for through October, 1862. Reported absent without leave in November-December, 1862. Returned to duty in January-February, 1863. Present or accounted for until July-August, 1863, when he was reported absent without leave. Returned to duty in September-October, 1863. Present or accounted for through August, 1864. Company records indicate that he was captured at or near Fort Harrison, Virginia, September 30, 1864; however, records of the Federal Provost Marshal do not substantiate that report. Presumably was killed at Fort Harrison.

NORRIS, WILLIAM INDY, Private
Resided in Columbus County and enlisted in New Hanover County at age 24, May 1, 1862, for the war. Present or accounted for through October, 1862. Reported absent sick in November-December, 1862. Returned to duty in January-February, 1863. Present or accounted for until May-August, 1864, when he was reported absent sick. Reported absent on detached service at the brigade hospital in September-December, 1864. Survived the war. [North Carolina pension records indicate that he was wounded in the chest and "privates" at Wilmington in February, 186(5).]

NORRIS, WILLIAM J., Private
Born in Columbus County where he resided as a farmer prior to enlisting in Columbus County at age 20, March 5, 1862. Present or accounted for until September-October, 1862, when he was reported absent sick. Returned to duty in November-December, 1862. Present or accounted for until July-August, 1863, when he was reported absent without leave. Returned to duty in September-October, 1863. Present or accounted for until December 1, 1863, when he was reported absent without leave. Returned to duty in January-February, 1864. Present or accounted for until September-December, 1864, when he was reported absent without leave.

POTTER, BENJAMIN W., Private
Born in Brunswick County and was by occupation a farmer prior to enlisting in Brunswick County at age 19, March 8, 1862. Present or accounted for until November-December, 1863, when he was reported sick in hospital in Wilmington. Returned to duty in January-February, 1864. Present or accounted for until captured at Cold Harbor, Virginia, May 31, 1864. Confined at Point Lookout, Maryland, June 8, 1864. Transferred to Elmira, New York, July 9, 1864. Paroled at Elmira on October 11, 1864. Received at Venus Point, Savannah River, Georgia, November 15, 1864, for exchange. Reported absent without leave on December 16, 1864. Apparently deserted to the enemy prior to December 24, 1864, when he was

admitted to a Federal field hospital with chronic diarrhoea. No further records.

POWERS, JORDAN, Private
Born in Columbus County where he resided as a farmer prior to enlisting in New Hanover County at age 30, May 1, 1862, for the war. Present or accounted for until wounded in the right arm at Fort Wagner, Charleston, South Carolina, July 18, 1863. Reported absent wounded through February, 1864. Dropped from the rolls of the company prior to May 1, 1864, by reason of disability from wounds. Survived the war.

PRINCE, ANDREW, Private
Resided in Columbus County and enlisted in New Hanover County at age 32, April 3, 1862. Present or accounted for through February, 1864. Reported absent sick in May-September, 1864. Hospitalized at Richmond, Virginia, October 5, 1864, with rheumatism. Furloughed for sixty days on February 20, 1865.

PRINCE, SOLOMON W., Private
Resided in Columbus County and enlisted at Camp Whiting, near Wilmington, at age 37, February 2, 1863, for the war. Present or accounted for until July-August, 1863, when he was reported absent without leave. Reported absent in jail in Charleston, South Carolina, in September-October, 1863. Reported present but under arrest in November-December, 1863. Returned to duty in January-February, 1864. Present or accounted for through December, 1864.

REAVES, JOHN T., Private
Born in New Hanover County and was by occupation a farmer prior to enlisting in New Hanover County at age 18, March 12, 1862. Discharged on or about April 1, 1862. Reason discharged not reported.

REDD, ZEPHANIAH W., Private
Born in Onslow County and was by occupation a farmer prior to enlisting in New Hanover County at age 18, March 28, 1862. Present or accounted for through October, 1862. Reported absent without leave in November-December, 1862. Returned to duty in January-February, 1863. Present or accounted for through December, 1864. Survived the war.

REGISTER, JOHN N., Private
Born in Brunswick County where he resided as a farmer prior to enlisting in Brunswick County at age 38, January 10, 1862. Present or accounted for until wounded in the right shoulder near Petersburg, Virginia, June 17, 1864. Hospitalized at Petersburg. Reported absent wounded until November 23, 1864, when he was reported absent without leave.

RITTER, HIRAM L., Private
Born in New Hanover County and was by occupation a farmer prior to enlisting in New Hanover County at age 34, March 18, 1862. Present or accounted for through February, 1864. Reported on duty as company cook in May-October, 1864. Reported present for duty in November-December, 1864. Survived the war.

ROBBINS, ELIJAH, Private

Born in Brunswick County and was by occupation a farmer or laborer prior to enlisting in New Hanover County at age 47, March 1, 1862. Present or accounted for until July-August, 1862, when he was reported absent sick. Returned to duty in September-October, 1862. Reported absent sick in November-December, 1862. Discharged on January 28, 1863, by reason of "debility consequent on old age. . . ."

ROBBINS, GEORGE W., Private

Born in Brunswick County where he resided as a farmer prior to enlisting in New Hanover County on March 3, 1862. Was about 17 years of age at time of enlistment. Reported absent sick in April-June, 1862. Returned to duty in July-August, 1862. Reported absent sick in September-October, 1862. Reported absent without leave in November-December, 1862. Returned to duty in January-February, 1863. Present or accounted for until May-June, 1863, when he was reported absent sick in the regimental hospital. Reported absent without leave from August 20 through October 31, 1863. Hospitalized at Wilmington on December 29, 1863, with debility from pneumonia. Furloughed for thirty days on an unspecified date. Reported absent sick during most of 1864. Hospitalized at Richmond, Virginia, December 23, 1864, with debility from pneumonia. Returned to duty on January 13, 1865. No further records.

ROBBINS, JAMES A., Private

Born in Brunswick County and resided in Robeson County where he was by occupation a farmer prior to enlisting in New Hanover County at age 25, March 5, 1862. Reported absent sick in April-June, 1862. Returned to duty in July-August, 1862. Reported absent without leave in November-December, 1862. Returned to duty in January-February, 1863. Present or accounted for through May, 1863. Reported absent sick from June 1, 1863, through June 30, 1864. Died in hospital at Kittrell's Springs (in present-day Vance County) on July 2, 1864. Cause of death not reported.

ROBBINS, JOEL A., Private

Born in Brunswick County where he resided as a farmer prior to enlisting in New Hanover County at age 47, March 6, 1862. Reported absent sick on or about April 21, 1862. No further records.

ROBERTS, EDMUND, Private

Born in Onslow County and was by occupation a farmer prior to enlisting in Columbus County at age 31, March 5, 1862. Present or accounted for through October, 1862. Reported sick in hospital at Goldsboro in November-December, 1862. Returned to duty in January-February, 1863. Present or accounted for until December 1, 1863, when he was reported absent without leave. Returned to duty on or about January 12, 1864. Present or accounted for until May-August, 1864, when he was reported absent sick at the brigade hospital. Returned to duty in November-December, 1864. No further records.

ROBERTS, GEORGE W., Private

Born in Brunswick County and was by occupation a farmer prior to enlisting in New Hanover County at age 18, March 3, 1862. Died at Fort Johnston, near Smithville (present-day Southport), June 29, 1862, of "fever."

SCARBOROUGH, JESSE C., Sergeant

Born in New Hanover County and was by occupation a farmer prior to enlisting in New Hanover County at age 30, March 5, 1862. Mustered in as Corporal. Reported absent sick in April-June, 1862. Returned to duty on July 8, 1862. Present or accounted for until January-February, 1864, when he was reported absent without leave. Returned to duty prior to September 1, 1864. Promoted to Sergeant in March-August, 1864. Present or accounted for through October, 1864. Reported sick in hospital at Wilmington in November-December, 1864.

SELLERS, JOSEPH C., Private

Born in Columbus County where he resided as a farmer prior to enlisting in Columbus County at age 32, March 5, 1862. Present or accounted for until November-December, 1862, when he was reported absent sick. Returned to duty in March-April, 1863. Present or accounted for until August 20, 1863, when he was reported absent without leave. Returned to duty in January-February, 1864. Present or accounted for until wounded in the left hand at Drewry's Bluff, Virginia, May 16, 1864. Reported absent wounded through October, 1864. Returned to duty in November-December, 1864. Present or accounted for through December, 1864. Survived the war.

SELLERS, WILLIAM W., Private

Born in Columbus County where he resided as a farmer prior to enlisting in Columbus County at age 35, March 5, 1862. Present or accounted for until he died in hospital at Charleston, South Carolina, on or about April 14, 1863. Cause of death not reported.

SHAW, DANIEL, Private

Born on July 9, 1817, and resided in Columbus County where he was by occupation a farmer prior to enlisting in New Hanover County on May 3, 1862, for the war. Present or accounted for until November-December, 1862, when he was reported absent without leave. Returned to duty in January-February, 1863. Present or accounted for until December 18, 1863, when he was reported absent without leave. Returned to duty on or about February 9, 1864. Present or accounted for until wounded in the right wrist and captured at Drewry's Bluff, Virginia, May 16, 1864. Sent to Fort Monroe, Virginia. Right arm amputated on an unspecified date. Confined at Point Lookout, Maryland, September 30, 1864. Paroled at Point Lookout and transferred to Venus Point, Savannah River, Georgia, where he was received on November 15, 1864, for exchange. Survived the war.

SIMMONS, ISAAC, Private

Previously served as Private in Company A of this regiment. Enlisted in this company in Columbus County on February 2, 1863, for the war. Present or accounted for until discharged on October 19, 1863. Reason discharged not reported. [North Carolina pension records indicate that he was wounded in the back and left hip by a piece of shell at Charleston, South Carolina, in 1863.]

SKIPPER, STEPHEN, Private
Born in Brunswick County and was by occupation a farmer prior to enlisting in New Hanover County at age 22, March 10, 1862. Present or accounted for through December, 1864. Hospitalized at Wilmington on February 18, 1865, with rheumatism. Transferred to another hospital on February 20, 1865. No further records.

SMITH, BRACY, Private
Born in Pitt County and resided in Columbus County where he was by occupation a cooper prior to enlisting in New Hanover County at age 24, May 2, 1862, for the war. Present or accounted for until captured at Cold Harbor, Virginia, June 1, 1864. Confined at Point Lookout, Maryland, June 11, 1864. Transferred to Elmira, New York, July 9, 1864. Died at Elmira on September 20, 1864, of "remittent fever."

SMITH, WILLIAM D., Private
Born in South Carolina and resided in Columbus County where he enlisted at age 35, February 2, 1863, for the war. Present or accounted for until wounded at Fort Wagner, Charleston, South Carolina, July 18, 1863. Returned to duty prior to September 1, 1863. Hospitalized at Petersburg, Virginia, January 13, 1864, with scabies. Returned to duty on March 12, 1864. Present or accounted for until captured at Cold Harbor, Virginia, June 1, 1864. Confined at Point Lookout, Maryland, June 11, 1864. Transferred to Elmira, New York, July 9, 1864. Paroled at Elmira on October 11, 1864. Received at Venus Point, Savannah River, Georgia, November 15, 1864, for exchange.

STRICKLAND, BETHEL P., Private
Resided in Columbus County and was by occupation a farmer prior to enlisting in New Hanover County at age 20, March 12, 1862. Present or accounted for until July-August, 1863, when he was reported absent without leave. Returned to duty prior to September 1, 1863. Present or accounted for through February, 1864. No further records.

STRICKLAND, MATTHEW L., Private
Born in Columbus County where he resided as a farmer prior to enlisting in New Hanover County at age 27, April 18, 1862, for the war. Present or accounted for until July-August, 1862, when he was reported in jail at Wilmington. Reason he was jailed not reported. Returned to duty in September-October, 1862. Present or accounted for until hospitalized at Wilmington on or about June 15, 1863, with dysentery. Furloughed for thirty days on July 11, 1863. Reported absent without leave on August 20, 1863. Returned to duty subsequent to February 29, 1864. Died in hospital at Petersburg, Virginia, April 23, 1864, of "pneumonia."

STRICKLAND, PHILIP, Private
Resided in Columbus County and was by occupation a farmer prior to enlisting in New Hanover County at age 25, April 5, 1862. Present or accounted for through February, 1863. Reported absent sick from March through December, 1863. Returned to duty in January-February, 1864. Killed at Drewry's Bluff, Virginia, May 16, 1864.

STRICKLAND, QUINCY, Private
Resided in Columbus County and was by occupation a farmer prior to enlisting in New Hanover County at age 16, April 18, 1862, for the war. Present or accounted for until July-August, 1862, when he was reported in jail at Wilmington. Reason he was jailed not reported. Returned to duty in September-October, 1862. Present or accounted for until hospitalized at Wilmington on June 14, 1863, with typhoid fever. Returned to duty on July 13, 1863. Reported absent without leave on August 20, 1863. Returned to duty in November-December, 1863. Present or accounted for through December, 1864.

STRICKLAND, WILLIAM T., Private
Resided in Columbus County and was by occupation a farmer prior to enlisting in New Hanover County at age 28, April 12, 1862. Present or accounted for until he died at Fort Johnston, near Smithville (present-day Southport), July 25, 1862, of "typh[oid] fever."

SUGGS, DOCTOR F., Corporal
Born in Columbus County where he resided as a merchant prior to enlisting in New Hanover County at age 33, May 16, 1862, for the war. Mustered in as Private. Promoted to Corporal in March-May, 1864. Present or accounted for until wounded in the back at or near Drewry's Bluff, Virginia, on or about May 15, 1864. Hospitalized at Richmond, Virginia. Furloughed for sixty days on May 27, 1864. Returned to duty prior to September 1, 1864. Wounded in the thigh and captured at Fort Harrison, Virginia, September 30, 1864. Apparently died in a Federal field hospital on or about the same date.

SUMMERSETT, JOHN M., Private
Born in Alabama and resided in Columbus County where he was by occupation a farmer prior to enlisting in New Hanover County at age 22, May 12, 1862, for the war. Reported absent sick in April-June, 1862. Returned to duty in July-August, 1862. Present or accounted for until August 20, 1863, when he was reported absent sick at Mount Pleasant, South Carolina. Returned to duty in November-December, 1863. Present or accounted for through December, 1864. Survived the war.

TEABOE, PHILIP, Private
Born in Columbus County and resided in Brunswick County where he was by occupation a farmer prior to enlisting in Columbus County at age 46, March 5, 1862. Present or accounted for until he died in hospital at Wilmington on or about September 7, 1862, of "typhoid fever."

TEABOE, WILLIAM W., Private
Born in Columbus County and resided in Brunswick County where he was by occupation a farmer prior to enlisting in Columbus County at age 19, March 5, 1862. Present or accounted for through June, 1863. Reported in jail at Charleston, South Carolina, in July-October, 1863, under charges of desertion. Reported present but under arrest in November-December, 1863. Hospitalized at Petersburg, Virginia, February 22, 1864, with scabies. Returned to duty on February 29, 1864. Captured at Cold Harbor, Virginia, on or about June 3, 1864. Confined at Point Lookout, Maryland, June 11, 1864. Released at

Point Lookout on June 22, 1864, after taking the Oath of
Allegiance and joining the U.S. Army. Assigned to
Company I, 1st Regiment U.S. Volunteer Infantry.

TEACHEY, WILLIAM, Private
Born in Duplin County and was by occupation a farmer
prior to enlisting in New Hanover County at age 17, March
15, 1862. Present or accounted for through April, 1863.
Reported in hospital at Wilmington on May 4, 1863, with
diarrhoea. Returned to duty in July-August, 1863. Present
or accounted for until captured at Cold Harbor, Virginia,
June 1, 1864. Confined at Point Lookout, Maryland, June
11, 1864. Transferred to Elmira, New York, where he
arrived on July 17, 1864. Died at Elmira on August 15,
1864, of "remittent fever."

TEW, SHERWOOD B., Private
Born in Sampson County where he resided as a farmer
prior to enlisting in New Hanover County at age 47,
March 11, 1862. Died in hospital at Wilmington on April
28, 1862, of "chills & fever."

THIGPEN, ALLEN, Private
Previously served as Private in Company I, 9th Regiment
N.C. State Troops (1st Regiment N.C. Cavalry).
Transferred to this company on August 31, 1864. Wounded
in the hip and captured at Fort Harrison, Virginia,
September 30, 1864. Confined at various Federal
hospitals. Confined at Camp Hamilton, Virginia,
November 25, 1864. Transferred to Point Lookout,
Maryland, on or about December 23, 1864. Released at
Point Lookout on May 13, 1865, after taking the Oath of
Allegiance.

THIGPEN, THOMAS, Private
Born in Duplin County and was by occupation a farmer
prior to enlisting in New Hanover County at age 19,
March 18, 1862. Present or accounted for through
December, 1864. Survived the war. [North Carolina
pension records indicate that he was wounded at Drewry's
Bluff, Virginia, "March 9, 1863," and at Petersburg,
Virginia, "June 19, 1863."]

THOMPSON, NATHAN J., Private
Previously served as Private in Company C, 20th
Regiment N.C. Troops (10th Regiment N.C. Volunteers).
Enlisted in this company in New Hanover County on May
1, 1862, for the war. Present or accounted for until
wounded at Goldsboro on December 17, 1862. Returned
to duty prior to January 1, 1863. Present or accounted for
until wounded in the hand at Drewry's Bluff, Virginia,
May 16, 1864. Returned to duty prior to September 1,
1864. Wounded in the left arm and captured at Fort
Harrison, Virginia, September 30, 1864. Hospitalized at
Fort Monroe, Virginia. Transferred to Camp Hamilton,
Virginia, on or about November 12, 1864. Transferred to
Point Lookout, Maryland, November 24, 1864. Paroled at
Point Lookout on January 17, 1865. Received at
Boulware's Wharf, James River, Virginia, January 21,
1865, for exchange. Survived the war.

TINDALL, AUSTIN, Private
Born in Sampson County and was by occupation a farm
laborer prior to enlisting in New Hanover County at age

18, March 11, 1862. Reported absent without leave on or
about April 1, 1862. No further records.

WALKER, JONES C., Private
Born in New Hanover County and was by occupation a
student prior to enlisting in New Hanover County at age
19, April 1, 1862. Discharged "by the surgeon" on May
15 or July 2, 1862. Reason discharged not reported.

WARD, ASA, Private
Born in Columbus County where he resided as a farmer
prior to enlisting in Columbus County at age 17, March
4, 1862. Present or accounted for until he died at Fort
Johnston, near Smithville (present-day Southport), July
20, 1862, of "ty[phoid] fever."

WARD, DANIEL, Private
Resided in Columbus County and was by occupation a
farmer prior to enlisting in New Hanover County at age
25, May 5, 1862, for the war. Reported absent without
leave through June, 1862. Reported for duty in July-
August, 1862. Reported absent sick in September-
October, 1862. Returned to duty in November-December,
1862. Present or accounted for until August 20, 1863,
when he was reported sick in hospital at Mount Pleasant,
South Carolina. Returned to duty in November-
December, 1863. Present or accounted for until wounded
and captured at Drewry's Bluff, Virginia, May 16, 1864.
Confined at Point Lookout, Maryland, May 20, 1864.
Died on an unspecified date while a prisoner of war.
Cause of death not reported; however, it appears probable
that he died of wounds received at the time of his capture
at Drewry's Bluff.

WARD, SAMUEL W., Private
Resided in Columbus County and enlisted in New
Hanover County at age 19, April 20, 1862, for the war.
Present or accounted for until November-December,
1862, when he was reported absent without leave.
Returned to duty in January-February, 1863. Present or
accounted for until November-December, 1863, when he
was reported absent without leave. Returned to duty in
January-February, 1864. Hospitalized at Richmond,
Virginia, August 13, 1864, with diarrhoea. Furloughed for
sixty days on August 27, 1864. Reported absent without
leave on October 26, 1864. Survived the war. [North
Carolina pension records indicate that he was wounded
in the head at Charleston, South Carolina, on an
unspecified date.]

WARD, WILLIAM A., Private
Enlisted in New Hanover County on April 9, 1862.
Present or accounted for until wounded at Goldsboro on
December 17, 1862. Returned to duty in March-April,
1863. Present or accounted for until wounded at Drewry's
Bluff, Virginia, May 16, 1864. Returned to duty prior to
September 1, 1864. Present or accounted for through
December, 1864.

WILLIAMS, JAMES BONEY, Private
Born in Duplin County and was by occupation a farmer
prior to enlisting in New Hanover County at age 18,
March 6, 1862. Present or accounted for until May-
August, 1864, when he was reported absent sick in the

brigade hospital. Returned to duty in September-October, 1864. Present or accounted for through December, 1864.

WILLIAMS, JOHN Q., Private

Resided in Columbus County and enlisted at Camp Whiting, near Wilmington, at age 17, January 31, 1863, for the war. Present or accounted for until July-August, 1863, when he was reported absent without leave. Returned to duty in September-October, 1863. Present or accounted for until wounded at Drewry's Bluff, Virginia, May 16, 1864. Returned to duty prior to September 1, 1864. Wounded in the finger at Fort Harrison, Virginia, September 30, 1864. Reported absent wounded until November 17, 1864, when he was reported absent without leave.

WILLIAMS, SOLOMON R., Private

Born in Brunswick County and was by occupation a farmer prior to enlisting in New Hanover County at age 19, March 3, 1862. Reported absent sick in April-June, 1862. Reported for duty in July-August, 1862. Present or accounted for until November-December, 1862, when he was reported absent without leave. Returned to duty in January-February, 1863. Present or accounted for until July-August, 1863, when he was reported absent without leave. Reported on detached service with the Engineer Corps at Wilmington in September-December, 1863. Rejoined the company in January-February, 1864. Captured at Drewry's Bluff, Virginia, May 16, 1864. Confined at Point Lookout, Maryland, May 21, 1864. Released at Point Lookout on June 7, 1864, after taking the Oath of Allegiance and joining the U.S. Army. Assigned to Company I, 1st Regiment U.S. Volunteer Infantry.

WILLIAMSON, J. M., ⸺

Resided in Duplin County. Place and date of enlistment not reported; however, he probably enlisted in January-April, 1865. Paroled at Goldsboro on May 15, 1865.

WILSON, JOSEPH J., Private

Enlisted at Petersburg, Virginia, at age 18, February 16, 1864, for the war. Present or accounted for until hospitalized at Richmond, Virginia, August 13, 1864, with an unspecified complaint. Reported absent sick in Duplin County in September-October, 1864. Reported absent without leave on December 30, 1864. Survived the war. [North Carolina pension records indicate that he was wounded in the right hand at Drewry's Bluff, Virginia, on an unspecified date.]

WILSON, WILLIAM W., Private

Born in Duplin County and was by occupation a farmer prior to enlisting in New Hanover County at age 21, March 6, 1862. Present or accounted for until November-December, 1862, when he was reported absent sick. Returned to duty in January-February, 1863. Present or accounted for until December 24, 1863, when he was reported absent without leave. Rejoined the company on or about January 23, 1864, and was placed under arrest. Returned to duty prior to May 16, 1864, when he was wounded in the left shoulder at Drewry's Bluff, Virginia. Hospitalized at Richmond, Virginia. Reported absent wounded until September 17, 1864, when he was reported

absent without leave. Returned to duty on or about December 3, 1864. No further records.

WOOD, UZ, Private

Born in Onslow County and resided in Columbus County where he was by occupation a merchant prior to enlisting in Columbus County at age 61, March 4, 1862. Discharged on April 7, 1862, probably by reason of being overage.

WOOD, WILLIAM THOMAS, Private

Born in New Hanover County and was by occupation a laborer prior to enlisting in New Hanover County at age 17, March 14, 1862. Reported absent sick in April-June, 1862. Returned to duty in July-August, 1862. Present or accounted for until transferred to Company A of this regiment in January, 1863.

WOODARD, JOSEPH, Private

Born in New Hanover or Brunswick County and was by occupation a laborer prior to enlisting in New Hanover County at age 18, March 5, 1862. Present or accounted for until wounded at or near Bermuda Hundred, Virginia, on or about May 20, 1864. Returned to duty prior to September 1, 1864. Deserted to the enemy on or about September 4, 1864.

WORLEY, MOSES, Private

Resided in Columbus County and was by occupation a farmer prior to enlisting in New Hanover County at age 27, May 1, 1862, for the war. Reported in jail at Wilmington in July-August, 1862. Reason he was jailed not reported. Returned to duty in September-October, 1862. Present or accounted for until July-August, 1863, when he was reported absent without leave. Reported in jail at Charleston, South Carolina, in September-October, 1863. Released on an unspecified date. Died in hospital at Tarboro on December 18, 1863, of meningitis.

COMPANY H

This company, known as the "Columbus Light Infantry," was raised in Columbus County and enlisted in Columbus County in March, 1862. It was mustered into state service at Wilmington on April 3, 1862, and assigned to the 51st Regiment N.C. Troops as Company H. After joining the regiment the company functioned as a part of the regiment, and its history for the remainder of the war is reported as a part of the regimental history.

The information contained in the following roster was compiled primarily from a company muster-in and descriptive roll dated April 3, 1862, and from company muster rolls for April 3, 1862-December 31, 1864. No company muster rolls were located for the period after December 31, 1864. Valuable information was obtained from primary records such as the North Carolina adjutant general's *Roll of Honor*, discharge certificates, medical records, prisoner of war records, *The War of the Rebellion: A Compilation of the Official Records of the Union and Confederate Armies*, militia records, newspaper casualty lists and obituaries, Confederate pension applications filed with the state of North Carolina, and the 1860 federal census of North Carolina. Secondary sources such as postwar rosters and histories, cemetery records, the *Confederate Veteran*, published genealogies, and records of the United Daughters of the Confederacy also provided useful information.

OFFICERS

CAPTAINS

KELLY, JOHN R.
Born in Columbus County and was by occupation a minister prior to enlisting at age 24. Appointed Captain on March 17, 1862. Reported absent sick in April-June, 1862. Returned to duty in July-August, 1862. Resigned on September 2, 1862, by reason of "an affection of the throat and lungs causing frequent though yet slight hemorrhages. . . ." Resignation accepted on September 16, 1862.

MAULTSBY, SAMUEL WHITE, SR.
Born in Columbus County on May 27, 1834. Resided in Columbus County where he was by occupation a farmer. Appointed 1st Lieutenant on March 17, 1862. Promoted to Captain on September 16, 1862. Present or accounted for until September-October, 1862, when he was reported absent sick at Kinston. Reported present but under arrest in November-December, 1862. Reason he was arrested not reported. Returned to duty in January-February, 1863. Present or accounted for until wounded in the right thigh at Drewry's Bluff, Virginia, May 16, 1864. Hospitalized at Richmond, Virginia. Furloughed on May 27, 1864. Reported absent without leave on October 15, 1864. Returned to duty in November-December, 1864. Present or accounted for through December, 1864. Survived the war.

LIEUTENANTS

BAMBERGER, JACOB, 1st Lieutenant
Born at Weismain, Bavaria, and resided in Columbus County where he was by occupation a merchant prior to enlisting in New Hanover County at age 22, March 7, 1862. Mustered in as 1st Sergeant. Appointed 2nd Lieutenant on October 7, 1862. Elected 1st Lieutenant on December 11, 1862. Present or accounted for until January-February, 1864, when he was reported sick in hospital at Wilmington. Resigned on March 14, 1864; however, his resignation was disapproved because "no reason [was] given." Reported absent without leave on April 8, 1864. Dropped from the rolls of the company on July 16, 1864.

HUGHES, JORDAN, 3rd Lieutenant
Born in Columbus County where he resided as a farmer prior to enlisting in New Hanover County at age 26, March 22, 1862. Mustered in as Private. Elected 3rd

Lieutenant on January 7, 1863. Present or accounted for until July-August, 1863, when he was reported sick at the regimental hospital. Reported absent without leave (overstayed sick furlough) on October 24, 1863. Returned to duty on November 28, 1863. Present or accounted for until April 8, 1864, when he was reported absent without leave. Dropped from the rolls of the company prior to September 1, 1864.

LENNON, JOHN CALE, 1st Lieutenant
Born in Columbus County on March 14, 1835, and was by occupation a farmer. Appointed 3rd Lieutenant on March 17, 1862. Promoted to 1st Lieutenant on September 16, 1862. Reported absent sick in September-November, 1862. Resigned on December 1, 1862, by reason of "a disease of the head and deafness" as well as "chronic rheumatism." Resignation accepted on December 11, 1862.

MEARES, JAMES A., 1st Lieutenant
Born in Columbus County on June 5, 1837. Resided in Columbus County where he was by occupation a clerk prior to enlisting in Columbus County on March 19, 1862. Mustered in as Private. Promoted to Sergeant in July-August, 1862. Appointed 3rd Lieutenant on October 16, 1862. Present or accounted for until August 22, 1863, when he was reported sick in hospital at Charleston, South Carolina. Returned to duty in November-December, 1863. Wounded at or near Petersburg, Virginia, in June, 1864. Promoted to 1st Lieutenant on July 16, 1864. Returned to duty in September, 1864. Wounded at Fort Harrison, Virginia, September 30, 1864. Returned to duty prior to November 1, 1864. Present or accounted for through December, 1864.

ROCKWELL, HENRY CLAY, 2nd Lieutenant
Born in Columbus County on July 2, 1834. Resided in Columbus County where he was by occupation a merchant. Appointed 2nd Lieutenant on March 17, 1862. Appointed Assistant Quartermaster (Captain) on April 30, 1862, and transferred to the Field and Staff of this regiment.

THOMPSON, WILLIAM M., 2nd Lieutenant
Born in Robeson County and resided in Columbus County where he was by occupation a farmer prior to enlisting in Columbus County at age 32, April 25, 1862, for the war. Mustered in as Private. Promoted to Corporal on August 1, 1863. Present or accounted for until May-August, 1864, when he was reported at home on sick furlough. Appointed 2nd Lieutenant on August 29, 1864. Returned to duty in November-December, 1864. Present or accounted for through December, 1864.

NONCOMMISSIONED OFFICERS AND PRIVATES

BAREFOOT, JOHN O., Private
Resided in Columbus County and was by occupation a farmer prior to enlisting in Columbus County at age 33, April 26, 1862, for the war. Present or accounted for until

September-October, 1862, when he was reported in hospital at Goldsboro. Returned to duty in January-February, 1863. Present or accounted for until July-August, 1863, when he was reported sick in hospital at Charleston, South Carolina. Returned to duty in September-October, 1863. Reported absent without leave in Columbus County on November 29, 1863. Returned to duty in March-April, 1864. Wounded in the right forearm at Drewry's Bluff, Virginia, May 16, 1864. Hospitalized at Richmond, Virginia. Furloughed for sixty days on June 3, 1864. Reported absent without leave on October 2, 1864. Hospitalized at Richmond on October 8, 1864 (presumably still suffering from wounds received at Drewry's Bluff). Returned to duty on December 27, 1864. No further records.

BATTEN, DANIEL, Private
Born in Columbus County where he resided as a farmer prior to enlisting in New Hanover County at age 47, April 2, 1862. Hospitalized at Wilmington on May 19, 1862, with rubeola. Returned to duty on May 26, 1862. Hospitalized at Wilmington on June 4, 1862, with acute rheumatism. Reported in hospital at Raleigh in September-October, 1862. Reported at home on sick furlough in November-December, 1862. Returned to duty in January-February, 1863. Discharged on April 10, 1863, after providing Private Edward W. Turner as a substitute.

BATTEN, DAVID J., _____
Resided in Columbus County and was by occupation a farmer. North Carolina pension records indicate that he served in this company. Served also as Private in Captain W. J. McDugald's Independent Company, Wilmington Railroad Guards.

BATTEN, WILLIAM, Private
Born in Columbus County and was by occupation a farmer prior to enlisting in New Hanover County at age 34, March 7, 1862. Present or accounted for until wounded at Goldsboro on December 17, 1862. Returned to duty prior to January 1, 1863. Present or accounted for until wounded in the right hand (fracture) and left ankle (fracture) and captured at Fort Harrison, Virginia, September 30, 1864. Confined at a Federal field hospital. Released on an unspecified date after taking the Oath of Allegiance.

BLACKBURN, WADE H., Private
Born in Horry District, South Carolina, and resided in Columbus County where he was by occupation a farmer prior to enlisting in New Hanover County at age 27, March 7, 1862. Present or accounted for until he died in Columbus County on June 26, 1863, of "fever."

BLACKMAN, ALPHA, Private
Born in Columbus County and was by occupation a tanner prior to enlisting in New Hanover County at age 30, March 7, 1862. Present or accounted for until wounded in the right arm during the bombardment of Sullivan's Island, Charleston, South Carolina, September 1, 1863. Right arm amputated. Hospitalized at Mount Pleasant, South Carolina, where he died on September 17, 1863, of "secondary hemorrhage."

BRIGHT, SAMUEL F., Private
Born in Columbus County where he resided as a farmer prior to enlisting in Columbus County at age 29, May 12, 1862, for the war. Present or accounted for until May-June, 1863, when he was reported sick in hospital at Wilmington. Returned to duty in July-August, 1863. Present or accounted for until he died in hospital at Petersburg, Virginia, on or about January 17, 1864, of "febris typhoides" and/or "pneumonia."

BRINSON, JOHN H., Private
Born in Horry District, South Carolina, and resided in Columbus County where he was by occupation a farmer prior to enlisting in New Hanover County at age 26, April 2, 1862. Present or accounted for until November-December, 1862, when he was reported sick in hospital at Wilmington. Returned to duty in January-February, 1863. Wounded slightly near Petersburg, Virginia, May 16-June 1, 1864. Transferred to Company K, 26th Regiment South Carolina Infantry, August 9, 1864.

BRINSON, JOSEPH, Private
Born in York District, South Carolina, and resided in Columbus County where he was by occupation a laborer prior to enlisting in New Hanover County at age 22, March 7, 1862. Present or accounted for until September-October, 1862, when he was reported in hospital at Raleigh. Discharged on December 1, 1862, by reason of "imbecility."

BROOKS, JOHN B., Sergeant
Born in Duplin County and was by occupation a mechanic prior to enlisting in New Hanover County at age 14, March 2, 1862. Mustered in as Sergeant. Present or accounted for until captured at Cold Harbor, Virginia, June 1, 1864. Confined at Point Lookout, Maryland, June 17, 1864. Transferred to Elmira, New York, July 12, 1864. Paroled at Elmira on or about February 20, 1865, and transferred to the James River, Virginia, for exchange. Hospitalized at Richmond, Virginia, March 3, 1865, with an unspecified complaint. Furloughed on March 11, 1865.

BROWN, COUNCIL L., Private
Born in Columbus County where he resided as a farmer prior to enlisting in New Hanover County at age 18, March 7, 1862. Died at Camp Davis, near Wilmington, June 16, 1862, of "fever."

BROWN, GEORGE MOORE, Sergeant
Born in Columbus County where he resided as a farmer prior to enlisting in New Hanover County at age 29, March 7, 1862. Mustered in as Private. Promoted to Corporal on June 1, 1862. Promoted to Sergeant in September-October, 1862. Present or accounted for until wounded at Goldsboro on December 17, 1862. Returned to duty prior to January 1, 1863. Present or accounted for until captured near Petersburg, Virginia, on or about June 16, 1864. Confined at Point Lookout, Maryland, June 19, 1864. Transferred to Elmira, New York, July 9, 1864. Paroled at Elmira on February 25, 1865, and transferred to the James River, Virginia, for exchange. Survived the war.

BUCK, BENJAMIN, Private

Born in Carteret County and resided in Columbus County where he was by occupation a farmer prior to enlisting in New Hanover County at age 21, April 23, 1862, for the war. Detailed as an oarsman on a ration boat at Charleston, South Carolina, September 25, 1863. Returned to duty with the company in November, 1863. Present or accounted for until wounded in the left knee at Cold Harbor, Virginia, on or about June 1, 1864. Hospitalized at Richmond, Virginia. Returned to duty on October 1, 1864. Hospitalized at Richmond on October 6, 1864, with wounds and diarrhoea. Returned to duty on December 27, 1864. Survived the war.

BURNEY, DANIEL, Private

Born in Bladen County on March 24, 1815. Resided in Columbus County where he was by occupation a farmer prior to enlisting in New Hanover County on March 2, 1862. Present or accounted for until September-October, 1863, when he was reported sick in the regimental hospital at Mount Pleasant, South Carolina. Returned to duty in November-December, 1863. Present or accounted for until captured near Petersburg, Virginia, on or about June 16, 1864. Confined at Point Lookout, Maryland, June 19, 1864. Transferred to Elmira, New York, July 9, 1864. Died at Elmira on February 27, 1865, of "chro[nic] diarr[hoea]."

BUTLER, LUKE H., Private

Born in Bladen County and resided in Columbus County where he was by occupation a farmer prior to enlisting in New Hanover County at age 28, March 7, 1862. Present or accounted for until captured near Petersburg, Virginia, on or about June 16, 1864. Confined at Point Lookout, Maryland, June 19, 1864. Transferred to Elmira, New York, July 9, 1864. Paroled at Elmira on March 2, 1865, and transferred to the James River, Virginia, for exchange. Hospitalized at Richmond, Virginia, March 7, 1865, with debilitas. Furloughed for thirty days on March 9, 1865. Survived the war.

BYRD, CHARLES, Private

Born in Columbus County and was by occupation a farmhand prior to enlisting in New Hanover County at age 24, March 7, 1862. Mustered in as Private. Promoted to Corporal on December 3, 1862. Reduced to ranks in May-June, 1863. Present or accounted for until May-June, 1863, when he was reported sick in hospital in Wilmington. Returned to duty in July-August, 1863. Present or accounted for through December, 1864. Survived the war.

CAMPBELL, JOHN E., 1st Sergeant

Born in Robeson County and resided in Columbus County where he was by occupation a carpenter prior to enlisting in New Hanover County at age 30, March 7, 1862. Mustered in as Private. Promoted to Corporal on June 1, 1862. Reduced to ranks in May-June, 1863. Present or accounted for until wounded in the left hand at or near Cold Harbor, Virginia, on or about June 1, 1864. Hospitalized at Petersburg, Virginia. Returned to duty on an unspecified date. Promoted to 1st Sergeant on August 29, 1864. Wounded in the head (skull fractured) and captured at Fort Harrison, Virginia, September 30, 1864.

Hospitalized at Fort Monroe, Virginia. Confined at Point Lookout, Maryland, December 27, 1864. Paroled at Point Lookout on February 18, 1865. Received at Boulware's Wharf, James River, Virginia, on or about February 21, 1865, for exchange. Survived the war.

CANADY, DERIAS CLINTON, Private

Resided in Columbus County and was by occupation a farmer prior to enlisting at Camp Hill, near Petersburg, Virginia, at age 16, March 15, 1864, for the war. Present or accounted for through December, 1864. Survived the war. [North Carolina pension records indicate that he was wounded at Fort Harrison, Virginia, in 186(4).]

CARTRETT, JOHN C., Private

Born in Columbus County and was by occupation a farmer prior to enlisting in New Hanover County at age 23, March 7, 1862. Present or accounted for until wounded at Goldsboro on December 17, 1862. Returned to duty prior to January 1, 1863. Present or accounted for until September-October, 1863, when he was reported absent on sick furlough in Columbus County. Returned to duty in November-December, 1863. Present or accounted for until killed at Drewry's Bluff, Virginia, May 16, 1864.

CARTRETT, LUKE R., Private

Resided in Columbus County and was by occupation a farmer prior to enlisting in Columbus County at age 30, April 25, 1862, for the war. Present or accounted for until transferred to Company H, 61st Regiment N.C. Troops, April 1, 1863, in exchange for Private Lucian Reynolds.

CARTRETT, MATTHEW, Private

Born in Columbus County and was by occupation a farmer prior to enlisting in New Hanover County at age 18, March 7, 1862. Present or accounted for until wounded in the elbow at or near Bermuda Hundred, Virginia, on or about May 20, 1864. Hospitalized at Petersburg, Virginia. Furloughed for sixty days on June 1, 1864. Returned to duty prior to September 30, 1864, when he was wounded in the right thigh (flesh) and captured at Fort Harrison, Virginia. Hospitalized at Fort Monroe, Virginia. Transferred to Point Lookout, Maryland, January 9, 1865. Released at Point Lookout on June 26, 1865, after taking the Oath of Allegiance.

CARTRETT, WILLIAM J., Private

Born in Columbus County where he resided as a farmer prior to enlisting in New Hanover County at age 24, March 7, 1862. Present or accounted for until wounded in the hand at Fort Harrison, Virginia, September 30, 1864. Reported absent wounded through December, 1864.

CLARK, ADDISON W., Private

Born in Columbus County on February 24, 1847. Resided in Columbus County where he was by occupation a farmhand prior to enlisting in Columbus County on April 30, 1862, for the war. Died in hospital at Wilmington on June 8, 1862, of "congestive fever."

CLARK, DANIEL D., Private

Born in Columbus County and was by occupation a farmhand prior to enlisting in New Hanover County at age

22, March 7, 1862. Present or accounted for until wounded in the breast and left thigh at Bermuda Hundred, Virginia, May 20, 1864. Reported absent wounded through December, 1864. Survived the war.

COLLIER, HANSOM B., Sergeant

Born in Wayne County and resided in Columbus or Johnston County where he was by occupation an overseer prior to enlisting in New Hanover County at age 30, March 7, 1862. Mustered in as Sergeant. Present or accounted for until hospitalized at Wilmington on or about May 29, 1863, with intermittent fever. Furloughed for thirty days on June 27, 1863. Returned to duty in September-October, 1863. Wounded in the head at Fort Harrison, Virginia, September 30, 1864. Returned to duty prior to November 1, 1864. Present or accounted for through December, 1864.

CORNISH, FRANKLIN W., Private

Born in Wayne County and resided in Columbus County where he was by occupation a laborer prior to enlisting in Columbus County at age 18, March 12, 1862. Present or accounted for until July-October, 1863, when he was reported absent on sick furlough in Columbus County. Reported sick in hospital at Wilson in November-December, 1863. Returned to duty in January-February, 1864. Present or accounted for through December, 1864. Hospitalized at Wilmington on January 10, 1865, with rheumatism. Transferred to hospital at Greensboro on January 15, 1865. Hospitalized at Richmond, Virginia, March 16, 1865. Transferred to another hospital the next day. Survived the war.

CORNISH, JOHN H., Private

Born in Wayne County and resided in Columbus County where he was by occupation a laborer prior to enlisting in Columbus County at age 16, March 12, 1862. Present or accounted for until September-October, 1862, when he was reported in hospital at Goldsboro. Returned to duty in November-December, 1862. Reported sick in hospital at Charleston, South Carolina, April 17, 1863. Returned to duty in July-August, 1863. Hospitalized at Wilmington on October 7, 1863, with otorrhoea. Returned to duty on October 24, 1863. Reported sick in hospital at Tarboro in November-December, 1863. Returned to duty in January-February, 1864. Wounded in the hand at Drewry's Bluff, Virginia, May 16, 1864. Hospitalized at Richmond, Virginia. Furloughed for sixty days on June 13, 1864. Reported absent wounded or absent sick until December 27, 1864, when he returned to duty.

CREECH, JOHN CALVIN, Private

Resided in Columbus County and was by occupation a farmer prior to enlisting at Petersburg, Virginia, at age 44, August 29, 1864, for the war. Present or accounted for through December, 1864.

CRIBB, ISHAM G., Private

Born in Marion District, South Carolina, October 13, 1844. Resided in Columbus County where he was by occupation a laborer prior to enlisting in Columbus County on March 20, 1862. Present or accounted for until September-October, 1863, when he was reported sick in hospital in Charleston, South Carolina. Reported absent

without leave in January-February, 1864. Returned to duty in March-April, 1864. Wounded and captured at Cold Harbor, Virginia, June 1, 1864. Confined at Point Lookout, Maryland, June 11, 1864. Transferred to Elmira, New York, July 12, 1864. Paroled at Elmira on March 2, 1865, and transferred to the James River, Virginia, for exchange. Hospitalized at Richmond, Virginia, March 6, 1865, with debilitas. Furloughed for thirty days on March 9, 1865. Survived the war.

DAVIS, SIMON, _____

North Carolina pension records indicate that he served in this company.

DOORS, JOHN W., Private

Born in Columbus County and was by occupation a farmer prior to enlisting in New Hanover County at age 38, March 7, 1862. Discharged "by Surgeon" on or about April 3, 1862. Reason discharged not reported.

DUNCAN, HARDY, Private

Born in Columbus County and was by occupation a farmer prior to enlisting in New Hanover County at age 36, March 7, 1862. Present or accounted for until he died in hospital at Wilmington on or about January 29, 1863, of "pneumonia."

EDWARDS, JOHN, Private

Born in Columbus County and was by occupation a farmer prior to enlisting in Columbus County at age 45, March 17, 1862. Present or accounted for until September-December, 1862, when he was reported absent on sick furlough in Columbus County. Returned to duty in January-February, 1863. Present or accounted for until December 2, 1863, when he was reported absent without leave. Returned to duty in January-February, 1864. Present or accounted for until November-December, 1864, when he was reported in hospital at Greensboro.

ELKINS, JAMES A., Private

Born in Columbus County on February 14, 1834. Resided in Columbus County where he was by occupation a laborer prior to enlisting in Columbus County on April 28, 1862, for the war. Present or accounted for through December, 1864. Served as a teamster during most of the war.

ELLIS, EVANDER, Private

Born in Columbus County and resided in Bladen County where he was by occupation a laborer prior to enlisting in Columbus County at age 45, March 12, 1862. Present or accounted for until December 2, 1863, when he was reported absent without leave. Reported absent without leave through April, 1864. Died in Bladen County on June 6, 1864. Cause of death not reported.

FIELDS, CLABON, Private

Born in Columbus County and was by occupation a fisherman prior to enlisting in New Hanover County at age 30, December 11, 1862, for the war. Present or accounted for through February, 1864. Reported on duty as a wagonmaster during most of that period. Reported sick in hospital at Petersburg, Virginia, in March-April,

1864. Reported absent on sick furlough in Columbus County in May-August, 1864. Reported absent in the division hospital in September-December, 1864. [May have served previously (probably as Private) in Company K, 20th Regiment N.C. Troops (10th Regiment N.C. Volunteers).]

FIELDS, JAMES K., Private

Born in Columbus County on December 24, 1820. Was by occupation a farmer prior to enlisting in New Hanover County on May 6, 1862, for the war. Present or accounted for until captured at Cold Harbor, Virginia, June 1, 1864. Confined at Point Lookout, Maryland, June 11, 1864. Transferred to Elmira, New York, July 12, 1864. Paroled at Elmira on March 14, 1865. Received at Boulware's Wharf, James River, Virginia, March 21, 1865, for exchange.

FLINN, DANIEL V., Private

Born in New Hanover County and resided in Columbus County where he was by occupation a farmer prior to enlisting in New Hanover County at age 26, March 7, 1862. Present or accounted for until killed at or near Petersburg, Virginia, June 18, 1864.

FLINN, GEORGE W., Private

Born in New Hanover County on September 9, 1837. Resided in Columbus County where he was by occupation a farmer prior to enlisting in Columbus County on April 25, 1862, for the war. Present or accounted for until he was injured when he fell from a train on the Northeastern Railroad (between Charleston and Florence, South Carolina) on July 14, 1863. Left leg and right arm "badly broken." Hospitalized at Charleston. Retired from service on January 10, 1865, by reason of disability.

FORMYDUVAL, COVAL LANE, Private

Born in Columbus County on June 22, 1845. Was by occupation a laborer prior to enlisting in New Hanover County on March 7, 1862. Present or accounted for until September-October, 1863, when he was reported absent on sick furlough in Columbus County. Returned to duty on December 29, 1863. Present or accounted for until captured at Drewry's Bluff, Virginia, May 16, 1864. Confined at Point Lookout, Maryland, May 19, 1864. Transferred to Elmira, New York, August 16, 1864. Paroled at Elmira on February 9, 1865. Received at Boulware's Wharf, James River, Virginia, on or about February 20, 1865, for exchange. Hospitalized at Richmond, Virginia, February 20, 1865, with an unspecified complaint. Furloughed on February 25, 1865. Survived the war. [North Carolina pension records indicate that he was "severely mashed" at Charleston, South Carolina, in May, 1863, when a cannon fell on him.]

FRINK, WILLIAM PINKNEY, Private

Born in Columbus County and was by occupation a farmer prior to enlisting in New Hanover County at age 26, March 7, 1862. Mustered in as Corporal. Reduced to ranks on May 31, 1862. Present or accounted for until killed at Goldsboro on December 17, 1862.

GANUS, JAMES S., Private

Born in Brunswick County and was by occupation a

laborer prior to enlisting in New Hanover County at age 16, April 2, 1862. Reported absent sick through October, 1862. Discharged on November 16, 1862, presumably by reason of his youth and poor health.

GANUS, JOHN C., Private

Born in Brunswick County and was by occupation a laborer prior to enlisting in New Hanover County at age 19, March 25, 1862. Present or accounted for through June, 1862. Deserted on an unspecified date. Reported under arrest awaiting trial for desertion in September-October, 1862. Returned to duty in November-December, 1862. Present or accounted for until wounded in the head at Cold Harbor, Virginia, June 1, 1864. Company records indicate that he was captured at Cold Harbor; however, records of the Federal Provost Marshal do not substantiate that report. His whereabouts for the remainder of the war are uncertain. Survived the war.

GAPPINS, JAMES J., Private

Born in Orange County and resided in Columbus County where he was by occupation a farmer prior to enlisting in Columbus County at age 33, March 12, 1862. Mustered in as Private. Appointed Musician (Fifer) in September-October, 1862. Reduced to ranks in January-February, 1863. Present or accounted for until transferred to Company G of this regiment on March 1, 1863.

GEORGE, FORNEY KELLY, Private

Born in Columbus County and was by occupation a student prior to enlisting in New Hanover County at age 17, March 7, 1862. Present or accounted for until July 13, 1863, when he was reported absent on sick furlough in Columbus County. Returned to duty in September-October, 1863. Reported sick in hospital at Wilmington in November-December, 1863. Returned to duty in January-February, 1864, and was detailed as a provost guard at Petersburg, Virginia. Reported absent without leave on August 11, 1864. Returned to duty on September 20, 1864. Company records indicate that he was captured at or near Fort Harrison, Virginia, September 30, 1864; however, records of the Federal Provost Marshal do not substantiate that report. Was presumably killed at Fort Harrison. [According to his tombstone, he died on an unspecified date in 1864.]

GORE, DANIEL RUSSELL, Private

Born in Columbus County on June 11, 1839. Resided in Columbus County where he was by occupation a farmer prior to enlisting in New Hanover County on March 7, 1862. Mustered in as Sergeant. Reduced to ranks on May 31, 1862. Reported absent sick in April-June, 1862. Returned to duty prior to November 1, 1862. Wounded at Goldsboro on December 17, 1862. Returned to duty in January-February, 1863. Present or accounted for until December 3, 1863, when he was reported absent without leave. Returned to duty in January-February, 1864, and was detailed as a provost guard at Petersburg, Virginia. Reported absent without leave on April 20, 1864. Returned to duty on August 13, 1864. Present or accounted for through December, 1864. Survived the war.

HAYNES, WARREN WENTWORTH, Private

Born in Columbus County in March, 1828. Resided in

Columbus County where he was by occupation a farmer prior to enlisting at Camp Holmes, near Raleigh, October 24, 1864, for the war. Reported absent on light duty in November-December, 1864. Hospitalized at Wilmington on January 23, 1865, with catarrhus. Furloughed for sixty days on February 8, 1865, by reason of debility following an attack of pneumonia. Survived the war.

HILL, ARMALIN BRYANT, Private
Resided in Columbus County and was by occupation a farmer prior to enlisting in Columbus County at age 33, April 27, 1862, for the war. Mustered in as Private. Promoted to Corporal in September-October, 1862. Reduced to ranks on December 3, 1862. Present or accounted for until discharged on April 24, 1863, after providing John Thomas Thompson as a substitute.

HOBBS, WILLIAM H. H., Sergeant
Born in Columbus or Bladen County and resided in Columbus County where he was by occupation a farmer prior to enlisting in New Hanover County at age 21, March 7, 1862. Mustered in as Private. Promoted to Corporal on December 3, 1862. Promoted to Sergeant on January 1, 1864. Present or accounted for until wounded in the right arm at Cold Harbor, Virginia, June 1, 1864. Right arm amputated. Hospitalized at Richmond, Virginia, until furloughed on July 31, 1864. Reported absent wounded until he was retired from service on January 13, 1865.

HOLTON, JAMES M., Private
Born in Bladen County and resided in Columbus County where he was by occupation a farmer prior to enlisting in New Hanover County at age 22, March 7, 1862. Present or accounted for until May-August, 1864, when he was reported absent on sick furlough in Columbus County. Returned to duty in September-October, 1864. Present or accounted for through December, 1864. Survived the war.

HOOKER, SAMUEL H., _____
North Carolina pension records indicate that he served in this company.

HOWELL, JOSEPH, Private
Born in Greene County and resided in Columbus County where he was by occupation a laborer prior to enlisting in Columbus County at age 16, April 2, 1862. Mustered in as Musician (Drummer). Reduced to ranks in March-April, 1863. Present or accounted for until killed at Cold Harbor, Virginia, June 1, 1864.

HUGGINS, WILLIAM J., Private
Resided in Columbus County and was by occupation a laborer prior to enlisting in Columbus County at age 25, April 29, 1862, for the war. Reported absent on sick leave in May-June, 1862. Returned to duty in September-October, 1862. Reported sick in hospital at Goldsboro in November-December, 1862. Reported absent on sick furlough in Columbus County in January-February, 1863. Returned to duty in March-April, 1863. Reported absent sick in July-October, 1863. Returned to duty in November-December, 1863. Present or accounted for until hospitalized at Richmond, Virginia, May 14, 1864, with debility. Furloughed for thirty days on July 30, 1864.

Reported absent without leave in September-October, 1864. Returned to duty in November-December, 1864. Present or accounted for through December, 1864. Survived the war.

JERNIGAN, DELANCY ALLEN, Private
Born in Columbus County on May 2, 1841. Resided in Columbus County where he was by occupation a farmer prior to enlisting in New Hanover County on March 7, 1862. Present or accounted for until September-October, 1863, when he was reported sick in the regimental hospital at Mount Pleasant, South Carolina. Returned to duty in November-December, 1863. Present or accounted for until captured at Cold Harbor, Virginia, June 1, 1864. Confined at Point Lookout, Maryland, June 11, 1864. Transferred to Elmira, New York, July 12, 1864. Died at Elmira on October 6, 1864, of "chronic diarrhoea."

JONES, DAVID J., Private
Resided in Columbus County where he enlisted at age 24, April 25, 1862, for the war. Present or accounted for until November-December, 1863, when he was reported sick in hospital at Florence, South Carolina. Returned to duty in January-February, 1864. Present or accounted for until captured at Cold Harbor, Virginia, June 1, 1864. Confined at Point Lookout, Maryland, June 11, 1864. Transferred to Elmira, New York, July 12, 1864. Paroled at Elmira on March 14, 1865. Received at Boulware's Wharf, James River, Virginia, on or about March 18, 1865, for exchange.

JONES, JAMES W., Private
Born in Columbus County where he resided as a laborer prior to enlisting in Columbus County at age 18, February 9, 1863, for the war. Present or accounted for until April 28, 1863, when he was reported absent on sick furlough in Columbus County. Returned to duty prior to July 1, 1863. Present or accounted for until September-October, 1863, when he was reported absent on sick furlough in Columbus County. Returned to duty on or about December 29, 1863. Died in hospital at Petersburg, Virginia, on or about January 25, 1864, of "pneumonia."

JOYNER, ROBERT T., Private
Resided in Columbus County and was by occupation an overseer prior to enlisting in Columbus County at age 27, April 25, 1862, for the war. Present or accounted for through August, 1864; however, he was reported absent on detail as a wagonmaster, foragemaster, and courier for General Thomas L. Clingman during much of that period. Rejoined the company in September-October, 1864. Present or accounted for through December, 1864.

KELLAHAN, ORREN, Private
Previously served as Private in Company A of this regiment. Transferred to this company on January 1, 1864. Wounded "by [his] own gun, in [his] own hands" near Petersburg, Virginia, May 16-June 1, 1864. Reported absent wounded through August, 1864. Reported absent without leave in September-December, 1864.

KELLIHAN, PINKNEY PURDIE, Private
Resided in Columbus County and was by occupation a cooper prior to enlisting in Columbus County at age 33,

May 12, 1862, for the war. Present or accounted for through October, 1862. Reported on duty as groom and hostler to the colonel of the regiment from November, 1862, through August, 1864. Wounded in the scalp and captured at Fort Harrison, Virginia, September 30, 1864. Hospitalized at Fort Monroe, Virginia. Confined at Point Lookout, Maryland, November 1, 1864. Released at Point Lookout on June 26, 1865, after taking the Oath of Allegiance.

LENNON, EZRA, Private
Born in Bladen County and resided in Columbus County where he was by occupation a farmer prior to enlisting in New Hanover County at age 18, March 7, 1862. Present or accounted for until he died in hospital at Mount Pleasant, South Carolina, September 10, 1863, of "typhoid fever."

LENNON, GEORGE W., Corporal
Born in Bladen County and resided in Columbus County where he was by occupation a farmer prior to enlisting in New Hanover County at age 30, March 7, 1862. Mustered in as Private. Reported absent on sick furlough in April-June, 1862. Returned to duty on an unspecified date. Reported present from September, 1862, through April, 1863. Promoted to Corporal in May-June, 1863. Reported sick in hospital at Wilmington in May-June, 1863. Returned to duty in July-August, 1863. Reported sick in hospital at Wilmington in November-December, 1863. Returned to duty in January-February, 1864. Present or accounted for until killed at or near Petersburg, Virginia, May 25, 1864.

LENNON, JOHN C., Private
Born in Bladen County and resided in Columbus County prior to enlisting at Camp Hill, near Petersburg, Virginia, at age 18, February 15, 1864, for the war. Present or accounted for until wounded at Drewry's Bluff, Virginia, May 16, 1864. Hospitalized at Richmond, Virginia, where he died on or about May 20, 1864, of wounds.

LENNON, JONATHAN, Private
Born in Bladen County and resided in Columbus County where he was by occupation a farmer prior to enlisting in Columbus County at age 32, April 25, 1862, for the war. Reported absent sick in May-June, 1862. Returned to duty on an unspecified date. Reported present in September-October, 1862. Discharged on December 9, 1862. Reason discharged not reported. Later served as Private in Captain W. J. McDugald's Independent Company, Wilmington Railroad Guards.

LITTLE, NATHAN, Private
Born in Brunswick County and resided in Columbus County where he was by occupation a farmer prior to enlisting in Columbus County at age 38, March 17, 1862. Present or accounted for until killed at Goldsboro on December 17, 1862.

LONG, LORENZO DOW, Private
Born in Columbus County on February 12, 1846. Resided in Columbus County where he was by occupation a farmer prior to enlisting at Camp Hill, near Petersburg, Virginia, March 1, 1864, for the war. Wounded in Virginia, June

2-23, 1864. Returned to duty in September-October, 1864. Present or accounted for through December, 1864.

McCOLSKEY, DANIEL, Private
Resided in Columbus County and was by occupation an apprentice blacksmith prior to enlisting in New Hanover County at age 22, May 12, 1862, for the war. Present or accounted for until November-December, 1863, when he was reported sick in hospital at Mount Pleasant, South Carolina. Reported absent on sick furlough in Columbus County in January-February, 1864. Returned to duty in March-April, 1864. Killed at Cold Harbor, Virginia, May 31, 1864.

MAULTSBY, NEILL ALEXANDER, 1st Sergeant
Resided in Columbus County and was by occupation a farmer prior to enlisting in Columbus County at age 29, April 29, 1862, for the war. Mustered in as Private. Promoted to Corporal on June 1, 1862. Present or accounted for until February 4, 1863, when he was reported absent on sick furlough in Columbus County. Returned to duty in May-June, 1863. Promoted to Sergeant on August 1, 1863. Promoted to 1st Sergeant on January 1, 1864. Present or accounted for until wounded in the right lung at or near Cold Harbor, Virginia, on or about June 1, 1864. Hospitalized at Petersburg, Virginia, where he died on July 17, 1864, of wounds.

MAULTSBY, THOMAS CARVER, Private
Born in Columbus County where he resided as a farmer prior to enlisting in New Hanover County at age 18, March 7, 1862. Present or accounted for until he died at home in Columbus County on February 14, 1863, of "typhoid fever."

MEARES, ERASMUS D., Private
Born in Columbus County on May 17, 1828. Resided in Columbus County where he was by occupation a farmer prior to enlisting in New Hanover County on May 14, 1862, for the war. Mustered in as Private. Promoted to Sergeant in September-October, 1862. Present or accounted for until April 26, 1863, when he was reported in hospital at Charleston, South Carolina. Reported absent on sick furlough in Columbus County from June 6 through August 31, 1863. Returned to duty in September-October, 1863. Reduced to ranks at his own request on January 1, 1864. Reported on duty as a teamster in January-October, 1864. Reported on detached service as brigade foragemaster in November-December, 1864. Survived the war.

MERCER, SAMUEL E., Private
Born in Columbus County in March, 1836. Resided in Columbus County where he was by occupation a farmer prior to enlisting in Columbus County on March 12, 1862. Present or accounted for until April 1, 1863, when he was reported absent on sick furlough. Returned to duty in May-June, 1863. Present or accounted for through December, 1864. Survived the war.

MILLICAN, SAUNDERS, Private
Previously served as Private in Company G of this regiment. Transferred to this company on March 1, 1863. Reported sick in hospital in May-August, 1863. Returned

to duty in September-October, 1863. Present or accounted for until captured at Cold Harbor, Virginia, June 1, 1864. Confined at Point Lookout, Maryland, June 11, 1864. Transferred to Elmira, New York, July 12, 1864. Died at Elmira on August 1, 1864, of "chronic diarrhoea."

MILLICAN, WILLIAM JAMES, Corporal

Born in Brunswick County on January 1, 1833. Resided in Columbus County where he was by occupation a farmer prior to enlisting in New Hanover County on March 7, 1862. Mustered in as Corporal. Promoted to Sergeant on June 1, 1862. Reduced to ranks on August 1, 1863. Promoted to Corporal on January 1, 1864. Present or accounted for until captured near Globe Tavern, Virginia, August 19, 1864. Confined at Point Lookout, Maryland, August 24, 1864. Paroled at Point Lookout on March 14, 1865. Received at Boulware's Wharf, James River, Virginia, March 16, 1865, for exchange.

NOBLES, ARCHIBALD, Private

Born in Columbus County where he resided as a farmer prior to enlisting in Columbus County at age 27, March 21, 1862. Present or accounted for until May-June, 1863, when he was reported sick in hospital at Wilmington. Returned to duty prior to July 18, 1863, when he was wounded at Fort Wagner, Charleston, South Carolina. Returned to duty in September-October, 1863. Present or accounted for until wounded in the breast at or near Drewry's Bluff, Virginia, May 16, 1864. Hospitalized at Richmond, Virginia. Returned to duty prior to September 30, 1864, when he was wounded in the right leg and right side and captured at Fort Harrison, Virginia. Hospitalized at Fort Monroe, Virginia, where he died on October 19, 1864, of wounds.

NOBLES, JAMES IRVIN, Private

Born in Columbus County where he resided as a farmer prior to enlisting in Columbus County at age 30, March 19, 1862. Present or accounted for until killed at Cold Harbor, Virginia, May 31, 1864.

NORRIS, DANIEL M., Private

Born in Columbus County where he resided as a farmer prior to enlisting in New Hanover County on March 7, 1862. Reported absent sick in April-June, 1862. Returned to duty on an unspecified date. Hospitalized at Wilmington on or about December 29, 1862, with abscesses. Reported absent on sick furlough for most of the period from January through August, 1863. Returned to duty in September-October, 1863. Reported sick in hospital at Petersburg, Virginia, in March-April, 1864. Reported absent on sick furlough in May-August, 1864. Returned to duty in September-October, 1864. Present or accounted for through December, 1864.

NORRIS, JENKINS, Private

Born in Columbus County where he resided as a farmer prior to enlisting in New Hanover County at age 20, March 7, 1862. Present or accounted for until September-October, 1862, when he was reported sick in hospital at Raleigh. Returned to duty in November-December, 1862. Present or accounted for until March-April, 1864, when he was reported sick in hospital at Petersburg, Virginia.

Returned to duty on an unspecified date. Reported present in September-December, 1864.

ODOM, CALVIN, Private

Born in Tennessee and resided in Columbus County where he was by occupation a farmer prior to enlisting in Columbus County at age 29, April 25, 1862, for the war. Present or accounted for until wounded at Goldsboro on December 17, 1862. Returned to duty prior to January 1, 1863. Present or accounted for until August 4, 1864, when he was reported absent without leave. Returned to duty on September 20, 1864. Wounded in the left thigh and buttock (flesh) and captured at Fort Harrison, Virginia, September 30, 1864. Hospitalized at Fort Monroe, Virginia. Transferred to Point Lookout, Maryland, February 1, 1865. Paroled at Point Lookout on March 17, 1865. Received at Boulware's Wharf, James River, Virginia, March 19, 1865, for exchange.

ODOM, JOHN, Private

Resided in Columbus County. Place and date of enlistment not reported; however, he probably enlisted in January-April, 1865. Paroled at Goldsboro on May 27, 1865.

PENNY, THOMAS, Private

Resided in Columbus County and was by occupation a farmer prior to enlisting in Columbus County at age 46, April 25, 1862, for the war. Present or accounted for until November-December, 1862, when he was reported at home on sick furlough. Returned to duty on an unspecified date. Reported present in March-April, 1863. Reported sick in hospital at Wilmington in May-June, 1863. Returned to duty in July-August, 1863. Reported sick in hospital in September-December, 1863. Reported absent without leave on February 29, 1864. Returned to duty in March-April, 1864. Reported absent sick at the brigade hospital in May-August, 1864. Hospitalized at Richmond, Virginia, October 5, 1864, with remittent fever. Returned to duty on January 3, 1865. No further records.

PENNY, WILLIAM, Private

Born in Columbus County where he resided as a laborer prior to enlisting in New Hanover County at age 45, March 7, 1862. Present or accounted for through October, 1862; however, he was reported absent sick during most of that period. Discharged on November 29, 1862, by the regimental surgeon. Reason discharged not reported.

PENNY, WILLIAM J., Private

Born in Columbus County where he resided as a farmer prior to enlisting in New Hanover County at age 21, March 7, 1862. Present or accounted for until May-June, 1863, when he was reported absent sick. Returned to duty in July-August, 1863. Reported sick in hospital at Mount Pleasant, South Carolina, in September-October, 1863. Returned to duty in November-December, 1863. Present or accounted for until captured at Cold Harbor, Virginia, on or about June 1, 1864. Confined at Point Lookout, Maryland, June 11, 1864. Transferred to Elmira, New York, where he arrived on August 14, 1864. Died at Elmira on January 22, 1865, of "pneumonia."

PIERCE, DANIEL GORE, Corporal

Born in Columbus County where he resided as a farmer prior to enlisting in Columbus County at age 17, April 30, 1862, for the war. Mustered in as Private. Promoted to Corporal in May-June, 1863. Present or accounted for until wounded and captured at Cold Harbor, Virginia, May 31, 1864. Confined at Point Lookout, Maryland, June 18, 1864. Transferred to Elmira, New York, July 9, 1864. Released at Elmira on June 30, 1865, after taking the Oath of Allegiance.

PORTER, CASWELL, Private

Born in Columbus County on February 28, 1829. Resided in Columbus County where he was by occupation a farmer prior to enlisting in New Hanover County on May 12, 1862, for the war. Reported absent sick in May-June, 1862. Returned to duty on an unspecified date. Reported present from September, 1862, through April, 1863. Reported sick in hospital in May-August, 1863. Returned to duty in September-October, 1863. Present or accounted for until hospitalized at Richmond, Virginia, on or about August 8, 1864, with typhoid fever. Furloughed for thirty days on September 22, 1864. Returned to duty prior to November 1, 1864. Present or accounted for through December, 1864. Wounded in the right foot at or near Bentonville on or about March 19-21, 1865. Reported in hospital at Raleigh on March 27, 1865. No further records.

PORTER, RICHARD, Private

Born in Columbus County on September 29, 1832. Resided in Columbus County where he was by occupation a farmer prior to enlisting in New Hanover County on May 12, 1862, for the war. Present or accounted for until hospitalized at Wilmington on February 21, 1863, with diarrhoea. Returned to duty on March 4, 1863. Present or accounted for until he died in hospital at Petersburg, Virginia, April 13, 1864, of "pneumonia."

POWELL, JOHN ELI, Private

Born in Columbus County on February 28, 1838. Resided in Columbus County where he was by occupation a farmer prior to enlisting in Columbus County on April 23, 1862, for the war. Present or accounted for through December, 1864. Reported on duty as a teamster during much of the war. Survived the war.

PRINCE, DANIEL F., Private

Born in Horry District, South Carolina, and was by occupation a farmer prior to enlisting in New Hanover County at age 18, April 2, 1862. Present or accounted for until November-December, 1862, when he was reported absent on sick furlough. Returned to duty in January-February, 1863. Present or accounted for until wounded in the head and right hand and captured at Cold Harbor, Virginia, on or about June 1, 1864. Hospitalized at Davids Island, New York Harbor, June 15, 1864. Transferred to Elmira, New York, October 9, 1864. Paroled at Elmira on February 9, 1865. Received at Boulware's Wharf, James River, Virginia, on or about February 20, 1865, for exchange.

PRINCE, SAMUEL W., Private

Born in Horry District, South Carolina, and resided in Columbus County where he was by occupation a farmer

prior to enlisting in New Hanover County at age 24, April 2, 1862. Present or accounted for until January-February, 1863, when he was left sick at Camp Whiting, near Wilmington. Returned to duty in March-April, 1863. Present or accounted for until hospitalized at Wilmington on June 3, 1863, with continued fever. Furloughed on June 27, 1863. Returned to duty in July-August, 1863. Present or accounted for until transferred to 1st Company B, Manigault's Battalion South Carolina Artillery, May 19, 1864.

REYNOLDS, BUNBERRY, Private

Born in Columbus County and was by occupation a farmer prior to enlisting in New Hanover County at age 26, March 7, 1862. Present or accounted for through August, 1864. Company records indicate that he was captured at Fort Harrison, Virginia, September 30, 1864; however, records of the Federal Provost Marshal do not substantiate that report. Was presumably killed at Fort Harrison.

REYNOLDS, DEMPSEY, Private

Born in Columbus County and was by occupation a farmer prior to enlisting in New Hanover County at age 31, March 7, 1862. Discharged on May 7, 1862, by reason of disability.

REYNOLDS, LUCIAN, Private

Previously served as Private in Company H, 61st Regiment N.C. Troops. Transferred to this company on April 1, 1863, in exchange for Private Luke R. Cartrett. Reported absent sick from April 18 until October 23, 1863, when he was reported absent without leave. Returned to duty on or about December 29, 1863. Hospitalized at Petersburg, Virginia, January 24, 1864, with pneumonia. Furloughed for thirty days on February 18, 1864. Reported absent without leave from April 2 through December 31, 1864.

REYNOLDS, PETER, Private

Born in Brunswick County and resided in Columbus County where he was by occupation a farmer prior to enlisting in Columbus County at age 31, April 25, 1862, for the war. Present or accounted for until September-October, 1862, when he was reported in hospital at Raleigh. Furloughed on January 1, 1863. Died at home in Columbus County on June 1, 1863, of "fever."

ROUSE, NOAH, Private

Previously served as Private in Company H, 18th Regiment N.C. Troops (8th Regiment N.C. Volunteers). Enlisted in this company in New Hanover County on March 7, 1862. Discharged on or about June 15, 1862, by reason of disability. Later served as Private in 2nd Company K, 40th Regiment N.C. Troops (3rd Regiment N.C. Artillery).

SASSER, CALVIN, Corporal

Born in Columbus County on May 11, 1827. Was by occupation a farmer prior to enlisting in New Hanover County on March 7, 1862. Mustered in as Private. Present or accounted for until wounded at or near Fort Wagner, Charleston, South Carolina, on or about July 18, 1863. Returned to duty prior to September 1, 1863. Promoted to Corporal on December 1, 1864. Present or accounted for through December, 1864. Survived the war.

SASSER, HELI, Private
Born in Columbus County where he resided as a farmer prior to enlisting in New Hanover County at age 44, March 7, 1862. Present or accounted for until wounded in the heel at Goldsboro on December 17, 1862. Hospitalized at Raleigh where he died on January 10, 1863, of wounds.

SASSER, MATTHEW G., Private
Born in Brunswick County and resided in Columbus County where he was by occupation a farmer prior to enlisting in New Hanover County at age 44, March 7, 1862. Mustered in as Sergeant. Reduced to ranks on May 31, 1862. Present or accounted for until reported absent sick at Mount Pleasant, South Carolina, in September-October, 1863. Returned to duty in November-December, 1863. Present or accounted for through December, 1864. Hospitalized at Raleigh on March 16, 1865, with a gunshot wound of the right arm. Place and date wounded not reported. Captured in hospital at Raleigh on April 13, 1865. Survived the war.

SASSER, SIMON, Private
Born in Columbus County in January, 1816. Resided in Columbus County where he was by occupation a farmer prior to enlisting in New Hanover County on March 7, 1862. Present or accounted for until discharged on January 28, 1863. Reason discharged not reported.

SELLERS, PITMAN E., Private
Born in Columbus County where he resided as a farmer or laborer prior to enlisting in Columbus County at age 20, March 15, 1862. Present or accounted for until April 24, 1863, when he was reported absent sick in Columbus County. Returned to duty in May-June, 1863. Present or accounted for until December 2, 1863, when he was reported absent without leave. "Killed as a deserter in the vicinity of his home" on February 12, 1864.

SHEPHERD, JAMES K., Private
Born in Columbus County where he resided as a farmer prior to enlisting in Columbus County at age 18, March 14, 1862. Present or accounted for until captured at Cold Harbor, Virginia, June 1, 1864. Confined at Point Lookout, Maryland, June 11, 1864. Transferred to Elmira, New York, July 12, 1864. Released at Elmira on July 3, 1865, after taking the Oath of Allegiance.

SIBBETT, JOHN WILLIAM, Private
Born in Robeson County and resided in Columbus County where he was by occupation a farmer prior to enlisting in New Hanover County at age 39, March 7, 1862. Present or accounted for until September-October, 1862, when he was reported absent on sick furlough. Returned to duty in November-December, 1862. Present or accounted for until wounded in the abdomen and captured at Cold Harbor, Virginia, May 31, 1864. Confined at various Federal hospitals until confined at Old Capitol Prison, Washington, D.C., July 2, 1864. Transferred to Elmira, New York, July 23, 1864. Paroled at Elmira on February

9, 1865. Received at Boulware's Wharf, James River, Virginia, on or about February 20, 1865, for exchange.

SIMMONS, AMAZIAH, Private
Resided in Columbus County and was by occupation a farmer prior to enlisting in New Hanover County at age 18, February 2, 1863, for the war. Present or accounted for until wounded in the abdomen and/or left hip near Petersburg, Virginia, on or about August 26, 1864. Hospitalized at Richmond, Virginia. Furloughed for sixty days on January 26, 1865. Survived the war.

SIMMONS, THOMAS, JR., Private
Born in Columbus County in May, 1817. Resided in Columbus County where he was by occupation a farmer prior to enlisting in Columbus County on March 10, 1862. Reported absent on sick furlough in April-June, 1862. Returned to duty in September-October, 1862. Present or accounted for until December 2, 1863, when he was reported absent without leave. Returned to duty in January-February, 1864. Reported absent sick in May-November, 1864. Hospitalized at Richmond, Virginia, December 9, 1864, with chronic diarrhoea. Returned to duty on December 16, 1864. Hospitalized at Richmond on December 22, 1864, with rheumatism. Returned to duty on January 26, 1865. Survived the war. [North Carolina pension records indicate that he was wounded at Petersburg, Virginia, in the autumn of 1863.]

SIMMS, DANIEL E., Private
Born in Cumberland County where he resided as an overseer prior to enlisting in New Hanover County at age 36, March 7, 1862. Mustered in as Corporal. Present or accounted for until September-October, 1862, when he was reported absent sick in Columbus County. Reduced to ranks on December 3, 1862. Reported absent sick from November, 1862, through August, 1864. Returned to duty in September-October, 1864. Present or accounted for until wounded in the middle finger of the left hand in a skirmish at or near Sugar Loaf Hill, near Wilmington, on or about January 16, 1865. Hospitalized at Wilmington. Returned to duty on January 20, 1865. Survived the war.

SINGLETARY, CALVIN, Private
Born in Columbus County where he resided as a laborer prior to enlisting in New Hanover County at age 19, March 7, 1862. Present or accounted for until May-August, 1864, when he was reported absent sick at the brigade hospital. Returned to duty prior to October 7, 1864, when he was captured on the Darbytown Road, near Richmond, Virginia. Confined at Bermuda Hundred, Virginia, October 8, 1864. Transferred to Point Lookout, Maryland, on or about November 24, 1864. Released at Point Lookout on June 20, 1865, after taking the Oath of Allegiance.

SINGLETARY, JOHN BRADLEY, Private
Born in Columbus County on April 4, 1846. Resided in Columbus County where he was by occupation a laborer prior to enlisting in New Hanover County on April 2, 1862. Present or accounted for until captured at or near Globe Tavern, Virginia, August 19, 1864. Confined at Point Lookout, Maryland, August 22, 1864. Paroled at Point Lookout on September 18, 1864. Received at Varina,

Virginia, September 22, 1864, for exchange. Returned to duty prior to September 30, 1864, when he was wounded at Fort Harrison, Virginia. Reported absent wounded or absent sick through December, 1864.

SINGLETARY, MONROE, Private
Born in Bladen County and was by occupation a farmer prior to enlisting in Columbus County at age 18, March 18, 1862. Present or accounted for until wounded at or near Cold Harbor, Virginia, on or about June 1, 1864. Hospitalized at Richmond, Virginia. Furloughed for sixty days on June 13, 1864. Reported on light duty as a hostler at the brigade headquarters in September-October, 1864. Reported absent on light duty in November-December, 1864. Rejoined the company on an unspecified date. Paroled at Greensboro on May 1, 1865.

SMITH, ISAIAH, Private
Born in Duplin County and resided in Columbus County where he was by occupation a farmer prior to enlisting in New Hanover County at age 53, March 12, 1862. Present or accounted for until November-December, 1862, when he was reported absent on sick furlough in Columbus County. Reported absent sick through June, 1863. Returned to duty in July-August, 1863. Reported absent sick from September, 1863, until August 31, 1864, when he was reported absent without leave.

SMITH, JOHN O., Corporal
Born in Columbus County where he resided as a "[man of] leisure" prior to enlisting in New Hanover County at age 15, March 7, 1862. Mustered in as Private. Present or accounted for until May-June, 1863, when he was reported absent sick in Columbus County. Returned to duty in July-August, 1863. Promoted to Corporal on December 1, 1864. Present or accounted for through December, 1864.

SMITH, SAMUEL H., Private
Resided in Columbus County and was by occupation a farmer prior to enlisting in New Hanover County at age 18, June 5, 1863, for the war. Present or accounted for until killed at Cold Harbor, Virginia, June 1, 1864.

SMITH, THOMAS J., Private
Resided in Columbus County and enlisted in New Hanover County on April 30, 1862, for the war. Present or accounted for until March-April, 1863, when he was reported sick in hospital at Charleston, South Carolina. Died at home in Columbus County on May 15, 1863, of "typhoid fever."

SMITH, WILLIAM HENRY, Private
Previously served as Private in Company H, 18th Regiment N.C. Troops (8th Regiment N.C. Volunteers). Enlisted in this company in Columbus County on April 28, 1862, for the war. Present or accounted for until wounded in the right hand at or near Cold Harbor, Virginia, on or about June 1, 1864. Index finger amputated. Hospitalized at Petersburg, Virginia. Furloughed for thirty days on June 16, 1864. Returned to duty in September-October, 1864. Present or accounted for through December, 1864. Survived the war.

SOLES, DANIEL W., Private
Resided in Columbus County and was by occupation a laborer prior to enlisting at Camp Pender, near Hamilton, at age 17, December 3, 1863, for the war. Present or accounted for through April, 1864. Reported absent on sick furlough in May-December, 1864.

SOLES, DRAKEFORD S., Private
Born in Columbus County where he resided as a farmer prior to enlisting in New Hanover County at age 19, April 30, 1862, for the war. Present or accounted for until hospitalized at Wilmington on or about December 18, 1862, with chronic rheumatism. Returned to duty in March-April, 1863. Present or accounted for until killed at Drewry's Bluff, Virginia, May 16, 1864.

SOLES, NATHANIEL, Private
Resided in Columbus County and was by occupation a laborer prior to enlisting in Columbus County at age 26, April 28, 1862, for the war. Reported absent sick in May-June, 1862. Reported for duty in September-October, 1862. Present or accounted for until hospitalized at Wilmington on or about July 10, 1863, with rheumatism. Returned to duty on February 8, 1864. Present or accounted for until March-April, 1864, when he was reported sick in hospital at Petersburg, Virginia. Reported absent sick through December, 1864. Paroled at Goldsboro on May 4, 1865.

SOLES, NEILL, Private
Born in Columbus County where he resided as a farmer prior to enlisting in New Hanover County at age 21, March 7, 1862. Reported absent sick through June 30, 1862. Dropped from the rolls of the company prior to September 1, 1862. Reason he was dropped not reported.

SPIVEY, OWEN, Private
Previously served as Private in Company D, 20th Regiment N.C. Troops (10th Regiment N.C. Volunteers). Enlisted in this company in New Hanover County on April 21, 1862, for the war. Present or accounted for until November-December, 1862, when he was reported sick in hospital in Wilmington. Discharged on January 23, 1863. Reason discharged not reported.

SPIVEY, WILLIAM P., Private
Born in Columbus County and was by occupation a laborer prior to enlisting in New Hanover County at age 19, March 7, 1862. Present or accounted for through December, 1864. Survived the war.

TAYLOR, WILEY JAMES, Private
Born in Greene County and resided in Columbus County where he was by occupation a mechanic prior to enlisting in Columbus County at age 28, April 25, 1862, for the war. Present or accounted for until December 5, 1862, when he was detached to work on gunboats at Wilmington. Rejoined the company on October 2, 1863. Present or accounted for until wounded "by [his] own gun, in [his] own hands" near Petersburg, Virginia, May 16-June 1, 1864. Returned to duty in November-December, 1864. Present or accounted for through December, 1864. Survived the war.

THOMPSON, JOHN T., Private

Born in Johnston County and resided in Columbus County where he was by occupation a farmer prior to enlisting in New Hanover County at age 42, March 24, 1862. Present or accounted for until hospitalized at Wilmington on May 26, 1863, with diarrhoea. Returned to duty in March-April, 1864. Wounded in the left hip (flesh) at Drewry's Bluff, Virginia, May 16, 1864. Hospitalized at Richmond, Virginia, where he died on May 25, 1864, of wounds.

THOMPSON, JOHN THOMAS, Private

Resided in Columbus County and was by occupation a farmer prior to enlisting at James Island, Charleston, South Carolina, at age 19, April 24, 1863, for the war as a substitute for Private Armalin Bryant Hill. Present or accounted for until wounded in the left leg (fracture) and pelvis and captured at Fort Harrison, Virginia, September 30, 1864. Hospitalized at Fort Monroe, Virginia, where he died on October 10, 1864, of "exhaustion following amputation l[eft] leg."

THOMPSON, NOAH McK., Private

Born in Columbus County and was by occupation a farmer prior to enlisting in New Hanover County at age 23, May 28, 1862, for the war. Present or accounted for through April, 1864. Wounded near Petersburg, Virginia, May 16-June 1, 1864. Died in hospital at Richmond, Virginia, July 3, 1864, of wounds.

THOMPSON, SAMUEL S. B., Private

Born in Robeson County and resided in Columbus County where he was by occupation a tenant farmer prior to enlisting in New Hanover County at age 28, May 8, 1862, for the war. Present or accounted for until July-August, 1863, when he was reported sick in hospital at Charleston, South Carolina. Returned to duty in September-October, 1863. Present or accounted for through December, 1864.

THOMPSON, WILLIAM P., Private

Resided in Columbus County and was by occupation a farmer prior to enlisting in New Hanover County at age 28, May 12, 1862, for the war. Present or accounted for until he died at Fort Johnston, near Smithville (present-day Southport), August 27, 1862, of "ty[phoid] fever."

TOON, LUTHER, Private

Born in Columbus County on April 28, 1844, and was by occupation a student. Enlistment date not reported; however, he enlisted prior to July 1, 1862. Appointed colonel's orderly in July, 1862. Drowned in the Cape Fear River on August 4, 1862, when he fell from the deck of the steamer *Congaree* near Smithville (present-day Southport). "It would appear [that he] had been asleep, and in waking up suddenly walked overboard." [*Wilmington Journal* (Weekly), August 7, 1862.] According to an eyewitness, Private Toon "swam well But the Boat was crowded so that the hands could not get to the light Boat in time to save him. I think he bore up fifteen minutes if not more. . . . He fell over ten [or] twelve miles from town. He cried for help as long as he could for stranglin." [Private William J. Burney to his father, August 6, 1862, Roster Document File Number 0473.]

TURNER, EDWARD W., Private

Enlisted at James Island, Charleston, South Carolina, April 10, 1863, for the war as a substitute for Private Daniel Batten. Present or accounted for until September-October, 1863, when he was reported sick in the regimental hospital at Mount Pleasant, South Carolina. Returned to duty in November-December, 1863. Transferred to Company A of this regiment on January 1, 1864.

TYSON, DANIEL, Private

Resided in Columbus County and enlisted at Camp Hill, near Petersburg, Virginia, April 13, 1864, for the war. Present or accounted for through August, 1864. Wounded in the left leg at Fort Harrison, Virginia, September 30, 1864. Reported absent wounded or absent sick through December, 1864.

TYSON, JOSEPH W., Private

Born in Bladen County and resided in Columbus County where he was by occupation a farmer prior to enlisting in Columbus County at age 18, March 12, 1862. Present or accounted for until he was left sick at Camp Whiting, near Wilmington, in January-February, 1863. Returned to duty in March-April, 1863. Present or accounted for until he was reported sick in hospital at Petersburg, Virginia, in March-April, 1864. Returned to duty prior to September 1, 1864. Wounded in the left leg (fracture) and captured at Fort Harrison, Virginia, September 30, 1864. Left leg amputated. Hospitalized at Fort Monroe, Virginia. Released on July 26, 1865, after taking the Oath of Allegiance.

VAUSE, AMOS R., Private

Born in Columbus County where he resided as a farmer prior to enlisting in New Hanover County at age 23, March 7, 1862. Present or accounted for until September-October, 1863, when he was reported sick in the regimental hospital at Mount Pleasant, South Carolina. Returned to duty in November-December, 1863. Present or accounted for until wounded at or near Cold Harbor, Virginia, on or about June 1, 1864. Hospitalized at Richmond, Virginia, where he died on July 11, 1864, of wounds.

VAUSE, JACOB McD., Private

Born in Columbus County where he resided as a farmer prior to enlisting in New Hanover County at age 21, March 7, 1862. Present or accounted for until September-October, 1862, when he was reported sick in hospital at Goldsboro. Reported absent sick until December 31, 1863, when he was dropped from the rolls of the company. Returned to duty on December 8, 1864. Hospitalized at Richmond, Virginia, December 11, 1864, with nephritis. Was apparently also suffering from chronic diarrhoea and debility. Returned to duty on January 10, 1865. Survived the war.

VAUSE, NATHAN L., Private

Born in Columbus County where he resided as a laborer prior to enlisting in New Hanover County at age 21, March 7, 1862. Present or accounted for until November-December, 1862, when he was reported absent without leave. Returned to duty in January-February, 1863.

Present or accounted for until he died at Camp Pender, near Hamilton, on or about December 20, 1863, of "pneumonia."

WARD, ABSALOM, Private
Born in Columbus County where he resided as an apprentice farmer prior to enlisting in Columbus County at age 17, March 7, 1862. Present or accounted for until hospitalized at Petersburg, Virginia, January 29, 1864, with typhoid fever. Returned to duty on March 12, 1864. Present or accounted for through December, 1864. Paroled at Greensboro on May 1, 1865.

WARD, JOHN, Private
Born in Columbus County where he resided as a farmer prior to enlisting in New Hanover County at age 37, March 7, 1862. Mustered in as Corporal. Reduced to ranks on May 31, 1862. Present or accounted for until hospitalized at Wilmington on or about June 9, 1863, with rheumatism. Returned to duty on June 24, 1863. Reported absent sick in the regimental hospital at Mount Pleasant, South Carolina, in July-October, 1863. Returned to duty in November-December, 1863. Died in hospital at Petersburg, Virginia, February 24, 1864, of "pneumonia."

WARD, JOHN DAVID, Private
Born in Columbus County and was by occupation a farmer prior to enlisting in Columbus County at age 19, March 12, 1862. Present or accounted for until February 8, 1863, when he was reported absent on sick furlough in Columbus County. Returned to duty in May-June, 1863. Present or accounted for until hospitalized at Petersburg, Virginia, February 23, 1864, with remittent fever. Returned to duty in March-April, 1864. Present or accounted for through December, 1864. Hospitalized at Wilmington on January 22, 1865, with erysipelas. Returned to duty on February 19, 1865.

WARD, SIMON, Private
Born in Columbus County where he resided as a farmer prior to enlisting in New Hanover County at age 20, March 7, 1862. Hospitalized at Wilmington on April 8, 1862, with "febris typhoides" and died on April 12, 1862.

WHITE, ALEXANDER, Private
Born in Columbus County where he resided as a farmer prior to enlisting in New Hanover County at age 37, March 7, 1862. Present or accounted for through December, 1864. Survived the war. [North Carolina pension records indicate that he was wounded in the right leg at Petersburg, Virginia, in June, 1863.]

WHITE, ALVA, Private
Born in Columbus County where he resided as a farmer prior to enlisting in New Hanover County at age 27, May 15, 1862, for the war. Present or accounted for until killed at Drewry's Bluff, Virginia, May 16, 1864.

WHITE, STEPHEN, Private
Born in Columbus County on November 20, 1831. Resided in Columbus County where he was by occupation a farmer prior to enlisting in New Hanover County on May 18,

1862, for the war. Present or accounted for until hospitalized at Richmond, Virginia, August 8, 1864, with diarrhoea. Furloughed for thirty days on August 27, 1864. Returned to duty in September-October, 1864, and was assigned to duty with the ambulance corps. Rejoined the company in November-December, 1864. Wounded in the head and right leg at Bentonville on March 19-21, 1865. Survived the war.

WIGGINS, JOSEPH D., Private
Enlisted in New Hanover County on April 30, 1862, for the war. Present or accounted for through December, 1862. Reported on detached duty as a teamster from January, 1863, through April, 1864. Reported absent sick in May-October, 1864. Returned to duty in November-December, 1864. Present or accounted for through December, 1864.

WILLIAMSON, JOHN, Private
Born in Columbus County where he resided as a farmer prior to enlisting in Columbus County at age 45, March 6, 1862. Present or accounted for through December, 1864.

YORK, C. W., Private
Resided in Surry County. Place and date of enlistment not reported (probably enlisted in January-April, 1865). Deserted to the enemy on an unspecified date. Confined at Louisville, Kentucky, April 2, 1865. Released at Louisville on or about April 10, 1865, after taking the Oath of Allegiance.

COMPANY I

This company was raised in Cumberland and Sampson counties and enlisted in Cumberland County in March-April, 1862. It was mustered into state service at Wilmington on April 23, 1862, and assigned to the 51st Regiment N.C. Troops as Company I. After joining the regiment the company functioned as a part of the regiment, and its history for the remainder of the war is reported as a part of the regimental history.

The information contained in the following roster was compiled primarily from a company muster-in and descriptive roll dated April 23, 1862, and from company muster rolls for April 23, 1862-February 29, 1864, and April 30-December 31, 1864. No company muster rolls were located for March 1-April 29, 1864, or for the period after December 31, 1864. Valuable information was obtained from primary records such as the North Carolina adjutant general's *Roll of Honor*, discharge certificates, medical records, prisoner of war records, *The War of the Rebellion: A Compilation of the Official Records of the Union and Confederate Armies*, militia records, newspaper casualty lists and obituaries, Confederate pension applications filed with the state of North Carolina, and the 1860 federal census of North Carolina. Secondary sources such as postwar rosters and histories, cemetery records, the *Confederate Veteran*, published genealogies, and records of the United Daughters of the Confederacy also provided useful information.

OFFICERS

CAPTAINS

McKETHAN, HECTOR McALLESTER

Previously served as 3rd Lieutenant of Company H, 1st Regiment N.C. Infantry (6 months, 1861). Appointed Captain of this company on March 19, 1862. Elected Major on April 30, 1862, and transferred to the Field and Staff of this regiment.

SLOAN, GEORGE

Previously served as Private in 2nd Company B, 36th Regiment N.C. Troops (2nd Regiment N.C. Artillery). Transferred to this company upon appointment as 1st Lieutenant on March 19, 1862. Promoted to Captain on April 30, 1862. Present or accounted for until wounded at Drewry's Bluff, Virginia, May 16, 1864. Returned to duty prior to June 1, 1864, when he was captured at Cold Harbor, Virginia. Confined at Point Lookout, Maryland, June 11, 1864. Transferred to Fort Delaware, Delaware, June 23, 1864. Released at Fort Delaware on June 17, 1865, after taking the Oath of Allegiance.

LIEUTENANTS

GUY, CHARLES THOMAS, 2nd Lieutenant

Born in Cumberland County where he resided as a farmer prior to enlisting in Cumberland County at age 24, April 1, 1862. Mustered in as 1st Sergeant. Elected 3rd Lieutenant on May 15, 1862. Present or accounted for until wounded at Goldsboro on December 17, 1862. Returned to duty prior to January 1, 1863. Reported present but under arrest in March-April, 1863. Reason he was arrested not reported. Returned to duty in May-June, 1863. Reported sick at home in July-August, 1863. Returned to duty in September-October, 1863. Promoted to 2nd Lieutenant on September 25, 1863. Present or accounted for until wounded in the right leg at Fort Harrison, Virginia, September 30, 1864. Hospitalized at Richmond, Virginia. Returned to duty in November-December, 1864. Present or accounted for through December, 1864. Survived the war.

McARTHUR, JOSEPH ALLAN, 1st Lieutenant

Previously served as Private in Company H, 1st Regiment N.C. Infantry (6 months, 1861). Appointed 2nd Lieutenant of this company on March 19, 1862. Promoted to 1st Lieutenant on April 30, 1862. Present or accounted for until July-August, 1862, when he was reported absent sick. Returned to duty in September-October, 1862. Present or accounted for until wounded in the chin, hip, right forearm, and left arm and captured at Drewry's Bluff, Virginia, May 16, 1864. Hospitalized at Bermuda Hundred, Virginia. Transferred to Fort Monroe, Virginia, May 17, 1864. Paroled at Fort Monroe on August 18, 1864, and transferred to Aiken's Landing, James River, Virginia, where he was received on August 22, 1864, for

exchange. Reported absent wounded or absent sick until March 3, 1865, when he was retired to the Invalid Corps by reason of "partial loss of use of hand."

McKENZIE, WILLIAM W., 2nd Lieutenant

Born in Cumberland County and enlisted at age 31. Appointed 2nd Lieutenant on March 19, 1862. Present or accounted for until November-December, 1862, when he was reported absent sick. Returned to duty in January-February, 1863. Present or accounted for until he resigned on September 7, 1863, by reason of "a hernia of the left side. . . ." Resignation accepted on September 17, 1863.

TAYLOR, JAMES H., 3rd Lieutenant

Previously served as Private in 2nd Company B, 36th Regiment N.C. Troops (2nd Regiment N.C. Artillery). Transferred to this company on June 19, 1862. Mustered in as 1st Sergeant. Appointed 3rd Lieutenant on October 1, 1863. Present or accounted for until appointed Adjutant (1st Lieutenant) on January 12, 1865, to rank from September 21, 1864, and transferred to the Field and Staff of this regiment.

NONCOMMISSIONED OFFICERS AND PRIVATES

ADAMS, JAMES C., Private

Enlisted in Cumberland County at age 25, April 26, 1862, for the war. Present or accounted for through June, 1863. Reported absent sick in July-October, 1863. Returned to duty in November-December, 1863. Present or accounted for until wounded in the breast at Drewry's Bluff, Virginia, May 16, 1864. Reported absent wounded or absent sick until October 1, 1864, when he was reported absent without leave. Survived the war.

ADAMS, WILLIAM H., Private

Enlisted in Cumberland County on October 4, 1862, for the war. Present or accounted for until wounded at Bermuda Hundred, Virginia, May 20, 1864. Wounded near Petersburg, Virginia, June 17, 1864. Reported absent wounded or absent sick through August, 1864. Reported on duty as a cattle guard in September-December, 1864. Paroled at Greensboro on May 1, 1865.

ALLEN, JOHN WILLIAM, Private

Born in Brunswick County and was by occupation a laborer prior to enlisting in Cumberland County at age 30, April 10, 1862. Present or accounted for until wounded in the arm and/or bowels at Goldsboro on December 17, 1862. Returned to duty in May-June, 1863. Reported absent sick in July-September, 1863. Reported absent without leave on October 21, 1863. Returned to duty in November-December, 1863. Reported absent without leave on February 1, 1864. Dropped from the rolls of the company in March-April, 1864.

ANDERSON, B. F., _____

North Carolina pension records indicate that he served in this company.

ANDERSON, WILLIAM JAMES, Private

Born in Houston County, Georgia, and was by occupation
a cabinetmaker prior to enlisting in Cumberland County
at age 28, March 29, 1862. Present or accounted for
through December, 1864. Served as a teamster (primarily
as an ambulance driver) during most of the war. Survived
the war.

AUTRY, DUNCAN, Private

Born in Cumberland County where he resided as a farmer
prior to enlisting in Cumberland County at age 28, April
1, 1862. Present or accounted for until wounded at
Bermuda Hundred, Virginia, May 20, 1864. Hospitalized
at Petersburg, Virginia, where he died on June 15, 1864,
of "pyaemia."

AVERITT, WILLIAM, Private

Enlisted in Cumberland County on October 4, 1862, for
the war. Present or accounted for until he died in hospital
at Wilmington on or about January 29, 1863, of
"pneumonia." [May have served previously as Private in
Company F, 24th Regiment N.C. Troops (14th Regiment
N.C. Volunteers).]

BAIN, ANGUS G., Private

Resided in Cumberland County and was by occupation a
farmer prior to enlisting in Cumberland County at age 27,
April 26, 1862, for the war. Present or accounted for until
wounded in the left side at Drewry's Bluff, Virginia, May
16, 1864. Hospitalized at Richmond, Virginia. Returned
to duty prior to September 30, 1864, when he was
captured at Fort Harrison, Virginia. Confined at Point
Lookout, Maryland, October 5, 1864. Paroled at Point
Lookout and transferred to Boulware's Wharf, James
River, Virginia, where he was received on March 19,
1865, for exchange. Survived the war.

BAIN, DANIEL D., JR., Private

Born in Cumberland County where he resided as a farmer
prior to enlisting in Cumberland County at age 32, March
26, 1862. Present or accounted for until November-
December, 1862, when he was reported sick in hospital
at Raleigh. Returned to duty in May-June, 1863. Present
or accounted for until hospitalized at Petersburg,
Virginia, October 21, 1864, with an unspecified
complaint. Returned to duty on December 29, 1864.
Captured at or near Wise's Forks on March 10, 1865.
Confined at Point Lookout, Maryland, March 16, 1865.
Released at Point Lookout on June 24, 1865, after taking
the Oath of Allegiance.

BAIN, DOUGALD A., Private

Born in Cumberland County and was by occupation a
farmer prior to enlisting in Cumberland County at age 18,
March 28, 1862. Present or accounted for until he died
in hospital at Sullivan's Island, Charleston, South
Carolina, August 16, 1863, of "congestion of the bowels."

BAIN, HUGH J., Private

Resided in Cumberland County where he enlisted on
April 26, 1862, for the war. Present or accounted for
through April, 1863; however, he was reported absent sick
during most of that period. Returned to duty in May-June,
1863. Present or accounted for until wounded at Cold

Harbor, Virginia, May 31, 1864. Wounded near
Petersburg, Virginia, June 17, 1864. Returned to duty
prior to September 1, 1864. Captured at Fort Harrison,
Virginia, September 30, 1864. Confined at Point Lookout,
Maryland, October 2, 1864. Paroled at Point Lookout and
transferred to Venus Point, Savannah River, Georgia,
where he was received on November 15, 1864, for
exchange.

BAREFOOT, SION McD., Private

Resided in Harnett County and enlisted in New Hanover
County on May 13, 1862, for the war. Present or
accounted for until wounded near Petersburg, Virginia,
June 16, 1864. Deserted on September 1, 1864.

BASS, URIAH, Private

Born in Sampson County and was by occupation a farmer
prior to enlisting in Cumberland County at age 17, March
31, 1862. Present or accounted for through July, 1862.
Reported on detached duty guarding stores at Fayetteville
from August 20, 1862, through February 28, 1863.
Rejoined the company in March-April, 1863. Present or
accounted for until wounded at Fort Wagner, Charleston,
South Carolina, July 18, 1863. Returned to duty prior to
September 1, 1863. Present or accounted for through
December, 1864. Paroled at Raleigh on May 27, 1865.

BEASLEY, GEORGE C., Private

Previously served as Private in Company B, 13th Battalion
N.C. Light Artillery. Transferred to this company on
December 16, 1863. Present or accounted for until
wounded in the right shoulder at Fort Harrison, Virginia,
September 30, 1864. Hospitalized at Richmond, Virginia,
where he died on or about October 26, 1864, of
"pneumonia."

BELL, JAMES, Private

Resided in Cumberland County where he enlisted at age
30, May 26, 1863, for the war. Present or accounted for
through August, 1863. Company records indicate that he
was captured at Fort Harrison, Virginia, September 30,
1864; however, records of the Federal Provost Marshal do
not substantiate that report. Was probably killed at Fort
Harrison.

BELL, RICHARD ROBERT, Private

Enlisted in Cumberland County at age 18, January 18,
1864, for the war. Wounded slightly in the foot near
Petersburg, Virginia, June 12, 1864. Captured at Fort
Harrison, Virginia, September 30, 1864. Confined at
Point Lookout, Maryland, October 5, 1864. Paroled at
Point Lookout on January 17, 1865. Received at
Boulware's Wharf, James River, Virginia, January 21,
1865, for exchange. Survived the war.

BLACKBURN, JAMES H., Private

Born in Sampson County and was by occupation a farmer
prior to enlisting in Cumberland County at age 17, March
29, 1862. Present or accounted for until he deserted on
or about December 27, 1863. Returned to duty prior to
March 1, 1864. Wounded slightly near Petersburg,
Virginia, June 17, 1864. Present or accounted for through
January 1, 1865. Survived the war.

BLUE, DANIEL, Private
Born in Sampson County in 1844 and was by occupation a farm laborer prior to enlisting in Cumberland County on November 12, 1863, for the war. Present or accounted for until wounded at Drewry's Bluff, Virginia, May 16, 1864. Died of wounds the same date.

BLUE, WILLIAM J., Corporal
Born in Sampson County and was by occupation a farmer prior to enlisting in Cumberland County at age 27, April 21, 1862, for the war. Mustered in as Private. Promoted to Corporal in November-December, 1862. Present or accounted for through June, 1863. Reported absent sick in July-October, 1863. Returned to duty in November-December, 1863. Present or accounted for until wounded in the breast near Petersburg, Virginia, June 21, 1864. Returned to duty prior to September 1, 1864. Wounded in the chest and captured at Fort Harrison, Virginia, September 30, 1864. Hospitalized at Fort Monroe, Virginia, where he died on October 15, 1864, of wounds. [Previously served as 2nd Lieutenant in the 24th Regiment N.C. Militia.]

BOLTON, HENRY H., Sergeant
Born in Cumberland County and was by occupation a farmer prior to enlisting in Cumberland County at age 23, April 21, 1862, for the war. Mustered in as Private. Promoted to Corporal prior to July 1, 1862. Present or accounted for until hospitalized at Wilmington on or about July 25, 1863, with rheumatism. Promoted to Sergeant on October 1, 1863. Returned to duty in November-December, 1863. Wounded slightly at Cold Harbor, Virginia, June 1, 1864. Captured at or near Globe Tavern, Virginia, August 19, 1864. Confined at Point Lookout, Maryland, August 22, 1864. Paroled at Point Lookout on March 14, 1865. Received at Boulware's Wharf, James River, Virginia, March 16, 1865, for exchange.

BOLTON, JOHN R., Private
Enlisted in Cumberland County on December 21, 1863, for the war. Present or accounted for until September-October, 1864, when he was reported sick in hospital at Richmond, Virginia. Returned to duty on or about December 20, 1864, but was reported absent sick on December 25, 1864. Captured near Fayetteville on March 12, 1865. Confined at Point Lookout, Maryland, March 30, 1865. Died at Point Lookout on May 1, 1865, of "catarrh."

BOLTON, PETER L., Private
Resided in Cumberland County where he enlisted at age 20, September 21, 1863, for the war. Present or accounted for until May-October, 1864, when he was reported sick in hospital at Fayetteville. Returned to duty in November-December, 1864. Captured near Fayetteville on March 12, 1865. Confined at Point Lookout, Maryland, March 30, 1865. Released at Point Lookout on June 24, 1865, after taking the Oath of Allegiance.

BREECE, JOSEPH, Private
Resided in Cumberland County and was by occupation a farmer prior to enlisting in Cumberland County at age 35, December 20, 1862, for the war. Present or accounted for

until wounded in the left hip at Drewry's Bluff, Virginia, May 16, 1864. Hospitalized at Richmond, Virginia. Furloughed for sixty days on June 22, 1864. Returned to duty prior to September 1, 1864. Company records indicate that he was captured at Fort Harrison, Virginia, September 30, 1864; however, records of the Federal Provost Marshal do not substantiate that report. Was probably killed at Fort Harrison.

BROCK, DAVID W., Private
Born in Cumberland or Sampson County and resided in Cumberland County where he was by occupation a farmer prior to enlisting in Cumberland County at age 32, March 31, 1862. Present or accounted for until wounded in the "body" at Bermuda Hundred, Virginia, May 20, 1864. Hospitalized at Petersburg, Virginia, where he died on May 31, 1864, of wounds.

BRYAN, KING, Private
Enlisted in Cumberland County on October 3, 1862, for the war. Present or accounted for through July, 1864. Company records indicate that he was captured at or near Globe Tavern, Virginia, August 19, 1864; however, records of the Federal Provost Marshal do not substantiate that report. Was probably killed at Globe Tavern.

BRYAN, LEVI, Private
Enlisted in Cumberland County at age 22, October 6, 1862, for the war. Reported absent on detached service as a courier for General Thomas L. Clingman from November 22, 1862, through October 31, 1863. Rejoined the company in November-December, 1863. Reported absent sick in May-October, 1864. Returned to duty in November-December, 1864. Present or accounted for through December, 1864. Survived the war.

BRYANT, ALDRIDGE M., Private
Enlisted in Cumberland County on October 20, 1864, for the war. Present or accounted for through December, 1864.

BRYANT, TRAVIS, Private
Born in Cumberland County where he resided as a farmer prior to enlisting in Cumberland County at age 35, March 5, 1863, for the war. Present or accounted for until captured at Cold Harbor, Virginia, June 1, 1864. Confined at Point Lookout, Maryland, June 11, 1864. Transferred to Elmira, New York, July 12, 1864. Killed in a railroad accident at Shohola, Pennsylvania, July 15, 1864, while en route to Elmira.

BUIE, DANIEL McD., Private
Enlisted in Cumberland County on December 6, 1862, for the war. Present or accounted for until May-August, 1864, when he was reported absent sick. Returned to duty in September-October, 1864. Present or accounted for through December, 1864. Survived the war.

BUIE, GEORGE McD., Private
Enlisted in Cumberland County on March 14, 1864, for the war. Present or accounted for until hospitalized at Richmond, Virginia, October 23, 1864, with chronic diarrhoea. Returned to duty on December 1, 1864. Present

or accounted for through December, 1864. Captured near Fayetteville on March 11, 1865. Confined at Point Lookout, Maryland, March 30, 1865. Released at Point Lookout on June 4, 1865, after taking the Oath of Allegiance.

BUIE, JOHN R., Sergeant

Born in Cumberland County and was by occupation a farmer prior to enlisting in Cumberland County at age 28, April 5, 1862. Mustered in as Private. Promoted to Sergeant prior to July 1, 1862. Reduced to the rank of Corporal prior to September 1, 1862. Present or accounted for until he was reported absent sick in September-October, 1862. Returned to duty in November-December, 1862. Promoted to Sergeant in March-April, 1863. Present or accounted for until wounded in the left arm at Drewry's Bluff, Virginia, May 16, 1864. Reported absent wounded through October, 1864. Returned to duty in November-December, 1864. Present or accounted for through December, 1864. Survived the war.

BUIE, MALCOLM J., JR., Private

Enlisted in Cumberland County on September 27, 1863, for the war. Present or accounted for through December, 1864.

BUIE, MALCOLM JAMES, Private

Resided in Cumberland County where he enlisted on December 31, 1862, for the war. Present or accounted for until August 18, 1863, when he was reported absent on sick furlough of thirty days. Returned to duty in September-October, 1863. Present or accounted for until wounded at or near Bermuda Hundred, Virginia, on or about May 20, 1864. Hospitalized at Petersburg, Virginia. Furloughed on May 29, 1864. Returned to duty on an unspecified date. Hospitalized at Richmond, Virginia, August 9, 1864, with debilitas. Furloughed on August 25, 1864. Reported sick in hospital at Fayetteville in September-December, 1864. Captured at or near Fayetteville on March 11, 1865. Confined at Point Lookout, Maryland, March 30, 1865. Released at Point Lookout on June 24, 1865, after taking the Oath of Allegiance.

BUNCE, HIRAM, Private

Born in Sampson County and was by occupation a farmer prior to enlisting in Cumberland County at age 30, March 30, 1862. Present or accounted for until July-August, 1862, when he was reported absent sick. Returned to duty in September-October, 1862. Present or accounted for until September 3, 1863, when he was reported absent without leave. Returned to duty on December 19, 1863. Present or accounted for until killed at Drewry's Bluff, Virginia, May 16, 1864.

CARROLL, JOHN W., Private

Born in Cumberland County and was by occupation a farmer prior to enlisting in Cumberland County at age 25, April 4, 1862. Present or accounted for until wounded at Fort Wagner, Charleston, South Carolina, July 18, 1863. Deserted on August 21, 1863. Reported under arrest at Charleston in September-December, 1863. Returned to duty in January-February, 1864. Present or accounted for until captured at Cold Harbor, Virginia, June 1, 1864.

Confined at Point Lookout, Maryland, June 11, 1864. Transferred to Elmira, New York, July 12, 1864. Killed in a railroad accident at Shohola, Pennsylvania, July 15, 1864, while en route to Elmira.

CARVER, CHARLES, Private

Born in Cumberland County and was by occupation a farmer prior to enlisting in Cumberland County at age 18, April 18, 1862, for the war. Present or accounted for until killed at Goldsboro on December 17, 1862.

CARVER, GEORGE W., Private

Born in Cumberland County and was by occupation a merchant prior to enlisting in Cumberland County at age 33, April 19, 1862, for the war. Present or accounted for until wounded by a sharpshooter near Petersburg, Virginia, June 26, 1864. Died in hospital at Richmond, Virginia, on or about July 29, 1864, presumably of wounds.

CORE, MALCOLM, Private

Born in Cumberland County and was by occupation a farmer prior to enlisting in Cumberland County at age 33, April 5, 1862. Present or accounted for until discharged on December 1, 1862, by reason of "phthisis pulmonalis & also a large fatty tumor between the shoulders."

CULBRETH, DUNCAN J., Private

Born in Cumberland County and was by occupation a farmer prior to enlisting in Cumberland County at age 24, March 31, 1862. Present or accounted for until he deserted at Sullivan's Island, Charleston, South Carolina, August 21, 1863. Returned to duty on September 18, 1863. Present or accounted for until wounded in the right hand at Drewry's Bluff, Virginia, May 16, 1864. Hospitalized at Richmond, Virginia. Returned to duty prior to June 15, 1864, when he was captured near Petersburg, Virginia. Confined at Point Lookout, Maryland, June 19, 1864. Transferred to Elmira, New York, July 9, 1864. Released at Elmira on or about May 13, 1865, after taking the Oath of Allegiance.

DAUGHTERY, HARDY J., Corporal

Born in Cumberland County and was by occupation a farmer prior to enlisting in Cumberland County at age 22, March 26, 1862. Mustered in as Private. Appointed Musician prior to July 1, 1862. Reduced to ranks in November-December, 1862. Promoted to Corporal in March-April, 1863. Present or accounted for until killed by a sharpshooter near Petersburg, Virginia, on the morning of June 17, 1864.

DAVIS, DEMPSEY, Private

Born in Bladen County and resided in Cumberland County where he was by occupation a farmer prior to enlisting in Cumberland County at age 37, April 9, 1862. Present or accounted for until wounded at Goldsboro on December 17, 1862. Returned to duty prior to January 1, 1863. Present or accounted for until hospitalized at Wilmington on June 24, 1863, with typhoid fever. Returned to duty on July 7, 1863, and was detailed as a provost guard at Fayetteville. Rejoined the company in September-October, 1863. Present or accounted for until December 25, 1864, when he was reported absent sick.

DAVIS, JOHN D., Private
Born in Cumberland County and was by occupation a farmer prior to enlisting in Cumberland County at age 18, March 29, 1862. Present or accounted for until September-December, 1862, when he was reported absent sick. Returned to duty in January-February, 1863. Present or accounted for until captured at Cold Harbor, Virginia, June 1, 1864. Confined at Point Lookout, Maryland, June 11, 1864. Transferred to Elmira, New York, July 12, 1864. Killed in a railroad accident at Shohola, Pennsylvania, July 15, 1864, while en route to Elmira.

DEAVER, NATHAN H., Private
Born in Bladen County and resided in Cumberland County where he was by occupation a farmer prior to enlisting in Cumberland County at age 27, April 11, 1862. Present or accounted for until February 11, 1863, when he was reported absent sick. Returned to duty in March-April, 1863. Present or accounted for until captured at Cold Harbor, Virginia, June 1, 1864. Confined at Point Lookout, Maryland, June 11, 1864. Transferred to Elmira, New York, July 12, 1864. Killed in a railroad accident at Shohola, Pennsylvania, July 15, 1864, while en route to Elmira.

DENNING, JOSIAH, Private
Resided in Cumberland County and was by occupation a farmer prior to enlisting in Cumberland County at age 18, March 3, 1864, for the war. Deserted on or about May 25, 1864. Listed as a deserter through December, 1864. Captured by the enemy near Fayetteville on March 16, 1865. Confined at Point Lookout, Maryland, March 30, 1865. Released at Point Lookout on June 26, 1865, after taking the Oath of Allegiance.

DORMAN, MARTIN, Private
Born in Cumberland County where he resided as a farmer prior to enlisting in Cumberland County at age 40, April 21, 1862, for the war. Present or accounted for until December 25, 1864, when he was reported absent sick.

DUDLEY, JOHN W., Private
Born in Sampson County and was by occupation a farmer prior to enlisting in Cumberland County at age 20, March 29, 1862. Reported absent sick in July-August, 1862. Reported absent on furlough (leg broken) in September, 1862. Returned to duty prior to November 1, 1862. Reported absent sick in November-December, 1862. Reported absent without leave in January-February, 1863. Returned to duty in March-April, 1863. Hospitalized at Wilmington on or about May 4, 1863, with typhoid fever. Discharged on May 23, 1863, by reason of "carditis."

DURDEN, DUNCAN J., Private
Born in Wayne County and was by occupation a farmer prior to enlisting in Cumberland County at age 32, April 9, 1862. Present or accounted for through December, 1862; however, he was reported absent sick during most of that period. Reported absent without leave in January-February, 1863. Reported absent sick in March-April, 1863. Dropped from the rolls of the company in May-June, 1863. Returned to duty subsequent to April 30, 1864. Wounded at Cold Harbor, Virginia, June 1, 1864.

Reported absent wounded through December, 1864. Survived the war.

ELLIS, ALEXANDER, Private
Born in Cumberland County and was by occupation a farmer prior to enlisting in Cumberland County at age 18, March 27, 1862. Present or accounted for until September-October, 1862, when he was reported absent sick. Returned to duty in November-December, 1862. Present or accounted for until he died in hospital at Petersburg, Virginia, May 24, 1864, of "anemia."

ELLIS, WILLIAM D. B., Private
Enlisted in Cumberland County on May 12, 1862, for the war. Present or accounted for until captured at Cold Harbor, Virginia, June 1, 1864. Confined at Point Lookout, Maryland, June 11, 1864. Transferred to Elmira, New York, July 12, 1864. Injured in a railroad accident at Shohola, Pennsylvania, July 15, 1864, while en route to Elmira. Paroled at Elmira on October 11, 1864, and transferred to Point Lookout. Received at Venus Point, Savannah River, Georgia, November 15, 1864, for exchange.

FISHER, GEORGE C., Private
Enlisted in Cumberland County at age 18, October 6, 1862, for the war. Present or accounted for until captured at Cold Harbor, Virginia, June 1, 1864. Confined at Point Lookout, Maryland, June 11, 1864. Transferred to Elmira, New York, July 12, 1864. Injured slightly in a railroad accident at Shohola, Pennsylvania, July 15, 1864, while en route to Elmira. Paroled at Elmira on October 11, 1864. Received at Venus Point, Savannah River, Georgia, November 15, 1864, for exchange. Survived the war.

GEDDIE, JOSEPH CARSON, Private
Resided in Cumberland County where he enlisted at age 17, December 15, 1862, for the war. Present or accounted for until wounded at Cold Harbor, Virginia, June 1, 1864. Returned to duty prior to September 30, 1864, when he was wounded in the right leg and captured at Fort Harrison, Virginia. Hospitalized at Fort Monroe, Virginia. Transferred to Point Lookout, Maryland, January 9, 1865. Paroled at Point Lookout on January 17, 1865. Received at Boulware's Wharf, James River, Virginia, January 21, 1865, for exchange. Hospitalized at Richmond, Virginia, January 22, 1865, and was furloughed on January 26, 1865. Survived the war.

GEDDIE, McDUFFIE, Sergeant
Born in Cumberland County where he resided as a farmer prior to enlisting in Cumberland County at age 19, April 3, 1862. Mustered in as Private. Promoted to Corporal prior to July 1, 1862. Promoted to Sergeant in March-April, 1863. Present or accounted for until wounded in the shoulder and captured at Drewry's Bluff, Virginia, May 16, 1864. Confined at Point Lookout, Maryland, on an unspecified date. Paroled at Point Lookout on January 17, 1865. Received at Boulware's Wharf, James River, Virginia, January 21, 1865, for exchange. Hospitalized at Richmond, Virginia, January 21, 1865, with catarrh. Furloughed for forty days on January 29, 1865. Survived the war.

GILMORE, STEPHEN, Private
Born in Cumberland County and was by occupation a farmer prior to enlisting in Cumberland County at age 24, April 21, 1862, for the war. Present or accounted for until September-October, 1862, when he was reported absent sick. Returned to duty in November-December, 1862. Present or accounted for until wounded at Drewry's Bluff, Virginia, May 16, 1864. Died on May 17, 1864, of wounds. Place of death not reported.

GLOVER, CALVIN T., Private
Enlisted in Cumberland County at age 35, November 8, 1864, for the war. Reported absent on sick leave on December 25, 1864. Survived the war.

GLOVER, WILLIAM R., Private
Born in Cumberland County where he resided as a farmer prior to enlisting in Cumberland County at age 30, March 31, 1862. Present or accounted for until November, 1862-February, 1863, when he was reported absent sick. Returned to duty in March-April, 1863. Present or accounted for until captured at Cold Harbor, Virginia, June 1, 1864. Confined at Point Lookout, Maryland, June 11, 1864. Transferred to Elmira, New York, July 12, 1864. Injured in a railroad accident at Shohola, Pennsylvania, July 15, 1864, while en route to Elmira. Paroled at Elmira on October 11, 1864. Received at Venus Point, Savannah River, Georgia, November 15, 1864, for exchange.

GRAHAM, DANIEL, Private
Born in Cumberland County where he resided as a farmer prior to enlisting in Cumberland County at age 27, March 29, 1862. Present or accounted for until captured at Cold Harbor, Virginia, June 1, 1864. Confined at Point Lookout, Maryland, June 11, 1864. Transferred to Elmira, New York, July 12, 1864. Suffered a broken leg in a railroad accident at Shohola, Pennsylvania, July 15, 1864, while en route to Elmira. Foot amputated on July 18, 1864. Died at Elmira on July 24, 1864, of injuries.

GUIN, ASA, Private
Born in Cumberland County and was by occupation a farmer prior to enlisting in Cumberland County at age 19, April 9, 1862. Present or accounted for through December, 1864.

GUY, AMOS J., Musician
Born in Cumberland County where he resided as a farmer prior to enlisting in Cumberland County at age 18, April 1, 1862. Mustered in as Private. Appointed Musician in November-December, 1862. Present or accounted for until hospitalized at Wilmington on or about June 13, 1863, with acute diarrhoea. Furloughed for thirty days on June 16, 1863. Returned to duty in September-October, 1863. Present or accounted for through December, 1864. Survived the war.

GUY, JAMES E., Private
Born in Cumberland County where he enlisted on February 22, 1864, for the war. Present or accounted for until wounded at Drewry's Bluff, Virginia, May 16, 1864. Hospitalized at Richmond, Virginia, where he died on May 21, 1864, of wounds.

GUY, JOHN ALEX, Private
Born in Cumberland County where he resided as a farmer prior to enlisting in Cumberland County at age 28, April 21, 1862, for the war. Present or accounted for until wounded in the foot at Goldsboro on December 17, 1862. Returned to duty prior to January 1, 1863. Present or accounted for until killed at Drewry's Bluff, Virginia, on or about May 16, 1864.

GUY, LEWIS H., Corporal
Born in Cumberland County where he resided as a farmer prior to enlisting in Cumberland County at age 26, April 1, 1862. Mustered in as Private. Present or accounted for until September-October, 1862, when he was reported absent sick. Returned to duty in November-December, 1862. Promoted to Corporal in March-April, 1863. Present or accounted for until hospitalized at Wilmington on June 17, 1863, with typhoid fever. Returned to duty on July 14, 1863. Present or accounted for until May-August, 1864, when he was reported absent sick. Returned to duty in September-October, 1864. Present or accounted for until wounded in the right thigh (fracture) at or near Wise's Forks in March, 1865. Hospitalized at Raleigh on March 11, 1865. Died in hospital at Raleigh on March 25, 1865, of "erysipelas and tetanus."

GUY, SAMUEL J., Private
Born in Cumberland County where he resided as a farmer prior to enlisting in Cumberland County at age 30, April 21, 1862, for the war. Present or accounted for until September-October, 1863, when he was reported sick in hospital at Charleston, South Carolina. Discharged on November 6, 1863, by reason of an injury to his left hip received in a prewar wagon accident.

GUY, WILLIAM ANTHONY, Private
Born in Cumberland County where he resided as a farmer prior to enlisting in Cumberland County at age 21, April 1, 1862. Present or accounted for until he was appointed Ensign (1st Lieutenant) on July 7, 1864, and transferred to the Field and Staff of this regiment.

HALL, HAYNES L., Sergeant
Born in Cumberland County where he resided as a farmer prior to enlisting in Cumberland or Sampson County at age 21, March 31, 1862. Mustered in as Private. Promoted to Sergeant prior to July 1, 1862. Present or accounted for until hospitalized at Wilmington on August 25, 1862, with dysentery. Furloughed on September 5, 1862. Returned to duty prior to November 1, 1862. Reported sick in hospital at Wilmington in November-December, 1862. Returned to duty in January-February, 1863. Present or accounted for until wounded at Drewry's Bluff, Virginia, May 16, 1864. Returned to duty prior to June 1, 1864, when he was captured at Cold Harbor, Virginia. Confined at Point Lookout, Maryland, June 11, 1864. Transferred to Elmira, New York, July 12, 1864. Released at Elmira on July 3, 1865, after taking the Oath of Allegiance.

HALL, JAMES MORRIS, Private
Born in Sampson County in 1847 and was by occupation a farm laborer prior to enlisting in Cumberland County

on October 20, 1864, for the war. Reported absent sick on December 25, 1864. No further records.

HALL, OLIVER, Private
Resided in Cumberland County where he enlisted on May 5, 1862, for the war. Present or accounted for until wounded in the hands and face at Goldsboro on December 17, 1862. Reported absent wounded or absent sick through April, 1863. Returned to duty in May-June, 1863. Present or accounted for until wounded at Drewry's Bluff, Virginia, May 16, 1864. Hospitalized at Richmond, Virginia. Furloughed for sixty days on May 26, 1864. Returned to duty in November-December, 1864. Reported absent sick on December 25, 1864.

HAM, GILES, JR., Private
Born in Cumberland County where he resided as a farmer prior to enlisting in Cumberland County at age 26, April 21, 1862, for the war. Reported absent sick in May-August, 1862. Returned to duty in September-October, 1862. Transferred to Company E, 8th Regiment N.C. State Troops, January 7, 1863.

HARDISON, JAMES J., Private
Previously served as Private in 2nd Company B, 36th Regiment N.C. Troops (2nd Regiment N.C. Artillery). Transferred to this company on September 24, 1863. Reported absent sick in October, 1863. Returned to duty in November-December, 1863. Present or accounted for until captured at Cold Harbor, Virginia, June 1, 1864. Confined at Point Lookout, Maryland, June 11, 1864. Transferred to Elmira, New York, July 12, 1864. Killed in a railroad accident at Shohola, Pennsylvania, July 15, 1864, while en route to Elmira.

HASH, LAZARUS, _____
North Carolina pension records indicate that he served in this company.

HEMMINGWAY, ISAAC W., Private
Previously served as Private in Company D, 41st Regiment N.C. Troops (3rd Regiment N.C. Cavalry). Transferred to this company on October 29, 1863. Present or accounted for until wounded ("fore-finger shot off") at Cold Harbor, Virginia, May 31, 1864. Reported absent wounded or absent sick through August, 1864. Reported absent on detached service with the brigade commissary department in September-December, 1864.

HOLLAND, WILLIAM H., Private
Resided in Cumberland County where he enlisted on October 20, 1864, for the war. Present or accounted for through December, 1864.

HOLLEY, SILAS, Private
Enlisted in Cumberland County on May 1, 1862, for the war. Present or accounted for until captured at Drewry's Bluff, Virginia, May 16, 1864. Confined at Point Lookout, Maryland, May 19, 1864. Transferred to Elmira, New York, in August, 1864. Paroled at Elmira on October 11, 1864. Received at Venus Point, Savannah River, Georgia, November 15, 1864, for exchange.

HOLLEY, WILLIAM, Private
Born in Sampson County where he resided as a farmer prior to enlisting in Sampson or Cumberland County at age 35, April 4, 1862. Present or accounted for until January-February, 1863, when he was reported absent sick at Wilmington. Returned to duty in March-April, 1863. Present or accounted for until September-October, 1863, when he was reported sick in hospital at Mount Pleasant, South Carolina. Returned to duty in November-December, 1863. Present or accounted for until wounded at Drewry's Bluff, Virginia, May 16, 1864. Reported absent wounded through August, 1864. Returned to duty on an unspecified date. Company records indicate that he was captured at Fort Harrison, Virginia, September 30, 1864; however, records of the Federal Provost Marshal do not substantiate that report. Was probably killed at Fort Harrison.

HOWARD, STEPHEN, Private
Born in Duplin County and resided in Cumberland County where he was by occupation a farmer prior to enlisting in Sampson or Cumberland County at age 34, March 27, 1862. Present or accounted for until he deserted on November 11, 1862. Returned to duty in March-April, 1863. Present or accounted for until he deserted at Sullivan's Island, Charleston, South Carolina, August 21, 1863. Returned to duty on October 30, 1863. Present or accounted for until captured at Drewry's Bluff, Virginia, May 16, 1864. Confined at Point Lookout, Maryland, May 19, 1864. Released at Point Lookout on June 7, 1864, after taking the Oath of Allegiance and joining the U.S. Army. Assigned to Company K, 1st Regiment U.S. Volunteer Infantry.

JACKSON, ALLEN T., Private
Born in Cumberland County and enlisted in New Hanover County on May 13, 1862, for the war. Present or accounted for until killed at Cold Harbor, Virginia, May 31, 1864.

JACKSON, ALMON T., Private
Resided in Harnett County and was by occupation a laborer prior to enlisting in New Hanover County at age 19, February 10, 1863, for the war. Present or accounted for until July-August, 1863, when he was reported sick in hospital at Wilmington. Returned to duty in September-October, 1863. Present or accounted for until captured at Drewry's Bluff, Virginia, May 16, 1864. Confined at Point Lookout, Maryland. Paroled at Point Lookout on March 15, 1865. Received at Boulware's Wharf, James River, Virginia, March 18, 1865, for exchange. Survived the war.

JACKSON, BRYANT B., Private
Enlisted in Cumberland County on January 12, 1863, for the war. Present or accounted for until he died in hospital at Charleston, South Carolina, on or about August 11, 1863, of "brain fever."

JACKSON, JAMES E., Private
Resided in Cumberland County where he enlisted at age 21, October 6, 1862, for the war. Present or accounted for until November-December, 1862, when he was reported sick in hospital at Wilmington. Returned to duty in January-February, 1863. Present or accounted for until

May-August, 1864, when he was reported sick in hospital at Fayetteville. Reported absent without leave on November 20, 1864. Survived the war.

JACKSON, JAMES W., Private
Enlisted in Cumberland County on May 6, 1862, for the war. Present or accounted for until captured at Cold Harbor, Virginia, June 1, 1864. Confined at Point Lookout, Maryland, June 11, 1864. Transferred to Elmira, New York, July 12, 1864. Injured in a railroad accident at Shohola, Pennsylvania, July 15, 1864, while en route to Elmira. Paroled at Elmira on October 11, 1864. Received at Venus Point, Savannah River, Georgia, November 15, 1864, for exchange.

JACKSON, JOHN W., Private
Enlisted in New Hanover County on May 13, 1862, for the war. Present or accounted for until captured at Cold Harbor, Virginia, June 1, 1864. Confined at Point Lookout, Maryland, June 11, 1864. Transferred to Elmira, New York, July 12, 1864. Injured in a railroad accident at Shohola, Pennsylvania, July 15, 1864, while en route to Elmira. Paroled at Elmira on October 11, 1864. Received at Venus Point, Savannah River, Georgia, November 15, 1864, for exchange.

JACKSON, JOHN W., Private
Was serving as Private in Company C, 54th Regiment N.C. Troops, when he enlisted in this company without permission on May 12, 1862. Returned to duty with the 54th Regiment on June 22, 1862.

JACKSON, RANSOM, Private
Resided in Harnett County and was by occupation a farm laborer prior to enlisting in Cumberland County at age 28, May 6, 1862, for the war. Mustered in as Musician. Reduced to ranks in July-August, 1862. Present or accounted for until killed "by fall from train at Hartsboro" on December 19, 1863.

JACKSON, YOUNG S., Private
Resided in Harnett County and was by occupation a cooper prior to enlisting in Cumberland County at age 23, May 6, 1862, for the war. Present or accounted for until May-August, 1864, when he was reported absent sick. Deserted on September 1, 1864. [North Carolina pension records indicate that he was wounded at New Bern on May 30, 1863, and was wounded at Fort Wagner, Charleston, South Carolina, on an unspecified date.]

JESSUP, WILLIAM S., Private
Born in Cumberland County where he resided as a student prior to enlisting in Cumberland County at age 16, March 26, 1862. Present or accounted for until transferred to Company B, 13th Battalion N.C. Light Artillery, December 16, 1863.

JOHNSON, ALEX M., Private
Enlisted in Cumberland County on December 7, 1864, for the war. Hospitalized at Wilmington on January 27, 1865, with "cardialgia." No further records.

JOHNSON, RICHARD, Sergeant
Born in Bladen County and was by occupation a farmer

prior to enlisting in Cumberland County at age 35, April 9, 1862. Mustered in as Private. Promoted to Sergeant prior to July 1, 1862. Present or accounted for until he died near Goldsboro on December 27, 1862, of disease.

JONES, BRYANT, Private
Born in Cumberland County where he resided as a farmer prior to enlisting in Cumberland County on May 2, 1862, for the war. Present or accounted for until February 16, 1863, when he was reported absent sick at Wilmington. Returned to duty in March-April, 1863. Present or accounted for until he died in hospital at Petersburg, Virginia, on or about May 15, 1864, of "pleuritis." Death records give his age as 36.

JONES, DANIEL, Private
Born in Duplin County and was by occupation a farmer prior to enlisting in Cumberland County at age 49, March 26, 1862. Present or accounted for until September-October, 1862, when he was reported absent sick. Returned to duty in November-December, 1862. Present or accounted for until March-April, 1863, when he was reported absent without leave. Dropped from the rolls of the company in May-June, 1863.

JONES, DAVID D., Private
Previously served as Private in 2nd Company B, 36th Regiment N.C. Troops (2nd Regiment N.C. Artillery). Transferred to this company on October 10, 1863. Present or accounted for until captured at Cold Harbor, Virginia, June 1, 1864. Confined at Point Lookout, Maryland, June 11, 1864. Transferred to Elmira, New York, July 12, 1864. Injured slightly in a railroad accident at Shohola, Pennsylvania, July 15, 1864, while en route to Elmira. Paroled at Elmira and transferred to Boulware's Wharf, James River, Virginia, where he was received on or about February 20, 1865, for exchange. Took the Oath of Allegiance at Raleigh on May 26, 1865.

JONES, HAYES, Private
Enlisted in Cumberland County at age 21, October 6, 1862, for the war. Present or accounted for until wounded in the head at Goldsboro on December 17, 1862. Returned to duty prior to January 1, 1863. Present or accounted for until hospitalized at Wilmington on or about June 14, 1863, with typhoid fever. Returned to duty on July 13, 1863. Present or accounted for until transferred to Company F, 24th Regiment N.C. Troops (14th Regiment N.C. Volunteers), in January, 1864.

JONES, IRVIN G., Private
Previously served as Private in 2nd Company B, 36th Regiment N.C. Troops (2nd Regiment N.C. Artillery). Transferred to this company on September 24, 1863. Present or accounted for until wounded in the side and/or chest at Fort Harrison, Virginia, September 30, 1864. Reported in hospital at Richmond, Virginia, through December, 1864. Survived the war.

JONES, JAMES, Private
Enlisted in Cumberland County on September 17, 1862, for the war as a substitute for R. N. Finly. Present or accounted for until March-April, 1863, when he was reported sick in hospital at Charleston, South Carolina.

Returned to duty in May-June, 1863. Reported absent sick in July-December, 1863. Returned to duty in January-February, 1864. Dropped from the rolls of the company in March-April, 1864. Reason he was dropped not reported.

JONES, THOMAS D., Private

Enlisted in Cumberland County at age 20, May 5, 1862, for the war. Present or accounted for through February, 1864. Wounded at Cold Harbor, Virginia, May 31, 1864. Reported absent wounded or absent sick through August, 1864. Returned to duty prior to September 30, 1864, when he was wounded in the right leg at Fort Harrison, Virginia. Hospitalized at Richmond, Virginia. Furloughed for sixty days on or about January 3, 1865. Survived the war.

LALAND, EDWARD, Private

Born in Paris, France, and was by occupation a painter prior to enlisting in Cumberland County at age 37, March 31, 1862. Present or accounted for through April, 1863; however, he was reported absent sick during most of that period. Discharged on May 10, 1863, by reason of "phthisis pulmonalis."

LEDBETTER, WILLIAM T., Private

Born in Dinwiddie County, Virginia, or in Cumberland County, North Carolina, and was by occupation a student prior to enlisting at age 14, March 28, 1862. Present or accounted for until July-October, 1863, when he was reported sick in hospital at Columbia, South Carolina. Returned to duty in November-December, 1863. Present or accounted for until killed by a sharpshooter near Petersburg, Virginia, June 12, 1864.

LEE, WILLIAM R., Private

Born in Sampson County and was by occupation a farmer prior to enlisting in Cumberland County at age 19, March 31, 1862. Present or accounted for until transferred to the C.S. Navy on April 23, 1863.

LOCKAMY, AARON, Private

Born in Sampson County in 1835 and was by occupation a farm laborer prior to enlisting in New Hanover County on May 9, 1862, for the war. Present or accounted for until July-August, 1863, when he was reported absent without leave. Reported absent sick in September-December, 1863. Returned to duty in January-February, 1864. Present or accounted for through December, 1864.

McCORQUEDALE, ANGUS, Private

Born in Sampson County where he resided as a farmer prior to enlisting in Cumberland County at age 47, March 31, 1862. Present or accounted for until March-April, 1863, when he was reported sick in hospital at Columbia, South Carolina. Returned to duty in May-June, 1863. Present or accounted for until discharged on or about March 1, 1864. Reason discharged not reported.

McCORQUEDALE, JOEL, Private

Born in Cumberland County and was by occupation a farmer prior to enlisting in Cumberland County at age 18, March 27, 1862. Present or accounted for through December, 1864.

McCORQUEDALE, MALCOLM, Private

Born in Cumberland County where he enlisted on May 23, 1863, for the war. Present or accounted for until captured at Cold Harbor, Virginia, June 1, 1864. Confined at Point Lookout, Maryland, June 11, 1864. Transferred to Elmira, New York, July 12, 1864. Killed in a railroad accident at Shohola, Pennsylvania, July 15, 1864, while en route to Elmira.

McDONALD, ARCHIBALD C., Private

Born in Cumberland County where he resided as a farmer prior to enlisting in Cumberland County at age 41, April 9, 1862. Present or accounted for until September-October, 1862, when he was reported absent sick. Returned to duty in November-December, 1862. Present or accounted for until wounded in the head at Charleston, South Carolina, July 18, 1863. Returned to duty prior to September 1, 1863. Present or accounted for until captured at Cold Harbor, Virginia, June 1, 1864. Confined at Point Lookout, Maryland. Transferred to Elmira, New York, July 12, 1864. Leg injured in a railroad accident at Shohola, Pennsylvania, July 15, 1864, while he was en route to Elmira. Paroled at Elmira on October 11, 1864, and transferred for exchange. Survived the war.

McINTYRE, DUGALD, Private

Born in Cumberland County and was by occupation a farmer prior to enlisting in Cumberland County at age 33, April 21, 1862, for the war. Present or accounted for until captured at Cold Harbor, Virginia, June 1, 1864. Confined at Point Lookout, Maryland, June 11, 1864. Transferred to Elmira, New York, July 12, 1864. Injured in a railroad accident at Shohola, Pennsylvania, July 15, 1864, while en route to Elmira. Arrived at Elmira on July 17, 1864. Paroled at Elmira on October 11, 1864. Received at Venus Point, Savannah River, Georgia, November 15, 1864, for exchange.

McKENZIE, ALEXANDER, Private

Previously served as Private in Company B, 18th Regiment Virginia Heavy Artillery. Transferred to this company on or about October 16, 1862. Reported absent without leave in November-December, 1862. Returned to duty in January-February, 1863. Present or accounted for until he deserted on December 17, 1863.

McLEAN, ANGUS, Private

Resided in Cumberland County where he enlisted on November 25, 1864, for the war. Captured at Wise's Forks on March 8, 1865. Confined at Point Lookout, Maryland, March 16, 1865. Released at Point Lookout on June 29, 1865, after taking the Oath of Allegiance.

McLELLAN, DANIEL G., 1st Sergeant

Born in Cumberland County and was by occupation a farmer prior to enlisting in Cumberland County at age 20, April 3, 1862. Mustered in as Private. Promoted to Corporal prior to July 1, 1862. Promoted to Sergeant in November-December, 1862. Promoted to 1st Sergeant on October 1, 1863. Present or accounted for until May-October, 1864, when he was reported absent on sick furlough. Returned to duty in November-December, 1864. Present or accounted for through December, 1864. Survived the war.

McMEANES, JONATHAN, _____
North Carolina pension records indicate that he served in this company.

McMILLAN, DANIEL A., Private
Enlisted in Cumberland County at age 18, February 22, 1864, for the war. Present or accounted for until wounded and captured at Drewry's Bluff, Virginia, May 16, 1864. Confined at Point Lookout, Maryland, May 19, 1864. Paroled at Point Lookout on or about September 18, 1864. Received at Varina, Virginia, September 22, 1864, for exchange. Reported absent sick through December, 1864. Survived the war.

McMILLAN, NEILL, Private
Born in Cumberland County where he resided as a farmer prior to enlisting in Cumberland County at age 43, March 31, 1862. Present or accounted for until discharged on March 11, 1864. Reason discharged not reported.

McPHAIL, DOUGALD, Private
Enlisted in New Hanover County at age 21, May 5, 1862, for the war. Present or accounted for through December, 1864. Served as a teamster during much of the war. Survived the war.

MANER, WILLIAM T., Private
Born in Sampson County and was by occupation a student prior to enlisting in Sampson County at age 16, March 29, 1862. Present or accounted for until November-December, 1862, when he was reported absent sick. Returned to duty in January-February, 1863. Reported absent on detached service at the brigade headquarters from September, 1863, through February, 1864. Rejoined the company prior to June 1, 1864, when he was captured at Cold Harbor, Virginia. Confined at Point Lookout, Maryland, June 11, 1864. Transferred to Elmira, New York, July 12, 1864. Injured slightly in a railroad accident at Shohola, Pennsylvania, July 15, 1864, while en route to Elmira. Paroled at Elmira on March 2, 1865, and transferred to the James River, Virginia, for exchange. Survived the war.

MELVIN, D. J., Private
Born in Cumberland County and was by occupation a farmer prior to enlisting in Cumberland County at age 19, April 14, 1862. Discharged on May 17, 1862. Reason discharged not reported.

MELVIN, ROBERT D., Private
Born in Cumberland County and resided in Bladen County where he was by occupation a farmer prior to enlisting in Cumberland County at age 28, April 10, 1862. Present or accounted for through July, 1862. Detailed for duty with the Signal Corps (probably as a telegraph operator) on August 6, 1862. Reported absent on detail with the Signal Corps through February, 1864. Dropped from the rolls of the company in March-April, 1864, presumably by reason of having been assigned to permanent duty with the Signal Corps. Transferred back to the company subsequent to December 31, 1864. Captured near Fayetteville on March 16, 1865. Confined at Point Lookout, Maryland, April 3, 1865. Released at

Point Lookout on June 3, 1865, after taking the Oath of Allegiance.

MONROE, DUNCAN, Private
Born in Cumberland County where he resided as a farmer prior to enlisting in Cumberland County at age 38, April 9, 1862. Present or accounted for through July, 1862. Reported absent on detached service guarding government stores at Fayetteville from August 20, 1862, through June 30, 1863. Rejoined the company in July-August, 1863. Present or accounted for until captured at Cold Harbor, Virginia, June 1, 1864. Confined at Point Lookout, Maryland, June 11, 1864. Transferred to Elmira, New York, July 12, 1864. Killed in a railroad accident at Shohola, Pennsylvania, July 15, 1864, while en route to Elmira.

MONROE, THOMAS, Private
Resided in Cumberland County and was by occupation a farmer prior to enlisting in Cumberland County at age 37, March 5, 1863, for the war. Present or accounted for through December, 1863; however, he was reported absent sick during most of that period. Returned to duty in January-February, 1864. Present or accounted for through August, 1864. Reported absent sick in September-December, 1864.

MOORE, ALDRIDGE, Private
Enlisted in Cumberland County on June 18, 1863, for the war. Present or accounted for until captured at Drewry's Bluff, Virginia, May 16, 1864. Confined at Point Lookout, Maryland, May 21, 1864. Released at Point Lookout on June 7, 1864, after taking the Oath of Allegiance and joining the U.S. Army. Assigned to Company I, 1st Regiment U.S. Volunteer Infantry.

MOORE, JOHN, Private
Previously served as Private in Company E, 8th Regiment N.C. State Troops. Transferred to this company on January 7, 1863. Present or accounted for until killed at Drewry's Bluff, Virginia, May 16, 1864.

NORRIS, WILLIAM J., Private
Resided in Sampson County and was by occupation a farm laborer prior to enlisting in Cumberland County at age 19, May 12, 1862, for the war. Present or accounted for until February 16, 1863, when he was reported sick at Washington, North Carolina. Returned to duty in March-April, 1863. Present or accounted for until captured at Cold Harbor, Virginia, June 1, 1864. Confined at Point Lookout, Maryland, June 11, 1864. Transferred to Elmira, New York, July 12, 1864. Injured in a railroad accident at Shohola, Pennsylvania, July 15, 1864, while en route to Elmira. Paroled at Elmira on October 11, 1864. Received at Venus Point, Savannah River, Georgia, November 15, 1864, for exchange.

NOTT, WILLIAM J., Private
Resided in Cumberland County where he enlisted at age 21, May 9, 1862, for the war. Present or accounted for until wounded slightly at Fort Harrison, Virginia, September 30, 1864. Returned to duty in November-December, 1864. Captured at Wise's Forks on March 8, 1865. Confined at Point Lookout, Maryland, March 16,

1865. Released at Point Lookout on June 28, 1865, after taking the Oath of Allegiance.

NUNNERY, HENRY, Private

Resided in Cumberland County where he enlisted at age 20, May 30, 1863, for the war. Present or accounted for until July-October, 1863, when he was reported absent sick. Returned to duty in November-December, 1863. Present or accounted for until he deserted on September 28, 1864. [North Carolina pension records indicate that he was wounded in the head at Cold Harbor, Virginia, June 1, 1864.]

NUNNERY, JOHN, Private

Enlisted in Cumberland County on May 3, 1862, for the war. Present or accounted for through August, 1862; however, he was reported absent sick during most of that period. Died at Wilmington on the morning of September 2, 1862, of "phthisis pulmonalis" and/or "brain fever." Was 22 years of age at the time of his death.

NUNNERY, WILLIAM, Private

Enlisted in Cumberland County on May 3, 1862, for the war. Present or accounted for until captured at Cold Harbor, Virginia, June 1, 1864. Confined at Point Lookout, Maryland, June 11, 1864. Transferred to Elmira, New York, July 12, 1864. Killed in a railroad accident at Shohola, Pennsylvania, July 15, 1864, while en route to Elmira.

PAGE, BRIGHT, Private

Born in Cumberland County. Place and date of enlistment not reported; however, he probably enlisted in the late spring or summer of 1864. Wounded in the hip (compound fracture) and captured near Globe Tavern, Virginia, August 19, 1864. Hospitalized at Washington, D.C., where he died on September 3, 1864, of wounds. Was 17 years of age at the time of his death.

PAGE, JESSE, Private

Resided in Cumberland County and was by occupation a farmer prior to enlisting in Cumberland County at age 36, October 20, 1864, for the war. Present or accounted for through December, 1864. Captured at Bentonville on March 19, 1865. Confined at Point Lookout, Maryland, March 30, 1865. Released at Point Lookout on June 17, 1865, after taking the Oath of Allegiance.

PAGE, WILLIAM, Private

Born in Cumberland County and was by occupation a farmer prior to enlisting in Cumberland County at age 20, March 31, 1862. Present or accounted for until he deserted at Sullivan's Island, Charleston, South Carolina, August 21, 1863. Reported under arrest at Charleston in September-December, 1863. Returned to duty in January-February, 1864. Present or accounted for through January 7, 1865.

PHARRIS, ALEXANDER, Private

Enlisted in Cumberland County at age 20, March 5, 1863, for the war. Present or accounted for until he deserted at Sullivan's Island, Charleston, South Carolina, August 21, 1863.

PHILLIPS, JARMON E., Private

Born in Sampson County and was by occupation a farmer prior to enlisting in Cumberland County at age 20, March 29, 1862. Present or accounted for until he was "knocked down by [an] exploding bomb shell" at Petersburg, Virginia, June 17, 1864. Returned to duty prior to September 1, 1864. Present or accounted for through December, 1864. Survived the war.

POPE, DOCTOR W., Private

Resided in Cumberland County where he enlisted on April 26, 1862, for the war. Present or accounted for until captured at Cold Harbor, Virginia, June 1, 1864. Confined at Point Lookout, Maryland, June 11, 1864. Released at Point Lookout on June 17, 1865, after taking the Oath of Allegiance. [North Carolina pension records indicate that he was wounded in the left eye at Drewry's Bluff, Virginia, in 1864.]

POPE, JAMES D., Private

Born in Sampson County and was by occupation a farmer prior to enlisting in Cumberland County at age 30, March 27, 1862. Present or accounted for until September-October, 1862, when he was reported absent sick. Returned to duty prior to December 17, 1862, when he was wounded in the thigh at Goldsboro. Returned to duty in March-April, 1863. Present or accounted for until captured at Cold Harbor, Virginia, June 1, 1864. Confined at Point Lookout, Maryland, June 4, 1864. Transferred to Elmira, New York, July 12, 1864. Injured in a railroad accident at Shohola, Pennsylvania, July 15, 1864, while en route to Elmira. Paroled at Elmira on March 2, 1865, and transferred to the James River, Virginia, for exchange. Hospitalized at Richmond, Virginia, March 6, 1865, with debilitas. Furloughed for thirty days on March 8, 1865. Survived the war.

POPE, JOSIAH, Private

Born in Sampson County and was by occupation a farmer prior to enlisting in Cumberland County at age 23, March 27, 1862. Present or accounted for through February, 1864. Reported absent on sick furlough in May-October, 1864. Reported absent without leave on December 20, 1864. Survived the war. [North Carolina pension records indicate that he suffered a fractured left hip at Petersburg, Virginia, May 10, 1864.]

POPE, LOUIS, Private

Born in Cumberland County and was by occupation a farmer prior to enlisting in Cumberland County at age 40, April 5, 1862. Present or accounted for until September-October, 1862, when he was reported absent sick. Returned to duty in November-December, 1862. Present or accounted for until he deserted on August 21, 1863. Returned to duty on May 25, 1864. Reported absent without leave on August 1, 1864. Listed as a deserter on October 18, 1864.

POPE, WILLIAM P., Private

Enlisted in Cumberland County on March 5, 1863, for the war. Present or accounted for until captured at Drewry's Bluff, Virginia, May 16, 1864. Confined at Point Lookout, Maryland, May 21, 1864. Paroled at Point Lookout on

March 14, 1865. Received at Boulware's Wharf, James River, Virginia, March 18, 1865, for exchange.

PORTER, MALCOLM, Private

Born in Cumberland County and was by occupation a farmer prior to enlisting in Cumberland County at age 28, March 29, 1862. Present or accounted for until wounded in the head at Fort Wagner, Charleston, South Carolina, July 18, 1863. Hospitalized at Summerville, South Carolina, where he died on August 4, 1863, of wounds.

PORTER, WILEY B., Private

Born in Cumberland County where he resided as a farmer prior to enlisting in Cumberland County at age 28, March 27, 1862. Present or accounted for until he deserted on August 21, 1863. Reported under arrest at Charleston, South Carolina, for desertion in September-December, 1863. Returned to duty in January-February, 1864. Present or accounted for until captured at Drewry's Bluff, Virginia, May 16, 1864. Confined at Point Lookout, Maryland, May 19, 1864. Transferred to Elmira, New York, August 16, 1864. Released at Elmira on May 29, 1865, after taking the Oath of Allegiance.

POWERS, MICHAEL M., Private

Enlisted in Cumberland County on July 31, 1864, for the war. Reported present in November-December, 1864.

POWERS, THOMAS J., Corporal

Resided in Cumberland County where he enlisted on April 29, 1862, for the war. Mustered in as Private. Present or accounted for until wounded in the thigh at Goldsboro on December 17, 1862. Returned to duty in May-June, 1863. Promoted to Corporal on October 1, 1863. Present or accounted for until captured near Globe Tavern, Virginia, August 19, 1864. Confined at Point Lookout, Maryland, August 24, 1864. Paroled at Point Lookout on or about February 10, 1865. Received at Cox's Wharf, James River, Virginia, February 14, 1865, for exchange. Survived the war.

RAIFORD, WILLIAM N., Private

Resided in Sampson County and enlisted in Brunswick County on July 7, 1862, for the war. Present or accounted for until November-December, 1862, when he was reported absent sick. Returned to duty in January-February, 1863. Present or accounted for until March-April, 1863, when he was reported sick in hospital at Columbia, South Carolina. Deserted from hospital at Columbia on April 28, 1863. Returned to duty on November 13, 1863. Wounded in the head near Petersburg, Virginia, June 17, 1864. Reported wounded or absent sick through August, 1864. Reported absent without leave on October 1, 1864. [Previously served as 1st Lieutenant in the 25th Regiment N.C. Militia.]

RASBURY, WILLIAM, Private

Born in Greene County and was by occupation a farmer prior to enlisting in Cumberland County at age 47, April 9, 1862. Present or accounted for until November-December, 1862, when he was reported absent sick. Returned to duty in January-February, 1863. Present or accounted for until discharged on June 11, 1863, by reason of a tumor.

ROYALS, ROBERT D., Private

Enlisted in Cumberland County on October 9, 1862, for the war. Present or accounted for until March-April, 1863, when he was reported absent sick. Returned to duty in May-June, 1863. Deserted at Sullivan's Island, Charleston, South Carolina, July 30, 1863. Brought into camp at Sullivan's Island on November 5, 1863, after being arrested at Tarboro. Returned to duty in January-February, 1864. Hospitalized at Petersburg, Virginia, March 28, 1864, with acute rheumatism. Transferred to Raleigh on June 18, 1864. Hospitalized at Fayetteville prior to September 1, 1864. Reported absent without leave on October 30, 1864.

RUSSELL, STEPHEN E., Private

Previously served as Private in Company H, 1st Regiment N.C. Infantry (6 months, 1861). Enlisted in this company in Cumberland County on April 29, 1862, for the war. Reported absent sick in July-August, 1862. Returned to duty in September-October, 1862. Present or accounted for until transferred to 2nd Company B, 36th Regiment N.C. Troops (2nd Regiment N.C. Artillery), September 24, 1863.

SANDY, JOHN A. W., Private

Resided in Cumberland County where he enlisted on September 5, 1863, for the war. Present or accounted for until wounded in the right arm at Drewry's Bluff, Virginia, May 16, 1864. Hospitalized at Richmond, Virginia. Returned to duty in September-October, 1864. Reported absent sick on December 25, 1864. Captured at Fayetteville on March 13, 1865. Confined at Point Lookout, Maryland, March 30, 1865. Released at Point Lookout on June 20, 1865, after taking the Oath of Allegiance.

SENTER, D. E., Private

North Carolina pension records indicate that he served in this company.

SIMMONS, MALCOLM L., Private

Enlisted in Cumberland County on May 25, 1864, for the war. Captured at Cold Harbor, Virginia, June 1, 1864. Confined at Point Lookout, Maryland, June 11, 1864. Transferred to Elmira, New York, July 12, 1864. While at Elmira it appears that he exchanged identities with Private Thaddeus D. Malpass of Company E, 18th Regiment N.C. Troops (8th Regiment N.C. Volunteers). One of the two men died at Elmira on or about November 28, 1864, of "hospital gangrene"; the other was paroled and transferred to Boulware's Wharf, James River, Virginia, where he was received on March 18-21, 1865, for exchange. It is not clear which of the two men survived the war.

SIMMONS, WILEY, Private

Resided in Cumberland County and was by occupation a turpentiner prior to enlisting in Cumberland County at age 32, October 20, 1864, for the war. Hospitalized at Wilmington on February 18, 1865. Died of disease on an unspecified date.

SKIPPER, WILLIAM L., Private

Born in Cumberland County and was by occupation a

farmer prior to enlisting in Cumberland County at age 30, March 29, 1862. Present or accounted for until September-October, 1862, when he was reported absent sick. Returned to duty in November-December, 1862. Present or accounted for until killed at Drewry's Bluff, Virginia, May 16, 1864.

SMITH, DAVID L., Private
Born in Wake County and was by occupation an apprentice prior to enlisting in Cumberland County at age 18, March 27, 1862. Present or accounted for until September-October, 1862, when he was reported absent sick. Returned to duty in November-December, 1862. Present or accounted for until transferred to 2nd Company B, 36th Regiment N.C. Troops (2nd Regiment N.C. Artillery), September 24, 1863.

SMITH, MALCOLM McI., Private
Born in Cumberland County where he enlisted on October 7, 1862, for the war. Present or accounted for until wounded at Fort Wagner, Charleston, South Carolina, July 18, 1863. Returned to duty prior to September 1, 1863. Present or accounted for until wounded at Drewry's Bluff, Virginia, May 16, 1864. Died "on the battlefield" the next day of wounds.

SMITH, PETER M., Private
Enlisted in Cumberland County on October 3, 1862, for the war. Present or accounted for until captured at Cold Harbor, Virginia, June 1, 1864. Confined at Point Lookout, Maryland, June 11, 1864. Transferred to Elmira, New York, July 12, 1864. Injured in a railroad accident at Shohola, Pennsylvania, July 15, 1864, while en route to Elmira. Paroled at Elmira on October 11, 1864. Received at Venus Point, Savannah River, Georgia, November 15, 1864, for exchange.

SOCKERINGE, AARON, _____
North Carolina pension records indicate that he served in this company.

STEWART, ALVIN, Private
Enlisted in Cumberland County on November 25, 1864, for the war. Reported absent without leave on December 28, 1864.

STEWART, DANIEL, Private
Born in Sampson County and resided in Cumberland County where he was by occupation a farm laborer prior to enlisting at Cumberland County at age 44, October 15, 1862, for the war. Present or accounted for until March-April, 1863, when he was reported sick in hospital at Charleston, South Carolina. Returned to duty in July-August, 1863. Present or accounted for until wounded in the right thigh at Cold Harbor, Virginia, June 1, 1864. Reported absent wounded or absent sick in hospital at Fayetteville through December, 1864.

STRICKLAND, THOMAS J., Private
Born in Sampson County and was by occupation a farmer prior to enlisting in Cumberland County at age 30, April 1, 1862. Present or accounted for until captured at Cold Harbor, Virginia, June 1, 1864. Confined at Point

Lookout, Maryland, June 11, 1864. Transferred to Elmira, New York, July 12, 1864. Killed in a railroad accident at Shohola, Pennsylvania, July 15, 1864, while en route to Elmira.

TAYLOR, ABRAM J., Private
Enlisted in Cumberland County on May 2, 1862, for the war. Hospitalized at Wilmington on January 28, 1863, with catarrhus. Returned to duty in March-April, 1863. Present or accounted for until reported sick in hospital at Charleston, South Carolina, in July-August, 1863. Returned to duty in September-October, 1863. Present or accounted for until wounded at Drewry's Bluff, Virginia, May 16, 1864. Returned to duty prior to June 1, 1864, when he was captured at Cold Harbor, Virginia. Confined at Point Lookout, Maryland, June 11, 1864. Transferred to Elmira, New York, July 12, 1864. Injured in a railroad accident at Shohola, Pennsylvania, July 15, 1864, while en route to Elmira. Paroled at Elmira on October 11, 1864. Received at Venus Point, Savannah River, Georgia, November 15, 1864, for exchange.

TAYLOR, JOHN H., Private
Born in Cumberland County where he enlisted on April 26, 1862, for the war. Reported absent sick in July-December, 1862. Returned to duty in January-February, 1863. Present or accounted for until killed at Bermuda Hundred, Virginia, May 20, 1864.

TAYLOR, WILLIAM ALFRED, Private
Born in Nash County and was by occupation a farmer prior to enlisting in Cumberland County at age 46, April 9, 1862. Present or accounted for until hospitalized at Wilmington on or about December 18, 1862, with hemoptysis. Returned to duty on January 27, 1863. Hospitalized at Wilmington on February 16, 1863. Transferred to the C.S. Navy on April 18, 1863.

TAYLOR, WILLIAM JAMES, Private
Born in Cumberland County where he resided as a farmer prior to enlisting in Cumberland County at age 34, April 3, 1862. Present or accounted for until September-October, 1862, when he was reported absent sick. Returned to duty in November-December, 1862. Present or accounted for until wounded at Fort Wagner, Charleston, South Carolina, July 18, 1863. Returned to duty prior to September 1, 1863. Present or accounted for until hospitalized at Wilmington on or about June 1, 1864, with a gunshot wound. Place and date wounded not reported. Reported absent wounded or absent sick through August, 1864. Returned to duty in September-October, 1864. Present or accounted for through December, 1864. Captured in Cumberland County on March 12, 1865. Sent to New Bern. Confined at Hart's Island, New York Harbor, April 10, 1865. Released at Hart's Island on June 19, 1865, after taking the Oath of Allegiance.

TEW, ALEXANDER, Private
Born in Sampson County in 1842 and resided in Sampson County where he was by occupation a farm laborer prior to enlisting in New Hanover County on May 9, 1862, for the war. Present or accounted for until captured at Cold Harbor, Virginia, June 1, 1864. Confined at Point

Lookout, Maryland, June 11, 1864. Transferred to Elmira, New York, July 12, 1864. Arrived at Elmira on July 17, 1864. Died at Elmira on November 2, 1864, of "chronic diarrhoea."

TEW, DANIEL C., Private
Born in Sampson County and resided in Wayne County where he was by occupation a farmer prior to enlisting in Cumberland County at age 16, April 7, 1862. Present or accounted for until November-December, 1862, when he was reported absent sick. Returned to duty in January-February, 1863. Present or accounted for until captured at Cold Harbor, Virginia, June 1, 1864. Confined at Point Lookout, Maryland, June 11, 1864. Transferred to Elmira, New York, July 12, 1864. Suffered a fractured breastbone, three broken ribs, and a dislocated left shoulder in a railroad accident at Shohola, Pennsylvania, July 15, 1864, while en route to Elmira. Released at Elmira on June 21, 1865, after taking the Oath of Allegiance.

TEW, JACKSON, Private
Born in Sampson County where he resided as a farmer prior to enlisting in Cumberland County at age 18, April 21, 1862, for the war. Present or accounted for until he was left sick at Wilmington in February, 1863. Returned to duty in March-April, 1863. Present or accounted for until wounded and captured at Cold Harbor, Virginia, May 31, 1864. Confined at Point Lookout, Maryland, June 11, 1864. Transferred to Elmira, New York, July 12, 1864. Died at Elmira on or about October 22, 1864, of "pneumonia."

TEW, JAMES MARTIN, Private
Enlisted in New Hanover County on May 9, 1862, for the war. Present or accounted for until captured at Cold Harbor, Virginia, June 1, 1864. Confined at Point Lookout, Maryland, June 11, 1864. Transferred to Elmira, New York, July 12, 1864. Died at Elmira on December 2, 1864, of "rheumatic carditis."

TEW, JEREMIAH, Private
Born in Sampson County in 1834 and resided in Sampson County where he was by occupation a farmer prior to enlisting in Cumberland County on September 14, 1863, for the war. Present or accounted for until hospitalized at Petersburg, Virginia, February 26, 1864, with "pneumonia typhoides." Returned to duty prior to September 1, 1864. Present or accounted for until he was reported absent sick on December 25, 1864.

TEW, JOHN, Private
Born in Sampson County where he resided as a farmer prior to enlisting in Sampson County at age 23, March 29, 1862. Present or accounted for until killed at Drewry's Bluff, Virginia, May 16, 1864.

TEW, JOHN R., Private
Born in Sampson County where he resided as a farmer prior to enlisting in Cumberland County at age 25, April 6, 1862. Present or accounted for until March-April, 1863, when he was reported absent without leave. Returned to duty in May-June, 1863. Present or accounted for until captured at Cold Harbor, Virginia, June 1, 1864. Confined at Point Lookout, Maryland, June 11, 1864.

Transferred to Elmira, New York, on or about July 12, 1864. "Left leg broken" and head "mashed" in a railroad accident at Shohola, Pennsylvania, July 15, 1864, while en route to Elmira. Paroled at Elmira on March 2, 1865, and transferred to the James River, Virginia, for exchange. Hospitalized at Richmond, Virginia, March 6, 1865, with debilitas and was furloughed for thirty days on March 9, 1865. Survived the war.

TEW, LEMICK J., Private
Born in Sampson County where he resided as a farmer prior to enlisting in Cumberland County at age 23, April 1, 1862. Mustered in as Private. Promoted to Sergeant prior to July 1, 1862. Reduced to ranks in March-April, 1863. Present or accounted for through February, 1864. Was reported on duty as acting sutler and as a wagon driver during part of that period. Captured at Cold Harbor, Virginia, June 1, 1864. Confined at Point Lookout, Maryland, June 11, 1864. Transferred to Elmira, New York, July 12, 1864. Paroled at Elmira on October 11, 1864. Received at Venus Point, Savannah River, Georgia, November 15, 1864, for exchange. Survived the war.

TEW, LOUDIN BLUE, Private
Born in Sampson County in 1834 and resided in Sampson County where he was by occupation a turpentine laborer prior to enlisting in Cumberland County on April 26, 1862, for the war. Present or accounted for until wounded in the side and/or right hip at Goldsboro on December 17, 1862. Returned to duty prior to January 1, 1863. Present or accounted for until May-August, 1864, when he was reported absent sick. Returned to duty in September-October, 1864. Present or accounted for through December, 1864. Hospitalized at Wilmington on February 3, 1865, with rheumatism and/or typhoid fever. Furloughed for sixty days on February 14, 1865. Survived the war.

TEW, WILLIAM H., Private
Enlisted in Cumberland County on March 5, 1863, for the war. Present or accounted for until July-August, 1863, when he was reported absent sick in hospital at Augusta, Georgia. Returned to duty in September-October, 1863. Present or accounted for through December, 1864. Survived the war.

THOMASON, WILLIAM G., Private
Born in Cumberland County and was by occupation a printer prior to enlisting in Cumberland County at age 17, March 26, 1862. Present or accounted for through July, 1862. Reported on detached service guarding government stores at Fayetteville from August 20, 1862, through February 28, 1863. Returned to duty in March-April, 1863. Present or accounted for until transferred to 2nd Company B, 36th Regiment N.C. Troops (2nd Regiment N.C. Artillery), September 24, 1863.

TOLAR, HIRAM, Private
Resided in Cumberland County and was by occupation a farmer prior to enlisting in Cumberland County at age 39, October 20, 1864, for the war. Present or accounted for until December 25, 1864, when he was reported absent sick.

TOLAR, ROBERT M., Private
Resided in Cumberland County where he enlisted on October 3, 1862, for the war. Present or accounted for until February 7, 1863, when he was reported absent sick. Returned to duty in May-June, 1863. Present or accounted for until transferred to 3rd Company B, 36th Regiment N.C. Troops (2nd Regiment N.C. Artillery), October 26, 1863. [He was one of nine brothers who served in the Confederate Army. A monument to the brothers was later erected at Cross Creek Cemetery, Fayetteville.]

WADE, JOHN LOUIS, Private
Enlisted in Cumberland County on October 20, 1864, for the war. Died in hospital at Raleigh on March 30, 1865, of "feb[ris] remittens."

WARREN, JAMES C., Private
Born in Sampson County where he resided as a farmer prior to enlisting in Sampson County at age 28, April 4, 1862. Present or accounted for until captured at Cold Harbor, Virginia, June 1, 1864. Confined at Point Lookout, Maryland, June 11, 1864. Transferred to Elmira, New York, July 12, 1864. Injured in a railroad accident at Shohola, Pennsylvania, July 15, 1864, while en route to Elmira. Paroled at Elmira on March 14, 1865. Received at Boulware's Wharf, James River, Virginia, March 18, 1865, for exchange. Survived the war.

WARREN, WILLIAM A., Private
Born in Sampson County where he resided as a farmer prior to enlisting in Sampson County at age 25, April 4, 1862. Present or accounted for until January 24, 1863, when he was reported absent sick in Sampson County. Returned to duty in March-April, 1863. Present or accounted for through February, 1864. Reported on detail as a guard at the medical purveying department at Charlotte from March 1, 1864, through February 7, 1865, by reason of disability. Paroled at Charlotte on May 3, 1865.

WEAVER, CHARLES J., Private
Previously served as Private in Company B, 10th Battalion N.C. Heavy Artillery. Enlisted in this company on April 21, 1862, while listed as a deserter from the 10th Battalion. Returned to duty with Company B, 10th Battalion N.C. Heavy Artillery, June 15, 1862.

WEST, JOSEPH, Private
Previously served as Private in Company F, 24th Regiment N.C. Troops (14th Regiment N.C. Volunteers). Transferred to this company in February, 1864. Wounded at Cold Harbor, Virginia, May 31, 1864. Reported absent wounded or absent sick at the division hospital in June-October, 1864. Reported absent on detached service at the division hospital in November-December, 1864. Hospitalized at Fayetteville on February 19, 1865, with an unspecified complaint. Reported still in hospital at Fayetteville on or about February 28, 1865.

WILLIAMS, HABRAN T., Private
Born in Sampson County and was by occupation a farmer prior to enlisting in Cumberland County at age 20, March 31, 1862. Present or accounted for until July-August, 1863, when he was reported sick in hospital at Charleston,

South Carolina. Returned to duty in November-December, 1863. Present or accounted for until he deserted to the enemy on or about April 1, 1865. Sent to Washington, D.C. Released at Washington on an unspecified date after taking the Oath of Allegiance.

WILLIAMS, HENRY, Private
Born in Sampson County and resided in Cumberland County where he was by occupation a farmer prior to enlisting in Cumberland County at age 38, March 27, 1862. Present or accounted for until November-December, 1862, when he was reported absent sick. Returned to duty in March-April, 1863. Present or accounted for until killed at Bermuda Hundred, Virginia, May 20, 1864.

WILLIAMS, JAMES DANIEL, Private
Born in Sampson County on June 17, 1823, and was by occupation a farmer prior to enlisting in Cumberland County on March 25, 1864, for the war. Wounded in the left leg (flesh) at Drewry's Bluff, Virginia, May 16, 1864. Hospitalized at Richmond, Virginia. Returned to duty prior to September 30, 1864. Company records indicate that he was captured at Fort Harrison, Virginia, on that date; however, records of the Federal Provost Marshal do not substantiate that report. Was presumably killed at Fort Harrison.

WILSON, EZEKIEL, Corporal
Born in Sampson County and was by occupation a farm laborer prior to enlisting in Sampson County at age 16, March 29, 1862. Mustered in as Private. Reported sick in hospital at Wilmington in September, 1862. Returned to duty prior to November 1, 1862. Promoted to Corporal in November-December, 1864. Present or accounted for through December, 1864.

WOOD, GARY, Private
Born in Cumberland County and resided in Sampson County where he was by occupation a farmer prior to enlisting in Cumberland County at age 32, March 27, 1862. Present or accounted for until he died in hospital at Wilmington on August 24, 1862, of "dysenteria acuta."

COMPANY K

This company, known as the "Confederate Stars," was raised in Sampson County and enlisted in Sampson County in March-April, 1862. It was mustered into state service at Camp Holmes, near Wilmington, on May 10, 1862, and assigned to the 51st Regiment N.C. Troops as Company K. After joining the regiment the company functioned as a part of the regiment, and its history for the remainder of the war is reported as a part of the regimental history.

The information contained in the following roster was compiled primarily from a company muster-in and descriptive roll dated May 10, 1862, and from company muster rolls for May 10, 1862-February 29, 1864, and April 30-December 31, 1864. No company muster rolls were located for March 1-April 29, 1864, or for the period after December 31, 1864. Valuable information was obtained from primary records such as the North Carolina adjutant general's *Roll of Honor*, discharge certificates, medical records, prisoner of war records, *The War of the Rebellion: A Compilation of the Official Records of the Union and Confederate Armies*, militia records, newspaper casualty lists and obituaries, Confederate pension applications filed with the state of North Carolina, and the 1860 federal census of North Carolina. Secondary sources such as postwar rosters and histories, cemetery records, the *Confederate Veteran*, published genealogies, and records of the United Daughters of the Confederacy also provided useful information.

OFFICERS

CAPTAINS

UNDERWOOD, JOSEPH B.
Born in Sampson County where he resided as a "gentleman" prior to enlisting at age 24. Appointed Captain on March 3, 1862. Present or accounted for until he resigned on September 5, 1863. Reason he resigned not reported. Resignation accepted on September 17, 1863.

MURPHY, WILLIAM F.
Previously served as Private in Company B of this regiment. Appointed 1st Lieutenant and transferred to this company on March 17, 1862. Promoted to Captain on September 17, 1863. Present or accounted for until November-December, 1863, when he was reported absent without leave. Reported absent on detached service in January-February, 1864. Rejoined the company prior to May 16, 1864, when he was captured at Drewry's Bluff, Virginia. Confined at Point Lookout, Maryland, May 19, 1864. Transferred to Fort Delaware, Delaware, June 23, 1864. Transferred to Hilton Head, South Carolina, August 20, 1864. Reported in confinement at Fort Pulaski, Georgia, October 20, 1864. Transferred back to Hilton Head on an unspecified date. Reported at Hilton Head on January 1, 1865. Transferred to Fort Delaware where he arrived on March 12, 1865. Released at Fort Delaware on June 16, 1865, after taking the Oath of Allegiance.

LIEUTENANTS

BOYKIN, SOLOMON, 2nd Lieutenant
Previously served as Sergeant in Company I, 46th Regiment N.C. Troops. Appointed 2nd Lieutenant on June 12, 1862, and transferred to this company. Present or accounted for until wounded by the explosion of a shell at Goldsboro on December 17, 1862. Died on December 18, 1862, of wounds. He was "a brave officer and good man, always punctual to every duty." [*Fayetteville Observer* (Weekly), January 12, 1863.]

DUDLEY, ELI, JR., 3rd Lieutenant
Born in Sampson County and was by occupation a farm

laborer prior to enlisting in Sampson County at age 25, April 28, 1862, for the war. Mustered in as Sergeant. Wounded in the left hand at or near Cold Harbor, Virginia, on or about June 1, 1864. Elected 3rd Lieutenant on July 20, 1864. Returned to duty prior to September 1, 1864. Present or accounted for through December, 1864.

ELLIOTT, ALEXANDER, JR., 3rd Lieutenant
Resided in Cumberland County and was by occupation a farmer prior to enlisting in Cumberland County at age 26, July 5, 1862, for the war. Mustered in with an unspecified rank (either Private or Corporal). Promoted to Sergeant on August 13, 1862. Wounded slightly in the left hand at Goldsboro on December 17, 1862. Returned to duty prior to January 1, 1863. Present or accounted for until he was promoted to Sergeant Major on April 23, 1863, and transferred to the Field and Staff of this regiment. Appointed 3rd Lieutenant on October 1, 1863, and transferred back to this company. Present or accounted for until mortally wounded at Cold Harbor, Virginia, on the evening of June 1, 1864. Died on the morning of June 2, 1864, of wounds. [For an account of his death, see a letter dated June 5, 1864, from an unknown writer to Sophie Mallett, George E. London Collection, PC 1275, North Carolina Division of Archives and History, Raleigh.]

McKETHAN, EDWIN TURNER, 1st Lieutenant
Born in Sampson County on February 8, 1840, and resided in Cumberland County. Appointed 2nd Lieutenant on July 12, 1862. Reported absent sick from November 7, 1862, through February 28, 1863. Returned to duty in March-April, 1863. Promoted to 1st Lieutenant on September 17, 1863. Present or accounted for until September-October, 1864, when he was reported sick in hospital at Fayetteville. Reported absent on furlough in November, 1864. Retired to the Invalid Corps on December 13, 1864.

TEW, JOHN JOEL, 2nd Lieutenant
Born in Sampson County where he resided as a farmer prior to enlisting in Sampson County at age 25, April 4, 1862. Mustered in as Sergeant. Elected 3rd Lieutenant on December 24, 1862. Promoted to 2nd Lieutenant on September 17, 1863. Present or accounted for until wounded in the left arm (fracture) at Cold Harbor, Virginia, May 31, 1864. Reported absent wounded until January 24, 1865, when he returned to duty. Survived the war.

NONCOMMISSIONED OFFICERS AND PRIVATES

AMMONS, DANIEL J., Private
Enlisted in Cumberland County on July 8, 1862, for the war. Present or accounted for until hospitalized at Wilmington on or about February 8, 1863, with continued fever. Returned to duty in May-June, 1863. Present or accounted for until December 28, 1864, when he was reported absent without leave.

ANDERSON, ALEXANDER, Private
Resided in Cumberland County where he enlisted on

March 4, 1863, for the war. Present or accounted for until May-August, 1864, when he was reported sick at home. Reported sick in hospital at Fayetteville in September-October, 1864. Returned to duty in November-December, 1864. Hospitalized at Raleigh on January 18, 1865, with chronic diarrhoea. Captured in hospital at Raleigh on April 13, 1865. Paroled at Raleigh on April 22, 1865.

BAIN, JOHN G., Private
Enlisted in Cumberland County on July 8, 1862, for the war. Present or accounted for until hospitalized at Petersburg, Virginia, June 17, 1864, with intermittent fever. Transferred to hospital at Farmville, Virginia, June 20, 1864. Furloughed for sixty days on July 29, 1864. Returned to duty in September-October, 1864. Present or accounted for through December, 1864. Survived the war.

BASDON, KINION H., Private
Enlisted in Johnston County on June 25, 1862, for the war. Present or accounted for until September-October, 1863, when he was reported absent sick at Mount Pleasant, South Carolina. Returned to duty in November-December, 1863. Present or accounted for until November-December, 1864, when he was reported absent sick.

BASDON, KINION H., Private
Enlisted in Johnston County on June 26, 1862, for the war. Present or accounted for until captured at Drewry's Bluff, Virginia, May 16, 1864. Confined at Point Lookout, Maryland, May 19, 1864. Transferred to Elmira, New York, August 15, 1864. Died at Elmira on April 5, 1865, of "chro[nic] diarr[hoea]."

BENNETT, FLEET S., Sergeant
Born in Sampson County where he resided as a farm laborer prior to enlisting in Sampson County at age 25, April 25, 1862, for the war. Mustered in as Sergeant. Present or accounted for until July-October, 1862, when he was reported absent sick in Sampson County. Discharged on December 5, 1862, by reason of "bronchial inflammation which . . . will [probably] resolve itself into consumption and [also a] single inguinal hernia which is aggravated by his cough. I [the medical examining officer] believe the bronchitis to be a sequela of typhoid fever."

BLACKBURN, FELIX, Private
Born in Bladen County where he resided as a farmer prior to enlisting in New Hanover County at age 32, March 7, 1862. Present or accounted for until September 20, 1862, when he was reported absent without leave. Reported absent in confinement at Wilmington in November-December, 1862. Returned to duty in January-February, 1863. Present or accounted for until hospitalized at Petersburg, Virginia, February 6, 1864, with an unspecified complaint. Deserted from hospital at Petersburg on July 11, 1864. Returned to duty prior to September 1, 1864. Present or accounted for through December, 1864.

BLACKBURN, JAMES R., Private
Enlisted in New Hanover County on June 6, 1863, for the war. Present or accounted for through February, 1864.

Reported absent sick in May-October, 1864. Returned to duty in November-December, 1864. Present or accounted for through December, 1864.

BLACKBURN, RESIN, Private
Born in Bladen County where he resided as a farmer prior to enlisting at "Smith's Mills" at age 36, April 13, 1862. Present or accounted for until September-October, 1862, when he was reported absent without leave. Shot and killed by the Sampson County militia on November 22, 1862, "in their attempt to arrest him."

BOON, DAVID M., Private
Born in Sampson County and was by occupation a farmer prior to enlisting in Duplin County at age 21, March 29, 1862. Present or accounted for until hospitalized at Wilmington on July 24, 1862, with rheumatism. Furloughed on August 4, 1862. Reported absent sick through April, 1863. Returned to duty in May-June, 1863. Reported sick in hospital at Petersburg, Virginia, in May-August, 1864. Returned to duty in September-October, 1864. Present or accounted for through December, 1864. Survived the war.

BOONE, JOHN A. D., Sergeant
Enlisted in Cumberland County on July 7, 1862, for the war. Mustered in as Private. Promoted to Corporal in July-August, 1863. Reduced to ranks on January 28, 1864. Promoted to Sergeant in May-August, 1864. Present or accounted for until hospitalized at Farmville, Virginia, June 20, 1864, with debilitas. Furloughed for sixty days on July 27, 1864. Returned to duty in September-October, 1864. Reduced to ranks on October 19, 1864. Promoted to Sergeant on October 27, 1864. Present or accounted for through December, 1864.

BOYER, DANIEL, _____
North Carolina pension records indicate that he served in this company.

BRADSHAW, JOHN T., Private
Born in Sampson County and was by occupation a farmer prior to enlisting in Sampson County at age 27, April 23, 1862, for the war. Present or accounted for through February, 1864. Reported absent on detached service in May-December, 1864.

BRADSHAW, MOSES L., Private
Born in Sampson County and was by occupation a farmer prior to enlisting in Sampson County at age 27, May 3, 1862, for the war. Present or accounted for until July-August, 1863, when he was reported sick in hospital at Charleston, South Carolina. Returned to duty in September-October, 1863. Present or accounted for until January 6, 1864, when he was reported absent without leave. Returned to duty on July 25, 1864. Wounded in the thigh at Fort Harrison, Virginia, September 30, 1864. Returned to duty on November 21, 1864. Survived the war.

BRADSHAW, S. T., _____
North Carolina pension records indicate that he served in this company.

BRANCH, ALCEY, Private
Born in Sampson County where he resided as a farmer and turpentine laborer prior to enlisting in New Hanover County at age 28, March 19, 1862. Present or accounted for until wounded at Goldsboro on December 17, 1862. Returned to duty in January-February, 1863. Present or accounted for until wounded at Fort Wagner, Charleston, South Carolina, July 18, 1863. Hospitalized at Charleston where he died on July 28, 1863, of wounds.

BRONSON, CHARLES H., Corporal
Born in Sampson County and was by occupation a farmer prior to enlisting in Duplin County at age 22, March 29, 1862. Mustered in as Corporal. Present or accounted for through August, 1862. Dropped from the rolls of the company in September-October, 1862. Reason he was dropped not reported. [Previously served as 1st Lieutenant in the 24th Regiment N.C. Militia.]

BRONSON, JULIAN, Private
Born in Sampson County and was by occupation a farmer prior to enlisting in Sampson County at age 19, March 29, 1862. Reported absent sick in July-October, 1862. Discharged in November-December, 1862, after providing a substitute. [Previously served as 2nd Lieutenant in the 24th Regiment N.C. Militia.]

BRONSON, JULIUS J., Private
Born in Sampson County and was by occupation a farmer prior to enlisting in Duplin County at age 19, March 29, 1862. Died at Camp French, near Wilmington, August 5, 1862. Cause of death not reported.

BULLARD, GILES M., Private
Enlisted in Cumberland County on July 8, 1862, for the war. Present or accounted for through December, 1864. Reported absent on detached duty with the regimental quartermaster and in the mining corps (possibly as a teamster) during much of that period. No further records.

CAIN, EVAN, Private
Resided in Bladen County and was by occupation a turpentiner prior to enlisting in New Hanover County at age 37, August 21, 1862, for the war. Present or accounted for until November-December, 1862, when he was reported sick in hospital at Wilmington. Reported absent without leave on February 18, 1863. Died in hospital at Florence, South Carolina, March 6, 1863, of "erysipelas."

CHESTNUTT, SAMUEL H., Private
Born in Sampson County where he resided as a farmer prior to enlisting in New Hanover County at age 40, March 7, 1862. Present or accounted for until wounded at Goldsboro on December 17, 1862. Returned to duty prior to January 1, 1863. Present or accounted for until August 15, 1863, when he was reported absent without leave. Reported under arrest in September-December, 1863. Returned to duty in January-February, 1864. Present or accounted for through December, 1864.

COOK, THOMAS M., Private
Born in Sampson County and was by occupation a farmer

prior to enlisting in Duplin County at age 44, March 28, 1862. Present or accounted for until September-October, 1862, when he was reported sick in hospital at Goldsboro. Hospitalized at Wilmington on December 29, 1862, with pneumonia. Returned to duty on January 4, 1863. Present or accounted for until transferred to Company A, 15th Battalion South Carolina Heavy Artillery (Lucas's), May 1, 1863.

CORNBOW, THOMAS, Private
Enlisted in Cumberland County on March 4, 1863, for the war. Present or accounted for until April 27, 1863, when he was reported absent sick. Returned to duty in May-June, 1863. Present or accounted for until captured near Globe Tavern, Virginia, August 19, 1864. Confined at Point Lookout, Maryland, August 24, 1864. Paroled at Point Lookout on March 14, 1865. Received at Boulware's Wharf, James River, Virginia, March 16, 1865, for exchange. Hospitalized at Richmond, Virginia, March 17, 1865, with scorbutus. Furloughed on March 19, 1865.

CRUMPLER, CHARLES H., Private
Born in Sampson County and enlisted in this company at age 20, April 23, 1862, for the war. Mustered in as Sergeant. Reduced to ranks and dropped from the rolls of the company prior to September 1, 1862. Was reported to be a deserter from the 7th Regiment N.C. State Troops; however, no evidence that he served in the 7th Regiment has been located.

DAWSON, JOHN C., Private
Born in Sampson County and was by occupation a farmer prior to enlisting in Sampson County at age 16, April 28, 1862, for the war. Present or accounted for until hospitalized at Petersburg, Virginia, February 22, 1864, with anemia. Transferred to another hospital on March 17, 1864. Hospitalized at Petersburg on August 20, 1864, with debilitas and was transferred to Raleigh on August 23, 1864. Reported present in September-December, 1864. Survived the war.

DIXON, DANIEL H., 1st Sergeant
Born in Sampson County and was by occupation a farmer prior to enlisting in Sampson County at age 20, April 4, 1862. Mustered in as Private. Promoted to Corporal on January 31, 1863. Present or accounted for until wounded in the breast and left arm at Fort Wagner, Charleston, South Carolina, July 18, 1863. Returned to duty prior to September 1, 1863. Present or accounted for until wounded in the side (two ribs fractured) at Drewry's Bluff, Virginia, May 16, 1864. Hospitalized at Richmond, Virginia. Furloughed for sixty days on May 31, 1864. Returned to duty in September-October, 1864. Promoted to 1st Sergeant on November 1, 1864. Present or accounted for through December, 1864. Survived the war.

EDWARDS, H. F., Private
Resided in Sampson County. Place and date of enlistment not reported; however, he probably enlisted subsequent to December 31, 1864. Paroled at Goldsboro on May 20, 1865.

FANN, RICHARD H., Private
Born in Sampson County in 1837 and was by occupation a

farm laborer prior to enlisting in Sampson County on October 11, 1862, for the war. Present or accounted for until hospitalized at Wilmington on May 29, 1863, with debility. Returned to duty on July 4, 1863. Reported absent on sick furlough in September-October, 1863. Returned to duty in November-December, 1863. Present or accounted for until captured near Globe Tavern, Virginia, August 19, 1864. Confined at Point Lookout, Maryland, August 24, 1864. Paroled at Point Lookout on March 14, 1865. Received at Boulware's Wharf, James River, Virginia, March 16, 1865, for exchange. Survived the war.

FANN, WILEY, Private
Born in Sampson County in 1839 and was by occupation a cooper prior to enlisting in Sampson County on October 11, 1862, for the war. Present or accounted for until February 17, 1863, when he was reported absent sick. Returned to duty in March-April, 1863. Present or accounted for until September-October, 1863, when he was reported sick in hospital at Mount Pleasant, South Carolina. Returned to duty in November-December, 1863. Present or accounted for until wounded at Cold Harbor, Virginia, on or about June 1, 1864. Hospitalized at Richmond, Virginia, where he died on June 23, 1864, of wounds.

GADDY, ISRAEL D., Private
Born in South Carolina and resided in Cumberland County where he was by occupation a farmer prior to enlisting in Cumberland County at age 35, March 4, 1863, for the war. Present or accounted for until transferred to Company A, 2nd Regiment Confederate Engineers, August 3, 1863.

GAINEY, J. H., Private
Enlisted in Wake County on October 23, 1864, for the war. Present or accounted for through December, 1864.

GIDDENS, HENRY C., Sergeant
Enlisted in New Hanover County on February 6, 1863, for the war. Mustered in as Private. Promoted to Sergeant in March-August, 1864. Present or accounted for through December, 1864.

GIDDENS, JAMES T., Private
Born in Wayne County and resided in Sampson County where he was by occupation a merchant prior to enlisting in Sampson County at age 23, April 23, 1862, for the war. Mustered in as 1st Sergeant. Reduced to ranks prior to June 30, 1862. Discharged on June 30, 1862, after providing Private David J. Gore as a substitute. [Previously served as 2nd Lieutenant in the 24th Regiment N.C. Militia.]

GIDDENS, JOHN W., Private
Born in Wayne County and resided in Sampson County where he was by occupation a farmer prior to enlisting in Sampson County at age 27, April 28, 1862, for the war. Present or accounted for until discharged on June 1, 1862, by reason of "a fractured foot [suffered some fifteen years previously] that renders him unfit for a march. . . ." [Previously served as 1st Lieutenant in the 24th Regiment N.C. Militia.]

GODWIN, HIRAM, Private
Born in Sampson County where he resided as a farmer prior to enlisting in Sampson County at age 31, April 4, 1862. Present or accounted for through February, 1864. Transferred to Company B, 56th Regiment N.C. Troops, March 7, 1864.

GODWIN, WILLIAM L., Private
Born in Georgia and resided in Sampson County where he was by occupation a farm laborer prior to enlisting in Sampson County at age 24, May 6, 1862, for the war. Present or accounted for until September-October, 1863, when he was reported in the regimental hospital at Mount Pleasant, South Carolina. Returned to duty in November-December, 1863. Present or accounted for until captured at Cold Harbor, Virginia, May 31, 1864. Confined at Point Lookout, Maryland, June 8, 1864. Transferred to Elmira, New York, July 9, 1864. Paroled at Elmira on February 20, 1865, and transferred to the James River, Virginia, for exchange. Survived the war.

GOFF, WILEY, Private
Born in 1822 and resided in Sampson County where he was by occupation a cooper prior to enlisting in New Hanover County on April 28, 1862, for the war. Present or accounted for until January 6, 1864, when he was reported absent without leave. Returned to duty in May-August, 1864. Present or accounted for through December, 1864. Survived the war. [North Carolina pension records indicate that he was wounded at Charleston, South Carolina, in 1863.]

GORE, DAVID J., Private
Born in Sampson County and was by occupation a farmer prior to enlisting in New Hanover County on June 14, 1862, for the war as a substitute for Private James T. Giddens. Present or accounted for until February 17, 1863, when he was reported absent without leave. Returned to duty in March-April, 1863. Reported on detached duty with the engineer department at Wilmington from July, 1863, through February, 1864. Transferred to Company A, 2nd Regiment Confederate Engineers, prior to September 1, 1864.

HARRIS, JOHN H., Private
Enlisted in Lenoir County on October 19, 1862, for the war. Reported absent without leave in November-December, 1862. Returned to duty in January-February, 1863. Reported absent sick on April 7, 1863. Furloughed for thirty days on April 24, 1863. Failed to return from furlough and was listed as a deserter on or about May 24, 1863.

HAWLEY, EDWARD, Private
Born in Sampson County and was by occupation a farmer prior to enlisting in Sampson County at age 27, April 4, 1862. Present or accounted for until wounded in the breast at Fort Wagner, Charleston, South Carolina, July 30-August 3, 1863. Returned to duty prior to September 1, 1863. Present or accounted for until December 28, 1864, when he was reported absent without leave.

HAWLEY, JONATHAN, Private
Born in Sampson County and was by occupation a farm

hand and student prior to enlisting in New Hanover County at age 16, May 6, 1862, for the war. Present or accounted for until November-December, 1862, when he was reported absent without leave. Reported absent sick on February 17, 1863. Reported absent without leave on March 17, 1863. Reported absent sick or absent without leave through February, 1864. Returned to duty in May-August, 1864. Present or accounted for until October, 1864, when he was reported absent without leave. Survived the war.

HAWLEY, SAMSON, Sergeant
Born in Sampson County and was by occupation a farmer prior to enlisting in New Hanover County at age 24, May 6, 1862, for the war. Mustered in as Corporal. Promoted to Sergeant on January 31, 1863. Present or accounted for until July-August, 1863, when he was reported sick in hospital at Mount Pleasant, South Carolina. Returned to duty in September-October, 1863. Present or accounted for until wounded at Cold Harbor, Virginia, May 31, 1864. Died on or about the same date of wounds.

HAWLEY, THOMAS JAMES, Private
Born in Sampson County in 1837 and was by occupation a farmer prior to enlisting in Sampson County on February 9, 1863, for the war. Sent to hospital sick on April 7, 1863. Furloughed for thirty days on April 22, 1863. Returned to duty prior to July 1, 1863. Reported absent sick in July-October, 1863. Returned to duty in November-December, 1863. Reported absent without leave on January 5, 1864. Rejoined the company on or about February 3, 1864, and was placed under arrest. Returned to duty prior to July 15, 1864, when he was reported absent without leave.

HOLLINGSWORTH, ALFRED, Private
Resided in Duplin County and was by occupation a farmer prior to enlisting in Duplin County at age 28, February 13, 1863, for the war. Present or accounted for until discharged on June 1, 1863. Reason discharged not reported.

HOLLINGSWORTH, BENJAMIN F., Corporal
Enlisted in Cumberland County on March 4, 1863, for the war. Mustered in as Private. Present or accounted for until hospitalized at Wilmington on May 27, 1863, with typhoid fever. Returned to duty on June 16, 1863. Reported in hospital at Charleston, South Carolina, in July-August, 1863. Returned to duty in September-October, 1863. Promoted to Corporal in March-August, 1864. Present or accounted for until wounded in the neck (flesh) and captured at Fort Harrison, Virginia, September 30, 1864. Hospitalized at Fort Monroe, Virginia. Transferred to Point Lookout, Maryland, on or about December 21, 1864. Paroled at Point Lookout on March 17, 1865. Received at Boulware's Wharf, James River, Virginia, March 19, 1865, for exchange.

HOUSLIVER, E., Private
Place and date of enlistment not reported. A regimental return dated May, 1862, states that he was absent on picket duty. No further records.

JACKSON, JOHN R., Private
Born in Sampson County and was by occupation a farmer prior to enlisting in Sampson County at age 20, April 5, 1862. Present or accounted for until February 3, 1863, when he was reported absent on sick furlough. Reported present but sick in March-April, 1863. Returned to duty in May-June, 1863. Reported sick in hospital at Augusta, Georgia, in July-December, 1863. Returned to duty in January-February, 1864. Present or accounted for until captured near Globe Tavern, Virginia, August 19, 1864. Confined at Point Lookout, Maryland, August 24, 1864. Exchanged on September 30, 1864. Hospitalized at Richmond, Virginia, with chronic diarrhoea. Furloughed on October 11, 1864. Reported absent sick through December, 1864. Survived the war.

JACKSON, LEWIS, Private
Born in Sampson County and resided in Duplin County where he was by occupation a farm laborer prior to enlisting in Sampson County at age 18, April 5, 1862. Present or accounted for until captured near Petersburg, Virginia, June 15, 1864. Confined at Point Lookout, Maryland, June 19, 1864. Transferred to Elmira, New York, July 9, 1864. Released at Elmira on July 3, 1865, after taking the Oath of Allegiance.

JACKSON, MONK L., Private
Born in Sampson County and was by occupation a farmer prior to enlisting in Sampson County at age 24, April 4, 1862. Present or accounted for until he deserted on October 15, 1862. [May have served previously as Private in Company D, 38th Regiment N.C. Troops.]

JACKSON, THOMAS, Private
Born in Sampson County and was by occupation a "mechanical farmer" prior to enlisting in Sampson County at age 26, March 27, 1862. Present or accounted for until September-October, 1863, when he was reported sick in hospital at Charleston, South Carolina. Reported absent without leave on December 31, 1863. Returned to duty in January-February, 1864. Present or accounted for until hospitalized at Richmond, Virginia, November 26, 1864, with chronic diarrhoea. Returned to duty on or about December 15, 1864. Survived the war.

JACKSON, W. H., Private
Enlisted in Wake County on May 15, 1862, for the war. Deserted prior to June 1, 1862.

JAMES, JOSEPH T., Private
Enlisted in Cumberland County at age 23, July 7, 1862, for the war. Mustered in as Private. Promoted to Corporal in September-October, 1862. Promoted to Sergeant on November 1, 1863. Reduced to ranks on January 28, 1864. Present or accounted for until wounded at or near Cold Harbor, Virginia, on or about June 1, 1864. Reported absent wounded or absent sick until January 5, 1865, when he returned to duty. Survived the war.

JOHNSON, DAVID CLARK, Private
Born in Sampson County on June 26, 1845, and was by occupation a farm laborer prior to enlisting in Sampson

County on February 10, 1863, for the war. Sent to hospital on April 27, 1863. Reported absent sick through June, 1863. Returned to duty in July-August, 1863. Present or accounted for until hospitalized at Petersburg, Virginia, in May-August, 1864, with an unspecified complaint. Returned to duty in September-October, 1864. Present or accounted for through December, 1864. Survived the war.

JOHNSON, GEORGE A., Private

Born in Sampson County in 1845 and was by occupation a farm laborer prior to enlisting in Sampson County on November 1, 1863, for the war. Present or accounted for until he died at Richmond, Virginia, July 28, 1864, of "diarrhoea."

JORDAN, HAYWOOD, Private

Born in Sampson County where he resided as a farmer prior to enlisting in Sampson County at age 32, March 27, 1862. Present or accounted for until July-October, 1862, when he was reported absent sick. Discharged on December 5, 1862, by reason of "phthisis pulmonalis."

JORDAN, JAMES ERVIN, Private

Born in Sampson County and was by occupation a farm laborer prior to enlisting in Sampson County at age 31, March 27, 1862. Reported absent on detached service at Wilmington with the quartermaster's department from January 17 through August 31, 1863. Returned to duty in September-October, 1863. Present or accounted for until captured near Petersburg, Virginia, on or about June 16, 1864. Confined at Point Lookout, Maryland, June 23, 1864. Paroled at Point Lookout on March 14, 1865. Received at Boulware's Wharf, James River, Virginia, March 16, 1865, for exchange. Survived the war. [North Carolina pension records indicate that he suffered frostbitten feet during the war.]

JORDAN, WILLIAM ROBB, Private

Born in Sampson County and resided in Duplin County where he was by occupation a farm laborer prior to enlisting in Sampson County at age 24, March 27, 1862. Present or accounted for until captured at Goldsboro on December 17, 1862. Paroled on or about the same date. Returned to duty in January-February, 1863. Reported absent sick in July-August, 1863. Returned to duty in September-October, 1863. Reported absent sick in November, 1863-February, 1864. Returned to duty prior to June 15, 1864, when he was captured near Petersburg, Virginia. Confined at Point Lookout, Maryland, June 19, 1864. Transferred to Elmira, New York, July 9, 1864. Released at Elmira on July 3, 1865, after taking the Oath of Allegiance.

JOYNER, DAVID, _____

North Carolina pension records indicate that he served in this company.

LAYTON, ISAAC W., Sergeant

Born in Sampson County and was by occupation a farmer prior to enlisting in Sampson County at age 21, April 4, 1862. Mustered in as Private. Promoted to Corporal on November 1, 1863. Reduced to ranks on or about January 28, 1864. Promoted to Corporal prior to June 1, 1864. Present or accounted for until wounded in Virginia, June

2-23, 1864. Returned to duty prior to September 1, 1864. Promoted to Sergeant on November 1, 1864. Present or accounted for through December, 1864.

LAYTON, SHERWOOD, Private

Born in Sampson County and was by occupation a farmer prior to enlisting in Sampson County at age 35, April 4, 1862. Present or accounted for until January 30, 1863, when he was hospitalized at Wilmington. Reported absent sick until June 1, 1863, when he was discharged by reason of "hypertrophy of the heart. . . ."

LEE, ERASMUS, Private

Resided in Cumberland County and was by occupation a farmer prior to enlisting in Cumberland County at age 22, July 8, 1862, for the war. Present or accounted for until he was sent to hospital sick on April 27, 1863. Returned to duty in May-June, 1863. Reported absent sick in July-August, 1863. Reported present but sick in September-October, 1863. Returned to duty in November-December, 1863. Present or accounted for until hospitalized at Richmond, Virginia, October 5, 1864, with remittent fever. Returned to duty on November 12, 1864. Present or accounted for through December, 1864. Survived the war.

LEE, JOHN B., Private

Born in Sampson County in 1846 and enlisted in Cumberland County on May 24, 1864, for the war. Died in Sampson County on October 16, 1864, of disease.

LEE, SIR WILLIAM, Private

Previously served as Private in Company B, 56th Regiment N.C. Troops. Transferred to this company on March 7, 1864. Captured at Cold Harbor, Virginia, June 1, 1864. Confined at Point Lookout, Maryland, June 11, 1864. Transferred to Elmira, New York, July 12, 1864. Killed in a railroad accident at Shohola, Pennsylvania, July 15, 1864, while en route to Elmira.

McDERMON, H. H., Private

Enlisted in Cumberland County on March 4, 1863, for the war. Deserted on May 1, 1863.

McKENZIE, ROBERT McK., Private

Born in Sampson County in 1837 and was by occupation a farm laborer prior to enlisting in Sampson County on March 21, 1862. Reported absent sick in May-August, 1862. Listed as a deserter in September-October, 1862. Dropped from the rolls of the company in November-December, 1862.

McKETHAN, AUGUSTUS A., JR., Private

Enlisted in Cumberland County on April 28, 1864, for the war. Wounded in Virginia, June 2-23, 1864. Returned to duty prior to September 1, 1864. Appointed 3rd Lieutenant on November 4, 1864, and transferred to Company B of this regiment.

McMILLAN, WILLIAM DOUGALD, Private

Enlisted at Camp Holmes, near Raleigh, February 8, 1864, for the war. Present or accounted for until promoted to Sergeant Major and transferred to the Field and Staff of this regiment on or about July 6, 1864. [North Carolina pension records indicate that he was wounded at Drewry's Bluff, Virginia, on an unspecified date.]

MORGAN, JOHN NATHAN, Private

Born in Sampson County in 1841 and was by occupation a student prior to enlisting in Sampson County on July 8, 1863, for the war. Present or accounted for through October, 1864; however, he was reported absent on detached service with the brigade quartermaster during that entire period. Rejoined the company in November-December, 1864. Paroled at Greensboro on May 1, 1865.

MUNNS, WASHINGTON W., Private

Enlisted in Cumberland County on March 4, 1863, for the war. Present or accounted for through June, 1863. Reported absent on sick furlough in July-October, 1863. Returned to duty in November-December, 1863. Present or accounted for until May-December, 1864, when he was reported on detached duty (probably as a teamster) at Petersburg, Virginia.

MURPHY, HUGH N., Private

Born in New Hanover County and was by occupation a farmer prior to enlisting in Duplin County at age 33, March 28, 1862. Present or accounted for until July 25, 1864, when he was reported absent without leave.

MURPHY, JOHN A., Private

Born in New Hanover County and was by occupation a farmer prior to enlisting in Duplin County at age 23, March 28, 1862. Appointed Ordnance Sergeant and transferred to the Field and Staff of this regiment on May 2, 1862. Reenlisted in this company at Camp Holmes, near Raleigh, October 16, 1864, for the war. Reported absent sick through December, 1864.

PARKER, JACK WYLIE, Private

Resided in Harnett County and enlisted in Sampson County on July 1, 1863, for the war. Reported sick in hospital at Charleston, South Carolina, in July-August, 1863. Reported absent on sick furlough in September-October, 1863. Returned to duty in November-December, 1863. Present or accounted for through December, 1864. Took the Oath of Allegiance at Raleigh on May 24, 1865.

PARKER, NOEL, Private

Born in Sampson County and was by occupation a farmer prior to enlisting in New Hanover County at age 42, May 6, 1862, for the war. Present or accounted for until November-December, 1862, when he was reported absent without leave. Left sick at Wilmington on February 12, 1863. Returned to duty in March-April, 1863. Reported absent without leave in May-June, 1863. Returned to duty on or about August 8, 1863. Present or accounted for until January-July, 1864, when he was reported absent sick. Reported absent without leave on August 10, 1864.

POPE, JAMES A., Private

Born in Sampson County and was by occupation a farmer prior to enlisting in Sampson County at age 42, March 26, 1862. Present or accounted for until September-October, 1862, when he was reported sick in hospital at Goldsboro. Returned to duty in November-December, 1862. Present or accounted for until September-October, 1863, when he was reported sick in hospital at Mount Pleasant, South Carolina. Reported sick in hospital at Wilmington in November-December, 1863. Reported absent without leave in January-February, 1864. Reported absent sick in April-October, 1864. Hospitalized at Richmond, Virginia, November 26, 1864, with chronic diarrhoea. Returned to duty on December 16, 1864. Reported absent sick on or about December 31, 1864.

POPE, MICHAEL S., Private

Born in Sampson County in 1845 and resided in Sampson County where he was by occupation a farm laborer prior to enlisting in Sampson County on April 15, 1862. Reported missing in the battle at the Neuse River Bridge, near Goldsboro, December 17, 1862. Returned to duty in January-February, 1863. Present or accounted for through December, 1864. Paroled at Greensboro on May 1, 1865.

POPE, MILTON, Private

Born in Sampson County in 1832 and resided in Sampson County where he was by occupation a farmer prior to enlisting in Sampson County on March 27, 1862. Present or accounted for until captured near Goldsboro on December 17, 1862. Paroled on an unspecified date. Returned to duty prior to January 1, 1863. Present or accounted for until wounded in the neck and shoulder at Cold Harbor, Virginia, June 1, 1864. Hospitalized at Richmond, Virginia. Furloughed for sixty days on June 7, 1864. Reported absent wounded until January 5, 1865, when he returned to duty.

POPE, OLLEN, Private

Born in Sampson County in 1815 and resided in Sampson County where he was by occupation a farmer prior to enlisting in Sampson County on March 14, 1862. Present or accounted for until he died at Camp Campbell, near Kinston, September 18, 1862, of "typhoid fever."

RICH, WILLIAM H., Private

Born in Sampson County where he resided as a farmer prior to enlisting in Duplin County at age 37, March 28, 1862. Present or accounted for until July 15, 1863, when he was reported absent without leave. Returned to duty in September-October, 1863. Present or accounted for until December 4, 1863, when he was reported absent without leave. Returned to duty on or about September 20, 1864. Wounded in the head at Fort Harrison, Virginia, September 30, 1864. Reported in hospital at Richmond, Virginia, on or about November 1, 1864. Reported absent without leave on December 10, 1864.

ROGERS, DAVID F., Private

Born in Sampson County and was by occupation a farmer prior to enlisting in Duplin County at age 21, March 29, 1862. Present or accounted for until September-December, 1862, when he was reported absent sick. Reported absent without leave on February 15, 1863. Returned to duty in March-April, 1863. Present or accounted for until captured near Globe Tavern, Virginia, August 19, 1864. Confined at Point Lookout, Maryland, August 24, 1864. Died at Point Lookout on March 24, 1865, of "acute dysentery."

ROGERS, JOSEPH, Private

Born in Sampson County or in South Carolina and was by occupation a farmer prior to enlisting in Sampson County at age 38, March 4, 1862. Present or accounted for until hospitalized at Wilmington on July 22, 1862, with chronic diarrhoea. Discharged on August 5, 1862, by reason of disability. Later served as Private in Company K, 31st Regiment N.C. Troops.

ROYAL, TOLBERT P., Private

Born in Sampson County where he resided as a farm laborer prior to enlisting in Sampson County at age 30, April 14, 1862. Reported absent sick in May-June, 1862. Returned to duty in July-August, 1862. Present or accounted for until wounded at Goldsboro on December 17, 1862. Reported absent wounded or absent sick through December, 1864.

RYALS, LEWIT W., Private

Enlisted in Cumberland County on July 8, 1862, for the war. Reported absent without leave in November-December, 1862. Returned to duty in January-February, 1863. Present or accounted for until August 15, 1863, when he was reported absent without leave. Reported in prison at Charleston, South Carolina, awaiting trial in September-October, 1863. Returned to duty in January-February, 1864. Died in hospital at Petersburg, Virginia, May 4, 1864, of "pneumonia."

SESSOMS, DICKSON, Private

Enlisted in New Hanover County on November 22, 1862, for the war. Hospitalized at Wilmington on February 17, 1863. Returned to duty in May-June, 1863. Present or accounted for until January-August, 1864, when he was reported absent sick. Returned to duty in September-October, 1864. Reported absent sick in November-December, 1864.

SILLS, DAVID, Private

Born in Sampson County where he resided as a farmer prior to enlisting in Sampson County at age 44, April 4, 1862. Reported absent without leave in September-October, 1862. Returned to duty in November-December, 1862. Present or accounted for until May-June, 1863, when he was reported to be awaiting trial at Wilmington (presumably for absence without leave). Returned to duty in July-August, 1863. Reported absent without leave on September 27, 1863. Returned to duty on October 30, 1863. Present or accounted for until December 28, 1864, when he was reported absent without leave.

SILLS, HENRY WASHINGTON, Private

Resided in Sampson County and was by occupation a farmer prior to enlisting in Sampson County at age 17, April 4, 1862. Present or accounted for until January-February, 1864, when he was reported under arrest. Reason he was arrested not reported. Returned to duty on an unspecified date. Reported present in May-December, 1864. Captured by Federal forces in Sampson County on March 16, 1865. Sent to New Bern. Confined at Hart's Island, New York Harbor, April 10, 1865. Released at Hart's Island on June 19, 1865, after taking the Oath of Allegiance.

SILLS, JOEL, _____

North Carolina pension records indicate that he served in this company.

SILLS, WILLIAM T., Private

Born in Sampson County where he resided as a farmer prior to enlisting in Sampson County at age 19, April 4, 1862. Present or accounted for until wounded in the left hand at Cold Harbor, Virginia, June 1, 1864. Returned to duty prior to September 1, 1864. Present or accounted for until captured in Sampson County on March 16, 1865. Confined at Hart's Island, New York Harbor, April 10, 1865. Released at Hart's Island on June 21, 1865, after taking the Oath of Allegiance.

SIMMONS, JAMES, Private

Born in Sampson County in 1839 and resided in Sampson County where he was by occupation a farm laborer prior to enlisting in Sampson County on March 27, 1862. Present or accounted for until hospitalized at Wilmington on or about July 22, 1862, with chronic diarrhoea. Returned to duty on August 4, 1862. Reported sick in hospital at Wilmington in September-October, 1862. Returned to duty in November-December, 1862. Present or accounted for until captured at Cold Harbor, Virginia, June 1, 1864. Confined at Point Lookout, Maryland, June 11, 1864. Transferred to Elmira, New York, July 12, 1864. Paroled at Elmira on October 11, 1864. Received at Venus Point, Savannah River, Georgia, November 15, 1864, for exchange.

SIMMONS, LEMON L., Private

Resided in Sampson County and was by occupation a farmer prior to enlisting in New Hanover County at age 27, March 19, 1862. Died in hospital at Wilmington on July 8, 1862, of a "congestive chill" following "typhoid fever."

SIMPSON, WILLIAM A., Private

Was by occupation a farmer prior to enlisting at Marietta, Georgia, March 1, 186[3], for the war. Hospitalized at Wilmington on June 5, 1863, with debility. Returned to duty on July 23, 1863. Present or accounted for through October, 1863. Hospitalized at Wilmington on an unspecified date with a gunshot wound of the right foot received from his own pistol. Transferred to Company C, 1st Regiment Georgia Infantry (Olmstead's), November 15, 1863.

STANLEY, ALFRED C., Private

Resided in Johnston County and enlisted in New Hanover County on February 6, 1863, for the war. Present or accounted for until wounded in the shoulder (collarbone broken) at Drewry's Bluff, Virginia, May 16, 1864. Hospitalized at Richmond, Virginia. Furloughed for sixty days on June 7, 1864. Returned to duty prior to September 1, 1864. Present or accounted for through December, 1864. Captured at or near Bentonville on or about March 22, 1865. Sent to New Bern. Confined at Hart's Island, New York Harbor, April 10, 1865. Released at Hart's Island on June 19, 1865, after taking the Oath of Allegiance.

STONE, JOHN P., Private
Born in Moore County and was by occupation a farmer prior to enlisting in Sampson County at age 24, April 4, 1862. Mustered in as Corporal. Present or accounted for until wounded at Goldsboro on December 17, 1862. Returned to duty in January-February, 1863. Promoted to Sergeant on April 23, 1863. Reported sick in hospital at Charleston, South Carolina, in July-August, 1863. Reported absent without leave on September 16, 1863. Reduced to ranks on October 8, 1863. Reported absent sick from November, 1863, through August, 1864. Discharged on September 9, 1864, by reason of disability. [Previously served as 1st Lieutenant in the 24th Regiment N.C. Militia.]

STRICKLAND, EDWIN B., Private
Born in Sampson County in 1841 and resided in Sampson County where he was by occupation a farm laborer prior to enlisting in Sampson County on April 23, 1862, for the war. Present or accounted for until he was left sick in camp on December 18, 1862. Reported absent without leave on April 25, 1863. Reported absent sick or absent without leave through December, 1863. Reported absent sick in January-December, 1864.

STRICKLAND, ROBERT M., Private
Born in Sampson County in 1831 and was by occupation a turpentine laborer prior to enlisting in Sampson County on April 23, 1862, for the war. Reported absent without leave in September-October, 1862. Returned to duty in November-December, 1862. Present or accounted for until May-June, 1864, when he was reported absent without leave for eighteen days. Returned to duty in July-August, 1863. Present or accounted for until December 28, 1864, when he was reported absent without leave. Survived the war.

STRICKLAND, WILLIAM A., Private
Born in Sampson County and was by occupation a laborer prior to enlisting in Sampson County at age 33, April 1, 1862. Present or accounted for until July-August, 1863, when he was reported absent on detached service in the engineer department at Wilmington. Reported sick in hospital at Wilmington in September-October, 1863. Reported absent without leave on November 23, 1863. Returned to duty subsequent to February 29, 1864. Reported absent on detached service near Petersburg, Virginia, in May-August, 1864. Reported absent on duty with the engineer department in September-December, 1864. Survived the war.

STRICKLAND, WILLIAM T., Private
Born in Sampson County and was by occupation a day laborer prior to enlisting in Sampson County at age 24, April 4, 1862. Present or accounted for until July 15, 1863, when he was reported absent without leave. Reported present but sick in September-October, 1863. Returned to duty in November-December, 1863. Present or accounted for until May-August, 1864, when he was reported in hospital near Petersburg, Virginia. Returned to duty in September-October, 1864. Present or accounted for through December, 1864. Wounded in the right hip at Bentonville on March 20, 1865. Survived the war.

SUTTON, PHILIP, Private
Born in Sampson County where he resided as a farmer prior to enlisting in Sampson County at age 41, March 28, 1862. Reported absent sick in July-August, 1862. Returned to duty in September-October, 1862. Reported sick in hospital at Wilmington on February 17, 1863. Returned to duty in March-April, 1863. Present or accounted for until January-February, 1864, when he was reported absent sick. Returned to duty on an unspecified date. Wounded in the chest and captured near Globe Tavern, Virginia, August 19, 1864. Died in hospital at City Point, Virginia, August 23, 1864, of wounds.

TEW, BEDFORD, Private
Born in Sampson County in 1838 and resided in Cumberland County where he was by occupation a laborer prior to enlisting in Cumberland County on July 10, 1862, for the war. Present or accounted for through February, 1863. Reported absent without leave for seventeen days in March-April, 1863. Reported absent on sick furlough in May-June, 1863. Reported absent without leave on July 28, 1863. Returned to duty on October 5, 1863. Present or accounted for until December 28, 1864, when he was reported absent without leave.

TEW, HOLLY, _____
North Carolina pension records indicate that he served in this company.

TEW, JOHN L., Private
Born in Sampson County where he resided as a farmer prior to enlisting in Sampson County at age 23, April 4, 1862. Present or accounted for until he died in hospital at Wilmington on May 16, 1863, of "pneumonia."

TEW, LEWIS M., Corporal
Born in Sampson County in 1835 and resided in Sampson County where he was by occupation a farmer prior to enlisting in New Hanover County on July 5, 1862, for the war. Mustered in as Private. Promoted to Corporal in March-August, 1864. Present or accounted for through December, 1864. Survived the war.

TEW, MARTIN B., Private
Born in Sampson County in 1842 and resided in Sampson County where he was by occupation a farm laborer prior to enlisting in Sampson County on April 26, 1862, for the war. Present or accounted for until November-December, 1862, when he was reported absent without leave. Returned to duty in January-February, 1863. Present or accounted for through December, 1864. Paroled at Greensboro on May 1, 1865.

TEW, MYUTT M., Private
Born in Sampson County in 1837 and was by occupation a farmer prior to enlisting in New Hanover County on July 5, 1862, for the war. Present or accounted for until September-October, 1863, when he was reported absent sick. Returned to duty in November-December, 1863. Present or accounted for through December, 1864.

TREADWELL, JOHN R., Private
Born in Sampson County in 1835 and resided in Sampson

County where he was by occupation a farmer prior to enlisting in Sampson County on March 28, 1862. Present or accounted for through June, 1862. Reported absent sick in July-December, 1862. Reported absent without leave on February 25, 1863. Returned to duty in March-April, 1863. Present or accounted for through June, 1863. Reported absent sick in July, 1863-February, 1864. Returned to duty on an unspecified date. Captured near Globe Tavern, Virginia, August 19, 1864. Confined at Point Lookout, Maryland, August 22, 1864. Paroled at Point Lookout on January 17, 1865. Received at Boulware's Wharf, James River, Virginia, January 21, 1865, for exchange.

VANN, CHESTER R., 1st Sergeant

Born in Sampson County where he resided as a farmer prior to enlisting in Duplin County at age 32, March 29, 1862. Mustered in as Private. Promoted to 1st Sergeant on July 1, 1862. Present or accounted for until hospitalized at Wilmington on May 29, 1863, with diarrhoea. Furloughed for twenty days on June 16, 1863. Returned to duty in July-August, 1863. Present or accounted for until captured at Cold Harbor, Virginia, June 1, 1864. Confined at Point Lookout, Maryland, June 11, 1864. Transferred to Elmira, New York, July 12, 1864. Died at Elmira on October 29, 1864, of "pneumonia."

WADE, DUNCAN B., Private

Resided in Cumberland County where he enlisted at age 22, July 4, 1862, for the war. Present or accounted for until he died at Wilmington on September 10, 1862, of "typhoid fever."

WADE, L. A., Private

Enlisted in Sampson County on June 9, 1863, for the war. Present or accounted for until he deserted on August 6, 1863.

WALKER, A. C., Private

Enlisted in Cumberland County on May 16, 1862, for the war. Reported absent without leave in July-August, 1862. Returned to duty in September-October, 1862. Present or accounted for until wounded at Cold Harbor, Virginia, on or about June 1, 1864. Died at Cold Harbor on or about the same date.

WARREN, JOHN T., Private

Born in Sampson County in 1839 and resided in Sampson County where he was by occupation a farmer prior to enlisting in Sampson County on February 9, 1863, for the war. Present or accounted for until July 10, 1863, when he was reported sick in hospital at Wilmington. Returned to duty in September-October, 1863. Present or accounted for until May-August, 1864, when he was reported absent wounded. Place and date wounded not reported. Reported sick at home in September-October, 1864. Reported absent without leave on December 10, 1864.

WARREN, RICHARD, Sergeant

Born in Sampson County where he resided as a farmer prior to enlisting in Sampson County at age 40, April 4, 1862. Mustered in as Private. Promoted to Sergeant in November-December, 1862. Wounded slightly at Goldsboro on December 17, 1862. Returned to duty in

January-February, 1863. Sent to hospital at Charleston, South Carolina, April 20, 1863. Returned to duty in May-June, 1863. Present or accounted for until wounded at Cold Harbor, Virginia, on or about June 1, 1864. Died on or about the same date of wounds. [Previously served as Captain in the 25th Regiment N.C. Militia.]

WATKINS, BLAKE, Private

Resided in Sampson County and was by occupation a farmer prior to enlisting in Duplin County at age 38, March 28, 1862. Present or accounted for until captured at Drewry's Bluff, Virginia, May 16, 1864. Confined at Point Lookout, Maryland, May 21, 1864. Paroled at Point Lookout and transferred to Cox's Wharf, James River, Virginia, where he was received on or about February 15, 1865, for exchange.

WATSON, THOMAS F., Private

Born in Sampson County in 1845 and was by occupation a laborer prior to enlisting in Sampson County on February 9, 1863, for the war. Reported absent on sick furlough in May-June, 1863. Returned to duty in July-August, 1863. Reported absent sick at Wilson in November-December, 1863. Reported absent without leave on February 14, 1864. Reported absent sick in May-October, 1864. Reported absent without leave on December 10, 1864. Survived the war.

WELLONS, J. D. T., Private

Resided in Johnston County and enlisted in Sampson County on July 5, 1862, for the war. Present or accounted for through December, 1864; however, he was reported on detail as a hospital nurse or hospital steward during most of that period. Paroled at Goldsboro on May 29, 1865.

WILLIFORD, JASON TOUNLEY, Private

Born in Sampson County where he resided as a farmer prior to enlisting in Sampson or Duplin County at age 18, April 4, 1862. Present or accounted for until captured at Fort Harrison, Virginia, September 30, 1864. Confined at Point Lookout, Maryland, where he died on February 11, 1865, of "chronic diarrhoea."

WILLIFORD, JOHN C., SR., Private

Resided in Cumberland County and was by occupation a turpentiner prior to enlisting in Cumberland County at age 28, July 8, 1862, for the war. Mustered in as Private. Present or accounted for until February 17, 1863, when he was reported absent sick. Returned to duty in March-April, 1863. Promoted to Corporal on April 23, 1863. Reported sick in hospital at Charleston, South Carolina, in July-August, 1863. Reduced to ranks on July 18, 1863. Reported absent without leave on October 28, 1863. Returned to duty in November-December, 1863. Present or accounted for until captured at Fort Harrison, Virginia, September 30, 1864. Confined at Point Lookout, Maryland, October 5, 1864. Paroled at Point Lookout on March 17, 1865. Received at Boulware's Wharf, James River, Virginia, March 19, 1865, for exchange. Hospitalized at Richmond, Virginia, March 19, 1865, with rheumatism. Furloughed for thirty days on March 20, 1865.

WILLIFORD, JOHN CAGER, Private
Born in Sampson County in 1830 and was by occupation a farmer prior to enlisting in Sampson County on November 1, 1863, for the war. Present or accounted for through December, 1864. Survived the war.

WILLIFORD, RICHARD, Private
Born in Sampson County in 1830 and resided in Sampson County where he was by occupation a farmer prior to enlisting in Sampson County on April 4, 1862. Present or accounted for through June, 1863. Reported absent on detached service at the regimental hospital in July-October, 1863. Returned to duty in November-December, 1863. Present or accounted for until captured at Cold Harbor, Virginia, June 1, 1864. Confined at Point Lookout, Maryland, June 11, 1864. Transferred to Elmira, New York, July 12, 1864. Paroled at Elmira on February 20, 1865, and transferred to the James River, Virginia, for exchange. Hospitalized at Richmond, Virginia, March 4, 1865, with rheumatism and was furloughed for thirty days on March 10, 1865. Survived the war.

WILLIFORD, SIR WILLIAM, Private
Resided in Sampson County and enlisted in Sampson or Duplin County at age 19, April 4, 1862. Reported absent sick in May-June, 1862. Returned to duty in July-August, 1862. Present or accounted for until wounded in the left leg at Drewry's Bluff, Virginia, May 16, 1864. Hospitalized at Richmond, Virginia. Furloughed for sixty days on May 27, 1864. Returned to duty in November-December, 1864. Captured in Sampson County on March 16, 1865. Confined at Hart's Island, New York Harbor, April 17, 1865. Released at Hart's Island on June 19, 1865, after taking the Oath of Allegiance.

WILLIFORD, TOWNLEY, Private
Resided in Sampson County and was by occupation a farmer prior to enlisting in Sampson or Duplin County at age 34, April 4, 1862. Present or accounted for until hospitalized at Wilmington on July 23, 1863, with dropsy.

Returned to duty on August 8, 1863. Reported absent sick in September-October, 1863. Returned to duty in November-December, 1863. Reported absent without leave from January 5 until February 17, 1864. Reported present in May-October, 1864. Reported absent without leave on December 28, 1864.

WILLIFORD, W. J. T., Private
Resided in Sampson County where he enlisted at age 19, May 2, 1862, for the war. Present or accounted for until wounded at Drewry's Bluff, Virginia, May 16, 1864. Died on the same date of wounds.

MISCELLANEOUS

Civil War records indicate that the following soldiers served in the 51st Regiment N.C. Troops; however, the companies in which they served are not reported.

IVEY, ELIJAH, _____
North Carolina pension records indicate that he served in this regiment.

_____, JIM, Cook
Previously served in Company H, 18th Regiment N.C. Troops (8th Regiment N.C. Volunteers). Deserted from that unit on June 18, 1864, and reportedly went to the 51st Regiment N.C. Troops. Records of the 51st Regiment do not indicate that he served herein.

MILLER, HARMON, _____
North Carolina pension records indicate that he served in this regiment.

SMITH, W. E., _____
North Carolina pension records indicate that he served in this regiment.

This placid image of Sergeant Manlove Kimrey, Company I, 52nd Regiment, belies what the future held in store for the thirty-year-old Stanly County farmer. He survived the Pickett-Pettigrew assault at Gettysburg on July 3, 1863, was captured during Lee's retreat from Pennsylvania, and spent most of the remainder of the war in two pestilential Federal prison camps. Sergeant Kimrey's service record appears on page 506 of this volume. Image furnished by Ervin Mauldin, Norwood, North Carolina.

Lieutenant Romulus Leedy Cox, a Forsyth County teacher in civilian life, strikes an inscrutable pose in his double-breasted officer's frock coat. He served as an officer in Company K, 52nd Regiment, from April, 1862, until he was wounded in the foot at Globe Tavern, Virginia, in August, 1864. His service record appears on page 439 of this volume. Image furnished by Ted Meredith, Boca Raton, Florida.

52ND REGIMENT N.C. TROOPS

The 52nd Regiment N.C. Troops was organized at Camp Mangum, near Raleigh, on April 28, 1862, and was composed of men recruited primarily in the counties of Cabarrus, Forsyth, Gates, Lincoln, Randolph, Richmond, Stanly, Stokes, and Wilkes. James K. Marshall, a Virgina-born resident of Chowan County and 1860 graduate of the Virginia Military Institute, was elected colonel. The regiment remained at Camp Mangum drilling and receiving instruction in various military skills and duties until about May 27, when it was issued arms.[1] At about the same time it was placed, along with the 44th and 47th Regiments N.C. Troops, in a brigade commanded by Brigadier General James G. Martin. On June 6 the regiment moved by rail to a point in Lenoir County near the present-day town of LaGrange, where the men cleared a sandy tract in a woods of longleaf pines and scrub oaks and established Camp Black Jack. Nine days later they marched to a site near Kinston and established Camp Johnston. On the 16th the regiment was detailed "by squads" to guard crossroads and "the most important points" just east of Kinston.[2] The men returned to Camp Johnston on the 24th. During that time there was much sickness in the regiment—mostly measles and colds. On June 30 the 52nd moved through Kinston to a point five miles down the New Bern road to meet an advancing enemy column. After word was received that the Federals had withdrawn, the regiment returned to Camp Johnston on July 1.[3]

On the night of July 10 the 52nd Regiment was sent by rail to Petersburg, where it rejoined Martin's brigade. Five days later the brigade was ordered seven miles south of Richmond to the James River bastion at Drewry's Bluff, which protected the Confederate capital from waterborne attack. At Drewry's Bluff, Martin's brigade established Camp Campbell, constructed fortifications, performed scouting and picket duty, and attempted to improve its skills in battlefield maneuver. In a letter to his wife dated July 27, Sergeant A. C. Myers of Company D reported that the regiment was in "a very healthy place" with "good water" drawn from wells the men had dug themselves. However, Myers complained, "we have to drill nearly all the time."[4] Writing again the next day Myers described the powerful Confederate defensive position at Drewry's Bluff in detail:

> [W]e are now about 1½ miles from Drewrys Bluff on [the] James River. . . . [W]e have a beautiful place for a camp[,] though . . . the yankees can shell us from the River if they can get [up it] high enough. . . . [W]e have an open view to the river[.] [T]he land is all cleared for two or three miles along the River & from this camp to a mile or two on the other side there is not a tree[.] [W]e are in the edge of the woods[.] [S]ome of the tents extend out in the field[.] [M]y tent is in the woods in a beautiful shade[.] [T]his Regt has been at work throwing up breast works ever since they have been here[.] [T]his hole country is well fortified[.] I went over to the Bluff yesterday & spent four hours looking at the Batries. . . . [T]here are 26 . . . cannon[,] all of which will throw a ball or shell five miles. . . . [T]he river is being Blockaded by sinking

---

[1]Two companies were armed with Enfield rifles and the rest with muskets. See Benjamin Franklin Little to his wife, June 17, 1862, B. F. Little Papers, Southern Historical Collection, University of North Carolina Library at Chapel Hill, hereinafter cited as Little Papers.

[2]B. F. Little to his wife, June 17, 1862, Little Papers.

[3]For further details concerning the movements of the 52nd Regiment on June 30, 1862, see B. F. Little to "My Dear Flax," July 3, 1862, Little Papers.

[4]A. C. Myers to his wife, July 27, 1862, Private Collections, A. C. Myers Papers, PC 114, Archives, Division of Archives and History, hereinafter cited as Myers Papers.

Boats[,] driving spiles [pilings] & filling in timbers & Rock[.] [T]here is no chance for the Yankees to pass the Bluff with their gun Boats.[5]

On August 20 the regiment returned to Petersburg, where it established a new camp, Camp French, at a point about three miles east of the city. There Brigadier General James J. Pettigrew was assigned to replace General Martin as commander of the brigade. The brigade was strengthened on August 26 by the addition of a new regiment, the 26th North Carolina. On September 14 the 52nd was sent by rail to Wakefield, about thirty miles southeast of Petersburg, to repair the track of the Norfolk and Petersburg Railroad. Five days later the regiment marched southward to the vicinity of Franklin, Virginia, where it arrived on September 22. It was then assigned to picket duty at Joyner's Ford on the Blackwater River. On October 4 three Federal gunboats steamed up river from Albemarle Sound in an unsuccessful attempt to destroy a pontoon bridge erected by Confederate engineers at Franklin. After penetrating within "10 or 15" miles of Franklin the gunboats encountered obstructions in the water. They then withdrew downstream under a bluff-top gauntlet of fire from the 52nd and 59th North Carolina regiments.[6] A Federal cavalry force, acting in conjunction with the gunboats, was repulsed by artillery fire. That evening the 52nd Regiment departed for Petersburg, where it remained for two weeks. On October 20 the regiment moved to City Point, about nine miles northeast of Petersburg on the James River, for guard duty. It returned to Petersburg on the 26th.

In early November the 52nd returned to the Blackwater River, in the vicinity of Franklin, and established picket posts at Joyner's Ford and other points. On November 18 an enemy unit of about 300 men forced a crossing at Joyner's Ford against a twenty-man picket detail and occupied the regiment's former camp. After the arrival of the remainder of the regiment, the outnumbered Federals lobbed a few shells into Franklin and retreated.[7]

The 52nd Regiment remained on picket duty along the Blackwater near Franklin until mid-December. For several weeks the men endured the cold without their tents and baggage, which had been left behind at Petersburg. A four-inch snowfall in early November and a rations shortage added further to their misery. "I would Rather go any where in the Southern Confederacy than to stay here," Sergeant Myers groaned in a letter to his wife. "[W]e are not drawing half enough to eat. . . . I have had to pay out a good deal of Money for provisions [but am] compeled to buy or do with out. . . ."[8] Writing to his wife again on November 25, Myers complained that

[T]here has been no arangement made as yet to put up winter quarters. . . . [W]e have not moved all of the Bagage from Petersburg[.] [S]everal tents is still there yet[.] [M]y trunk & all of my clothes is at the Old Camp. . . . I had to buy a shirt & pair of draw[er]s since I came here for a change of clothes. . . . [T]he different companys has petitioned to send one man home for each company to get Blankets[,] shoes[,] clothing[,] &c. [T]his was disapproved & no man allowed to go home & the government cannot furnish Blankets [or] overcoats and has not as yet furnished but one hundred & eighty pairs of shoes for the Regt & that only furnished those who was barefooted. . . .[9]

---

[5]A. C. Myers to his wife, July 28, 1862, Myers Papers.

[6]R. N. Scott and others (eds.), *The War of the Rebellion: A Compilation of the Official Records of the Union and Confederate Armies* (Washington: Government Printing Office, 70 volumes, 1880-1901), Series I, XVIII, 16-19, hereinafter cited as *Official Records (Army)*; A. C. Myers to his son Joe, October 14, 1862, Myers Papers.

[7]*Official Records (Army)*, Series I, XVIII, 33-34.

[8]A. C. Myers to his wife, November 11, 1862, Myers Papers.

[9]A. C. Myers to his wife, November 25, 1862, Myers Papers.

The regiment remained on the Blackwater until December 16. On that date it moved by rail to Goldsboro to assist in defending the important Neuse River railroad bridge against an enemy force advancing from New Bern under Major General John G. Foster. When Foster arrived at Goldsboro the next day the 52nd Regiment was in position to cover the railroad bridge. The 8th Regiment N.C. Troops of Brigadier General Thomas L. Clingman's brigade was covering a nearby road bridge, and the 51st Regiment N.C. Troops, also of Clingman's brigade, was equidistant between the two bridges. The Confederate force of perhaps 2,000 men, commanded by Clingman, found itself confronted by a small army five times its size that promptly opened fire on the 52nd with artillery and musketry and advanced a "heavy force" of converging columns.[10] Unable to hold their ground against "the increasing volleys of musketry" and the "rapid[ly] falling" shells of the enemy, the 52nd Regiment fell back.[11] Thereupon the Federals "applied the torch" to the bridge, which was soon burning rapidly.[12] At that juncture the shaken men of the 52nd found themselves the recipients of a nerve-shattering volley from the 51st Regiment, which had hurried to their assistance but had mistaken them for the enemy in the smoke and confusion. The Federals having in the meantime fortuitously halted their advance, the 52nd regrouped. General Foster, after concentrating his artillery fire on the bridge long enough to foreclose any attempt to save it, detailed a brigade under Colonel H. C. Lee as rear guard and began withdrawing toward New Bern.

In the late afternoon General Clingman, bolstered by the arrival of reinforcements, ordered a counterattack by the 51st and 52nd Regiments. Advancing steadily in line across an open, 1,000-yard-wide field "swept by heavy batteries supported by large masses of infantry," the two regiments reached a point 300 yards from Colonel Lee's position. There, raked by "showers" of canister and musketry, some of the men flung themselves down in search of shelter while others fell back in "the wildest confusion."[13] Sergeant Myers, writing to his wife the next day, reported that he was unhurt but "very tired" and "nearly Broke down."

[W]e arived here the night of the 16th at 12 oclock [Myers continued,] staid til morning by the side of the R.R. & yesterday morning the 17th we was called out in line of Battle [at] 8 oclock AM. [T]he yankees was five hundred yards from us in a field in fair view[.] [W]e only had 3 Regts here at that time[.] [O]ur pickets was sent out to draw on the fire [and] our Regt sent to the R Road Bridge. . . . [O]ur company & one other compa[ny] (Co A & D) was sent out as skirmishers. [W]e held our position til we was nearly surrounded. [W]e was [then] ordered to fall back & join the Regt[.] [A]bout that time the fight became general[.] [W]e was engaged in

---

[10]Walter Clark (ed.), *Histories of the Several Regiments and Battalions from North Carolina in the Great War, 1861-'65* (Raleigh and Goldsboro: State of North Carolina, 5 volumes, 1901), III, 230, hereinafter cited as Clark, *Histories of the North Carolina Regiments*.

[11]*Official Records (Army)*, Series I, XVIII, 118.

[12]Clark, *Histories of the North Carolina Regiments*, III, 230; *Official Records (Army)*, Series I, XVIII, 58. Although Foster's claim that the bridge was fired by hand has generally been accepted and is confirmed by some Confederate witnesses, at least one Confederate officer at the scene told a different story. Captain J. J. Bradbury of the Wilmington and Weldon Railroad Guards (an independent company) stated in a letter dated December 27, 1862, that the brigade was fired "on the top [roof] within 20 feet of the Southern end, by the bursting of a shell thereon by the enemy. . . . Three out of the six men who are said to have fired the bridge, fell by the fire of my men and none of them got within 50 yards. . . ." *Wilmington Journal* (Weekly), January 1, 1863. See also the *Wilmington Journal* (Weekly), January 8, 1863, for a description of the battlefield by one "A. A. McB," a traveler who visited it on about December 27.

[13]*Official Records (Army)*, Series I, XVIII, 119; Private Henry A. Clapp to John P. Clapp, December 22, 1862, Letterbook of Private Henry A. Clapp of Company F, 44th Regiment Massachusetts Volunteers (TP.84.5.1), 139, Tryon Palace Restoration Complex, New Bern, North Carolina, hereinafter cited as Clapp Letterbook.

all theaoters of the fight til about 4 oclock PM when we was ordered to charge on the yankee bateries. . . . [W]e made a charge three quarters of a mile across a open field. . . . [O]ur Regt . . . charged up in 2 hundred yards of the yankees . . . [who were] firing 9 pieces artilery into the 52 [and] throwing grape & canister & shells. . . . [Y]ou ma[y] know we was in a close place. . . . [T]he loss of the 52 Regt was 79 killed[,] wounded and missing[.] [W]e lost the most of this number . . . in the charge[.] [A]fter we had charged [with]in 200 yards of the yankees Battery . . . [—]they standing firm & cutting us down[—]the Regt all fell to the ground[.] [W]e laid their nearly ½ hour waiting for . . . suport. . . . [W]e then had to rise & retreat. . . . [B]y this time it was nearly sun set[.][14]

The exhausted, sweat-drenched men were then formed in line of battle, where they remained shivering with cold until about nine o'clock.[15] Shortly after nightfall Colonel Lee withdrew down the road to New Bern. According to a report filed on December 18 by the regimental adjutant, the 52nd Regiment lost 8 men killed, 58 wounded, and 13 missing at Goldsboro.[16]

The regiment remained in the vicinity of Goldsboro for several more days before returning to its camp on the Blackwater River near Franklin on December 24. At about that time Pettigrew's brigade was further strengthened by the addition of the 11th Regiment N.C. Troops (1st Regiment N.C. Volunteers). On December 26 the 52nd Regiment was detailed on a foraging expedition across the Blackwater into territory occupied by Federal forces. After gathering a "considerable quantity" of forage and driving two enemy cavalry companies from Windsor with artillery fire, the 52nd returned to its Blackwater camp on January 1, 1863.[17] On January 3—the day after a disgusted Sergeant Myers and several comrades completed work on a cabin they had built for winter quarters—the 52nd Regiment was ordered to Rocky Mount. There the brigade was reunited and, "to the delight of the entire regiment," the men came once again under the command of General Pettigrew.[18] On the 20th the brigade was ordered to Magnolia, in Duplin County. After several weeks of daily drill and "rigid inspection," the 52nd moved to Goldsboro on February 13. It remained there until March 9 when it departed to participate, with the remainder of Pettigrew's brigade, in Major General D. H. Hill's attempt to recapture New Bern and Washington, North Carolina.[19]

Lying at the confluence of the Neuse and Trent rivers, New Bern was the most important Federal base in eastern North Carolina and the jumping-off point for destructive raids that were depriving the Confederacy of valuable supplies and devastating civilian morale. Determined to punish the "marauding" Federal "hosts" and, as he assured the members of the 52nd Regiment and other units in a speech on February 25, "cut down to six feet by two, the dimensions of the farms which these plunderers propose to appropriate," Hill planned a

[14]A. C. Myers to his wife, December 18, 1862, Myers Papers.
[15]A. C. Myers to his wife, December 18, 1862, Myers Papers.
[16]Clark, *Histories of the North Carolina Regiments*, III, 231-232. Casualty figures compiled from the rosters contained in this volume indicate that the regiment lost 16 men killed, 43 wounded, and 8 captured at Goldsboro. Unless otherwise indicated, casualty figures cited in this history are derived from the accompanying rosters. Mortally wounded men, including those who were captured and those who died of their wounds weeks or months after they were injured, are included in the "killed" category. Men who were wounded (not mortally) and captured are included in the "captured" category. For battles in which a substantial number of captured men were also wounded, as at Gettysburg, a separate "wounded and captured" figure is cited.
[17]Clark, *Histories of the North Carolina Regiments*, III, 232. Further details concerning this expedition appear in A. C. Myers to his wife, January 2, 1863, Myers Papers.
[18]Clark, *Histories of the North Carolina Regiments*, III, 232.
[19]Clark, *Histories of the North Carolina Regiments*, III, 232. The regiment's departure date from Goldsboro is confirmed in A. C. Myers to his wife, March 5, 1863, and A. C. Myers to his son Joe, March 25, 1863, Myers Papers.

three-column attack on New Bern.[20] One column, under Brigadier General Junius Daniel, was to move directly against the town along the north side of the Trent while two flanking columns, commanded by Pettigrew and Brigadier General Beverly H. Robertson, were to advance down the north bank of the Neuse and the south side of the Trent. Pettigrew's orders were to bombard Fort Anderson, across the Neuse from New Bern, and shell Federal gunboats on the river; Robertson's cavalry command was to tear up the track of the Atlantic and North Carolina Railroad. On March 13, after a brief skirmish, Daniel's force captured the Federal entrenchments at Deep Gully, about eight miles east of New Bern. In the meantime, Pettigrew, whose bombardment of Fort Anderson was supposed to have started the same day, found himself all but immobilized in marshy terrain:

[H]eavy rain . . . had swollen the swamps and put the roads in very bad condition [he later reported]. Many of the bridges broke down under the 20-pounders, all causing great delay. . . . The infantry reached the camp, 8 miles from Barrington's [Ferry, near Fort Anderson], at dark [on the 12th], and I intended to start at midnight for the ferry, but a swamp some 3 miles in rear of the halt changed under the [artillery] train into quicksand. The men vainly worked all night in the freezing water to repair it. It was [finally] necessary to bridge the whole swamp in a new place. . . . About 3 p.m. Friday [the 13th] the bridge was finished. The infantry arrived at the ferry early in the night, but the 20-pounders having mired, the artillery was detained until late in the morning [of the 14th].[21]

Having reached his assigned position at last, Pettigrew found Fort Anderson to be a unprepossessing and lightly manned earthwork protected on three sides by swamps and the Neuse River and approachable only over a narrow causeway. Unwilling to storm the fort at a cost he estimated at "50 or 100 men," Pettigrew decided to "display" his force, "demoralize [the enemy] . . . by a heavy fire, and demand a surrender. . . ."[22] When it became evident that the Federals were using Pettigrew's surrender demand to stall for time, the artillery bombardment resumed, with ludicrous results:

I now devoted my attention to the 20-pounders. I regret to say that their performance was execrable. . . . Half of the shells . . . burst just outside of the guns. They turned over in the air and were perfectly harmless to the enemy. At length the axle of one of these guns broke and it became unserviceable. Then another burst, wounding 3 men, 1 of them mortally. These four 20-pounders were our sole agents for accomplishing the object of the expedition. It was now painfully evident that they were worse than useless.[23]

Unable to inflict any damage on the fort and, more significantly, on the heavily armed gunboats that had gotten up steam and were now coming around from the Trent, the 52nd Regiment spent much of the day, in the words of Captain B. F. Little of Company E, "flat on our faces" under the nerve-racking if largely ineffective fire of the gunboats.[24] The next day, perceiving that Daniel's attack had been canceled and that he was in danger of being cut off, Pettigrew fell back eight miles to a point near Swift Creek, where he received orders to

[20]*Charlotte Daily Bulletin*, March 7, 1863.
[21]*Official Records (Army)*, Series I, XVIII, 192.
[22]*Official Records (Army)*, Series I, XVIII, 193.
[23]*Official Records (Army)*, Series I, XVIII, 193.
[24]B. F. Little to "My Dear Flax," March 17, [1863], Little Papers.

retreat to Greenville. Still fearful of entrapment, the brigade "moved by stealth" all through the night of the 15th with some of the men, according to Captain Little, literally sleeping as they marched.[25] The brigade reached Greenville on the 17th. The exhausted men had, according to Pettigrew's report:

> [M]arched 127 miles, waded swamps, worked in them by night and day, bivouacked in the rain, sometimes without fire, [and] never enjoyed a full night's rest after the first, besides undergoing a furious shelling. . . .[26]

Casualties in Pettigrew's brigade totaled, according to Pettigrew's report, two men killed, two mortally wounded, five seriously wounded, and fourteen slightly wounded.[27]

Frustrated at New Bern, General Hill then turned his attention to the Federal-occupied town of Washington, on the Pamlico River. Pettigrew's brigade was ordered to take part in the planned attack. After advancing from Greenville on the 18th the brigade reached Tranter's Creek, about eight miles west of Washington, the next day. There a rainfall lasting three days and nights began. By the time the deluge ended, Sergeant Myers reported, "the waters was so high & the roads so muddy we could not get along," and the brigade withdrew to Greenville.[28] On March 28 Hill tried again, and by March 30 Washington was under siege. Hoping to prevent the arrival of Federal reinforcements by the Pamlico, Hill positioned batteries at key points around the town and attempted to block the river with sunken hulks and pilings cut off below the waterline. Pettigrew's and Daniel's brigades were stationed west of the town to engage any Federal relief force that might advance from New Bern. Handicapped by an inadequate supply of artillery ammunition and under orders not to attempt to capture Washington by storm, Hill opened a sporadic shelling and settled down to starve the Unionists into submission. For its part the Federal garrison, which possessed adequate numbers, weapons, and munitions but was already on short rations, returned the Confederate battery fire and prepared for what it hoped would be a short siege.

In the meantime the 52nd Regiment had erected a heavy earthwork on a bluff on the south bank of the Pamlico below Washington and was attempting to block the river to Federal reinforcements.[29] From this edifice, called Fort Hill, the Confederates, armed only with light caliber field artillery, exchanged a desultory and ineffective daily fire with Federal gunboats. The latter, made wary of the fort's firepower by the Confederate ruse of occasionally hauling up two of the heavier cannon bombarding Washington, kept a respectful distance.

> Ever since we have been here [wrote Sergeant Myers] there has been from 5 to 18 yankee Gun Boats laying off down the river[.] [T]hey give us a few Balls accasionally[.] [T]hey some times comence shelling & shell about an hour & come up in 2 miles with 3 or four Boats[.] [T]hen we give them a few shots & they go Back. . . . [O]ur guns generally throw about 3 shot & always strike the Boat with 1 or 2 of them[.][30]

On April 9 the 52nd Regiment, with the rest of Pettigrew's brigade, took part in the bloodless repulse of a Federal relief column at Blount's Creek. The column's commander, a

[25]B. F. Little to "My Dear Flax," March 17, [1863], Little Papers.
[26]*Official Records (Army)*, Series I, XVIII, 194.
[27]*Official Records (Army)*, Series I, XVIII, 194. See also A. C. Myers to his son Joe, March 25, 1863, Myers Papers. During the New Bern campaign the 52nd Regiment apparently suffered only one casualty, Private Lee Gibson of Company D, who was wounded.
[28]A. C. Myers to his son Joe, March 25, 1863, Myers Papers.
[29]Clark, *Histories of the North Carolina Regiments*, III, 233.
[30]A. C. Myers to his wife, April 8, 1863, Myers Papers.

political general named F. B. Spinola, in the disgusted but accurate words of one member of the New Bern garrison, literally "got frightened at nothing and ran home."[31] That small Confederate victory was negated on the evening of April 13 when the Federal steamer *Escort*, her decks piled with hay bales to protect her from artillery fire, ran Hill's Pamlico River gauntlet, bringing supplies and the 5th Regiment Rhode Island Infantry. Although fired upon "repeatedly," the damage to the vessel from the Confederate field guns was "trifling."[32] Two days later the *Escort* steamed safely past Fort Hill on her return trip, this time in broad daylight. Convinced that Washington could not be taken, General Hill raised the siege on April 16.

From Washington the 52nd Regiment was ordered to Hookerton, in Greene County, where it remained until it marched to Kinston on the 25th. On the evening of May 2 the regiment departed by rail for Virginia, arriving too late to take part in the great battle near Chancellorsville. Several tense days were spent in the Richmond fortifications looking, according to Private W. D. Patterson of Company E, "for and attack every minit" by raiding Federal cavalrymen. The regiment was then sent to Hanover Junction on May 7 to escort 2,000 Federal prisoners to Richmond.[33] A few days later five companies were dispatched to build fortifications at the Virginia Central Railroad bridge over the South Anna River, about sixteen miles north of Richmond near Hanover Court House. Two other companies were detailed for picket duty on the Richmond and Fredericksburg Railroad. When not engaged in various details, the regiment was drilled daily and had attained "the finest condition" by the time it was assigned with the rest of Pettigrew's brigade to Major General Henry Heth's division of Lieutenant General A. P. Hill's corps about June 1.[34] On June 8 the 52nd Regiment joined Hill's command at Fredericksburg where it found everything, Captain Little assured his wife, "as quiet as a Sabbath morning."[35]

Five days earlier, on June 3, the Army of Northern Virginia, under the command of General Robert E. Lee, had moved toward the Shenandoah Valley to begin the campaign that would end at Gettysburg. Lieutenant General Richard S. Ewell's corps moved first and was followed by the corps of Lieutenant General James Longstreet. Hill's corps remained temporarily at Fredericksburg to watch the Federal forces opposite the town. On June 13 Ewell defeated an enemy force at Winchester, and Longstreet occupied Culpeper Court House. The Federals evacuated their Fredericksburg position the same day, and Hill's corps was ordered to move north. Ewell's corps crossed the Potomac into Maryland on June 16 and was followed by Hill, whose men began fording the river at Shepherdstown, West Virginia, on June 24. On the afternoon of June 27 Hill's corps arrived at Fayetteville, Pennsylvania. Longstreet's corps was at Chambersburg, just west of Fayetteville, that day, and Ewell's corps was advancing on Carlisle, about thirty miles to the northeast. Hill's corps was ordered to Cashtown, about twelve miles southeast of Fayetteville, on June 29, and Longstreet was directed to follow on June 30. Ewell was instructed to rejoin the army at Cashtown or Gettysburg, as developments the next day dictated.

Heth's division reached Cashtown on June 29, and the next day Pettigrew's brigade was sent to Gettysburg to procure supplies. Finding the town occupied by the enemy, Pettigrew withdrew to Cashtown. During the evening of June 30 General Hill arrived at Cashtown with

[31]H. A. Clapp to Mary Clapp, April 19, 1863, Clapp Letterbook, 347.
[32]Clark, *Histories of the North Carolina Regiments*, III, 234.
[33]W. D. Patterson to his wife, May 5, 1863, Roster Document File Number 0349, Civil War Roster Project, Division of Archives and History, Raleigh.
[34]Clark, *Histories of the North Carolina Regiments*, III, 235.
[35]B. F. Little to "My Dear Flax," June 8, 1863, Little Papers.

Major General William D. Pender's division and decided to advance on Gettysburg with Heth's and Pender's divisions the next morning. At daylight on June 1 the two divisions, with Heth's men in the lead, moved toward Gettysburg.

Approaching the town from the west via the Chambersburg Pike, Heth topped a height known as Herr Ridge to find himself confronted by dismounted Federal cavalrymen. This thin blue line extended from the base of a hill southward across an unfinished railroad cut and the Chambersburg Pike and thence through a woods and along the far bank of a shallow creek called Willoughby Run. Pitching into the Federals with the brigades of Brigadier Generals James J. Archer and Joseph R. Davis, Heth made a slow but costly progress against the rapid fire of the troopers' breechloaders until Federal infantry arrived. A furious fight in the woods with the Federal Iron Brigade, tough Westerners from Wisconsin, Indiana, and Michigan, then sent Archer's men reeling back across Willoughby Run. North of the pike Davis's brigade, after flanking the Federal defenders and forcing a precipitate retreat to Seminary Ridge, just west of Gettysburg, was in turn flanked. Part of the brigade was driven into the railroad cut, which in some places was as much as twenty feet deep, and forced to surrender.

The focus of the fighting then shifted to Heth's left, where the division of Major General Robert Rodes of Ewell's corps, after being momentarily in a position to roll up the enemy flank, received a bloody repulse from the frantically improvising Federals. The arrival of Major General Jubal A. Early's division of Ewell's corps on Rodes's left then presented a new opportunity to turn the Federal flank, and General Lee, who had reached the battlefield, ordered Heth to renew his attack. Pettigrew's brigade was ordered up from its reserve position and placed in the center of Heth's line between the brigades of Archer and Colonel J. M. Brockenbrough. Opposite Heth's division, the black-hatted Iron Brigade was still holed up in the woods. "Yelling like demons," Pettigrew's men sprinted through the wheat field covering the east slope of Herr Ridge, pushed their way through the briery underbrush skirting the banks of Willoughby Run, and, after crossing the torpid little creek, charged into the woods, where a murderous conflict ensued.[36] "The brigade moved forward in beautiful style" to a point near the run, Major John T. Jones of the 26th Regiment reported, where a "heavy force" of the enemy began pouring

> a galling fire into the left of the brigade from the opposite bank. . . . The Forty-seventh and Fifty-second, although exposed to a hot fire from artillery and infantry, lost but few in comparison with the Eleventh and Twenty-sixth. On went the command across the branch and up the opposite slope, driving the enemy at the point of the bayonet back upon their second line. This . . . line was encountered by our left (the Twenty-sixth), while the other regiments were exposed to a heavy shelling. . . . The enemy did not perceive the Fifty-second, which flanked their left, until they [the 52nd] discovered themselves by a raking and destructive fire into their [the Federals'] ranks, by which they were broken. On this second line the fighting was terrible— our men advancing, the enemy stubbornly resisting, until the two lines were pouring volleys into each other at a distance not greater than 20 paces. At last the enemy were compelled to give way. They again made a stand in the woods, and the third time they were driven from their position. . . .[37]

Falling back to high ground on Seminary Ridge, the Federals attempted to re-form their lines. Meantime, below their position, Pender's fresh division passed over Heth's bloodied

---

[36] *Official Records (Army)*, Series I, XXVII, Part I, 268.
[37] *Official Records (Army)*, Series I, XXVII, Part II, 643.

ranks and, with the "howls" of the wounded ringing in their ears, stormed up the slopes of Seminary Ridge.[38] There frenzied Federal cannoneers greeted them with full-face blasts of double-shotted canister. "Up and down the line," wrote one of the Federal gunners,

> men reeling and falling; splinters flying from wheels and axles where bullets hit; in rear, horses tearing and plunging, mad with wounds or terror; drivers yelling, shells bursting, shot shrieking overhead, howling about our ears or throwing up great clouds of dust where they struck; the musketry crashing . . . bullets hissing, humming, and whistling everywhere; cannon roaring . . . smoke, dust, splinters, blood; wreck and carnage indescribable.[39]

Recoiling momentarily before this inferno, Pender's men quickly came on again, driving the exhausted Federals pell-mell from their position. On the Federal right a similar rout was in progress. Thousands of Federal soldiers fell back through the streets of Gettysburg to new positions on Cemetery and Culp's hills. There the disorganized men re-formed as best they could, anticipating a new Confederate assault that, because of a misinterpretation of orders by the sluggish Ewell, was not to be forthcoming. Darkness fell over a scene of purgatorial suffering. The two armies attempted to care for their casualties and prepared to renew the contest the next day. During the night Longstreet's corps arrived, bringing the Confederate strength up to about 50,000 men. The Federals were even more heavily reinforced. By morning, Lee faced a wounded but unbowed, determined, and well-led army of at least 60,000 in a position of daunting natural strength.

The three-mile-long, fishhook-shaped Federal position on July 2 was solidly anchored at the hook's point by Culp's Hill, which rose some 180 feet above the neighboring terrain. The line then curved sharply to the left to 100-foot-high Cemetery Hill. From there it extended southward down the long, low, undulating brow of Cemetery Ridge to the base of another hill, known as Little Round Top, which formed the hook's "eye." Several thousand yards away, across an open, sloping plain, the Army of Northern Virginia was in a sickle-like line anchored on Seminary Ridge and conforming roughly to the Federal dispositions. Longstreet's corps held the south (right) end of the line, Hill's the middle, and Ewell's the north. Under orders from Lee, Longstreet and Ewell launched powerful, bloody attacks on July 2 that, particularly in the case of Longstreet, narrowly failed to achieve decisive results. Some fighting occurred on Hill's front, but the 52nd Regiment, along with the other regiments of Pettigrew's brigade, was in reserve and saw no action.

Having failed in assaults at either end of the Federal line, Lee ordered a 13,000-man attack against the center on July 3. Heth's division, under the command of Pettigrew since the wounding of Heth on July 1, was ordered to take a position on the left of Major General George E. Pickett's newly arrived division. After a spectacular but ineffective two-hour bombardment by some 140 Confederate cannon, forty-two regiments, including the 52nd North Carolina, stepped out of the woods atop Seminary Ridge. Having methodically formed ranks for their assault, the men advanced at a steady pace across coverless ground sloping down to the Emmitsburg Road, which fronted the Federal position on Cemetery Ridge. Shortly, enfilading artillery fire from Cemetery Hill and Little Round Top began tearing gaping holes in the Confederate ranks. As the men approached the Emmitsburg Road, a crashing volley at short range by an isolated Ohio regiment well in advance of the Federal line sent Brockenbrough's brigade, on the extreme left of the Confederate line, fleeing for safety.

[38]Clark, *Histories of the North Carolina Regiments*, V, 119.
[39]Richard Wheeler, *Voices of the Civil War* (New York: Thomas Y. Crowell Company, 1976), 296.

Davis's brigade, the next in line, also began to waver and crumble. On Davis's right, Pettigrew's brigade, under the command of Colonel James K. Marshall of the 52nd Regiment, and the brigade of Archer continued to struggle gamely forward. As the men clambered over the rail fences on either side of the Emmitsburg Road, Federal cannon and infantry on Cemetery Ridge opened fire. "A dense cloud of smoke and dust," a Federal officer reported, immediately enveloped the Confederate line. "Arms, heads, blankets, guns, and knapsacks" went flying into the air, and a moan went up from the field that was distinctly heard amid the storm of battle.[40] Colonel Marshall, who had remounted after being knocked from his horse by an explosion a few moments earlier, was shot dead.

Staggered, and under fire on both flanks from Federal infantry units that had moved out to enfilade their rapidly telescoping and diminishing line, the Confederate survivors charged up the gentle, smoke-shrouded slope of Cemetery Ridge towards a copse of trees and the Federal infantry blazing away from behind a low stone wall. Lethal blasts of double-shotted canister delivered at a point-blank range by Federal cannoneers scythed down scores of the attackers but failed to stop the survivors from clearing the wall. A desperate, frenzied melee ensued, but Federal reinforcements were quickly on the scene and those battered Confederates who were still on their feet surrendered. Those beyond the reach of the Federal infantry fell back to Seminary Ridge still taking terrible punishment from Federal battery fire. Some of the wounded were dragged or carried back by their comrades. Others who were able to crawl came into the lines that night.

The precise events that befell the 52nd Regiment during the great charge of July 3, 1863, are difficult to ascertain from surviving records and manuscripts, but the report of Major Jones on the activities of Pettigrew's brigade as a whole suggests the ferocity of the fighting and the severity of the casualties:

When about half across the intervening space [Jones wrote] the enemy opened on us a most destructive fire of grape and canister. When within about 250 or 300 yards of the stone wall behind which the enemy was posted, we were met by a perfect hail-storm of lead from their small-arms. The brigade dashed on, and many had reached the wall, when we received a deadly volley from the left. The whole line on the left had given way, and we were being rapidly flanked. With our thinned ranks and in such a position, it would have been folly to stand, and against such odds. We therefore fell back to our original position in rear of the batteries. After this day's fight, but one field officer was left in the brigade. Regiments that went in with colonels came out commanded by lieutenants.[41]

Adjutant John H. Robinson of the 52nd, writing many years after the war, stated only that

[Our regiment] moved gallantly and steadily forward under the [covering] fire of our guns until it reached a point beyond which it was unsafe to fire over our heads. Steadily the advance was made, and as steadily and coolly met with a murderous fire from the enemy's cannon, charged with grape, shrapnel and canister. Still the line advanced, and at every step our comrades fell on every side, killed or wounded. Still we advanced under the incessant discharge of the cannon, assisted by the infantry's rifles, and had almost attained success, when by the overpowering force and almost impregnable position of the enemy, our lines were forced back, and then the

---

[40]Clark, *Histories of the North Carolina Regiments*, V, 126.
[41]*Official Records (Army)*, Series I, XXVII, Part II, 644.

slaughter was terrific. We fell back to the point from which the attack was made, rallying all whom it was possible to reach, and reforming our shattered lines.[42]

Whatever the specifics of the 52nd Regiment's part in the fighting on July 3, its casualties during the three-day battle were appalling. According to the Army of Northern Virginia's chief medical officer in a report filed on September 1, 1863, the regiment lost 33 men killed and 114 wounded. However, these figures apparently omit men who were mortally wounded. In actuality, 77 members of the regiment were killed or mortally wounded and 63 more received nonfatal wounds. Perhaps equally important, particularly insofar as the regiment's fighting capacity was concerned, 206 men were captured, of whom 112 were wounded. Although most of these captured men and many of the wounded eventually returned to duty, it seems probable, as casualty figures for later battles suggest, that the 52nd's strength and battlefield effectiveness were never the same again.[43]

Following the failure of the assault on July 3 the Army of Northern Virginia remained briefly in position to receive an expected but unforthcoming Federal attack. The next afternoon the army began its retreat. Presently, a heavy rain began to fall that continued off and on for days. Churned by the passage of hundreds of supply wagons, artillery pieces, caissons, ambulances, and other wheeled vehicles in a train that stretched for miles, the roads became quagmires, slowing progress to a crawl. On July 7 the army reached Hagerstown, where a defensive line was established to wait for the rain-swollen waters of the Potomac to subside. Major General George G. Meade's Federal army, itself severely battered by the three days of carnage at Gettysburg, trailed cautiously behind the retreating Confederates. Only the Federal cavalry showed any aggressiveness, harrying the wagon trains. Almost out of ammunition and with an army reduced to less than half the size of its opponent, Lee entrenched at Falling Waters with his back to the river and began improvising a pontoon bridge from demolished warehouses. On the wild, rainy night of July 13, which Lee himself described as, for the season, "one of the most inclement . . . I have ever known," the bulk of the army crossed safely. However, Heth's division, acting as rear guard, was surprised by Federal cavalry north of the river on the morning of July 14.[44] Rousing themselves from a sleep of exhaustion to find many of their rain-drenched muskets inoperable and the Federal horsemen upon them, the 52nd Regiment and other units of Heth's division fought with clubbed muskets, axes, and fence rails. In the melee, General Pettigrew was mortally wounded. Heth's men then conducted a fighting withdrawal to the pontoon bridge, which they crossed just as it was being cut. Losses in the 52nd Regiment at Falling Waters were two men wounded and seventy-one captured.

After crossing the Potomac, Pettigrew's brigade marched to Bunker Hill, West Virginia, where it rested for several days. It then moved south by way of Winchester to Culpeper Court

---

[42]Clark, *Histories of the North Carolina Regiments*, III, 238.

[43]*Official Records (Army)*, Series I, XXVII, Part II, 333, 344. The 52nd Regiment also lost its flag, which was captured by Corporal Christopher Flynn, Company K, 14th Regiment Connecticut Volunteers. See *Official Records (Army)*, Series I, XXVII, Part I, 468, and Series III, IV, 815. The combat efficiency of the regiment probably was reduced not only by its heavy overall casualties but also by the loss of all three of its field officers. Colonel Marshall and Major John Q. Richardson were both killed, and Lieutenant Colonel Marcus A. Parks was wounded and captured. Although Parks was promoted in absentia to the rank of colonel, he remained in Federal hands until March 22, 1865. From July 3, 1863, until April 15, 1864, the regiment was commanded by Captain B. F. Little of Company E. On the latter date Little was appointed Lieutenant Colonel. He resigned on July 15, 1864, and was replaced by Lieutenant Colonel Eric Erson, who was promoted from the rank of major the same date. Among its ten captains the 52nd Regiment lost 3 killed, 3 wounded, and 2 wounded and captured at Gettysburg; among its thirty lieutenants the regiment lost 2 killed, 4 wounded, and 5 captured (of whom four were wounded).

[44]Salem *People's Press*, August 6, 1863.

House, where it went into camp on July 25. About a week later the brigade departed for Orange Court House. By August 4 the Army of Northern Virginia occupied a line in the vicinity of the Rapidan River, and the Army of the Potomac had taken position on the Rappahannock. The 44th Regiment, which had been on detached duty during the Gettysburg campaign, rejoined the brigade at about that time and its colonel, Thomas C. Singletary, assumed temporary command of the brigade in place of the fallen Pettigrew. Singletary was replaced on September 7, 1863, by Brigadier General William W. Kirkland. The brigade continued to serve in Heth's division of A. P. Hill's corps.

The 52nd Regiment remained in camp near Orange Court House "doing picket duty and drilling daily" until September 20, when it moved with the rest of the brigade to Rapidan Station.[45] In early October Lee, who had recently dispatched most of Longstreet's corps to the assistance of General Braxton Bragg in north Georgia, learned that the Army of the Potomac had also sent reinforcements to the West. He therefore took the offensive and attempted to strike Meade's right flank in the vicinity of the Rapidan, thereby compelling the Federal commander to retire northeastward in the direction of Centreville. As one corps of Meade's rear guard was crossing Broad Run, near Bristoe Station, on October 14, Heth's division of Hill's corps arrived on the field. Without waiting for the rest of his command to come up or to reconnoiter, Hill, with characteristic audacity, ordered an immediate attack. Unaware that an entire corps of the enemy was concealed behind a railroad embankment to their right, the brigades of Kirkland and Brigadier General John R. Cooke charged down an open hillside toward the retreating Federal column. Immediately, a furious blast of artillery and rifle fire from behind the embankment raked the two brigades. Wheeling toward the embankment, the Confederates charged into the murderous fire and were sent stumbling back with severe losses. According to the casualty report filed by Hill, the two brigades lost at least 109 men killed, 659 wounded, and about 445 missing. Cooke's brigade, on the right, suffered the most heavily, but Kirkland's losses totaled at least 50 killed and 220 wounded.[46] Casualties in the 52nd Regiment were, according to figures compiled for this volume, 6 men killed, 20 wounded, and 46 captured. General Kirkland was wounded also, and Colonel Singletary again assumed temporary command of the brigade.

No further attempts were made to attack the enemy at Bristoe Station, and during the night the Federal rear guard continued its march to Centreville. Lee followed briefly but began retreating to the Rappahannock on the 17th. After battles at Rappahannock Bridge and Kelly's Ford on November 7 in which the 52nd Regiment was not engaged, Lee fell back to the Rapidan. On November 26 Meade began moving his army across the Rapidan in an attempt to turn Lee's right flank. Advancing with extreme prudence, Meade allowed the Confederate commander time to reinforce and fortify his right wing. By November 29 Lee's men were strongly entrenched along a ridge behind a creek known as Mine Run, and Meade, unable to locate a vulnerable point against which to launch an attack, also began entrenching. Perceiving that the Federals would not attack him in his formidable works, Lee sent two divisions against what he believed to be an exposed Federal flank on the morning of December 2. However, by that time the Federals had retreated, and the blow landed in the air. A pursuit was undertaken, but Meade recrossed the Rapidan unmolested. During the Federal commander's cautious, pantomimic campaign along Mine Run, the 52nd Regiment was involved in a brief skirmish on November 29. Its casualties, if any, were light.

[45]Clark, *Histories of the North Carolina Regiments*, III, 241.
[46]*Official Records (Army)*, Series I, XXIX, Part I, 428.

On December 3 the 52nd Regiment moved to Camp Marshall, near Orange Court House, where it went into winter quarters. After two months of such "drilling and general camp duty" as the weather permitted, the regiment was detailed for picket duty on the Rapidan on February 3, 1864.[47] On February 20 General Kirkland, who had recovered from the wound he received at Bristoe Station, resumed command of the brigade. In the meantime the men of the 52nd patrolled the segment of the Rapidan to which they were assigned and built cabins. On April 27 the regiment moved, "as a sanitary measure," to a new encampment about one mile from the previous site.[48]

Kirkland's brigade was still in camp near Orange Court House when the Army of the Potomac, under the strategic direction of General Ulysses S. Grant, began crossing the lower Rapidan in two powerful columns on the morning of May 4, 1864, and entered an area of dense woods and tangled undergrowth known as the Wilderness. When news of Grant's crossing was received Lee ordered Hill's corps to move eastward from Orange Court House by the Orange Plank Road and Ewell's corps, south of Morton's Ford, to advance on Hill's left down the Orange Turnpike. Longstreet's corps, a two-day march away near Gordonsville, was instructed to hurry to the scene and move up on Hill's right on the Catharpin Road.

Early on the morning of May 5 Hill's column, with Kirkland's brigade in the lead, came upon Federal cavalry at Parker's Store and forced the enemy back to a point near the junction of the Orange Plank and Brock roads. There the advance was halted by Federal infantry. Hill then ordered Heth's division to deploy across the Plank Road, and Kirkland's brigade was placed in reserve behind the brigade of Cooke, which held the center of Heth's line. Groping their way forward through the thickets and brambles, the Federals were met by a blast of musketry from a distance of fifty yards that halted them in their tracks and sent them reeling back in confusion. Hill then went over to the attack and resumed his slow progress toward the junction.

At about 4:00 p.m. the arrival of reinforcements allowed Grant to return to the offensive, and Hill ordered Kirkland's brigade forward to assist Cooke's hard-pressed men. That Federal attack and another one an hour later were shredded by Confederate musketry, but fresh Federal units continued to join the fighting, and the Confederate line began to waver. Battling desperately and almost blindly in the gloomy, smoke-filled, nearly impenetrable woods, Hill's tired men managed to hang on until nightfall. The 52nd Regiment, which had been detailed to guard the division's wagon train, missed most of the day's fighting but rejoined Kirkland's brigade at about five o'clock. "As we approached the lines," wrote one member of the regiment,

> we were met by great numbers of our men wounded and seeking the rear for shelter and relief. These men were wounded in every conceivable manner—some slightly, others severely and not a few mortally. Nothing daunted by this spectacle, the . . . Fifty-second moved rapidly forward and took its position in the brigade, and at once became hotly engaged. The ground over which we were fighting was covered with dense undergrowth, and the enemy could scarcely be seen, in many places, one hundred yards in our front. From the time we joined the brigade . . . until nightfall there was one continuous roll of musketry. . . . The regiment spent the night upon the

[47]Clark, *Histories of the North Carolina Regiments*, III, 244.
[48]Clark, *Histories of the North Carolina Regiments*, III, 244.

ground on which it had ceased to fight in the evening, and the exhausted men sought what rest they could.[49]

At 5:00 o'clock the next morning, May 6, Federal columns struck Heth's line in the center and on the left flank. The division on Kirkland's left was quickly driven from its position, and Hill's entire line began to disintegrate. The 52nd Regiment, finding itself flanked and under fire from the rear, fell back in disorder with Hill's other units. An attempt to rally on Cooke's reserve brigade was momentarily successful, but the Federals came on again and a general rout followed. Only the timely arrival of Longstreet's corps, moving up at the double-quick on the Orange Plank Road to reinforce Hill, prevented the collapse of the right wing of Lee's army. The Federal assault, which had already lost cohesiveness in the burning woods, was blunted and driven back. Hill's men, after re-forming behind Longstreet, were dispatched to close a gap between Longstreet and Ewell in the vicinity of Chewning Plateau. Throughout the day the battle continued on Longstreet's front with unremitting fury. By nightfall Longstreet's men, assisted by Hill's regrouped command, had restored the Confederate right, while an attack by Ewell on the left had spoiled another major assault planned by Grant. An uneasy silence fell over the smoldering Wilderness. Fires continued to blaze here and there, and wounded soldiers, lying helpless between the lines, died screaming in the flames, adding to the usual battlefield horrors the stench of burning flesh. The 52nd Regiment lost five men wounded and thirty-nine captured in the Wilderness battle of May 5-6.

Late on the evening of May 7, following a day of relative quiet, it became apparent that Grant's army was moving around Lee's right and was on the march to Spotsylvania Court House, a strategic road junction whose possession would give the Federals control of the shortest route to Richmond and force Lee to either run an unequal race to the Confederate capital or attack the superior Federal army on its own terms. Throughout the night of May 7 the Confederates pushed southeastward through the grim, fire-blackened woods, narrowly beating the Federals to Spotsylvania the next morning. A strong defensive line was quickly constructed. Hill's corps, temporarily commanded by Early, held the right, Ewell's corps the center, and Longstreet's corps, under the temporary command of Major General Richard H. Anderson since the wounding of Longstreet on May 6, the left. Heth's division, including the 52nd Regiment, occupied the extreme right of the Confederate line. After attempting unsuccessfully to dent the positions of Anderson and Early on May 8, Grant spent the next day deploying his army and probing the Confederate defenses.

In the meantime the Confederates dug in with a vengeance. On May 10 the Federals launched several heavy but unsuccessful attacks against Anderson and against a convex, U-shaped salient known as the "Mule Shoe" in the center of the Confederate line. Heth's division was moved from its position on the right extremity of the Confederate works and marched to Anderson's left flank, which had been turned by a weak but potentially dangerous Federal force. Underestimating the potential afforded by this flanking gambit, Grant ordered a withdrawal that was already in progress when Heth's men arrived. A sharp fight with the two brigades of the Federal rear guard ensued. We "charged on the enemy through the open field," wrote Private John A. Foster of Company F, 52nd Regiment,

[49]Clark, *Histories of the North Carolina Regiments*, III, 245. "I never have seen and heard such musketry in my life," wrote Corporal James W. Wright of the 26th Regiment, one of the 52nd Regiment's sister units in Kirkland's brigade. "[I]t looked like a man could not live." James W. Wright to his father, mother, and Fanny, May 9, 1864, Private Collections, John Wright Family Papers, PC 1594, Archives, Division of Archives and History, Raleigh, hereinafter cited as Wright Papers.

then raleighed [rallied] and charged up on them . . . and drove them out of thare brest works and . . . raleighed and formed in the rode[.] [W]e then lay in the rode and rested for a while[,] the enemy shelling us verry heavy all the time. Then . . . we maid the second charge[.] The 52nd Regt charged . . . all the way through the open field & the enemy throwing grape all the time[.] [V]erry fast we charged to thare second brest works and drove them out . . . and then moved off to the right and come back to the rode. . . .[50]

Heth's men returned to their original position on the Confederate right on the morning of May 11. There the 52nd Regiment was "shell[ed] . . . some" by the enemy, and its skirmishers spent the day exchanging shots with their Federal counterparts.[51] An early morning drizzle developed by evening into a steady downpour, and the regiment spent a miserable night in the mud and water.

Early on the morning of May 12 the Federals launched a sudden attack against the Mule Shoe salient. Overwhelmed by the onslaught of twenty-four brigades against a segment of their line measuring no more than a few hundred yards long, the Confederates fell back. After vicious, hand-to-hand fighting, Confederate reinforcements managed to check the Federal assault while a new line was constructed across the base of the salient. The regiments of Kirkland's brigade had been detached earlier to defend various artillery positions around the courthouse, and the 52nd, although subjected to heavy shelling, was not directly involved in the fighting.

Following several more unsuccessful attempts against the Spotsylvania line during the next week, Grant abandoned the muddy, pestilential battlefield, loathsome with the stench of hundreds of unburied bodies, and began moving southeastward.[52] Lee then fell back to the North Anna River to a point just north of Hanover Junction, where he blocked the Federal route of advance. On May 23 the Federals crossed the river with three divisions at Jericho Ford. Major General Cadmus M. Wilcox's division of Hill's corps surprised one of the Federal units in the act of deployment and sent it stampeding for safety, but Wilcox was unable to budge the other Federal units. Heth's division, including the 52nd Regiment, was sent to Wilcox's assistance and was shelled by Federal artillery but arrived too late to take part in the battle. Several days of inconclusive fighting, in which Heth's division was not directly involved, convinced Grant of the tactical inferiority of his position on the North Anna, and on the night of May 26 he recrossed the river and moved southeastward toward the Pamunkey.

Lee began moving his army southward as soon as he learned that Grant was again on the march, and on May 27 Ewell's corps, temporarily commanded by General Early (General Hill had returned to the command of his own corps on May 21), went into position behind Totopotomoy Creek, near Atlee's Station, about eight miles northeast of Richmond. There it was joined the same day by Hill's and Longstreet's corps (the latter still under Anderson). On May 30, in an effort to prevent another sidle to the south by Grant, Early's corps attacked the Federal left but was driven back after failing to exploit its initial advantage.

In the meantime, Grant dispatched cavalry units under Major General Phil Sheridan a few miles further south to seize Cold Harbor, a strategic road junction whose capture would afford the Federals a shorter route to their supply base at White House Landing, on the

---

[50]Diary of John A. Foster, May 10, 1864, Alfred M. and John A. Foster Papers, Manuscript Department, Duke University Library, Durham, hereinafter cited as Foster Diary.

[51]Foster Diary, May 11, 1864.

[52]Casualties in the 52nd Regiment during the fighting at Spotsylvania Court House were 3 men killed, 8 wounded, and 11 captured.

Pamunkey, and open a new avenue of advance against Richmond. Finding Cold Harbor occupied by Confederate cavalry under Major General Fitzhugh Lee on the morning of May 31, Sheridan began a day-long struggle for possession of that dismal hamlet. The arrival of infantry support in the form of a brigade of Major General Robert F. Hoke's division, just up from Petersburg to reinforce Lee, failed to swing the battle against the Federal troopers and their rapid-firing Spencer carbines, and Sheridan's horsemen seized the place in the late afternoon. An attempt to retake Cold Harbor by Major General Joseph B. Kershaw's division of Anderson's corps the next day was turned aside by murderous blasts of grape and canister and sheets of fire from the seven-shot Spencers. A green South Carolina regiment, spearheading the attack, panicked and fled the field, unnerving the rest of Kershaw's command. To complete the shambles, Hoke's division, which was supposed to support Kershaw, failed to move at all. Stymied, the Confederates began entrenching. That afternoon, following the arrival of reinforcements on both sides, the Federals attacked. A near breakthrough was achieved at one point, but the fire of the defenders was so withering, according to Private Foster, that the Yankees soon went reeling back "faster than they come."[53]

Convinced that the Confederate infantry were sufficiently weakened and demoralized by the events of the last month to deliver a decisive blow, Grant planned a massive assault on the entire Confederate line for the morning of June 2. However, one of his corps missed its way during the night and arrived in such a state of exhaustion that the attack had to be temporarily delayed. A Confederate probing attack in which the 52nd Regiment took part further disrupted the timetable.[54] In the late afternoon a heavy rain began to fall, causing the assault to be postponed until the next day. In the meantime, Lee's entire army arrived on the field and busied itself with the construction of a virtually impregnable line of fortifications anchored on Totopotomoy Creek on the left and the Chickahominy River on the right. Early on the cool, misty morning of June 3, 50,000 Federals, many of whom rightly sensed that they were being sent to their deaths, advanced through the mud into a curtain of fire whose thunderous roar was clearly audible in Richmond eight miles away. Staggered by the hail of musketry and storm of case shot and double-shotted canister that raked them from several angles, the Federals milled in confusion and agony, unable to advance or, because of their comrades charging up behind them, retreat. In a matter of minutes the attack was over, with at least 7,000 Federals dead or wounded. Heth's division, on the extreme left of the Confederate line, was subjected to three separate assaults delivered with minimal determination and aggressiveness. Losses in the 52nd Regiment on June 3 were practically nil; during the four-day battle at Cold Harbor the regiment lost 4 men killed, 12 wounded, and 2 captured. Heth was ordered to the right to rejoin the rest of Hill's corps at Turkey Hill that afternoon.

The 52nd Regiment remained in the Confederate line at Cold Harbor until June 9, when it was ordered to Bottom's Bridge, on the Chickahominy River, for picket duty. After several quiet days "talking and trading with [the] yankees," the regiment moved five miles south on the 14th for picket duty at White Oak Swamp.[55] On the same day the Army of the Potomac began crossing the James River and prepared to attack Petersburg, whose formidable but badly undermanned works were commanded by General P. G. T. Beauregard. On June 18 the 52nd Regiment, under orders to go to the aid of the frantic Beauregard, marched ten miles to the James River, crossed on a pontoon bridge, and moved by rail to Petersburg where it

---

[53]Foster Diary, June 1, 1864.
[54]The 52nd Regiment lost two men killed and seven wounded in this attack.
[55]Foster Diary, June 10, 1864.

arrived "dusty and very fatigu[ed]" that evening.[56] During the next three days the regiment was engaged in skirmishing with the enemy and suffered a few casualties, but by then the Army of Northern Virginia had moved south of the James and the crisis passed. During the fighting near Petersburg the 52nd Regiment lost four men wounded.

On the afternoon of the 21st the regiment was ordered to a position four miles north of Petersburg to guard the railroad and pike bridges over Swift Creek. Three days later it returned to the Petersburg lines, where it remained for the next month. A selection of June and July entries from the diary of Private Foster gives a sketchy but clear picture of conditions in the trenches and the activities of the 52nd Regiment during that period:

> June 25 — [A]fter dark fortified[.] Cannonading and small arms heard in the direction of Petersburg[.] June 26 — [Q]uiet along our front — cannonading on or right in the direction of Petersburg. . . . [R]ained enough to [illegible] lay the dust. June 27 — Skirmishing on our right and very slow cannonading. [V]erry warm & dry. July 4 — [A]t dark was relieved from picket and ordered to report to our command[.] [M]arched 3 miles. July 7 — Skirmishing & ocasionaly shelling of the city. July 8 — Formed in line of Battle at the Weldon Rail-road. Heavy cannonading in the evening and during the night. Skirmishing. July 13 — Skirmishing and cannonading. . . . Very dry and hot. July 17 — Quiet until dark. Usual skirmishing and cannonading through the night. July 20 — Nothing of importance. Crowse and Tharp disappeared [deserted]. July 21 — Cannonading and skirmishing.[57]

During this period Colonel William MacRae of the 15th Regiment N.C. Troops (5th Regiment N.C. Volunteers) was appointed acting brigadier general to rank from June 22, 1864, and assigned to command the brigade in place of General Kirkland, who had been wounded at Cold Harbor on June 2. MacRae was promoted to the permanent rank of brigadier general on November 4, 1864. The brigade continued to serve in Heth's division of Hill's corps.

On July 27 MacRae's brigade moved from its position south of Petersburg to Chaffin's Bluff, about twelve miles north of Petersburg on the James River, where a new Federal thrust against Richmond seemed in the offing. In actuality, the dual purposes of this Federal operation were to draw Confederate forces from south of the James prior to the detonation of the great Petersburg mine on July 30 and to prevent those forces from interfering with a Federal cavalry raid designed to cut the Virginia Central Railroad, over which supplies continued to reach Richmond from the Shenandoah Valley. Thus the infantry operation near Chaffin's Bluff was primarily a feint, and the Federals, finding themselves confronted by formidable, well-manned fortifications, soon withdrew. On the morning of July 31, following the explosion of the mine on the previous day and the ensuing Battle of the Crater, MacRae's men returned to their former position south of Petersburg. On August 2 the brigade was moved further to the west and placed in reserve until the 9th, when it relieved Cooke's brigade in the trenches. There the sharpshooters on both sides, being only some 200 yards apart, kept up a "constant" firing day and night, inflicting a mounting toll of casualties and making it difficult for the men to rest.[58] The brigade was relieved again on the 13th and returned to camp.

In mid-August Grant ordered a westward extension of his lines south of Petersburg in order to sever another of Lee's vital supply arteries, the Weldon Railroad. On August 18 a Federal

---

[56]Clark, *Histories of the North Carolina Regiments*, III, 247.
[57]Foster Diary, dates as indicated in text.
[58]Clark, *Histories of the North Carolina Regiments*, III, 248.

corps under Major General G. K. Warren seized Globe Tavern, three miles south of Petersburg, and began tearing up track. A surprise attack through thick woods by elements of Heth's division, including the 52nd Regiment, drove the Federals back temporarily, but by nightfall they had repulsed the Confederates and recovered their lost ground.[59] Both sides received reinforcements that night and the following morning, and heavy fighting broke out again late on the afternoon of the 19th. Two Federal brigades were overrun and most of their members captured, but again Warren's men rallied and regained possession of the field. The 52nd Regiment was not involved in the fighting on the 19th. After a rainy day of relative quiet during which the Federals threw up a line of entrenchments, Confederate units under the command of A. P. Hill and Major General William Mahone attacked again on August 21. A noisy but ineffective bombardment by thirty cannon was followed by a headlong Confederate assault that was wrecked by heavy artillery fire. Private Foster reported somewhat dolefully that

[We] charged the yankees through the open field and woods[,] mud and swamps. The most sevear cannonading I ever witnessed. We drove the enemy [pickets?] 1 mile. Charged them out of thir works [not the main ones.] [G]ot in them in mud and water knee deep. This day will be long remembered.[60]

Casualties in the 52nd Regiment were, in view of Foster's diary account, unexpectedly light: a combined total of four men killed and eight wounded for the fighting on both the 18th and 21st.

Now firmly astride the Weldon Railroad, Grant gave orders that the track be torn up as far south of Globe Tavern as prudence allowed. A Federal corps under Major General W. S. Hancock immediately undertook that assignment and by the evening of the 24th had progressed as far as Reams' Station, five miles south of Globe Tavern. Determined to limit the extent of the incursion, Lee dispatched Hill with seven infantry brigades, two cavalry divisions, and an ample artillery contingent to "punish" the Federals.[61] Two early afternoon assaults in which the 52nd Regiment did not take part were narrowly staved off by Hancock's weary, outnumbered men, many of whom were taking part in their first battle. Another attack that afternoon, preceded by a mind-numbing bombardment that enfiladed part of the Federal line, sawed off trees, and flattened some ill-constructed breastworks, terminated in a wild melee inside the enemy trenches. Hundreds of the untried, demoralized Federal soldiers fled the field, and more than 2,000 threw down their weapons and surrendered. "It was a compleat victory," wrote Private Foster. "[W]e killed some and taken nearly all the [others]. . . ."[62] Casualties in the 52nd Regiment were three men killed and seven wounded. The regiment returned to the Petersburg defenses with the rest of MacRae's brigade that night and went into position just east of the Weldon Railroad.

---

[59]Apparently the regiment suffered no casualties in this engagement.

[60]Foster Diary, August 21, 1864.

[61]Clifford Dowdey and Louis H. Manarin, *The Wartime Papers of Robert E. Lee* (Boston: Little, Brown and Company, 1961), 845.

[62]Foster Diary, August 25, 1864. "[W]e . . . charge[d] and captured the yankee breastworks at the point of the bayonet," wrote Corporal James W. Wright of the 26th North Carolina. "[W]hen they saw us coming at a double quick they threw down their guns and commenced waving their hats." Some of the Federals came over their breastworks to greet Kirkland's men in the open and, with the clear intention of putting quick distance between themselves and their captors, marched off to the Confederate rear. James W. Wright to his father and Fanny, August 27, 1864, Wright Papers. See also Charles M. Stedman, "Battle at Reams' Station," *Southern Historical Society Papers*, XIX (1891), 113-120.

For the next three weeks the brigade was occupied in constructing fortifications.[63] On September 16 MacRae's men moved to a position about three miles southwest of Petersburg and about a half mile south of the Boydton Plank Road, where it resumed digging. On the 29th the brigade moved a few miles northeastward to replace the units that were sent north of the James to counter a Federal thrust against Fort Harrison. Immediately, Grant made a westward lunge against the weakened Confederate defenses southwest of Petersburg, and MacRae's men were sent back to their original positions the next day. On the afternoon of the 30th, while the brigade was making an attack, a Federal force smashed into the flank of the 52nd Regiment and sent it reeling in confusion. Rebounding briskly, the 52nd and the 11th North Carolina made a gallant countercharge and captured about 600 Federal prisoners. The next morning the men of the 44th and 52nd, either because they misunderstood their orders or were temporarily out of the control of their officers, made an unauthorized attack in a rainstorm against Federal entrenchments but escaped with light casualties. During the course of the three-day battle, known variously as Jones' Farm and Peebles' Farm, the Confederates regained some lost ground but were unable to completely dislodge the Federals. The result was a three-mile extension of the Federal lines to the west. The 52nd Regiment lost three men killed and twenty-six wounded in the fighting.

MacRae's brigade was then assigned to a position on the extreme right of the Petersburg defenses and began throwing up fortifications to cover the newly extended Federal line. On October 27, following a month of relative quiet, a powerful Federal force consisting of a cavalry division and parts of three infantry corps moved westward toward Burgess' Mill in an attempt to cut the Boydton Plank Road and the Southside Railroad. Although outnumbering their Confederate opponents by a margin of at least two to one, lack of coordination among the Federals and swampy, heavily wooded terrain in which several units lost their way slowed the advance to a crawl. A counterattack by MacRae's brigade (temporarily commanded by General Mahone) and other units drove a deep wedge in the Federal line, but the Confederates were forced to "cut [their] way out" after enemy units appeared in their rear.[64] The Federal offensive ground to a halt, and the Boydton Plank Road and Southside Railroad remained in Confederate hands. Losses in the 52nd Regiment were 3 men killed, 5 wounded, and 34 captured.

On October 29 MacRae's brigade returned to its position in the lines south of Petersburg near the Hart house. New works, closer to Petersburg, were constructed, and the men built cabins for the winter. On December 8 the 52nd Regiment and the rest of Hill's corps were ordered to Belfield, about forty miles south of Petersburg on the Weldon Railroad, where a Federal corps was busily ripping up track and burning crossties. In weather that may well have inflicted the greatest suffering endured by the 52nd in a noncombat situation during the entire war, the hungry, ill-clothed men set out in a high wind and cold rain that was soon succeeded by hail and sleet. After a miserable night huddled around fires in a "semi-conscious, half-freezing condition," Hill's men arrived the next day at Jarratt's Station, about nine miles north of Belfield, where they learned that the enemy had retired.[65] A brief pursuit having inflicted about 100 casualties on the Federals, the men bivouacked for another

---

[63]A report by Lieutenant Colonel H. E. Peyton, Assistant Adjutant and Inspector General of the Army of Northern Virginia, dated September 23, 1864, states that MacRae's brigade was in "specially good order" and commanded by a "most excellent officer" who was "devoting himself with great energy to the comfort and efficiency of his command and the improvement and strengthening of his line. General MacRae is a strict disciplinarian, but has secured in an eminent degree the confidence of his men, as was shown in his successful charge at Reams' Station on 25th of August." *Official Records (Army)*, Series I, XLII, Part II, 1274-1275.

[64]Letter from an unidentified member of the 11th Regiment N.C. Troops (a sister unit to the 52nd Regiment in MacRae's brigade), Raleigh *Daily Confederate*, November 5, 1864.

[65]W. S. Dunlop, *Lee's Sharpshooters: or, the Forefront of Battle* (Little Rock: Tunnah and Pittard, 1899), 222.

wretched night. The 52nd Regiment arrived back at its camp near Petersburg on December 14. It remained there, drilling and doing picket duty in the trenches, through January of the new year.

Early in February, 1865, Grant ordered a thrust southwest of Petersburg to interdict Confederate supply wagon traffic on the Boydton Plank Road near Hatcher's Run. Heth's division, including the 52nd Regiment, and a division commanded by General Clement A. Evans clashed with the Federal intruders on the icy afternoon of February 5 but were unable to dislodge them. New fighting, in which the 52nd Regiment did not take part, broke out the following day along Hatcher's Run. Units from both sides, inspired by a combination of exhaustion, inexperience, and ammunition shortages, fled the field in disorder at virtually the first sign of opposition. During the night a blizzard roared in from the north, burying the combatants under a blanket of sleet and snow and putting a merciful end to the battle. Grant then extended his lines to the Vaughn Road crossing of Hatcher's Run, and Lee ordered his own badly undermanned works extended to match those of the Federals. During the fighting on February 5 the 52nd Regiment lost three men wounded.

The regiment then returned to its position in the fortifications southwest of Petersburg, where it remained for almost two months. The clatter of small arms fire, interspersed with the explosion of artillery and mortar shells, seldom ceased day or night, and enemy snipers, deadly and resourceful, brought an abrupt conclusion to the career of many a momentarily careless Confederate. The virtual breakdown of the Confederate commissary resulted in a severe food shortage and, if not starvation, a degree of hunger that made the men long for the days when they subsisted on half rations. Although the coming of spring brought an improvement in the food situation, demoralization deepened along with the malodorous mud. Unable to endure the privations and hopelessness, scores of ragged, louse-ridden, exhausted Confederates, many of whom had served faithfully for months or years, deserted to the Federal lines every night.

On March 25 Lee, well aware that the end was near, launched a desperate, forlorn-hope assault against Fort Stedman, east of Petersburg, hoping to weaken the Federal grip long enough for at least part of the Army of Northern Virginia to escape and join forces under General Joseph E. Johnston in North Carolina. Although momentarily successful, a resolute counterattack by the massive Federal army quickly overpowered the Confederates, inflicting more than 4,000 casualties. The 52nd Regiment was not involved in the attack on Fort Stedman but took part in some of the peripheral fighting, loosing eight men wounded and twenty-two captured.

Two days later General Sheridan's victorious Army of the Shenandoah, having devastated the Shenandoah Valley and virtually destroyed the army of General Early with which it had been contending since the summer of 1864, joined Grant. Anticipating an immediate attack on the vital Southside Railroad, Lee concentrated most of his cavalry west of Petersburg and shortly thereafter ordered Confederate infantry units under the overall command of Major General George E. Pickett to reinforce them.

On the 29th the expected movement began with Sheridan's cavalrymen making a wide detour well to the southwest of Petersburg before turning northwest. At the same time, a powerful Federal infantry force under Major General G. K. Warren advanced slowly westward, crossing the Boydton Plank Road. By the morning of April 1 the Federal infantry were about four miles east of a crossroads known as Five Forks, where Pickett's force was concentrated. Sheridan was at Dinwiddie Court House about six miles to the southeast. Late that afternoon the combined commands of Sheridan and Warren, numbering almost 50,000 men, attacked, crushing the left flank of Pickett's 19,000-man force, routing the Confederates from the field, and taking more than 5,000 prisoners.

Swiftly following up his advantage, Grant unleashed a massive assault against the Confederate line south of Petersburg on the morning of April 2, broke through, and swept down the trenches. Most of Heth's division, including the 52nd Regiment, was in position between the Boydton Plank and White Oak roads, near Hatcher's Run. Falling back in some disorder after the Confederate lines to their left were breached, Heth's division and that of Major General C. M. Wilcox rallied on a ridge near Sutherland's Station, on the Southside Railroad, beating off two attacks before their line buckled under a third. The 52nd then retreated with "little, if any, organization" in the direction of the Appomattox River, having lost eighty-six men captured.[66]

With Richmond and Petersburg irredeemably lost, Lee ordered the remnants of his army to evacuate the two cities that night and march westward to Amelia Court House. There an ample stock of badly needed rations supposedly awaited, and the army could use the Richmond and Danville Railroad to move to Danville and unite with Joseph E. Johnston's army moving up from North Carolina.

Lee's desperate plan floundered at its first step when no supplies were found at Amelia Court House. Although most of his units reached the town on the 4th, the absence of rations caused a delay of twenty-four hours while foraging parties were sent out. Meanwhile, Federal cavalry and infantry, paralleling Lee's line of retreat to the south, slipped ahead of the Confederates and occupied Jetersville, thereby cutting the Richmond and Danville Railroad. Abandoning the railroad, Lee's army moved out of Amelia Court House about noon on the 5th, looping to the north to avoid Jetersville. After marching all night in a driving rain the 52nd Regiment, at the head of the Confederate column with other units under Longstreet and Heth, reached Rice's Station on the Southside Railroad around noon on the 6th.

In the meantime the Confederate rear guard, under Major General John B. Gordon, had become separated from the center of Lee's column, while the center, under Ewell and Anderson, had in turn lost contact with the van. In heavy fighting in the vicinity of Sayler's Creek, more than 8,000 men under the three generals were killed, wounded, or captured, reducing the size of Lee's force by at least a fourth. Harassed by Federal cavalry, the army moved on, marching all night to reach Farmville, where boxcars loaded with provisions waited. In the midst of a hurried, half-cooked breakfast, word was received of the approach of Federal cavalry and infantry, forcing a hasty retreat over the Farmville bridges to the north side of the rain-swollen Appomattox River. There, about three miles north of Farmville, the rear guard under General Mahone was attacked on the morning of the 7th near Cumberland Church. Although lacking sufficient numbers to defeat Mahone, the attackers delayed the Confederate retreat for the rest of the day. In the meantime the 52nd Regiment and other units of MacRae's brigade, after assisting Fitz Lee in the successful defense of a wagon train under attack by Federal horsemen near Farmville, fell back to the vicinity of Cumberland Church. The regiment's part in Mahone's fight at that place, if any, is unclear.

During the night of April 7 Lee's bone-weary men were on the move again, this time headed for Appomattox Station, on the Southside Railroad, where supplies sent from Lynchburg were waiting. The haggard, disintegrating army continued its march throughout the next day in a welcome if ominous absence of serious harassment; the enemy units in Lee's rear failed to catch up with their quarry, while to the south the Federals were hurrying forward to get across Lee's line of march at Appomattox Station. Gordon's men took the lead, while Longstreet's command, including what was left of the 52nd Regiment, formed the rear guard. Three miles from Appomattox Station the army bivouacked for the night. At about 9

---

[66]Clark, *Histories of the North Carolina Regiments*, III, 252.

o'clock a short burst of cannon fire was heard from the southwest, followed by silence. Presently, Lee's worst fear was confirmed: Federal forces had captured the vital supplies at Appomattox Station and were across his line of retreat.

Later that night Lee and his generals held their last council of war. The essential questions now became: how strong was the Federal force that had seized Appomattox Station, and did it include infantry? Cavalry might be swept aside, but if infantry units were present in sizable numbers it would be impossible for Lee, with his wrecked, starving army, reduced to an organized force of perhaps 12,000 men, to break through. In that case, surrender would be the only rational choice. On the morning of April 9 Confederate units under Gordon and Fitz Lee attacked and succeeded in driving a line of dismounted Federal cavalrymen from their temporary breastworks. At that moment of apparent deliverance, Federal infantry units, some of which had marched for twenty-one hours in the last twenty-four to reach Appomattox Station, began arriving on the field. Shortly, Gordon found himself under attack from three sides and cut off from Fitz Lee. In the Confederate rear, Longstreet's command, including the 52nd Regiment, also braced for an attack by a newly arrived Federal corps. Trapped and hopelessly outnumbered, Lee surrendered the Army of Northern Virginia at the nearby hamlet of Appomattox Court House that afternoon. On April 12, sixty-six members of the 52nd Regiment were paroled.

FIELD AND STAFF

COLONELS

MARSHALL, JAMES KEITH
Previously served as Captain of Company M, 1st Regiment N.C. Infantry (6 months, 1861). Appointed Colonel of this regiment on April 23, 1862. Killed at Gettysburg, Pennsylvania, July 3, 1863.

PARKS, MARCUS A.
Previously served as Captain of Company F of this regiment. Appointed Major on April 18, 1862, and transferred to the Field and Staff. Promoted to Lieutenant Colonel on April 25, 1862. Wounded in both thighs and captured at Gettysburg, Pennsylvania, July 3, 1863. Hospitalized at Gettysburg. Transferred to Johnson's Island, Ohio, where he arrived on July 24, 1863. Paroled at Johnson's Island on March 14, 1865. Received at Cox's Wharf, James River, Virginia, March 22, 1865, for exchange. [Was promoted to Colonel in July, 1863, while a prisoner of war.]

LIEUTENANT COLONELS

LITTLE, BENJAMIN F.
Previously served as Captain of Company E of this regiment. Appointed Lieutenant Colonel on April 15, 1864, to rank from July 3, 1863, and transferred to the Field and Staff. Resigned on July 15, 1864, by reason of disability from wounds received at Gettysburg, Pennsylvania, July 3, 1863. Resignation accepted on August 30, 1864.

ERSON, ERIC
Previously served as Captain of Company H of this regiment. Appointed Major on April 15, 1864, and transferred to the Field and Staff. Wounded in the right thigh at Reams' Station, Virginia, August 25, 1864. Hospitalized at Richmond, Virginia, August 28, 1864. Promoted to Lieutenant Colonel on August 30, 1864. Furloughed from hospital on September 18, 1864. Reported absent wounded through December, 1864. Returned to duty on an unspecified date. Surrendered at Appomattox Court House, Virginia, April 9, 1865.

MAJOR

RICHARDSON, JOHN Q.
Appointed Major on April 29, 1862. "Killed instantly by a rifle ball" while leading the left wing of his regiment at Gettysburg, Pennsylvania, July 3, 1863. He was "brave and dashing."

ADJUTANTS

WARREN, LEWELLYN P.
Previously served as 1st Lieutenant of Company M, 1st Regiment N.C. Infantry (6 months, 1861). Appointed Adjutant (1st Lieutenant) of this regiment on July 11, 1862, to rank from June 6, 1862. Appointed Surgeon of the 26th Regiment N.C. Troops on October 14, 1862, to rank from August 28, 1862, and transferred.

ROBINSON, JOHN H.
Previously served as 2nd Lieutenant of Company B of this regiment. Appointed Adjutant (1st Lieutenant) on March 16, 1863, to rank from November 1, 1862, and transferred to the Field and Staff. Reported on duty as acting Assistant Adjutant General of General William MacRae's brigade on March 21, 1865. Surrendered at Appomattox Court House, Virginia, April 9, 1865.

ASSISTANT QUARTERMASTERS

McCORKLE, JAMES M.
Previously served as Sergeant in Company I of this regiment. Appointed Assistant Quartermaster (Captain) on July 11, 1862, to rank from June 6, 1862, and transferred to the Field and Staff. Resigned on October 29, 1862, while under charges of "drunken conduct" and failure to return to camp when ordered to do so. Resignation accepted on November 15, 1862.

GATLING, JOHN T., JR.
Previously served as 2nd Lieutenant of Company C of this regiment. Appointed Assistant Quartermaster (Captain) on December 2, 1862, to rank from December 1, 1862, and transferred to the Field and Staff. Appointed Assistant Quartermaster (Captain) of General William Kirkland's brigade on September 15, 1864, and transferred.

ASSISTANT COMMISSARY OF SUBSISTENCE

COKE, GEORGE H.
Appointed Assistant Commissary of Subsistence (1st Lieutenant) on July 11, 1862, to rank from June 6, 1862. Dropped from the rolls of the regiment on February 5, 1863.

SURGEONS

FOULKES, JAMES F.
Previously served as Captain of Company B of this regiment. Appointed Surgeon on September 26, 1862, to rank from June 28, 1862, and transferred to the Field and

Staff. Present or accounted for until he was assigned to hospital duty at Richmond, Virginia, on an unspecified date (probably in November-December, 1864).

LILLY, WILLIAM H.

Born in Montgomery County and was by occupation a physician prior to enlisting at age 28. Appointed Assistant Surgeon on September 26, 1862, to rank from June 27, 1862. Promoted to Surgeon on or about December 8, 1864. Surrendered at Appomattox Court House, Virginia, April 9, 1865.

CHAPLAINS

CLINE, JAMES M.

Methodist Episcopalian. Appointed Chaplain on July 11, 1862, to rank from June 6, 1862. Resigned on August 24, 1863, by reason of the illness of his wife. Resignation accepted on August 28, 1863.

SANFORD, WILLIAM FRANK

Previously served as Private in Company E of this regiment. Appointed Chaplain on October 27, 1864, and transferred to the Field and Staff. No further records.

ENSIGN

JAMES, PHILIP A.

Previously served as Sergeant in Company D of this regiment. Appointed Ensign (1st Lieutenant) on April 30, 1864, and transferred to the Field and Staff. Captured at Hatcher's Run, Virginia, April 2, 1865. Confined at Old Capitol Prison, Washington, D.C., April 5, 1865. Transferred to Johnson's Island, Ohio, April 9, 1865. Released at Johnson's Island on June 18, 1865, after taking the Oath of Allegiance.

SERGEANTS MAJOR

WARREN, JOHN CRITTENDEN

Previously served as Private in Company C of this regiment. Promoted to Sergeant Major on or about April 24, 1862, and transferred to the Field and Staff. Appointed 2nd Lieutenant on September 13, 1862, and transferred back to Company C.

BAINES, ROBERT G.

Previously served as Sergeant in Company K of this regiment. Promoted to Sergeant Major in September-October, 1862, and transferred to the Field and Staff. Wounded in the knee (probably also in the hand) and captured at Gettysburg, Pennsylvania, July 3, 1863. Hospitalized at Gettysburg. Leg amputated. Died in hospital at Gettysburg on July 13, 1863, of wounds.

TURNER, HENRY CLAY

Previously served as Commissary Sergeant of this regiment. [See Commissary Sergeants' section below.] Promoted to Sergeant Major on July 8, 1863. Present or accounted for until wounded at or near Globe Tavern, Virginia, on or about August 21, 1864. Hospitalized at Richmond, Virginia. Returned to duty on or about November 1, 1864. Elected 2nd Lieutenant on January 19, 1865, and transferred to Company K, 28th Regiment N.C. Troops.

QUARTERMASTER SERGEANTS

ROBINSON, JOHN T.

Previously served as Private in Company I of this regiment. Appointed Quartermaster Sergeant on April 28, 1862, and transferred to the Field and Staff. Discharged on June 6, 1862, by reason of disability.

RUSSELL, WALTER R.

Previously served as Private in Company C of this regiment. Appointed Quartermaster Sergeant in May-June, 1864, and transferred to the Field and Staff. Captured at Petersburg, Virginia, April 3, 1865. Confined at Hart's Island, New York Harbor, April 11, 1865. Released at Hart's Island on June 21, 1865, after taking the Oath of Allegiance.

COMMISSARY SERGEANTS

TURNER, HENRY CLAY

Previously served as Sergeant in Company I of this regiment. Appointed Commissary Sergeant on May 1, 1862, and transferred to the Field and Staff. Present or accounted for until promoted to Sergeant Major on July 8, 1863. [See Sergeants Major's section above.]

BROOKSHIRE, WILLIAM F.

Previously served as 1st Sergeant of Company E of this regiment. Appointed Commissary Sergeant in July-August, 1863, and transferred to the Field and Staff. Present or accounted for through December, 1864. Captured at Farmville, Virginia, April 6, 1865. Confined at Point Lookout, Maryland, April 14, 1865. Released at Point Lookout on June 10, 1865, after taking the Oath of Allegiance.

ORDNANCE SERGEANTS

RICHARDSON, THOMAS N.

Previously served as Private in Company C of this regiment. Appointed Ordnance Sergeant in September, 1862-February, 1863, and transferred to the Field and Staff. Discharged on September 13, 1863. Reason discharged not reported.

PEPPER, JOHN KERR

Previously served as Sergeant in Company D of this regiment. Appointed Ordnance Sergeant in September-October, 1864, and transferred to the Field and Staff. Reported absent sick in November-December, 1864.

HOSPITAL STEWARD

DeBERRY, EDMUND J.

Previously served as Sergeant in Company E of this regiment. Appointed Hospital Steward in July-October, 1864, and transferred to the Field and Staff. Surrendered at Appomattox Court House, Virginia, April 9, 1865.

BAND

DECAMP, CHARLES, Chief Musician

Previously served as Private in Company C of this regiment. Appointed Chief Musician (Drum Major) in September-October, 1864, and transferred to the regimental band. Paroled at Charlotte on May 20, 1865.

PIERCE, JOHN H. C., Musician

Previously served as Musician in Company F of this regiment. Transferred to the regimental band in August-November, 1864. Captured near Petersburg, Virginia, April 2, 1865. Confined at Point Lookout, Maryland, April 4, 1865. Released at Point Lookout on June 17, 1865, after taking the Oath of Allegiance.

SHAW, WILEY H., Musician

Previously served as Musician (Drummer) in Company B of this regiment. Transferred to the regimental band in July-October, 1864. Reported absent in hospital in November-December, 1864. No further records.

WARREN, ROBERT F., Chief Musician

Previously served as Chief Musician of Company F of this regiment. Transferred to the regimental band on an unspecified date (probably in July-October, 1864). Reported present in November-December, 1864.

COMPANY A

This company, known as the "Cabarrus Riflemen," was raised in Cabarrus County and enlisted at Concord in March-April, 1862. It was mustered into state service at Camp Mangum, near Raleigh, on April 28, 1862, and assigned to the 52nd Regiment N.C. Troops as Company A. After joining the regiment the company functioned as a part of the regiment, and its history for the remainder of the war is reported as a part of the regimental history.

The information contained in the following roster was compiled primarily from a company muster-in and descriptive roll dated April 28, 1862, and from company muster rolls for May 1-June 30, 1862; October 31, 1862-February 28, 1863; and July 1, 1863-December 31, 1864. No company muster rolls were located for July 1-September 30, 1862; March 1-June 30, 1863; or for the period after December 31, 1864. Valuable information was obtained from primary records such as the North Carolina adjutant general's *Roll of Honor*, discharge certificates, medical records, prisoner of war records, *The War of the Rebellion: A Compilation of the Official Records of the Union and Confederate Armies*, militia records, newspaper casualty lists and obituaries, Confederate pension applications filed with the state of North Carolina, and the 1860 federal census of North Carolina. Secondary sources such as postwar rosters and histories, cemetery records, the *Confederate Veteran*, published genealogies, and records of the United Daughters of the Confederacy also provided useful information.

OFFICERS

CAPTAINS

PROPST, GEORGE A.

Born in Cabarrus County where he resided as a farmer prior to enlisting at age 41. Appointed Captain on April 28, 1862. Resigned on August 12, 1862. Resignation accepted on November 25, 1862.

ALEXANDER, JOHN MARION

Born in Cabarrus County where he resided as a tailor prior to enlisting at age 33. Appointed 1st Lieutenant on April 28, 1862. Promoted to Captain on November 25, 1862. Present or accounted for until wounded in the right arm at Gettysburg, Pennsylvania, on or about July 3, 1863. Hospitalized at Richmond, Virginia. Returned to duty on July 30, 1863. Present or accounted for through December, 1864. Surrendered at Appomattox Court House, Virginia, April 9, 1865.

LIEUTENANTS

BLACK, JAMES A., 3rd Lieutenant

Resided in Cabarrus County and was by occupation a merchant's clerk prior to enlisting at age 31. Appointed 3rd Lieutenant on April 28, 1862. Died at Concord on July 4, 1862, of "sickness contracted in the camp."

COOK, JAMES M., 1st Lieutenant

Previously served as Sergeant in Company B, 20th Regiment N.C. Troops (10th Regiment N.C. Volunteers). Transferred to this company on March 20, 1862. Mustered in as 1st Sergeant. Appointed 2nd Lieutenant on August 26, 1862. Promoted to 1st Lieutenant on November 25, 1862. Killed at Gettysburg, Pennsylvania, July 3, 1863.

CORRELL, PHILLIP A., 2nd Lieutenant

Born in Cabarrus County where he resided as a farmer

prior to enlisting at age 34. Appointed 2nd Lieutenant on April 28, 1862. Resigned on August 15, 1862, by reason of "calculus in his bladder." Resignation accepted on August 26, 1862.

HILL, JOSEPH CORNELIUS, 3rd Lieutenant
Born in Cabarrus County where he resided as a carpenter prior to enlisting in Cabarrus County at age 27, March 21, 1862. Mustered in as Sergeant. Appointed 3rd Lieutenant on November 25, 1862. Wounded at Goldsboro on December 17, 1862. Returned to duty prior to March 1, 1863. Reported present from July, 1863, through April, 1864. Hospitalized at Richmond, Virginia, June 5, 1864, with a gunshot wound. Place and date wounded not reported (probably wounded at or near Cold Harbor, Virginia, May 31-June 3, 1864). Returned to duty in July-August, 1864. Wounded at Burgess' Mill, Virginia, October 27, 1864. Hospitalized at Richmond. Furloughed for sixty days on December 24, 1864. Returned to duty on an unspecified date. Captured at or near Sutherland's Station, Virginia, April 2, 1865. Confined at Old Capitol Prison, Washington, D.C., April 5, 1865. Transferred to Johnson's Island, Ohio, April 9, 1865. Released at Johnson's Island on June 18, 1865, after taking the Oath of Allegiance.

HURLEY, ALEXANDER F., 1st Lieutenant
Born in Montgomery County and resided in Cabarrus County where he was by occupation a deputy sheriff prior to enlisting in Cabarrus County at age 34, March 21, 1862. Mustered in as Corporal. Promoted to Sergeant prior to July 1, 1862. Appointed 2nd Lieutenant on November 25, 1862. Wounded in the head at Gettysburg, Pennsylvania, July 3, 1863. Promoted to 1st Lieutenant the same date. Returned to duty in November-December, 1863. Present or accounted for through December, 1864. Surrendered at Appomattox Court House, Virginia, April 9, 1865.

NONCOMMISSIONED OFFICERS AND PRIVATES

ALEXANDER, JOHN M., Private
Born in Cabarrus County and enlisted on August 1, 1864, for the war. Died "at home" on December 11, 1864, of disease.

ALLEN, LEE S., Private
Resided in Cabarrus County and enlisted at age 38, October 15, 1862, for the war. Company records indicate that he was absent sick through December, 1864.

BAKER, JOHN C., Private
Born in Rowan County and resided in Cabarrus County where he was by occupation a farmer prior to enlisting in Cabarrus County at age 43, March 8, 1862. Deserted to the enemy at or near Gettysburg, Pennsylvania, on or about July 2, 1863. Confined at Fort Mifflin, Pennsylvania. Released at Fort Mifflin on November 17, 1863, after taking the Oath of Allegiance.

BARNHARDT, ADAM A., Private
Born in Cabarrus County where he resided as a farmer prior to enlisting in Cabarrus County at age 22, March 21, 1862. Reported absent sick on or about July 1, 1862. Returned to duty prior to March 1, 1863. Present or accounted for through December, 1864. Served as a teamster during most of that period. Deserted to the enemy on or about March 25, 1865. Sent to City Point, Virginia. Transferred to Washington, D.C., where he arrived on March 30, 1865. Released at Washington on or about the same date after taking the Oath of Allegiance.

BARNHARDT, BENTON, Private
Born in Cabarrus County where he resided as a farmer prior to enlisting in Cabarrus County at age 19, March 21, 1862. Captured at Bristoe Station, Virginia, October 14, 1863. Confined at Point Lookout, Maryland, October 28, 1863. Paroled at Point Lookout on January 17, 1865. Received at Boulware's Wharf, James River, Virginia, January 21, 1865, for exchange. Paroled at Salisbury on May 16, 1865.

BARNHARDT, DAVID C., Private
Born in Cabarrus County where he resided as a farmer. Was about 32 years of age at time of enlistment. Enlisted prior to April 28, 1862, when he was reported absent with leave. No further records.

BARNHARDT, JOHN F., Private
Enlisted prior to April 28, 1862. No further records.

BARNHARDT, TOBIAS, Private
Born in Cabarrus County where he resided as a farmer prior to enlisting in Cabarrus County at age 29, March 21, 1862. Wounded and captured at Gettysburg, Pennsylvania, on or about July 3, 1863. Confined at Fort Delaware, Delaware. Transferred to Point Lookout, Maryland, October 20, 1863. Died at Point Lookout on November 3, 1863, of "chr[onic] diarrh[oea] & scorbutus."

BEATY, JUNIUS F., Private
Born in Cabarrus County where he resided as a manufacturer prior to enlisting in Cabarrus County at age 19, March 21, 1862. Reported present or accounted for on surviving records through April, 1864. Hospitalized at Richmond, Virginia, May 27, 1864, with diarrhoea. Furloughed for thirty days on August 27, 1864. Returned to duty prior to October 27, 1864, when he was captured at Burgess' Mill, Virginia. Confined at Point Lookout, Maryland, October 30, 1864. Died in hospital at Point Lookout on March 13, 1865, of "chronic diarrhoea."

BENSON, WILLIAM L. D., Corporal
Born in Cabarrus County where he resided as a farmer prior to enlisting in Cabarrus County at age 37, March 21, 1862. Mustered in as Corporal. Discharged on May 30, 1862, by reason of being overage.

BLACKWELDER, ALLISON J., Private
Resided in Cabarrus County and was by occupation a farmer prior to enlisting in Cabarrus County at age 34, April 26, 1862, for the war. Wounded and captured at

Gettysburg, Pennsylvania, July 3, 1863. Hospitalized at Davids Island, New York Harbor. Paroled at Davids Island and transferred to City Point, Virginia, where he was received on September 16, 1863, for exchange. Detailed for light duty in North Carolina on February 22, 1864. Rejoined the company in May-June, 1864. Retired from service on July 27, 1864, presumably by reason of disability from wounds received at Gettysburg.

BLACKWELDER, CHARLES M., Private
Resided in Cabarrus County and was by occupation a farmer prior to enlisting in Cabarrus County at age 30, April 26, 1862, for the war. Wounded in the leg and captured at Gettysburg, Pennsylvania, July 3, 1863. Hospitalized at Gettysburg. Transferred to hospital at Chester, Pennsylvania, on or about July 27, 1863. Died in hospital at Chester on September 21, 1863, of "pyaemia."

BLACKWELDER, COLUMBUS, Private
Born in Cabarrus County where he resided as a farmer prior to enlisting in Cabarrus County at age 18, March 21, 1862. Reported present or accounted for on surviving company muster rolls through August, 1863. Captured at Bristoe Station, Virginia, October 14, 1863. Confined at Old Capitol Prison, Washington, D.C. Transferred to Point Lookout, Maryland, October 27, 1863. Paroled at Point Lookout on February 18, 1865. Received at Boulware's Wharf, James River, Virginia, on or about February 20, 1865, for exchange. Survived the war.

BLACKWELDER, GEORGE W., Private
Resided in Cabarrus County and was by occupation a farmhand prior to enlisting in Cabarrus County at age 20, April 26, 1862, for the war. Died in hospital at Petersburg, Virginia, September 8, 1862, of "cont[inued] fever."

BLACKWELDER, RANSOM C., Private
Resided in Cabarrus County and was by occupation a "livery stable [worker?]" prior to enlisting in Cabarrus County at age 23, April 26, 1862, for the war. Reported present or accounted for on surviving company muster rolls through November, 1864. Transferred to Company G, 9th Regiment N.C. State Troops (1st Regiment N.C. Cavalry), December 8, 1864.

BLUME, GEORGE C., Corporal
Born in Cabarrus County where he resided as a farmer prior to enlisting in Cabarrus County at age 22, March 24, 1862. Mustered in as Private. Promoted to Corporal prior to March 1, 1863. Wounded and captured at Gettysburg, Pennsylvania, July 3, 1863. Hospitalized at Gettysburg. Transferred to Fort Delaware, Delaware, on or about July 10, 1863. Transferred to Point Lookout, Maryland, October 20, 1863. Paroled at Point Lookout on February 18, 1865. Received at Boulware's Wharf, James River, Virginia, on or about February 20, 1865, for exchange.

BLUME, JOSEPH W., Private
Resided in Cabarrus County and was by occupation a wagonmaker prior to enlisting in Cabarrus County at age 22, September 1, 1862, for the war. Reported sick in

hospital at Goldsboro on or about March 1, 1863. Returned to duty prior to July 3, 1863, when he was wounded in the left arm and captured at Gettysburg, Pennsylvania. Hospitalized at Davids Island, New York Harbor. Paroled at Davids Island and transferred to City Point, Virginia, where he was received on September 16, 1863, for exchange. Reported absent wounded through February, 1864. Reported absent on light duty in North Carolina in March-April, 1864. Rejoined the company prior to July 1, 1864. Reported present until November-December, 1864, when he was reported absent on sick furlough. Survived the war.

BLUME, WILLIAM HARVEY, JR., Private
Resided in Cabarrus County and was by occupation a wagonmaker prior to enlisting in Cabarrus County at age 20, October 15, 1862, for the war. Wounded and captured at Gettysburg, Pennsylvania, on or about July 3, 1863. Hospitalized at Gettysburg. Transferred to Fort Delaware, Delaware, on or about July 10, 1863. Transferred to Point Lookout, Maryland, October 20, 1863. Paroled at Point Lookout on February 18, 1865. Received at Boulware's Wharf, James River, Virginia, on or about February 20, 1865, for exchange.

BLUME, WILLIAM HARVEY, SR., Private
Resided in Cabarrus County and was by occupation a farmhand prior to enlisting in Cabarrus County at age 22, September 1, 1862, for the war. Wounded and captured at Gettysburg, Pennsylvania, July 3, 1863. Transferred to hospital at Davids Island, New York Harbor, on or about July 20, 1863. Paroled at Davids Island and transferred to City Point, Virginia, where he was received on September 16, 1863, for exchange. Returned to duty in January-February, 1864. Present or accounted for through December, 1864. Survived the war.

BOSTIAN, JESSE J., Sergeant
Born in Rowan County and resided in Cabarrus County where he was by occupation a farmer prior to enlisting in Cabarrus County at age 20, March 21, 1862. Mustered in as Private. Promoted to Corporal prior to July 1, 1862. Promoted to Sergeant prior to September 6, 1862. Died in hospital at Petersburg, Virginia, September 6, 1862, of "con[tinued] fever."

BRAMBLE, WILLIAM W., Private
Previously served as Private in Company D, 19th Regiment N.C. Troops (2nd Regiment N.C. Cavalry). Transferred to this company on December 7, 1864. Furloughed from hospital at Richmond, Virginia, February 25, 1865. No further records.

BROWN, JAMES NAPOLEON, Private
Resided in Cabarrus County and was by occupation a postmaster prior to enlisting in Cabarrus County at age 34, April 6, 1863, for the war. Wounded and captured at Gettysburg, Pennsylvania, on or about July 3, 1863. Confined at Fort McHenry, Maryland. Transferred to Fort Delaware, Delaware, prior to August 1, 1863. Paroled at Fort Delaware and transferred to Cairo, Illinois, April 10, 1865. Transferred to New Orleans, Louisiana, where he arrived on April 22, 1865. Transferred to the Red River, Louisiana, where he was exchanged on May 4, 1865.

Hospitalized at Shreveport, Louisiana, May 11, 1865. Released from hospital on May 17, 1865.

BROWN, JOHN H. C., Corporal

Born in Cabarrus County where he resided as a farmer prior to enlisting in Cabarrus County at age 19, March 21, 1862. Mustered in as Private. Promoted to Corporal in July, 1862-February, 1863. Present or accounted for on surviving company muster rolls through April, 1864. Captured at or near Wilderness, Virginia, on or about May 6, 1864. Confined at Point Lookout, Maryland. Transferred to Elmira, New York, July 29, 1864. Died at Elmira on June 6, 1865, of "chro[nic] diarr[hoea]."

BROWN, PHILIP J., Private

Resided in Cabarrus County and enlisted in Guilford County on October 24, 1864, for the war. Reported sick in hospital on or about January 1, 1865. Captured near Petersburg, Virginia, March 25, 1865. Confined at Point Lookout, Maryland, March 28, 1865. Released at Point Lookout on June 23, 1865, after taking the Oath of Allegiance.

CLINE, ADAM, Private

Born in Cabarrus County where he resided as a farmer prior to enlisting in Cabarrus County at age 23, March 21, 1862. Reported absent on detached service on or about July 1, 1862. Hospitalized at or near Petersburg, Virginia, December 3, 1862, with pneumonia. Returned to duty on March 1, 1863. Reported sick in hospital on or about September 1, 1863. Reported absent without leave on or about November 1, 1863. Returned to duty prior to January 1, 1864. Present or accounted for until wounded in the left leg and/or left hand at Jones' Farm, Virginia, on or about September 30, 1864. Hospitalized at Richmond, Virginia, October 2, 1864. Furloughed for sixty days on October 28, 1864. Reported absent wounded through December, 1864. Paroled at Salisbury on May 12, 1865. Took the Oath of Allegiance at Salisbury on June 14, 1865.

CLINE, JOHN N., Private

Born in Cabarrus County where he resided as a farmer prior to enlisting in Cabarrus County at age 25, March 21, 1862. Reported present or accounted for on surviving company muster rolls through August, 1863. Captured at, Bristoe Station, Virginia, October 14, 1863. Confined at Old Capitol Prison, Washington, D.C. Transferred to Point Lookout, Maryland, October 27, 1863. Paroled at Point Lookout on February 18, 1865. Received at Boulware's Wharf, James River, Virginia, on or about February 20, 1865, for exchange.

COCHRAN, WILLIAM, Private

Born in Mecklenburg County and resided in Cabarrus County where he was by occupation a farmer prior to enlisting in Cabarrus County at age 33, March 21, 1862. Died in hospital at Raleigh on June 7, 1862, of "pneumonia and rubeola."

COOKE, RICHARD F., Corporal

Born in Cabarrus County where he resided as a farmer prior to enlisting in Cabarrus County at age 17, March 21, 1862. Mustered in as Private. Promoted to Corporal in

September-October, 1863. Reported present on surviving company muster rolls through August, 1864. Hospitalized at Richmond, Virginia, October 29, 1864, with a gunshot wound. Place and date wounded not reported (probably wounded at Burgess' Mill, Virginia, October 27, 1864). Furloughed for sixty days on November 29, 1864. Returned to duty subsequent to January 1, 1865. Surrendered at Appomattox Court House, Virginia, April 9, 1865.

CORZINE, JAMES O., Private

Born in Cabarrus County where he resided as a farmer prior to enlisting in Cabarrus County at age 27, March 21, 1862. Died in hospital at Raleigh on or about May 28, 1862, of "rubeola and pneumonia."

CRESS, JEREMIAH, Private

Resided in Cabarrus County and was by occupation a farm laborer prior to enlisting in Cabarrus County at age 24, October 15, 1862, for the war. Reported present or accounted for on surviving company muster rolls through August, 1863. Wounded in the right leg at Bristoe Station, Virginia, October 14, 1863. Right leg amputated. Hospitalized at Gordonsville, Virginia, where he died on November 7, 1863, of "pyaemia."

CRESS, JOHN MONROE, Private

Resided in Cabarrus County and was by occupation a drayman prior to enlisting in Cabarrus County at age 32, September 1, 1862, for the war. Died in hospital at Petersburg, Virginia, October 17, 1862, of "typhoid fever."

DeMARCUS, WILLIAM A., Private

Born in Cabarrus County where he resided as a farmer prior to enlisting in Cabarrus County at age 48, March 21, 1862. Reported present or accounted for on surviving company muster rolls through December, 1864. Served as an ambulance driver during much of the war. Surrendered at Appomattox Court House, Virginia, April 9, 1865.

DOVE, JULIUS C., Private

Born in Cabarrus County where he resided as a farmer prior to enlisting in Cabarrus County at age 18, March 21, 1862. Died at Petersburg, Virginia, July 29 or August 8, 1862. Cause of death not reported.

DRY, WILLIAM E., Private

Resided in Cabarrus County and was by occupation a farm laborer prior to enlisting in Cabarrus County at age 22, March 21, 1862. Wounded at Goldsboro on December 17, 1862. Returned to duty prior to March 1, 1863. Captured at Bristoe Station, Virginia, October 14, 1863. Confined at Old Capitol Prison, Washington, D.C. Transferred to Point Lookout, Maryland, October 27, 1863. Paroled at Point Lookout on February 24, 1865. Received at Aiken's Landing, James River, Virginia, on or about February 28, 1865, for exchange. Survived the war.

EASOM, DAVID, Private

Previously served as Private in Company D, 19th Regiment N.C. Troops (2nd Regiment N.C. Cavalry). Transferred to this company in November-December,

1864. Captured at Sutherland's Station, Virginia, April 2, 1865. Confined at Point Lookout, Maryland, April 14, 1865. Released at Point Lookout on June 12, 1865, after taking the Oath of Allegiance.

EASOM, JAMES, Private
Previously served as Private in Company D, 19th Regiment N.C. Troops (2nd Regiment N.C. Cavalry). Transferred to this company in November-December, 1864. Deserted to the enemy on December 30, 1864. Confined at Washington, D.C., January 4, 1865. Released on or about the same date after taking the Oath of Allegiance.

EASOM, JOHN E., Private
Previously served as Private in Company D, 19th Regiment N.C. Troops (2nd Regiment N.C. Cavalry). Transferred to this company in November-December, 1864. Deserted to the enemy on or about December 30, 1864. Confined at Washington, D.C., January 4, 1865. Released on or about the same date after taking the Oath of Allegiance.

EDDLEMAN, DANIEL W., Private
Born in Rowan County and resided in Cabarrus County where he was by occupation a farmer prior to enlisting in Cabarrus County at age 20, March 21, 1862. Reported absent sick on or about July 1, 1862. Returned to duty on an unspecified date. Sent to hospital at Winchester, Virginia, on or about July 17, 1863. Not heard from after that date and was dropped from the rolls of the company in July-August, 1864.

EUDY, WILLIAM, Private
Born in Cabarrus County where he resided as a farmer prior to enlisting in Cabarrus County at age 34, March 21, 1862. Captured at Gettysburg, Pennsylvania, July 3, 1863. Confined at Fort Delaware, Delaware, on or about July 10, 1863. Transferred to Point Lookout, Maryland, October 20, 1863. Paroled at Point Lookout on February 18, 1865. Received at Boulware's Wharf, James River, Virginia, on or about February 20, 1865, for exchange. Paroled at Salisbury on May 19, 1865.

EURY, ANDREW J., Private
Resided in Cabarrus County and was by occupation a farmer prior to enlisting in Cabarrus County at age 28, October 15, 1862, for the war. Hospitalized at Richmond, Virginia, July 11, 1863, with chronic diarrhoea. Returned to duty on August 11, 1863. Captured at or near Wilderness, Virginia, on or about May 6, 1864. Confined at Point Lookout, Maryland, May 17, 1864. Transferred to Elmira, New York, August 8, 1864. Paroled at Elmira on October 11, 1864. Received at Venus Point, Savannah River, Georgia, November 15, 1864, for exchange. Returned to duty on an unspecified date. Captured at Sutherland's Station, Virginia, April 2, 1865. Confined at Point Lookout on April 4, 1865. Released at Point Lookout on June 12, 1865, after taking the Oath of Allegiance.

FETZER, JOHN W., 1st Sergeant
Born in Page County, Virginia, and resided in Cabarrus or Rowan County where he was by occupation a school teacher prior to enlisting in Cabarrus County at age 18, March 21, 1862. Mustered in as Corporal. Promoted to Sergeant prior to July 1, 1862. Promoted to 1st Sergeant on October 1, 1863. Reported present or accounted for on surviving company muster rolls through December, 1864. Surrendered at Appomattox Court House, Virginia, April 9, 1865. Took the Oath of Allegiance at Salisbury on July 8, 1865.

FINK, ADAM H., Private
Resided in Cabarrus County and was by occupation a farmhand prior to enlisting in Cabarrus County at age 27, March 21, 1862. Captured at Gettysburg, Pennsylvania, July 3, 1863. Confined at Fort Delaware, Delaware, on or about July 10, 1863. Transferred to Point Lookout, Maryland, October 20, 1863. Paroled at Point Lookout on April 27, 1864. Received at City Point, Virginia, April 30, 1864, for exchange. Hospitalized at Richmond, Virginia, May 1, 1864, with dysentery. Furloughed for thirty days on May 12, 1864. Returned to duty prior to September 1, 1864. Wounded in the leg on an unspecified date. Leg amputated. Hospitalized at Richmond until November 8, 1864, when he was furloughed for sixty days.

FLEMING, THOMAS A., Sergeant
Resided in Cabarrus County and was by occupation a farmer prior to enlisting in Cabarrus County at age 32, May 14, 1862, for the war. Mustered in as Private. Promoted to Corporal prior to July 1, 1862. Promoted to Sergeant in July, 1862-February, 1863. Wounded at Gettysburg, Pennsylvania, July 1, 1863. Returned to duty prior to July 14, 1863, when he was captured at Falling Waters, Maryland. Confined at Old Capitol Prison, Washington, D.C. Transferred to Point Lookout, Maryland, August 8, 1863. Paroled at Point Lookout on March 3, 1864. Received at City Point, Virginia, March 6, 1864, for exchange. Returned to duty in July-August, 1864. Hospitalized at Richmond, Virginia, October 23, 1864, with typhoid fever. Furloughed for sixty days on December 9, 1864. Survived the war.

FURR, TOBIAS, Private
Born in Cabarrus County where he resided as a farmer prior to enlisting in Cabarrus County at age 47, March 21, 1862. Wounded at Goldsboro on December 17, 1862. Returned to duty prior to March 1, 1863. Hospitalized at Farmville, Virginia, July 15, 1863, with debilitas. Returned to duty on September 21, 1863. Present or accounted for until wounded in the thigh near Petersburg, Virginia, in August, 1864. Hospitalized at Petersburg where he died prior to November 1, 1864, of wounds and/or disease.

GALLIMORE, JOSEPH S., Private
Resided in Cabarrus County and was by occupation a farm laborer prior to enlisting in Cabarrus County at age 19, May 14, 1862, for the war. Died in hospital at Richmond, Virginia, June 19, 1863, of "typhoid fever."

GOODNIGHT, HENRY W., Private
Born in Cabarrus County and resided in Cabarrus or Alexander County where he was by occupation a farmer prior to enlisting in Cabarrus County at age 42, March 21, 1862. Reported present on surviving company muster

rolls through August, 1863. Captured at Bristoe Station, Virginia, October 14, 1863. Confined at Point Lookout, Maryland. Paroled at Point Lookout on March 16, 1864. Received at City Point, Virginia, March 20, 1864, for exchange. Returned to duty in May-June, 1864. Reported present or accounted for through December, 1864. Captured near Petersburg, Virginia, March 25, 1865. Confined at Point Lookout on March 28, 1865. Released at Point Lookout on June 11, 1865, after taking the Oath of Allegiance.

GOODSON, MATTHEW, 1st Sergeant

Resided in Cabarrus County and was by occupation a merchant prior to enlisting in Cabarrus County at age 34, May 14, 1862, for the war. Mustered in as Private. Promoted to Sergeant on May 14, 1862. Promoted to 1st Sergeant prior to March 1, 1863. Wounded in the lungs and captured at Gettysburg, Pennsylvania, July 3, 1863. Hospitalized at Gettysburg where he died on July 12, 1863, of wounds.

HAGLER, CALEB, Private

Born in Cabarrus County where he resided as a farmer prior to enlisting in Cabarrus County at age 21, March 21, 1862. Killed at Gettysburg, Pennsylvania, July 3, 1863.

HALL, JAMES A., Private

Born in Montgomery County and resided in Cabarrus County where he was by occupation a farmer prior to enlisting in Cabarrus County at age 19, March 21, 1862. Reported present on surviving company muster rolls from May, 1862, through February, 1863. Reported absent sick in July-December, 1863. Returned to duty in January-February, 1864. Present or accounted for through December, 1864.

HAMILTON, JOHN F., Private

Born in Mecklenburg or Cabarrus County and resided in Cabarrus County where he was by occupation a farmer prior to enlisting in Cabarrus County at age 19, March 21, 1862. Captured at Gettysburg, Pennsylvania, July 3, 1863. Confined at Fort Delaware, Delaware, on or about July 10, 1863. Transferred to Point Lookout, Maryland, October 20, 1863. Died at Point Lookout on May 27, 1864. Cause of death not reported.

HARKEY, CLARK W., Private

Resided in Union County and was by occupation a farmer prior to enlisting at age 32, October 15, 1862, for the war. Hospitalized at or near Petersburg, Virginia, on or about December 3, 1862, with rheumatism. Returned to duty on December 25, 1862. Reported sick in hospital at Goldsboro on or about March 1, 1863. Detailed for light duty in hospital at Wilmington on or about August 25, 1863, by reason of disability from rheumatism. Reported on detail at Wilmington through August, 1864. Rejoined the company in September-October, 1864. Reported present in November-December, 1864. Captured at Sutherland's Station, Virginia, April 2, 1865. Confined at Point Lookout, Maryland, April 4, 1865. Released at Point Lookout on June 27, 1865, after taking the Oath of Allegiance.

HINSEMAN, LEVI, Private

Resided in Cabarrus County and was by occupation a farmhand prior to enlisting in Cabarrus County at age 34, October 15, 1862, for the war. Reported present on surviving company muster rolls through April, 1864. Captured at or near Wilderness, Virginia, on or about May 6, 1864. Confined at Point Lookout, Maryland. Transferred to Elmira, New York, July 27, 1864. Released at Elmira on or about June 12, 1865, after taking the Oath of Allegiance.

HURLOCKER, MONROE, Private

Born in Cabarrus County where he resided as a farmer prior to enlisting in Cabarrus County at age 30, March 21, 1862. Reported present or accounted for on surviving company muster rolls through April, 1864. Captured at or near Wilderness, Virginia, on or about May 6, 1864. Confined at Point Lookout, Maryland, May 18, 1864. Died at Point Lookout on or about September 9, 1864. Cause of death not reported.

ISENHOUR, HENRY W., Private

Born in Cabarrus County where he resided as a farmer prior to enlisting in Cabarrus County at age 20, March 21, 1862. Wounded at Goldsboro on December 17, 1862. Returned to duty prior to March 1, 1863. Reported present or accounted for on surviving company muster rolls through December, 1864. Captured at Sutherland's Station, Virginia, April 2, 1865. Confined at Point Lookout, Maryland, April 4, 1865. Released at Point Lookout on June 14, 1865, after taking the Oath of Allegiance.

JOHNSTON, ROBERT ALLISON, Private

Born in Cabarrus County where he resided as a farmer prior to enlisting in Cabarrus County at age 34, April 6, 1863, for the war. Hospitalized at Richmond, Virginia, October 9, 1863, with an unspecified complaint. Reported absent on furlough on or about January 1, 1864. Reported absent sick on or about March 1, 1864. Detailed for hospital duty at Richmond on or about April 15, 1864. Hospitalized at Richmond on April 21, 1864, with "chron[ic] diarrhoea" and died on May 3, 1864.

JOHNSTON, ROBERT W., JR., Private

Born in Cabarrus County and resided in Cabarrus or Mecklenburg County where he was by occupation a farmer prior to enlisting in Cabarrus County at age 19, March 21, 1862. Wounded and captured at Gettysburg, Pennsylvania, on or about July 3, 1863. Confined at Fort Delaware, Delaware, on or about July 10, 1863. Transferred to Point Lookout, Maryland, October 20, 1863. Paroled at Point Lookout on September 18, 1864. Received at Varina, Virginia, September 22, 1864, for exchange. Returned to duty prior to November 1, 1864. Captured at Sutherland's Station, Virginia, April 2, 1865. Confined at Point Lookout on April 4, 1865. Released at Point Lookout on June 28, 1865, after taking the Oath of Allegiance.

JOHNSTON, ROBERT WILSON, SR., Private

Born in Cabarrus County where he resided as a farmer prior to enlisting in Cabarrus County at age 34, May 14, 1862, for the war. Reported present or accounted for on surviving company muster rolls through October, 1864. Transferred to Company G, 9th Regiment N.C. State Troops (1st Regiment N.C. Cavalry), December 8, 1864.

JOYNER, ADDISON M., Private
Born in Cabarrus County where he resided as a farmer prior to enlisting in Cabarrus County at age 38, March 21, 1862. Captured at Falling Waters, Maryland, July 14, 1863. Hospitalized at Baltimore, Maryland, August 3, 1863, with an unspecified complaint. Transferred to Fort McHenry, Maryland, on or about September 12, 1863. Transferred to Point Lookout, Maryland, September 15, 1863. Paroled at Point Lookout on or about February 10, 1865. Received at Cox's Wharf, James River, Virginia, on or about February 14, 1865, for exchange.

JOYNER, WILLIAM B., Private
Born in Cabarrus County where he resided as a blacksmith prior to enlisting in Cabarrus County at age 18, March 20, 1862. Reported present or accounted for on surviving company muster rolls through February, 1863. Detailed to work as a blacksmith in the workshops of the Virginia Central Railroad on August 26, 1863. Reported absent on detail through December, 1864. Paroled at Richmond on or about April 24, 1865.

KETNER, JOHN, Private
Resided in Cabarrus County and was by occupation a farmer prior to enlisting in Cabarrus County at age 33, March 21, 1862. Died at Hanover Junction, Virginia, on or about June 13, 1863, of "ty[phoid] fever."

KETNER, JOHN P., Private
Born in Rowan County and resided in Cabarrus County where he was by occupation a farmer prior to enlisting in Cabarrus County at age 26, March 21, 1862. Reported present on surviving company muster rolls through April, 1864. Captured at or near Wilderness, Virginia, on or about May 6, 1864. Confined at Point Lookout, Maryland, May 17, 1864. Transferred to Elmira, New York, July 27, 1864. Died at Elmira on or about September 19, 1864, of "chronic diarrhoea & scorbutus."

KEZIAH, JAMES H., Private
Previously served as Private in Company C, 33rd Regiment N.C. Troops. Enlisted in this company in Cabarrus County on March 21, 1862. Captured at Falling Waters, Maryland, July 14, 1863. Sent to Baltimore, Maryland. Confined at Point Lookout, Maryland, August 21, 1863. Paroled at Point Lookout on December 24, 1863. Received at City Point, Virginia, December 28, 1863, for exchange. Returned to duty prior to March 1, 1864. Wounded "on skirmish line" on May 30, 1864. Reported absent wounded through December, 1864. Returned to duty on an unspecified date. Surrendered at Appomattox Court House, Virginia, April 9, 1865.

KNOTTS, JAMES G., Private
Born in Anson County and resided in Cabarrus County where he was by occupation a miner prior to enlisting in Cabarrus County at age 25, March 21, 1862. Hospitalized at Charlottesville, Virginia, June 28, 1863, with acute rheumatism. Returned to duty on August 1, 1863. Captured at or near Wilderness, Virginia, on or about May 6, 1864. Confined at Point Lookout, Maryland, May 18, 1864. Transferred to Elmira, New York, August 10, 1864. Released at Elmira on May 29, 1865, after taking the Oath of Allegiance.

KRIMINGER, THOMAS C., Private
Resided in Cabarrus County and was by occupation a farmhand prior to enlisting in Cabarrus County at age 23, April 4, 1863, for the war. Present or accounted for through April, 1864. Hospitalized at Richmond, Virginia, May 22, 1864, with a gunshot wound. Place and date wounded not reported. Returned to duty on July 13, 1864. Hospitalized at Richmond on or about August 8, 1864, with continued fever. Furloughed for thirty days on August 27, 1864. Returned to duty prior to November 1, 1864. Captured at Sutherland's Station, Virginia, April 2, 1865. Confined at Point Lookout, Maryland, April 4, 1865. Released at Point Lookout on June 28, 1865, after taking the Oath of Allegiance.

LINN, MOSES, Private
Born in Rowan County and resided in Cabarrus County where he was by occupation a farmer prior to enlisting in Cabarrus County at age 31, March 21, 1862. Killed at Goldsboro on December 17, 1862.

LIPE, DANIEL M., Private
Resided in Cabarrus County where he enlisted at age 18, March 21, 1862. Reported present on surviving company muster rolls through August, 1863. Captured at Bristoe Station, Virginia, October 14, 1863. Confined at Old Capitol Prison, Washington, D.C. Transferred to Point Lookout, Maryland, October 27, 1863. Paroled at Point Lookout on February 24, 1865. Received for exchange on or about February 28, 1865.

LITTLE, THOMAS, Private
Born in Cabarrus County where he resided as a farmer prior to enlisting in Cabarrus County at age 17, March 10, 1862. Discharged on May 26, 1862, by reason of being under 18 years of age.

LUDWIG, THOMAS BENTON STANHOPE, Private
Born in Cabarrus County where he resided as a farmer prior to enlisting in Cabarrus County at age 19, March 21, 1862. Reported present or accounted for on surviving company muster rolls through August, 1863. Captured at Bristoe Station, Virginia, October 14, 1863. Confined at Old Capitol Prison, Washington, D.C. Transferred to Point Lookout, Maryland, October 27, 1863. Paroled at Point Lookout and transferred to Cox's Wharf, James River, Virginia, where he was received on or about February 14, 1865, for exchange.

MELTON, JOSEPH C., Private
Previously served as Private in Company D, 19th Regiment N.C. Troops (2nd Regiment N.C. Cavalry). Transferred to this company in November-December, 1864. No further records.

MICHAEL, GEORGE W., Private
Born in Lincoln County and resided in Cabarrus County where he was by occupation a carpenter prior to enlisting

in Cabarrus County at age 35, March 8, 1862. Discharged on May 26, 1862, by reason of being overage.

MILLER, JOSEPH Mc., Private
Resided in Cabarrus County where he enlisted at age 32, April 6, 1863, for the war. Captured at Gettysburg, Pennsylvania, July 3, 1863. Died in hospital at Gettysburg on or about July 21, 1863, presumably of wounds.

MISENHEIMER, CALEB, Private
Born in Cabarrus County where he resided as a farmer prior to enlisting in Cabarrus County at age 35, March 19, 1862. Discharged on May 26, 1862, by reason of being overage.

MISENHEIMER, GEORGE A., Corporal
Born in Cabarrus County where he resided as a farmer prior to enlisting in Cabarrus County at age 18, March 21, 1862. Mustered in as Private. Promoted to Corporal in July, 1862-February, 1863. Wounded in both legs (both legs fractured) and captured at Gettysburg, Pennsylvania, July 3, 1863. Reported in hospital at Chester, Pennsylvania, July 17, 1863. Transferred to Point Lookout, Maryland, October 2, 1863. Paroled at Point Lookout on March 16, 1864. Received at City Point, Virginia, March 20, 1864, for exchange. Hospitalized at Richmond, Virginia, March 20, 1864, with wounds received at Gettysburg. Furloughed for sixty days on March 31, 1864. Reported absent wounded through December, 1864. Survived the war.

MISENHEIMER, JAMES M., Private
Resided in Cabarrus County and was by occupation a farmhand prior to enlisting in Cabarrus County at age 28, September 1, 1862, for the war. Mortally wounded at Gettysburg, Pennsylvania, July 3, 1863. Place and date of death not reported.

MORRISON, JOHN WILSON, Private
Resided in Cabarrus County and was by occupation a farm laborer prior to enlisting in Cabarrus County at age 22, September 1, 1862, for the war. Reported present on surviving company muster rolls through April, 1864. Captured at or near Wilderness, Virginia, on or about May 6, 1864. Confined at Point Lookout, Maryland, May 17, 1864. Transferred to Elmira, New York, July 27, 1864. Released at Elmira on June 12, 1865, after taking the Oath of Allegiance.

NESBITT, GIBSON R., Private
Born in Cabarrus County where he resided as a tanner prior to enlisting in Cabarrus County at age 16, March 21, 1862. Reported present on surviving company muster rolls through April, 1864. Reported sick in hospital at Richmond, Virginia, on or about July 1, 1864. Reported absent on sick furlough on or about September 1, 1864. Wounded in the right hand at Jones' Farm, Virginia, on or about September 30, 1864. Returned to duty prior to November 1, 1864. Hospitalized at Richmond on December 20, 1864, with dysentery or colitis. Furloughed for sixty days on February 3, 1865. Paroled at Salisbury on May 13, 1865.

O'QUINN, WILLIAM, Private
Previously served as Private in Company D, 19th Regiment N.C. Troops (2nd Regiment N.C. Cavalry). Transferred to this company in November-December, 1864. No further records.

PAGE, JOHN C., Private
Born in Cabarrus County where he resided as a farmer prior to enlisting in Cabarrus County at age 19, March 21, 1862. Reported missing at Gettysburg, Pennsylvania, July 3, 1863. Records of the Federal Provost Marshal do not indicate that he was captured at Gettysburg, and he was presumably killed.

PATTERSON, CALEB W., Private
Born in Cabarrus County where he resided as a farmer prior to enlisting in Cabarrus County at age 28, March 21, 1862. Wounded at Goldsboro on December 17, 1862. Reported absent wounded or absent sick through December, 1863. Discharged on or about February 10, 1864, presumably by reason of disability from wounds.

PHILLIPS, JACOB M., Private
Resided in Cabarrus County and was by occupation a farmhand prior to enlisting at age 20, October 15, 1862, for the war. Discharged on February 26, 1863, by reason of disability. Took the Oath of Allegiance at Salisbury on May 24, 1865.

PLESS, HENRY J., Private
Born in Rowan County and resided in Cabarrus County where he was by occupation a farmer prior to enlisting in Cabarrus County at age 20, March 24, 1862. Hospitalized at Richmond, Virginia, June 19, 1863, with an unspecified complaint. Returned to duty on August 12, 1863. Captured at Bristoe Station, Virginia, October 14, 1863. Confined at Old Capitol Prison, Washington, D.C. Transferred to Point Lookout, Maryland, October 27, 1863. Released at Point Lookout on February 25, 1864, after taking the Oath of Allegiance and joining the U.S. Army. Unit to which assigned not reported.

POPE, LEROY W., Sergeant
Born in Cabarrus County where he resided as a farmer prior to enlisting in Cabarrus County at age 20, March 21, 1862. Mustered in as Sergeant. Died at Camp Mangum, near Raleigh, May 13, 1862, of disease.

POTEAT, JOHN W., Private
Born in Cabarrus County where he resided as a farmer prior to enlisting in Cabarrus County at age 34, March 21, 1862. Captured at or near Goldsboro on or about December 17, 1862. Paroled the same date. Returned to duty prior to March 1, 1863. Reported present or accounted for on surviving company muster rolls through February, 1864. Hospitalized at Richmond, Virginia, April 4, 1864, with an unspecified complaint. Furloughed for thirty days on April 5, 1864. Returned to duty in May-June, 1864. Present or accounted for through December, 1864. Surrendered at Appomattox Court House, Virginia, April 9, 1865.

POTEAT, THOMAS J., Private

Born in Cabarrus County where he resided as a farmer prior to enlisting in Cabarrus County at age 22, March 21, 1862. Wounded in the right thigh (possibly also in the left arm) and captured at Gettysburg, Pennsylvania, July 3, 1863. Hospitalized at Gettysburg. Transferred to hospital at Chester, Pennsylvania, on or about July 14, 1863. Paroled at Chester and transferred to City Point, Virginia, where he was received on August 20, 1863, for exchange. Hospitalized at Farmville, Virginia, August 28, 1863. Furloughed for thirty days on September 12, 1863. Reported absent wounded or absent sick through December, 1864. Deserted to the enemy on an unspecified date. Took the Oath of Allegiance at City Point on February 9, 1865.

POWLES, HENRY, Private

Born in Cabarrus County where he resided as a farmer prior to enlisting in Cabarrus County at age 23, March 21, 1862. Captured at or near Gettysburg, Pennsylvania, on or about July 4, 1863. Confined at Fort Delaware, Delaware, on or about July 10, 1863. Transferred to Point Lookout, Maryland, October 20, 1863. Released at Point Lookout on January 24, 1864, after taking the Oath of Allegiance and joining the U.S. Army. Assigned to Company B, 1st Regiment U.S. Volunteer Infantry.

RICE, GEORGE W., Private

Born in Cabarrus County where he resided as a farmer prior to enlisting in Cabarrus County at age 16, March 21, 1862. Reported present on surviving company muster rolls through December, 1864. Wounded in the left shoulder by the explosion of a shell and captured at Sutherland's Station, Virginia, April 2, 1865. Confined at Point Lookout, Maryland, April 4, 1865. Released at Point Lookout on June 17, 1865, after taking the Oath of Allegiance.

RICE, WILLIAM, Private

Born in Stanly County and resided in Cabarrus County where he was by occupation a farmer prior to enlisting in Cabarrus County at age 18, March 21, 1862. Wounded and captured at Gettysburg, Pennsylvania, July 3, 1863. Hospitalized at Gettysburg. Transferred to hospital at Chester, Pennsylvania, where he arrived on July 18, 1863. Died in hospital at Chester on August 20, 1863, of "secondary hemorrhage."

RODGERS, JAMES M., Private

Born in Cabarrus County and was by occupation a farmer prior to enlisting in Cabarrus County at age 38, March 8, 1862. Discharged on May 26, 1862, by reason of being overage.

ROSS, HUGH D., Private

Born in Cabarrus or Union County* and resided in Cabarrus County where he was by occupation a carpenter or farmer prior to enlisting in Cabarrus County at age 42, March 21, 1862. Reported present or accounted for on surviving company muster rolls through April, 1864.

Wounded in the left foot at Cold Harbor, Virginia, June 2, 1864. Reported absent wounded through December, 1864. Retired from service on January 30, 1865, by reason of disability from wounds.

SAFRIT, RUFUS A., Corporal

Born in Rowan County and resided in Cabarrus County where he was by occupation a farmer prior to enlisting in Cabarrus County at age 19, March 21, 1862. Mustered in as Private. Promoted to Corporal in July-August, 1864. Reported present on surviving company muster rolls through August, 1864. Captured at Burgess' Mill, Virginia, October 27, 1864. Confined at Point Lookout, Maryland. Paroled and transferred to Cox's Wharf, James River, Virginia, where he was received on or about February 14, 1865, for exchange. Hospitalized at Richmond, Virginia, February 15, 1865, with chronic diarrhoea. Furloughed for sixty days on February 24, 1865. Took the Oath of Allegiance at Salisbury on June 7, 1865.

SCOTT, ALLISON J., Corporal

Born in Cabarrus County where he resided as a farmer prior to enlisting in Cabarrus County at age 26 on or about March 21, 1862. Mustered in as Private. Promoted to Corporal prior to July 1, 1862. Died in hospital at Petersburg, Virginia, September 8, 1862, of "febris remittens."

SIMPSON, JESSE, Private

Previously served as Private in Company E, 19th Regiment N.C. Troops (2nd Regiment N.C. Cavalry). Transferred to this company on December 7, 1864. Captured at Sutherland's Station, Virginia, April 2, 1865. Confined at Point Lookout, Maryland, April 4, 1865. Released at Point Lookout on June 20, 1865, after taking the Oath of Allegiance.

SMITH, ALFRED HARRIS, Sergeant

Born in Cabarrus County where he resided as a farmer prior to enlisting in Cabarrus County at age 31, March 21, 1862. Mustered in as Private. Promoted to Sergeant in July, 1862-February, 1863. Wounded and captured at Gettysburg, Pennsylvania, July 3, 1863. Hospitalized at Chester, Pennsylvania, on an unspecified date. Paroled and transferred to City Point, Virginia, August 17, 1863, for exchange. Returned to duty in November-December, 1863. Present or accounted for until captured at or near Wilderness, Virginia, on or about May 6, 1864. Confined at Point Lookout, Maryland, May 17, 1864. Transferred to Elmira, New York, July 27, 1864. Released at Elmira on June 12, 1865, after taking the Oath of Allegiance.

SMITH, JOHN R., Private

Born in Cabarrus County where he resided prior to enlisting in Cabarrus County at age 27, May 14, 1862, for the war. Reported present or accounted for on surviving company muster rolls through October, 1864. Died in hospital at Richmond, Virginia, November 15, 1864. Cause of death not reported.

SMITH, MATHIAS H., Private

Resided in Cabarrus County and was by occupation a day laborer prior to enlisting at age 26, October 15, 1862, for the war. Hospitalized at or near Petersburg, Virginia, October 27, 1862, with diarrhoea. Returned to duty on November 30, 1862. Captured at Gettysburg, Pennsylvania, on or about July 3, 1863. Confined at Fort Delaware, Delaware, on or about July 10, 1863. Transferred to Point Lookout, Maryland, October 20, 1863. Died at Point Lookout on November 12, 1863, of "chronic diarrhoea."

SOLOMON, JAMES, Private

Born in Mecklenburg County and resided in Cabarrus County where he was by occupation a farmer prior to enlisting in Cabarrus County at age 57, March 13, 1862. Discharged on May 30, 1862, by reason of being overage.

STANCIL, JACKSON, Private

Born in Union County* and resided in Cabarrus County where he was by occupation a farmer prior to enlisting in Cabarrus County at age 29, March 28, 1862. Wounded in the right elbow and captured at Gettysburg, Pennsylvania, July 3, 1863. Confined at Fort Delaware, Delaware, on or about July 10, 1863. Paroled at Fort Delaware on September 14, 1864. Received at Varina, Virginia, on or about September 21, 1864, for exchange. No further records. Survived the war.

STARNES, MARTIN, Private

Born in Cabarrus County where he resided as a farmer prior to enlisting in Cabarrus County at age 22, March 21, 1862. Wounded in the right shoulder at Gettysburg, Pennsylvania, on or about July 3, 1863. Returned to duty prior to September 1, 1863. Present or accounted for through December, 1864. Surrendered at Appomattox Court House, Virginia, April 9, 1865.

STEEL, JAMES H., Private

Born in Mecklenburg County and resided in Cabarrus County where he was by occupation a farmer prior to enlisting in Cabarrus County at age 37, March 8, 1862. Discharged on May 30, 1862, by reason of being overage.

STILLER, DANIEL, Private

Resided in Cabarrus County and was by occupation a shoemaker prior to enlisting in Guilford County at age 39, October 24, 1864, for the war. Hospitalized at Richmond, Virginia, November 26, 1864, with an unspecified complaint. Transferred to another hospital on November 27, 1864. Survived the war.

SUTHER, GREENBURY R., Private

Born in Cabarrus County where he resided as a farmer prior to enlisting in Cabarrus County at age 20, March 21, 1862. Reported present or accounted for on surviving company muster rolls through December, 1864. Captured at Sutherland's Station, Virginia, April 2, 1865. Confined at Point Lookout, Maryland, April 3, 1865. Released at

Point Lookout on June 20, 1865, after taking the Oath of Allegiance. Records of the Federal Provost Marshal indicate that he was blind in the left eye.

SUTHER, JOHN P., Private

Born in Cabarrus County where he resided as a mechanic prior to enlisting in Cabarrus County at age 31, March 21, 1862. Reported present or accounted for on surviving company muster rolls through April, 1864. Wounded in the head at or near Spotsylvania Court House, Virginia, on or about May 12, 1864. Hospitalized at Richmond, Virginia. Furloughed on or about May 26, 1864. Returned to duty in November-December, 1864. Captured at Sutherland's Station, Virginia, April 2, 1865. Confined at Point Lookout, Maryland, April 4, 1865. Released at Point Lookout on June 20, 1865, after taking the Oath of Allegiance.

SUTHER, RICHARD M., Private

Born in Cabarrus County where he resided as a farmer prior to enlisting in Cabarrus County at age 20, March 21, 1862. Reported present on surviving company muster rolls through April, 1864. Hospitalized at Richmond, Virginia, May 25, 1864, with intermittent fever. Returned to duty on June 27, 1864. Hospitalized at Richmond on the same date with a gunshot wound. Returned to duty on September 28, 1864. Reported present through December, 1864. Surrendered at Appomattox Court House, Virginia, April 9, 1865.

TUCKER, DARLIN, Private

Resided in Cabarrus County and enlisted in Guilford County at age 44, October 24, 1864, for the war. Surrendered at Appomattox Court House, Virginia, April 9, 1865.

VANPELT, CHARLES, Private

Born in Mecklenburg County and resided in Cabarrus County where he was by occupation a farmer prior to enlisting in Cabarrus County at age 25, March 21, 1862. Wounded in the left shoulder and left leg at Goldsboro on December 17, 1862. Returned to duty prior to March 1, 1863. Reported present on surviving company muster rolls through December, 1864. Surrendered at Appomattox Court House, Virginia, April 9, 1865.

VANPELT, THOMAS S., Sergeant

Resided in Cabarrus County and was by occupation a "land renter" prior to enlisting in Cabarrus County at age 28, March 21, 1862. Mustered in as Private. Promoted to Corporal in July-December, 1862. Wounded at Goldsboro on December 17, 1862. Returned to duty prior to March 1, 1863. Promoted to Sergeant in September-October, 1863. Reported present or accounted for on surviving company muster rolls through August, 1864. Captured at Burgess' Mill, Virginia, October 27, 1864. Confined at Point Lookout, Maryland, October 31, 1864. Released at Point Lookout on June 21, 1865, after taking the Oath of Allegiance.

VANPELT, WILLIAM C., Private

Born in Cabarrus County where he resided as a farmer

prior to enlisting in Cabarrus County at age 28, March 21, 1862. Reported present or accounted for on surviving company muster rolls through December, 1864. Surrendered at Appomattox Court House, Virginia, April 9, 1865.

WALLACE, JAMES H., Private

Born in Cabarrus County where he resided as a farmer prior to enlisting in Cabarrus County at age 24, March 21, 1862. Wounded at Gettysburg, Pennsylvania, July 3, 1863. Reported absent wounded through October, 1863. Reported sick in hospital at Raleigh in November, 1863-February, 1864. Hospitalized at Richmond, Virginia, March 7, 1864, with heart disease. Returned to duty on March 25, 1864. Killed near Globe Tavern, Virginia, August 21, 1864.

WALLACE, JOHN B., Private

Resided in Cabarrus County where he enlisted at age 22, September 1, 1862, for the war. Reported absent on sick furlough in July-August, 1863. Reported sick in hospital in September, 1863-February, 1864. Detailed for light duty as a hospital nurse at Richmond, Virginia, March 25, 1864. Reported absent on detail at Richmond through February, 1865. Captured in hospital at Richmond on April 3, 1865. Paroled on May 3, 1865.

WALTER, CHARLES F., Sergeant

Born in Cabarrus County where he resided as a farmer prior to enlisting in Cabarrus County at age 22, March 21, 1862. Mustered in as Corporal. Promoted to Sergeant in July, 1862-February, 1863. Hospitalized at Petersburg, Virginia, December 3, 1862, with an abscess. Furloughed on February 14, 1863. Returned to duty prior to March 1, 1863. Reported present on surviving company muster rolls through April, 1864. Wounded in the right leg at Cold Harbor, Virginia, on or about June 2, 1864. Returned to duty in July-August, 1864. Captured at Sutherland's Station, Virginia, April 2, 1865. Confined at Point Lookout, Maryland, April 4, 1865. Released at Point Lookout on June 21, 1865, after taking the Oath of Allegiance.

WALTER, MARTIN CRAWFORD, Private

Born in Cabarrus County where he resided as a farmer prior to enlisting in Cabarrus County at age 17, March 21, 1862. Wounded in the forearm (fracture) and captured at Gettysburg, Pennsylvania, July 3, 1863. Hospitalized at Davids Island, New York Harbor, on or about July 20, 1863. Paroled at Davids Island and transferred to City Point, Virginia, where he was received on September 27, 1863, for exchange. Detailed for light duty in North Carolina on February 22, 1864. Rejoined the company in May-June, 1864. Retired to the Invalid Corps on December 15, 1864, presumably by reason of wounds received at Gettysburg.

WEAVER, JACOB, Private

Born in Rowan County and resided in Cabarrus County where he was by occupation a machinist prior to enlisting in Cabarrus County at age 47, March 26, 1862. Reported present or accounted for on surviving company muster rolls through April, 1864; however, he was reported absent sick during much of that period. Hospitalized at Charlotte on June 26, 1864, with chronic diarrhoea. Returned to duty on August 26, 1864. Detailed as a hospital guard at Richmond, Virginia, September 27, 1864. Reported absent on detail through November, 1864. Hospitalized at Richmond on December 23, 1864, with pneumonia. Returned to duty on January 27, 1865.

WINECOFF, GEORGE, Private

Born in Cabarrus County where he resided as a farmer prior to enlisting in Cabarrus County at age 38, March 12, 1862. Mustered in as Sergeant. Reduced to ranks on an unspecified date. Discharged on May 26, 1862, by reason of being overage.

WINECOFF, GEORGE W., Private

Born in Cabarrus County where he resided as a farmer prior to enlisting in Cabarrus County at age 20, March 21, 1862. Killed at Goldsboro on December 17, 1862.

WINECOFF, HARVEY, Private

Born in Cabarrus County and was by occupation a farmer prior to enlisting in Cabarrus County at age 42, March 12, 1862. Discharged on May 26, 1862, by reason of being overage.

WINECOFF, JOHN M., Private

Resided in Cabarrus County and was by occupation a wagon- and buggymaker prior to enlisting in Cabarrus County at age 28, June 26, 1863, for the war. Wounded at Bristoe Station, Virginia, October 14, 1863. Returned to duty in January-February, 1864. Captured at or near Wilderness, Virginia, on or about May 6, 1864. Confined at Point Lookout, Maryland, May 17, 1864. Transferred to Elmira, New York, July 27, 1864. Paroled at Elmira on October 11, 1864. Received at Venus Point, Savannah River, Georgia, November 15, 1864, for exchange.

YATES, JOHN W., Private

Enlisted on August 1, 1864, for the war. Wounded in the right arm (fracture) at Reams' Station, Virginia, August 25, 1864. Hospitalized at Richmond, Virginia. Returned to duty on December 9, 1864. Surrendered at Appomattox Court House, Virginia, April 9, 1865.

YOST, HENRY W., Corporal

Born in Cabarrus County where he resided as a farmer prior to enlisting in Cabarrus County at age 21, March 21, 1862. Mustered in as Private. Promoted to Corporal in July-December, 1862. Killed at Goldsboro on December 17, 1862.

COMPANY B

This company, known as the "Randolph Guards," was raised in Randolph County and enlisted at Asheboro in March, 1862. It was mustered into state service at Camp Mangum, near Raleigh, on April 28, 1862, and assigned to the 52nd Regiment N.C. Troops as Company B. After joining the regiment the company functioned as a part of the regiment, and its history for the remainder of the war is reported as a part of the regimental history.

The information contained in the following roster was compiled primarily from a company muster-in and descriptive roll dated April 28, 1862, and from company muster rolls for May 1-June 30, 1862; September 1, 1862-February 28, 1863; and August 17, 1863-December 31, 1864. No company muster rolls were located for July 1-August 31, 1862; March 1-August 16, 1863; or for the period after December 31, 1864. Valuable information was obtained from primary records such as the North Carolina adjutant general's *Roll of Honor*, discharge certificates, medical records, prisoner of war records, *The War of the Rebellion: A Compilation of the Official Records of the Union and Confederate Armies*, militia records, newspaper casualty lists and obituaries, Confederate pension applications filed with the state of North Carolina, and the 1860 federal census of North Carolina. Secondary sources such as postwar rosters and histories, cemetery records, the *Confederate Veteran*, published genealogies, and records of the United Daughters of the Confederacy also provided useful information.

OFFICERS

CAPTAINS

FOULKES, JAMES F.
Born in Guilford County and resided in Cumberland County where he was by occupation a physician prior to enlisting in Wake County at age 33. Appointed Captain on March 1, 1862. Appointed Surgeon on September 26, 1862, to rank from June 28, 1862, and transferred to the Field and Staff of this regiment.

KYLE, JESSE KNEEDER
Previously served as Private in Company H, 1st Regiment N.C. Infantry (6 months, 1861). Appointed 1st Lieutenant of this company on March 15, 1862. Promoted to Captain on July 11, 1862. Reported present or accounted for on surviving company muster rolls through April, 1864. Captured near the North Anna River, Virginia, May 22, 1864. Confined at Old Capitol Prison, Washington, D.C., May 29, 1864. Transferred to Fort Delaware, Delaware, June 15, 1864. Transferred to Hilton Head, South Carolina, August 20, 1864. Received at Fort Pulaski, Georgia, October 20, 1864. Transferred back to Hilton Head subsequent to December 26, 1864. Transferred to Fort Delaware where he arrived on March 12, 1865. Released at Fort Delaware in June, 1865, after taking the Oath of Allegiance.

LIEUTENANTS

HARDISTER, LINDSEY C., 2nd Lieutenant
Born in Randolph County where he resided as a farmer prior to enlisting in Randolph County at age 19, March 12, 1862. Mustered in as Sergeant. Appointed 2nd Lieutenant on July 21, 1862. Died in hospital at

Petersburg, Virginia, August 7, 1862, of "febris typhoides."

HUSKE, JAMES WILL, 2nd Lieutenant
Previously served as Private in Company A, 63rd Regiment N.C. Troops (5th Regiment N.C. Cavalry). Transferred to this company upon appointment as 2nd Lieutenant to rank from October 28, 1862. Wounded at Gettysburg, Pennsylvania, July 3, 1863. Returned to duty in January-February, 1864. Killed "while gallantly leading the left wing of the regiment" in a charge at Burgess' Mill, Virginia, October 27, 1864. "Behaved with conspicuous gallantry" at Burgess' Mill.

KYLE, WILLIAM EMMETT, 1st Lieutenant
Previously served as Private in Company H, 1st Regiment N.C. Infantry (6 months, 1861). Appointed 3rd Lieutenant of this company on March 15, 1862. Promoted to 1st Lieutenant on November 1, 1862. Wounded in the head at Gettysburg, Pennsylvania, on or about July 3, 1863. Returned to duty prior to November 1, 1863. Present or accounted for until wounded in the hip at Spotsylvania Court House, Virginia, in May, 1864. Returned to duty prior to July 1, 1864. Wounded in the leg at Petersburg, Virginia, on an unspecified date. Surrendered at Appomattox Court House, Virginia, April 9, 1865.

ROBINSON, JOHN H., 2nd Lieutenant
Previously served as Sergeant in Company H, 1st Regiment N.C. Infantry (6 months, 1861). Appointed 2nd Lieutenant of this company on March 15, 1862. Appointed Adjutant (1st Lieutenant) on March 16, 1863, to rank from November 1, 1862, and transferred to the Field and Staff of this regiment.

NONCOMMISSIONED OFFICERS AND PRIVATES

ALDRED, DAVID L., Private
Born in Randolph County and was by occupation a farmer prior to enlisting in Randolph County at age 28, March 7, 1862. Reported present or accounted for on surviving company muster rolls through December, 1864. Captured at Sutherland's Station, Virginia, April 2, 1865. Confined at Point Lookout, Maryland, April 4, 1865. Released at Point Lookout on June 22, 1865, after taking the Oath of Allegiance.

ALDRED, RICHARD, Private
Born in Randolph County where he resided as a miner prior to enlisting in Randolph County at age 19, March 12, 1862. Deserted on January 17, 1863. Apprehended on or about June 27, 1863, and returned to duty. Reported present or accounted for on surviving company muster rolls through June, 1864. Reported present but on duty as a courier for General William MacRae in July-December, 1864. Surrendered at Appomattox Court House, Virginia, April 9, 1865. [North Carolina pension records indicate that he was wounded at Drewry's Bluff, Virginia, in August, 1862.]

ASHWORTH, ELIAS, Private

Born in Randolph County where he resided as a farmer prior to enlisting in Randolph County at age 19, March 6, 1862. Listed as a deserter in May-June, 1862. Returned from desertion in September, 1864. Deserted to the enemy on or about December 10, 1864. Sent to City Point, Virginia. Transferred to Washington, D.C. Released at Washington on or about December 15, 1864, after taking the Oath of Allegiance.

AUMAN, FLETCHER H., Private

Resided in Randolph County and was by occupation a farm laborer prior to enlisting in Wake County at age 20, October 10, 1862, for the war. Wounded and captured at Goldsboro on December 17, 1862. Paroled the same date. Listed as a deserter on January 12, 1863. Apprehended on June 21, 1863, and returned to duty. Reported present on surviving company muster rolls through April, 1864. Captured at Wilderness, Virginia, May 6, 1864. Confined at Point Lookout, Maryland, May 17, 1864. Transferred to Elmira, New York, July 23, 1864. Released at Elmira on May 29, 1865, after taking the Oath of Allegiance.

AUMAN, HENRY, Private

Born in Randolph County where he resided as a farm laborer prior to enlisting in Randolph County at age 24, March 6, 1862. Deserted prior to July 1, 1862. Returned to duty prior to December 17, 1862, when he was captured in battle at Goldsboro. Paroled on or about the same date. Listed as a paroled prisoner through February, 1863. Dropped from the rolls of the company prior to September 1, 1863. Reason he was dropped not reported. [Previously served as 2nd Lieutenant in the 63rd Regiment N.C. Militia.]

AUMAN, JACOB, Private

Resided in Randolph County and was by occupation a farm laborer prior to enlisting at age 18, October 10, 1862, for the war. No further records.

BELL, MILTON, Private

Born in Randolph County where he resided as a farmer prior to enlisting in Randolph County at age 22, March 12, 1862. Captured at or near Gettysburg, Pennsylvania, on or about July 5, 1863. Confined at Fort Delaware, Delaware. Paroled at Fort Delaware on July 30, 1863. Received at City Point, Virginia, August 1, 1863, for exchange. Reported absent on furlough from hospital in September-October, 1863. Reported absent in hospital in January-February, 1864. Hospitalized at Richmond, Virginia, April 9, 1864, with chronic diarrhoea. Furloughed for sixty days on April 27, 1864. Reported absent without leave on or about July 1, 1864.

BELL, ZIMRI, Corporal

Born in Randolph County where he resided as a farmer prior to enlisting in Randolph County at age 19, March 12, 1862. Mustered in as Private. Promoted to Corporal on December 1, 1862. Hospitalized at Danville, Virginia, May 14, 1863, with chronic rheumatism. Returned to duty on August 18, 1863. Captured at Bristoe Station, Virginia, October 14, 1863. Confined at Old Capitol Prison, Washington, D.C. Released at Old Capitol Prison on March 15, 1864, after taking the Oath of Allegiance.

BINGHAM, ALVERY, Sergeant

Born in Randolph County where he resided as a farmer prior to enlisting in Randolph County at age 32, March 12, 1862. Mustered in as Sergeant. Died at home in Randolph County on September 23 or October 10, 1862, of disease.

BIRD, HARTWELL, Private

Resided in Randolph County and enlisted in Wake County at age 21, November 7, 1862, for the war. Deserted prior to September 1, 1863. Returned to duty on September 20, 1864. Wounded at Jones' Farm, Virginia, on or about September 30, 1864. Reported absent wounded in November-December, 1864.

BOLEN, KERNEY, Private

Resided in Guilford County and enlisted in Wake County at age 30, October 10, 1862, for the war. Mentioned in dispatches for "good conduct" at the siege of Washington, North Carolina, in March-April, 1863. Wounded and captured at Gettysburg, Pennsylvania, on or about July 3, 1863. Confined at Fort Delaware, Delaware, on or about July 10, 1863. Transferred to Point Lookout, Maryland, October 20, 1863. Died in hospital at Point Lookout on January 3, 1864, of "chronic diarrhoea."

BROOKSHIRE, THOMAS F., Private

Born in Randolph County where he resided as a painter prior to enlisting in Randolph County at age 38, March 12, 1862. Reported absent without leave on or about April 28, 1862. Returned to duty prior to July 1, 1862. Reported present on surviving company muster rolls through February, 1863. No further records.

BROWN, ADAM, Private

Resided in Randolph County and enlisted at age 35, November 1, 1862, for the war. Dropped from the rolls of the company prior to March 1, 1863. Reason he was dropped not reported. Paroled at Greensboro on May 17, 1865.

BROWN, ELI, Private

Resided in Randolph County and enlisted at age 27, November 1, 1862, for the war. Dropped from the rolls of the company prior to March 1, 1863. Reason he was dropped not reported. Paroled at Greensboro on May 13, 1865.

BROWN, REUBEN, Private

Resided in Randolph County and enlisted at age 25, November 1, 1862, for the war. Dropped from the rolls of the company prior to March 1, 1863. Reason he was dropped not reported.

BRUNELL, STANTON, Private

Place and date of enlistment not reported (probably enlisted in March-June, 1863). Wounded in the knee and captured at Gettysburg, Pennsylvania, on or about July 3, 1863. Exchanged on an unspecified date. Died in Richmond County prior to August 19, 1864. Cause of death not reported.

CALLICOTT, ASA, Private

Resided in Randolph County and enlisted in Wake County

at age 25, October 21, 1862, for the war. Present or accounted for through February, 1863. Deserted prior to September 1, 1863.

CALLICOTT, JACOB, Private
Born in Randolph County where he resided as a farmer prior to enlisting in Randolph County at age 19, March 6, 1862. Mentioned in dispatches for "good conduct" at the siege of Washington, North Carolina, in March-April, 1863. Wounded and captured at Gettysburg, Pennsylvania, on or about July 3, 1863. Confined at Fort Delaware, Delaware. Released at Fort Delaware on October 1, 1863, after taking the Oath of Allegiance and joining the U.S. Army. Assigned to Company F, 1st Regiment Connecticut Cavalry.

CALLICOTT, PLEASANT, Private
Resided in Randolph County and enlisted in Wake County at age 21, October 21, 1862, for the war. Present or accounted for through February, 1863. Deserted prior to September 1, 1863.

CASHATT, J. F., Private
Resided in Randolph County and enlisted at age 24, November 7, 1862, for the war. Wounded at Gettysburg, Pennsylvania, on or about July 3, 1863. Captured at Falling Waters, Maryland, July 14, 1863. Confined at Old Capitol Prison, Washington, D.C. Released at Old Capitol Prison on December 13, 1863, after taking the Oath of Allegiance.

COLE, EVAN, Private
Resided in Randolph County and was by occupation a farmer prior to enlisting in Wake County at age 30, October 10, 1862, for the war. Present or accounted for through February, 1863. Deserted prior to September 1, 1863. Hospitalized at Charlottesville, Virginia, November 9, 1863, with debilitas. Returned to duty on December 31, 1863. Reported present or accounted for until May-June, 1864, when he was reported absent wounded. Place and date wounded not reported. Reported absent wounded through December, 1864.

COLE, J. MILTON, Private
Resided in Randolph County and enlisted in Wake County at age 25, October 10, 1862, for the war. Reported absent in hospital on or about March 1, 1863. Deserted prior to September 1, 1863.

COOPER, GEORGE W., Corporal
Born in Randolph County where he resided as a carpenter prior to enlisting in Randolph County at age 39, March 6, 1862. Mustered in as Corporal. Discharged prior to July 1, 1862, by reason of being overage.

COOPER, JOHN, Private
Born in Randolph County where he resided as a farmer prior to enlisting in Randolph County at age 23, March 12, 1862. Reported absent without leave on or about July 1, 1862. Dropped from the rolls of the company prior to March 1, 1863.

COOPER, MATHEW, Private
Born in Randolph County where he resided as a farmer

prior to enlisting in Randolph County at age 27, March 12, 1862. Reported absent on sick furlough on or about July 1, 1862. No further records.

COOPER, ROBERT, Private
Born in Randolph County where he resided as a farmer prior to enlisting in Randolph County at age 20, March 12, 1862. Deserted prior to July 1, 1862.

DUNNING, JOHN, Private
Born in Randolph County where he resided as a farmer prior to enlisting in Randolph County at age 25, March 7, 1862. Captured at Falling Waters, Maryland, July 14, 1863. Confined at Old Capitol Prison, Washington, D.C. Transferred to Point Lookout, Maryland, October 27, 1863. Released at Point Lookout on February 25, 1864, after taking the Oath of Allegiance and joining the U.S. Army. Assigned to Company F, 1st Regiment U.S. Volunteer Infantry.

EDGERTON, NATHAN, Private
Resided in Wake County and enlisted at age 28, October 10, 1862, for the war. Discharged prior to March 1, 1863, by reason of being a Quaker.

EDWARDS, G. W., _____
North Carolina pension records indicate that he served in this company.

FESMIRE, REUBEN C., Sergeant
Born in Randolph County where he resided as a farmer prior to enlisting in Randolph County at age 35, March 12, 1862, as a substitute. Mustered in as Corporal. Reported absent without leave in May-June, 1862. Returned to duty prior to October 28, 1862, and was promoted to Sergeant. Reported present through February 28, 1863. Deserted prior to September 1, 1863.

FINCHER, OSBORNE, Private
Previously served as Private in Company F, 49th Regiment N.C. Troops. Transferred to this company on or about February 4, 1863, in exchange for Private Marion L. Harkey. Died in hospital at Staunton, Virginia, September 29, 1863, of "chronic diarrhoea."

FLOYD, BENJAMIN F., Private
Born in Randolph County where he resided as a farmer prior to enlisting in Randolph County at age 30, March 12, 1862. Deserted prior to July 1, 1862. Returned to duty in November, 1863-February, 1864. Deserted on March 18, 1864.

FLOYD, MILES, Private
Born in Wake County and resided in Randolph County where he was by occupation a farmer prior to enlisting in Randolph County at age 52, March 12, 1862. Deserted prior to July 1, 1862. Returned to duty prior to March 1, 1863. Deserted prior to September 1, 1863.

FOARD, ZEBULON M., Private
Resided in Mecklenburg County and enlisted in Wake County at age 23, October 1, 1862, for the war. Reported present or accounted for on surviving company muster

rolls through April, 1864. Captured at Wilderness, Virginia, May 6, 1864. Confined at Point Lookout, Maryland, May 11, 1864. Transferred to Elmira, New York, July 8, 1864. Paroled at Elmira on March 2, 1865, and transferred to the James River, Virginia, for exchange. Hospitalized at Richmond, Virginia, March 7, 1865, with debilitas and was furloughed for thirty days on March 9, 1865.

GALLAHORN, ALPHEUS, Private
Born in Randolph County where he resided as a farmer prior to enlisting in Randolph County at age 18, March 7, 1862. Mustered in as Corporal. Reported absent on sick furlough on or about July 1, 1862. Dropped from the rolls of the company prior to March 1, 1863, probably for absence without leave. Reduced to ranks prior to September 1, 1863. Listed as a deserter on or about the same date.

GATTIS, JOHN, Private
Resided in Davidson County and enlisted on November 7, 1862, for the war. Deserted prior to March 1, 1863. Returned to duty in September, 1864. Deserted to the enemy on or about December 28, 1864. Confined at Washington, D.C., January 4, 1865. Released at Washington on or about the same date after taking the Oath of Allegiance.

GLASGOW, WILLIAM W., Sergeant
Born in Randolph County where he resided as a farmer prior to enlisting in Randolph County at age 24, April 8, 1862. Mustered in as Sergeant. Died at Murfreesboro on October 23, 1862, of disease.

GOINS, ANDREW J., Corporal
Born in Randolph County where he resided as a farmer prior to enlisting in Randolph County at age 26, March 7, 1862. Mustered in as Private. Deserted prior to July 1, 1862. Returned to duty prior to March 1, 1863. Promoted to Corporal in November, 1863-January, 1864. Reported absent wounded in July-August, 1864. Place and date wounded not reported (probably wounded at Globe Tavern, Virginia, August 19-21, 1864). Furloughed on or about August 29, 1864. Returned to duty prior to November 1, 1864. Surrendered at Appomattox Court House, Virginia, April 9, 1865.

GOWINS, MANLY C., Private
Born in Randolph County and was by occupation a farmer prior to enlisting in Randolph County at age 36, March 11, 1862. Discharged prior to July 1, 1862, by reason of being overage.

GREEN, ROBERT, Private
Born in Sampson County and was by occupation a farmer prior to enlisting in Randolph County at age 38, March 12, 1862. Discharged prior to July 1, 1862, by reason of being overage.

GRISSOM, THOMAS A., Private
Born in Tennessee and resided in Randolph County where he was by occupation a farmer prior to enlisting in Randolph County at age 25, March 12, 1862. Reported

present on surviving company muster rolls through August, 1863. Wounded at Bristoe Station, Virginia, October 14, 1863. Hospitalized at Richmond, Virginia. Furloughed on November 5, 1863. Reported absent wounded through April, 1864. Reported on detail for light duty at Raleigh in May-August, 1864. Reported absent on detached service (probably as a teamster) in July-October, 1864. Rejoined the company in November-December, 1864. Captured at the Appomattox River, Virginia, April 3, 1865. Confined at Point Lookout, Maryland, April 13, 1865. Released on June 27, 1865, after taking the Oath of Allegiance.

HADDOCK, BENJAMIN F., Private
Resided in Randolph County and enlisted in Wake County at age 25, October 21, 1862, for the war. Died in hospital at Staunton, Virginia, June 1, 1863, of "febris typhoides."

HADDOCK, THOMAS W., Private
Resided in Randolph County and enlisted in Wake County at age 22, October 21, 1862, for the war. Wounded at Goldsboro on December 17, 1862. Returned to duty prior to March 1, 1863. Deserted on April 2, 1863. Arrested on November 21, 1863. Court-martialed and sentenced to be shot. Executed on February 1, 1864, for desertion.

HAGER, JOHN T., _____
Enlisted on December 12, 1864, for the war. Survived the war.

HALL, ALEXANDER W., Sergeant
Born in Randolph County where he resided as a carpenter prior to enlisting in Randolph County at age 26, March 7, 1862. Mustered in as Private. Promoted to Sergeant on October 1, 1862. Wounded in the leg (fracture) and captured at Gettysburg, Pennsylvania, July 3, 1863. Leg amputated. Hospitalized at Gettysburg. Transferred to hospital at Baltimore, Maryland, September 16, 1863. Paroled at Baltimore on September 25, 1863. Received at City Point, Virginia, September 27, 1863, for exchange. Retired from service on February 14, 1865.

HALL, LOVELACE N., Sergeant
Born in Montgomery County and resided in Randolph County where he was by occupation a farmer prior to enlisting in Randolph County at age 18, April 8, 1862. Mustered in as Private. Promoted to Corporal on December 1, 1862. Reported present on surviving company muster rolls through August, 1863. Captured at Bristoe Station, Virginia, October 14, 1863. Confined at Point Lookout, Maryland. Paroled at Point Lookout on February 24, 1865. Received at Aiken's Landing, James River, Virginia, on or about February 28, 1865, for exchange. Promoted to Sergeant while a prisoner of war. Survived the war.

HAMMOND, WILLIAM, Private
Born in Randolph County where he resided as a farmer prior to enlisting in Randolph County at age 30, March 12, 1862. Listed as a deserter prior to July 1, 1862. Returned to duty prior to March 1, 1863. Wounded and captured at Gettysburg, Pennsylvania, on or about July 1, 1863. Died at Winchester, Virginia, July 22, 1863, of wounds.

HANCOCK, ALBERT, Private

Resided in Randolph County and enlisted at age 19, November 7, 1862, for the war. Wounded at Goldsboro on December 17, 1862. Reported absent wounded through February, 1863. Dropped from the rolls of the company prior to September 1, 1863. Reason he was dropped not reported. Returned to duty in July-August, 1864. Surrendered at Appomattox Court House, Virginia, April 9, 1865.

HANCOCK, DAVID, Private

Born in Randolph County where he resided as a farmer prior to enlisting in Randolph County at age 24, March 6, 1862. Died in hospital at Petersburg, Virginia, on or about August 16, 1862, of "febris remittens."

HARGETT, D. A., Private

Resided in Mecklenburg County and enlisted in Wake County at age 27, October 1, 1862, for the war. Discharged at Wilson on or about April 1, 1863, by reason of "disease of spinal column and great difficulty of walking."

HARKEY, MARION L., Private

Resided in Mecklenburg County and enlisted at age 21, October 1, 1862, for the war. Transferred to Company F, 49th Regiment N.C. Troops, on or about February 4, 1863, in exchange for Private Osborne Fincher.

HARPER, JOHN B., Private

Born in Chatham County and resided in Randolph County where he was by occupation a farmer prior to enlisting in Randolph County at age 20, March 12, 1862. Deserted on May 20, 1862. Apprehended on October 21, 1862. Deserted on January 20, 1863. Apprehended on July 21, 1863. Deserted on August 2, 1863. Apprehended on August 12, 1863. Reported present on surviving company muster rolls from September, 1863, through August, 1864. Captured at Burgess' Mill, Virginia, October 27, 1864. Confined at Point Lookout, Maryland, October 31, 1864. Died at Point Lookout on April 12, 1865, of "chronic diarrhoea."

HOOVER, WILLIAM M., Private

Resided in Randolph County and enlisted in Wake County at age 26, November 7, 1862, for the war. Wounded at Gettysburg, Pennsylvania, July 3, 1863. Reported absent wounded through April, 1864. Detailed for light duty at Raleigh in May-June, 1864. Reported absent on detail through December, 1864. Rejoined the company prior to March 25, 1865, when he was captured near Petersburg, Virginia. Confined at Point Lookout, Maryland, March 27, 1865. Released at Point Lookout on June 28, 1865, after taking the Oath of Allegiance.

HULAND, JOHN, Private

Resided in Randolph County where he enlisted at age 36, June 22, 1863, for the war. Captured at Bristoe Station, Virginia, October 14, 1863. Confined at Old Capitol Prison, Washington, D.C. Transferred to Point Lookout, Maryland, October 27, 1863. Released at Point Lookout on January 25, 1864, after taking the Oath of Allegiance and joining the U.S. service. Unit to which assigned not reported.

HURLEY, CALVIN, Private

Born in Randolph County where he resided as a farmer prior to enlisting in Randolph County at age 21, March 12, 1862. Died in Randolph County on April 19, 1862, of disease.

JACKSON, MICAJAH C., Private

Resided in Randolph County and enlisted in Wake County on November 21, 1863, for the war. Captured at or near Wilderness, Virginia, on or about May 6, 1864. Confined at Point Lookout, Maryland, May 17, 1864. Transferred to Elmira, New York, July 23, 1864. Released at Elmira on May 13, 1865, after taking the Oath of Allegiance.

JERRALD, ABSALOM, Private

Born in Randolph County where he resided as a farmer prior to enlisting in Randolph County at age 51, March 12, 1862, as a substitute. Deserted prior to July 1, 1862. Returned to duty prior to March 1, 1863. Reported present or accounted for on surviving company muster rolls through August, 1864. Captured at Burgess' Mill, Virginia, October 27, 1864. Confined at Point Lookout, Maryland, October 31, 1864. Paroled at Point Lookout on January 17, 1865. Received at Boulware's Wharf, James River, Virginia, January 21, 1865, for exchange. Hospitalized at Richmond, Virginia, January 22, 1865, with phthisis. Transferred to another hospital on January 26, 1865. No further records.

JERRALD, WILLIAM B., Private

Born in Randolph County where he resided as a farmer prior to enlisting in Randolph County at age 24, March 21, 1862. Reported absent without leave on or about July 1, 1862. Dropped from the rolls of the company prior to March 1, 1863. Returned to duty prior to July 14, 1863, when he was captured at Falling Waters, Maryland. Confined at Old Capitol Prison, Washington, D.C. Released on December 13, 1863, after taking the Oath of Allegiance.

JONES, ALVIS, Private

Resided in Guilford County and enlisted at age 24, November 7, 1862, for the war. No further records.

JONES, AMOS, Private

Born in Randolph County where he resided as a laborer prior to enlisting in Randolph County at age 36, March 6, 1862. Reported present through June 30, 1862. Dropped from the rolls of the company prior to March 1, 1863. Reason he was dropped not reported (was probably discharged by reason of being overage).

JONES, BARTLEY, Private

Born in Wake County and resided in Randolph County where he was by occupation a farmer prior to enlisting in Randolph County at age 53, March 24, 1862. Hospitalized at Richmond, Virginia, June 23, 1863, with rheumatism. Transferred to another hospital on August 13, 1863. Returned to duty prior to November 1, 1863. Reported on duty as an ambulance driver in January-February, 1864. Discharged on April 19, 1864, by reason of "his age."

JONES, WILLIAM H., Private
Born in Guilford County and resided in Randolph County where he was by occupation a farmer prior to enlisting in Randolph County at age 18, March 6, 1862. Died at or near Petersburg, Virginia, on or about August 27, 1862, of disease.

KEARNES, ISAAC, Private
Born in Randolph County and resided in Randolph or Guilford County where he was by occupation a farmer prior to enlisting in Randolph County at age 33, March 7, 1862. Wounded and captured at Falling Waters, Maryland, July 14, 1863. Exchanged subsequent to November 1, 1863. Returned to duty prior to March 1, 1864. Wounded in the hand in September-October, 1864. Place and date wounded not reported. Hospitalized at Richmond, Virginia, where he was captured on April 3, 1865. Transferred to Newport News, Virginia, April 23, 1865. Released at Newport News on June 30, 1865, after taking the Oath of Allegiance.

KEARNES, THOMAS S., Private
Resided in Randolph County and enlisted in Wake County at age 20, May 13, 1862, for the war. Reported present on surviving company muster rolls through August, 1863. Captured at Bristoe Station, Virginia, October 14, 1863. Confined at Old Capitol Prison, Washington, D.C. Transferred to Point Lookout, Maryland, October 27, 1863. Released at Point Lookout on February 25, 1864, after taking the Oath of Allegiance and joining the U.S. Army. Assigned to Company F, 1st Regiment U.S. Volunteer Infantry.

KERNEGAY, JAMES H., Private
Resided in Duplin County and enlisted in Wake County at age 23, October 1, 1862, for the war. Wounded and captured at Gettysburg, Pennsylvania, July 3, 1863, or at Falling Waters, Maryland, July 14, 1863. Confined at Old Capitol Prison, Washington, D.C. Transferred to Point Lookout, Maryland, August 8, 1863. Transferred to Elmira, New York, August 16, 1864. Paroled at Elmira on March 10, 1865. Received at Boulware's Wharf, James River, Virginia, on or about March 15, 1865, for exchange. Survived the war.

KING, JAMES, Private
Born in Randolph County where he resided as a farmer prior to enlisting in Randolph County at age 30, March 6, 1862. Listed as a deserter prior to July 1, 1862. Returned to duty subsequent to February 28, 1863. Captured at or near Gettysburg, Pennsylvania, on or about July 4, 1863. Confined at Fort Delaware, Delaware, on or about July 10, 1863. Died at Fort Delaware on August 10, 1863, of "inflam[mation] of lungs."

LAMB, WILLIAM H. H., Private
Resided in Duplin County and enlisted in Wake County at age 21, October 1, 1862, for the war. Reported present or accounted for on surviving company muster rolls through December, 1864. Surrendered at Appomattox Court House, Virginia, April 9, 1865.

LEDWELL, JASON, Private
Resided in Randolph County and enlisted at age 19,

December 1, 1862, for the war. Dropped from the rolls of the company prior to March 1, 1863. Roll of Honor states that he was wounded at Falling Waters, Maryland, July 14, 1863. No further records.

LEDWELL, JOHN W., Private
Resided in Randolph County and was by occupation a farm laborer prior to enlisting at Camp French, near Petersburg, Virginia, at age 20, October 6, 1862, for the war. Reported present through February, 1863. Deserted prior to September 1, 1863.

LEDWELL, THOMAS, Private
Resided in Randolph County and enlisted at age 53, December 1, 1862, for the war as a substitute. Captured at Falling Waters, Maryland, July 14, 1863. Sent to Baltimore, Maryland. Transferred to Point Lookout, Maryland, August 16, 1863. Released at Point Lookout on August 12, 1864, after taking the Oath of Allegiance.

LEDWELL, THOMAS W., Sergeant
Born in Randolph County where he resided as a farmer prior to enlisting in Randolph County at age 21, March 7, 1862. Mustered in as Private. Promoted to Sergeant in November, 1862. Wounded at Goldsboro on December 17, 1862. Returned to duty prior to March 1, 1863. Wounded and captured at Gettysburg, Pennsylvania, July 3, 1863. Confined at Fort Delaware, Delaware, on or about July 10, 1863. Released at Fort Delaware on May 3, 1865, after taking the Oath of Allegiance.

LEWALLEN, JOHN, Private
Resided in Randolph County and was by occupation a laborer prior to enlisting in Wake County at age 30, November 7, 1862, for the war. Deserted on November 23, 1862. Apprehended on May 21, 1863, and was returned to duty. Died in hospital at Lynchburg, Virginia, November 18, 1863, of "diarrhoea chron[ic]."

LEWIS, CALVIN B., Sergeant
Born in Randolph County where he resided as a farmer prior to enlisting in Randolph County at age 31, March 12, 1862. Mustered in as Sergeant. Died in hospital at Petersburg, Virginia, August 11, 1862, of "continued fever."

LOFLIN, JOHN, Private
Resided in Randolph County and enlisted at age 29, November 7, 1862, for the war. Dropped from the rolls of the company (presumably for desertion) prior to March 1, 1863. Company records do not indicate whether he returned to duty; however, he went over to the enemy on or about October 28, 1864. Confined at Camp Hamilton, Virginia. Released on November 13, 1864, after taking the Oath of Allegiance.

LONG, JAMES G., _____
North Carolina pension records indicate that he served in this company.

LOWDERMILK, REUBEN, Corporal
Born in Randolph County where he resided as a farmer prior to enlisting in Randolph County at age 25, March

12, 1862. Mustered in as Corporal. Reported present through June, 1862. Dropped from the rolls of the company prior to March 1, 1863. Reason he was dropped not reported. Paroled at Greensboro on May 16, 1865.

LUTHER, BARNEY R., Private
Born in Randolph County where he resided as a farmer prior to enlisting in Randolph County at age 24, March 7, 1862. Died in hospital at Petersburg, Virginia, August 10, 1862, of "febris typhoides."

LUTHER, COLLIER, Sergeant
Born in Randolph County where he resided as a blacksmith prior to enlisting in Randolph County at age 32, March 6, 1862. Mustered in as Private. Promoted to Sergeant on December 1, 1862. Wounded at Goldsboro on December 17, 1862. Returned to duty prior to March 1, 1863. Hospitalized at Richmond, Virginia, June 21, 1863, with chronic rheumatism. Furloughed for thirty days on August 8, 1863. Surviving company muster rolls indicate that he was absent sick through December, 1864.

LUTHER, FRANKLIN, Corporal
Born in Randolph County where he resided as a farmer prior to enlisting in Randolph County at age 21, March 12, 1862. Mustered in as Private. Promoted to Corporal on December 1, 1862. Wounded in the right leg and captured at Gettysburg, Pennsylvania, on or about July 3, 1863. Right leg amputated. Hospitalized at Gettysburg where he died on or about September 14, 1863, of wounds.

LYNDON, JOSIAH W., Private
Born in Randolph County where he resided as a farmer prior to enlisting in Randolph County at age 31, March 14, 1862. Died in hospital at Richmond, Virginia, August 11, 1862, of "typhoid fever."

MANUS, ENOCH, Private
Born in Moore County and resided in Chatham County where he was by occupation a farmer prior to enlisting in Moore County at age 45, March 12, 1862. Deserted on June 19, 1862. Apprehended on January 20, 1863, and was returned to duty. Died on September 30, 1863, of disease. Place of death not reported.

MEDLEY, JAMES H., Private
Born in Wake County and resided in Randolph County where he was by occupation a farmer prior to enlisting in Randolph County on March 6, 1862. Died at Raleigh on or about May 25, 1862, of disease.

MEDLEY, JOHN, Private
Born in Wake County and resided in Randolph County where he was by occupation a farmer prior to enlisting in Randolph County at age 41, March 10, 1862. Deserted prior to July 1, 1862. Returned to duty prior to March 1, 1863. Wounded in the head at Gettysburg, Pennsylvania, July 3, 1863. Captured on or about the same date. Hospitalized at Gettysburg. Transferred to hospital at Davids Island, New York Harbor, where he arrived on or about July 20, 1863. Paroled at Davids Island on August 24, 1863. Received at City Point, Virginia, August 28, 1863, for exchange. Reported absent wounded through

October, 1863. Returned to duty in November, 1863-February, 1864. Present or accounted for through December, 1864. Survived the war. [North Carolina pension records indicate that he was blinded in one eye as a result of wounds received at Gettysburg.]

MESSICK, JAMES J., Private
Resided in Yadkin County and enlisted in Wake County at age 25, October 8, 1862, for the war. Present or accounted for through February, 1863. Wounded and captured at Gettysburg, Pennsylvania, on or about July 3, 1863. Confined at Fort Delaware, Delaware, on or about July 10, 1863. Released at Fort Delaware on May 5, 1865, after taking the Oath of Allegiance.

MILLER, ALSON, Private
Resided in Chatham County and enlisted at age 37, November 7, 1862, for the war. Dropped from the rolls of the company prior to March 1, 1863. Reason he was dropped not reported. Died at or near Shepherdstown, West Virginia, June 26, 1863, of disease.

MILLER, WILLIAM MASH, Private
Resided in Randolph County and was by occupation a farmer prior to enlisting in Wake County at age 30, November 7, 1862, for the war. Deserted prior to March 1, 1863. Returned to duty on September 20, 1864. Deserted to the enemy on or about December 28, 1864. Confined at Washington, D.C., January 4, 1865. Released at Washington on or about the same date after taking the Oath of Allegiance.

MUNROE, M. L. J., Sergeant
Resided in Randolph County and enlisted in Wake County at age 27, October 10, 1862, for the war. Mustered in as Private. Hospitalized at or near Petersburg, Virginia, November 12, 1862, with hepatitis. Promoted to Corporal on December 1, 1862. Released from hospital and returned to duty on December 11, 1862. Hospitalized at Wilmington on April 30, 1863, with typhoid fever. Returned to duty on November 21, 1863. Promoted to Sergeant in May-June, 1864. Reported present or accounted for through August, 1864. Reported absent wounded in September-December, 1864. Place and date wounded not reported.

MURRAY, P. G., Private
Resided in Guilford County and enlisted in Wake County at age 27, October 21, 1862, for the war. Wounded in the right leg at Gettysburg, Pennsylvania, July 3, 1863. Captured on or about the same date. Hospitalized at Gettysburg. Transferred to Fort Delaware, Delaware, where he arrived on or about July 10, 1863. Transferred to Point Lookout, Maryland, October 20, 1863. Released at Point Lookout on January 24, 1864, after taking the Oath of Allegiance and joining the U.S. Army. Assigned to the 1st Regiment U.S. Volunteer Infantry.

NELSON, JAMES, _____
North Carolina pension records indicate that he served in this company.

NELSON, MORRIS, Private
Born in Montgomery County and resided in Randolph

County where he was by occupation a farmer prior to enlisting in Randolph County at age 20, March 24, 1862. Wounded at Gettysburg, Pennsylvania, July 3, 1863. Captured on or about the same date. Confined at Fort Delaware, Delaware, on or about July 10, 1863. Released at Fort Delaware on or about October 4, 1863, after taking the Oath of Allegiance and joining the U.S. Army. Assigned to Company F, 1st Regiment Connecticut Cavalry.

OWENS, WILLIAM, Private
Born in Moore County where he resided as a farmer prior to enlisting in Randolph County at age 33, March 7, 1862. Deserted prior to July 1, 1862.

PARISH, D. M., Private
Resided in Randolph County and enlisted at age 19, November 7, 1862, for the war. Dropped from the rolls of the company prior to March 1, 1863. Reason he was dropped not reported.

PEARCE, LOVETT, Private
Resided in Randolph County and was by occupation a farmer prior to enlisting in Randolph County at age 44, March 11, 1862. Discharged on May 14, 1862, by reason of being overage.

PEARCE, WILLIAM, Private
Resided in Randolph County and enlisted in Wake County at age 27, October 10, 1862, for the war. Captured at Waynesboro, Pennsylvania, on or about July 9, 1863. Confined at Fort Delaware, Delaware. Released at Fort Delaware on or about October 4, 1863, after taking the Oath of Allegiance and joining the U.S. Army. Assigned to the 1st Regiment Connecticut Cavalry.

PERKINS, SAMUEL, Private
Resided in Wake County and enlisted at age 31, October 1, 1862, for the war. Because he was a Quaker he was discharged on October 2, 1862, after paying a $500 fee as required by law.

PHILLIPS, JAMES, Private
Born in Moore County and resided in Randolph County where he was by occupation a farmer prior to enlisting in Randolph County at age 28, March 12, 1862. Deserted prior to July 1, 1862. Returned to duty in March-May, 1864. Captured at Cold Harbor, Virginia, June 3, 1864. Confined at Point Lookout, Maryland, June 11, 1864. Released at Point Lookout on June 20, 1864, after taking the Oath of Allegiance and joining the U.S. Army. Assigned to Company F, 1st Regiment U.S. Volunteer Infantry.

PIGGOTT, J. H., Private
Resided in Randolph County and enlisted at age 28, October 1, 1862, for the war. Because he was a Quaker he was discharged on March 20, 1863, after paying a $500 fee as required by law.

PIKE, MARK E., Private
Resided in Wake County and enlisted at age 30, October 1, 1862, for the war. Because he was a Quaker he was discharged on October 2, 1862, after paying a $500 fee as required by law.

POPE, JOHN R., Private
Enlisted in Wake County on January 1, 1864, for the war. Present or accounted for until hospitalized at Richmond, Virginia, November 29, 1864. Died in hospital at Richmond on December 25, 1864. Cause of death not reported.

PRESNELL, JAMES M., Private
Born in Randolph County where he resided as a laborer prior to enlisting in Randolph County at age 33, March 24, 1862. Killed at Gettysburg, Pennsylvania, July 3, 1863.

PRESNELL, STANTON, Private
Born in Randolph County where he resided as a farmer prior to enlisting in Randolph County at age 21, March 12, 1862. Wounded in the right knee and right hand and captured at Gettysburg, Pennsylvania, July 3, 1863. Hospitalized at Chester, Pennsylvania. Transferred to Point Lookout, Maryland, where he arrived on October 4, 1863. Paroled at Point Lookout on April 27, 1864. Received at City Point, Virginia, April 30, 1864, for exchange. Hospitalized at Richmond, Virginia, May 1, 1864, with chronic rheumatism. Furloughed for thirty days on May 5, 1864. Dropped from the company rolls prior to July 1, 1864. Reason he was dropped not reported. Survived the war.

REAVES, JESSE, Private
Resided in Duplin County and enlisted in Wake County at age 19, October 1, 1862, for the war. Wounded at Gettysburg, Pennsylvania, July 3, 1863. Captured at or near Cashtown, Pennsylvania, July 4, 1863. Hospitalized at Chester, Pennsylvania. Paroled and transferred to City Point, Virginia, where he was received on August 20, 1863, for exchange. Reported absent wounded through October, 1863. Died in hospital at Richmond, Virginia, December 31, 1863, of "typhoid pneumonia."

REVELLS, ANDREW H., Private
Resided in Randolph County where he enlisted at age 18, June 22, 1863, for the war. Died in hospital at Gordonsville, Virginia, August 30, 1863, of "febris typhoides."

RIDGE, WILLIS, Private
Resided in Randolph County and enlisted at age 40, November 7, 1862, for the war. Dropped from the rolls of the company prior to March 1, 1863. Reason he was dropped not reported.

ROBBINS, AHI C., Private
Resided in Randolph County where he enlisted at age 24, June 22, 1863, for the war. Reported present or accounted for on surviving company muster rolls through April, 1864. Captured at or near Bottom's Bridge, on the Chickahominy River, Virginia, on or about June 13, 1864. Sent to City Point, Virginia. Confined at Point Lookout, Maryland, June 24, 1864. Released at Point Lookout on June 27, 1864, after taking the Oath of Allegiance and

joining the U.S. Army. Assigned to Company K, 1st Regiment U.S. Volunteer Infantry.

ROBBINS, ALEX S., Private
Resided in Randolph County and was by occupation a farmer prior to enlisting at age 28, November 7, 1862, for the war. Dropped from the rolls of the company prior to March 1, 1863. Reason he was dropped not reported. Paroled at Greensboro on May 11, 1865.

ROBBINS, CLARKSON, Private
Resided in Randolph County and was by occupation a farmer prior to enlisting at age 25, November 7, 1862, for the war. Dropped from the rolls of the company (probably for desertion) prior to March 1, 1863.

ROBBINS, CLARKSON L., Private
Born in Randolph County where he resided as a farmer prior to enlisting in Randolph County at age 18, March 12, 1862. Present or accounted for through June, 1862. Deserted prior to March 1, 1863. Returned to duty on April 28, 1864. Wounded in the left hand at Jones' Farm, Virginia, September 30, 1864. Returned to duty in November-December, 1864. Captured at Sutherland's Station, Virginia, April 2, 1865. Confined at Point Lookout, Maryland, April 4, 1865. Released at Point Lookout on June 17, 1865, after taking the Oath of Allegiance.

ROBBINS, ELIAS, Private
Resided in Randolph County and was by occupation a farmer prior to enlisting at age 30, November 7, 1862, for the war. Dropped from the rolls of the company prior to March 1, 1863. Reason he was dropped not reported. Captured at or near Bottom's Bridge, on the Chickahominy River, Virginia, June 12, 1864. Confined at Point Lookout, Maryland, June 24, 1864. Transferred to Elmira, New York, July 23, 1864. Died at Elmira on December 24, 1864, of "chronic diarrhoea."

ROBBINS, JOHN, Private
Resided in Randolph County where he enlisted at age 37, June 22, 1863, for the war. Reported present on surviving company muster rolls through December, 1864. Captured near Petersburg, Virginia, March 25, 1865. Confined at Point Lookout, Maryland, March 27, 1865. Released at Point Lookout on June 17, 1865, after taking the Oath of Allegiance.

ROBBINS, MICAJAH, Private
Resided in Randolph County and enlisted in Wake County at age 20, November 7, 1862, for the war. Deserted on November 23, 1862. Apprehended on June 20, 1863, and was returned to duty. Captured at Bristoe Station, Virginia, October 14, 1863. Confined at Old Capitol Prison, Washington, D.C. Released at Old Capitol Prison on March 14, 1864, after taking the Oath of Allegiance.

RODGERS, JOHN, Private
Born in Randolph County where he resided as a farmer prior to enlisting in Randolph County at age 45, March 12, 1862. Reported absent without leave on or about July 1, 1862. Dropped from the rolls of the company prior to

March 1, 1863. Returned to duty on an unspecified date but deserted on April 28, 1863. Killed in Randolph County (presumably by troops hunting deserters) on June 1, 1863.

RUSH, ALSON J., 1st Sergeant
Born in Randolph County where he resided as a farmer prior to enlisting in Randolph County at age 20, March 12, 1862, as a substitute. Mustered in as Private. Promoted to 1st Sergeant on December 1, 1862. Wounded at Goldsboro on December 17, 1862. Returned to duty prior to March 1, 1863. Reported present on surviving company muster rolls through December, 1864. Survived the war.

RUSH, ARCHIBALD F., Private
Born in Randolph County where he resided as a blacksmith prior to enlisting in Randolph County at age 44, March 12, 1862. Captured near Gettysburg, Pennsylvania, on or about July 7, 1863. Confined at Fort Delaware, Delaware, on or about July 10, 1863. Released at Fort Delaware on September 22, 1863, after taking the Oath of Allegiance and joining the U.S. Army. Assigned to Company G, 3rd Regiment Maryland Cavalry.

RUSH, AZEL G., Private
Born in Randolph County and was by occupation a farmer prior to enlisting in Randolph County at age 38, March 7, 1862. Discharged prior to July 1, 1862, by reason of being overage.

RUSH, CALVIN J., 1st Sergeant
Born in Randolph County where he resided as a farmer prior to enlisting in Randolph County at age 20, March 12, 1862, as a substitute. Mustered in as 1st Sergeant. Died in hospital at Petersburg, Virginia, on or about September 1, 1862, of "phthisis."

RUSH, GEORGE, Private
Resided in Randolph County and was by occupation a farmer prior to enlisting at age 40, March 12, 1862. Discharged on May 20, 1862, by reason of being overage.

RUSSELL, DANIEL, Private
Born in Randolph County where he resided as a blacksmith prior to enlisting in Randolph County at age 44, March 12, 1862. Discharged on May 25, 1862, by reason of being overage.

SCOTT, BENJAMIN L., Private
Resided in Randolph County and was by occupation a farmer prior to enlisting at age 28, November 7, 1862, for the war. Dropped from the rolls of the company prior to March 1, 1863. Reason he was dropped not reported. Paroled at Greensboro on May 13, 1865.

SCOTT, WILLIAM B., Private
Born in Randolph County where he resided as a farmer prior to enlisting in Randolph County at age 28, March 24, 1862. Wounded at Gettysburg, Pennsylvania, July 3, 1863. Captured at Gettysburg on or about the same date. Confined at Fort Delaware, Delaware, on or about July 10, 1863. Paroled at Fort Delaware on October 30, 1864.

Received at Venus Point, Savannah River, Georgia, November 15, 1864, for exchange. Survived the war.

SHAW, WILEY H., Musician

Born in Randolph County where he resided as a farmer prior to enlisting in Randolph County at age 18, April 8, 1862. Mustered in as Private. Appointed Musician (Drummer) in May-June, 1864. Reported present or accounted for on company muster rolls through June, 1864. Transferred to the regimental band in July-October, 1864.

SMITH, LEROY, Private

Resided in Mecklenburg County and enlisted in Wake County at age 19, October 1, 1862, for the war. Wounded at Gettysburg, Pennsylvania, July 3, 1863. Captured on or about the same date. Confined at Fort Delaware, Delaware, on or about July 10, 1863. Died at Fort Delaware on October 7, 1863. Cause of death not reported.

STALEY, CALVIN, Private

Born in Randolph County where he resided as a farmer prior to enlisting in Randolph County at age 20, March 6, 1862. Deserted in March-August, 1863.

STEED, THOMAS J., Private

Enlisted in Wake County on November 21, 1863, for the war. Died on May 2, 1864. Place and cause of death not reported.

STRIDER, ANDREW, Private

Born in Randolph County where he resided as a farmer prior to enlisting in Randolph County at age 21, March 6, 1862. Hospitalized at or near Petersburg, Virginia, September 24, 1862, with remittent fever. Returned to duty on November 11, 1862. Wounded at Bristoe Station, Virginia, October 14, 1863. Died on October 17, 1863, of wounds. Place of death not reported.

STRIDER, JOEL, Private

Born in Randolph County where he resided as a farmer prior to enlisting in Randolph County at age 27, March 7, 1862. Captured at Falling Waters, Maryland, July 14, 1863. Confined at Old Capitol Prison, Washington, D.C. Transferred to Point Lookout, Maryland, August 8, 1863. Transferred to Elmira, New York, August 16, 1864. Died at Elmira on September 20, 1864, of "chronic diarrhoea."

STUTTS, WILLIAM, Private

Resided in Randolph County and enlisted in Wake County at age 25, October 10, 1862, for the war. Deserted on January 21, 1863. Apprehended on or about November 3, 1863. Court-martialed and sentenced to be shot. Executed at or near Orange Court House, Virginia, February 1, 1864, for desertion. [For further details concerning his execution, see a letter dated February 1, 1864, in the John Wright Family Papers, Private Collection 1594, North Carolina Division of Archives and History, Raleigh.]

SURRATT, JOSIAH, Private

Born in Davidson County and resided in Randolph or Guilford County where he was by occupation a farmer

prior to enlisting in Randolph County at age 16, March 25, 1862. Wounded at Goldsboro on December 17, 1862. Returned to duty prior to March 1, 1863. Reported present on surviving company muster rolls through April, 1864. Deserted to the enemy at or near Bottom's Bridge, Chickahominy River, Virginia, on or about June 13, 1864. Confined at Point Lookout, Maryland, June 24, 1864. Transferred to Elmira, New York, on or about July 25, 1864. Released at Elmira on June 19, 1865, after taking the Oath of Allegiance.

TADLOCK, JOHN W., Private

Resided in Guilford County and enlisted in Wake County on November 7, 1862, for the war. Reported present or accounted for on surviving company muster rolls through April, 1864. Captured at or near Wilderness, Virginia, on or about May 6, 1864. Confined at Point Lookout, Maryland, May 17, 1864. Transferred to Elmira, New York, July 23, 1864. Released at Elmira on May 29, 1865, after taking the Oath of Allegiance.

TADLOCK, JOSEPH C., Private

Born in Randolph County where he resided as a farmer prior to enlisting in Randolph County at age 32, March 12, 1862. Deserted on May 12, 1862. Returned to duty on November 1, 1863. Deserted on March 18, 1864.

THAYER, KENDRICK, _____

Place and date of enlistment not reported; however, he probably enlisted in March-June, 1863. Died in hospital at Wilson prior to June 25, 1863, of wounds received near Suffolk, Virginia, on an unspecified date.

TROTTER, JOHN M., Corporal

Born in Randolph County where he resided as a farmer prior to enlisting in Randolph County at age 18, March 26, 1862. Mustered in as Private. Reported present or accounted for on surviving company muster rolls through June, 1864. Promoted to Corporal in November, 1863-February, 1864. Hospitalized at Richmond, Virginia, August 29, 1864, with a gunshot wound of the hand. Forefinger amputated. Place and date wounded not reported (was probably wounded at Reams' Station, Virginia, August 25, 1864). Furloughed for thirty days on September 8, 1864. Returned to duty on or about October 8, 1864. Hospitalized at Richmond on March 28, 1865, with a gunshot wound of the right hip. Place and date wounded not reported (was probably wounded near Petersburg, Virginia, March 25, 1865). Captured in hospital at Richmond on April 3, 1865. Paroled on May 30, 1865.

VANDERFORD, JOSEPH J., Private

Born in Chatham County and resided in Randolph County where he was by occupation a laborer prior to enlisting in Randolph County at age 24, March 6, 1862. Hospitalized at Danville, Virginia, August 13, 1862, with typhoid fever. Returned to duty on October 16, 1862. Reported present or accounted for on surviving company muster rolls through December, 1864. Served as a teamster during part of the war. Was also detailed "to work in the mines" near Petersburg, Virginia.

VANDERFORD, WILLIAM B., Private

Born in Chatham County and resided in Randolph County where he was by occupation a farmer prior to enlisting in Randolph County at age 21, March 6, 1862. Reported present or accounted for on surviving company muster rolls through December, 1864. Paroled at Burkeville Junction, Virginia, on or about April 14, 1865.

VUNCANNON, JOHN, Private

Resided in Randolph County where he enlisted at age 38, November 7, 1862, for the war. Reported present on surviving company muster rolls through August, 1863. Wounded in the left foot at Bristoe Station, Virginia, October 14, 1863. Hospitalized at Richmond, Virginia. Furloughed for thirty days on October 31, 1863. Reported absent wounded through April, 1864. Reported on detail "to hunt deserters" in May-August, 1864. Returned to duty in November-December, 1864. Deserted to the enemy on or about March 3, 1865. Confined at Washington, D.C., March 7, 1865. Released on or about the same date after taking the Oath of Allegiance.

WALKER, NATHAN S., Private

Born in Randolph County where he resided as a farmer prior to enlisting in Randolph County at age 25, March 12, 1862. Reported present on surviving company muster rolls through August, 1863. Captured at Bristoe Station, Virginia, October 14, 1863. Confined at Old Capitol Prison, Washington, D.C. Transferred to Point Lookout, Maryland, October 27, 1863. Exchanged in September, 1864. Hospitalized at Richmond, Virginia, in early October, 1864, with chronic diarrhoea. Furloughed on October 11, 1864.

WEBSTER, ARCHIBALD M., Private

Born in Randolph County where he resided as a farmer prior to enlisting in Randolph County at age 23, March 12, 1862. Deserted prior to July 1, 1862.

WHISENHUNT, HENRY H., Private

Previously served as Private in Company F, 2nd Battalion N.C. Infantry. Attached himself to this company after most of the 2nd Battalion N.C. Infantry was captured at Roanoke Island on February 8, 1862. Formally enlisted in this company on March 26, 1862. Died in hospital at Raleigh on March 22, 1863, of "pneumonia" and/or "continued fever."

WHITE, JOSEPH A., Private

Place and date of enlistment not reported. Paroled at Greensboro on May 15, 1865.

WILLIAMS, A. SPAIN, Private

Born in Moore County and resided in Randolph County where he was by occupation a farmer prior to enlisting in Randolph County at age 29, March 24, 1862. Deserted prior to July 1, 1862. Returned to duty prior to March 1, 1863. Wounded at Gettysburg, Pennsylvania, on or about July 3, 1863. Reported absent without leave from October 1, 1863, through August 31, 1864. Returned to duty prior to October 27, 1864, when he was captured at Burgess' Mill, Virginia. Confined at Point Lookout, Maryland, October 31, 1864. Released at Point Lookout on March 23, 1865, after taking the Oath of Allegiance.

WILLIAMS, JESSE, Private

Born in Randolph County where he resided prior to enlisting at age 22, November 7, 1862, for the war. Died in hospital at Petersburg, Virginia, November 25, 1862, of "pneumonia."

WILLIAMS, REUBEN, Private

Resided in Randolph County and was by occupation a farmer prior to enlisting at age 29, December 1, 1862, for the war. No further records.

WILLIAMS, SAMUEL, Private

Resided in Randolph County and enlisted in Wake County at age 24, November 7, 1862, for the war. Reported present or accounted for on surviving company muster rolls through April, 1864. Captured at or near Wilderness, Virginia, May 6, 1864. Confined at Point Lookout, Maryland. Transferred to Elmira, New York, July 9, 1864. Died at Elmira on August 20, 1864, of "chronic diarrhoea."

WILLIAMSON, NOAH, Private

Enlisted in Wake County on January 1, 1863, for the war. Reported present through February, 1863. Dropped from the rolls of the company prior to September 1, 1863. Reason he was dropped not reported.

YATES, ANDREW L., Private

Resided in Randolph County and was by occupation a carpenter prior to enlisting in Wake County at age 25, November 7, 1862, for the war. Wounded at Gettysburg, Pennsylvania, on or about July 1, 1863. Captured at or near Gettysburg prior to July 6, 1863. Hospitalized at Gettysburg. Transferred to hospital at Davids Island, New York Harbor, where he arrived on or about July 20, 1863. Paroled at Davids Island on August 24, 1863. Received at City Point, Virginia, August 28, 1863, for exchange. Returned to duty in November, 1863-February, 1864. Hospitalized at Danville, Virginia, May 13, 1864, with acute diarrhoea. Transferred to another hospital on May 25, 1864. Died near Petersburg, Virginia, February 9, 1865. Cause of death not reported.

YATES, WILLIAM BAILEY, Private

Resided in Randolph County and was by occupation a farmer prior to enlisting in Wake County at age 20, November 7, 1862, for the war. Deserted prior to March 1, 1863. Returned to duty on September 20, 1864. Deserted to the enemy on or about December 28, 1864. Confined at Washington, D.C., January 4, 1865. Released on or about the same date after taking the Oath of Allegiance.

COMPANY C

This company, known as the "Orapeake Guards," was raised in Gates County and enlisted at Gatesville on February 27, 1862. It was mustered into state service at Camp Mangum, near Raleigh, on April 28, 1862, and assigned to the 52nd Regiment N.C. Troops as Company C. After joining the regiment the company functioned as a part of the regiment, and its history for the remainder of the war is reported as a part of the regimental history.

The information contained in the following roster was compiled primarily from a company muster-in and descriptive roll dated April 28, 1862, and from company muster rolls for May 1-June 30, 1862; August 31, 1862-February 28, 1863; and July 1, 1863-December 31, 1864. No company muster rolls were located for July 1-August 30, 1862; March 1-June 30, 1863; or for the period after December 31, 1864. Valuable information was obtained from primary records such as the North Carolina adjutant general's *Roll of Honor*, discharge certificates, medical records, prisoner of war records, *The War of the Rebellion: A Compilation of the Official Records of the Union and Confederate Armies*, militia records, newspaper casualty lists and obituaries, Confederate pension applications filed with the state of North Carolina, and the 1860 federal census of North Carolina. Secondary sources such as postwar rosters and histories, cemetery records, the *Confederate Veteran*, published genealogies, and records of the United Daughters of the Confederacy also provided useful information.

OFFICERS

CAPTAINS

GILLIAM, JULIAN

Born in Gates County and resided in Chowan County where he was by occupation a farmer prior to enlisting in Chowan County at age 25. Appointed Captain on March 7, 1862. Resigned on April 1, 1863. Reason he resigned not reported.

GILLIAM, GEORGE

Born in Gates County and resided in Northampton County where he was by occupation a merchant prior to enlisting in Chowan County at age 27. Appointed 1st Lieutenant on March 7, 1862. Promoted to Captain on April 1, 1863. Wounded in the thigh and captured at Gettysburg, Pennsylvania, July 3, 1863. Hospitalized at Gettysburg. Transferred to hospital at Davids Island, New York Harbor, where he arrived on or about July 20, 1863. Transferred to Johnson's Island, Ohio, September 18, 1863. Paroled at Johnson's Island on or about March 14, 1865. Received at Cox's Wharf, James River, Virginia, March 22, 1865, for exchange. Survived the war.

GOSLEN, JUNIUS W.

Served as Captain of Company K of this regiment. Reported on duty as acting commander of this company on November 17, 1863, and in January-April, 1864.

COX, ROMULUS LEEDY

Served as 1st Lieutenant of Company K of this regiment. Reported on duty as acting commander of this company in May-June, 1864.

ELLIOTT, LAURISTON F.

Served as Corporal in Company K of this regiment. Reported on duty as acting commander of this company in September-December, 1864.

LIEUTENANTS

GATLING, JOHN T., JR., 2nd Lieutenant

Born in Gates County and was by occupation a farmer prior to enlisting at age 22. Appointed 2nd Lieutenant on April 8, 1862. Appointed Assistant Quartermaster (Captain) on December 2, 1862, to rank from December 1, 1862, and transferred to the Field and Staff of this regiment. [Previously served as 2nd Lieutenant in the 7th Regiment N.C. Militia.]

HARRELL, JAMES NOAH, 2nd Lieutenant

Born in Gates County and was by occupation a merchant prior to enlisting in Gates County at age 23. Appointed 2nd Lieutenant on or about March 7, 1862. Resigned on August 22, 1862. Reason he resigned not reported. [Previously served as 1st Lieutenant in the 7th Regiment N.C. Militia.]

PARKER, DAVID W., 3rd Lieutenant

Born in Gates County and was by occupation a farmer prior to enlisting in Gates County at age 19, February 27, 1862. Mustered in as Sergeant. Promoted to 1st Sergeant on September 26, 1862. Elected 3rd Lieutenant on December 10, 1862. Captured at Falling Waters, Maryland, July 14, 1863. Confined at Old Capitol Prison, Washington, D.C. Transferred to Johnson's Island, Ohio, August 8, 1863. Released at Johnson's Island on June 11, 1865, after taking the Oath of Allegiance.

WARREN, JOHN CRITTENDEN, 1st Lieutenant

Born in Chowan County and enlisted at Camp Mangum, near Raleigh, at age 17, April 24, 1862, for the war. Mustered in as Private. Promoted to Sergeant Major on or about April 24, 1862, and transferred to the Field and Staff of this regiment. Appointed 2nd Lieutenant on September 13, 1862, and transferred back to this company. Promoted to 1st Lieutenant on April 1, 1863. Mentioned in dispatches for "good conduct" during the siege of Washington, North Carolina, in March-April, 1863. Wounded in the lung, right wrist, and left thigh and captured at Gettysburg, Pennsylvania, July 3, 1863. Hospitalized at Gettysburg. Transferred to hospital at Baltimore, Maryland, October 6, 1863. Transferred to Fort McHenry, Maryland, October 22, 1863. Transferred to Point Lookout, Maryland, January 23, 1864. Paroled at Point Lookout on March 3, 1864. Received at City Point, Virginia, March 6, 1864, for exchange. Reported absent wounded through October, 1864. Retired from service prior to January 1, 1865. Took the Oath of Allegiance on or about August 5, 1865.

NONCOMMISSIONED OFFICERS AND PRIVATES

ARNOLD, RICHARD, Corporal
Born in Gates County and was by occupation a merchant prior to enlisting in Gates County at age 27, February 27, 1862. Mustered in as Corporal. Deserted at Franklin, Virginia, November 8, 1862.

BAGLEY, ERASTUS, Private
Born in Perquimans County where he resided as a farmer prior to enlisting in Chowan County at age 28, March 19, 1862. Failed to report for duty and was dropped from the rolls of the company on or about July 1, 1862.

BAKER, ELIJAH, Private
Born in Gates County where he resided as a farmer prior to enlisting in Gates County at age 32, February 27, 1862. Deserted at Franklin, Virginia, October 3, 1862. Returned to duty on February 25, 1863. Captured at or near Gettysburg, Pennsylvania, on or about July 3, 1863. Confined at Fort Delaware, Delaware, on or about July 10, 1863. Transferred to Point Lookout, Maryland, October 20, 1863. Died at Point Lookout on October 30, 1863, of "erysipelas in face."

BARNES, THOMAS J., Private
Born in Gates County where he resided as a farmer prior to enlisting in Gates County at age 45, February 27, 1862. Discharged on May 26, 1862, presumably by reason of being overage.

BENTON, JACOB, Private
Born in Gates County where he resided as a farmer prior to enlisting in Gates County at age 44, February 27, 1862. Discharged on May 24, 1862, presumably by reason of being overage.

BENTON, JAMES, Private
Born in Gates County and was by occupation a farmer prior to enlisting in Gates County at age 33, February 27, 1862. Deserted at Franklin, Virginia, October 3, 1862.

BENTON, WILLIAM T., Private
Born in Gates County where he resided as a farmer prior to enlisting in Gates County at age 33, February 27, 1862. Reported sick in hospital at Raleigh on or about July 1, 1862. No further records.

BLANCHARD, ELDRIDGE S., Private
Enlisted in Gates County on May 10, 1862, for the war. Captured at or near Gettysburg, Pennsylvania, on or about July 3, 1863. Confined at Fort Delaware, Delaware, on or about July 10, 1863. Transferred to Point Lookout, Maryland, October 20, 1863. Died at Point Lookout on February 3, 1865, of "chronic hepatitis."

BLANCHARD, J. CALVIN, Corporal
Enlisted in Gates County on May 10, 1862, for the war. Mustered in as Private. Promoted to Corporal on December 10, 1862. Wounded in the hip and captured at Gettysburg, Pennsylvania, July 3, 1863. Hospitalized at

Gettysburg. Transferred to hospital at Baltimore, Maryland, September 14, 1863. Paroled at Baltimore on September 25, 1863. Received at City Point, Virginia, September 27, 1863, for exchange. Returned to duty in January-February, 1864. Reported absent wounded in May-December, 1864.

BLANCHARD, JAMES R., Private
Born in Gates County and was by occupation a farmer prior to enlisting in Gates County at age 17, February 27, 1862. Reported present in May-June, 1862. No further records.

BRATTEN, JOHN, Private
Born in Perquimans County and was by occupation a farmer prior to enlisting in Perquimans County at age 41, March 1, 1862. Discharged on May 21, 1862, presumably by reason of being overage.

BRISCOE, EASTON, Private
Born in Gates County where he resided as a farmer prior to enlisting in Gates County at age 41, February 27, 1862. Discharged on May 24, 1862, presumably by reason of being overage.

BUNCH, CULLEN, Private
Born in Chowan County where he resided as a farmer prior to enlisting in Chowan County at age 26, March 1, 1862. Captured at Falling Waters, Maryland, July 14, 1863. Sent to Baltimore, Maryland. Confined at Point Lookout, Maryland, August 17, 1863. Paroled at Point Lookout on March 3, 1864. Received at City Point, Virginia, March 6, 1864, for exchange.

BUTLER, OLIVER, Private
Enlisted at Wakefield, Virginia, September 17, 1862, for the war. Deserted at Petersburg, Virginia, October 15, 1862. Apprehended and was returned to the company on January 30, 1863. Reported in confinement on or about February 28, 1863. No further records.

BYRD, MOSES, Private
Born in Nansemond County, Virginia, and was by occupation a farmer prior to enlisting in Gates County at age 31, February 27, 1862. Captured at Gettysburg, Pennsylvania, on or about July 3, 1863. Reported in hospital at Davids Island, New York Harbor, on or about July 20, 1863. Paroled at Davids Island on an unspecified date. Received at City Point, Virginia, September 16, 1863, for exchange. No further records.

CARTER, ALFRED M., Private
Born in Gates County and was by occupation a farmer prior to enlisting in Gates County at age 18, February 27, 1862. Killed at Goldsboro on December 17, 1862.

CARTER, HENRY, Private
Born in Gates County where he enlisted on February 27, 1862. Failed to report for duty and was dropped from the rolls of the company on or about July 1, 1862.

CARTER, LEWIS W., Private
Born in Gates County where he resided as a farmer prior

to enlisting in Gates County at age 26, February 27, 1862. Wounded in the shoulder and abdomen and captured at Gettysburg, Pennsylvania, July 3, 1863. Hospitalized at Gettysburg where he died on July 27, 1863, of wounds.

CHAPEL, JOHN, Private
Born in Chowan County and enlisted in Wake County on March 8, 1862. Failed to report for duty and was dropped from the rolls of the company on or about July 1, 1862.

CHAPEL, WESLEY, Private
Born in Chowan County and was by occupation a farmer prior to enlisting in Gates County at age 20, February 27, 1862. Died in hospital at Petersburg, Virginia, October 28, 1862, of "pneumonia."

CORBETT, ROBERT J., Private
Born in Southampton County, Virginia, and was by occupation a farmer prior to enlisting in Gates County at age 28, February 27, 1862. Deserted at Franklin, Virginia, November 8, 1862.

DAIL, JOSEPH, Private
Born in Perquimans County where he resided as a farmer prior to enlisting in Chowan County at age 27, March 19, 1862. Discharged "by surgeon" prior to July 1, 1862.

DAIL, NATHAN, Private
Born in Perquimans County where he resided as a farmer prior to enlisting in Perquimans County at age 42, March 1, 1862. Discharged prior to July 1, 1862, presumably by reason of being overage.

DAVENPORT, AARON, Private
Enlisted at Franklin, Virginia, November 17, 1862, for the war. Deserted at Rocky Mount on January 12, 1863.

DAVENPORT, HENDERSON, Private
Born in Chowan County where he resided as a farmer prior to enlisting in Chowan County at age 18, February 27, 1862. Detailed as colonel's orderly on April 15, 1862. Reported absent on detail through February, 1863. No further records.

DAVIS, EDWARD H., Quartermaster Sergeant
Previously served as Private in Company L, 17th Regiment N.C. Troops (1st Organization). Enlisted in this company in March-August, 1863. Mustered in as Quartermaster Sergeant. Appointed Adjutant on February 19, 1864, and transferred to the Field and Staff of the 17th Regiment N.C. Troops (2nd Organization).

DECAMP, CHARLES, Private
Enlistment date reported as August 25, 1862; however, he was not listed in the records of this company until July-August, 1864, when he was reported absent wounded. Place and date wounded not reported. Appointed Chief Musician (Drum Major) in September-October, 1864, and transferred to the regimental band.

DUMFORD, JESSE, Private
Born in Gates County and was by occupation a farmer prior to enlisting in Gates County at age 45, February 27,

1862. Reported present in May-June, 1862. Dropped from the rolls of the company on or about July 1, 1862. Reason he was dropped not reported.

EDMONDSON, CHARLES, Private
Born in England and was by occupation a sailor prior to enlisting in Chowan County on March 1, 1862. Failed to report for duty and was dropped from the rolls of the company on or about July 1, 1862.

ELLIS, JAMES N., Private
Born in Gates County and was by occupation a farmer prior to enlisting in Gates County at age 18, February 27, 1862. Killed at the Blackwater River, Virginia, November 9, 1863, "by accidental discharge of a gun."

ELLIS, JOSIAH, Private
Born in Gates County and was by occupation a farmer prior to enlisting in Gates County at age 21, February 27, 1862. Wounded in the foot and captured at Gettysburg, Pennsylvania, on or about July 1, 1863. Foot amputated. Hospitalized at Gettysburg. Transferred to hospital at Davids Island, New York Harbor, on an unspecified date. Paroled at Davids Island and transferred to City Point, Virginia, where he was received on October 28, 1863, for exchange. Survived the war.

EURE, DANIEL D., Corporal
Resided in Gates County and was by occupation a farmer prior to enlisting in Gates County at age 40, February 27, 1862. Mustered in as Private. Promoted to Corporal on December 10, 1862. Captured at Gettysburg, Pennsylvania, on or about July 1, 1863. Sent to Baltimore, Maryland. Paroled at Baltimore on August 23, 1863. Received at City Point, Virginia, August 24, 1863, for exchange.

EURE, ELMORE, Private
Born in Gates County and was by occupation a farmer prior to enlisting in Gates County at age 20, February 27, 1862. Reported present on surviving company muster rolls through November 17, 1863. Reported absent sick in January-December, 1864.

EURE, HENRY C., Private
Born in Gates County and was by occupation a farmer prior to enlisting in Gates County at age 20, February 27, 1862. Died at Raleigh on May 26, 1862. Cause of death not reported.

EURE, JAMES R., Private
Born in Gates County and was by occupation a farmer prior to enlisting in Gates County at age 22, February 27, 1862. Wounded in the hand and captured at Gettysburg, Pennsylvania, on or about July 3, 1863. Hospitalized at Gettysburg. Transferred to hospital at Chester, Pennsylvania, where he arrived on July 18, 1863. Died in hospital at Chester on September 20, 1863, of "pyaemia."

EURE, JETHRO H., Private
Born in Gates County where he resided as a farmer prior to enlisting in Gates County at age 25, February 27, 1862. Deserted at Camp Mangum, near Raleigh, June 3, 1862.

EURE, NOAH, Private

Born in Gates County where he resided as a farmer prior to enlisting in Gates County at age 24, February 27, 1862. Reported at home on sick furlough on or about July 1, 1862. Dropped from the rolls of the company prior to March 1, 1863. Reason he was dropped not reported. Restored to the rolls in March-April, 1864, and was reported present through December, 1864. Captured at Sutherland's Station, Virginia, April 2, 1865. Confined at Point Lookout, Maryland, April 3, 1865. Released at Point Lookout on June 12, 1865, after taking the Oath of Allegiance.

EURE, PRESTON, Private

Born in Gates County where he resided as a farmer prior to enlisting in Gates County at age 21, February 27, 1862. Reported present or accounted for on surviving company muster rolls through December, 1864.

FAIRLESS, JOHN A., Private

Born in Gates County where he resided as a carpenter prior to enlisting at age 23, February 27, 1862. Failed to report for duty. Dropped from the rolls of the company and was listed as a deserter to the enemy on or about July 1, 1862. Shortly thereafter he became the commander of a group of pro-Union irregulars, known as "Buffaloes," with headquarters at Wingfield, in Chowan County. This group "pillaged, plundered, burned, and decoyed off slaves" in Chowan, Bertie, Perquimans, Hertford, and Gates counties. Fairless was killed in October, 1862, in a fight with one of his own men. [John G. Barrett, *The Civil War in North Carolina* (Chapel Hill: University of North Carolina Press, 1963), 174-175. See also T. C. Parramore, "The Roanoke-Chowan Story," Chapter 10 ("Five Days in July"), Ahoskie, North Carolina, *Daily Roanoke-Chowan News*, Civil War Supplement, 1960, 109-113.]

FELTON, JOHN, Private

Born in Gates County and was by occupation a farmer prior to enlisting in Gates County at age 21, February 27, 1862. Discharged "by the surgeon" at Camp Mangum, near Raleigh, prior to July 1, 1862.

FERRELL, WILLIAM, Private

Enlisted at Orange Court House, Virginia, December 7, 1863, for the war. Captured at or near Wilderness, Virginia, on or about May 6, 1864. Confined at Point Lookout, Maryland, May 17, 1864. Hospitalized at Point Lookout on May 22, 1864, with debilitas. Died at Point Lookout on September 9, 1864.

FLOYD, JAMES J., Private

Born in Chowan County and was by occupation a landlord prior to enlisting in Chowan County at age 22, February 27, 1862. Reported present or accounted for on surviving company muster rolls through February, 1864. Detailed to work in the subsistence department on April 11, 1864. Reported absent on detail through March 10, 1865.

GRAY, EDWIN, Private

Born in Gates County and was by occupation a farmer prior to enlisting in Gates County at age 26, February 27,

1862. Deserted at Camp Mangum, near Raleigh, June 6, 1862.

GREEN, JAMES, Private

Born in Gates County and was by occupation a farmer prior to enlisting in Gates County at age 42, February 27, 1862. Reported present in May-June, 1862. Dropped from the rolls of the company on or about July 1, 1862. Reason he was dropped not reported.

GREEN, WILLIAM G., Private

Born in Chowan County and was by occupation a farmer prior to enlisting in Franklin County on November 19, 1862, for the war. Discharged on July 6, 1863, by reason of "necrosis of femur and debility from extreme youth. . . ." Discharge certificate gives his age as 15.

GREEN, WILLIAM J., Private

Enlisted in Franklin County. Enlistment date reported as March 17, 1862; however, he was not listed on the rolls of this company until May-June, 1864, when he was reported absent. No further records.

GREEN, WILLIAM T., Private

Born in Gates County and was by occupation a farmer prior to enlisting in Gates County at age 19, February 27, 1862. Deserted at Franklin, Virginia, November 3, 1862.

HARRELL, GEORGE, Private

Born in Gates County and was by occupation a farmer prior to enlisting in Gates County at age 19, February 27, 1862. Reported present on surviving company muster rolls through April, 1864. Wounded in the right hip in an unspecified battle in May-June, 1864. Reported absent wounded through October, 1864. Discharged on March 14, 1865, by reason of disability from wounds.

HARRELL, WILLIAM HENRY, Private

Born in Gates County where he resided as a miller prior to enlisting in Chowan County at age 18, February 27, 1862. Captured at Goldsboro on December 17, 1862. Paroled the same date. Returned to duty on an unspecified date. Captured at Gettysburg, Pennsylvania, on or about July 3, 1863. Confined at Fort Delaware, Delaware, July 10, 1863. Transferred to Point Lookout, Maryland, October 20, 1863. Transferred to Fort Monroe, Virginia, March 7, 1864. Released at Fort Monroe on or about April 25, 1864, after taking the Oath of Allegiance.

HAUGHTON, JOHN P., Private

Born in Chowan County where he resided as a sailor prior to enlisting in Chowan County at age 32, March 1, 1862. Failed to report for duty and was dropped from the rolls of the company on or about July 1, 1862.

HAYES, CALEB M., Sergeant

Born in Gates County where he resided as a farmer prior to enlisting in Gates County at age 29, February 27, 1862. Mustered in as Sergeant. Wounded in the right thigh (fracture) and captured at Gettysburg, Pennsylvania, on or about July 3, 1863. Hospitalized at Gettysburg. Confined at Fort Delaware, Delaware, on or about July 10, 1863. Transferred to Point Lookout, Maryland,

October 20, 1863. Paroled at Point Lookout on February 18, 1865. Received at Boulware's Wharf, James River, Virginia, February 20, 1865, for exchange.

HOFLER, JACOB, Private

Born in Gates County and was by occupation a farmer prior to enlisting in Gates County at age 19, February 27, 1862. Captured at Gettysburg, Pennsylvania, on or about July 3, 1863. Confined at Fort Delaware, Delaware, July 10, 1863. Died at Fort Delaware on November 3, 1863, of "typhoid fever."

HOFLER, JOB, 1st Sergeant

Born in Gates County where he resided as a farmer prior to enlisting in Gates County at age 25, February 27, 1862. Mustered in as 1st Sergeant. Died in hospital at Petersburg, Virginia, September 25, 1862, of "febris typhoides."

HOFLER, PETERSON, Corporal

Born in Gates County where he resided as a farmer prior to enlisting in Gates County at age 36, February 27, 1862. Mustered in as Corporal. Discharged prior to July 1, 1862, presumably by reason of being overage.

HOFLER, TOWNSEND, Private

Enlisted on or about May 10, 1862, for the war. Reported sick in hospital at Raleigh on or about July 1, 1862. No further records.

HOFLER, WILLIAM A., Corporal

Born in Gates County where he resided as a farmer prior to enlisting in Gates County at age 28, February 27, 1862. Mustered in as Corporal. Died in hospital at Petersburg, Virginia, October 24, 1862, of "febris typhoides."

HOWELL, ALBERT J., Private

Born in Gates County where he resided as a farmer prior to enlisting in Gates County at age 38, February 27, 1862. Reported present or accounted for on surviving company muster rolls through January 23, 1864. Reported as a prisoner of war on company muster roll dated March-April, 1864; however, records of the Federal Provost Marshal do not substantiate that report. Reported absent sick in hospital in May-December, 1864.

HOWELL, RENSELEAR, Private

Born in Gates County where he resided as a farmer prior to enlisting in Gates County at age 29, February 27, 1862. Broke his right ankle on or about December 24, 1862, when the railroad car in which he was riding caught fire and he jumped from the train. Reported absent in hospital or absent sick through December, 1864. Survived the war.

HURDLE, ELISHA N., Private

Born in Gates County where he resided as a blacksmith prior to enlisting at age 39, February 27, 1862. Failed to report for duty and was dropped from the rolls of the company on or about July 1, 1862.

HYATT, JESSE PRESTON, Private

Born in Gates County where he resided as a farmer prior to enlisting in Gates County at age 30, February 27, 1862.

Deserted prior to July 1, 1862. Hospitalized at or near Petersburg, Virginia, September 5, 1862, with dysentery. Returned to duty on September 23, 1862. Hospitalized at or near Petersburg on January 31, 1863, with scabies. Returned to duty on April 29, 1863. Captured at Gettysburg, Pennsylvania, on or about July 3, 1863. Confined at Fort Delaware, Delaware, on or about July 10, 1863. Transferred to Point Lookout, Maryland, October 20, 1863. Paroled at Point Lookout on February 18, 1865. Received at Boulware's Wharf, James River, Virginia, on or about February 20, 1865, for exchange.

JACKSON, ALFRED, Private

Enlisted on December 7, 1862, for the war. Captured at Goldsboro on December 17, 1862. Paroled on or about the same date. No further records.

JONES, JOSHUA, Private

Born in Chowan County and was by occupation a farmer prior to enlisting in Gates County at age 19, February 27, 1862. Captured at Gettysburg, Pennsylvania, July 3, 1863. Confined at Fort Delaware, Delaware, on or about July 10, 1863. Died at Fort Delaware on February 3, 1864, of "fever."

JORDAN, EDWARD M., Private

Enlisted in Gates County on February 27, 1862. Transferred to another unit prior to July 1, 1862.

JORDAN, RICHARD, Private

Born in Chowan County and was by occupation a farmer prior to enlisting in Chowan County at age 18, February 27, 1862. Transferred to another company prior to July 1, 1862. [The company to which he was transferred was probably Company B, 3rd Battalion N.C. Light Artillery.]

LASSITER, ALLEN A., Private

Born in Gates County and was by occupation a farmer prior to enlisting in Gates County at age 22, February 27, 1862. Wounded at Goldsboro on December 17, 1862. Returned to duty prior to March 1, 1863. Wounded in the head and left leg at Gettysburg, Pennsylvania, on or about July 2, 1863. Returned to duty prior to September 1, 1863. Captured at Bristoe Station, Virginia, October 14, 1863. Confined at Old Capitol Prison, Washington, D.C., October 15, 1863. Transferred to Point Lookout, Maryland, October 27, 1863. Paroled at Point Lookout on or about February 10, 1865. Received at Cox's Wharf, James River, Virginia, February 14, 1865, for exchange. Hospitalized at Richmond, Virginia, February 16, 1865, with an unspecified complaint. Transferred to another hospital on February 27, 1865. Survived the war.

LASSITER, HENRY E., Private

Born in Gates County and was by occupation a farmer prior to enlisting in Gates County on February 27, 1862. Failed to report for duty. Listed as a deserter and dropped from the rolls of the company on or about July 1, 1862.

LASSITER, JOSIAH, Private

Enlisted in Gates County on May 10, 1862, for the war. Reported absent without leave on February 3, 1863.

LASSITER, REUBEN B., Private
Born in Gates County where he enlisted on February 27, 1862. Failed to report for duty. Listed as a deserter and was dropped from the rolls of the company on or about July 1, 1862.

LASSITER, RICHARD H., Private
Born in Gates County and was by occupation a farmer prior to enlisting in Gates County at age 19, February 27, 1862. Captured at Gettysburg, Pennsylvania, July 3, 1863. Confined at Fort Delaware, Delaware, on or about July 10, 1863. Paroled at Fort Delaware on July 30, 1863. Received at City Point, Virginia, August 1, 1863, for exchange. Reported absent in hospital in January-February, 1864. Returned to duty in March-April, 1864. Wounded at Cold Harbor, Virginia, on or about June 1, 1864. Died on June 21, 1864, of wounds. Place of death not reported.

LEE, ISAAC, Private
Born in Gates County and was by occupation a farmer prior to enlisting in Gates County at age 19, February 27, 1862. Captured at Gettysburg, Pennsylvania, on or about July 3, 1863. Confined at Fort Delaware, Delaware, on or about July 10, 1863. Transferred to Point Lookout, Maryland, October 20, 1863. Paroled at Point Lookout on September 18, 1864. Received at Varina, Virginia, September 22, 1864, for exchange. Hospitalized at Richmond, Virginia, where he died on October 13, 1864, of "diarr[hoea] chron[ic]."

MATHIAS, THOMAS, Corporal
Born in Gates County and was by occupation a mason prior to enlisting in Gates County at age 26, February 27, 1862. Mustered in as Private. Promoted to Corporal on December 10, 1862. Captured at Gettysburg, Pennsylvania, on or about July 3, 1863. Confined at Fort Delaware, Delaware, on or about July 10, 1863. Transferred to Point Lookout, Maryland, October 20, 1863. Took the Oath of Allegiance at Point Lookout on or about February 17, 1864. Hospitalized at Point Lookout on March 7, 1864, with pneumonia. Released from hospital on April 17, 1864. Was apparently released at Point Lookout on or about the same date and assigned to a U.S. military unit. Unit to which assigned not reported.

MATTHEWS, RIDDICK O., Private
Born in Gates County and was by occupation an overseer prior to enlisting in Gates County at age 33, February 27, 1862. Deserted at Rocky Mount on January 12, 1863.

MITCHELL, JOHN E., Private
Born in Chowan County and enlisted on or about March 19, 1862. Died in hospital at Raleigh on August 12, 1862, of "erysipelas, diarrhoea, & pneumonia."

MITCHELL, WILLIAM, Private
Enlisted in Chowan County on May 10, 1862, for the war. Deserted on June 6, 1862. Returned to duty in July-August, 1864. Deserted to the enemy on or about August 22, 1864. Confined at Washington, D.C. Released on or about August 29, 1864, after taking the Oath of Allegiance.

MUNROE, THOMAS J., Corporal
Born in Caroline County, Maryland, and was by occupation a sailor prior to enlisting in Chowan County at age 19, February 27, 1862. Mustered in as Corporal. Present or accounted for through June, 1862. Dropped from the rolls of the company on or about July 1, 1862. Reason he was dropped not reported.

NEWBY, THOMAS, Private
Born in Perquimans County and enlisted in Gates County on March 1, 1862. Reported absent without leave on or about April 28, 1862. Dropped from the rolls of the company on or about July 1, 1862.

OWENS, BENJAMIN P., Private
Born in Gates County and was by occupation a farmer prior to enlisting in Gates County at age 28, February 27, 1862. Detailed for seventeen days as a drummer on May 15, 1862. Reported on duty as a wagoner from August 31, 1862, through August 31, 1864. Rejoined the company in September-October, 1864. Reported absent sick in November-December, 1864. Survived the war.

PARKER, ISAAC, Private
Born in Gates County and was by occupation a farmer prior to enlisting in Gates County at age 18, February 27, 1862. Dropped from the rolls of the company prior to July 1, 1862. Reason he was dropped not reported.

PARKER, JETHRO W., Private
Born in Gates County and was by occupation a farmer prior to enlisting in Gates County at age 33, February 27, 1862. Dropped from the rolls of the company prior to July 1, 1862. Reason he was dropped not reported.

PARKER, SETH, Private
Born in Gates County and was by occupation a farmer prior to enlisting in Gates County at age 45, February 27, 1862. Discharged at Camp Mangum, near Raleigh, May 24, 1862, presumably by reason of being overage.

PEEL, WILLIAM R., Private
Born in Gates County where he resided as a carpenter prior to enlisting in Gates County at age 33, February 27, 1862. Reported present on surviving company muster rolls through February, 1864. Transferred to the C.S. Navy on April 1, 1864.

PERRY, ALLAN A., Private
Born in Chowan County and was by occupation a farmer prior to enlisting in Gates County at age 18, February 27, 1862. Reported present or accounted for through December, 1864. Survived the war. [North Carolina pension records indicate that he was wounded at Cold Harbor, Virginia, in 1864.]

PIERCE, JAMES, Private
Born in Gates County and was by occupation a farmer prior to enlisting in Gates County at age 40, February 27, 1862. Died at Franklin, Virginia, October 6, 1862. Cause of death not reported.

RABY, LUKE, Private
Born in Nansemond County, Virginia, and was by

occupation a farmer prior to enlisting in Gates County at age 32, February 27, 1862. Company records indicate that he was captured at Goldsboro on December 17, 1862; however, records of the Federal Provost Marshal do not substantiate that report. No further records.

RAWLES, JOHN B., Private
Born in Gates County and was by occupation a farmer prior to enlisting in Gates County at age 18, February 27, 1862. Wounded in the right hip at Gettysburg, Pennsylvania, July 3, 1863. Hospitalized at Richmond, Virginia. Returned to duty in March-April, 1864. Reported on detail in hospital at Richmond in May-December, 1864. Hospitalized at Richmond on March 21, 1865, with an unspecified complaint. Transferred to another hospital on March 22, 1865.

REDD, ROBERT, Private
Enlisted in Gates County on February 27, 1862. Reported present or accounted for on surviving company muster rolls through August, 1864. Served as a teamster during much of that period. Reported absent without leave in September-December, 1864.

RHEA, JAMES N., Private
Born in Hertford County and enlisted in Gates County at age 44, February 27, 1862. Discharged at Camp Mangum, near Raleigh, May 24, 1862, presumably by reason of being overage.

RICHARDSON, CHARLES E., Sergeant
Previously served as Private in Company K, 9th Regiment Virginia Infantry. Transferred to this company on July 29, 1862. Discharged on August 25, 1862, by reason of "rheumatism, hernia, and hemorrhages from his lungs."

RICHARDSON, THOMAS N., Private
Enlisted at Camp Johnston, near Kinston, July 5, 1862, for the war. Appointed Ordnance Sergeant in September, 1862-February, 1863, and transferred to the Field and Staff of this regiment.

RIDDICK, SIMON, Private
Born in Gates County and was by occupation a farmer prior to enlisting in Gates County at age 18, February 27, 1862. Wounded in the right leg (flesh) at Bristoe Station, Virginia, October 14, 1863. Hospitalized at Richmond, Virginia. Furloughed for thirty days on December 18, 1863. Returned to duty prior to March 1, 1864. Reported present or accounted for through December, 1864. Surrendered at Appomattox Court House, Virginia, April 9, 1865.

RIDDICK, THOMAS J., Private
Born in Gates County and was by occupation a farmer prior to enlisting in Gates County at age 18, February 27, 1862. Reported present or accounted for through April, 1864; however, he was reported absent sick during much of that period. Died in hospital at Richmond, Virginia, May 23, 1864, of "peritonitis."

ROBINSON, JEREMIAH, Private
Enlisted in Gates County on May 10, 1862, for the war. Deserted at Camp Mangum, near Raleigh, June 6, 1862.

ROUNTREE, SETH, _____
North Carolina pension records indicate that he served in this company.

RUSSELL, WALTER R., Private
Previously served as Private in Company L, 17th Regiment N.C. Troops (1st Organization). Enlisted in this company in March-August, 1863. Appointed Quartermaster Sergeant in May-June, 1864, and transferred to the Field and Staff of this regiment.

SAVAGE, DAVID W., Sergeant
Born in Chowan County and was by occupation a farmer prior to enlisting in Gates County on February 27, 1862. Mustered in as Private. Promoted to Corporal on May 24, 1862. Promoted to Sergeant on or about December 10, 1862. Reported missing at Gettysburg, Pennsylvania, July 3, 1863. Was probably killed at Gettysburg.

SAWYER, JESSE, Private
Enlisted at Franklin, Virginia, November 17, 1862, for the war. Captured at Goldsboro on December 17, 1862. Paroled the same date. No further records.

SINNETT, JOHN, Private
Enlisted at Franklin, Virginia, November 17, 1862, for the war. Deserted to the enemy at Plymouth in April, 1863. Released on an unspecified date after taking the Oath of Allegiance.

SMALL, DAVID, Private
Born in Gates County and was by occupation a farmer prior to enlisting in Gates County at age 40, February 27, 1862. Discharged at Camp Mangum, near Raleigh, May 24, 1862, presumably by reason of being overage.

SMALL, THOMAS A., Private
Born in Gates County where he resided as a farmer prior to enlisting in Gates County at age 49, February 17, 1862. Discharged on May 24, 1862, presumably by reason of being overage.

SMITH, JAMES P., Private
Born in Gates County and was by occupation a fisherman prior to enlisting in Gates County at age 26, February 27, 1862. Deserted to the enemy in Pennsylvania on June 28, 1863. Confined at Fort Delaware, Delaware, on or about July 10, 1863. No further records.

SPEIGHT, EDWARD, Private
Born in Gates County and was by occupation a farmer prior to enlisting in Gates County at age 34, February 27, 1862. Deserted at Franklin, Virginia, October 3, 1862.

SPEIGHT, WILLIAM W., Sergeant
Resided in Gates County and was by occupation a farmer prior to enlisting in Gates County at age 31, May 10, 1862, for the war. Mustered in as Private. Promoted to Sergeant on September 5, 1862. Reported present on surviving company muster rolls through December, 1864. Reported on detail in the commissary department during most of that period. Captured at Farmville, Virginia, April 6, 1865. Confined at Point Lookout, Maryland, April 14,

1865. Released at Point Lookout on June 19, 1865, after taking the Oath of Allegiance.

SPRUILL, WILLIAM, Private

Enlisted in Chowan or Gates County on May 10, 1862, for the war. Captured at Gettysburg, Pennsylvania, July 3, 1863. Confined at Fort Delaware, Delaware, on or about July 10, 1863. Transferred to Point Lookout, Maryland, October 26, 1863. Paroled at Point Lookout on March 3, 1864. Received at City Point, Virginia, March 6, 1864, for exchange. Transferred to Company G, 19th Regiment N.C. Troops (2nd Regiment N.C. Cavalry), in July-August, 1864. Transferred back to this company in December, 1864. No further records.

TOMKINS, J. P., Corporal

Place and date of enlistment not reported (probably enlisted in May-September, 1864). Promotion record not reported. Reported in hospital at Richmond, Virginia, on or about September 12, 1864. Last reported in the records of this company on January 29, 1865.

TROTMAN, DANIEL W., Corporal

Born in Gates County and resided in Perquimans County where he was by occupation a farmer prior to enlisting in Chowan County at age 29, February 27, 1862. Mustered in as Private. Promoted to Corporal on December 10, 1862. Wounded at Gettysburg, Pennsylvania, July 1, 1863. Listed as a prisoner of war in company records dated January-April, 1864; however, records of the Federal Provost Marshal do not substantiate that report. Reported absent without leave in May-December, 1864.

TROTMAN, JAMES E., Private

Born in Gates County where he resided prior to enlisting in Gates County at age 30, February 27, 1862. Reported absent without leave on or about April 28, 1862. Dropped from the rolls of the company on or about July 1, 1862.

UMPHLET, BRYANT, Private

Born in Gates County where he resided as a farmer prior to enlisting in Gates County at age 32, February 27, 1862. Captured at Bristoe Station, Virginia, October 14, 1863. Confined at Old Capitol Prison, Washington, D.C., October 15, 1863. Transferred to Point Lookout, Maryland, October 27, 1863. Paroled at Point Lookout on or about February 24, 1865. Received at Aiken's Landing, James River, Virginia, on or about February 28, 1865, for exchange. Reported in hospital at Richmond, Virginia, on or about March 6, 1865. Survived the war. [North Carolina pension records indicate that he was wounded in the hip by a piece of shell and was also struck on the head by a falling limb at Goldsboro in December, 186(2).]

WALKER, WILLIAM, Private

Enlisted in Wayne County on February 28, 186[3], for the war. Wounded in the right leg (flesh) and captured at Gettysburg, Pennsylvania, on or about July 3, 1863. Hospitalized at Gettysburg. Transferred to hospital at Davids Island, New York Harbor, where he arrived on or about July 23, 1863. Paroled at Davids Island on August 24, 1863. Received at City Point, Virginia, August 28, 1863, for exchange. Captured by the enemy at Hatteras Mills or at Edenton on May 22 or June 4, 1864. Sent to Fort Monroe, Virginia. Transferred to Point Lookout, Maryland, June 30, 1864. Transferred to Elmira, New York, July 23, 1864. Transferred back to Point Lookout where he arrived on October 14, 1864. Died at Point Lookout on January 31, 1865, of "chronic diarrhoea."

WARD, ANDERSON J., Sergeant

Born in Chowan County where he resided prior to enlisting in Chowan County on March 19, 1862. Mustered in as Private. Promoted to Sergeant on September 26, 1862. Captured at Gettysburg, Pennsylvania, July 3, 1863. Confined at Fort Delaware, Delaware, on or about July 10, 1863. Paroled at Fort Delaware and transferred to Cairo, Illinois, April 10, 1865. Received at New Orleans, Louisiana, April 22, 1865. Transferred "to the mouth of the Red River," Louisiana, May 2, 1865, for exchange.

WARD, AUGUSTUS, Private

Born in Chowan County where he enlisted on March 17, 1862. Wounded at Gettysburg, Pennsylvania, July 1, 1863. Hospitalized at Staunton, Virginia. Returned to duty in March-April, 1864. Detailed as a provost guard at Salem, Virginia, September 6, 1864. Reported absent on detail through February, 1865. Paroled at Farmville, Virginia, April 23, 1865.

WESCOTT, SAMUEL P., Private

Born in Gates County and enlisted in Chowan County on February 27, 1862. Reported absent sick on or about April 28, 1862. No further records.

WHITE, ROBERT, Private

Born in Gates County where he resided as a farmer prior to enlisting in Gates County at age 38, February 27, 1862. Reported absent without leave on or about April 28, 1862. No further records.

WIGGINS, JAMES, Private

Born in Gates County where he enlisted on February 27, 1862. Died in hospital at Wilmington on July 2, 1862, of "dis[en]t[ary] ac[u]te."

WIGGINS, WILLIS, Private

Born in Gates County and was by occupation a farmer prior to enlisting in Gates County at age 43, February 27, 1862. Discharged at Camp Mangum, near Raleigh, May 24, 1862, presumably by reason of being overage.

WILLIAMS, THOMAS E., Private

Born in Chowan County where he enlisted on March 19, 1862. Transferred to Company B, 3rd Battalion N.C. Light Artillery, April 19, 1862.

COMPANY D

This company, known as "McCulloch's Avengers," was raised in Stokes County and enlisted in Stokes County in March, 1862. It was mustered into state service at Camp Mangum, near Raleigh, on April 28, 1862, and assigned to the 52nd Regiment N.C. Troops as Company D. After joining the regiment the company functioned as a part of the regiment, and its history for the remainder of the war is reported as a part of the regimental history.

The information contained in the following roster was compiled primarily from a company muster-in and descriptive roll dated April 28, 1862, and from company muster rolls for May 1-June 30, 1862; November 1, 1862-March 1, 1863; and July 1, 1863-December 31, 1864. No company muster rolls were located for July 1-October 31, 1862; April 1-June 30, 1863; or for the period after December 31, 1864. Valuable information was obtained from primary records such as the North Carolina adjutant general's *Roll of Honor*, discharge certificates, medical records, prisoner of war records, *The War of the Rebellion: A Compilation of the Official Records of the Union and Confederate Armies*, militia records, newspaper casualty lists and obituaries, Confederate pension applications filed with the state of North Carolina, and the 1860 federal census of North Carolina. Secondary sources such as postwar rosters and histories, cemetery records, the *Confederate Veteran*, published genealogies, and records of the United Daughters of the Confederacy also provided useful information.

OFFICERS

CAPTAIN

GIBSON, LEONIDAS R.
Born in Stokes County where he resided as a farmer prior to enlisting in Stokes County at age 32. Appointed Captain on March 19, 1862. Wounded slightly in the head and leg at Gettysburg, Pennsylvania, July 3, 1863. Returned to duty prior to September 1, 1863. Reported absent sick or absent with leave in September, 1863-February, 1864. Returned to duty in March-April, 1864. Wounded at or near Spotsylvania Court House, Virginia, May 10, 1864. Died on May 11, 1864, of wounds. Place of death not reported.

LIEUTENANTS

FOWLER, JOHN HENRY, 2nd Lieutenant
Born in Stokes County and resided in Forsyth County where he was by occupation a farmer prior to enlisting in Stokes County at age 37. Appointed 2nd Lieutenant on March 15, 1862. Survived the war.

NELSON, ISAAC H., 1st Lieutenant
Born in Stokes County where he resided as a farmer prior to enlisting in Stokes County at age 23. Appointed 1st Lieutenant on March 19, 1862. Captured at Gettysburg, Pennsylvania, July 3, 1863. Confined at Fort Delaware, Delaware, July 7, 1863. Transferred to Johnson's Island, Ohio, July 18, 1863. Paroled at Johnson's Island on March 14, 1865. Received at Cox's Wharf, James River, Virginia, March 22, 1865, for exchange. Survived the war.

POINDEXTER, DAVID, 2nd Lieutenant
Born in Stokes County and was by occupation a farmer prior to enlisting in Stokes County at age 26. Appointed 2nd Lieutenant on or about March 19, 1862. Reported absent with leave on or about July 1, 1862. No further records.

RIERSON, SAMUEL M., 2nd Lieutenant
Born in Stokes County where he resided as a farmer prior to enlisting in Stokes County at age 19, March 19, 1862. Mustered in as Sergeant. Appointed 2nd Lieutenant on March 7, 1863. Captured at Bristoe Station, Virginia, October 14, 1863. Confined at Old Capitol Prison, Washington, D.C., October 15, 1863. Transferred to Johnson's Island, Ohio, November 11, 1863. Arrived at Johnson's Island on November 14, 1863. Released at Johnson's Island on June 12, 1865, after taking the Oath of Allegiance.

NONCOMMISSIONED OFFICERS AND PRIVATES

ADAMS, JOHN L., _____
North Carolina pension records indicate that he served in this company.

ALLEN, ANDREW JACKSON, Private
Born in Stokes County where he resided as a farmer prior to enlisting in Stokes County at age 26, March 19, 1862. Reported absent without leave in May-June, 1862. Returned to duty prior to March 2, 1863. Killed at Spotsylvania Court House, Virginia, May 12, 1864, "by a cannonball striking his head. . . ."

ALLEN, JOHN M., 1st Sergeant
Born in Stokes County where he resided as a farmer prior to enlisting in Stokes County at age 24, March 19, 1862. Mustered in as Private. Promoted to Corporal on November 1, 1862. Wounded at Gettysburg, Pennsylvania, July 1, 1863. Returned to duty prior to September 1, 1863. Promoted to Sergeant in September-October, 1863. Wounded in the right leg (flesh) at Jones' Farm, Virginia, on or about September 30, 1864. Hospitalized at Richmond, Virginia. Furloughed for sixty days on October 28, 1864. Promoted to 1st Sergeant on December 1, 1864.

BARKER, ELI C., Private
Resided in Stokes County and enlisted at Camp French, near Petersburg, Virginia, at age 19, October 1, 1862, for the war. Captured at Gettysburg, Pennsylvania, July 3, 1863. Confined at Fort Delaware, Delaware, on or about July 10, 1863. Transferred to Point Lookout, Maryland, October 20, 1863. Paroled at Point Lookout on February 10, 1865. Received at Cox's Wharf, James River, Virginia, on or about February 14, 1865, for exchange. Hospitalized at Richmond, Virginia, February 14, 1865, with chronic diarrhoea. Furloughed for sixty days on February 24, 1865. Survived the war.

BEARD, WILLIAM H., Private

Born in Cabarrus County and resided in Stokes County where he was by occupation a tailor prior to enlisting in Stokes County at age 35, March 19, 1862. Mustered in as Corporal. Reduced to ranks prior to May 25, 1862. Discharged on May 25, 1862, by reason of being overage.

BIBY, JOHN P., Private

Born in Stokes County where he resided as a farmer prior to enlisting in Stokes County at age 32, March 19, 1862. Hospitalized at Richmond, Virginia, July 12, 1863, with chronic rheumatism. Transferred to Danville, Virginia, July 20, 1863. Reported absent sick through December, 1863. Returned to duty in January-February, 1864. Reported absent sick in March-August, 1864. Returned to duty in September-October, 1864. Reported present in November-December, 1864. Hospitalized at Richmond on February 24, 1865, with ulcers. Transferred to Farmville, Virginia, April 1, 1865. Paroled at Lynchburg, Virginia, April 15, 1865.

BOWDEN, R. W., Private

Enlisted in Stokes County on May 1, 1862, for the war. Died in hospital at Raleigh on June 18, 1862, of "meningitis and pneumonia."

BOWDIN, DRURY, Private

Born in Stokes County where he resided as a farmer prior to enlisting in Stokes County at age 38, March 19, 1862. Died in hospital at Raleigh on or about June 3, 1862, of "typhoid fever."

BOWDIN, HENRY, Private

Born in Stokes County and was by occupation a farmer prior to enlisting in Stokes County at age 32, March 13, 1862. Reported absent sick on or about April 28, 1862. No further records.

BOWDIN, JOHN, Private

Born in Stokes County where he resided as a farmer prior to enlisting in Stokes County at age 35, March 19, 1862. Reported present on surviving company muster rolls through October, 1864. Died near Petersburg, Virginia, February 19, 1865. Cause of death not reported.

BOWMAN, DAVID H., Private

Resided in Stokes County where he enlisted at age 19, February 20, 1863, for the war. Wounded in the right leg at Gettysburg, Pennsylvania, July 3, 1863. Captured at Gettysburg on July 4, 1863. Hospitalized at Baltimore, Maryland, July 13, 1863. Transferred to hospital at Chester, Pennsylvania, on an unspecified date. Transferred to Point Lookout, Maryland, where he arrived on October 4, 1863. Died at Point Lookout on November 18, 1863. Cause of death not reported.

BOWMAN, JOSEPH H., Private

Born in Washington County, Virginia, and resided in Stokes County where he was by occupation a farmer prior to enlisting in Stokes County at age 27, March 19, 1862. Mustered in as Corporal. Reduced to ranks in April-June, 1863. Captured at Gettysburg, Pennsylvania, July 3, 1863. Confined at Fort Delaware, Delaware, on or about July 10,

1863. Released at Fort Delaware on June 19, 1865, after taking the Oath of Allegiance.

BRANSON, JAMES S., Private

Resided in Stokes County where he enlisted at age 18, February 20, 1863, for the war. Wounded in the leg and captured at Gettysburg, Pennsylvania, July 1, 1863. Hospitalized at Gettysburg. Exchanged (or escaped) prior to July 20, 1863, when he was hospitalized at Richmond, Virginia. Transferred to Raleigh on July 25, 1863. Reported absent wounded through December, 1863. Returned to duty in January-February, 1864. Reported absent sick or absent on furlough in March-June, 1864. Returned to duty in July-August, 1864. Reported present through December, 1864. Paroled at Greensboro on May 17, 1865.

BREWER, ALLEN C., Private

Born in Stokes County where he resided as a farmer prior to enlisting in Stokes County at age 17, March 19, 1862. Wounded at Bristoe Station, Virginia, October 14, 1863. The exact nature of his wound is not reported; however, it appears that his liver was injured. Hospitalized at Richmond, Virginia. Furloughed for sixty days on November 17, 1863. Died in hospital at Richmond on or about June 30, 1864, of wounds.

BROWN, B. F., Private

Born in Stokes County where he enlisted at age 27, October 21, 1862, for the war. Reported absent without leave in November, 1862-February, 1863. Dropped from the rolls of the company prior to September 1, 1863.

BROWN, JACOB, Private

Resided in Stokes County and enlisted at Camp French, near Petersburg, Virginia, at age 24, October 21, 1862, for the war. Reported absent without leave in November, 1862-February, 1863, and in July-August, 1863. Dropped from the rolls of the company prior to November 1, 1863.

BROWN, WILLIAM, Private

Born in Henry County, Virginia, and resided in Stokes County where he was by occupation a teamster prior to enlisting in Stokes County at age 40, March 19, 1862. Discharged on May 25, 1862, by reason of being overage. Reenlisted in the company on April 1, 1863. Wounded in the right thigh (hamstring severed) and captured at Gettysburg, Pennsylvania, July 3, 1863. Hospitalized at Gettysburg. Transferred to hospital at Baltimore, Maryland, where he arrived on July 25, 1863. Paroled on or about August 22, 1863, and transferred for exchange. Received at City Point, Virginia, August 24, 1863, for exchange. Reported absent on parole through February, 1864. Reported absent without leave in March-December, 1864. Paroled at Charlotte on May 12, 1865.

CAPE, CLAIBORN U., Private

Born in Orange County and resided in Stokes County where he was by occupation a farmer prior to enlisting in Stokes County at age 48, March 13, 1862. Reported absent without leave (furlough expired) on or about July 1, 1862. Returned to duty prior to March 2, 1863. Captured at Gettysburg, Pennsylvania, July 3, 1863. Confined at Fort Delaware, Delaware, on or about July 10,

1863. Paroled at Fort Delaware on September 18, 1864. Received at Varina, Virginia, September 23, 1864, for exchange. Reported absent on parole through December, 1864.

CARMICHAEL, J. W., Private

Resided in Forsyth County and enlisted at Camp French, near Petersburg, Virginia, at age 34, October 21, 1862, for the war. Reported present or accounted for on surviving company muster rolls through April, 1864; however, he was reported absent on detached service during much of that period. Captured at Wilderness, Virginia, May 6, 1864. Confined at Point Lookout, Maryland, May 18, 1864. Transferred to Elmira, New York, July 25, 1864. Released at Elmira on May 15, 1865, after taking the Oath of Allegiance.

CHAPMAN, ROBERT W., Private

Born in Halifax County, Virginia, and was by occupation a farmer prior to enlisting in Stokes County at age 25, March 19, 1862. Reported absent sick on surviving company muster rolls through March, 1863. Hospitalized at Richmond, Virginia, July 12, 1863, with neuralgia. Transferred to hospital at Danville, Virginia, July 20, 1863. Furloughed for thirty days from hospital at Danville on September 8, 1863. Reported absent sick through April, 1864. Returned to duty in May-June, 1864. Present or accounted for through December, 1864; however, he was reported absent sick during most of that period.

COFER, BENJAMIN F., Private

Born in Stokes County and was by occupation a farmer prior to enlisting in Stokes County at age 17, March 19, 1862. Wounded at Goldsboro on December 17, 1862. Returned to duty prior to March 2, 1863. Wounded in the right arm and captured at Gettysburg, Pennsylvania, July 3, 1863. Hospitalized at Gettysburg. Transferred to hospital at Chester, Pennsylvania, where he arrived on July 21, 1863. Paroled at Chester on or about August 17, 1863, and transferred to City Point, Virginia, for exchange. Was reportedly transferred to the 21st Regiment N.C. Troops (11th Regiment N.C. Volunteers) in March-April, 1864; however, records of the 21st Regiment do not indicate that he served therein. Company records dated May-December, 1864, indicate that he had been absent without leave since the date of his return from Federal confinement.

CORDLE, JAMES C., Private

Born in Halifax County, Virginia, and resided in Stokes County where he was by occupation a farmer prior to enlisting in Stokes County at age 23, March 19, 1862. Died in hospital at or near Wilson on an unspecified date (probably in July-August, 1863). Cause of death not reported.

DAVIS, ISAAC, Private

Enlisted at Camp French, near Petersburg, Virginia, at age 20, October 21, 1862, for the war. Reported missing and presumed killed at Gettysburg, Pennsylvania, July 3, 1863.

DAVIS, LAWRENCE D., 1st Sergeant

Born in Halifax County, Virginia, and resided in Forsyth County where he was by occupation a farmer prior to enlisting in Stokes County at age 26, March 19, 1862. Mustered in as 1st Sergeant. Discharged on May 27, 1862, after providing a substitute.

DAVIS, ROBERT W., Private

Born in Forsyth County* and was by occupation a farmer prior to enlisting in Stokes County at age 19, March 19, 1862. Reported missing at Gettysburg, Pennsylvania, July 3, 1863. Was probably killed at Gettysburg.

DAVIS, YANCY B., Private

Born in Stokes County where he resided as a farmer prior to enlisting in Stokes County at age 41, March 19, 1862. Discharged on May 25, 1862, by reason of being overage.

DENNEY, ADAM M., Private

Born in Guilford County and resided in Forsyth County where he was by occupation a mechanic prior to enlisting in Stokes County at age 34, March 19, 1862. Reported present or accounted for on surviving company muster rolls through October, 1864. Captured near Petersburg, Virginia, March 25, 1865. Confined at Point Lookout, Maryland, March 28, 1865. Released at Point Lookout on June 12, 1865, after taking the Oath of Allegiance.

FLETCHER, HENRY, Private

Born in Stokes County where he resided as a mechanic prior to enlisting in Stokes County at age 29, March 19, 1862. Died in hospital at Petersburg, Virginia, September 3, 1862, of "cerebro meningitis."

FULTON, JAMES MATTHEW, Private

Resided in Stokes County and enlisted at age 29, May 1, 1862, for the war. Wounded in the breast at Gettysburg, Pennsylvania, July 3, 1863. Returned to duty prior to September 1, 1863. Reported present or accounted for on surviving company muster rolls through December, 1864. Deserted to the enemy on or about March 31, 1865. Confined at Washington, D.C., April 4, 1865. Released on or about the same date after taking the Oath of Allegiance.

FULTON, WILLIAM, Private

Born in Stokes County where he resided as a farmer prior to enlisting in Stokes County at age 37, March 19, 1862. Discharged on May 25, 1862, by reason of being overage. [May have served later as Private in Company G, 21st Regiment N.C. Troops (11th Regiment N.C. Volunteers).]

GEORGE, REUBEN, Private

Resided in Stokes County and enlisted in Wake County at age 41, May 12, 1862, for the war as a substitute. Captured at Gettysburg, Pennsylvania, July 3, 1863. Confined at Fort Delaware, Delaware, on or about July 10, 1863. Released at Fort Delaware on February 13, 1865, after taking the Oath of Allegiance.

GIBSON, D. N., Private

Enlisted in Stokes County on May 1, 1862, for the war. Died in hospital at Richmond, Virginia, August 6, 1862, of "typhoid fever."

GIBSON, LEE, Private

Born in Stokes County where he resided as a farmer prior

to enlisting in Stokes County at age 18, March 19, 1862. Captured at Gettysburg, Pennsylvania, July 3, 1863. Confined at Fort Delaware, Delaware, on or about July 10, 1863. Transferred to hospital at Chester, Pennsylvania, July 19, 1863. Paroled at Chester on an unspecified date. Received at City Point, Virginia, September 23, 1863, for exchange. Returned to duty in January-April, 1864. Hospitalized at Richmond, Virginia, on an unspecified date. Reason he was hospitalized not reported. Furloughed for sixty days on November 15, 1864. Survived the war. [North Carolina pension records indicate that he was wounded at New Bern on March 1, 1863.]

GIBSON, WILLIAM N., Musician
Born in Stokes County where he resided as a doctor prior to enlisting in Stokes County at age 28, March 19, 1862. Mustered in as Private. Appointed Musician (Drum Major) on May 23, 1862. Ordered to report to Richmond, Virginia, on or about February 10, 1863, apparently for reassignment. Survived the war.

GOLDING, ROBERT W., Private
Born in Stokes County where he resided as a farmer prior to enlisting in Stokes County at age 22, March 19, 1862. Captured at Falling Waters, Maryland, July 14, 1863. Sent to Baltimore, Maryland. Transferred to Point Lookout, Maryland, August 20, 1863. Paroled at Point Lookout on March 16, 1864. Received at City Point, Virginia, March 20, 1864, for exchange. Reported absent without leave in May-June, 1864. Returned to duty in July-August, 1864. Present or accounted for through November, 1864. Hospitalized at Richmond, Virginia, December 29, 1864, with chronic diarrhoea. Furloughed for sixty days on January 28, 1865. Survived the war. [North Carolina pension records indicate that he was wounded at Gettysburg, Pennsylvania, in July, 1863.]

GOODE, HENRY, Private
Resided in Stokes County where he enlisted at age 26, May 15, 1862, for the war. Died at Hanover Junction, Virginia, or at Gordonsville, Virginia, in March-August, 1863. Cause of death not reported.

HALL, R. W., Private
Enlisted at Camp French, near Petersburg, Virginia, October 21, 1862, for the war. Reported absent without leave on surviving company muster rolls through August, 1863. Dropped from the rolls of the company in September-October, 1863.

HANCOCK, JOHN H., Private
Enlisted at Camp French, near Petersburg, Virginia, October 21, 1862, for the war. Killed at Gettysburg, Pennsylvania, July 1, 1863.

HARGRAVES, RUFUS M., Corporal
Born in Stokes County and was by occupation a farmer prior to enlisting in Stokes County at age 18, March 19, 1862. Mustered in as Corporal. Died in hospital at Petersburg, Virginia, August 6, 1862, of "febris typhoides."

HELMS, WILLIAM, Private
Resided in Stokes or Mecklenburg County and enlisted at Camp French, near Petersburg, Virginia, at age 34, October 21, 1862, for the war. Reported present or accounted for until wounded slightly in the right side at Jones' Farm, Virginia, on or about September 30, 1864. Returned to duty in November-December, 1864. Hospitalized at Charlotte on January 13, 1865, with an unspecified complaint. Returned to duty on February 1, 1865. Captured at Sutherland's Station, Virginia, April 2, 1865. Confined at Point Lookout, Maryland, April 4, 1865. Released at Point Lookout on June 27, 1865, after taking the Oath of Allegiance.

HOPKINS, B. J., Private
Resided in Stokes County where he enlisted at age 25, April 28, 1862, for the war. Reported absent sick on surviving company muster rolls through February, 1863. Hospitalized at Richmond, Virginia, May 9, 1863, with phthisis and scorbutus and was furloughed for sixty days on June 9, 1863. Reported absent sick through April, 1864. Died prior to December 17, 1864. Place and cause of death not reported.

HOPKINS, WILLIAM P., Private
Resided in Stokes County where he enlisted at age 25, February 20, 1863, for the war. Wounded in the left ankle (flesh) and captured at Gettysburg, Pennsylvania, July 3, 1863. Hospitalized at Chester, Pennsylvania. Transferred to hospital at Point Lookout, Maryland, where he arrived on October 4, 1863. Paroled at Point Lookout on October 11, 1864. Received at Cox's Wharf, James River, Virginia, October 15, 1864, for exchange. Returned to duty subsequent to December 31, 1864. Surrendered at Appomattox Court House, Virginia, April 9, 1865.

ISOM, SPENCER, Private
Born in Virginia and resided in Alleghany County where he was by occupation a farmer prior to enlisting in Stokes County at age 50, May 1, 1862, for the war. Captured at Bristoe Station, Virginia, October 14, 1863. Confined at Point Lookout, Maryland, October 28, 1863. Paroled at Point Lookout on March 16, 1864. Received at City Point, Virginia, March 20, 1864, for exchange. Reported absent without leave in May-December, 1864.

JACKSON, GEORGE W., Private
Born in Rockingham County and was by occupation a farmer prior to enlisting in Stokes County at age 17, March 19, 1862. Reported present or accounted for on surviving company muster rolls through December, 1864. Served as a teamster during much of the war. Survived the war.

JAMES, PHILIP A., Sergeant
Born in Davidson County and resided in Forsyth County where he was by occupation a farmer prior to enlisting in Stokes County at age 22, March 19, 1862. Mustered in as Sergeant. Wounded in the arm at Gettysburg, Pennsylvania, July 3, 1863. Returned to duty in September-October, 1863. Appointed Ensign (1st Lieutenant) on April 30, 1864, and transferred to the Field and Staff of this regiment.

JESTER, ALEXANDER Z., Private

Enlisted at Camp French, near Petersburg, Virginia, at age 20, October 21, 1862, for the war. Wounded and captured at Gettysburg, Pennsylvania, July 3, 1863. Confined at Fort Delaware, Delaware, on or about July 10, 1863. Transferred to hospital at Chester, Pennsylvania, July 19, 1863. Paroled at Chester on an unspecified date. Received at City Point, Virginia, September 23, 1863, for exchange. Reported absent on parole through April, 1864. Reported absent without leave in May-December, 1864.

KNOTT, JESSE CHARLES, Private

Born in Guilford County and resided in Stokes County where he was by occupation a farmer prior to enlisting in Stokes County at age 20, March 19, 1862. Reported present on surviving company muster rolls through March 1, 1863. Hospitalized at Richmond, Virginia, June 21, 1863, with intermittent fever. Furloughed for thirty days on August 8, 1863. Returned to duty in November-December, 1863. Hospitalized at Richmond on March 30, 1864, with bronchitis. Transferred to another hospital on May 15, 1864. Returned to duty in July-August, 1864. Captured at Burgess' Mill, Virginia, October 27, 1864. Confined at Point Lookout, Maryland, October 31, 1864. Paroled at Point Lookout on March 28, 1865. Received at Boulware's Wharf, James River, Virginia, March 30, 1865, for exchange. Survived the war.

KRAUSE, SAMUEL A., Sergeant

Born in Stokes County where he resided as a mechanic and/or stage driver prior to enlisting in Stokes County at age 23, March 19, 1862. Mustered in as Private. Promoted to Sergeant in April-July, 1862. Captured at Gettysburg, Pennsylvania, July 3, 1863. Confined at Fort Delaware, Delaware, on or about July 10, 1863. Transferred to Point Lookout, Maryland, October 20, 1863. Released at Point Lookout on January 29, 1864, after taking the Oath of Allegiance and joining the U.S. Army. Assigned to Company D, 1st Regiment U.S. Volunteer Infantry.

LANDERS, ISAAC, Private

Resided in Stokes County where he enlisted at age 26, May 1, 1862, for the war. Wounded in the right hand and right leg and captured at Gettysburg, Pennsylvania, July 3, 1863. Confined at Fort Delaware, Delaware, on or about July 10, 1863. Transferred to Point Lookout, Maryland, October 20, 1863. Paroled at Point Lookout on March 15, 1865. Received at Boulware's Wharf, James River, Virginia, March 18, 1865, for exchange. Survived the war.

LANDERS, JOHN F., Corporal

Resided in Stokes County where he enlisted at age 33, March 13, 1862. Mustered in as Private. Promoted to Corporal on December 1, 1864. Reported present or accounted for on surviving company muster rolls through December, 1864. Captured at Sutherland's Station, Virginia, April 2, 1865. Confined at Point Lookout, Maryland, April 4, 1865. Released at Point Lookout on June 29, 1865, after taking the Oath of Allegiance.

LANDERS, ZACHARIAH J., Private

Resided in Stokes County where he enlisted at age 23,

March 13, 1862. Reported present or accounted for on surviving company muster rolls through April, 1864. Captured at or near Wilderness, Virginia, on or about May 6, 1864. Confined at Point Lookout, Maryland, May 17, 1864. Paroled at Point Lookout on September 18, 1864. Received at Varina, Virginia, on or about September 21, 1864, for exchange.

LAWSON, JAMES W., Private

Born in Stokes County and resided in Guilford County where he was by occupation a farmer prior to enlisting in Stokes County at age 25, March 19, 1862. Reported present or accounted for on surviving company muster rolls through March 1, 1863. Reported present but under arrest in November-December, 1863. Reason he was arrested not reported. Returned to duty in January-February, 1864. Deserted to the enemy at the Chickahominy River, Virginia, on or about June 13, 1864. Confined at Point Lookout, Maryland, June 23, 1864. Transferred to Elmira, New York, July 23, 1864. Released at Elmira on May 29, 1865, after taking the Oath of Allegiance.

LEAMAN, JAMES D., Private

Resided in Yadkin County and enlisted at age 35, October 21, 1862, for the war. Killed at Gettysburg, Pennsylvania, July 1, 1863.

LIGON, WILLIAM E., Private

Born in Halifax County, Virginia, and resided in Stokes County where he was by occupation a farmer prior to enlisting in Stokes County at age 18, March 19, 1862. Reported missing at Gettysburg, Pennsylvania, July 3, 1863. Apparently died of wounds in the hands of the enemy.

MARLER, H. FRANKLIN, Private

Resided in Yadkin County and enlisted at Camp French, near Petersburg, Virginia, at age 32, October 21, 1862, for the war. Reported absent without leave on surviving company muster rolls through August, 1863. Dropped from the rolls of the company in September-October, 1863.

MARSHALL, MATTHEW, Private

Born in Stokes County where he resided as a farmer prior to enlisting in Stokes County at age 21, March 19, 1862. Reported present or accounted for on surviving company muster rolls through August, 1864. Hospitalized at Richmond, Virginia, on or about September 10, 1864, with anasarca. Furloughed for thirty days on September 22, 1864. Returned to duty in November-December, 1864. Captured at Sutherland's Station, Virginia, April 2, 1865. Confined at Point Lookout, Maryland, April 4, 1865. Released at Point Lookout on June 29, 1865, after taking the Oath of Allegiance.

MARSHALL, RICHARD, Private

Born in Stokes County where he resided as a farmer prior to enlisting in Stokes County at age 37, March 13, 1862. Wounded in the right leg (fracture) at Bristoe Station, Virginia, October 14, 1863. Hospitalized at Richmond, Virginia. Furloughed for forty days on December 18, 1863. Reported absent wounded or absent sick through

October, 1864. Returned to duty in November-December, 1864. Captured at Sutherland's Station, Virginia, April 2, 1865. Confined at Point Lookout, Maryland, April 4, 1865. Released at Point Lookout on June 29, 1865, after taking the Oath of Allegiance.

MORRIS, LEWIS, Private

Born in Stokes County where he resided as a farmer prior to enlisting in Stokes County at age 41, March 19, 1862. Discharged on May 25, 1862, by reason of being overage.

MYERS, ADERSON C., 1st Sergeant

Born in Davidson County and resided in Stokes County where he was by occupation a farmer prior to enlisting in Stokes County at age 30, March 19, 1862. Mustered in as Private. Promoted to 1st Sergeant on May 28, 1862. Wounded in the left arm and left hip and captured at Gettysburg, Pennsylvania, July 3, 1863. Hospitalized at Gettysburg. Transferred to hospital at Baltimore, Maryland, October 6, 1863. Paroled at Baltimore on or about November 12, 1863. Received at City Point, Virginia, November 17, 1863, for exchange. Reported absent wounded until August 18, 1864, when he was retired to the Invalid Corps.

NELSON, JOHN H., Sergeant

Born in Stokes County where he resided prior to enlisting at age 17, March 19, 1862. Mustered in as Sergeant. Wounded and captured at Gettysburg, Pennsylvania, July 3, 1863. Died at or near Gettysburg on or about July 5, 1863, of wounds.

PEELE, A. E., _____

North Carolina pension records indicate that he served in this company.

PEPPER, JOHN KERR, Sergeant

Previously served as 2nd Lieutenant of Company F, 21st Regiment N.C. Troops (11th Regiment N.C. Volunteers). Enlisted in this company at Orange Court House, Virginia, September 1, 1863, for the war. Mustered in as Sergeant. Reduced to ranks in November-December, 1863. Promoted to Sergeant in July-August, 1864. Appointed Ordnance Sergeant in September-October, 1864, and transferred to the Field and Staff of this regiment.

REDMAN, FRANKLIN, Private

Born in Stokes County where he resided as a farmer prior to enlisting in Stokes County at age 44, March 19, 1862. Discharged on May 25, 1862, by reason of being overage.

RICHARDSON, GREEN L., Private

Enlisted in camp on September 1, 1864, for the war. Wounded in the chest and right hand near Petersburg, Virginia, on or about March 25, 1865. Hospitalized at Richmond, Virginia. Captured in hospital at Richmond on April 3, 1865. Took the Oath of Allegiance on an unspecified date.

RICHARDSON, R. F., Private

Resided in Stokes County where he enlisted at age 22, February 20, 1863, for the war. Reported present on

surviving company muster rolls through December, 1864; however, he was reported absent sick during much of that period. Hospitalized at Richmond, Virginia, January 2, 1865, with remittent fever. Furloughed for sixty days on January 28, 1865.

SIMMONS, WILLIAM M., Private

Born in Surry County and resided in Stokes County where he was by occupation a farmer prior to enlisting in Stokes County at age 18, March 19, 1862. Wounded at Gettysburg, Pennsylvania, July 1, 1863. Returned to duty prior to September 1, 1863. Reported absent sick in November-December, 1863. Hospitalized at Richmond, Virginia, January 29, 1864, with a gunshot wound of the left knee. Place and date wounded not reported. Reported absent wounded or absent sick until December 15, 1864, when he was retired to the Invalid Corps.

SOUTHERN, GEORGE W., Private

Born in Stokes County where he resided as a farmer prior to enlisting in Stokes County at age 40, March 19, 1862. Discharged on or about May 28, 1862, by reason of being overage.

SOUTHERN, JOHN W., Private

Born in Stokes County where he resided as a farmer prior to enlisting in Stokes County at age 30, March 13, 1862. Reported absent without leave on or about April 28, 1862. Discharged prior to July 1, 1862. Reason discharged not reported.

SPENCER, ISHAM, Private

Resided in Stokes County and enlisted at age 32, March 13, 1862. No further records.

STANFIL, RICHARD B., Private

Born in Halifax County, Virginia, and resided in Stokes County where he was by occupation a tailor prior to enlisting in Stokes County at age 37, March 19, 1862. Discharged on May 28, 1862, by reason of being overage.

STARNES, DULIN, Private

Enlisted in this company on October 21, 1862, while listed as a deserter from Company F, 35th Regiment N.C. Troops, and Company I, 37th Regiment N.C. Troops. Captured by the enemy at Goldsboro on December 17, 1862. Paroled on or about the same date. Shot for desertion prior to September 1, 1863.

STARNES, JOHN L., Private

Resided in Union County and enlisted at Camp French, near Petersburg, Virginia, at age 38, October 21, 1862, for the war. Captured at Bristoe Station, Virginia, October 14, 1863. Confined at Old Capitol Prison, Washington, D.C., October 15, 1863. Transferred to Point Lookout, Maryland, October 27, 1863. Exchanged on March 17, 1865.

STRICKLAND, BYTHAN ELBERT, _____

North Carolina pension records indicate that he served in this company.

THREAT, BENJAMIN, Private
Resided in Union County and enlisted at Camp French, near Petersburg, Virginia, October 21, 1862, for the war. Reported present through March 1, 1863. Shot for desertion prior to September 1, 1863.

TUTTLE, CALVIN, Private
Born in Stokes County where he resided as a farmer prior to enlisting in Stokes County at age 31, March 19, 1862. Died at Camp Mangum, near Raleigh, May 17, 1862, of disease.

TUTTLE, DEWITT P., Sergeant
Born in Stokes County where he resided as a farmer prior to enlisting in Stokes County at age 18, March 19, 1862. Mustered in as Sergeant. Reported present on surviving company muster rolls through June, 1864. Killed at Reams' Station, Virginia, August 25, 1864.

TUTTLE, GIDEON JEFF, Private
Born in Stokes County where he resided as a farmer prior to enlisting in Stokes County at age 23, March 19, 1862. Wounded and captured at or near Falling Waters, Maryland, on or about July 14, 1863. Sent to Baltimore, Maryland. Transferred to Point Lookout, Maryland, August 20, 1863. Paroled at Point Lookout on March 16, 1864. Received at City Point, Virginia, March 20, 1864, for exchange. Reported absent without leave in May-June, 1864. Returned to duty in July-August, 1864. Captured at Burgess' Mill, Virginia, October 27, 1864. Confined at Point Lookout, Maryland, October 31, 1864. Released at Point Lookout on May 14, 1865, after taking the Oath of Allegiance.

TUTTLE, JEFFERSON G., Private
Born in Stokes County where he resided as a farmer prior to enlisting in Stokes County at age 21, March 19, 1862. Wounded in the right arm and captured at Gettysburg, Pennsylvania, July 3, 1863. Right arm amputated. Hospitalized at Gettysburg. Transferred to hospital at Baltimore, Maryland, in September, 1863. Paroled at Baltimore on September 25, 1863. Received at City Point, Virginia, September 27, 1863, for exchange. Reported absent wounded until February 17, 1864, when he was retired from service.

TUTTLE, JOHN W., Sergeant
Born in Stokes County where he resided as a farmer prior to enlisting in Stokes County at age 20, March 19, 1862. Mustered in as Musician (Fifer). Reduced to ranks prior to July 1, 1862. Promoted to Corporal in May, 1863. Promoted to Sergeant on December 1, 1864. Reported present or accounted for on surviving company muster rolls through December, 1864. Captured at Sutherland's Station, Virginia, April 2, 1865. Confined at Point Lookout, Maryland, April 4, 1865. Released at Point Lookout on June 20, 1865, after taking the Oath of Allegiance.

TUTTLE, PETER H., Private
Born in Stokes County where he resided as a farmer prior to enlisting in Stokes County at age 28, March 19, 1862. Reported present or accounted for on surviving company muster rolls through October, 1864. Captured at

Sutherland's Station, Virginia, April 2, 1865. Confined at Point Lookout, Maryland, April 4, 1865. Released at Point Lookout on June 20, 1865, after taking the Oath of Allegiance.

VAUGHN, ALEXANDER S., Private
Born in Halifax County, Virginia, and resided in Stokes County where he was by occupation a farmer prior to enlisting in Stokes County at age 31, March 19, 1862. Died at Petersburg, Virginia, July 19, 1862. Cause of death not reported.

WALL, DRURY BENJAMIN WESLEY, Private
Born in Halifax County, Virginia, and resided in Stokes County where he was by occupation a farmer prior to enlisting in Stokes County at age 19, March 19, 1862. Wounded in the leg at Gettysburg, Pennsylvania, July 3, 1863. Captured at or near Gettysburg on July 4-5, 1863. Leg amputated. Hospitalized at Chester, Pennsylvania, on or about July 12, 1863. Transferred to Point Lookout, Maryland, on an unspecified date. Paroled at Point Lookout on March 16, 1864. Received at City Point, Virginia, March 20, 1864, for exchange. Hospitalized at Richmond, Virginia, March 20, 1864. Furloughed on March 31, 1864. Died at home on May 21, 1864.

WALL, EVY, Private
Born in Halifax County, Virginia, and resided in Stokes County where he was by occupation a blacksmith prior to enlisting in Stokes County at age 52, March 19, 1862. Reported present on surviving company muster rolls through April, 1864. Died at Farmville, Virginia, June 27, 1864, of "dropsy."

WALL, JOHN RICHARD FRANCIS, Private
Enlisted in Stokes County at age 18, February 20, 1863, for the war. Captured at or near Falling Waters, Maryland, July 14, 1863. Confined at Point Lookout, Maryland, where he died on October 9, 1863. Cause of death not reported.

WALL, WILLIAM ANDREW WATKINS, Private
Born in Halifax County, Virginia, and resided in Stokes County where he was by occupation a farmer prior to enlisting in Stokes County at age 21, March 19, 1862. Reported absent with leave on or about July 1, 1862. Died at home in Stokes County prior to September 21, 1863. Cause of death not reported.

WESTMORELAND, DAVID F., Private
Born in Stokes County where he resided as a farmer prior to enlisting in Stokes County at age 20, March 19, 1862. Captured at Gettysburg, Pennsylvania, July 3, 1863. Confined at Fort Delaware, Delaware, July 10, 1863. Transferred to Point Lookout, Maryland, October 20, 1863. Released at Point Lookout on January 29, 1864, after taking the Oath of Allegiance and joining the U.S. Army. Assigned to Company C, 1st Regiment U.S. Volunteer Infantry.

WHITE, JOHN GIDEON, Corporal
Born in Stokes County where he resided as a mechanic prior to enlisting in Stokes County at age 26, March 19,

1862. Mustered in as Private. Promoted to Corporal in May, 1863. Wounded at Gettysburg, Pennsylvania, July 1, 1863. Returned to duty prior to September 1, 1863. Wounded at or near Cold Harbor, Virginia, on or about June 2, 1864. Returned to duty in September-October, 1864. Detailed as a shoemaker at Richmond, Virginia, November 21, 1864. Furloughed on January 28, 1865.

WILLIAMS, CHARLES M., Corporal
Born in Stokes County where he resided as a mechanic prior to enlisting in Stokes County at age 18, March 19, 1862. Mustered in as Corporal. Reported present on surviving company muster rolls through December, 1864. Surrendered at Appomattox Court House, Virginia, April 9, 1865.

YOUNG, D. ED., Private
Resided in Stokes County and enlisted at Camp Campbell, Drewry's Bluff, Virginia, at age 28, August 28, 1862, for the war. Captured at Falling Waters, Maryland, July 14, 1863. Sent to Baltimore, Maryland. Confined at Point Lookout, Maryland, August 21, 1863. Paroled at Point Lookout on March 16, 1864. Received at City Point, Virginia, March 20, 1864, for exchange. Reported absent without leave in May-June, 1864. Returned to duty in July-August, 1864. Hospitalized at Richmond, Virginia, November 20, 1864, with anasarca. Furloughed for sixty days on December 16, 1864.

YOUNG, EDWARD H., Sergeant
Resided in Stokes County where he enlisted at age 39, April 1, 1863, for the war. Mustered in as Private. Captured at Gettysburg, Pennsylvania, July 3, 1863. Confined at Fort Delaware, Delaware, on or about July 10, 1863. Transferred to hospital at Chester, Pennsylvania, August 10, 1863. Paroled at Chester on an unspecified date. Received at City Point, Virginia, September 23, 1863, for exchange. Returned to duty in January-February, 1864. Promoted to Sergeant in November-December, 1864. Present or accounted for through December, 1864. Survived the war.

YOUNG, ROBERT W., Private
Resided in Stokes County where he enlisted at age 38, February 20, 1863, for the war. Captured at Gettysburg, Pennsylvania, on or about July 3, 1863. Confined at Fort Delaware, Delaware, on or about July 10, 1863. Paroled at Fort Delaware on July 30, 1863. Received at City Point, Virginia, August 1, 1863, for exchange. Died in hospital at Petersburg, Virginia, August 22, 1863, of "diarrhoea chronic."

ZEIGLER, BENJAMIN J., Private
Born in Stokes County where he resided as a farmer prior to enlisting in Stokes County at age 22, March 19, 1862. Wounded at Goldsboro on December 17, 1862. Returned to duty prior to March 2, 1863. Captured at Gettysburg, Pennsylvania, July 3, 1863. Confined at Fort Delaware, Delaware, on or about July 10, 1863. Transferred to Point Lookout, Maryland, October 20, 1863. Died at Point Lookout on December 10, 1863, of "chronic diarrhoea."

ZEIGLER, SAMUEL M., Private
Born in Stokes County where he resided as a farmer prior

to enlisting in Stokes County at age 20, March 19, 1862. Wounded in the head at Gettysburg, Pennsylvania, July 3, 1863. Returned to duty in September-October, 1863. Wounded at or near Spotsylvania Court House, Virginia, on or about May 12, 1864. Hospitalized at Richmond, Virginia, where he died on or about May 21, 1864, of wounds.

COMPANY E

This company, known as the "Richmond Regulators," was raised in Richmond County and enlisted in Richmond County in March-April, 1862. It was mustered into state service at Camp Mangum, near Raleigh, on April 28, 1862, and assigned to the 52nd Regiment N.C. Troops as Company E. After joining the regiment the company functioned as a part of the regiment, and its history for the remainder of the war is reported as a part of the regimental history.

The information contained in the following roster was compiled primarily from a company muster-in and descriptive roll dated April 28, 1862, and from company muster rolls for May 1-June 30, 1862; November 1, 1862-February 28, 1863; and July 1, 1863-December 31, 1864. No company muster rolls were located for July 1-October 31, 1862; March 1-June 30, 1863; or for the period after December 31, 1864. Valuable information was obtained from primary records such as the North Carolina adjutant general's *Roll of Honor*, discharge certificates, medical records, prisoner of war records, *The War of the Rebellion: A Compilation of the Official Records of the Union and Confederate Armies*, militia records, newspaper casualty lists and obituaries, Confederate pension applications filed with the state of North Carolina, and the 1860 federal census of North Carolina. Secondary sources such as postwar rosters and histories, cemetery records, the *Confederate Veteran*, published genealogies, and records of the United Daughters of the Confederacy also provided useful information.

OFFICERS

CAPTAINS

LITTLE, BENJAMIN F.
Born in Richmond County where he resided as a farmer prior to enlisting in Richmond County at age 31. Appointed Captain on March 12, 1862. Wounded in the left arm and captured at Gettysburg, Pennsylvania, July 3, 1863. Left arm amputated. Hospitalized at Gettysburg. Transferred to hospital at Baltimore, Maryland, September 28, 1863. Transferred to Fort McHenry, Maryland, October 22, 1863. Transferred to Point Lookout, Maryland, January 23, 1864. Paroled at Point Lookout on March 3, 1864. Received at City Point, Virginia, March 6, 1864, for exchange. Appointed Lieutenant Colonel on April 15, 1864, to rank from July 3, 1863, and transferred to the Field and Staff of this regiment.

AUSTIN, MILTON S.

Resided in Richmond County and was by occupation a merchant prior to enlisting at age 34. Appointed 1st Lieutenant on March 19, 1862. Promoted to Captain to rank from July 3, 1863. Wounded in the right foot at Gettysburg, Pennsylvania, July 3, 1863. Hospitalized at Richmond, Virginia. Furloughed for thirty days on August 17, 1863. Returned to duty prior to November 1, 1863. Present or accounted for until wounded in the right arm at Burgess' Mill, Virginia, October 27, 1864. Arm amputated. Resigned on an unspecified date.

LIEUTENANTS

BALDWIN, THOMAS ROPER, 3rd Lieutenant

Born in Montgomery County and resided in Richmond County where he was by occupation a farmer prior to enlisting in Richmond County at age 29. Appointed 3rd Lieutenant on April 14, 1862. Reported present or accounted for on surviving company muster rolls through August, 1863. Resigned on August 31, 1863, by reason of "disease of the chords [sic] of his testicles. . . ." Resignation accepted on September 11, 1863.

McDONALD, MARTIN ROBESON, 2nd Lieutenant

Born in Richmond County on October 1, 1830. Resided in Richmond County where he was by occupation a farmer prior to enlisting in Richmond County. Appointed 2nd Lieutenant on March 19, 1862. Wounded and captured at Gettysburg, Pennsylvania, July 3, 1863. Hospitalized at Gettysburg. Transferred to hospital at Davids Island, New York Harbor, where he arrived on or about July 20, 1863. Transferred to Johnson's Island, Ohio, September 18, 1863. Paroled at Johnson's Island on March 14, 1865. Received at Cox's Wharf, James River, Virginia, March 22, 1865, for exchange.

NONCOMMISSIONED OFFICERS AND PRIVATES

BALDWIN, DANIEL W., Private

Resided in Richmond County where he enlisted at age 28, May 3, 1862, for the war. Captured on the march from Gettysburg, Pennsylvania, to Hagerstown, Maryland, on or about July 5, 1863. Confined at Fort Delaware, Delaware, on or about July 10, 1863. Died at Fort Delaware on November 25, 1863, of "diarrhoea chronic."

BALDWIN, MADISON, Private

Born in Richmond County and was by occupation a farmer prior to enlisting in Richmond County at age 31, March 8, 1862. Captured on the march from Gettysburg, Pennsylvania, to Hagerstown, Maryland, on or about July 5, 1863. Confined at Fort Delaware, Delaware, on or about July 10, 1863. Transferred to Point Lookout, Maryland, October 20, 1863. Died at Point Lookout on November 1, 1863, of "erysipelas, dysentery, & scorbutus."

BALLARD, ISAIAH W., Private

Resided in Montgomery County and was by occupation a farmer prior to enlisting in Richmond County at age 38, February 16, 1863, for the war. Reported present or accounted for on surviving company muster rolls through December, 1864; however, he was reported absent sick during most of that period. Survived the war.

BARMER, WILLIAM J., Private

Resided in Richmond County and was by occupation a field hand prior to enlisting in Richmond County at age 17, May 12, 1862, for the war as a substitute for John M. Scales of Anson County. Captured at Falling Waters, Maryland, July 14, 1863. Confined at Old Capitol Prison, Washington, D.C. Transferred to Point Lookout, Maryland, August 8, 1863. Transferred to Elmira, New York, August 16, 1864. Paroled at Elmira on March 10, 1865. Received at Boulware's Wharf, James River, Virginia, March 15, 1865, for exchange.

BARRENTINE, CHARLES A., Private

Enlisted at age 24, October 17, 186[2], for the war. Transferred to Company D, 12th Battalion Virginia Light Artillery, November 20, 1862, in exchange for Private Cameron Smith. Later served as Private in Company A, 13th Battalion N.C. Light Artillery.

BLAKE, JAMES T., Private

Resided in Montgomery County and enlisted at age 23, October 11, 1862, for the war. Deserted on April 27, 1863. Returned to duty in September, 1864. Deserted to the enemy on or about November 1, 1864. Sent to Fort Monroe, Virginia. Hospitalized at Fort Monroe on November 12, 1864, with diarrhoea. Released from confinement on December 7, 1864, after taking the Oath of Allegiance.

BOLTON, JAMES H., Private

Enlisted in Richmond County at age 27, April 30, 1862, for the war. Hospitalized at or near Petersburg, Virginia, September 15, 1862, with stricture of the urethra. Furloughed on December 19, 1862. Reported absent sick or absent on furlough on surviving company muster rolls through February, 1864. Returned to duty in March-April, 1864. Reported absent in hospital in May-June, 1864. Discharged in July-August, 1864, probably by reason of stricture of the urethra.

BOROUGHS, MATTHEW W., Sergeant

Born in Moore County and resided in Montgomery County where he was by occupation a farmer prior to enlisting in Richmond County at age 48, April 4, 1862. Mustered in as Sergeant. Discharged on May 23, 1862, by reason of being overage.

BOSTICK, THOMAS T., Private

Born in Richmond County on January 18, 1841. Resided in Richmond County where he was by occupation a farmer prior to enlisting in Richmond County on March 19, 1862. Mustered in as Private. Promoted to Sergeant on April 14, 1862. Reduced to ranks in July, 1862-February, 1863. Reported absent without leave in November, 1862-February, 1863. Returned to duty in July-August, 1863. Present or accounted for until captured at or near

Wilderness, Virginia, on or about May 6, 1864. Confined at Point Lookout, Maryland, May 17, 1864. Transferred to Elmira, New York, August 8, 1864. Released at Elmira on June 12, 1865, after taking the Oath of Allegiance.

BROOKSHIRE, WILLIAM F., 1st Sergeant
Born in Randolph County and resided in Richmond County where he was by occupation a farmer prior to enlisting in Richmond County at age 31, April 4, 1862. Mustered in as Private. Promoted to 1st Sergeant on April 14, 1862. Appointed Commissary Sergeant in July-August, 1863, and transferred to the Field and Staff of this regiment. [Previously served as 1st Lieutenant in the 61st Regiment N.C. Militia.]

BULLARD, GEORGE W., Private
Enlisted at age 18, October 17, 1862, for the war. Reported absent without leave in November, 1862-February, 1863. Dropped from the rolls of the company prior to September 1, 1863. May have enlisted later in another unit.

BUNNELL, STEPHEN PINKNEY, Private
Enlisted in Richmond County at age 42, May 14, 1862, for the war as a substitute for William B. Little of Anson County. Deserted on June 21, 1863. Returned to duty on July 15, 1863. Reported present in September-December, 1863. Reported absent without leave in January-February, 1864. Died at Rockingham on March 17, 1864, of disease.

CAPEL, THOMAS R., Sergeant
Resided in Richmond County where he enlisted at age 25, May 2, 1862, for the war. Mustered in as Corporal. Promoted to Sergeant prior to March 1, 1863. Wounded at Gettysburg, Pennsylvania, July 1, 1863. Returned to duty prior to September 1, 1863. Present or accounted for until he deserted on July 27, 1864. "Found dead nine days afterwards in Appomattox River."

CARMICHAEL, JOHN M., Private
Enlisted in Wake County at age 48, June 4, 1862, for the war as a substitute for Private John F. Gibson of this company. Died at Petersburg, Virginia, May 21, 1863. Cause of death not reported.

CHAPPELL, A. TERRILL, Private
Resided in Montgomery County and enlisted in Richmond County at age 36, February 16, 1863, for the war. Deserted on June 21, 1863. Returned to duty on October 24, 1863. Hospitalized at Richmond, Virginia, April 10, 1864, with chronic diarrhoea. Transferred to Farmville, Virginia, May 2, 1864. Furloughed for sixty days on May 21, 1864. Reported absent sick through August, 1864. Died prior to November 1, 1864. Place and cause of death not reported.

CHAPPELL, MARTIN, Private
Born in Montgomery County and resided in Richmond County where he was by occupation a farmer prior to enlisting in Richmond County at age 32, March 10, 1862. Wounded in the right thigh (flesh) and captured at Gettysburg, Pennsylvania, July 3, 1863. Hospitalized at Gettysburg. Transferred to hospital at Baltimore, Maryland, where he arrived on July 25, 1863. Paroled at Baltimore on August 23, 1863. Received at City Point,

Virginia, August 24, 1863, for exchange. Returned to duty in January-February, 1864. Present or accounted for through December, 1864. Captured near Petersburg, Virginia, March 25, 1865. Confined at Point Lookout, Maryland, March 28, 1865. Released at Point Lookout on June 26, 1865, after taking the Oath of Allegiance.

CHAPPELL, ROLIN, Private
Previously served as Private in Company H, 44th Regiment N.C. Troops. Transferred to this company on December 28, 1862. Wounded at Gettysburg, Pennsylvania, July 1-3, 1863. Captured near Gettysburg on or about July 6, 1863. Hospitalized at Gettysburg. Transferred to hospital at Chester, Pennsylvania, where he arrived on July 19, 1863. Died in hospital at Chester on July 23, 1863, of "chronic diarrhoea."

COVINGTON, ANDREW J., Private
Resided in Richmond County and was by occupation a farmer prior to enlisting at age 38. Place and date of enlistment not reported. First listed in the records of this company on May 6, 1863, when he was hospitalized at Richmond, Virginia, with "typh[oid] febris." Died in hospital at Richmond on or about May 13, 1863.

COVINGTON, BENJAMIN F., Corporal
Born in Richmond County where he resided as a farmer prior to enlisting in Richmond County at age 22, April 4, 1862. Mustered in as Private. Wounded and captured at Falling Waters, Maryland, July 14, 1863. Hospitalized at Baltimore, Maryland, August 3, 1863. Paroled at Baltimore on August 23, 1863. Received at City Point, Virginia, August 24, 1863, for exchange. Returned to duty in November-December, 1863. Promoted to Corporal on January 1, 1864. Wounded at Cold Harbor, Virginia, June 2, 1864. Reported absent wounded through December, 1864. Retired to the Invalid Corps on February 10, 1865.

COVINGTON, HENRY A., Private
Enlisted in Richmond County at age 25, April 28, 1862, for the war. Died in hospital at Richmond, Virginia, June 13, 1863. Cause of death not reported.

COVINGTON, HENRY H., Private
Born in Richmond County where he resided as a farmer prior to enlisting in Richmond County at age 19, March 8, 1862. Reported absent without leave in November, 1862-February, 1863. Returned to duty prior to September 1, 1863. Reported present or accounted for until November-December, 1864, when he was reported absent without leave.

COVINGTON, JOHN B., Private
Born in Richmond County where he resided as a farmer prior to enlisting in Richmond County at age 16, March 10, 1862. Captured at Falling Waters, Maryland, July 14, 1863. Confined at Old Capitol Prison, Washington, D.C. Transferred to Point Lookout, Maryland, August 8, 1863. Died at Point Lookout on November 28, 1863, of "smallpox."

COVINGTON, JOSEPH E., Corporal
Born in Marlboro District, South Carolina, and was by

occupation a farmer prior to enlisting in Richmond County at age 17, March 8, 1862. Mustered in as Private. Wounded at Bristoe Station, Virginia, October 14, 1863. Returned to duty prior to November 1, 1863. Promoted to Corporal in September-October, 1864. Captured at Burgess' Mill, Virginia, October 27, 1864. Confined at Point Lookout, Maryland, October 31, 1864. Paroled at Point Lookout on January 17, 1865. Received at Boulware's Wharf, James River, Virginia, January 21, 1865, for exchange.

COVINGTON, THOMAS J., Private
Born in Richmond County where he resided as a farmer prior to enlisting in Richmond County at age 21, March 8, 1862. Wounded at Gettysburg, Pennsylvania, July 1-3, 1863. Returned to duty prior to September 1, 1863. Present or accounted for until wounded at or near Jones' Farm, Virginia, on or about September 30, 1864. Reported absent wounded through December, 1864. Survived the war.

COVINGTON, THOMAS T., Private
Resided in Richmond County and was by occupation a field hand prior to enlisting in Richmond County at age 18, February 16, 1863, for the war. Reported present or accounted for on surviving company muster rolls through June, 1864. Died in hospital at Richmond, Virginia, July 29, 1864. Cause of death not reported.

COVINGTON, WILLIAM RILEY, Private
Born in Richmond County where he resided as a farmer prior to enlisting in Richmond County at age 53, March 19, 1862, as a substitute. Captured at Gettysburg, Pennsylvania, July 3, 1863. Confined at Fort Delaware, Delaware, on or about July 10, 1863. Paroled at Fort Delaware on or about July 30, 1863. Received at City Point, Virginia, August 1, 1863, for exchange. Reported absent on parole or absent with leave until March-April, 1864, when he was reported absent without leave.

CROUCH, SAMUEL C., Sergeant
Born in Richmond County where he resided as a farmer prior to enlisting in Richmond County at age 33, March 8, 1862. Mustered in as Corporal. Wounded at Gettysburg, Pennsylvania, July 1, 1863. Captured near Gettysburg on or about July 5, 1863. Confined at Fort Delaware, Delaware, on or about July 10, 1863. Transferred to Point Lookout, Maryland, October 20, 1863. Promoted to Sergeant in January-February, 1864, while a prisoner of war. Died at Point Lookout on August 10, 1864. Cause of death not reported.

DAWKINS, GEORGE, Private
Born in Richmond County where he resided as a farmer prior to enlisting in New Hanover County at age 37, March 14, 1862. Discharged on May 23, 1862, by reason of being overage.

DAWKINS, SAMUEL C. B., Private
Born in Richmond County and was by occupation a farmer prior to enlisting in New Hanover County at age 26, March 14, 1862. Died near Drewry's Bluff, Virginia, August 10, 1862. Cause of death not reported.

DeBERRY, EDMUND J., Sergeant
Previously served as Sergeant in Company K, 26th Regiment N.C. Troops. Transferred to this company on May 1, 1862. Mustered in as Private. Promoted to Sergeant prior to March 1, 1863. Accidentally wounded in the shoulder (flesh) near Greenville by members of his own regiment on March 15, 1863. Returned to duty and was reduced to ranks prior to September 1, 1863. Promoted to Sergeant in November-December, 1863. Reduced to ranks in May-June, 1864. Promoted to Sergeant in July-August, 1864. Appointed Hospital Steward in July-October, 1864, and transferred to the Field and Staff of this regiment. Served as acting Hospital Steward for about two years prior to his appointment and during that period he was reported to have "given entire satisfaction."

DRIGGERS, ANDERSON, Private
Born in Richmond County and was by occupation a farmer prior to enlisting in Richmond County at age 31, March 8, 1862. Captured at Gettysburg, Pennsylvania, July 3, 1863. Confined at Fort Delaware, Delaware, on or about July 10, 1863. Died at Fort Delaware on October 31, 1863, of "dropsy."

EWING, JOHN WESLEY, 1st Sergeant
Born in Richmond County where he resided as a farmer prior to enlisting in Richmond County at age 23, March 8, 1862. Mustered in as Sergeant. Promoted to 1st Sergeant on April 25, 1862. Wounded in the knee and captured at Gettysburg, Pennsylvania, July 3, 1863. Hospitalized at Gettysburg. Transferred to hospital at Davids Island, New York Harbor, July 22, 1863. Paroled at Davids Island on August 24, 1863. Received at City Point, Virginia, August 28, 1863, for exchange. Reported absent without leave in January-February, 1864. Returned to duty in March-April, 1864. Reported on detail for light duty in May-August, 1864. Reported absent on detail as a guard and nurse in hospital at Fayetteville from September 15 through December 31, 1864.

GALLOWAY, JOHN, Private
Resided in Richmond County where he enlisted at age 23, April 28, 1862, for the war. Deserted on June 21, 1863. Returned to duty on July 15, 1863. Present or accounted for until captured at or near Wilderness, Virginia, on or about May 6, 1864. Confined at Point Lookout, Maryland, May 17, 1864. Transferred to Elmira, New York, August 8, 1864. Died at Elmira on February 13, 1865, of "variola."

GALLOWAY, WILLIAM H., Private
Resided in Richmond or Montgomery County and enlisted in Richmond County at age 26, April 28, 1862, for the war. Captured at Goldsboro on December 17, 1862. Paroled the same date. Hospitalized at Richmond, Virginia, July 12, 1863, with chronic rheumatism. Transferred to Raleigh on July 28, 1863. Deserted from hospital at Raleigh on August 19, 1863. Returned to duty on or about October 29, 1863. Deserted on July 27, 1864. Returned to duty in September, 1864. Deserted to the enemy on or about December 7, 1864. Sent to Washington, D.C. Released at Washington on or about December 15, 1864, after taking the Oath of Allegiance.

GATELY, ISAAC, Sergeant
Born in Richmond County where he resided as a farmer prior to enlisting in Richmond County at age 28, March 8, 1862. Mustered in as Corporal. Promoted to Sergeant on or about April 14, 1862. Reported present or accounted for on surviving company muster rolls through August, 1864. Wounded in the left leg at or near Jones' Farm, Virginia, on or about September 30, 1864. Hospitalized at Richmond, Virginia. Furloughed for sixty days on November 4, 1864. Survived the war.

GAY, DANIEL ODOM, Corporal
Born in Richmond County on February 17, 1841. Resided in Richmond County where he was by occupation a farmer prior to enlisting in Richmond County on March 19, 1862. Mustered in as Private. Promoted to Corporal on June 13, 1862. Wounded at Gettysburg, Pennsylvania, July 1, 1863. Returned to duty in March-April, 1864. Wounded in the left leg near Globe Tavern, Virginia, August 21, 1864. Left leg amputated. Reported absent wounded through December, 1864. Survived the war.

GAY, SAMUEL L., Private
Resided in Anson County where he enlisted on January 5, 1864, for the war. Present or accounted for through December, 1864. Captured at Sutherland's Station, Virginia, April 2, 1865. Confined at Point Lookout, Maryland, April 4, 1865. Released at Point Lookout on June 19, 1865, after taking the Oath of Allegiance.

GIBSON, ELIJAH, Private
Resided in Richmond County and was by occupation a farmhand prior to enlisting at age 28, October 17, 1862, for the war. Reported absent without leave on or about March 1, 1863. Returned to duty on an unspecified date. Deserted on July 21, 1863. Dropped from the rolls of the company prior to November 1, 1863. Captured by the enemy in Richmond County on March 17, 1865. Confined at Point Lookout, Maryland, March 30, 1865. Released at Point Lookout on June 27, 1865, after taking the Oath of Allegiance.

GIBSON, JOHN F., Private
Enlisted in Wake County at age 18, May 14, 1862, for the war. Discharged on June 4, 1862, after providing Private John M. Carmichael as a substitute.

GIBSON, PLEASANT, Private
Resided in Richmond County and enlisted in Wake County at age 22, May 14, 1862, for the war. Discharged prior to March 1, 1863, after providing a substitute.

GIBSON, ROBERT FLETCHER, Sergeant
Resided in Richmond County and was by occupation a farmer prior to enlisting in Wake County at age 25, May 14, 1862, for the war. Mustered in as Private or Corporal. Promoted to Sergeant on June 2, 1862. Wounded at Goldsboro on December 17, 1862. Returned to duty prior to March 1, 1863. Wounded at Gettysburg, Pennsylvania, July 1, 1863. Captured on the march from Gettysburg to Hagerstown, Maryland, on or about July 5, 1863. Confined at Fort Delaware, Delaware. Released at Fort Delaware on June 19, 1865, after taking the Oath of Allegiance.

GIBSON, SAMUEL, Private
Born in Richmond County where he resided as a farmer prior to enlisting in Richmond County at age 43, March 19, 1862. Discharged on May 23, 1862, by reason of being overage.

GRAHAM, WILLIAM, Private
Resided in Richmond County and enlisted at age 22, October 17, 1862, for the war. Reported absent without leave on or about March 1, 1863. No further records.

GREEN, GEORGE, Private
Enlisted in Richmond County at age 33, May 3, 1862, for the war. Deserted at Camp Mangum, near Raleigh, May 8, 1862. Returned to duty prior to March 1, 1863. Captured at Bristoe Station, Virginia, October 14, 1863. Confined at Old Capitol Prison, Washington, D.C. Transferred to Point Lookout, Maryland, October 27, 1863. Released at Point Lookout on January 25, 1864, after taking the Oath of Allegiance and joining the U.S. service. Unit to which assigned not reported.

GREEN, WILLIAM B., Private
Place and date of enlistment not reported (probably enlisted in March, 1862). Reported absent without leave on or about April 28, 1862.

HAIR, THOMAS K., _____
North Carolina pension records indicate that he served in this company.

HALL, ALLISON GRAY, Private
Resided in Richmond County where he enlisted at age 28, April 28, 1862, for the war. Died in hospital at Wilson on February 24, 1863, of "febris typhoides."

HARVELL, GEORGE H., Private
Born in Moore County and resided in Richmond County where he was by occupation a farmer prior to enlisting in Richmond County at age 50, April 4, 1862. Wounded and captured at Gettysburg, Pennsylvania, on or about July 3, 1863. Confined at Fort Delaware, Delaware, on or about July 10, 1863. Died at Fort Delaware on November 3, 1863, of "smallpox."

HASTY, JAMES, Private
Born in Richmond County where he resided as a farmer prior to enlisting in Richmond County at age 20, March 8, 1862. Died in hospital at Raleigh on May 7, 1862, of "brain fever."

HASTY, JOHN C., Private
Born in Richmond County where he resided as a farmer prior to enlisting in Richmond County at age 22, March 8, 1862. Captured at Gettysburg, Pennsylvania, July 3, 1863. Confined at Fort Delaware, Delaware, on or about July 10, 1863. Released at Fort Delaware on May 19, 1865, after taking the Oath of Allegiance.

HENRY, HENRY HENRY, Private
Born in Richmond County where he resided as a farmer prior to enlisting in Richmond County at age 24, March 8, 1862. Deserted on June 21, 1863. Returned to duty on

July 15, 1863. Present or accounted for through December, 1864. Survived the war.

HICKS, CHARLES C., Private
Previously served as Private in Company E, 38th Regiment N.C. Troops. Transferred to this company in March-April, 1864. Killed at Reams' Station, Virginia, August 25, 1864.

HICKS, EDWARD L., Private
Born in Richmond County where he resided as a farmer prior to enlisting in Richmond County at age 18, March 8, 1862. Reported present on surviving company muster rolls through December, 1864. Served as a teamster during part of the war. Survived the war. [North Carolina pension records indicate that he was wounded at Stony Creek, Virginia, March 28, 1865.]

HINSON, W. BRINKLEY, Private
Resided in Richmond County where he enlisted at age 19, May 12, 1862, for the war as a substitute. Wounded at Gettysburg, Pennsylvania, July 1, 1863. Captured at Gettysburg on July 5, 1863. Hospitalized at Davids Island, New York Harbor, July 9, 1863. Died in hospital at Davids Island on July 28, 1863, of wounds.

HOGANS, DAVID, Private
Resided in Montgomery County and enlisted at age 21, October 11, 1862, for the war. Died in hospital at Wilson on May 19, 1863, of "febris typhoides."

HOGANS, ZACHARIAH, Private
Born in Montgomery County and resided in Richmond County where he was by occupation a farmer prior to enlisting in Richmond County at age 45, March 19, 1862. Discharged on May 28, 1862, by reason of being overage.

HOLDEN, BENJAMIN FRANKLIN, _____
North Carolina pension records indicate that he served in this company.

JERNIGAN, LOUIS, Private
Born on October 19, 1830, and resided in Richmond County where he enlisted on April 28, 1862, for the war. Reported absent without leave on or about July 1, 1862. Returned to duty prior to March 1, 1863. Deserted on June 18, 1863. Returned to duty in the summer of 1864. Captured at Burgess' Mill, Virginia, October 27, 1864. Confined at Point Lookout, Maryland. Paroled at Point Lookout on January 17, 1865. Received at Boulware's Wharf, James River, Virginia, January 21, 1865, for exchange.

JOHNSON, ISHAM H., Private
Born in Montgomery County and resided in Richmond County where he was by occupation a farmer prior to enlisting in Richmond County at age 26, March 8, 1862. Wounded at Goldsboro on December 17, 1862. Died in hospital at Goldsboro on December 18, 1862, of wounds.

JOHNSON, JOHN J., Private
Resided in Richmond County where he enlisted at age 28, April 28, 1862, for the war. Deserted on June 18, 1863.

Returned to duty on July 24, 1863. Transferred to Company E, 38th Regiment N.C. Troops, April 9, 1864.

JOHNSON, WILLIAM L., Private
Resided in Richmond County where he enlisted at age 26, May 2, 1862, for the war. Hospitalized at or near Petersburg, Virginia, October 6, 1862, with a gunshot wound. Place and date wounded not reported. Returned to duty on December 7, 1862. Deserted on June 1, 1863.

JONES, HUGH, Private
Born in Chesterfield District, South Carolina, and resided in Richmond County where he was by occupation a farmer prior to enlisting in New Hanover County at age 24, March 14, 1862. Died in hospital at Petersburg, Virginia, November 4, 1862, of "typhoid fever."

KELLY, JOHN, Private
Resided in Richmond County and was by occupation a farmer prior to enlisting in Richmond County at age 30, March 8, 1862. Deserted on June 1, 1863, "and had his brains shot out while in the woods."

KENNEDY, WILLIAM M., Private
Born in Moore County and resided in Richmond County where he was by occupation a farmer prior to enlisting in Richmond County at age 20, March 8, 1862. Mustered in as Private. Promoted to Corporal prior to March 1, 1863. Reported absent without leave from November 1, 1863, until October 31, 1864. Reduced to ranks on January 1, 1864. Dropped from the rolls of the company in November-December, 1864.

LISK, ROBINSON, Private
Previously served as Private in Company E, 38th Regiment N.C. Troops. Enlisted in this company on or about March 17, 1862. Died in hospital at Petersburg, Virginia, October 16, 1862, of "catarrh."

LOWE, DANIEL, Private
Resided in Richmond County and enlisted in Chesterfield County, Virginia, at age 18, August 14, 1862, for the war as a substitute for his father, Private Isaac Lowe. Hospitalized at Wilmington on August 7, 1863, with debility. Returned to duty on October 14, 1863. Captured at or near Wilderness, Virginia, on or about May 6, 1864. Confined at Point Lookout, Maryland, May 17, 1864. Transferred to Elmira, New York, August 8, 1864. Released at Elmira on May 29, 1865, after taking the Oath of Allegiance.

LOWE, ISAAC, Private
Born in Anson County and resided in Richmond County where he was by occupation a farmer prior to enlisting in Richmond County at age 56, March 8, 1862. Discharged on or about August 14, 1862, after providing his son, Private Daniel Lowe, as a substitute.

LUNCEFORD, ARIS, Private
Resided in Richmond County and enlisted at age 40, April 4, 1862. Discharged on April 21, 1862, presumably by reason of being overage.

McDONALD, STARLING C., Private

Resided in Richmond County where he enlisted at age 19, May 5, 1862, for the war. Wounded in the left shoulder and captured at Gettysburg, Pennsylvania, July 3, 1863. Hospitalized at Gettysburg. Transferred to hospital at Davids Island, New York Harbor, where he arrived on or about July 10, 1863. Paroled at Davids Island on an unspecified date. Received at City Point, Virginia, September 8, 1863, for exchange. Hospitalized at Petersburg, Virginia, September 8, 1863. Furloughed for sixty days on September 16, 1863. Reported absent on furlough until January-February, 1864, when he was reported absent without leave. Returned to duty in March-April, 1864. Retired from service (presumably by reason of disability from wounds) in May-June, 1864.

McDUFFIE, JOHN W., Private

Born in Anson County and resided in Richmond County where he was by occupation a farmer prior to enlisting in Richmond County at age 26, April 10, 1862. Hospitalized at or near Petersburg, Virginia, September 24, 1862, with typhoid fever. Furloughed for forty days on November 3, 1862. Returned to duty prior to March 1, 1863. Captured at Falling Waters, Maryland, July 14, 1863. Sent to Baltimore, Maryland. Confined at Point Lookout, Maryland, August 17, 1863. Paroled at Point Lookout on March 3, 1864. Received at City Point, Virginia, March 6, 1864, for exchange. Returned to duty in May-June, 1864. Hospitalized at Richmond, Virginia, December 20, 1864, with continued fever. Furloughed for sixty days on February 24, 1865.

McDUFFIE, MURDOCK, Private

Resided in Richmond County and was by occupation a farmer prior to enlisting in Richmond County at age 35, February 16, 1863, for the war. Captured at Bristoe Station, Virginia, October 14, 1863. Confined at Old Capitol Prison, Washington, D.C. Transferred to Point Lookout, Maryland, October 27, 1863. Paroled at Point Lookout on an unspecified date. Received at Aiken's Landing, James River, Virginia, on or about February 28, 1865, for exchange.

McKAY, LAUCHLIN L., Private

Born in Richmond County where he resided as a farmer prior to enlisting in Richmond County at age 50, April 4, 1862. Hospitalized at or near Petersburg, Virginia, October 13, 1862, with "ueterns[?]." Returned to duty on December 23, 1862. Killed at Gettysburg, Pennsylvania, July 3, 1863.

McKAY, WILLIAM, Private

Enlisted at age 18, October 11, 1862, for the war. Hospitalized at Farmville, Virginia, April 11, 1863, with diarrhoea. Died in hospital at Farmville on July 6, 1863, of "phthisis pulmonalis."

McKINNON, ALEXANDER, Private

Born in Chesterfield District, South Carolina, and resided in Richmond County where he was by occupation a farmer prior to enlisting in Richmond County at age 31, March 8, 1862. Died in hospital at Petersburg, Virginia, September 2, 1862, of "ty[phoid] fever."

McKINNON, LAUCHLIN C., Private

Born in Montgomery County and resided in Richmond County where he was by occupation a farmer prior to enlisting in Richmond County at age 21, March 13, 1862. Reported present on surviving company muster rolls through December, 1864. Served as a teamster during most of the war. Survived the war.

McLANE, DANIEL, Private

Born in Richmond County where he resided as a farmer prior to enlisting in Richmond County at age 22, March 19, 1862. Died in hospital at Goldsboro on July 18, 1862, of "fever."

McLENDON, BENJAMIN, Private

Previously served as Private in Company E, 38th Regiment N.C. Troops. Transferred to this company on April 22, 1863. Reported present on surviving company muster rolls through June, 1864. Wounded on an unspecified date. Furloughed on or about August 27, 1864. Returned to duty in November-December, 1864. Surrendered at Appomattox Court House, Virginia, April 9, 1865.

McLENDON, JOEL, Private

Born in Richmond County where he resided as a farmer prior to enlisting in Richmond County at age 41, March 8, 1862. Discharged on May 23, 1862, by reason of being overage.

McLENDON, ZACHARIAH, Private

Born in Richmond County where he resided as a farmer prior to enlisting in Richmond County at age 24, March 8, 1862. Died in hospital at Wilson on April 22, 1863, of "ty[phoid] fever."

McNAIR, JOHN A., Private

Born in Richmond County where he resided as a farmer prior to enlisting in Richmond County at age 23, March 8, 1862. Reported present or accounted for on surviving company muster rolls through April, 1864. Wounded at or near Wilderness, Virginia, on or about May 6, 1864. Returned to duty in July-October, 1864. Surrendered at Appomattox Court House, Virginia, April 9, 1865.

McNAIR, WILLIAM, Private

Born in Montgomery County and resided in Richmond County where he was by occupation a farmer prior to enlisting in Richmond County at age 29, March 8, 1862. Reported present or accounted for on surviving company muster rolls through December, 1864. Captured at Sutherland's Station, Virginia, April 2, 1865. Confined at Fort Delaware, Delaware, April 4, 1865. Released at Fort Delaware on June 19, 1865, after taking the Oath of Allegiance.

MANER, JAMES, Private

Born in Montgomery County and resided in Richmond County where he was by occupation a farmer prior to enlisting in Richmond County at age 34, March 8, 1862. Mortally wounded at Gettysburg, Pennsylvania, July 3, 1863. Died on or about the same date.

MARTIN, WILLIAM K., Private
Born in Anson County and was by occupation a farmer prior to enlisting in Richmond County at age 15, April 10, 1862, as a substitute. Wounded at Goldsboro on December 17, 1862. Died in hospital at Goldsboro on December 18, 1862, of wounds. He was a "promising and most gallant boy. . . ." [*Fayetteville Observer* (Semiweekly), February 5, 1863.]

MASON, JOHN H., Corporal
Born in Richmond County on May 21, 1843. Was by occupation a farmer prior to enlisting in Richmond County on March 8, 1862. Mustered in as Private. Promoted to Corporal on January 1, 1864. Present or accounted for until killed at Jones' Farm, Virginia, on or about September 30, 1864.

MEACHAM, DANIEL H., Private
Born in Montgomery County and resided in Wake County where he was by occupation a farmer prior to enlisting at Camp Mangum, near Raleigh, at age 32, April 16, 1862, for the war. Reported present on surviving company muster rolls through August, 1863. Captured at Bristoe Station, Virginia, October 14, 1863. Confined at Old Capitol Prison, Washington, D.C. Transferred to Point Lookout, Maryland, October 27, 1863. Paroled at Point Lookout on or about February 24, 1865. Received at Aiken's Landing, James River, Virginia, February 28, 1865, for exchange.

MEACHAM, ROBERT C., Private
Previously served as Sergeant in Company E, 38th Regiment N.C. Troops. Transferred to this company with the rank of Private on February 10, 1863. Captured at Falling Waters, Maryland, July 14, 1863. Confined at Old Capitol Prison, Washington, D.C. Transferred to Point Lookout, Maryland, August 8, 1863. Transferred to Elmira, New York, August 16, 1864. Paroled at Elmira on October 11, 1864. Received at Venus Point, Savannah River, Georgia, on or about November 15, 1864, for exchange.

MEACHAM, WILLIAM L., Private
Place and date of enlistment not reported (enlisted prior to April 28, 1862, when he was reported absent without leave). Failed to report for duty and was dropped from the rolls of the company in September-October, 1863.

MOORE, WILLIAM H., Private
Enlisted in Richmond County on April 16, 1863, for the war. Captured at Gettysburg, Pennsylvania, July 3, 1863. Confined at Fort Delaware, Delaware, on or about July 10, 1863. Died at Fort Delaware on September 20, 1863, of "chronic diarrhoea."

MORGAN, JOHN H., Private
Born in Richmond County where he resided as a farmer prior to enlisting in Richmond County at age 30, March 8, 1862. Captured at Falling Waters, Maryland, July 14, 1863. Confined at Baltimore, Maryland. Transferred to Point Lookout, Maryland, August 20, 1863. Released at Point Lookout on August 23, 1863, after taking the Oath of Allegiance.

NICHOLS, JOHN HAMER, Sergeant
Born in Richmond County where he resided as a farmer prior to enlisting in Richmond County at age 29, March 8, 1862. Mustered in as Sergeant. Hospitalized at or near Petersburg, Virginia, October 6, 1862, with typhoid fever. Returned to duty on March 24, 1863. Captured at Gettysburg, Pennsylvania, on or about July 3, 1863. Confined at Fort Delaware, Delaware, on or about July 10, 1863. Died at Fort Delaware on September 21, 1863, of "acute dysentery."

O'BRIEN, DENNIS, Private
Resided in Richmond County where he enlisted at age 39, March 19, 1862. Discharged on May 23, 1862, by reason of being overage.

PARSONS, MUMFORD, Private
Resided in Richmond County where he enlisted at age 24, April 28, 1862, for the war. Hospitalized at Raleigh on or about May 30, 1862. Died in hospital at Raleigh on July 31, 1862, of "chronic diarrhoea." [May have served previously as Private in Company E, 38th Regiment N.C. Troops.]

PATTERSON, WILLIAM D., Private
Born in Moore County and resided in Richmond County where he was by occupation a farmer prior to enlisting in Richmond County at age 22, March 8, 1862. Wounded in the right leg at Gettysburg, Pennsylvania, July 3, 1863. Hospitalized at Richmond, Virginia. Died in hospital at Richmond on October 18, 1863, of "diarrhoea ch[ronic]."

PAUL, JOHN, Private
Born in Anson County and resided in Richmond County where he was by occupation a farmer prior to enlisting in Richmond County at age 47, March 8, 1862. Captured at Falling Waters, Maryland, July 14, 1863. Sent to Baltimore, Maryland. Transferred to Point Lookout, Maryland, August 20, 1863. Died at Point Lookout on or about October 11, 1863, of "diarrhoea chronic."

POOL, SETH, Corporal
Born in Montgomery County and resided in Richmond County where he was by occupation a mechanic prior to enlisting in Richmond County at age 40, March 8, 1862. Mustered in as Private. Promoted to Corporal on April 14, 1862. Discharged on May 23, 1862, by reason of being overage.

POWELL, R. JAMES, 1st Sergeant
Resided in Richmond County and enlisted in Wake County at age 22, May 16, 1862, for the war. Mustered in as Private. Promoted to Sergeant on May 25, 1862. Promoted to 1st Sergeant on June 24, 1862. Transferred to Company H, 44th Regiment N.C. Troops, December 28, 1862.

RICHARDSON, ALEXANDER H., Private
Previously served as Private in Company H, 44th Regiment N.C. Troops. Transferred to this company on April 15, 1862. Died in hospital at Goldsboro on July 8, 1862, of "typhoid fever."

RICHARDSON, LLOYD M., Private
Born in Richmond County where he resided as a farmer

prior to enlisting in Richmond County at age 40, March 8, 1862. Discharged on May 23, 1862, by reason of being overage.

ROBINSON, CHARLES, Private
Resided in Richmond County where he enlisted on April 4, 1862. Wounded and captured at Gettysburg, Pennsylvania, July 3, 1863. Died at Gettysburg on July 5, 1863, of wounds.

ROPER, WILLIAM T., Corporal
Born in Randolph County, Georgia, and resided in Richmond County where he was by occupation a farmer prior to enlisting in Richmond County at age 16, March 19, 1862. Mustered in as Private. Captured at Gettysburg, Pennsylvania, July 3, 1863. Confined at Fort Delaware, Delaware, on or about July 10, 1863. Transferred to Point Lookout, Maryland, October 20, 1863. Paroled at Point Lookout on December 24, 1863. Received at City Point, Virginia, December 28, 1863, for exchange. Returned to duty in March-April, 1864. Promoted to Corporal on April 1, 1864. Present or accounted for until wounded in the head at Burgess' Mill, Virginia, October 27, 1864. Hospitalized at Richmond, Virginia. Furloughed for sixty days on November 29, 1864. Survived the war.

SANDFORD, KELITA, Private
Born in Richmond County where he resided as a farmer prior to enlisting in New Hanover County at age 26, March 14, 1862. Discharged on May 30, 1862, by reason of disability.

SANFORD, DENNIS B., Private
Resided in Richmond County and enlisted in Beaufort County at age 17, April 15, 1863, for the war. Captured at Bristoe Station, Virginia, October 14, 1863. Confined at Old Capitol Prison, Washington, D.C. Transferred to Point Lookout, Maryland, October 27, 1863. Released at Point Lookout on February 26, 1864, after taking the Oath of Allegiance and joining the U.S. Army. Assigned to Company F, 1st Regiment U.S. Volunteer Infantry.

SANFORD, WILLIAM FRANK, Private
Born in Richmond County where he resided as a farmer prior to enlisting in Richmond County at age 21, April 10, 1862. Captured at Gettysburg, Pennsylvania, July 3, 1863. Confined at Fort Delaware, Delaware, on or about July 10, 1863. Paroled at Fort Delaware on July 30, 1863. Received at City Point, Virginia, August 1, 1863, for exchange. Returned to duty in November-December, 1863. Wounded at Cold Harbor, Virginia, on or about June 2, 1864. Returned to duty on or about October 27, 1864. Appointed Chaplain on October 27, 1864, and transferred to the Field and Staff of this regiment.

SCARBOROUGH, WILLIAM S., Private
Resided in Montgomery County and enlisted in Richmond County at age 28, March 19, 1862. Died in hospital at Goldsboro on July 15, 1862. Cause of death not reported.

SEDBERRY, DANIEL W., Private
Born in Montgomery County and resided in Richmond County where he was by occupation a mechanic prior to

enlisting in Richmond County at age 38, March 8, 1862. Reported present on surviving company muster rolls through August, 1863. Captured at Bristoe Station, Virginia, October 14, 1863. Confined at Old Capitol Prison, Washington, D.C. Transferred to Point Lookout, Maryland, October 27, 1863. Paroled at Point Lookout on an unspecified date. Received at Venus Point, Savannah River, Georgia, November 15, 1864, for exchange.

SHANKLE, WILLIS, Private
Born in Stanly County* and resided in Montgomery County where he was by occupation a farmer prior to enlisting in Richmond County at age 37, March 19, 1862. Wounded in the thigh at Gettysburg, Pennsylvania, July 3, 1863. Hospitalized at Richmond, Virginia. Furloughed on August 6, 1863. Returned to duty in November-December, 1863. Captured near Petersburg, Virginia, March 25, 1865. Confined at Point Lookout, Maryland, March 31, 1865. Released at Point Lookout on May 14, 1865, after taking the Oath of Allegiance.

SHEPHERD, CALVIN, Private
Resided in Richmond County where he enlisted at age 19, May 13, 1862, for the war. Variously reported to have been captured at or near Gettysburg, Pennsylvania, on or about July 5, 1863, and at Falling Waters, Maryland, July 14, 1863. Apparently died prior to March 1, 1864. Place, date, and cause of death not reported.

SHEPHERD, ELI, Private
Born in Richmond County where he resided as a farmer prior to enlisting in Richmond County at age 17, March 25, 1862. Captured at Falling Waters, Maryland, July 14, 1863. Sent to Baltimore, Maryland. Transferred to Point Lookout, Maryland, August 16, 1863. Died in hospital at Point Lookout on January 4, 1864, of "chronic diarrhoea."

SHEPHERD, MARTIN, Private
Born in Richmond County where he resided as a farmer prior to enlisting in Richmond County at age 21, April 10, 1862. Reported present on surviving company muster rolls through August, 1864. Reported absent sick in September-December, 1864. Survived the war.

SHEPHERD, NOAH R., Private
Born in Richmond County where he resided as a farmer prior to enlisting in Richmond County at age 27, April 4, 1862. Deserted on June 25, 1863. Returned to duty on July 27, 1863. Died at Lynchburg, Virginia, on an unspecified date (probably prior to November 1, 1863). Cause of death not reported.

SHEPHERD, WILLIAM H., Private
Born in Richmond County where he resided as a farmer prior to enlisting in Richmond County at age 22, April 4, 1862, as a substitute. Transferred to Company E, 38th Regiment N.C. Troops, February 1, 1863.

SHEPHERD, WILSON C., Private
Resided in Richmond County where he enlisted at age 35, February 16, 1863, for the war. Deserted on June 23, 1863. Returned to duty on July 27, 1863. Present or accounted

for until captured at Burgess' Mill, Virginia, October 27, 1864. Confined at Point Lookout, Maryland, October 31, 1864. Released at Point Lookout on June 30, 1865, after taking the Oath of Allegiance.

SMITH, CAMERON, Private
Previously served as Private in Company D, 12th Battalion Virginia Light Artillery. Transferred to this company on November 20, 1862, in exchange for Private Charles A. Barrentine. Reported absent without leave on company records dated November 1, 1862-February 28, 1863. Captured by the enemy in Richmond County on March 7, 1865. Sent to New Bern. Confined at Point Lookout, Maryland, March 30, 1865. Released at Point Lookout on June 19, 1865, after taking the Oath of Allegiance.

SMITH, ENOS, Private
Enlisted in Lenoir County on July 4, 1862, for the war. Reported present on surviving company muster rolls through December, 1864. Surrendered at Appomattox Court House, Virginia, April 9, 1865. Served as a blacksmith during part of the war.

STEIN, COLSON, Private
Resided in South Carolina and enlisted in Richmond County at age 45, May 14, 1862, for the war as a substitute for Robert L. Nichols. Reported absent without leave on or about March 1, 1863. Returned to duty prior to September 1, 1863. Reported under arrest in November-December, 1863. Reason he was arrested not reported. Returned to duty in January-February, 1864. Present or accounted for through December, 1864; however, he was reported absent sick during much of that period.

STRICKLAND, JONATHAN, Private
Born in Richmond County where he resided as a farmer prior to enlisting in Richmond County at age 20, March 8, 1862, as a substitute. Captured at Gettysburg, Pennsylvania, July 3, 1863. Confined at Fort Delaware, Delaware, on or about July 10, 1863. Transferred to Point Lookout, Maryland, October 20, 1863. Hospitalized at Point Lookout on November 10, 1863, with smallpox. Discharged from hospital on December 18, 1863. Released at Point Lookout on February 21, 1864, after taking the Oath of Allegiance and joining the U.S. Army. Assigned to Company E, 1st Regiment U.S. Volunteer Infantry.

SWINK, GEORGE W., Private
Born in Anson County and resided in Montgomery County where he was by occupation a farmer prior to enlisting in Richmond County at age 36, March 8, 1862. Discharged on May 23, 1862, by reason of being overage. Reenlisted in the company in Richmond County on November 8, 1862. Wounded in the right foot and captured at Gettysburg, Pennsylvania, July 3, 1863. Hospitalized at Gettysburg. Transferred to hospital at Baltimore, Maryland, where he arrived on July 25, 1863. Paroled at Baltimore on August 22, 1863. Received at City Point, Virginia, August 24, 1863, for exchange. Returned to duty in November-December, 1863. Captured at Sutherland's Station, Virginia, April 2, 1865. Confined

at Fort Delaware, Delaware, April 4, 1865. Died at Fort Delaware in May, 1865, of "chronic diarrhoea."

TERRY, CHAMP G., Private
Born in Richmond County where he resided as a farmer prior to enlisting in New Hanover County at age 36, March 14, 1862. Deserted on June 18, 1863. Returned to duty in September, 1864. Captured by the enemy at Burgess' Mill, Virginia, October 27, 1864. Confined at Point Lookout, Maryland, October 31, 1864. Paroled at Point Lookout on January 17, 1865. Received at Boulware's Wharf, James River, Virginia, January 21, 1865, for exchange.

THOMAS, BENJAMIN M., Private
Born in Richmond County on April 11, 1829. Resided in Montgomery County where he was by occupation a farmer prior to enlisting in Richmond County on April 4, 1862. Wounded in the back by a piece of shell at Gettysburg, Pennsylvania, July 3, 1863. Hospitalized at Richmond, Virginia. Furloughed on August 6, 1863. Reported on detached duty as a guard at Charlotte in November-December, 1863. Rejoined the company in January-February, 1864. Deserted on July 27, 1864. Returned to duty in September-October, 1864. Captured near Petersburg, Virginia, March 25, 1865. Confined at Point Lookout, Maryland, March 30, 1865. Released at Point Lookout on May 14, 1865, after taking the Oath of Allegiance.

THOMAS, JAMES, Private
Born in Richmond County where he resided as a farmer prior to enlisting in Richmond County at age 39, March 8, 1862. Died in hospital at Wilson on or about January 21, 1863, of "pneumonia."

THOMAS, JAMES K., Private
Resided in Montgomery County and enlisted in Beaufort County at age 18, April 15, 1863, for the war. Died in hospital at Richmond, Virginia, on or about June 14, 1864, of "gastritis."

THOMAS, ROBERT, Private
Resided in Richmond County where he enlisted at age 29, May 3, 1862, for the war. "Left on battlefield" at Gettysburg, Pennsylvania, July 3, 1863, and was believed to have been killed.

THOMPSON, GEORGE, Private
Born in Richmond County where he resided as a farmer prior to enlisting in Richmond County at age 18, April 4, 1862. Reported present on surviving company muster rolls through April, 1864. Killed on a skirmish line near Petersburg, Virginia, June 22, 1864.

THOMPSON, STEPHEN, Private
Born in Richmond County where he resided as a farmer prior to enlisting in Richmond County at age 16, April 4, 1862. Reported present or accounted for on surviving company muster rolls through December, 1864. Surrendered at Appomattox Court House, Virginia, April 9, 1865.

THOMPSON, WILLIAM, Private

Resided in Richmond County and enlisted at age 60, April 10, 1862, as a substitute. Discharged prior to November 1, 1862, by reason of disability.

THROWER, WILLIAM H., Private

Resided in Richmond County and was by occupation a nurseryman prior to enlisting in Richmond County at age 21, May 5, 1862, for the war. Reported missing and presumed killed at Gettysburg, Pennsylvania, July 3, 1863.

TINER, JAMES, Private

Born in Robeson County and resided in Richmond County where he was by occupation a farmer prior to enlisting in Richmond County at age 44, March 19, 1862. Deserted from Camp Mangum, near Raleigh, May 27, 1862. Returned to duty subsequent to February 28, 1863. Deserted on June 18, 1863. Returned to duty on July 25, 1863. Present or accounted for until captured at or near Wilderness, Virginia, on or about May 6, 1864. Confined at Point Lookout, Maryland, May 17, 1864. Transferred to Elmira, New York, August 8, 1864. Died at Elmira on March 13, 1865, of "pneumonia."

WADE, JOHN V., Corporal

Born in Richmond County where he resided as a farmer prior to enlisting in Richmond County at age 32, March 8, 1862. Mustered in as Private. Promoted to Corporal in July, 1862-February, 1863. Captured at Gettysburg, Pennsylvania, on or about July 3, 1863. Confined at Fort Delaware, Delaware, on or about July 10, 1863. Transferred to Point Lookout, Maryland, October 20, 1863. Died at Point Lookout on February 2, 1864, of "chro[nic] diarrhoea."

WATSON, JOHN G., Corporal

Born in Richmond County where he resided as a farmer prior to enlisting in Richmond County at age 40, March 8, 1862. Mustered in as Private. Promoted to Corporal on April 14, 1862. Discharged on May 23, 1862, by reason of being overage.

WEBB, ATLAS L., Private

Resided in Richmond County and was by occupation a farmer prior to enlisting in Richmond County at age 30, March 19, 1862. Captured at Falling Waters, Maryland, July 14, 1863. Sent to Baltimore, Maryland. Transferred to Point Lookout, Maryland, on or about August 16, 1863. Transferred to Elmira, New York, August 16, 1864. Died at Elmira on February 9, 1865, of "chronic diarrhoea."

WEBB, HENRY C., Sergeant

Enlisted in Richmond County on March 9, 1864, for the war. Mustered in as Private. Reported present or accounted for through December, 1864. Promoted to Sergeant subsequent to December 31, 1864. Surrendered at Appomattox Court House, Virginia, April 9, 1865.

WEBB, JOHN L., Private

Born in Richmond County where he resided as a farmer prior to enlisting in Richmond County at age 21, March

17, 1862. Captured at Gettysburg, Pennsylvania, July 3, 1863. Confined at Fort Delaware, Delaware. Transferred to hospital at Chester, Pennsylvania, July 19, 1863. Paroled at Chester on an unspecified date. Received at City Point, Virginia, September 23, 1863, for exchange. Reported absent without leave in January-February, 1864. Returned to duty in March-April, 1864. Captured at or near Wilderness, Virginia, on or about May 6, 1864. Confined at Point Lookout, Maryland, May 17, 1864. Transferred to Elmira, New York, August 8, 1864. Paroled at Elmira and transferred to the James River, Virginia, February 20, 1865, for exchange.

WEBB, LEONARD J., Private

Born in Richmond County where he resided as a farmer prior to enlisting in Richmond County at age 18, April 10, 1862. Reported absent sick on surviving company muster rolls through October, 1863. Returned to duty in November-December, 1863. Died in hospital at Richmond, Virginia, March 26, 1864, of "bronchitis" and "diarrhoea chron[ic]."

WEBB, ROBERT C., Private

Born in Richmond County where he resided as a farmer prior to enlisting in Richmond County at age 24, April 10, 1862. Captured at Gettysburg, Pennsylvania, July 3, 1863. Confined at Fort Delaware, Delaware, on or about July 10, 1863. Died at Fort Delaware on or about September 21, 1863, of "chronic dysentery."

WEBB, WILLIAM C., Sergeant

Born in Richmond County where he resided as a farmer prior to enlisting in Richmond County at age 18, April 10, 1862. Mustered in as Private. Promoted to Sergeant in November-December, 1864. Reported present or accounted for on surviving company muster rolls through December, 1864. Surrendered at Appomattox Court House, Virginia, April 9, 1865.

WOODARD, THOMAS, Private

Born in Richmond County where he resided prior to enlisting in Richmond County at age 22, October 17, 1862, for the war. Wounded and captured at Gettysburg, Pennsylvania, July 3, 1863. Confined at Fort Delaware, Delaware, on or about July 10, 1863. Paroled at Fort Delaware on July 30, 1863. Received at City Point, Virginia, August 1, 1863, for exchange. Died in hospital at Petersburg, Virginia, August 22, 1863, of "febris typhoides."

YARBROUGH, DAVID B., Private

Resided in Montgomery County and was by occupation a farmer prior to enlisting in Montgomery County at age 43, December 3, 186[4], for the war. Wounded in the left leg at Hatcher's Run, Virginia, on or about February 6, 1865. Hospitalized at Richmond, Virginia. Captured in hospital at Richmond on April 3, 1865. Transferred to Libby Prison, Richmond, on an unspecified date. Transferred to Newport News, Virginia, April 23, 1865. Released at Newport News on June 15, 1865, after taking the Oath of Allegiance.

COMPANY F

This company, known as the "Wilkes Grays," was raised in Wilkes County and enlisted at Wilkesboro in March-April, 1862. It was mustered into state service at Camp Mangum, near Raleigh, on April 28, 1862, and was assigned to the 52nd Regiment N.C. Troops as Company F. After joining this regiment the company functioned as a part of the regiment, and its history for the remainder of the war is reported as a part of the regimental history.

The information contained in the following roster was compiled primarily from a company muster-in and descriptive roll dated April 28, 1862, and from company muster rolls for May 1-June 30, 1862, and July 1, 1863-December 31, 1864. No company muster rolls were located for July 1, 1862-June 30, 1863, or for the period after December 31, 1864. Valuable information was obtained from primary records such as the North Carolina adjutant general's *Roll of Honor*, discharge certificates, medical records, prisoner of war records, *The War of the Rebellion: A Compilation of the Official Records of the Union and Confederate Armies*, militia records, newspaper casualty lists and obituaries, Confederate pension applications filed with the state of North Carolina, and the 1860 federal census of North Carolina. Secondary sources such as postwar rosters and histories, cemetery records, the *Confederate Veteran*, published genealogies, and records of the United Daughters of the Confederacy also provided useful information.

OFFICERS

CAPTAINS

PARKS, MARCUS A.
Previously served as 1st Lieutenant of Company B, 1st Regiment N.C. State Troops. Appointed Captain of this company to rank from March 14, 1862. Appointed Major on April 18, 1862, and transferred to the Field and Staff of this regiment. Later served as Colonel of this regiment.

FOSTER, NATHANIEL A.
Born in Wilkes County where he resided as a merchant prior to enlisting in Wilkes County at age 30. Appointed 1st Lieutenant on March 14, 1862. Promoted to Captain on April 18, 1862. Captured at Falling Waters, Maryland, July 14, 1863. Confined at Old Capitol Prison, Washington, D.C. Transferred to Johnson's Island, Ohio, August 8, 1863. Transferred to Point Lookout, Maryland, April 22, 1864. Arrived at Point Lookout on April 26, 1864. Transferred back to Old Capitol Prison on August 9, 1864. Transferred to Fort Delaware, Delaware, August 11, 1864. Released at Fort Delaware on June 12, 1865, after taking the Oath of Allegiance.

CARMICHAEL, WILLIAM W.
Born in Wilkes County where he resided as a merchant prior to enlisting in Wilkes County at age 18. Appointed

2nd Lieutenant on March 14, 1862. Promoted to 1st Lieutenant on April 18, 1862. Reported on duty as acting commander of this company in March-April and July-October, 1864. Reported on duty as acting commander of the regiment in July-October, 1864. Promoted to Captain subsequent to December 31, 1864. Captured at Sutherland's Station, Virginia, April 2, 1865. Confined at Old Capitol Prison, Washington, D.C. Transferred to Johnson's Island, Ohio, April 9, 1865. Released at Johnson's Island on June 18, 1865, after taking the Oath of Allegiance.

LIEUTENANTS

HALL, JOSEPH GAITHER, 3rd Lieutenant
Born in Iredell County and resided in Wilkes County where he was by occupation a merchant prior to enlisting in Wilkes County at age 18, March 14, 1862. Mustered in as 1st Sergeant. Appointed 3rd Lieutenant on April 19, 1862. Reported present on surviving company muster rolls through August, 1864. Wounded in the right arm (flesh) at or near Jones' Farm, Virginia, on or about October 1, 1864. Hospitalized at Richmond, Virginia. Returned to duty in November-December, 1864.

PARLEIR, JACOB J., 2nd Lieutenant
Born in Wilkes County where he resided as a farmer prior to enlisting in Wilkes County at age 23. Appointed 3rd Lieutenant on March 14, 1862. Promoted to 2nd Lieutenant on April 15, 1862. Reported present or accounted for on surviving company muster rolls through December, 1864. Resigned on January 23, 1865, by reason of his desire to serve as a Private in the 9th Regiment N.C. State Troops (1st Regiment N.C. Cavalry). Resignation accepted on February 4, 1865. [No evidence was located of later service by this officer in the 9th Regiment N.C. State Troops.]

NONCOMMISSIONED OFFICERS AND PRIVATES

ABSHER, ABRAM, Private
Resided in Wilkes County and was by occupation a farmer prior to enlisting at Camp French, near Petersburg, Virginia, at age 33, September 22, 1862, for the war. Wounded at Gettysburg, Pennsylvania, July 3, 1863. Deserted from an unspecified hospital on August 10, 1863. Returned to duty on September 29, 1863. Present or accounted for through December, 1864.

ABSHER, ADAM, Private
Resided in Wilkes County and was by occupation a farmer prior to enlisting at Camp French, near Petersburg, Virginia, at age 32, September 22, 1862, for the war. Wounded at Globe Tavern, Virginia, August 21, 1864. Hospitalized at Richmond, Virginia, where he died on or about September 9, 1864, of wounds.

ABSHER, ALFRED, Private
Resided in Wilkes County and enlisted at Camp French, near Petersburg, Virginia, at age 32, September 22, 1862, for the war. Died in hospital at Goldsboro prior to November 1, 1863. Date and cause of death not reported.

ABSHER, BENJAMIN F., Private
Resided in Wilkes County and enlisted at Camp French, near Petersburg, Virginia, at age 28, September 22, 1862, for the war. Captured at Falling Waters, Maryland, July 14, 1863. Confined at Old Capitol Prison, Washington, D.C. Transferred to Baltimore, Maryland. Paroled at Baltimore on August 23, 1863. Received at City Point, Virginia, August 24, 1863, for exchange. Hospitalized at Charlottesville, Virginia, November 17, 1863, with pneumonia. Furloughed for sixty days on January 5, 1864. Reported absent without leave in March-August, 1864. Returned to duty on October 4, 1864. Captured by the enemy at Burgess' Mill, Virginia, October 27, 1864. Confined at Point Lookout, Maryland, October 31, 1864. Paroled at Point Lookout on or about March 17, 1865. Received at Boulware's Wharf, James River, Virginia, March 19, 1865, for exchange.

ABSHER, LEWIS W., _____
North Carolina pension records indicate that he served in this company.

ABSHER, TOBIAS L., Private
Resided in Wilkes County and enlisted at Camp French, near Petersburg, Virginia, at age 22, September 22, 1862, for the war. Reported absent wounded in May, 1864. Battle in which wounded not reported. Returned to duty in September-October, 1864. Captured at Sutherland's Station, Virginia, April 2, 1865. Confined at Point Lookout, Maryland, April 4, 1865. Released at Point Lookout on June 23, 1865, after taking the Oath of Allegiance.

ABSHIRE, OWEN J., Private
Resided in Wilkes County and was by occupation a farmer prior to enlisting at age 24, September 22, 1862, for the war. Killed at Goldsboro on December 17, 1862.

ADAMS, CALVIN, Private
Resided in Wilkes County and was by occupation a farmer prior to enlisting at Camp Holmes, near Raleigh, at age 52, November 4, 1863, for the war. Died "in camp" on December 16, 1863. Cause of death not reported.

ADAMS, CHARLES, Private
Born in Wilkes County and resided in Wilkes or Iredell County where he was by occupation a farmer prior to enlisting in Wilkes County at age 20, April 5, 1862. Reported absent without leave in May-June, 1862. Returned to duty on an unspecified date. Deserted on June 20, 1863. Returned to duty on October 7, 1863. Captured at or near Wilderness, Virginia, on or about May 6, 1864. Confined at Point Lookout, Maryland, May 17, 1864. Transferred to Elmira, New York, August 8, 1864. Released at Elmira on June 12, 1865, after taking the Oath of Allegiance.

ADAMS, GENERAL J., Private
Born in Wilkes County where he resided as a farmer prior to enlisting in Wilkes County at age 22, April 5, 1862. Reported absent without leave in May-June, 1862. Reported absent sick in November-December, 1863. Died in hospital at Charlottesville, Virginia, January 7, 1864, of "typhoid fever."

ADAMS, JACKSON, Private
Place and date of enlistment not reported (probably enlisted in July-December, 1862). Wounded at Goldsboro on December 17, 1862. Died of wounds. Place and date of death not reported.

ADAMS, JOHN M., Private
Enlisted at Camp Holmes, near Raleigh, November 4, 1863, for the war. Deserted on April 18, 1864.

ADAMS, JOSEPH H., Private
Resided in Wilkes County and was by occupation a farmer prior to enlisting at Petersburg, Virginia, at age 38, December 19, 1864, for the war. Captured at Sutherland's Station, Virginia, April 2, 1865. Confined at Point Lookout, Maryland, April 13, 1865. Released at Point Lookout on June 23, 1865, after taking the Oath of Allegiance.

ANDERSON, AUSBURN, Private
Resided in Wilkes County and enlisted at Camp French, near Petersburg, Virginia, at age 33, September 22, 1862, for the war. Wounded and captured at Gettysburg, Pennsylvania, July 3, 1863. Hospitalized at Chester, Pennsylvania. Paroled at Chester on or about September 17, 1863. Received at City Point, Virginia, September 23, 1863, for exchange. Returned to duty in January-February, 1864. Present or accounted for through August, 1864. Died in hospital at Richmond, Virginia, October 7, 1864, of "dysenteria acuta."

BILLINGS, HIRAM, Private
Resided in Wilkes County and enlisted at age 19, September 22, 1862, for the war. No further records.

BISHOP, HORTON A., Private
Born in Wilkes County where he resided as a farmer prior to enlisting in Wilkes County at age 19, March 14, 1862. Died in hospital at Lynchburg, Virginia, August 16, 1863, of "febris typhoides."

BISHOP, LARKIN, Private
Born in Wilkes County where he resided as a farmer prior to enlisting in Wilkes County at age 21, March 14, 1862. Captured at Falling Waters, Maryland, July 14, 1863. Confined at Old Capitol Prison, Washington, D.C. Transferred to Point Lookout, Maryland, August 8, 1863. Died in hospital at Point Lookout on or about November 20, 1863, of "diarrhoea chronic."

BOWLES, ELAM, Private
Born in Iredell County and resided in Wilkes County where he was by occupation a farmer prior to enlisting in Wilkes County at age 19, April 5, 1862. Wounded at or near Bristoe Station, Virginia, on or about October 14,

1863. Hospitalized at Charlottesville, Virginia. Returned to duty on November 5, 1863. Present or accounted for through December, 1864. Captured at Sutherland's Station, Virginia, April 2, 1865. Confined at Point Lookout, Maryland, April 4, 1865. Released at Point Lookout on June 23, 1865, after taking the Oath of Allegiance.

BOWLES, SIMPSON, Private
Born in Iredell County and resided in Wilkes County where he was by occupation a farmer prior to enlisting in Wilkes County at age 24, April 5, 1862. Wounded at Gettysburg, Pennsylvania, July 3, 1863. Returned to duty in September-October, 1863. Captured at Bristoe Station, Virginia, October 14, 1863. Confined at Old Capitol Prison, Washington, D.C. Transferred to Point Lookout, Maryland, October 27, 1863. Paroled at Point Lookout on February 13, 1865. Received at Cox's Wharf, James River, Virginia, on or about February 15, 1865, for exchange.

BROOKS, JAMES M., Private
Born in Iredell County on November 2, 1844, and was by occupation a farmer prior to enlisting at Richmond, Virginia, January 8, 1864, for the war. Died on May 27, 1864. Place and cause of death not reported.

BROOKS, JAMES W., Private
Born in Wilkes County where he resided as a farmer prior to enlisting in Wilkes County at age 35, March 14, 1862. Wounded in the left thigh (flesh) at Goldsboro on December 17, 1862. Returned to duty on an unspecified date. Deserted on June 28, 1863. Returned to duty on October 3, 1863. Wounded in the left knee ("bursting the knee cap") at Spotsylvania Court House, Virginia, May 10, 1864. Reported absent wounded through December, 1864. Survived the war.

BROOKS, JOHN N., Private
Enlisted at Camp Holmes, near Raleigh, at age 19, November 12, 1863, for the war. Hospitalized at Farmville, Virginia, April 30, 1864, with chronic diarrhoea. Furloughed for sixty days on June 3, 1864. Reported absent without leave in July-December, 1864. Survived the war.

BROOKS, NATHAN MATTHEW, Private
Born in Wilkes County where he resided as a farmer prior to enlisting in Wilkes County at age 35, March 14, 1862. Wounded at Goldsboro on December 17, 1862. No further records.

BROOKS, ROBERT P., Private
Born in Wilkes County where he resided as a farmer prior to enlisting in Wilkes County at age 25, March 14, 1862. Deserted on June 20, 1863. Returned to duty on October 19, 1863. Captured at or near Wilderness, Virginia, on or about May 6, 1864. Confined at Point Lookout, Maryland, May 17, 1864. Transferred to Elmira, New York, August 8, 1864. Paroled at Elmira and transferred to the James River, Virginia, February 20, 1865, for exchange. Died while en route to the James River. Place, date, and cause of death not reported.

BROTHERTON, JOHN M. C., Private
Resided in Wilkes County and was by occupation a farmer prior to enlisting at Camp Holmes, near Raleigh, at age 38, November 26, 1863, for the war. Transferred to Company C, 26th Regiment N.C. Troops, March 1, 1864.

BROWN, AARON P., Private
Resided in Wilkes County and was by occupation a farmer prior to enlisting at Camp Holmes, near Raleigh, at age 41, October 17, 1863, for the war. Deserted on December 9, 1863. Died in hospital at Gordonsville, Virginia, January 28, 1864, of "typhoid pneumonia."

BROWN, ABRAM, Private
Born in Wilkes County where he resided as a farmer prior to enlisting in Wilkes County at age 23, March 14, 1862. Deserted on June 20, 1863. Returned to duty on October 3, 1863. Wounded in the left side at Spotsylvania Court House, Virginia, May 10, 1864. Reported absent wounded or absent sick through December, 1864. Survived the war.

BROWN, BENJAMIN RUFUS, Corporal
Born in Wilkes County where he resided as a farmer prior to enlisting in Wilkes County at age 23, March 14, 1862. Mustered in as Private. Promoted to Corporal on November 1, 1862. Died in hospital at Petersburg, Virginia, February 18, 1863, of "ty[phoid] fever."

BROWN, ELIJAH, Private
Resided in Wilkes County and enlisted at Camp French, near Petersburg, Virginia, at age 22, September 22, 1862, for the war. Deserted on November 14, 1862. Returned to duty on January 13, 1864. Captured at Burgess' Mill, Virginia, October 27, 1864. Confined at Point Lookout, Maryland, October 31, 1864. Died at Point Lookout on December 19, 1864, of "chronic diarrhoea."

BROWN, G. JACKSON, Private
Resided in Wilkes County and enlisted at age 25, September 22, 1862, for the war. Discharged in November, 1862, after providing a substitute.

BROWN, GEORGE H., Private
Resided in Wilkes County and enlisted at Camp French, near Petersburg, Virginia, at age 25, September 22, 1862, for the war. Deserted on November 14, 1862. Returned to duty on November 27, 1863. Wounded in the eye and left cheek at Spotsylvania Court House, Virginia, May 10, 1864. Returned to duty on an unspecified date. Wounded in the left leg at or near Jones' Farm, Virginia, on or about October 1, 1864. Hospitalized at Richmond, Virginia. Furloughed for forty days on October 26, 1864. Survived the war.

BROWN, JAMES W., Private
Resided in Wilkes County and enlisted at Camp French, near Petersburg, Virginia, at age 22, September 22, 1862, for the war. Deserted on November 14, 1862. Returned to duty on October 8, 1863. Reported present through December, 1864. Captured at Farmville, Virginia, April 6, 1865. Confined at Point Lookout, Maryland, April 14, 1865. Released at Point Lookout on June 23, 1865, after taking the Oath of Allegiance.

BROWN, JESSE F., Private
Born in Wilkes County where he resided as a farmer prior to enlisting in Wilkes County at age 31, March 14, 1862. Reported present or accounted for on surviving company muster rolls through December, 1864. Captured at Sutherland's Station, Virginia, April 2, 1865. Confined at Point Lookout, Maryland, April 4, 1865. Released at Point Lookout on June 23, 1865, after taking the Oath of Allegiance.

BROWN, JOHN J., Private
Resided in Wilkes County and enlisted at age 24, September 22, 1862, for the war. Died in camp on the Blackwater River, Virginia, December 13, 1862. Cause of death not reported.

BROWN, JOHN L., Private
Resided in Wilkes County and enlisted at Camp French, near Petersburg, Virginia, at age 27, September 22, 1862, for the war. Deserted on November 14, 1862. Returned to duty on January 13, 1864. Captured at or near Wilderness, Virginia, on or about May 6, 1864. Confined at Point Lookout, Maryland, May 17, 1864. Died at Point Lookout on July 28, 1864. Cause of death not reported.

BROWN, JOHN T., Private
Born in Wilkes County where he resided as a farmer prior to enlisting in Wilkes County at age 28, April 5, 1862. Wounded at Goldsboro on December 17, 1862. Listed as a deserter on an unspecified date. Returned to duty on October 10, 1863. Captured at or near Wilderness, Virginia, on or about May 6, 1864. Confined at Point Lookout, Maryland, May 17, 1864. Transferred to Elmira, New York, August 8, 1864. Died at Elmira on February 9, 1865, of "pneumonia."

BROWN, REUBEN, Private
Resided in Wilkes County and enlisted at age 20, September 22, 1862, for the war. Wounded in the back by a shell at Goldsboro on December 17, 1862. Dropped from the rolls of the company prior to September 1, 1863. Reason he was dropped not reported. Survived the war.

BROWN, WILLIAM B., Private
Resided in Wilkes County and enlisted at Camp French, near Petersburg, Virginia, at age 18, September 22, 1862, for the war. Hospitalized at or near Petersburg on October 27, 1862, with typhoid fever. Returned to duty on November 20, 1862. Deserted on June 20, 1863. Returned to duty on or about September 25, 1864. Captured near Petersburg on March 25, 1865. Confined at Point Lookout, Maryland, March 27, 1865. Released at Point Lookout on June 23, 1865, after taking the Oath of Allegiance.

BROWN, WILLIAM H., Private
Resided in Wilkes County and enlisted at age 19, September 22, 1862, for the war. Killed at Goldsboro on December 17, 1862.

BROYHILL, JOHNSON, Private
Born in Wilkes County where he resided as a farmer prior to enlisting in Wilkes County at age 17, April 5, 1862.

Reported present or accounted for on surviving company muster rolls through April, 1864. Deserted to the enemy on or about June 11, 1864. Sent to Fort Monroe, Virginia. Released on June 27, 1864, after taking the Oath of Allegiance.

BULLIS, DAVID W., Private
Born in Wilkes County where he resided as a farmer prior to enlisting in Wilkes County at age 21, March 14, 1862. Wounded and captured at Gettysburg, Pennsylvania, July 1, 1863. Hospitalized at Gettysburg. Transferred to hospital at Davids Island, New York Harbor, where he arrived on July 19, 1863. Died at Davids Island on August 3, 1863, of "pyaemia."

BULLIS, JAMES SIDNEY, Private
Born in Wilkes County where he resided as a farmer prior to enlisting in Wilkes County at age 35, March 14, 1862. Died in hospital at Raleigh on June 14, 1862, of "typhoid fever."

BUMGARNER, SIMEON N., Private
Born in Wilkes County where he resided as a farmer prior to enlisting in Wilkes County at age 26, March 14, 1862. Died in hospital at Petersburg, Virginia, August 10, 1862, of "febris typhoides."

BURCHETT, ISHAM, Private
Born in Wilkes County where he resided as a blacksmith prior to enlisting in Wilkes County at age 32, March 14, 1862. Reported present or accounted for on surviving company muster rolls through December, 1864. Reported on detached duty as a blacksmith during much of that period. Survived the war. [North Carolina pension records indicate that he was severely shocked by the explosion of a shell at Gettysburg, Pennsylvania, July 2, 1863, and the hearing in his right ear was almost entirely destroyed.]

BYERS, JAMES A., Private
Resided in Wilkes County and enlisted at age 34, September 22, 1862, for the war. No further records.

BYERS, JAMES S., Private
Born in Wilkes County where he resided as a farmer prior to enlisting in Wilkes County at age 35, April 5, 1862. Deserted on June 20, 1863. Returned to duty on October 11, 1863. Present or accounted for through December, 1864.

CAIN, ANDERSON, Corporal
Born in Orange County and resided in Wilkes County where he was by occupation a farmer prior to enlisting in Wilkes County at age 23, March 14, 1862. Mustered in as Private. Promoted to Corporal in July-August, 1863. Wounded in the right leg at Jones' Farm, Virginia, October 1, 1864. Right leg amputated. Hospitalized at Richmond, Virginia. Furloughed for sixty days on November 29, 1864. Survived the war.

CAMPBELL, WILLIAM F., Private
Born in Alexander County* where he resided as a farmer prior to enlisting in Wilkes County at age 24, April 5,

1862. Mustered in as Sergeant. Reduced to ranks prior to July 1, 1862. Wounded at Goldsboro on December 17, 1862. Reported absent without leave in July-December, 1863. Discharged on January 8, 1864. Reason discharged not reported.

CARLTON, CHARLES, Private
Born in Wilkes County where he resided as a farmer prior to enlisting in Wilkes County at age 43, March 14, 1862. Mustered in as Sergeant. Reduced to ranks prior to May 24, 1862. Discharged on May 24, 1862, by reason of being overage.

CARLTON, JAMES S., Private
Previously served as Private in Company K, 53rd Regiment N.C. Troops. Transferred to this company on September 13, 1863. Present or accounted for until he died in hospital at Richmond, Virginia, on or about October 27, 1864, of "phthisis pulmonalis."

CARLTON, P. J., Private
Place and date of enlistment not reported (probably enlisted in January-March, 1865). Hospitalized at Richmond, Virginia, March 24, 1865, with phthisis pulmonalis. Captured in hospital at Richmond on April 3, 1865. Died in hospital at Richmond on or about April 14, 1865, of "remittent fever."

CARLTON, THOMAS C., Corporal
Born in Wilkes County where he resided as a farmer prior to enlisting in Wilkes County at age 21, March 14, 1862. Mustered in as Private. Hospitalized at or near Petersburg, Virginia, October 11, 1862, with typhoid fever. Furloughed for forty days on December 9, 1862. Returned to duty on an unspecified date. Promoted to Corporal on September 23, 1863. Wounded slightly in the left hand at Jones' Farm, Virginia, on or about September 30, 1864. Returned to duty in November-December, 1864.

CAUDILL, ABNER, Private
Born in Wilkes County where he resided as a farmer prior to enlisting in Wilkes County at age 18, March 14, 1862. Captured at Falling Waters, Maryland, July 14, 1863. Confined at Old Capitol Prison, Washington, D.C. Transferred to Point Lookout, Maryland, August 8, 1863. Released at Point Lookout on February 22, 1864, after taking the Oath of Allegiance and joining the U.S. Army. Assigned to Company F, 1st Regiment U.S. Volunteer Infantry.

CHAPEL, MARION C., Private
Born in Surry County and resided in Wilkes County where he was by occupation a farmer prior to enlisting in Wilkes County at age 23, March 14, 1862. Reported present or accounted for on surviving company muster rolls through December, 1864. Reported absent sick during most of that period. Surrendered at Appomattox Court House, Virginia, April 9, 1865.

CHAPPELL, SOLOMON C., Private
Born in Yadkin County* and resided in Wilkes County where he was by occupation a farmer prior to enlisting in Wilkes County at age 19, April 5, 1862. Wounded in the

right side and captured at Gettysburg, Pennsylvania, July 3, 1863. Hospitalized at Gettysburg. Transferred to hospital at Davids Island, New York Harbor, where he arrived on or about July 20, 1863. Paroled at Davids Island and transferred to City Point, Virginia, where he was received on September 8, 1863, for exchange. Returned to duty in January-February, 1864. Reported present through December, 1864. Captured at or near Amelia Court House, Virginia, April 4, 1865. Confined at Point Lookout, Maryland, April 13, 1865. Released at Point Lookout on June 24, 1865, after taking the Oath of Allegiance.

CHURCH, GABRIEL, Private
Resided in Wilkes County and enlisted at Camp Johnston, near Kinston, at age 47, in June, 1862, for the war as a substitute for A. Chatham. Reported present in May-June, 1862. Reported absent sick in September-October, 1863. Reported absent without leave in November-December, 1863. Reported absent sick in May-June, 1864. Reported absent without leave in July-December, 1864.

CHURCH, JAMES WILSON, Private
Born in Wilkes County where he resided as a farmer prior to enlisting in Wilkes County at age 26, March 14, 1862. Hospitalized at or near Petersburg, Virginia, September 24, 1862, with bronchitis. Returned to duty on November 20, 1862. Captured at Falling Waters, Maryland, July 14, 1863. Confined at Point Lookout, Maryland. Paroled at Point Lookout on March 3, 1864. Received at City Point, Virginia, March 6, 1864, for exchange. Reported absent without leave in May-August, 1864. Returned to duty in September-October, 1864. Captured at Sutherland's Station, Virginia, April 2, 1865. Confined at Point Lookout on April 4, 1865. Released on June 24, 1865, after taking the Oath of Allegiance.

CHURCH, JOHN A., Private
Born in Wilkes County where he resided as a farmer prior to enlisting in Wilkes County at age 21, March 14, 1862. Reported present or accounted for on surviving company muster rolls through June, 1864. Captured "while scouting" on or about August 10, 1864. Confined at Point Lookout, Maryland, August 22, 1864. Paroled at Point Lookout on March 14, 1865. Received at Boulware's Wharf, James River, Virginia, March 16, 1865, for exchange. Survived the war. [North Carolina pension records indicate that he was wounded on July 3, 1864.]

CHURCH, WILLIAM H., Corporal
Born in Wilkes County where he resided as a farmer prior to enlisting in Wilkes County at age 17, March 14, 1862. Mustered in as Private. Wounded in the right thigh and captured at Gettysburg, Pennsylvania, on or about July 3, 1863. Hospitalized at Gettysburg. Transferred to Baltimore, Maryland. Transferred to Davids Island, New York Harbor. Paroled at Davids Island and transferred to City Point, Virginia, where he was received on September 8, 1863, for exchange. Returned to duty in January-February, 1864. Promoted to Corporal on March 1, 1864. Captured at or near Wilderness, Virginia, on or about May 6, 1864. Confined at Point Lookout, Maryland, May 17, 1864. Transferred to Elmira, New York, August 8, 1864. Released at Elmira on June 11, 1865, after taking the Oath of Allegiance.

COCKERHAM, ELIJAH, _____
North Carolina pension records indicate that he served in this company.

COCKERHAM, FRANKLIN, Private
Resided in Wilkes County and enlisted at Orange Court House, Virginia, at age 15, March 10, 1864, for the war. Wounded at Globe Tavern, Virginia, August 21, 1864. Reported absent wounded through December, 1864. Returned to duty prior to April 2, 1865, when he was captured at Sutherland's Station, Virginia. Confined at Point Lookout, Maryland, April 4, 1865. Released at Point Lookout on June 24, 1865, after taking the Oath of Allegiance.

COCKERHAM, JOSEPH, Private
Born in Wilkes County where he resided as a farmer prior to enlisting in Wilkes County at age 35, March 14, 1862. Captured at Bristoe Station, Virginia, October 14, 1863. Confined at Old Capitol Prison, Washington, D.C. Transferred to Point Lookout, Maryland, October 27, 1863. Released at Point Lookout on February 22, 1864, after taking the Oath of Allegiance and joining the U.S. Army. Unit to which assigned not reported.

CROUSE, HAMPTON, Private
Resided in Wilkes County and was by occupation a day laborer prior to enlisting at age 30, April 5, 1862. Reported present in May-June, 1862. Dropped from the rolls of the company (probably for desertion) in July-December, 1863. Returned to duty in January-February, 1864, and was court-martialed. Deserted on July 20, 1864. Returned to duty subsequent to December 31, 1864. Captured near Petersburg, Virginia, March 25, 1865. Confined at Point Lookout, Maryland, March 27, 1865. Released at Point Lookout on June 24, 1865, after taking the Oath of Allegiance.

CURRY, SAMUEL, Private
Born in Wilkes County where he resided as a farmer prior to enlisting at Camp French, near Petersburg, Virginia, at age 32, September 22, 1862, for the war. Reported absent on expired furlough on August 27, 1863. Reported absent sick in September-October, 1863. Discharged on November 30, 1863, by reason of "phthisis pulmonalis."

DANCY, JAMES M., Private
Born in Wilkes County where he resided as a farmer prior to enlisting in Wilkes County at age 21, March 14, 1862. Died in hospital at Petersburg, Virginia, November 11, 1862, of "febris typhoides."

DARNALL, JOHN S., Private
Resided in Wilkes County and enlisted at age 14, April 5, 1862. Discharged at Camp Mangum, near Raleigh, prior to July 1, 1862, by reason of being underage.

DARNALL, JOSEPH M., Private
Born in Wilkes County where he resided as a farmer prior to enlisting in Wilkes County at age 23, March 14, 1862. Wounded at Gettysburg, Pennsylvania, July 3, 1863. Reported absent wounded until August 28, 1863, when he was reported absent without leave. Survived the war.

DARNALL, MORGAN S., Private
Born in Wilkes County and was by occupation a farmer prior to enlisting in Wilkes County at age 15, April 5, 1862. Discharged on June 2, 1862, by reason of being underage.

DAVIDSON, JOHN P., Private
Resided in Alexander County and enlisted in February, 1865, for the war. Captured at Sutherland's Station, Virginia, April 2, 1865. Confined at Point Lookout, Maryland, April 4, 1865. Released at Point Lookout on June 26, 1865, after taking the Oath of Allegiance.

DAVIS, ELIJAH, Private
Born in Wilkes County where he resided as a farmer prior to enlisting in Wilkes County at age 35, April 5, 1862. Wounded in the left leg at Goldsboro on December 17, 1862. Left leg amputated. Discharged on December 7, 1863, by reason of disability.

DILLARD, JACOB, Private
Born in Ashe County and resided in Wilkes County where he was by occupation a farmer prior to enlisting in Wilkes County at age 35, April 15, 1862. Reported present or accounted for on surviving company muster rolls through February, 1864. Hospitalized at Richmond, Virginia, March 18, 1864, with phthisis pulmonalis. Furloughed for sixty days on April 27, 1864. Reported absent without leave in July-August, 1864. Reported absent sick in September-October, 1864. Returned to duty in November-December, 1864. Captured at Sutherland's Station, Virginia, April 2, 1865. Confined at Point Lookout, Maryland, April 4, 1865. Released at Point Lookout on June 11, 1865, after taking the Oath of Allegiance.

DIMETT, JOEL, Private
Resided in Wilkes County and enlisted at Petersburg, Virginia, November 8, 1864, for the war. Captured at Sutherland's Station, Virginia, April 2, 1865. Confined at Point Lookout, Maryland, April 4, 1865. Released on June 12, 1865, after taking the Oath of Allegiance.

DOWEL, COLUMBUS F., Private
Born in Yadkin County* and resided in Wilkes County where he was by occupation a farmer prior to enlisting in Wilkes County at age 21, March 14, 1862. Hospitalized at or near Petersburg, Virginia, February 4, 1863, with intermittent fever. Returned to duty on April 1, 1863. Reported absent without leave on September 15, 1863. Returned to duty on October 5, 1863. Present or accounted for through June, 1864. Deserted on an unspecified date. Apprehended prior to July 17, 1864, when he was confined at Castle Thunder Prison, Richmond, Virginia. Reported absent sick or absent under arrest through September, 1864. Hospitalized at Richmond on October 29, 1864 (probably with chronic diarrhoea). Returned to duty on January 12, 1865. No further records.

DOWEL, EMERAL, Private
Resided in Wilkes County and was by occupation a farm laborer prior to enlisting in Wilkes County at age 38, April 5, 1862. Reported absent without leave in May-June, 1862. Dropped from the rolls of the company on an unspecified date (probably in the summer of 1862).

DUNCAN, JAMES W., Private
Born in Yancey County and resided in Wilkes County where he was by occupation a farmer prior to enlisting in Wilkes County at age 17, March 14, 1862. Wounded at Goldsboro on December 17, 1862. Returned to duty prior to September 1, 1863. Wounded near Petersburg, Virginia, June 19, 1864. Returned to duty in July-August, 1864. Captured at Amelia Court House, Virginia, April 4, 1865. Confined at Point Lookout, Maryland, April 13, 1865. Released at Point Lookout on June 11, 1865, after taking the Oath of Allegiance.

ELLER, FRANCIS, Private
Resided in Wilkes County and enlisted at Camp French, near Petersburg, Virginia, at age 25, September 22, 1862, for the war. Transferred to Company K, 53rd Regiment N.C. Troops, September 13, 1863.

ELLIOTT, JONATHAN CEBERN, _____
North Carolina pension records indicate that he served in this company.

EMERSON, JOHN W., Sergeant
Born in Rowan County and resided in Wilkes County where he was by occupation a farmer prior to enlisting in Wilkes County at age 18, April 5, 1862. Mustered in as Private. Promoted to Corporal in November, 1862. Wounded at Gettysburg, Pennsylvania, July 3, 1863. Returned to duty prior to September 1, 1863. Promoted to Sergeant on March 1, 1864. Wounded in the left elbow at Jones' Farm, Virginia, on or about October 1, 1864. Hospitalized at Richmond, Virginia. Furloughed for thirty days on October 13, 1864. Returned to duty subsequent to December 31, 1864. Wounded in the thigh near Petersburg, Virginia, March 25, 1865. Hospitalized at Richmond. Captured in hospital at Richmond on April 3, 1865. Transferred to Point Lookout, Maryland, May 2, 1865. Released at Point Lookout on June 26, 1865, after taking the Oath of Allegiance.

EVANS, JOHN, Private
Born in Wilkes County where he resided as a farmer prior to enlisting in Wilkes County at age 25, March 14, 1862. Wounded at Gettysburg, Pennsylvania, July 1, 1863. Returned to duty in September-October, 1863. Hospitalized at Richmond, Virginia, May 16, 1864, with a gunshot wound of the knee. Place and date wounded not reported. Died in hospital at Raleigh on June 25, 1864, of "diarrhoea chronic."

FAW, MARTIN, Private
Resided in Wilkes County and was by occupation a farmer prior to enlisting in Wake County at age 38, October 17, 1863, for the war. Present or accounted for until he was discharged on October 14, 1864. Reason discharged not reported.

FAW, WILLIAM H., Private
Resided in Wilkes County and was by occupation a farmer. Place and date of enlistment not reported (probably enlisted in January, 1865). Was about 18 years of age at time of enlistment. Wounded in the right leg at Hatcher's Run, Virginia, February 5, 1865. Hospitalized

at Richmond, Virginia. Furloughed for sixty days on or about March 8, 1865.

FOSTER, ACHILLES E., Private
Resided in Wilkes County and enlisted at Camp French, near Petersburg, Virginia, at age 32, September 22, 1862, for the war. Wounded at Goldsboro on December 17, 1862. Deserted on June 20, 1863. Returned to duty on October 1, 1863. Wounded at Spotsylvania Court House, Virginia, May 10, 1864. Returned to duty in July-August, 1864. Present or accounted for through December, 1864. Captured near Petersburg on March 25, 1865. Confined at Point Lookout, Maryland, March 27, 1865. Released at Point Lookout on June 26, 1865, after taking the Oath of Allegiance.

FOSTER, HUGH AKILLIS, Private
Resided in Wilkes County. Place and date of enlistment not reported (probably enlisted in January-March, 1865). Wounded near Petersburg, Virginia, in March, 1865. Hospitalized at Richmond, Virginia. Captured in hospital at Richmond on April 3, 1865. Transferred to Libby Prison, Richmond, on an unspecified date. Transferred to Newport News, Virginia, April 23, 1865. Released at Newport News on June 30, 1865, after taking the Oath of Allegiance.

FOSTER, JESSE M., Private
Enlisted in Wilkes County on February 8, 1864, for the war. Present or accounted for through December, 1864. Surrendered at Appomattox Court House, Virginia, April 9, 1865.

FOSTER, JOHN A., 1st Sergeant
Born in Wilkes County where he resided as a farmer prior to enlisting in Wilkes County at age 18, March 14, 1862. Mustered in as Private. Promoted to Sergeant on June 10, 1862. Wounded at Bristoe Station, Virginia, October 14, 1863. Returned to duty in January-February, 1864. Promoted to 1st Sergeant on March 1, 1864. Wounded in the right forearm at Reams' Station, Virginia, August 25, 1864. Hospitalized at Richmond, Virginia. Furloughed for thirty days on September 8, 1864. Returned to duty on November 4, 1864. Wounded in the right leg near Petersburg, Virginia, on or about March 25, 1865. Right leg amputated. Hospitalized at Richmond. Captured in hospital at Richmond on April 3, 1865. Took the Oath of Allegiance on June 6, 1865.

FOSTER, JOHN S., Private
Previously served as Private in Company G, 54th Regiment N.C. Troops. Transferred to this company on or about October 20, 1862. Wounded at Bristoe Station, Virginia, October 14, 1863. Returned to duty on an unspecified date. Wounded in the left wrist at Cold Harbor, Virginia, on or about June 1, 1864. Reported absent wounded through December, 1864. Retired from service on February 17, 1865, by reason of disability from wounds.

FOSTER, JOHN T., Private
Resided in Wilkes County and enlisted at Camp French, near Petersburg, Virginia, at age 21, September 22, 1862, for the war. Wounded at Goldsboro on December 17, 1862.

Returned to duty on an unspecified date. Wounded at Bristoe Station, Virginia, October 14, 1863. Returned to duty in November-December, 1863. Present or accounted for until wounded at Wilderness, Virginia, May 6, 1864. Returned to duty in November-December, 1864. Deserted to the enemy on or about March 25, 1865. Confined at Washington, D.C., March 30, 1865. Released on or about the same date after taking the Oath of Allegiance.

FOSTER, WILLIAM A., Sergeant

Born in Wilkes County where he resided as a farmer prior to enlisting in Wilkes County at age 23, March 14, 1862. Mustered in as Sergeant. Wounded at Goldsboro on December 17, 1862. Returned to duty on an unspecified date. Wounded and captured at Gettysburg, Pennsylvania, on or about July 3, 1863. Hospitalized at Gettysburg. Transferred to hospital at Davids Island, New York Harbor, where he arrived on or about July 20, 1863. Paroled at Davids Island and transferred to City Point, Virginia, where he was received on September 27, 1863, for exchange. Returned to duty in March-April, 1864, but was apparently found unfit for service. Retired to the Invalid Corps on September 8, 1864. [Previously served as 2nd Lieutenant in the 92nd Regiment N.C. Militia.]

GAMBILL, B. F., _____

North Carolina pension records indicate that he served in this company.

GAMBILL, WILLIAM BOURNE, Private

Born in Wilkes County where he resided prior to enlisting at Petersburg, Virginia, at age 20, December 27, 1864, for the war. Wounded in the hand near Petersburg on March 25, 1865. Hospitalized at Richmond, Virginia. Captured in hospital at Richmond on April 3, 1865. Transferred to Libby Prison, Richmond, on an unspecified date. Transferred to Newport News, Virginia, April 23, 1865. Released at Newport News on June 30, 1865, after taking the Oath of Allegiance.

GILBREATH, ETHELBERT J. N., Private

Born in Wilkes County where he resided as a farmer prior to enlisting in Wilkes County at age 22, March 14, 1862. Died in hospital at Raleigh on May 20, 1862. Cause of death not reported.

GILBREATH, JAMES P., Private

Born in Wilkes County where he resided as a farmer prior to enlisting in Wilkes County at age 28, March 14, 1862. Mustered in as Corporal. Reduced to ranks in July, 1862-August, 1863, "for bad health." Reported absent without leave in July-August, 1863. Returned to duty in September-October, 1863. Present or accounted for through December, 1864; however, he was reported absent sick during much of that period. Surrendered at Appomattox Court House, Virginia, April 9, 1865.

GLASS, WILLIAM R., Private

Resided in Wilkes County and was by occupation a farmer prior to enlisting at Camp French, near Petersburg, Virginia, at age 26, September 22, 1862, for the war. Deserted on August 22, 1863.

HALL, DANIEL M., Private

Resided in Wilkes County and was by occupation a farmer prior to enlisting at Camp French, near Petersburg, Virginia, at age 24, September 22, 1862, for the war. Captured at or near Funkstown, Maryland, July 6, 1863. Sent to Baltimore, Maryland. Confined at Point Lookout, Maryland, August 21, 1863. Paroled at Point Lookout on March 16, 1864. Received at City Point, Virginia, March 20, 1864, for exchange. Reported absent without leave in May-December, 1864.

HALL, NATHAN C., Private

Born in Wilkes County where he resided as a farmer prior to enlisting in Wilkes County at age 18, March 14, 1862. Wounded in the left leg (fracture) and captured at Gettysburg, Pennsylvania, on or about July 1, 1863. Left leg amputated. Hospitalized at Gettysburg. Transferred to Fort Delaware, Delaware, September 16, 1863. Died at Fort Delaware on October 12, 1863, presumably of wounds.

HALL, NATHANIEL, Private

Born in Wilkes County where he resided as a farmer prior to enlisting in Wilkes County at age 18, April 5, 1862. Deserted prior to September 1, 1863. Reported present but under arrest in March-April, 1864. Wounded at Spotsylvania Court House, Virginia, May 10, 1864. Reported absent wounded through August, 1864. Reported absent without leave in September-December, 1864.

HALL, WILLIAM A., Private

Born in Wilkes County where he resided as a farmer prior to enlisting in Wilkes County at age 20, April 5, 1862. Mustered in as Private. Promoted to Sergeant on June 10, 1862. Hospitalized at or near Petersburg, Virginia, September 24, 1862, with typhoid fever. Returned to duty on November 23, 1862. Wounded and captured at Gettysburg, Pennsylvania, July 3, 1863. Confined at Fort Delaware, Delaware, on or about July 10, 1863. Transferred to Point Lookout, Maryland, October 20, 1863. Paroled at Point Lookout on March 16, 1864. Received at City Point, Virginia, March 20, 1864, for exchange. Reported absent without leave in May-December, 1864. Reduced to ranks on December 1, 1864.

HALL, WILLIAM H., Private

Born in Wilkes County where he resided as a farmer prior to enlisting in Wilkes County at age 19, April 5, 1862. Captured at Bristoe Station, Virginia, October 14, 1863. Confined at Old Capitol Prison, Washington, D.C. Transferred to Point Lookout, Maryland, October 27, 1863. Released at Point Lookout on February 21, 1864, after taking the Oath of Allegiance and joining the U.S. Army. Assigned to Company F, 1st Regiment U.S. Volunteer Infantry.

HAMBY, JOHN H., Private

Born in Wilkes County where he resided as a farmer prior to enlisting in Wilkes County at age 22, March 14, 1862. Reported present or accounted for on surviving company muster rolls through October, 1863. Reported present but under arrest in November-December, 1863. Reason he was arrested not reported. Returned to duty in January-

February, 1864. Captured at or near Wilderness, Virginia, on or about May 6, 1864. Confined at Point Lookout, Maryland, on or about May 17, 1864. Transferred to Elmira, New York, August 8, 1864. Paroled at Elmira on February 20, 1865, and transferred to the James River, Virginia, for exchange. Survived the war.

HANDY, JOHN T., Private

Resided in Wilkes County and enlisted at Camp French, near Petersburg, Virginia, at age 24, September 22, 1862, for the war. Captured at Gettysburg, Pennsylvania, on or about July 3, 1863. Confined at Fort McHenry, Maryland, August 14, 1863. Transferred to Point Lookout, Maryland, August 22, 1863. Paroled at Point Lookout on May 3, 1864. Received at Aiken's Landing, James River, Virginia, May 8, 1864, for exchange. Hospitalized at Richmond, Virginia, May 8, 1864, with chronic diarrhoea. Furloughed for thirty days on May 20, 1864. Reported absent without leave in July-December, 1864. Survived the war.

HANDY, MARCUS H., Private

Resided in Wilkes County and enlisted at Camp French, near Petersburg, Virginia, at age 20, September 22, 1862, for the war. Wounded and captured at Gettysburg, Pennsylvania, July 3, 1863. Confined at Fort Delaware, Delaware, on or about July 10, 1863. Transferred to Point Lookout, Maryland, October 20, 1863. Paroled at Point Lookout on February 18, 1865. Received at Boulware's Wharf, James River, Virginia, on or about February 20, 1865, for exchange.

HARRALD, WILLIAM M., Private

Resided in Wilkes County and enlisted at age 21, September 22, 1862, for the war. Dropped from the rolls of the company prior to September 1, 1863. Reason he was dropped not reported. Survived the war. [North Carolina pension records indicate that he was wounded at the Blackwater River, Virginia, June 7, 1863.]

HARRIS, OREN J., Corporal

Born in Wilkes County where he resided as a farmer prior to enlisting in Wilkes County at age 26, March 14, 1862. Mustered in as Corporal. Transferred to Company G, 54th Regiment N.C. Troops, in October, 1862.

HARRIS, WYATT M., Private

Born in Wilkes County where he resided as a farmer prior to enlisting in Wilkes County at age 22, March 14, 1862. Wounded in the leg and captured at Gettysburg, Pennsylvania, July 3, 1863. Hospitalized at Gettysburg. Transferred to Fort Delaware, Delaware, where he arrived on or about July 10, 1863. Transferred to Point Lookout, Maryland, October 20, 1863. Paroled at Point Lookout on March 16, 1864. Received at City Point, Virginia, March 20, 1864, for exchange. Reported absent without leave in May-December, 1864. Transferred to Company G, 54th Regiment N.C. Troops, February 10, 1865.

HAVENER, JESSE L., Private

Born in Wilkes County where he resided as a farmer prior to enlisting in Wilkes County at age 19, March 14, 1862. Wounded and captured at Gettysburg, Pennsylvania, on or

about July 1, 1863. Confined at Fort Delaware, Delaware, on or about July 10, 1863. Paroled at Fort Delaware on July 30, 1863. Received at City Point, Virginia, August 1, 1863, for exchange. Reported absent on parole through February, 1864. Reported absent without leave in March-December, 1864. Survived the war.

HENDREN, JABEZ E., Private

Born in Wilkes County where he resided as a farmer prior to enlisting in Wilkes County at age 19, April 5, 1862. Killed at Gettysburg, Pennsylvania, July 3, 1863.

HIGGINS, JOHN F., Private

Born in Wilkes County where he resided as a farmer prior to enlisting in Wilkes County at age 15, April 5, 1862. Reported present or accounted for on surviving company muster rolls through June, 1864. Reported absent without leave in July-August, 1864. Returned to duty in September, 1864. Wounded in the back and left side at or near Jones' Farm, Virginia, on or about October 2, 1864. Hospitalized at Richmond, Virginia. Furloughed for sixty days on October 21, 1864. Survived the war.

HIX, JOHN S., Private

Resided in Wilkes County where he enlisted at age 34, April 5, 1862. Captured at Falling Waters, Maryland, July 14, 1863. Confined at Old Capitol Prison, Washington, D.C. Transferred to Point Lookout, Maryland, where he arrived on August 23, 1863. Died at Point Lookout on or about January 13, 1864. Cause of death not reported.

HOBBS, J. R., _____

North Carolina pension records indicate that he served in this company.

HOLDER, JOHN, Private

Born in Wilkes County where he resided as a farmer prior to enlisting in Wilkes County at age 26, April 5, 1862. Reported absent on furlough in May-June, 1862. No further records.

HOOTS, JAMES HARRISON, Private

Born in Wilkes County where he resided as a farmer prior to enlisting in Wilkes County at age 18, March 14, 1862. Died in hospital at Petersburg, Virginia, July 29, 1862, of "meningitis."

HOOTS, WILLIAM, Private

Born in Wilkes County where he resided as a farmer prior to enlisting in Wilkes County at age 24, March 14, 1862. Died in hospital at Raleigh on June 6, 1862, of "pneumonia abscess."

HUTCHINSON, FRANCIS A., Private

Born in Wilkes County where he resided as a farmer prior to enlisting in Wilkes County at age 21, April 5, 1862. Died at Goldsboro on June 30, 1862, of "pneumonia."

HUTCHISON, WILLIAM E., Private

Resided in Wilkes County and enlisted at Camp French, near Petersburg, Virginia, at age 19, September 22, 1862, for the war. Killed at Gettysburg, Pennsylvania, July 3, 1863.

JENNINGS, HENRY, Private
Resided in Wilkes County and was by occupation a farmer prior to enlisting at age 34, September 22, 1862, for the war. No further records.

JENNINGS, PRESSLEY B., Corporal
Born in Wilkes County where he resided as a farmer prior to enlisting in Wilkes County at age 19, March 14, 1862. Mustered in as Private. Promoted to Corporal in September, 1862. Died in hospital at Petersburg, Virginia, October 20, 1862, of "febris typhoides."

JOHNSON, DAVID, Private
Resided in Wilkes County and enlisted at Camp French, near Petersburg, Virginia, at age 34, September 22, 1862, for the war. Reported present or accounted for on surviving company muster rolls through June, 1864. Reported absent without leave in July-August, 1864. Reported absent sick in July-December, 1864.

JOHNSON, JAMES F., Private
Born in Guilford County and resided in Wilkes County where he was by occupation a farmer prior to enlisting in Wilkes County at age 30, March 14, 1862. Wounded in the left leg and captured at Gettysburg, Pennsylvania, July 1, 1863. Exchanged on an unspecified date. Hospitalized at Richmond, Virginia, October 28, 1863. Furloughed on or about October 31, 1863. Reported absent wounded or absent sick through October, 1864. Reported absent without leave in November-December, 1864.

JONES, ELBERT W., Private
Born in Wilkes County where he resided as a farmer prior to enlisting in Wilkes County at age 54, March 14, 1862. Transferred to Company F, 26th Regiment N.C. Troops, September 1, 1862.

JORDAN, ELIAS ALEXANDER, Private
Born in Iredell County and resided in Wilkes County where he was by occupation a farmer prior to enlisting in Wilkes County at age 20, April 5, 1862. Died in hospital at Petersburg, Virginia, September 22, 1862, of fever.

JOYNER, JOHN, Private
Born in Surry County and resided in Wilkes County where he was by occupation a miller prior to enlisting in Wilkes County at age 59, April 5, 1862. Discharged on May 24, 1862, by reason of being overage.

KILBY, HENRY G., Private
Born in Wilkes County where he resided as a farmer prior to enlisting in Wilkes County at age 15, March 14, 1862. Discharged on May 18, 1862, by reason of being underage.

KILBY, JAMES C., Private
Enlisted at Orange Court House, Virginia, November 15, 1863, for the war. Present or accounted for through December, 1864.

KILBY, JOHN H., Private
Resided in Wilkes County and enlisted at age 24, September 22, 1862, for the war. No further records.

KILBY, JOHN J., Private
Born in Wilkes County where he resided as a farmer prior to enlisting in Wilkes County at age 19, April 5, 1862. Wounded and captured at Gettysburg, Pennsylvania, July 3, 1863. Hospitalized at Gettysburg. Transferred to hospital at Baltimore, Maryland, on an unspecified date. Paroled at Baltimore on August 23, 1863. Received at City Point, Virginia, August 24, 1863, for exchange. Returned to duty in November-December, 1863. Captured near Petersburg, Virginia, April 3, 1865. Confined at Hart's Island, New York Harbor, April 7, 1865. Released at Hart's Island on June 17, 1865, after taking the Oath of Allegiance.

KILBY, SAMUEL, Private
Resided in Wilkes County and enlisted at age 33, September 22, 1862, for the war. No further records.

KILBY, WILLIAM J., Private
Born in Wilkes County where he resided as a farmer prior to enlisting in Wilkes County at age 21, March 14, 1862. Hospitalized at Richmond, Virginia, July 27, 1862, with typhoid fever. Died at Richmond on an unspecified date.

KILBY, WILLIAM N., Private
Resided in Wilkes County and enlisted at age 20, September 22, 1862, for the war. Died at home in Wilkes County on July 4, 1863. Cause of death not reported.

LANE, THOMAS, Private
Born in Wilkes County where he resided as a farmer prior to enlisting in Wilkes County at age 37, March 14, 1862. Discharged on May 24, 1862, by reason of being overage.

LUNDY, JOSEPH A., Private
Born in Grayson County, Virginia, and resided in Wilkes County where he was by occupation a farmer prior to enlisting in Wilkes County at age 18, March 14, 1862. Captured at Bristoe Station, Virginia, October 14, 1863. Confined at Old Capitol Prison, Washington, D.C. Transferred to Point Lookout, Maryland, October 27, 1863. Paroled at Point Lookout on an unspecified date. Received at Aiken's Landing, James River, Virginia, on or about February 28, 1865, for exchange.

LUNDY, ZEBEDEE FREELAND, Private
Born in Grayson County, Virginia, and resided in Wilkes County where he was by occupation a carpenter prior to enlisting in Wilkes County at age 21, March 14, 1862. Wounded at Gettysburg, Pennsylvania, July 3, 1863. Returned to duty prior to September 1, 1863. Captured at Bristoe Station, Virginia, October 14, 1863. Confined at Old Capitol Prison, Washington, D.C. Transferred to Point Lookout, Maryland, October 27, 1863. Paroled at Point Lookout on or about February 24, 1865. Received at Aiken's Landing, James River, Virginia, on or about February 28, 1865, for exchange.

McDANIEL, THOMAS, Private
Previously served as Private in Company C, 26th Regiment N.C. Troops. Transferred to this company in January-February, 1864. Captured at Burgess' Mill, Virginia, October 27, 1864. Confined at Point Lookout,

Maryland, October 31, 1864. Paroled at Point Lookout on February 18, 1865. Received at Boulware's Wharf, James River, Virginia, on or about February 20, 1865, for exchange. Died in hospital at Danville, Virginia, March 2, 1865, of "diarrhoea chronica."

McGRADY, JOHN, Private
Resided in Wilkes County and was by occupation a farmer prior to enlisting at Petersburg, Virginia, at age 33, December 19, 1864, for the war. Captured at Sutherland's Station, Virginia, April 2, 1865. Confined at Point Lookout, Maryland, April 4, 1865. Died at Point Lookout on June 2, 1865, of "infl[ammation] of lungs."

MARLEY, JOHN F., Private
Born in Wilkes County where he resided as a farmer prior to enlisting in Wilkes County at age 32, March 14, 1862. Reported present or accounted for on surviving company muster rolls through April, 1864. Died in hospital at Lynchburg, Virginia, on or about May 27, 1864, of "diarrhoea chronica."

MARLEY, MILTON J., Private
Born in Alexander County* and resided in Wilkes County where he was by occupation a farmer prior to enlisting in Wilkes County at age 21, April 5, 1862. Died at Camp Mangum, near Raleigh, May 24, 1862. Cause of death not reported.

MARLOW, HARVEY, Private
Born in Wilkes County where he resided as a farmer prior to enlisting in Wilkes County at age 34, March 14, 1862. Captured at Falling Waters, Maryland, July 14, 1863. Sent to Baltimore, Maryland. Confined at Point Lookout, Maryland, August 17, 1863. Released at Point Lookout on February 10, 1864, after taking the Oath of Allegiance and joining the U.S. Army. Unit to which assigned not reported.

MATHIAS, JOHN, Private
Enlisted at Petersburg, Virginia, September 18, 1864, for the war. Present or accounted for through December, 1864.

MILAM, ADAM, Private
Born in Wilkes County where he resided as a farmer prior to enlisting in Wilkes County at age 44, March 14, 1862. Died in hospital at Weldon on January 12, 1863, of "pneumonia typh[oid]."

MILAM, THOMAS C., Private
Born in Wilkes County where he resided as a farmer prior to enlisting in Wilkes County at age 28, March 14, 1862. Reported absent without leave on or about June 20, 1863. Returned to duty in January-February, 1864. Wounded in the hand at or near Cold Harbor, Virginia, on or about June 2, 1864. Returned to duty prior to September 1, 1864. Hospitalized at Richmond, Virginia, February 10, 1865, with a gunshot wound of the right foot. Place and date wounded not reported (probably wounded at Hatcher's Run, Virginia, February 5, 1865). Furloughed for sixty days on April 1, 1865.

MINTON, JOEL, Private
Born in Wilkes County where he resided as a farmer prior to enlisting in Wilkes County at age 22, March 14, 1862. Present or accounted for through June 30, 1862. No further records.

MINTON, JOHN H., Private
Born in Wilkes County where he resided as a farmer prior to enlisting in Wilkes County at age 17, March 14, 1862. Wounded at Falling Waters, Maryland, July 14, 1863. Returned to duty prior to September 1, 1863. Killed in the trenches near Petersburg, Virginia, August 8, 1864.

MINTON, PURVIS, Private
Born in Wilkes County where he resided as a farmer prior to enlisting in Wilkes County at age 17, March 14, 1862. Discharged on May 24, 1862, by reason of being underage.

MOCK, JAMES A., Corporal
Born in Surry County and resided in Wilkes County where he was by occupation a farmer prior to enlisting in Wilkes County at age 26, March 14, 1862. Mustered in as Private. Promoted to Corporal in February, 1863. Captured at or near Gettysburg, Pennsylvania, on or about July 3, 1863. Confined at Fort Delaware, Delaware, on or about July 10, 1863. Paroled at Fort Delaware on July 30, 1863. Received at City Point, Virginia, August 1, 1863, for exchange. Returned to duty in September-October, 1863. Wounded in the leg at Spotsylvania Court House, Virginia, May 10, 1864. Leg amputated. Hospitalized at Richmond, Virginia. Furloughed for sixty days on July 18, 1864. No further records.

NANCE, WILBORN, Private
Resided in Wilkes County and was by occupation a farmer prior to enlisting at Camp Holmes, near Raleigh, at age 36, November 26, 1863, for the war. Died in hospital at Charlottesville, Virginia, January 26, 1864, of "typhoid fever."

OLIVER, JAMES R., Private
Born in Wilkes County where he resided as a farmer prior to enlisting in Wilkes County at age 19, March 14, 1862. Reported present or accounted for on surviving company muster rolls through June, 1864; however, he was absent sick during much of that period. Reported absent without leave in July-August, 1864. Returned to duty in September-October, 1864. Captured at Sutherland's Station, Virginia, April 2, 1865. Confined at Point Lookout, Maryland, April 4, 1865. Released at Point Lookout on June 29, 1865, after taking the Oath of Allegiance. [North Carolina pension records indicate that he was wounded in the leg at "Wilderness, Virginia, June 1, 1863."]

OWENS, GEORGE F., Private
Resided in Wilkes County and was by occupation a farmer prior to enlisting at Camp French, near Petersburg, Virginia, at age 28, September 22, 1862, for the war. Deserted on June 20, 1863. Returned to duty on October 20, 1863. Wounded at or near Cold Harbor, Virginia, on or about June 2, 1864. Reported absent wounded through December, 1864.

OWENS, JOHN C., Private
Born in Wilkes County where he resided as a farmer prior to enlisting in Wilkes County at age 26, April 5, 1862. Reported absent without leave on July 25, 1863. Returned to duty on August 14, 1863. Hospitalized at Charlottesville, Virginia, May 6, 1864, with erysipelas. Returned to duty on June 19, 1864. Captured at Burgess' Mill, Virginia, October 27, 1864. Confined at Point Lookout, Maryland, October 31, 1864. Died at Point Lookout on December 13, 1864, of "acute dysentery."

OWENS, REUBEN H., Private
Resided in Wilkes County and was by occupation a miller prior to enlisting at age 25, January 21, 1863, for the war. Killed in October, 1864. Place of death not reported.

OWENS, WILLIAM T., Private
Resided in Wilkes County and was by occupation a farmer prior to enlisting at age 24, September 22, 1862, for the war. Died in hospital at Petersburg, Virginia, January 15, 1863, of "cong fever" and/or "bronchitis."

PARKS, MARTIN G., Private
Born in Wilkes County where he resided as a farmer prior to enlisting in Wilkes County at age 19, March 14, 1862. Reported present or accounted for on surviving company muster rolls through April, 1864. Killed at or near Cold Harbor, Virginia, on or about June 2, 1864.

PARLEIR, ELBERT A., Private
Born in Wilkes County where he resided as a farmer prior to enlisting in Wilkes County at age 23, March 14, 1862. Died in hospital at Petersburg, Virginia, August 1, 1862, of "feb[ris] typhoides."

PARLEIR, GEORGE WESLEY, Private
Born in Wilkes County where he resided as a farmer prior to enlisting in Wilkes County at age 46, March 14, 1862. Died at Camp Mangum, near Raleigh, May 22, 1862. Cause of death not reported.

PIERCE, JOHN H. C., Musician
Previously served as Private in Company C, 26th Regiment N.C. Troops. Enlisted in this company at Franklin, Virginia, November 15, 1862, for the war as a substitute. Mustered in as Musician. Reported present or accounted for on surviving company muster rolls through May, 1864. Hospitalized at Richmond, Virginia, June 25, 1864, with chronic diarrhoea. Furloughed for forty days on August 4, 1864. Transferred to the regimental band prior to November 1, 1864.

PRESNELL, WILLIAM R., Private
Born in Iredell County and was by occupation a farmer prior to enlisting in Wilkes County at age 41, April 5, 1862. Discharged on May 24, 1862, presumably by reason of being overage.

PRICE, JOHN, Private
Born in Alexander County* and resided in Wilkes County where he was by occupation a farmer prior to enlisting in Wilkes County at age 38, March 14, 1862. Died at Camp Johnston, near Kinston, July 1, 1862. Cause of death not reported.

PRICE, SMITH, Private
Born in Alexander County* and resided in Wilkes County where he was by occupation a farmer prior to enlisting in Wilkes County at age 26, March 14, 1862. Wounded at Bristoe Station, Virginia, October 14, 1863. Returned to duty in January-February, 1864. Captured at or near Wilderness, Virginia, on or about May 6, 1864. Confined at Point Lookout, Maryland, on or about May 17, 1864. Transferred to Elmira, New York, August 8, 1864. Paroled at Elmira on March 2, 1865, and transferred to the James River, Virginia, for exchange.

QUEEN, FINLEY A., Private
Born in Alexander County* and resided in Wilkes County where he was by occupation a farmer prior to enlisting in Wilkes County at age 23, April 5, 1862. Reported present or accounted for on surviving company muster rolls through April, 1864. Reported absent without leave in May-December, 1864.

QUEEN, JAMES, Private
Resided in Wilkes County and was by occupation a farmer prior to enlisting at Petersburg, Virginia, at age 44, December 24, 1864, for the war. Deserted to the enemy on or about March 8, 1865. Confined at Washington, D.C., March 10, 1865. Released on or about the same date after taking the Oath of Allegiance.

QUEEN, WILLIAM R., Private
Born in Wilkes County where he resided as a farmer prior to enlisting in Wilkes County at age 19, April 5, 1862. Captured at Falling Waters, Maryland, July 14, 1863. Confined at Old Capitol Prison, Washington, D.C. Transferred to Point Lookout, Maryland, August 8, 1863. Paroled at Point Lookout on March 3, 1864. Received at City Point, Virginia, March 6, 1864, for exchange. Reported absent without leave in May-December, 1864.

RASH, REUBEN A., Private
Born in Wilkes County where he resided as a farmer prior to enlisting in Wilkes County at age 22, March 14, 1862. Wounded in the legs at Goldsboro on December 17, 1862. Both legs amputated. Died in hospital at Goldsboro on January 8, 1863, of wounds.

RASH, ZENO MELVIN, Corporal
Born in Wilkes County where he resided as a farmer prior to enlisting in Wilkes County at age 21, March 14, 1862. Mustered in as Corporal. Died near Drewry's Bluff, Virginia, August 5, 1862. Cause of death not reported.

REAVES, SAMUEL, Private
Resided in Wilkes County and enlisted at age 22, September 22, 1862, for the war. Hospitalized at or near Petersburg, Virginia, December 3, 1862, with typhoid fever. Furloughed on April 29, 1863. Failed to return to duty. Dropped from the rolls of the company (presumably for absence without leave) prior to September 1, 1863.

REAVIS, ANDREW H., Private
Born in Yadkin County* and resided in Wilkes County where he was by occupation a mechanic prior to enlisting in Wilkes County at age 22, March 14, 1862. Reported

present on surviving company muster rolls through December, 1863. Hospitalized at Petersburg, Virginia, February 18, 1864, with an unspecified complaint. Furloughed on April 20, 1864. Reported absent without leave in May-June, 1864. Returned to duty in September-October, 1864. Captured at Sutherland's Station, Virginia, April 2, 1865. Confined at Point Lookout, Maryland, April 4, 1865. Released at Point Lookout on June 19, 1865, after taking the Oath of Allegiance.

RICHARDSON, WILLIAM B., Private
Born in Virginia and resided in Wilkes County where he was by occupation a farmer prior to enlisting at Camp Holmes, near Raleigh, at age 25, December 25, 1863, for the war. Reported present or accounted for on surviving company muster rolls through October, 1864. Died in hospital at Richmond, Virginia, November 26, 1864. Cause of death not reported.

RODGERS, WILLIAM R., Private
Enlisted in Wilkes County on March 14, 1862. Reported absent without leave on or about July 1, 1862. No further records.

ROOP, CHRISTIAN, Private
Resided in Wilkes County and was by occupation a farmer prior to enlisting at Petersburg, Virginia, at age 37, December 19, 1864, for the war. Died at or near Petersburg on February 4, 1865. Cause of death not reported.

RUSSELL, JOHN M., Private
Born in Wilkes County where he resided as a farmer prior to enlisting in Wilkes County at age 18, March 14, 1862. Died in hospital at Raleigh on July 4, 1862, of "typhoid fever."

St. CLAIR, JAMES, Private
Born in Wilkes County where he resided as a farmer prior to enlisting in Wake County at age 18, October 2, 1863, for the war. Wounded in the right arm (fracture) at Wilderness, Virginia, May 5, 1864. Reported absent wounded through December, 1864. Retired from service on February 28, 1865, by reason of disability from wounds producing "permanent anchylosis of elbow joint. . . ."

St. CLAIR, JOHN, Private
Resided in Wilkes County and enlisted at Camp French, near Petersburg, Virginia, at age 19, September 22, 1862, for the war. Deserted on July 25, 1863. Returned to duty on August 14, 1863. Reported present or accounted for through December, 1863. Died in hospital at Richmond, Virginia, January 16, 1864, of "typhoid fever."

SEBASTIAN, HENRY C., Sergeant
Born in Wilkes County where he resided as a farmer prior to enlisting in Wilkes County at age 23, April 5, 1862. Mustered in as Private. Promoted to Corporal in September, 1862. Wounded in the head and thigh and captured at Gettysburg, Pennsylvania, July 3, 1863. Exchanged on an unspecified date. Returned to duty prior to September 1, 1863. Promoted to Sergeant on September 23, 1863. Present or accounted for until wounded at Globe

Tavern, Virginia, August 21, 1864. Reported absent wounded in September-October, 1864. Reported absent without leave in November-December, 1864. Survived the war.

SEBASTIAN, MARTIN H., Private
Resided in Wilkes County and enlisted at Camp French, near Petersburg, Virginia, at age 21, September 22, 1862, for the war. Wounded in the right leg (fracture) and captured at Gettysburg, Pennsylvania, July 3, 1863. Hospitalized at Gettysburg. Transferred to hospital at Chester, Pennsylvania, where he arrived on or about July 17, 1863. Transferred to Point Lookout, Maryland, October 2, 1863. Paroled at Point Lookout on an unspecified date. Received at City Point, Virginia, March 6, 1864, for exchange. Reported absent wounded through December, 1864. Survived the war.

SEBASTIAN, WILLIAM GRAY, Private
Resided in Wilkes County and enlisted at Camp French, near Petersburg, Virginia, at age 22, September 22, 1862, for the war. Reported absent sick in July-August, 1863. Reported absent without leave in September-October, 1863. Reported under arrest for desertion in November-December, 1864. Returned to duty prior to April 2, 1865, when he was captured at Sutherland's Station, Virginia. Confined at Point Lookout, Maryland, April 4, 1865. Released at Point Lookout on June 20, 1865, after taking the Oath of Allegiance.

SHATLEY, DAVID, Private
Born in Virginia and resided in Wilkes County where he was by occupation a farmer prior to enlisting in Wilkes County at age 22, March 14, 1862. Died at home in Wilkes County on May 31, 1862. Cause of death not reported.

SHEPHERD, JOHN W., Private
Enlisted in Alleghany County[?]. Enlistment date reported as August 10, 1861; however, he was not listed in the records of this company until March-April, 1864, when he was reported present. Reported absent wounded in May-June, 1864. Place and date wounded not reported. Returned to duty in July-August, 1864. Died in hospital at Richmond, Virginia, on or about November 16, 1864, of "colitis."

SHUMATE, DANIEL, Private
Resided in Wilkes County and enlisted at Camp French, near Petersburg, Virginia, at age 24, September 22, 1862, for the war. Deserted on January 20, 1863. Returned to duty on October 16, 1863. Present or accounted for until captured at or near Wilderness, Virginia, on or about May 6, 1864. Confined at Point Lookout, Maryland, May 17, 1864. Transferred to Elmira, New York, August 8, 1864. Died at Elmira on January 6, 1865, of "pneumonia."

SHUMATE, JASPER, Private
Born in Virginia and resided in Wilkes County where he was by occupation a farmer prior to enlisting at Camp Holmes, near Raleigh, at age 36, November 4, 1863, for the war. Hospitalized at Richmond, Virginia, February 16, 1864, with pneumonia. Returned to duty on February 23, 1864. Hospitalized at Richmond on April 21, 1864,

with chronic diarrhoea. Furloughed for sixty days on April 30, 1864. Reported absent without leave in July-December, 1864.

SHUMATE, JESSE HARDIN, Private
Resided in Wilkes County and was by occupation a farmer prior to enlisting at age 30, September 22, 1862, for the war. Wounded in the right arm (fracture) by a shell at Goldsboro on December 17, 1862. Dropped from the rolls of the company prior to September 1, 1863. Reason he was dropped not reported. Survived the war.

SHUMATE, WESLEY, Private
Resided in Wilkes County and enlisted at age 19, September 22, 1862, for the war. Dropped from the rolls of the company prior to September 1, 1863. Reason he was dropped not reported.

SHUMATE, WILLIAM J., _____
North Carolina pension records indicate that he served in this company.

SMITHEY, HARVEY, Private
Previously served as Private in Company G, 54th Regiment N.C. Troops. Transferred to this company on February 10, 1865. Surrendered at Appomattox Court House, Virginia, April 9, 1865.

SMITHY, WILLIAM S., Private
Resided in Wilkes County and enlisted at Camp French, near Petersburg, Virginia, at age 28, September 22, 1862, for the war. Wounded in the left leg at Gettysburg, Pennsylvania, on or about July 1, 1863. Reported absent wounded or absent sick through December, 1863. Reported absent without leave in January-February, 1864. Reported absent sick in March-April, 1864. Reported absent without leave in May-December, 1864. Survived the war.

SPRINKLE, LINDSEY, Private
Born in Wilkes County where he resided as a farmer prior to enlisting in Wilkes County at age 17, March 14, 1862. Wounded at Goldsboro on December 17, 1862. Returned to duty prior to September 1, 1863. Present or accounted for until killed at Burgess' Mill, Virginia, October 27, 1864.

STOKES, HUGH MONTGOMERY, Private
Born in Rowan County and resided in Wilkes County where he was by occupation a teacher prior to enlisting in Wilkes County at age 65, March 14, 1862. Discharged in August, 1862, presumably by reason of being overage.

SUMERLIN, JESSE C., Private
Born in Wilkes County where he resided as a farmer prior to enlisting in Wilkes County at age 35, April 5, 1862. Captured at Gettysburg, Pennsylvania, July 5, 1863, after being left behind as a nurse for the wounded. Confined at Fort Delaware, Delaware, on or about July 10, 1863. Transferred to Point Lookout, Maryland, October 20, 1863. Paroled at Point Lookout on February 18, 1865. Received at Boulware's Wharf, James River, Virginia, on or about February 20, 1865, for exchange.

TEDDER, HOUSTON, Private
Born in Wilkes County where he resided as a farmer prior to enlisting in Wilkes County at age 36, March 14, 1862. Died in hospital at Petersburg, Virginia, October 3, 1862, of "ty[phoid] fever."

TEDDER, JAMES, Private
Born in Wilkes County where he resided as a farmer prior to enlisting in Wilkes County at age 37, March 14, 1862. Deserted on June 20, 1863. Returned to duty on September 29, 1863. Died at Orange Court House, Virginia, in January, 1864. Cause of death not reported.

THARPE, HANSON H., Private
Enlisted at Orange Court House, Virginia, April 9, 1864, for the war. Reported absent without leave on July 20, 1864. Returned to duty in September-October, 1864. Captured at Burgess' Mill, Virginia, October 27, 1864. Confined at Point Lookout, Maryland, October 31, 1864. Died at Point Lookout on February 9, 1865, of "consumption."

THOMPSON, ROBERT, Private
Born in Lincoln County and resided in Wilkes County where he was by occupation a stonemason prior to enlisting in Wilkes County at age 57, April 5, 1862. Hospitalized at or near Petersburg, Virginia, October 18, 1862, with debility. Died in hospital at Petersburg on January 24, 1863, of "smallpox."

THOMPSON, WESLEY, Private
Resided in Transylvania County and enlisted at Petersburg, Virginia, December 27, 1864, for the war. Captured at Sutherland's Station, Virginia, April 2, 1865. Confined at Point Lookout, Maryland, April 4, 1865. Released at Point Lookout on June 21, 1865, after taking the Oath of Allegiance.

TUCKER, AARON A., Private
Born in Wilkes County where he resided as a farmer prior to enlisting in Wilkes County at age 23, April 5, 1862. Reported present or accounted for on surviving company muster rolls through June, 1864. Wounded in the right shoulder at Ream's Station, Virginia, August 25, 1864. Returned to duty on or about November 1, 1864. Wounded in the left hand near Petersburg, Virginia, March 25, 1865. Hospitalized at Richmond, Virginia. Captured in hospital at Richmond on April 3, 1865. Transferred to Point Lookout, Maryland, May 2, 1865. Released at Point Lookout on June 26, 1865, after taking the Oath of Allegiance.

VANNOY, ELIJAH ROSS, 1st Sergeant
Born in Cherokee County and resided in Wilkes County where he was by occupation a merchant prior to enlisting in Wilkes County at age 18, April 5, 1862. Mustered in as Sergeant. Promoted to 1st Sergeant on April 19, 1862. Killed at Gettysburg, Pennsylvania, July 3, 1863.

VONCANNON, ABRAM B., Private
Born in Randolph County and resided in Wilkes County where he was by occupation a farmer prior to enlisting in Wilkes County at age 26, March 14, 1862. Captured at

Falling Waters, Maryland, July 14, 1863. Confined at Baltimore, Maryland. Transferred to Point Lookout, Maryland, where he arrived on August 17, 1863. Released at Point Lookout on February 10, 1864, after taking the Oath of Allegiance and joining the U.S. Army. Unit to which assigned not reported.

WAGGONER, WILLIAM R., Private
Resided in Ashe County and enlisted in Wake County at age 19, June 3, 1862, for the war. Reported present or accounted for on surviving company muster rolls through October, 1863. Reported absent without leave in November-December, 1863.

WALLACE, RICHARD H., Private
Resided in Wilkes County and was by occupation a blacksmith prior to enlisting at Petersburg, Virginia, at age 27, December 27, 1864, for the war. Captured at Sutherland's Station, Virginia, April 2, 1865. Confined at Point Lookout, Maryland, April 4, 1865. Died at Point Lookout on July 6, 1865, of "chronic diarrhoea."

WARREN, DANIEL B., Private
Enlisted in Wilkes County on December 24, 1863, for the war. Hospitalized at Richmond, Virginia, May 26, 1864, with pneumonia. Furloughed for forty days on July 19, 1864. Reported absent sick through December, 1864. Captured in hospital at Richmond on April 3, 1865. Died in hospital at Richmond on April 29, 1865, of a gunshot wound of the right arm. Place and date wounded not reported.

WARREN, JAMES H., Sergeant
Born in Wilkes County where he resided as a farmer prior to enlisting in Wilkes County at age 18, April 5, 1862. Mustered in as Private. Wounded in the left shoulder and right thigh at Gettysburg, Pennsylvania, July 3, 1863. Returned to duty in November-December, 1863. Reported present but on detail as a provost guard in March-October, 1864. Reported absent on furlough in November-December, 1864. Promoted to Sergeant on December 1, 1864. Surrendered at Appomattox Court House, Virginia, April 9, 1865.

WARREN, JAMES P., Sergeant
Born in Wilkes County where he resided as a farmer prior to enlisting in Wilkes County at age 19, March 14, 1862. Mustered in as Sergeant. Discharged in June, 1863, "by Civil Authority." Reason discharged not reported.

WARREN, ROBERT F., Chief Musician
Born in Wilkes County where he resided as a farmer prior to enlisting in Wilkes County at age 18, March 14, 1862. Mustered in as Private. Appointed Musician (Drummer) prior to July 1, 1862. Appointed Chief Musician in July, 1862-August, 1863. Transferred to the regimental band on an unspecified date (probably in July-October, 1864).

WARREN, S. M., _____
North Carolina pension records indicate that he served in this company.

WATTS, ELI, Private
Born in Wilkes County where he resided as a farmer prior

to enlisting in Wilkes County at age 31, April 5, 1862. Killed at Goldsboro on December 17, 1862.

WATTS, JAMES MADISON, Private
Born in Wilkes County where he resided as a farmer prior to enlisting in Wilkes County at age 20, March 14, 1862. Wounded in the left elbow at Gettysburg, Pennsylvania, July 1, 1863. Reported absent wounded or absent sick through December, 1863. Detailed for light duty at Gordonsville, Virginia, on or about February 2, 1864. Rejoined the company in March-April, 1864. Present or accounted for through October, 1864. Reported absent on detached service in November-December, 1864. Survived the war.

WATTS, JOHN, Private
Born in Wilkes County where he resided as a farmer prior to enlisting in Wilkes County at age 20, March 14, 1862. Wounded in the right shoulder at Gettysburg, Pennsylvania, on or about July 3, 1863. Returned to duty prior to September 1, 1863. Wounded in the right leg at Globe Tavern, Virginia, August 21, 1864. Returned to duty prior to September 1, 1864. Surrendered at Appomattox Court House, Virginia, April 9, 1865.

WATTS, WESLEY C., Private
Born in Wilkes County where he resided as a farmer prior to enlisting in Wilkes County at age 23, March 14, 1862. Hospitalized at or near Petersburg, Virginia, August 29, 1862, with pneumonia. Transferred to another hospital on October 23, 1862. Reported absent sick in July-December, 1863. Returned to duty in January-February, 1864. Reported absent sick in May-June, 1864. Reported present in July-December, 1864. Captured near Petersburg on March 25, 1865. Confined at Point Lookout, Maryland, March 27, 1865. Released at Point Lookout on June 21, 1865, after taking the Oath of Allegiance.

WELLS, H. C., Private
Resided in Wilkes County and enlisted at age 24, September 22, 1862, for the war. No further records.

WHITE, TERRELL, _____
North Carolina pension records indicate that he served in this company.

WILCOXEN, DANIEL, Corporal
Born in Iredell County and resided in Wilkes County where he was by occupation a farmer prior to enlisting in Wilkes County at age 24, March 14, 1862. Mustered in as Corporal. Died at Drewry's Bluff, Virginia, July 25, 1862, of disease.

WILLIAMS, FRANKLIN, Private
Born in Wilkes County where he resided as a farmer prior to enlisting in Wilkes County at age 22, April 5, 1862. Wounded and captured at Gettysburg, Pennsylvania, July 3, 1863. Confined at Fort Delaware, Delaware, on or about July 10, 1863. Died at Fort Delaware on October 18, 1863, of "remitt[ent] fever."

WILLIAMS, JOHN, Private
Born in Wilkes County where he resided as a farmer prior

to enlisting in Wilkes County at age 19, April 5, 1862. Killed at Gettysburg, Pennsylvania, July 3, 1863.

WOODS, JAMES M., Private
Resided in Wilkes County and was by occupation a farmer prior to enlisting at age 28, September 22, 1862, for the war. Dropped from the rolls of the company prior to September 1, 1863. Reason he was dropped not reported. Survived the war.

WOODS, JOSEPH, Private
Resided in Wilkes County where he enlisted at age 36, March 14, 1862. Captured at Falling Waters, Maryland, July 14, 1863. Sent to Baltimore, Maryland. Confined at Point Lookout, Maryland, August 17, 1863. Died at Point Lookout on January 5, 1864. Cause of death not reported.

WOOTEN, REUBEN, Private
Born in Yadkin County* and resided in Wilkes County where he was by occupation a carpenter prior to enlisting at Camp Mangum, near Raleigh, at age 34, May 12, 1862, for the war. Died in hospital at Petersburg, Virginia, August 8, 1862, of "febris typhoides."

YOUNGER, PHLEGM H., Private
Enlisted at Camp Holmes, near Raleigh, November 26, 1863, for the war. Transferred to Company D, 26th Regiment N.C. Troops, March 1, 1864.

COMPANY G

This company, known as the "Dry Pond Dixies," was raised in Lincoln County and enlisted in Lincoln County in March, 1862. It was mustered into state service at Camp Mangum, near Raleigh, on April 28, 1862, and assigned to the 52nd Regiment N.C. Troops as Company G. After joining the regiment the company functioned as a part of the regiment, and its history for the remainder of the war is reported as a part of the regimental history.

The information contained in the following roster was compiled primarily from a company muster-in and descriptive roll dated April 28, 1862, and from company muster rolls for May 1-June 30, 1862; November 1, 1862-March 1, 1863; and July 1, 1863-December 31, 1864. No company records were located for July 1-October 31, 1862; March 2-June 30, 1863; or for the period after December 31, 1864. Valuable information was obtained from primary records such as the North Carolina adjutant general's *Roll of Honor*, discharge certificates, medical records, prisoner of war records, *The War of the Rebellion: A Compilation of the Official Records of the Union and Confederate Armies*, militia records, newspaper casualty lists and obituaries, Confederate pension applications filed with the state of North Carolina, and the 1860 federal census of North Carolina. Secondary sources such as postwar rosters and histories, cemetery records, the *Confederate Veteran*, published genealogies, and records of the United Daughters of the Confederacy also provided useful information.

OFFICERS

CAPTAINS

SHELTON, JOSEPH B.
Born in Lincoln County where he resided as a farmer prior to enlisting at age 38. Appointed Captain on March 25, 1862. Resigned on or about August 16, 1862, by reason of "chronic diarrhoea." Resignation accepted on August 28, 1862.

KINCAID, JAMES M.
Resided in Lincoln County and enlisted at age 24. Appointed 1st Lieutenant on March 25, 1862. Promoted to Captain on August 28, 1862. Wounded in the left thigh and captured at Gettysburg, Pennsylvania, July 3, 1863. Hospitalized at Gettysburg. Died in hospital at Gettysburg on August 27, 1863, of wounds.

WELLS, JAMES DANIEL
Previously served as Musician in Company K, 1st Regiment N.C. Infantry (6 months, 1861). Appointed 3rd Lieutenant on March 25, 1862. Promoted to 2nd Lieutenant on May 24, 1862. Promoted to 1st Lieutenant on August 28, 1862. Promoted to Captain on August 27, 1863. Reported present or accounted for on surviving company muster rolls through April, 1864. Captured at or near Wilderness, Virginia, on or about May 6, 1864. Confined at Point Lookout, Maryland, May 14, 1864. Transferred to Fort Delaware, Delaware, June 23, 1864. Released at Fort Delaware on June 16, 1865, after taking the Oath of Allegiance.

LIEUTENANTS

ASBURY, DANIEL M., 2nd Lieutenant
Born in Lincoln County where he resided as a farmer prior to enlisting at age 38. Appointed 2nd Lieutenant on March 25, 1862. Resigned on an unspecified date. Reason he resigned not reported. Resignation accepted on May 23, 1862.

GATENS, JOHN E., 1st Lieutenant
Previously served as Private in Company K, 1st Regiment N.C. Infantry (6 months, 1861). Enlisted in this company on April 26, 1862, for the war. Mustered in as Private. Appointed 3rd Lieutenant on November 25, 1862. Wounded slightly at Bristoe Station, Virginia, October 14, 1863. Promoted to 1st Lieutenant on November 1, 1863. Reported present or accounted for on surviving company muster rolls through April, 1864. Wounded in the neck at or near Cold Harbor, Virginia, on or about June 1, 1864. Hospitalized at Petersburg, Virginia. Returned to duty on or about July 12, 1864. Wounded in the right shoulder and arm (flesh) at or near Jones' Farm, Virginia, on or about October 1, 1864. Reported absent wounded through December, 1864. Captured at Sutherland's Station, Virginia, April 2, 1865. Confined at

Old Capitol Prison, Washington, D.C., April 5, 1865. Transferred to Johnson's Island, Ohio, April 9, 1865. Released at Johnson's Island on June 18, 1865, after taking the Oath of Allegiance.

HOUSTON, ROBERT B. B., 3rd Lieutenant
Resided in Lincoln County and enlisted at age 22, May 8, 1862, for the war. Mustered in as Private. Elected 3rd Lieutenant on June 11, 1862. Resigned on February 12, 1863, by reason of "hypertrophy and solidification of the right lung complicated with bronchitis." Resignation accepted on February 20, 1863.

WELLS, HENRY W., 3rd Lieutenant
Born in Lincoln County where he resided as a mason prior to enlisting at age 25, March 22, 1862. Mustered in as Private. Promoted to Corporal on June 14, 1862. Promoted to Color Sergeant prior to February 26, 1863. Appointed 3rd Lieutenant on February 26, 1863. Hospitalized at Richmond, Virginia, August 24, 1863, with remittent fever. Returned to duty subsequent to November 17, 1863. Reported present in January-April, 1864. Reported at home on furlough in May-June, 1864. Retired to the Invalid Corps on August 1, 1864. [North Carolina pension records indicate that he died (possibly was killed in action) on April 1, 1865.]

NONCOMMISSIONED OFFICERS AND PRIVATES

ABERNATHY, DAVID A., Private
Born in Catawba County* and resided in Lincoln County where he was by occupation a farmer prior to enlisting at age 24, March 21, 1862. Killed at Gettysburg, Pennsylvania, July 3, 1863.

ABERNATHY, MILTON M., Private
Born in Lincoln County and resided in Iredell County where he was by occupation a farmer prior to enlisting at age 27, March 23, 1862. Reported present on surviving company muster rolls through November 17, 1863. Reported absent without leave in January-February, 1864. Returned to duty in March-April, 1864. Present or accounted for through December, 1864. Captured by the enemy on an unspecified date. Confined at Hart's Island, New York Harbor, April 11, 1865. Released at Hart's Island on June 19, 1865, after taking the Oath of Allegiance. [North Carolina pension records indicate that he was wounded at or near Gettysburg, Pennsylvania, July 3, 1863.]

ALLEN, JOHN ALEXANDER, Private
Born in South Carolina and resided in Burke County where he was by occupation a day laborer prior to enlisting at age 31, April 28, 1862, for the war. Reported present or accounted for on surviving company muster rolls through December, 1864; however, he was reported absent sick during much of that period. Captured near Petersburg, Virginia, March 25, 1865. Confined at Point Lookout, Maryland, March 28, 1865. Released at Point

Lookout on or about June 8, 1865, after taking the Oath of Allegiance.

ARMSTRONG, JOHN, Private
Resided in Lincoln County and was by occupation a farm laborer prior to enlisting at age 53, October 27, 1864, for the war. Present or accounted for through December, 1864.

ARMSTRONG, JOHN G., Private
Born in Lincoln County where he resided as a blacksmith prior to enlisting at age 41, March 23, 1862. Discharged on or about May 29, 1862, by reason of being overage.

ASBURY, OSBURN W., Private
Born in Lincoln County where he resided as a carpenter prior to enlisting at age 26, March 21, 1862. Reported present on surviving company muster rolls through August, 1864. Captured at Burgess' Mill, Virginia, October 27, 1864. Confined at Point Lookout, Maryland, October 31, 1864. Paroled at Point Lookout on March 28, 1865. Received at Boulware's Wharf, James River, Virginia, March 30, 1865, for exchange.

BALLARD, JAMES A., Private
Born in Lincoln County where he resided as a farmer prior to enlisting at age 21, March 23, 1862. Died in hospital at Richmond, Virginia, August 26, 1862, of "intermittent fever."

BALLARD, JOHN F., Private
Born in Lincoln County where he resided as a farmer prior to enlisting at age 39, March 23, 1862. Discharged on May 6, 1862, by reason of being overage.

BARKER, CYRUS, Private
Quaker. Resided in Randolph County and was conscripted at age 30, November 3, 1862, for the war. Refused to perform military duty but was forced to remain with the company. Captured at Gettysburg, Pennsylvania, July 5, 1863, after he was left behind as a nurse for the wounded. Confined at Fort Delaware, Delaware. Released at Fort Delaware on July 25, 1863, and was furnished transportation to Philadelphia, Pennsylvania.

BARKER, NATHAN, Private
Quaker. Resided in Randolph County and was conscripted at age 21, November 3, 1862, for the war. Refused to perform military duty but was forced to remain with the company. Captured at Gettysburg, Pennsylvania, July 5, 1863, after he was left behind as a nurse for the wounded. Confined at Fort Delaware, Delaware, on or about July 10, 1863. Released at Fort Delaware on July 25, 1863, and was furnished transportation to Philadelphia, Pennsylvania.

BROTHERTON, HENRY, Private
Born in Lincoln County where he resided as a farmer prior to enlisting at age 20, March 23, 1862. Reported absent wounded and in hospital at Richmond, Virginia, in July-August, 1863. Place and date wounded not reported (probably wounded at or near Gettysburg, Pennsylvania, on or about July 3, 1863). Returned to duty

prior to October 14, 1863, when he was captured at Bristoe Station, Virginia. Confined at Old Capitol Prison, Washington, D.C. Transferred to Point Lookout, Maryland, October 27, 1863. Released at Point Lookout on January 28, 1864, after taking the Oath of Allegiance and joining the U.S. Army. Assigned to Company C, 1st Regiment U.S. Volunteer Infantry.

BROTHERTON, JAMES, Private
Resided in Lincoln County and enlisted at Orange Court House, Virginia, at age 18, August 21, 1863, for the war. Present or accounted for through December, 1864. Surrendered at Appomattox Court House, Virginia, April 9, 1865.

BRYANT, J. B., Private
Enlisted at Orange Court House, Virginia, October 8, 1863, for the war. Died in hospital at Richmond, Virginia, November 25, 1863. Cause of death not reported.

BRYANT, PHILLIP W., Private
Born in Lincoln County where he resided as a farmer prior to enlisting at Orange Court House, Virginia, at age 43, October 8, 1863, for the war. Died in hospital at Charlottesville, Virginia, December 30, 1863, of "typhoid fever."

CALDWELL, JAMES F., Sergeant
Born in Lincoln County where he resided as a farmer prior to enlisting at age 19, March 23, 1862. Mustered in as Private. Wounded and captured at Gettysburg, Pennsylvania, July 3, 1863. Hospitalized at Davids Island, New York Harbor, on or about July 20, 1863. Paroled at Davids Island on an unspecified date. Received at City Point, Virginia, September 8, 1863, for exchange. Returned to duty in January-February, 1864. Promoted to Sergeant in March-April, 1864. Reported present or accounted for through December, 1864. Surrendered at Appomattox Court House, Virginia, April 9, 1865. [Was probably promoted to Corporal at about the time of his capture at Gettysburg.]

CALDWELL, MOSES A., Private
Born in Iredell County where he resided as a clerk prior to enlisting at age 24, March 21, 1862. Mustered in as Corporal. Reduced to ranks on or about December 10, 1862, by reason of "ill health." Reported present or accounted for on surviving company muster rolls through August, 1863; however, he was reported absent sick during much of that period. Hospitalized at Charlottesville, Virginia, November 3, 1863, with intermittent fever. Returned to duty on December 8, 1863. Hospitalized at Richmond, Virginia, February 15, 1864, with rheumatism. Furloughed for thirty days on February 27, 1864. Died in March, 1864. Place and cause of death not reported.

CASHION, FRANKLIN, Private
Enlisted at Orange Court House, Virginia, October 8, 1863, for the war. Present or accounted for through October, 1864. Transferred to Company K, 63rd Regiment N.C. Troops (5th Regiment N.C. Cavalry), in November-December, 1864.

CASHION, JAMES H., Private
Resided in Lincoln County and enlisted at age 27, April 25, 1862, for the war. Reported present or accounted for on surviving company muster rolls through October, 1864. Served as a teamster during much of that period. Transferred to Company K, 63rd Regiment N.C. Troops (5th Regiment N.C. Cavalry), in November-December, 1864.

CHERRY, DAVID, Private
Born in Lincoln County where he resided as a farmer prior to enlisting at Orange Court House, Virginia, at age 54, October 8, 1863, for the war. Present or accounted for through December, 1864; however, he was reported absent sick during much of that period. Captured at Sutherland's Station, Virginia, April 2, 1865. Confined at Point Lookout, Maryland, April 4, 1865. Released at Point Lookout on June 24, 1865, after taking the Oath of Allegiance.

COX, NATHANIEL, Private
Quaker. Resided in Randolph County and was conscripted at age 35, November 3, 1862, for the war. Refused to perform military duty but was forced to remain with the company. Discharged on February 14, 1863, after having paid the required tax.

CRANFORD, J. P., Private
Resided in Randolph County and enlisted at Franklin, Virginia, at age 31, November 3, 1862, for the war. Wounded and captured at Gettysburg, Pennsylvania, July 3, 1863. Confined at Fort Delaware, Delaware, on or about July 10, 1863. Exchanged prior to August 1, 1863, when he was hospitalized at Petersburg, Virginia, with chronic diarrhoea. Furloughed for thirty days on August 26, 1863. Reported absent without leave in January-December, 1864. Survived the war.

CRANFORD, LEVI, Private
Resided in Randolph County and enlisted at Franklin, Virginia, at age 28, November 3, 1862, for the war. Deserted on or about June 29, 1863.

CRANFORD, P. C., Private
Resided in Randolph County and enlisted at Franklin, Virginia, at age 30, November 3, 1862, for the war. Deserted on November 24, 1862. Returned to duty subsequent to March 1, 1863. Deserted to the enemy at or near Gettysburg, Pennsylvania, on or about July 2, 1863. Confined at Fort Mifflin, Pennsylvania, where he died on September 29, 1863. Cause of death not reported.

DAVIS, HENRY, Private
Resided in Randolph County and enlisted at Franklin, Virginia, at age 25, November 3, 1862, for the war. Reported present on surviving company muster rolls through April, 1864. Captured at or near Wilderness, Virginia, on or about May 6, 1864. Confined at Point Lookout, Maryland, May 17, 1864. Died at Point Lookout on August 6, 1864, of disease.

DELLINGER, LEROY M., 1st Sergeant
Born in Lincoln County where he resided as a farmer

prior to enlisting in Lincoln County at age 25, March 23, 1862. Mustered in as Private. Promoted to Sergeant on June 30, 1863. Wounded at Gettysburg, Pennsylvania, July 3, 1863. Returned to duty prior to September 1, 1863. Promoted to 1st Sergeant on December 10, 1863. Reported absent wounded in May-June, 1864. Place and date wounded not reported. Returned to duty in July-August, 1864. Captured at or near Amelia Court House, Virginia, April 4, 1865. Confined at Hart's Island, New York Harbor, April 11, 1865. Released at Hart's Island on June 19, 1865, after taking the Oath of Allegiance.

DELLINGER, LORENZO D., Private
Resided in Lincoln County and enlisted at Camp French, near Petersburg, Virginia, at age 19, September 22, 1862, for the war. Hospitalized at Richmond, Virginia, December 24, 1863, with anasarca. Furloughed on February 12, 1864. Reported absent sick through August, 1864. Hospitalized at Danville, Virginia, October 31, 1864, with pneumonia. Furloughed on March 24, 1865.

EDWARDS, JACOB O., Private
Born in Lincoln County where he resided as a farmer prior to enlisting at age 19, March 23, 1862. Captured at Gettysburg, Pennsylvania, on or about July 3, 1863. Confined at Fort Delaware, Delaware, on or about July 10, 1863. Died at Fort Delaware on October 28, 1863, of "diarrhoea chronic."

EDWARDS, LEWIS, Private
Resided in Lincoln County and enlisted at Orange Court House, Virginia, at age 36, August 10, 1863, for the war. Captured at Bristoe Station, Virginia, October 14, 1863. Confined at Old Capitol Prison, Washington, D.C. Transferred to Point Lookout, Maryland, October 27, 1863. Died at Point Lookout on January 9, 1864, of "smallpox."

EDWARDS, WILLIAM E., Corporal
Born in Lincoln County where he resided as a farmer prior to enlisting in Lincoln County at age 18, March 23, 1862. Mustered in as Private. Promoted to Corporal on December 10, 1863. Reported present on surviving company muster rolls through April, 1864. Killed at Cold Harbor, Virginia, June 3, 1864.

FLEMING, DAVID C., Private
Enlisted on April 25, 1862, for the war. Killed at Goldsboro on December 17, 1862.

GANT, HARRISON G., Private
Born in Lincoln County where he resided as a farmer prior to enlisting at age 22, March 20, 1862. Reported present or accounted for on surviving company muster rolls through August, 1864. Captured at Burgess' Mill, Virginia, October 27, 1864. Confined at Point Lookout, Maryland, October 31, 1864. Paroled at Point Lookout on March 28, 1865. Received at Boulware's Wharf, James River, Virginia, March 30, 1865, for exchange. Paroled at Charlotte on May 17, 1865.

GANT, O. JEFFERSON, Private
Resided in Lincoln County where he enlisted at age 39,

March 12, 1863, for the war. Captured at Gettysburg, Pennsylvania, July 3, 1863. Confined at Fort Delaware, Delaware, on or about July 10, 1863. Died at Fort Delaware on September 23, 1863, of "bronchitis acute."

GOODSON, JOEL, Private
Born in Lincoln County where he resided as a farmer prior to enlisting in Lincoln County at age 21, March 23, 1862. Reported present or accounted for on surviving company muster rolls through February, 1864. Hospitalized at Richmond, Virginia, April 15, 1864, with debilitas. Transferred to hospital at Farmville, Virginia, April 29, 1864. Died in hospital at Farmville on May 11, 1864, of "chr[onic] diarrhoea."

GOODSON, JOHN F., Private
Born in Lincoln County where he resided as a farmer prior to enlisting in Lincoln County at age 24, March 20, 1862. Hospitalized at or near Petersburg, Virginia, September 24, 1862, with remittent fever. Returned to duty on December 4, 1862. Captured at Gettysburg, Pennsylvania, July 3, 1863. Confined at Fort Delaware, Delaware, on or about July 10, 1863. Transferred to Point Lookout, Maryland, October 20, 1863. Released at Point Lookout on February 5, 1864, after taking the Oath of Allegiance and joining the U.S. Army. Assigned to Company C, 1st Regiment U.S. Volunteer Infantry. [Prior to his service in the 52nd Regiment N.C. Troops he may have served as 2nd Lieutenant of Company K, 23rd Regiment N.C. Troops (13th Regiment N.C. Volunteers).]

GOODSON, JOHN W., Private
Born in Lincoln County where he resided as a farmer prior to enlisting in Lincoln County at age 18, March 20, 1862. Wounded at Bristoe Station, Virginia, October 14, 1863. Returned to duty in January-February, 1864. Reported absent wounded in May-August, 1864. Place and date wounded not reported. Reported absent on detached service at Raleigh in September-October, 1864. Rejoined the company in November-December, 1864. Captured near Petersburg, Virginia, March 25, 1865. Confined at Point Lookout, Maryland, March 28, 1865. Released at Point Lookout on June 27, 1865, after taking the Oath of Allegiance.

GOODSON, REUBEN, Private
Born in Lincoln County where he resided as a farmer prior to enlisting in Lincoln County at age 21, March 20, 1862. Reported present on surviving company muster rolls through April, 1864. Died in hospital at Richmond, Virginia, on or about June 6, 1864, of "dysentery acute."

HAGAR, JAMES H., Private
Resided in Lincoln County and enlisted on October 27, 1864, for the war. Captured at Sutherland's Station, Virginia, April 2, 1865. Confined at Point Lookout, Maryland, April 4, 1865. Released at Point Lookout on June 27, 1865, after taking the Oath of Allegiance.

HAGAR, JAMES W., Private
Resided in Lincoln County and enlisted on October 27, 1864, for the war. Captured near Petersburg, Virginia, March 25, 1865. Confined at Point Lookout, Maryland,

March 28, 1865. Released at Point Lookout on June 27, 1865, after taking the Oath of Allegiance.

HAGAR, THOMAS F., Private
Resided in Lincoln County where he enlisted at age 25, March 9, 1863, for the war. Reported present on surviving company muster rolls through August, 1864. Wounded slightly in the left arm at Jones' Farm, Virginia, on or about September 30, 1864. Reported absent wounded or absent sick until December 19, 1864, when he was furloughed for sixty days.

HAGER, ADAM MILLER, Private
Born in Lincoln County where he resided as a farmer prior to enlisting in Lincoln County at age 26, March 17, 1862. Reported absent without leave in May-June, 1862. Returned to duty prior to March 2, 1863. Captured at Gettysburg, Pennsylvania, July 3, 1863. Confined at Fort Delaware, Delaware, on or about July 10, 1863. No further records.

HAGER, CHRISTOPHER W., Private
Born in Lincoln County where he resided as a farmer prior to enlisting at age 42, March 17, 1862. Discharged on or about May 29, 1862, by reason of being overage. [May have served later as Private in Company K, 23rd Regiment N.C. Troops (13th Regiment N.C. Volunteers).]

HAGER, J. F., Private
Enlisted at Orange Court House, Virginia, October 8, 1863, for the war. Died in hospital at Richmond, Virginia, June 23, 1864, of "febris typh[oid]."

HAGER, J. MONROE, Private
Resided in Lincoln County and enlisted at age 27, September 22, 1862, for the war. Captured at Falling Waters, Maryland, July 14, 1863. Confined at Old Capitol Prison, Washington, D.C. Transferred to Point Lookout, Maryland, August 8, 1863. Released at Point Lookout on or about January 25, 1864, after taking the Oath of Allegiance and joining the U.S. Army. Assigned to Company C, 1st Regiment U.S. Volunteer Infantry.

HAGER, JAMES HENRY, Private
Born in Lincoln County where he resided as a farmer prior to enlisting at age 35, March 19, 1862. Discharged on May 29, 1862, by reason of being overage.

HAGER, JAMES R., Private
Born in Lincoln County where he resided as a farmer prior to enlisting at age 48, March 19, 1862. Discharged on or about May 29, 1862, by reason of being overage.

HAGER, JAMES R., Private
Born in Lincoln County where he resided as a farmer prior to enlisting in Lincoln County at age 23, March 17, 1862. Reported present on surviving company muster rolls through June, 1864. Died prior to November 1, 1864. Place, exact date, and cause of death not reported.

HAGER, JOHN, Private
Resided in Lincoln County where he enlisted at age 26, March 9, 1863, for the war. Reported present or accounted

for on surviving company muster rolls through February, 1864. Died in hospital at Richmond, Virginia, April 7, 1864. Cause of death not reported.

HAGER, PHILIP, Private
Born in Lincoln County where he resided as a farmer prior to enlisting in Lincoln County at age 38, March 17, 1862. Reported present or accounted for on surviving company muster rolls through October, 1864. Died in hospital at Richmond, Virginia, November 25, 1864, of "diarrhoea."

HAGER, ROBERT D., Private
Born in Lincoln County where he resided as a farmer prior to enlisting in Lincoln County at age 19, March 17, 1862. Reported present or accounted for on surviving company muster rolls through April, 1864. Captured at or near Wilderness, Virginia, on or about May 6, 1864. Confined at Point Lookout, Maryland, May 17, 1864. Transferred to Elmira, New York, August 8, 1864. Paroled at Elmira on October 11, 1864. Received at Venus Point, Savannah River, Georgia, November 15, 1864, for exchange. Died at Savannah on November 18, 1864. Cause of death not reported.

HAGER, SIMEON S., Private
Enlisted at Orange Court House, Virginia, October 8, 1863, for the war. Reported present or accounted for on surviving company muster rolls through October, 1864. Transferred to Company A, 19th Regiment N.C. Troops (2nd Regiment N.C. Cavalry), in November-December, 1864.

HARWELL, JOSEPH M., Private
Enlisted at Orange Court House, Virginia, October 8, 1863, for the war. Present or accounted for through April, 1864. Reported absent wounded in May-June, 1864. Place and date wounded not reported. Reported absent wounded through October, 1864. Retired to the Invalid Corps on December 15, 1864.

HIGLEY, GEORGE, Private
Born in Lincoln County and resided in Catawba County where he was by occupation a farmer prior to enlisting at age 24, March 19, 1862. Reported absent without leave on or about April 28, 1862.

HINKLE, CYRUS, Private
Born in Lincoln County where he resided as a farmer prior to enlisting at age 45, March 23, 1862. Discharged on or about May 29, 1862, by reason of being overage.

HINSHAW, JACOB, Private
Quaker. Resided in Randolph County and was by occupation a farmer. Conscripted at age 28, November 3, 1862, for the war. Refused to perform military duty but was forced to remain with the company. Captured at Gettysburg, Pennsylvania, July 5, 1863, after he was left behind as a nurse for the wounded. Confined at Fort Delaware, Delaware, on or about July 10, 1863. Released on July 25, 1863, and was furnished transportation to Philadelphia, Pennsylvania.

HINSHAW, THOMAS, Private

Quaker. Resided in Randolph County and was conscripted at age 31, November 3, 1862, for the war. Refused to perform military duty but was forced to remain with the company. Captured at Gettysburg, Pennsylvania, July 5, 1863, after he was left behind as a nurse for the wounded. Confined at Fort Delaware, Delaware, on or about July 10, 1863. Released on July 25, 1863, and was furnished transportation to Philadelphia, Pennsylvania.

HOUSTON, WILLIAM G. P., Private

Born in Lincoln County where he resided as a merchant prior to enlisting in Lincoln County at age 25, March 21, 1862. Mustered in as Corporal. Reduced to ranks on December 10, 1862, by reason of "ill health." Reported present or accounted for on surviving company muster rolls through December, 1864; however, he was reported absent sick during most of that period.

HOWARD, ALLEN, Private

Born in Lincoln County where he resided as a farmer prior to enlisting at age 19, March 19, 1862. Died at Drewry's Bluff, Virginia, August 8, 1862. Cause of death not reported.

HOWARD, JOSEPH, Private

Born in Lincoln County where he resided as a farmer prior to enlisting at age 22, March 19, 1862. Killed at Gettysburg, Pennsylvania, July 3, 1863.

HOWARD, WILLIAM G., Private

Resided in Lincoln County and enlisted in Wayne County at age 30, February 22, 1863, for the war. Wounded in the thigh at Gettysburg, Pennsylvania, July 1, 1863. Captured at Gettysburg on or about July 4, 1863. Hospitalized at Gettysburg. Confined at Davids Island, New York Harbor, on or about July 20, 1863. Paroled at Davids Island and transferred to City Point, Virginia, where he was received on September 8, 1863, for exchange. Reported absent wounded or absent on parole through August, 1864. Retired from service in September-October, 1864. [May have served previously as Private in Company K, 23rd Regiment N.C. Troops (13th Regiment N.C. Volunteers).]

HUNT, McDONALD, Private

Resided in Lincoln County where he enlisted at age 27, June 30, 1862, for the war. Reported present on surviving company muster rolls through June, 1864. Killed at Globe Tavern, Virginia, August 21, 1864.

HUNT, SIMON W., Private

Born in Lincoln County where he resided as a farmer prior to enlisting at age 40, March 23, 1862. Died in hospital at Petersburg, Virginia, October 23, 1862, of "febris typhoides."

KIDDS, W. SIDNEY, Private

Resided in Lincoln County and enlisted at Camp French, near Petersburg, Virginia, at age 27, September 22, 1862, for the war. Captured at Falling Waters, Maryland, July 14, 1863. Sent to Baltimore, Maryland. Confined at Point Lookout, Maryland, August 21, 1863. Released at Point

Lookout on January 29, 1864, after taking the Oath of Allegiance and joining the U.S. Army. Assigned to Company C, 1st Regiment U.S. Volunteer Infantry.

KING, ALEXANDER, Private

Born in Lincoln County where he resided as a blacksmith prior to enlisting at Hanover Junction, Virginia, at age 38, May 20, 1863, for the war. Reported present or accounted for on surviving company muster rolls through April, 1864. Died in hospital near Spotsylvania Court House, Virginia, May 20, 1864, of "pneumonia."

LILLEY, JOHN W., Sergeant

Born in York District, South Carolina, and resided in Lincoln County where he was by occupation a carpenter prior to enlisting at age 24, March 22, 1862. Mustered in as Sergeant. Died in hospital at Petersburg, Virginia, October 27, 1862, of "ty[phoid] fever."

LINEBARGER, FREDERICK H., Sergeant

Born in Lincoln County where he resided as a farmer prior to enlisting at age 40, March 22, 1862. Mustered in as Sergeant. Discharged on or about May 24, 1862, by reason of being overage.

LITTLE, JOHN F., Sergeant

Born in Lincoln County where he resided as a farmer prior to enlisting in Lincoln County at age 26, March 22, 1862. Mustered in as Sergeant. Captured at Gettysburg, Pennsylvania, July 3, 1863. Confined at Fort Delaware, Delaware, on or about July 10, 1863. Transferred to Point Lookout, Maryland, October 20, 1863. Paroled at Point Lookout on or about February 13, 1865. Received at Cox's Wharf, James River, Virginia, on or about February 15, 1865, for exchange.

LITTLE, SAMUEL C., Private

Resided in Lincoln County and was by occupation a farmer prior to enlisting in Lincoln County at age 33, April 26, 1862, for the war. Reported present or accounted for on surviving company muster rolls through April, 1864. Died in May, 1864, of wounds. Place and date wounded not reported. Place of death not reported.

LITTLE, WILLIAM, Corporal

Born in Lincoln County where he resided as a farmer prior to enlisting at age 47, March 21, 1862. Mustered in as Corporal. Discharged on or about May 24, 1862, by reason of being overage.

LOCKMAN, JOHN, Private

Born in Lincoln County and enlisted at Camp French, near Petersburg, Virginia, September 8, 1862, for the war. Died in hospital at Petersburg on January 15, 1863, of "diarrhoea chronica."

LUCKY, ARCHIBALD C., Private

Resided in Lincoln County where he enlisted at age 38, March 9, 1863, for the war. Captured at Falling Waters, Maryland, July 14, 1863. Confined at Baltimore, Maryland. Transferred to Point Lookout, Maryland, August 20, 1863. Hospitalized at Point Lookout on October 23, 1863, with rubeola. Discharged from hospital on or about March 17, 1864. Paroled at Point Lookout and transferred to City Point, Virginia, where he was received on March 20, 1864, for exchange. Returned to duty in May-June, 1864, and was wounded in action. Place and date wounded not reported. Reported absent wounded through August, 1864. Returned to duty prior to October 27, 1864, when he was captured at Burgess' Mill, Virginia. Confined at Point Lookout on October 31, 1864. Paroled at Point Lookout on March 28, 1865. Received at Boulware's Wharf, James River, Virginia, March 30, 1865, for exchange. Hospitalized at Richmond, Virginia, March 30, 1865, with chronic diarrhoea. Transferred to another hospital on April 1, 1865.

LUCKY, DAVID, Private
Born in Lincoln County where he resided as a farmer prior to enlisting in Lincoln County at age 34, March 23, 1862. Reported present on surviving company muster rolls through April, 1864. Captured at or near Wilderness, Virginia, on or about May 6, 1864. Confined at Point Lookout, Maryland, May 17, 1864. Transferred to Elmira, New York, August 8, 1864. Died at Elmira on or about February 28, 1865, of "chro[nic] diarrhoea."

LUCKY, JOHN, Private
Born in Lincoln County where he resided as a farmer prior to enlisting in Lincoln County at age 26, March 23, 1862. Captured at Falling Waters, Maryland, July 14, 1863. Sent to Baltimore, Maryland. Paroled at Baltimore on August 23, 1863. Received at City Point, Virginia, August 24, 1863, for exchange. Returned to duty prior to March 1, 1864. Reported absent wounded in July-August, 1864. Place and date wounded not reported. Reported absent wounded through December, 1864. Paroled at Charlotte on May 17, 1865.

McINTOSH, WILLIAM, Private
Born in Mecklenburg County and resided in Gaston County where he was by occupation a farmer prior to enlisting at Orange Court House, Virginia, at age 42, October 8, 1863, for the war. Reported present or accounted for on surviving company muster rolls through December, 1864. Captured at Sutherland's Station, Virginia, April 2, 1865. Confined at Point Lookout, Maryland, April 4, 1865. Released at Point Lookout on June 29, 1865, after taking the Oath of Allegiance.

MELTON, ZACHARIAH, Private
Previously served as Private in Company I, 28th Regiment N.C. Troops. Transferred to this company on September 22, 1864. Reported present in November-December, 1864.

MOORE, JAMES A., Private
Born in Lincoln County where he resided as a farmer prior to enlisting at age 42, March 23, 1862. Discharged on May 29, 1862, by reason of being overage.

MOORE, JAMES M., Private
Enlisted at Orange Court House, Virginia, October 8, 1863, for the war. Reported present or accounted for on surviving company muster rolls through June, 1864. Variously reported to have died in July, 1864, and on

September 19, 1864, of disease. Place of death not reported.

MUNDAY, JAMES D., Private
Born in Lincoln County where he resided as a student prior to enlisting in Lincoln County at age 17, March 23, 1862. Reported present on surviving company muster rolls through December, 1864.

MUNDAY, JEREMIAH F., Private
Born in Lincoln County where he resided as a farmer prior to enlisting in Lincoln County at age 19, March 23, 1862. Wounded at Goldsboro on December 17, 1862. Returned to duty in March-August, 1863. Wounded in the hand (finger amputated) at Bristoe Station, Virginia, October 14, 1863. Reported absent wounded through April, 1864. Reported absent on detail at Salisbury in May-August, 1864. Reported absent on detached service at Concord in July-December, 1864. Paroled at Salisbury on May 3, 1865.

MUNDAY, WILLIAM F., Private
Born in Lincoln County where he resided as a farmer prior to enlisting at age 21, March 23, 1862. Captured at Gettysburg, Pennsylvania, July 3, 1863. Confined at Fort Delaware, Delaware, on or about July 10, 1863. Died at Fort Delaware on October 10, 1863. Cause of death not reported.

NANCE, ALBERT C., Private
Born in Lincoln County where he resided as a farmer prior to enlisting at age 26, October 27, 1864, for the war. Captured at or near Amelia Court House, Virginia, April 4, 1865. Confined at Hart's Island, New York Harbor, April 11, 1865. Released at Hart's Island on or about June 19, 1865, after taking the Oath of Allegiance.

NIXON, ALBERT M., Private
Born in Lincoln County where he resided as a farmer prior to enlisting in Lincoln County at age 25, March 21, 1862. Captured at Falling Waters, Maryland, July 14, 1863. Confined at Old Capitol Prison, Washington, D.C. Transferred to Point Lookout, Maryland, August 8, 1863. Released at Point Lookout on or about January 28, 1864, after taking the Oath of Allegiance and joining the U.S. Army. Assigned to Company C, 1st Regiment U.S. Volunteer Infantry.

NIXON, ARCHIBALD, Private
Born in Lincoln County where he resided as a farmer prior to enlisting at age 39, March 25, 1862. Wounded in the thigh and captured at Gettysburg, Pennsylvania, on or about July 3, 1863. Leg amputated. Hospitalized at Gettysburg where he died on July 19, 1863, of wounds.

NIXON, FRANKLIN, Private
Born in Lincoln County where he resided as a farmer prior to enlisting in Lincoln County at age 36, March 12, 1863, for the war. Captured at Gettysburg, July 3, 1863. Confined at Fort Delaware, Delaware, on or about July 10, 1863. Paroled at Fort Delaware on July 30, 1863. Received at City Point, Virginia, August 1, 1863, for exchange. Returned to duty in January-February,

1864. Captured at or near Wilderness, Virginia, on or about May 6, 1864. Confined at Point Lookout, Maryland, May 17, 1864. Transferred to Elmira, New York, August 8, 1864. Exchanged in September-October, 1864. Reported absent sick in November-December, 1864.

NIXON, GEORGE, Private
Born in Lincoln County where he resided as a farmer prior to enlisting at age 34, March 25, 1862. Wounded in the head and captured at Gettysburg, Pennsylvania, July 3, 1863. Hospitalized at Gettysburg where he died on July 20, 1863, of wounds.

NIXON, JAMES TURNER, Private
Born in Lincoln County where he resided as a farmer prior to enlisting at age 45, October 27, 1864, for the war. Captured at Sutherland's Station, Virginia, April 2, 1865. Confined at Point Lookout, Maryland, April 4, 1865. Released at Point Lookout on June 21, 1865, after taking the Oath of Allegiance.

NIXON, JOHN MONROE, Private
Born in Lincoln County where he resided as a farmer prior to enlisting in Lincoln County at age 34, March 25, 1862. Wounded in the left shoulder at Gettysburg, Pennsylvania, July 3, 1863. Returned to duty in September-October, 1863. Captured at Bristoe Station, Virginia, October 14, 1863. Confined at Old Capitol Prison, Washington, D.C. Transferred to Point Lookout, Maryland, October 27, 1863. Paroled at Point Lookout on or about March 16, 1864. Received at City Point, Virginia, March 20, 1864, for exchange. Returned to duty in May-June, 1864. Present or accounted for through December, 1864. Died in 1865. Place, exact date, and cause of death not reported.

NIXON, SIDNEY G., Private
Born in Lincoln County where he resided as a farmer prior to enlisting in Lincoln County at age 35, March 17, 1862. Captured at Falling Waters, Maryland, July 14, 1863. Sent to Baltimore, Maryland. Transferred to Point Lookout, Maryland, August 20, 1863. Paroled at Point Lookout on or about March 16, 1864. Received at City Point, Virginia, March 20, 1864, for exchange. Returned to duty in May-June, 1864. Captured at Burgess' Mill, Virginia, October 27, 1864. Confined at Point Lookout. Died at Point Lookout on February 8, 1865, of "dropsy."

NORWOOD, JAMES T., Corporal
Born in Lincoln County where he resided as a farmer prior to enlisting in Lincoln County at age 45, March 25, 1862. Mustered in as Private. Promoted to Corporal on December 11, 1862. Wounded at Gettysburg, Pennsylvania, July 3, 1863. Returned to duty in September-October, 1863. Captured at Bristoe Station, Virginia, October 14, 1863. Confined at Old Capitol Prison, Washington, D.C. Transferred to Point Lookout, Maryland, October 27, 1863. Paroled at Point Lookout on or about March 16, 1864. Received at City Point, Virginia, March 20, 1864, for exchange. Returned to duty in May-June, 1864. Reported absent wounded in July-October, 1864. Place and date wounded not reported. Returned to duty on an unspecified date. Surrendered at Appomattox Court House, Virginia, April 9, 1865.

NORWOOD, THOMAS S., Private
Born in Lincoln County where he resided as a farmer prior to enlisting in Lincoln County at age 28, March 27, 1862. Captured at Falling Waters, Maryland, July 14, 1863. Sent to Baltimore, Maryland. Transferred to Point Lookout, Maryland, August 20, 1863. Paroled at Point Lookout on or about March 16, 1864. Received at City Point, Virginia, March 20, 1864, for exchange. Returned to duty in May-June, 1864. Captured at Burgess' Mill, Virginia, October 27, 1864. Confined at Point Lookout on October 31, 1864. Died at Point Lookout on January 23, 1865, of "dysentery."

PENDERGRASS, JOHN, Private
Enlisted at Petersburg, Virginia, July 12, 1864, for the war. Present or accounted for through October, 1864. Hospitalized at Richmond, Virginia, December 5, 1864, with chronic diarrhoea. Returned to duty on March 24, 1865. Surrendered at Appomattox Court House, Virginia, April 9, 1865.

PERKINS, HENRY, Private
Born in Lincoln County where he resided as a farmer prior to enlisting at age 35, March 23, 1862. Died in hospital at Petersburg, Virginia, November 9, 1862, of "typhoid fever."

POTTS, WILLIAM T., Private
Resided in Lincoln County and enlisted at age 18, June 30, 1862, for the war. Captured at Bristoe Station, Virginia, October 14, 1863. Confined at Old Capitol Prison, Washington, D.C. Transferred to Point Lookout, Maryland, October 27, 1863. Died at Point Lookout on or about December 25, 1863. Cause of death not reported.

PRIM, WILLIAM A., Private
Born in Lincoln County where he resided as a farmer prior to enlisting in Lincoln County at age 22, March 17, 1862. Wounded in the right ankle and captured at Gettysburg, Pennsylvania, on or about July 1, 1863. Hospitalized at Gettysburg. Transferred to hospital at Davids Island, New York Harbor, where he arrived on or about July 20, 1863. Paroled at Davids Island on or about October 22, 1863. Received at City Point, Virginia, October 28, 1863, for exchange. Reported absent wounded or absent on parole through December, 1864. Survived the war.

PROCTOR, EDWARD A., Private
Resided in Lincoln County and enlisted at Orange Court House, Virginia, April 8, 1864, for the war. Captured at Burgess' Mill, Virginia, October 27, 1864. Confined at Point Lookout, Maryland, October 31, 1864. Released at Point Lookout on June 16, 1865, after taking the Oath of Allegiance.

REAGAN, JAMES L., Private
Resided in Lincoln County and enlisted in Wayne County at age 18, March 1, 1863, for the war. Reported present or accounted for on surviving company muster rolls through June, 1864. Wounded in the groin at or near Reams' Station, Virginia, on or about August 25, 1864. Returned to duty in November-December, 1864. Captured

at Petersburg, Virginia, April 3, 1865. Confined at Hart's Island, New York Harbor, April 11, 1865. Released at Hart's Island on June 19, 1865, after taking the Oath of Allegiance.

REDDING, MICHAEL F., Private

Resided in Randolph County and enlisted at Franklin, Virginia, at age 26, November 3, 1862, for the war. Deserted on November 24, 1862. Returned to duty subsequent to March 1, 1863. Deserted to the enemy near Gettysburg, Pennsylvania, on or about July 5, 1863. Confined at Fort Delaware, Delaware, on or about July 10, 1863. Released at Fort Delaware on September 22, 1863, after taking the Oath of Allegiance and joining the U.S. Army. Assigned to Company E, 3rd Regiment Maryland Cavalry.

REED, JAMES H., Private

Resided in Iredell or Mecklenburg County and enlisted in Lincoln County at age 19, April 28, 1862, for the war. Wounded in the right arm at Gettysburg, Pennsylvania, July 3, 1863. Returned to duty prior to September 1, 1863. Reported present through December, 1864. Captured at Sutherland's Station, Virginia, April 2, 1865. Confined at Point Lookout, Maryland, April 4, 1865. Released at Point Lookout on June 19, 1865, after taking the Oath of Allegiance.

REED, THOMAS L., Private

Resided in Lincoln County and enlisted at age 28, April 26, 1862, for the war. Wounded in the right thigh and left hand and captured at Gettysburg, Pennsylvania, on or about July 3, 1863. Hospitalized at Gettysburg. Transferred to hospital at Chester, Pennsylvania, where he arrived on July 19, 1863. Transferred to Point Lookout, Maryland, October 2, 1863. Paroled at Point Lookout on March 17, 1864. Received at City Point, Virginia, March 20, 1864, for exchange. Returned to duty in July-August, 1864. Wounded in the left foot (flesh) at Jones' Farm, Virginia, on or about September 30, 1864. Reported absent wounded through December, 1864. Paroled at Greensboro on May 1, 1865.

REYNOLDS, JOHN C., Private

Enlisted on October 27, 1864, for the war. Captured at Sutherland's Station, Virginia, April 2, 1865. Confined at Point Lookout, Maryland, April 4, 1865. Released at Point Lookout on June 8, 1865, after taking the Oath of Allegiance.

RILEY, JAMES, Private

Born in Lincoln County where he resided as a farmer prior to enlisting in Lincoln County at age 39, March 23, 1862. Deserted on June 24, 1863. Returned to duty on April 29, 1864. Reported absent sick in July-December, 1864. Reported absent without leave on March 11, 1865.

ROBINSON, FRANCIS C., Private

Resided in Lincoln County and enlisted at Orange Court House, Virginia, April 8, 1864, for the war. Reported present or accounted for through December, 1864. Captured at Sutherland's Station, Virginia, April 2, 1865. Confined at Point Lookout, Maryland, April 4, 1865.

Released at Point Lookout on June 16, 1865, after taking the Oath of Allegiance.

ROBINSON, JOHN C., Private

Born in Lincoln County and resided in Lincoln or Gaston County where he was by occupation a farmer prior to enlisting in Lincoln County at age 24, March 23, 1862. Captured at Gettysburg, Pennsylvania, July 3, 1863. Confined at Fort Delaware, Delaware, on or about July 10, 1863. Paroled at Fort Delaware on September 14, 1864. Received at Varina, Virginia, September 22, 1864, for exchange. Returned to duty in November-December, 1864. Captured at Sutherland's Station, Virginia, April 2, 1865. Confined at Point Lookout, Maryland, April 4, 1865. Released at Point Lookout on June 19, 1865, after taking the Oath of Allegiance.

ROBINSON, JOHN H., Corporal

Born in Lincoln County where he resided as a farmer prior to enlisting in Lincoln County at age 24, March 23, 1862. Mustered in as Private. Promoted to Corporal on September 1, 1864. Reported present or accounted for on surviving company muster rolls through December, 1864.

ROBINSON, JOSEPH B., Corporal

Born in Lincoln County where he resided as a farmer prior to enlisting at age 22, March 23, 1862. Mustered in as Private. Promoted to Corporal on December 11, 1862. Wounded in the left arm, right shoulder, and right thigh and captured at Gettysburg, Pennsylvania, on or about July 3, 1863. Hospitalized at Gettysburg. Died in hospital at Gettysburg on September 9, 1863, of wounds.

ROBINSON, THOMAS M., Private

Born in Lincoln County where he resided as a merchant prior to enlisting in Lincoln County at age 20, March 23, 1862. Captured near Hagerstown, Maryland, July 12, 1863. Sent to Baltimore, Maryland. Transferred to Point Lookout, Maryland, August 20, 1863. Paroled at Point Lookout on March 16, 1864. Received at City Point, Virginia, March 20, 1864, for exchange. Returned to duty in May-June, 1864. Reported absent wounded in July-October, 1864. Place and date wounded not reported. Was reportedly transferred to Barringer's cavalry brigade in November-December, 1864; however, no record of his service in the cavalry was located.

RUSSELL, HENRY COLUMBUS, Private

Resided in Randolph or Montgomery County and enlisted at Franklin, Virginia, at age 25, November 3, 1862, for the war. Captured at Gettysburg, Pennsylvania, July 3, 1863. Confined at Fort Delaware, Delaware, on or about July 10, 1863. Released at Fort Delaware on June 19, 1865, after taking the Oath of Allegiance.

SEXTON, JOHN, Private

Resided in Randolph County and enlisted at Franklin, Virginia, at age 26, November 3, 1862, for the war. Deserted on November 21, 1862. Returned to duty subsequent to March 1, 1863. Deserted on July 7, 1863.

SHELTON, LEVI M., Sergeant

Born in Lincoln County where he resided as a farmer

prior to enlisting in Lincoln County at age 32, March 22, 1862. Mustered in as Private. Promoted to Sergeant on June 14, 1862. Captured at Falling Waters, Maryland, July 14, 1863. Sent to Baltimore, Maryland. Confined at Point Lookout, Maryland, August 21, 1863. Paroled at Point Lookout on or about March 17, 1864. Received at City Point, Virginia, March 20, 1864, for exchange. Returned to duty in May-June, 1864. Reported absent wounded in July-October, 1864. Place and date wounded not reported. Returned to duty in November-December, 1864. Captured at Sutherland's Station, Virginia, April 2, 1865. Confined at Point Lookout on April 4, 1865. Released at Point Lookout on June 20, 1865, after taking the Oath of Allegiance. [North Carolina pension records indicate that he was wounded at Gettysburg, Pennsylvania, July 3, 1863, and at Richmond, Virginia, on unspecified dates.]

SHERRILL, JAMES M., Private
Born in Lincoln County where he resided as a farmer prior to enlisting in Lincoln County at age 18, March 25, 1862. Reported present or accounted for on surviving company muster rolls through August, 1864. Captured at Burgess' Mill, Virginia, October 27, 1864. Confined at Point Lookout, Maryland, October 31, 1864. Paroled at Point Lookout on January 17, 1865. Received at Boulware's Wharf, James River, Virginia, January 21, 1865, for exchange.

SHERRILL, JOHN A., Private
Born in Lincoln County where he resided as a farmer prior to enlisting at Orange Court House, Virginia, at age 18, August 21, 1863, for the war. Present or accounted for until wounded in the left arm at Jones' Farm, Virginia, October 1, 1864. Left arm amputated. Reported absent wounded through December, 1864. Retired from service on February 17, 1865.

SHERRILL, WILLIAM, Private
Resided in Lincoln County and enlisted in Wayne County at age 18, March 1, 1863, for the war. Reported present or accounted for on surviving company muster rolls through October, 1864. Died at or near Richmond, Virginia, on or about November 13, 1864. Cause of death not reported.

SIFFORD, JOHN FRANK, Private
Born in Lincoln County where he resided as a farmer prior to enlisting in Lincoln County at age 37, March 23, 1862. Hospitalized at Petersburg, Virginia, August 5, 1862, with acute rheumatism. Returned to duty on November 14, 1862. Captured at or near Falling Waters, Maryland, on or about July 14, 1863. Sent to Baltimore, Maryland. Confined at Point Lookout, Maryland, on or about August 17, 1863. Died at Point Lookout on February 20, 1864. Cause of death not reported.

SIFFORD, ROBERT J., Private
Resided in Lincoln County where he enlisted at age 24, April 10, 1862. Mustered in as Private. Promoted to Corporal on December 11, 1862. Wounded in the right leg and captured at Gettysburg, Pennsylvania, on or about July 3, 1863. Hospitalized at Gettysburg. Transferred to hospital at Chester, Pennsylvania, where he arrived on July 17, 1863. Transferred to hospital at Baltimore,

Maryland, where he arrived on or about October 4, 1863. Reduced to ranks in November, 1863-February, 1864, while a prisoner of war. Released at Point Lookout on May 14, 1865, after taking the Oath of Allegiance.

SIFFORD, WILLIAM A., Private
Resided in Lincoln County where he enlisted at age 35, March 10, 1863, for the war. Wounded in the left leg and captured at Gettysburg, Pennsylvania, on or about July 3, 1863. Hospitalized at Chester, Pennsylvania, on or about July 17, 1863. Transferred to hospital at Point Lookout, Maryland, where he arrived on or about October 4, 1863. Paroled at Point Lookout on March 16, 1864. Received at City Point, Virginia, March 20, 1864, for exchange. Reported absent on parole or absent sick through December, 1864. Paroled at Charlotte on May 3, 1865.

SMITH, JACKSON, Private
Resided in Lincoln County and enlisted at Camp French, near Petersburg, Virginia, at age 21, September 22, 1862, for the war. Wounded in the left arm at Goldsboro on December 17, 1862. Reported absent wounded through March 1, 1863. Company records do not indicate whether he returned to duty; however, he was listed as a deserter on August 26, 1863. Returned to duty on April 29, 1864. Present or accounted for through December, 1864. Surrendered at Appomattox Court House, Virginia, April 9, 1865.

SMITH, WILLIAM H., Corporal
Born in Lincoln County where he resided as a farmer prior to enlisting in Lincoln County at age 30, March 22, 1862. Mustered in as Private. Promoted to Corporal on December 10, 1863. Reported present on surviving company muster rolls through December, 1864.

THOMPSON, DANIEL G., Sergeant
Born in Lincoln County where he resided as a farmer prior to enlisting in Lincoln County at age 18, March 22, 1862. Mustered in as Private. Wounded in the groin and right thigh and captured at Gettysburg, Pennsylvania, July 3, 1863. Hospitalized at Gettysburg. Transferred to hospital at Baltimore, Maryland, July 25, 1863. Paroled at Baltimore on August 23, 1863. Received at City Point, Virginia, August 24, 1863, for exchange. Returned to duty on an unspecified date (probably in November-December, 1863). Promoted to Sergeant on December 10, 1863. Present or accounted for until transferred to Company I, 28th Regiment N.C. Troops, November 1, 1864.

THOMPSON, JOHN, Private
Born in Lincoln County where he resided as a farmer prior to enlisting in Lincoln County at age 19, March 22, 1862. Captured at Gettysburg, Pennsylvania, on or about July 3, 1863. Confined at Fort Delaware, Delaware, on or about July 10, 1863. Transferred to Point Lookout, Maryland, October 20, 1863. Died at Point Lookout on December 24, 1863, of "chronic diarrhoea."

THOMPSON, THOMAS B., Sergeant
Born in Lincoln County where he resided as a farmer prior to enlisting at age 28, March 22, 1862. Mustered

in as Sergeant. Wounded in the left thigh (fracture) and captured at Gettysburg, Pennsylvania, July 3, 1863. Hospitalized at Gettysburg where he died on August 10, 1863, of wounds.

THOMPSON, WILLIAM D., 1st Sergeant
Born in Lincoln County where he resided as a farmer prior to enlisting at age 32, March 23, 1862. Mustered in as 1st Sergeant. Killed at Gettysburg, Pennsylvania, July 3, 1863.

TUCKER, DAVID C., Private
Born in Lincoln County where he resided as a farmer prior to enlisting at age 22, March 22, 1862. Died in hospital at Petersburg, Virginia, September 5, 1862, of "typhoid fever."

TUCKER, JOHN C., Private
Resided in Lincoln County where he enlisted at age 27, April 28, 1862, for the war. Captured at Hagerstown, Maryland, July 12, 1863. Sent to Baltimore, Maryland. Confined at Point Lookout, Maryland, August 21, 1863. Hospitalized at Point Lookout on October 29, 1863, with chronic diarrhoea. Reported in hospital at Point Lookout until March 3, 1864, when he was paroled and transferred for exchange. Received at City Point, Virginia, March 6, 1864, for exchange. Returned to duty in May-June, 1864. Killed on June 8, 1864. Place of death not reported.

TUCKER, ROBERT A., Private
Born in Lincoln County where he resided as a farmer prior to enlisting at age 30, March 22, 1862. Died at home on or about June 3, 1862. Cause of death not reported.

WILKERSON, JAMES SIDNEY, Private
Born in Catawba County* and resided in Lincoln County where he was by occupation a farmer prior to enlisting at age 21, March 22, 1862. Captured at Gettysburg, Pennsylvania, on or about July 3, 1863. Confined at Fort Delaware, Delaware, on or about July 10, 1863. Transferred to Point Lookout, Maryland, October 20, 1863. Died in the smallpox hospital at Point Lookout on November 17, 1863.

WILLIAMS, JAMES, Private
Born in Cleveland County and was by occupation a blacksmith prior to enlisting at age 19, March 23, 1862. Reported absent without leave prior to July 1, 1862.

WILLIAMSON, JAMES D., Corporal
Born in Lincoln County where he resided as a tanner prior to enlisting in Lincoln County at age 38, March 22, 1862. Mustered in as Private. Deserted on June 24, 1863. Returned to duty on October 22, 1863. Promoted to Corporal on September 1, 1864. Captured at Burgess' Mill, Virginia, October 27, 1864. Confined at Point Lookout, Maryland, October 31, 1864. Died at Point Lookout on December 27, 1864, of "chronic diarrhoea."

WOMACK, STARLING, Private
Resided in Lincoln County and enlisted at Orange Court House, Virginia, at age 42, October 8, 1863, for the war. Hospitalized at Charlottesville, Virginia, December 25,

1863, with hemorrhoids. Furloughed for sixty days on March 9, 1864. Returned to duty in May-June, 1864. Captured at Sutherland's Station, Virginia, April 2, 1865. Confined at Point Lookout, Maryland, April 4, 1865. Released at Point Lookout on June 21, 1865, after taking the Oath of Allegiance. [North Carolina pension records indicate that he was wounded in the head near Petersburg, Virginia, October 4, 1864.]

YOUNG, SOLOMON, Private
Resided in Lincoln County and enlisted at Camp French, near Petersburg, Virginia, at age 27, September 22, 1862, for the war. Reported present or accounted for on surviving company muster rolls through December, 1864. Reported on duty as an ambulance driver during much of that period.

COMPANY H

This company, known as the "Spring Hill Guards," was raised in Lincoln County and enlisted in Lincoln County on March 25, 1862. It was mustered into state service at Camp Mangum, near Raleigh, on April 28, 1862, and assigned to the 52nd Regiment N.C. Troops as Company H. After joining the regiment the company functioned as a part of the regiment, and its history for the remainder of the war is reported as a part of the regimental history.

The information contained in the following roster was compiled primarily from a company muster-in and descriptive roll dated April 28, 1862, and from company muster rolls for May 31-June 30, 1862; October 31, 1862-February 28, 1863; and July 1, 1863-December 31, 1864. No company muster rolls were located for April 29-May 30, 1862; July 1-October 30, 1862; March 1-June 30, 1863; or for the period after December 31, 1864. Valuable information was obtained from primary records such as the North Carolina adjutant general's *Roll of Honor*, discharge certificates, medical records, prisoner of war records, *The War of the Rebellion: A Compilation of the Official Records of the Union and Confederate Armies*, militia records, newspaper casualty lists and obituaries, Confederate pension applications filed with the state of North Carolina, and the 1860 federal census of North Carolina. Secondary sources such as postwar rosters and histories, cemetery records, the *Confederate Veteran*, published genealogies, and records of the United Daughters of the Confederacy also provided useful information.

OFFICERS

CAPTAIN

ERSON, ERIC
Previously served as Corporal in Company K, 1st Regiment N.C. Infantry (6 months, 1861). Appointed Captain of this company on March 25, 1862. Wounded in the right hand (index finger fractured) at Gettysburg,

Pennsylvania, July 3, 1863. Index finger amputated. Returned to duty in January-February, 1864. Appointed Major on April 15, 1864, and transferred to the Field and Staff of this regiment.

LIEUTENANTS

ARENT, WILLIAM R., 3rd Lieutenant
Born in Lincoln County and was by occupation a farmer prior to enlisting in Lincoln County at age 22. Appointed 3rd Lieutenant on March 25, 1862. Wounded in the right leg at Gettysburg, Pennsylvania, on or about July 3, 1863. Captured at or near Gettysburg on July 5, 1863. Hospitalized at Gettysburg where he died on or about August 6, 1863, of wounds.

BEAL, PETER S., 3rd Lieutenant
Born in Lincoln County where he resided as a farmer prior to enlisting in Lincoln County at age 26, March 25, 1862. Mustered in as Sergeant. Appointed 3rd Lieutenant on October 1, 1862. Reported present or accounted for on surviving company muster rolls through April, 1864. Captured at or near Wilderness, Virginia, on or about May 6, 1864. Confined at Point Lookout, Maryland, May 14, 1864. Transferred to Fort Delaware, Delaware, June 23, 1864. Released at Fort Delaware on June 16, 1865, after taking the Oath of Allegiance.

DELLINGER, LAWSON ALEXANDER, 1st Lieutenant
Previously served as Sergeant in Company K, 1st Regiment N.C. Infantry (6 months, 1861). Appointed 2nd Lieutenant of this company on March 25, 1862. Promoted to 1st Lieutenant on August 19, 1862. Wounded and captured at Gettysburg, Pennsylvania, July 3, 1863. Confined at Fort Delaware, Delaware, on or about July 17, 1863. Transferred to Johnson's Island, Ohio, July 27, 1863. Paroled at Johnson's Island on an unspecified date. Received at City Point, Virginia, on or about February 24, 1865, for exchange. Survived the war. [It appears probable that he was appointed Captain subsequent to April 15, 1864; however, it also appears that his promotion was not confirmed.]

RANDLEMAN, SAMUEL H., 3rd Lieutenant
Born in Lincoln County where he resided as a farmer prior to enlisting in Lincoln County at age 21, March 25, 1862. Mustered in as Sergeant. Elected 3rd Lieutenant on February 1, 1864. Reported present on surviving company muster rolls through April, 1864. Hospitalized at Petersburg, Virginia, June 21, 1864, with a gunshot wound. Place and date wounded not reported. Returned to duty prior to July 1, 1864. Hospitalized at Richmond, Virginia, on or about October 17, 1864, with chronic diarrhoea. Returned to duty on November 25, 1864. No further records.

SUMMEROW, WILLIAM A., 1st Lieutenant
Previously served as Corporal in Company K, 1st Regiment N.C. Infantry (6 months, 1861). Appointed 1st Lieutenant of this company on March 25, 1862. Hospitalized at Petersburg, Virginia, on an unspecified

date with typhoid fever. Died on August 18, 1862, of "injuries received by falling from a window in the upper story of the Hospital."

NONCOMMISSIONED OFFICERS AND PRIVATES

ABERNATHY, ENOCH, _____
North Carolina pension records indicate that he served in this company.

ABERNATHY, WILLIAM F., Private
Resided in Lincoln County where he enlisted at age 28, November 11, 1862, for the war. Reported absent wounded on August 31, 1863. Place and date wounded not reported. Returned to duty in November, 1863-February, 1864. Killed at Cold Harbor, Virginia, on or about June 2, 1864.

ANDERSON, DAVID TROY, Private
Resided in Ashe County where he enlisted at age 23, November 11, 1862, for the war. Reported present or accounted for on surviving company muster rolls through December, 1864. Surrendered at Appomattox Court House, Virginia, April 9, 1865.

ARMSTRONG, JAMES MONROE, Private
Born in Lincoln County where he resided as a farmer prior to enlisting in Lincoln County at age 22, March 25, 1862. Died in hospital at Raleigh on or about April 29, 1862, of "pneumonia."

BALLARD, LAWSON A., Private
Born in Lincoln County where he resided as a farmer prior to enlisting in Lincoln County at age 18, March 25, 1862. Reported present or accounted for on surviving company muster rolls through December, 1864; however, he was reported absent sick during much of that period. Captured at Sutherland's Station, Virginia, April 2, 1865. Confined at Point Lookout, Maryland, April 4, 1865. Released at Point Lookout on June 22, 1865, after taking the Oath of Allegiance.

BLACK, DAVIDSON M., Private
Resided in Lincoln County where he enlisted at age 37, November 5, 1863, for the war. Hospitalized at Richmond, Virginia, February 20, 1864, with intermittent fever. Returned to duty on April 7, 1864. Reported present through June, 1864. Reported absent sick in July-December, 1864.

BROTHERTON, HIRAM, Private
Resided in Lincoln County and was by occupation a farmer prior to enlisting in Lincoln County at age 35, November 5, 1863, for the war. Reported present or accounted for on surviving company muster rolls through December, 1864. Surrendered at Appomattox Court House, Virginia, April 9, 1865.

BYNUM, ALBERT A., Private
Resided in Lincoln County where he enlisted at age 23, July 6, 1862, for the war. Deserted on July 25, 1863.

BYNUM, JAMES, Private
Born in Lincoln County where he resided as a farmer prior to enlisting in Lincoln County at age 22, March 25, 1862. Captured at or near Williamsport, Maryland, on or about July 5, 1863. Confined at Fort Delaware, Delaware. Paroled at Fort Delaware on July 30, 1863. Received at City Point, Virginia, August 1, 1863, for exchange. Returned to duty in January-February, 1864. Present or accounted for through December, 1864. Captured at or near Sayler's Creek, Virginia, on or about April 6, 1865. Sent to City Point, Virginia. Hospitalized at Washington, D.C., April 23, 1865, with chronic diarrhoea. Released at Washington on or about June 14, 1865, after taking the Oath of Allegiance.

BYNUM, JAMES FRANKLIN, Private
Resided in Lincoln County where he enlisted at age 21, July 8, 1862, for the war. Present or accounted for until wounded at Gettysburg, Pennsylvania, on or about July 3, 1863. No further records.

BYNUM, JOHN A., Private
Born in Lincoln County where he resided as a farmer prior to enlisting in Lincoln County at age 17, March 25, 1862. Discharged on an unspecified date, presumably by reason of being underage. Reenlisted in the company on July 10, 1863. Deserted on July 25, 1863. Returned to duty on November 7, 1863. Reported present or accounted for through October, 1864; however, he was reported absent sick during much of that period. Hospitalized at Richmond, Virginia, December 6, 1864, with dysentery. Furloughed for sixty days on December 31, 1864.

BYNUM, WILLIAM LAFAYETTE, Private
Born in Lincoln County where he resided as a farmer prior to enlisting in Lincoln County at age 18, March 25, 1862. Captured at Gettysburg, Pennsylvania, on or about July 3, 1863. Confined at Fort Delaware, Delaware, on or about July 10, 1863. Transferred to Point Lookout, Maryland, October 20, 1863. Died at Point Lookout on January 11, 1864. Cause of death not reported.

CALDWELL, JULIUS A., Private
Born in Lincoln County where he resided as a farmer prior to enlisting in Lincoln County at age 28, March 25, 1862. Died in hospital at Raleigh on April 29, 1862, of "pneumonia."

CALDWELL, MARCUS, Private
Born in Lincoln County where he resided as a farmer prior to enlisting in Lincoln County at age 26, March 25, 1862. Wounded in the right hand and captured at Gettysburg, Pennsylvania, on or about July 3, 1863. One finger amputated. Hospitalized at Gettysburg. Transferred to hospital at Baltimore, Maryland, on an unspecified date. Died in hospital at Baltimore on October 30, 1863. Cause of death not reported.

CARPENTER, WILLIAM P., Private
Born in Lincoln County where he resided as a farmer prior to enlisting in Lincoln County at age 18, March 25, 1862. Died at or near Winchester, Virginia, July 18, 1863, of wounds. Place and date wounded not reported.

CHESSER, EPHRAIM, Private
Born in Lincoln County where he resided as a farmer prior to enlisting in Lincoln County at age 28, March 25, 1862. Deserted on July 25, 1863. Apprehended on an unspecified date. Reported present but under arrest awaiting trial on January 7, 1864. Returned to duty prior to March 1, 1864. Reported present or accounted for through December, 1864. Captured at Sutherland's Station, Virginia, April 2, 1865. Confined at Point Lookout, Maryland, April 4, 1865. Released at Point Lookout on June 10, 1865, after taking the Oath of Allegiance.

CLARK, TOM, _____
Negro. Worked as a servant during the war.

CLIPPARD, D. ELAM, Private
Born in Lincoln County where he resided as a millwright prior to enlisting in Lincoln County at age 25, April 29, 1862, for the war. Died at Goldsboro on July 3, 1862. Cause of death not reported.

CLIPPARD, JOHN A., Private
Born in Lincoln County where he resided as a farmer prior to enlisting in Lincoln County at age 20, March 25, 1862. Died in hospital at Raleigh on or about May 11, 1863, of "pneumonia."

CLONINGER, ELI A., Private
Resided in Lincoln County where he enlisted at age 24, October 2, 1862, for the war. Hospitalized at Richmond, Virginia, June 24, 1863, with debilitas. Returned to duty on or about July 29, 1863. Captured at Bristoe Station, Virginia, October 14, 1863. Confined at Old Capitol Prison, Washington, D.C. Transferred to Point Lookout, Maryland, October 27, 1863. Died at Point Lookout on August 13, 1864. Cause of death not reported.

CODY, PERRY, Private
Previously served as Private in Company B, 7th Regiment Georgia Volunteer Infantry. Transferred to this company on September 1, 1864. Wounded slightly in the head at Jones' Farm, Virginia, on or about September 30, 1864. Captured at Sutherland's Station, Virginia, April 2, 1865. Confined at Point Lookout, Maryland, April 4, 1865. Released at Point Lookout on June 5, 1865, after taking the Oath of Allegiance.

DELLINGER, ALBERT P., Private
Born in Lincoln County where he resided as a farmer prior to enlisting in Lincoln County at age 18, March 25, 1862. Reported present or accounted for on surviving company muster rolls through December, 1864. Survived the war.

DELLINGER, ISAAC, Private
Resided in Lincoln County where he enlisted at age 28, July 6, 1862, for the war. Captured at Gettysburg, Pennsylvania, July 5, 1863, after he was left behind to help attend to the wounded. Confined at Fort Delaware, Delaware, on or about July 10, 1863. Transferred to Point Lookout, Maryland, where he arrived on October 15, 1863. Paroled at Point Lookout on February 18, 1865.

Received at Boulware's Wharf, James River, Virginia, February 20, 1865, for exchange. Survived the war.

DELLINGER, JOHN CALVIN, Sergeant
Previously served as Private in Company K, 1st Regiment N.C. Infantry (6 months, 1861). Enlisted in this company in Lincoln County on March 25, 1862. Mustered in as Corporal. Promoted to Sergeant on March 21, 1864. Reported present or accounted for on surviving company muster rolls through October, 1864. Hospitalized at Charlotte on November 27, 1864, with necrosis. Returned to duty on December 30, 1864. Captured near Petersburg, Virginia, March 25, 1865. Confined at Point Lookout, Maryland, March 28, 1865. Released at Point Lookout on June 12, 1865, after taking the Oath of Allegiance.

DELLINGER, JOHN F., Private
Born in Lincoln County where he resided as a farmer prior to enlisting in Lincoln County at age 20, March 25, 1862. Died in hospital at Raleigh on or about May 2, 1862, of "pneumonia."

DELLINGER, MICHAEL P., Private
Born in Lincoln County where he resided as a farmer prior to enlisting in Lincoln County at age 21, March 25, 1862. Reported present or accounted for on surviving company muster rolls through December, 1864; however, he was reported absent sick during much of that period. Survived the war.

DELLINGER, MONROE D., Private
Resided in Lincoln County where he enlisted at age 24, July 6, 1862, for the war. Captured at Falling Waters, Maryland, July 14, 1863. Confined at Old Capitol Prison, Washington, D.C. Transferred to Point Lookout, Maryland, August 8, 1863. Transferred to Elmira, New York, August 16, 1864. Paroled at Elmira on March 10, 1865. Received at Boulware's Wharf, James River, Virginia, March 15, 1865, for exchange. Survived the war.

DELLINGER, NOAH, Private
Born in Lincoln County where he resided as a farmer prior to enlisting in Lincoln County at age 18, March 25, 1862. Hospitalized at Charlottesville, Virginia, October 18, 1863, with a gunshot wound. Place and date wounded not reported (probably wounded at Bristoe Station, Virginia, October 14, 1863). Furloughed for thirty days on November 17, 1863. Returned to duty in January-February, 1864. Captured at Burgess' Mill, Virginia, October 27, 1864. Confined at Point Lookout, Maryland, October 31, 1864. Paroled at Point Lookout on March 28, 1865. Received at Boulware's Wharf, James River, Virginia, March 30, 1865, for exchange.

DELLINGER, SAMUEL W., Private
Previously served as Private in Company K, 1st Regiment N.C. Infantry (6 months, 1861). Enlisted in this company on May 11, 1862. Reported absent without leave on or about July 1, 1862.

EARNEY, ADMIRAL P., Private
Born in Lincoln County where he resided prior to enlisting in Lincoln County at age 23, April 19, 1862, for

the war. Hospitalized at Charlottesville, Virginia, October 18, 1863, with an unspecified wound. Place and date wounded not reported (probably wounded at Bristoe Station, Virginia, October 14, 1863). Returned to duty on November 24, 1863. Reported present or accounted for through December, 1864. Wounded in the right foot and captured at Sutherland's Station, Virginia, April 2, 1865. Right foot amputated. Hospitalized at Washington, D.C., April 12, 1865. Released at Washington on July 10, 1865, after taking the Oath of Allegiance.

EARNEY, LAFAYETTE, Private
Previously served as Private in Company K, 1st Regiment N.C. Infantry (6 months, 1861). Enlisted in this company in Lincoln County on March 25, 1862. Captured at Falling Waters, Maryland, July 14, 1863. Confined at Old Capitol Prison, Washington, D.C. Transferred to Point Lookout, Maryland, August 8, 1863. Transferred to Fort Monroe, Virginia, March 2, 1864. Released at Fort Monroe on March 3, 1864, after taking the Oath of Allegiance.

EDDLEMAN, DAVID F., Private
Born in Lincoln County and resided in Gaston County where he was by occupation a farmer prior to enlisting in Lincoln County at age 30, March 25, 1862. Captured at Gettysburg, Pennsylvania, on or about July 3, 1863. Confined at Fort Delaware, Delaware, on or about July 10, 1863. Transferred to Point Lookout, Maryland, October 20, 1863. Hospitalized at Point Lookout on October 27, 1863, with chronic diarrhoea. Returned to duty on January 12, 1864. Paroled at Point Lookout on May 3, 1864. Received at Aiken's Landing, James River, Virginia, May 8, 1864, for exchange. Returned to duty prior to July 1, 1864. Captured at Sutherland's Station, Virginia, April 2, 1865. Confined at Point Lookout on April 4, 1865. Released at Point Lookout on June 11, 1865, after taking the Oath of Allegiance.

EDDLEMAN, WILLIAM P., Private
Born in Lincoln County and resided in Gaston County where he was by occupation a farmer prior to enlisting in Lincoln County at age 26, March 25, 1862. Died in hospital at Petersburg, Virginia, October 16, 1862, of "gastritis acuta."

ELLIOTT, SAMUEL T., Private
Place and date of enlistment not reported (probably enlisted in January-March, 1865). Surrendered at Appomattox Court House, Virginia, April 9, 1865.

ERVIN, LAWSON A., Private
Enlisted in Lincoln County at age 18, April 20, 1864, for the war. Reported present through December, 1864. Survived the war. [North Carolina pension records indicate that he was wounded (knocked down and stunned by a cannonball) at Burgess' Mill, Virginia, on or about October 28, 1864. North Carolina pension records also indicate that he was wounded in the head, hand, and hip at Hatcher's Run, Virginia, on an unspecified date.]

FISHER, DAVID, Private
Resided in Lincoln County where he enlisted at age 34, January 30, 1863, for the war. Captured at Falling Waters,

Maryland, July 14, 1863. Confined at Baltimore, Maryland. Transferred to Point Lookout, Maryland, where he arrived on August 17, 1863. Paroled at Point Lookout on March 3, 1864. Received at City Point, Virginia, March 6, 1864, for exchange. Reported present through December, 1864. Captured at Sutherland's Station, Virginia, April 2, 1865. Confined at Point Lookout, Maryland, April 4, 1865. Released at Point Lookout on June 27, 1865, after taking the Oath of Allegiance. [North Carolina pension records indicate that he was wounded at Reams' Station, Virginia, in 1864. May have served previously as Private in Company B, 23rd Regiment N.C. Troops (13th Regiment N.C. Volunteers).]

FISHER, JAMES, Private
Born in Lincoln County where he resided as a farmer prior to enlisting in Lincoln County at age 18, March 25, 1862. Deserted on July 25, 1863. Returned to duty on November 7, 1863. Reported present through December, 1864. Survived the war.

FORNEY, JACOB G., Private
Enlisted in Lincoln County on February 8, 1862. No further records.

FORNEY, SIDNEY J., Corporal
Born in Lincoln County where he resided as a farmer prior to enlisting in Lincoln County at age 18, March 25, 1862. Mustered in as Private. Promoted to Corporal on February 2, 1864. Reported present or accounted for on surviving company muster rolls through December, 1864. Survived the war. [North Carolina pension records indicate that he was wounded at Globe Tavern, Virginia, August 21, 186(4).]

FRIDAY, JOHN CALEB, Private
Born in Lincoln County and resided in Gaston County where he was by occupation a farmer prior to enlisting in Lincoln County at age 18, March 25, 1862. Reported present or accounted for on surviving company muster rolls through December, 1864. Surrendered at Appomattox Court House, Virginia, April 9, 1865. [Wounded in the hand at Petersburg, Virginia, on an unspecified date and lost two fingers.]

FRIDAY, WILLIAM A., Private
Born in Lincoln County and resided in Gaston County where he was by occupation a farmer prior to enlisting in Lincoln County at age 19, March 25, 1862. Reported present or accounted for on surviving company muster rolls through June, 1864. Served as an orderly to an unspecified general during most of that period. Hospitalized at Richmond, Virginia, July 30, 1864, with chronic diarrhoea. Furloughed for thirty days on August 4, 1864. Returned to duty prior to November 1, 1864. Surrendered at Appomattox Court House, Virginia, April 9, 1865.

GARRISON, EPHRAIM, Sergeant
Born in Lincoln County where he resided as a farmer prior to enlisting in Lincoln County at age 21, March 25, 1862. Mustered in as Sergeant. Died in hospital at

Petersburg, Virginia, on or about October 27, 1862, of "febris typhoides."

GARRISON, HENRY, Private
Resided in Lincoln County and enlisted at age 30. Enlistment date not reported (probably enlisted in the spring of 1863). Discharged on May 28, 1863. Reason discharged not reported.

GARRISON, SIDNEY, Private
Born in Lincoln County where he resided as a farmer prior to enlisting in Lincoln County at age 16, March 25, 1862. Died in hospital at Goldsboro on March 16, 1863, of "typhoid fever."

GIBSON, GEORGE, Private
Born in Lincoln County and resided in Gaston County where he was by occupation a farmer prior to enlisting in Lincoln County at age 48, March 25, 1862. Captured at Falling Waters, Maryland, July 14, 1863. Sent to Baltimore, Maryland. Confined at Point Lookout, Maryland, August 11, 1863. Paroled at Point Lookout on March 3, 1864. Received at City Point, Virginia, March 6, 1864, for exchange. Returned to duty prior to July 1, 1864. Reported present through December, 1864. Survived the war.

GOODSON, ABNER, Private
Resided in Lincoln County where he enlisted at age 26, July 6, 1862, for the war. Wounded in the left leg (fracture) and captured at Gettysburg, Pennsylvania, July 3, 1863. Hospitalized at Gettysburg. Transferred to hospital at Baltimore, Maryland, September 14, 1863. Paroled at Baltimore on September 25, 1863. Received at City Point, Virginia, September 27, 1863, for exchange. Returned to duty in January-February, 1864. Reported present through December, 1864. Captured near Petersburg, Virginia, March 25, 1865. Confined at Point Lookout, Maryland, March 28, 1865. Released at Point Lookout on June 27, 1865, after taking the Oath of Allegiance.

GOODSON, GEORGE W., Sergeant
Resided in Lincoln County where he enlisted at age 31, July 6, 1862, for the war. Mustered in as Private. Promoted to Corporal on February 2, 1864. Reported present or accounted for on surviving company muster rolls through April, 1864. Hospitalized at Richmond, Virginia, May 18, 1864, with a gunshot wound. Place and date wounded not reported. Furloughed for thirty days on June 9, 1864. Returned to duty prior to November 1, 1864. Promoted to Sergeant subsequent to December 31, 1864. Captured at Sutherland's Station, Virginia, April 2, 1865. Confined at Point Lookout, Maryland, April 4, 1865. Released at Point Lookout on June 27, 1865, after taking the Oath of Allegiance. [Recommended for promotion to 2nd Lieutenant on March 29, 1865, for "gallantry and general good conduct"; however, it appears that his appointment was never confirmed.]

GOODSON, JEREMIAH, Private
Born in Lincoln County where he resided as a farmer prior to enlisting in Lincoln County at age 23, March 25,

1862. Died at Company Shops (present-day Burlington) on December 1, 1862. Cause of death not reported.

GOODSON, JOHN C., Sergeant
Born in Lincoln County where he resided as a farmer prior to enlisting in Lincoln County at age 24, March 25, 1862. Mustered in as Corporal. Wounded at Goldsboro on December 17, 1862. Returned to duty prior to March 1, 1863. Promoted to Sergeant on February 2, 1864. Reported present or accounted for on surviving company muster rolls through June, 1864. Hospitalized at Richmond, Virginia, August 16, 1864, with chronic diarrhoea. Returned to duty on August 19, 1864. "Died in the field" on October 5, 1864. Cause of death not reported.

GOODSON, RUFUS L., Private
Resided in Lincoln County where he enlisted at age 25, July 6, 1862, for the war. Reported present or accounted for on surviving company muster rolls through June, 1864. Hospitalized at Richmond, Virginia, on or about July 14, 1864, with chronic diarrhoea. Furloughed for thirty days on July 30, 1864. Returned to duty prior to November 1, 1864. Wounded in both legs near Petersburg, Virginia, March 25, 1865. Hospitalized at Richmond. Captured in hospital at Richmond on April 3, 1865. Survived the war.

GUTHERY, COLUMBUS, Private
Born in Union District, South Carolina, and resided in Gaston County where he was by occupation a farmer prior to enlisting at age 16, March 25, 1862. Discharged at Raleigh on May 28, 1862, presumably by reason of being underage.

HAWKINS, WILLIAM P., Private
Born in Lincoln County where he resided as a farmer prior to enlisting in Lincoln County at age 22, March 25, 1862. Captured (and possibly wounded) at Gettysburg, Pennsylvania, on or about July 3, 1863. Confined at Fort Delaware, Delaware, July 10, 1863. Transferred to Point Lookout, Maryland, October 20, 1863. Released at Point Lookout on February 5, 1864, after taking the Oath of Allegiance and joining the U.S. Army. Unit to which assigned not reported.

HAYNES, JOHN C., Private
Previously served as Private in Company K, 1st Regiment N.C. Infantry (6 months, 1861). Enlisted in this company in Lincoln County on March 25, 1862. Reported present or accounted for on surviving company muster rolls through January 7, 1864. Hospitalized at Richmond, Virginia, February 16, 1864, with chronic diarrhoea. Transferred to Farmville, Virginia, May 2, 1864. Died in hospital at Farmville on June 7, 1864, of "chr[onic] diarrhoea." Served as a teamster during much of the war.

HEDGEPETH, A., Private
Place and date of enlistment not reported (probably enlisted in January-March, 1865). Surrendered at Appomattox Court House, Virginia, April 9, 1865.

HELDERMAN, ABLE J., Private
Resided in Lincoln County where he enlisted at age 24,

November 5, 1863, for the war. Reported present or accounted for on surviving company muster rolls through December, 1864. Hospitalized at Richmond, Virginia, March 13, 1865, with chronic diarrhoea. Captured in hospital at Richmond on April 3, 1865. Transferred to Libby Prison, Richmond, on an unspecified date. Transferred to Newport News, Virginia, April 23, 1865. Transferred back to Richmond on an unspecified date. Reported in hospital at Richmond on May 28, 1865. [Surviving records suggest that this soldier died in 1865 while still in Federal hands.]

HELDERMAN, GEORGE F., Private
Born in Lincoln County where he resided as a farm laborer prior to enlisting in Lincoln County at age 28, October 11, 1862, for the war. Wounded at Goldsboro on December 17, 1862. Returned to duty prior to March 1, 1863. Captured at Bristoe Station, Virginia, October 14, 1863. Confined at Old Capitol Prison, Washington, D.C. Transferred to Point Lookout, Maryland, October 27, 1863. Paroled at Point Lookout on or about February 12, 1865. Received at Cox's Wharf, James River, Virginia, on or about February 14, 1865, for exchange.

HELDERMAN, JOHN F., Private
Born in Lincoln County where he resided as an overseer prior to enlisting in Lincoln County at age 33, April 25, 1862, for the war. Detailed to work as a mechanic in the armory at Petersburg, Virginia, on or about September 5, 1862. Rejoined the company in July-August, 1864. Reported present through December, 1864. Survived the war.

HELDERMAN, RUFUS M., Corporal
Previously served as Private in Company K, 1st Regiment N.C. Infantry (6 months, 1861). Enlisted in this company on April 28, 1862, for the war. Mustered in as Private. Promoted to Corporal on November 1, 1862. Reported missing at Gettysburg, Pennsylvania, on or about July 3, 1863. Was presumably killed at Gettysburg.

HELMS, AUSTIN, Private
Born in Mecklenburg County and resided in Lincoln County where he was by occupation a farmer prior to enlisting in Lincoln County at age 48, March 25, 1862. Reported present or accounted for on surviving company muster rolls through December, 1864. Captured at Sutherland's Station, Virginia, April 2, 1865. Confined at Point Lookout, Maryland, April 4, 1865. Released at Point Lookout on June 27, 1865, after taking the Oath of Allegiance.

HONEYCUT, JOHN H., Private
Resided in Lincoln County and enlisted at age 22, July 6, 1862, for the war. Killed at Bristoe Station, Virginia, October 14, 1863.

HOPE, CHRISTOPHER D., Private
Born in Lincoln County and resided in Gaston County where he was by occupation a brickmason prior to enlisting in Lincoln County at age 31, March 25, 1862. Wounded in the right leg and captured at Gettysburg, Pennsylvania, July 3, 1863. Hospitalized at Gettysburg.

Transferred to hospital at Baltimore, Maryland, July 19, 1863. Exchanged on or about August 28, 1863. Returned to duty prior to November 1, 1863. Reported present until May 6, 1864, when he was captured at Wilderness, Virginia. Confined at Point Lookout, Maryland. Paroled at Point Lookout on or about September 18, 1864. Received at Aiken's Landing, James River, Virginia, September 22, 1864, for exchange. Hospitalized at Richmond, Virginia, September 23, 1864, with chronic diarrhoea and scorbutus. Furloughed for thirty days on October 14, 1864. Returned to duty in November-December, 1864. Captured at Sutherland's Station, Virginia, April 2, 1865. Confined at Point Lookout on April 4, 1865. Released at Point Lookout on June 27, 1865, after taking the Oath of Allegiance.

HOPE, JOHN, Private
Born in Lincoln County where he resided as a farmer prior to enlisting in Lincoln County at age 46, March 25, 1862. Died at Raleigh on or about May 16, 1862. Cause of death not reported.

HOPE, WILLIAM, Private
Born in Lincoln County where he resided as a farmer prior to enlisting in Lincoln County at age 39, March 25, 1862. Reported absent without leave in June, 1862. Returned to duty prior to March 1, 1863. Reported present or accounted for on surviving company muster rolls through December, 1864. Served as a teamster during much of the war. Survived the war. [North Carolina pension records indicate that he was wounded in the leg at the Weldon Railroad on August 27 (correct date was probably August 25), 1864.]

HOVIS, MOSES, Private
Born in Lincoln County where he resided as a farmer prior to enlisting in Lincoln County at age 19, March 25, 1862. Wounded and captured at Gettysburg, Pennsylvania, July 3, 1863. Hospitalized at Baltimore, Maryland. Paroled at Baltimore on September 25, 1863. Received at City Point, Virginia, September 27, 1863, for exchange. Returned to duty in March-April, 1864. Captured at or near Spotsylvania Court House, Virginia, on or about May 12, 1864. Confined at Point Lookout, Maryland, May 17, 1864. Transferred to Elmira, New York, August 12, 1864. Released at Elmira on June 12, 1865, after taking the Oath of Allegiance.

HOVIS, WESTLEY, Private
Resided in Lincoln County and was by occupation a farmer prior to enlisting at age 30, July 6, 1862, for the war. Wounded in the thumb at Gettysburg, Pennsylvania, July 3, 1863. Returned to duty in September-October, 1863. Reported present through December, 1864. Captured at Sutherland's Station, Virginia, April 2, 1865. Confined at Point Lookout, Maryland, April 4, 1865. Released at Point Lookout on June 27, 1865, after taking the Oath of Allegiance.

KEENER, CEPHAS, Private
Born in Lincoln County where he resided as a farmer prior to enlisting in Lincoln County at age 31, March 10, 1863, for the war. Reported present or accounted for on surviving company muster rolls through August, 1864. Killed at Burgess' Mill, Virginia, October 27, 1864.

KEENER, DAVID A., Private
Born in Lincoln County where he resided as a farmer prior to enlisting in Lincoln County at age 21, March 25, 1862. Wounded in the left thigh at Bristoe Station, Virginia, October 14, 1863. Hospitalized at Richmond, Virginia. Furloughed for sixty days on December 1, 1863. Reported on detail for light duty at Charlotte in March-December, 1864. Survived the war.

KEEVER, DAVID A., Private
Resided in Lincoln County where he enlisted at age 25, July 6, 1862, for the war. Reported present on surviving company muster rolls through April, 1864. Reported absent wounded in May-June, 1864. Place and date wounded not reported. Returned to duty in September-October, 1864. Captured near Petersburg, Virginia, March 25, 1865. Confined at Point Lookout, Maryland, March 28, 1865. Released at Point Lookout on June 28, 1865, after taking the Oath of Allegiance. [Postwar records indicate that he was shot through the body in an unspecified battle but survived even though such a wound was "usually mortal."]

KEEVER, THOMAS, Private
Enlisted in Lincoln County on January 3, 1864, for the war. Died in hospital at Richmond, Virginia, April 25, 1864, of "chron[ic] diarrhoea" and "typh[oid] febris."

LANEY, JOHN S., Private
Resided in Lincoln County where he enlisted at age 20, July 6, 1862, for the war. Wounded at Gettysburg, Pennsylvania, July 1, 1863. Hospitalized at Richmond, Virginia. Transferred to hospital at Raleigh on or about July 24, 1863. Died in hospital at Raleigh on August 26, 1863, of wounds, "typhoid fever," and "diarrhoea."

LAWING, JOHN M., Private
Born in Mecklenburg County and resided in Lincoln County where he was by occupation a farmer prior to enlisting in Lincoln County at age 20, March 25, 1862. Wounded at Gettysburg, Pennsylvania, July 3, 1863. Returned to duty in November, 1863-February, 1864. Reported present or accounted for on surviving company muster rolls through December, 1864.

LAWING, WILLIAM A., Private
Resided in Lincoln County where he enlisted at age 25, October 24, 1862, for the war. Wounded in the left leg and captured at Gettysburg, Pennsylvania, July 3, 1863. Hospitalized at Gettysburg. Transferred to hospital at Chester, Pennsylvania, on or about July 14, 1863. Hospitalized at Point Lookout, Maryland, October 4, 1863. Paroled at Point Lookout on or about March 3, 1864. Received at City Point, Virginia, March 6, 1864, for exchange. Hospitalized at Richmond, Virginia. Furloughed for thirty days on March 15, 1864. Reported on detail as a hospital nurse in July-December, 1864. Reported on duty as an "agent" in hospital at Kittrell Springs on February 15, 1865. Survived the war.

LEE, WILLIAM, Private
Resided in Lincoln County and enlisted at age 35, March 25, 1862. Discharged on May 28, 1862, presumably by reason of being overage.

LEWIS, MANUEL, Private
Resided in Ashe County and enlisted in Lincoln County at age 20, November 11, 1862, for the war. Deserted on November 25, 1862.

LOFTIN, LANGDON A., Private
Born in Lincoln County where he resided as a farmer prior to enlisting at age 36, March 25, 1862. Discharged on May 28, 1862, presumably by reason of being overage. Later served as Private in Company B, 23rd Regiment N.C. Troops (13th Regiment N.C. Volunteers).

LOFTIN, MARCUS LAFAYETTE, Sergeant
Born in Lincoln County where he resided as a farmer prior to enlisting in Lincoln County at age 30, March 25, 1862. Mustered in as Corporal. Promoted to Sergeant in July-October, 1862. Captured at Falling Waters, Maryland, July 14, 1863. Sent to Baltimore, Maryland. Transferred to Point Lookout, Maryland, August 16, 1863. Paroled at Point Lookout on April 27, 1864. Received at City Point, Virginia, April 30, 1864, for exchange. Returned to duty in July-August, 1864. Captured at Sutherland's Station, Virginia, April 2, 1865. Confined at Point Lookout on April 4, 1865. Released at Point Lookout on June 28, 1865, after taking the Oath of Allegiance.

LOWE, FRANKLIN, Private
Born in Lincoln County where he resided as a farmer prior to enlisting in Lincoln County at age 17, March 25, 1862. Died at Raleigh on May 28, 1862. Cause of death not reported.

LYNCH, EPHRAIM MILTON, Private
Resided in Lincoln County where he enlisted at age 34, July 6, 1862, for the war. Reported present or accounted for on surviving company muster rolls through December, 1864. Captured at Sutherland's Station, Virginia, April 2, 1865. Confined at Point Lookout, Maryland. Released at Point Lookout on June 28, 1865, after taking the Oath of Allegiance.

McCALL, JOHN C., Sergeant
Born in Lincoln County where he resided as a farmer prior to enlisting in Lincoln County at age 28, March 25, 1862. Mustered in as Sergeant. Wounded at Goldsboro on December 17, 1862. Returned to duty prior to March 1, 1863. Captured at Gettysburg, Pennsylvania, on or about July 3, 1863. Confined at Fort Delaware, Delaware, July 10, 1863. Transferred to Point Lookout, Maryland, October 20, 1863. Paroled at Point Lookout on May 3, 1864. Received at Aiken's Landing, James River, Virginia, May 8, 1864, for exchange. Returned to duty prior to July 1, 1864. Captured at Burgess' Mill, Virginia, October 27, 1864. Confined at Point Lookout on October 31, 1864. Died at Point Lookout on March 6, 1865. Cause of death not reported.

McCAUL, JAMES, Private
Resided in Lincoln County where he enlisted at age 19, March 11, 1863, for the war. Died in hospital at Richmond, Virginia, September 18, 1863, of "typhoid fever."

McCORKLE, RICHARD A., Private
Born in Lincoln County where he resided as a farmer prior to enlisting in Lincoln County at age 38, March 25, 1862. Mustered in as Corporal. Wounded in the left forearm at Gettysburg, Pennsylvania, July 3, 1863. Reported absent wounded through February, 1864. Reported on detail for light duty at Salisbury in March-April, 1864. Reduced to ranks in March-April, 1864. Retired from service on February 14, 1865, by reason of disability from wounds received at Gettysburg "producing partial paralysis of hand [and] loss of rotatory motion."

MAIN, LEMUEL, Private
Resided in Ashe County where he enlisted at age 20, November 11, 1862, for the war. Deserted on November 25, 1862.

MOORE, ANDREW F., Corporal
Born in Lincoln County where he resided as a farmer prior to enlisting in Lincoln County at age 20, March 25, 1862. Mustered in as Private. Promoted to Corporal on March 21, 1864. Reported present or accounted for on surviving company muster rolls through December, 1864. Survived the war. [North Carolina pension records indicate that he was wounded in the head near Petersburg, Virginia, in 1864.]

NANCE, ALBERT, Private
Resided in Gaston County and was by occupation a farm laborer prior to enlisting in Lincoln County at age 18, October 14, 1863, for the war. Present or accounted for until he died in hospital at or near Richmond, Virginia, on or about July 7, 1864. Cause of death not reported.

NANCE, CLABERN, Private
Born in Lincoln County and resided in Gaston County where he was by occupation a farmer prior to enlisting in Lincoln County at age 23, March 25, 1862. Captured at Falling Waters, Maryland, July 14, 1863. Sent to Baltimore, Maryland. Confined at Point Lookout, Maryland, August 17, 1863. Paroled at Point Lookout on March 3, 1864. Received at City Point, Virginia, March 6, 1864, for exchange. Returned to duty prior to July 1, 1864. Reported absent on sick furlough in July-December, 1864. Survived the war. [North Carolina pension records indicate that he was wounded in the left foot near Petersburg, Virginia, August 21, 1864.]

NANCE, JAMES, Private
Resided in Gaston County and enlisted in Lincoln County at age 30, October 16, 1862, for the war. Deserted on May 24, 1863. Returned to duty on October 19, 1863. Died in hospital at Richmond, Virginia, February 4, 1864, of "typhoid fever."

NANCE, LAWSON, Private
Born in Lincoln County and resided in Gaston County

where he was by occupation a farm laborer prior to enlisting in Lincoln County at age 21, March 25, 1862. Deserted on July 25, 1863. Returned to duty on October 19, 1863. Reported present until November-December, 1864, when he was reported absent without leave.

NANCE, LEVI, Private
Resided in Gaston County and enlisted in Lincoln County at age 32, November 12, 1863, for the war. Captured at or near Spotsylvania Court House, Virginia, on or about May 12, 1864. Confined at Point Lookout, Maryland, May 17, 1864. Transferred to Elmira, New York, August 8, 1864. Paroled at Elmira on October 11, 1864. Received at Venus Point, Savannah River, Georgia, November 15, 1864, for exchange. Died in April, 1865. Place and cause of death not reported.

NANCE, WILLIAM, Private
Born in Lincoln County and resided in Gaston County prior to enlisting in Lincoln County at age 22, March 25, 1862. Deserted on May 24, 1863. Returned to duty on October 19, 1863. Died in hospital at Charlottesville, Virginia, January 23, 1864, of "typhoid fever."

NANTZ, D. L., _____
North Carolina pension records indicate that he served in this company.

PAINTER, JOHN L., Private
Resided in Lincoln County where he enlisted at age 31, October 17, 1862, for the war. Died at Orange Court House, Virginia, January 13, 1864. Cause of death not reported.

PAINTER, PINKNEY, Private
Resided in Lincoln County where he enlisted at age 26, October 17, 1862, for the war. Hospitalized at Richmond, Virginia, July 25, 1863, with "irritatio spinalis." Returned to duty on September 4, 1863. Present or accounted for until hospitalized at Richmond on November 4, 1864, with an unspecified complaint. Furloughed for sixty days on December 19, 1864.

PARKER, HOSEA P., Private
Born in Spartanburg District, South Carolina, and resided in Lincoln County where he was by occupation a farm laborer prior to enlisting in Lincoln County at age 25, July 6, 1862, for the war. Reported present on surviving company muster rolls through December, 1864. Surrendered at Appomattox Court House, Virginia, April 9, 1865.

PARKER, JOHN M., Private
Born in Lincoln County where he resided as a farmer prior to enlisting in Lincoln County at age 23, March 25, 1862. Wounded in the chest at Gettysburg, Pennsylvania, on or about July 3, 1863. Returned to duty in September-October, 1863. Wounded in the left leg at or near Jones' Farm, Virginia, on or about October 1, 1864. Left leg amputated. Hospitalized at Richmond, Virginia. Furloughed for sixty days on February 24, 1865. Survived the war.

PATTERSON, CALVIN, Private
Resided in Lincoln County where he enlisted at age 35, November 19, 1863, for the war. Present or accounted for through December, 1864. Surrendered at Appomattox Court House, Virginia, April 9, 1865.

PATTERSON, JAMES A., Private
Born in Ashe County and resided in Lincoln County where he enlisted at age 31, March 25, 1862. Mustered in as 1st Sergeant. Reported present on surviving company muster rolls through February, 1863. Reported absent sick in July-October, 1863. Reduced to ranks in November, 1863-February, 1864. Detailed as a carpenter at Gordonsville, Virginia, on or about December 18, 1863. Transferred to the quartermaster's department on January 27, 1864.

PERKINS, J. FRANKLIN, Private
Resided in Lincoln County where he enlisted at age 23, October 24, 1862, for the war. Reported present or accounted for on surviving company muster rolls through December, 1864. Surrendered at Appomattox Court House, Virginia, April 9, 1865. [North Carolina pension records indicate that he was wounded in the left shoulder at Petersburg, Virginia, in 1864.]

PERKINS, LEANDER P., Private
Enlisted in Lincoln County at age 23, April 20, 1864, for the war. Present or accounted for through December, 1864. Wounded in the right thigh near Petersburg, Virginia, March 25, 1865. Hospitalized at Richmond, Virginia. Captured in hospital at Richmond on April 3, 1865. Released on or about June 5, 1865, after taking the Oath of Allegiance.

POPE, JAMES L., Private
Resided in Ashe County where he enlisted at age 30, November 11, 1862, for the war. Reported present or accounted for through November, 1863; however, he was reported absent sick during much of that period. Deserted in December, 1863.

QUEEN, JAMES A., Private
Born in Lincoln County where he resided as a farmer prior to enlisting in Lincoln County at age 32, March 25, 1862. Reported present on surviving company muster rolls through April, 1864. Wounded in the neck and leg at Wilderness, Virginia, on or about May 6, 1864. Returned to duty prior to July 1, 1864. Reported present through December, 1864. Surrendered at Appomattox Court House, Virginia, April 9, 1865. [Was apparently captured briefly at Wilderness, Virginia, on or about May 6, 1864.]

REEL, DANIEL R., Private
Born in Lincoln County where he resided prior to enlisting in Lincoln County at age 28, March 25, 1862. Died at Raleigh on May 2, 1862. Cause of death not reported.

RENDLEMAN, JOHN M., Private
Born in Lincoln County where he resided as an overseer prior to enlisting in Lincoln County at age 25, April 28,

1862, for the war. Reported absent without leave on or about July 1, 1862.

RICHARDSON, JOSEPH, Private
Resided in Ashe County where he enlisted at age 26, November 11, 1862, for the war. Captured at Falling Waters, Maryland, July 14, 1863. Sent to Baltimore, Maryland. Transferred to Point Lookout, Maryland, August 20, 1863. Died at Point Lookout on April 5, 1864, of "chilblains & diarrhoea."

ROARK, ALVIN, Private
Resided in Ashe County where he enlisted at age 25, November 11, 1862, for the war. Deserted on November 25, 1862.

ROARK, DAVID, Private
Resided in Ashe County where he enlisted at age 27, November 11, 1862, for the war. Deserted on November 25, 1862.

ROARK, HARVEY J., Private
Resided in Ashe County where he enlisted at age 23, November 11, 1862, for the war. Died in hospital at Lynchburg, Virginia, June 9, 1863, of "febris typhoides."

ROARK, ISAAC, Private
Resided in Ashe County where he enlisted at age 23, November 11, 1862, for the war. Deserted on January 6, 1863.

ROARK, NATHANIEL W., Private
Resided in Ashe County where he enlisted at age 27, November 11, 1862, for the war. Deserted on January 6, 1863.

ROBINSON, HENRY, Private
Born in Lincoln County where he resided as a farmer prior to enlisting in Lincoln County at age 21, March 25, 1862. Died in hospital at Petersburg, Virginia, September 17, 1862, of "contin[ued] fever."

ROBINSON, PHILO, Private
Enlisted in Lincoln County on March 3, 1864, for the war. Reported present or accounted for through December, 1864.

ROBINSON, WESLEY, Private
Resided in Lincoln County where he enlisted on January 3, 1864, for the war. Reported present or accounted for through December, 1864. Captured at Sutherland's Station, Virginia, April 2, 1865. Confined at Point Lookout, Maryland, April 4, 1865. Released at Point Lookout on June 17, 1865, after taking the Oath of Allegiance.

RUTLEDGE, WILLIAM G., 1st Sergeant
Resided in Lincoln County where he enlisted at age 23, April 25, 1862, for the war. Mustered in as Private. Promoted to Corporal in July-October, 1862. Promoted to Sergeant on November 1, 1862. Promoted to 1st Sergeant in January-February, 1864. Reported present or accounted for through April, 1864. Wounded in the right knee at

Wilderness, Virginia, on or about May 6, 1864. Reported absent wounded or absent sick through December, 1864. Paroled at Charlotte in May, 1865.

SAUNDERS, JAMES, Private
Born in Lincoln County where he resided as a farmer prior to enlisting in Lincoln County at age 18, March 25, 1862. Wounded in the thigh (fracture) and captured at Gettysburg, Pennsylvania, on or about July 3, 1863. Hospitalized at Gettysburg where he died on July 19, 1863, of wounds.

SAUNDERS, THOMAS J., Private
Born in Lincoln County where he resided as a farmer prior to enlisting in Lincoln County at age 20, March 25, 1862. Wounded in the left thigh at Gettysburg, Pennsylvania, July 3, 1863. Reported absent wounded through April, 1864. Reported absent on detail in May-August, 1864. Returned to duty in September-October, 1864. Captured at Sutherland's Station, Virginia, April 2, 1865. Confined at Point Lookout, Maryland, April 4, 1865. Released at Point Lookout on or about July 1, 1865, after taking the Oath of Allegiance.

SENTER, CALEB O., Private
Born in Lincoln County where he resided as a farmer prior to enlisting in Lincoln County at age 32, March 25, 1862. Deserted on May 24, 1863. Returned to duty on October 19, 1863. Captured at Cold Harbor, Virginia, June 1, 1864. Confined at Point Lookout, Maryland, June 11, 1864. Transferred to Elmira, New York, July 12, 1864. Killed in a railroad accident at Shohola, Pennsylvania, July 15, 1864, while en route to Elmira.

SHRUM, HENRY, Private
Resided in Lincoln County where he enlisted on October 26, 1864, for the war. Captured at Sutherland's Station, Virginia, April 2, 1865. Confined at Point Lookout, Maryland, April 4, 1865. Released at Point Lookout on June 20, 1865, after taking the Oath of Allegiance.

SIFFORD, MILES L., Private
Resided in Lincoln County where he enlisted at age 25, July 6, 1862, for the war. Reported on detail as a shoemaker at Richmond, Virginia, from October 31, 1862, through December, 1864. Assigned to duty with Company B, 2nd Battalion Virginia Infantry (Local Defense), while on detail at Richmond.

SPARGO, JAMES, Private
Born in Cornwall, England, and resided in Lincoln County where he was by occupation a miner prior to enlisting in Lincoln County at age 39, March 25, 1862. Reported on detail as a miner in Lincoln County from October 20, 1862, through August, 1864. No further records.

SRONCE, SIDNEY J., Private
Born in Lincoln County where he resided as a farmer prior to enlisting in Lincoln County at age 25, March 25, 1862. Hospitalized at Richmond, Virginia, June 22, 1863, with rheumatism. Returned to duty on August 4, 1863. Reported present or accounted for on surviving company muster rolls through December, 1864.

STEWART, THOMAS W., Private
Born in Lincoln County where he resided as a farmer prior to enlisting in Lincoln County at age 19, March 25, 1862. Killed at Gettysburg, Pennsylvania, on or about July 3, 1863.

STOWE, JOHN M., Private
Enlisted in Lincoln County on May 15, 1864, for the war. Present or accounted for through December, 1864.

STROUP, ANDREW JACKSON, Private
Resided in Lincoln County where he enlisted at age 31, July 6, 1862, for the war. Reported absent sick on surviving company muster rolls through February, 1863. Wounded at Franklin, Virginia, on an unspecified date. Reported absent wounded from August 31, 1863, through January 7, 1864. No further records.

STROUP, CALEB, Private
Born in Lincoln County and resided in Gaston County where he was by occupation a farmer prior to enlisting in Lincoln County at age 44, January 3, 1864, for the war. Died in hospital at Richmond, Virginia, on or about June 17, 1864, of "dysenteria chron[ic]."

STROUP, DAVID C., Private
Resided in Lincoln County where he enlisted at age 26, July 6, 1862, for the war. Deserted on May 24, 1863. Returned to duty on December 8, 1863. Captured at or near Spotsylvania Court House, Virginia, on or about May 12, 1864. Confined at Point Lookout, Maryland, May 17, 1864. Transferred to Elmira, New York, August 8, 1864. Paroled at Elmira on February 20, 1865, and transferred to the James River, Virginia, for exchange. Survived the war.

STROUP, HOSEA, Private
Resided in Lincoln County and was by occupation a farmer prior to enlisting in Lincoln County at age 35, May 5, 1863, for the war. Deserted on May 24, 1863. Returned to duty on October 19, 1863. Reported present or accounted for on surviving company muster rolls through August, 1864. Captured at Burgess' Mill, Virginia, October 27, 1864. Confined at Point Lookout, Maryland, where he died on December 5, 1864, of "typhoid fever."

STROUP, LAFAYETTE, Private
Resided in Lincoln County where he enlisted at age 20, July 6, 1862, for the war. Captured by the enemy on an unspecified date (probably at or near Gettysburg, Pennsylvania, on or about July 3, 1863). Confined at Point Lookout, Maryland, where he died on or about February 17, 1864. Cause of death not reported.

STROUP, ROBERT, Private
Born in Lincoln County where he resided as a farmer prior to enlisting in Lincoln County at age 20, March 25, 1862. Captured at Falling Waters, Maryland, July 14, 1863. Confined at Old Capitol Prison, Washington, D.C. Transferred to Point Lookout, Maryland, August 8, 1863. Died at Point Lookout on or about February 13, 1864. Cause of death not reported.

STROUP, ROBERT B., Private
Resided in Lincoln County where he enlisted at age 24, July 6, 1862, for the war. Reported present or accounted for on surviving company muster rolls through April, 1864. Hospitalized at Petersburg, Virginia, June 24, 1864, with acute diarrhoea. Furloughed for thirty days on August 4, 1864. Reported absent sick through December, 1864.

STROUP, WESLEY C., Private
Born in Lincoln County where he resided as a farmer prior to enlisting in Lincoln County at age 27, March 25, 1862. Wounded in the right foot (fracture) and captured at Gettysburg, Pennsylvania, on or about July 3, 1863. Right foot amputated. Hospitalized at Gettysburg. Transferred to hospital at Baltimore, Maryland, on an unspecified date. Paroled at Baltimore on or about November 12, 1863. Received at City Point, Virginia, November 17, 1863, for exchange. Reported absent wounded until November 8, 1864, when he was retired to the Invalid Corps.

SUMMEROW, DAVID F., Private
Resided in Lincoln County where he enlisted at age 19, February 10, 1863, for the war. Captured at Gettysburg, Pennsylvania, on or about July 3, 1863. Confined at Fort Delaware, Delaware, on or about July 10, 1863. Transferred to Point Lookout, Maryland, October 20, 1863. Paroled at Point Lookout on or about September 30, 1864, and transferred for exchange. Returned to duty prior to November 1, 1864. Reported present in November-December, 1864.

SUMMEROW, FRANK, Private
Born in Lincoln County and was by occupation a farmer prior to enlisting in Lincoln County at age 17, March 25, 1862. No further records.

SUMMEROW, HENRY M., Corporal
Resided in Lincoln County where he enlisted at age 23, April 29, 1862, for the war. Mustered in as Private. Wounded in the leg at Gettysburg, Pennsylvania, July 3, 1863. Returned to duty in September-October, 1863. Promoted to Corporal on March 21, 1864. Reported absent sick in July-December, 1864. Surrendered at Appomattox Court House, Virginia, April 9, 1865.

SUMMEY, DAVID A., Private
Born in Lincoln or Gaston* county and resided in Lincoln County where he was by occupation a farmer prior to enlisting in Lincoln County at age 17, March 25, 1862. Wounded in the jaw (fracture) and right leg at Gettysburg, Pennsylvania, on or about July 3, 1863. Returned to duty on or about September 1, 1863. Present or accounted for until wounded in the right arm (fracture) at or near Jones' Farm, Virginia, on or about October 2, 1864. Hospitalized at Richmond, Virginia. Furloughed for sixty days on November 14, 1864. Survived the war.

SUMMEY, JONAS F., Private
Resided in Lincoln County where he enlisted at age 35, November 19, 1863, for the war. Reported present or accounted for on surviving company muster rolls through

December, 1864. Captured near Petersburg, Virginia, March 25, 1865. Confined at Point Lookout, Maryland, March 28, 1865. Released at Point Lookout on June 20, 1865, after taking the Oath of Allegiance.

THOMPSON, SIDNEY J., Private

Born in Lincoln County where he resided as a farmer prior to enlisting in Lincoln County at age 25, March 25, 1862. Captured at Gettysburg, Pennsylvania, July 3, 1863. Confined at Fort Delaware, Delaware, on or about July 10, 1863. Died at Fort Delaware on October 30, 1863, of "jaundice."

VARNER, ALBERT RANKIN, Private

Enlisted in Lincoln County on March 9, 1864, for the war. Captured at Burgess' Mill, Virginia, October 27, 1864. Confined at Point Lookout, Maryland, October 31, 1864. Died at Point Lookout on April 7, 1865, of "scurvy."

WEATHERS, JOHN A., Private

Born in Lincoln County where he resided as a farmer prior to enlisting in Lincoln County at age 26, April 27, 1862, for the war. Wounded in the left arm and captured at Gettysburg, Pennsylvania, July 3, 1863. Left arm amputated. Hospitalized at Gettysburg. Transferred to hospital at Chester, Pennsylvania, on an unspecified date. Paroled at Chester and transferred to City Point, Virginia, where he was received on August 20, 1863, for exchange. Reported absent wounded until he was retired to the Invalid Corps on April 18 or October 17, 1864.

WEATHERS, OLIVER W., Private

Born in Lincoln County where he resided as a farmer prior to enlisting in Lincoln County at age 24, March 25, 1862. Wounded at Goldsboro on December 17, 1862. Returned to duty in March-August, 1863. Reported present or accounted for on surviving company muster rolls through June, 1864. Reported absent sick in July-August, 1864. Died in hospital at Richmond, Virginia, September 23, 1864, of wounds. Place and date wounded not reported.

WEATHERS, PINKNEY, Private

Enlisted in Lincoln County on April 1, 1864, for the war. Present or accounted for through April 30, 1864. No further records.

WHITE, WILLIAM H., Private

Born in Hertford County and was by occupation a farmer prior to enlisting in Lincoln County at age 33, October 19, 1863, for the war. Transferred to the C.S. Navy on or about April 1, 1864.

WILLIAMS, ISAAC C., Private

Born in Lincoln County where he resided as a farmer prior to enlisting in Lincoln County at age 18, March 25, 1862. Reported present on surviving company muster rolls through December, 1864. Survived the war.

COMPANY I

This company, known as the "Stanly Rebels," was raised in Stanly County and enlisted at Albemarle on March 25, 1862. It was mustered into state service at Camp Mangum, near Raleigh, on April 28, 1862, and assigned to the 52nd Regiment N.C. Troops as Company I. After joining the regiment the company functioned as a part of the regiment, and its history for the remainder of the war is reported as a part of the regimental history.

The information contained in the following roster was compiled primarily from a company muster-in and descriptive roll dated April 28, 1862, and from company muster rolls for May 1-June 30, 1862; August 31, 1862-February 28, 1863; and July 1, 1863-December 31, 1864. No company muster rolls were located for July 1-August 30, 1862; March 1-June 30, 1863; or for the period after December 31, 1864. Valuable information was obtained from primary records such as the North Carolina adjutant general's *Roll of Honor*, discharge certificates, medical records, prisoner of war records, *The War of the Rebellion: A Compilation of the Official Records of the Union and Confederate Armies*, militia records, newspaper casualty lists and obituaries, Confederate pension applications filed with the state of North Carolina, and the 1860 federal census of North Carolina. Secondary sources such as postwar rosters and histories, cemetery records, the *Confederate Veteran*, published genealogies, and records of the United Daughters of the Confederacy also provided useful information.

OFFICERS

CAPTAINS

McCAIN, JOHN C.

Born in Stanly County* where he resided as a farmer prior to enlisting in Stanly County at age 30. Appointed Captain on March 29, 1862. Killed at Gettysburg, Pennsylvania, July 1, 1863.

HEARNE, JAMES D.

Born in Stanly County* where he resided as a merchant prior to enlisting in Stanly County at age 27. Appointed 1st Lieutenant on March 29, 1862. Promoted to Captain on July 1, 1863. Furloughed in February, 1864. Tendered his resignation while at home on furlough. Reason he resigned not reported. His resignation was not accepted; however, he failed to return to duty and was reported absent without leave on or about March 10, 1864. Dropped from the rolls of the company on December 9, 1864, for prolonged absence without leave.

PARLEIR, JACOB J.

Served as 2nd Lieutenant of Company F of this regiment. Reported on duty as acting commander of this company in May-June, 1864.

LILLY, SAMUEL S.
Born in Stanly County* where he resided as a farmer prior to enlisting in Stanly County at age 27. Appointed 2nd Lieutenant on March 29, 1862. Promoted to 1st Lieutenant on July 1, 1863. Wounded at or near Cold Harbor, Virginia, on or about June 3, 1864. Returned to duty in September-October, 1864. Promoted to Captain on December 1, 1864. Surrendered at Appomattox Court House, Virginia, April 9, 1865.

LIEUTENANT

RANDALL, WILLIS, 3rd Lieutenant
Born in Stanly County* where he resided as a farmer prior to enlisting in Stanly County at age 26. Appointed 3rd Lieutenant on March 29, 1862. Wounded in the left hand at Gettysburg, Pennsylvania, July 3, 1863. Captured at Gettysburg on or about July 4, 1863. Hospitalized at Gettysburg. Confined at Fort McHenry, Maryland, July 9, 1863. Transferred to Fort Delaware, Delaware, where he arrived on July 14, 1863. Transferred to Johnson's Island, Ohio, July 27, 1863. Died at Johnson's Island on December 31, 1864. Cause of death not reported.

NONCOMMISSIONED OFFICERS AND PRIVATES

ALLEN, A. S., Private
Resided in Stanly County and enlisted at Camp French, near Petersburg, Virginia, at age 28, September 8, 1862, for the war. Captured at Bristoe Station, Virginia, October 14, 1863. Confined at Old Capitol Prison, Washington, D.C. Transferred to Point Lookout, Maryland, October 27, 1863. Released at Point Lookout on February 25, 1864, after taking the Oath of Allegiance and joining the U.S. Army. Assigned to Company F, 1st Regiment U.S. Volunteer Infantry.

ALMOND, NATHAN, Private
Born in Stanly County* where he resided as a farmer prior to enlisting in Stanly County at age 24, March 25, 1862. Captured at Bristoe Station, Virginia, October 14, 1863. Confined at Old Capitol Prison, Washington, D.C. Transferred to Point Lookout, Maryland, February 3, 1864. Died at Point Lookout on October 15, 1864, of "acute diarrhoea."

AUSTIN, BENJAMIN P., Corporal
Born in Stanly County* where he resided as an artist prior to enlisting in Stanly County at age 28, March 25, 1862. Mustered in as Corporal. Reported absent on detail as an overseer on the "public works" near Petersburg, Virginia, from August 22, 1862, until September 9, 1863, when he rejoined the company. Wounded at Bristoe Station, Virginia, October 14, 1863. Died near the Rappahannock River on October 17, 1863, of wounds.

AUSTIN, JOHN M., Private
Born in Stanly County* where he resided as a farmer prior to enlisting in Stanly County at age 24, March 25, 1862. Wounded in the left hand and captured at Gettysburg, Pennsylvania, July 3, 1863. Hospitalized at Gettysburg. Transferred to hospital at Davids Island, New York Harbor, where he arrived on July 20, 1863. Paroled at Davids Island and transferred to City Point, Virginia, where he was received on October 28, 1863, for exchange. Reported absent wounded or absent on parole through October, 1864. Retired to the Invalid Corps on December 22, 1864.

AVETT, J. M., Private
Resided in Stanly County and enlisted at Camp French, near Petersburg, Virginia, at age 26, September 25, 1862, for the war. Reported present or accounted for on surviving company muster rolls through October, 1863. Hospitalized at Charlottesville, Virginia, December 4, 1863, with acute diarrhoea. Returned to duty on May 4, 1864. Captured at Sutherland's Station, Virginia, April 2, 1865. Confined at Point Lookout, Maryland, April 4, 1865. Released at Point Lookout on June 22, 1865, after taking the Oath of Allegiance.

BARRINGER, HENRY H., Private
Born in Stanly County where he resided as a farmer prior to enlisting in Stanly County at age 20, March 25, 1862. Wounded at Gettysburg, Pennsylvania, July 3, 1863. Died on or about the same date.

BECK, WILLIAM S., Private
Previously served as Private in Company B, 19th Regiment N.C. Troops (2nd Regiment N.C. Cavalry). Transferred to this company on December 5, 1864. Deserted to the enemy on or about December 21, 1864. Confined at Washington, D.C. Released at Washington on or about December 27, 1864, after taking the Oath of Allegiance.

BIRD, JACKSON D., Private
Resided in Stanly County and was by occupation a carpenter prior to enlisting in Stanly County at age 31, April 26, 1862, for the war. Wounded in the right shoulder and captured at Gettysburg, Pennsylvania, July 3, 1863. Hospitalized at Gettysburg. Transferred to hospital at Davids Island, New York Harbor, on or about July 20, 1863. Paroled at Davids Island on an unspecified date. Received at City Point, Virginia, September 8, 1863, for exchange. Returned to duty in January-February, 1864. Captured at or near Spotsylvania Court House, Virginia, on or about May 12, 1864. Confined at Point Lookout, Maryland, May 17, 1864. Transferred to Elmira, New York, August 8, 1864. Paroled at Elmira on February 20, 1865, and transferred to the James River, Virginia, for exchange. Died "on the boat" while en route to the James River. Date and cause of death not reported.

BIRD, MARTIN, Private
Born in Stanly County* where he resided as a farmer prior to enlisting in Stanly County at age 26, March 25, 1862. Discharged at Goldsboro on February 28, 1863, by reason of disability (probably rheumatism).

BLALOCK, EDMOND D., Private
Born in Stanly County* where he resided as a farmer prior to enlisting in Stanly County at age 26, March 25, 1862. Detailed as a teamster on December 19, 1862. Rejoined the company in March-August, 1863. Reported present on surviving company muster rolls through December, 1864. Captured at or near Amelia Court House, Virginia, April 4, 1865. Confined at Point Lookout, Maryland, April 13, 1865. Released at Point Lookout on June 23, 1865, after taking the Oath of Allegiance.

BLALOCK, HENRY W., Private
Born in Stanly County* where he resided as a farmer prior to enlisting in Stanly County at age 28, March 25, 1862. Died in hospital at Richmond, Virginia, July 31, 1862, of "continued fever."

BLALOCK, MERRITT E., Private
Born in Stanly County where he resided as a farmer prior to enlisting in Stanly County at age 20, March 25, 1862. Detailed as a teamster on or about December 26, 1862. Reported on detail as a teamster through August, 1863. Reported absent sick on November 17, 1863. Returned to duty prior to March 1, 1864. Wounded in the right hand (thumb amputated) at Spotsylvania Court House, Virginia, May 10, 1864. Hospitalized at Richmond, Virginia. Returned to duty prior to July 1, 1864. Reported present through December, 1864.

BLALOCK, ZACHARIAH D., Private
Born in Stanly County* and resided in Stanly or Rowan County where he was by occupation a farmer prior to enlisting in Stanly County at age 22, March 25, 1862. Wounded at Goldsboro on December 17, 1862. Reported absent wounded or absent sick on surviving company muster rolls through February, 1864. Returned to duty in March-April, 1864. Captured at or near Spotsylvania Court House, Virginia, on or about May 12, 1864. Confined at Point Lookout, Maryland, May 17, 1864. Transferred to Elmira, New York, August 8, 1864. Released at Elmira on June 12, 1865, after taking the Oath of Allegiance.

BLAYLOCK, SIDNEY, Private
Enlisted in Wake County on December 24, 1863, for the war. Killed at Burgess' Mill, Virginia, October 27, 1864.

BLAYLOCK, W. C., Private
Resided in Stanly County and was by occupation a farmer prior to enlisting in Rowan County at age 37, March 17, 1863, for the war. Died in hospital at Lynchburg, Virginia, June 3, 1863, of "pneumonia."

BROOKS, CORNELIUS B., Private
Born in Stanly County* where he resided as a farmer prior to enlisting in Stanly County at age 28, March 25, 1862. Wounded at Goldsboro on December 17, 1862. Died at Goldsboro on December 22, 1862, of wounds.

CALAWAY, GEORGE W., Private
Born in Stanly County* where he resided as a farmer prior to enlisting in Stanly County at age 22, March 25, 1862.

Discharged at Camp Mangum, near Raleigh, May 24, 1862, after providing a substitute.

CALLAWAY, AGRIPPA G., Private
Born in Stanly County* where he resided as a farmer prior to enlisting in Stanly County at age 38, March 25, 1862. Discharged at Camp Mangum, near Raleigh, May 24, 1862, presumably by reason of being overage.

CALLAWAY, JOHN C., Private
Born in Stanly County* where he resided as a farmer prior to enlisting in Stanly County at age 25, March 25, 1862. Captured at Falling Waters, Maryland, July 14, 1863. Sent to Baltimore, Maryland. Confined at Point Lookout, Maryland, August 17, 1863. Transferred to Elmira, New York, on or about August 10, 1864. Died at Elmira on April 8, 1865, of "pneumonia."

CARTER, GEORGE A., Private
Born in Stanly County where he resided prior to enlisting in Stanly County at age 19, April 28, 1862, for the war. Died in hospital at Petersburg, Virginia, October 14, 1862, of "typhoid fever."

CARTER, JOHN D., Private
Resided in Stanly County where he enlisted at age 22, April 28, 1862, for the war. Died in hospital at Goldsboro on June 22, 1862. Cause of death not reported.

CAUBLE, FRANKLIN, Private
Born in Stanly County* where he resided as a farmer prior to enlisting in Stanly County at age 36, March 25, 1862. Discharged at Camp Mangum, near Raleigh, May 26, 1862, presumably by reason of being overage.

CAUBLE, WILLIAM P., Private
Born in Stanly County* where he resided as a farmer prior to enlisting in Stanly County at age 31, March 25, 1862. Transferred to Company F, 44th Regiment N.C. Troops, October 15, 1862, in exchange for Private John Giles Christian.

CHRISTIAN, JOHN GILES, Private
Previously served as Private in Company F, 44th Regiment N.C. Troops. Transferred to this company on or about October 15, 1862, in exchange for Private William P. Cauble. Accidentally wounded in the right thigh near Greenville by a member of his own regiment on March 15, 1863. Returned to duty in January-February, 1864; however, his wound failed to heal properly and he was detail as an "agriculturist" on or about July 28, 1864. Reported absent on detail through December, 1864. Paroled at Albemarle on May 19, 1865.

COLSON, T. K., JR., Private
Born in Stanly County where he resided as a farmer prior to enlisting in Stanly County at age 18, March 1, 1863, for the war. Wounded in the left foot and captured at Gettysburg, Pennsylvania, July 3, 1863. Hospitalized at Gettysburg. Transferred to hospital at Davids Island, New York Harbor, where he arrived on or about July 20, 1863. Paroled at Davids Island and transferred to City Point, Virginia, where he was received on September 16, 1863,

for exchange. Reported absent wounded or absent on parole through December, 1864. Retired from service on February 14, 1865, by reason of disability from wounds.

COLSON, T. K., SR., Private
Resided in Stanly County and enlisted at age 38, March 25, 1862. "Got tired and went home from Camp Mangum," near Raleigh. Roll of Honor states that he "didn't regularly belong to the company." Dropped from the rolls of the company prior to July 1, 1862.

CREPS, JULIUS ALEXANDER, Private
Born in Stanly County where he resided as a farmer prior to enlisting in Stanly County at age 18, March 25, 1862. Captured at Gettysburg, Pennsylvania, July 3, 1863. Confined at Fort Delaware, Delaware, on or about July 10, 1863. Transferred to Point Lookout, Maryland, where he arrived on October 15, 1863. Hospitalized at Point Lookout on November 21, 1863, with chronic diarrhoea and pneumonia. Reported in hospital until March 17, 1864, when he was paroled. Received at City Point, Virginia, March 20, 1864, for exchange. Returned to duty in May-June, 1864. Hospitalized at Richmond, Virginia, on or about November 23, 1864, with chronic diarrhoea. Returned to duty on December 29, 1864. Paroled at Albemarle on March 19, 1865.

CROWELL, BUCKNER KIMBALL, 1st Sergeant
Born in Stanly County* where he resided as a farmer prior to enlisting in Stanly County at age 24, March 25, 1862. Mustered in as 1st Sergeant. Wounded in the right thigh and captured at Gettysburg, Pennsylvania, July 3, 1863. Hospitalized at Gettysburg. Transferred to hospital at Chester, Pennsylvania, where he arrived on July 17, 1863. Transferred to Point Lookout, Maryland, October 2, 1863. Paroled at Point Lookout on April 27, 1864. Received at City Point, Virginia, April 30, 1864, for exchange. Reported absent wounded until November 3, 1864, when he was retired to the Invalid Corps.

CROWELL, GEORGE W., Private
Resided in Stanly County and was by occupation a farmer prior to enlisting in Stanly County at age 33, April 28, 1862, for the war. Wounded at Gettysburg, Pennsylvania, July 3, 1863. Hospitalized at Richmond, Virginia, July 14, 1863. Furloughed for thirty days on July 30, 1863. Reported absent wounded through October, 1864. Reported absent sick without leave in November-December, 1864. Died on January 21, 1865, of wounds.

DeBERRY, EDMUND P., Private
Born in Stanly County where he resided as a farmer prior to enlisting in Stanly County at age 20, March 25, 1862. Wounded and captured at Gettysburg, Pennsylvania, July 3, 1863. Confined at Fort Delaware, Delaware, on or about July 10, 1863. Transferred to hospital at Chester, Pennsylvania, August 10, 1863. Paroled at Chester on or about September 17, 1863. Received at City Point, Virginia, September 23, 1863, for exchange. Returned to duty in January-February, 1864. Reported present through December, 1864. Captured at Sutherland's Station, Virginia, April 2, 1865. Confined at Point Lookout, Maryland, April 4, 1865. Released at Point Lookout on June 10, 1865, after taking the Oath of Allegiance.

DEES, JAMES A., Private
Born in Stanly County where he resided prior to enlisting at Camp French, near Petersburg, Virginia, September 25, 1862, for the war. Died in hospital at Petersburg on October 25, 1862, of "febris congestiva." Was 29 years of age at the time of his death.

DEES, W. BOGGAN, Private
Resided in Stanly County and enlisted at Camp French, near Petersburg, Virginia, at age 36, September 25, 1862, for the war. Deserted on August 5, 1863. Returned to duty on October 3, 1863. Captured at Bristoe Station, Virginia, October 14, 1863. Confined at Old Capitol Prison, Washington, D.C. Transferred to Point Lookout, Maryland, October 27, 1863. Died at Point Lookout on January 19, 1865, of "chronic diarrhoea."

DRY, CHRISTOPHER, Private
Born in Stanly County* where he resided as a farmer prior to enlisting in Stanly County at age 31, March 25, 1862. Killed at Gettysburg, Pennsylvania, July 3, 1863.

DRY, DANIEL, Private
Born in Cabarrus County and resided in Stanly County where he was by occupation a day laborer prior to enlisting at age 34, April 28, 1862, for the war. Killed in camp on the Blackwater River, near Franklin, Virginia, November 12, 1862, "by the accidental discharge of a gun."

DRY, GEORGE A., Private
Born in Stanly County* where he resided as a farmer prior to enlisting in Stanly County at age 25, March 25, 1862. Captured at Gettysburg, Pennsylvania, July 3, 1863. Confined at Fort Delaware, Delaware, on or about July 10, 1863. Died at Fort Delaware on December 22, 1863, of "bronchitis chronic."

FARMER, WILLIAM M., Private
Born in Stanly County* where he resided as a farmer prior to enlisting in Stanly County at age 28, March 25, 1862. Reported present or accounted for on surviving company muster rolls through December, 1864.

FESPERMAN, HENRY P., Private
Born in Stanly County where he resided as a farmer prior to enlisting in Stanly County at age 19, March 25, 1862. Died in hospital at Petersburg, Virginia, August 5, 1862, of "feb[ris] typhoides."

FOREMAN, STEPHEN D., Private
Born in Stanly County* where he resided as a farmer prior to enlisting in Stanly County at age 36, March 25, 1862. Discharged at Camp Mangum, near Raleigh, May 29, 1862, presumably by reason of being overage. Later served as Private in Company A, 27th Regiment N.C. Troops.

FORREST, JAMES D., Sergeant
Born in Stanly County* where he resided as a farmer prior to enlisting in Stanly County at age 25, March 25, 1862. Mustered in as Private. Promoted to Sergeant on June 26, 1862. Hospitalized at Richmond, Virginia, July 23, 1862,

with continued fever. Transferred to Salisbury on September 13, 1862. Returned to duty prior to March 1, 1863. Reported present or accounted for on surviving company muster rolls through December, 1864. Surrendered at Appomattox Court House, Virginia, April 9, 1865.

FORREST, JOSEPH H., Private
Enlisted in Stanly County on February 1, 1864, for the war. Reported present or accounted for through December, 1864. Captured at Sutherland's Station, Virginia, April 2, 1865. Confined at Point Lookout, Maryland, April 4, 1865. Released at Point Lookout on June 6, 1865, after taking the Oath of Allegiance.

FRY, EBEN, Private
Born in Stanly County* where he resided as a farmer prior to enlisting in Stanly County at age 38, March 25, 1862. Wounded in the shoulder and captured at Gettysburg, Pennsylvania, July 3, 1863. Hospitalized at Gettysburg. No further records.

FRY, JOHN C., Private
Born in Stanly County* where he resided as a farmer prior to enlisting in Stanly County at age 35, March 25, 1862. Reported present or accounted for on surviving company muster rolls through January 23, 1864. Hospitalized at Richmond, Virginia, February 8, 1864, with chronic diarrhoea. Furloughed for sixty days on March 19, 1864. Returned to duty in September-October, 1864. Reported absent sick in November-December, 1864. Hospitalized at Richmond on March 2, 1865, with "fistula in ano." Transferred to Farmville, Virginia, April 1, 1865. Paroled at Albemarle on May 19, 1865.

FRY, NATHAN, Private
Born in Stanly County* where he resided as a farmer prior to enlisting in Stanly County at age 48, March 25, 1862. Discharged on May 24, 1862, presumably by reason of being overage.

FRY, WILLIAM, Private
Born in Stanly County where he resided as a farmer prior to enlisting in Stanly County at age 18, March 25, 1862. Died at Camp Mangum, near Raleigh, May 29, 1862, of "typhoid fever."

GREEN, JOHN R., Private
Previously served as Private in Company F, 19th Regiment N.C. Troops (2nd Regiment N.C. Cavalry). Transferred to this company on December 5, 1864. Deserted to the enemy on or about December 22, 1864. Sent to Washington, D.C. Released at Washington on or about December 27, 1864, after taking the Oath of Allegiance.

HARRIS, JOHN M., Private
Born in Stanly County* where he resided as a farmer prior to enlisting in Stanly County at age 37, March 25, 1862. Discharged at Camp Mangum, near Raleigh, May 29, 1862, presumably by reason of being overage.

HARRIS, REUBEN, Sergeant
Born in Stanly County* where he resided as a farmer prior

to enlisting in Stanly County at age 35, March 25, 1862. Mustered in as Sergeant. Wounded and captured at Gettysburg, Pennsylvania, July 3, 1863. Confined at Point Lookout, Maryland, on an unspecified date. Died at Point Lookout on November 11, 1863, of "chronic diarrhoea."

HASKELL, JOSEPH T., 1st Sergeant
Resided in Stanly County where he enlisted at age 22, April 28, 1862, for the war. Mustered in as Private. Promoted to Sergeant on February 1, 1864. Promoted to 1st Sergeant on November 1, 1864. Reported present on surviving company muster rolls through December, 1864. Surrendered at Appomattox Court House, Virginia, April 9, 1865.

HATLEY, ALFRED, Private
Born in Stanly County* where he resided as a farmer prior to enlisting in Stanly County at age 27, March 25, 1862. Wounded in the leg and captured at Gettysburg, Pennsylvania, July 3, 1863. Leg amputated. Hospitalized at Gettysburg where he died on July 17, 1863, of wounds.

HENLEY, GREEN B., Private
Born in Stanly County where he resided as a farmer prior to enlisting in Stanly County at age 17, March 25, 1862. Reported present or accounted for on surviving company muster rolls through December, 1864. Surrendered at Appomattox Court House, Virginia, April 9, 1865.

HINSON, DOCTOR F., Private
Born in Stanly County where he resided as a farmer prior to enlisting in Stanly County at age 17, March 25, 1862. Captured at Falling Waters, Maryland, July 14, 1863. Sent to Baltimore, Maryland. Confined at Point Lookout, Maryland, August 17, 1863. Released at Point Lookout on January 24, 1864, after taking the Oath of Allegiance and joining the U.S. Army. Assigned to Company B, 1st Regiment U.S. Volunteer Infantry.

HINSON, ISAAC, Private
Resided in Stanly County and was by occupation a farmer prior to enlisting in Stanly County at age 25, April 28, 1862, for the war. Wounded at Goldsboro on December 17, 1862. Died at Goldsboro on December 19, 1862, of wounds.

HOWELL, JULIUS A., Private
Resided in Stanly County where he enlisted at age 28, April 28, 1862, for the war. Captured at Falling Waters, Maryland, July 14, 1863. Confined at Old Capitol Prison, Washington, D.C. Transferred to Point Lookout, Maryland, August 8, 1863. Transferred to Elmira, New York, August 16, 1864. Paroled at Elmira on October 11, 1864. Received at Venus Point, Savannah River, Georgia, November 15, 1864, for exchange. Returned to duty subsequent to December 31, 1864. Captured at Sutherland's Station, Virginia, April 2, 1865. Confined at Point Lookout on April 4, 1865. Released at Point Lookout on June 27, 1865, after taking the Oath of Allegiance.

HUDSON, LEWIS, Private
Born in Stanly County* where he resided as a farmer prior

to enlisting in Stanly County at age 35, March 25, 1862. Captured at Bristoe Station, Virginia, October 14, 1863. Confined at Old Capitol Prison, Washington, D.C. Transferred to Point Lookout, Maryland, prior to November 1, 1863. Paroled at Point Lookout on October 11, 1864. Received at Cox's Wharf, James River, Virginia, October 15, 1864, for exchange. Survived the war.

HURLOCKER, SIMEON, Private
Born in Catawba County and resided in Stanly County where he was by occupation a farmer prior to enlisting in Stanly County at age 20, March 25, 1862. Died in hospital at Goldsboro on June 28, 1862. Cause of death not reported.

IVY, ISAAC T., Private
Born in Stanly County* where he resided as a farmer prior to enlisting in Stanly County at age 26, March 25, 1862. Captured at Gettysburg, Pennsylvania, July 3, 1863. Confined at Fort Delaware, Delaware, on or about July 10, 1863. Paroled at Fort Delaware on July 30, 1863. Died on board the steamer *New York* at City Point, Virginia, August 1, 1863, while being transferred for exchange. Cause of death not reported.

KENDALL, JULIUS A., Private
Enlisted in Stanly County at age 33, March 1, 1863, for the war. Left on the battlefield (presumably mortally wounded) at Gettysburg, Pennsylvania, July 3, 1863. [May have served previously as 2nd Lieutenant of Company H, 14th Regiment N.C. Troops (4th Regiment N.C. Volunteers).]

KIMREY, MANLOVE, Sergeant
Born in Stanly County* where he resided as a farmer prior to enlisting in Stanly County at age 30, March 25, 1862. Mustered in as Private. Promoted to Sergeant on May 7, 1862. Captured at Falling Waters, Maryland, July 14, 1863. Sent to Baltimore, Maryland. Transferred to Point Lookout, Maryland, August 16, 1863. Transferred to Elmira, New York, August 16, 1864. Paroled at Elmira on or about February 13, 1865. Received at Boulware's Wharf, James River, Virginia, February 20, 1865, for exchange.

KINDALL, J. A., Private
Resided in Stanly County where he enlisted at age 33, March 1, 1863, for the war. Killed at Gettysburg, Pennsylvania, July 3, 1863.

KIRK, GEORGE E., Private
Born in Stanly County* where he resided as a farmer prior to enlisting in Stanly County at age 31, March 25, 1862. Captured at Falling Waters, Maryland, July 14, 1863. Sent to Baltimore, Maryland. Confined at Point Lookout, Maryland, August 17, 1863. Died at Point Lookout on March 13, 1864. Cause of death not reported.

KIRK, JAMES C., Private
Resided in Stanly County and was by occupation a farmer prior to enlisting in Wake County at age 44, October 22, 1864, for the war. Captured at Sutherland's Station, Virginia, April 2, 1865. Confined at Point Lookout,

Maryland, April 4, 1865. Released at Point Lookout on June 28, 1865, after taking the Oath of Allegiance.

KIRK, PARHAM S., Private
Resided in Stanly County and was by occupation a farmer prior to enlisting in Stanly County at age 32, April 28, 1862, for the war. Left on the battlefield (presumably mortally wounded) at Gettysburg, Pennsylvania, July 3, 1863. [May have served previously as Private in Company K, 28th Regiment N.C. Troops.]

KIRK, WILLIAM A., Private
Born in Stanly County* where he resided as a farmer prior to enlisting in Stanly County at age 27, March 25, 1862. Discharged on March 1, 1863, after providing a substitute. [May have served later as Private in Company K, 28th Regiment N.C. Troops.]

LANIER, J. T., Private
Resided in Stanly County and enlisted at Camp French, near Petersburg, Virginia, at age 18, September 25, 1862, for the war. Mortally wounded and left on the battlefield at Gettysburg, Pennsylvania, July 3, 1863.

LILLY, ROBERT N., Private
Born in Stanly County* where he resided as a farmer prior to enlisting in Stanly County at age 22, March 25, 1862. Reported present or accounted for on surviving company muster rolls through November 17, 1863. Died at home in Stanly County on December 14, 1863. Cause of death not reported.

LITTLETON, ENOCH A. J., Private
Born in Stanly County* where he resided as a farmer prior to enlisting in Stanly County at age 23, March 25, 1862. Captured at Gettysburg, Pennsylvania, July 3, 1863. Confined at Fort Delaware, Delaware, on or about July 10, 1863. Released at Fort Delaware on June 19, 1865, after taking the Oath of Allegiance.

LITTLETON, JAMES R., Private
Resided in Stanly County where he enlisted at age 29, April 28, 1862, for the war. Discharged at Camp Mangum, near Raleigh, July 29, 1862, by reason of disability.

LOWDER, ARCHIBALD C., Private
Resided in Stanly County where he enlisted at age 28, April 28, 1862, for the war. Captured at Bristoe Station, Virginia, October 14, 1863. Confined at Old Capitol Prison, Washington, D.C. Transferred to Point Lookout, Maryland, October 27, 1863. Died at Point Lookout on September 16, 1864. Cause of death not reported.

LOWDER, DANIEL, Corporal
Born in Stanly County* where he resided as a farmer prior to enlisting in Stanly County at age 28, March 25, 1862. Mustered in as Private. Promoted to Corporal in March-July, 1863. Captured at Falling Waters, Maryland, July 14, 1863. Confined at Old Capitol Prison, Washington, D.C., July 23, 1863. Transferred to Point Lookout, Maryland, August 8, 1863. Transferred to Elmira, New York, August 16, 1864. Paroled at Elmira on March 10,

1865. Received at Boulware's Wharf, James River, Virginia, on or about March 14, 1865, for exchange.

LOWDER, GEORGE WILLIAM, JR., Private
Born in Stanly County where he resided as a farmer prior to enlisting in Stanly County at age 19, March 25, 1862. Wounded in the right hand (fracture) and right arm at Gettysburg, Pennsylvania, July 3, 1863. Reported absent wounded until July 28, 1864, when he was detailed for light duty. Retired to the Invalid Corps on August 18, 1864. Paroled at Albemarle on May 19, 1865.

LOWDER, WILLIAM P., Private
Resided in Stanly County and was by occupation a farmer prior to enlisting in Stanly County at age 31, May 14, 1862, for the war. Wounded and captured at Gettysburg, Pennsylvania, July 3, 1863. Hospitalized at Davids Island, New York Harbor, on or about July 20, 1863. Paroled at Davids Island and transferred to City Point, Virginia, where he was received on September 16, 1863, for exchange. Returned to duty in March-April, 1864. Reported absent wounded in July-December, 1864. Place and date wounded not reported. No further records.

McCORKLE, JAMES M., Sergeant
Born in Anson County and resided in Stanly County where he was by occupation an attorney prior to enlisting in Stanly County at age 36, March 28, 1862. Mustered in as Sergeant. Appointed Assistant Quartermaster (Captain) on July 11, 1862, to rank from June 6, 1862, and transferred to the Field and Staff of this regiment.

McINNIS, JOHN D., Sergeant
Born in Stanly County where he resided as a farmer prior to enlisting in Stanly County at age 16, March 25, 1862. Mustered in as Private. Wounded at Gettysburg, Pennsylvania, July 3, 1863. Returned to duty in January-February, 1864. Promoted to Sergeant on October 20, 1864. Captured at Burgess' Mill, Virginia, October 27, 1864. Confined at Point Lookout, Maryland, October 31, 1864. Paroled at Point Lookout on March 28, 1865. Received at Boulware's Wharf, James River, Virginia, March 30, 1865, for exchange.

McLESTER, SILAS M., Private
Resided in Stanly County where he enlisted at age 32, May 1, 1862, for the war. Reported present or accounted for on surviving company muster rolls through November 17, 1863. Detailed to guard government trains on November 18, 1863. Rejoined the company in September, 1864. Wounded in the abdomen and/or left leg at or near Jones' Farm, Virginia, on or about October 1, 1864. Hospitalized at Richmond, Virginia. Furloughed for sixty days on October 28, 1864. Returned to duty on an unspecified date. Captured near Petersburg, Virginia, March 25, 1865. Confined at Point Lookout, Maryland, March 27, 1865. Released at Point Lookout on June 29, 1865, after taking the Oath of Allegiance.

MANERS, HAMMET J., Private
Born in Stanly County where he resided as a farmer prior to enlisting in Stanly County at age 18, March 25, 1862. Captured at Falling Waters, Maryland, July 14, 1863.

Confined at Old Capitol Prison, Washington, D.C. Transferred to Point Lookout, Maryland, August 8, 1863. Transferred to Elmira, New York, August 16, 1864. Paroled at Elmira on October 11, 1864. Received at Venus Point, Savannah River, Georgia, November 15, 1864, for exchange.

MARBRY, JAMES E., Private
Born in Stanly County* where he resided as a farmer prior to enlisting in Stanly County at age 26, March 25, 1862. Wounded at Gettysburg, Pennsylvania, July 3, 1863. Captured in hospital at Gettysburg on July 5, 1863. Hospitalized at Baltimore, Maryland, where he died on July 26, 1863, presumably of wounds.

MARTIN, EZEKIEL, _____
Place and date of enlistment not reported (probably enlisted in March-June, 1863). Was probably killed at Gettysburg, Pennsylvania, on or about July 3, 1863.

MASON, JAMES A., Private
Born in Stanly County where he resided as a farmer prior to enlisting in Stanly County at age 20, March 25, 1862. Reported present on surviving company muster rolls through April, 1864. Captured at or near Wilderness, Virginia, on or about May 6, 1864. Confined at Point Lookout, Maryland, May 17, 1864. Transferred to Elmira, New York, August 8, 1864. Released on an unspecified date after taking the Oath of Allegiance.

MASON, WILLIAM D. A., Corporal
Born in Stanly County* where he resided as a farmer prior to enlisting in Stanly County at age 25, March 25, 1862. Mustered in as Corporal. Killed at Gettysburg, Pennsylvania, July 3, 1863.

MELTON, ATLAS D., Private
Previously served as Private in Company H, 14th Regiment N.C. Troops (4th Regiment N.C. Volunteers). Enlisted in this company in Stanly County on March 1, 1863, for the war. Captured at Falling Waters, Maryland, July 14, 1863. Confined at Old Capitol Prison, Washington, D.C. Transferred to Point Lookout, Maryland, August 8, 1863. Released at Point Lookout on January 23, 1864, after taking the Oath of Allegiance and joining the U.S. Army. Assigned to Company A, 1st Regiment U.S. Volunteer Infantry.

MELTON, EBEN, Private
Resided in Stanly County where he enlisted on February 1, 1864, for the war. Present or accounted for through December, 1864. Captured at Sutherland's Station, Virginia, April 2, 1865. Confined at Point Lookout, Maryland, April 4, 1865. Released at Point Lookout on June 15, 1865, after taking the Oath of Allegiance.

MELTON, JOSEPH, Private
Resided in Stanly County and enlisted in Pitt County at age 50, March 25, 1863, as a substitute. Hospitalized at Richmond, Virginia, July 18, 1863, with a gunshot wound of the left side. Place and date wounded not reported. Returned to duty on August 1, 1863. Captured at Bristoe Station, Virginia, October 14, 1863. Confined at Old

Capitol Prison, Washington, D.C. Transferred to Point Lookout, Maryland, October 27, 1863. Released at Point Lookout on February 1, 1864, after taking the Oath of Allegiance and joining the U.S. Army. Unit to which assigned not reported.

MICHAUX, DANIEL M., Private
Previously served as Private in Company F, 19th Regiment N.C. Troops (2nd Regiment N.C. Cavalry). Transferred to this company on December 5, 1864. Captured at Sutherland's Station, Virginia, April 2, 1865. Confined at Point Lookout, Maryland, April 4, 1865. Released at Point Lookout on June 29, 1865, after taking the Oath of Allegiance.

MOOSE, GEORGE, Private
Resided in Stanly County and was by occupation a farmer prior to enlisting in Stanly County at age 29, April 26, 1862, for the war. Reported present in May-June, 1862. Reported on detail as an overseer of public works near Petersburg, Virginia, on or about March 1, 1863. Died at home in Stanly County on December 14, 1863, while absent on furlough. Cause of death not reported.

MORGAN, MARTIN, Private
Resided in Stanly County where he enlisted at age 29, May 1, 1862, for the war. Captured at Gettysburg, Pennsylvania, July 3, 1863. Confined at Fort Delaware, Delaware, on or about July 10, 1863. Transferred to Point Lookout, Maryland, October 20, 1863. Died at Point Lookout on September 14, 1864. Cause of death not reported.

MORRIS, ROBERT, Private
Resided in Stanly County and was by occupation a carpenter prior to enlisting in Stanly County at age 31, April 26, 1862, for the war. Wounded and captured at Gettysburg, Pennsylvania, July 3, 1863. Confined at Fort Delaware, Delaware, on or about July 10, 1863. Died at Fort Delaware on January 15, 1864, of "compression of brain."

MORTON, EZEKIEL, Private
Resided in Stanly County and was by occupation a farmer prior to enlisting at Camp French, near Petersburg, Virginia, at age 33, September 25, 1862, for the war. Killed at Gettysburg, Pennsylvania, July 3, 1863.

MOYER, DANIEL M., Private
Born in Stanly County* where he resided as a harnessmaker prior to enlisting in Stanly County at age 43, March 25, 1862, as a substitute. Reported on duty as a wagonmaster and foragemaster from January 1, 1863, through April 30, 1864. Rejoined the company in May-June, 1864. Killed at Globe Tavern, Virginia, August 21, 1864.

PARKER, GEORGE P., Sergeant
Born in Stanly County* where he resided as a mechanic prior to enlisting in Stanly County at age 23, March 25, 1862. Mustered in as Sergeant. Died at Camp Mangum, near Raleigh, April 26, 1862, of "brain fever."

PENCE, HENRY, Private
Resided in Stanly County and was by occupation a day laborer prior to enlisting in Wayne County at age 48, March 6, 1863, for the war as a substitute. Captured at Gettysburg, Pennsylvania, on or about July 3, 1863. Confined at Fort Delaware, Delaware, on or about July 10, 1863. Paroled at Fort Delaware on September 14, 1864. Received at Aiken's Landing, James River, Virginia, September 18, 1864, for exchange. Reported absent sick through December, 1864.

PENCE, NOAH FRANKLIN, Private
Resided in Stanly County where he enlisted at age 27, April 25, 1862, for the war. Wounded in the left arm and captured at Gettysburg, Pennsylvania, July 3, 1863. Left arm amputated. Hospitalized at Davids Island, New York Harbor, on or about July 20, 1863. Paroled at Davids Island on an unspecified date. Received at City Point, Virginia, September 27, 1863, for exchange. Retired to the Invalid Corps on July 29, 1864.

PERRY, JAMES, Private
Born in Stanly County* where he resided as a farmer prior to enlisting in Stanly County at age 21, March 25, 1862. Left on the battlefield (presumably mortally wounded) at Gettysburg, Pennsylvania, July 3, 1863.

PICKLER, JOHN CALHOUN, Private
Born in Stanly County where he resided as a farmer prior to enlisting in Stanly County at age 21, March 25, 1862. Wounded and captured at Gettysburg, Pennsylvania, July 3, 1863. Confined at Fort Delaware, Delaware, on or about July 10, 1863. Died at Fort Delaware on October 23, 1863, of "dysentery chronic."

PICKLER, JOHN WHITSON, Private
Born in Stanly County* where he resided as a farmer prior to enlisting in Stanly County at age 28, March 25, 1862. Captured at Falling Waters, Maryland, July 14, 1863. Sent to Baltimore, Maryland. Confined at Point Lookout, Maryland, August 17, 1863. Transferred to Elmira, New York, on or about August 16, 1864. Paroled at Elmira on March 14, 1865. Received at Boulware's Wharf, James River, Virginia, March 18, 1865, for exchange. Hospitalized at Richmond, Virginia, March 18, 1865, with scorbutus. Deserted on March 20, 1865.

POPLIN, JAMES A., Private
Born in Stanly County* where he resided as a farmer prior to enlisting in Stanly County at age 27, March 25, 1862. Wounded in the right thigh and captured at Gettysburg, Pennsylvania, July 3, 1863. Hospitalized at Davids Island, New York Harbor, on or about July 20, 1863. Transferred to Fort Delaware, Delaware, August 19, 1864. Paroled at Fort Delaware on September 14, 1864. Received at Aiken's Landing, James River, Virginia, September 18, 1864, for exchange. Hospitalized at Richmond, Virginia, on or about September 22, 1864, still suffering from the gunshot wound he received at Gettysburg. Furloughed for sixty days on October 5, 1864. Returned to duty subsequent to December 31, 1864. Surrendered at Appomattox Court House, Virginia, April 9, 1865.

RANDLE, WILLIAM, Private
Resided in Stanly County and enlisted at Camp Campbell, Drewry's Bluff, Virginia, at age 34, July 21, 1862, for the war. Reported present or accounted for on surviving company muster rolls through August, 1863. Died at Gordonsville, Virginia, September 2, 1863, of "diarrhoea chr[onic]."

RICH, GEORGE W., Private
Previously served as Private in Company F, 19th Regiment N.C. Troops (2nd Regiment N.C. Cavalry). Transferred to this company on December 5, 1864. Wounded in the back and right shoulder and captured at Sutherland's Station, Virginia, April 2, 1865. Hospitalized at Washington, D.C. Released at Washington on or about June 14, 1865, after taking the Oath of Allegiance.

ROBINSON, JOHN L., Private
Previously served as Private in Company F, 19th Regiment N.C. Troops (2nd Regiment N.C. Cavalry). Transferred to this company on December 5, 1864. Captured at Sutherland's Station, Virginia, April 2, 1865. Confined at Point Lookout, Maryland, April 4, 1865. Died at Point Lookout on May 28, 1865, of "chro[nic] diarrhoea."

ROBINSON, JOHN T., Private
Born in Stanly County* where he resided as a farmer prior to enlisting in Stanly County at age 25, March 25, 1862. Appointed Quartermaster Sergeant on April 28, 1862, and transferred to the Field and Staff of this regiment.

ROGERS, DAVID D., Corporal
Born in Stanly County* where he resided as a farmer prior to enlisting in Stanly County at age 26, March 25, 1862. Mustered in as Corporal. Died at Camp Campbell, Drewry's Bluff, Virginia, July 19, 1862. Cause of death not reported.

ROGERS, JOHN H., Private
Resided in Stanly County and enlisted at Camp Vance at age 28, December 4, 1862, for the war. Killed at Gettysburg, Pennsylvania, July 1, 1863.

RUMAGE, HARRIS, Private
Resided in Stanly County and was by occupation a farmer prior to enlisting in Stanly County at age 34, April 26, 1862, for the war. Mustered in as Private. Promoted to Corporal in August, 1862-February, 1863. Broke a leg when he fell from a train on December 23, 1862. Returned to duty in January-February, 1864. Reduced to ranks on August 1, 1864. Captured near Petersburg, Virginia, March 25, 1865. Confined at Point Lookout, Maryland, March 27, 1865. Released at Point Lookout on June 3, 1865, after taking the Oath of Allegiance.

SAUNDERS, ROMULUS W., Private
Previously served as 1st Lieutenant of Company F, 19th Regiment N.C. Troops (2nd Regiment N.C. Cavalry). Assigned to duty with this company with the rank of Private on December 5, 1864. Captured at Sutherland's Station, Virginia, April 2, 1865. Confined at Point

Lookout, Maryland, April 4, 1865. Released at Point Lookout on June 1, 1865, after taking the Oath of Allegiance.

SELL, JACOB, Private
Born in Stanly County where he resided as a farmer prior to enlisting in Stanly County at age 17 on or about March 25, 1862, as a substitute. Discharged on June 24, 1862, presumably by reason of being underage. Reenlisted in the company on or about March 1, 1863. Killed at Gettysburg, Pennsylvania, July 3, 1863.

SELL, JOHN, Private
Born in Stanly County* where he resided as a farmer prior to enlisting in Stanly County at age 36, March 25, 1862. Wounded mortally and left on the battlefield at Gettysburg, Pennsylvania, July 3, 1863.

SELL, SOLOMON, Private
Born in Stanly County* where he resided as a farmer prior to enlisting at Camp Mangum, near Raleigh, at age 56, May 17, 1862, for the war as a substitute. Wounded in the hip and captured at Gettysburg, Pennsylvania, July 3, 1863. Hospitalized at Chester, Pennsylvania. Paroled at Chester on an unspecified date. Received at City Point, Virginia, September 23, 1863, for exchange. Discharged on March 26, 1864, by reason of disability from wounds.

SHANKLE, JACOB, Private
Born in Stanly County* where he resided as a farmer prior to enlisting in Stanly County at age 34, March 25, 1862. Reported present or accounted for on surviving company muster rolls through December, 1864. Surrendered at Appomattox Court House, Virginia, April 9, 1865.

SHANKLE, JAMES W., Private
Previously served as Private in Company H, 14th Regiment N.C. Troops (4th Regiment N.C. Volunteers). Enlisted in this company in Stanly County on March 1, 1863, for the war. Wounded and captured at Gettysburg, Pennsylvania, July 3, 1863. Died at Gettysburg on July 6, 1863, of wounds.

SHANKLE, JOHN N., Corporal
Born in Stanly County* where he resided as a farmer prior to enlisting in Stanly County at age 48, March 25, 1862. Mustered in as Private. Captured at Falling Waters, Maryland, July 14, 1863. Confined at Old Capitol Prison, Washington, D.C. Transferred to Point Lookout, Maryland, August 8, 1863. Paroled at Point Lookout on March 3, 1864. Received at City Point, Virginia, March 6, 1864, for exchange. Returned to duty in May-June, 1864. Promoted to Corporal on October 20, 1864. Captured at Burgess' Mill, Virginia, October 27, 1864. Confined at Point Lookout on October 31, 1864. Paroled at Point Lookout on or about February 10, 1865. Received at Cox's Wharf, James River, Virginia, on or about February 15, 1865, for exchange. Hospitalized at Richmond, Virginia, February 15, 1865, with debilitas. Furloughed for sixty days on March 2, 1865.

SHAVER, NOAH, Private
Born in Stanly County* where he resided as a farmer prior

to enlisting in Stanly County at age 32, March 25, 1862. Killed at Gettysburg, Pennsylvania, July 3, 1863.

SIDES, D. A., Private

Resided in Stanly County and enlisted at Camp Vance at age 34, December 4, 1862, for the war. Captured at Gettysburg, Pennsylvania, July 3, 1863. Confined at Fort Delaware, Delaware, on or about July 10, 1863. Transferred to Point Lookout, Maryland, October 20, 1863. Paroled at Point Lookout on February 18, 1865. Received at Boulware's Wharf, James River, Virginia, on or about February 20, 1865, for exchange.

SMITH, ARTHUR A., Private

Born in Stanly County where he resided as a farmer prior to enlisting in Stanly County at age 21, March 25, 1862. Died in hospital at Petersburg, Virginia, September 27, 1862, of "typhoid fever."

SMITH, CLARK C., Private

Resided in Stanly County where he enlisted at age 23, April 28, 1862, for the war. Died at Goldsboro on July 5, 1862. Cause of death not reported.

SMITH, ELI M., Corporal

Born in Stanly County* where he resided as a farmer prior to enlisting in Stanly County at age 28, March 25, 1862. Mustered in as Private. Captured at Gettysburg, Pennsylvania, July 3, 1863. Hospitalized at Davids Island, New York Harbor, July 20, 1863. Paroled at Davids Island on August 24, 1863. Received at City Point, Virginia, August 28, 1863, for exchange. Returned to duty prior to November 18, 1863. Promoted to Corporal on November 1, 1864. Captured at Sutherland's Station, Virginia, April 2, 1865. Confined at Point Lookout, Maryland, April 4, 1865. Released at Point Lookout on June 20, 1865, after taking the Oath of Allegiance.

SMITH, GREEN B., Private

Born in Stanly County* where he resided as a farmer prior to enlisting in Stanly County at age 27, March 25, 1862. Mustered in as Private. Promoted to Corporal on August 1, 1864. Reported present or accounted for on surviving company muster rolls through August, 1864. Wounded in the left leg at Jones' Farm, Virginia, on or about September 30, 1864. Leg amputated. Reduced to ranks on or about October 20, 1864. Died in hospital at Richmond, Virginia, on or about October 30, 1864, of wounds.

SMITH, REUBEN K., Private

Born in Stanly County where he resided as a farmer prior to enlisting in Stanly County at age 17, March 25, 1862. Wounded in the right thigh at Gettysburg, Pennsylvania, July 3, 1863. Captured at Gettysburg on or about July 5, 1863. Hospitalized at Gettysburg. Transferred to hospital at Baltimore, Maryland, July 19, 1863. Transferred to hospital at Chester, Pennsylvania, on or about July 21, 1863. Paroled and transferred to City Point, Virginia, where he was received on August 20, 1863, for exchange. Hospitalized at Farmville, Virginia, August 28, 1863. Furloughed for thirty days September 7, 1863. Returned to duty prior to November 18, 1863. Reported absent wounded in May-June, 1864. Place and date wounded not

reported. Died on June 15, 1864, of wounds. Place of death not reported.

SMITH, S. A., Private

Resided in Stanly County and enlisted at Orange Court House, Virginia, at age 18, September 1, 1863, for the war. Reported present or accounted for on surviving company muster rolls through August, 1864. Wounded slightly in the left leg at Jones' Farm, Virginia, on or about September 30, 1864. Returned to duty in November-December, 1864. Captured at Sutherland's Station, Virginia, April 2, 1865. Confined at Point Lookout, Maryland, April 4, 1865. Released at Point Lookout on June 8, 1865, after taking the Oath of Allegiance.

SMITH, WILLIAM A., Sergeant

Born in Stanly County where he resided as a clerk prior to enlisting in Stanly County at age 21, March 25, 1862. Mustered in as Corporal. Promoted to Sergeant in March-June, 1863. Killed at Bristoe Station, Virginia, October 14, 1863.

SWARINGEN, ELI S., Sergeant

Born in Stanly County* where he resided as a farmer prior to enlisting in Stanly County at age 23, March 25, 1862. Mustered in as Private. Promoted to Sergeant on November 1, 1864. Reported present or accounted for on surviving company muster rolls through December, 1864. Surrendered at Appomattox Court House, Virginia, April 9, 1865.

THOMPSON, NATHAN, Private

Resided in Stanly County and was by occupation a farmer prior to enlisting in Stanly County at age 43, September 29, 1863, for the war. Reported present or accounted for on surviving company muster rolls through December, 1864. Captured at Sutherland's Station, Virginia, April 2, 1865. Confined at Point Lookout, Maryland, April 4, 1865. Released at Point Lookout on June 20, 1865, after taking the Oath of Allegiance.

THOMPSON, RISDEN N., Private

Born in Stanly County where he resided as a farmer prior to enlisting in Stanly County at age 18, March 25, 1862. Wounded in the left thigh (fracture) and captured at Gettysburg, Pennsylvania, July 3, 1863. Hospitalized at Gettysburg where he died on or about September 25, 1863, of wounds.

THOMPSON, WILLIAM R., Private

Born in Stanly County where he resided as a farmer prior to enlisting in Stanly County at age 18, March 25, 1862. Hospitalized at Richmond, Virginia, June 21, 1863, with chronic diarrhoea. Transferred to another hospital on August 15, 1863. Returned to duty prior to November 18, 1863. Hospitalized at Richmond on November 18, 1864, with an unspecified complaint. Furloughed for thirty days on January 26, 1865. Returned to duty prior to April 2, 1865, when he was captured at Sutherland's Station, Virginia. Confined at Point Lookout, Maryland, April 4, 1865. Released at Point Lookout on or about June 20, 1865, after taking the Oath of Allegiance.

TOLBERT, JOHN C., Private

Resided in Stanly County where he enlisted at age 33, April 26, 1862, for the war. Deserted on August 5, 1863. Returned to duty on October 3, 1863. Captured at Bristoe Station, Virginia, October 14, 1863. Confined at Old Capitol Prison, Washington, D.C. Transferred to Point Lookout, Maryland, October 27, 1863. Hospitalized at Point Lookout on November 8, 1863, with scorbutus. Returned to duty on January 10, 1864. Paroled at Point Lookout on or about November 1, 1864. Died on board the U.S. Hospital Steamer *Baltic* on November 11, 1864, of "pneumonia" while being transferred for exchange. Buried at Hilton Head, South Carolina.

TROUTMAN, JOHN, Private

Resided in Stanly County where he enlisted at age 30, April 28, 1862, for the war. Hospitalized at Richmond, Virginia, June 22, 1863, with debility. Transferred to another hospital on July 29, 1863. Returned to duty in November, 1863-February, 1864. Transferred to Company G, 19th Regiment N.C. Troops (2nd Regiment N.C. Cavalry), December 5, 1864.

TROUTMAN, THOMAS J., Private

Born in Stanly County where he resided as a farmer prior to enlisting in Stanly County at age 18, March 25, 1862. Died in hospital at Wilson on March 1, 1863, of "pneumonia."

TURNER, HENRY CLAY, Sergeant

Born in Stanly County where he resided as a student prior to enlisting in Stanly County at age 18, March 25, 1862. Mustered in as Sergeant. Appointed Commissary Sergeant on May 1, 1862, and transferred to the Field and Staff of this regiment.

UPCHURCH, WILLIAM R., Corporal

Born in Stanly County* where he resided as a farmer prior to enlisting in Stanly County at age 36, March 25, 1862. Mustered in as Private. Wounded and captured at Gettysburg, Pennsylvania, July 3, 1863. Hospitalized at Gettysburg. Transferred to hospital at Davids Island, New York Harbor, where he arrived on or about July 20, 1863. Paroled at Davids Island on an unspecified date. Received at City Point, Virginia, September 8, 1863, for exchange. Returned to duty in March-April, 1864. Hospitalized at Richmond, Virginia, August 29, 1864, with a grapeshot wound of the left hand. Place and date wounded not reported (probably wounded at Reams' Station, Virginia, August 25, 1864). Furloughed for thirty days on September 8, 1864. Returned to duty in October, 1864. Promoted to Corporal on November 1, 1864. Captured at Sutherland's Station, Virginia, April 2, 1865. Confined at Point Lookout, Maryland, April 4, 1865. Released at Point Lookout on June 21, 1865, after taking the Oath of Allegiance.

WALLER, JOHN R., Private

Resided in Stanly County where he enlisted at age 28, April 28, 1862, for the war. Wounded in the thigh and captured at Gettysburg, Pennsylvania, July 3, 1863. Hospitalized at Gettysburg where he died on or about July 23, 1863, of wounds.

WATKINS, JAMES D., Private

Born in Stanly County where he resided as a farmer prior to enlisting in Stanly County at age 21, March 25, 1862. Mustered in as Private. Promoted to Sergeant on May 7, 1862. Wounded in the left thigh at Goldsboro on December 17, 1862. Leg amputated. Reduced to ranks on March 4, 1863. Reported absent wounded until April 15, 1864, when he was retired to the Invalid Corps.

COMPANY K

This company, known as the "Fighting Boys," was raised in Forsyth County and enlisted at Winston in March, 1862. It was mustered into state service at Camp Mangum, near Raleigh, on April 28, 1862, and assigned to the 52nd Regiment N.C. Troops as Company K. After joining the regiment the company functioned as a part of the regiment, and its history for the remainder of the war is reported as a part of the regimental history.

The information contained in the following roster was compiled primarily from a company muster-in and descriptive roll dated April 28, 1862, and from company muster rolls for May 1-June 30, 1862; October 31, 1862-February 28, 1863; and July 1, 1863-December 31, 1864. No company muster rolls were located for July 1, 1862-October 30, 1862; March 1-June 30, 1863; or for the period after December 31, 1864. Valuable information was obtained from primary records such as the North Carolina adjutant general's *Roll of Honor*, discharge certificates, medical records, prisoner of war records, *The War of the Rebellion: A Compilation of the Official Records of the Union and Confederate Armies*, militia records, newspaper casualty lists and obituaries, Confederate pension applications filed with the state of North Carolina, and the 1860 federal census of North Carolina. Secondary sources such as postwar rosters and histories, cemetery records, the *Confederate Veteran*, published genealogies, and records of the United Daughters of the Confederacy also provided useful information.

OFFICERS

CAPTAINS

BLACKBURN, AURELIUS C.

Born in Forsyth County* where he resided as a student prior to enlisting at age 22. Appointed Captain on April 3, 1862. Killed at Gettysburg, Pennsylvania, July 1, 1863. He was "young and chivalrous."

GOSLEN, JUNIUS W.

Born in Forsyth County* where he resided as a student prior to enlisting in Forsyth County at age 21. Appointed 1st Lieutenant on April 3, 1862. Promoted to Captain to rank from July 1, 1863. Reported present or accounted for on surviving company muster rolls through June, 1864. Furloughed for sixty days on or about August 1, 1864, by reason of "insanity." Returned to duty prior to October 27, 1864, when he was captured at Burgess' Mill, Virginia. Confined at Old Capitol Prison, Washington, D.C. Transferred to Fort Delaware, Delaware, December 16, 1864. Released at Fort Delaware on June 17, 1865, after taking the Oath of Allegiance. [Reported on duty as acting commander of Company C of this regiment on November 17, 1863, and in January-April, 1864.]

LIEUTENANTS

COX, ROMULUS LEEDY, 1st Lieutenant
Born in Forsyth County* where he resided as a teacher prior to enlisting in Forsyth County at age 27. Appointed 2nd Lieutenant on April 3, 1862. Promoted to 1st Lieutenant to rank from July 1, 1863. Reported present or accounted for on surviving company muster rolls through June, 1864. Wounded in the bottom of the left foot near Globe Tavern, Virginia, August 21, 1864. Hospitalized at Richmond, Virginia. Furloughed for thirty days on or about August 27, 1864. Reported absent on furlough through December, 1864. Hospitalized at Richmond on March 4, 1865, with nephritis. Furloughed for thirty days on March 22, 1865. Paroled at Greensboro on May 9, 1865. [Reported on duty as acting commander of Company C of this regiment in May-June, 1864.]

WALKER, VIRGIL H., 3rd Lieutenant
Born in Forsyth County* where he resided as a teacher prior to enlisting in Forsyth County at age 22. Appointed 3rd Lieutenant on April 3, 1862. Reported present or accounted for on surviving company muster rolls through September, 1864. Captured at Burgess' Mill, Virginia, October 27, 1864. Confined at Old Capitol Prison, Washington, D.C. Transferred to Fort Delaware, Delaware, December 16, 1864. Released at Fort Delaware on June 17, 1865, after taking the Oath of Allegiance.

NONCOMMISSIONED OFFICERS AND PRIVATES

BAINES, ROBERT G., Sergeant
Resided in Virginia and enlisted in Wake County at age 20, May 5, 1862, for the war. Mustered in as Private. Promoted to Sergeant on June 10, 1862. Promoted to Sergeant Major in September-October, 1862, and transferred to the Field and Staff of this regiment.

BECK, JOHN W., 1st Sergeant
Born in Forsyth County* where he resided as a farmer prior to enlisting in Forsyth County at age 27, March 22, 1862. Mustered in as 1st Sergeant. Discharged on May 30, 1862, after providing Private Alexander B. Everett as a substitute. Later served as Private in Company D, 21st Regiment N.C. Troops (11th Regiment N.C. Volunteers).

BOWEN, HENRY R., Private
Resided in Forsyth County where he enlisted at age 30,

March 22, 1862. Wounded in the thigh and ankle and captured at Gettysburg, Pennsylvania, July 3, 1863. Hospitalized at Chester, Pennsylvania, July 17, 1863. Transferred to Point Lookout, Maryland, October 2, 1863. Released at Point Lookout on February 2, 1864, after taking the Oath of Allegiance and joining the U.S. Army. Assigned to Company D, 1st Regiment U.S. Volunteer Infantry.

BROWN, MICAJAH, Private
Resided in Wilkes County and enlisted at Camp French, near Petersburg, Virginia, at age 20, October 30, 1862, for the war. Reported absent on detail in the quartermaster department from August 8, 1863, through February 29, 1864. Reported on detail as a teamster in March-August, 1864. Reported absent without leave in July-December, 1864.

BROWNING, WILLIAM, Private
Born in Caswell County and resided in Forsyth County where he was by occupation a farmer prior to enlisting in Forsyth County at age 16, March 22, 1862. Captured at Falling Waters, Maryland, July 14, 1863. Sent to Baltimore, Maryland. Confined at Point Lookout, Maryland, August 17, 1863. Died at Point Lookout on May 3, 1864. Cause of death not reported.

BRUNER, GEORGE M., Private
Born in Forsyth County* where he resided as a farmer prior to enlisting in Forsyth County at age 48, March 22, 1862. Discharged at Raleigh on May 28, 1862, by reason of being overage.

CARMICHAEL, ALEXANDER B., Private
Born in Forsyth County* where he resided as a farmer prior to enlisting in Forsyth County at age 20, March 22, 1862. Reported present or accounted for on surviving company muster rolls through August, 1864.

CARMICHAEL, JOHN W., Private
Born in Forsyth County* where he resided as a farmer prior to enlisting in Forsyth County at age 22, March 22, 1862. Reported present or accounted for on surviving company muster rolls through August, 1864. Reported on detail as a baker in September-December, 1864. Hospitalized at Richmond, Virginia, March 2, 1865, with chronic diarrhoea. Captured in hospital at Richmond on April 3, 1865. Transferred to Libby Prison, Richmond, on an unspecified date. Transferred to Newport News, Virginia, April 23, 1865. Arrived at Newport News on April 24, 1865. Died in hospital at Newport News on June 5, 1865, of "diarrhoea chr[onic]."

CARMICHAEL, THOMAS E., Private
Resided in Forsyth County and enlisted at Drewry's Bluff, Virginia, at age 18, August 7, 1862, for the war. Captured at Gettysburg, Pennsylvania, July 3, 1863. Transferred to hospital at Davids Island, New York Harbor, where he arrived on July 20, 1863. Paroled at Davids Island on an unspecified date. Received at City Point, Virginia, September 16, 1863, for exchange. Returned to duty in January-February, 1864. Present or accounted for through December, 1864.

CHEEK, AARON, Private

Enlisted at Orange Court House, Virginia, at age 33, November 20, 1863, for the war. Reported present through August, 1864. Wounded in the right ankle at Jones' Farm, Virginia, on or about September 30, 1864. Reported absent wounded through December, 1864. Survived the war.

CLAYTON, GIDEON E., Private

Born in Forsyth County* where he resided as a farmer prior to enlisting in Forsyth County at age 25, March 22, 1862. Mustered in as Sergeant. Wounded and captured at Gettysburg, Pennsylvania, July 3, 1863. Hospitalized at Gettysburg. Transferred to hospital at Davids Island, New York Harbor, where he arrived on or about July 20, 1863. Paroled at Davids Island and transferred to City Point, Virginia, where he was received on September 8, 1863, for exchange. Returned to duty in January-February, 1864. Hospitalized at Lynchburg, Virginia, May 7, 1864, with acute rheumatism. Returned to duty on June 18, 1864. Reported absent sick in July-August, 1864. Reduced to ranks in September, 1864. Killed at Jones' Farm, Virginia, October 1, 1864.

COLEY, CHARLES M., Private

Enlisted in Forsyth County on October 31, 1864, for the war. Surrendered at Appomattox Court House, Virginia, April 9, 1865. [North Carolina pension records indicate that he was wounded at Hatcher's Run, Virginia, in 1865.]

CORDELL, WILLIAM, Private

Born in Stokes County and resided in Forsyth County where he was by occupation a farmer prior to enlisting in Forsyth County at age 55, March 26, 1862. Deserted on April 27, 1862. Returned to duty prior to July 1, 1862. Captured at Falling Waters, Maryland, July 14, 1863. Sent to Baltimore, Maryland. Confined at Point Lookout, Maryland, August 17, 1863. Released at Point Lookout on January 29, 1864, after taking the Oath of Allegiance and joining the U.S. service.

COX, PAYTON A., _____,

North Carolina pension records indicate that he served in this company.

CRAFT, NATHAN L., Private

Resided in Forsyth County and was by occupation a carpenter prior to enlisting in Wayne County at age 26, January 18, 1863, for the war. Captured at Bristoe Station, Virginia, October 14, 1863. Confined at Old Capitol Prison, Washington, D.C. Died in hospital at Washington on January 11, 1864, of "diarrhoea chronica."

CREWS, JOHN M., Sergeant

Born in Forsyth County* where he resided as a farmer prior to enlisting in Forsyth County at age 40, March 22, 1862. Mustered in as Sergeant. Discharged on May 5, 1862, after providing Private Yancey Crews as a substitute.

CREWS, YANCEY, Private

Resided in Forsyth County and enlisted in Wake County at age 17, May 5, 1862, for the war as a substitute for

Sergeant John M. Crews. Captured at Gettysburg, Pennsylvania, July 5, 1863, after he was left behind as a nurse for the wounded. Confined at Fort Delaware, Delaware, on or about July 10, 1863. Transferred to Point Lookout, Maryland, October 20, 1863. Released at Point Lookout on February 2, 1864, after taking the Oath of Allegiance and joining the U.S. Army. Assigned to Company D, 1st Regiment U.S. Volunteer Infantry.

CROMMER, BENJAMIN F., Private

Resided in Forsyth County where he enlisted at age 37, February 10, 1863, for the war. Reported present or accounted for on surviving company muster rolls through December, 1864; however, he was reported absent sick with typhoid fever and remittent fever during much of that period. Survived the war.

DAVIS, HAMILTON, Private

Born in Forsyth County* where he resided as a blacksmith prior to enlisting in Forsyth County at age 30, March 22, 1862. Wounded in the ankle and captured at Gettysburg, Pennsylvania, on or about July 3, 1863. Hospitalized at Gettysburg where he died on or about July 13, 1863, of wounds.

DAVIS, JOHN W., Private

Born in Forsyth County* where he resided as a farmer prior to enlisting in Forsyth County at age 35, March 22, 1862. Discharged at Raleigh on or about May 22, 1862, by reason of being overage.

DAVIS, THOMAS R., Corporal

Born in Forsyth County* where he resided as a farmer prior to enlisting in Forsyth County at age 19, March 22, 1862. Mustered in as Corporal. Captured at Gettysburg, Pennsylvania, July 3, 1863. Confined at Fort Delaware, Delaware, on or about July 10, 1863. Transferred to Point Lookout, Maryland, October 20, 1863. Died at Point Lookout on November 11, 1863, of "scorbutus."

DAWSON, WILLIAM P., Sergeant

Born in Forsyth County* where he resided as a farmer prior to enlisting in Forsyth County at age 27, March 22, 1862. Mustered in as Sergeant. Killed at Gettysburg, Pennsylvania, July 1, 1863.

DULL, GEORGE T., Private

Born in Forsyth County* where he resided as a farmer prior to enlisting in Forsyth County at age 23, March 13, 1862. Wounded in the left leg (flesh) and captured at Gettysburg, Pennsylvania, July 3, 1863. Hospitalized at Gettysburg. Transferred to hospital at Davids Island, New York Harbor, where he arrived on or about July 20, 1863. Paroled at Davids Island on an unspecified date. Received at City Point, Virginia, September 8, 1863, for exchange. Failed to returned to duty and was reported absent without leave in March-December, 1864. Survived the war.

DULL, HENDERSON, Private

Born in Forsyth County* where he resided as a farmer prior to enlisting in Forsyth County at age 25, March 13, 1862. Company records indicate that he was wounded and captured at Gettysburg, Pennsylvania, July 3, 1863;

however, records of the Federal Provost Marshal do not substantiate that report. Reported absent without leave in March-December, 1864.

ELLIOTT, LAURISTON F., Corporal
Born in Forsyth County* where he resided as a farmer prior to enlisting in Forsyth County at age 20, March 26, 1862. Mustered in as Corporal. Wounded in the right forearm (fracture) and captured at Gettysburg, Pennsylvania, July 3, 1863. Hospitalized at Gettysburg. Transferred to hospital at Davids Island, New York Harbor, where he arrived on or about July 20, 1863. Paroled at Davids Island on an unspecified date. Received at City Point, Virginia, September 8, 1863, for exchange. Returned to duty in November, 1863-February, 1864. Reported present through December, 1864. Captured at Sutherland's Station, Virginia, April 2, 1865. Confined at Point Lookout, Maryland, April 4, 1865. Released at Point Lookout on June 11, 1865, after taking the Oath of Allegiance. [Reported on duty as acting commander of Company C of this regiment in May-June, 1864.]

ELLIOTT, LEROY S., Private
Resided in Forsyth County where he enlisted at age 18, July 10, 1862, for the war. Wounded in the arm and captured at Gettysburg, Pennsylvania, July 3, 1863. Exchanged on an unspecified date. Returned to duty in January-February, 1864. Discharged on March 24, 1864, presumably by reason of disability from wounds.

EVERETT, ALEXANDER B., Private
Born in Virginia and resided in Forsyth County where he was by occupation a farmer prior to enlisting in Forsyth County at age 48, March 18, 1862, as a substitute for 1st Sergeant John W. Beck. Discharged on May 30, 1862, by reason of being overage. Reenlisted in the company on March 18, 1863. Reported present or accounted for on surviving company muster rolls through December, 1864. Paroled at Greensboro on May 22, 1865.

GLASSCOCK, JAMES R., Private
Born in Halifax County, Virginia, and resided in Forsyth County where he was by occupation a farmer prior to enlisting in Forsyth County at age 26, March 18, 1862. Captured at Falling Waters, Maryland, July 14, 1863. Confined at Old Capitol Prison, Washington, D.C. Transferred to Point Lookout, Maryland, August 8, 1863. Hospitalized at Point Lookout on October 28, 1863, with chronic diarrhoea. Paroled in hospital at Point Lookout on March 17, 1864. Received at City Point, Virginia, March 20, 1864, for exchange. Reported absent without leave in July-December, 1864. Survived the war.

GRUBBS, JAMES W., Private
Resided in Guilford County and enlisted in Forsyth County on November 1, 1863, for the war. Hospitalized at Richmond, Virginia, January 29, 1864, with intermittent fever. Furloughed for thirty days on February 4, 1864. Returned to duty in March-April, 1864. Captured at Spotsylvania Court House, Virginia, May 12, 1864. Confined at Point Lookout, Maryland, May 17, 1864. Transferred to Elmira, New York, July 27, 1864. Released at Elmira on June 12, 1865, after taking the Oath of Allegiance.

GRUBBS, JOHN E., Private
Born in Forsyth County* where he resided as a farmer prior to enlisting in Forsyth County at age 26, March 18, 1862. Wounded at or near Goldsboro on or about December 17, 1862. Returned to duty prior to March 1, 1863. Reported present or accounted for on surviving company muster rolls through December, 1864; however, he was reported absent sick during most of that period. Paroled at Greensboro on May 16, 1865.

HAMPTON, SILAS, Private
Born in Wilkes County where he resided as a farmer prior to enlisting at Camp French, near Petersburg, Virginia, at age 30, October 30, 1862, for the war. Wounded slightly in the leg at Gettysburg, Pennsylvania, on or about July 3, 1863. Captured at Falling Waters, Maryland, July 14, 1863. Confined at Old Capitol Prison, Washington, D.C. Transferred to Point Lookout, Maryland, August 8, 1863. Paroled at Point Lookout on March 3, 1864. Received at City Point, Virginia, March 6, 1864, for exchange. Reported absent without leave in July-December, 1864. Survived the war.

HARDGROVE, FRANCIS M., Sergeant
Born in Forsyth County* where he resided as a farmer prior to enlisting in Forsyth County at age 19, March 22, 1862. Mustered in as Private. Promoted to Sergeant on April 25, 1863. Wounded in the left hip at Bristoe Station, Virginia, October 14, 1863. Hospitalized at Richmond, Virginia. Returned to duty in July-August, 1864. Reported on detail at the division infirmary in July-December, 1864. Surrendered at Appomattox Court House, Virginia, April 9, 1865.

HARDGROVE, LEWIS F., Private
Born in Forsyth County* where he resided as a farmer prior to enlisting in Forsyth County at age 22, March 18, 1862. Captured at Gettysburg, Pennsylvania, July 3, 1863. Confined at Fort Delaware, Delaware, on or about July 10, 1863. Transferred to Point Lookout, Maryland, October 20, 1863. Released at Point Lookout on February 2, 1864, after taking the Oath of Allegiance and joining the U.S. Army. Assigned to Company D, 1st Regiment U.S. Volunteer Infantry.

HARDGROVE, THOMAS M., Private
Born in Forsyth County* and resided in Forsyth or Guilford County where he was by occupation a farmer prior to enlisting in Forsyth County at age 21, March 22, 1862. Captured at Falling Waters, Maryland, July 14, 1863. Hospitalized at Baltimore, Maryland, August 3, 1863. Paroled at Baltimore on August 23, 1863. Received at City Point, Virginia, August 24, 1863, for exchange. Returned to duty in January-February, 1864. Captured at or near Wilderness, Virginia, on or about May 6, 1864. Confined at Point Lookout, Maryland, May 17, 1864. Transferred to Elmira, New York, August 8, 1864. Released at Elmira on July 11, 1865, after taking the Oath of Allegiance.

HAUSER, MOSES EDWIN, Private
Born in Forsyth County* where he resided as a farmer prior to enlisting at age 34, March 18, 1862, as a substitute. Wounded in the right hand and left thigh at

Gettysburg, Pennsylvania, July 3, 1863. Returned to duty in January-February, 1864. Reported present or accounted for through December, 1864. Survived the war.

HENDERSON, JOHN, Private
Resided in Forsyth County where he enlisted at age 31, May 19, 1862, for the war as a substitute. Present or accounted for until January-February, 1864, when he was reported to be "lost." No further records.

HINE, EDWARD A., Private
Born in Forsyth County* where he resided as a farmer prior to enlisting in Lenoir County at age 29, March 18, 1862. Captured at Gettysburg, Pennsylvania, July 3, 1863. Confined at Fort Delaware, Delaware, on or about July 10, 1863. Exchanged on an unspecified date. Returned to duty in November, 1863-February, 1864. Captured at Spotsylvania Court House, Virginia, May 12, 1864. Confined at Point Lookout, Maryland, May 17, 1864. Transferred to Elmira, New York, July 27, 1864. Released at Elmira on June 12, 1865, after taking the Oath of Allegiance.

HINE, THEODORE T., Private
Resided in Forsyth County and was by occupation a farmer prior to enlisting in Forsyth County at age 32, February 10, 1863, for the war. Captured at Gettysburg, Pennsylvania, July 3, 1863. Confined at Fort Delaware, Delaware, on or about July 10, 1863. Paroled at Fort Delaware on July 30, 1863. Received at City Point, Virginia, on or about August 2, 1863, for exchange. Returned to duty in January-February, 1864. Captured at or near Spotsylvania Court House, Virginia, on or about May 12, 1864. Confined at Point Lookout, Maryland. Transferred to Elmira, New York, July 27, 1864. Released at Elmira on June 12, 1865, after taking the Oath of Allegiance.

HOLDER, WILLIAM J., Private
Born in Forsyth County* where he resided as a farmer prior to enlisting in Lenoir County at age 18, March 18, 1862. Reported present or accounted for on surviving company muster rolls through October, 1863. Died in hospital at Petersburg, Virginia, December 3, 1863, of "diarrhoea chronica."

HUDGINS, ANDREW J., Private
Enlisted at Orange Court House, Virginia, December 1, 1863, for the war. Died in hospital at Lynchburg, Virginia, May 11, 1864, of "rubeola."

HUNT, WILLIAM, Private
Born in Guilford County and resided in Forsyth County where he was by occupation a farmer prior to enlisting at age 48, March 13, 1862. Discharged at Raleigh on May 24, 1862, by reason of being overage.

INGRAM, JAMES R., Corporal
Born in Stokes County and resided in Forsyth County where he was by occupation a farmer prior to enlisting in Forsyth County at age 26, March 22, 1862. Mustered in as Corporal. Captured at Falling Waters, Maryland, July 14, 1863. Confined at Old Capitol Prison,

Washington, D.C. Transferred to Point Lookout, Maryland, August 8, 1863. Paroled at Point Lookout on March 3, 1864. Received at City Point, Virginia, March 6, 1864, for exchange. Returned to duty in May-June, 1864. Killed at Reams' Station, Virginia, August 25, 1864.

JENNINGS, SAMUEL, Private
Resided in Wilkes County and was by occupation a clerk prior to enlisting at Camp French, near Petersburg, Virginia, at age 26, October 30, 1862, for the war. Hospitalized at Richmond, Virginia, June 22, 1863, with debility. Returned to duty on or about November 1, 1863. Reported present or accounted for through December, 1864. Captured at Sutherland's Station, Virginia, April 2, 1865. Confined at Point Lookout, Maryland, April 4, 1865. Released at Point Lookout on June 28, 1865, after taking the Oath of Allegiance.

JENNINGS, THOMAS, Private
Resided in Wilkes County and was by occupation a farmer prior to enlisting at Camp French, near Petersburg, Virginia, at age 30, October 30, 1862, for the war. Reported present or accounted for on surviving company muster rolls through August, 1864. Captured at Burgess' Mill, Virginia, October 27, 1864. Confined at Point Lookout, Maryland, October 31, 1864. Paroled at Point Lookout on or about March 28, 1865. Received at Boulware's Wharf, James River, Virginia, March 30, 1865, for exchange.

JOHNSON, JESSE B., Private
Resided in Forsyth County and was by occupation a farmer prior to enlisting in Forsyth County at age 22, March 18, 1862. Wounded in the thigh and captured at Gettysburg, Pennsylvania, July 3, 1863. Confined at Fort Delaware, Delaware, on or about July 10, 1863. Transferred to Point Lookout, Maryland, October 20, 1863. Released at Point Lookout on January 29, 1864, after taking the Oath of Allegiance and joining the U.S. Army. Assigned to Company C, 1st Regiment U.S. Volunteer Infantry.

JOHNSON, JOHN A., Private
Born in Forsyth County* where he resided as a farmer prior to enlisting in Forsyth County at age 19, March 22, 1862. Wounded at Goldsboro on December 17, 1862. Returned to duty prior to March 1, 1863. Hospitalized at Charlottesville, Virginia, December 1, 1863, with acute diarrhoea. Returned to duty on February 6, 1864. Reported absent sick in July-October, 1864. Returned to duty in November-December, 1864. Paroled at Greensboro on May 20, 1865.

JOHNSON, WILLIAM M. H., Private
Resided in Forsyth County and was by occupation a farmer prior to enlisting in Forsyth County at age 25, March 22, 1862. Wounded at Goldsboro on December 17, 1862. Returned to duty prior to March 1, 1863. Wounded in the thigh and captured at Gettysburg, Pennsylvania, on or about July 3, 1863. Hospitalized at Gettysburg. Transferred to hospital at Davids Island, New York Harbor, where he arrived on or about July 20, 1863. Paroled at Davids Island on an unspecified date. Received at City Point, Virginia, September 8, 1863, for exchange.

Returned to duty in January-February, 1864. Captured at Spotsylvania Court House, Virginia, May 12, 1864. Confined at Point Lookout, Maryland, May 17, 1864. Transferred to Elmira, New York, July 29, 1864. Died at Elmira on January 18, 1865, of "pneumonia."

JONES, JOHN T., Private
Resided in Forsyth County where he enlisted at age 18, March 18, 1862. Wounded at Gettysburg, Pennsylvania, July 3, 1863. Captured at Williamsport, Maryland, July 14, 1863. Hospitalized at Hagerstown, Maryland. Transferred to hospital at Chester, Pennsylvania, on or about September 14, 1863. Transferred to Point Lookout, Maryland, on or about October 1, 1863. Paroled at Point Lookout on or about March 17, 1864. Received at City Point, Virginia, March 20, 1864, for exchange. Reported absent wounded through December, 1864. [According to the Salem People's Press of July 24, 1863, one of his legs was amputated as a result of wounds received at Gettysburg.]

JONES, SIMON P., Private
Enlisted at Salem on May 10, 1864, for the war. Wounded prior to July 1, 1864. Reported absent wounded until November-December, 1864, when he was reported absent without leave.

JORDAN, S. H., _____
North Carolina pension records indicate that he served in this company.

JOYNER, LEWIS, Private
Enlisted in Forsyth County on May 10, 1864, for the war. Present or accounted for until September-December, 1864, when he was reported absent sick.

KIGER, ADAM, Private
Born in Forsyth County* where he resided as a farmer prior to enlisting in Forsyth County at age 22, March 18, 1862. Reported present or accounted for on surviving company muster rolls through December, 1864. Survived the war. [North Carolina pension records indicate that he was wounded at the Chickahominy River, Virginia, in July, 1862.]

LEDFORD, WILLIAM F., Private
Resided in Forsyth County and was by occupation a farmer prior to enlisting in Forsyth County at age 39, February 10, 1863, for the war. Reported present or accounted for on surviving company muster rolls through October, 1864; however, he was reported absent sick or absent on furlough during most of that period. Paroled at Greensboro on May 17, 1865.

LIVENGOOD, SOLOMON, Private
Resided in Forsyth County and was by occupation a day laborer prior to enlisting in Forsyth County at age 36, February 10, 1863, for the war. Captured at Gettysburg, Pennsylvania, July 3, 1863. Confined at Fort Delaware, Delaware, on or about July 10, 1863. Died at Fort Delaware on August 4, 1863, of "typhoid pneumonia."

LUPER, THEOPHILUS H., Private
Born in Forsyth County* where he resided as a farmer

prior to enlisting in Forsyth County at age 23, March 18, 1862. Died at the Blackwater River, Virginia, November 25, 1862, of disease.

McGEE, ALBERT, Private
Born in Forsyth County* where he resided as a farmer prior to enlisting in Forsyth County at age 21, March 26, 1862. Reported present or accounted for on surviving company muster rolls through December, 1864; however, he was reported absent sick or absent on furlough during most of that period. Paroled at Greensboro on or about May 22, 1865.

McGEE, JOSEPH, Private
Resided in Forsyth County and was by occupation a farmer prior to enlisting in Forsyth County at age 30, February 10, 1863, for the war. Reported present or accounted for on surviving company muster rolls through December, 1864; however, he was reported absent sick or absent on furlough during most of that period. Captured at Sutherland's Station, Virginia, April 2, 1865. Confined at Point Lookout, Maryland, April 4, 1865. Released at Point Lookout on June 29, 1865, after taking the Oath of Allegiance.

McGEE, WILLIAM, Private
Born in Forsyth County* where he resided as a farmer prior to enlisting in Forsyth County at age 25, March 22, 1862. Wounded in the left hip at Goldsboro on December 17, 1862. Returned to duty in March-August, 1863. Reported absent wounded in September-October, 1863. Place and date wounded not reported. Returned to duty in November, 1863-February, 1864. Present or accounted for through December, 1864; however, he was reported absent sick during much of that period. Surrendered at Appomattox Court House, Virginia, April 9, 1865.

McKNIGHT, JOHN W., Private
Born in Forsyth County* where he resided as a farmer prior to enlisting in Forsyth County at age 22, March 22, 1862, as a substitute. Wounded in the leg and captured at Gettysburg, Pennsylvania, July 3, 1863. Hospitalized at Chester, Pennsylvania. Transferred to Point Lookout, Maryland, October 2, 1863. Died in hospital at Point Lookout on May 25, 1864. Cause of death not reported.

McMILLAN, JOHN W., Private
Born in Stokes County and resided in Forsyth County where he was by occupation a farmer prior to enlisting in Forsyth County at age 36, March 18, 1862. Reported present or accounted for on surviving company muster rolls through December, 1864; however, he was reported absent sick for almost that entire period.

MANN, ANIAS, _____
North Carolina pension records indicate that he served in this company.

MARTIN, JAMES T., Private
Born in Chatham County and resided in Forsyth County where he was by occupation a farmer prior to enlisting in Forsyth County at age 21, March 14, 1862. Captured at Falling Waters, Maryland, July 14, 1863. Confined at

Old Capitol Prison, Washington, D.C. Transferred to Point Lookout, Maryland, August 8, 1863. Paroled at Point Lookout on March 3, 1864. Received at City Point, Virginia, March 6, 1864, for exchange. Returned to duty in July-August, 1864. Wounded in the left thigh (flesh) at Jones' Farm, Virginia, on or about September 30, 1864. Returned to duty on January 11, 1865.

MARTIN, JOHN T., Private
Born in Chatham County and resided in Forsyth County where he was by occupation a farmer prior to enlisting in Forsyth County at age 19, March 14, 1862. Wounded in the right thigh (flesh) at Bristoe Station, Virginia, October 14, 1863. Hospitalized at Richmond, Virginia. Furloughed for sixty days on or about November 9, 1863. Returned to duty in May-June, 1864. Reported absent sick or absent on furlough in July-December, 1864. Captured at Sutherland's Station, Virginia, April 2, 1865. Confined at Point Lookout, Maryland, April 4, 1865. Released at Point Lookout on June 29, 1865, after taking the Oath of Allegiance.

MARTIN, WILLIAM O. K., Private
Born in Chatham County and resided in Forsyth County where he was by occupation a farmer prior to enlisting in Forsyth County at age 49, March 22, 1862, as a substitute. Reported present or accounted for on surviving company muster rolls through December, 1864; however, he was reported absent sick for almost that entire period. Survived the war.

MECUM, MATTHEW W., Private
Born in Forsyth County* where he resided as a farmer prior to enlisting in Forsyth County at age 40, March 26, 1862. Died in hospital at Petersburg, Virginia, August 24, 1862, of "continued fever."

MERRITT, ALEXANDER R., Private
Resided in Mecklenburg County and enlisted at Camp French, near Petersburg, Virginia, at age 21, October 8, 1862, for the war. Captured at Gettysburg, Pennsylvania, July 3, 1863. Confined at Fort Delaware, Delaware, on or about July 10, 1863. Died at Fort Delaware on October 6, 1863. Cause of death not reported.

MICKEY, LOWELL P., Private
Born in Forsyth County* where he resided as a farmer prior to enlisting in Forsyth County at age 24, March 22, 1862. Died in hospital at Raleigh on May 13, 1862, of disease.

MICKEY, THOMAS I., Private
Born in Forsyth County* where he resided as a farmer prior to enlisting in Forsyth County at age 31, March 18, 1862. Wounded in the foot (fracture) and captured at Gettysburg, Pennsylvania, July 3, 1863. Hospitalized at Gettysburg where he died on or about July 24, 1863, of wounds.

MILLER, HENRY L., Private
Born in Forsyth County* where he resided as a farmer prior to enlisting in Forsyth County at age 16, April 3,

1862. Discharged at Raleigh prior to July 1, 1862, presumably by reason of being underage.

MOORE, HENRY H., Private
Resided in Davidson County and enlisted at Camp French, near Petersburg, Virginia, at age 19, October 8, 1862, for the war. Captured at Gettysburg, Pennsylvania, July 3, 1863. Confined at Fort Delaware, Delaware, on or about July 10, 1863. Died at Fort Delaware on November 25, 1864, of "intermitt[ent] fever."

MOSER, E. A., Private
Enlisted in Forsyth County at age 19, December 30, 1863, for the war. Reported absent wounded in May-June, 1864. Place and date wounded not reported. Returned to duty in July-August, 1864. Wounded in the right foot at or near Jones' Farm, Virginia, on or about October 1, 1864. Reported absent wounded through December, 1864. Paroled at Greensboro on May 16, 1865.

MOSER, EMANUEL, Private
Born in Forsyth County* where he resided as a farmer prior to enlisting in Forsyth County at age 38, March 22, 1862. Reported present on surviving company muster rolls through August, 1864. Reported sick in hospital in September-December, 1864.

MOSER, JOHN A., Private
Born in Forsyth County* where he resided as a farmer prior to enlisting in Forsyth County at age 15, March 22, 1862. Discharged at Raleigh prior to July 1, 1862, presumably by reason of being underage.

MOSER, JOSIAH, _____
North Carolina pension records indicate that he served in this company.

MOSER, ROBERT W., Private
Born in Forsyth County* and resided in Forsyth or Guilford County where he was by occupation a farmer prior to enlisting in Forsyth County at age 21, March 22, 1862. Reported present or accounted for on surviving company muster rolls through April, 1864. Captured at Spotsylvania Court House, Virginia, May 12, 1864. Confined at Point Lookout, Maryland, May 17, 1864. Transferred to Elmira, New York, July 27, 1864. Released at Elmira on June 12, 1865, after taking the Oath of Allegiance.

NEWMAN, JOSEPH E., _____
North Carolina pension records indicate that he served in this company.

NEWSOM, GEORGE W., Private
Born in South Carolina and resided in Forsyth County where he was by occupation a farmer prior to enlisting in Forsyth County at age 29, March 18, 1862. Discharged at Raleigh on May 24, 1862. Reason discharged not reported.

PADGETT, A. C., _____
North Carolina pension records indicate that he served in this company.

PADGETT, MARVILL S., Private

Resided in Rowan County and enlisted at Camp French, near Petersburg, Virginia, at age 25, October 8, 1862, for the war. Captured at Gettysburg, Pennsylvania, July 3, 1863. Confined at Fort Delaware, Delaware, on or about July 10, 1863. Released at Fort Delaware on June 19, 1865, after taking the Oath of Allegiance.

PARHAM, BENJAMIN F., Private

Resided in Forsyth County and enlisted at Camp Johnston, near Kinston, at age 22, July 8, 1862, for the war. Reported present or accounted for through January 23, 1864; however, he was reported absent sick during most of that period. Reported absent without leave in January-February, 1864. Returned to duty in March-April, 1864. Reported absent on sick furlough in May-August, 1864. Returned to duty in September-October, 1864. Captured in hospital at Richmond, Virginia, April 3, 1865. Transferred to Libby Prison, Richmond, on or about April 14, 1865. Transferred to Newport News, Virginia, April 23, 1865. Released at Newport News on June 30, 1865, after taking the Oath of Allegiance.

PARHAM, THOMAS P., Private

Born in Granville County and resided in Forsyth County where he was by occupation a farmer prior to enlisting in Forsyth County at age 28, March 18, 1862. Wounded in the right arm and captured at Gettysburg, Pennsylvania, July 3, 1863. Hospitalized at Gettysburg. Transferred to hospital at Davids Island, New York Harbor, where he arrived on or about July 20, 1863. Confined at Fort Wood, Bedloe's Island, New York Harbor, on or about October 24, 1863. Transferred to Fort Delaware, Delaware, July 15, 1864. Paroled at Fort Delaware on September 14, 1864. Received at Aiken's Landing, James River, Virginia, September 18, 1864, for exchange. Reported absent wounded or absent on parole through December, 1864.

PEGRAM, JACOB Y., Private

Born in Guilford County and resided in Forsyth County where he was by occupation a farmer prior to enlisting in Forsyth County at age 19, March 18, 1862. Reported present or accounted for on surviving company muster rolls through October, 1863. Hospitalized at Richmond, Virginia, January 29, 1864, with syphilis. Returned to duty on April 1, 1864. Hospitalized at Danville, Virginia, October 13, 1864, with ascites. Hospitalized at Raleigh on November 26, 1864, with eczema. Furloughed for sixty days on December 12, 1864. Hospitalized at Richmond on February 24, 1865, with an ulcer on one of his feet and was furloughed on March 16, 1865. Paroled at Greensboro on May 20, 1865.

PEGRAM, JOSEPH E., Private

Resided in Forsyth County and was by occupation a farm laborer prior to enlisting at Camp French, near Petersburg, Virginia, at age 23, October 8, 1862, for the war. Wounded in the hand and captured at Gettysburg, Pennsylvania, on or about July 3, 1863. Hand amputated. Hospitalized at Gettysburg. Transferred to hospital at Davids Island, New York Harbor, where he arrived on July 9, 1863. Died at Davids Island on August 1, 1863, of "ch[ronic] diarrhoea."

PENDRY, JOHN H., Private

Resided in Forsyth County and was by occupation a day laborer prior to enlisting in Forsyth County at age 30, March 22, 1862. Wounded in the breast by a shell at Gettysburg, Pennsylvania, on or about July 1, 1863. Captured at Gettysburg on or about July 5, 1863. Hospitalized at Gettysburg. Transferred to Fort Delaware, Delaware, where he arrived on or about July 10, 1863. Transferred to Point Lookout, Maryland, October 20, 1863. Died in hospital at Point Lookout on November 10, 1863, of "pneumonia."

PERDUE, MAJOR, Private

Resided in Wilkes County and was by occupation a farmer prior to enlisting at age 35, October 30, 1862, for the war. Deserted on or about December 5, 1862.

PETREE, JACOB, Private

Born in Forsyth County* where he resided as a farmer prior to enlisting in Forsyth County at age 36, March 22, 1862. Captured at Gettysburg, Pennsylvania, July 3, 1863. Confined at Fort Delaware, Delaware, on or about July 10, 1863. Died at Fort Delaware on September 17, 1863, of "remittent fever."

PINSTON, W. F., Private

Place and date of enlistment not reported (probably enlisted in January-March, 1865). Paroled at Salisbury on May 3, 1865.

POWERS, JAMES E., Private

Born in Guilford County and resided in Forsyth County where he was by occupation a farmer prior to enlisting in Forsyth County at age 22, March 18, 1862. Reported missing at Gettysburg, Pennsylvania, July 3, 1863. Presumably killed at Gettysburg.

PRATT, FRANCIS MARION, Private

Resided in Forsyth County where he enlisted at age 28, May 10, 1862, for the war. Captured at Falling Waters, Maryland, July 14, 1863. Sent to Baltimore, Maryland. Confined at Point Lookout, Maryland, August 17, 1863. Paroled at Point Lookout on March 3, 1864. Received at City Point, Virginia, March 6, 1864, for exchange. Returned to duty in May-June, 1864. Reported on detail with the division wagon train in July-December, 1864.

PRATT, THOMAS, Sergeant

Born in Forsyth County* where he resided as a farmer prior to enlisting in Forsyth County at age 21, March 22, 1862. Mustered in as Private. Promoted to Sergeant in July, 1862-February, 1863. Killed at Gettysburg, Pennsylvania, on or about July 3, 1863.

PRATT, WILLIAM R., Corporal

Born in Forsyth County* where he resided as a farmer prior to enlisting in Forsyth County at age 21, March 22, 1862. Mustered in as Private. Promoted to Corporal in July, 1862-February, 1863. Captured at Gettysburg, Pennsylvania, July 3, 1863. Confined at Fort Delaware, Delaware, on or about July 10, 1863. Transferred to Point Lookout, Maryland, October 20, 1863. Died at Point Lookout on March 6, 1864. Cause of death not reported.

PRESNELL, H. C., _____
North Carolina pension records indicate that he served in this company.

RANSOM, RICHARD, Private
Born in Forsyth County* where he resided as a farmer prior to enlisting in Forsyth County on March 22, 1862, as a substitute. Reported present or accounted for on surviving company muster rolls through August, 1863. Reported absent wounded in September-October, 1863. Place and date wounded not reported (probably wounded at Bristoe Station, Virginia, October 14, 1863). Reported on detail as a hospital nurse at Staunton, Virginia, in January-February, 1864. Rejoined the company in March-April, 1864. Reported sick in hospital in May-June, 1864. No further records.

REEDY, WILLIAM, Private
Resided at Forsyth County and enlisted at Camp French, near Petersburg, Virginia, at age 23, October 10, 1862, for the war. Reported present on surviving company muster rolls through June, 1864. Wounded in "the lower right extremities" in July-August, 1864. Place and date wounded not reported. Reported on detail in hospital at Charlotte in November-December, 1864. Paroled at Charlotte in May, 1865.

SAMS, EDMUND W., Private
Born in Forsyth County* where he resided as a farmer prior to enlisting in Forsyth County at age 26, March 22, 1862. Captured at Gettysburg, Pennsylvania, on or about July 3, 1863. Confined at Fort Delaware, Delaware, on or about July 10, 1863. Died at Fort Delaware on September 29, 1863, of "acute diarrhoea."

SAPP, JOHN H., Private
Born in Forsyth County* where he resided as a farmer prior to enlisting in Forsyth County at age 18, March 18, 1862. Captured at Bristoe Station, Virginia, October 14, 1863. Confined at Old Capitol Prison, Washington, D.C. Transferred to Point Lookout, Maryland, February 3, 1864. Released at Point Lookout on February 17, 1864, after taking the Oath of Allegiance and joining the U.S. Army. Assigned to Company G, 1st Regiment U.S. Volunteer Infantry.

SAPP, MICHAEL A., Private
Born in Forsyth County* where he resided as a farmer prior to enlisting in Forsyth County at age 21, March 18, 1862. Wounded at Goldsboro on December 17, 1862. Returned to duty prior to March 1, 1863. Captured at Bristoe Station, Virginia, October 14, 1863. Confined at Old Capitol Prison, Washington, D.C. Transferred to Point Lookout, Maryland, October 27, 1863. Released at Point Lookout on February 2, 1864, after taking the Oath of Allegiance and joining the U.S. Army. Assigned to Company G, 1st Regiment U.S. Volunteer Infantry.

SHORES, MEREDITH, Private
Resided in Wilkes County and was by occupation a day laborer prior to enlisting at Camp French, near Petersburg, Virginia, at age 23, October 30, 1862, for the war. Deserted on or about December 5, 1862. Dropped

from the rolls of the company prior to September 1, 1863. Hospitalized at Richmond, Virginia, December 7, 1863 (probably suffering from pneumonia). Returned to duty on February 27, 1864. Wounded in the right foot near Petersburg in June, 1864. Reported absent wounded through August, 1864. Reported absent without leave in September-December, 1864. Survived the war.

SHOUSE, JOHN H., Private
Resided in Forsyth County and was by occupation a farmer prior to enlisting in Forsyth County at age 33, February 10, 1863, for the war. Captured at Gettysburg, Pennsylvania, July 3, 1863. Confined at Fort Delaware, Delaware, on or about July 10, 1863. Transferred to Point Lookout, Maryland, October 20, 1863. Paroled at Point Lookout on February 18, 1865. Received at Boulware's Wharf, James River, Virginia, on or about February 21, 1865, for exchange. Hospitalized at Richmond, Virginia, February 21, 1865, with scorbutus. Furloughed for thirty days on March 11, 1865.

SIZEMORE, JAMES, Private
Born in Stokes County and resided in Forsyth County where he was by occupation a farmer prior to enlisting in Forsyth County at age 30, March 22, 1862. Died in hospital at Raleigh on May 13, 1862. Cause of death not reported.

SNIPES, JAMES, Private
Born in Forsyth County* where he resided as a farmer prior to enlisting in Forsyth County at age 31, March 22, 1862. Reported present or accounted for on surviving company muster rolls through December, 1864. Captured near Petersburg, Virginia, March 25, 1865. Confined at Point Lookout, Maryland, March 31, 1865. Released at Point Lookout on May 14, 1865, after taking the Oath of Allegiance.

SNIPES, JOHN F., Private
Resided in Forsyth County where he enlisted at age 22, May 10, 1862, for the war. Reported present or accounted for on surviving company muster rolls through December, 1864.

SNIPES, WILEY T., Private
Resided in Forsyth County where he enlisted at age 20, May 10, 1862, for the war. Wounded at Goldsboro on December 17, 1862. Returned to duty subsequent to February 28, 1863. Captured at Gettysburg, Pennsylvania, July 3, 1863. Confined at Fort Delaware, Delaware, on or about July 10, 1863. Transferred to Point Lookout, Maryland, October 20, 1863. Died at Point Lookout on or about December 8, 1863, of "diarrh[oea] chron[ic]."

SPAINHOWER, C. T., Private
Resided in Forsyth County and was by occupation a farmer prior to enlisting at Petersburg, Virginia, November 1, 1864, for the war. Was about 51 years of age at time of enlistment. Hospitalized at Richmond, Virginia, March 13, 1865, with scorbutus. Transferred to Farmville, Virginia, April 1, 1865. Paroled at Lynchburg, Virginia, April 15, 1865.

SPRINKLE, BENNETT, Private

Resided in Forsyth County where he enlisted at age 38, February 10, 1863, for the war. Captured at Falling Waters, Maryland, July 14, 1863. Confined at Old Capitol Prison, Washington, D.C. Hospitalized at Washington on August 3, 1863, with typhoid fever. Transferred to Baltimore, Maryland, October 14, 1863. Confined at Point Lookout, Maryland, October 28, 1863. Paroled at Point Lookout on February 24, 1865. Received on or about February 28, 1865, for exchange.

STARBUCK, JOHN W., Private

Resided in Forsyth County where he enlisted at age 19, February 10, 1863, for the war. Wounded in the left thigh and captured at Gettysburg, Pennsylvania, July 3, 1863. Hospitalized at Chester, Pennsylvania. Transferred to Point Lookout, Maryland, on or about October 3, 1863. Paroled at Point Lookout on or about March 3, 1864. Received at City Point, Virginia, March 6, 1864, for exchange. Hospitalized at Richmond, Virginia. Furloughed for sixty days on March 12, 1864. Returned to duty on or about November 1, 1864. Reported on detail in the quartermaster's department in November-December, 1864. Rejoined the company on an unspecified date. Surrendered at Appomattox Court House, Virginia, April 9, 1865.

STILLY, ALBERT, Private

Resided in Forsyth County and was by occupation a shoemaker prior to enlisting at age 40, March 22, 1862. "Discharged on examination" prior to July 1, 1862.

TERRY, EPHRAIM B., Private

Born in Forsyth County* where he resided as a farmer prior to enlisting in Forsyth County at age 26, March 22, 1862. Mustered in as Corporal. Reduced to ranks on August 1, 1862. Reported present or accounted for on surviving company muster rolls through December, 1864.

TRANSOU, AMOS E., Sergeant

Resided in Forsyth County where he enlisted at age 18, February 10, 1863, for the war. Mustered in as Private. Wounded in the head at Gettysburg, Pennsylvania, on or about July 1, 1863. Returned to duty in January-February, 1864. Promoted to Sergeant in March-April, 1864. Hospitalized at Richmond, Virginia, June 27, 1864, with rubeola. Returned to duty on July 27, 1864. Reported absent sick in September-December, 1864. Survived the war.

WALKER, ALFRED B., Private

Resided in Forsyth County where he enlisted at age 18, May 16, 1862, for the war. Reported present on surviving company muster rolls through April, 1864. Captured at Spotsylvania Court House, Virginia, May 21, 1864. Confined at Point Lookout, Maryland, May 30, 1864. Transferred to Elmira, New York, July 24, 1864. Records of the Federal Provost Marshal indicate both that he died at Elmira on January 11, 1865, and that he was released on the same date. No further records.

WALLACE, WILLIAM D., 1st Sergeant

Resided in Craven County and enlisted in Wake County

at age 21, May 16, 1862, for the war. Mustered in as Private. Promoted to 1st Sergeant on or about June 10, 1862. Reported present or accounted for on surviving company muster rolls through August, 1864. Wounded in the right side of the chest at Jones' Farm, Virginia, on or about September 30, 1864. Reported absent wounded through December, 1864. Survived the war.

WALLS, DRURY, Private

Born in Halifax County, Virginia, and resided in Forsyth County where he was by occupation a farmer prior to enlisting in Forsyth County at age 35, March 18, 1862. Died at Black and White's, Virginia, May 28, 1863. Cause of death not reported.

WESTMORELAND, DAVID, Private

Born in Forsyth County* where he resided as a farmer prior to enlisting in Forsyth County at age 21, March 22, 1862. Killed at Gettysburg, Pennsylvania, July 3, 1863.

WESTMORELAND, OLIVER T., Private

Born in Forsyth County* where he resided as a farmer prior to enlisting in Forsyth County at age 18, March 22, 1862. Captured at Falling Waters, Maryland, July 14, 1863. Confined at Old Capitol Prison, Washington, D.C. Transferred to Point Lookout, Maryland, where he arrived on August 28, 1863. Released at Point Lookout on January 25, 1864, after taking the Oath of Allegiance and joining the U.S. Army. Assigned to Company C, 1st Regiment U.S. Volunteer Infantry.

YEATES, GEORGE THOMAS, Private

Born in Forsyth County* where he resided as a farmer prior to enlisting in Forsyth County at age 22, March 18, 1862. Captured at Gettysburg, Pennsylvania, July 3, 1863. Confined at Fort Delaware, Delaware, on or about July 10, 1863. Records of the Federal Provost Marshal indicate both that he died while a prisoner and that he was exchanged. No further records.

YEATES, THOMAS E., Private

Born in Randolph County and resided in Forsyth County where he was by occupation a farmer prior to enlisting in Forsyth County at age 41, March 18, 1862. Discharged at Raleigh on May 28, 1862, by reason of being overage.

MISCELLANEOUS

Civil War records indicate that the following soldiers served in the 52nd Regiment N.C. Troops; however the companies in which they served are not reported.

ADAMS, JOHN P., _____

North Carolina pension records indicate that he served in this regiment.

CLINTON, JOHN, Private

Resided in Wilkes County. Place and date of enlistment not reported. Took the Oath of Allegiance at City Point, Virginia, February 1, 1865.

DANIELS, E. P., Private

Resided in Alexander County. Place and date of enlistment not reported. Deserted to the enemy on or about January 30, 1865. Sent to Washington, D.C. Released at Washington on or about February 4, 1865, after taking the Oath of Allegiance.

DeBERRY, B. G., Private

Served as Private in Company K, 26th Regiment N.C.

Troops. Was reportedly transferred to the 52nd Regiment N.C. Troops on June 2, 1862; however, records of the 52nd Regiment do not indicate that he served therein. No further records.

LITTLER, JEREMIAH, _____

Quaker. Conscripted into the regiment on an unspecified date (probably in the summer of 1862). Discharged after a few weeks by reason of "infirmity."

PIGGOTT, SIMON, _____

Quaker. Conscripted into the regiment in the summer of 1862. Discharged a few weeks later after promising to pay a $500 tax.

INDEX

This index contains citations for soldiers listed in the foregoing rosters and for a variety of entries, including all persons, places, regiments, and battalions, that appear in the regimental histories. Alternate spellings of some surnames are cross-referenced. Because this index is composed primarily of personal names, a modified form of the letter-by-letter method of alphabetization has been employed whereby each entry is *initially* alphabetized to the point where the first comma appears; words that follow the first comma are alphabetized separately as a *secondary* category. That method permits the placement of entries such as "Franklin Rifles" at the end, rather than awkwardly in the middle, of the Franklin surname section.

Depending on the information available concerning their initials and given names, soldiers with the same surname are divided into one of two individually alphabetized groups composed of (1) soldiers for whom initials only (W. Franklin, W. M. Franklin) are available or for whom an initial plus a given name (W. Melvin Franklin) are available, and (2) soldiers for whom a given name (William Franklin), a given name plus an initial (William M. Franklin), or two or more given names (William Melvin Franklin) are available. Place names are placed *after* identical surnames; for example, an entry for Franklin, North Carolina, would follow an entry for Franklin, William Melvin. Regiments and battalions are listed numerically under entries in which the word "units" is preceded by the name of the state of origin.

A

Abernathy, David A., 481
Abernathy, Enoch, 491
Abernathy, Milton A., 117
Abernathy, Milton M., 481
Abernathy, William F., 491
Abrams, H. P., 248
Absher. *See also* Abshire
Absher, Abram, 465
Absher, Adam, 465
Absher, Alfred, 466
Absher, Benjamin F., 466
Absher, John, 164
Absher, Lewis W., 466
Absher, Tobias L., 466
Abshire. *See also* Absher
Abshire, Owen J., 466
Ackley. *See also* Rackley
Ackley, J. R., 279
Acock. *See* Adcock, Aycock
Adair, Columbus C., 216
Adair, Govan, 216
Adair, J. W., 216
Adams, Alsey, 188
Adams, Calvin, 466
Adams, Charles, 466
Adams, D. H., 175
Adams, David H., 176
Adams, E. W., 104
Adams, Edward W., 149
Adams, General J., 466
Adams, Hinton C., 188
Adams, Jackson, 466
Adams, James, 256
Adams, James C., 367
Adams, James E., 188
Adams, James T., 127
Adams, John L., 447
Adams, John M., 466

Adams, John P., 520
Adams, Joseph, 279
Adams, Joseph E., 188
Adams, Joseph H., 466
Adams, N. H., 91
Adams, Richard, 30
Adams, William H., 367
Adams, William Henry, 188
Adams, William M., 188
Adcock. *See also* Aycock
Adcock, J. W., 248
Adkinson. *See* Atkinson
Albemarle, North Carolina, 501
Albemarle Sound, North Carolina, 13, 394
Albertson, Peter H., 299
Albright, Elias, 248
Albright, George, 55
Albright, John G., 147
Albright, Michael, 55
Albright, R. H., 28, 73
Aldred, David L., 428
Aldred, Richard, 428
Alexander, Charles, 73
Alexander, David M., 128
Alexander, Elias A., 248
Alexander, Enoch E., 80
Alexander, John F., 128
Alexander, John J., 80
Alexander, John M., 418
Alexander, John Marion, 417
Alexander, Major R., 248
Alexander, Robert N., 80
Alexander, T. P., 91
Alexander, Theophilus B., 81
Alexander, William P., 81
Alfin. *See also* Alphin
Alfin, D. J., 332
Alford, James B., 277
Allen, A. S., 502

Allen, Adolphus, 204
Allen, Amzi W., 81
Allen, Andrew Jackson, 447
Allen, Charles G., 204
Allen, David, Jr., 91
Allen, Elijah P., 236
Allen, Forney, 204
Allen, James, 204
Allen, James W., 236
Allen, John Alexander, 481
Allen, John M., 447
Allen, John William, 367
Allen, Josiah G., 176
Allen, Julius, 188
Allen, Larkin, 91
Allen, Lee S., 418
Allen, Lovit Green, 188
Allen, M. A., 91
Allen, Monroe S., 153
Allen, Ransom G., 188
Allen, Sir William, 188
Allen, Thomas, 205
Allen, W. H., 189
Allen, William A., 276, 299
Allen, William S., 91
Allgard, Thomas, 256
Allison. *See* Ellison
Almond, Nathan, 502
Alphin. *See also* Alfin
Alphin, Daniel J., 299
Alphin, William, 299
Altman, John J., 176
Amelia Court House, Virginia, 23-24, 413
Ammon. *See also* Auman
Ammon, A. J., 164
Ammons, Cameron, 321
Ammons, Daniel J., 382
Anders. *See also* Andrews
Anders, E. M., 104

Anders, L. Clark, 104
Anderson, Alexander, 382
Anderson, Ausburn, 466
Anderson, B. F., 367
Anderson, David Troy, 491
Anderson, Richard, 197
Anderson, Richard H., 24, 268, 406-408, 413
Anderson, William James, 368
Andrews. *See also* Anders
Andrews, DeWitt Quincey, 216
Andrews, George W., 215
Andrews, William, 164
Andrews, William H., 41
Annier, John, 205
Anthony, E., 128
Anthony, Gideon C., 128
Anthony, J. David, 28, 46
Anthony, James Carson, 104
Anthony, Vardrey, 128
Antietam Creek, Maryland, 4-6
Appomattox Court House, Virginia, 25, 414
Appomattox River, Virginia, 13, 24, 267, 413
Appomattox Station, Virginia, 24, 413-414
Archer, James J., 400, 402
Ardrey, James P., 79
Arent. *See also* Arnett
Arent, William R., 491
Armstrong, Edward, 289
Armstrong, James Monroe, 491
Armstrong, John, 289, 481
Armstrong, John G., 481
Arnett. *See also* Arent
Arnett, Frederick, 164
Arnett, Warren C., 164
Arney. *See* Earney
Arnold, John, 341
Arnold, Richard, 440
Arwood, B. F., 236
Asbury, Daniel M., 480
Asbury, Osburn W., 481
Ashby's Gap, Virginia, 6
Asheboro, North Carolina, 427
Ashley, Andrew Jackson, 320
Ashley, James Robeson, 321
Ashley, James W., 153
Ashley, Stephen W., 164
Ashley, William A., 81
Ashley River, South Carolina, 261
Ashpole True Boys, 331
Ashworth, Elias, 429
Aston. *See also* Austin
Aston, Leander, 279
Atkinson, Atlas, 163
Atkinson, Bright, 151, 164

Atkinson, E. C., 163
Atkinson, John C., 164
Atkinson, Joseph Henry, 226
Atkinson, Thomas, 279
Atkinson, W. H., 176
Atlantic and North Carolina Railroad, 10, 142-143, 266, 397
Atlee's Station, Virginia, 407
Atwood, Joel P., 277, 300
Augusta, Georgia, 144
Auman. *See also* Ammon
Auman, Fletcher H., 429
Auman, Henry, 429
Auman, Jacob, 429
Ausley, James W., 41
Austin. *See also* Aston
Austin, Benjamin P., 502
Austin, Elbert, 176
Austin, James, 176
Austin, James E., 176
Austin, John M., 502
Austin, Joseph, 176
Austin, Milton S., 455
Autry, Duncan, 368
Autry, John H., 226
Autry, Wiley, 226
Avent. *See* Arent
Averasboro, North Carolina, 146, 274
Averitt. *See also* Everett, Everitt
Averitt, William, 368
Avery, John T., 176
Avett, J. M., 502
Aycock. *See also* Adcock
Aycock, Lawrence A., 176

B

Baber. *See also* Baker, Barber
Baber, Campbell S., 236
Baber, James L., 248
Bachelor, James M., 341
Bagley, Erastus, 440
Bailes. *See* Bales
Bailey, Daniel, 55
Bailey, Milas Alexander, 28, 73
Bailey, Richard A., 72
Bailey, W. H., 256
Bain, Angus G., 368
Bain, Daniel D., Jr., 368
Bain, Dougald A., 368
Bain, Hugh, 226
Bain, Hugh J., 368
Bain, John G., 383
Bain, William A., 226
Baines, Robert G., 416, 512
Baker. *See also* Baber, Barker

Baker, Allen R., 189
Baker, Archibald M., 341
Baker, Bennett A., 128
Baker, Elijah, 440
Baker, Jesse E., 332
Baker, John C., 418
Baker, John H., 128
Baker, Jonathan, 189
Baker, Joseph, 226
Baker, Laurence S., 145
Baker, Matthew M., 189
Baker, Neill A., 205
Baker, Randal J., 279
Baldwin, Cephas, 104
Baldwin, Daniel W., 455
Baldwin, John, 164
Baldwin, Madison, 455
Baldwin, R. W., 256
Baldwin, Thomas Roper, 455
Bales, William B., 227
Ballance, Aaron, 176
Ballard. *See also* Bullard
Ballard, Isaiah W., 455
Ballard, James A., 481
Ballard, John F., 481
Ballard, Lawson A., 491
Ballard, Solomon, 248
Bamberger, Jacob, 354
Bane. *See* Bain, Boon
Banner. *See* Danner
Banter, Joel F., 248
Barber. *See also* Baber
Barber, Ervin G., 176
Barber, G. I., 176
Barber, Jesse M., 189
Barber, John R., 55
Barber, Noah, 332
Barber, Pulia P., 176
Barber, R. A., 176
Barber, W. G., 91, 189
Barber, William R. A., 176
Barden. *See* Borden
Barefoot, Bythan B., 189
Barefoot, John O., 354
Barefoot, Sion McD., 368
Barfield, Goolsbury, 164
Barfield, Jeremiah, 197
Barfield, Willis A., 164
Barger, Jacob A., 55
Barger, Monroe, 56
Barker. *See also* Baker
Barker, Anderson R., 309
Barker, Cyrus, 481
Barker, Eli C., 447
Barker, Nathan, 481
Barker, Riley A., 321
Barlow, Eliphet, 248
Barmer, William J., 455
Barnes. *See also* Burns

Barnes, Aldred A., 321
Barnes, Canada, 164
Barnes, E. H., 177
Barnes, E. P. D., 164
Barnes, H. H., 165
Barnes, Harvey A., 91
Barnes, Henry P., 321
Barnes, Jethro, 165
Barnes, John F., 165
Barnes, Joseph P., 165
Barnes, Moore, 165
Barnes, Oliver M., 165
Barnes, Richard Rhodes, 165
Barnes, Thomas J., 440
Barnes, Timothy, 165
Barnes, W. H., 165
Barnes, Willis P., 165
Barnett. See also Barrett,
  Burnett
Barnett, John W., 80
Barnett, William P., 80
Barnhardt, Adam A., 418
Barnhardt, Benton, 418
Barnhardt, David C., 418
Barnhardt, John F., 418
Barnhardt, Tobias, 418
Barnum. See Bynum
Barrentine, Charles A., 455
Barrett. See also Barnett
Barrett, Alexander, 64
Barrett, David Samuel, 64
Barrett, John F., 73
Barrett, Perry, 91
Barrett, Robert G., 27
Barrett, William A., 64
Barrett, William R., 65
Barringer, Henry H., 502
Barrington's Ferry, North
  Carolina, 397
Barton. See also Batten, Batton,
  Burton
Barton, J., 257
Barton, Seth M., 10-12, 266
Basdon, Kinion H., 383
Bass. See also Bess
Bass, E. C., 300
Bass, Frederick, 332
Bass, Gilson, 321
Bass, Jacob, 197
Bass, Jesse, 197
Bass, Lemon, 165
Bass, Nevill, 321
Bass, Thomas, 321
Bass, Uriah, 368
Bass, William, 165, 197
Batchelder's Creek, North
  Carolina, 10-11, 266
Batten. See also Barton, Batton,
  Bratten

Batten, Daniel, 355
Batten, David J., 355
Batten, William, 355
Battery Beauregard, Sullivan's
  Island, Charleston, South
  Carolina, 261
Battery Bee, Sullivan's Island,
  Charleston, South Carolina,
  261
Battery Gregg, Morris Island,
  Charleston, South Carolina,
  261-263
Battle of the Crater, Virginia,
  409
Batton. See also Barton, Batten,
  Bratten, Patton
Batton, Hardy, 177
Batton, James C., 197
Batton, William H., 177
Baumgardner. See Bumgarner
Baxley, Archibald C., 332
Baxley, Ervin H., 309
Baxley, Henry J., 332
Baxley, Henry L., 332
Baxley, Miles S., 333
Baxley, Peter D., 333
Baxley, Samuel W., 165
Baxley, William H., 165
Baxley, William H. R., 333
Baxter, Aaron F., 30
Baxter, Milton, 309
Baxter, Peter Z., 127
Baxter, Thomas H., 128
Bayles. See Bales
Beach, Thomas E., 91
Beal. See also Bell, Deal
Beal, Peter S., 491
Beam. See also Bean
Beam, David C., 128
Beam, George W., 127
Bean. See also Beam, Dean
Bean, Eli C., 65
Beard. See also Bird, Byrd
Beard, William H., 448
Beasley, Ephraim Oxford, 189
Beasley, George C., 368
Beasley, William Jackson, 341
Beason, Archibald, 91, 128
Beatie, William C., 104
Beaty, John W., 30
Beaty, Junius F., 418
Beaufort, North Carolina, 10,
  266
Beauregard, P. G. T., 13-15,
  261-262, 264, 270, 408
Beck. See also Buck, Deck
Beck, Alexander, 138
Beck, John W., 512
Beck, Philip, 138

Beck, William S., 502
Becker. See Beeker
Beckerstaff. See also Biggerstaff
Beckerstaff, A., 216
Bedwell, Alfred, 279
Beeker, Philip S., 56
Belfield, Virginia, 411
Bell. See also Beal
Bell, Elias, 289
Bell, Felix, 289
Bell, James, 368
Bell, James H., 153
Bell, Martin, 104
Bell, Milton, 429
Bell, Owen, 341
Bell, Richard Robert, 368
Bell, Robert C., 81
Bell, Thomas, 289
Bell, Thomas L., 73
Bell, Walter R., 288
Bell, Zimri, 429
Bender, John L., 341
Benfield, Wesley P., 117
Benfrem, T. N., 197
Bennett, Alvin, 41
Bennett, Doctor G., 81
Bennett, Fleet S., 383
Bennett, Gardner, 65
Bennett, James G., 41
Bennett, Jehu S., 41
Bennett, John, 129
Bennett, Manath A., 41
Bennett, Robert F., 129
Bennett, William Benjamin, 41
Bennick, George, 236
Bennick, Henry J., 236
Bennick, J. S., 236
Bennitt House (near Durham),
  North Carolina, 148, 275
Benson, John U., 189
Benson, Robert L., 56
Benson, Samuel S., 56
Benson, William L. D., 418
Benton, Jacob, 440
Benton, James, 440
Benton, Nelson, 341
Benton, Simeon, 341
Benton, William T., 440
Bentonville, North Carolina,
  146-148, 274-275
Bermuda Hundred, Virginia,
  13-15, 267-268, 270
Berrier, Andrew, 46
Berry. See also Perry
Berry, Enos M., 104
Berry, William, 248
Berryhill, Pinkney L., 129
Bess. See also Bass, Best
Bess, Thomas, 129

Bessent, James H., 341
Best. *See also* Bess, Bost
Best, Benjamin S., 289
Best, William Bright, 187
Best, William R., 289
Bevener, J., 197
Biby, John P., 448
Biggerstaff. *See also* Beckerstaff
Biggerstaff, Baruch, 216
Biggerstaff, Benjamin Franklin, 216
Biggerstaff, Elijah, Jr., 216
Biggerstaff, Elijah, Sr., 216
Biggerstaff, Jacob, 216
Biggerstaff, Thomas, 216
Biggs. *See also* Boggs, Briggs
Biggs, H. H., 321
Bigham, William W., 236
Billings, Hiram, 466
Bingham, Alvery, 429
Bird. *See also* Beard, Byrd
Bird, Hartwell, 429
Bird, Jackson D., 502
Bird, James A., 30
Bird, James H., 30
Bird, Martin, 502
Bird, William H., 91
Birksley, I. M., 138
Bishop, Asa, 227
Bishop, Horton A., 466
Bishop, Larkin, 466
Bishop, Nathan M., 227
Black. *See also* Blake
Black, Archibald, 65
Black, Archibald M., 65
Black, Davidson M., 491
Black, Duncan, 65, 227
Black, G. L., 216
Black, James A., 417
Black, James H., 216
Black, Samuel A., 92
Black, William, 81
Black, William Martin, 64
Black, William W., 217
Blackard. *See also* Blanchard
Blackard, Lawrence H., 153
Blackard, Thomas W., 153
Blackburn, Aurelius C., 511
Blackburn, Daniel, 129
Blackburn, David A., 129
Blackburn, Felix, 383
Blackburn, James, 165
Blackburn, James H., 368
Blackburn, James R., 383
Blackburn, Resin, 383
Blackburn, Wade H., 355
Blackley. *See* Bleckley
Blackman. *See also* Blackmon
Blackman, Alpha, 355

Blackman, Dillen, 321
Blackman, H. S., 189
Blackman, James B., 341
Blackman, Jesse Fordham, 205
Blackman, John C., 321
Blackman, McDaniel, 342
Blackman, William, 321
Blackmon. *See also* Blackman
Blackmon, Ashley, 189
Blackmon, Richard J., 189
Blackwater River, Virginia, 9, 394-396
Blackwelder, Allison J., 418
Blackwelder, Charles M., 419
Blackwelder, Columbus, 419
Blackwelder, George W., 419
Blackwelder, Ransom C., 419
Blackwell, Calvin, 248
Blackwell, James William, 248
Blackwell, Levi, 279
Blackwell, Marion, 248
Blackwood, Joseph, 104
Bladenboro, North Carolina, 144
Blake. *See also* Black
Blake, Alva Franklin, 342
Blake, James T., 455
Blake, John, 41
Blake, John Beaty, 342
Blalock. *See also* Blaylock, Blayluff
Blalock, C., 153
Blalock, Columbus C., 153
Blalock, Edmond D., 503
Blalock, Green W., 153
Blalock, Hardy, 342
Blalock, Hasten, 153
Blalock, Henry W., 503
Blalock, Joseph B., 30
Blalock, Merritt E., 503
Blalock, Thomas, 154
Blalock, Weldon Dewitt, 154
Blalock, William·A., 153-154
Blalock, William P., 154
Blalock, Zachariah D., 503
Blanchard. *See also* Blackard
Blanchard, David J., 289
Blanchard, Eldridge S., 440
Blanchard, Henry, 309
Blanchard, J. Calvin, 440
Blanchard, James R., 440
Bland, Jacob C., 236
Bland, Thomas R., 236
Blankenship, Hezekiah, 217
Blankenship, James, 236
Blankenship, Joseph B., 236
Blankinship, William W., 217
Blanks, James W., 333
Blanton, Enoch, 342
Blanton, John W., 342

Blanton, Joseph J., 342
Blanton, Joseph R., 31
Blanton, Moses, 300, 342
Blanton, William J., 31
Blaylock. *See also* Blalock, Blayluff
Blaylock, Sidney, 503
Blaylock, W. C., 503
Blayluff. *See also* Blalock, Blaylock
Blayluff, M. M., 279
Bleckley, J. M., 117
Bleckley, William L., 117
Blevins, Harrison, 189
Block. *See* Black, Brock
Bloom. *See* Blume
Blount. *See also* Blunt
Blount, James W., 333
Blount's Creek, North Carolina, 143, 398
Blue. *See also* Blume
Blue, Daniel, 369
Blue, Neill C., 64
Blue, William J., 369
Blue Ridge Mountains, 6
Blume. *See also* Blue
Blume, George C., 419
Blume, Joseph W., 419
Blume, William Harvey, Jr., 419
Blume, William Harvey, Sr., 419
Blunt. *See also* Blount
Blunt, George W., 129
Bobbitt, Richard M., 205
Boggs. *See also* Biggs
Boggs, Noah Elias, 46
Bolen. *See also* Bolin
Bolen, Kerney, 429
Boles. *See* Bools, Bowles
Bolick, A. P., 248
Bolick, Noah, 81
Bolin. *See also* Bolen
Bolin, Alexander, 204
Bolivar Heights, West Virginia, 4
Bolton, Henry H., 369
Bolton, Jackson, 237
Bolton, James H., 455
Bolton, John R., 369
Bolton, Peter L., 369
Bools. *See also* Bowles
Bools, Bartlett, 154
Boon. *See also* Boone
Boon, David M., 383
Boon, Henry J., 177
Boon, Jackson, 333
Boon, John H., 289
Boon, Joseph F., 290
Boon, William, 333
Boon, William R., 309

Boone. *See also* Boon
Boone, Andrew C., 217
Boone, James W., 321
Boone, John A. D., 383
Boone, Lafayette, 217
Boone, Sampson, 342
Boone, Thomas, 217
Boone's Mill, North Carolina, 10
Borden, Edwin B., 149
Borden, William H., 149, 196
Boroughs. *See also* Burroughs
Boroughs, Matthew W., 455
Bost. *See also* Best
Bost, Lawson O., 73
Bost, Manuel, 73
Bostian, Jesse J., 419
Bostick, Daniel, 300
Bostick, Daniel J., 300
Bostick, David R., 300
Bostick, Elijah, 300
Bostick, George, 237
Bostick, Samuel E., 235
Bostick, Thomas T., 455
Boswell, Amos, 342
Boteler's Ford, Maryland, 5-6
Bottom's Bridge, Virginia, 10, 14, 408
Bowden. *See also* Bowdin, Dowden
Bowden, Madison, 154
Bowden, R. W., 448
Bowden, William B., 300
Bowdin. *See also* Bowden
Bowdin, Drury, 448
Bowdin, Henry, 448
Bowdin, John, 448
Bowen, George W., 290
Bowen, Henry R., 512
Bowers. *See also* Powers
Bowers, Giles, 55
Bowers, John Anderson, 31
Bowes, J. Samuel, 154
Bowles. *See also* Bools, Boyles
Bowles, Elam, 466
Bowles, Simpson, 467
Bowman, David H., 448
Bowman, Henry, 321
Bowman, Joseph H., 448
Boyd, Robert Franklin, 104
Boydton Plank Road, Virginia, 22, 411-413
Boyer, Daniel, 383
Boyette, John Ankrum, 290
Boykin, Ellington B., 197
Boykin, Hillory, 177
Boykin, Jacob, 197
Boykin, John M., 177
Boykin, Jonathan, 177

Boykin, Solomon, 382
Boykin's Depot, Virginia, 13
Boyles. *See also* Bowles
Boyles, William B., 227
Brack. *See also* Brock
Brack, Robert F., 248
Bracket, Joseph, 46
Bracket, Robert, 46
Bracket, William, 237
Brackett, George W., 129
Bradford, David L., 73
Bradford, James S., 73
Bradley. *See also* Brady
Bradley, A. Hampton, 237
Bradley, Absalom B., 249
Bradley, Augustus, 249
Bradley, B. F., 249
Bradley, E., 154
Bradley, James, 237
Bradley, Thomas D., 237
Bradley, Wilson, 237
Bradshaw. *See also* Bradsher
Bradshaw, Daniel J., 290
Bradshaw, John T., 383
Bradshaw, Moses L., 383
Bradshaw, S. T., 383
Bradsher. *See also* Bradshaw
Bradsher, James M., 154
Bradsher, John W., 154
Brady. *See also* Bradley
Brady, Alfred, 249
Brady, George A., 117
Brady, John F., 117
Brady, Joseph M., 73
Bragg, Braxton, 146-147, 273-275, 404
Bramble, William W., 419
Brammer, T. P., 309
Branch, Alcey, 384
Branch, Alden, 165
Branch, Amon J., 321
Branch, Ethemore T. C., 322
Branch, James G., 299
Branch, Talton D., 322
Branch, Thomas, 300
Branchville, South Carolina, 145
Brandle, Noah R., 217
Branson. *See also* Brinson, Bronson
Branson, James S., 448
Brantly, Benjamin F., 226
Brantly, John, 226
Braswell, Lewis, 177
Bratten. *See also* Batten, Batton
Bratten, John, 440
Brawley, Peter W., 117
Breece, Joseph, 369
Brem, T. H., 141
Brett. *See* Britt

Brewer. *See also* Bruner
Brewer, Allen C., 448
Brewer, Eli H., 129
Brewer, H. L., 129
Brewer, Jesse A., 333
Brewer, Jesse J., 197
Brewer, John C., 333
Brewer, Nathaniel M., 129
Brewer, Richard, 333
Brewer, Samuel W., 42
Brewer, Solomon, 198
Brewer, William, 333
Briant. *See* Bryant, O'Briant
Brice, Charles, 177
Bridges, John L., 92
Briggs. *See also* Biggs
Briggs, John W., 129
Briggs, Thomas W., 130
Briggs, William B., 127
Bright, Samuel F., 355
Brightwell, John J., 154
Brigman, Alexander B., 333
Brigman, Wellington, 333
Brimer, Andrew T., 104
Brindle. *See* Brandle
Brinkley, D., 46
Brinkley, Harrison, 46
Brinkley, J. B., 342
Brinkley, John Hamilton, 46
Brinson. *See also* Branson, Brison, Bronson
Brinson, John, 280
Brinson, John H., 355
Brinson, Joseph, 355
Briscoe, Easton, 440
Brison. *See also* Brinson
Brison, H. B., 104
Brison, J. B. P., 104
Brison, Joseph W., 28, 104
Brison, S. B. A., 105
Brison, T. L., 105
Bristoe Station, Virginia, 404-405
Britt, A. A., 166
Britt, Alexander, Jr., 166
Britt, Alexander C., Sr., 166
Britt, Alfred, 166
Britt, Alva G., 166
Britt, Andrew J., 65
Britt, Archibald, 322
Britt, C. C., 166
Britt, Calvin C., 322
Britt, Caswell, 322
Britt, Colen L., 166
Britt, Edmund, 166
Britt, Enoch W., 166
Britt, Henry L., 166
Britt, Henry P., 166

Britt, James E., 166
Britt, Joel, 322
Britt, John J., 322
Britt, John W., 166
Britt, Joseph, Jr., 167
Britt, Joseph B., 167
Britt, Kenneth, 227
Britt, Labon, 322
Britt, Oliver P., 167
Broach, John H., 154
Broach, Pleasant, 154
Broach, Richard H., 154
Broadhurst, John C., 280
Broad Run, Virginia, 404
Broadwell, J. H., 177
Brock. *See also* Brack
Brock, David W., 369
Brock, G. T., 290
Brockenbrough, J. M., 400-401
Brock Road, Virginia, 405
Brogden, William, 322
Bronson. *See also* Branson,
  Brinson
Bronson, Charles H., 384
Bronson, Julian, 384
Bronson, Julius J., 384
Brooks, A. W., 154
Brooks, C. C., 151
Brooks, Cornelius B., 503
Brooks, H. C., 277
Brooks, James J., 154
Brooks, James M., 467
Brooks, James W., 467
Brooks, Job Terrell, 205
Brooks, John B., 355
Brooks, John N., 467
Brooks, John W. T., 154
Brooks, Nathan Matthew, 467
Brooks, Robert P., 467
Brooks, Robert W., 227
Brooks, William Marsh, 205
Brooks, Wyatt H., 155
Brookshire, John, 249
Brookshire, Thomas F., 429
Brookshire, William F., 416, 456
Brothers, John R., 280
Brotherton, Henry, 481
Brotherton, Hiram, 491
Brotherton, Hugh, 117
Brotherton, James, 482
Brotherton, John M. C., 467
Broughton, John W., 177
Brown, Aaron P., 467
Brown, Abram, 467
Brown, Adam, 429
Brown, Albert, 42
Brown, Andrew Elbert, 28, 117
Brown, Archibald, 309
Brown, B. F., 448

Brown, Barden, 198
Brown, Benjamin Rufus, 467
Brown, Brantly, 155
Brown, Calvin, 155
Brown, Council L., 355
Brown, Eli, 429
Brown, Elijah, 467
Brown, Elisha B., 42
Brown, G. Jackson, 467
Brown, G. W., 205
Brown, George H., 467
Brown, George Moore, 355
Brown, George W., 290
Brown, Green Daniel, 155
Brown, Hosea, 117
Brown, Jacob, 117, 448
Brown, James Arthur, 290
Brown, James G., 81
Brown, James Napoleon, 419
Brown, James W., 467
Brown, Jesse F., 468
Brown, John, 198
Brown, John H. C., 420
Brown, John J., 468
Brown, John L., 468
Brown, John T., 468
Brown, Joseph A., 42
Brown, Kilby, 343
Brown, Micajah, 512
Brown, Monroe, 105
Brown, Owen T., 290
Brown, Peter B., 309
Brown, Philip J., 420
Brown, Reuben, 429, 468
Brown, Thompson, 118
Brown, W. H., 155
Brown, Warren H., 81
Brown, William, 448
Brown, William A., 65
Brown, William B., 468
Brown, William H., 468
Brown, William J., 118
Brown, William P., 65
Browning, Samuel J., 280
Browning, William, 512
Broyhill, Johnson, 468
Bruce, S. C., 27
Brunell, Stanton, 429
Bruner. *See also* Brewer
Bruner, George M., 512
Bryan. *See also* Bryant
Bryan, A. H., 249
Bryan, King, 369
Bryan, Levi, 369
Bryan, Redin, 205
Bryant. *See also* Bryan
Bryant, Aldridge M., 369
Bryant, J. B., 482
Bryant, Major, 189

Bryant, Nicholas F., 290
Bryant, Phillip W., 482
Bryant, Travis, 369
Buchanan, A. J., 205
Buchanan, Cerney, 205
Buchanan, Elbert, 205
Buchanan, Hilliard S., 205
Buchanan, J. Ruffe, 205
Buchanan, J. W., 205
Buchanan, Joseph, 206
Buchanan, Riley, 206
Buchanan, Ruffin, 206
Buchanan, Samuel R. B., 206
Buck. *See also* Beck
Buck, Benjamin, 356
Buffkin, Elias J., 343
Buford's Bridge, South Carolina,
  145
Buie, Daniel McD., 369
Buie, George McD., 369
Buie, John R., 370
Buie, Malcolm J., Jr., 370
Buie, Malcolm James, 370
Bullard. *See also* Ballard,
  Bullock
Bullard, Doget, 280
Bullard, George W., 456
Bullard, Giles M., 384
Bullard, James Thomas, 167
Bullard, John J., 322
Bullard, Joseph, 167
Bullard, William H., 280
Bullis, David W., 468
Bullis, James Sidney, 468
Bullock. *See also* Bullard
Bullock, Atlas, 322
Bullock, Charles Baker, 334
Bullock, Colon E., 322
Bullock, Davis, 322
Bullock, Henry Johnson, 334
Bullock, Jesse, 334
Bullock, John, 322
Bullock, John L., 322
Bullock, Joseph H., 322
Bullock, Meredith, 323
Bullock, Michael R., 323
Bullock, William A., 320
Bumgarner, Andrew, 130
Bumgarner, James M., 118
Bumgarner, Simeon N., 468
Bunce. *See also* Bunch, Burch
Bunce, Hiram, 370
Bunch. *See also* Bunce, Burch
Bunch, Cullen, 440
Bunker Hill, West Virginia, 403
Bunn. *See also* Dunn
Bunn, A. G., 177
Bunn, James Caid, 56
Bunnell, Stephen Pinkney, 456

Burch. *See also* Bunce, Bunch
Burch, James A., 153
Burch, Thomas B., 155
Burchett, Isham, 468
Burgess' Mill, Virginia, 19, 22, 411
Burgin, R. L., 249
Burgwyn, W. H. S., 267, 271-272
Burnett. *See also* Barnett
Burnett, Carter, 235
Burnett, Landrum, 237
Burney, Charles H., 309
Burney, Daniel, 356
Burney, James, 309
Burncy, W. A., 249
Burney, William James, 258-261, 263, 343
"Burney Place" (Craven County), North Carolina, 143-144
Burns. *See also* Barnes
Burns, Duncan, 198
Burnside, Ambrose E., 6-8, 16
Burroughs. *See also* Boroughs
Burroughs, Elijah B., 65
Burton. *See also* Barton
Burton, Dudley, 155
Burwell, Philip L., 196
Butler, Benjamin F., 13-15, 266-268, 270, 273
Butler, Elisha, 31
Butler, Isham R., 323
Butler, Luke H., 356
Butler, Oliver, 440
Butler, Othiel, 237
Butler, Steven R., 237
Butler, William, 334
Button. *See* Burton
Butts, Samuel, 198
Byas, Vedo, 249
Byas, William, 249
Byerly, George Lindsay, 46
Byers, James A., 468
Byers, James S., 468
Byers, William M., 74
Bynum, Albert A., 491
Bynum, James, 492
Bynum, James Franklin, 492
Bynum, John A., 492
Bynum, William Lafayette, 492
Byrd. *See also* Beard, Bird
Byrd, Aquilla, Sr., 227
Byrd, Bright D., 227
Byrd, Charles, 356
Byrd, David S., 226-227
Byrd, Edward D., 227
Byrd, Elijah, 334
Byrd, Isaac, 323

Byrd, James F., 280
Byrd, James L., 227
Byrd, John H., 227
Byrd, Joshua, 334
Byrd, Lemuel W., 227
Byrd, Moses, 440
Byrd, Needham T., 190
Byrd, Reddin, 228
Byrd, Timothy S., 280
Byrd, William Benjamin, 280
Byrum. *See* Bynum

C

Cabaniss, F. W., 9, 47
Cabaniss, Harvey D., 47
Cabarrus Riflemen, 417
Caddell. *See also* Cordle
Caddell, Archibald B., 65
Caddell, Neill B., 65
Cain, Anderson, 468
Cain, Evan, 384
Caison. *See also* Cashion
Caison, Lewis, 300
Caison, William B., 300
Calaway. *See also* Callaway, Calloway
Calaway, George W., 503
Calder, Peter, 167
Calder, W. C., 167
Calder, William H., 167
Caldwell, Abel, 118
Caldwell, James, 118
Caldwell, James C., 118
Caldwell, James F., 482
Caldwell, Julius A., 492
Caldwell, Lawson, 118
Caldwell, Marcus, 492
Caldwell, Moses A., 482
Caldwell, Thomas C., 81
Caldwell, William J., 118
Calk, Fate, 92
Calk, Henry, 280
Callaway. *See also* Calaway, Calloway
Callaway, Agrippa G., 503
Callaway, James M., 190
Callaway, John C., 503
Callicott, Asa, 429
Callicott, Jacob, 430
Callicott, Pleasant, 430
Calloway. *See also* Calaway, Callaway
Calloway, James, 217
Cameron, Dugald C., 206
Cameron, James R., 310
Cameron, John F., 28
Camp, L. A., 92

Camp, Richard L., 31
Campbell, Angus, 65
Campbell, Daniel, 65
Campbell, George P., 74
Campbell, John E., 356
Campbell, William, 217
Campbell, William F., 468
Camps—Military
    Camp Battle (near Tarboro), North Carolina, 265
    Camp Black Jack (Lenoir County), North Carolina, 393
    Camp Campbell, Drewry's Bluff, Virginia, 393
    Camp Campbell (near Kinston), North Carolina, 258
    Camp Clingman (near Wilmington), North Carolina, 259
    Camp Davis (near Wilmington), North Carolina, 258, 261
    Camp Florida (near Wilmington), North Carolina, 261
    Camp French (near Petersburg), Virginia, 394
    Camp French (near Wilmington), North Carolina, 258
    Camp Hill (near Petersburg), Virginia, 266
    Camp Holmes (near Wilmington), North Carolina, 258, 340, 381
    Camp Johnston (near Kinston), North Carolina, 393
    Camp Lamb (near Wilmington), North Carolina, 258
    Camp Leventhorpe (near Wilmington), North Carolina, 258
    Camp McKethan (near Charleston), South Carolina, 261
    Camp Mangum (near Raleigh), North Carolina, 1, 29, 40, 54, 64, 72, 79, 90, 102, 116, 126, 140, 152, 163, 175, 187, 196, 204, 215, 225, 235, 246, 308, 393, 417, 427, 438, 446, 454, 465, 480, 490, 501, 511
    Camp Marshall (near Orange Court House), Virginia, 405
    Camp Mears (near Wilmington), North Carolina, 259

Camp Morgan (near Wilmington), North Carolina, 258
Camp Pender (near Hamilton), North Carolina, 265
Camp Whiting (near Wilmington), North Carolina, 259-261
Canada, Thomas, 249
Canady, Derias Clinton, 356
Candler. See Chandler
Canfel, John, 280
Canipe. See also Cape
Canipe, Eli, 31
Cannady. See Canada, Canady
Cannon. See also Connor
Cannon, Robert T., 343
Cantrell, George, 249
Cantwell, John Lucas, 258, 276
Cape. See also Canipe
Cape, Claiborn U., 448
Cape Fear River, North Carolina, 258, 273
Capel, Thomas R., 456
Capps. See Creps
Caraway, Daniel M., 31
Caraway, James D. Lafayette, 31
Carlisle, Atlas, 310
Carlisle, David Blount, 310
Carlisle, Dennis L., 310
Carlisle, Ervin, 310
Carlisle, Pennsylvania, 399
Carlton, Charles, 469
Carlton, Henry J., 290
Carlton, James S., 469
Carlton, P. J., 469
Carlton, Thomas C., 469
Carmack, Samuel, 280
Carmichael, Alexander B., 512
Carmichael, J. W., 449
Carmichael, John M., 456
Carmichael, John W., 512
Carmichael, Thomas E., 512
Carmichael, William W., 465
Carothers, Thomas M., 28, 81
Carpenter, Joe, 290
Carpenter, John Christenbury, 237
Carpenter, John N., 56
Carpenter, Kinchen Jahu, 237
Carpenter, Robert, 228
Carpenter, William A. J., 92
Carpenter, William P., 492
Carr. See Kerr
Carraway. See Caraway
Carrigan, Robert A., 74
Carrigan, Thomas W., 280
Carroll. See also Correll
Carroll, John C., 290

Carroll, John W., 370
Carroll, Robert J., 300
Carroll, William D., 291
Carroll, William S., 291
Carson, Edward W., 105
Carson, John C., 217
Carter, Alexander, 167
Carter, Alfred M., 440
Carter, George A., 503
Carter, Henry, 440
Carter, James C., 47
Carter, John D., 503
Carter, Leonard H., 300
Carter, Lewis W., 440
Carter, Moses, 177
Carter, Neill, 323
Carter, Zachariah, 323
Carthage, North Carolina, 64
Cartrett. See also Cartwright
Cartrett, John C., 356
Cartrett, Luke R., 356
Cartrett, Matthew, 356
Cartrett, William J., 356
Cartwright. See also Cartrett
Cartwright, David J., 343
Cartwright, George W., 343
Cartwright, Jacob, 343
Carver. See also Craver
Carver, Charles, 370
Carver, George W., 370
Carver, Joshua, 310
Carver, Reuben C., 155
Case. See Chase
Cash, Preston, 155
Cashatt, J. F., 430
Cashion. See also Caison
Cashion, Franklin, 482
Cashion, James H., 482
Cashtown, Pennsylvania, 399
Cason. See Caison, Cashion
Catawba Marksmen, 116
Cates. See also Coats
Cates, Columbus C., 155
Cates, Ephraim, 155
Cates, John D., 155
Cates, Richard H., 155
Cates, Samuel H., 155
Cates, Thomas, 206
Catharpin Road, Virginia, 405
Cauble, Franklin, 503
Cauble, William P., 503
Caudill, Abner, 469
Caudle. See Cauble, Caudill
Caulder. See Calder
Cavaness, Thomas, 281
Caviness, Thomas, 42
Cedar Run, Virginia, 7
Cemetery Hill, Gettysburg, Pennsylvania, 401

Cemetery Ridge, Gettysburg, Pennsylvania, 401-402
Center. See Senter
Centreville, Virginia, 404
Chaffin's Bluff, Virginia, 14-15, 409
Chamberlain, S. W., 150
Chambers, Henry Alexander, 8, 11, 15-16, 18, 21-23, 55
Chambers, Pinckney Brown, 26, 54
Chambers, Richard M., 56
Chambersburg, Pennsylvania, 399
Champion, James, 228
Chancellorsville, Virginia, 13, 266, 399
Chandler, Jesse, 155
Chandler, Stephen D., 155
Chapel. See also Chappell
Chapel, Daniel, 81
Chapel, John, 441
Chapel, M. C., 206
Chapel, Marion C., 469
Chapel, Wesley, 441
Chapman, Robert W., 449
Chappell. See also Chapel
Chappell, A. Terrill, 456
Chappell, Martin, 456
Chappell, Rolin, 456
Chappell, Solomon C., 469
Charles, N. L., 47
Charles, R. Fulton, 47
Charleston, South Carolina, 146, 261-262, 265
Charleston and Savannah Railroad, 145
Charlotte, North Carolina, 79
Chase, William H., 291
Chatham Cossacks, 40
Cheek, Aaron, 513
Chenault, William W., 116
Cheraw, South Carolina, 145
Cherry, Albert, 105
Cherry, David, 482
Cherry, Workman H., 105
Chesapeake and Ohio Canal, 4
Chesnutt. See also Chestnut, Chestnutt
Chesnutt, Daniel H., 291
Chesnutt, Jacob L., 291
Chesnutt, John K., 300
Chesser, Ephraim, 492
Chestnut. See also Chesnutt, Chestnutt
Chestnut, James M., 343
Chestnutt. See also Chesnutt, Chestnut
Chestnutt, D. J., 300

Chestnutt, G. Franklin, 300
Chestnutt, Nicholas P., 300
Chestnutt, Samuel H., 384
Chestnutt, William N., 291
Chewning Plateau, Virginia, 406
Chickahominy River, Virginia, 2, 10, 14, 408
Childress, William B., 155
Chinnis, Samuel R., 340
Chowan River, North Carolina, 13
Chrisown, Burton, 31
Christian, George W., 206
Christian, John Giles, 503
Church, Charles F., 217
Church, Gabriel, 469
Church, James Wilson, 469
Church, John A., 469
Church, William B., 237
Church, William H., 469
City Point, Virginia, 2, 13, 266, 394
Clapp, Sidney P., 310
Clark, Addison W., 356
Clark, Daniel D., 356
Clark, David J., 118
Clark, James Mel, 28, 74
Clark, John B., 66
Clark, M. Y., 47
Clark, R. F., 47
Clark, Thomas C., 42
Clark, Tom, 492
Clark, William, 257
Clayton, Gideon E., 513
Clayton, Henderson, 156
Clayton, J. B., 156
Clayton, James H., 156
Clayton, John D., 156
Clayton, L. G., 156
Clayton, Solomon C., 156
Clayton, William D., 156
Clay Valley Rangers, 319
Claywell, John H., 74
Clear. See Cloar
Clements, John A., 217
Clements, Samuel, 334
Clemmer. See also Glemmer
Clemmer, George P., 105
Clemmer, J. L., 105
Cleveland Mountain Boys, 45
Clifton, G. W., 190
Clifton, George B., 190
Clifton, James H., 190
Clifton, Joel R., 190
Clifton, Samuel, 249
Cline, Adam, 420
Cline, James M., 416
Cline, John N., 420
Clingman, Thomas L., 259-

262, 267-268, 270-272, 275, 395
Clinton, John, 521
Clippard, D. Elam, 492
Clippard, John A., 492
Cloar. See also Core
Cloar, William F., 74
Clodfelter, George R., 47
Clodfelter, J., 47
Cloninger, Eli A., 492
Clover. See Cloar
Coats. See also Cates
Coats, D. A., 190
Coats, P. P., 190
Cobb, James, 291
Cobb, John H., 92
Cobb, R. J., 92
Cobb, Stephen J., Jr., 310
Cobb, William Wesley, Jr., 92
Coble. See Cauble
Cochran. See also Cockerham
Cochran, James Reid, 217
Cochran, John R., 217
Cochran, William, 420
Cochran, William C., 217
Cockerham. See also Cochran
Cockerham, Elijah, 470
Cockerham, Franklin, 470
Cockerham, Joseph, 470
Cody, Perry, 492
Cofer, Benjamin F., 449
Coffey, Benjamin L., 81
Coggins. See also Collins, Scoggins
Coggins, John W., 31
Coke. See also Cook, Cooke
Coke, George H., 415
Cold Harbor, Virginia, 14-15, 268, 270, 407-409
Coldwell. See Caldwell
Cole. See also Coles
Cole, David, 249
Cole, Duncan, 66
Cole, Evan, 430
Cole, J. Milton, 430
Cole, James Brandon, 56
Cole, James M., 42
Cole, Jason, 238
Cole, John, 42
Cole, Malcolm, 66
Coleman, Lott Caswell, 343
Coles. See also Cole, Cowles
Coles, W., 218
Coley. See also Conley, Cooly
Coley, Charles M., 513
Collier. See also Colyer
Collier, Hansom B., 357
Collins. See also Coggins
Collins, F. W., 167

Collins, G. R., 167
Collins, Henry, 118
Collins, J. William, 47
Collins, James Pink, 118
Collins, John H., 167
Collins, John S., 92
Collins, Martin, 92
Collins, Randall P., 163
Collins, Samuel S., 167
Collins, Thomas D., 167
Collins, William T., 167
Colson. See also Gholson
Colson, T. K., Jr., 503
Colson, T. K., Sr., 504
Columbus Light Infantry, 353
Colwell. See Caldwell
Colyer. See also Collier
Colyer, T. E., 177
Combest, William, 105
Combs, Calvin, 130
Compton, W., 156
Conaway, William H., 343
Concord, North Carolina, 417
Condry, David C., 31
Condry, Joseph, 31
Conely. See also Conley, Connelly
Conely, D. G., 118
Confederate Stars, 381
Conley. See also Coley, Conely, Connelly, Cooly
Conley, H. Clay, 30
Conley, John A., 310
Conley, John C., 310
Conley, Thomas J., 310
Conley, William Scott, 310
Connelly. See also Conely, Conley
Connelly, Francis H., 310
Conner. See also Connor
Conner, Samuel L., 31
Connor. See also Cannon, Conner
Connor, Caswell Augustus, 116
Connor, Charles Fulton, 116
Connor, James P., 130
Conrad, Lindsey Lemuel, 47
Contentnea Creek (Greene County), North Carolina, 13
Cook. See also Coke, Cooke
Cook, H., 167
Cook, James M., 417
Cook, James Madison, 47, 105
Cook, John B., 105
Cook, Madison, 105
Cook, Thomas M., 56, 384
Cook, W. D., 238
Cook, William P., 42
Cooke. See also Coke, Cook

Cooke, John R., 404-406, 409
Cooke, Richard F., 420
Cooly. *See also* Coley, Conley
Cooly, J. C., 249
Coombs. *See* Combs
Coon. *See* Koon, Koone
Cooper, George W., 430
Cooper, James Daniel, 42
Cooper, John, 430
Cooper, John O., 238
Cooper, Mathew, 430
Cooper, Robert, 430
Cooper River, South Carolina, 261
Cope. *See* Cape
Copeland, John N., 66
Corbett, Robert J., 441
Corbett, William M., 235
Corbett, William S., 45
Cordell. *See also* Cordle, Cottle
Cordell, William, 513
Cordle. *See also* Caddell, Cordell, Cottle
Cordle, James C., 449
Core. *See also* Cloar, Corn, Gore
Core, Malcolm, 370
Core Creek, North Carolina, 9, 143
Corn. *See also* Core, Kern
Corn, Noah W., 249
Cornbow, Thomas, 384
Cornish, Franklin W., 357
Cornish, Jacob, 48
Cornish, John H., 357
Correll. *See also* Carroll
Correll, Phillip A., 417
Corse, Montgomery D., 267
Corzine, James O., 420
Costner, A. W., 92
Costner, Aaron C., 106
Costner, Christopher, 130
Costner, E. S., 106
Costner, Joseph M., 106
Costner, Joseph W., 106
Costner, M. S. P., 106
Costner, W. F., 106
Costner, Zimri, 106
Cottle. *See also* Cordell, Cordle
Cottle, Nixon, 343
Cottle, W. Henry, 301
Couch. *See* Crouch
Council, D. A., 138
Council, James, 310
Council, John M., 311
Council, William, 311
Covington, Andrew J., 456
Covington, Benjamin F., 456
Covington, Henry A., 456

Covington, Henry H., 456
Covington, John B., 456
Covington, John T., 90
Covington, Joseph E., 456
Covington, Thomas J., 457
Covington, Thomas T., 457
Covington, William Riley, 457
Cowan. *See also* Gowan
Cowan, Hugh M., 281
Cowles. *See also* Coles
Cowles, Charles L., 277, 288
Cowley. *See* Cooly
Cowper. *See* Cofer, Cooper
Cox, Alexander H., 151, 206
Cox, Benton Petty, 206
Cox, Edward A., 31
Cox, Eli, 167
Cox, Harmon M., 32
Cox, Henry A., 151, 206
Cox, Isham, 228
Cox, John A., 66
Cox, Joseph W., 228
Cox, McDonald, 66
Cox, Nathaniel, 482
Cox, Payton A., 513
Cox, Romulus Leedy, 439, 512
Cox, Sandy, 206
Cox, Stephen D., 228
Cox, Thomas C., 206
Cox, W. W., 177
Cox, William J., 151, 206
Cox, William P., 167
Coxey, Richard, 218
Craft, Nathan L., 513
Craig, Charles M., 343
Cramer. *See* Crommer
Crane, Job S., 82
Crane, Mark W., 250
Cranford. *See also* Crawford
Cranford, J. P., 482
Cranford, Levi, 482
Cranford, P. C., 482
Craton, Marshall D., 140, 142, 149
Crause. *See* Crouse, Krause
Craver. *See also* Carver
Craver, F., 48
Craver, G. N., 48
Crawford. *See also* Cranford
Crawford, Abram L., 74
Crawford, James, 106
Crawford, James Alexander, 106
Crawford, James M., 74
Crawford, John B., 343
Crawford, John Thomas, 72
Crawford, R. N., 92
Crawford, Thomas O., 106
Crawford, W. H., 190
Creech, Ezekiel, 190

Creech, James W., 190
Creech, John Calvin, 357
Creech, Levi P., 178
Creech, Robert G., 190
Creech, Romulus H., 190
Crenshaw, John, 82
Creps, Julius Alexander, 504
Cress, Jeremiah, 420
Cress, John Monroe, 420
Cress, Lawson, 56
Crews. *See also* Cruise
Crews, John M., 513
Crews, Robert Martin, 74
Crews, Yancey, 513
Cribb, Isham G., 357
Crider. *See* Krider
Criminger. *See* Kriminger
Crocker, Barden, 178
Crocker, Berry F., 198
Crocker, Bridgers, 198
Crocker, James W., 178
Crocker, Joseph, 198
Crocker, Madison, 250
Crocker, William H., 178
Croft. *See* Craft
Crommer, Benjamin F., 513
Crook, Silas D., 66
Croom, Judson W., 281
Cross. *See* Cress
Crossland, Sabastian T., 301
Crouch, Jacob, 48
Crouch, Samuel C., 457
Crouse. *See also* Krause
Crouse, Hampton, 470
Crow, James L., 32
Crow, John, 32
Crowder, J. W., 48
Crowell, Buckner Kimball, 504
Crowell, George W., 504
Cruise. *See also* Crews
Cruise, John W., 74
Crumpler, Charles H., 384
Crumpler, R. W., 198
Cruse. *See* Crews, Cruise
Culbreath, William M., 238
Culbreth, Duncan J., 370
Culbreth, Marshall B., 281
Culp, John, 82
Culp, John H., 92
Culp, L. A., 93
Culpeper Court House, Virginia, 6-7, 399, 403
Culp's Hill, Gettysburg, Pennsylvania, 401
Cumberland Church, Virginia, 24, 413
Cummings, James M., 301
Cummings, John, 228
Currie. *See also* Curry

Currie, Archibald, 66
Currie, Archibald M., 311
Currie, Daniel J., 311
Currie, Daniel McG., 311
Currie, Francis S., 309
Currie, Gilbert G., 311
Currie, Randal M., 311
Curry. *See also* Currie
Curry, David H., 218
Curry, Samuel, 470

D

Daffron, George W., 278, 323
Daggett. *See* Doggett
Dail. *See also* Deal, Dull
Dail, Joseph, 441
Dail, Julius V., 301
Dail, Lemuel L., 301
Dail, Nathan, 441
Dail, Thomas F., 301
Dail, W. M., 301
Dallas, Hugh, 311
Dallas, North Carolina, 102
Dalrymple, James, 149-151, 204
Dalrymple, Malcolm, 206
Dalrymple, William M., 206
Damron, John D., 127
Dancey, Calvin, 130
Dancy, James M., 470
Dandridge, T. W., 16
Daniel. *See also* Daniels
Daniel, Calvin, 156
Daniel, F. M., 156
Daniel, Francis L., 250
Daniel, John R., 198
Daniel, John W., 343
Daniel, Joseph C., 250
Daniel, Junius, 140-143, 397-398
Daniel, Needham, 198
Daniel, William H., 198
Daniel, Wylie B., 56
Daniels. *See also* Daniel
Daniels, E. P., 521
Daniels, Leroy R., 334
Danner, James Monroe, 118
Danner, John Lemuel Franklin, 118
Danville, Virginia, 273, 413
Darden. *See* Durden
Darnall, John S., 470
Darnall, Joseph M., 470
Darnall, Morgan S., 470
Darroch, J. L., 228
Darroch, Malcolm, Jr., 228
Darroch, Malcolm, Sr., 228
Darroch, Neill, 228

Daugherty. *See also* Daughtrey, Daughtry, Dorety
Daugherty, William A., 130
Daughery, Hardy J., 370
Daughtrey. *See also* Daugherty, Daughtry, Dorety
Daughtrey, John, 178
Daughtry. *See also* Daugherty, Daughtrey, Dorety
Daughtry, George William, 178
Davenport, Aaron, 441
Davenport, Henderson, 441
Davenport, James D., 156
Daves. *See also* Davis
Daves, William S., 218
David, James, 344
Davidson, John, 66
Davidson, John P., 470
Davis. *See also* Daves
Davis, Andrew L., 119
Davis, Barney W., 238
Davis, Bartlett, 198
Davis, Dempsey, 370
Davis, Drury Dobbins, 93
Davis, Edward H., 441
Davis, Elias P., 168
Davis, Elias S., 311
Davis, Elijah, 470
Davis, Elisha, 190
Davis, Ervin Q., 311
Davis, H. H., 82
Davis, Hamilton, 513
Davis, Hanson, 311
Davis, Henry, 482
Davis, Henry P., 168
Davis, Isaac, 449
Davis, Isaiah I., 28, 130
Davis, J. C., 106
Davis, J. M., 311
Davis, J. T., 178
Davis, Jacob L., 238
Davis, James, 106, 119
Davis, James T., 323
Davis, James Taylor, 26, 79
Davis, Jefferson, 148, 275
Davis, John A., 32
Davis, John B., 93
Davis, John D., 371
Davis, John L., 323
Davis, John W., 513
Davis, Joseph R., 400, 402
Davis, Josiah, 178
Davis, Lawrence D., 449
Davis, Logan C., 32
Davis, R. H., 168
Davis, Robert W., 449
Davis, Simon, 357
Davis, Stephen D., 66
Davis, T. L., 106

Davis, Thomas A., 32
Davis, Thomas R., 513
Davis, William B., 32
Davis, William H., 178
Davis, William J., 311
Davis, William Jasper, 32
Davis, Yancy B., 449
Dawkins, George, 457
Dawkins, Samuel C. B., 457
Dawson, Amos, 344
Dawson, John C., 384
Dawson, Joseph, 42
Dawson, William P., 513
Day, George W., 74
Day, Robert O., 75
Day, William Albertus, 1-3, 7, 17-20, 119
Deal. *See also* Beal, Dail
Deal, Daniel, 93
Dean. *See also* Bean
Dean, Green L., 228
Dean, J. A., 228
Dean, William P., 228
Dean, William R., 228
Deans, Jesse, 198
Dearing, James, 10, 12, 266
DeArmond, James Boyce, 82
Deas. *See* Dees
Deaver, Nathan H., 371
DeBerry, B. G., 521
DeBerry, Edmund J., 417, 457
DeBerry, Edmund P., 504
DeBose. *See* DuBose
Decamp, Charles, 417, 441
Deck. *See also* Beck
Deck, Eusebius, 107
Deep Gully, North Carolina, 142, 397
Dees, James A., 504
Dees, Robert, 334
Dees, W. Boggan, 504
Dellinger. *See also* Dillinger
Dellinger, Adam, 130
Dellinger, Albert P., 492
Dellinger, Isaac, 492
Dellinger, John Calvin, 493
Dellinger, John F., 493
Dellinger, Lawson Alexander, 491
Dellinger, Leroy M., 482
Dellinger, Lorenzo D., 483
Dellinger, Michael P., 493
Dellinger, Monroe D., 493
Dellinger, Noah, 493
Dellinger, Noah H., 48
Dellinger, Philip F., 130
Dellinger, Samuel W., 493
DeMarcus, William A., 420
Denney. *See also* Denny

Denney, Adam M., 449
Denning. *See also* Dunning
Denning, Josiah, 371
Denny. *See also* Denney
Denny, Nathaniel A., 156
DePriest, J. G., 238
DePriest, James Bynum, 250
DePriest, Thomas Baxter, 238
Deviney. *See also* Divinny
Deviney, J. G., 48
Dicken. *See also* Dickens
Dicken, James T., 206
Dicken, Thomas, 206
Dickens. *See also* Dicken, Dinkins
Dickens, J. K., 190
Dickens, John T., 207
Dickinson. *See also* Dickson, Dixon
Dickinson, James, 198
Dickson. *See also* Dickinson, Dixon
Dickson, Calvin L., 291
Dickson, James A., 93
Dickson, James Joshua, 32
Dickson, Major Everitt, 281
Dickson, William A., 32
Dillard, Jacob, 470
Dilling, Freno, 107
Dillinger. *See also* Dellinger
Dillinger, J. D., 93
Dillingham, A. G., 93
Dimett, Joel, 470
Dingle, William, 56
Dinkins. *See also* Dickens
Dinkins, Henry H., 26-27
Dinwiddie Court House, Virginia, 22, 412
Disher, H., 48
Disher, Thomas, 48
Dismal Swamp Canal, North Carolina and Virginia, 12
Divinny. *See also* Deviney
Divinny, William G., 48
Dixon. *See also* Dickinson, Dickson
Dixon, Benjamin F., 21, 90
Dixon, Columbus H., 90
Dixon, Daniel H., 384
Dixon, John, 130
Dixon, Robert W., 130
Dixon, William, Jr., 93
Dixon, William W., 93
Dobbins, Christopher C., 238
Dobbins, George R., 238
Dobbins, Jeff J., 238
Dobbins, William Ballard, 238
Dodd, H. L., 178
Dodd, I. B., 178

Dodd, James M., 178
Dodd, John W., 178
Dodd, Q. B., 178
Dodge, M., 257
Doggett, James G., 238
Doggett, James Lewis, 238
Doggett, John Hugh, 238
Doggett, William D., 238
Donaldson, A. J., 198
Doors, John W., 357
Dorety. *See also* Daugherty, Daughtrey, Daughtry
Dorety, John Henry, 130
Dorman, Calvin L., 228
Dorman, Isaac B., 229
Dorman, John T., 229
Dorman, Martin, 371
Douglas, Elam L., 119
Douglas, George, 334
Douglas, Nathan, 204
Douglas, R. B., 207
Douglass, James E., 334
Douvet, John L., 229
Dove, Julius C., 420
Dowden. *See also* Bowden
Dowden, Ezekiel, 190
Dowel, Columbus F., 470
Dowel, Emeral, 470
Downey, Thomas J., 239
Drake, Silas A., 156
Draughon, George Theophilus, 229
Draughon, William G., 229
Drewry's Bluff, Virginia, 3, 9-10, 13-14, 140-142, 267, 393
Driggers, Anderson, 457
Driver, Wesley, 229
Drum, J. Philip, 119
Drum, John W., 10, 119
Drum, Peter Monroe, 119
Drum, Rufus L., 119
Drum, Thomas F., 119
Dry, Christopher, 504
Dry, Daniel, 504
Dry, George A., 504
Dry, William C., 420
Dry Pond Dixies, 480
DuBose, Jacob W., 281
Dudley, Eli, Jr., 382
Dudley, John W., 371
Duffy, Charles, Jr., 27
Duffy, Walter, 150
Dull. *See also* Dail
Dull, George T., 513
Dull, Henderson, 513
Dumford, Jesse, 441
Dunahoe, Cruck, 250
Duncan, A. R., 178
Duncan, Hardy, 357

Duncan, Isaiah T., 156
Duncan, James Henry, 178
Duncan, James W., 156, 471
Duncan, Ransom H., 178
Duncan, W. S., 179
Duncan, William Henry, 179
Dunden, _____, 239
Dunn. *See also* Bunn
Dunn, James R., 82
Dunn, John B., 250
Dunn, Sampson, 190
Dunn, Sir William, 190
Dunning. *See also* Denning
Dunning, John, 430
Duplin Stars, 298
Durden, Duncan J., 371
Durham, Cicero A., 13, 26
Durham Station, North Carolina, 148, 275
Dyer, Elisha, 250
Dyson, James T., 344
Dyson, Solomon Asberry, 344

E

Earl, B. G., 93
Earl, L. G., 93
Earles, John, 93
Earles, John W., 218
Earles, Martin L., 218
Earley, John, 239
Earls, Isaac H., 93
Early, Frank, 32
Early, Jubal A., 22, 400, 406-407, 412
Early, William, 218
Earney, Admiral P., 493
Earney, Lafayette, 493
Earnhardt, Moses G., 56
Earp, James Henderson, 179
Earp, John E., 179
Easom. *See also* Eason
Easom, David, 420
Easom, James, 421
Easom, John E., 421
Eason. *See also* Easom
Eason, John William, 179
Eatman, Harris H., 179
Eatmon, W. H., 179
Eaves, Andrew J., 235
Eaves, John B., 235
Eaves, Spencer, 150
Eddins, C., 138
Eddleman, Daniel W., 421
Eddleman, David F., 493
Eddleman, William P., 493
Edge, Simeon B., 311
Edgerton, Nathan, 430

Edisto River, South Carolina, 145
Edmondson, Charles, 441
Edmondson, J. N., 157
Edmundson, Jesse W., 149-150, 198
Edwards, Alexander, 168
Edwards, Benjamin, 198
Edwards, Bryant, 179
Edwards, Erastus, 199
Edwards, G. W., 430
Edwards, H. F., 384
Edwards, Henry T., 199
Edwards, Jacob O., 483
Edwards, Jesse, 191
Edwards, John, 357
Edwards, Levi, 179, 281
Edwards, Lewis, 483
Edwards, Nicholas, 191
Edwards, W. Pinckney, 344
Edwards, Washington, 281
Edwards, Wheeler Simeon, 119
Edwards, William E., 483
Edwards, William L., 196
Elevation, North Carolina, 146
Eliason. See also Ellison
Eliason, William Adlai, 26
Elkins, James A., 357
Eller, Alexander, 119
Eller, Francis, 471
Eller, Samuel F., 48
Ellington, Jesse Thompson, 175
Ellington, Joseph Crittenden, 140, 142-144, 147, 175
Elliocutt, T. C., 48
Elliott, Alexander, Jr., 277, 382
Elliott, James A., 82
Elliott, John A., 130
Elliott, John L., 119
Elliott, Jonathan Cebern, 471
Elliott, Julius A., 29, 56
Elliott, Lauriston F., 439, 514
Elliott, Leroy S., 514
Elliott, Samuel C., 48
Elliott, Samuel H., 80
Elliott, Samuel T., 493
Elliott, Stephen, 16
Elliott, Thomas William, 138
Ellis. See also Ennis
Ellis, Alexander, 371
Ellis, Don Juan, 179
Ellis, Evander, 357
Ellis, George Washington, 179
Ellis, Jacob, 179
Ellis, James, 344
Ellis, James N., 441
Ellis, John C., 179
Ellis, Josiah, 441
Ellis, William D. B., 371

Ellis, William H., 49
Ellison. See also Eliason
Ellison, E. Byrd, 157
Elmore, Eli A., 130
Elmore, Ephraim A., 130
Elms, James H., 80
Emerson, John W., 471
England, Johial, 32
Ennis. See also Ellis
Ennis, James, 157
Ennis, James F., 281
Ennis, John Allen, 191
Ennis, Levi, 191
Erson, Eric, 415, 490
Ervin. See also Irvin
Ervin, Lawson A., 493
Erwin, William M., 218
Escort, 143, 399
Essick, Ransom, 49
Essick, Thomas, 49
Etters, Henry, 93
Eudy. See also Eury
Eudy, William, 421
Eure, Daniel D., 441
Eure, Elmore, 441
Eure, Henry C., 441
Eure, James R., 441
Eure, Jethro H., 441
Eure, Noah, 442
Eure, Preston, 442
Eury. See also Eudy
Eury, Andrew J., 421
Evans, Anchram H., 344
Evans, Clement A., 412
Evans, Davidson, 334
Evans, Duncan C., 311
Evans, Jacob A., 340
Evans, James A., 311
Evans, John, 471
Evans, John B., 344
Evans, Michael, 334
Evans, William C., 281
Evans, William W., 344
Everett. See also Averitt, Everitt
Everett, Alexander B., 514
Everhart, A., 49
Everhart, Britton, 49
Everhart, C., 49
Everhart, Hamilton, 49
Everhart, Michael, 49
Everhart, William, 49
Everitt. See also Averitt, Everett
Everitt, D. E., 199
Ewell, Richard S., 24, 399-401, 405-407, 413
Ewing, John Wesley, 457
Exum, William D., 199

Ezzell, Chesnutt J., 291
Ezzell, Curtis H., 291
Ezzell, Elisha Henry, 291
Ezzell, James A., 82
Ezzell, Joseph C., 291
Ezzell, Lewis T., 291
Ezzell, Lewis W., 291
Ezzell, Rabon J., 292
Ezzell, Thomas, 301
Ezzell, William W., 292
Ezzell, Zachariah, 292

F

Faircloth, Daniel, 168
Faires. See also Farris
Faires, Jesse A., 107
Fairfax, Thomas A., 344
Fairless, John A., 442
Falk. See Faulk
Falling Waters, Maryland, 403
Falls, Alfred V., 90
Falls, Francis M., 93
Falls, J. C., 94
Falls, James F., 94
Falls, James H., 94
Falls, Robert W., 127
Falls, William, 107
Falmouth, Virginia, 7
Fann, Richard H., 384
Fann, Wiley, 385
Faris. See also Farris, Pharris
Faris, John A., 82
Farley. See Furley
Farmer, Moses B., 281
Farmer, William M., 504
Farmville, Virginia, 24, 413
Farr. See Furr
Farrell. See Ferrell
Farris. See also Faires, Faris, Pharris
Farris, John T., 29, 75
Faucette, Thomas B., 229
Faulk, Daniel Ashbury, 335
Faulk, James C., 335
Faw, Martin, 471
Faw, William H., 471
Fayetteville, North Carolina, 145, 274
Fayetteville, Pennsylvania, 399
Feadwell, W. C., 301
Fears. See Faires
Felker, William, 57
Felton. See also Fulton
Felton, John, 442
Ferguson, Alfred, 107
Ferguson, Columbus, 107
Ferguson, James, 107

Ferguson, L. B., 107
Ferguson, Thomas W., 107
Ferrell. *See also* Perrell, Terrell
Ferrell, J. D., 179
Ferrell, John A., 157
Ferrell, John W., 157
Ferrell, William, 442
Fesmire, Reuben C., 430
Fesperman, Henry P., 504
Fetzer, John W., 421
Few. *See* Faw
Fields, Clabon, 357
Fields, James K., 358
Fields, Minos A., 82
Fields, William B., 301
Fighting Boys, 511
Finch, William H., 57
Fincher, John E., 82
Fincher, Osborne, 82, 430
Fink, Adam H., 421
Finlay, Robert W., 32
Fish, Elcanah, 119
Fisher, David, 493
Fisher, Elcany, 119
Fisher, George C., 371
Fisher, J. G., 292
Fisher, James, 494
Fisher, Joseph, 120
Fisher, Lawson, 131
Fisher, Reuben, 120
Fisher, Thomas M., 120
Fisher, William J., 120
Fitch. *See* Futch
Five Forks, Virginia, 22-23, 412
Flack, C. J., 218
Flack, John P., 215
Flack, Lewis B., 218
Flack, W. G., 168
Flannagan, Lee B., 82
Fleming. *See also* Flemming
Fleming, David C., 483
Fleming, John H., 30
Fleming, Thomas A., 421
Flemming. *See also* Fleming
Flemming, James Greenlee, 30
Flemming, John A., 26, 29
Flemming, William J., 32
Fletcher, Henry, 449
Flinn. *See also* Flynn
Flinn, Daniel V., 358
Flinn, George W., 358
Flinn, John, 239
Florence, South Carolina, 145
Flowers, Exum, 199
Flowers, Robert G., 107
Floyd, Benjamin F., 430
Floyd, Charles Johnson, 323
Floyd, Faulkner J., 335
Floyd, Francis Fulton, 320

Floyd, James J., 442
Floyd, Memory J., 335
Floyd, Miles, 430
Floyd, William Pinkney, 323
Flynn. *See also* Flinn
Flynn, Thomas J., 239
Foard. *See also* Ford
Foard, Zebulon M., 430
Folly Island, Charleston, South Carolina, 262
Foltege, Samuel, 42
Forbes, Joseph T., 49, 131
Forbush, David R.', 239
Forbush, Franklin, 239
Ford. *See also* Foard
Ford, A. P., 107
Ford, Belton, 131
Ford, George B., 247
Ford, James H., 107
Ford, John M., 107
Ford, John Wesley, 131
Ford, Pinkney B., 247
Ford, Thomas P., 335
Foreman, Stephen D., 504
Formyduval, Coval Lane, 358
Forney, Jacob G., 494
Forney, Sidney J., 494
Forrest, James D., 504
Forrest, Joseph H., 505
Forrest, Sidney, 281
Fortenberry, William, 94
Forts
Fort Anderson (near New Bern), North Carolina, 10, 12, 142, 266, 397
Fort Fisher (near Wilmington), North Carolina, 273
Fort Harrison (near Richmond), Virginia, 271-272, 411
Fort Hill (near Washington), North Carolina, 398-399
Fort Johnston (near Smithville; present-day Southport), North Carolina, 258
Fort McAllister, Savannah, Georgia, 261
Fort Moultrie, Sullivan's Island, Charleston, South Carolina, 261
Fort Stedman (near Petersburg), Virginia, 21-22, 412
Fort Sumter, Charleston, South Carolina, 261-263, 265
Fort Wagner, Morris Island, Charleston, South Carolina, 261-264, 273
Fortune, William Pinckney, 218
Fortune, Williamson M., 218
Forty-Five Mile Station,

Georgia, 145
Foster, Achilles E., 471
Foster, Hugh Akillis, 471
Foster, Jesse M., 471
Foster, John A., 406, 408-410, 471
Foster, John G., 259, 395
Foster, John S., 471
Foster, John T., 471
Foster, Nathaniel A., 465
Foster, William A., 472
Foulkes. *See also* Fultz
Foulkes, James F., 415, 428
Fouts, A., 49
Fowler, A. Benjamin, 250
Fowler, Harmon, 344
Fowler, John Henry, 447
Fowler, Laban, 344
Fowler, William H., 311
Fowler, Zachariah, 250
Fox, Lee Allison, 120
Foy. *See also* Fry
Foy, James L., 107
Foy, John F., 108
Foy, Solomon E., 108
Francis, John M., 239
Francis, T. A., 94
Franklin, William B., 8
Franklin, Virginia, 12-13, 394, 396
Frasier, David, 250
Frederick, Erasmus D., 157
Frederick, Simon P., 292
Frederick, Maryland, 4
Fredericksburg, Virginia, 7-8, 399
Freeland, Charles, 49
Freeland, Silas A., 75
Freeman, Evan, 168
Freeman, George H., 157
Freeman, John C., 120, 168
Freeman, Riley W., 131
Freeze, Edward L., 75
Freeze, Jacob, 57
Freeze, John F., 75
Freeze, Peter, 75
Freeze, S. Andrew, 75
Freeze, William, 75
French, William, 82
French, William R., 277, 323
Friday, John Caleb, 494
Friday, William A., 494
Frink, William Pinkney, 358
Fritts, Henderson, 50
Froneberger, Lewis, 108
Fry. *See also* Foy
Fry, Alexander M., 66
Fry, Eben, 505
Fry, Grafton R., 66

Fry, Jacob B., 66
Fry, John C., 505
Fry, Joseph, 67
Fry, Murdoch P., 67
Fry, Nathan, 505
Fry, Neill A., 65
Fry, Thomas M., 67
Fry, William, 505
Fulgum, Robert L., 282
Fulmore, Andrew C., 332
Fulton. *See also* Felton
Fulton, Horatio D., 94
Fulton, James Matthew, 449
Fulton, James Preston, 90
Fulton, William, 449
Fultz. *See also* Foulkes
Fultz, A., 50
Fultz, Francis, 50
Fuquay, George W., 229
Fuquay, John, 207
Fuquay, John A., 229
Fuquay, Stephen W., 229
Furley, J. B., 179
Furmage, John J., 292
Furr, Tobias, 421
Fussell, William H., 301
Futch, Jacob, 282

G

Gable. *See* Goble
Gaddis. *See* Gattis
Gaddy. *See also* Gately, Geddie
Gaddy, Israel D., 385
Gaines. *See* Goins
Gainey, J. H., 385
Galbreath. *See also* Gilbreath
Galbreath, Malcolm, 312
Gallahorn, Alpheus, 431
Gallaway. *See* Galloway
Gallimore, Joseph S., 421
Gallimore, W. B., 57
Gallimore, William F., 57
Galloway, John, 457
Galloway, William H., 457
Gambill. *See also* Gamble
Gambill, B. F., 472
Gambill, William Bourne, 472
Gamble. *See also* Gambill
Gamble, A. J., 108
Gamble, Robert F., 108
Gamble, W. F., 94
Gant. *See also* Grant
Gant, Harrison G., 483
Gant, O. Jefferson, 483
Ganus. *See also* Gurganious
Ganus, James S., 358
Ganus, John C., 358

Gappins, James J., 344, 358
Gardner. *See also* Garner
Gardner, Daniel, 94
Gardner, James, 199
Gardner, James L., 94
Gardner, Jeremiah A., 32
Gardner, R. M., 94
Gardner, W. J., 199
Gardner, William T., 196
Garman. *See* Gearman, German
Garner. *See also* Gardner
Garner, Francis M., 301
Garner, Simeon, 301
Garris. *See also* Garriss, Harris
Garris, Jonathan G., 199
Garrison. *See also* Harrison
Garrison, Aaron, 83
Garrison, Ephraim, 494
Garrison, Henry, 494
Garrison, Sidney, 494
Garrison, William N., 75
Garriss. *See also* Garris
Garriss, George W., 282
Garvin. *See also* Gavin
Garvin, Thomas W., 33
Gary. *See* Geary
Garysburg, North Carolina, 10, 140
Gaskill, Furney, 344
Gaston Rangers, 102
Gately. *See also* Gaddy
Gately, Isaac, 458
Gatens, John E., 480
Gates. *See* Cates
Gatesville, North Carolina, 12, 438
Gatling, John T., Jr., 415, 439
Gattis, John, 431
Gattis, William, 250
Gaum, Daniel H., 301
Gavin. *See also* Garvin
Gavin, William A., 292
Gay. *See also* Gray, Guy
Gay, Daniel Odom, 458
Gay, Samuel L., 458
Gaylor, John B., 292
Gaylor, Lewis, 292
Gearman. *See also* German
Gearman, Gabriel, 229
Geary, Sampson, 57
Geddie. *See also* Gaddy
Geddie, Joseph Carson, 371
Geddie, McDuffie, 371
Geisler, John, 57
George, Edward Payson, 27
George, Forney Kelly, 358
George, Reuben, 449
Georgia Central Railroad, 145
German. *See also* Gearman

German, John H., 18, 120
Getty. *See* Gaddy, Geddie
Gettysburg, Pennsylvania, 9-10, 399-401, 403
Gholson. *See also* Colson, Goodson
Gholson, Durell B., 199
Gibbons. *See also* Gibson
Gibbons, A. I., 94
Gibbons, John H., 94
Gibson. *See also* Gibbons
Gibson, D. N., 449
Gibson, E., 323
Gibson, Elijah, 458
Gibson, George, 494
Gibson, Hugh S., 75
Gibson, John F., 458
Gibson, Lee, 449
Gibson, Leonidas R., 447
Gibson, Oliver P., 50
Gibson, Pleasant, 458
Gibson, Robert Fletcher, 458
Gibson, Samuel, 458
Gibson, William N., 75, 450
Giddens, Henry C., 385
Giddens, James T., 385
Giddens, John W., 385
Gilbert, Henry T., 229
Gilbert, William D., 229
Gilbreath. *See also* Galbreath
Gilbreath, Ethelbert J. N., 472
Gilbreath, James P., 472
Gilchrest, Charles A., 207
Gill, G. R., 94
Gillean, Hezekiah C., 57
Gillean, John N., 57
Gilleland. *See also* Gilliland
Gilleland, Henderson Albert, 120
Gilliam, George, 439
Gilliam, Julian, 439
Gilliland. *See also* Gilleland
Gilliland, Marcus, 120
Gilliland, Reuben, 120
Gilliland, Thomas, 120
Gillmore, Quincy A., 262
Gilmore, Jasper H., 207
Gilmore, Stephen, 372
Gipson. *See* Gibson
Givens. *See* Giddens
Gladden, Henry J., 95
Gladden, James A., 50
Gladden, Rufus C., 95
Gladden, W. H., 50
Glascock. *See* Glasscock
Glasgow, William W., 431
Glass, William R., 472
Glasscock, James R., 514
Glemmer. *See also* Clemmer

Glemmer, G. P., 108
Globe Tavern, Virginia, 18-19, 271, 410
Glover, Calvin T., 372
Glover, William R., 372
Goar. *See* Gore
Goble, Lawson, 120
Goble, William Davidson F., 120
Goddin. *See also* Godwin
Goddin, Stephen, 199
Goddin, Theophilus, 199
Godfrey, Henry A., 207
Godfrey, John, 207
Godwin. *See also* Goddin, Goodwin
Godwin, Avera E., 180
Godwin, Guy W., 345
Godwin, Hiram, 385
Godwin, Jacob H., 180
Godwin, James A., 180
Godwin, Ollin, 312
Godwin, William B., 180
Godwin, William L., 385
Goff, Wiley, 385
Goforth, A. J., 95
Goforth, G. W., 29, 95
Goforth, Henry P., 95
Goforth, Isaac W., 95
Goforth, John Wesley, 95
Goforth, Samuel, 95
Goforth, Wash LaFayette, 95
Goforth, William C., 95
Goins. *See also* Gowins
Goins, Andrew J., 431
Goins, Michael H., 50
Golding, Robert W., 450
Goldsboro, North Carolina, 1, 9, 142, 145, 147, 196, 259-260, 273-275, 395-396
Goode, Frank M., 239
Goode, Henry, 450
Goode, James Milton Webb, 239
Goode, Reginald H., 27
Goodman, James, 199
Goodman, Robert Franklin, 121
Goodnight, Henry W., 421
Goodnight, Peter A., 75
Goodrich, George W., 292
Goodson. *See also* Gholson
Goodson, Abner, 494
Goodson, Andrew J., 335
Goodson, Charles P., 335
Goodson, George W., 494
Goodson, Jeremiah, 494
Goodson, Joel, 483
Goodson, John C., 495
Goodson, John F., 483
Goodson, John W., 483

Goodson, Matthew, 422
Goodson, Reuben, 483
Goodson, Rufus L., 495
Goodson, William A., 33
Goodwin. *See also* Godwin
Goodwin, George, 199
Goodwin, Wesley, 42
Goodwin, Winship, 42
Goore. *See also* Gore
Goore, Isaac, Jr., 292
Gordon, Adam E., 83
Gordon, John B., 24-25, 413-414
Gordonsville, Virginia, 405
Gore. *See also* Core, Goore
Gore, Daniel Russell, 358
Gore, David J., 385
Goslen, Junius W., 439, 511
Gouger, James H., 28, 83
Gowan. *See also* Cowan
Gowan, Benjamin A., 340
Gowan, James T., 345
Gowens, Martin, 218
Gowins. *See also* Goins
Gowins, Manly C., 431
Gracie, Archibald, 15
Grady, D., 301
Grady, Frederick, 301
Grady, William Henry, 301
Graham. *See also* Grantham
Graham, Archibald, 312
Graham, Calvin, 168
Graham, Daniel, 372
Graham, Duncan J., 312
Graham, George, 67
Graham, George A., 312
Graham, Hector R., 312
Graham, Henry Clay, 57
Graham, James Calvin, 312
Graham, Joseph, 57
Graham, Joseph C., 57, 324
Graham, Richard S., 57
Graham, Robert, 312
Graham, Thomas, 168
Graham, William, 458
Grahamville, South Carolina, 145
Grant. *See also* Gant
Grant, Ulysses S., 13-14, 16, 18, 21-22, 266, 269-271, 405-413
Grantham. *See also* Graham
Grantham, Stephen, 335
Graves. *See* Groves
Gray. *See also* Gay
Gray, Augustus M., 157
Gray, David Jasper, 250
Gray, Edwin, 442
Gray, George Thomas, 157
Grayson, Alfred M., 33
Grayson, John S., 33

Grayson, William G., 218
Green, Albert, 239
Green, Andrew J., 239
Green, C. P., 151, 239
Green, Elias G., 250
Green, G. M., 50
Green, George, 458
Green, Henry, 33
Green, Henry H., 312
Green, J. G., 239
Green, James, 442
Green, John A., 150, 199
Green, John R., 505
Green, Levi, 345
Green, Nathan G., 180
Green, Oliver, 239
Green, Robert, 431
Green, Sanders Donehew, 240
Green, William B., 458
Green, William G., 442
Green, William J., 442
Green, William T., 442
Greenlee, David W., 251
Greenlee, Tilman, 251
Green River Rifles, 246
Greensboro, North Carolina, 146, 148, 273, 275
Greenville, North Carolina, 13, 143, 398
Greenway, John W., 240
Greenway, L. E., 240
Greer. *See* Grier
Gregg. *See* Grigg
Gregory, Alexander D., 229
Gregory, Matthew, 324
Gregory, Matthew W., 229
Gregory, William, 324
Gresham. *See* Grissom
Grice. *See also* Grist, Rice
Grice, James, 200
Grice, William H., 200
Grier, John C., 23, 79
Grier, Lawrence, 83
Grier, Robert H., 80
Griffin. *See also* Griffith
Griffin, Egbert, 83
Griffin, Isaac G., 83
Griffin, Thomas J., 57
Griffith. *See also* Griffin
Griffith, Jonathan Wallace, 83
Griffith, Thomas D., 83
Grigg, Abner M., 131
Grigg, Eli C., 131
Grigg, William D., 131
Grimsley, Andrew J., 324
Grimsley, Bright, 324
Grimsley, Everett, 324
Grimsley, George, 324
Grimsley, James, 335

Grimsley, Lewis, 324
Grimsley, Travis L., 168
Grissom, Thomas A., 431
Grist. *See also* Grice
Grist, Commodore D., 33
Grist, Doc, 33
Griswold, George C., 197
Griswold, John B., 196
Groves, George F., 302
Groves, J. B., 240
Grubb, R., 50
Grubbs, James W., 514
Grubbs, John E., 514
Guffey. *See also* Guffy
Guffey, Samuel R., 219
Guffey, Thomas A., 219
Guffey, William T., 131
Guffy. *See also* Guffey
Guffy, Elijah P., 33
Guffy, John, 219
Guin. *See also* Gwinn
Guin, Asa, 372
Guin, John, 191
Gum Swamp, North Carolina, 9
Gunter, Ambrose A., 207
Gurganious. *See also* Ganus
Gurganious, David, 259, 282
Gurganious, John D., 282
Guthery, Columbus, 495
Guy. *See also* Gay
Guy, Alexander, 292
Guy, Amos J., 372
Guy, Charles Thomas, 367
Guy, David T., 292
Guy, James E., 372
Guy, John Alex, 372
Guy, John J., 282
Guy, Lewis H., 372
Guy, Samuel J., 372
Guy, William Anthony, 277, 372
Gwinn. *See also* Guin
Gwinn, William, 180

H

Hackney, Albert J., 42
Hackney, Basil A., 29, 42
Hackney, Basil M., 42
Hackney, Jesse E., 42
Hackney, Joshua H., 43
Haddock. *See also* Hancock
Haddock, Benjamin F., 431
Haddock, Daniel A., 259, 345
Haddock, Thomas W., 431
Hafner, George W., 131
Hafner, Lawson, 131
Hagans, Warren S., 131
Hagar. *See also* Hager, Hagler

Hagar, James H., 483
Hagar, James W., 483
Hagar, Thomas F., 484
Hager. *See also* Hagar, Hagler
Hager, Adam Miller, 484
Hager, Christopher W., 484
Hager, J. F., 484
Hager, J. Monroe, 484
Hager, James, 121
Hager, James Henry, 484
Hager, James R., 484
Hager, John, 484
Hager, John C., 121
Hager, John T., 431
Hager, Philip, 484
Hager, Robert D., 484
Hager, Simeon S., 484
Hager, Thomas O., 121
Hager, William H., 121
Hagerstown, Maryland, 4, 403
Hagler. *See also* Hagar, Hager
Hagler, Caleb, 422
Hahn, Francis, 230
Haigwood, Kenneth, 230
Haines. *See* Haynes
Hainey. *See* Haney
Hair. *See also* Hare
Hair, D. J., 230, 335
Hair, Hugh, 335
Hair, Robert, 335
Hair, Thomas K., 458
Hair, William James, 312
Hall. *See also* Hill, Hull
Hall, Alexander W., 431
Hall, Allison Gray, 458
Hall, Daniel M., 472
Hall, Edward James, 302
Hall, George W., 240
Hall, Harrison, 28, 108
Hall, Haynes L., 372
Hall, Henry, 138
Hall, James A., 422
Hall, James Morris, 372
Hall, Jeremiah P., 282
Hall, John A., 58
Hall, John G., 268-269, 345
Hall, Joseph Gaither, 465
Hall, Lovelace N., 431
Hall, N. C., 83
Hall, Nathan C., 472
Hall, Nathaniel, 472
Hall, Oliver, 373
Hall, R. W., 450
Hall, Thomas F., 58
Hall, William A., 472
Hall, William H., 472
Ham, Giles, Jr., 373
Ham, Richard, 200
Ham, W. N., 75

Ham, William, 200
Hambleton. *See* Hamilton
Hamby. *See also* Handy
Hamby, John H., 472
Hamby, Millington P., 33
Hamilton. *See also* Hampton
Hamilton, John F., 422
Hamilton, Larkin H., 108
Hamilton, Leonidas D., 121
Hamilton, Stephen J., 251
Hamilton, Thomas S., 251
Hamilton, North Carolina, 13, 265
Hamlin, J. D., 157
Hamlin, William P., 157
Hammond. *See also* Hammonds
Hammond, John, 324
Hammond, Sidney P., 324
Hammond, William, 431
Hammonds. *See also* Hammond
Hammonds, Dougald, 335
Hammonds, Wiley F., 345
Hampton. *See also* Hamilton
Hampton, A. S., 240
Hampton, B. F. C., 240
Hampton, Joseph L., 247
Hampton, Samuel D., 215
Hampton, Silas, 514
Hampton, Thomas J., 251
Hamrick, A. B., 251
Hamrick, Elias, 240
Hamrick, Robert B., 251
•Hance, Thomas W., 95
Hancock. *See also* Haddock
Hancock, Albert, 432
Hancock, David, 432
Hancock, John H., 450
Hancock, W. S., 410
Handy. *See also* Hamby, Hanley, Hansley
Handy, John T., 473
Handy, Marcus H., 473
Haney, William, 33
Hanley. *See also* Handy
Hanley, D. M., 207
Hanna, Q. T., 131
Hanna, William Dixon, 108
Hannon. *See also* Harmon
Hannon, James J., 83
Hanover Court House, Virginia, 258, 399
Hanover Junction, Virginia, 399, 407
Hansley. *See also* Handy, Hensley
Hansley, John D., 345
Hantz. *See* Hance
Hardee, William J., 145-147, 274-275

Hardeeville, South Carolina, 145
Harden. *See also* Hardin
Harden, Jesse, 168
Hardgrove. *See also* Hargrove
Hardgrove, Francis M., 514
Hardgrove, Lewis F., 514
Hardgrove, Thomas M., 514
Hardin. *See also* Harden
Hardin, Berry P., 240
Hardin, Hugh, 312
Hardin, James B., 240
Hardin, Jesse N., 240
Hardin, John E., 240
Hardin, LaFayette C., 240
Hardin, Louis, 312
Hardin, R. H., 95
Hardin, Thomas C., 95
Hardison, James J., 373
Hardister, Lindsey C., 428
Hardy, John, 345
Hardy, Washington M., 145
Hare. *See also* Hair
Hare, H. H., 180
Hargett, D. A., 432
Hargis, R., 157
Hargraves, Rufus M., 450
Hargrove. *See also* Hardgrove
Hargrove, Alvin, 292
Hargrove, Benjamin, Jr., 293
Harkey, Clark W., 422
Harkey, David E., 83
Harkey, James J., 83
Harkey, Marion L., 83, 432
Harkey, Milas, 58
Harkey, Washington, 84
Harmon. *See also* Hannon, Harrison
Harmon, Alfred, 240
Harmon, Andrew, 240
Harmon, Frederick, 157
Harmon, Jacob H., 132
Harmon, John G., 95
Harmon, John L., 132
Harmon, Joseph, 241
Harmon, Samuel, 95
Harmon, T. W., 29, 96
Harmon, W. W., 96
Harmon, William Henry, 96
Harper, John, 67
Harper, John B., 432
Harper, John R., 180
Harpers Ferry, West Virginia, 4, 6
Harrald, William M., 473
Harrel, David, 241
Harrell, Alfred W., 241
Harrell, Elisha, 312
Harrell, George, 442
Harrell, James Noah, 439

Harrell, John W. U., 282
Harrell, William H., 324
Harrell, William Henry, 442
Harrell, William T., 293
Harrellsville, North Carolina, 13
Harrelson, Aaron B., 282, 345
Harrington. *See also* Herrington
Harrington, A. M., 207
Harrington, Charles Turner, 335
Harris. *See also* Garris, Hovis
Harris, Alexander B., 157
Harris, Anderson, 241
Harris, Calvin B., 251
Harris, Coleman B., 251
Harris, Edwin Victor, 72
Harris, Elias, 251
Harris, Francis M., 33
Harris, G. B., 251
Harris, G. W., 251
Harris, Herbert, 251
Harris, J. D., 157
Harris, John E., 157
Harris, John H., 385
Harris, John M., 505
Harris, Joseph H., 247
Harris, Kelsey, 251
Harris, Oren J., 473
Harris, Reuben, 505
Harris, Robert W., 96
Harris, William, 207, 251
Harris, William A., 157
Harris, Wyatt M., 473
Harrison. *See also* Garrison, Harmon
Harrison, Bennett A., 58
Harrison, J. W., 33
Harrison's Landing, Virginia, 3, 141
Hartgrove. *See* Hardgrove, Hargrove
Hartis, James L., 84
Hartis, John S., 84
Hartman, Jacob W., 332
Hartman, John A., 50
Hartman, John B., 58
Hartman, John E., 336
Hartman, Nathan C., 132
Harvell. *See also* Harwell
Harvell, George H., 458
Harvey, Allen, 241
Harvey, Henry, 282
Harvey, William, 282
Harwell. *See also* Harvell
Harwell, Elbert, 121
Harwell, James T., 121
Harwell, John, 121
Harwell, Joseph M., 484
Harwell, N. A., 121
Hash, Lazarus, 373

Haskell, Joseph T., 505
Hasty, James, 458
Hasty, John C., 458
Hatcher, Henry C., 345
Hatcher's Run, Virginia, 19, 412-413
Hatley. *See also* Shatley
Hatley, Alfred, 505
Hatley, Simeon W., 58
Haughton, John P., 442
Haughton, Thomas Benbury, 150
Hauser. *See also* Houser, Howser
Hauser, Moses Edwin, 514
Havener, Jesse L., 473
Havner, Daniel, 108
Hawes. *See also* Hayes, Hughes
Hawes, Asa W., 345
Hawes, Reuben J. T., 278
Hawfield, James W., 84
Hawkins, Calvin, 157
Hawkins, Hampton P., 219
Hawkins, William L., 219
Hawkins, William P., 495
Hawley. *See also* Holley, Holly
Hawley, Edward, 385
Hawley, John Allen, 207
Hawley, Jonathan, 385
Hawley, Samson, 386
Hawley, Thomas James, 386
Haws. *See* Hawes
Hayes. *See also* Hawes, Haynes, Hays
Hayes, Bennet J., 336
Hayes, Caleb M., 442
Hayes, J. H., 108
Hayes, J. J., 108
Hayes, John W., 168
Hayes, Jonathan J., 96
Hayes, Levi C., 336
Hayles, John, 180
Haynes. *See also* Hayes
Haynes, Benjamin G., 251
Haynes, Francis Marion, 168
Haynes, John C., 495
Haynes, Warren Wentworth, 358
Hays. *See also* Hayes
Hays, James J., 96
Hays, John H., 191
Hays, W. D., 96
Hazlewood, Hiram G., 336
Head, Philip, 252
Head, Thomas W., 200
Hearne. *See also* Horn, Horne
Hearne, James D., 501
Hedalston. *See also* Huddleston
Hedalston, John H., 219
Hedes, W. H., 257
Hedgepeth, A., 495

Hedgepeth, Arch B., 168
Hedgepeth, Daniel, 168
Hedgepeth, Joel D., 168
Hedgepeth, Joseph H., 169
Hedgepeth, Stephen W., 169
Helderman, Able J., 495
Helderman, George F., 495
Helderman, John F., 495
Helderman, Rufus M., 495
Helms, Austin, 495
Helms, J. T., 108
Helms, William, 132, 450
Helton. See also Holton
Helton, Milton B., 108
Hemmingway, Isaac W., 373
Hemphill, Thomas Posey, 219, 241
Henderson, J. W., 108
Henderson, Jepsey, 336
Henderson, John, 43, 515
Henderson, Jonathan, 109
Henderson, Robert F., 109
Henderson, W. J., 109
Hendren. See also Herndon
Hendren, Jabez E., 473
Henley. See also Hensley, Hurley
Henley, Green B., 505
Henley, John D., 58
Hennigan, James E., 84
Henry, Henry Henry, 458
Hensley. See also Hansley, Henley
Hensley, W. M., 219
Henson. See Hinson
Herndon. See also Hendren
Herndon, Sidney Lucien, 43
Herring, Dawsey, 324
Herring, Isaac W., 293
Herring, Jack G., 169
Herring, James E., 282
Herring, Joel, 169
Herring, John, 180
Herring, Lewis, 169
Herring, Louis, 207
Herring, Michael B., 169
Herring, Oliver, 336
Herring, Thomas James, 288
Herrington. See also Harrington
Herrington, Leonard A., 90
Herr Ridge, Gettysburg, Pennsylvania, 400
Hester, James M., 252
Heth, Henry, 399-401, 403-410, 412-413
Hicks. See also Hix
Hicks, Charles C., 459
Hicks, Daniel M., 207
Hicks, David A., 158

Hicks, David W., 158
Hicks, Edward L., 459
Hicks, Francis Y., 46
Hicks, James Washington, 158
Hicks, Solomon D., 158
Hicks, T. W., 158
Hicks, William G., 219
Higby. See Higley
Higgins. See also Huggins
Higgins, James Marion, 29
Higgins, Jesse B., 345
Higgins, John F., 473
Higgins, William L., 219
Highsmith, Samuel L., 282
Hight, James H., 207
Higley, George, 484
Higley, Gilbert P., 332
Hill. See also Hall, Hull
Hill, A. C., 219
Hill, A. P., 6, 18, 399, 401, 404-411
Hill, Armalin Bryant, 359
Hill, C. J., 219
Hill, D. H., 5-6, 9, 142-143, 273, 396, 398-399
Hill, Isaac L., 121
Hill, John C., 121
Hill, Joseph Cornelius, 418
Hill, Moses, 180
Hill, W. S., 219
Hill, William G., 200
Hill, William J., 58
Hill, William M., 169
Hillard, Jesse, 236
Hilliard, David, 230
Hilliard, William J., 325
Hilton. See Helton, Holton
Hine, Edward A., 515
Hine, Theodore T., 515
Hinkle, Cyrus, 484
Hinman, Samuel, 132
Hinseman, Levi, 422
Hinshaw, Jacob, 484
Hinshaw, Thomas, 485
Hinson, Asa Kelly, 345
Hinson, Doctor F., 505
Hinson, Edward P., 346
Hinson, Elijah, 283
Hinson, Isaac, 505
Hinson, John L., 346
Hinson, John P., 346
Hinson, Robert R., 346
Hinson, W. Brinkley, 459
Hinton, Francis M., 200
Hinton, Jesse W., 180
Hipps, James G., 252
Hix. See also Hicks
Hix, John S., 473
Hobbs, J. R., 473

Hobbs, James R., 230
Hobbs, John W., 230
Hobbs, Lewis, 230
Hobbs, William H. H., 359
Hobby, James I., 230
Hobson, Caleb B., 276, 288
Hobson, Lewis H., 230
Hocut, James A., 180
Hocut, William B., 181
Hodge, Benjamin, 336
Hodge, Mathew, 336
Hodge, William, 181
Hodges, John, 325
Hoffman, R. W., 109
Hoffner, Atlas, 58
Hofler, Jacob, 443
Hofler, Job, 443
Hofler, Peterson, 443
Hofler, Townsend, 443
Hofler, William A., 443
Hogan, Warren, 132
Hogan, William, 33
Hogans, David, 459
Hogans, Zachariah, 459
Hoke, Robert F., 10-11, 13, 15, 147-148, 266-268, 270-275, 408
Holden, Benjamin Franklin, 459
Holden, John Thomas, 325
Holder, Ithra, 230
Holder, Jacob, 230
Holder, John, 473
Holder, Malikiah, 181
Holder, Riley, 230
Holder, Thomas, 230
Holder, William, 230
Holder, William H., 230
Holder, William J., 515
Holdsclaw, William J., 121
Holdshouser, John, 58
Holland, Franklin, 109
Holland, James R., 28, 109
Holland, Jesse, 109
Holland, John F., 75
Holland, Julius A., 109
Holland, Remus W., 75
Holland, William C., 241
Holland, William H., 373
Holley. See also Hawley, Holly
Holley, Silas, 373
Holley, William, 373
Hollifield, James, 241
Holliman, C. M., 181
Hollingsworth, Alfred, 386
Hollingsworth, Benjamin F., 386
Hollingsworth, Leonard W., 293
Holloman. See Holliman
Holly. See also Hawley, Holley
Holly, David, 191
Holly, John C., 191

Holmes, Brazil, 191
Holmes, Edward, 283
Holmes, Frederick, 191
Holmes, James W., 191
Holmes, John, Sr., 191
Holmes, John H., Jr., 191
Holmes, John W., 191
Holmes, Theophilus H., 1, 140
Holsomback, George W., 158
Holsomback, William T., 158
Holton. See also Helton
Holton, James M., 359
Homan, John, 283
Honeycut. See also Hunnicutt
Honeycut, John H., 495
Honey Hill, South Carolina, 145
Hood, B., 200
Hood, John B., 5
Hooker, Joseph, 5
Hooker, Samuel H., 359
Hookerton, North Carolina, 399
Hooks, Albert, 200
Hooper. See Hopper
Hoots, James Harrison, 473
Hoots, William, 473
Hoover, William M., 432
Hope, Christopher D., 495
Hope, James, 109
Hope, John, 496
Hope, William, 496
Hopis. See also Hovis
Hopis, Joel, 29, 34
Hopkins, B. J., 450
Hopkins, William P., 450
Hopper, Clayton C., 96
Horan, George P., 90
Horde, Richard M., 29, 46
Horn. See also Hearne, Horne
Horn, James H., 200
Horne. See also Hearne, Horn,
   Thorne
Horne, Ashley, 181
Horne, Samuel R., 181
Horne, William F., 346
Horton, Elijah M., 158
Horton, James W., 43
Horton, William M., 158
House. See Shouse
Houser. See also Hauser,
   Howser
Houser, Daniel R., 132
Houser, Emanuel, 132
Houser, Franklin A., 132
Houser, Jacob, 132
Houser, Joseph, 132
Houser, Lawson, 132
Houser, Thomas, 132
Housliver, E., 386
Houston. See also Hudson

Houston, Hiram V., 299, 320
Houston, Robert B. B., 481
Houston, William G. P., 485
Hovis. See also Harris, Hopis
Hovis, Jacob J., 109
Hovis, Moses, 496
Hovis, Westley, 496
Howard, Allen, 485
Howard, Edmond, 181
Howard, Harris, 293
Howard, John, 200
Howard, John T., 293
Howard, Jonathan M., 84
Howard, Joseph, 485
Howard, Oliver O., 145-147, 274
Howard, Stephen, 373
Howard, William G., 485
Howel, Aaron, Jr., 283
Howell, Albert J., 443
Howell, Amos, 312
Howell, John J., 96
Howell, John W., 200
Howell, Joseph, 359
Howell, Julius A., 505
Howell, Renselear, 443
Howell, S. H., 96
Howell, Thomas, 96
Howell, W. E., 96
Howell, William H., 200
Howser. See also Hauser,
   Houser
Howser, D. R., 96
Howser, William H. C., 219
Hoyle, B. W., 132
Hoyle, Daniel A., 50
Hoyle, John S., 133
Hoyle, Peter C., 133
Hoyle, Samuel J., 133
Hoyles, John, 181
Huddleston. See also Hedalston
Huddleston, J. H., 219
Hudgins, Andrew J., 515
Hudgins, James W., 252
Hudgins, William B., 158
Hudgins, William D., 252
Hudson. See also Houston
Hudson, Lewis, 505
Hudson, Wilson M., 84
Huffman. See Hoffman
Huffstetler. See also Huffstutler
Huffstetler, Alexander Caleb, 97
Huffstetler, Eli, 109
Huffstetler, Ephraim C., 97
Huffstetler, Henry C., 133
Huffstetler, Jacob, 109
Huffstutler. See also Huffstetler
Huffstutler, Albert, 34
Huffstutler, Henry, 34
Huger, Benjamin, 2

Huggins. See also Higgins
Huggins, Thomas, 336
Huggins, William J., 359
Hughes. See also Hawes
Hughes, Braswell, 181
Hughes, Jordan, 354
Hughes, Orin Turner, 207
Hughes, Spencer, 207
Hughes, William, 200, 208
Huland, John, 432
Hull. See also Hall, Hill
Hull, William, 133
Humphrey, Duncan C., 313
Humphrey, John, 346
Humphrey, Lewis, 313
Humphrey, Matthew, 313
Humphrey, William James, 313
Humphrey, William P., 336
Hunnicutt. See also Honeycut
Hunnicutt, Richard N., 76
Hunsucker, Calvin A., 121
Hunsucker, William W., 67
Hunt, Absalom, 219
Hunt, Alfred W., 219
Hunt, Calvin, 283
Hunt, John, 241
Hunt, L., 50
Hunt, McDonald, 485
Hunt, Simon W., 485
Hunt, Thomas C., 50
Hunt, William, 515
Hunt, William H., 51
Hunter, Benjamin W., 208
Hunter, Hogan, 302
Hunter, John E., 241
Hunter, John G., 208
Hunter, John M., 208
Huntsinger, Noah, 252
Huntsinger, Toliver, 252
Huntsinger, William, 241
Hurdle, Elisha N., 443
Hurley. See also Henley
Hurley, Alexander F., 418
Hurley, Calvin, 432
Hurlocker, Monroe, 422
Hurlocker, Simeon, 506
Hurt, James R., 34
Huske, James Will, 428
Huskins, Alex, 252
Huss, Jacob, 133
Hussey, John E., 302
Hutchens, John C., 220
Hutchinson, David W., 133
Hutchinson, Francis A., 473
Hutchison, William E., 473
Hutson. See Hudson
Hyatt, Jesse Preston, 443
Hyden, W. H., 241
Hyder, William H., 158

I

Icenhour. *See* Isenhour
Ikener, Ward, 346
Ingram, Isaac, 191
Ingram, James R., 515
Ingram, Nathan, 192
Inman, Floyd H., 325
Inman, Henry W., 325
Inman, Jesse, 346
Irby, J. R., Jr., 51
Irvin. *See also* Ervin
Irvin, A. H., 51
Irvin, J. J., 51
Irwin. *See* Ervin
Isenhour, Henry W., 422
Isom, Spencer, 450
Israel, John, 325
Israel, Wright, 336
Ivey. *See also* Ivy
Ivey, Archibald, 169
Ivey, Arren, 169
Ivey, Elijah, 392
Ivey, Enoch, 169
Ivey, Henry, 169
Ivey, Hugh R., 325
Ivey, Kader, 169
Ivey, Kibben, 169
Ivey, Oliver McKay, 169
Ivey, William Berry, 169
Ivey, Zephanias, 170
Ivor Station, Virginia, 9, 266
Ivy. *See also* Ivey
Ivy, Isaac T., 506

J

Jackson, Alfred, 443
Jackson, Allen T., 263, 373
Jackson, Almon T., 373
Jackson, Andrew, 133
Jackson, Bryant B., 373
Jackson, Drury S., 133
Jackson, Gabriel, 34
Jackson, George W., 450
Jackson, James E., 373
Jackson, James W., 374
Jackson, John R., 386
Jackson, John W., 374
Jackson, Joseph G., 293
Jackson, Lewis, 386
Jackson, Micajah C., 432
Jackson, Monk L., 386
Jackson, Ransom, 374
Jackson, Solomon L., 133
Jackson, Thomas, 386
Jackson, Thomas J., 4-8
Jackson, W. H., 386

Jackson, Young S., 374
Jackson, North Carolina, 10
James, David Hinton, 302
James, Elisha, 76
James, Francis A., 34
James, Godfrey, 76
James, John J., 302
James, Joseph T., 386
James, Kenneth, 302
James, Philip A., 416, 450
James, Robinson C., 299
James, Thomas A., 72
James, William L., 29, 34
James Island, Charleston, South
  Carolina, 261-262
James River, Virginia, 1-3,
  13-15, 140-141, 266-267,
  270-272, 393-394, 408-409, 411
Jamison, Emory, 84
Jammer, G., 257
Jarman. *See* German
Jarratt's Station, Virginia, 13,
  411
Jarrell. *See also* Jerrald
Jarrell, Adam, 220
Jarrell, Dock J., 220
Jarvis, Martin, 241
Jasser. *See also* Jester
Jasser, D., 200
Jenkins, Alfred L., 76
Jenkins, Elias, 170
Jenkins, Henry P., 170
Jenkins, Irvin, 170
Jenkins, John, 252
Jenkins, John T., 110
Jenkins, John W., 170
Jenkins, Levi, 252
Jenkins, Lewis, 170
Jenkins, William, 252
Jenkins, William B., 163
Jenkins, William M., 121
Jennings, Henry, 474
Jennings, Pressley B., 474
Jennings, Samuel, 515
Jennings, Thomas, 515
Jenrette, John H., 346
Jericho Ford, Virginia, 407
Jernigan, Delancy Allen, 359
Jernigan, Jesse L., 192
Jernigan, Joseph Martin, 230
Jernigan, Keder, 181
Jernigan, L. M., 192
Jernigan, Louis, 459
Jernigan, Willis, 346
Jerrald. *See also* Jarrell
Jerrald, Absalom, 432
Jerrald, William B., 432
Jessup, William S., 374
Jester. *See also* Jasser

Jester, Alexander Z., 451
Jetersville, Virginia, 24, 413
Jetton, Charles P., 133
Jetton, George M., 133
Jillwan, W., 181
_____, Jim, 392
Johnson. *See also* Johnston
Johnson, A. L., 192
Johnson, A. T., 133
Johnson, Aaron, 220
Johnson, Alex M., 374
Johnson, Alexander, Jr., 67
Johnson, Alexander, Sr., 67
Johnson, Andy J., 252
Johnson, Archibald McGregor,
  313
Johnson, Bushrod R., 14-16, 22,
  267, 270
Johnson, C., 133
Johnson, Curtis, 181
Johnson, Daniel J., 84
Johnson, David, 474
Johnson, David Clark, 386
Johnson, E. A., 231
Johnson, George A., 387
Johnson, Haywood H., 181
Johnson, Hezekiah W., 220
Johnson, Isham H., 459
Johnson, J. J., 133
Johnson, James A., 84
Johnson, James F., 474
Johnson, Jesse B., 515
Johnson, John A., 133, 515
Johnson, John J., 459
Johnson, John M., 325
Johnson, M. B., 181
Johnson, Marion, 181
Johnson, Mitchell, 293
Johnson, Nathan, 181
Johnson, R., 220
Johnson, Richard, 374
Johnson, Sandy, 67
Johnson, Thomas, 192
Johnson, William, 34
Johnson, William L., 459
Johnson, William M. H., 515
Johnson, Willis, 200
Johnston. *See also* Johnson
Johnston, David, 208
Johnston, George W., 58
Johnston, Joseph E., 21, 23,
  145-148, 273-275, 412-413
Johnston, Robert Allison, 422
Johnston, Robert W., Jr., 422
Johnston, Robert Wilson, Sr.,
  422
Johnston, William, 58
Joiner. *See* Joyner
Jolly, Daniel Jasper, 346

Jolly, Hugh J., 336
Jolly, Jesse R., 346
Jones, Alvi, 336
Jones, Alvis, 432
Jones, Amos, 432
Jones, Bartley, 432
Jones, Bedford, 122, 158
Jones, Bryant, 374
Jones, Calvin, 158, 283
Jones, Claudius B., 181
Jones, Daniel, 374
Jones, David D., 374
Jones, David H., 192
Jones, David J., 359
Jones, Doctor T., 231
Jones, Elbert, 122
Jones, Elbert W., 474
Jones, Elkin D., 67
Jones, Evlin H., 122
Jones, G. W., 122
Jones, George T., 197
Jones, George W., 192
Jones, Hayes, 374
Jones, Hugh, 459
Jones, Irvin G., 374
Jones, James, 200, 302, 374
Jones, James T., 158
Jones, James W., 359
Jones, Jason, 192
Jones, Jeptha A., 122
Jones, Jesse, 170
Jones, Jesse B., 336
Jones, John Calvin, 182
Jones, John T., 400, 402, 516
Jones, John Troy, 182
Jones, Jonas, 302
Jones, Joshua, 443
Jones, Josiah F., 122
Jones, Julius T., 122
Jones, Levi, 201
Jones, Lewis R., 302
Jones, Milton H., 122
Jones, Nathan J., 302
Jones, Nehemiah H., 170
Jones, Pinkney Lafayette, 122
Jones, Robert, 158, 283
Jones, Robert Y., 241
Jones, Samuel J., 252
Jones, Simon P., 516
Jones, Stephen, 293
Jones, Thomas D., 375
Jones, William, 122, 220, 293, 302
Jones, William Benton, 182
Jones, William H., 182, 433
Jones, William L., 34
Jones, Wilson, 122
Jones' Farm, Virginia, 19, 411
Jordan, Edward M., 443

Jordan, Elias Alexander, 474
Jordan, Haywood, 387
Jordan, James Ervin, 387
Jordan, James M., 34
Jordan, James S., 58
Jordan, P. C., 76
Jordan, Richard, 443
Jordan, S. H., 516
Jordan, William Robb, 387
Jordan, William W., 159
Journegan. See Jernigan
Joyner, Addison M., 423
Joyner, David, 387
Joyner, George W., 336
Joyner, John, 474
Joyner, Lewis, 516
Joyner, Meredith, 337
Joyner, Robert T., 359
Joyner, William B., 423
Joyner's Ford, Virginia, 394
Justice, T. L., 252
Justice, William A., 34

K

Kale. See also Kyle
Kale, Ephraim, 122
Kale, Sidney, 122
Kale, Thomas J., 122
Kanipe, Henry, 134
Kanipe, John, 97
Kearnes, Isaac, 433
Kearnes, Thomas S., 433
Keathley. See also Ketchie
Keathley, Archelaus, 302
Keathley, Elisha Herring, 303
Keathly, Lewis, 303
Keen, Wiley, 201
Keenan, David G., 84
Keener. See also Keeter, Keever
Keener, Cephas, 496
Keener, David A., 496
Keeter. See also Keener, Keever
Keeter, James A., 220
Keeter, William H., 220
Keever. See also Keener, Keeter
Keever, Andrew, 123
Keever, David A., 496
Keever, Thomas, 496
Kellahan. See also Kellihan
Kellahan, Orren, 283, 359
Kelley. See Kelly
Kellihan. See also Kellahan
Kellihan, Pinkney Purdie, 359
Kelly, Archibald A., 208
Kelly, Archibald C., 67
Kelly, Benjamin, 208
Kelly, H. B., 67

Kelly, H. M., 208
Kelly, Henry, 208
Kelly, Hugh, 208
Kelly, J. David, 208
Kelly, James Oscar Abner, 204
Kelly, John, 459
Kelly, John B., 208
Kelly, John R., 354
Kelly, Joseph D., 151, 208
Kelly, O. W., 208
Kelly, Roderick, 208
Kelly, Spencer, 208
Kelly, Stephen, 209
Kelly, Thomas M., 151, 209
Kelly, William Joseph, 151, 209
Kelly's Ford, Virginia, 404
Kenan. See Keenan
Kenansville, North Carolina, 9
Kendall, Julius A., 506
Kenerly. See Kennerly
Kenier, John Right, 84
Kenier, William, 84
Kennedy, Bright, 201
Kennedy, C. A., 241
Kennedy, J. T., 144
Kennedy, J. W., 123
Kennedy, James H., 182
Kennedy, Jesse Thomas, 283
Kennedy, John A., 67
Kennedy, John Bunyan, 182
Kennedy, John R., 231
Kennedy, Neill, 67
Kennedy, William M., 459
Kennerly, E. William, 76
Kenon. See Kinion
Kent, Robert, 347
Kern. See also Corn
Kern, Daniel, Jr., 58
Kernegay, James H., 433
Kerr, J. A., 85
Kerr, James, 85
Kerr, Milton, 283
Kerr, Samuel, 85
Kerr, William D., 283
Kershaw, Joseph B., 268, 408
Kester, John, 34
Ketcham. See Ketchum
Ketchie. See also Keathley
Ketchie, Noah, 59
Ketchum, David W., 276, 341
Ketchum, James F., 347
Ketner, John, 423
Ketner, John P., 423
Keyser. See Kiser
Keziah, James H., 423
Kidds, W. Sidney, 485
Kiger, Adam, 516
Kilby, Henry G., 474
Kilby, James C., 474

Kilby, John H., 474
Kilby, John J., 474
Kilby, Samuel, 474
Kilby, William J., 474
Kilby, William N., 474
Kimmy, James M., 303
Kimrey, Manlove, 506
Kincaid, James M., 480
Kindall, J. A., 506
King, Alexander, 485
King, Christopher C., 347
King, D. C., 192
King, George G., 192
King, James, 433
King, Marsden, 347
King, Warren D., 182
King, William, 220
Kings Mountain Tigers, 90
King's School House, Virginia, 2
Kinion, Jacob, 283
Kinlaw, Oliver, 283
Kinlaw, Pinkney G., 313
Kinston, North Carolina, 9-10, 12-13, 142-143, 258-259, 266, 273, 393, 399
Kirby, Wiley L., 43
Kirk, George E., 506
Kirk, James C., 506
Kirk, Parham S., 506
Kirk, William A., 506
Kirkland, William W., 148, 404-407, 409
Kirkpatrick, Silas A., 85
Kirksey, Jackson W., 123
Kirksey, William F., 123
Kiser, William H., 110
Kittner. See Ketner
Kizer. See Kiser
Knight, Cleveland, 110
Knight, James L., 209
Knight, John L., 209
Knott. See also Knotts, Nott
Knott, Jesse Charles, 451
Knotts. See also Knott, Nott
Knotts, James G., 423
Knowles, Marion, 110
Knowles, Stephen, 347
Koon, L., 220
Koone, Calvin, 220
Koone, Dewalt, 220
Koone, Elisha, 220
Koone, James, 220
Kornegay. See Kernegay
Krause. See also Crouse
Krause, Samuel A., 451
Krider, Charles Cornelius, 55
Kriminger, Thomas C., 423
Kyle. See also Kale
Kyle, Jesse Kneeder, 428

Kyle, William Emmett, 428

L

Lackey. See also Leaky, Leckie, Luckey, Lucky
Lackey, David, 134
Lackey, J. A., 97
LaGrange, North Carolina, 393
Laland, Edward, 375
Lamb, Alexander, 170
Lamb, Barnabas, 170
Lamb, Hugh, 170
Lamb, Isham, 170
Lamb, McIntyre, 170
Lamb, Michael, 170
Lamb, Peter, 325
Lamb, William H. H., 433
Lambert, Eli, 67
Landers, Isaac, 451
Landers, John F., 451
Landers, Zachariah J., 451
Lane, Joseph C., 325
Lane, Thomas, 474
Lane, William, 175
Laney. See also Lundy
Laney, John S., 496
Langdon, E. H., 192
Langdon, J. H., 192
Langdon, Jacob M., 192
Langdon, Zachariah, 134
Langly, Nathan, 201
Langston, David, 201
Lanier, Bryant, 293
Lanier, David, 293
Lanier, Hosea F., 303
Lanier, J. T., 506
Lanier, Joseph J., 303
Lanier, Stephen, 294
Lansford. See Lunsford
Largin, Joseph A., 220
Lashley, John L., 209
Lassiter, Allen A., 443
Lassiter, H. C., 85
Lassiter, Henry E., 443
Lassiter, Josiah, 443
Lassiter, Reuben B., 444
Lassiter, Richard H., 444
Latham. See also Layton
Latham, Norfleet Franklin, 201
Latta, Adam G., 347
Latta, John C., 268
Latta, John R., 276
Lattimore, Daniel D., 46
Lattimore, John L., 51
Laughlin. See Loflin
Laurence. See also Lawrence, Lowrance

Laurence, Joseph T., 209
Lawhorn, John H., 283
Lawing, John M., 496
Lawing, William A., 496
Lawrence. See also Laurence, Lowrance
Lawrence, D. K., 209
Lawrence, John A., 110
Lawrence, William J. H., 347
Lawson, James W., 451
Lawson, Jesse, 347
Lawson, W. D., 170
Lay. See also Loy
Lay, A. S., 110
Lay, John C., 110
Lay, N. J., 138
Lay, W. J., 110
Layton. See also Latham
Layton, Isaac W., 387
Layton, Sherwood, 387
Lea. See also Lee
Lea, Addisen, 159
Lea, Calvin, 159
Lea, James H., 159
Lea, John B., 159
Lea, S. M., 159
Lea, W. F., 159
Lea, William A., 159
Leaky. See also Lackey, Leckie, Luckey, Lucky
Leaky, J. S., 34
Leaman, James D., 451
Leckie. See also Lackey, Leaky, Luckey, Lucky
Leckie, John H., 76
Ledbetter, A. B., 252
Ledbetter, Andrew, 252
Ledbetter, Jonathan, 253
Ledbetter, William T., 375
Ledford, Daniel H., 253
Ledford, Frederick, 253
Ledford, J. A., 253
Ledford, James E., 134
Ledford, Jeff C., 134
Ledford, William, 51
Ledford, William F., 516
Ledwell, Jason, 433
Ledwell, John W., 433
Ledwell, Thomas, 433
Ledwell, Thomas W., 433
Lee. See also Lea
Lee, Asa C., 325
Lee, B. R., 192
Lee, David L., 325
Lee, Edward, 192
Lee, Erasmus, 387
Lee, Fitzhugh, 24-25, 268, 408, 413-414
Lee, H. C., 260, 395-396

Lee, Isaac, 444
Lee, J. T., 182
Lee, J. W., 193
Lee, James, 171, 193
Lee, James L., 325
Lee, James S., 123
Lee, Jerry A., 193
Lee, Jesse, 325
Lee, John, Jr., 193
Lee, John B., 387
Lee, John I., 182
Lee, John J., 193
Lee, John Walker, 241
Lee, Marion Washington, 182
Lee, Robert E., 2, 4-6, 8-10,
    13-15, 18, 21-25, 148, 268-272,
    399-401, 403-410, 412-414
Lee, Robert G., 123
Lee, Sir William, 387
Lee, William, 497
Lee, William Bizzell, 303
Lee, William H., 193
Lee, William O., 325
Lee, William R., 375
Lee, Young J., 188
Leeper. See also Luper
Leeper, Andrew, 110
Leesburg, Virginia, 4
Leggett, George W., 313
Leggett, Robert, 171
Leggett, William, 171
Leggett, Wright, 171
Lenhardt. See also Leonhardt
Lenhardt, Jacob N., 134
Lenhardt, John W., 134
Lenhardt, Joseph, 134
Lenhardt, Lawrence K., 110
Lennon, Ezra, 360
Lennon, George W., 360
Lennon, John C., 360
Lennon, John Cale, 354
Lennon, John P., 347
Lennon, Jonathan, 360
Lentz, Caleb A., 59
Lentz, Eli Crawford, 29, 59
Leonard, Felix W., 51
Leonard, Franklin J., 134
Leonard, Ransom, 139
Leonhardt. See also Lenhardt
Leonhardt, Calvin, 134
Lett, William D., 209
Lewallen, John, 433
Lewis, Alfred, 284
Lewis, Calvin B., 433
Lewis, Charles Rufus, 241
Lewis, Dawson, 171
Lewis, Dwight W., 171
Lewis, Henry P., 171
Lewis, Hillsman, 284

Lewis, James, 34
Lewis, John H., 171
Lewis, John P., 171
Lewis, McThomas, 284
Lewis, Manuel, 497
Lewis, Nelson L., 76
Lewis, Warren A., 171
Lewis, William E., 201
Lieupo, John, 313
Ligon, William E., 451
Lilley, John W., 485
Lillington, North Carolina, 225
Lilly, Robert N., 506
Lilly, Samuel S., 502
Lilly, William H., 416
Linback, W. R., 313
Lincoln, Abraham, 6-7, 141
Lindsay, Thomas Watkin, 127
Linebarger. See also Lineberger
Linebarger, Frederick H., 485
Lineberger. See also Linebarger
Lineberger, James Wellington,
    103
Lineberger, John F., 103
Lineberger, Lewis M., 110
Lineberger, R. A., 110
Lineberger, W. C., 111
Lineberger, W. V., 111
Linhardt. See Lenhardt
Link, James M., 59
Linn. See also Lynn
Linn, Moses, 423
Lipe, Daniel M., 423
Lippitt, James Wright, 340
Lippitt, Thomas B., 341
Lisk, Robinson, 459
Litten. See Litton
Little. See also Lytle
Little, Benjamin F., 397-399,
    415, 454
Little, Duncan, 313
Little, Gilbert G., 313
Little, James A., 313
Little, John F., 485
Little, Nathan, 360
Little, Robert F., 313
Little, Samuel C., 485
Little, Thomas, 423
Little, William, 485
Littlejohn, Francis F., 253
Littlejohn, William Herbert, 279
Littler, Jeremiah, 521
Little Round Top, Gettysburg,
    Pennsylvania, 401
Littleton, Enoch A. J., 506
Littleton, James R., 506
Litton, A. Jackson, 123
Litton, Elcanah C., 123
Litton, Elijah, 123

Litton, Isaac, 134
Livengood, Solomon, 516
Livingston, Peter, 313
Lock, Stephen, 337
Lockamy, Aaron, 375
Lockman, John, 485
Locuss, James A., 337
Loflin, John, 433
Loftin, Langdon A., 497
Loftin, Marcus Lafayette, 497
Loftis, John B., 159
Loftis, W. M., 159
Lofton, James Franklin, 123
Logan, Joseph C., 242
Logan, Reuben F., 215
Lollar, Thomas D., 253
London, John R., 27, 51
London, William T., 201
Lonergan, Patrick, 111
Long, Daniel M., 347
Long, Francis M., 220
Long, I. I., 67
Long, James G., 433
Long, John A., 253
Long, John J., 159
Long, Lorenzo Dow, 360
Long, R. J., 97
Long, Stephen M., 159
Long, Thomas J., 215
Long, Watson, 242
Long, William L., 221
Long, William M., 159
Long, William T., 123
Long, Z. T., 159
Long Island, Charleston, South
    Carolina, 265
Longstreet, James, 4-8, 15,
    24-25, 399, 401, 404-407,
    413-414
Loudoun Heights, Virginia, 4
Louis. See Lewis
Love. See also Lowe
Love, Andrew J., 103
Love, Edmond, 67
Love, John A., 111
Love, Richard A., 68
Lovelace, Cicero, 253
Lovelace, J. L., 242
Lovitt, Aldridge, 171
Lovitt, Benjamin, 171
Lovitt, Doson, 171
Lovitt, Joel, 171
Lovitt, John, 171
Lovitt, Mizel, 171
Lovitt, William, 172
Lowder, Archibald C., 506
Lowder, Daniel, 506
Lowder, George William, Jr.,
    507

Lowder, William P., 507
Lowdermilk, Reuben, 433
Lowe. *See also* Love
Lowe, Daniel, 459
Lowe, Franklin, 497
Lowe, Isaac, 459
Lowe, John, 134
Lowe, John A., 134
Lowe, Marcus, 134
Lowery. *See also* Lowrey
Lowery, William, 97
Lowrance. *See also* Laurence, Lawrence
Lowrance, Nerius Clinton, 123
Lowrance, Sidney Nelson, 123
Lowrey. *See also* Lowery
Lowrey, Alex W., 34
Loy. *See also* Lay
Loy, William M., 159
Lucas, William, 193
Luckey. *See also* Lackey, Leaky, Leckie, Lucky
Luckey, John A., 76
Lucky. *See also* Lackey, Leaky, Leckie, Luckey
Lucky, Archibald C., 485
Lucky, David, 486
Lucky, John, 486
Ludwick, Alfred F., 59
Ludwig, Thomas Benton Stanhope, 423
Lumberton, North Carolina, 163, 319, 331
Lumsden, William McK., 313
Lunceford. *See also* Lunsford
Lunceford, Aris, 459
Lunceford, Robert Darius, 175
Lundy. *See also* Laney
Lundy, Joseph A., 474
Lundy, Zebedee Freeland, 474
Lunsford. *See also* Lunceford
Lunsford, Allen H., 153
Luper. *See also* Leeper
Luper, Theophilus H., 516
Luther, Barney R., 434
Luther, Collier, 434
Luther, Franklin, 434
Luther, George W., 209
Lyerly, Isaac, 59
Lyerly, Julius A., 59
Lynch, Ephraim Milton, 497
Lynch, William A., 182
Lynchburg, Virginia, 24, 413
Lyndon, Josiah W., 434
Lynn. *See also* Linn
Lynn, S. M., 97
Lyons, W. D., 277
Lytle. *See also* Little
Lytle, George W., 29

Lytle, M. P., 35
Lytle, Thomas Y., 30

M

Mabry. *See* Marbry
Mabury, John T., 134
McAfee, August A., 97
McAfee, LeRoy Mangum, 20, 26
McAllister, A. M., 111
McAllister, Henry B., 29, 85
McAllister, John W., 279
McArthur, Andrew L., 111
McArthur, J. A., 111
McArthur, John T., 294
McArthur, Joseph Allan, 367
McArthur, William A., 294
McAuley, James D., 209
McBrier, John, 253
McBryde, Thomas, 209
McCain, John C., 501
McCall. *See also* McCaul
McCall, John C., 497
McCallister. *See* McAllister
McCallum, Angus, 68
McCallum, Henry H., 314
McCallum, James B., 309
McCanless, David A., 59
McCanless, John D., 59
McCannon, Harvey, 253
McCarn, George W., 59
McCarver, Harvey P., 111
McCarver, J. E., 111
McCaskill, Malcolm, 68
McCaul. *See also* McCall
McCaul, James, 497
McClellan. *See also* McClelland, McLellan, McLelland
McClellan, E. T., 59
McClellan, George B., 1-2, 4-7
McClelland. *See also* McClellan, McLellan, McLelland
McClelland, Thomas, 76
McClelland, William Augustus, 76
McCollins, S., 257
McColskey, Daniel, 360
McCorkle, James M., 415, 507
McCorkle, Richard A., 497
McCormick, Philip B., 326
McCormick, Wesley, 326
McCormick, William, 314
McCorquedale, Angus, 375
McCorquedale, Joel, 375
McCorquedale, Malcolm, 375
McCoy, Daniel M., 35

McCoy, James A., 123
McCraw, James Asberry, 253
McCray. *See* McRae
McCulloch's Avengers, 446
McCullough, Vincent A., 111
McCurrie, H. C., 242
McCurry, J. C., 257
McCurry, Kaja J., 35
McDade, Franklin G., 253
McDade, Spartan, 253
McDaniel, Andrew Hudlow, 242
McDaniel, David, 97
McDaniel, G. E., 242
McDaniel, John W., 60
McDaniel, Lewis, 242
McDaniel, Matthew McBee, 242
McDaniel, Reuben, 242
McDaniel, Thomas, 474
McDermon, H. H., 387
McDonald, Alfred M., 97
McDonald, Archibald C., 375
McDonald, Archibald N., 314
McDonald, Franklin M., 337
McDonald, George P., 314
McDonald, Henry J., 314
McDonald, J. W., 139
McDonald, James Alexander, 314
McDonald, James R., 276, 308
McDonald, John, 314
McDonald, John A., 209
McDonald, John T., 68
McDonald, Kenneth M., 68
McDonald, Malcolm J., 314
McDonald, Martin Robeson, 455
McDonald, Murdoch Sween, 68
McDonald, Randolph J., 68
McDonald, Starling C., 460
McDonald, Stephen J., 135
McDougald, Malcolm A., 314
McDuffie, John W., 460
McDuffie, Murdock, 460
McEachern, Hector, 309
McEachern, Robert J., 308
McEachin, S. M., 242
McEntire. *See also* McIntyre
McEntire, R. M., 51
McFarland, Dugald, 68
McFarland, James R., 326
McFarland, James S., 221
McFarland, John B., 209
McFarland, John M., 35
McFarland, John W., 326
McFarland, William F., 326
McFarland, William M., 209
McGeachy, Alexander Currie, 314
McGeachy, John David, 314
McGee, Albert, 516

McGee, James W., 277, 303
McGee, Joseph, 516
McGee, William, 516
McGill, Alexander D., 97
McGill, T. J., 97
McGill, William O., 97
McGougan, Daniel A., 314
McGougan, Hugh, 314
McGowan, George M., 76
McGrady, John, 475
McGuiness. *See* Magness
McIlwinnin, James, 68
McInnis, Duncan, 68
McInnis, John, 68
McInnis, John D., 507
McInnis, John M., 315
McIntosh, Asa S., 68
McIntosh, William, 486
McIntyre. *See also* McEntire
McIntyre, Dugald, 375
McIntyre, S., 210
McKay. *See also* Mickey
McKay, George A., 315
McKay, Lauchlin L., 460
McKay, William, 460
McKee, Augustus A., 111
McKennis, A., 68
McKennon. *See* McKinnon
McKenzie, Alexander, 375
McKenzie, Robert McK., 387
McKenzie, William M., 278, 315
McKenzie, William W., 367
McKethan, Augustus A., Jr.,
   271, 289, 387
McKethan, Edwin Turner, 382
McKethan, Hector McAllester,
   267, 276, 367
McKinnie. *See also* McKinny
McKinnie, John L., 231
McKinnon, Alexander, 460
McKinnon, John A., 68
McKinnon, Lauchlin C., 460
McKinny. *See also* McKinnie
McKinny, Henry, Jr., 35
McKinny, Henry, Sr., 35
McKinny, Joseph, 35
McKinny, Sampson, 35
McKnight, John W., 516
McKolsky. *See* McColskey
McLane. *See also* McLean
McLane, Daniel, 460
McLaws, Lafayette, 4-5, 145,
   147-148
McLean. *See also* McLane
McLean, Alexander, 326
McLean, Angus, 375
McLean, Archibald S., 326
McLean, Daniel, 315
McLean, E. C., 111

McLean, Eli, 303
McLean, Hector R., 326
McLean, Hugh, 210
McLean, John, 231
McLean, John A., 315
McLean, John Craig, 29, 111
McLean, John Peabody, 226
McLean, Kenneth, 68
McLean, Martin, 315
McLean, Neill B., 337
McLean, Weston G., 326
McLellan. *See also* McClellan,
   McClelland, McLelland
McLellan, Daniel B., 337
McLellan, Daniel G., 375
McLellan, William B., 337
McLelland. *See also* McClellan,
   McClelland, McLellan
McLelland, Isaac, 124
McLendon, Benjamin, 460
McLendon, Joel, 460
McLendon, Zachariah, 460
McLeod, William A., 326
McLester, Silas M., 507
McMeanes, Jonathan, 376
McMercer, Saul, 315
McMillan, Archibald, 69
McMillan, Daniel A., 376
McMillan, Daniel J., 315
McMillan, George Delaney, 315
McMillan, Hector J., 315
McMillan, John W., 516
McMillan, Malcolm, 315
McMillan, Neill, 376
McMillan, Neill A., 315
McMillan, William Dougald,
   277, 387
McMillan, William James, 315
McNair, E. A., 111
McNair, John A., 460
McNair, William, 460
McNatt, Edward, 69
McNeill, Alexander, 210
McNeill, Andrew J., 210
McNeill, Emory D., 326
McNeill, James A., 315
McNeill, James S., 326
McNeill, John, Jr., 210
McNeill, John, Sr., 210
McNeill, John A., 210
McNeill, Neill, 210
McNeill, Neill A., 210
McNeill, Torquill, 210
McPaul, Timothy D., 315
McPhail, Dougald, 376
McPhail, Dougle A., 231
McPhail, George Vincent, 231
McPhail, John L., 231
McPhalter, Alex, 284

McPhatter, Alexander S., 172
McPhaul. *See* McPaul
McPherson, John A., 347
McPherson, Joshua, 347
McQuaig, W. D., 139
McRae, John S., 231
McRae, Malcolm L., 316
McRae, Malcolm W., 316
McRae, Peter P., 316
McRae, Roderick S., 316
MacRae, William, 409-411, 413
McRainy, Samuel, 85
McRimmon, Murdock, 316
McRimmon, Neill, 316
McSwain, Samuel O., 98
Maddox, James T., 152, 210
Madison Court House, Virginia,
   7
Magee. *See* McGee
Magness. *See also* Maness,
   Manus
Magness, Judson Jordan, 45
Magness, S. P., 51
Magnolia, North Carolina, 261,
   396
Magruder, John B., 2
Mahone, William, 17-18, 24,
   410-411, 413
Main, Lemuel, 497
Mainor. *See* Maner
Mallard. *See* Millard
Malloy, John Douglas, 308
Malone, John P., 159
Malone, Willis, 316
Malpass, Hanson, 284
Malpass, Owen M., 284
Malpass, Richard T., 284
Malvern Hill, Virginia, 2-3
Maner, James, 460
Maner, William T., 376
Maners, Hammet J., 507
Maness. *See also* Magness,
   Manus
Maness, Bartimeus, 69
Maness, John W., 69
Maness, Shadrack, 69
Mann, Anias, 516
Mann, Benjamin M., 35
Mann, Carney C., 43
Mann, Henry A., 43
Mann, Joseph B., 27
Manner. *See* Maner
Manors, Crayter J., 35
Manors, James B., 35
Mansfield, Joseph, 5
Manson. *See also* Mason
Manson, William L., 85
Manus. *See also* Magness,
   Maness

Manus, Enoch, 434
Marbry, James E., 507
Marks, James A., 43
Marks, Thomas B., 43
Marler. See also Marley
Marler, H. Franklin, 451
Marley. See also Marler,
  Marlow
Marley, John F., 475
Marley, Milton J., 475
Marlow. See also Marley
Marlow, Elijah W., 35
Marlow, Harvey, 475
Marshall, James A., 159
Marshall, James Keith, 393,
  402, 415
Marshall, Matthew, 451
Marshall, Richard, 451
Marshall, W. Clark, 124
Marshburn. See also Mashburn
Marshburn, J. S., 210
Martin, Bryan, 51
Martin, Ezekiel, 507
Martin, James G., 143, 393-394
Martin, James T., 516
Martin, John T., 517
Martin, Robert H., 327
Martin, William D., 111
Martin, William K., 461
Martin, William O. K., 517
Martinsburg, West Virginia, 6
Marvin, James, 242
Marye's Heights, Virginia, 7-8
Maryland Heights, Maryland, 4
Mashburn. See also Marshburn
Mashburn, Baxter, 35
Mashburn, J. H., 221
Mask, Marion, 60
Mason. See also Manson
Mason, Daniel A., 231
Mason, E., 76
Mason, James A., 507
Mason, John H., 461
Mason, Levi, 316
Mason, William D. A., 507
Massachusetts Units
  54th Regt. Mass. Infantry,
    263-264
Massagee, Abner, 135
Massengill. See also Massingill
Massengill, Joel Henry, 193
Massey. See also Massie
Massey, Emmit S., 76
Massey, John D., 151, 182, 188
Massey, P. T., 182
Massey, W. G., 112
Massie. See also Massey
Massie, R. B., 51
Massingill. See also Massengill

Massingill, Henry, 193
Massingill, Needham G., 193
Massingill, William R., 193
Matheson, Cornelius, 69
Mathews. See Mathias, Mathis,
  Matthews
Mathias. See also Mathis,
  Matthews
Mathias, John, 475
Mathias, Thomas, 444
Mathis. See also Mathias,
  Matthews
Mathis, Benjamin D., 303
Mathis, Bryan, 303
Mathis, Fleet C., 303
Mathis, Jacob Edward, 303
Mathis, Louis H., 284
Mathis, Luther R., 303
Mathis, Peyton P., 303
Mathis, Richard, 284
Mathis, Thomas B., 303
Matthews. See also Mathias,
  Mathis
Matthews, Riddick O., 444
Matthews, Thomas, 182
Mattox. See Maddox
Mauldin, James, 69
Maultsby, Neill Alexander, 360
Maultsby, Samuel White, Sr.,
  354
Maultsby, Thomas Carver, 360
Mauney. See also Money,
  Mooney
Mauney, Franklin H., 60
Mauney, Lawson, 127
Mauney, Noah H., 135
May. See Moye
Mayfield, John M., 98
Mayfield, Robert N., 135
Mayfield, Thomas, 135
Mayfield, William N., 135
Mayhew, David, 98
Maynard, William Henry, 182
Meacham. See also Mecum,
  Mitcham, Mitchell
Meacham, Daniel H., 461
Meacham, Robert C., 461
Meacham, William L., 461
Meade, George G., 403-404
Meares. See also Myers
Meares, Erasmus D., 360
Meares, James A., 354
Mecklenburg Guards, 79
Mecum. See also Meacham,
  Mitcham
Mecum, Matthew W., 517
Medford, William Riley, 36
Medley, James H., 434
Medley, John, 434

Medlin, Benjamin J., 69
Melton, Alfred, 36
Melton, Atlas D., 507
Melton, David H., 221
Melton, Eben, 507
Melton, Elijah D., 221
Melton, Elijah R., 36
Melton, Jesse G., 221
Melton, John M., 221
Melton, Joseph, 507
Melton, Joseph C., 423
Melton, Joseph G., 221
Melton, Joshua S., 221
Melton, Josiah S., 221
Melton, Philip H., 221
Melton, S. L., 36
Melton, Samuel, 36
Melton, W. Landrum, 36
Melton, William, 221
Melton, Zachariah, 486
Melvin, D. J., 376
Melvin, Robert D., 376
Mendenhall, Cyrus Erastus,
  27-28, 103
Menis, Andrew, 60
Menis, James F., 60
Mercer. See also Messer
Mercer, John Picket, 316
Mercer, John Q., 347
Mercer, Miles V., 316
Mercer, Samuel E., 360
Mercer, William, 347
Merchant's Hope Church,
  Virginia, 141
Merritt, Alexander R., 517
Merritt, Alsa, 304
Merritt, Francis M., 294
Merritt, George W., 294
Merritt, Hiram, 304
Merritt, Hubbard, 304
Merritt, Isaac, 294
Merritt, James A., 347
Merritt, James Thomas, 294
Merritt, Kenan, 294
Merritt, Levi, 304
Merritt, Lewis W., 304
Merritt, Marley, 348
Merritt, Mordecai M., 294
Merritt, Payton, 294
Merritt, Richard, 294
Merritt, Robert, 304
Merritt, Robert Hooks, 304
Merritt, Thomas W., 294
Merritt, William James, 294
Merritt, William M., 348
Messemore, George W., 60
Messer. See also Mercer
Messer, Dushia A., 231
Messer, Whitley, 231

Messick, James J., 434
Michael. *See also* Mitchell
Michael, George W., 423
Michael, John M., 135
Michaux, Daniel M., 508
Mickey. *See also* McKay
Mickey, Lowell P., 517
Mickey, Thomas I., 517
Middle Sound, North Carolina, 261
Milam, Adam, 475
Milam, Thomas C., 475
Millard, Joseph, 253
Mill Creek, North Carolina, 147-148, 274-275
Miller. *See also* Minler
Miller, Alexander M., 60
Miller, Alson, 434
Miller, Aspasia Earl, 242
Miller, Daniel Franklin, 242
Miller, George W., 60
Miller, Harmon, 392
Miller, Henry L., 517
Miller, Isaiah, 77
Miller, James, 60
Miller, James A., 247
Miller, Joseph Mc., 424
Miller, Kerr Boyce, 253
Miller, Levan M., 77
Miller, Robert J., 294
Miller, William H., 304
Miller, William Mash, 434
Miller, William T., 85
Miller, Zachariah H., 327
Millican, Saunders, 348, 360
Millican, William James, 361
Millis, Alonzo, 304
Mills, John, 77
Mills, Joseph D., 304
Milton. *See* Melton
Milwood, John, 253
Mincey, George, 337
Mine Run, Virginia, 404
Minler. *See also* Miller
Minler, W. G., 242
Minton, Joel, 475
Minton, John H., 475
Minton, Purvis, 475
Misenheimer, Caleb, 424
Misenheimer, George A., 424
Misenheimer, James M., 424
Mitcham. *See also* Meacham, Mecum, Mitchell
Mitcham, R. J., 98
Mitchell. *See also* Meacham, Michael, Mitcham
Mitchell, Christopher, 124
Mitchell, Hiram J., 247
Mitchell, Hugh G., 327

Mitchell, John E., 444
Mitchell, R. S., 159
Mitchell, William, 444
Mitchell, William E., 160
Mitchum. *See* Mitcham
Mock, James A., 475
Mode, A. F., 51
Mode, Devaney, 51
Mode, James C., 52
Mode, Joseph T., 52
Modlin. *See* Mauldin
Moffett. *See also* Moffitt
Moffett, J. R., 36
Moffett, William P., 36
Moffitt. *See also* Moffett
Moffitt, James J., 36
Moffitt, John N., 36
Moile, Matthew, 139
Monday. *See* Munday
Monds. *See* Munns
Money. *See also* Mauney, Mooney
Money, J. L., 160
Money, Joseph, 160
Monocacy Junction, Maryland, 4
Monocacy River, Maryland, 4
Monroe. *See also* Munroe
Monroe, Benjamin F., 69
Monroe, Duncan, 376
Monroe, Hugh B., 69
Monroe, James C., 69
Monroe, Levi D., 69
Monroe, Thomas, 376
Monroe, William J., 69
Monteith, G. W., 221
Monteith, John C., 221
Moody, B. Frank, 124
Moody, Richard, 327
Mooney. *See also* Mauney, Money
Mooney, George W., 36
Mooney, James M., 221
Mooney, John, 36
Mooney, Robert J., 36
Moore. *See also* Moose
Moore, Aldridge, 376
Moore, Alexander Davis, 72
Moore, Americus V., 284
Moore, Andrew F., 497
Moore, Andrew J., 254
Moore, Briant, 69
Moore, Charles A., 348
Moore, Charles H., 284
Moore, Francis, 236
Moore, George W., 160
Moore, Green W., 327
Moore, Haywood, 193
Moore, Henry H., 517
Moore, J., 295

Moore, James A., 284, 486
Moore, James M., 486
Moore, John, 135, 160, 193, 376
Moore, John Terrell, 254
Moore, Levi, 193
Moore, Luther W., 284
Moore, R. H., 37
Moore, Richard H., 327
Moore, Thomas McGee, 278, 304
Moore, Walter R., 193
Moore, William, 160
Moore, William H., 461
Moore, William S., 69
Moore, William W., 85
Moore, Willis P., 320
Moore Sharpshooters, 204
Moose. *See also* Moore
Moose, Daniel P., 77
Moose, George, 508
Moose, George H., 77
Moran, Robert S., 150
Morehead City, North Carolina, 10, 266
Morgan, A. F., 242
Morgan, Elijah Merrimon, 242
Morgan, Humphrey P., 221
Morgan, J. F., 222
Morgan, Jackson, 194
Morgan, James, 222
Morgan, Jethro, 222
Morgan, John, 43
Morgan, John D., 37
Morgan, John H., 461
Morgan, John Nathan, 388
Morgan, Kenneth T., 337
Morgan, Martin, 508
Morgan, Porter O., 222
Morris. *See also* Norris
Morris, Abraham, 337
Morris, George W., 242
Morris, Green C., 85
Morris, James, 243
Morris, James M., 337
Morris, John C., 327
Morris, John W., 85
Morris, Joseph B., 243
Morris, Lewis, 452
Morris, Robert, 337, 508
Morris, William, 85
Morrisey, Samuel Bunting, 276
Morris Island, Charleston, South Carolina, 261-262, 265
Morrison, Daniel A., 316
Morrison, Ephraim, 77
Morrison, I. M., 37
Morrison, John A., 215
Morrison, John Wilson, 424
Morrison, Perry M., 222

Morrison, Robert P., 222
Morrison, William C., 77
Morrow. *See also* Murray
Morrow, Alfred, 243
Morrow, David, 243
Morrow, Elbert G., 243
Morrow, Hugh M., 77
Morrow, James, 243
Morrow, McKibbin, 37
Morrow, W. B., 98
Morton. *See also* Moton
Morton, Ezekiel, 508
Morton, John, 52
Morton's Ford, Virginia, 405
Moseley Creek, North Carolina, 9
Moser, E. A., 517
Moser, Emanuel, 517
Moser, John A., 517
Moser, Josiah, 517
Moser, Robert W., 517
Moss. *See also* Muse
Moss, Abner C., 37
Moss, G. W., 124
Moton. *See also* Morton
Moton, R. Andy, 112
Mower, Joseph A., 148, 275
Moye, William E., 201
Moyer, Daniel M., 508
Moyle, William, 60
Mozingo, Calvin, 201
Mozingo, Mark, 201
Muckle, Benjamin, 210
Muldoon, John, 172
Mule Shoe, Virginia, 406-407
Mull, Samuel, 254
Mullinaux, John W., 98
Munday, James D., 486
Munday, Jeremiah F., 486
Munday, William F., 486
Munns, Samuel, 183
Munns, Washington W., 388
Munroe. *See also* Monroe
Munroe, M. L. J., 434
Munroe, Thomas J., 444
Murfreesboro, North Carolina, 10, 13
Murphy. *See also* Murray
Murphy, Hugh N., 388
Murphy, John A., 278, 388
Murphy, William F., 295, 382
Murray. *See also* Morrow, Murphy
Murray, P. G., 434
Murray, Samuel, 284
Murray, W. D., 37
Murrell, John P., 348
Murry. *See* Murray
Muse. *See also* Moss

Muse, John B., 69
Muse, Kindred, 70
Muse, Wesley B., 70
Musslewhite, Abel, 316
Musslewhite, Archibald, 316
Musslewhite, Augustus, 316
Musslewhite, Calvin, 317
Musslewhite, Jacob, 317
Musslewhite, John R., 337
Musslewhite, Lewis, 317
Musslewhite, Nathan, 317
Musslewhite, Randall, 317
Musslewhite, Rhodes, 337
Musslewhite, Wiley M., 337
Myers. *See also* Meares
Myers, Aderson C., 393-396, 398, 452

N

Nabors, Asbury H., 215
Nance. *See also* Nantz
Nance, Albert, 497
Nance, Albert C., 486
Nance, Clabern, 497
Nance, James, 497
Nance, Lawson, 497
Nance, Levi, 498
Nance, Vinsen, 98
Nance, Wilborn, 475
Nance, William, 498
Nanney, Amos, 222
Nanney, Coburn, 222
Nanney, George Washington, 243
Nanney, William, 222
Nanny, Martin, 86
Nantz. *See also* Nance
Nantz, D. L., 498
Nash, Abraham, 60
Nash, Wylie A., 60
Nashville, 258
Neagle, J. E., 103
Neagle, John L., 28, 112
Neal. *See also* Neel, Neil
Neal, Elisha M., 43
Neal, J. C., 98
Neal, J. W., 98
Neal, Joseph Camp, 30
Neal, Joseph Grayson, 37
Neal, Larkin M., 86
Neal, William A., 43
Nealy. *See also* Neely
Nealy, John Allen, 348
Neel. *See also* Neal, Neil
Neel, Samuel R., 80
Neel, Thomas W., 86
Neel, William B., 86

Neely. *See also* Nealy
Neely, William Amzie, 86
Neil. *See also* Neal, Neel
Neil, Charles, 139
Nelson, Isaac H., 447
Nelson, James, 434
Nelson, John H., 452
Nelson, Morris, 434
Nelson, Neill L. McF., 317
Nelson, William A., 348
Nesbitt, Benjamin, 37
Nesbitt, Gibson R., 424
Neuse River, North Carolina, 10-13, 142, 265-266, 395-397
New Bern, North Carolina, 9-11, 13, 142-144, 258-261, 265-266, 273, 393, 395-399
Newby, Thomas, 444
Newell, William A., 86
Newman, Joseph E., 517
Newsom, George W., 517
Newton, William B., 348
Nichols, John Hamer, 461
Nicholson. *See also* Nixon
Nicholson, Peter C., 27
Nifong, Wylie, 60
Niven, David, 210
Nix, Enoch P., 222
Nix, William F., 222
Nixon. *See also* Nicholson
Nixon, Albert M., 486
Nixon, Archibald, 486
Nixon, Franklin, 486
Nixon, George, 487
Nixon, James Turner, 487
Nixon, John Monroe, 487
Nixon, Sidney G., 487
Noah, Milus A., 61
Nobles, Archibald, 361
Nobles, Averitt, 348
Nobles, Emanuel, 348
Nobles, James Irvin, 361
Nobles, John Crawford, 348
Nodine, Charles C., 254
Nodine, Thomas, 254
Noggle, Sylvanus J., 98
Nolen, John, 222
Norfolk and Petersburg Railroad, 9, 394
Norman, I. F., 150
Norman, W. A., 337
Norman, Willis P., 337
Norment, William Stokes, 332
Norris. *See also* Morris
Norris, Amos, 194
Norris, Daniel M., 361
Norris, Elcaney, 348
Norris, Elijah, 160
Norris, Ephraim, 160

Norris, Jenkins, 361
Norris, John S., 160
Norris, Solomon, 349
Norris, William, 160
Norris, William Indy, 349
Norris, William J., 349, 376
North Anna River, Virginia, 407
North Carolina Units
  1st Regt. N.C. Artillery. See
    10th Regt. N.C. State Troops
  1st Regt. N.C. Volunteers. See
    11th Regt. N.C. Troops
  4th Regt. N.C. Cavalry. See
    59th Regt. N.C. Troops
  5th Regt. N.C. Volunteers. See
    15th Regt. N.C. Troops
  7th Regt. N.C. Junior
    Reserves. See 77th Regt.
    N.C. Troops
  8th Regt. N.C. State Troops,
    259, 264-265, 268, 271, 395
  10th Bn. N.C. Heavy Artillery,
    145, 148
  10th Regt. N.C. State Troops,
    1
  11th Regt. N.C. Troops, 396,
    400, 411
  13th Bn. N.C. Infantry, 258
  14th Regt. N.C. Volunteers.
    See 24th Regt. N.C. Troops
  15th Regt. N.C. Troops, 409
  17th Regt. N.C. Troops (2nd
    Organization), 143, 148
  24th Regt. N.C. Troops, 1-2,
    4, 9-10, 14, 16, 23
  25th Regt. N.C. Troops, 1-2,
    4, 9, 23
  26th Regt. N.C. Troops, 1-2,
    4, 394, 400
  27th Regt. N.C. Troops, 4
  31st Regt. N.C. Troops, 259,
    262, 264, 267-268
  32nd Regt. N.C. Troops, 141
  35th Regt. N.C. Troops, 1-2,
    4, 9-10, 140
  42nd Regt. N.C. Troops, 143,
    148
  43rd Regt. N.C. Troops, 140
  44th Regt. N.C. Troops, 393,
    404, 411
  45th Regt. N.C. Troops, 140
  47th Regt. N.C. Troops, 393,
    400
  48th Regt. N.C. Troops, 1, 4
  49th Regt. N.C. Troops, 1-25
  50th Regt. N.C. Troops,
    140-148
  51st Regt. N.C. Troops,
    258-275, 395

  52nd Regt. N.C. Troops,
    259-260, 393-414
  53rd Regt. N.C. Troops, 141
  56th Regt. N.C. Troops, 9,
    14-15, 23
  59th Regt. N.C. Troops, 394
  60th Regt. N.C. Troops, 145
  61st Regt. N.C. Troops, 259,
    269, 271
  66th Regt. N.C. Troops, 148
  77th Regt. N.C. Troops, 145
Northeast Cape Fear River,
  North Carolina, 273
Norton, Augustus, 172
Norton, Joshua, 172
Norton, Nicholas A., 77
Norville. See also Nowell
Norville, Samuel, 243
Norville, William A., 243
Norwood, James T., 487
Norwood, Thomas S., 487
Nott. See also Knott, Knotts,
  Nutt
Nott, William J., 376
Nottoway River, Virginia, 22
Nowell. See also Norville
Nowell, James A., 183
Null, George, 124
Nunnery, Henry, 377
Nunnery, John, 377
Nunnery, William, 377
Nutt. See also Nott
Nutt, William Henry, 152, 160,
  172, 231

O

Oates, Thomas M., 112
Oates, William S. A., 98
O'Briant. See also O'Brien
O'Briant, Albert, 153
O'Briant, Alexander, 151, 160
O'Briant, Henry, 160
O'Briant, John, 160
O'Briant, William, 160
O'Brien. See also O'Briant
O'Brien, Dennis, 461
O'Brien, John, 37
O'Daniel, Cornelius M., 112
Odom, Calvin, 361
Odom, John, 361
Odum, Jeremiah, 337
Ogeechee River, Georgia, 145
Oldham, Thomas S., 43
Oldham, Wesley A., 43
Oldham, William E., 43
Oldham, Younger A., 41
Olive, Calvin, 44

Oliver, Alfred C., 210
Oliver, E. M., 183
Oliver, Festus, 201
Oliver, James R., 475
Oliver, John, 210
Oliver, M. T., 210
Oliver, Moses H., 211
Oliver, Willis M., 211
O'Quinn, Alexander, 231
O'Quinn, Burrel B., 231
O'Quinn, William, 424
Orange Court House, Virginia,
  3, 404-405
Orange Plank Road, Virginia,
  405-406
Orange Turnpike, Virginia, 405
Orapeake Guards, 438
Ord, E. O. C., 16-17
Orr, Turley W., 284
Osborne, Jonathan Hudson, 86
Overby, James T., 257
Overcash, Caleb, 135
Overman, John, 201
Overton, Jackson, 317
Owen, Thomas B., 77
Owens, Adam C., 37
Owens, Andrew, 135
Owens, Benjamin P., 444
Owens, Gabriel, 304
Owens, George F., 475
Owens, John C., 476
Owens, Reuben H., 476
Owens, Richard, 254
Owens, Thomas, 254
Owens, William, 435
Owens, William H., 201
Owens, William T., 476
Owensby, Francis M., 98
Oxendine, William, 338

P

Padgett, A. C., 517
Padgett, Barney, 243
Padgett, Hix, 243
Padgett, J. C., 243
Padgett, Leander, 243
Padgett, Mansel, 243
Padgett, Marvill S., 518
Padgett, Morris, 243
Padgett, Noah, 243
Padgett, Tirrel, 244
Padgett, W. L., 244
Page, Bright, 377
Page, David, 338
Page, Elias, 135
Page, Jesse, 377
Page, John, 284

Page, John C., 424
Page, John E., 304
Page, John J., 338
Page, Stephen, 254
Page, Truscan Cheves, 244
Page, W., 295
Page, William, 377
Paine. See Payne
Painter. See also Panter, Panther
Painter, John L., 498
Painter, Pinkney, 498
Palmer, James B., 86
Palmer, William M., 338
Pamlico River, North Carolina, 142-143, 398-399
Pamunkey River, Virginia, 407-408
Pannel. See also Parnel, Pernell
Pannel, J. M., 244
Panter. See also Painter, Panther
Panter, Wyatt, 160
Panther. See also Painter, Panter
Panther, George W., 254
Panther, Joseph, 254
Pardew. See also Perdue
Pardew, Elbert M., 135
Parham, Benjamin F., 518
Parham, Thomas P., 518
Parham, William H., 317, 338
Parish. See also Parrish
Parish, D. M., 435
Parish, David, 70
Parish, J. B., 70
Parker, A. J., 52
Parker, Anthony L., 226
Parker, B. F., 231
Parker, Daniel W., 295
Parker, David W., 439
Parker, Duncan H., 232
Parker, Edward Sanders, 149
Parker, Everett, 327
Parker, George P., 508
Parker, Hosea P., 498
Parker, Isaac, 444
Parker, Jackson, 135
Parker, Jack Wylie, 388
Parker, James, 232
Parker, Jethro W., 444
Parker, John M., 498
Parker, Joseph, 37, 52, 327
Parker, Joseph W., 232
Parker, Larkin Newby, 295
Parker, Nicholas, 295
Parker, Noel, 388
Parker, Redmond, 194
Parker, Richard, 172
Parker, Samuel N., 232
Parker, Seth, 444
Parker, William J., 232

Parker, William L., 278, 295
Parker, Young E., 194
Parker's Store, Virginia, 405
Parks, Marcus A., 415, 465
Parks, Martin G., 476
Parleir, Elbert A., 476
Parleir, George Wesley, 476
Parleir, Jacob J., 465, 501
Parnel. See also Pannel, Pernell
Parnel, Isaac, 304
Parrish. See also Parish
Parrish, James, 194
Parrish, Justice, 183
Parrish, Ransom, 194
Parrish, Richard, 183
Parsons. See also Person
Parsons, Mumford, 461
Partin. See also Parton, Patton
Partin, Benjamin F., 44
Parton. See also Partin, Patton
Parton, John, 222
Pasour, Adam M., 112
Pasour, Andrew, 112
Pasour, F. M., 112
Pasour, John P., 112
Pasour, Joseph A., 112
Pasour, Moses Eli, 112
Patten. See Patton
Patterson. See also Peterson
Patterson, Archibald B., 232
Patterson, Caleb W., 424
Patterson, Calvin, 498
Patterson, D. C., 98
Patterson, James A., 498
Patterson, John A., 70
Patterson, John O., 295
Patterson, John W., 232
Patterson, Joseph Robert Grier, 77
Patterson, Malloy, 317
Patterson, Milen M., 98
Patterson, Pinkney D., 29, 99
Patterson, Robert J., 232
Patterson, Robert M., 317
Patterson, S. Crowder, 99
Patterson, Samuel D., 70
Patterson, W. W., 99
Patterson, William D., 399, 461
Patterson, William J., 295
Patton. See also Batton, Partin, Parton
Patton, John D., 150
Patton, William, 37
Paul, Abraham, 327
Paul, Hector C., 317
Paul, John, 461
Paxton, Samuel L., 86
Payne, Joseph D., 112
Payne, Thomas L., 112

Payseur. See Pasour
Peacock, John, 183
Peal. See Peel
Pearce. See also Pierce
Pearce, Lovett, 435
Pearce, William, 435
Pearson. See also Person
Pearson, B. B., 183
Pearson, J. J., 112
Pearson, W. A., 112
Pearson, William H., 232
Peebles' Farm, Virginia, 411
Pee Dee River, South Carolina, 145
Peedin, Hilbert F., 183
Peel, Mark, 295
Peel, William, 201
Peel, William R., 444
Peele, A. E., 452
Pegram, Jacob Y., 518
Pegram, Joseph E., 518
Pell. See Peel
Pence, Henry, 508
Pence, Noah Franklin, 508
Pender, William D., 400-401
Pendergrass, John, 487
Pendergrass, Michael G., 37
Pendry, John H., 518
Pennington, Jackson, 44
Pennington, William, 201
Penny, John G., 52
Penny, Joseph James, 188
Penny, Thomas, 361
Penny, William, 361
Penny, William J., 361
Pepper, John Kerr, 417, 452
Perdue. See also Pardew
Perdue, Major, 518
Perkins, Henry, 487
Perkins, J. Franklin, 498
Perkins, Leander P., 498
Perkins, Samuel, 435
Pernell. See also Pannel, Parnel
Pernell, Anson B., 338
Perrell. See also Ferrell, Terrell
Perrell, C. S., 172
Perry. See also Berry
Perry, Allan A., 444
Perry, Jacob B., 86
Perry, James, 508
Person. See also Parsons, Pearson
Person, Benjamin T., 201
Petersburg, Virginia, 1-3, 8-10, 12-13, 15, 18-23, 140, 265-267, 269-271, 393-394, 408-413
Petersburg and Weldon Railroad, 13, 18, 270-271, 409-411
Peterson. See also Patterson

Peterson, Henry S., 285
Peterson, John, 327
Peterson, W. S., 304
Petree, Jacob, 518
Pettigrew, James J., 4, 142-143, 259, 394, 396-404
Petty, Charles Q., 26, 102
Petty, James F., 52
Pharris. *See also* Faris, Farris
Pharris, Alexander, 377
Phifer, Edward X., 128
Phifer, Elijah M., 86
Phifer, George L., 27, 127
Philbeck, Amos H., 52
Philbeck, P. H., 52
Philbeck, T. G., 52
Phillips, Absalom, 295
Phillips, Jacob M., 424
Phillips, James, 435
Phillips, Jarmon E., 377
Phillips, Thomas, 285
Pickard, Alvis, 44
Pickett, George E., 10-12, 22-24, 265-266, 401, 412
Pickett, John L., 304
Pickler, John Calhoun, 508
Pickler, John Whitson, 508
Pierce. *See also* Pearce
Pierce, Daniel Gore, 362
Pierce, James, 444
Pierce, John, 86
Pierce, John A., 113
Pierce, John H. C., 417, 476
Pierce, Leonidas M., 86
Pierson. *See* Pearson
Piggott, J. H., 435
Piggott, Simon, 521
Pike, Mark E., 435
Pinkerton, James R., 37
Pinston, W. F., 518
Pintuff, Barney B., 244
Pintuff, Michael P., 244
Pipkin, John E. J., 211
Pipkin, Stephen I., 295
Pipkin, William, 211
Pitman. *See also* Pittman, Putnam
Pitman, Isham, 327
Pitman, James P., 320
Pitman, John, 172
Pitman, Lewis, 172
Pittman. *See also* Pitman, Putnam
Pittman, James B., 338
Pittman, Randolph, 328
Pleasant Home Guards, 126
Pless, Henry J., 424
Plummer, Matthew, 61
Plymouth, North Carolina, 13, 144

Pocotaligo, South Carolina, 145
Poindexter, David, 447
Polk. *See* Pope
Pollard, Benjamin J., 194
Pollard, John W., 183
Pollard, Samuel J., 194
Pollard, W. H., 194
Pollock, Alfred C., 295
Pollock, Luke, 295
Pollocksville, North Carolina, 11-12
Pool. *See also* Poole
Pool, Seth, 461
Pool, Thomas, 285
Pool, William H., 183
Pool, William S., 124
Poole. *See also* Pool
Poole, A. S., 183
Poole, John W., 28
Poole, Perrin P., 152, 183
Poole, S. C., 183
Poole, W. C., 183
Pope, Albert, 37
Pope, David, 124
Pope, Doctor W., 377
Pope, Elkanah, 37
Pope, Franklin G., 38
Pope, I. S., 244
Pope, J. S., 223
Pope, James A., 388
Pope, James D., 377
Pope, James K., 184
Pope, James L., 498
Pope, Jerry, 194
Pope, John R., 435
Pope, John W., 38
Pope, Josiah, 377
Pope, Leroy W., 424
Pope, Louis, 377
Pope, Michael S., 388
Pope, Milton, 388
Pope, Ollen, 388
Pope, Silas, 124
Pope, William Frank, 124
Pope, William P., 377
Pope, Willis H., 320
Poplin, James A., 508
Porter, Caswell, 362
Porter, James A., 285
Porter, James H., 285
Porter, Joseph M., 99
Porter, Malcolm, 378
Porter, Richard, 362
Porter, Robert A., 86
Porter, Samuel L., 86
Porter, Wiley B., 378
Porter, Zenas, 87
Porterfield, David R., 161
Poteat, John W., 424

Poteat, Thomas J., 425
Poteet, Francis M., 38
Potomac River, 4-6, 399, 403
Potter, Benjamin W., 349
Potter, Edward E., 143-144
Potter, Francis W., 150
Potts, John G., 80
Potts, William T., 487
Pouch, John, 257
Powell, Andrew B., 124
Powell, George Tate, 124
Powell, John Eli, 362
Powell, O. D., 172
Powell, Patrick M., 328
Powell, R. James, 461
Powell, Wiley, 295
Powell, William, 295
Powers. *See also* Bowers, Powlas, Powles
Powers, Henry T., 317
Powers, James, 317
Powers, James E., 518
Powers, Jordan, 349
Powers, Michael M., 378
Powers, Thomas J., 378
Powlas. *See also* Powers, Powles
Powlas, Eli, 61
Powlas, Jesse, 61
Powles. *See also* Powers, Powlas
Powles, Henry, 425
Prather, Augustus R., 87
Prather, Silas F., 87
Pratt, Francis Marion, 518
Pratt, Thomas, 518
Pratt, William R., 518
Presnell, H. C., 519
Presnell, James M., 435
Presnell, Stanton, 435
Presnell, William R., 476
Prevatt. *See also* Previtt
Prevatt, Alfred R., 328
Prevatt, Andrew J., 328
Prevatt, Charles, 172
Prevatt, Elias, 328
Prevatt, Henry C., 328
Prevatt, James P., 328
Prevatt, Jordan, 328
Prevatt, Michael, 328
Prevatt, Peter P., 328
Prevatt, William W., 328
Prevatt, Willis P., 329
Previtt. *See also* Prevatt
Previtt, Allen, 87
Prevo, W. Henry B., 285
Price. *See also* Prince
Price, Eden, 304
Price, George L., 184
Price, Gideon, 184
Price, H. G., 184

Price, Joel, 304
Price, John, 476
Price, N. G., 184
Price, Quilla, 184
Price, Smith, 476
Price, William P., 52
Prichard, Henry, 38
Pridgeon, Bryant, 338
Prim, William A., 487
Prince. *See also* Price
Prince, Andrew, 349
Prince, Daniel F., 362
Prince, Samuel W., 362
Prince, Solomon W., 349
Pritchard. *See* Prichard
Privette. *See* Prevatt, Previtt
Proctor, Edward A., 487
Proctor, Rufus, 254
Proctor's Creek, Virginia, 141
Propst, George A., 417
Pruit, P. H., 99
Pugh, William E., 266, 305
Pulliam, James, 194
Purvis, John, 172
Putnam. *See also* Pitman, Pittman
Putnam, A. C., 99, 135
Putnam, D. C., 99
Putnam, E. L., 52
Putnam, Elias W., 99
Putnam, J. H., 8, 99
Putnam, John Berry, 99
Putnam, L. D., 99
Putnam, Martin, 53
Putnam, P. G., 99
Putnam, Samuel, 53
Putnam, W. H., 99
Putnam, William A., 53
Putnam, William Roswell, 99

Q

Queen. *See also* Quinn
Queen, Finley A., 476
Queen, George W., 38
Queen, James, 476
Queen, James A., 498
Queen, Jeremiah M., 38
Queen, Richard, 254
Queen, William, 38
Queen, William N., 223
Queen, William R., 476
Quesenberry, D., 244
Quinn. *See also* Queen
Quinn, Ichabod, 305
Quinn, Thomas F., 113, 285
Quinn, W. F., 113

R

Rabb, William M., 135
Raby, Luke, 444
Rackley. *See also* Ackley, Ratley
Rackley, Joseph R., 285
Rackley, Joshua A., 285
Rackley, Sherman, 295
Rackley, William E., 296
Radford. *See also* Ratchford
Radford, George W., 201
Radford, Rufus W., 202
Radford, Stephen, 202
Ragan. *See* Reagan
Raiford, William N., 378
Rains, John T., 184
Rains, William, 254
Raleigh, North Carolina, 1, 140, 145, 148, 274-275, 393
Ralzamon, Musslewhite, 318
Ramseur, Stephen Dodson, 1, 26
Ramsey, Robert D., 153
Randall, Willis, 502
Randle, William, 509
Randleman. *See also* Rendleman
Randleman, Samuel H., 491
Randolph Guards, 427
Rankin, Ephraim L., 113
Rankin, Lawson Lafayette, 103
Rankin, Wade D., 113
Rankin, Wallace A., 103
Ransom, Arthur, 329
Ransom, Matt W., 9-10, 12-15, 18-20, 22, 24, 270
Ransom, Richard, 519
Ransom, Robert, 1-4, 6-9, 267
Raper, Robinson, 202
Rapidan River, Virginia, 404-405
Rapidan Station, Virginia, 3, 404
Rappahannock Bridge, Virginia, 404
Rappahannock River, Virginia, 7-8, 404
Rasbury, William, 378
Rash. *See also* Rush
Rash, Reuben A., 476
Rash, Zeno Melvin, 476
Ratchford. *See also* Radford
Ratchford, W. A., 113
Ratley. *See also* Rackley
Ratley, Calvin, 338
Ratley, Joseph, 338
Ratley, Richard C., 329
Ratterree, William L., 87
Ratts, Burrell R., 61
Rawles. *See also* Ryals
Rawles, John B., 445

Ray. *See also* Rea, Rhea, Wray
Ray, Brantley M., 44
Ray, Cornelius, 232
Ray, David, 232
Ray, Francis, 44
Ray, James T., 61
Ray, John, 232
Ray, Nelson, 161
Ray, Nivin, 232
Ray, William A., 70
Rayford. *See* Raiford
Rea. *See also* Ray, Rhea, Wray
Rea, David J., 87
Reagan, James L., 487
Real. *See* Reel
Reams' Station, Virginia, 410
Reaves. *See also* Reeves
Reaves, Jesse, 435
Reaves, John, 44
Reaves, John T., 349
Reaves, Robert D., 232
Reaves, Samuel, 476
Reaves, Timothy, 305
Reavis, Andrew H., 476
Redd. *See also* Reed, Reid
Redd, Robert, 445
Redd, Zephaniah W., 349
Redden, Thomas Calvin, 70
Redding, Michael F., 488
Redford. *See* Radford, Raiford
Redman, Franklin, 452
Reed. *See also* Redd, Reid
Reed, Henry S., 211
Reed, James H., 488
Reed, Thomas L., 488
Reedy, William, 519
Reel, Daniel R., 498
Reel, John H., 38
Reep, George, 135
Reeves. *See also* Reaves
Reeves, Joel P., 61
Register, Burrell M., 296
Register, Cullen, 285
Register, George R., 296
Register, James E., 305
Register, John N., 349
Register, Richard J., 305
Register, Robert Marshal, 305
Register, Samuel R., 296
Reid. *See also* Redd, Reed
Reid, Alfred L., 77
Reid, J. B., 99
Reid, Marten, 99
Reid, William N., 87
Rendleman. *See also* Randleman
Rendleman, John M., 498
Renfrow, William Cary, 184
Rentfro, James I., 202
Revells, Andrew H., 435

Revels, Eli, 338
Revels, Henry, 338
Revels, Hinson, 338
Revels, Jonathan, 338
Revis. See Reavis
Reynolds, Bunberry, 362
Reynolds, Dempsey, 362
Reynolds, John C., 488
Reynolds, Lucian, 362
Reynolds, Peter, 362
Reynolds, William T., 124
Rhea. See also Ray, Rea, Wray
Rhea, James N., 445
Rhew, J. T., 161
Rhode Island Units
 5th Regt. Rhode Island
  Infantry, 143, 399
Rhodes, Daniel, 113
Rhodes, Hezekiah, 172
Rhom, Robert, 38
Rhyne, Abel Brown, 113
Rhyne, Abel Peterson, 113
Rhyne, Eli S., 113
Rhyne, Jacob E., 113
Rhyne, John Bunyan, 113
Rhyne, John Leroy, 113
Rhyne, M. H., 113
Rhyne, M. S., 113
Rice. See also Grice
Rice, George W., 425
Rice, Joseph A., 61
Rice, William, 425
Rice, William G., 61
Rice's Station, Virginia, 24, 413
Rich, George W., 509
Rich, William H., 388
Richardson, Alexander H., 461
Richardson, Charles E., 445
Richardson, Green L., 452
Richardson, James Hiram, 87
Richardson, John H., 124
Richardson, John Q., 415
Richardson, Joseph, 499
Richardson, Lloyd M., 461
Richardson, R. F., 452
Richardson, Thomas N., 416, 445
Richardson, William B., 477
Richey. See Ritchie
Richmond, Stephen D., 26
Richmond, Virginia, 1-3, 6-7,
 9-10, 13-15, 20, 23, 140-141,
 267-271, 393, 399, 406-409,
 413
Richmond and Danville
 Railroad, 24, 413
Richmond and Fredericksburg
 Railroad, 399
Richmond and York River
 Railroad, 14

Richmond Regulators, 454
Riddick, Simon, 445
Riddick, Thomas J., 445
Riddle, J. L., 100
Ridge, Willis, 435
Ried. See Reed, Reid
Rierson, Samuel M., 447
Rieves. See Reaves, Reeves
Riggsbee, Alexander J., 44
Riggsbee, Elbert, 44
Riggsbee, John Alvis, 44
Riggsbee, John M., 41, 44
Riggsbee, John W., 44
Riggsbee, Jones E., 29, 44
Riggsbee, Larkins J., 44
Riggsbee, Revel, 44
Riggsbee, Thomas S., 44
Riggsbee, William L., 44
Riley. See also Ryley
Riley, James, 488
Rimmer, Adderson, 161
Rimmer, Hasten, 161
Rimmer, Samuel R., 161
Rimmer, William, 161
Ritchie, George M., 61
Ritter, Hiram L., 349
Rivenbark, Benjamin R., 305
Rivenbark, Daniel J., 296
River's Bridge, South Carolina,
 145
Roan, Wiley M., 285
Roanoke River, North Carolina,
 10, 13, 140
Roark, Alvin, 499
Roark, David, 499
Roark, Harvey J., 499
Roark, Isaac, 499
Roark, Nathaniel W., 499
Robb. See Rabb
Robbards. See Roberts
Robbins, Ahi C., 435
Robbins, Alex S., 436
Robbins, Clarkson, 436
Robbins, Clarkson L., 436
Robbins, Elias, 436
Robbins, Elijah, 350
Robbins, George W., 350
Robbins, James A., 350
Robbins, Joel A., 350
Robbins, John, 436
Robbins, Micajah, 436
Roberson. See also Robertson,
 Robeson, Robinson, Robison
Roberson, Smith, 244
Roberts, Abel H., 254
Roberts, Edmund, 350
Roberts, Elcana, 202
Roberts, Franklin N., 226
Roberts, George W., 350

Roberts, Harvey C., 254
Roberts, John Edmond, 100
Roberts, John R., 285
Roberts, Rufus, 90
Roberts, W. A. E., 254
Robertson. See also Roberson,
 Robinson, Robison
Robertson, Beverly H., 142, 397
Robeson. See also Roberson,
 Robertson, Robinson, Robison
Robeson, Albert T., 278
Robinson. See also Roberson,
 Robertson, Robeson, Robison
Robinson, Charles, 462
Robinson, Francis C., 488
Robinson, Henry, 499
Robinson, James M., 125
Robinson, James P., 202
Robinson, Jeremiah, 445
Robinson, John, 202
Robinson, John C., 488
Robinson, John H., 402, 415,
 428, 488
Robinson, John L., 509
Robinson, John T., 416, 509
Robinson, Joseph B., 488
Robinson, Josiah, 305
Robinson, Philo, 499
Robinson, S. M., 114
Robinson, Thomas M., 488
Robinson, Wesley, 499
Robinson, William E., 114, 305
Robison. See also Roberson,
 Robertson, Robeson, Robinson
Robison, James H., 61
Robison, Thomas T., 61
Roby. See Raby
Rockwell, Henry Clay, 276, 354
Rocky Mount, North Carolina,
 10, 143-144, 396
Rodes, Robert, 400
Rodgers. See also Rogers
Rodgers, Henry H., 62
Rodgers, J. E., 305
Rodgers, James M., 425
Rodgers, John, 436
Rodgers, William R., 477
Rodgers, William S., 338
Roe. See Rowe
Rogers. See also Rodgers
Rogers, David D., 509
Rogers, David F., 388
Rogers, John H., 509
Rogers, Joseph, 389
Rogers, Simeon A., 161
Rogers, William, 244
Rohrbach Bridge, Maryland, 5
Rollins, S. R., 53
Roop, Christian, 477

Roope, King M., 194
Roper, William T., 462
Rose. *See also* Rouse
Rose, Elias, 184
Rose, H. C., 184
Rose, J. C., 184
Roseman, Cyrus P., 78
Roseman, Theodore A., 78
Ross, Hugh D., 425
Ross, Spencer, 38
Ross, William A., 87
Rost, M., 139
Roulhac, Thomas R., 17, 23, 27, 65
Rountree, Seth, 445
Rouse. *See also* Rose
Rouse, Noah, 362
Rowe, William F., 285
Royal, Tolbert P., 389
Royals, Robert D., 378
Royster, Solomon, 161
Rozier, Amos L., 318
Rozier, Evander C., 318
Rozier, N. Russel, 285
Rozier, Oliver, 286
Rozier, Robert A., 318
Rudd. *See* Redd
Ruffin, John Kirkland, 27
Rufty, Michael, 125
Rumage, Harris, 509
Rumfelt, James S., 38
Rumfelt, John L., 38, 114
Runyan, J. P., 100
Rush. *See also* Rash
Rush, Alson J., 436
Rush, Archibald F., 436
Rush, Azel G., 436
Rush, Calvin J., 436
Rush, George, 436
Russell, Daniel, 436
Russell, Henry Columbus, 488
Russell, John M., 477
Russell, Stephen E., 378
Russell, Walter R., 416, 445
Russell, Wesley Soule, 318
Rutherford Farmers, 215
Rutherford Regulars, 235
Rutherford Regulators, 235
Rutledge, William G., 499
Ryals. *See also* Rawles
Ryals, Henry J., 149, 187
Ryals, John W., 194
Ryals, Lewit W., 389
Ryals, Richard B., 194
Ryals, William M., 194
Ryan. *See* Rhyne
Ryley. *See also* Riley
Ryley, James, 45

S

Safriet, James A., 62
Safrit, Rufus A., 425
St. Clair, James, 477
St. Clair, John, 477
Salkehatchie River, South Carolina, 145
Sally, James R., 257
Salmon. *See also* Solomon
Salmon, Edward A., 233
Salmon, James P., 233
Sampson. *See* Simpson
Sams. *See also* Seams
Sams, Edmund W., 519
Sanderford. *See* Sanford
Sanders. *See also* Saunders
Sanders, Ashley S., 194
Sanders, D. C., 100
Sanderson, Isaac, 296
Sandford. *See also* Sanford, Stanford
Sandford, Kelita, 462
Sandlin, George L., 38
Sandlin, Hiram L., 296
Sands. *See* Sams
Sandy, John A. W., 378
Sandy Ridge, North Carolina, 9
Sanford. *See also* Sandford, Stanford
Sanford, Dennis B., 462
Sanford, William Frank, 416, 462
Sapp, John H., 519
Sapp, Michael A., 519
Sarvis, Alexander, 100
Sarvis, Thomas, 100
Sasser, Calvin, 362
Sasser, Heli, 363
Sasser, Hilliard, 202
Sasser, Matthew G., 363
Sasser, Simon, 363
Sasser, Wiley, 202
Satterfield, William D., 161
Sauls, William J., 305
Saunders. *See also* Sanders
Saunders, James, 499
Saunders, Romulus W., 509
Saunders, Thomas J., 499
Savage, David W., 445
Savannah, Georgia, 144-145, 261
Sawyer, Jesse, 445
Sayler's Creek, Virginia, 24, 413
Scarborough, Jesse C., 350
Scarborough, William S., 462
Scarbrough, James C., 211
Scoggins. *See also* Coggins
Scoggins, J. J. W., 161
Scoggins, Joseph, 244

Scotch Tigers, 308
Scott, Allison J., 425
Scott, Benjamin L., 436
Scott, William B., 436
Scott, William H., 318
Scriven, Thomas James, 318
Scruggs, Robert, 244
Sealey, Nicholas T., 329
Sealy, Emcoin, 172
Sealy, Isham, 173
Sealy, Jackson, 173
Sealy, John R., 173
Sealy, Melvin, 173
Sealy, Nephison, 329
Seams. *See also* Sams
Seams, John, 257
Sebastian, Henry C., 477
Sebastian, Martin H., 477
Sebastian, William Gray, 477
Second Manassas, Virginia, 4
Sedberry, Daniel W., 462
Seldon. *See* Shelton
Sell. *See also* Shell, Shull
Sell, Jacob, 509
Sell, John, 509
Sell, Solomon, 509
Sellers, David G., 296
Sellers, George L., 286
Sellers, Joseph C., 350
Sellers, Pitman E., 363
Sellers, Richard, 202
Sellers, William W., 350
Selton. *See also* Shelton
Selton, C. P., 136
Seminary Ridge, Gettysburg, Pennsylvania, 400-402
Sennett. *See* Sinnett
Senter, Caleb O., 499
Senter, D. E., 378
Senter, John W., 233
Service. *See* Sarvis
Sessoms, Dickson, 389
Setzer, James Pink, 125
Seven Days Battles, 2
Sewell, Thomas, 286
Sexton, John, 488
Seymour, Leonidas B., 202
Shaffer. *See* Shaver
Shankle, Jacob, 509
Shankle, James W., 509
Shankle, John N., 509
Shankle, Willis, 462
Sharpe, Abner Clayton, 72
Sharpe, Francis M., 78
Sharpe, Leander Davidson, 78
Sharpe, William P., 78
Sharpsburg, Maryland, 4-6, 142
Shatley. *See also* Hatley
Shatley, David, 477

Shaver, Alvin W., 62
Shaver, M. A., 62
Shaver, Noah, 509
Shaw, Archibald James, 318
Shaw, Colin, 277
Shaw, Daniel, 318, 350
Shaw, John A., 318
Shaw, Jones Newton, 87
Shaw, Lock W. A., 87
Shaw, Malcolm, 318
Shaw, Norman, 318
Shaw, Wiley H., 417, 437
Shehan, Edward, 244, 254
Shehan, Edward A., 39
Shehan, Henry, 254
Shehan, Hodge, 39
Shehan, Jackson, 244
Shehan, James, 244
Shehan, John, Jr., 255
Shelby, North Carolina, 90
Shell. See also Sell, Shull
Shell, William Henry, 136
Shella, T. H., 257
Shelton. See also Selton
Shelton, Joseph B., 480
Shelton, Levi M., 488
Shelton, Meacon J., 29, 125
Shenandoah River, Virginia, 4
Shenandoah Valley, Virginia, 6,
  22, 399, 409, 412
Shepherd. See also Sheppard
Shepherd, Calvin, 462
Shepherd, Eli, 462
Shepherd, James K., 363
Shepherd, John W., 477
Shepherd, Martin, 462
Shepherd, Noah R., 462
Shepherd, William H., 462
Shepherd, William R., 136
Shepherd, Wilson C., 462
Shepherdstown, West Virginia,
  399
Sheppard. See also Shepherd
Sheppard, James L., 151, 211
Sheppard, John A., 211
Sheridan, Phil, 22, 407-408, 412
Sherman, William T., 21,
  144-145, 147-148, 273-275
Sherrell, Leland, 78
Sherrell, W., 39
Sherrill, Adam Elliott, 125
Sherrill, Adam T., 53
Sherrill, David J., 125
Sherrill, Gabriel Powell, 136
Sherrill, Jacob W., 116
Sherrill, James H., 29, 116
Sherrill, James M., 489
Sherrill, Jeptha, 116
Sherrill, John A., 489

Sherrill, John Nelson, 136
Sherrill, Silas Wodford, 125
Sherrill, William, 489
Shields, Alexander M., 100
Shields, R. D., 53
Shores, Meredith, 519
Short, James, 53
Short, Wade H., 53
Shouse, John H., 519
Shrum, Henry, 499
Shull. See also Sell, Shell
Shull, Charles W., 136
Shull, Moses, 136
Shull, Pearson, 136
Shumate, Daniel, 477
Shumate, Jasper, 477
Shumate, Jesse Hardin, 478
Shumate, Wesley, 478
Shumate, William J., 478
Shuping, Andrew, 62
Shupping, Jeremiah A., 78
Shupping, Smith A., 78
Sibbett, John William, 363
Sides, D. A., 510
Sides, Ransom, 62
Sifford. See also Stafford
Sifford, John Frank, 489
Sifford, Miles L., 499
Sifford, Robert J., 489
Sifford, William A., 489
Sigmon, Henry, 125
Sigmon, James Washington, 125
Sigmon, Julius A., 125
Sigmon, Martin A., 125
Sikes, Charles M., 305
Sillivent. See also Sullivan
Sillivent, Lemuel, 202
Sills, David, 389
Sills, Henry Washington, 389
Sills, Joel, 389
Sills, William T., 389
Simmons, Amaziah, 363
Simmons, Isaac, 286, 350
Simmons, James, 389
Simmons, Lemon L., 389
Simmons, Malcolm L., 378
Simmons, Thomas, Jr., 363
Simmons, Wiley, 378
Simmons, William M., 452
Simms. See also Sims
Simms, Daniel E., 363
Simons. See Simmons
Simpson, Even, 136
Simpson, H. W., 152
Simpson, Jesse, 425
Simpson, William A., 389
Sims. See also Simms
Sims, Joseph P., 223
Singletary, Calvin, 363

Singletary, John Bradley, 363
Singletary, Monroe, 364
Singletary, Thomas C., 404
Sinnett, John, 445
Sipe. See Lipe
Sisk, A. J., 223
Sizemore, James, 519
Skeen, Jesse, 62
Skinker's Neck, Virginia, 7
Skipper, Stephen, 351
Skipper, William L., 378
Sloan, David M., 152, 211
Sloan, George, 367
Slocum, Henry W., 145-147, 274
Small, Alfred B., 173
Small, David, 445
Small, Thomas A., 445
Small, William S., 173
Smart, Henry Kerr, 223
Smart, Philow Whitefield, 39
Smart, William G., 39
Smiley, M., 223
Smith, Albert O., 296
Smith, Alfred Harris, 425
Smith, Amos J., 296
Smith, Anderson H., 70
Smith, Arthur A., 510
Smith, Bracy, 351
Smith, C. A. D., 223
Smith, Cameron, 463
Smith, Clark C., 510
Smith, David J., 296
Smith, David L., 379
Smith, Doc Miller, 244
Smith, Edley Martin, 244
Smith, Eli, 114
Smith, Eli M., 510
Smith, Ellison, 87
Smith, Enos, 463
Smith, George A., 329
Smith, George W., 245
Smith, Green B., 510
Smith, Henry, 255
Smith, Henry C., 70
Smith, Henry E., 202
Smith, Huey, 255
Smith, Isaiah, 364
Smith, Jackson, 489
Smith, James A., 318
Smith, James P., 329, 445
Smith, James W., 114
Smith, Jesse T., 289
Smith, John, 286
Smith, John C., 62
Smith, John G., 233
Smith, John L., 114
Smith, John O., 364
Smith, John R., 425
Smith, Joseph B., 184

Smith, Josiah, 203
Smith, Leroy, 437
Smith, Lewis H., 296
Smith, M. L., 245
Smith, Malcolm McI., 379
Smith, Martin Alexander, 152, 211
Smith, Mathias H., 426
Smith, O. P., 257
Smith, Peter M., 379
Smith, Reuben K., 510
Smith, Richard R., 329
Smith, S. A., 510
Smith, Samuel H., 364
Smith, Thomas, 203
Smith, Thomas C., 151, 245
Smith, Thomas J., 364
Smith, W. E., 392
Smith, W. F., 15, 270
Smith, W. M., 257
Smith, William A., 510
Smith, William D., 255, 351
Smith, William H., 489
Smith, William Henry, 364
Smith, William J. B., 88
Smith, William T., 184
Smith, Willis H., 70
Smithey, Harvey, 478
Smithfield, North Carolina, 148, 175, 273-275
Smithville (present-day Southport), North Carolina, 258
Smithy, William S., 478
Snavely's Ford, Maryland, 4
Sneed, W. B., 173
Snipes, Hugh G., 329
Snipes, James, 519
Snipes, John F., 519
Snipes, Nelson, 329
Snipes, Wiley T., 519
Snowden, Thomas F., 255
Snowden, W. G., 136
Snyder, William H., 286
Sockeringe, Aaron, 379
Soles, Daniel W., 364
Soles, Drakeford S., 364
Soles, Nathaniel, 364
Soles, Neill, 364
Solomon. See also Salmon
Solomon, James, 426
Sommers. See Summers
Sorrells, Charles H., 245
Sorrells, Israel P., 223
Sorrels, Jesse C., 223
South Anna River, Virginia, 399
South Carolina Units
    17th Regt. S.C. Infantry, 16
Southerland. See also Sullivan

Southerland, Abraham, 305
Southerland, Bryan, 305
Southerland, Edward, 278
Southerland, George N., 305
Southerland, Hugh, 286
Southerland, James, 306
Southerland, Thomas J., 306
Southerland, William J., 279
Southern, George W., 452
Southern, John W., 452
South Mills, North Carolina, 12
South Mountain, Maryland, 4
Southside Railroad, Virginia, 22, 24, 411-413
Southwest Creek, North Carolina, 273
Sowles. See Soles
Spainhower, C. T., 519
Spang, Wiley, 62
Spargo, James, 499
Sparkman, George A., 338
Sparkman, William P., 339
Sparks, A. Crighton, 100
Sparks, Merit R., 245
Sparrow, William H., 100
Speck, J. P., 53
Speight, Edward, 445
Speight, William W., 445
Spence, Neill A., 233
Spencer, Isham, 452
Spencer, J. Rufus, 184
Spide, S. S., 318
Spinola, F. B., 399
Spivey, Aikin, 339
Spivey, Charles, 173
Spivey, Henry, 339
Spivey, John, 173
Spivey, John Q., 339
Spivey, Jordan, 211
Spivey, Lewis J., 339
Spivey, Owen, 364
Spivey, Samuel, 339
Spivey, William P., 364
Spotsylvania Court House, Virginia, 13, 406-407
Spratt, Andrew Pinkney, 88
Spratt, Joseph L., 136
Spratt, Samuel L., 223
Spring Hill Guards, 490
Springs, Jacob, 296
Sprinkle, Bennett, 520
Sprinkle, Lindsey, 478
Spruill, William, 446
Squires, Marcus D., 88
Sronce, Sidney J., 499
Stafford. See also Sifford
Stafford, Nathaniel, 39
Staley. See also Stanley, Stanly
Staley, Calvin, 437

Stallings, James B., 184
Stamper, George W., 78
Stamper, L. Franklin, 78
Stancil, Jackson, 426
Stanfield, William A., 161
Stanfil, Richard B., 452
Stanford. See also Sandford, Sanford
Stanford, Charles L., 88
Stanford, George W., 277, 306
Stanford, Henry C., 306
Stanford, Leonidas, 306
Stanford, Samuel M., 299
Stanley. See also Staley, Stanly
Stanley, Alfred C., 389
Stanley, William B., 173
Stanly. See also Staley, Stanley
Stanly, Elijah, 195
Stanly, Gideon, 195
Stanly, Jacob H., 185
Stanly, Nicholas, 195
Stanly Rebels, 501
Stansel. See Stancil
Starbuck, John W., 520
Starkey. See Harkey
Starling, Daniel A., 203
Starling, John, 203
Starnes, Dulin, 452
Starnes, John L., 452
Starnes, Martin, 426
Starnes, Rufus P., 100
Statesville, North Carolina, 72
Stearns. See Starnes
Stedman, Andrew J., 45
Stedman, Jason, 255
Steed, Thomas J., 437
Steel, James H., 426
Stein, Colson, 463
Stephens. See also Stevens
Stephens, Ancel, 173
Stephens, Benjamin F., 233
Stephens, David S., 185
Stephens, Francis, 329
Stephens, J. Marshall, 152, 211
Stephens, James M., 277
Stephens, John L., 233
Stephens, Joseph S., 233
Stephens, Kelly, 233
Stephenson, J. E., 195
Stephenson, Jonathan, 195
Stephenson, Manly, 195
Stephenson, William J., 88
Sterling. See Starling
Stevens. See also Stephens
Stevens, James William, 195
Stevens, John C., 185
Stevens, John T., 306
Stewart. See also Stuart
Stewart, A. P., 146-147, 274

Stewart, Alexander, 233
Stewart, Alvin, 379
Stewart, Andrew Jackson, 211
Stewart, C. E., 211
Stewart, Daniel, 379
Stewart, Daniel R., 233
Stewart, Drewry, 211
Stewart, G. A., 233
Stewart, J. F., 152, 212
Stewart, J. Franklin, 125
Stewart, James, 318
Stewart, Jeptha P., 125
Stewart, John, 255
Stewart, John A., 212, 233
Stewart, John H., 223
Stewart, Neill A., 233
Stewart, Thomas W., 500
Stewart, William H., 212
Stikeleather, John McK., 62
Stiles, John H., 126
Stiles, Marcus, 126
Stiller, Daniel, 426
Stilly, Albert, 520
Stitt. See also Stutts
Stitt, James Morrison, 88
Stogner, Holden, 136
Stokes, Aaron, 286
Stokes, Hugh Montgomery, 478
Stone. See also Stowe
Stone, Andrew J., 319
Stone, Archibald, 212
Stone, Benjamin E., 173
Stone, Elias B., 173
Stone, Hardy J., 173
Stone, Isham, 173
Stone, J., 286
Stone, J. S., 233
Stone, Jacob, 174
Stone, James P., 174
Stone, Joel, 174
Stone, John P., 390
Stone, John S., 233
Stone, Joshua, 174
Stone, Richard A., 62
Stone, Robert J., 62
Stone, Rufus A., 72
Stone, William A., 174
Stowe. See also Stone
Stowe, Green P., 114
Stowe, J. Green, 114
Stowe, John M., 500
Stowe, William I., 114
Street, Anthony, 223
Street, David D., 39
Street's Ferry, North Carolina, 144
Strickland, Bethel P., 351
Strickland, Bythan Elbert, 452
Strickland, Calvin M., 296

Strickland, Edwin B., 390
Strickland, Henry J., 203
Strickland, Isaac, 286
Strickland, Jeremiah, 297
Strickland, John, 233
Strickland, Jonathan, 463
Strickland, Josiah, 297
Strickland, Julius W., 195
Strickland, Matthew L., 351
Strickland, Philip, 351
Strickland, Quincy, 351
Strickland, Robert M., 390
Strickland, Thomas J., 379
Strickland, Washington, 185
Strickland, Wiley, 195
Strickland, William A., 390
Strickland, William H., 195, 297
Strickland, William T., 351, 390
Strider, Andrew, 437
Strider, Joel, 437
Stroup, Andrew Jackson, 500
Stroup, Caleb, 500
Stroup, David C., 500
Stroup, Hosea, 500
Stroup, Johann H., 3, 114
Stroup, Lafayette, 500
Stroup, Robert, 500
Stroup, Robert B., 500
Stroup, W. W., 114
Stroup, Wesley C., 500
Stuart. See also Stewart
Stuart, Enoch, 70
Stuart, J. E. B., 7
Stuart, John L., 70
Stutts. See also Stitt
Stutts, William, 437
Styers, William O., 62
Suffolk, Virginia, 12, 266
Sugard, D. J., 339
Sugar Loaf Hill (near Fort Fisher), North Carolina, 273
Sugg, Aquilla, 195
Suggs, Doctor F., 351
Suit, John S., 161
Sullivan. See also Sillivent, Southerland
Sullivan, Adam, 306
Sullivan, Andrew McI., 299
Sullivan, Elias, 306
Sullivan, Henry, 185
Sullivan, John Haywood, 185
Sullivan, Lemuel L., 306
Sullivan, Wiley, 185
Sullivan, William, 185
Sullivan's Island, Charleston, South Carolina, 261, 265
Sumerlin, Jesse C., 478
Summerlin, David C., 306
Summerlin, James Louis, 306

Summerlin, John D., 306
Summerlin, John J., 307
Summerlin, Levi, 307
Summerlin, Thomas, 307
Summerow, David F., 500
Summerow, Frank, 500
Summerow, Henry M., 500
Summerow, William A., 491
Summers, John N., 62
Summers, John Stephenson, 73
Summersett, John M., 351
Summey, David A., 500
Summey, Jonas F., 500
Sumner, Edwin, 5
Surls, D. H., 195
Surratt, Josiah, 437
Suther, Greenbury R., 426
Suther, John P., 426
Suther, Richard M., 426
Sutherland. See Southerland
Sutherland's Station, Virginia, 413
Suttle, John H., 223
Suttle, William, 223
Suttles, Joseph, 255
Suttles, Robert, 255
Suttles, William, 255
Sutton, Michael Wesley, 297
Sutton, Philip, 390
Swann, John B., 88
Swaringen, Eli S., 510
Swift Creek, Virginia, 15, 397, 409
Swink, George W., 463
Swinson, John E., 289
Sykes. See Sikes

T

Tadlock, John W., 437
Tadlock, Joseph C., 437
Talbert. See Tolbert
Talton, James D., 185
Talton, James T., 185
Talton, Lewis, Jr., 185
Talton, William J., 185
Tarboro, North Carolina, 10, 143-144, 265
Tar River, North Carolina, 143
Tart, William T., 234
Tate, Albert, 245
Taylor. See also Tyler
Taylor, A. Jackson, 137
Taylor, Abram J., 379
Taylor, Amos, 329
Taylor, Benjamin, 329
Taylor, David D., 339
Taylor, Edward S., 88

Taylor, Isaac, 319
Taylor, James H., 276, 367
Taylor, James P., 88
Taylor, John Archibald R., 88
Taylor, John F., 307
Taylor, John H., 379
Taylor, Kenan, 307
Taylor, Mitchell, 307
Taylor, Napoleon B., 70
Taylor, Paul, 307
Taylor, Robert C., 245
Taylor, Stephen, 339
Taylor, Wiley James, 364
Taylor, William Alfred, 379
Taylor, William James, 379
Taylor, Willis, 329
Taylor's Ferry, North Carolina, 13
Tays, Samuel L., 78
Teaboe, Philip, 351
Teaboe, William W., 351
Teachey, William, 352
Teague, Baldin T. Kirby, 114
Tedder, Houston, 478
Tedder, James, 478
Temple, Caswell, 195
Terrell. See also Ferrell, Perrell
Terrell, Joel L., 255
Terrell, John, 63
Terry, Alfred H., 273
Terry, Champ G., 463
Terry, Ephraim B., 520
Tevepaugh, J. L., 88
Tevepaugh, William A., 88
Tew, Alexander, 379
Tew, Bedford, 390
Tew, Daniel C., 380
Tew, Holly, 390
Tew, Jackson, 380
Tew, James Martin, 380
Tew, Jeremiah, 380
Tew, John, 380
Tew, John Joel, 382
Tew, John L., 390
Tew, John R., 380
Tew, Lemick J., 380
Tew, Lewis M., 390
Tew, Loudin Blue, 380
Tew, Martin B., 390
Tew, Myutt M., 390
Tew, Sherwood B., 352
Tew, William H., 380
Tharpe. See also Thorpe
Tharpe, Hanson H., 478
Thayer, Kendrick, 437
Themegley, T. F., 297
Thigpen, Allen, 352
Thigpen, Thomas, 352
Thomas, Benjamin M., 463

Thomas, Benjamin W., 212
Thomas, David A., 212
Thomas, Henry Peyton, 212
Thomas, J. W., Sr., 212
Thomas, Jackson J., 212
Thomas, James, 63, 286, 463
Thomas, James A., 234
Thomas, James K., 463
Thomas, Jasper, 212
Thomas, Jesse, 70
Thomas, John C., 71
Thomas, John G., 114
Thomas, John Ivey, 307
Thomas, John L., 212
Thomas, John M. B., 212
Thomas, John P., 213
Thomas, John W., Jr., 213
Thomas, Jonathan, 203
Thomas, Joseph H., 213
Thomas, Joseph P., 71
Thomas, Luther, 234
Thomas, Luther R., 213
Thomas, Robert, 463
Thomas, Robert B., 213
Thomas, Wiley F., 71
Thomason. See also Thompson, Thomson
Thomason, John, 53
Thomason, Turner P., 63
Thomason, William A., 63
Thomason, William G., 380
Thompson. See also Thomason, Thomson
Thompson, Benjamin Turner, 63
Thompson, Daniel G., 489
Thompson, George, 463
Thompson, Giles W., 320
Thompson, Hosea H., 245
Thompson, James P., 330
Thompson, John, 330, 489
Thompson, John Easy, 330
Thompson, John N., Jr., 63
Thompson, John Nelson, Sr., 55
Thompson, John S., 330
Thompson, John T., 330
Thompson, John Thomas, 365
Thompson, Nathan, 510
Thompson, Nathan J., 352
Thompson, Noah McK., 365
Thompson, Oliver T., 330
Thompson, Risden N., 510
Thompson, Robert, 478
Thompson, Samuel S. B., 365
Thompson, Sidney J., 501
Thompson, Stephen, 463
Thompson, Theodore Ashley, 330
Thompson, Thomas B., 489
Thompson, Thomas L., 63

Thompson, Wesley, 478
Thompson, William, 464
Thompson, William A., 63, 330
Thompson, William D., 490
Thompson, William Henry, 63
Thompson, William M., 354
Thompson, William P., 365
Thompson, William R., 510
Thomson. See also Thomason, Thompson
Thomson, W., 330
Thorne. See also Horne
Thorne, J. F., 114
Thornton, Richard, 174
Thornton, Thomas J., 297
Thornton, William E., 195
Thorpe. See also Tharpe
Thorpe, H. R., 27
Threat, Benjamin, 453
Thrower, John T., 71
Thrower, William H., 464
Tidwell, F. A., 88
Tidwell, William T. A., 88
Timms, Benjamin, 137
Timms, John, 137
Tindall, Austin, 352
Tiner. See also Tyner
Tiner, Bythan, 185
Tiner, James, 464
Tolar, Hiram, 380
Tolar, Robert M., 381
Tolbert, John C., 511
Tomberlin, John H., 223, 255
Tomberlin, V. B., 224
Tomkins, J. P., 446
Tomlinson, Nathaniel M., 185
Toney, John, 224
Toole, Bithan L., 196
Toon, Luther, 365
Topsail Sound, North Carolina, 261
Torrence, John N., 103
Torrence, William Marcus, 114
Totopotomoy Creek, Virginia, 407-408
Towe. See Tew
Towery. See also Towry
Towery, George W., 137
Towery, Joseph, 137
Townsend, Charles F., 330
Townsend, Floyd, 339
Townsend, Fuller C., 330
Townsend, Jackson, 330
Townsend, Jacob, 257
Towry. See also Towery
Towry, Joseph, 39
Towry, Martin S., 39
Towry, R. P., 53
Traffenstedt, Absalom, 126

Traffenstedt, Daniel, 126
Traffenstedt, Noah, 126
Trammel, James, 137
Trammel, Samuel, 137
Trammel, Thomas, 137
Transou, Amos E., 520
Tranter's Creek, North Carolina, 398
Treadwell, John R., 390
Trenton, North Carolina, 11, 13, 259
Trent River, North Carolina, 10-11, 13, 142, 265-266, 396-397
Trimm, Robert B., 161
Tripp, Benjamin F., 203
Tripp, William, 203
Trotman, Daniel W., 446
Trotman, James E., 446
Trotter, John M., 437
Trout, William Gaither, 245
Troutman, John, 511
Troutman, Thomas J., 511
Troutman, Travis, 63
Troy, Edmond, 286
Truelove, Timothy, 234
Truley, Joel Benton, 185
Tucker, A., 297
Tucker, Aaron A., 478
Tucker, Calvin, 297
Tucker, Darlin, 426
Tucker, David C., 490
Tucker, John C., 490
Tucker, Kilby, 297
Tucker, Robert A., 490
Tucker, William, 297
Turbyfield, Jackson, 126
Turkey Bend, Virginia, 3
Turkey Hill, Virginia, 408
Turley. See Truley
Turner, David W., 277, 307
Turner, Edward W., 286, 365
Turner, Francis M., 89
Turner, G. R., 114
Turner, G. T., 319
Turner, George W., 152, 213
Turner, H. C., 152, 213
Turner, Henry Clay, 416, 511
Turner, James, 126
Turner, John W., 286
Turner, Thomas J., 213
Turnidge, John James, 297
Tuttle, Calvin, 453
Tuttle, Dewitt P., 453
Tuttle, Gideon Jeff, 453
Tuttle, Jefferson G., 453
Tuttle, John W., 453
Tuttle, Peter H., 453
Tyler. See also Taylor

Tyler, John, 174
Tyner. See also Tiner
Tyner, Nicholas, 339
Tyner, Wiley J., 330
Tyner, William, 339
Tyson, Daniel, 365
Tyson, Joseph W., 365

U

Umberger, C. W., 307
Umphlet, Bryant, 446
Underwood, Acy J., 319
Underwood, Joseph B., 382
Unger, Lawrence, 224
Upchurch, William, 245
Upchurch, William R., 511
Upperville, Virginia, 6-7
Upton, Benjamin B., 224
Upton, Edward, 224
Usery, Hampton, 137

V

Vancannon. See also Voncannon, Vuncannon
Vancannon, John W., 286
Vanderburg, Francis, 63
Vanderford, Joseph J., 437
Vanderford, William B., 438
Van Hook, John C., 149, 152
Vann, Chester R., 391
Vann, John R., 286
Vann, William T., 287
Vannoy, Elijah Ross, 478
Vanpelt, Charles, 426
Vanpelt, Thomas S., 426
Vanpelt, William C., 426
Varner. See also Warner
Varner, Albert Rankin, 501
Vaughn, Alexander S., 453
Vaughn, John W., 161
Vaughn Road, Virginia, 412
Vause, Amos R., 365
Vause, Jacob McD., 365
Vause, Nathan L., 365
Vick, John A., 203
Vick, Samuel, 287
Vickers, Alexander R., 224
Vickers, J. N., 224
Vickers, J. W., 224
Vickers, Thomas J., 224
Vickers, W. B., 224
Vickers, William A., 115
Virginia Central Railroad, 399, 409
Virginia Creek, North Carolina, 144

Virginia Units
30th Regt. Virginia Infantry, 4
Voncannon. See also Vancannon, Vuncannon
Voncannon, Abram B., 478
Vuncannon. See also Vancannon, Voncannon
Vuncannon, John, 438

W

Wacaster, Stephen M., 39
Wacaster, William W., 39
Waddle, Camull D., 45
Wade, Aretos I., 297
Wade, Clark M., 307
Wade, Duncan B., 391
Wade, John Louis, 381
Wade, John V., 464
Wade, L. A., 391
Wadkins. See also Watkins
Wadkins, John M., 39
Waggoner, William R., 479
Wakefield, Virginia, 394
Walker, A. C., 391
Walker, A. R., 224
Walker, Alfred, 39
Walker, Alfred B., 520
Walker, Edward J., 287
Walker, Elias, 224
Walker, Elijah, 245
Walker, Elijah M., 89
Walker, George F., 278
Walker, James W., 39, 224
Walker, Jeremiah S., 224
Walker, Jerry, Sr., 40
Walker, Jerry L., 40
Walker, Jesse R., 245
Walker, John, 40
Walker, John G., 4-7
Walker, Jonathan, 40
Walker, Jones C., 352
Walker, Moses, 161, 287
Walker, Nathan S., 438
Walker, Richard Allen, 224
Walker, Samuel J., 287
Walker, Virgil H., 512
Walker, Washington, 40
Walker, Washington H., 279
Walker, William, 245, 446
Wall. See also Walls
Wall, A. C., 245
Wall, Drury Benjamin Wesley, 453
Wall, Evy, 453
Wall, George G., 186
Wall, J. N., 245
Wall, John Richard Francis, 453

Wall, M. W., 246
Wall, T. J., 297
Wall, William Andrew Watkins, 453
Wallace. *See also* Wallis
Wallace, A. K., 224
Wallace, David H., 115
Wallace, Francis L., 225
Wallace, James H., 427
Wallace, John B., 427
Wallace, John D., 225
Wallace, John P., 287
Wallace, Joseph L., 225
Wallace, Lawson A., 225
Wallace, Monroe, 115
Wallace, Richard H., 479
Wallace, Tristram L., 319
Wallace, W. H., 23
Wallace, William D., 520
Waller, John R., 511
Wallis. *See also* Wallace
Wallis, Hiram, 71
Wallis, Isham, 71
Walls. *See also* Wall, Wells
Walls, Drury, 520
Walter. *See also* Walters
Walter, Alfred B., 331
Walter, Charles F., 427
Walter, Martin Crawford, 427
Walters. *See also* Walter, Waters
Walters, Isaac, 174
Walters, Lucus, 339
Walters, Philip, 174
Walters, Thomas F., 174, 287
Walters, William, 174, 225
Walters, William P., 163
Walters, Zeb, 174
Ward, Absalom, 366
Ward, Anderson J., 446
Ward, Asa, 352
Ward, Augustus, 446
Ward, Daniel, 352
Ward, Edward H., 41
Ward, James H., 27
Ward, Jethro, 40
Ward, John, 366
Ward, John David, 366
Ward, John F., 330
Ward, Joseph, 287
Ward, Miles A., 137
Ward, Samuel W., 352
Ward, Simon, 366
Ward, William A., 352
Ware. *See also* Weir
Ware, J. F., 100
Ware, James A., 100
Ware, James G., 101
Ware, James W., 101
Ware, John C., 101

Ware, M. L., 101
Ware, Martin S., 101
Ware, Rufus A., 101
Ware, William O., 101
Warlick. *See also* Warwick
Warlick, Rufus M., 128
Warner. *See also* Varner, Warren
Warner, Edward, 71
Warner, Neill R., 71
Warner, Swain, 71
Warren. *See also* Warner
Warren, Achilles, 255
Warren, Archibald, 255
Warren, Daniel B., 479
Warren, G. K., 16-17, 22, 410, 412
Warren, James C., 381
Warren, James H., 479
Warren, James P., 479
Warren, John Crittenden, 416, 439
Warren, John Q., 161
Warren, John T., 391
Warren, Killis B., 256
Warren, Lewellyn P., 415
Warren, Richard, 391
Warren, Robert F., 417, 479
Warren, S. M., 479
Warren, W. C. P., 115
Warren, William A., 381
Warrenton, Virginia, 7
Warsaw, North Carolina, 9, 261
Warsaw Sampsons, 288
Warwick. *See also* Warlick
Warwick, George, 234
Warwick, James Morrison, 89
Warwick, John J., 234
Washington, James A., 142, 144, 149
Washington, North Carolina, 9, 13, 142-144, 396, 398-399
Waters. *See also* Walters
Waters, Benajah, 297
Waters, J. E., 307
Waters, John A., 53
Waters, John M., 101
Waters, Jonathan, 54, 225
Waters, Matthew J., 297
Waters, W. P., 101
Waterson. *See* Watterson
Watkins. *See also* Wadkins
Watkins, Blake, 391
Watkins, Commodore, 196
Watkins, George E., 40
Watkins, James D., 511
Watkins, John W., 234
Watkins, Philip, 256
Watkins, Robert R., 307
Watson, Alexander, 213

Watson, Benjamin, 298
Watson, Daniel W., 225
Watson, David F., 63
Watson, David R., 307
Watson, Edward L., 299
Watson, Garner, 213
Watson, George Washington, 140-141, 149, 175
Watson, Giles, 186
Watson, Henry, 234
Watson, James Adolphus, 89
Watson, James F., 63
Watson, James Winfield, 225
Watson, John B., 63, 89
Watson, John G., 464
Watson, John H., 186
Watson, M. K., 213
Watson, Malcolm McFarland, 204
Watson, Neill T., 213
Watson, Noah, 330
Watson, Quincy, 186
Watson, Richard E., 162
Watson, Robert R., 203
Watson, Samuel Allison, 225
Watson, Samuel D., 340
Watson, Thomas F., 391
Watson, Thomas T., 63
Watson, William Andrew, 162
Watson, William H., 203
Watson, Z., 174
Watt. *See also* Watts
Watt, William T., 79
Watters. *See* Waters, Walters
Watterson, John, 101
Watterson, P. H., 101
Watterson, Robert N., 101
Watts. *See also* Watt
Watts, Alva, 174
Watts, Eli, 479
Watts, J. Silas, 89
Watts, James Madison, 479
Watts, John, 479
Watts, Wesley C., 479
Waugh, Simeon A., 79
Weathers, John A., 501
Weathers, Martin A., 246
Weathers, Oliver W., 501
Weathers, Pinkney, 501
Weaver, Charles J., 381
Weaver, Jacob, 427
Weaver, Sylvester J., 91
Webb, Atlas L., 464
Webb, Henry C., 464
Webb, James, 102
Webb, John, 186
Webb, John E., 319
Webb, John L., 464
Webb, Leonard J., 464

Webb, Noel, 126
Webb, Patillo P., 246
Webb, Robert C., 464
Webb, Sylvester, 102
Webb, William C., 464
Weber, G. W., 79
Webster, Archibald M., 438
Weeks. *See also* Wicks
Weeks, Joseph L., 89
Wehunt, Caleb, 137
Weir. *See also* Ware
Weir, J. W., 102
Weldon, John J., 213
Weldon, North Carolina, 1,
   8-10, 12-13, 140
Weldon Railroad. *See* Petersburg
   and Weldon Railroad
Wellons, J. D. T., 391
Wells. *See also* Walls
Wells, H. C., 479
Wells, Henry W., 481
Wells, James Daniel, 480
Wells, James H., 287
Wescott, Samuel P., 446
West, Alexander, 40
West, David James, 287
West, E. P., 257
West, James, 319
West, Joseph, 381
West, Thaddeus L., 298
West, Thomas, 40
Westbrooks, John, 162
Westbrooks, William A., 162
Westmoreland, David, 520
Westmoreland, David F., 453
Westmoreland, Oliver T., 520
Wetherington. *See* Witherington
Whaley. *See also* Wheeler,
   Wheeley
Whaley, Braddock, 308
Wheeler. *See also* Whaley,
   Wheeley
Wheeler, Henry, 196
Wheeler, Jacob, 186
Wheeler, John H., 186
Wheeley. *See also* Whaley,
   Wheeler
Wheeley, Ephraim, 162
Wheeley, Obadiah, 162
Wheeley, Samuel, 162
Wheeling, Carson, 256
Whetstine, George W., 137
Whetstine, W. F., 102
Whisenhunt, Henry H., 438
Whisnant, Archibal, 256
Whisnant, Eli, 30
Whisnant, Elkanah, 40
Whisnant, Ephraim, 40
White, Alexander, 366

White, Alva, 366
White, Calvin, 137
White, Daniel, 319
White, David, 137
White, Edward, 272
White, Henry P., 102
White, John B., 28, 115
White, John Gideon, 453
White, Joseph A., 438
White, L. S., 115
White, Lewis M., 319
White, Neill D., 319
White, R. M., 319
White, Robert, 446
White, Stephen, 366
White, Terrell, 479
White, Thomas, 54
White, Weston, 234
White, William H., 501
Whitefield. *See also* Whitfield
Whitefield, Alexander, 162
Whitefield, E., 162
Whitefield, Thomas Livingston,
   162
Whitefield, Yancy W., 162
White House Landing, Virginia,
   407
White Oak Road, Virginia, 413
White Oak Swamp, Virginia,
   408
Whitesides, Edward W., 115
Whitesides, J. F., 115
Whitesides, John Gamble, 115
Whitesides, Robert G., 115
Whitesides, William H., 89
Whitfield. *See also* Whitefield
Whitfield, Benjamin H., 308
Whitfield, Canny L., 45
Whitfield, D. F., 162
Whitfield, George W., 298
Whitfield, J. T., 308
Whitfield, J. W., 162
Whitfield, William T., 45
Whitley, Jesse Phillip, 186
Wicker, Benjamin Parker, 214
Wicker, David Warren, 214
Wicker, Elijah M., 214
Wicker, Elisha, 214
Wicker, Green B., 214
Wicker, J. A., 214
Wicker, Thomas R., 214
Wicker, William W., 214
Wicks. *See also* Weeks
Wicks, James A., 45
Wiggins, James, 446
Wiggins, Joseph D., 366
Wiggins, R. M., 54
Wiggins, William M., 54
Wiggins, Willis, 446

Wiggs, Arthur T., 151, 186
Wiggs, John, 186
Wiggs, John T., 196
Wiggs, Needham M., 186
Wilcox, Cadmus M., 407, 413
Wilcox, Redden, 331
Wilcox, Richard B., 331
Wilcoxen, Daniel, 479
Wilder, Joseph H., 186
Wilderness, Virginia, 13, 266,
   405-406
Wiley, James, 298
Wilfong, J. H., 71
Wilfong, John W., 126
Wilford. *See* Williford
Wilkerson. *See also* Wilkinson
Wilkerson, James Sidney, 490
Wilkes, Angus J., 319
Wilkesboro, North Carolina, 465
Wilkes Grays, 465
Wilkie, Oliver J., 256
Wilkie, Washington J., 246
Wilkins, Daniel, 331
Wilkins, John, 246
Wilkins, John M., 331
Wilkins, Lewis, 247
Wilkins, M. A., 246
Wilkins, Phillip, 186
Wilkins, Richard, 162
Wilkins, Samuel, 247
Wilkins, William I., 246
Wilkinson. *See also* Wilkerson
Wilkinson, James, 331
Wilkinson, John V., 256
Wilkinson, Malcolm, 331
Williams. *See also* Williamson
Williams, A. Spain, 438
Williams, Addison J., 45
Williams, B. B., 102
Williams, Benajah B., 187
Williams, Benjamin B., 203
Williams, Charles M., 454
Williams, Cicero, 187
Williams, Franklin, 479
Williams, Giles B., 331
Williams, Habran T., 381
Williams, Harllee, 174
Williams, Harvey C., 246
Williams, Henry, 381
Williams, Isaac C., 501
Williams, J. E., 102
Williams, J. H., 214
Williams, James, 490
Williams, James Boney, 352
Williams, James Daniel, 381
Williams, Jesse, 438
Williams, John, 479
Williams, John G., 64
Williams, John Henry, 331

Williams, John Q., 353
Williams, Marshal, 71
Williams, O. P., 256
Williams, Reuben, 438
Williams, Robert K., 298
Williams, Rowland F., 331
Williams, Samuel, 438
Williams, Sandy, 54
Williams, Smith W., 162
Williams, Solomon R., 353
Williams, Thomas, 214
Williams, Thomas E., 446
Williams, William T., 203
Williamson. *See also* Williams
Williamson, J. M., 353
Williamson, James D., 490
Williamson, Jasper B., 298
Williamson, Jesse R., 298
Williamson, John, 366
Williamson, Matthew, 71
Williamson, Noah, 438
Williamson, Page, 298
Williamson, Patrick, 71
Williamson, William, 287
Williamson, Wyatt, 71
Williford, Jason Tounley, 391
Williford, John C., Sr., 391
Williford, John Cager, 392
Williford, Richard, 392
Williford, Sir William, 392
Williford, Townley, 392
Williford, W. J. T., 392
Willis, John W., 319
Willis, W. J., 138
Willoughby, Solomon, 257
Willoughby Run, Pennsylvania, 400
Wills. *See* Walls, Wells
Wilmington, North Carolina, 9, 144, 258-262, 273, 278, 288, 298, 319, 331, 340, 353, 366
Wilmington and Weldon Railroad, 8, 143, 261
Wilson, Alexander H., 138
Wilson, Allen, 187
Wilson, Anderson, 234
Wilson, Athen E., 246
Wilson, Ezekiel, 381
Wilson, James D., 308
Wilson, James W., 26
Wilson, Jerry, 115
Wilson, John J., 298
Wilson, John Tyler Monroe, 234
Wilson, Joseph, 256
Wilson, Joseph G., 246
Wilson, Joseph J., 353
Wilson, Josiah J., 29, 115
Wilson, Maxwell, 138
Wilson, Monroe A., 234

Wilson, N. B., 138
Wilson, Neill A., 234
Wilson, Robert Newton, 103
Wilson, Samuel M., 29, 115
Wilson, William, 115
Wilson, William W., 353
Wilton, William R., 287
Winchester, Virginia, 6-7, 399, 403
Windsor, North Carolina, 13, 396
Winecoff, Daniel, 138
Winecoff, George, 427
Winecoff, George W., 427
Winecoff, Harvey, 427
Winecoff, John M., 427
Winfield, Minos A., 139
Wingate, John Planner, 89
Wingate, William C., 89
Winn, David, 203
Winston, North Carolina, 511
Winters, John A., 102
Winters, John W., 138
Winton, North Carolina, 13
Wise, Alexander, 64
Wise, Edward, 64
Wise's Forks, North Carolina, 9, 273
Witherington, Stephen, 116
Withrow, J. C., 54
Withrow, Thomas J., 54
Withrow, William P., 54
Wolfe, John W., 89
Womack, John B., 214
Womack, Landrun, 246
Womack, Noah W., 246
Womack, Starling, 490
Womick, Thomas, 246
Wood. *See also* Woods
Wood, Alfred B., 319
Wood, Andes, 256
Wood, Archibald, 214
Wood, Augustus, 256
Wood, Calvin, 234
Wood, Frederick A., 298
Wood, Gary, 381
Wood, Henry H., 234
Wood, James, 234
Wood, John, 256, 319
Wood, T. F., 235
Wood, Uz, 353
Wood, Wesley W., 71
Wood, William M., 298
Wood, William Thomas, 287, 353
Woodall, James D., 187
Woodall, William H., 196
Woodard. *See also* Woodward
Woodard, Joseph, 353

Woodard, Thomas, 464
Woodcock, Hanson M., 288
Woodcock, Nelson, 288
Woodcock, William L., 288
Woodell, Andrew Jackson, 319
Woodell, Troy, 235
Woodell, Zachariah, 235
Woods. *See also* Wood
Woods, James M., 480
Woods, James R., 79
Woods, Joseph, 480
Woodsides, John Fruno, 79
Woodward. *See also* Woodard
Woodward, George W., 340
Wooten, Reuben, 480
Word. *See* Ward
Workman, Addison F., 45
Workman, E. J., 115
Worley, Moses, 353
Wortham, George, 144, 149
Wray. *See also* Ray, Rea, Rhea
Wray, James Calvin, 138
Wray, William Arthur, 102
Wrenn, George Warren, 162
Wright, A. R., 2
Wright, Bryson P., 54
Wright, C. G., 149
Wright, Council B., 150, 203
Wright, Henry, 138
Wright, J. B., 162
Wrightsville Sound, North Carolina, 259
Wyckoff, John Wesley, 126
Wycoff, Andrew A., 126

Y

Yarbrough, David, 163
Yarbrough, David B., 464
Yarbrough, Elias G., 214
Yarbrough, G., 246
Yarbrough, Henderson, 163
Yarbrough, James, 214
Yarbrough, Jordan W., 163
Yarbrough, William T., 214
Yates. *See also* Yeates
Yates, Andrew L., 438
Yates, John W., 427
Yates, William Bailey, 438
Yeates. *See also* Yates
Yeates, George Thomas, 520
Yeates, Thomas E., 520
Yelton, W. J., 225
Yelvington, Bennett, 187
Yelvington, Ransom H., 150, 187
Yopp, Franklin V. B., 341
York, C. W., 366
York River, Virginia, 1

Yost, Henry W., 427
Young, D. Ed., 454
Young, Edward H., 454
Young, Robert W., 454
Young, Solomon, 490

Youngblood, D. H., 187
Youngblood, Thomas Rice, 175
Younger, Phlegm H., 480
Younts, Julius L., 64

Z

Zay, James, 288
Zeigler, Benjamin J., 454
Zeigler, Samuel M., 454

ALLEGHANY
ASHE
Mount Airy
STOKES
Danbury
SURRY
Germantown
WATAUGA
Deep Gap
Boone
WILKES
FORSYTH
GUIL
Blowing Rock
Yadkin R.
YADKIN
Salem
Wilkesboro
MITCHELL
CALDWELL
YANCEY
ALEXANDER
DAVIE
Lenoir
Mocksville
MADISON
BURKE
Taylorsville
DAVIDSON
Burnsville
Catawba R.
Mars Hill
Camp Vance
Statesville
C. S. Nitre & Mining Bureau
Marshall
McDOWELL
WESTERN NORTH CAROLINA R.R.
C. S. Smelting Wo
Lexington
Camp Patton
Camp
Morganton
IREDELL
C. S. Prison
Battery Hill Battery
Clingman
Swannanoa
CATAWBA
ROWAN
Camp Hill
HAYWOOD
Arsenal
Gap
Salisbury
Armory
Asheville
Marion
Beaucatcher Battery
BUNCOMBE
LINCOLN
Waynesville
RUTHERFORD
CABARRUS
W. C. S.
CHEROKEE
HENDERSON
STANLY
MACON
JACKSON
POLK
Mecklenburg
MONTG
Hendersonville
CLEVELAND
GASTON
Franklin
TRANSYLVANIA
Howard's Gap
C. S. Navy Yard
ANSON
Murphy
Camp Stokes
CLAY
Charlotte
UNION

Map of North Carolina, 1861–1865

Drawn by James R. Vogt

This map locates the principal camps, for s,
towns, railroads, and engagements fought in
the State during the Civil War.

LEGEND

● – Towns
■ – Forts and batteries
▲ – Camps
★ – Engagements
✕ – Railroads